NURSES' CLINICAL CONSULT TO

Psychopharmacology

Jacqueline Rhoads, PhD, ACNP-BC,
ANP-C, GNP, CCRN

Patrick J. M. Murphy, PhD

SPRINGER PUBLISHING COMPANY

NEW YORK

Springer Publishing Company, LLC
11 West 42nd Street
New York, NY 10036
www.springerpub.com

Acquisitions Editor: Margaret Zuccarini
Composition: Newgen Imaging

ISBN: 978-0-8261-0503-5
E-book ISBN: 978-0-8261-0504-2

12 13 14 15 / 5 4 3 2

The author and the publisher of this Work have made every effort to use sources believed to be reliable to provide information that is accurate and compatible with the standards generally accepted at the time of publication. Because medical science is continually advancing, our knowledge base continues to expand. Therefore, as new information becomes available, changes in procedures become necessary. We recommend that the reader always consult current research and specific institutional policies before performing any clinical procedure; to check the package insert especially for new and infrequently used drugs; and to consider drugs and dosages in light of the patient's medical condition. The author and publisher shall not be liable for any special, consequential, or exemplary damages resulting, in whole or in part, from the readers' use of, or reliance on, the information contained in this book. The publisher has no responsibility for the persistence or accuracy of URLs for external or third-party Internet Web sites referred to in this publication and does not guarantee that any content on such Web sites is, or will remain, accurate or appropriate.

Library of Congress Cataloging-in-Publication Data

Rhoads, Jacqueline, 1948-
  Nurses' clinical consult to psychopharmacology / Jacqueline Rhoads,
Patrick J.M. Murphy.
    p. ; cm.
  Includes bibliographical references and index.
  ISBN 978-0-8261-0503-5 —ISBN 978-0-8261-0504-2 (e-book)
  I. Murphy, Patrick J. M. II. Title.
  [DNLM: 1. Mental Disorders—drug therapy. 2. Mental Disorders—nursing.
3. Psychotropic Drugs—pharmacology. 4. Psychotropic Drugs—therapeutic
use. WM 402]
  616.89'18—dc23   2011036135

Printed in the United States of America by Gasch Printing.

I dedicate this book to all of the students to whom I have had the pleasure of teaching the art of nursing. With thanks for hours of enjoyment, years of inspiration, and a lifetime of admiration.

    —Jackie Rhoads

To Dean Mary K. Walker and the students—past and future—of the Seattle University College of Nursing.

    —Patrick Murphy

Contents

Contributors

Sandra S. Bauman, PhD, ARNP, LMHC
North Miami Beach, FL
Chapter 6: Treatment of Psychotic Disorders

Deonne J. Brown-Benedict, DNP, ARNP, FNP-BC
Assistant Professor, Family Nurse Practitioner Track Clinical Coordinator, Seattle
    University College of Nursing, Seattle, WA
Chapter 5: Treatment of Mood Disorders

Angela Chia-Chen Chen, PhD, RN, PMHNP-BC
Assistant Professor, Arizona State University, College of Nursing & Healthcare
    Innovation, Phoenix, AZ
Chapter 6: Treatment of Psychotic Disorders

Karen Crowley, DNP, APRN-BC, WHNP, ANP
Chapter 10: Treatment of Eating Disorders

Deborah Gilbert-Palmer, EdD, FNP-BC
Associate Professor, Arkansas State University
Chapter 11: Treatment of Behavioral and Psychological Disorders in the Elderly
Chapter 13: Treatment of Sleep Disorders

Lori S. Irelan, FNP, APRN, MSN
Wilmington University, New Castle, DE
Chapter 8: Treatment of Childhood and Adolescent Disorders

Mitsi H. Lizer, PharmD, BCPP, CGP
Associate Professor Pharmacy Practice, Shenandoah University School of Pharmacy,
    Winchester, VA
Chapter 4: Emergency Psychiatry

JoAnn Marrs, EdD, FNP-BC
East Tennessee State University, Johnson City, TN
Chapter 14: Treatment of Dissociative Disorders

Patrick J. M. Murphy, PhD
Assistant Professor, Seattle College of Nursing, Seattle, WA
Chapter 3: Principles of Pharmacokinetics and Pharmacodynamics in Psychopharmacology

Stephanie Ann Plummer, DNP, APRN, PMHNP-BC
Assistant Clinical Professor, UCLA School of Nursing, Fayetteville, AR;
    Department of Psychiatry, VAMC—Jay CBOC, Jay, Oklahoma
Chapter 1: The Relationship of Psychopharmacology to Neurotransmitters, Receptors, Signal Transduction,
    and Second Messengers

Jacqueline Rhoads, PhD, ACNP-BC, ANP-C, GNP, CCRN
Professor of Nursing, University of Texas at Galveston Health Science Center School of
    Nursing, Galveston, TX
Chapter 2: Clinical Neuroanatomy as It Relates to Pharmacology With Emphasis on Psychoactive Drugs

Ester Ruiz, PhD, RN
Professor Emeritus, Arizona State University, Tempe, AZ

Barbara Sartell, EdD, RN, CANP
Wilmington University, New Castle, DE
Chapter 7: Treatment of Anxiety Disorders

Antiqua Smart, BSN, MN, APRN, FNP-BC, CPE
Southern University and A&M College, Baton Rouge, LA
Chapter 13: Treatment of Sleep Disorders

Sandra J. Wiggins Petersen, DNP, FNP, GNP-BC
Program Track Administrator, UTMB Masters in Nursing Leadership Program, UTMB
    School of Nursing, Galveston, TX
Chapter 12: Treatment of Personality Disorders

Hsin-Yi (Jean) Tang, PhD, APRN-BC, PMHNP
Assistant Professor, College of Nursing, Seattle University, Seattle, WA
Chapter 5: Treatment of Mood Disorders

Kristen M. Vandenberg, DNP, ARNP
Nursing Faculty, University of North Florida
Chapter 9: Treatment of Substance-Related Disorder

Lisa Waggoner, DNP, FNP-BC
Arkansas State University, State University, AR
Chapter 11: Treatment of Behavioral and Psychological Disorders in the Elderly

Veronica Wilbur, PhD, FNP-BC, CNE
Associate Professor, Wilmington University, New Castle, DE
Chapter 7: Treatment of Anxiety Disorder

Reviewers

Melanie Blunk, DNP, Adult/Family PMHNP, APRN
Adjunct Clinical Faculty, University of Missouri, Columbia, MO; Psychiatric Consultant,
    Long Term Care Facilities and Personal Care Homes, Parkview
    Psychiatric Services, Bowling Green, KY

JoEllen Kubik, MSN, MA, ARNP/PMHNP-BC, LMHC
Associate Professor of Nursing, Allen College, Waterloo, IA

Martha Kuhlmann, MSN, FNP, PMHCNS
Clinical Assistant Professor and Specialty Coordinator, Family Psychiatric Mental
    Health Nurse Practitioner Program, UAMS College of Nursing, Little Rock, AR

Adrianne D. Linton, PhD, RN
Professor of Nursing (Tenured), Chair, Department of Family and Community
    Health Systems, University of Texas Health Science Center at San Antonio,
    Graduate School of Biomedical Sciences, San Antonio, TX

Cynthia Luther, DSN, GNP-BC, FNP-BC
Assistant Professor of Nursing, Director, Mississippi Educational Consortium
    for Specialized Advanced Practice Nursing (MECSAPN); Director, Gerontological and
    Psychiatric Mental Health Nurse Practitioner Tracks, University of Mississippi
    Medical Center School of Nursing, Jackson, MS

Evelyn Parrish, PhD, APRN
Professor of Nursing, Eastern Kentucky University, Richmond, KY

Preface

The main intent in writing this clinical reference was to present to both primary care providers and psychiatric/mental health specialists a wide-ranging guide to psychopharmacology in relation to its application in practice. It is hoped that the contents of this text will offer providers and nurses in advanced practice the basic concepts and in-depth prescribing guidelines that are necessary for the clinical management of those patients with mental health disorders. Compiled by expert practitioners in psychiatric care, this work provides an overview of the management of the major *Diagnostic and Statistical Manual of Mental Disorders, Fourth Edition, Text Revision* (American Psychiatric Association, 2000), disorders across the lifespan, and complete clinical guidelines for their psychopharmacologic management for use by nurse practitioners and others caring for patients in clinical practice. Not every mental health disorder is listed. The disorders chosen are those where drugs can play a significant therapeutic role in altering the course or progression of the disease.

We have constructed each chapter in a bullet format for quick reference using a structured approach. The book is organized into two major sections: The first is the overview of the principles of clinical psychopharmacology; the second is the treatment section, where the major disorders that benefit from drug intervention are used to organize and present drugs that are appropriate to prescribe for their management.

In the treatment section, handy psychopharmacology drug selection tables present first- and second-line drug therapies, along with adjunctive therapy, that can be beneficial to support optimal functioning of the individual with a mental health disorder. Drugs are then presented in monograph format, organized according to the drug classifications in the tables. More than 90 drugs are clearly presented.

It is important to note that, *in the drug tables, the order in which drugs are listed within the classification is significant and will help guide drug choice for specific disorders.* Note, too, that not every drug within a classification is included for all disorders; rather, *only drugs that have been shown to have clinical efficacy are listed in a priority fashion,* again to help guide the drug choice by the prescriber.

Essential drug information that is needed to safely prescribe and monitor the patient's response to those drugs includes drug names (generic and brand names), drug class, usual and customary dosage, administration of the drug, availability (e.g., tablet, injection, intravenous, capsule), side effects, drug interaction, pharmacokinetics, precautions, patient and family education, and special populations. The special populations section includes management of pregnant, breastfeeding, elderly, child, and adolescent populations, and patients with impaired renal, hepatic, or cardiac function.

Pharmacology knowledge and applied clinical practices are constantly evolving owing to new research and applied science that expand our diagnostic capabilities and treatments. Therefore, it must be emphasized that practitioners carry an important responsibility to ensure that the selected treatment reflects current research and is appropriate according to manufacturer drug information and that dosages, routes of administration, side effects/precautions, drug interactions, and use in special populations have been taken into consideration and are accurate and appropriate for each patient. The practitioner is ultimately responsible to know each patient's history, to conduct a thorough physical examination, and to consult appropriate diagnostic test results to ascertain the best possible pharmacotherapeutic actions for optimal patient outcomes and appropriate safety procedures.

The contributors to this text have worked hard to present current and applicable content that is of therapeutic value in the understanding of specific mental health disorders. We are very grateful to the contributors of this text for their hard work and focused support.

Jackie Rhoads
Patrick Murphy

Acknowledgments

The publication of this book would not have been possible without the generous help and support of many people. The contributors were among the most accomplished advanced practice nurses in the discipline of nursing. They were selected because each is recognized to be among the most accomplished in their fields. They provided up-to-date information on their topics, discussing both personal and best-practice principles.

A special thank you also goes to Dr. Patrick Murphy for critiquing chapters in the book for specific pharmacological content and providing many beneficial suggestions. The textbook was greatly enhanced by his focused and timely input.

Last and most important, I would like to acknowledge the support of Margaret Zuccarini, Publisher, Nursing, at Springer Publishing Company. Her ongoing support and encouragement made this work possible during a time in my life when I didn't think I could possibly pursue this endeavor.

Jackie Rhoads

Abbreviations

ABA	applied behavior analysis	EPS	extrapyramidal symptoms
ACE	angiotension-converting enzyme	ER	extended release
AD	Alzheimer's disease	ESRD	end-stage renal disease
ADHD	attention-deficit hyperactivity disorder	ETT	endotracheal tube
AIDS	acquired immunodeficiency syndrome	exam	examination
ALT	alanine aminotransferase		
AMI	acute myocardial infarction	FDA	Food and Drug Administration
ANA	antinuclear antibody	FGAs	first-generation antipsychotics
ANC	absolute neutrophil count		
ANS	autonomic nervous system	GABA	gamma-amino butyric acid
ASA	acetylsalicylic acid	GAD	general anxiety disorder
ASAP	as soon as possible	GGT	gamma-glutamyl transpeptidase
ASD	acute stress disorder	GI	gastrointestinal
AST	aspartate aminotransferase	GPCRs	G protein-coupled receptors
		GU	genitourinary
BDNF	brain-derived neurotropic factor		
bid	two times a day	H	histamine
BMI	body mass index	HD	heart disease
BP	blood pressure	HHS	Health and Human Services
BPH	benign prostatic hyperplasia	HLA	human leukocyte antigen
BUN	blood urea nitrogen	HR	heart rate
BZD	benzodiazepine	HTN	hypertension
Ca^{2+}	calcium	IM	intramuscular
cAMP	cyclic adenosine monophosphate	IO	intraosseous
CBC	complete blood count	IOP	intraocular pressure
CBT	cognitive–behavioral therapy	IP3	triphosphate
CHF	congestive heart failure	IR	immediate release
CK	creatine kinase	IV	intravenous
CMI	clomipramine		
CNS	central nervous system	LFT	liver function test
COPD	chronic obstructive pulmonary disease		
CrCl	creatinine clearence	MAOI	monoamine oxidase inhibitor
CSF	cerebrospinal fluid	MDD	major depressive disorder
CSID	critical incident stress debriefing	MFO	mixed-function oxidases
CT	computed tomography	MI	myocardial infarction
CV	cardiovascular	MRI	magnetic resonance imaging
CYP	cytochrome P450		
		NaSSA	noradrenergic and specific serotonergic antidepressants
DBT	dialectical behavior therapy		
DDI	drug–drug interaction	NDRI	norepinephrine and dopamine reuptake inhibitor
DEA	Drug Enforcement Administration		
		NE	norepinephrine
ECG	electrocardiogram	NMDA	N-methyl-D-aspartate
ECT	electroconvulsive therapy	NMS	neuroleptic malignant syndrome
EEG	electroencephalogram	NOS	not otherwise specified
EENT	eye, ear, nose, and throat	NREM	nonrapid eye movement
EKG	electrocardiogram	NRT	nicotine replacement therapy

NSAID	nonsteroidal anti-inflammatory drugs		SARI	serotonin antagonist and reuptake inhibitor
			SC	subcutaneous
OCD	obsessive–compulsive disorder		SIADH	syndrome of inappropriate anti diuretic hormone
ODD	oppositional defiant disorder			
ODT	orally disintegrating tablet		SNRI	serotonin and norepinephrine reuptake inhibitor
OTC	over the counter			
OTP	opioid treatment programs		SNS	sympathetic nervous system
			SSNRI	selective serotonin norepinephrine reuptake inhibitor
PD	panic disorder			
PKU	phenylketonuria		SSRI	selective serotonin reuptake inhibitor
PMDD	premenstrual dysphoric disorder			
PNS	peripheral nervous system		TCA	tricyclic antidepressant
PO	orally		TD	tardive dyskinesia
PSNS	parasympathetic nervous system		tid	three times a day
PTSD	posttraumatic stress disorder		TZD	thiazolidinediones
RBC	red blood cell		UA	uric acid
RDA	recommended dietary allowances		UCD	urea cycle disorder
REM	rapid eye movement		UTI	urinary tract infection
RPR	rapid plasma reagin			
SAMHSA	Substance Abuse and Mental Health Services Administration		WBC	white blood cell

The Relationship of Psychopharmacology to Neurotransmitters, Receptors, Signal Transduction, and Second Messengers

The last 20 years have afforded scientists with a greater understanding of the brain. Extreme changes in psychopharmacology have produced newer medicines with fewer side effects and greater benefits than ever before. These changes translate into improved wellness for patients with mental health disorders.

This chapter presents:
- A basic outline of the currently understood processes by which the brain communicates
- Information to support an improved understanding of the inner brain mechanisms from synaptic and cellular viewpoints in regard to psychopharmacology
- The signaling pathways associated with the six neurotransmitters most commonly altered in modern psychopharmacological therapy
- A strong scientific background on which to base psychopharmacological prescribing practices

NEUROTRANSMITTERS
These are the molecules that mediate intracellular signaling of the brain.
- Neurotransmitters are chemicals that communicate their messages to the interior of the neurons:
  - Through their release from the presynaptic terminal
  - By diffusing across the synaptic cleft
  - To further bind to receptors in the postsynaptic membrane
- There are more than several dozen known or suspected neurotransmitters in the brain.
- Theoretically there may be several hundred neurotransmitters based on the amount of genetic materials in the neurons.
- Neurotransmitters are endogenous molecules; examples include various peptides and hormones (Table 1.1).
- Psychoactive drugs act by increasing, decreasing, or otherwise modulating the actions of neurotransmitters at their receptor sites.
- *Ligand* is a generic term referring to either endogenous or exogenous receptor binding partner proteins to which neurotransmitters bind, resulting in changes to downstream cellular processes.
- Six neurotransmitter systems are the major targets for psychotropic drugs:
  - **Serotonergic neurons** (neurotransmitter = serotonin) originating primarily in the raphe nuclei of the reticular formation extending from the medulla to the midbrain
  - **Noradrenergic neurons** (neurotransmitter = norepinephrine) originating in the locus coeruleus
  - **Dopaminergic neurons** (neurotransmitter = dopamine) originating primarily in the ventral tegmental area
  - **Muscarinic cholinergic neurons** (neurotransmitter = acetylcholine), one of the principal neurotransmitters in the ANS
  - **Glutamatergic neurons** (neurotransmitter = glutamate), an amino acid transmitter synthesized by the brain from glucose and other nutrients for motor activity
  - **GABAergic neurons** (neurotransmitter = GABA), an inhibitory amino acid neurotransmitter, which is synthesized from glutamate in the brain and decreases activity in nerve cells
- These six neurotransmitters are relatively low-molecular-weight amines or amino acids.
- Multiple neurons that release more than one neurotransmitter may converge at a single synapse.
- Co-transmission involves a monoamine coupled with a neuropeptide.
  - This natural combination of multiple signaling molecules at the synapse is the basis for the modern treatment rationale of prescribing drugs affecting multiple neuronal signaling pathways.

Table 1.1 Major Neurotransmitters in the CNS

NEUROTRANSMITTER	EFFECTS
Acetylcholine (ACh)	Cognition, learning, memory, alertness, muscle contraction
Dopamine	Pleasure, pain, movement control, emotional response
GABA	Psychomotor agitation/retardation, stress, anxiety
Glutamate	Memory, energy
Norepinephrine	Arousal, dreaming, depressed mood, suicide, apathy, psychomotor agitation/retardation, constricts blood vessels, increases heart rate and blood pressure, affects attention and the sleep/wake cycle
Serotonin	Mood control, temperature regulation, impulsiveness, aggression, cognitive problems, depressed mood, suicide, apathy, psychomotor agitation/retardation

SIX NEUROTRANSMITTERS MOST COMMONLY AFFECTED BY PSYCHOPHARMACOLOGY TREATMENT REGIMENS*

Communication within the brain happens in three ways: anterograde, retrograde, or nonsynaptic. Chemical neurotransmission is the foundation of psychopharmacology.

- **Anterograde neurotransmission:**
  - Most predominant means of excitation-coupling and synapses.
  - Occurs in one direction (i.e., presynaptic to postsynaptic), from the cell body, down the axon, to the synaptic cleft.
  - Involves stimulation of a presynaptic neuron causing electrical impulses to be sent to its axon terminal (may be regarded as "classic" neurotransmission).
  - Electrical impulses are converted into chemical messengers, known as neurotransmitters.
  - Chemical messengers (neurotransmitters) are released to stimulate the receptors of the postsynaptic neuron.
  - Communication *within* a neuron is mediated by electrical conduction of an action potential from the cell body down the axon of the neuron where it ends at the synaptic cleft.
  - Communication *between* neurons is chemical and mediated by one of several neurotransmitters described earlier.
  - Excitation–secretion coupling is the process by which an electrochemical signal in the first (i.e., presynaptic) neuron is converted from a chemical impulse into the release of a chemical signal at the synapse.
  - Electrical impulses result from the opening of *ion channels* in the neuronal cell membrane along the axon, causing a change in net charge of the neuron. The difference in charge between the inside of the cell and the outside of the cell is referred to as an *action potential.*
    - Voltage-sensitive sodium channels
    - Voltage-sensitive potassium channels
  - This all happens very quickly once the electrical impulse enters the presynaptic neuron.
  - Occurs predominately in one direction (from the cell body, down the axon, to the synaptic cleft).
- **Retrograde neurotransmission:**
  - Postsynaptic neurons can talk back directly and indirectly.
    - Indirectly through a long neuronal feedback loop
    - Directly through retrograde neurotransmission from postsynaptic to presynaptic
  - Examples of retrograde neurotransmitters synthesized in the postsynaptic neuron, released, and diffused into the presynaptic neuron are:
    - Endocannabinoids (endogenous compounds similar to marijuana, also known as cannabis)
    - Nitric oxide

- **Nonsynaptic neurotransmission:**
  - No neurotransmission across a synaptic cleft
  - Chemical messengers sent by one neuron diffuse to compatible receptor sites distant to the synapse

RECEPTORS

These are proteins to which neurotransmitters bind, resulting in changes to downstream cellular processes.

- Found within plasma membranes and cytoplasm of a cell
- Affected by psychoactive drugs
- Located on cell membranes of neurons

Receptors Specific to Psychopharmacology

Psychotropic medications are developed to target these various receptor sites.

Serotonin

RECEPTOR TYPE	DISTRIBUTION	EFFECTS
5HT1, 5HT1A, 1B, 1D, 1E, 1F	Brain, blood vessels, intestinal nerves	*Inhibitory:* neuronal inhibition, cerebral vasoconstriction *Behavioral effects:* addiction, aggression, anxiety, appetite, impulsivity, learning, memory, mood, sexual behavior, sleep
5HT2, 2A, 2B, 2C	Brain, blood vessels, heart, lungs, smooth muscle control, GI system, blood vessels, platelets	*Excitatory:* neuronal excitation, vasoconstriction *Behavioral effects:* addiction, anxiety, appetite, mood, sexual behavior, sleep
5HT3	Limbic system, CNS, PNS, GI system	*Excitatory:* nausea *Behavioral effects:* addiction, anxiety, learning, memory
5HT4	CNS, smooth muscle, GI system	*Excitatory:* neuronal excitation, GI *Behavioral effects:* anxiety, appetite, learning, memory, mood
5HT5, 5A, 6, 7	Brain	*Inhibitory:* may be linked to BDNF *Behavioral effects:* sleep
5HT6	CNS	*Excitatory:* may be linked to BDNF *Behavioral effects:* anxiety, cognition, learning, memory, mood
5HT7	CNS, blood vessels GI system	*Excitatory:* may be linked to BDNF *Behavioral effects:* anxiety, memory, sleep, mood

---

*Currently prescribed psychotropic medications are developed to target these neurotransmitter signaling pathways.

- **Serotonin:** Binds to 5HT1A, 5HT1B, 5HT1D, 5HT1E, 5HT1F, 5HT2, 5HT2A, 5HT2B, 5HT2C, 5HT3, 5HT4, and 5HT5A receptors

- **Norepinephrine:** Binds to alpha$_1$ and alpha$_2$, beta$_1$, beta$_2$, and beta$_3$ receptors

Norepinephrine

RECEPTOR TYPE	DISTRIBUTION	EFFECTS
Alpha$_1$	Brain, heart, smooth muscle	*Excitatory:* vasoconstriction, smooth muscle contraction
Alpha$_2$	Presynaptic neurons in brain, pancreas, smooth muscle	*Inhibitory:* vasoconstriction, GI relaxation presynaptically
Beta$_1$	Heart, brain	*Excitatory:* increased heart rate
Beta$_2$	Lungs, brain, skeletal muscle	*Excitatory:* bronchial relaxation, vasodilation, smooth muscle relaxation
Beta$_3$	Adipose tissue	*Excitatory:* stimulation of effector cells

- **Dopamine:** Binds to D1, D2, D3, D4, and D5 receptors

Dopamine

RECEPTOR TYPE	DISTRIBUTION	EFFECTS
D1	Brain, smooth muscle	*Excitatory:* possible role in schizophrenia and Parkinson's
D2	Brain, cardiovascular system, presynaptic nerve terminals	*Inhibitory:* possible role in schizophrenia
D3	Brain, cardiovascular system, presynaptic nerve terminals	*Inhibitory:* possible role in schizophrenia
D4	Brain, cardiovascular system, presynaptic nerve terminals	*Inhibitory:* possible role in schizophrenia
D5	Brain, smooth muscle	*Excitatory:* possible role in schizophrenia and Parkinson's

- **Acetylcholine:** Binds to nicotinic (N) and muscarinic (M) receptors

Acetlycholine

RECEPTOR TYPE	DISTRIBUTION	EFFECTS
M1	Ganglia, secretory glands	*Excitatory:* CNS excitation, gastric acid secretion
M2	Heart, nerves, smooth muscle	*Inhibitory:* cardiac inhibition, neural inhibition
M3	Glands, smooth muscle, endothelium, secretory glands	*Excitatory:* smooth muscle contraction, vasodilation
M4	CNS, PNS, smooth muscle, secretory glands	*Inhibitory*
M5	CNS	*Inhibitory*
N$_M$	Skeletal muscle, neuromuscular junction	*Excitatory:* neuromuscular transmission
N$_N$	Postganglionic cell body dendrites	*Excitatory:* ganglionic transmission

- **GABA:** Binds to GABA$_A$ and GABA$_B$ receptors

GABA

RECEPTOR TYPE	DISTRIBUTION	EFFECTS
GABA$_A$	CNS	Inhibitory
GABA$_B$	ANS	Excitatory

Glutamate: Binds to AMPA, kainate, and NMDA receptors

Glutamate

RECEPTOR TYPE	DISTRIBUTION	EFFECTS
AMPA	CNS	Excitatory
Kainate	CNS	Excitatory
NMDA	CNS	Excitatory

SIGNAL TRANSDUCTION

It is the movement of signals from the outside of a cell to the inside.

- Signal → receptor → change in cell function
- Plays a very specific role through messaging and activation of an inactive molecule
  - Starts a reaction that cascades through chemical neurotransmission via numerous molecules
    - Long-term effects of late gene products and many more messages

– Can occur over the time course of minutes, hours, days, or weeks
– Effects may be temporary or permanent
- Signal transduction translates into the following diverse biological responses:
  - Gene expression
  - Synaptogenesis

SECOND MESSENGERS

These are synthesized and activated by enzymes, and help mediate intracellular signaling in response to a ligand binding to its receptor.
- Relay and amplify signals received by receptors such as cAMP, IP_3, and Ca^{2+}.

ENDOGENOUS NEUROTRANSMITTERS
- See Table 1.2.

Table 1.2 Endogenous Neurotransmitters

NEUROTRANSMITTER	RECEPTOR	SIGNAL TRANSDUCTION	SECOND MESSENGER
Acetylcholine	Muscarinic	G-protein linked	cAMP or IP_3
	Nicotinic	Ion channel linked	Calcium
Dopamine	D1, D2, D3, D4, D5	G-protein linked	cAMP or IP_3
	alpha$_1$, beta$_2$	G-protein linked	cAMP or IP_3
GABA	GABA$_A$	Ion channel linked and ligand-gated ion channels	Calcium
	GABA$_B$	G-protein linked	cAMP or IP_3
Glutamate	AMPA, Kainate, and NMDA	Ion channel linked	Calcium
	Metabotropic	G-protein linked	cAMP or IP_3
Norepinephrine	alpha$_1$, alpha$_2$	G-protein linked	cAMP or IP_3
	beta$_1$	G-protein linked	cAMP or IP_3
Epinephrine	alpha$_1$, alpha$_2$	G-protein linked	cAMP or IP_3
	beta$_1$, beta$_2$	G-protein linked	cAMP or IP_3
Serotonin	5HT1A, 5HT1B, 5HT1D, 5HT1E, 5HT1F	G-protein linked	cAMP or IP_3
	5HT2, 5HT2A, 5HT2B, 5HT2C	G-protein linked	cAMP or IP_3
	5HT3	Ion channel linked	Calcium
	5HT4	G-protein linked	cAMP or IP_3
	5HT5A	G-protein linked	cAMP or IP_3

Clinical Neuroanatomy as It Relates to Pharmacology With Emphasis on Psychoactive Drugs

2

Clinical neuroanatomy is the method of studying lesions of the human nervous system as a tool to reinforce and amplify learning of the structure and organization of the CNS.

Clinical neuropharmacology is the study of drugs that alter processes controlled by the nervous system.

This chapter deals with the basic anatomy and physiology of the CNS, PNS, somatic nervous system, blood–brain barrier, basal ganglia, hippocampus, hypothalamus, and neurotransmitters.

Nervous System

CNS
- Composed of the brain and spinal cord, which are covered by protective membranes (meninges) and have fluid-filled spaces; weighs less than most desktop computers; receives and interprets sensory information and controls simple/complex motor behaviors

PNS
- Composed of cranial and spinal nerves; the nerves contain nerve fibers, which conduct information to (afferent) and from (efferent) the CNS; efferent fibers are involved in motor function, such as contraction of muscles or activation of secretory glands; afferent fibers convey sensory stimuli from the skin, mucous membranes, and deeper structures
- *Somatic nervous system*: Part of PNS; innervates the structures of the body wall (muscles, skin, and mucous membranes)
- *Autonomic nervous system*: Part of PNS; contains the SNS ("fight or flight") and PSNS; controls activities of the smooth muscles, glands, and internal organs, including blood vessels, and returns sensory information to the brain.

CENTRAL NERVOUS SYSTEM
Brain and Spinal Cord
- CNS drugs are used medically to treat psychiatric disorders, seizures, and pain, and as anesthetics; nonmedically, they are used as stimulants, depressants, euphoriants, and mind-altering substances.
- The CNS drugs include at least 21 neurotransmitters.
  - *Monoamines*: NE, epinephrine, dopamine DA, serotonin
  - *Amino acids*: Aspartate, glutamate, GABA, glycine
  - *Purines*: Adenosine, adenosine monophosphate, and triphosphate

- *Peptides*: Dynorphins, endorphins, enkephalins, neurotensin, somatostatin, substance P, oxytocin, and vasopressin
- *Others*: Ach, histamine

Blood–Brain Barrier
The blood–brain barrier blocks the entry of some drugs and substances into the brain.
- *Elements*: Supporting cells (neuralgia), particularly the astrocytes, and tight junctions between endothelial cells.
- *Function*: Selectively inhibits certain substances in the blood from entering the interstitial spaces of the brain or CSF. Certain metabolites, electrolytes, and chemicals have differing abilities to cross the blood–brain barrier. This has substantial implications for drug therapy because some antibiotics and chemotherapeutic drugs show a greater ability than others for crossing the barrier.
- *P-glycoprotein*: A protective element of the blood–brain barrier and a transport molecule that pumps various types of drugs out of cells. In capillaries of the CNS, P-glycoprotein pumps drugs back into the blood, thus limiting their access to the brain.
- Passage limited to lipid-soluble substances and drugs that cross by means of transport systems (protein-bound and highly ionized substances cannot cross).
- Protects brain from injury due to toxic substances but also acts as an obstacle to entry of therapeutic drugs.

THE BRAIN
The brain is able to adapt to prolonged drug exposure, which can alter the therapeutic effects and side effects of some drugs (adaptive changes are often beneficial but can be harmful).
- Increased therapeutic effects, decreased side effects, tolerance, and physical dependences may occur.

- Acts as a control center by receiving, interpreting, and directing sensory information throughout the body.
- Composed of cerebrum (*telencephalon*–cerebral cortex, subcortical white matter, commissures, basal ganglia; *diencephalon*–thalamus, hypothalamus, epithalamus, subthalamus), brain stem (midbrain, pons, medulla oblongata), and cerebellum (cerebellar cortex, cerebellar nuclei). Cerebrum and cerebellum are organized into right and left hemispheres.
- There are *three major divisions* of the brain—the forebrain, the midbrain, and the hindbrain.
  - The forebrain is responsible for receiving and processing sensory information, thinking, perceiving, producing and understanding language, and controlling motor function.
  - The midbrain is responsible for auditory and visual responses and motor function.
  - The hindbrain is responsible for maintaining balance and equilibrium, movement coordination, and the conduction of sensory information.
- *The limbic system* is often called the "pleasure center."
  - It is the group of structures that governs emotions and behavior.
  - It connects to all areas of the brain, especially the frontal cortex, which is the learning center.

PERIPHERAL NERVOUS SYSTEM

PNS is divided into the *somatic nervous system* (controls movement of skeletal muscles) and the *autonomic nervous system*. The autonomic nervous system is further divided into the parasympathetic nervous system (PSN) and the sympathetic nervous system (SNS).
- *PSNS*—housekeeping chores of the body, and stimulation of these nerves slows heart rate, increases gastric secretions, empties bladder and bowel, focuses eye for near vision, constricts pupil, and contracts bronchial smooth muscle.
- *SNS*—three main functions: regulates the cardiovascular system, regulates body temperature, and implements the fight-or-flight response.
  The PNS uses three neurotransmitters to exert its actions: Ach (released by all preganglionic neurons of the PSNS and SNS, all postganglionic neurons of the PSNS, all motor neurons of the skeletal muscles, and most postganglionic neurons of the SNS that supply the sweat glands), NE (released by almost all postganglionic neurons of SNS with the exception of postganglionic neurons that supply sweat glands), and epinephrine (released by adrenal medulla).
- Two basic categories of PNS receptors and their subtypes (receptor subtypes make it possible for drugs to act selectively):
  - Cholinergic-mediated responses to ACh subtypes include the following:
    - Nicotinic$_N$ activation stimulates parasympathetic and sympathetic postganglionic nerves and causes release of epinephrine from adrenal medulla.
    - Nicotinic$_M$ activation causes contraction of skeletal muscle.
    - Muscarinic activation causes focus of lens for near vision, miosis, decreased heart rate, constriction of bronchi, promotion of secretions, increase in bladder pressure, urination, salivation, increased gastric secretions, increased intestinal tone and motility, sweating, erection, and vasodilation.
  - Adrenergic-mediated responses to epinephrine and NE subtypes include the following:
    - Alpha$_1$ activation by epinephrine, NE, or dopamine causes mydriasis, vasoconstriction, ejaculation, and prostate contraction.
    - Alpha$_2$ activation by epinephrine or NE causes *inhibition* of subsequent neurotransmitter release.
    - Beta$_1$ activation by epinephrine, NE, or dopamine causes increased heart rate, force of contraction, atrioventricular conduction, and increased renin release from the kidney.
    - Beta$_2$ activation (only by epinephrine) causes vasodilation, bronchial dilation, uterine relaxation, glycogenolysis, and enhanced contraction of skeletal muscle.
    - Dopamine (responds only to dopamine) activation causes dilation of kidney vasculature.

SOMATIC NERVOUS SYSTEM

- *Elements:* Motor neurons arising from the spinal cord and brain and the neuromuscular junction.
- *Neuromuscular junction:* Formed by the terminal of the motor neuron and the motor end plates (special sites on the muscle's membrane). Motor neurons release neurotransmitter ACh to the junction; subsequently, ACh activates its receptor (nicotinic$_M$ receptor) on the motor end plates and causes muscle contraction.
- *Drugs that target the neuromuscular junction:* Cholinesterase inhibitors, nondepolarizing neuromuscular blockers, and depolarizing neuromuscular blockers.

Basal Ganglia (or Basal Nuclei)

It is a group of nuclei situated at the base of the forebrain and strongly connected to the cerebral cortex, thalamus, and other areas.
- *Elements:* Striatum, pallidum, substantia nigra, and subthalamic nucleus.
- *Function:* They are associated with motor control and learning functions. The substantia nigra provides dopaminergic input to the striatum. The basal ganglia play a central role in a number of neurological conditions, including several movement disorders. The most notable are Parkinson's disease, which involves degeneration of the dopamine-producing cells in the substantia nigra, and Huntington's disease, which primarily involves damage to the striatum.
- Drugs are used for Parkinson's disease to increase the dopamine level at the striatum.

Hippocampus

The hippocampus belongs to the limbic system that forms the inner border of the cortex.

- *Function*: Emotion, behavior, and long-term memory. Beta-amyloid, neuritic plaques and neurofibrillary tangles, and tau in the hippocampus and cerebral cortex are the prominent features of Alzheimer's disease (AD). Another characteristic of AD is that the level of ACh, an important neurotransmitter in the hippocampus and cerebral cortex, is significantly below normal.
- Drugs used to treat AD include cholinesterase inhibitors and NMDA receptor antagonist.

Hypothalamus

It is located below the thalamus and above the brainstem.

- The *pituitary gland* is located below the third ventricle of the brain and the hypothalamus, composed of anterior pituitary (adenohypophysis) and posterior pituitary (neurohypophysis). The pituitary stalk connects the hypothalamus to the pituitary gland.
- *Function:* The hypothalamus controls the anterior pituitary by hypothalamic releasing factors, while it synthesizes oxytocin and antidiuretic hormone and projects its neuronal axon to the posterior pituitary. The hypothalamus controls body temperature, hunger, thirst, fatigue, and circadian cycles.
- Drugs that target the pituitary stimulate or inhibit the synthesis and release of hormones from the anterior pituitary gland. In addition, some drugs act as agonists or antagonists of pituitary gland hormone receptors.

Both in the PNS and CNS, neurons regulate physiologic processes in the same way through two steps:

- *Axonal conduction*—an action potential is sent down the axon of a neuron.
  - Drugs that influence axonal conduction are not selective, so they stop transmission in the axon of any neuron they reach.
  - The only group of drugs that affect axonal conduction are local anesthetics.
- *Synaptic transmission*—a transmitter is released from the neuron carrying information across a synapse, or gap, to a postsynaptic cell receptor causing a change in that cell.
  - Most drugs work by affecting synaptic transmission.
  - Drugs that work by affecting synaptic transmission are very selective due to different types of transmitters and receptor sites.

- To work, drugs must have either a direct or an indirect effect on target cell receptors.

Synaptic transmission includes five steps:

- *Transmitter synthesis*—synthesis of the transmitter in the neuron
  - Drugs work here by:
    - Increasing amount of transmitter synthesized
    - Decreasing amount of transmitter synthesized
    - Synthesizing a "super" transmitter that is more potent than the naturally occurring transmitter
- *Transmitter storage*—the transmitter is stored in vesicles in the axon terminal for later use.
  - Drugs work here by:
    - Reducing amount of transmitter stored
- *Transmitter release*—axonal conduction causes release of the transmitter into the synapse between the neuron and the target cell.
  - Drugs work here by:
    - Increasing amount of transmitter released
    - Decreasing amount of transmitter released
- *Receptor binding*—the transmitter binds to receptor sites on the postsynaptic, or target, cell causing a change in that cell.
  - Drugs work here by:
    - Mimicking the natural transmitter and binding to additional target cell receptor sites to increase the effects on a target cell (agonist)
    - Binding to target cell receptor sites to block the naturally occurring transmitter from binding to the target cell and decreasing the effect the naturally occurring transmitter has on the target cell (antagonist)
    - Binding to the same target cell receptor sites together with the naturally occurring transmitter to increase the target cell's response to the transmitter
- *Termination of transmission*—the transmitter is depleted by reuptake, enzymatic degradation, or diffusion.
  - Drugs work here by:
    - Stopping the reuptake of the transmitter allowing more transmitter to be available to bind to the target cell receptor sites
    - Stopping the enzymatic degradation of the transmitter allowing more transmitter to be available to bind to the target cell receptor sites

Neurotransmitters

Neurotransmitters are chemicals that account for the transmission of signals from one neuron to the next across a synapse. They are also found at the axon endings of motor neurons, where they stimulate the muscle fibers to contract.

- Chemical substances stored in the terminal end of a neuron, released when the storing neuron

"fires"; have the potential to influence the activity of a receiving cell (either increasing or decreasing likelihood of action).

- Present in the synaptic terminal.
- Action may be blocked by pharmacologic agents.
- Examples of CNS neurotransmitters:

- *ACh*—Widely distributed throughout the CNS and is the primary transmitter at the neuromuscular junction.
- *Dopamine*—Involved in a wide variety of behaviors and emotions associated with parkinsonism and perhaps schizophrenia.
- *Serotonin*—Involved in sleep regulation, dreaming, mood, eating, pain, and aggression and associated with depression (i.e., selective serotonin reuptake inhibitor).
- *Glutamate*—An excitatory transmitter, associated in memory, arousal, and pain.
- *GABA*—Widely distributed, largely an inhibitory transmitter.

NEUROTRANSMITTER	FOCUSED AREAS

ACh	Neuromuscular junction, autonomic ganglia, parasympathetic neurons, motor nuclei of cranial nerves, caudate nucleus and putamen, basal nucleus of Meynert, portions of the limbic system
	Receptor: N, action: excitatory
	Receptor: M, action: excitatory or inhibitory
	Action: CNS—memory, sensory processing, motor coordination
	■ Muscarinic—found at postganglionic parasympathetic endings (heart, smooth muscle, glands). Five subtypes of muscarinic receptors:
	    M_1 receptors found in ganglia and secretory glands
	    M_2 receptors predominate in myocardium and in smooth muscle
	    M_3 and M_4 receptors found in smooth muscle and secretory glands
	    M_5 receptors have been identified in the CNS along with the other 4 types
	■ Nicotinic receptors found in ganglia and at neuromuscular junction. Identified as:
	    N_M receptors found at the neuromuscular junction in skeletal muscle
	    N_G receptors found in autonomic ganglia, adrenal medulla, and CNS

NE	SNS, locus coeruleus, lateral tegmentum *Action:* CNS—positive mood and reward, orienting and alerting responses, basic instincts (sex, eating, thirst) *C-receptors:* ■ Alpha$_1$ (postsynaptic) (causes contraction of blood vessels, sphincters, radial muscle of eye) ■ Alpha$_2$ (presynaptic): negative feedback loop inhibiting subsequent release of neurotransmitter: up- and downregulation occur in response to decreased or increased activation of receptors; present at extrasynaptic sites in blood vessels and the CNS; stimulation in the brain stem decreases sympathetic outflow; stimulation in the pancreas inhibits insulin release. ■ Beta$_1$ (predominately cardiac) stimulation increases heart rate or strength of contraction ■ Beta$_2$ (predominately noncardiac) found on smooth muscle (bronchi; large blood vessels) causes relaxation and promotes insulin release, liver and muscle gluconeogenesis and glycogenolysis and lipolysis in fat cells. ■ Beta$_3$ receptors are expressed in visceral adipocytes
Dopamine	Hypothalamus, midbrain nigrostriatal system *Receptors:* D1 and D2, action: inhibitory ■ Dopamine$_1$ (postsynaptic) receptors responsible for vasodilation in splanchnic and renal circulations. Stimulation in chemoreceptor trigger zone causes nausea and vomiting. ■ Dopamine$_2$ (presynaptic) receptors initiate a negative feedback loop. Five forms are found in the brain. *Action:* Regulation of hormonal balance, voluntary movement, reward
Serotonin (5-HT)	Parasympathetic neurons in gut, pineal gland, nucleus raphe magnus of pons *Action:* CNS— sleep and emotional arousal, impulse control, cognition, pain processing, dreaming, homeostatic processes
GABA	Cerebellum, hippocampus, cerebral cortex, striatonigral system *Receptor:* GABAa, action: inhibitory (postsynaptic) *Receptor:* GABAb, action: inhibitory (presynaptic)
Glycine	Spinal cord *Action:* inhibitory
Glutamic acid	Spinal cord, brainstem, cerebellum, hippocampus, cerebral cortex

Neuropharmacology

Neuropharmacology is the study of drugs that alter processes regulated by the nervous system. The nervous system regulates almost all bodily processes and therefore almost all bodily processes can be influenced by drugs that alter neuron regulation. By blocking (antagonist) or mimicking (agonist) neuron regulation, neuropharmacological drugs can modify skeletal muscle contraction, cardiac output, vascular tone, respiration, gastrointestinal function, uterine motility, glandular secretion, and functions of CNS, such as pain perception, ideation, and mood.

- Neurons regulate physiological processes through a two-step process involving axonal conduction and synaptic transmission.
  - *Axonal conduction*—process of conducting an action potential down the axon of the neuron.
    - Drugs (local anesthetics) that alter this conduction are not very selective because the process of axonal conduction is almost the same in all neurons; therefore, a drug that alters conduction will alter conduction in all cells.
  - *Synaptic transmission*—process of carrying information across the synapse between the neuron and the postsynaptic cell and requires release of neurotransmitters and binding of these transmitters to receptors on the postsynaptic cell.
    - Most drugs act by altering this synaptic transmission because they are able to produce more selective effects by altering the following:
      - Transmitter synthesis and receptor activation can be increased; transmitter synthesis and receptor activation can be decreased; or transmitters that are more effective than the natural transmitter, which will cause receptor activation to increase, can be synthesized.
      - Transmitter storage can cause receptor activation to decrease by decreasing the amount of transmitter available.
      - Transmitter release can promote release and increase receptor activation or can inhibit release and reduce receptor activation.
      - Termination of transmitter action blocks transmitter reuptake or inhibition of transmitter degradation; both will increase concentration of transmitter and cause receptor activation to increase.
    - In order for a drug to exert its effect, it must be able to directly or indirectly influence the receptor activity on the target cell. Drugs act on receptors by:
      - Binding to them and causing activation (agonist)
      - Binding to them and blocking their activation by other agents (antagonists)
      - Binding to their components and indirectly enhancing their activation by the natural transmitter

CLINICAL NEUROANATOMY: RATIONALE FOR UNDERSTANDING

- Understanding neuroanatomy helps guide pharmacological approaches to treatment. A key goal of pharmacotherapy is to modify a patient's pathogenic nervous system activity.
  - The nervous system (CNS and PNS) regulates our bodily processes. Therefore, our body processes can be affected by the drugs that regulate neuronal activity. Understanding clinical neuroanatomy helps in the development of neuropharmacological drugs and treatment selection to modify a patient's pathogenic nervous system activity.

CLINICAL NEUROANATOMY: ASSOCIATION WITH DRUG ACTION

- Drug enters the body through various *routes of administration:* injection; oral; sublingual; inhalation; transdermal
- What the body does to the drug (*pharmacokinetics*)
  - *Absorption* (transfer of drug from the site of application to the blood stream)
    - Affected by the rate of dissolution, surface area, blood flow, lipid solubility, and pH partitioning
    - Bioavailability (the fraction of unchanged drug that reaches site of action) affected by anything that alters absorption, distribution, or metabolism
  - *Distribution* (drug leaves blood stream → interstitial space of tissues → target cells responsible for therapeutic and adverse effects)
    - Determined by the blood flow to tissues, ability to exit the vascular system (capillary beds, blood–brain barrier, placental drug transfer, and protein binding), and ability to enter cells (lipid solubility and presence of transport system)
  - *Metabolism* (enzymatic alteration of drug structure or "bagging the trash," usually by liver)
    - Hepatic drug-metabolizing enzymes
  - *Excretion* (removal of drugs from body)
- What the drug does to the body (*pharmacodynamics*)
  - Dose–response relationship
    - Size of administered dose
    - Intensity of the response produced
  - *Drug–receptor interactions* (drugs interact with chemical)

– *Receptor* (chemicals in the body to which the drug binds to produce effects)
  - Regulated by endogenous compounds or macromolecules (body's own receptors for hormones, neurotransmitters, and other regulatory molecules
  - Can be turned on or off
  - Turned on by interaction with other molecules
  - When the drug binds to receptors, it either mimics (*agonists*) or blocks (*antagonists*) the action of endogenous regulatory molecules such as neurotransmitters (supplied to receptors by neurons of the nervous system)
  - There are receptors for each neurotransmitter, each hormone, and all other regulatory molecules
  - Drugs are selective to specific receptors (a receptor is analogous to a lock and a drug is analogous to a key for that lock), so only drugs with proper size, shape, and properties can bind to a receptor

Principles of Pharmacokinetics and Pharmacodynamics in Psychopharmacology

3

Pharmacokinetics and pharmacodynamics comprise the collective interactions between a drug and a patient.

- *Pharmacokinetics* refers to the effects of the patient on the drug. The four primary pharmacokinetic processes are absorption, distribution, metabolism, and excretion.
- *Pharmacodynamics* refers to the effects of the drug on the patient.

Pharmacokinetic Principles

- The four pharmacokinetic processes of absorption, distribution, metabolism, and excretion describe the effects the patient's organ systems have on the drug from the time it enters until the time it leaves the body.
- The extent to which a psychoactive drug will undergo each process is dependent on drug-specific and patient-specific variables.
  - Examples of drug-specific variables include the *chemical structure* and *route of administration*.
  - Examples of patient-specific variables include any *comorbidities*, overall *health*, the patient's *age*, and *concurrent pharmacotherapy*.

ABSORPTION

- *Absorption* refers to the movement of a drug from its site of administration into the circulatory system.
- Drug absorption is affected by the chemical properties of the drug as well as the route of drug administration.
  - Movement of drugs into the circulatory system most commonly requires drugs to pass across and through cellular compartments.
  - This movement occurs by active transport, passive diffusion, or direct penetration through the cell membranes.
  - Chemical properties of the drug, drug concentration, presence of drug-transporter molecules, and pH affect intercellular drug movement.
  - The dosage requirements for a drug may be noticeably different based on its route of administration.
  - Dosing differences are often necessary to ensure that *bioequivalence* is achieved when two different routes of administration of the same drug are employed.
- Absorption following *oral administration*
  - Drugs enter the GI tract and are absorbed through the stomach or small intestine. They travel via the portal vein first to the liver and then through the heart and into general circulation.
  - Oral administration results in more variable drug absorption and drug bioavailability than other administration routes.
  - *First-pass metabolism* (also known as the *first-pass effect*) refers to the inactivation of an orally administered drug by liver enzymes immediately following absorption from the GI tract and prior to the drug reaching general circulation.
  - *Enterohepatic recirculation* refers to the cyclical movement of orally administered drugs from the GI tract to the liver, then packaged into bile and secreted into the small intestine, and then reabsorbed back into the liver.
  - Drug dissolution may be protracted up to approx. 8 hr by formulating sustained-release, extended-release, and controlled-release preparations. Sustained-release formulations (e.g., controlled-release paroxetine [Paxil CR]) may minimize GI distress, decrease the number of daily dosages, and provide more uniform drug absorption.
    – Many CR formulations are available only as brand name medications at a substantially increased price over standard-release formulations.
  - Drugs that are inactivated by gastric acid or that cause gastric irritation may be prepared with an *enteric coating*, which permits drug absorption to be delayed until the drug passes through the stomach and enters the intestine.
  - Patients with GI distress may have impaired oral absorption.
- Absorption following *transdermal administration*
  - Suitable formulation and route of administration for drugs able to permeate intact skin.
  - Toxic effects may occur during transdermal absorption if drugs are highly lipid soluble.

- Controlled-release transdermal formulations (e.g., nicotine patches) are becoming increasingly available for various medications.
■ Absorption following *intramuscular (IM) administration* and *subcutaneous (SC) administration*
  - Many similarities exist between IM and SC injections. Both provide relatively rapid absorption of aqueous solutions and relatively slow absorption of lipophilic solutions.
  - The rate of absorption and drug bioavailability following an IM or SC injection are dependent on the lipophilicity of the drug, fat content, and blood flow at the injection site.
  - Injections may provide even, prolonged absorption. A drug may be prepared in a depot formulation that is gradually absorbed over time. Coadministration of a vasoconstricting medication may prolong absorption.
  - SC injections may result in pain if irritant is present.
■ Administration via *intravenous (IV) injection*
  - Absorption is essentially instantaneous, as the drug is delivered directly into the circulatory system.
  - It is useful when rapid drug effect is needed and allows for administration of poorly lipid-soluble drugs and irritants.
  - Continued and repeated IV administration requires accessibility to patent veins.
■ Absorption may involve passive diffusion or active transport.
  - *Passive diffusion* is the movement of a drug across a cell membrane down its concentration gradient.
  - Drugs that are smaller, less protein bound, and more lipophilic can be more readily absorbed via passive diffusion. Most psychotherapeutic drugs are absorbed via passive diffusion.
  - *Active transport* is the facilitated movement of a drug across a cell membrane.
  - Drugs unable to be absorbed via passive diffusion—either because of their chemical properties or the drug concentration gradient—require active transport in order to be absorbed.
  - Active transport mechanisms include membrane-spanning proteins that facilitate the movement of drugs across cell membranes and into the circulatory system. Active transport of drugs is limited to those medications structurally related to endogenous compounds for which active transport mechanisms already exist (e.g., ions, amino acids, and simple carbohydrates).
■ *Ion trapping* occurs when a drug classified as a weak acid transfers from a body compartment that is more acidic to one that is more alkaline (e.g., from the stomach to the plasma) or, conversely, when a weak base transfers from a more alkaline to a more basic compartment.
■ Absorption-related *drug–drug* or *food–drug interactions* should be closely monitored. Antacids, for example, may impair the absorption of orally coadministered psychiatric drugs, leading to subtherapeutic concentrations of the coadministered drug (MacDonald, Foster, & Akhtar, 2009).

DISTRIBUTION

■ *Distribution* refers to the movement of a drug from the circulatory system to its site(s) of action. Drugs are distributed to sites in the body responsible for producing both therapeutic effects and adverse effects.
■ The variables affecting drug distribution—and delivery of the drug to its site of action—include blood flow to the target tissue, lipid solubility, and plasma protein binding.
  - Tissues of the body with *high blood flow* (e.g., the brain and muscle) will receive higher concentrations of a drug faster than tissues with low blood flow (e.g., adipose tissue).
  - Drugs with *high lipid solubility* (e.g., nonpolar molecules) will more readily cross cell membranes, including the blood–brain barrier and placenta. These drugs will more readily localize in tissues with high lipid content (e.g., brain and adipose tissue).
  - Drugs with a *low level of plasma protein binding* (e.g., lithium) have a less encumbered movement and have generally increased bioavailability than drugs with a high level of plasma protein binding (e.g., valproic acid). Table 3.1 identifies psychiatric drugs with high and low plasma protein binding.
  - The most abundant plasma protein is *albumin*, and the terms *plasma protein binding* and *albumin binding* are often used interchangeably.
  - The biochemical properties that make a drug more readily absorbed into the circulatory system (e.g., high lipid solubility and low molecular weight) also make the drug more readily distributed throughout the body (Gupta, Chatelain, Massingham, Jonsson, & Hammarlund-Udenaes, 2006).
■ The total accumulation of lipid-soluble drugs in *adipose tissue* is dependent on the fat content of an individual. Adipose tissue may serve as a drug reservoir, which may result in redistribution during instances of profound weight loss.
■ The *blood–brain barrier* results from brain capillary endothelial cells possessing continuous

Table 3.1 Relative Plasma Protein Binding

HIGH PROTEIN-BINDING PSYCHIATRIC DRUGS	LOW PROTEIN-BINDING PSYCHIATRIC DRUGS
aripiprazole (>99%)	lithium (0%)
ziprasidone (>99%)	gabapentin (3%)
atomoxetine (99%)	levetiracetam (10%)
diazepam (99%)	topiramate (15%)
sertraline (98%)	methylphenidate (15%)
buspirone (95%)	clonidine (20%)
valproic acid (93%)	venlafaxine (28%)

tight junctions, which impede drug movement from the circulatory system into the CNS. Drugs passing into the CNS require specific transporter proteins or high drug lipophilicity.

- Variables affecting *in utero drug distribution*
  - For women who are pregnant, special considerations should be given to the potential for maternal–fetal drug transfer via the *placenta*.
  - Similar properties dictate passive diffusion across the placenta as the blood–brain barrier. Often drugs are able to cross the placenta first.
  - Drugs that have a high degree of lipid solubility, low molecular weight, and low serum protein binding cross the placenta more readily than drugs with a low degree of lipid solubility, high molecular weight, and high serum protein binding.
  - Because fetal plasma is slightly more acidic than maternal plasma, ion trapping of alkaline drugs may result in the increased accumulation of drug in the placenta.
- Patients suffering from malnutrition or acute or chronic inflammatory responses may present with *hypoalbuminemia*. The decrease in serum protein caused by hypoalbuminemia may result in greater drug bioavailability, particularly for drugs that are highly protein bound, leading to potentially toxic effects.
- Distribution-related drug–drug or food–drug interactions should be closely monitored. Warfarin, for example, may compete for albumin binding with other highly protein-bound psychiatric drugs, leading to an *increased* bioavailable plasma concentration of either the psychiatric drug or warfarin. These increased drug levels may be toxic and thus require dosage adjustments (Hisaka, Ohno, Yamamoto, & Suzuki, 2010).

METABOLISM

- *Metabolism* refers to the chemical modification of the administered drug by enzymes in the patient's body. Drug metabolism may take place before or after the drug reaches its site of action.
- Drugs may be metabolized (a) from active to inactive compounds, or (b) from inactive to active compounds, or (c) from an active compound to a slightly less active compound (or vice versa).
  - Most commonly, drug metabolism leads to the *biotransformation* of a more lipophilic parent drug to a more hydrophilic metabolite, which is often essential to increase the rate of excretion from the body.
  - The chemically modified variant of the administered drug is referred to as a *metabolite*.
  - Metabolites of several commonly administered drugs are therapeutically active at the same sites as their parent drug (e.g., s-desmethylcitalopram, the metabolite of escitalopram).
  - Metabolites of other drugs produce effects different from their parent drug (e.g., desipramine, the metabolite of imipramine, blocks noradrenaline uptake, whereas imipramine itself inhibits serotonin reuptake).

- *Cytochrome P450 (CYP)* refers to the large family of enzymes, found primarily in the liver, responsible for facilitating the majority of drug metabolism in the body.
  - Each CYP family member has a unique collection of substrates (i.e., drugs and other exogenous compounds) that it metabolizes.
  - Metabolism of one psychotherapeutic drug may increase or decrease the metabolism of a second medication (Azzaro, Ziemniak, Kemper, Campbell, & VanDenBerg, 2007). This is often a consequence of alterations in CYP activity.
  - Identification of a drug's CYP metabolism is routinely established in preclinical and clinical testing. This information is generally included in the pharmacokinetics sections of printed drug guides or online/PDA-based clinical management software (e.g., Lexi-Comp or ePocrates).
  - Individual drug effects on or by P450s may also be included as drug side effects or as drug–drug or food–drug interactions.
  - The standard nomenclature for specific CYP isozymes includes a 3- to 4-digit number-letter-number sequence, which identifies each isoform's sequence homologies.
  - The primary CYP isozymes present in humans and involved in metabolizing psychiatric drugs are CYP1A2, 2B6, 2C19, 2D6, and 3A4.
  - In addition to being substrates for specific CYPs, drugs may induce or inhibit P450 activity. Grapefruit juice, for example, specifically inhibits the drug metabolizing activity of CYP3A4. This leads to an increase in plasma concentration of other drugs that would have normally been metabolized by CYP3A4.
- The majority of drug metabolism occurs via P450s in the liver; however, in addition to hepatic P450s, notable amounts of drug metabolism also take place in the small intestine, kidney, and lungs.
- Patients with impaired liver function, such as those suffering from hepatitis or cirrhosis, are at risk of having impaired drug metabolizing activity. This may lead to an increase in bioactive drug concentrations and require a decrease in dosing in order to avoid drug toxicity.
- Metabolism-related drug–drug or food–drug interactions should be closely monitored. Grapefruit juice inhibits the metabolism of buspirone and other CYP 3A4 metabolites, leading to an *increased* plasma concentration of buspirone.
- *Therapeutic drug monitoring* improves the quality and safety of psychiatric drug therapy. Valid specimens must be collected during a specific time window. Appropriate pharmacokinetic interpretation of monitoring data can decrease costs and improve therapeutic outcomes (Llorente Fernández, Parés, Ajuria, et al., 2010).
- The term *half-life* (t½) refers to the amount of time necessary to decrease the concentration of the drug in the patient by 50%. The term *plateau*

refers to the steady-state drug levels achieved in the body with continual drug administration.

  - Due to the unique pharmacodynamic properties of psychiatric drugs (e.g., antidepressants), it is possible for there to be a significant delay in therapeutic response even after a plateau drug level has been reached.
  - Since psychoactive drugs often have delayed neurochemical effects (e.g., receptor remodeling), it is possible that physiologic changes will be observed even after most of the medication has been removed from the body.
  - Drugs of the same pharmacologic class may have very different half-lives (Table 3.2).

Table 3.2 Comparison of Half-Lives of Commonly Administered SSRIs and Atypical Antipsychotics

SSRIs	ATYPICAL ANTIPSYCHOTICS
paroxetine ($t_{1/2}$ = 17 hr)	ziprasidone ($t_{1/2}$ = 3 hr)
fluvoxamine ($t_{1/2}$ = 15 hr)	risperidone ($t_{1/2}$ = 3 hr)
sertraline ($t_{1/2}$ = 23 hr)	quetiapine ($t_{1/2}$ =6 hr)
citalopram ($t_{1/2}$ = 33 hr)	clozapine ($t_{1/2}$ = 23 hr)
escitalopram ($t_{1/2}$ = 33 hr)	olanzapine ($t_{1/2}$ = 33 hr)
fluoxetine ($t_{1/2}$ = 53 hr)	aripiprazole ($t_{1/2}$ = 47 hr)

EXCRETION

  - *Excretion* refers to the removal of the drug and any drug metabolites from the patient's body. Of particular concern is the excretion of (1) a therapeutically active parent drug, (2) any bioactive metabolites, and (3) any toxic metabolites.
  - The primary organs facilitating drug excretion are the kidneys. Renal excretion includes (a) glomerular filtration, (b) active tubular secretion, and (3) passive tubular reabsorption.
  - Non–protein-bound drug is filtered through the glomerulus. Transporter proteins facilitate active reabsorption.
  - Drugs may also be excreted through the *GI tract* via sequestration in bile or directly into the intestines. Drugs may also be excreted through the skin (e.g., sweat), oral mucosa (e.g., saliva), breast (e.g., lactation), and lungs (e.g., expiration).
  - Enterohepatic recirculation may impede excretion. Patients with impaired kidney function may have impaired drug excretion.
  - Although most drugs undergo hepatic metabolism, some drugs (e.g., lithium) are excreted in their active form.

Pharmacodynamic Principles

Pharmacodynamics refers to the effects of the drug on the patient. Pharmacodynamic effects can be observed at the molecular and cellular levels, as well as tissue and organ system levels.

MECHANISMS OF DRUG ACTION OR MOLECULAR DRUG TARGETS

  - Drugs most commonly produce their physiologic effects through interactions with cellular drug targets, known as *receptors*. Receptors are most typically proteins and are expressed on a variety of tissues.
  - The term *ligand* refers to drugs and endogenous molecules (e.g., neurohormones).
  - Drug–receptor interactions account for the majority of *drug side effects* as well as *therapeutic effects*. A drug may interact with one or more receptors.
    - The drug–receptor interaction responsible for the therapeutic drug effect may be the same or different from the drug–receptor interaction responsible for specific drug side effects.
    - An example of therapeutic and adverse drug reactions being caused by the same drug–receptor interaction is illustrated by morphine: Both analgesia (therapeutic effect) and respiratory sedation (drug side effect) are caused by the binding of morphine to the mu opioid receptor.
    - An example of therapeutic and adverse drug reactions being caused by different

drug–receptor interactions is illustrated by imipramine: The antidepressant effects result from interactions with serotonin and norepinephrine transporters and receptors; its side effects result from binding to cholinergic receptors (dry mouth, blurred vision, constipation) and histamine receptors (weight gain).

  - Drug receptors can be classified into five classes based on their cellular location and general function. The five classes are G protein-coupled receptors (GPCRs), ligand-gated ion channels, cell membrane–embedded enzymes and transporters, intracellular enzymes and signaling proteins, and nuclear transcription factors.
  - GPCRs comprise a superfamily of proteins, each containing seven membrane-spanning alpha helices and coupled to a GTP-binding protein, which alters the activity of a cellular enzyme or ion channel.
  - Examples of GPCRs include muscarinic acetylcholine receptors, histamine receptors, serotonin receptors, and dopamine receptors.
  - *Ligand-gated ion channels* are located across cell membranes and permit a specific ion to cross into or out of a cell, down its concentration gradient.
    - Examples of ligand-gated ion channels include nicotinic acetylcholine receptors and gamma-aminobutyric acid receptors.

- *Cell membrane–embedded enzymes and transporters* span the cell membrane and have catalytic activity. Examples include the insulin receptor and neurotransmitter reuptake pumps.
- *Intracellular enzymes and signaling proteins,* such as monoamine oxidase, alter the cellular environment by catalyzing chemical reactions or conveying chemical messages.
- *Nuclear transcription factors,* such as the glucocorticoid receptor and thyroid hormone receptor, bind to DNA and alter the transcription rates of specific gene families.

DRUG–RECEPTOR INTERACTIONS

- A drug or endogenous chemical that activates a receptor is referred to as an *agonist.* Agonists may be classified as producing maximal receptor activation (full agonist) or less than that (partial agonist). A partial agonist may impede the actions of a full agonist, thus diminishing receptor activity.
- A drug or endogenous chemical that inhibits a receptor from being activated is referred to as an *antagonist.* Antagonists block the actions of both drugs and endogenous chemicals (e.g., neurotransmitters).
  - While the effects of *competitive antagonists* can be overcome by the increased concentration of an agonist, the effects of other antagonists, referred to as *noncompetitive antagonists,* will persist even if more agonist is present.
- Drugs often act on more than one receptor, causing a multitude of both therapeutic and adverse drug effects.
- The description of a drug binding to a receptor simply indicates a physical interaction. This may lead to either receptor agonism or antagonism.

- Prolonged stimulation of a receptor may result in *desensitization,* in which the same concentration of a drug produces diminished therapeutic effects.
- The amount of observed therapeutic effect produced by a drug is a measure of *efficacy.* Maximal efficacy is the greatest response produced.
- The amount of effect a drug produces at a specific drug concentration is a measure of *potency.* High-potency drugs produce effects even when a small dose is given. Low-potency drugs may be nonetheless efficacious; however, they may require a greater dose to be administered.
- The difference between high-potency and low-potency psychiatric drugs are exemplified by first-generation antipsychotics (FGAs), where high-potency FGAs such as haloperidol produce their therapeutic effects at 1/10 to 1/100 the dose of low-potency FGAs (e.g., chlorpromazine).

PHARMACODYNAMIC DRUG–DRUG INTERACTIONS AND SIDE EFFECTS

- Pharmacodynamic drug–drug interactions occur when one drug affects the physiologic activity of another drug unrelated to a direct chemical interaction or pharmacokinetic process. Most pharmacodynamic drug–drug interactions occur at the cellular or receptor level.
  - An example of a pharmacodynamic drug–drug interaction is serotonin syndrome produced by the coadministration of a monoamine oxidase inhibitor (e.g., phenelzine) and an SSRI (e.g., fluoxetine). Both drugs contribute to a toxic accumulation of serotonin due to their actions on their respective drug targets.

Interpatient Variability

PHARMACOKINETIC AND PHARMACODYNAMIC CHANGES ACROSS THE LIFE SPAN

- Life span considerations affect both pharmacokinetic and pharmacodynamic drug properties.
- In general, pediatric and geriatric patients are more at risk of experiencing increased sensitivity to therapeutic and adverse drug actions.
- Pregnancy causes alterations in the pharmacokinetic actions of certain drugs, primarily by altering the rates of drug absorption and excretion.

PHARMACOGENETIC IMPLICATIONS TO PHARMACOKINETICS AND PHARMACODYNAMICS

- *Pharmacogenetics* refers to the effect a patient's genetic profile has on the patients response to drug therapy.

- Slight changes in the genetic code, referred to as *polymorphisms,* have been identified in DNA that direct the production of proteins that affect drug metabolism, leading to pharmacokinetic variability. Polymorphisms that direct the production of drug receptors have also been identified in DNA, leading to pharmacodynamic drug variability.
- An example of a genetic alteration affecting psychiatric drug pharmacokinetics is a polymorphism in CYP 3A4, leading to the rapid or delayed metabolism of CYP substrates.
- An example of a genetic alteration affecting pharmacodynamics is referred to as the short allele polymorphism of the serotonin (5-HT) transporter. Patients with short allele 5-HT transporter experienced insomnia and agitation at higher rates during treatment with fluoxetine (Perlis, Mischoulon, Smoller, et al., 2010).

DEFINITION

A psychiatric emergency is any disturbance in thoughts, feelings, or actions for which immediate therapeutic intervention is necessary.

- *Major emergencies:* Suicidal patients; agitated and aggressive patients
- *Minor emergencies:* Grief reaction; rape; disaster; panic attack
- *Medical emergencies:* Delirium; neuroleptic malignant syndrome; serotonin syndrome; MAOI/tyramine reactions; overdosages of common psychiatric medications; overdosages and withdrawal from addicting substances

ETIOLOGY/BACKGROUND

- Approx. 29–30% of psychiatric emergency patients are suicidal, approx. 10% are violent, and approx. 40% require hospitalization.
- Psychiatric emergencies peak between 6 and 10 p.m. when family members are home together and conflicts arise; substance use increases and aggravates disruptive behavior. Family physicians, pastors, counselors, and other resources are difficult to reach.
- Patients present with severe changes in mood, thoughts, or behavior; those experiencing severe drug adverse effects need urgent psychiatric assessment and treatment.
- Psychiatric emergencies often erupt suddenly. A person may curse, hit, throw objects, or brandish a weapon.
- Patients may neglect self-care, stop eating, exhibit confusion, wander into traffic, or appear unclothed in public.
- Because psychiatric emergencies can be concomitant with medical illnesses, it is imperative that the ED physician establish if the patient's symptoms are caused or exacerbated by a medical disease, such as infection, metabolic abnormality, seizure, or diabetic crisis.
- Emergency psychiatry includes specialized problems such as substance abuse, child abuse, and spousal abuse, as well as violence (suicide, homicide, and rape) and social issues (homelessness, aging, and competence). People with mental illness often lack a primary care physician and seek health care in crisis. Often uninsured, they have been denied coverage due to medical illness.

INCIDENCE

- Psychiatric emergencies from acute psychotic disturbances, manic episodes, major depression, bipolar disorder, and substance abuse are responsible for approx. 6% of all ED admissions in the USA.
- In bipolar mania, agitation occurs with a frequency of approx. 90%; in schizophrenia, agitation accounts for approx. 20% of psychiatric emergency visits.
- Drug and alcohol intoxication or withdrawal is the most common diagnosis in combative patients.
- In 2006, there were 1,742,887 drug-related ED visits nationwide.
  - 31% involved illicit drugs only.
  - 28% involved misuse or abuse of pharmaceuticals (i.e., prescription or OTC medications, dietary supplements) only.
  - 13% involved illicit drugs with alcohol.

SUICIDAL STATE

Suicidal ideation and behavior are the most serious and common psychiatric emergencies.

- Each year approximately 30,000 people in the USA and 1 million worldwide commit suicide; 650,000 receive emergency treatment after attempting suicide. It is the 10th leading cause of death worldwide.
- Suicide is highly prevalent in the adolescent population. Confounding comorbidities include depression, antisocial behavior, and alcohol abuse.
- A history of suicide attempts increases the odds of completing suicide more than any other risk factor.
- Most people who commit suicide reportedly never made a prior attempt and have never seen a mental health professional.
- People who attempt suicide more than once and later complete the act tend to be more anxious and socially withdrawn.
- In the USA, the majority of suicides are completed with firearms, followed by hanging among men and poisoning among women.
- Risk factors for suicide include:
  - Psychiatric illnesses
    - More than 90% of persons who attempt suicide have a major psychiatric disorder.
    - The most common mental disorders leading to suicide include major depression, substance abuse, schizophrenia, and severe personality disorders.
  - Impulsivity and hopelessness
  - History of previous suicide attempts

- Age, sex, and race
  - Risk increases with age.
  - Young adults attempt suicide more frequently.
  - Elderly (85+ years) White males have the highest suicide rate.
  - Suicide rates have traditionally been higher among Whites compared with Blacks. The incidence of suicide attempts among young Blacks is rising.
- Marital status
  - Whatever the family structure, living alone increases risk of suicide.
- Occupation
  - Unemployed and unskilled persons are at higher risk.
- Health status
  - Risk increases with physical illness such as chronic or terminal illness, chronic pain, and recent surgery.

VIOLENT BEHAVIOR

Certain features can serve as warning signs that a patient may be escalating toward physically violent behavior. The following list is not exhaustive:

- Facial expressions are tense and angry
- Increased or prolonged restlessness, body tension, pacing
- General overarousal of body systems (increased breathing and heart rate, muscle twitching, dilating pupils)
- Increased volume of speech, erratic movements
- Prolonged eye contact
- Discontentment, refusal to communicate, withdrawal, fear, irritation
- Thought processes unclear, poor concentration
- Delusions or hallucinations with violent content
- Verbal threats or gestures
- Reporting anger or violent feelings
- Blocking escape routes

AGITATION AND AGGRESSION

- Aggressive, violent patients are often psychotic and diagnosed with schizophrenia, delusional disorder, delirium, acute mania, and dementia, but these behaviors can also result from intoxication with alcohol or other substances of abuse, such as cocaine, PCP, and amphetamines.
- Medical disorders associated with violent behavior include (not all inclusive):
  - *Neurologic illnesses*—Seizure disorders, hepatic encephalopathy, cerebral infarcts, encephalitis, Wilson's disease, Parkinson's disease, intracranial bleeds
  - *Endocrinopathies*—Hypothyroidism, Cushing's syndrome, thyrotoxicosis, diabetic crisis
  - *Metabolic disorders*—Hypoglycemia, hypoxia, electrolyte imbalance
  - *Infections*—AIDS, syphilis, tuberculosis
  - *Vitamin deficiencies*—Folic acid, pyridoxine, vitamin B12
  - *Temperature disturbances*—Hypothermia, hyperthermia
  - *Poisoning*
- Behavioral signs of agitation include excessive motor restlessness, irritability, jitteriness, and purposeless and repetitive motor or verbal activity.
- Precautions should be taken to modify the environment to maximize safety.
  - Ensure that patient is physically comfortable
  - Minimize waiting time
  - Communicate in a safe, respectful attitude
  - Remove all dangerous objects
- Aggressive behavior is usually managed with some combination of seclusion, physical restraints, monitoring with constant observation by a sitter, and drug therapy.
  - Seclusion offers a decrease in external stimuli that may be enough to reduce aggressiveness.
  - Restraints may be needed to obtain a thorough assessment.
- Drug therapy such as tranquilization should target control of specific symptoms.
- Rapid calming or tranquilization of a patient is achieved with benzodiazepine or antipsychotic given IM or IV.
  - Typical or atypical antipsychotic may be used.
  - Benzodiazepines act more quickly but often have erratic IM absorption.
  - A combination of both drugs can be very effective.
- If oral medications are appropriate, orally disintegrating or liquid formulations are available for haloperidol, risperidone, olanzapine, and aripiprazole.

DRUG THERAPY FOR AGITATION IN PSYCHIATRIC EMERGENCIES

- It is better for a patient to take medication voluntarily and orally before the behavior escalates than to be involuntarily medicated after a crisis.
- The decision on which medication to use is often based on the underlying diagnosis. If the patient is known to be schizophrenic or bipolar and most likely is in a psychotic or manic state, then an antipsychotic should be used. If the diagnosis is unclear or the result of intoxication with drugs or alcohol, then lorazepam, a benzodiazepine, is most often administered.
- Medications discussed are those that have injectable dosage forms. There are other antipsychotics in liquids or disintegrating tablet forms that would work as well in the appropriate patient.

DIAGNOSTIC WORKUP

- Mental status exam to rule out contributing mental illness to psychiatric emergency
- Physical exam to rule out physical explanation for psychiatric emergency
- Laboratory evaluation:
  - *WBC*—to look for infectious contribution
  - *Serum electrolytes, creatinine, BUN*—to rule out electrolyte abnormalities such as hyponatremia, dehydration, and renal insufficiency, which can contribute to agitation
  - *Liver function tests*—hepatic encephalopathy and hyperammonemia can present with agitation and aggression
  - *Toxicologic analysis of serum and urine*—substance abuse contribution to emergency
  - *Neuroimaging (CT/MRI)*—rule out stroke, tumor
  - *EEG*—if seizure disorder suspected

MEDICAL/LEGAL PITFALLS

- Involuntary administration of psychotropic medications is allowed in emergencies that are considered life threatening. Wide variations exist in the legal definition of life threatening and in the practice of administering involuntary medication.
- Timely documentation of the need for restraint and involuntary medication is essential.
- Informed consent: The most important element of informed consent is the assessment of decisional capacity, e.g., through the use of the Mini-Mental State Examination.

- If the patient is suffering from either an organic or a functional acute change in mental status and is a danger to self or others, then the patient should undergo emergency medical evaluation. If the patient will not voluntarily submit to this evaluation, then a request for an emergency medical evaluation from a judge, justice of the peace, or police officer is obtained.
- Chemical or physical restraints may be necessary in the combative patient. Chemical restraints typically include benzodiazepines and/or antipsychotics. Physical restraints include soft restraints, leather restraints, and handcuffs and foot chains placed by police.
  - Protocols for restraints will vary by community.
  - Physical restraints should be used in the least restrictive manner and for the least amount of time possible.
  - As required by the Joint Commission, institutions must have policies in place that deal with the use of restraints.
- A person with capacity cannot be confined or restrained against his or her will. Doing so can lead to a legal charge of false imprisonment or battery.
- Duty to warn:
  - Requires a clinician to warn a person who may be in danger from a combative patient
  - Failure to do so may make the clinician liable for injury to the third party

CLASS	DRUG
Benzodiazepines (BZDs)	
	lorazepam (*Ativan*)
	midazolam (*Versed*)
First-Generation (Typical) Antipsychotics	
	haloperidol (*Haldol*)
	droperidol (*Inapsine*)
Second-Generation (Atypical) Antipsychotics	
	aripiprazole (*Abilify*)
	olanzapine (*Zyprexa*)
	ziprasidone (*Geodon*)
Antihistamine	
	cyproheptadine (*Periactin*)
Skeletal Muscle Relaxant	
	dantrolene (*Dantrium*)
Dopamine Agonist	
	bromocriptine (*Parlodel*)

Class: Benzodiazepines (BZDs)

lorazepam   *Ativan*

AVAILABLE FORMS: Tablet, oral liquid, injectable

DOSAGE: 0.5–2 mg PO, IM, IV

ADMINISTRATION: q1 hr PO, IM, or IV; dilute with equal volume of compatible diluent. Rate of injection should not exceed 2 mg/min. Good IM absorption

DRUG INTERACTIONS: Few drug–drug interactions; no involvement of the cytochrome P450 system. CNS depressant effects will be increased with co-administration of alcohol, barbiturates, antipsychotics, anxiolytics, narcotic analgesics, anesthetics, or anticonvulsants. Valproic acid and probenecid may decrease the metabolism of lorazepam

PHARMACOKINETICS:
Absorption: 90% bioavailable
Onset: IM, 15–30 min; IV, 5–20 min; PO, 30–60 min
Duration: ~8 hr
Metabolism: Hepatic; 85% protein binding
Half-life: 13 hr

PRECAUTIONS:
- Loss of consciousness
- Combination with other CNS depressants may lead to respiratory depression
- Caution must be exercised in patients with compromised respiratory function or renal or hepatic impairment

PATIENT AND FAMILY EDUCATION:
- Do not increase dose or frequency.
- May cause physical or psychological dependence
- Do not use alcohol or other prescription or OTC medications such as pain medicines, sedatives, antihistamines, or hypnotics without consulting prescriber
- Do not get pregnant or breast feed

SPECIAL POPULATIONS:
- *Elderly:* Elderly or debilitated may be more susceptible to sedative effects. Initial dose not to exceed 2 mg.
- *Pregnancy:* Pregnancy category D.
- *Lactation:* Breast feeding not recommended.

midazolam   *Versed*

AVAILABLE FORMS: Syrup (liquid); injectable

DOSAGE: IM, 0.07–0.08 mg/kg; usual dose, 5 mg IM; IV, 0.02–0.04 mg/kg every 5 min prn up to 0.1–0.2 mg/kg; PO, 0.25–0.5 mg/kg as single dose; max, 20 mg (PO not recommended for emergency use)

ADMINISTRATION: IM, IV, PO

DRUG INTERACTIONS: Substrate of CYP3A4 (major). Avoid concomitant use with efavirenz, protease inhibitors, fluconazole, isoniazid, macrolide antibiotics, propofol, and certain statins. Avoid grapefruit juice with oral syrup.

PHARMACOKINETICS:
Absorption: Oral = rapid
Onset: IM, 15 min; IV, 1–5 min; PO, 30–60 min
Duration: Mean = 2 hr; up to 6 hr
Metabolism: Hepatic via CYP3A4; 95% protein binding
Half-life: 1–4 hr; prolonged in cirrhosis, CHF, obesity, elderly

PRECAUTIONS:
- Loss of consciousness
- May cause severe respiratory depression or apnea; appropriate resuscitative equipment must be available

(cont.)

midazolam (cont.)

- Titrate dose cautiously
- Decrease dose by 30% if narcotics or other CNS depressants are given. Caution must be exercised in patients with compromised respiratory function or renal or hepatic impairment

PATIENT AND FAMILY EDUCATION:
- Avoid use of alcohol or prescription or OTC sedatives; driving; or tasks that require alertness for a minimum of 24 hr after administration.

- There may be some loss of memory following administration.

SPECIAL POPULATIONS:
- *Elderly:* Elderly or debilitated may be more susceptible to the sedative effects. Use conservative dosing.
- *Pregnancy:* Pregnancy category D.
- *Lactation:* No breast feeding for 24 hr after administration.
- *Other:* Obese patients may have prolonged action.

Class: First-Generation (Typical) Antipsychotics

Haldol   **haloperidol**

AVAILABLE FORMS: Tablets, liquid concentrate; injectable

DOSAGE: 5–10 mg IM or IV q30 min prn (EKG monitoring recommended with IV use); 5–10 mg PO. Average total dose for rapid tranquilization 10–20 mg

ADMINISTRATION: IM, IV, PO, avoid diluting liquid with coffee or tea

DRUG INTERACTIONS: Dopamine agonists may diminish therapeutic effect. Carbamazepine increases metabolism of haloperidol. Caution must be exercised with other agents that prolong QT interval with IV haloperidol. Haloperidol is a CYP2D6 inhibitor.

PHARMACOKINETICS:
Absorption: Injection, 100%; oral, 60–70%
Onset: IM and IV, 30–60 min
Duration: 2–6 hr
Metabolism: Hepatic 50–60% glucuronidation
Half-life: 18 hr

PRECAUTIONS:
- Keep patient recumbent for at least 30 min following injection to minimize hypotensive effects
- No respiratory depression.
- May alter cardiac conduction and prolong QT interval
- Risk of EPS and tardive dyskinesia and hyperprolactinemia
- Seizures
- Excessive sedation

PATIENT AND FAMILY EDUCATION:
- Maintain adequate hydration
- Avoid contact (liquid) with skin; may cause contact dermatitis
- Do not take within 2 hr of antacid

SPECIAL POPULATIONS:
- *Elderly:* Elderly patients are at an increased risk of death compared with placebo.
- *Pregnancy:* Pregnancy category C.
- *Lactation:* Breast feeding not recommended.
- *Other:* Use with caution in patients with myasthenia gravis, Parkinson's disease, and seizures.

Inapsine   **droperidol**

AVAILABLE FORMS: Solution for injection

DOSAGE: Initial, 0.625–2.5 mg; additional doses of 1.25 mg may be given to desired effect

ADMINISTRATION: IM, IV (slowly)

DRUG INTERACTIONS: Caution with other agents that prolong QTc interval. Avoid use with artemether, dronedarone, lumefantrine, metoclopramide, nilotinib, pimozide, quinine, tetrabenazine, thioridazine, and ziprasidone.

PHARMACOKINETICS:
Absorption: Injection 100%
Onset: 30 min
Duration: 2–4 hr
Metabolism: Hepatic; extensive protein binding
Half-life: 2–3 hr

PRECAUTIONS:
- Risk of QT prolongation and torsades de pointes

- Limit use to prevention of surgical nausea and vomiting
- Usage outside of labeled indication not recommended
- Excessive sedations
- Seizures

PATIENT AND FAMILY EDUCATION:
- May cause orthostatic hypotension. Use caution when changing from lying to sitting position.
- Immediately report any palpitations, confusion, loss of thought processes, and respiratory difficulty.

SPECIAL POPULATIONS:
- *Elderly:* Caution in elderly due to increased risk of adverse reactions.
- *Pregnancy:* Pregnancy category C.
- *Lactation:* Breast feeding not recommended.

Class: Second-Generation (Atypical) Antipsychotics

aripiprazole   *Abilify*

AVAILABLE FORMS: Tablets, orally disintegrating tablet, liquid concentrate; injectable. Injectable used in emergency situations.

DOSAGE: *Aggression:* IM 9.75 mg as a single dose (range 5.25–15 mg). Repeated doses may be given at >2 hr intervals to max of 30 mg/day; *bipolar acute*: oral, 15 mg once daily

ADMINISTRATION: IM or PO; do not administer IV or SC; inject slowly into deep muscle mass

DRUG INTERACTIONS: Major substrate of CYP2D6 and 3A4. Caution with other CYP2D6 inhibitors or CYP3A4 inhibitors. Avoid with metoclopramide. May increase effects of alcohol, CNS depressants, and methylphenidate.

PHARMACOKINETICS:
Absorption: IM, 100%; PO, 87%
Onset: IM, 1 hr; PO, 1–3 weeks

Duration: 2 hr for injectable
Metabolism: Hepatic 50–60% glucuronidation
Half-life: 75 hr

PRECAUTIONS: Cardiovascular disease; dementia; seizures; Parkinson's disease; sedation

PATIENT AND FAMILY EDUCATION:
- Oral disintegrating tablet contains phenylalanine
- Avoid alcohol. Maintain adequate hydration; caution when changing position from lying to sitting

SPECIAL POPULATIONS:
- *Elderly:* Elderly patients should be administered the lower end of the dosing range.
- *Pregnancy:* Pregnancy category C.
- *Lactation:* Excretion in breast milk unknown/breast-feeding not recommended

olanzapine   *Zyprexa*

AVAILABLE FORMS: Tablets, orally disintegrating tablet, powder for solution injection, powder for injection extended-release formulation (not for acute use)

DOSAGE: *Acute agitation:* 5–10 mg IM may repeat in 2–4 hr; max, 30 mg (2.5 mg if clinical factors warrant); *bipolar mania (acute)*: 10–15 mg PO qd

ADMINISTRATION: IM or PO; inject slowly IM deep into muscle; not for IV administration; see Precautions.

DRUG INTERACTIONS: Concurrent use of IM/IV BZD is not recommended. Major substrate of CYP1A2; caution with CYP1A2 inhibitors or inducers. Avoid with metoclopramide. May increase effects of alcohol, CNS depressants, and methylphenidate. Levels of olanzapine may be increased by fluvoxamine, lamotrigine, and tetrabenazine. Levels may be decreased by smoking and other CYP1A2 inducers.

PHARMACOKINETICS:
Absorption: IM, 100%; PO, well absorbed
Onset: IM, 15–45 min; PO, 6 hr

Duration: 2 hr for injectable
Metabolism: Via CYP1A2 (major) and CYP2D6 (minor) + direct glucuronidation
Half-life: 21–54 hr

PRECAUTIONS: Postinjection delirium/sedation syndrome; cardiac conduction alterations; anticholinergic effects, cerebrovascular events, EPS, NMS, orthostatic hypotension, temperature regulation, and sedation, seizures.

PATIENT AND FAMILY EDUCATION
- Oral disintegrating tablet contains phenylalanine
- Avoid alcohol. Maintain adequate hydration; caution when changing position from lying to sitting

SPECIAL POPULATIONS:
- *Elderly:* Elderly patients should be administered the lower end of the dosing range.
- *Pregnancy:* Pregnancy category C.
- *Lactation:* Breastfeeding is not recommended. Breast-fed infant may be exposed to 2% of the maternal dose.

ziprasidone   *Geodon*

AVAILABLE FORMS: Capsule; powder for reconstitution

DOSAGE: *Acute agitation*: 10 mg IM q2 hr or 20 mg q4 hr; max: 40 mg/day; *bipolar mania (acute)*: 40 mg PO bid with food

ADMINISTRATION: IM or PO

DRUG INTERACTIONS: Avoid concomitant use with dronedarone, artemether, lumefantrine, metoclopramide, nilotinib, primozide, quinine,

thioridazine, tetrabenazine, and QTc-prolonging agents

PHARMACOKINETICS:
Absorption: IM, 100%; must be given orally with food to obtain 60% bioavailability
Onset: IM, < 1 hr; PO, 6–8 hr
Duration: 2 hr for injectable
Metabolism: Hepatic via aldehyde oxidase, less than 1/3 is via cytochrome P450 system
Half-life: 2–7 hr

(cont.)

ziprasidone (*cont.*)

PRECAUTIONS: Contraindicated with a history of prolonged QT
- Congenital long QT syndrome, recent MI, uncompensated heart failure, or other QTc-prolonging agents
- EPS, NMS, temperature regulation, dementia class warning, electrolyte imbalance
- Use IM formulation with caution in patients with renal impairment due to accumulation of cyclodextrin
- Seizures, excessive sedation

PATIENT AND FAMILY EDUCATION:
- Take oral formulation with food.
- Avoid alcohol. Maintain adequate hydration; caution when changing position from lying to sitting

SPECIAL POPULATIONS:
- *Elderly:* Elderly patients should be administered the lower end of the dosing range.
- *Pregnancy:* Pregnancy category C.
- *Lactation:* Excretion in breast milk unknown/breast-feeding not recommended.

Class: Antihistamines
Periactin   **cyproheptadine**

AVAILABLE FORMS: Tablets

DOSAGE: 12 mg PO followed by 2 mg q2 hr until symptoms improve

ADMINISTRATION: PO; take with food to avoid GI distress

DRUG INTERACTIONS: No interactions to avoid concomitant use

PHARMACOKINETICS:
Absorption: Complete
Metabolism: Hepatic
Half-life: 1–4 hr

PRECAUTIONS:
- Contraindicated in narrow-angle glaucoma
- Concurrent use of MAOIs

- Bladder neck obstruction, GI obstruction
- May cause CNS depression

PATIENT AND FAMILY EDUCATION: Avoid use with other depressants, sleep-inducing medications unless approved by prescriber. Possible dizziness and drowsiness (caution when driving or engaging in tasks requiring alertness)

SPECIAL POPULATIONS:
- *Elderly:* May be inappropriate in the elderly due to anticholinergic effects although for short-term use, weigh risk versus benefit.
- *Pregnancy:* Pregnancy category B.
- *Lactation:* Excretion in breast milk unknown.
- *Outcome:* Symptoms improve in 24 hr although mental confusion can last for several days.

Class: Skeletal Muscle Relaxants
Dantrium   **dantrolene**

USE: It is a direct-acting skeletal muscle relaxant. There is a risk of hepatotoxicity

AVAILABLE FORMS: Capsules; powder for reconstitution (contains mannitol)

DOSAGE: *NMS:* IV, 1 mg/kg; may repeat up to a maximum cumulative dose of 10 mg/kg; then switch to oral therapy. Use for up to 10 days

ADMINISTRATION: IV or PO; use within 6 hr of reconstitution

DRUG INTERACTIONS: No interactions but it is recommended to avoid concomitant use. Dantrolene may increase the effects of alcohol, CNS depressants. Levels of dantrolene may be increased by CYP3A4 inhibitors and decreased by strong CYP3A4 inducers

PHARMACOKINETICS:
Absorption: IV: 100%; PO: slow but complete

Onset: IV, immediate; PO, 6 hr
Metabolism: CYP3A4 substrate
Half-life: 8.7 hr

PRECAUTIONS: Active hepatic disease; IV administration requires cardiac monitoring; extravasation monitoring

PATIENT AND FAMILY EDUCATION:
- Do not use alcohol, prescription or OTC antidepressants, or sedatives or pain medications without consulting prescriber.
- Drowsiness, dizziness, and lightheadedness (avoid driving or engaging in tasks that require alertness)

SPECIAL POPULATIONS:
- *Pregnancy:* Pregnancy category C.
- *Lactation:* Breast-feeding is not recommended

Class: Dopamine Agonists

bromocriptine	*Parlodel*

USE: Dopamine agonist, restores dopaminergic tone.

AVAILABLE FORMS: Tablets

DOSAGE: PO, 2.5–10 mg q6–8 hr. Continue therapy until NMS is controlled, then taper slowly. Maximum dose is 40 mg/day

ADMINISTRATION: PO; take with food to avoid GI distress

DRUG INTERACTIONS: Avoid concomitant use with efavirenz, itraconazole, posaconazole, protease inhibitors, serotonin 5HT1D agonists; sibutramine; voriconazole
- Major substrate of CYP3A4. Caution with other CYP3A4 strong inducers or inhibitors

PHARMACOKINETICS:
Absorption: 28% bioavailable
Onset: 1–3 hr

Metabolism: Via CYP3A4 (major)
Half-life: 15 hr

PRECAUTIONS:
- Contraindicated with potent inhibitors of CYP3A4
- Patients with cardiac valvular fibrosis and other CV disease
- May cause impulse control disorders. Increased risk of melanoma

PATIENT AND FAMILY EDUCATION: Do not discontinue this medicine without consulting prescriber. Take with meals to avoid GI distress. Urine or perspiration may appear darker

SPECIAL POPULATIONS:
- *Pregnancy*: Pregnancy category B
- *Location*: Breast-feeding is not recommended
- *Outcome*: Mortality is estimated between 10% and 20%. Recovery is approx. 2 weeks

Guidelines

Annals of Emergency Medicine

HIGHLIGHTS OF TREATMENT
- Use a benzodiazepine (lorazepam [*Ativan*]) or midazolam (*Versed*) or a typical antipsychotic *Inapsine* (droperidol) or *Haldol* (haloperidol) as effective monotherapy for the initial treatment of the acutely agitated, undifferentiated patient in the ED.
- If rapid sedation is required, use droperidol instead of haloperidol.

- Use an antipsychotic (typical or atypical) as effective monotherapy for both management of agitation and initial drug therapy for the patient with known psychiatric illness where antipsychotics are indicated.
- Use a combination of an oral benzodiazepine (lorazepam) and an oral antipsychotic (*Risperdal*; risperidone) for agitated but cooperative patients.

American Psychiatric Association

HIGHLIGHTS OF TREATMENT
- When sedation is indicated and the patient is unwilling to accept oral medication, IM injection of a typical (haloperidol 5 mg) or atypical antipsychotic (i.e., ziprasidone [*Geodon*] 10 mg IM) can be given with or without a concomitant dose of 1–2 mg of oral or IM lorazepam.

- ▶ **Alert:** If olanzapine (*Zyprexa*) IM is used, concomitant benzodiazepines should NOT be given due to increased fatalities from cardiorespiratory depression.
- Droperidol (*Inapsine*) 2.5–5.0 mg IM can be used in selected situations of extreme emergency or in highly agitated patients.

Expert Consensus Guidelines

TREATMENT OF BEHAVIORAL EMERGENCIES: HIGHLIGHTS OF TREATMENT
- Support the use of oral formulations (liquid concentrate, rapidly dissolving tablets) of atypical antipsychotics as first-line therapy for the

initial management of agitation or aggression in the emergency setting. Provide faster times to peak concentration.
- Reserve IM injections for patients unable to cooperate with oral therapy.

Other Medical Emergencies in Psychiatry

Delirium

Clinical Presentation: A condition of impaired attention, changes in behavior, and a clouded sensorium, which follows a waxing and waning course. The patient may be agitated, disoriented, and confused. It is a disturbance of attention not a disturbance of memory. It is acute in onset and may have concomitant neurologic disturbances such as tremor, increased muscle tone, visual hallucinations, and impaired speech.

Etiology: Delirium is often caused by changes in acetylcholine balance. It can be caused by medications such as anticholinergics, narcotics, or steroids, or an underlying medical condition such as a urinary tract infection, liver failure, drug or alcohol abuse, or electrolyte/metabolic abnormalities. People with delirium need immediate medical attention.

Incidence: It occurs in 30% of all elderly medical patients. The risk of delirium increases for people who are demented, dehydrated, and taking drugs that affect the nervous system.

Treatment: Treatment depends on the condition causing the delirium. The underlying medical condition should be treated first. Eliminate or change medications that can worsen confusion or that are unnecessary. Medications may be needed to control aggressive or agitated behaviors. These are usually started at very low doses and adjusted as needed. Most often antipsychotics and sedatives are selected but should be titrated slowly in the elderly and selected to target the symptom. It should be kept in mind that benzodiazepine usage in the elderly can worsen confusion and delirium.

Outcome: Delirium often lasts about 1 week although it may take several weeks for mental function to return to normal levels. Full recovery is common.

Neuroleptic Malignant Syndrome (NMS)

Clinical Presentation: NMS is a rare but life-threatening neurologic emergency associated with the use of antipsychotic agents and characterized by a clinical syndrome of mental status change, rigidity, fever, and dysautonomia. Mortality results from systemic complications and dysautonomia. The cardinal features include muscular rigidity, hyperthermia, autonomic dysfunction, and altered consciousness. Rigidity and akinesia usually develop initially or concomitantly with a temperature elevation as high as 41°C. Autonomic dysfunction includes tachycardia, labile BP, diaphoresis, dyspnea, and urinary incontinence. Creatine kinase, CBC, and LFTs are usually increased. Symptoms develop over 24–72 hr.

Etiology: The cause of NMS is unknown but is thought to be related to central dopamine blockade. The risk appears to be lower for the atypical antipsychotics than for the typical.

Incidence: It occurs in 0.2–3.2% of patients. Most patients are young adults, but the disease has been described in all age groups. It can occur hours to months after initial drug exposure.

Treatment: Discontinue any neuroleptic agent or precipitating drug. Maintain cardiorespiratory and euvolemic stability. Benzodiazepines can be used for agitation. Lower fever using cooling blankets.

Serotonin Syndrome

It is a potential life-threatening syndrome associated with increased serotonergic activity in the CNS, such as from the combination of an selective serotonin reuptake inhibitor and an MAOI. Can be seen with therapeutic use, drug interactions, or intentional self-poisoning. Classically, it is a triad of mental status changes, autonomic hyperactivity, and neuromuscular abnormalities. It is a clinical diagnosis; no laboratory test can confirm the diagnosis.

Clinical Presentation: It can manifest a wide range of clinical symptoms from mild tremor to life-threatening hyperthermia and shock. Examination findings can include hyperthermia, agitation, ocular clonus, tremor, akathisia, deep tendon hyperreflexia, inducible or spontaneous clonus, muscle rigidity, dilated pupils, dry mucous membranes, increased bowel sounds, flushed skin, and diaphoresis. Neuromuscular findings are typically more pronounced in the lower extremities.

Etiology: It occurs due to increased serotonin in the CNS. Postsynaptic 5HT1A and 5HT2A receptors are implicated. Occurs most commonly with the concomitant use of serotonergic drugs, with drugs that impair metabolism of serotonin including MAOIs or with antipsychotics or other dopamine antagonists.

Treatment: Discontinue serotonergic agents. Provide supportive care such as IV fluids for hydration and benzodiazepines for agitation, myoclonus, hyperreflexia, and hyperthermia.

Specific agents: Periactin (cyproheptadine) is an antihistamine with serotonergic antagonist properties. It should be considered in moderate to severe cases.

Treatment of Mood Disorders

Bipolar Disorders

OVERVIEW

- Characterized by episodic fluctuations in mood, including one or more episodes of mania or hypomania.
- *DSM-IV-TR* considers mood disorders as a spectrum of disorders and includes bipolar I, bipolar II, and bipolar disorder not otherwise specified.
- Bipolar I disorder includes at least one episode of mania or mixed mood. Bipolar II disorder includes at least one episode of hypomania and one episode of major depression. Cyclothymia includes hypomanic episodes with periods of low-grade depression.
- Patients presenting with depressive symptoms or elevated mood should be evaluated for bipolar disorder. Depressive episodes in patients with both bipolar I and bipolar II may result in misdiagnosis of MDD.
- Lifetime incidence of bipolar I disorder in the USA is 1.0–2.4%. Lifetime incidence of bipolar II disorder is 0.2–5%.
- Common comorbidities include anxiety and substance abuse.
- Individuals with bipolar type I disorder are thought to have a prognosis similar to those with the bipolar subtype of schizoaffective disorder.
- Diagnostic work-up includes a complete physical examination, thorough mental status examination including mood disorder questionnaire and laboratory studies (CBC, rapid plasma reagent, thyroid function, UA, pregnancy test if female and of childbearing age, lipid panel, HIV test). Abnormal neurologic findings if any, may be indicated by a CT or MRI, and/or EEG. Psychological testing may assist with diagnosis.
- Differential diagnosis includes: psychotic disorder due to a general medical condition (delirium or dementia), substance-induced psychotic disorder, substance-induced delirium, schizophrenia, schizoaffective disorder, and major depression with psychotic symptoms.
- Common ICD-9 codes used for diagnosed bipolar disorder include: 296.5 (Bipolar I disorder, most recent episode [or current] depressed; 296.6, (Bipolar I disorder, most recent episode [or current] mixed; 296.7 (Bipolar I disorder, most recent episode [or current] unspecified; and 296.8 (other and unspecified bipolar disorders).

Psychopharmacology of Bipolar Disorder

OVERVIEW

- *Mood stabilizers*, including mood-stabilizing anticonvulsants and lithium, are identified as first-line treatment approaches. Lithium is recommended for bipolar depression. Mood-stabilizing anticonvulsants (e.g., valproate) are preferred for rapid cycling disorders.
- For patients unresponsive to monotherapy, a combination of lithium plus mood-stabilizing anticonvulsant or mood-stabilizer plus atypical antipsychotic may be considered.
- Hypomanic episodes and mild depressive episodes are generally managed with a single mood stabilizer. Acute manic and severe depressive episodes often require two or three medications.
- A benzodiazepine (e.g., diazepam or lorazepam) may be considered as an adjunct short-term treatment for reducing insomnia or agitation.
- Use of antidepressants by primary care providers for treating bipolar patients should be avoided. Antidepressant monotherapy may precipitate mania or induce rapid cycling disorders between mania and depression.
- Dosage adjustments may be required if the patient experiences a partial response or breakthrough symptoms.
- Electroconvulsive therapy (ECT) may be considered for treatment-resistant or severe mania. In general, mood stabilizer treatment has produced better outcomes than ECT.

BIPOLAR DISORDERS

CLASS	DRUG
Mood-Stabilizing Anticonvulsants	**First-Line Drug Therapy**
	valproate sodium, valproic acid, divalproex sodium (*Depacon, Depakene, Depakote, Depakote ER, Depakote Sprinkle*) carbamazepine (*Tegretol, Carbatrol, Tegretol XR*) topiramate (*Topamax*) lamotrigine (*Lamictal, Lamictal XR*)
Non-Anticonvulsant Mood Stabilizer	**First-Line Drug Therapy for Bipolar Depression**
	lithium (*Eskalith, Lithobid*)
Atypical Antipsychotics (Second Generation)	
	aripiprazole (*Abilify*) olanzapine (*Zyprexa*) risperidone (*Risperdal, Risperdal Consta*) quetiapine (*Seroquel, Seroquel XR*) ziprasidone (*Geodon*)

Class: Mood-Stabilizing Anticonvulsants

valproate sodium, valproic acid, divalproex sodium — *Depacon, Depakene, Depakote, Depakote ER, Depakote Sprinkle*

AVAILABLE FORMS: *Valproate sodium:* Syrup, 250 mg/5 mL; capsule, 250 mg; tablet (extended release), 250 and 500 mg. *Divalproex sodium*: Capsule (sprinkle), 125 mg; tablet (delayed-release), 125, 250 and 500 mg; tablet (extended-release), 250 and 500 mg

DOSAGE: *Adults:* Initially, 750 mg *Depakote* daily PO in divided doses, or 25 mg/kg *Depakote ER* once daily. Adjust dosage based on patient's response; maximum dose of 60 mg/kg daily.

ADMINISTRATION:
- Give PO drug with food or milk to reduce adverse GI effects.
- Do not mix syrup with carbonated beverages as the mixture may be irritating to oral mucosa.
- Capsules may be swallowed whole or opened and contents sprinkled on a teaspoonful of soft food. Patient should swallow the capsule immediately without chewing.
- Monitor drug level, and adjust dosage as needed.

SIDE EFFECTS:
- *CNS:* Asthenia, dizziness, headache, insomnia, nervousness, somnolence, tremor, abnormal thinking, amnesia, ataxia, depression, emotional upset, fever, sedation.
- *CV:* Chest pain, edema, hypertension, hypotension, tachycardia.
- *EENT:* Blurred vision, diplopia, nystagmus, pharyngitis, rhinitis, tinnitus
- *GI:* Abdominal pain, anorexia, diarrhea, dyspepsia, nausea, vomiting, pancreatitis, constipation, increased appetite.
- *Hematologic:* Bone marrow suppression, hemorrhage, thrombocytopenia, bruising, petechiae.
- *Hepatic:* Hepatotoxicity.
- *Metabolic:* Hyperammonemia, weight gain.
- *Musculoskeletal:* Back and neck pain.
- *Respiratory:* Bronchitis, dyspnea.
- *Skin:* Alopecia, flu syndrome, infection, erythema multiforme, hypersensitivity reactions, Stevens-Johnson syndrome, rash, photosensitivity reactions, pruritus

DRUG INTERACTIONS: Aspirin, chlorpromazine, clonazepam, topiramate, cimetidine, erythromycin, felbamate, carbamazepine, lamotrigine, phenobarbital, phenytoin, rifampin, warfarin, zidovudine. Alcohol use is discouraged.

PHARMACOKINETICS:
Peak action: Oral, between 15 min and 4 hr. Facilitates the effects of the inhibitory neurotransmitter GABA.
Half-life: 6–16 hr

PRECAUTIONS:
- May increase ammonia, ALT, AST, and bilirubin lab levels.
- May increase eosinophil count and bleeding time. May decrease platelet, RBC, and WBC.
- May cause false-positive results for urine ketone levels.
- Contraindicated in patients hypersensitive to the drug, with hepatic disease or significant hepatic dysfunction, and, with a UCD.
- Safety and efficacy of *Depakote ER* in children less than 10 years have not been established.
- Obtain liver function test results, platelet count, and PT and INR before starting therapy, and monitor these values periodically.
- Adverse reactions may not be caused by valproic acid alone because it is usually used with other anticonvulsants.
- When changing the drug from *Depakote* to *Depakote ER* for adults and children aged 10 and above with seizures, ensure that the extended-release dose is 8–20% higher than the regular dose administered previously. The manufacturer's PI should be checked for more details.

(cont.)

valproate sodium, valproic acid, divalproex sodium (cont.)

- Divalproex sodium has a lower risk of adverse GI reactions.
- Never withdraw a drug suddenly as this may worsen seizures. Call the prescriber at once if adverse reactions develop.
- Patients at high risk for hepatotoxicity include those with congenital metabolic disorders, mental retardation, or organic brain disease; those taking multiple anticonvulsants; and children younger than 2 years of age.
- Notify the prescriber if tremors occur; a dosage reduction may be needed.
- weight gain is common. Monitor BMI and assess for pre-diabetes and dyslipidemia.
- sedation is common.
- When changing the drug from a brand-name to a generic one for patients, caution must be exercised as breakthrough seizures may occur.
- May cause thrombocytopenia or tremors

▶**Alert:** Sometimes fatal, hyperammonemic encephalopathy may occur when starting valproate therapy in patients with UCD. Evaluate patients with UCD risk factors before starting valproate therapy. Patients who develop symptoms of unexplained hyperammonemic encephalopathy during valproate therapy should stop taking the drug, undergo prompt appropriate treatment, and be evaluated for underlying UCD.

▶**Alert:** Fatal hepatotoxicity may follow nonspecific symptoms, such as malaise, fever, and lethargy. If these symptoms occur during therapy, notify the prescriber at once because the patient who might be developing hepatic dysfunction must stop taking the drug.

▶**Alert:** Life-threatening pancreatitis has been reported following initiation of therapy as well as after prolonged use. Monitor the patient for developing symptoms and discontinue treatment if pancreatitis is suspected.

PATIENT AND FAMILY EDUCATION:
- Take the drug with food or milk to reduce adverse GI effects.
- It may take several weeks or longer to optimize mood stabilizing effects
- Capsules may either be swallowed whole or carefully opened and contents sprinkled on a teaspoonful of soft food. Swallow the capsule immediately without chewing.
- Keep drugs out of children's reach.
- Warn about the consequences of stopping drug therapy abruptly.
- Avoid driving and indulging in other potentially hazardous activities that require mental alertness until the drug's effects on the CNS are known.
- Call the prescriber if malaise, weakness, lethargy, facial swelling, loss of appetite, or vomiting occurs.
- Instruct women to inform the prescriber if they become pregnant or have plans to start a family during the course of therapy.

SPECIAL POPULATIONS:
- *Elderly:* Caution is advised when using this drug in the elderly due to more sensitivity to the drug. Initiate treatment at a lower dose and then escalate the dose more slowly.
- *Pregnancy:* Category D. This medication should only be used when required utmost during pregnancy as the drug is secreted into breast milk. Increased risk of neural tube defects (1 in 20) and other major birth defects have been reported, especially when the fetus is exposed during first 12 weeks of pregnancy.
- *Children:* Caution must be exercised when using this drug in a child or adolescent as a balance must be established between the potential risks and the clinical need. The drug is not recommended for use in children or adolescents under 18 years of age who are suffering from bipolar disorder.

Tegretol, Carbatrol, Tegretol XR   **carbamazepine**

AVAILABLE FORMS: Tablet, 200 and 400 mg; chewable tablet, 100 mg; XR capsule, 100, 200 and 400 mg; oral suspension, 100 mg/5 mL

DOSAGES: *Adults:* 400 mg/day in divided doses for initial therapy. Increase the dosage by 200 mg/day to a maximum of 1,600 mg/day. Increase dosage based on blood levels to achieve optimum dosage. *Elderly:* May be initiated at a lower dose and the dosage gradually increased.

ADMINISTRATION:
- Store the oral suspension and tablets at room temperature.
- Give with meals to reduce the risk of GI distress.
- Shake the oral suspension well.
- Do not administer with grapefruit juice
- Do not crush the extended-release capsules or tablets.

SIDE EFFECTS:
- Drowsiness; dizziness; nausea; vomiting; visual abnormalities; dry mouth; tongue irritation; headache; fluid retention; diaphoresis; constipation; behavioral changes in children

DRUG INTERACTIONS:
- May decrease effects of anticoagulants, clarithromycin, dilitiazem, erythromycin, estrogens, propoxyphene, quinidine, and steroids.
- May increase CNS depressant effects of antipsychotic medications, haloperidol, and TCAs.
- May increase metabolism of other anticonvulsants, barbiturates, benzodiazepines, and valproic acid.
- Cimetidine, itraconazole, ketoconazole, and isoniazid may increase serum concentration and toxicity of the drug.

(cont.)

BIPOLAR DISORDERS: Mood-Stabilizing Anticonvulsants

carbamazepine (cont.)

- May increase the metabolism of isoniazid.
- MAOIs may cause seizures and hypertensive crisis.

PHARMACOKINETICS:
Onset: 3–5 weeks
Peak: 1.5 hr (oral suspension); 4–5 hr (tablets); metabolized in the liver by CYP3A4
Half-life: 25–60 hr

PRECAUTIONS:
Contraindications:
- Concomitant use of MAOIs
- History of myelosuppression
- Hypersensitivity to TCAs

Cautions:
- Mental illness
- Increased IOP
- Cardiac/hepatic/renal impairment

PATIENT AND FAMILY EDUCATION:
- Do not abruptly discontinue this drug after long-term use.
- Avoid tasks that require alertness and motor skills until response to the drug is established.
- Report visual disturbances.
- Report the results for frequent blood tests during the first 3 months of therapy and at monthly intervals thereafter for 2–3 years.
- Do not take oral suspension simultaneously with other liquid medicine.
- Do not take with grapefruit juice.

SPECIAL POPULATIONS:
- *Elderly:* More susceptible to confusion, agitation, AV block, bradycardia, and syndrome of inappropriate antidiuretic hormone.
- *Pregnancy/Lactation:* Category D: Positive evidence of human fetal harm. Patients should discontinue prior to anticipated pregnancy. Crosses placenta. Distributed in breast milk. Accumulates in fetal tissue.
- *Children:* Behavioral changes more likely to occur

topiramate   *Topamax*

AVAILABLE FORMS: Tablet, 25, 50, 100 and 200 mg; sprinkle capsule, 15 and 25 mg

DOSAGE:
- *Adults:* 25–50 mg/day for 1 week initially, then increase by 25–50 mg/day at weekly intervals. Usual maintenance dose, 100–200 mg twice per day
- *Elderly:* 25–50 mg/day for 1 week initially, then increase by 25–50 mg/day at weekly intervals. Usual maintenance dose is 100–200 mg twice per day

ADMINISTRATION:
- Do not break tablets.
- Give irrespective of meal timings.
- Capsules may be swallowed whole or contents sprinkled on a teaspoonful of soft food and swallowed immediately. Do not chew.

SIDE EFFECTS: Drowsiness; dizziness; ataxia; nystagmus; diplopia; paresthesia; nausea; tremor; confusion; dyspepsia; depression; weight loss; mood disturbances

DRUG INTERACTIONS:
- Alcohol and other CNS depressants may increase CNS depression.
- Carbamazepine, phenytoin, and valproic acid may decrease serum concentration.
- Carbonic anhydrase inhibitors may increase risk of renal calculi formation.
- May decrease the effectiveness of oral contraceptives.

PHARMACOKINETICS:
Onset: 4 days
Peak: 2 hr
Duration: 2–3 months
Half-life: 21 hr

PRECAUTIONS:
Contraindications:
- Bipolar disorder

Cautions:
- Sensitivity to topiramate
- Hepatic/renal impairment
- Predisposition to renal calculi

PATIENT AND FAMILY EDUCATION:
- Avoid tasks that require alertness and motor skills until response to drug is established.
- Avoid use of alcohol and other CNS depressants.
- Do not abruptly discontinue this drug.
- Tablet should be swallowed whole.
- Maintain adequate fluid intake.
- Inform the health care provider if blurred vision or eye pain occurs.

SPECIAL POPULATIONS:
- *Elderly:* Dosage adjustment may be required to prevent age-related renal impairment.
- *Pregnancy/Lactation:* Unknown whether it is distributed in breast milk.
- *Children:* Safety and efficacy have not been established in pediatric patients.

BIPOLAR DISORDERS: Mood-Stabilizing Anticonvulsants

Lamictal, Lamictal XR   **lamotrigine**

AVAILABLE FORMS: Tablet, 25, 100, 150, and 200 mg; chewable tablet, 2, 5, and 25 mg

DOSAGE: Starting dose for adults, 25 mg orally every day for 2 weeks, then 50 mg every day for 2 weeks, then 100 mg every day for 1 week. Maximum dose, 200 mg/day.

ADMINISTRATION:
- Discontinue medicine at first sign of a rash.
- This medicine should be taken as directed as it is well-tolerated in the recommended doses. Individuals taking this medicine should carry an identification card with them to alert medical personnel who might be caring for them.
- The potential carcinogenic, mutagenic, and fertility effects are unknown.

SIDE EFFECTS: Common reactions to the drug include dizziness, headache, diplopia, ataxia, asthenia, nausea, blurred vision, somnolence, rhinitis, rash, pharyngitis, vomiting, cough, flu syndrome, dysmenorrheal, incoordination, insomnia, diarrhea, fever, abdominal pain, depression, tremor, anxiety, vaginitis, speech disturbance, seizures, weight loss, photosensitivity, nystagmus, constipation, and dry mouth.

DRUG INTERACTIONS: Avoid using the following drugs with this medicine: oral progesterone contraceptives (may decrease hormonal contraceptive levels), etonogestrel subdermal implant (may decrease hormonal contraceptive levels), ginkgo biloba such as Eun-haeng, fossil tree, ginkyo, icho, ityo, Japanese silver apricot kew tree, maidenhair tree, salisburia, silver apricot (may decrease anticonvulsant efficacy), medroxyprogesterone acetate (may decrease hormonal contraceptive levels), St. John's wort (may decrease lamotrigine levels as clearance is increased).

PHARMACOKINETICS: This drug is metabolized by the liver (CYP450); 94% of it is excreted in the urine and 2% in the feces.
Half-life: 25 hr.

PRECAUTIONS: Caution should be exercised when administering this medicine to patients with suicide risk, pregnancy, hepatic impairment, renal impairment, and hypersensitivity to antiepileptic drugs.

PATIENT AND FAMILY EDUCATION: Do not stop taking this drug abruptly; it must be tapered by the health care provider. If depression symptoms increase, notify the health care provider immediately.

SPECIAL POPULATIONS:
- *Elderly:* Caution should be exercised when administering this drug to the elderly.
- *Impaired renal function:* If creatinine clearance is 10–50, then decrease dose by 25%. If creatinine clearance is less than 10, then give 100 mg every other day. Give 100 mg after dialysis or 100 mg every other day.
- *Impaired liver function:* For moderate to severe impairment, decrease dose by 25%. If severe impairment, decrease the dose by 50%.
- *Pregnancy:* Category C drug. Animal studies show adverse fetal effect(s) but no controlled human studies. It is considered unsafe for breastfeeding mothers. Medication administration requires cessation of breastfeeding.
- *Children:* Serious rashes requiring hospitalization and discontinuance of treatment in patients with Stevens-Johnson syndrome; rare cases of toxic epidermal necrolysis and rash-related deaths. Incidence is 0.8% in children 2–6 years of age and 0.3% in adults. Most life-threatening rashes occur in the first 2–8 weeks of treatment.

Class: Non-Anticonvulsant Mood Stabilizers

Eskalith, Lithobid   **lithium**

AVAILABLE FORMS: Capsule, 150, 300, and 600 mg; slow-release tablet, 300 mg; controlled-release tablet, 300 and 450 mg; syrup, 300 mg (8 mEq/5 mL)

DOSAGE: *Adults:* 300–600 mg/day to qid or 900 mg controlled-release tablets every 12 hr. Increase dosage based on blood levels. Recommended therapeutic lithium levels are 1–1.5 mEq/L for acute mania and 0.6–1.2 mEq/L for maintenance therapy.

ADMINISTRATION:
- PO
- Give the drug after meals with plenty of water to minimize GI upset.
- Do not crush controlled-release tablets.

SIDE EFFECTS:
- *CNS:* Fatigue, lethargy, coma, epileptiform seizures, tremors, drowsiness, headache, confusion, restlessness, dizziness, psychomotor retardation, blackouts, EEG changes, impaired speech, ataxia, incoordination
- *CV:* Arrhythmias, bradycardia, reversible EKG changes, hypotension.
- *EENT:* Tinnitus, blurred vision.
- *GI:* Vomiting, anorexia, diarrhea, thirst, nausea, metallic taste, dry mouth, abdominal pain, flatulence, indigestion.
- *GU:* Polyuria, renal toxicity with long-term use, glycosuria, decreased creatinine clearance, albuminuria.
- *Hematologic:* Leukocytosis with leukocyte count of 14,000 to 18,000/mm.
- *Metabolic:* Transient hyperglycemia, goiter, hypothyroidism, hyponatremia.
- *Musculoskeletal:* Muscle weakness.

(cont.)

lithium (cont.)

- *Skin:* Pruritus, rash, diminished or absent sensation, drying and thinning of hair, psoriasis, acne, alopecia.
- *Other:* Ankle and wrist edema

DRUG INTERACTIONS:

- ACE inhibitors, aminophylline, sodium bicarbonate, urine alkalizers, calcium channel blockers (verapamil), carbamazepine, fluoxetine, methyldopa, NSAIDs, probenecid, neuromuscular blockers, thiazide diuretics.
- Diuretics, especially loop diuretics, may inhibit lithium elimination and increase lithium toxicity.
- Caffeine may decrease lithium levels and drug effects. Advise patients who ingest large amounts of caffeine.

PHARMACOKINETICS:

- Probably alters chemical transmitters in the CNS, possibly by interfering with ionic pump mechanisms in brain cells, and may compete with or replace sodium ions. With PO dose onset the duration of action is unknown. The peak action is between 30 min and 1 hr.

Half-life: 18 hr (adolescents) to 36 hr (elderly).

PRECAUTIONS:

- May increase glucose and creatinine levels. May decrease sodium, T3, T4, and protein-bound iodine levels.
- May increase WBC and neutrophil counts.
- Contraindicated if therapy can't be closely monitored.
- Avoid using in pregnant patients unless benefits outweigh risks.
- Use with caution in patients receiving neuromuscular blockers and diuretics; in elderly or debilitated patients; and in patients with thyroid disease, seizure disorder, infection, renal or CV disease, severe debilitation or dehydration, or sodium depletion.

▶**Alert:** Drug has a narrow therapeutic margin of safety. Determining drug level is crucial to the safe use of the drug. Don't use the drug in patients who can't have regular tests done. Monitor levels 8–12 hr after the first dose, the morning before the second dose is given, two or three times weekly for the first month, and then weekly to monthly during maintenance therapy.

- When the drug level is less than 1.5 mEq/L, adverse reactions are usually mild.
- Monitor baseline EKG, thyroid studies, renal studies, and electrolyte levels.

- Check fluid intake and output, especially when surgery is scheduled.
- Weigh patient daily; check for edema or sudden weight gain.
- Adjust fluid and salt ingestion to compensate if excessive loss occurs from protracted diaphoresis or diarrhea. Under normal conditions, patient's fluid intake should be 2 to 3 L daily, with a balanced diet with adequate salt intake.
- Check urine specific gravity and report levels below 1.005, which may indicate diabetes insipidus.
- Drug alters glucose tolerance in diabetics. Monitor glucose level closely.
- Perform outpatient follow-up of thyroid and renal functions every 6–12 months. Palpate thyroid to check for enlargement.

PATIENT AND FAMILY EDUCATION:

- Tell the patient to take the drug with plenty of water and after meals to minimize GI upset.
- Explain the importance of having regular blood tests to determine drug levels; even slightly high values can be dangerous.
- Warn patients and caregivers to expect transient nausea, large amounts of urine, thirst, and discomfort during the first few days of therapy and to watch for evidence of toxicity (diarrhea, vomiting, tremor, drowsiness, muscle weakness, incoordination).
- Instruct patients to withhold one dose and call the prescriber if signs and symptoms of toxicity appear, but not to stop drug abruptly.
- Warn patients to avoid hazardous activities that require alertness and good psychomotor coordination until the CNS effects of drug are known.
- Tell patients not to switch brands or take other prescription or OTC drugs without the prescriber's guidance.
- Tell patients to wear or carry medical identification at all times.

SPECIAL POPULATIONS:

- *Elderly:* Initial dose reduction and possibly lower maintenance doses due to age-related changes and sensitivity to side effects.
- *Pregnancy:* Category D. Positive evidence of fetal harm has been demonstrated.
- *Children:* Not approved in children less than 12 years of age; use with caution and monitor closely for side effects and suicidality. Children may experience more frequent and severe side effects.

Class: Atypical Antipsychotics (Second Generation)

Abilify **aripiprazole**

AVAILABLE FORMS: Tablet, 2, 5, 10, 15, 20, and 30 mg; tablet, orally disintegrating: 10 and 15 mg; solution, oral, 1 mg/mL

DOSAGE: 10–15 mg/day, up to 15–30 mg/day. Dosages exceeding 10–15 mg/day have not demonstrated greater efficacy

ADMINISTRATION:
- Tablets may be given with or without food.
- Parenteral administration is intended for IM use only; inject slowly, deep into the muscle mass. IM injection has not been evaluated in children.
- Do not give IV or SC.
- Oral solution may be substituted for tablets on a mg-per-mg basis up to a 25 mg dose. Patients receiving 30 mg tablets should receive 25 mg of the solution.
- Dosing for the orally disintegrating tablet is the same as the oral tablet.
- Do not open the orally disintegrating tablets until ready to administer. The orally disintegrating tablet should be taken without liquid. Do not split the orally disintegrating tablet.
- Use oral aripiprazole 10–30 mg/day instead of IM aripiprazole as soon as possible if ongoing therapy is indicated.

SIDE EFFECTS: Nausea, vomiting; dizziness; insomnia, akathisia, activation; headache, asthenia; sedation; weight gain; constipation; orthostatic hypotension (occasionally during initial phase); increased risk of death and cerebrovascular events in elderly with dementia-related psychosis; tardive dyskinesia; neuroleptic malignant syndrome (rare); seizures (rare)

DRUG INTERACTIONS:
- CYP450 3A4 inhibitors (e.g., nefazodone, fluvoxamine, fluoxetine), CYP40 2D6 inhibitors (e.g., paroxetine, fluoxetine, duloxetine), and quinidine may increase plasma levels of aripiprazole
- Carbamazepine and other CYP450 3A4 inducers may decrease plasma levels of aripiprazole
- Aripiprazole may enhance effects of antihypertensive medications
- Aripiprazole may antagonize levodopa, dopamine agonists
▶**Alert:** This list may not describe all possible interactions. Instruct the patient to provide a list of all the medicines, herbs, nonprescription drugs, or dietary supplements being used. Also instruct clients to inform health care providers if they smoke, drink alcohol, or use illegal drugs.

PHARMACOKINETICS:
- Primarily metabolized by CYP450 2D6 and CYP450 3A4
- About 25% of a single oral dose is excreted in urine (less than 1% unchanged) and 55% in feces (18% as unchanged drug).

Mean elimination half-life: 75 hr (aripiprazole) and 94 hr (active metabolite)

PRECAUTIONS:
- Dysphagia is associated with the use of aripiprazole. Use with caution in patients who are at risk for aspiration pneumonia
- Use with caution in patients with conditions who may develop hypotension (dehydration, overheating etc.)
▶**Alert:** Patients who are allergic to aripiprazole.

PATIENT AND FAMILY EDUCATION:
- Store aripiprazole at 59–86°F. An opened bottle can be used for up to 6 months. Protect solution from light by storing in a carton until use.
- If pregnant, contact the health care provider. Discuss the benefits and risks of using aripiprazole orally-disintegrating tablets while pregnant.
- Dose adjustment or special tests to safely take aripiprazole may be needed with: liver or kidney disease; heart disease, high blood pressure, heart rhythm problems; history of heart attack or stroke; history of high WBC counts; history of breast cancer; seizures or epilepsy; personal or family history of diabetes; problems swallowing; PKU.
- Contact health care provider if signs of hyperglycemia such as increased thirst or urination, excessive hunger, or weakness. If diabetic, check blood sugar levels on a regular basis while taking aripiprazole.

SPECIAL POPULATIONS:
- *Elderly:* Dosage adjustment is generally not required. Elderly with dementia-related psychosis who are treated with atypical antipsychotics such as aripiprazole are at a higher risk of death and cerebrovascular events.
- *Renal impairment:* No dosage adjustment is needed.
- *Hepatic impairment:* No dosage adjustment required.
- *Cardiac impairment:* Use with caution because of the risk of orthostatic hypotension
- *Pregnancy:* Category C. It is not known if aripiprazole orally disintegrating tablets can cause harm to the fetus.
- *Lactation:* Although there are no data on the excretion of aripiprazole into human milk, it is suggested that women receiving aripiprazole should not breast-feed.
- *Children and adolescents:* Aripiprazole is approved for children with schizophrenia (aged 13 and older) and manic/mixed episodes (age 10 and older). Should be monitored more frequently than adults. May tolerate lower doses better.
▶**Alert:** Not approved for children with depression.

BIPOLAR DISORDERS: Atypical Antipsychotics (Second Generation)

olanzapine   *Zyprexa*

AVAILABLE FORMS: Tablet, 2.5, 5, 7.5, 10, 15 and 20 mg; orally disintegrating tablet, 5, 10, 15 and 20 mg

DOSAGE: 10–20 mg/day PO

ADMINISTRATION:
- Tablets may be given with or without food.
- Advise patients to take the missed dose as soon as remembered. Skip the missed dose if almost time for the next scheduled dose. Do not take extra medicine to make up for the missed dose.
- Store at room temperature away from moisture, heat, and light.

SIDE EFFECTS:
- Can increase the risk for diabetes and dyslipidemia
- Dizziness, sedation; weight gain; dry mouth, constipation, dyspepsia; peripheral edema; joint pain, back pain, chest pain, extremity pain, abnormal gait, ecchymosis; tachycardia; orthostatic hypotension (usually during initial dose titration); hyperglycemia; increased risk of death and cerebrovascular events in elderly with dementia-related psychosis
- *Rare:* Tardive dyskinesia; rash on exposure to sunlight; neuroleptic malignant syndrome; seizures

DRUG INTERACTIONS:
- May increase effects of antihypertensive medications
- May antagonize levodopa, dopamine agonists
- May need to reduce dose if given with CYP450 1A2 inhibitors (e.g., fluvoxamine)
- May need to increase dose if given with CYP450 1A2 inducers (e.g., cigarette smoke, carbamazepine)
- This list may not describe all possible interactions. Instruct clients to provide a list of all the medicines, herbs, nonprescription drugs, or dietary supplements that they use.

PHARMACOKINETICS:
- Metabolites are inactive
Half-life: 21–54 hr

PRECAUTIONS:
- Use with caution in patients with conditions that predispose them to hypotension (dehydration, overheating). Watch closely for symptoms of hypotension if IM formulation is given.
- Use with caution in patients with prostatic hypertrophy, narrow angle-closure glaucoma, paralytic ileus.
- Use with caution in patients who are at risk for aspiration pneumonia.
- IM formulation is not recommended to be given with parenteral benzodiazepines. If patients need a parenteral benzodiazepine, give at least 1 hr after intramuscular formulation olanzapine.
- Do not use if there is a proven allergy
- Do not give IM formulation.
- Do not give if patient's medical condition is unstable (e.g., AMI, unstable angina pectoris, severe hypotension and/or bradycardia, sick sinus syndrome, recent heart surgery).
- Do not give if the patient has known risks of narrow angle-closure glaucoma.

PATIENT AND FAMILY EDUCATION:
- Take exactly as prescribed by the health care provider. Do not take in larger or smaller amounts or for longer than recommended.
- Can be taken with or without food.
- For olanzapine orally disintegrating tablets, keep the tablet in its blister pack until the patient is ready to take it. Open the package and peel back the foil from the tablet blister. Do not push a tablet through the foil. Using dry hands, remove the tablet and place it in the mouth; it will begin to dissolve immediately.
- Do not swallow the tablet whole. Allow it to dissolve in the mouth without chewing. If desired, drink liquid to help swallow the dissolved tablet.
- If the patient has diabetes, check blood sugar levels on a regular basis
- The patient can gain weight or have high cholesterol and triglycerides (types of fat) while taking this drug, especially if teenaged. Blood will need to be tested often.
- Do not stop taking the drug suddenly without first talking to the health care provider, even if feeling fine. Serious side effects may occur if drug is stopped suddenly.
- Call the health care provider if symptoms do not improve, or get worse.
- Store at room temperature away from moisture, heat, and light.

SPECIAL POPULATIONS:
- *Elderly:*
  - May tolerate lower doses better. Elderly with dementia-related psychosis treated with atypical antipsychotics are at higher risk of death and cerebrovascular events. Can increase the incidence of stroke.
  - If IM formulation is given, the recommended starting dose is 2.5–5 mg. A second injection of 2.5–5 mg may be given 2 hr after the first injection. No more than three injections should be administered within 24 hr.
- *Renal impairment:* No dose adjustment is required for oral formulation. Consider the lower starting dose (5 mg) for IM formulation. Not removed by hemodialysis.
- *Hepatic impairment:* Start oral dose at 5 mg for patients with moderate to severe hepatic function impairment; increase dose with caution. Consider the lower starting dose (5 mg) for IM formulation. Check the patient's report for liver function tests a few times a year.
- *Cardiac impairment:* Use with caution because of the risk of orthostatic hypotension.
- *Pregnancy:* Category C. Some animal studies show adverse effects. No controlled studies
(cont.)

olanzapine (cont.)

have been performed in humans. Should be used only when the potential benefits outweigh potential risks to the fetus. This drug may be preferable to anticonvulsant mood stabilizers if treatment is required during pregnancy.

- *Lactation*: It is unknown whether this is secreted in human breast milk. It is recommended to discontinue the drug or bottle feed. Infants of women who choose to breastfeed while tak-

ing this drug should be monitored for possible adverse effects.

- *Children and adolescents:*
  - Probably safe and effective for behavioral disturbances in this population.
  - IM formulation has not been studied in patients under 18 years of age and is not recommended for use in this population.
  - Should be monitored more frequently than adults.

Risperdal, Risperdal Consta   **risperidone**

AVAILABLE FORMS: Tablet, 0.25, 0.5, 1, 2, 3, 4 and 6 mg; orally disintegrating tablet, 0.5, 1 and 2 mg; liquid, 1 mg/mL (30 mL bottle).

DOSAGE: 2–8 mg/day PO for adults. 0.5–2.0 mg/day PO for the elderly

ADMINISTRATION:
- Tablets may be given with or without food.
- Advise patients to take the missed dose as soon as remembered. Skip the missed dose if it is almost time for the next scheduled dose. Do not take extra medicine to make up for the missed dose.
- Measure the liquid form of risperidone (*Risperdal*) with a special dose-measuring spoon or cup, not a regular tablespoon.
- Do not mix the liquid form with cola or tea.

SIDE EFFECTS:
- Can increase risk for diabetes and dyslipidemia
- Extrapyramidal symptoms (dose dependent)
- Hyperprolactinemia (dose dependent)
- Dizziness, insomnia, headache, anxiety
- Nausea, sedation, weight gain, constipation, abdominal pain; tachycardia; sexual dysfunction; hyperglycemia
- Increased risk of death and cerebrovascular events in elderly with dementia-related psychosis
- *Rare:* Tardive dyskinesia; orthostatic hypotension (usually during initial dose titration); neuroleptic malignant syndrome; seizures

DRUG INTERACTIONS:
- May increase the effects of antihypertensive medications
- May antagonize levodopa, dopamine agonists
- Plasma levels of risperidone may be reduced if given in conjunction with carbamazepine.
- Plasma levels of risperidone may be increased if given in conjunction with fluoxetine or paroxetine
- Plasma levels of risperidone may be increased if given in conjunction with clozapine but no dose adjustment is required.
- This list may not describe all possible interactions. Instruct clients to provide a list of all the medicines, herbs, nonprescription drugs, or dietary supplements that they use.

PHARMACOKINETICS:
- Elimination at 7–8 weeks after last injection (long-acting formulation)
- Metabolites are active
- Metabolized by CYP450 2D6

Half-life: 20–24 hr (oral formulation); 3–6 days (long-acting formulation)

PRECAUTIONS:
- Use with caution in patients with conditions that predispose them to hypotension (dehydration, overheating).
- Use with caution in patients at risk for aspiration pneumonia.
- Priapism has been reported to occur in patients taking this drug. Severe cases may require surgical intervention.
- Do not use if there is a proven allergy.

PATIENT AND FAMILY EDUCATION:
- Take exactly as prescribed by the health care provider. Do not take in larger or smaller amounts, or for longer than recommended.
- Can be taken with or without food.
- Patients may become more sensitive to temperature extremes (very hot or cold conditions) when taking this medication. Avoid getting too cold, or becoming overheated or dehydrated.
- Drink plenty of fluids, especially in hot weather and during exercise.
- Risperidone can cause side effects that may impair thinking or reactions. Be careful if driving or doing anything that requires alertness.
- Risperidone may cause high blood sugar (hyperglycemia). Talk to the provider if any signs of hyperglycemia such as increased thirst or urination, excessive hunger, or weakness. If diabetic, check blood sugar levels on a regular basis.
- Risperidone orally disintegrating tablet may contain phenylalanine. Talk to the provider before using this form of risperidone with PKU.
- Avoid drinking alcohol. It can increase some of the side effects.
- Do not mix the liquid form with cola or tea.
- Stop using this medication and call the health care provider immediately if fever, stiff muscles, confusion, sweating, fast or uneven heartbeats,

(cont.)

BIPOLAR DISORDERS: Atypical Antipsychotics (Second Generation)

risperidone (*cont.*)

restless muscle movements in face or neck, tremor (uncontrolled shaking), trouble swallowing, feeling light-headed, or fainting.
- Do not stop taking the drug suddenly without first talking to the provider, even if feeling fine. Serious side effects may occur if the drug is stopped suddenly.
- Call the health care provider if symptoms do not improve, or get worse.
- Store at room temperature away from moisture, light, and heat. Do not freeze the liquid form of risperidone.

SPECIAL POPULATIONS:
- *Elderly:*
  - Initial dose of 0.5 mg orally twice a day, then increase to 0.5 mg bid. Titrate once a week for doses above 1.5 mg bid.
  - Long-acting: 25 mg should be given every 2 weeks. Oral administration should be continued for 3 weeks after the first injection.
  - Elderly with dementia-related psychosis treated with atypical antipsychotics are at higher risk of death and cerebrovascular events.
- *Renal impairment:*
  - Initial dose of 0.5 mg PO bid for the first week. Increase to 1 mg bid during the second week.
  - Long-acting risperidone should not be given to patients with renal function impairment unless patients can tolerate at least 2 mg/day orally.
  - Long-acting risperidone should be given at a dose of 25 mg every 2 weeks. Oral administration should be continued for 3 weeks after the first injection.

- *Hepatic impairment:*
  - Initial dose of 0.5 mg PO bid for the first week. Increase to 1 mg bid during the second week.
  - Long-acting risperidone should not be given to the patient with renal function impairment unless the patient can tolerate at least 2 mg/day orally.
  - Long-acting risperidone should be given at a dose of 25 mg every 2 weeks. Oral administration should be continued for 3 weeks after the first injection.
- *Cardiac impairment:* Use with caution because of the risk of orthostatic hypotension. The drug can increase the risk of stroke if given to elderly patients with atrial fibrillation.
- *Pregnancy:* Category C. Some animal studies show adverse effects. No controlled studies have been performed in humans. Should be used only when the potential benefits outweigh potential risks to the fetus. Risperidone may be preferable to anticonvulsant mood stabilizers if treatment is required during pregnancy. Effects of hyperprolactinemia on the fetus are unknown.
- *Lactation:* Drug is secreted in human breast milk. It is recommended to either discontinue drug or bottle feed. Infants of women who choose to breastfeed while on this drug should be monitored for possible adverse effect.
- *Children and adolescents:*
  - Safe and effective for behavioral disturbances in this population.
  - Risperidone is the most frequently used atypical antipsychotic medication in this population.

quetiapine   *Seroquel, Seroquel XR*

AVAILABLE FORMS: Tablet, 25, 50, 100, 200, 300 and 400 mg; extended-release tablet, 200, 300 and 400 mg

DOSAGE: 200–800 mg/day in 1 XR or 2 standard release doses

ADMINISTRATION:
- Tablets may be given with or without food.
- Take with full glass of water.
- Advise patient not to crush, chew, or break extended-release tablet. Swallow the pill whole. Breaking the pill may cause too much of the drug to be released at one time.
- Advise patient to take the missed dose as soon as remembered. Skip the missed dose if it is almost time for the next scheduled dose. Do not take extra medicine to make up for the missed dose.

SIDE EFFECTS:
- Can increase the risk for diabetes and dyslipidemia
- Dizziness; sedation; weight gain; dry mouth, constipation, dyspepsia, abdominal pain; tachycardia; hyperglycemia

- Increased risk of death and cerebrovascular events in elderly with dementia-related psychosis
- Orthostatic hypotension (usually during initial dose titration)
- *Rare:* Neuroleptic malignant syndrome; seizures

DRUG INTERACTIONS:
- May increase the effects of antihypertensive medications
- Plasma levels of quetiapine may be increased if given in conjunction with CYP450 3A4 and CYP450 2D6 inhibitors. However, no dose adjustment is required.

PHARMACOKINETICS:
- Metabolites are inactive
Half-life: 6–7 hr

PRECAUTIONS:
- Use with caution in patients who are at risk for aspiration pneumonia.
- Manufacturer recommends examination for cataracts before and every 6 months after starting quetiapine.
- Do not use if there is a proven allergy.

(cont.)

quetiapine (*cont.*)

PATIENT AND FAMILY EDUCATION:
- Take exactly as prescribed by the health care provider. Do not take in larger or smaller amounts or for longer than recommended.
- Can be taken with or without food.
- Quetiapine can cause side effects that may impair thinking or reactions. Be careful if driving or doing anything that requires you to be awake and alert.
- Quetiapine may cause high blood sugar (hyperglycemia). Talk to the provider if any signs of hyperglycemia such as increased thirst or urination, excessive hunger, or weakness. If diabetic, check blood sugar levels on a regular basis.
- Avoid becoming overheated or dehydrated during exercise and in hot weather. May be more prone to heat stroke.
- Avoid getting up too fast from a sitting or lying position. Get up slowly and steady yourself to prevent a fall.
- Avoid drinking alcohol.
- Stop using this medication and call the provider immediately if very stiff (rigid) muscles, high fever, sweating, confusion, fast or uneven heartbeats, tremors; feeling faint or may pass out, uncontrollable jerky muscle movements; trouble swallowing, problems with speech; blurred vision, eye pain, or seeing halos around lights; increased thirst and urination, excessive hunger, fruity breath odor, weakness, nausea and vomiting; fever, chills, body aches, flu symptoms; or white patches or sores inside mouth or on lips.
- Do not stop taking the drug suddenly without first talking to provider, even if feeling fine. Serious side effects may occur if the drug is stopped suddenly.
- Call the provider if symptoms do not improve or get worse.

- Store at room temperature away from moisture and heat.

SPECIAL POPULATIONS:
- *Elderly:*
  - Generally lower dose is used (e.g., 25–100 mg bid). Higher dose can be used if tolerated.
  - Elderly with dementia-related psychosis treated with atypical antipsychotics are at higher risk of death and cerebrovascular events.
- *Renal impairment:* No dose adjustment is required.
- *Hepatic impairment:* May need to reduce dose.
- *Cardiac impairment:* Use with caution because of the risk of orthostatic hypotension.
- *Pregnancy:* Category C. Some animal studies show adverse effects. No controlled studies have been performed in humans. Should be used only when the potential benefits outweigh potential risks to the fetus. Quetiapine may be preferable to anticonvulsant mood stabilizers if treatment is required during pregnancy.
- *Lactation:* It is unknown whether the drug is secreted in human breast milk. It is recommended to either discontinue the drug or bottle-feed. Infants of nursing mothers who choose to breastfeed while on this drug should be monitored for possible adverse effects.
- *Children and adolescents:*
  - Not officially recommended for patients under the age of 18.
  - Probably safe and effective for behavioral disturbances in this population.
  - Should be monitored more frequently than adults. May tolerate lower doses better.
  - Watch for activation of suicidal ideation. Inform parents or guardian of this risk so that they can help monitor the risk.

Geodon   **ziprasidone**

AVAILABLE FORMS: Tablet, 20, 40, 60 and 80 mg

DOSAGE: 80–160 mg/day in divided doses

ADMINISTRATION:
- Take this medication with a meal.
- Dosing at 20–40 bid is too low and activating, perhaps due to potent 5HT2C antagonist properties. Reduce activation by increasing the dose to 60–80 mg bid.
- Best efficacy in schizophrenia and bipolar disorder is at doses > 120 mg/day.
- Monitor BMI monthly for 3 months, then quarterly.
- Monitor fasting triglycerides monthly for several months in patients at high risk for metabolic complications.
- Monitor blood pressure, fasting plasma glucose, fasting lipids within 3 months and then annually, but earlier and more frequently for patients

with diabetes or who have gained >5% of initial weight.

SIDE EFFECTS:
- Dizziness, sedation, and hypotension especially at high doses
- Motor side effects (rare)
- Possible increased incidence of diabetes or dyslipidemia is unknown

DRUG INTERACTIONS:
- May enhance the effects of antihypertensive drugs
- May antagonize levodopa, dopamine agonists
- May enhance QT prolongation of other drugs capable of prolonging QT interval

PHARMACOKINETICS:
- Protein binding >99%
- Metabolized by CYP450 3A4
- **Mean Half-life:** 6.6 hr

(cont.)

BIPOLAR DISORDERS: Atypical Antipsychotics (Second Generation)

ziprasidone (cont.)

PRECAUTIONS:
- Prolongs QT interval more than some other antipsychotics
- Use with caution in patients with conditions that predispose them to hypotension (dehydration, overheating)
- Priapism has been reported to occur in patients taking this drug. Severe cases may require surgical intervention.
- Dysphagia has been associated with antipsychotic use, and should be used cautiously in patients at risk for aspiration pneumonia
- Do not use if the patient is taking agents capable of prolonging QT interval (pimozide, thioridazine, selected antiarrhythmics, moxifloxacin, sparfloxacin)
- Do not use if there is a history of QT prolongation, cardiac arrhythmia, recent AMI, uncompensated heart failure
- Do not use if there is a proven allergy to ziprasidone

PATIENT AND FAMILY EDUCATION:
- Take with a meal of a few hundred calories (turkey sandwich and a piece of fruit) to enhance the absorption.
- Avoid becoming overheated or dehydrated during exercise and in hot weather. May be more prone to heat stroke.
- Avoid getting up too fast from a sitting or lying position. Get up slowly and steady yourself to prevent a fall.
- Avoid drinking alcohol.
- Stop using this medication and call the provider immediately if very stiff (rigid) muscles, high fever, sweating, confusion, fast or uneven heartbeats, tremors; feeling like you might pass out; jerky muscle movements you cannot control, trouble swallowing, problems with speech; blurred vision, eye pain, or seeing halos around lights; increased thirst and urination, excessive hunger, fruity breath odor, weakness, nausea and vomiting; fever, chills, body aches, flu symptoms; or white patches or sores inside mouth or on lips.
- Do not stop taking the drug suddenly without first talking to the provider, even if feeling fine. You may have serious side effects if you stop taking the drug suddenly.
- Call the provider if the symptoms do not improve, or get worse.
- Store at room temperature away from moisture and heat.

SPECIAL POPULATIONS:
- *Elderly:* Some patients may tolerate lower doses better. Elderly patients with dementia-related psychosis treated with atypical antipsychotics are at an increased risk of death compared to placebo.
- *Cardiac impairment:* Contraindicated in patients with a known history of QT prolongation, recent AMI, and uncompensated heart failure.
- *Pregnancy:* Category C. Some animal studies show adverse effects; no controlled studies have been performed in humans.
- *Lactation:* It is unknown whether it is secreted in human breast milk. Recommend either to discontinue drug or bottlefeed.
- *Children and adolescents:* Not recommended for patients under the age of 18. Early data suggest it may be safe and effective for behavioral disturbances in children and adolescents.

Major Depressive Disorder (MDD)

OVERVIEW

- Overwhelming sadness or lack of enjoyment, along with hopelessness and a sense of feeling overwhelmed, fatigue, and somatic symptoms.
- Often follows chronic stress or significant acute stressor(s).
- Negatively impacts social functioning, such as getting out of bed, going to work, attending school and having positive relationships, and is a recurrent illness.

Psychopharmacology of MDD

OVERVIEW
Acute Phase

- Psychotropic medication should be selected based on relative efficacy, tolerability and anticipated side effects, co-occurring psychiatric or general medical conditions, half-life, cost, potential drug interactions, and the patient's preference and prior response to medication.
- The onset of benefit from pharmacologic treatment may be more gradual in MDD than the onset of benefit in nonchronic depression.
- Treatment nonresponsive patients should be re-evaluated for accuracy of diagnosis, unaddressed co-occurring medical or psychiatric disorders, such as substance abuse, the need for a change in treatment modalities, inadequate dose or duration of medical treatment, the need to augment medical treatment (with a second antidepressant from a different pharmacological class, or use of an adjunctive such as second generation atypical antipsychotic, anticonvulsant or thyroid hormone), inadequate frequency of psychotherapy, complicating psychosocial factors, nonadherence to treatment, and poor "fit" between patient and therapist.
- Common combinations of medications include an SSRI with the addition of bupropion or the combination of mirtazapine and an SSRI or venlafaxine.
- Pharmacotherapy may increase the potential of suicidal ideation, particularly in patients less than 25 years of age. General guidelines include:
  - Depressed patients with suicidal ideation, plan, and intent should be hospitalized, especially if they have current psychosocial stressors and access to lethal means.
  - Depressed patients with suicidal ideation and a plan but without intent may be treated on an outpatient basis with close follow-up, especially when they have good social support and no access to lethal means.
  - Depressed patients who express suicidal ideation but deny a plan should be assessed carefully for psychosocial stressors. Remove weapons from the environment.

- Pay careful attention in the first 1–4 weeks of treatment to a sudden lift of depression, or to worsening mood as initial response to antidepressant therapy as these could be signs of increased risk for suicide.
- Pharmacotherapy for MDD should begin at the lowest dosage and gradually be increased, if needed, following a 4-week evaluation for therapeutic response. Patients should be observed 1–2 weeks after initiation of therapy for evaluation of adverse drug effects. Frequency of monitoring should be determined based on symptom severity, co-occurring disorders, availability of social support, patient cooperation with treatment, and side effects of medication.

Chronic or Continuation Phase

- Once the patient has reached remission of symptoms, the patient is monitored for an additional 4–9 months prior to tapering the medication, or, in the case of three or more episodes, the patient is placed on maintenance treatment.
- In cases where medication loses its effectiveness, alternative regimens and diagnoses should be explored.
- ECT is recommended as the treatment of choice for patients with severe MDD that is not responsive to pharmacologic treatment and psychotherapy.
- Pharmacologic education should include frequency of dosing, the likelihood that side effects will occur prior to improvement of symptoms, expectations that it will take 2–4 weeks prior to beneficial effects and 4–8 weeks prior to full effects of the dosage, the importance of taking medication even after feeling better, consulting with the health care provider before discontinuing medication, correcting misconceptions about medication use, and explaining what to do if side effects, questions, or worsening symptoms arise. Nonpharmacologic recommendations should also be made such as sleep hygiene, decreased use or elimination of caffeine, tobacco, and alcohol, light therapy, and regular exercise.

MAJOR DEPRESSIVE DISORDER

MAJOR DEPRESSIVE DISORDER

CLASS	DRUG
Selective Serotonin Reuptake Inhibitors (SSRIs)	**First-Line Drug Therapy**
	fluoxetine (*Prozac*)
	sertraline (*Zoloft*)
	paroxetine (*Paxil, Paxil CR*)
	citalopram (*Celexa*)
	escitalopram (*Lexapro*)
	fluvoxamine (*Luvox*)
Serotonin/Norepinephrine Reuptake Inhibitors (SNRIs)	
	venlafaxine (*Effexor*);
	venlafaxine XR (*Effexor XR*)
	duloxetine (*Cymbalta*)
	desvenlafaxine (*Pristiq*)
Serotonin-2 Antagonist/Reuptake Inhibitors (SARIs)	**Second-Line Drug Therapy**
	nefazodone (*Serzone*)
	trazodone (*Desyrel*)
Noradrenergic and Specific Serotonergic Antidepressants (NaSSAs)	**Alternative Therapy Option**
	mirtazapine (*Remeron*)
Norepinephrine/Dopamine Reuptake Inhibitors (NDRIs)	**Alternative Therapy Option**
	bupropion (*Wellbutrin, Zyban*),
	bupropion SR (*Wellbutrin SR*), and
	bupropion XL (*Wellbutrin XL*)
Tricyclic Antidepressants (TCAs)	
	amitriptyline (*Elavil*)
	clomipramine (*Anafranil*)
	desipramine (*Norpramin*)
	imipramine (*Tofranil*)
	nortriptyline (*Pamelor*)
Monoamine Oxidase Inhibitors (MAOIs)	
	phenelzine (*Nardil*)
	isocarboxazid (*Marplan*)
	tranylcypromine (*Parnate*)

Class: Selective Serotonin Reuptake Inhibitors (SSRIs)

MAJOR DEPRESSIVE DISORDER: SSRIs

- SSRIs are one of the more commonly used medications for MDD.
- Typically display fewer side effects than TCAs and MAOIs, with minimal risk of death in an intentional overdose. Treatment decisions should take into consideration patient symptoms and medication side effect profile.
- With the exception of fluoxetine, SSRI medications may be helpful for patients with co-existing anxiety disorders or panic attacks.
- SSRI medications may not be preferred for patients with sexual dysfunction or who find sexual dysfunction as an intolerable side effect.
- Limited or no cholinergic, histaminergic, dopaminergic, or adrenergic receptor activity (i.e., they do not cause hypotension or anticholinergic response).
- May be of benefit to perimenopausal women experiencing hot flashes.
- Patients reporting intolerable side effects to one SSRI may benefit from switching to another SSRI.

Prozac, Sarafem   **fluoxetine**

INDICATIONS: Has the most data in treatment of bulimia nervosa.

AVAILABLE FORMS: Capsule, 10, 20 and 40 mg; tablet, 10, 15 and 20 mg; pellets, 90 mg ps; delayed release, enteric coated (*Prozac* weekly); solution, 5 mL and 120 mL, 20 mg/5 mL. *Note:* Availability of certain formulations may be limited to brand-name versions of the drug.

DOSAGE: Starting dose 20 mg/day; maintenance dose 20–60 mg, adjust in 20 mg increments

ADMINISTRATION:
- Oral, with or without food.
- Capsules may be diluted into water or apple juice. Grapefruit juice should not be used due to cytochrome P450 effects.

SIDE EFFECTS:
- May cause CNS depression (sedation, fatigue) or activation (insomnia)
- Tends to be weight neutral or approximately 2 pounds of weight gain in a year
- Nervousness, agitation; headache and nausea, particularly early in treatment; insomnia; excess perspiration; serotonin syndrome; diarrhea; sexual dysfunction (>50% in men and women); hyponatremia (e.g., in geriatric patients taking diuretics)
- Withdrawal syndrome (including neonatal withdrawal syndrome): Symptoms may include dizziness, muscle aches, headache, nausea, vomiting, gait instability, agitation, and/or "electric shock" sensations.
- Side effects are most common during the first or second week of therapy. Starting with a lower dosage and gradually increasing it, and taking the medication with food will limit some of these side effects.

DRUG INTERACTIONS:
- *MAOIs:* Extreme risk for serotonin syndrome. Requires a 5–6 week washout period or longer before use of an MAOI.
- *TCAs:* Plasma levels may be increased by SSRIs, so add with caution in low doses
- *ASA and NSAIDs:* Increased risk of bleeding
- *CNS depressants:* May increase depressant effects
- *SSRIs or SARIs:* May cause serotonin syndrome in combination with other medications such as tramadol, high-dose triptans, or the antibiotic linezolid.
- Use with caution in patients taking blood thinners (*Coumadin*), other antidepressants, antihistamines, lithium, TCAs, and certain antibiotics, such as erythromycin, clarithromycin, or azithromycin.

PHARMACOKINETICS:
- Metabolized in the liver by cytochrome P-450 microsomal enzymes.
- Highly bound to plasma proteins and have a large volume of distribution.

- Readily absorbed in the GI tract, metabolized in the liver, and excreted in the urine. Dosages may be decreased in patients with liver or kidney disease.
- Caution advised in elderly clients.

Peak plasma levels: 2–10 hr

Half-life: Variable, but most SSRIs have half-lives of 20–24 hr. A notable exception is fluoxetine (*Prozac*), and its active metabolite, norfluoxetine, which have half-lives of 2–4 days and 8–9 days, respectively. Hence, addition of serotonergic medications to a patient's regimen must not occur until 2–3 weeks after discontinuation of an SSRI (some recommend a 5-week "washout" period for fluoxetine prior to initiation of an MAOI).

PRECAUTIONS:
- May cause sedation and mental clouding
- Use with caution in patients with liver, kidney, or cardiovascular disease
- *Elderly patients:* May require decreased dosage
- Adverse effects and side effects are commonly observed before therapeutic effects
- Many side effects are dose-dependent and may improve over time
- Taper discontinuation to avoid withdrawal symptoms

PATIENT AND FAMILY EDUCATION:
- Should be taken about the same time every day, morning or evening, and can be taken with or without food (with food if there is any stomach upset)
- May start with half of lowest effective dose for 3–7 days, then increase to lowest effective dose to diminish side effects.
- Administration time may be adjusted based on observed sedating or activating drug effects
- May take up to 4–8 weeks to reach its full effect at this dose, but some may see symptoms of depression improving in as little as 2 weeks.
- If planning or are pregnant, discuss the benefits versus the risks of using this medicine while pregnant.
- Because this medicine is excreted in the breast milk, nursing mothers should not breastfeed while taking this medicine without prior consultation with a psychiatric nurse practitioner or psychiatrist. Newborns may develop symptoms including feeding or breathing difficulties, seizures, muscle stiffness, jitteriness, or constant crying.
- Do not stop taking this medication unless the health care provider directs. Report side effects or worsening symptoms to the health care provider promptly.
- The medication should be tapered gradually when changing or discontinuing therapy.
- Dosage should be adjusted to reach remission of symptoms and treatment should continue for at least 4–9 months following remission of symptoms

(cont.)

MAJOR DEPRESSIVE DISORDER: Selective Serotonin Reuptake Inhibitors (SSRIs)

fluoxetine (*cont.*)

- Caution is advised when using this drug in the elderly because they may be more sensitive to the effects of the drug. Elderly patients should receive a lower starting dose.
- Keep these medications out of the reach of children and pets.

SPECIAL POPULATIONS:

- *Elderly:* Avoid use in the elderly. Older individuals tend to be more sensitive to medication side effects such as hypotension and anticholinergic effects. They often require adjustment of medication doses for hepatic or renal dysfunction. SSRIs with shorter half-lives or less P-450 inhibition may be more desirable (e.g., citalopram) for geriatric populations. SSRIs have been associated with increased risk of falls in nursing home residents and neurologic effects in patients with Parkinson's disease. Geriatric patients are more prone to SSRI-induced hyponatremia. Paroxetine shows greater anticholinergic and sedating effects than other SSRIs.

- *Pregnancy:* Psychotherapy is the initial choice for most pregnant patients with mild to moderate MDD. Most SSRIs are category C drugs due to adverse effects observed in animal studies. Thus, an individual risk-benefit analysis must be done to determine appropriate treatment in pregnant women with MDD. Paroxetine is a category D drug. If continued during pregnancy, SSRI dosage may need to be increased to maintain euthymia due to physiologic changes associated with pregnancy.
- *Children:* FDA approved for use in children with depression. Initial SSRI dosing in children typically begins at approx. 50% adult dosing. Increasing doses may require more gradual increments, and discontinuation may require a more gradual taper. Psychiatric consultation is recommended due to black box warning of increased suicidal ideation using SSRI therapy in children.

sertraline   *Zoloft*

AVAILABLE FORMS: Tablet, 25, 50 and 100 mg; solution, 20 mg/mL (60 mL) concentrate

DOSAGE: Starting dose 50 mg/day; maintenance dose 50–200 mg

ADMINISTRATION: PO, with or without food. Concentrate solution must be diluted immediately prior to use with water or juice (other than grapefruit juice).

SIDE EFFECTS: Displays some inhibition of dopamine reuptake, which may be beneficial to some patients (e.g., those experiencing hypersomnia, low energy, or mood reactivity), but problematic to others (e.g., causing overactivation in patients with panic disorder). May see a little more GI side effect (diarrhea) than others in class

- Nervousness; headache and nausea; insomnia; serotonin syndrome; dry mouth, easy bruising, or excess perspiration; diarrhea; sexual dysfunction (>50% in men and women); hyponatremia (e.g., in geriatric patients taking diuretics)
- Withdrawal syndrome (including neonatal withdrawal syndrome): Symptoms may include dizziness, muscle aches, headache, nausea, vomiting, gait instability, agitation, and/or "electric shock" sensations.
- Side effects are most common during the first or second week of therapy. Starting with a lower dosage and gradually increasing it, and taking the medication with food will limit some of these side effects.

DRUG INTERACTIONS:

- *MAOIs:* Extreme risk for serotonin syndrome. Allow 2-week washout period post-MAOI prior to initiating

- *TCAs:* Plasma levels may be increased by SSRIs, so add with caution in low doses
- *ASA and NSAIDs:* Increased risk of bleeding
- *CNS depressants:* May increase depressant effects
- *SSRIs or SARIs:* May cause serotonin syndrome in combination with other medications such as tramadol, high-dose triptans, or the antibiotic linezolid.
- Use with caution in patients taking blood thinners (*Coumadin*), other antidepressants, antihistamines, lithium, TCAs, and certain antibiotics, such as erythromycin, clarithromycin, or azithromycin.

PHARMACOKINETICS:

- Metabolized in the liver by cytochrome P-450 microsomal enzymes.
- Patients reporting intolerable side effects to one SSRI may benefit from switching to another SSRI
- Highly bound to plasma proteins and have a large volume of distribution.
- Readily absorbed in the GI tract, metabolized in the liver, and excreted in the urine. Dosages may be decreased in patients with liver or kidney disease.

Peak plasma levels: 2–10 hr.

Half-life: Variable, but most SSRIs have half-lives of 20–24 hr. A notable exception is fluoxetine (*Prozac*), and its active metabolite, norfluoxetine, which have half-lives of 2–4 days and 8–9 days, respectively. Hence, addition of serotonergic medications to a patient's regimen must not occur until 2–3 weeks after discontinuation of an SSRI (some recommend a 5-week "washout" period for fluoxetine prior to initiation of an MAOI).

- Caution advised in elderly clients.

(cont.)

sertraline (cont.)

PRECAUTIONS:
- May cause sedation and mental clouding
- Use with caution in patients with liver, kidney, or cardiovascular disease
- *Elderly patients:* May require decreased dosage
- Adverse effects and side effects are commonly observed before therapeutic effects
- Many side effects are dose-dependent and may improve over time
- Taper discontinuation to avoid withdrawal symptoms

PATIENT AND FAMILY EDUCATION:
- Should be taken about the same time every day, morning or evening, and can be taken with or without food (with food if there is any stomach upset)
- May start with half of lowest effective dose for 3–7 days, then increase to lowest effective dose to diminish side effects.
- Administration time may be adjusted based on observed sedating or activating drug effects
- May take up to 4–8 weeks to reach its full effect at this dose, but some may see symptoms of depression improving in as little as 2 weeks.
- If planning or are pregnant, discuss the benefits versus the risks of using this medicine while pregnant.
- Because this medicine is excreted in the breast milk, nursing mothers should not breastfeed while taking this medicine without prior consultation with a psychiatric nurse practitioner or psychiatrist. Newborns may develop symptoms including feeding or breathing difficulties, seizures, muscle stiffness, jitteriness, or constant crying.
- Do not stop taking this medication unless the health care provider directs. Report side effects or worsening symptoms to the health care provider promptly.
- The medication should be tapered gradually when changing or discontinuing therapy.
- Dosage should be adjusted to reach remission of symptoms and treatment should continue

for at least 4–9 months following remission of symptoms
- Caution is advised when using this drug in the elderly because they may be more sensitive to the effects of the drug. Elderly patients should receive a lower starting dose.
- Keep these medications out of the reach of children and pets.

SPECIAL POPULATIONS:
- *Elderly:* Older individuals tend to be more sensitive to medication side effects such as hypotension and anticholinergic effects. They often require adjustment of medication doses for hepatic or renal dysfunction. SSRIs with shorter half-lives or less P-450 inhibition may be more desirable (e.g., citalopram) for geriatric populations than SSRIs with longer half-lives (e.g., fluoxetine). SSRIs have been associated with increased risk of falls in nursing home residents and neurologic effects in patients with Parkinson's disease. Elderly patients are more prone to SSRI-induced hyponatremia. Paroxetine shows greater anticholinergic and sedating effects than other SSRIs
- *Pregnancy:* Psychotherapy is the initial choice for most pregnant patients with mild to moderate MDD. Most SSRIs are category C drugs due to adverse effects observed in animal studies. Sertraline has been found to have lower cord blood levels than other SSRIs, although the clinical significance is unknown. Thus, an individual risk-benefit analysis must be done to determine appropriate treatment in pregnant women with MDD. Paroxetine is a category D drug. If continued during pregnancy, SSRI dosage may need to be increased to maintain euthymia due to physiologic changes associated with pregnancy.
- *Children:* Initial SSRI dosing in children typically begins at approx. 50% adult dosing. Increasing doses may require more gradual increments, and discontinuation may require a more gradual taper. Psychiatric consultation is recommended due to black box warning of increased suicidal ideation using SSRI therapy in children.

Paxil, Paxil CR   **paroxetine**

AVAILABLE FORMS: Controlled release (CR) is formulated to dissolve in lower intestine and minimize GI distress. Tablet, 10, 20, 30 and 40 mg; suspension, 10 mg/5 mL (250 mL); controlled release ECTs, 12.5, 25 and 37.5 mg. *Note:* Some formulations may be only available as trade name formulations.

DOSAGE: Starting dose 20 mg/day; maintenance dose 20–60 mg

ADMINISTRATION: PO, with or without food. Controlled release tables must remain intact and not be split or crushed prior to administration.

SIDE EFFECTS: Due to short half-life, may observe greater withdrawal side effects than others in its class. Also may notice more weight gain than other medications in its class.
- May cause CNS depression (sedation, fatigue) or activation (insomnia); weight gain; nervousness; headache and nausea, particularly early in treatment; dry mouth; excess perspiration; insomnia; serotonin syndrome; diarrhea; sexual dysfunction (>50% in men and women); hyponatremia (e.g., in geriatric patients taking diuretics).
- Withdrawal syndrome (including neonatal withdrawal syndrome): May include dizziness,
(cont.)

MAJOR DEPRESSIVE DISORDER: Selective Serotonin Reuptake Inhibitors (SSRIs)

paroxetine (*cont.*)

muscle aches, headache, nausea, vomiting, gait instability, agitation, and/or "electric shock" sensations.

- Side effects are most common during the first or second week of therapy. Starting with a lower dosage and gradually increasing it, and taking the medication with food will limit some of these side effects.

DRUG INTERACTIONS:

- *MAOIs:* Extreme risk for serotonin syndrome. Allow 2-week washout period post-MAOI prior to initiation
- *TCAs:* Plasma levels may be increased by SSRIs, so add with caution in low doses
- *ASA and NSAIDs:* Increased risk of bleeding
- *CNS depressants:* May increase depressant effects
- *SSRIs or SARIs:* May cause serotonin syndrome in combination with other medications such as tramadol, high-dose triptans, or the antibiotic linezolid.
- Use with caution in patients taking blood thinners (*Coumadin*), other antidepressants, antihistamines, lithium, TCAs, and certain antibiotics, such as erythromycin, clarithromycin, or azithromycin.

PHARMACOKINETICS:

- Metabolized in the liver by cytochrome P-450 microsomal enzymes.
- Highly bound to plasma proteins and have a large volume of distribution.
- Readily absorbed in the GI tract, metabolized in the liver, and excreted in the urine. Dosages may be decreased in patients with liver or kidney disease.
- Caution advised in elderly clients.

Peak plasma levels: 2–10 hr

Half-life: Variable, but most SSRIs have half-lives of 20–24 hr. A notable exception is fluoxetine (*Prozac*), and its active metabolite, norfluoxetine, which have half-lives of 2–4 days and 8–9 days, respectively. Hence, addition of serotonergic medications to a patient's regimen must not occur until 2–3 weeks after discontinuation of an SSRI (some recommend a 5-week "washout" period for fluoxetine prior to initiation of an MAOI).

PRECAUTIONS:

- May cause sedation and mental clouding
- Use with caution in patients with liver, kidney, or cardiovascular disease
- *Elderly patients:* May require decreased dosage
- Adverse effects and side effects are commonly observed before therapeutic effects
- Many side effects are dose-dependent and may improve over time
- Taper discontinuation to avoid withdrawal symptoms

PATIENT AND FAMILY EDUCATION:

- Should be taken about the same time every day, morning or evening, and can be taken with or without food (with food if there is any stomach upset)
- May start with half of lowest effective dose for 3–7 days, then increase to lowest effective dose to diminish side effects.
- Administration time may be adjusted based on observed sedating or activating drug effects
- May take up to 4–8 weeks to reach its full effect at this dose, but some may see symptoms of depression improving in as little as 2 weeks.
- If planning or are pregnant, discuss the benefits versus the risks of using this medicine while pregnant.
- Because this medicine is excreted in the breast milk, nursing mothers should not breastfeed while taking this medicine without prior consultation with a psychiatric nurse practitioner or psychiatrist. Newborns may develop symptoms including feeding or breathing difficulties, seizures, muscle stiffness, jitteriness, or constant crying.
- Do not stop taking this medication unless the health care provider directs. Report side effects or worsening symptoms to the health care provider promptly.
- The medication should be tapered gradually when changing or discontinuing therapy.
- Dosage should be adjusted to reach remission of symptoms and treatment should continue for at least 4–9 months following remission of symptoms
- Caution is advised when using this drug in the elderly because they may be more sensitive to the effects of the drug. Elderly patients should receive a lower starting dose.
- Keep these medications out of the reach of children and pets.

SPECIAL POPULATIONS:

- *Elderly:* Older individuals tend to be more sensitive to medication side effects such as hypotension and anticholinergic effects. They often require adjustment of medication doses for hepatic or renal dysfunction. SSRIs with shorter half-lives or less P-450 inhibition may be more desirable (e.g., citalopram) for geriatric populations than SSRIs with longer half-lives (e.g., fluoxetine). SSRIs have been associated with increased risk of falls in nursing home residents and neurologic effects in patients with Parkinson's disease. Elderly patients are more prone to SSRI-induced hyponatremia. Paroxetine shows greater anticholinergic and sedating effects than other SSRIs
- *Pregnancy:* Psychotherapy is the initial choice for most pregnant patients with mild to moderate MDD. Most SSRIs are category C drugs due to adverse effects observed in animal studies. Thus, an individual risk-benefit analysis must be done to determine appropriate treatment in pregnant women with MDD. Paroxetine is a category D drug. If continued during pregnancy, *(cont.)*

MAJOR DEPRESSIVE DISORDER: Selective Serotonin Reuptake Inhibitors (SSRIs)

paroxetine (cont.)

SSRI dosage may need to be increased to maintain euthymia due to physiologic changes associated with pregnancy.

- *Children:* Initial SSRI dosing in children typically begins at approx. 50% adult dosing. Increasing doses may require more gradual increments, and discontinuation may require a more gradual taper. Psychiatric consultation is recommended due to black box warning of increased suicidal ideation using SSRI therapy in children.

Celexa   **citalopram**

AVAILABLE FORMS: Tablet, 10, 20, and 40 mg; solution, 10 mg/5 mL (240 mL)

DOSAGE: Starting dose 20 mg/day; maintenance dose 20–60 mg, adjust in 20 mg increments

ADMINISTRATION: Oral, with or without food.

SIDE EFFECTS:

- May cause CNS depression (sedation, fatigue) or activation (insomnia)
- Tends to be weight neutral or approximately 2 pounds of weight gain in a year
- Nervousness; headache and nausea, particularly early in treatment; insomnia; excess perspiration; serotonin syndrome; diarrhea; sexual dysfunction; hyponatremia (e.g., in geriatric patients taking diuretics)
- Withdrawal syndrome (including neonatal withdrawal syndrome): Symptoms may include dizziness, muscle aches, headache, nausea, vomiting, gait instability, agitation, and/or "electric shock" sensations.
- Side effects are most common during the first week or two of therapy. Starting with a lower dosage and gradually increasing it, and taking the medication with food will limit some of these side effects.

DRUG INTERACTIONS:

- *MAOIs:* Extreme risk for serotonin syndrome. Allow 2-week washout period post-MAOI prior to initiating
- *TCAs:* Plasma levels may be increased by SSRIs, so add with caution in low doses
- *ASA and NSAIDs:* Increased risk of bleeding
- *CNS depressants:* May increase depressant effects
- *SSRIs or SARIs:* May cause serotonin syndrome in combination with other medications such as tramadol, high-dose triptans, or the antibiotic linezolid.
- Use with caution in patients taking blood thinners (*Coumadin*), other antidepressants, antihistamines, lithium, TCAs, and certain antibiotics, such as erythromycin, clarithromycin, or azithromycin.

PHARMACOKINETICS:

- Metabolized in the liver by cytochrome P-450 microsomal enzymes.
- Highly bound to plasma proteins and have a large volume of distribution.
- Readily absorbed in the GI tract, metabolized in the liver, and excreted in the urine. Dosages may be decreased in patients with liver or kidney disease.
- Caution advised in elderly clients.

Peak plasma levels: 2–10 hr.

Half-life: Variable, but most SSRIs have half-lives of 20–24 hr. A notable exception is fluoxetine (*Prozac*), and its active metabolite, norfluoxetine, which have half-lives of 2–4 days and 8–9 days, respectively. Hence, addition of serotonergic medications to a patient's regimen must not occur until 2–3 weeks after discontinuation of an SSRI (some recommend a 5-week "washout" period for fluoxetine prior to initiation of an MAOI).

PRECAUTIONS:

- May cause sedation and mental clouding
- Use with caution in patients with liver, kidney, or cardiovascular disease
- *Elderly patients:* May require decreased dosage
- Adverse effects and side effects are commonly observed before therapeutic effects
- Many side effects are dose-dependent and may improve over time
- Taper discontinuation to avoid withdrawal symptoms

PATIENT AND FAMILY EDUCATION:

- Should be taken about the same time every day, morning or evening, and can be taken with or without food (with food if there is any stomach upset)
- May start with half of lowest effective dose for 3–7 days, then increase to lowest effective dose to diminish side effects.
- Administration time may be adjusted based on observed sedating or activating drug effects
- May take up to 4–8 weeks to reach its full effect at this dose, but some may see symptoms of depression improving in as little as 2 weeks.
- If planning or are pregnant, discuss the benefits versus the risks of using this medicine while pregnant.
- Because this medicine is excreted in the breast milk, nursing mothers should not breastfeed while taking this medicine without prior consultation with a psychiatric nurse practitioner or psychiatrist. Newborns may develop symptoms including feeding or breathing difficulties, seizures, muscle stiffness, jitteriness, or constant crying.
- Do not stop taking this medication unless the health care provider directs. Report side effects
(cont.)

MAJOR DEPRESSIVE DISORDER: Selective Serotonin Reuptake Inhibitors (SSRIs)

citalopram (cont.)

or worsening symptoms to the health care provider promptly.

- The medication should be tapered gradually when changing or discontinuing therapy.
- Dosage should be adjusted to reach remission of symptoms and treatment should continue for at least 4–9 months following remission of symptoms
- Caution is advised when using this drug in the elderly because they may be more sensitive to the effects of the drug. Elderly patients should receive a lower starting dose.
- Keep these medications out of the reach of children and pets.

SPECIAL POPULATIONS:

- *Elderly:* Older individuals tend to be more sensitive to medication side effects such as hypotension and anticholinergic effects. They often require adjustment of medication doses for hepatic or renal dysfunction. SSRIs with shorter half-lives or less P-450 inhibition may be more desirable (e.g., citalopram) for geriatric populations than SSRIs with longer half-lives (e.g., fluoxetine). SSRIs have been associated with increased risk of falls in nursing home residents and neurologic effects in patients with Parkinson's disease. Elderly patients are more prone to SSRI-induced hyponatremia. Paroxetine shows greater anticholinergic and sedating effects than other SSRIs

- *Pregnancy:* Psychotherapy is the initial choice for most pregnant patients with mild to moderate MDD. Most SSRIs are category C drugs due to adverse effects observed in animal studies. Thus, an individual risk-benefit analysis must be done to determine appropriate treatment in pregnant women with MDD. Paroxetine is a category D drug. If continued during pregnancy, SSRI dosage may need to be increased to maintain euthymia due to physiologic changes associated with pregnancy.

- *Children:* Initial SSRI dosing in children typically begins at approx. 50% adult dosing. Increasing doses may require more gradual increments, and discontinuation may require a more gradual taper. Psychiatric consultation is recommended due to black box warning of increased suicidal ideation using SSRI therapy in children.

escitalopram   *Lexapro*

AVAILABLE FORMS: Tablet, 5, 10, and 20 mg; solution: 1 mg/mL (240 mL)

DOSAGE: Starting dose, 10 mg/day; maintenance dose, 10–20 mg

ADMINISTRATION: Oral, once daily, with or without food

SIDE EFFECTS:

- *CNS:* Headache, agitation or restlessness, insomnia, sedation, changes in sexual desire, sexual performance and sexual satisfaction; excess perspiration; withdrawal syndrome if not tapered; lower incidence of side effects than citalopram;
- *GI:* Nausea, constipation, dry mouth

DRUG INTERACTIONS:

- *MAOIs:* Extreme risk for serotonin syndrome. Allow 2-week washout period post-MAOI prior to initiation
- *TCAs:* Plasma levels may be increased by SSRIs, so add with caution in low doses
- *ASA and NSAIDs:* Increased risk of bleeding
- *CNS depressants:* May increase depressant effects
- *SSRIs or SARIs:* May cause serotonin syndrome in combination with other medications such as tramadol, high-dose triptans, or the antibiotic linezolid.
- Use with caution in patients taking blood thinners (*Coumadin*), other antidepressants, antihistamines, lithium, TCAs, and certain antibiotics, such as erythromycin, clarithromycin, or azithromycin.

PHARMACOKINETICS:

- Metabolized in the liver by cytochrome P-450 microsomal enzymes. Paroxetine, fluoxetine, and sertraline may have greater P-450 enzyme effect than citalopram and escitalopram.
- Highly bound to plasma proteins and have a large volume of distribution.
- Absorbed in the GI tract, metabolized in the liver, and excreted in the urine. Dosages may be decreased in patients with liver or kidney disease.
- Caution advised in elderly clients.

Peak plasma levels: 2–10 hr

Half-life: Variable, but most have half-lives of 20–24 hr. Notable exception is fluoxetine (*Prozac*), and its active metabolite, norfluoxetine, which have half-lives of 2–4 days and 8–9 days, respectively. Hence, addition of serotonergic medications to a patient's regimen must not occur until 2–3 weeks after discontinuation of an SSRI (some recommend a 5-week "washout" period for fluoxetine prior to initiation of an MAOI).

PRECAUTIONS:

- May cause sedation and mental clouding
- Use with caution in patients with liver, kidney, or cardiovascular disease
- *Elderly:* May require decreased dosage
- Adverse effects and side effects are commonly observed before therapeutic effects
- Many side effects are dose-dependent and may improve over time

(cont.)

MAJOR DEPRESSIVE DISORDER: Selective Serotonin Reuptake Inhibitors (SSRIs)

escitalopram (*cont.*)

- Taper discontinuation to avoid withdrawal symptoms

PATIENT AND FAMILY EDUCATION:
- Should be taken about the same time every day, morning or evening, and can be taken with or without food (with food if there any stomach upset).
- May start with half of lowest effective dose for 3–7 days, then increase to lowest effective dose to diminish side effects.
- Administration time may be adjusted based on observed sedating or activating drug effects
- May take up to 4–8 weeks to reach its full effect at this dose, but some may see symptoms of depression improving in as little as 2 weeks.
- If planning or are pregnant, discuss benefits versus risks of using this medicine while pregnant.
- Because this medicine is excreted in the breast milk, nursing mothers should not breastfeed while taking this medicine without prior consultation with a psychiatric nurse practitioner or psychiatrist. Newborns may develop symptoms including feeding or breathing difficulties, seizures, muscle stiffness, jitteriness, or constant crying.
- Do not stop taking this medication unless the health care provider directs. Report side effects or worsening symptoms to the health care provider promptly.
- The medication should be tapered gradually when changing or discontinuing therapy.
- Dosage should be adjusted to reach remission of symptoms and treatment should continue for at least 4–9 months following remission of symptoms.
- Caution is advised when using this drug in the elderly because they may be more sensitive to the effects of the drug. Elderly patients should receive a lower starting dose.
- Keep these medications out of the reach of children and pets.

SPECIAL POPULATIONS:
- *Elderly:* Older individuals tend to be more sensitive to medication side effects such as hypotension and anticholinergic effects. They often require adjustment of medication doses for hepatic or renal dysfunction. SSRIs with shorter half-lives or less P-450 inhibition may be more desirable (e.g., citalopram, escitalopram) for geriatric populations than SSRIs with longer half-lives (e.g., fluoxetine). SSRIs have been associated with increased risk of falls in nursing home residents and neurologic effects in patients with Parkinson's disease. Elderly patients are more prone to SSRI-induced hyponatremia. Paroxetine shows greater anticholinergic and sedating effects than other SSRIs.
- *Pregnancy:* Psychotherapy is the initial choice for most pregnant patients with mild to moderate MDD. Most SSRIs are category C drugs due to adverse effects observed in animal studies. Thus, an individual risk-benefit analysis must be done to determine appropriate treatment in pregnant women with MDD. Paroxetine is a category D drug. If continued during pregnancy, SSRI dosage may need to be increased to maintain euthymia due to physiologic changes associated with pregnancy.
- *Children:* Initial SSRI dosing in children typically begins at approx. 50% of adult dosing. Increasing doses may require more gradual increments, and discontinuation may require a more gradual taper. Psychiatric consultation is recommended due to black box warning of increased suicidal ideation using SSRI therapy in children.

Luvox **fluvoxamine**

AVAILABLE FORMS: Tablet, 25, 50 and 100 mg; extended-release capsule, 100 and 150 mg. *Note:* Some formulations are not available as generic medications

DOSAGE: Starting dose 50 mg/day; maintenance dose 50–300 mg

ADMINISTRATION: Oral, with or without food. Controlled release tables must remain intact and not be split or crushed prior to administration.

SIDE EFFECTS: May cause significant sedation (unique among SSRIs); administer at bedtime due to sedation; side effects similar to paroxetine and other SSRIs also observed. May be used for clients with co-existing OCD or other anxiety disorders. May be associated with less sexual side effect than other SSRIs.

DRUG INTERACTIONS
- *MAOIs:* Extreme risk for serotonin syndrome. Allow 2-week washout period post-MAOI prior to initiation
- *TCAs:* Plasma levels may be increased by SSRIs, so add with caution in low doses
- *ASA and NSAIDs:* Increased risk of bleeding
- *CNS depressants:* May increase depressant effects
- *SSRIs or SARIs:* May cause serotonin syndrome in combination with other medications such as tramadol, high-dose triptans, or the antibiotic linezolid.
- Use with caution in patients taking blood thinners (*Coumadin*), other antidepressants, antihistamines, lithium, TCAs, and certain antibiotics, such as erythromycin, clarithromycin, or azithromycin.

(cont.)

MAJOR DEPRESSIVE DISORDER: Selective Serotonin Reuptake Inhibitors (SSRIs)

fluvoxamine (*cont.*)

PHARMACOKINETICS:
- Metabolized in the liver by cytochrome P-450 microsomal enzymes.
- Highly bound to plasma proteins and have a large volume of distribution.
- Readily absorbed in the GI tract, metabolized in the liver, and excreted in the urine. Dosages may be decreased in patients with liver or kidney disease.
- Caution advised in elderly clients.

Peak plasma levels: 2–10 hr

Half-life: Variable, but most SSRIs have half-lives of 20–24 hr. A notable exception is fluoxetine (*Prozac*), and its active metabolite, norfluoxetine, which have half-lives of 2–4 days and 8–9 days, respectively. Hence, addition of serotonergic medications to a patient's regimen must not occur until 2–3 weeks after discontinuation of an SSRI (some recommend a 5-week "washout" period for fluoxetine prior to initiation of an MAOI).

PRECAUTIONS:
- Adverse effects and side effects are commonly observed before therapeutic effects
- Many side effects are dose-dependent and may improve over time
- Taper discontinuation to avoid withdrawal symptoms

PATIENT AND FAMILY EDUCATION:
- Should be taken about the same time every day, morning or evening, and can be taken with or without food (with food if there is any stomach upset)
- May start with half of lowest effective dose for 3–7 days, then increase to lowest effective dose to diminish side effects.
- Administration time may be adjusted based on observed sedating or activating drug effects
- May take up to 4–8 weeks to reach its full effect at this dose, but some may see symptoms of depression improving in as little as 2 weeks.
- If planning or are pregnant, discuss the benefits versus the risks of using this medicine while pregnant.
- Because this medicine is excreted in the breast milk, nursing mothers should not breastfeed while taking this medicine without prior consultation with a psychiatric nurse practitioner

or psychiatrist. Newborns may develop symptoms including feeding or breathing difficulties, seizures, muscle stiffness, jitteriness, or constant crying.
- Do not stop taking this medication unless the health care provider directs. Report side effects or worsening symptoms to the health care provider promptly.
- The medication should be tapered gradually when changing therapy or discontinuing.
- Dosage should be adjusted to reach remission of symptoms and treatment should continue for at least 4–9 months following remission of symptoms.
- Caution is advised when using this drug in the elderly because they may be more sensitive to the effects of the drug. Elderly patients should receive a lower starting dose.
- Keep these medications out of the reach of children and pets.

SPECIAL POPULATIONS:
- *Elderly:* Older individuals tend to be more sensitive to medication side effects such as hypotension and anticholinergic effects. They often require adjustment of medication doses for hepatic or renal dysfunction. SSRIs with shorter half-lives (e.g., paroxetine) may be more desirable geriatric populations than SSRIs with longer half-lives (e.g., fluoxetine). SSRIs have been associated with increased risk of falls in nursing home residents and neurologic effects in patients with Parkinson's disease. Elderly patients are more prone to SSRI-induced hyponatremia. Paroxetine shows greater anticholinergic and sedating effects than other SSRIs
- *Pregnancy:* Psychotherapy is the initial choice for most pregnant patients with mild to moderate MDD. Most SSRIs are category C drugs due to adverse effects observed in animal studies. Paroxetine is a category D drug. If continued during pregnancy, dosage may need to be increased to maintain euthymia due to physiologic changes associated with pregnancy.
- *Children:* Initial SSRI dosing in children typically begins approx. 50% adult dosing. Increasing doses may require more gradual increments, and discontinuation may require a more gradual taper.

Class: Serotonin/Norepinephrine Reuptake Inhibitors (SNRIs)

- SNRIs are a common alternative to SSRIs, with particular use in those clients with chronic pain disorders and atypical symptoms characterized by fatigue and difficulty with concentration. May be of benefit to perimenopausal women experiencing hot flashes. May be less preferred in patients with pre-existing hypertension.
- Inhibition of NE reuptake may increase CNS stimulation and produce anti-sedative effects. Higher drug concentrations tend to produce more NE effects; lower concentrations produce more serotonergic effects.

MAJOR DEPRESSIVE DISORDER: Serotonin/Norepinephrine Reuptake Inhibitors (SNRIs)

Effexor, Effexor XR | **venlafaxine, venlafaxine XR**

AVAILABLE FORMS: Tablet, 25, 37.5, 50, 75 and 100 mg; extended-release capsule, 37.5, 50, 75 and 150 mg; extended-release tablet, 37.5, 75, 150 and 225 mg.

▶ **Note:** Preference for XR formulation due to possibly increased potential for side effects, particularly withdrawal syndrome, of non-extended release formulation with short half-life

DOSAGE: Starting dose 37.5 mg/day; maintenance dose 75–225 mg/day, adjusted in 37.5–75 mg increments; maximum dose of 375 mg/day may be used for unresponsive MDD

ADMINISTRATION: PO, with food. Extended release tablets should not be crushed or chewed. Capsules may be opened and sprinkled on applesauce.

SIDE EFFECTS: Increased anxiety, nervousness; impaired platelet aggregation (easy bruising); CNS depression; hypertension; nausea, weight loss, or occasionally weight gain; headache, nausea; muscle weakness; insomnia; serotonin syndrome
- Withdrawal syndrome (including neonatal withdrawal syndrome); sexual dysfunction; hyponatremia (e.g., geriatric patients taking diuretics)

DRUG INTERACTIONS
- *ASA and NSAIDs:* Increased risk of bleeding
- *CNS depressants:* May increase or decrease effects
- *MAOI:* May cause serotonin syndrome. Allow 2-week washout period post-MAOI prior to initiating venlafaxine
- *SSRIs or SARIs:* May cause serotonin syndrome
- *TCAs:* Plasma levels may be increased by SNRIs
- Alcohol may substantially increase potential for hepatotoxicity

PHARMACOKINETICS
- Metabolized to the active metabolite desvenlafaxine by CYP450 2D6, leading to a prolonged duration of action.
- Well absorbed and readily distributed throughout the body. Renal excretion accounts for nearly 90% of drug removal.

Half-life: non-enteric coated formulation, 2 hr; extended-release formulation, 6 hr

PRECAUTIONS
- Not FDA approved for use in children
- Monitor for BP elevations
- *Seizure disorders:* Use with caution
- *Hepatic impairment:* Reduce dosage
- *Renal impairment:* Reduce dosage
- *Narrow-angle glaucoma or elevated IOP:* Use with caution
- Pharmacokinetic properties similar to SSRIs.
- Adverse effects and side effects are commonly observed before therapeutic effects
- Many side effects are dose-dependent and may improve over time

PATIENT AND FAMILY EDUCATION:
- Should be taken about the same time every day, morning or evening, although typically it is started in the morning, and can be taken with or without food (with food if there is any stomach upset)
- May start with half of lowest effective dose for 3–7 days, then increase to lowest effective dose to diminish side effects.
- Administration time may be adjusted based on observed sedating or activating drug effects
- May take up to 4–8 weeks to reach its full effect at this dose, but some may see symptoms of depression improving in as little as 2 weeks.
- If planning or are pregnant, discuss the benefits versus the risks of using this medicine while pregnant.
- Because this medicine is excreted in the breast milk, nursing mothers should not breastfeed while taking this medicine without prior consultation with a psychiatric nurse practitioner or psychiatrist. Newborns may develop symptoms including feeding or breathing difficulties, seizures, muscle stiffness, jitteriness, or constant crying.
- Do not stop taking this medication unless the health care provider directs. Report side effects or worsening symptoms to the health care provider promptly.
- The medication should be tapered gradually when changing therapy or discontinuing.
- Dosage should be adjusted to reach remission of symptoms and treatment should continue for at least 4–9 months following remission of symptoms.
- Caution is advised when using this drug in the elderly because they may be more sensitive to the effects of the drug. Elderly patients should receive a lower starting dose.
- Keep these medications out of the reach of children and pets.

SPECIAL POPULATIONS:
- *Elderly:* Older individuals tend to be more sensitive to medication side effects such as hypotension and anticholinergic effects. They often require adjustment of medication doses for hepatic or renal dysfunction. Elderly patients may tolerate lower doses better and there is a reduced risk of suicide. May assist in treatment of chronic or depression-related physical pain.
- *Pregnancy:* Psychotherapy is the initial choice for most pregnant patients with mild to moderate MDD. Category C drug, as there are no adequate studies during pregnancy. Particular caution with exposure (avoid if possible) during first trimester. An individual risk-benefit analysis must be done to determine appropriate treatment in pregnant women with MDD.
- *Children:* Monitor closely, as risk of suicidal ideation is greatest in adolescents. Monitor for excessive activation effects or undiagnosed bipolar disorder. Obtain consultation with a pediatric psychiatric specialist.

MAJOR DEPRESSIVE DISORDER: Serotonin/Norepinephrine Reuptake Inhibitors (SNRIs)

duloxetine   *Cymbalta*

AVAILABLE FORMS: Delayed-release enteric coated capsule, 20, 30 and 60 mg

DOSAGE: Starting dose 30 mg/day; maintenance dose 40–60 mg/day

ADMINISTRATION: PO, with or without food. Do not crush or chew capsules. May start as twice-daily or once daily administration (typically in the morning)

SIDE EFFECTS:
- GI distress, particularly nausea at onset of treatment, sexual dysfunction, and urinary retention. Others similar to venlafaxine.
- Recommended for treating depression that has accompanying physical pain. May be associated with lower incidence of hypertension and have milder withdrawal symptoms than other SNRIs.

DRUG INTERACTIONS: Similar to other SNRIs, can cause elevated response in TCAs and fatal interaction if combined with MAOIs.

PHARMACOKINETICS: Metabolized by CYP450 1A2 and 2D6.

PRECAUTIONS:
- Not recommended for patients with renal impairment or hepatic impairment
- Closely monitor patients with a history of seizures
- Avoid stimulants, such as caffeine, as may amplify the drug's activating side effects

PATIENT AND FAMILY EDUCATION:
- Should be taken about the same time every day, morning or evening, although typically it is started in the morning, and can be taken with or without food (with food if there is any stomach upset)
- May start with half of lowest effective dose for 3–7 days, then increase to lowest effective dose to diminish side effects.
- Administration time may be adjusted based on observed sedating or activating drug effects
- May take up to 4–8 weeks to reach its full effect at this dose, but some may see symptoms of depression improving in as little as 2 weeks.
- If planning or are pregnant, discuss the benefits versus the risks of using this medicine while pregnant.

- Because this medicine is excreted in the breast milk, nursing mothers should not breastfeed while taking this medicine without prior consultation with a psychiatric nurse practitioner or psychiatrist. Newborns may develop symptoms including feeding or breathing difficulties, seizures, muscle stiffness, jitteriness, or constant crying.
- Do not stop taking this medication unless the health care provider directs. Report side effects or worsening symptoms to the health care provider promptly.
- The medication should be tapered when changing or discontinuing therapy.
- Dosage should be adjusted to reach remission of symptoms and treatment should continue for at least 4–9 months following remission of symptoms.
- Caution is advised when using this drug in the elderly because they may be more sensitive to the effects of the drug. Elderly patients should receive a lower starting dose.
- Keep these medications out of the reach of children and pets.

SPECIAL POPULATIONS:
- *Elderly:* Older individuals tend to be more sensitive to medication side effects such as hypotension and anticholinergic effects. They often require adjustment of medication doses for hepatic or renal dysfunction. Elderly patients may tolerate lower doses better and there is a reduced risk of suicide. May assist in treatment of chronic or depression-related physical pain.
- *Pregnancy:* Psychotherapy is the initial choice for most pregnant patients with mild to moderate MDD. Category C drug, as there are no adequate studies during pregnancy. Particular caution with exposure (avoid if possible) during first trimester. An individual risk-benefit analysis must be done to determine appropriate treatment in pregnant women with MDD.
- *Children:* Monitor closely, as risk of suicidal ideation is greatest in adolescents. Monitor for excessive activation effects or undiagnosed bipolar disorder. Obtain consultation with a pediatric psychiatric specialist.

desvenlafaxine   *Pristiq*

AVAILABLE FORMS: Extended-release tablet, 50 and 100 mg

DOSAGE: Starting dose 50 mg/day; maintenance dose 50–400 mg/day. Doses greater than 50 mg/day not found to have additional benefit and may be associated with greater side effects.

ADMINISTRATION: PO, with or without food. Do not crush or chew tablet.

SIDE EFFECTS: GI distress, sexual dysfunction, and urinary retention; increased blood pressure.

DRUG INTERACTIONS: Similar to other NRIs, can cause elevated response in TCAs and fatal interaction if combined with MAOIs.

PHARMACOKINETICS:
- Not metabolized by P450s, so more predictable plasma levels than many other antidepressants, including venlafaxine.

(cont.)

desvenlafaxine (cont.)

Half-life: 9–13 hr

PRECAUTIONS:
- Similar to other SNRIs.
- Do not administer with MAOIs and use caution when combining with other drugs that have activating properties.
- Use with caution in patients with a history of seizures or heart disease.

PATIENT AND FAMILY EDUCATION: Similar to other SNRIs.

SPECIAL POPULATIONS:
- *Elderly:* Older individuals tend to be more sensitive to medication side effects such as hypotension and anticholinergic effects. Often require adjustment of medication doses for hepatic or renal dysfunction. Elderly patients may tolerate lower doses better and there is a reduced risk of suicide. May assist in treatment of chronic or depression-related physical pain.
- *Pregnancy:* Psychotherapy is the initial choice for most pregnant patients with mild to moderate MDD. Category C drug, as there are no adequate studies during pregnancy. Particular caution with exposure (avoid if possible) during first trimester. An individual risk-benefit analysis must be done to determine appropriate treatment in pregnant women with MDD.
- *Children:* Psychotherapy is the initial choice for most pregnant patients with MDD. Monitor closely, as risk of suicidal ideation is greatest in adolescents. Monitor for excessive activation effects or undiagnosed bipolar disorder. Obtain consultation with a pediatric psychiatric specialist.

Class: Serotonin-2 Antagonist/Reuptake Inhibitors (SARIs)

- Alternative to SSRIs, with particular use in clients with co-occurring insomnia or anxiety.
- Inhibits serotonin 2A receptor and serotonin reuptake. Receptor inhibition produces sedating effect.
- Second-line medications that may be used in combination with SSRIs or SNRIs.

Serzone   **nefazodone**

AVAILABLE FORMS: Tablet, 50, 100, 150, 200 and 250 mg

DOSAGE: Starting dose, 50 mg/day; maintenance dose, 100–400 mg/day, typically administered in divided doses

ADMINISTRATION: Administration with or after food may decrease side effects, but may impair drug absorption.

SIDE EFFECTS: Anticholinergic effects; hepatotoxicity; orthostatic hypotension; headache, drowsiness, insomnia, agitation, dizziness, or sedation; priapism; dry mouth, nausea, and constipation; muscle weakness; sexual dysfunction, significantly less than with SSRIs

DRUG INTERACTIONS:
- Sedative effects may be exacerbated by use of other sedatives
- May be used as adjunct to SSRI therapy
- *MAOIs:* Extreme risk for drug toxicity

PHARMACOKINETICS:
- Inhibits activity of CYP450 3A4, which may alter metabolism of other medications

Half-life: Parent compound, 2–4 hr. Metabolized to an active metabolite that has a half-life of 12 hr, which is inactivated by CYP450 2D6

PRECAUTIONS:
- Use with caution in patients with renal impairment
- Avoid in patients with hepatic impairment or pre-existing liver disease and avoid combining with other medications with hepatic effects
- Monitor with routine serum liver function tests
- Caution in patients at risk for seizure disorders; may lower seizure threshold.
- Extremely low but life-threatening potential for liver damage (1:300,000 patient-years)
- Adverse effects and side effects are commonly observed before therapeutic effects

PATIENT AND FAMILY EDUCATION:
- Should be taken about the same time every day, morning or evening, although typically it is started in the morning, and can be taken with or without food (with food if there is any stomach upset)
- May take up to 4–8 weeks to reach its full effect at this dose, but some may see symptoms of depression improving in as little as 2 weeks.
- If planning or are pregnant, discuss the benefits versus the risks of using this medicine while pregnant.
- Because this medicine is excreted in the breast milk, nursing mothers should not breastfeed while taking this medicine without prior consultation

(cont.)

nefazodone (cont.)

with a psychiatric nurse practitioner or psychiatrist. Newborns may develop symptoms including feeding or breathing difficulties, seizures, muscle stiffness, jitteriness, or constant crying.

- Do not stop taking this medication unless the health care provider directs. Report side effects or worsening symptoms to the health care provider promptly.
- The medication should be tapered when changing or discontinuing therapy.
- Dosage should be adjusted to reach remission of symptoms and treatment should continue for at least 4–9 months following remission of symptoms.
- Caution is advised when using this drug in the elderly because they may be more sensitive to the effects of the drug. Elderly patients should receive a lower starting dose.
- Keep these medications out of the reach of children and pets.

SPECIAL POPULATIONS:

- *Elderly:* Older individuals tend to be more sensitive to medication side effects such as hypotension and anticholinergic effects. They often require adjustment of medication doses for hepatic or renal dysfunction. Begin treatment at half the standard dose. Do not use in clients with hepatic disease. Caution regarding sedative effects.
- *Pregnancy:* Psychotherapy is the initial choice for most pregnant patients with MDD. Category C drug; not recommended for use during pregnancy, especially during the first trimester, as there are no adequate studies during pregnancy.
- *Children:* Psychiatric consultation is recommended due to black box warning of increased suicidal ideation using SSRI therapy in children.

trazodone   *Desyrel*

AVAILABLE FORMS: Tablet, 50, 100, 150, and 300 mg; extended-release tablet (scored), 150 and 300 mg

DOSAGE: Starting dose 50 mg/day; maintenance dose 75–400 mg

ADMINISTRATION: Orally; taking with food decreases some side effects. Scored extended relief tablets may be broken in half, but should not be crushed or chewed.

SIDE EFFECTS: Sedation, hypotension, nausea; may aid patients experiencing SSRI/SNRI-induced insomnia. Rare occurences of priapism have been reported. This should be discussed with male clients.

DRUG INTERACTIONS: SSRIs may increase plasma concentrations. May inhibit full effect of antihypertensive medications. Patients taking MAOIs should not take this.

PHARMACOKINETICS: Metabolized by CYP450 3A4 to an active metabolite.
Half-life: Parent drug, 7–8 hr; active metabolite, 5–9 hr

PRECAUTIONS:

- Do not use with MAOIs.
- Use with caution in patients with history of seizures.
- Use with caution in patients at risk for undiagnosed bipolar disorder.

SPECIAL POPULATIONS:

- *Elderly:* Older individuals tend to be more sensitive to medication side effects such as hypotension and anticholinergic effects. They often require adjustment of medication doses for hepatic or renal dysfunction. May be more sensitive to side effects and require a lower dosing regimen. Caution due to sedative effects.
- *Pregnancy:* Psychotherapy is the initial choice for most pregnant patients with mild to moderate MDD. Category C. Not advised during pregnancy, as there are no adequate studies (similar to nefazodone).
- *Children:* Typically require a lower initial dosing and prolonged titration. Increased risk of suicidal ideation than in adults

Class: Noradrenergic and Specific Serotonergic Antidepressants (NaSSAs)

NaSSAs and NDRIs are additional alternative MDD treatment options, with a tendency for fewer sexual side effects. They are often used as adjuncts to SSRIs or SNRIs, for specific presentations, when other medications are not effective, or when side effects from other medications are intolerable.

- These antidepressants work through poorly defined mechanisms or mechanisms other than the SSRIs and SNRIs. They do not appear to inhibit serotonergic or histaminergic signaling. Some anticholingeric effects have been reported.

- May be combined with SSRI to offset some SSRI side effects (e.g., sexual dysfunction) or for augmentation of antidepressant effect.
- Mirtazapine antagonizes central presynaptic alpha-2 receptors. Exhibits both noradrenergic and serotonergic activity.
- Bupropion inhibits dopamine and norepinephrine reuptake. It is also nicotininic agonist.
- Buproprion aids in smoking cessation. It is weight neutral and may assist in weight loss. It may be more likely to improve symptoms of fatigue and sleepiness than SSRIs. It should not be used in patients with seizure disorders, eating disorders, or alcohol abuse.

MAJOR DEPRESSIVE DISORDER: Noradrenergic and Specific Serotonergic Antidepressants (NaSSAs)

Remeron   **mirtazapine**

INDICATIONS: Alternative antidepressant medication with particular use in patients who are underweight, anxious, or who have insomnia.

AVAILABLE FORMS: Tablet, 7.5, 15, 30 and 45 mg

DOSAGE: Starting dose 5–15 mg nightly, titrate up to 15–45 mg/day

ADMINISTRATION: Orally, with or without food, at bedtime.

SIDE EFFECTS:
- *Serious:* Agranulocytosis
- Anticholinergic effects
- *Blood dyscrasias:* Neutropenia and agranulocytosis
- Orthostatic hypotension or hypertension
- *CNS:* Somnolence and sedation, dizziness, tremor, confusion
- Increased risk for hyperlipidemia
- Dry mouth
- Significant appetite increase and weight gain (greater than 7% body mass)
- Asthenia

DRUG INTERACTIONS:
- *Sedatives:* Effects may be exacerbated by use of other sedatives
- *MAOIs:* Risk for drug toxicity
- *CNS stimulants* (e.g., amphetamines): May lower seizure threshold
- *Anticholinergic drugs (e.g., antihistamines):* increase effects

PHARMACOKINETICS: Prolonged half-life 20–40 hr, which is increased further in patients with hepatic or renal impairment.

PRECAUTIONS:
- Use with caution in patients with hepatic impairment or renal impairment
- May lower seizure threshold in patients at risk for seizure disorders
- Monitor with CBC and history for signs of agranulocytosis or severe neutropenia
- Low incidence of sexual dysfunction
- Usually dosed at hs due to associated drowsiness (may be helpful in patients with insomnia or anxiety)
- May alter liver function
- Adverse effects and side effects are commonly observed before therapeutic effects

PATIENT AND FAMILY EDUCATION:
- Take 60–90 minutes prior to bedtime, due to associated drowsiness. Do not drive until you know the effect of this medication.
- May cause stomach upset or blood pressure changes (particularly with getting up suddenly).
- This medication may increase appetite or craving for carbohydrates. Monitoring diet and exercise is important.
- May take up to 4–8 weeks to reach its full effect at this dose, but some may see symptoms of depression improving in as little as 2 weeks.
- If planning or are pregnant, discuss the benefits versus the risks of using this medicine while pregnant.
- Because this medicine is excreted in the breast milk, nursing mothers should not breastfeed while taking this medicine without prior consultation with a psychiatric nurse practitioner or psychiatrist. Newborns may develop symptoms including feeding or breathing difficulties, seizures, muscle stiffness, jitteriness, or constant crying.
- Do not stop taking this medication unless the health care provider directs. Report side effects or worsening symptoms to the health care provider promptly.
- Dosage should be adjusted to reach remission of symptoms and treatment should continue for at least 4–9 months following remission of symptoms.
- Caution is advised when using this drug in the elderly because they may be more sensitive to the effects of the drug. Elderly patients should receive a lower starting dose.
- Keep these medications out of the reach of children and pets.

SPECIAL POPULATIONS:
- *Elderly:* Older individuals tend to be more sensitive to medication side effects such as hypotension and anticholinergic effects. They often require adjustment of medication doses for hepatic or renal dysfunction. Recommended to begin at lower dosage.
- *Pregnancy:* Psychotherapy is the initial choice for most pregnant patients with MDD. Category C. Not recommended during pregnancy, especially during the first trimester
- *Children:* Not approved by the FDA for use in children. Use only after consultation with psychiatric specialist.

MAJOR DEPRESSIVE DISORDER: Noradrenergic and Specific Serotonergic Antidepressants (NaSSAs)

Class: Norepinephrine/Dopamine Reuptake Inhibitors (NDRIs)

bupropion, **buproprion SR,** **buproprion XL**	*Wellbutrin, Zyban,* *Wellbutrin SR,* *Wellbutrin XL*

INDICATIONS: Particular use in depressed patients with fatigue, difficulty in concentrating, or who are obese. Common adjunctive agent.

AVAILABLE FORMS: Tablet, 75 and 100 mg; sustained release tablet, 100 and 150 mg; extended-release tablet, 100, 150, 200 and 300 mg

DOSAGE: Starting dose, 150 mg/day; maintenance dose, 150–450 mg/day

ADMINISTRATION: Depending upon formulation prescribed, taken tid (rapid release); bid, second dose not to be given within 5–6 hr of hs in order to avoid insomnia (SR); or once daily in the morning (XL). SR and XL formulations are most commonly used, and XL formulation is recommended if available.

SIDE EFFECTS:
- *Seizures:* Seizure threshold significantly decreased particularly at >300–450 mg/day dosage. Use of SR or XL formulation also helpful in reducing risk of seizure.
- *CNS stimulation:* Headache, anxiety, tremor, tachycardia, and insomnia
- Cognitive impairment and mental clouding
- Delayed hypersensitivity reactions
- Nausea; increased sweating; blurred vision; dry mouth; weight loss

DRUG INTERACTIONS:
- Can elevate TCA activity; therefore, use with caution
- Can be fatal when combined with MAOIs
- Potentially increases plasma levels of other 2D6 metabolites
- Risk of seizure may be increased by concomitant use of inhibitors of CYP2B6 (e.g., desipramine, sertraline, paroxetine, fluoxetine), due to increased bupropion blood levels.

PHARMACOKINETICS:
- Inhibits activity of CYP450 2D6, potentially increasing plasma levels of other 2D6 metabolites
- Converted to an active metabolite.

Half-life: Parent compound, 10–24 hr; active metabolite, 20–24 hr

PRECAUTIONS:
- Use with caution in patients with cardiovascular disease, hepatic impairment, or renal impairment
- Do not use in patients with seizure disorders, alcoholism, or anorexia nervosa
- The incidence of sexual dysfunction occurring from taking this drug is relatively low.

- It may lower the seizure threshold in patients who are at risk for seizure disorders
- Avoid combinations with other CNS stimulants

PATIENT AND FAMILY EDUCATION:
- Should be taken about the same time every day, preferably in the morning (for XL formulation) with or without food.
- If taking rapid release or SR formulation, take last dose more than 5–6 hr from bedtime, as late dosing can precipitate insomnia.
- May take up to 4–8 weeks to reach full effect, but some may see symptoms of depression improving in as little as 2 weeks.
- If planning or are pregnant, discuss the benefits versus the risks of using this medicine while pregnant.
- Because this medicine is excreted in the breast milk, nursing mothers should not breastfeed while taking this medicine without prior consultation with a psychiatric nurse practitioner or psychiatrist. Newborns may develop symptoms including feeding or breathing difficulties, seizures, muscle stiffness, jitteriness, or constant crying.
- Do not stop taking this medication unless the health care provider directs. Report side effects or worsening depression symptoms to the health care provider promptly. Dosage should be adjusted to reach remission of symptoms and treatment should continue for at least 4–9 months following remission of symptoms.
- Keep these medications out of the reach of children and pets.

SPECIAL POPULATIONS:
- *Elderly:* Older individuals tend to be more sensitive to medication side effects such as hypotension and anticholinergic effects. They often require adjustment of medication doses for hepatic or renal dysfunction. Begin at lower dosage; XL formulation recommended
- *Pregnancy:* Psychotherapy is the initial choice for most pregnant patients with mild to moderate MDD. Category C drug. No adequate studies in pregnancy. Particular caution with exposure (avoid if possible) during the first trimester.
- *Children:* Recommended to begin at a lower dosage. Monitor closely for suicidal ideation. Psychiatric consultation is recommended due to black box warning of increased suicidal ideation using SSRI therapy in children. May be useful in treating children with comorbid ADHD.

Class: Tricyclic Antidepressants (TCAs)

TCAs are older antidepressants that are infrequently used for the primary treatment of depression, but sometimes used as an adjunct for patients with comorbid chronic pain or insomnia.

- TCAs are infrequently used for the treatment of MDD due to risk for cardiac arrhythmia and significant side effects. Pre-treatment EKG is indicated in patients with significant cardiac risk factors or in patients older than 50 years of age. Follow-up EKGs may be indicated to identify development of conduction changes shortly after the initiation of TCA use. Persons with QT prolongation are predisposed to develop ventricular tachycardia.

- TCAs are sometimes used adjunctively off label for sleep problems or neuropathic pain syndromes associated with MDD.
- TCAs may be considered for treatment of MDD when all other medications fail to work.
- Common adverse effects result from anticholinergic effects (e.g., blurred vision [mydriasis and cycloplegia], dry mucous membranes, elevated IOP, hyperthermia, constipation, and urinary retention).
- Extrapyramidal effects including tardive dyskinesia, pseudoparkinsonism, akathisia, and dystonia commonly occur.

Elavil — **amitriptyline**

AVAILABLE FORMS: Tablet, 10, 25, 50, 75, 100 and 150 mg

DOSAGE: Starting dose 25–50 mg/day; maintenance dose, 100–300 mg/day

ADMINISTRATION: Orally at bedtime or in divided doses

SIDE EFFECTS: Cardiotoxicity (particularly in overdose), cardiac arrhythmias, and QT interval prolongation; anticholinergic effects; orthostatic hypotension; hypomania; sedation and drowsiness; increased potential for seizures; extrapyramidal effects

DRUG INTERACTIONS
- *MAOIs:* Risk for extreme hypertension
- *CNS depressants* (e.g., alcohol): TCAs increase effects
- *Direct-acting adrenergic agonists* (e.g., epinephrine): TCAs increase effects
- *Anticholinergic drugs* (e.g., antihistamines): TCAs increase effects. Do not use in combination.
- Antiarrhythmic agents
- *SSRIs and other medications:* serotonin syndrome

PHARMACOKINETICS:
- Nicotine use (smoking) increases drug metabolism and may diminish drug potency
- Metabolized by CYP450 2D6 and 1A2, converted to the active metabolite nortriptyline.
- Blood levels may be checked to ensure that levels are not excessive.
Half-life: Approx. 15 hr

PRECAUTIONS:
- Adverse effects and side effects are commonly observed before therapeutic effects
- Many side effects are dose-dependent and may improve over time
- Overdose may result in lethal cardiotoxicity or seizure
- Use with caution in patients with a history of seizure or heart disease
- Avoid in patients with a history of cardiac arrhythmia.
- Monitor with EKG

PATIENT AND FAMILY EDUCATION:
- Should be taken about the same time every day, typically in the evening, and can be taken with

or without food. May cause prolonged sedation. Do not drive until you know the effect of this medication.
- Administration time may be adjusted based on observed sedating or activating drug effects
- May take up to 4–8 weeks to show its maximum effect, but patient may see symptoms of depression improving in as little as 2 weeks.
- If patient plans on becoming pregnant, discuss the benefits versus the risks of using this medicine while pregnant.
- Because this medicine is excreted in the breast milk, nursing mothers should not breastfeed while taking this medicine. Newborns may develop symptoms including feeding or breathing difficulties, seizures, muscle stiffness, jitteriness, or constant crying.
- Do not stop taking this medication unless the health care provider directs. Report symptoms to the health care provider promptly.
- Drug should be tapered gradually when discontinued
- Dosage should be adjusted to reach remission of symptoms and treatment should continue for at least 4–9 months following remission of symptoms
- Keep these medications out of the reach of children and pets.

SPECIAL POPULATIONS:
- *Elderly:* Older individuals tend to be more sensitive to medication side effects such as hypotension and anticholinergic effects. They often require adjustment of doses for hepatic or renal dysfunction. TCAs have been shown in at least one controlled clinical trial to be more effective than SSRIs in hospitalized geriatric patients, and in patients with melancholia and unipolar depression. However, cardiac side effects and fall risk are of great concern in this population. Side effects may be more pronounced and require decreased dosage
- *Pregnancy:* Psychotherapy is the initial choice for most pregnant patients with MDD. Category C. Not recommended in most cases.
- *Children:* Not recommended for children under the age of 12.

MAJOR DEPRESSIVE DISORDER: Tricyclic Antidepressants (TCAs)

clomipramine   *Anafranil*

AVAILABLE FORMS: Tablet, 25, 50 and 75 mg

DOSAGE: Starting dose, 25–50 mg/day; maintenance dose, typically 100–250 mg/day if used for antidepressive effects

ADMINISTRATION: PO, at bedtime as a single dose (once tolerated)

SIDE EFFECTS: Similar to amitriptyline.
- Anticholinergic effects of dry mouth, constipation, and blurred vision
- Cardiac arrhythmias
- Fatigue, sedation, and weight gain
- Sexual dysfunction

DRUG INTERACTIONS:
- *MAOIs:* Risk for extreme hypertension
- *CNS depressants* (e.g., alcohol): TCAs increase effects
- *Direct-acting adrenergic agonists* (e.g., epinephrine): TCAs increase effects
- *Anticholinergic drugs* (e.g., antihistamines): TCAs increase effects. Do not use in combination.
- *SSRIs and other medications:* serotonin syndrome
- Antiarrhythmic agents

PRECAUTIONS:
- Adverse effects and side effects commonly observed before therapeutic effects
- Many side effects are dose dependent and may improve over time
- Overdose may result in lethal cardiotoxicity
- Use with caution in patients with a history of seizure or heart disease
- Avoid in patients with a history of cardiac arrhythmia.
- Monitor with EKG.

PHARMACOKINETICS:
Metabolism: Metabolized to an inactive form by CYP450 2D6 and 1A2
Half-life: Approx. 24 hr

PATIENT AND FAMILY EDUCATION:
- Should be taken about the same time every day, typically in the evening, and can be taken with or without food. May cause prolonged sedation. Do not drive until the effect of this medication is known.
- Administration time may be adjusted based on observed sedating or activating drug effects
- May take up to 4–8 weeks to show its maximum effect, but patient may see symptoms of depression improving in as little as 2 weeks.
- If patient plans on becoming pregnant, discuss benefits versus risks of using this medicine while pregnant.
- Because this medication is excreted in breast milk, nursing mothers should not breastfeed while taking this medicine without prior consultation with a psychiatric nurse practitioner or psychiatrist. Newborns may develop symptoms including feeding or breathing difficulties, seizures, muscle stiffness, jitteriness, or constant crying.
- Do not stop taking this medication unless the health care provider directs. Report symptoms to the health care provider promptly.
- Drug should be tapered gradually when discontinued. Dosage should be adjusted to reach remission of symptoms and treatment should continue for at least 4–9 months following remission of symptoms.
- Keep these medications out of the reach of children and pets.

SPECIAL POPULATIONS:
- *Elderly:* Older individuals tend to be more sensitive to side effects such as hypotension and anticholinergic effects. Often require adjustment of medication doses for hepatic or renal dysfunction. TCAs have been shown in at least one controlled clinical trial to be more effective than SSRIs in hospitalized geriatric patients, and in patients with melancholia and unipolar depression. However, cardiac side effects and fall risk are of great concern in this population. Side effects may be more pronounced and require decreased dosage
- *Pregnancy:* Psychotherapy is the initial choice for most pregnant patients with MDD. Category C; not recommended in most cases.
- *Children:* Not recommended for children under the age of 12.

despiramine   *Norpramin*

AVAILABLE FORMS: Tablet, 10, 25, 50, 75, 100 and 150 mg

DOSAGE: Starting dose, 25–50 mg/day; maintenance dose, typically 75–300 mg/day if used for antidepressant effect

ADMINISTRATION: PO in divided doses; may be administered as single dose once tolerated

SIDE EFFECTS: Similar to amitriptyline; cardiac arrhythmias; fatigue, sedation, and weight gain; sexual dysfunction

DRUG INTERACTIONS:
- *MAOIs:* Risk for extreme hypertension
- *CNS depressants* (e.g., alcohol): TCAs increase effects
- *Direct-acting adrenergic agonists* (e.g., epinephrine): TCAs increase effects
- *Anticholinergic drugs* (e.g., antihistamines): TCAs increase effects
- *SSRIs and other medications:* serotonin syndrome
- Antiarrhythmic agents

(cont.)

desipramine (cont.)

PHARMACOKINETICS:
Metabolism: Metabolized to an inactive form by CYP450 2D6 and 1A2
Half-life: Approx. 24 hr

PRECAUTIONS:
- Drug overdose has resulted in higher death rate in comparison to other TCAs. Overdose may result in lethal cardiotoxicity or seizure.
- Avoid in patients with a family history of cardiac arrhythmias and/or seizures.
- Monitor for cardiac effects with EKG.

PATIENT AND FAMILY EDUCATION:
- Should be taken about the same time every day, typically in the evening, and can be taken with or without food. May cause prolonged sedation. Do not drive until the effect of this medication is known.
- Administration time may be adjusted based on observed sedating or activating drug effects.
- May take up to 4–8 weeks to show its maximum effect, but patient may see symptoms of depression improving in as little as 2 weeks.
- If patient plans on becoming pregnant, discuss the benefits versus the risks of using this medicine while pregnant.
- Because this medicine is excreted in the breast milk, nursing mothers should not breastfeed while taking this medicine without prior consultation with a psychiatric nurse practitioner or psychiatrist. Newborns may develop symptoms including feeding or breathing difficulties, seizures, muscle stiffness, jitteriness, or constant crying.
- Do not stop taking this medication unless the health care provider directs. Report symptoms to the health care provider promptly.
- Drug should be tapered gradually when discontinued. Dosage should be adjusted to reach remission of symptoms and treatment should continue for at least 4–9 months following remission of symptoms
- Keep these medications out of the reach of children and pets.

SPECIAL POPULATIONS:
- *Elderly:* Older individuals tend to be more sensitive to medication side effects such as hypotension and anticholinergic effects. Often require adjustment of medication doses for hepatic or renal dysfunction. TCAs have been shown in at least one controlled clinical trial to be more effective than SSRIs in hospitalized geriatric patients and in patients with melancholia and unipolar depression. However, cardiac side effects and fall risk are of great concern in this population. Side effects may be more pronounced and require decreased dosage
- *Pregnancy:* Psychotherapy is the initial choice for most pregnant patients with MDD. Category C; not recommended in most cases.
- *Children:* Not recommended for children under the age of 12.

Tofranil   **imipramine**

AVAILABLE FORMS: Capsule, 75, 100, 125 and 150 mg; tablet, 10, 25 and 50 mg

DOSAGE: Starting dose, 25–50 mg/day; maintenance dose, typically in divided doses, 75–300 mg/day if used for antidepressant effect

ADMINISTRATION: PO formulations require tid-qid dosing

SIDE EFFECTS: Similar to amitriptyline; cardiac arrhythmias; fatigue, sedation, and weight gain; sexual dysfunction

DRUG INTERACTIONS:
- *MAOIs:* Risk for extreme hypertension
- *CNS depressants* (e.g., alcohol): TCAs increase effects
- *Direct-acting adrenergic agonists* (e.g., epinephrine): TCAs increase effects
- *SSRIs and other medications:* serotonin syndrome
- *Anticholinergic drugs* (e.g., antihistamines): TCAs increase effects. Do not use in combination.

PHARMACOKINETICS:
Metabolism: Metabolized to the active metabolite desipramine form by CYP450 2D6. Also metabolized by CYP450 1A2
Half-life: Approx. 2–3 days

PRECAUTIONS: Overdose may result in lethal cardiotoxicity or seizure
- Use with caution in patients with a history of seizure or heart disease
- Avoid in patients with a history of cardiac arrhythmia.
- Monitor with EKG

PATIENT AND FAMILY EDUCATION:
- Should be taken about the same time every day, with or without food. May cause prolonged sedation. Do not drive until the effect of this medication is known.
- Administration time may be adjusted based on observed sedating or activating drug effects
- May take up to 4–8 weeks to show its maximum effects, but patient may see symptoms of depression improving in as little as 2 weeks.
- If patient plans on becoming pregnant, discuss the benefits versus the risks of using this medicine while pregnant.
- Because this medicine is excreted in the breast milk, nursing mothers should not breastfeed while taking this medicine without prior consultation with a psychiatric nurse practitioner or psychiatrist. Newborns may develop symptoms including feeding or breathing

(cont.)

MAJOR DEPRESSIVE DISORDER: Tricyclic Antidepressants (TCAs)

imipramine (*cont.*)

difficulties, seizures, muscle stiffness, jitteriness, or constant crying.

- Do not stop taking this medication unless the health care provider directs. Report symptoms to the health care provider promptly.
- Drug should be tapered gradually when discontinued.
- Keep these medications out of the reach of children and pets.
- Dosage should be adjusted to reach remission of symptoms and treatment should continue for at least 4–9 months following remission of symptoms

SPECIAL POPULATIONS:

- *Elderly:* Older individuals tend to be more sensitive to medication side effects such as hypotension and anticholinergic effects. Often require adjustment of medication doses for hepatic or renal dysfunction. TCAs have been shown in at least one controlled clinical trial to be more effective than SSRIs in hospitalized geriatric patients and in patients with melancholia and unipolar depression. However, cardiac side effects and fall risk are of great concern in this population. Side effects may be more pronounced and require decreased dosage.
- *Pregnancy:* Psychotherapy is the initial choice for most pregnant patients with MDD. Category D; not recommended in pregnancy.
- *Children:* Not recommended for children under the age of 12.

nortriptyline   *Pamelor*

AVAILABLE FORMS: Capsule, 10, 25, 50, and 75 mg; oral solution, 10 mg/5 mL (480 mL)

DOSAGE: Starting dose, 25 mg/day; maintenance dose, typically 50–200 mg/day if used for antidepressive effects

ADMINISTRATION: PO in 3–4 divided doses. May be given once per day once tolerated

SIDE EFFECTS: Similar to amitriptyline; cardiac arrhythmias, fatigue, sedation, and weight gain; sexual dysfunction

DRUG INTERACTIONS:

- *MAOIs:* Risk for extreme hypertension
- *CNS depressants* (e.g., alcohol): TCAs increase effects
- *Direct-acting adrenergic agonists* (e.g., epinephrine): TCAs increase effects
- *Anticholinergic drugs* (e.g., antihistamines): TCAs increase effects

PHARMACOKINETICS:

Metabolism: Metabolized to an inactive form by CYP450 2D6
Half-life: Approx. 36 hr

PRECAUTIONS:

- Adverse effects and side effects are commonly observed before therapeutic effects
- Many side effects are dose dependent and may improve over time
- Overdose may result in lethal cardiotoxicity
- Monitor with routine EKG

PATIENT AND FAMILY EDUCATION:

- Should be taken about the same time every day, with or without food. May cause prolonged sedation. Do not drive until the effect of this medication is known.
- Administration time may be adjusted based on observed sedating or activating drug effects.
- May take up to 4–8 weeks to to show its effects, but patient may see symptoms of depression improving in as little as 2 weeks.

- If patient plans on becoming pregnant, discuss the benefits versus the risks of using this medicine while pregnant.
- Because this medicine is excreted in the breast milk, nursing mothers should not breastfeed while taking this medicine without prior consultation with a psychiatric nurse practitioner or psychiatrist. Newborns may develop symptoms including feeding or breathing difficulties, seizures, muscle stiffness, jitteriness, or constant crying.
- Do not stop taking this medication unless the health care provider directs. Report symptoms to the health care provider promptly.
- Drug should be tapered gradually when discontinued.
- Dosage should be adjusted to reach remission of symptoms and treatment should continue for at least 4–9 months following remission of symptoms.
- Keep these medications out of the reach of children and pets.

SPECIAL POPULATIONS:

- *Elderly:* Older individuals tend to be more sensitive to medication side effects such as hypotension and anticholinergic effects. Often require adjustment of medication doses for hepatic or renal dysfunction. TCAs have been shown in at least one controlled clinical trial to be more effective than SSRIs in hospitalized geriatric patients, and in patients with melancholia and unipolar depression. However, cardiac side effects and fall risk are of great concern in this population. Side effects may be more pronounced and require decreased dosage.
- *Pregnancy:* Psychotherapy is the initial choice for most pregnant patients with MDD. Category D; not recommended in pregnancy.
- *Children:* Not recommended for children under the age of 12.

MAJOR DEPRESSIVE DISORDER: Tricyclic Antidepressants (TCAs)

Class: Monoamine Oxidase Inhibitors (MAOIs)

MAOIs are older antidepressants that rarely are used, but may be an option when other medical therapy has failed.
- Rarely used for depression due to serious side effects and interactions with other medications and foods.

- May be particularly effective in patients with atypical features such as reactive mood and sensitivity to rejection.
- Should only be prescribed by a psychiatrist who is experienced in their use.

Nardil   **phenelzine**

AVAILABLE FORMS: Tablet, 15 mg

DOSAGE: Starting dose, 15 mg/day; maintenance dose, 15–90 mg/day in divided doses

ADMINISTRATION: PO, bid-tid dosing

SIDE EFFECTS:
- Orthostatic hypotension
- Hypertensive crisis, secondary to excessive consumption of dietary tyramine (e.g., soft cheeses, aged fish, aged meat, and avocados) or tryptophan-rich foods
- CNS stimulation
- Sexual dysfunction

DRUG INTERACTIONS:
- *High potential for interactions:* Do not use with other MAOI or antidepressants
- Avoid products containing sympathomimetic stimulants or dextromethorphan
- Concurrent use with antihypertensive agents may lead to exaggeration of hypotensive effects.
- Examples of drugs to avoid include alpha$_1$-agonists, amphetamines, buproprion, buspirone, dextromethorphan, linezolid, meperidine, methyldopa, methylphenidate, mirtazapine, SSRIs, SARIs, SNRIs, and TCAs
- *SSRIs, SNRIs, and TCAs:* Risk for extreme hypertension
- Indirect-acting adrenergic agonists (e.g., ephedrine) increase MAOI effects
- Antihypertensive drugs may dangerously lower blood pressure

PHARMACOKINETICS:
Duration of action: May last 2–3 weeks following discontinuation
Half-life: Approx. 11 hr, but irreversible MAO inhibition prolongs effects

PRECAUTIONS:
- Not approved by the FDA for the treatment of depression in children ≤16 years of age.
- *Diabetic patients:* Use with caution and monitor blood glucose
- *Glaucoma:* Potential increase in IOP

- *Patients at risk for seizure disorders:* May lower seizure threshold
- *Patients with hyperthyroidism or being treated with thyroid hormone:* Increased risk for proarrhythmias
- Generally well tolerated in elderly patients with controlled diet
- Adverse effects and side effects are commonly observed before therapeutic effects
- Dietary restrictions require substantial patient adherence

PATIENT AND FAMILY EDUCATION:
- Should be taken about the same time every day, with or without food.
- Substantial education required on dietary changes and importance of dietary adherence.
- Patient should advise all health care providers that he/she is on an MAOI prior to initiating new medications.
- Administration time may be adjusted based on observed sedating or activating drug effects.
- May take up to 4–8 weeks to show its maximum effect, but some may see symptoms of depression improving in as little as 2 weeks.
- Do not take if risk of pregnancy or pregnant.
- Because this medicine is excreted in the breast milk, nursing mothers should not breastfeed while taking this medication. Newborns may develop symptoms including feeding or breathing difficulties, seizures, muscle stiffness, jitteriness, or constant crying.
- Report potential side effects to the health care provider promptly.
- Keep these medications out of the reach of children and pets.

SPECIAL POPULATIONS:
- *Elderly:* Requires 1/3 drug dose in adult patients over 65 years old. Due to common need for polypharmacy, it is not recommended.
- *Pregnancy:* Psychotherapy is the initial choice for most pregnant patients with MDD. Generally not recommended during pregnancy.
- *Children:* Not recommended for children less than 16 years of age

---

Marplan   **isocarboxazid**

AVAILABLE FORMS: Tablet, 10 mg

DOSAGE: Starting dose, 20 mg/day; maintenance dose, 20–60 mg/day, in divided doses

ADMINISTRATION: PO, tid-qid dosing

SIDE EFFECTS:
- Hypertensive crisis, secondary to excessive consumption of dietary tyramine (e.g., soft cheeses, aged fish, aged meat, and avocados)

(cont.)

isocarboxazid (cont.)

- CNS stimulation
- Orthostatic hypotension
- Sexual dysfunction

DRUG INTERACTIONS:
- *SSRIs, SNRIs, and TCAs:* Risk for extreme hypertension
- *Indirect-acting adrenergic agonists* (e.g., ephedrine): Increases MAOI effects
- Antihypertensive drugs may dangerously lower blood pressure

PHARMACOKINETICS:
Duration of action: May last 2–3 weeks following discontinuation due to irreversible MAO inhibition

PRECAUTIONS:
- Adverse effects and side effects are commonly observed before therapeutic effects
- Dietary restrictions require substantial patient adherence

PATIENT AND FAMILY EDUCATION:
- Should be taken about the same time every day, with or without food.
- Substantial education required on dietary changes and importance of dietary adherence.
- Patient should advise all health care providers that he/she is on an MAOI prior to initiating new medications.
- Administration time may be adjusted based on observed sedating or activating drug effects.
- May take up to 4–8 weeks to show its maximum effect, but some may see symptoms of depression improving in as little as 2 weeks.
- Do not take if risk of pregnancy or pregnant.
- Because this medicine is excreted in the breast milk, nursing mothers should not breastfeed while taking this medicine. Newborns may develop symptoms including feeding or breathing difficulties, seizures, muscle stiffness, jitteriness, or constant crying.
- Report potential side effects to health care provider promptly.
- Keep these medications out of the reach of children and pets.

SPECIAL POPULATIONS:
- *Elderly:* Requires lower drug dose in adult patients over 65 years old. Due to common need for polypharmacy, it is not recommended.
- *Pregnancy:* Psychotherapy is the initial choice for most pregnant patients with MDD. Generally not recommended during pregnancy.
- *Children:* Not recommended for children less than 16 years of age

tranylcypromine   *Parnate*

AVAILABLE FORMS: Tablet, 10 mg

DOSAGE: Starting dose, 10 mg/day; maintenance dose, 10–60 mg/day in divided doses

ADMINISTRATION: PO, bid-tid dosing

SIDE EFFECTS:
- Hypertensive crisis, secondary to excessive consumption of dietary tyramine (e.g., soft cheeses, aged fish, aged meat, and avocados)
- CNS stimulation
- Orthostatic hypotension
- Sexual dysfunction

DRUG INTERACTIONS:
- *SSRIs, SNRIs, and TCAs:* Risk for extreme hypertension
- *Indirect-acting adrenergic agonists* (e.g., ephedrine): Increase MAOI effects
- Antihypertensive drugs may dangerously lower blood pressure

PHARMACOKINETICS:
Duration of action: May last 2–3 weeks following discontinuation
Half-life: 1–3 hr, but irreversible MAO inhibition prolongs effects

PRECAUTIONS:
- Adverse effects and side effects are commonly observed before therapeutic effects
- Dietary restrictions require substantial patient adherence

PATIENT AND FAMILY EDUCATION:
- Should be taken about the same time every day, with or without food.
- Substantial education required on dietary changes and importance of dietary adherence.
- Patient should advise all health care providers that he/she is on an MAOI prior to initiating new medications.
- Administration time may be adjusted based on observed sedating or activating drug effects.
- May take up to 4–8 weeks to show its maximum effect, but some may see symptoms of depression improving in as little as 2 weeks.
- Do not take if risk of pregnancy or pregnant.
- Because this medicine is excreted in the breast milk, nursing mothers should not breastfeed while taking this medicine. Newborns may develop symptoms including feeding or breathing difficulties, seizures, muscle stiffness, jitteriness, or constant crying.
- Report potential side effects to the health care provider promptly.
- Keep these medications out of the reach of children and pets.

(cont.)

MAJOR DEPRESSIVE DISORDER: Monoamine Oxidase Inhibitors (MAOIs)

tranylcypromine (*cont.*)

SPECIAL POPULATIONS:

- *Elderly:* Requires lower drug dose in adult patients older than 65 years old. Due to common need for polypharmacy, it is not recommended.

- *Pregnancy:* Psychotherapy is the initial choice for most pregnant patients with MDD. Generally not recommended during pregnancy.
- *Children:* Not recommended for children less than 18 years of age

Dysthymic Disorder (DD)

OVERVIEW

- Dysthymic disorder (DD) is a chronic mood disorder characterized by a depressed mood occurring on more days than not, but not meeting the criteria for MDD.
- Associated with increased morbidity from physical disease.
- Patients with DD often possess a pessimistic outlook on life, use ruminative coping strategies, and have a tendency toward self-criticism and inadequacy.
- Research suggests that those with DD spend limited time in leisure activities, experience decreased quality of relationships, and an increased likelihood of unemployment.
- Often starts in childhood or adolescence with an early sense of unhappiness without clear cause.

- Approximately 77% lifetime risk for adult patients with DD to develop MDD.
- 76% of children or adolescents with dysthymia develop MDD in follow up over 3–12 years and 13% develop bipolar disorder.
- Due to the chronicity and severity, there may be a higher risk of suicide attempts among patients with DD than patients with episodic MDD.
- Pharmacotherapy may increase the potential of suicidal ideation, particularly in patients less than 25 years old.
- Patients with bipolar disorder (diagnosed or undiagnosed) are at increased risk of CNS activating effects of most DD pharmacotherapy options

Psychopharmacology of DD

OVERVIEW

- Psychotropic medication should be selected based on relative efficacy, tolerability and anticipated side effects, co-occurring psychiatric or general medical conditions, half-life, cost, potential drug interactions, and the patient's preference and prior response to medication.
- Pharmacotherapy for DD should begin at the lowest dosage and gradually increase, if needed, following 4-week evaluation for therapeutic response.
- Patients should be examined 1–2 weeks after initiation of therapy for evaluation of adverse drug effects.
- Patients with DD must be evaluated on an ongoing basis for the development of MDD and for suicide risk.
- Pharmacologic education should include frequency of dosing, the likelihood that side effects will occur prior to improvement of symptoms, expectations that it will take 2–4 weeks prior to beneficial effects and 4–8 weeks prior to full effects of the dosage, the importance of taking medication even after feeling better, consulting with the health care provider before discontinuing medication, correcting misconceptions about medication use, and explaining what to do if side effects, questions, or worsening symptoms arise. Nonpharmacologic recommendations should

also be made such as sleep hygiene; decreased use or elimination of caffeine, tobacco, and alcohol; light therapy; and regular exercise.

- The onset of benefit from pharmacologic treatment may be more gradual in DD than the onset of benefit in nonchronic depression.
- Treatment of nonresponsive patients should be re-evaluated for accuracy of diagnosis, unaddressed co-occurring medical or psychiatric disorders such as substance abuse, the need for a change in treatment modalities, inadequate dose or duration of medical treatment, the need to augment medical treatment (with a second antidepressant from a different pharmacological class, or use of an adjunctive such as second generation atypical antipsychotic, anticonvulsant, or thyroid hormone), inadequate frequency of psychotherapy, complicating psychosocial factors, nonadherence to treatment, and poor "fit" between patient and therapist.
- Common combinations of medications include an SSRI with the addition of bupropion or the combination of mirtazapine and an SSRI or venlafaxine.
- Because of the chronic nature of DD, long-term medication use, along with interpersonal therapy, is advised. In cases where medication loses its effectiveness, alternative regimens should be considered.

DYSTHYMIC DISORDER

CLASS	DRUG
Selective Serotonin Reuptake Inhibitors (SSRIs)	**First-Line Drug Therapy**
	escitalopram (*Lexapro*) citalopram (*Celexa*) fluoxetine (*Prozac, Sarafem*) fluvoxamine (*Luvox*) paroxetine (*Paxil, Paxil CR*) sertraline (*Zoloft*)
Serotonin/Norepinephrine Reuptake Inhibitors (SNRIs)	**First-Line Drug Therapy**
	venlafaxine (*Effexor*); venlafaxine XR (*Effexor XR*) duloxetine (*Cymbalta*) desvenlafaxine (*Pristiq*)
Serotonin-2 Antagonist/Reuptake Inhibitors (SARIs)	**Second-Line Drug Therapy; may be used as adjunctive to SSRI or SNRI**
	nefazodone (*Serzone*) trazodone (*Desyrel*)
Norepinephrine/Dopamine Reuptake Inhibitors (NDRIs)	
	bupropion (*Wellbutrin, Zyban*); bupropion SR (*Wellbutrin SR*); bupropion XL (*Wellbutrin XL*)
Noradrenergic and Specific Serotonergic Antidepressants (NaSSAs)	
	mirtazapine (*Remeron*)
Tricyclic Antidepressants (TCAs)	
	amitriptyline (*Elavil*) clomipramine (*Anafranil*) desipramine (*Norpramin*) imipramine (*Tofranil*) nortriptyline (*Pamelor*)
Monoamine Oxidase Inhibitors (MAOIs)	
	phenelzine (*Nardil*) isocarboxazid (*Marplan*) tranylcypromine (*Parnate*)

Class: Selective Serotonin Reuptake Inhibitors (SSRIs)

This class of drugs is one of the more commonly used for DD.

- Typically display fewer side effects than TCAs and MAOIs, with minimal risk of death in intentional overdose. Treatment decisions should take into consideration patient symptoms and medication side-effect profile.
- SSRIs are currently the first-line treatment option in adolescents, adults, and elderly patients.
- With the exception of fluoxetine, SSRI medications may be helpful for patients with co-existing anxiety disorders or panic attacks.

- SSRI medications may not be preferred for patients with sexual dysfunction or who find sexual dysfunction as an intolerable side effect.
- Limited or no cholinergic, histaminergic, dopaminergic, or adrenergic receptor activity (i.e., do not cause hypotension or anticholinergic response).
- Patients reporting intolerable side effects to one SSRI may benefit from switching to another SSRI.

escitalopram	*Lexapro*

AVAILABLE FORMS: Tablet, 5, 10 and 20 mg; solution, 1 mg/mL (240 mL)

DOSAGE: Starting dose, 10 mg/day; maintenance dose, 10–20 mg

ADMINISTRATION: PO, once daily, with or without food

SIDE EFFECTS:
- *CNS:* Headache, agitation or restlessness, insomnia, sedation
- Changes in sexual desire, sexual performance and sexual satisfaction
- Excess perspiration; withdrawal syndrome if not tapered

(cont.)

escitalopram (*cont.*)

- Lower incidence of side effects than citalopram
- *GI:* Nausea, constipation, dry mouth

DRUG INTERACTIONS:
- *MAOIs:* Extreme risk for serotonin syndrome. Allow 2-week washout period post-MAOI prior to initiation
- *TCAs:* Plasma levels may be increased by SSRIs, so add with caution in low doses
- *ASA and NSAIDs:* Increased risk of bleeding
- *CNS depressants:* May increase depressant effects
- *SSRIs or SARIs:* May cause serotonin syndrome in combination with other medications such as tramadol, high-dose triptans, or the antibiotic linezolid
- Use with caution in patients taking blood thinners (*Coumadin*), other antidepressants, antihistamines, lithium, TCAs, and certain antibiotics, such as erythromycin, clarithromycin, or azithromycin

PHARMACOKINETICS:
- Metabolized in the liver by cytochrome P-450 microsomal enzymes. Paroxetine, fluoxetine, and sertraline may have greater P-450 enzyme effect than citalopram and escitalopram.
- Highly bound to plasma proteins and have a large volume of distribution.

Absorption: Readily absorbed in the GI tract, metabolized in the liver, and excreted in the urine. Dosages may be decreased in patients with liver or kidney disease.

Peak plasma levels: Reached in 2–10 hr

Half-life: Variable, but most SSRIs have half-lives of 20–24 hr. A notable exception is fluoxetine (*Prozac*), and its active metabolite, norfluoxetine, which have half-lives of 2–4 days and 8–9 days, respectively. Hence, addition of serotonergic medications to a patient's regimen must not occur until 2–3 weeks after discontinuation of an SSRI (some recommend a 5-week "washout" period for fluoxetine prior to initiation of an MAOI).

PRECAUTIONS:
- May cause sedation and mental clouding
- Use with caution in patients with liver, kidney, or cardiovascular disease
- Adverse effects and side effects are commonly observed before therapeutic effects
- Many side effects are dose-dependent and may improve over time
- Taper discontinuation to avoid withdrawal symptoms
- *Elderly:* May require decreased dosage

PATIENT AND FAMILY EDUCATION:
- Should be taken about the same time every day, morning or evening, with or without food (with food if there is any stomach upset)
- May start with half of lowest effective dose for 3–7 days, then increase to lowest effective dose to diminish side effects.
- Administration time may be adjusted based on observed sedating or activating drug effects

- May take up to 4–8 weeks to show its maximum effect at this dose, but some may see symptoms of DD improving in as little as 2 weeks.
- If patient plans on becoming pregnant or is pregnant, discuss the benefits versus the risks of using this medicine while pregnant.
- Because this medicine is excreted in the breast milk, nursing mothers should not breastfeed while taking this medicine without prior consultation with a psychiatric nurse practitioner or psychiatrist. Newborns may develop symptoms including feeding or breathing difficulties, seizures, muscle stiffness, jitteriness, or constant crying.
- Do not stop taking this medication unless the health care provider directs. Report side effects or worsening symptoms to the health care provider promptly.
- The medication should be tapered gradually when changing or discontinuing therapy.
- Dosage should be adjusted to reach remission of symptoms and treatment should continue for at least 6–12 months following last reported dysthymic experience.
- Caution is advised when using this drug in the elderly because they may be more sensitive to the effects of the drug. Elderly patients should receive a lower starting dose.

SPECIAL POPULATIONS:
- *Elderly:* ▶ **Caution:** Older individuals tend to be more sensitive to medication side effects such as hypotension and anticholinergic effects and often require adjustment of medication doses for hepatic or renal dysfunction. SSRIs with shorter half-lives or less P-450 inhibition may be more desirable (e.g., citalopram, escitalopram) for geriatric populations than SSRIs with longer half-lives (e.g., fluoxetine). SSRIs have been associated with increased risk of falls in nursing home residents and neurologic effects in patients with Parkinson's disease. Elderly patients are more prone to SSRI-induced hyponatremia. Paroxetine shows greater anticholinergic and sedating effects than other SSRIs.
- *Pregnancy:* Psychotherapy is the initial choice for most pregnant patients with DD. Most SSRIs are Category C drugs due to adverse effects observed in animal studies. Thus, an individual risk-benefit analysis must be done to determine appropriate treatment in pregnant women with DD. If continued during pregnancy, SSRI dosage may need to be increased to maintain euthymia due to physiologic changes associated with pregnancy.
- *Children:* Initial SSRI dosing in children typically begins at approx. 50% adult dosing. Increasing doses may require more gradual increments, and discontinuation may require a more gradual taper. Psychiatric consultation is recommended due to black box warning of increased suicidal ideation using SSRI therapy in children.

DYSTHYMIC DISORDER: Selective Serotonin Reuptake Inhibitors (SSRIs)

citalopram   *Celexa*

AVAILABLE FORMS: Tablet, 10, 20 and 40 mg; solution, 10 mg/5 mL (240 mL)

DOSAGE: Starting dose, 20 mg/day: maintenance dose, 20–60 mg, adjust in 20 mg increments

ADMINISTRATION: PO, with or without food.

SIDE EFFECTS:
- May cause CNS depression (sedation, fatigue) or activation (insomnia)
- Tends to be weight neutral or approximately 2 pounds of weight gain in one year
- Nervousness
- Headache and nausea, particularly early in treatment
- Insomnia
- Excess perspiration
- Serotonin syndrome
- Withdrawal syndrome (including neonatal withdrawal syndrome): Symptoms may include dizziness, muscle aches, headache, nausea, vomiting, gait instability, agitation, and/or "electric shock" sensations
- Diarrhea
- Sexual dysfunction
- Hyponatremia (e.g., in geriatric patients taking diuretics)
- Side effects are most common during the first or second week of therapy. Starting with a lower dosage and gradually increasing it, and taking the medication with food will limit some of these side effects.

DRUG INTERACTIONS:
- *MAOIs:* Extreme risk for serotonin syndrome. Allow 2-week washout period post-MAOI prior to initiating
- *TCAs:* Plasma levels may be increased by SSRIs, so add with caution in low doses
- *ASA and NSAIDs:* Increased risk of bleeding
- *CNS depressants:* May increase depressant effects
- *SSRIs or SARIs:* May cause serotonin syndrome in combination with other medications such as tramadol, high-dose triptans, or the antibiotic linezolid.
- Use with caution in patients taking blood thinners (*Coumadin*), other antidepressants, antihistamines, lithium, TCAs, and certain antibiotics, such as erythromycin, clarithromycin, or azithromycin.

PHARMACOKINETICS:
- Highly bound to plasma proteins and have a large volume of distribution.
- Caution advised in elderly clients.

Metabolism: Metabolized in the liver by cytochrome P-450 microsomal enzymes.

Absorption: Readily absorbed in the GI tract, metabolized in the liver, and excreted in the urine. Dosages may be decreased in patients with liver or kidney disease.

Peak plasma levels: Reached in 2–10 hr.

Half-life: Variable, but most SSRIs have half-lives of 20–24 hr. A notable exception is fluoxetine (*Prozac*), and its active metabolite, norfluoxetine, which have half-lives of 2–4 days and 8–9 days, respectively. Hence, addition of serotonergic medications to a patient's regimen must not occur until 2–3 weeks after discontinuation of an SSRI (some recommend a 5-week "washout" period for fluoxetine prior to initiation of an MAOI).

PRECAUTIONS:
- May cause sedation and mental clouding
- Use with caution in patients with liver, kidney, or cardiovascular disease
- Adverse effects and side effects are commonly observed before therapeutic effects
- Many side effects are dose-dependent and may improve over time
- Taper discontinuation to avoid withdrawal symptoms
- *Elderly:* May require decreased dosage

PATIENT AND FAMILY EDUCATION:
- Should be taken about the same time every day, morning or evening, with or without food (with food if there is any stomach upset)
- May start with half of lowest effective dose for 3–7 days, then increase to lowest effective dose to diminish side effects.
- Administration time may be adjusted based on observed sedating or activating drug effects
- May take up to 4–8 weeks to show its maximum effect at this dose, but some may see symptoms of DD improving in as little as 2 weeks.
- If planning on becoming pregnant or are pregnant, discuss the benefits versus the risks of using this medicine while pregnant.
- Because this medicine is excreted in the breast milk, nursing mothers should not breastfeed while taking this medicine without prior consultation with a psychiatric nurse practitioner or psychiatrist. Newborns may develop symptoms including feeding or breathing difficulties, seizures, muscle stiffness, jitteriness, or constant crying.
- Do not stop taking this medication unless the health care provider directs. Report side effects or worsening symptoms to the health care provider promptly.
- The medication should be tapered gradually when changing or discontinuing therapy.
- Dosage should be adjusted to reach remission of symptoms and treatment should continue for at least 6–12 months following last reported dysthymic experience.
- Caution is advised when using this drug in the elderly because they may be more sensitive to the effects of the drug. Elderly patients should receive a lower starting dose.

SPECIAL POPULATIONS:
- *Elderly:* Older individuals tend to be more sensitive to medication side effects such as hypotension and anticholinergic effects. They often require adjustment of medication doses for hepatic or renal dysfunction. SSRIs

(cont.)

citalopram (*cont.*)

with shorter half-lives or less P-450 inhibition may be more desirable (e.g., citalopram) for geriatric populations than SSRIs with longer half-lives (e.g., fluoxetine). SSRIs have been associated with increased risk of falls in nursing home residents and neurologic effects in patients with Parkinson's disease. Elderly patients are more prone to SSRI-induced hyponatremia.

- *Pregnancy:* Psychotherapy is the initial choice for most pregnant patients with DD. Most SSRIs are Category C drugs due to adverse

effects observed in animal studies. Thus, an individual risk-benefit analysis must be done to determine appropriate treatment in pregnant women with DD.

- *Children:* Initial SSRI dosing in children typically begins at approx. 50% adult dosing. Increasing doses may require more gradual increments, and discontinuation may require a more gradual taper. Psychiatric consultation is recommended due to black box warning of increased suicidal ideation using SSRI therapy in children.

Prozac, Sarafem   **fluoxetine**

INDICATIONS: Has the most data in the treatment of bulimia nervosa.

AVAILABLE FORMS: Capsule, 10, 20 and 40 mg; tablet, 10, 15 and 20 mg; pellet, delayed release, enteric coated (*Prozac Weekly*), 90 mg; solution, 5 mL and 120 mL (20 mg/5 mL). *Note:* Availability of certain formulations may be limited to brandname versions of the drug.

DOSAGE: Starting dose, 20 mg/day; maintenance dose, 20–60 mg, adjust in 20 mg increments

ADMINISTRATION:
- PO, with or without food.
- Capsules may be diluted into water or apple juice. Grapefruit juice should not be used due to cytochrome P450 effects.

SIDE EFFECTS:
- May cause CNS depression (sedation, fatigue) or activation (insomnia)
- Tends to be weight neutral or approximately 2 pounds of weight gain in one year
- Nervousness, agitation
- Headache and nausea, particularly early in treatment
- Insomnia
- Excess perspiration
- Serotonin syndrome
- Withdrawal syndrome (including neonatal withdrawal syndrome): Symptoms may include dizziness, muscle aches, headache, nausea, vomiting, gait instability, agitation, and/or "electric shock" sensations
- Diarrhea
- Sexual dysfunction (approx. 50% of men and women)
- Hyponatremia (e.g., in geriatric patients taking diuretics)
- Side effects are most common during the first or second week of therapy. Starting with a lower dosage and gradually increasing, and taking the medication with food will limit some of these side effects.

DRUG INTERACTIONS:
- *MAOIs:* Extreme risk for serotonin syndrome. Requires a 5- to 6-week washout period or longer before use of an MAOI.
- *TCAs:* Plasma levels may be increased by SSRIs, so add with caution in low doses
- *ASA and NSAIDs:* Increased risk of bleeding
- *CNS depressants:* May increase depressant effects
- *SSRIs or SARIs:* May cause serotonin syndrome in combination with other medications such as tramadol, high-dose triptans, or the antibiotic linezolid
- Use with caution in patients taking blood thinners (*Coumadin*), other antidepressants, antihistamines, lithium, TCAs, and certain antibiotics, such as erythromycin, clarithromycin, or azithromycin

PHARMACOKINETICS:
- Highly bound to plasma proteins and have a large volume of distribution.
- Readily absorbed in the GI tract, metabolized in the liver, and excreted in the urine. Dosages may be decreased in patients with liver or kidney disease.
- Caution advised in elderly clients.

Peak plasma levels: Reached in 2–10 hr.

Metabolism: Metabolized in the liver by cytochrome P-450 microsomal enzymes.

Half-life: Variable, but most SSRIs have half-lives of 20–24 hr. A notable exception is fluoxetine (*Prozac*), and its active metabolite, norfluoxetine, which have half-lives of 2–4 days and 8–9 days, respectively. Hence, addition of serotonergic medications to a patient's regimen must not occur until 2–3 weeks after discontinuation of an SSRI (some recommend a 5-week "washout" period for fluoxetine prior to initiation of an MAOI).

PRECAUTIONS:
- Use with caution in patients with liver, kidney, or cardiovascular disease.
- *Elderly:* May require decreased dosage
- Adverse effects and side effects are commonly observed before therapeutic effects

(cont.)

fluoxetine (cont.)

- Many side effects are dose dependent and may improve over time
- Taper discontinuation to avoid withdrawal symptoms (although fluoxetine has fewer withdrawal symptoms than other SSRIs due to long half-life).

PATIENT AND FAMILY EDUCATION:
- Should be taken about the same time every day, morning or evening; can be taken with or without food (with food if there is any stomach upset).
- May start with half of lowest effective dose for 3–7 days, then increase to lowest effective dose to diminish side effects.
- Administration time may be adjusted based on observed sedating or activating drug effects.
- May take up to 4–8 weeks to show its maximum effect at this dose, but some may see symptoms of dysthymia improving in as little as 2 weeks.
- If patient plans on becoming pregnant or is pregnant, discuss the benefits versus the risks of using this medicine while pregnant.
- Because this medicine is excreted in the breast milk, nursing mothers should not breastfeed while taking this medicine without prior consultation with a psychiatric nurse practitioner or psychiatrist. Newborns may develop symptoms including feeding or breathing difficulties, seizures, muscle stiffness, jitteriness, or constant crying.
- Do not stop taking this medication unless the health care provider directs. Report side effects or worsening symptoms to the health care provider promptly.
- The medication should be tapered gradually when changing or discontinuing therapy.

- Dosage should be adjusted to reach remission of symptoms and treatment should continue for at least 6–12 months following last reported dysthymic experience.

SPECIAL POPULATIONS:
- *Elderly:* Avoid use in the elderly if possible. Older individuals tend to be more sensitive to medication side effects such as hypotension and anticholinergic effects. They often require adjustment of medication doses for hepatic or renal dysfunction. SSRIs with shorter half-lives or less P-450 inhibition may be more desirable (e.g., citalopram) for geriatric populations. SSRIs have been associated with increased risk of falls in nursing home residents and neurologic effects in patients with Parkinson's disease. Geriatric patients are more prone to SSRI-induced hyponatremia.
- *Pregnancy:* Psychotherapy is the initial choice for most pregnant patients with DD. Most SSRIs are Category C drugs, due to adverse effects observed in animal studies. Thus, an individual risk-benefit analysis must be done to determine appropriate treatment in pregnant women with DD.
- *Children:* It has been approved by the FDA for use in children with depression. Initial SSRI dosing in children typically begins at approx. 50% adult dosing. Increasing doses may require more gradual increments, and discontinuation may require a more gradual taper. Psychiatric consultation is recommended due to black box warning of increased suicidal ideation using SSRI therapy in children.

---

fluoxamine   *Luvox*

AVAILABLE FORMS: Tablet, 25, 50 and 100 mg; extended release capsule, 100 and 150 mg. *Note:* Some formulations not available as generic medications.

DOSAGE: Starting dose, 50 mg/day; maintenance dose, 50–300 mg/day

ADMINISTRATION: PO, with or without food. Controlled release tables must remain intact and not be split or crushed prior to administration.

SIDE EFFECTS: May cause significant sedation (unique among SSRIs); administer at bedtime due to sedation; side effects similar to paroxetine and other SSRIs also observed. May be used for clients with co-existing OCD or other anxiety disorders. May be associated with less sexual side effects than other SSRIs.

DRUG INTERACTIONS
- *MAOIs:* Extreme risk for serotonin syndrome. Allow 2-week washout period post-MAOI prior to initiation.
- *TCAs:* Plasma levels may be increased by SSRIs, so add with caution in low doses.
- *ASA and NSAIDs:* Increased risk of bleeding

- *CNS depressants:* May increase depressant effects.
- *SSRIs or SARIs:* May cause serotonin syndrome in combination with other medications such as tramadol, high-dose triptans, or the antibiotic linezolid.
- Use with caution in patients taking blood thinners (*Coumadin*), other antidepressants, antihistamines, lithium, TCAs, and certain antibiotics, such as erythromycin, clarithromycin, or azithromycin.

PHARMACOKINETICS:
- Highly bound to plasma proteins and have a large volume of distribution.
- Readily absorbed in the GI tract, metabolized in the liver, and excreted in the urine. Dosages may be decreased in patients with liver or kidney disease.
- Caution advised in elderly clients.

Metabolism: Metabolized in the liver by cytochrome P-450 microsomal enzymes.

Peak plasma levels: Reached in 2–10 hr

Half-life: Variable, but most SSRIs have half-lives of 20–24 hr. A notable exception is fluoxetine (*Prozac*),

(cont.)

fluvoxamine (cont.)

and its active metabolite, norfluoxetine, which have half-lives of 2–4 days and 8–9 days, respectively. Hence, addition of serotonergic medications to a patient's regimen must not occur until 2–3 weeks after discontinuation of an SSRI (some recommend a 5-week "washout" period for fluoxetine prior to initiation of an MAOI).

PRECAUTIONS:
- Adverse effects and side effects are commonly observed before therapeutic effects.
- Many side effects are dose dependent and may improve over time.
- Taper discontinuation to avoid withdrawal symptoms.

PATIENT AND FAMILY EDUCATION:
- Should be taken about the same time every day, morning or evening, and can be taken with or without food (with food if there is any stomach upset).
- May start with half of lowest effective dose for 3–7 days, then increase to lowest effective dose to diminish side effects.
- Administration time may be adjusted based on observed sedating or activating drug effects.
- May take up to 4–8 weeks to show its maximum effect at this dose, but some may see symptoms of dysthymia improving in as little as 2 weeks.
- If patient plans on becoming pregnant or is pregnant, discuss the benefits versus the risks of using this medicine while pregnant.
- Because this medicine is excreted in the breast milk, nursing mothers should not breastfeed while taking this medicine without prior consultation with a psychiatric nurse practitioner or psychiatrist. Newborns may develop symptoms including feeding or breathing difficulties, seizures, muscle stiffness, jitteriness, or constant crying.
- Do not stop taking this medication unless the health care provider directs. Report side effects

or worsening symptoms to the health care provider promptly.
- The medication should be tapered gradually when changing or discontinuing therapy.
- Dosage should be adjusted to reach remission of symptoms and treatment should continue for at least 6–12 months following last reported dysthymic experience.
- Caution is advised when using this drug in the elderly because they may be more sensitive to the effects of the drug. Elderly patients should receive a lower starting dose.
- Keep these medications out of the reach of children and pets.

SPECIAL POPULATIONS:
- *Elderly:* ▶ **Caution:** Older individuals tend to be more sensitive to medication side effects such as hypotension and anticholinergic effects. They often require adjustment of medication doses for hepatic or renal dysfunction. SSRIs with shorter half-lives (e.g., paroxetine) may be more desirable for geriatric populations than SSRIs with longer half-lives (e.g., fluoxetine). SSRIs have been associated with increased risk of falls in nursing home residents and neurologic effects in patients with Parkinson's disease. Elderly patients are more prone to SSRI-induced hyponatremia.
- *Pregnancy:* Psychotherapy is the initial choice for most pregnant patients with DD. Most SSRIs are Category C drugs, due to adverse effects observed in animal studies. If continued during pregnancy, dosage may need to be increased to maintain euthymia due to physiologic changes associated with pregnancy.
- *Children:* Initial SSRI dosing in children typically begins approx. 50% adult dosing. Increasing doses may require more gradual increments, and discontinuation may require a more gradual taper.

Paxil, Paxil CR   **paroxetine**

AVAILABLE FORMS: Tablet, 10, 20, 30 and 40 mg; suspension, 10 mg/5 mL (250 mL); controlled-release enteric coated tablet, 12.5, 25 and 37.5 mg.
▶ **Note:** Controlled-release (CR) formulations dissolve in lower intestine and minimize GI distress. Some formulations may be only available as trade name formulations.

DOSAGE: starting dose, 20 mg/day; maintenance dose, 20–60 mg.

ADMINISTRATION: PO, with or without food. Controlled release tables must remain intact and not be split or crushed prior to administration.

SIDE EFFECTS: Due to short-half life, may see greater withdrawal side effects than other drugs

in its class. Also may see more weight gain than other medications in its class.
- May cause CNS depression (sedation, fatigue) or activation (insomnia)
- Weight gain
- Nervousness
- Headache and nausea, particularly early in treatment
- Dry mouth
- Excess perspiration
- Serotonin syndrome
- Withdrawal syndrome (including neonatal withdrawal syndrome): Symptoms may include dizziness, muscle aches, headache, nausea, vomiting, gait instability, agitation, and/or "electric shock" sensations.

(cont.)

DYSTHYMIC DISORDER: Selective Serotonin Reuptake Inhibitors (SSRIs)

paroxetine *(cont.)*

- Diarrhea
- Sexual dysfunction (approx. 50% of men and women)
- Hyponatremia (e.g., in geriatric patients taking diuretics)
- Side effects are most common during the first or second week of therapy. Starting with a lower dosage and gradually increasing, and taking the medication with food will limit some of these side effects.

DRUG INTERACTIONS:

- *MAOIs:* Extreme risk for serotonin syndrome. Allow 2-week washout period post-MAOI prior to initiation
- *TCAs:* Plasma levels may be increased by SSRIs, so add with caution in low doses
- *ASA and NSAIDs:* Increased risk of bleeding
- *CNS depressants:* May increase depressant effects
- *SSRIs or SARIs:* May cause serotonin syndrome in combination with other medications such as tramadol, high-dose triptans, or the antibiotic linezolid.
- Use with caution in patients taking blood thinners (*Coumadin*), other antidepressants, antihistamines, lithium, TCAs, and certain antibiotics, such as erythromycin, clarithromycin, or azithromycin.

PHARMACOKINETICS:

- Highly bound to plasma proteins and have a large volume of distribution.
- Readily absorbed in the GI tract, metabolized in the liver, and excreted in the urine. Dosages may be decreased in patients with liver or kidney disease.
- Caution advised in elderly clients.

Metabolism: Metabolized in the liver by cytochrome P-450 microsomal enzymes.

Peak plasma levels: Reached in 2–10 hr.

Half-life: Variable, but most SSRIs have half-lives of 20–24 hr. A notable exception is fluoxetine (*Prozac*), and its active metabolite, norfluoxetine, which have half-lives of 2–4 days and 8–9 days, respectively. Hence, addition of serotonergic medications to a patient's regimen must not occur until 2–3 weeks after discontinuation of an SSRI (some recommend a 5-week "washout" period for fluoxetine prior to initiation of an MAOI).

PRECAUTIONS:

- May cause sedation and mental clouding.
- Use with caution in patients with liver, kidney, or cardiovascular disease.
- *Elderly:* May require decreased dosage.
- Adverse effects and side effects are commonly observed before therapeutic effects.
- Many side effects are dose dependent and may improve over time.
- Taper discontinuation to avoid withdrawal symptoms.

PATIENT AND FAMILY EDUCATION:

- Should be taken about the same time every day, morning or evening, and can be taken with or without food (with food if there is any stomach upset).
- May start with half of lowest effective dose for 3–7 days, then increase to lowest effective dose to diminish side effects.
- Administration time may be adjusted based on observed sedating or activating drug effects.
- May take up to 4–8 weeks to show its maximum effect at this dose, but some may see symptoms of dysthymia improving in as little as 2 weeks.
- If patient plans on becoming pregnant or is pregnant, discuss the benefits versus the risks of using this medicine while pregnant.
- Because this medicine is excreted in the breast milk, nursing mothers should not breastfeed while taking this medicine without prior consultation with a psychiatric nurse practitioner or psychiatrist. Newborns may develop symptoms including feeding or breathing difficulties, seizures, muscle stiffness, jitteriness, or constant crying.
- Do not stop taking this medication unless the health care provider directs. Report side effects or worsening symptoms to the health care provider promptly.
- The medication should be tapered gradually when changing therapy or discontinuing.
- Dosage should be adjusted to reach remission of symptoms and treatment should continue for at least 6–12 months following last reported dysthymic experience.
- Caution is advised when using this drug in the elderly because they may be more sensitive to the effects of the drug. Elderly patients should receive a lower starting dose.

SPECIAL POPULATIONS:

- *Elderly:* ▶ **Caution**: Older individuals tend to be more sensitive to medication side effects such as hypotension and anticholinergic effects. Often require adjustment of medication doses for hepatic or renal dysfunction. SSRIs with shorter half-lives or less P-450 inhibition may be more desirable (e.g., citalopram) for geriatric populations than SSRIs with longer half-lives (e.g., fluoxetine). SSRIs have been associated with increased risk of falls in nursing home residents and neurologic effects in patients with Parkinson's disease. Elderly patients are more prone to SSRI-induced hyponatremia. Paroxetine shows greater anticholinergic and sedating effects than other SSRIs
- *Pregnancy:* Psychotherapy is the initial choice for most pregnant patients with DD. Most SSRIs are Category C drugs, due to adverse effects observed in animal studies. Thus, an individual risk-benefit analysis must be done to determine appropriate treatment in pregnant women with DD. Paroxetine is a Category D drug. If continued during pregnancy, SSRI
(cont.)

paroxetine (*cont.*)

dosage may need to be increased to maintain euthymia due to physiologic changes associated with pregnancy.

- *Children:* Initial SSRI dosing in children typically begins at approx. 50% adult dosing. Increasing doses may require more gradual

increments, and discontinuation may require a more gradual taper. Psychiatric consultation is recommended due to black box warning of increased suicidal ideation using SSRI therapy in children.

Zoloft   **sertraline**

AVAILABLE FORMS: Tablet, 25, 50 and 100 mg; concentrate solution, 20 mg/mL (60 mL)

DOSAGE: Starting dose, 50 mg/day; maintenance dose, 50–200 mg

ADMINISTRATION: PO, with or without food. Concentrate solution must be diluted immediately prior to use with water or juice (other than grapefruit juice).

SIDE EFFECTS: Displays some inhibition of dopamine reuptake, which may be beneficial to some patients (e.g., those experiencing hypersomnia, low energy, or mood reactivity), but problematic to others (e.g., causing overactivation in patients with panic disorder). May see a little more GI side effect (diarrhea) than others in class

- Nervousness, headache and nausea, insomnia; serotonin syndrome; dry mouth, easy bruising, or excess perspiration; diarrhea.
- Withdrawal syndrome (including neonatal withdrawal syndrome): Symptoms may include dizziness, muscle aches, headache, nausea, vomiting, gait instability, agitation, and/or "electric shock" sensations.
- Sexual dysfunction (more than 50% of men and women)
- Hyponatremia (e.g., in geriatric patients taking diuretics)
- Side effects are most common during the first or second week of therapy. Starting with a lower dosage and gradually increasing it, and taking the medication with food will limit some of these side effects.

DRUG INTERACTIONS:

- *MAOIs:* Extreme risk for serotonin syndrome. Allow 2-week washout period post-MAOI prior to initiation
- *TCAs:* Plasma levels may be increased by SSRIs, so add with caution in low doses
- *ASA and NSAIDs:* Increased risk of bleeding
- *CNS depressants:* May increase depressant effects
- *SSRIs or SARIs:* May cause serotonin syndrome in combination with other medications such as tramadol, high-dose triptans, or the antibiotic linezolid.
- Use with caution in patients taking blood thinners (*Coumadin*), other antidepressants, antihistamines, lithium, TCAs, and certain antibiotics, such as erythromycin, clarithromycin, or azithromycin.

PHARMACOKINETICS:

- Highly bound to plasma proteins and have a large volume of distribution.
- Readily absorbed in the GI tract, metabolized in the liver, and excreted in the urine. Dosages may be decreased in patients with liver or kidney disease.
- Caution advised in elderly clients.

Metabolism: Metabolized in the liver by cytochrome P-450 microsomal enzymes.

Peak plasma levels: 2–10 hr.

Half-life: Variable, but most SSRIs have half-lives of 20–24 hr. A notable exception is fluoxetine (*Prozac*), and its active metabolite, norfluoxetine, which have half-lives of 2–4 days and 8–9 days, respectively. Hence, addition of serotonergic medications to a patient's regimen must not occur until 2–3 weeks after discontinuation of an SSRI (some recommend a 5-week "washout" period for fluoxetine prior to initiation of an MAOI).

PRECAUTIONS:

- May cause sedation and mental clouding.
- Use with caution in patients with liver, kidney, or cardiovascular disease.
- Adverse effects and side effects are commonly observed before therapeutic effects.
- Many side effects are dose dependent and may improve over time.
- Taper discontinuation to avoid withdrawal symptoms.
- *Elderly:* May require decreased dosage.

PATIENT AND FAMILY EDUCATION:

- Should be taken about the same time every day, morning or evening, and can be taken with or without food (with food if there is any stomach upset).
- May start with half of lowest effective dose for 3–7 days, then increase to lowest effective dose to diminish side effects.
- Administration time may be adjusted based on observed sedating or activating drug effects.
- May take up to 4–8 weeks to show its maximum effect at this dose, but some may see symptoms of dysthymia improving in as little as 2 weeks.
- If patient plans on becoming pregnant or is pregnant, discuss the benefits versus the risks of using this medicine while pregnant.
- Because this medicine is excreted in the breast milk, nursing mothers should not breastfeed while taking this medicine without prior consultation with a psychiatric nurse practitioner or

(cont.)

DYSTHYMIC DISORDER: Selective Serotonin Reuptake Inhibitors (SSRIs)

sertraline (*cont.*)

psychiatrist. Newborns may develop symptoms including feeding or breathing difficulties, seizures, muscle stiffness, jitteriness, or constant crying.

- Do not stop taking this medication unless the health care provider directs. Report side effects or worsening symptoms to the health care provider promptly.
- The medication should be tapered gradually when changing or discontinuing therapy.
- Dosage should be adjusted to reach remission of symptoms and treatment should continue for at least 6–12 months following last reported dysthymic experience.
- Caution is advised when using this drug in the elderly because they may be more sensitive to the effects of the drug. Elderly patients should receive a lower starting dose.
- Keep these medications out of the reach of children and pets.

SPECIAL POPULATIONS:

- *Elderly:* Older individuals tend to be more sensitive to medication side effects such as hypotension and anticholinergic effects. They often require adjustment of medication doses for hepatic or renal dysfunction. SSRIs with shorter half-lives or less P-450 inhibition may

be more desirable (e.g., citalopram) for geriatric populations than SSRIs with longer half-lives (e.g., fluoxetine). SSRIs have been associated with increased risk of falls in nursing home residents and neurologic effects in patients with Parkinson's disease. Elderly patients are more prone to SSRI-induced hyponatremia.

- *Pregnancy:* Psychotherapy is the initial choice for most pregnant patients with DD. Most SSRIs are Category C drugs, due to adverse effects observed in animal studies. Sertraline has been found to have lower cord blood levels than other SSRIs, although the clinical significance is unknown. Thus, an individual risk-benefit analysis must be done to determine appropriate treatment in pregnant women with DD. If continued during pregnancy, SSRI dosage may need to be increased to maintain euthymia due to physiologic changes associated with pregnancy.
- *Children:* Initial SSRI dosing in children typically begins at approx. 50% adult dosing. Increasing doses may require more gradual increments, and discontinuation may require a more gradual taper. Psychiatric consultation is recommended due to black box warning of increased suicidal ideation using SSRI therapy in children.

Class: Serotonin and Norepinephrine Reuptake Inhibitors (SNRIs)

Common alternative to SSRIs, with particular use in clients with chronic pain disorders and atypical symptoms characterized by fatigue and difficulty in concentrating. May be less preferred in patients with pre-existing hypertension.

- Inhibition of norepinephrine reuptake may increase CNS stimulation and produce antisedative effects
- Higher drug concentrations tend to produce more NE effects; lower concentrations produce more serotonergic effects

venlafaxine venlafaxine XR	*Effexor* *Effexor XR*

AVAILABLE FORMS: Tablet, 25, 37.5, 50, 75 and 100 mg; extended release capsule, 37.5, 50, 75 and 150 mg; extended release tablet, 37.5, 75, 150 and 225 mg.
▶**Note:** Preference for XR formulation due to possibly increased potential for side effects, particularly withdrawal syndrome, of non-extended release formulation with short half-life.

DOSAGE: Starting dose, 37.5 mg/day; maintenance dose, 75–225 mg/day, adjusted in 37.5–75 mg increments; maximum dose 375 mg/day may be used for unresponsive MDD.

ADMINISTRATION: PO; take with food. Extended-release tablets should not be crushed or chewed. Capsules may be opened and sprinkled on applesauce.

SIDE EFFECTS: Increased anxiety; impaired platelet aggregation (easy bruising); CNS depression; hypertension; nausea, weight loss, or occasionally weight gain; withdrawal syndrome; headache,

nausea; muscle weakness; nervousness; insomnia; serotonin syndrome; withdrawal syndrome (including neonatal withdrawal syndrome); sexual dysfunction; hyponatremia (e.g., geriatric patients taking diuretics)

DRUG INTERACTIONS:

- *ASA and NSAIDs:* Increased risk of bleeding
- *CNS depressants:* May increase or decrease effects
- *MAOIs:* May cause serotonin syndrome. Allow 2-week washout period post-MAOI prior to initiating venlafaxine
- *SSRIs or SARIs:* May cause serotonin syndrome
- *TCAs:* Plasma levels may be increased by SNRIs
- Alcohol may substantially increase potential for hepatotoxicity

PHARMACOKINETICS:

- Well absorbed and readily distributed throughout the body. Renal excretion accounts for nearly 90% of drug removal.

(cont.)

venlafaxine, venlafaxine XR (*cont.*)

Metabolism: Metabolized to the active metabolite desvenlafaxine by CYP450 2D6, leading to a prolonged duration of action.

Half-life: Non-enteric coated formulation, 2 hr; extended release formulation, 6 hr

PRECAUTIONS:
- Not approved by the FDA for use in children
- Monitor for BP elevations
- *Seizure disorders:* Use with caution
- *Hepatic impairment:* Reduce dosage
- *Renal impairment:* Reduce dosage
- *Narrow-angle glaucoma or elevated IOP:* Use with caution
- Pharmacokinetic properties similar to SSRIs.
- Adverse effects and side effects are commonly observed before therapeutic effects
- Many side effects are dose dependent and may improve over time

PATIENT AND FAMILY EDUCATION:
- Should be taken about the same time every day, morning or evening, although typically it is started in the morning; can be taken with or without food (with food if there is any stomach upset)
- May start with half of lowest effective dose for 3–7 days, then increase to lowest effective dose to diminish side effects.
- Administration time may be adjusted based on observed sedating or activating drug effects.
- May take up to 4–8 weeks to show its maximum effect at this dose, but some may see symptoms of dysthymia improving in as little as 2 weeks.
- If patient plans on becoming pregnant or is pregnant, discuss the benefits versus the risks of using this medicine while pregnant.
- Because this medicine is excreted in the breast milk, nursing mothers should not breastfeed while taking this medicine without prior consultation with a psychiatric nurse practitioner or psychiatrist. Newborns may develop symptoms including feeding or breathing difficulties, seizures, muscle stiffness, jitteriness, or constant crying.
- Do not stop taking this medication unless the health care provider directs. Report side effects or worsening symptoms to the health care provider promptly.
- The medication should be tapered gradually when changing or discontinuing therapy.
- Dosage should be adjusted to reach remission of symptoms and treatment should continue for at least 6–12 months following last reported dysthymic experience.
- Caution is advised when using this drug in the elderly because they may be more sensitive to the effects of the drug. Elderly patients should receive a lower starting dose.
- Keep these medications out of the reach of children and pets.

SPECIAL POPULATIONS:
- *Elderly:* Older individuals tend to be more sensitive to medication side effects such as hypotension and anticholinergic effects. They often require adjustment of medication doses for hepatic or renal dysfunction. Elderly patients may tolerate lower doses better and there is a reduced risk of suicide. May assist in treatment of chronic or depression-related physical pain.
- *Pregnancy:* Category C. Generally not recommended during pregnancy, especially during first trimester, as there are no adequate studies during pregnancy. An individual risk-benefit analysis must be done to determine appropriate treatment in pregnant women with DD.
- *Children:* Monitor closely, as risk of suicidal ideation is greatest in adolescents. Monitor for excessive activation effects or undiagnosed bipolar disorder. Obtain consultation with a pediatric psychiatric specialist.

Cymbalta   **duloxetine**

AVAILABLE FORMS: Delayed-release enteric coated capsule, 20, 30 and 60 mg

DOSAGE: Starting dose, 30 mg/day; maintenance dose, 40–60 mg/day

ADMINISTRATION: PO, with or without food. Do not crush or chew capsules. May start as twice-daily or once daily administration (typically in the morning)

SIDE EFFECTS: GI distress, particularly nausea at onset of treatment, sexual dysfunction, and urinary retention. Others similar to venlafaxine. Recommended for treating dysthymia that has accompanying physical pain. May be associated with lower incidence of hypertension and have milder withdrawal symptoms than other SNRIs.

DRUG INTERACTIONS: Similar to other SNRIs, can cause elevated response in TCAs and fatal interaction if combined with MAOIs.

PHARMACOKINETICS: Metabolized by CYP450 1A2 and 2D6

PRECAUTIONS:
- Not recommended for patients with renal impairment or hepatic impairment
- Closely monitor patients with a history of seizures
- Avoid stimulants, such as caffeine, as they may amplify the drug's activating side effects

PATIENT AND FAMILY EDUCATION:
- Should be taken about the same time every day, morning or evening, although typically it is
(cont.)

DYSTHYMIC DISORDER: Serotonin and Norepinephrine Reuptake Inhibitors (SNRIs)

duloxetine (cont.)

started in the morning, and can be taken with or without food (with food if there is any stomach upset).

- May start with half of lowest effective dose for 3–7 days, then increase to lowest effective dose to diminish side effects.
- Administration time may be adjusted based on observed sedating or activating drug effects.
- May take up to 4–8 weeks to show its maximum effect at this dose, but some may see symptoms of dysthymia improving in as little as 2 weeks.
- If patient plans on becoming pregnant or is pregnant, discuss the benefits versus the risks of using this medicine while pregnant.
- Because this medicine is excreted in the breast milk, nursing mothers should not breastfeed while taking this medicine without prior consultation with a psychiatric nurse practitioner or psychiatrist. Newborns may develop symptoms including feeding or breathing difficulties, seizures, muscle stiffness, jitteriness, or constant crying.
- Do not stop taking this medication unless the health care provider directs. Report side effects or worsening symptoms to the health care provider promptly.
- The medication should be tapered when changing or discontinuing therapy.
- Dosage should be adjusted to reach remission of symptoms and treatment should continue

for at least 6–12 months following last reported dysthymic experience.

- Caution is advised when using this drug in the elderly because they may be more sensitive to the effects of the drug. Elderly patients should receive a lower starting dose.
- Keep these medications out of the reach of children and pets.

SPECIAL POPULATIONS:
- *Elderly:* Older individuals tend to be more sensitive to medication side effects such as hypotension and anticholinergic effects. They often require adjustment of medication doses for hepatic or renal dysfunction. Elderly patients may tolerate lower doses better and there is a reduced risk of suicide. May assist in treatment of chronic or depression-related physical pain.
- *Pregnancy:* Psychotherapy is the initial choice for most pregnant patients with DD. Category C drug. Generally not recommended during pregnancy, especially during first trimester, as there are no adequate studies during pregnancy. An individual risk-benefit analysis must be done to determine appropriate treatment in pregnant women with DD.
- *Children:* Monitor closely, as risk of suicidal ideation is greatest in adolescents. Monitor for excessive activation effects or undiagnosed bipolar disorder. Obtain consultation with a pediatric psychiatric specialist.

desvenlafaxine   *Pristiq*

AVAILABLE FORMS: Extended-release tablet, 50 and 100 mg

DOSAGE: Starting dose, 50 mg/day; maintenance dose, 50–400 mg/day, although doses greater than 50 mg/day not found to have additional benefit and may be associated with greater side effects.

ADMINISTRATION: PO, with or without food. Do not crush or chew tablet.

SIDE EFFECTS: GI distress, sexual dysfunction, and urinary retention; increased blood pressure.

DRUG INTERACTIONS: Similar to other SNRIs, can cause elevated response in TCAs and fatal interaction if combined with MAOIs.

PHARMACOKINETICS: Not metabolized by P450s, so more predictable plasma levels than many other antidepressants, including venlafaxine.
Half-life: 9–13 hr

PRECAUTIONS:
- Similar to other SNRIs.
- Do not administer with MAOIs and use caution when combining with other drugs that have activating properties.

- Use with caution in patients with a history of seizures or heart disease

PATIENT AND FAMILY EDUCATION: Similar to other SNRIs.

SPECIAL POPULATIONS:
- *Elderly:* Older individuals tend to be more sensitive to medication side effects such as hypotension and anticholinergic effects. They often require adjustment of medication doses for hepatic or renal dysfunction. Elderly patients may tolerate lower doses better and there is a reduced risk of suicide. May assist in treatment of chronic or depression-related physical pain.
- *Pregnancy:* Category C drugs. Generally not recommended during pregnancy, especially during first trimester, as there are no adequate studies during pregnancy. An individual risk-benefit analysis must be done to determine appropriate treatment in pregnant women with DD.
- *Children:* Psychotherapy is the initial choice for most pregnant patients with DD. Monitor closely, as risk of suicidal ideation is greatest in adolescents. Monitor for excessive activation effects or undiagnosed bipolar disorder. Obtain consultation with a pediatric psychiatric specialist.

Class: Serotonin-2 Antagonist/Reuptake Inhibitors (SARIs)

Alternative to SSRIs, with particular use in clients with co-occurring insomnia or anxiety.
- Inhibits serotonin 2A receptor and serotonin reuptake.

- Receptor inhibition produces sedating effect
- Second-line medications that may be used in combination with SSRIs or SNRIs

---

Serzone   **nefazodone**

AVAILABLE FORMS: Tablet, 50, 100, 150, 200 and 250 mg

DOSAGE: Starting dose, 50 mg/day; maintenance dose, 100–400 mg/day; typically administered in divided doses

ADMINISTRATION: Administration with or after food may decrease side effects, but may impair drug absorption.

SIDE EFFECTS: Anticholinergic effects; hepatotoxicity; orthostatic hypotension; headache, drowsiness, insomnia, agitation, dizziness, or sedation; priapism; dry mouth, nausea, and constipation; muscle weakness; sexual dysfunction, significantly less than with SSRIs

DRUG INTERACTIONS:
- *Sedatives:* Effects may be exacerbated by use of other sedatives
- *MAOIs:* Extreme risk for drug toxicity
- May be used as adjunct to SSRI therapy

PHARMACOKINETICS:
- Inhibits activity of CYP450 3A4, which may alter metabolism of other medications.

Metabolism: Metabolized to an active metabolite that has a half-life of 12 hr, which is inactivated by CYP450 2D6.

Half-life: Parent compound, 2–4 hr

PRECAUTIONS:
- Use with caution in patients with renal impairment
- Avoid in patients with hepatic impairment or pre-existing liver disease and avoid combining with other medications with hepatic effects
- Monitor with routine serum liver function tests
- Caution in patients at risk for seizure disorders: May lower seizure threshold.
- Extremely low but life-threatening potential for liver damage (1:300,000 patient-years)
- Adverse effects and side effects are commonly observed before therapeutic effects

PATIENT AND FAMILY EDUCATION:
- Should be taken about the same time every day, morning or evening, although typically it is started in the morning, and can be taken with or without food (with food if there is any stomach upset).

- May take up to 4–8 weeks to show its maximum effect at this dose, but some may see symptoms of dysthymia improving in as little as 2 weeks.
- If patient plans on becoming pregnant or is pregnant, discuss the benefits versus the risks of using this medicine while pregnant.
- Because this medicine is excreted in the breast milk, nursing mothers should not breastfeed while taking this medicine without prior consultation with a psychiatric nurse practitioner or psychiatrist. Newborns may develop symptoms including feeding or breathing difficulties, seizures, muscle stiffness, jitteriness, or constant crying.
- Do not stop taking this medication unless the health care provider directs. Report side effects or worsening symptoms to the health care provider promptly.
- The medication should be tapered when changing or discontinuing therapy.
- Dosage should be adjusted to reach remission of symptoms and treatment should continue for at least 6–12 months following last reported dysthymic experience.
- Caution is advised when using this drug in the elderly because they may be more sensitive to the effects of the drug. Elderly patients should receive a lower starting dose.
- Keep these medications out of the reach of children and pets.

SPECIAL POPULATIONS:
- *Elderly:* Older individuals tend to be more sensitive to medication side effects such as hypotension and anticholinergic effects. They often require adjustment of medication doses for hepatic or renal dysfunction. Begin treatment at half the standard dose. Do not use in clients with hepatic disease. Be cautious as the drug has sedative effects.
- *Pregnancy:* Psychotherapy is the initial choice for most pregnant patients with DD. Category C drug, not recommended for use during pregnancy, especially during the first trimester, as there are no adequate studies during pregnancy.
- *Children:* Psychiatric consultation is recommended due to black box warning of increased suicidal ideation using SSRI therapy in children.

Desyrel   **trazodone**

AVAILABLE FORMS: Tablet, 50, 100, 150, and 300 mg; extended-release tablet (scored), 150 and 300 mg

DOSAGE: Starting dose, 50 mg/day; maintenance dose, 75–400 mg

ADMINISTRATION: PO, with food decreases some side effects. Scored extended-relief tablets may be broken in half but should not be crushed or chewed.

(cont.)

DYSTHYMIC DISORDER: Serotonin-2 Antagonist/Reuptake Inhibitors (SARIs)

trazodone (cont.)

SIDE EFFECTS: Sedation, hypotension, nausea; may aid patients experiencing SSRI/SNRI-induced insomnia. Priapism has been reported (rare). This should be discussed with male clients.

DRUG INTERACTIONS: May increase plasma concentrations. May inhibit full effect of antihypertensive medications. Patients taking MAOIs should not use this drug.

PHARMACOKINETICS:
Metabolism: Metabolized by CYP450 3A4 to an active metabolite.
Half-life: Parent drug, 7–8 hr; active metabolite, 5–9 hr

PRECAUTIONS: Do not use with MAOIs. Use with caution in patients having a history of seizures and in patients at risk for undiagnosed bipolar disorder.

SPECIAL POPULATIONS:
- *Elderly:* Older individuals tend to be more sensitive to medication side effects such as hypotension and anticholinergic effects. They often require adjustment of medication doses for hepatic or renal dysfunction. May be more sensitive to side effects and require a lower dosing regimen. Be cautious as the drug has sedative effects.
- *Pregnancy:* Psychotherapy is the initial choice for most pregnant patients with DD. Category C, not advised during pregnancy (similar to nefazodone).
- *Children:* Typically require a lower initial dosing and prolonged titration. Increased risk of suicidal ideation than in adults

Class: Norepinephrine/Dopamine Reuptake Inhibitors (NDRIs)

These are additional alternative dysthymia treatment options, with a tendency for fewer sexual side effects. Often used as adjuncts to SSRIs or SNRIs. Used for specific presentations, when other medications are not effective, or when side effects from other medications are intolerable.
- These antidepressants work through poorly defined mechanisms or mechanisms other than the SSRIs and SNRIs. They do not appear to inhibit serotinergic or histaminergic signaling. Some anticholingeric effects reported.
- May be combined with SSRIs to offset some SSRI side effects (e.g., sexual dysfunction) or for augmentation of antidepressant effect.

- Mirtazapine antagonizes central presynaptic alpha$_2$-receptors. Exhibits both noradrenergic and serotonergic activity.
- Bupropion inhibits neuronal dopamine reuptake in addition to weak SNRIs. Binds to nicotininic receptor.
- Buproprion aids with smoking cessation. It is weight neutral and may assist with weight loss. It may be more likely to improve symptoms of fatigue and sleepiness than SSRIs. It should not be used in patients with seizure disorders, eating disorders, or alcohol abuse.

bupropion / buproprion SR / buproprion XL — Wellbutrin, Zyban / Wellbutrin SR / Wellbutrin XL

AVAILABLE FORMS: Tablet, 75 and 100 mg; sustained-release tablet, 100 and 150 mg; extended-release tablet, 100, 150, 200 and 300 mg

DOSAGE: Starting dose, 150 mg/day; maintenance dose, 150–450 mg/day

ADMINISTRATION: Depending upon formulation prescribed, taken tid (rapid release), bid; second dose not to be given within 5–6 hr of hs in order to avoid insomnia (SR), or once daily in the morning (XL). SR and XL formulations are most commonly used, and XL formulation is recommended if available.

SIDE EFFECTS:
- Seizure threshold significantly decreased particularly at >300–450 mg/day dosage. Use of SR or XL formulation also helpful in reducing risk of seizure.
- Headache, anxiety, tremor, tachycardia, and insomnia; cognitive impairment and mental clouding; delayed hypersensitivity reactions; tachycardia; nausea; increased sweating; blurred vision; dry mouth; weight loss

DRUG INTERACTIONS:
- Can elevate TCA activity; use with caution.
- Can be fatal when combined with MAOIs.
- Potentially increases plasma levels of other 2D6 metabolites.
- Risk of seizure may be increased by concomitant use of inhibitors of CYP2B6 (e.g., desipramine, sertraline, paroxetine, fluoxetine), due to increased bupropion blood levels.

PHARMACOKINETICS:
- Inhibits activity of CYP450 2D6, potentially increasing plasma levels of other 2D6 metabolites
- Converted to an active metabolite.
Half-life: Parent compound, 10–24 hr; active metabolite, 20–24 hr

PRECAUTIONS:
- Use with caution in patients with cardiovascular disease, hepatic impairment, or renal impairment.
- Do not use in patients with seizure disorders, alcoholism, or anorexia nervosa.

(cont.)

bupropion, buproprion SR, buproprion XL (*cont.*)

- Low incidence of sexual dysfunction.
- *Patients at risk for seizure disorders:* May lower seizure threshold.
- Avoid combinations with other CNS stimulants.

PATIENT AND FAMILY EDUCATION:
- Should be taken about the same time every day, preferably in the morning (for XL formulation) with or without food.
- If taking rapid release or SR formulation, take last dose more than 5–6 hr from bedtime, as late dosing can precipitate insomnia.
- May take up to 4–8 weeks to show its maximum effect, but some may see symptoms of dysthymia improving in as little as 2 weeks.
- If patient plans on becoming pregnant, discuss the benefits versus the risks of using this medicine while pregnant.
- Because this medicine is excreted in the breast milk, nursing mothers should not breastfeed while taking this medicine without prior consultation with a psychiatric nurse practitioner or psychiatrist. Newborns may develop symptoms including feeding or breathing difficulties, seizures, muscle stiffness, jitteriness, or constant crying.
- Do not stop taking this medication unless your health care provider directs you to do so. Report side effects or worsening dysthymia symptoms to your health care provider promptly.
- Treatment should continue for 6–12 months following last reported dysthymic experience.
- Keep these medications out of the reach of children and pets.

SPECIAL POPULATIONS:
- *Elderly:* Older individuals tend to be more sensitive to medication side effects such as hypotension and anticholinergic effects. They often require adjustment of medication doses for hepatic or renal dysfunction. Begin at lower dosage; XL formulation recommended
- *Pregnancy:* Psychotherapy is the initial choice for most pregnant patients with DD. Category C; not recommended during pregnancy, especially first trimester, as there are no adequate studies during pregnancy.
- *Children:* Recommended to begin at lower dosage. Monitor closely for suicidal ideation. Psychiatric consultation is recommended due to black box warning of increased suicidal ideation using SSRI therapy in children. May be useful in treating children with comorbid ADHD

Class: Noradrenergic and Specific Serotonergic Antidepressants (NaSSAs)

These are additional alternative dysthymia treatment options, with a tendency for fewer sexual side effects. Often used as adjuncts to SSRIs or SNRIs. Used for specific presentations, when other medications are not effective, or when side effects from other medications are intolerable.
- These antidepressants work through poorly defined mechanisms or mechanisms other than the SSRIs and SNRIs. They do not appear to inhibit serotinergic or histaminergic signaling. Some anticholingeric effects reported.
- May be combined with SSRIs to offset some SSRI side effects (e.g., sexual dysfunction) or for augmentation of antidepressant effect.
- Mirtazapine antagonizes central presynaptic alpha2-receptors. Exhibits both noradrenergic and serotonergic activity.
- Bupropion inhibits neuronal dopamine reuptake in addition to weak SNRIs. Binds to nicotininic receptor.
- Buproprion aids with smoking cessation. It is weight neutral and may assist with weight loss. It may be more likely to improve symptoms of fatigue and sleepiness than SSRIs. It should not be used in patients with seizure disorders, eating disorders, or alcohol abuse.

| *Remeron* | mitazapine |

AVAILABLE FORMS: Tablet, 7.5, 15, 30 and 45 mg

DOSAGE: Starting dose, 5–15 mg nightly; titrate up to 15–45 mg/day

ADMINISTRATION: PO, with or without food, at bedtime.

SIDE EFFECTS:
- *Serious:* Agranulocytosis
- Anticholinergic effects; *blood dyscrasias:* neutropenia and agranulocytosis; orthostatic hypotension or hypertension; somnolence and sedation, dizziness, tremor, confusion; increased risk for hyperlipidemia; dry mouth; significant appetite increase and weight gain (greater than 7% body mass); asthenia

DRUG INTERACTIONS:
- *Sedatives:* Effects may be exacerbated by use of other sedatives
- *MAOIs:* Risk for drug toxicity
- *CNS stimulants* (e.g., amphetamines): May lower seizure threshold
- *Anticholinergic drugs* (e.g., antihistamines): Increase effects

PHARMACOKINETICS: Prolonged half-life of 20–40 hr, which is increased further in patients with hepatic or renal impairment.

PRECAUTIONS:
- Use with caution in patients with hepatic impairment or renal impairment

(cont.)

DYSTHYMIC DISORDER: Noradrenergic and Specific Serotonergic Antidepressants (NaSSAs)

mirtazapine (cont.)

- *Patients at risk for seizure disorders:* May lower seizure threshold.
- Monitor with CBC and history for signs of agranulocytosis or severe neutropenia
- Low incidence of sexual dysfunction
- Usually dosed at hs due to associated drowsiness (may be helpful in patients with insomnia or anxiety)
- May alter liver function
- Adverse effects and side effects are commonly observed before therapeutic effects

PATIENT AND FAMILY EDUCATION:

- Take 60–90 minutes prior to bedtime, due to associated drowsiness. Do not drive until the effect of this medication is known.
- May cause stomach upset or blood pressure changes (particularly with getting up suddenly).
- This medication may increase appetite or craving for carbohydrates. Monitoring diet and exercise is important.
- May take up to 4–8 weeks to show its maximum effect at this dose, but some may see symptoms of depression improving in as little as 2 weeks.
- If planning on becoming pregnant or are pregnant, discuss the benefits versus the risks of using this medicine while pregnant.
- Because this medicine is excreted in the breast milk, nursing mothers should not breastfeed while taking this medicine without prior consultation with a psychiatric nurse practitioner or psychiatrist. Newborns may develop symptoms including feeding or breathing difficulties, seizures, muscle stiffness, jitteriness, or constant crying.
- Do not stop taking this medication unless the health care provider directs. Report side effects or worsening symptoms to the health care provider promptly.
- Dosage should be adjusted to reach remission of symptoms and treatment should continue for at least 4–9 months following remission of symptoms.
- Caution is advised when using this drug in the elderly because they may be more sensitive to the effects of the drug. Elderly patients should receive a lower starting dose.
- Keep these medications out of the reach of children and pets.

SPECIAL POPULATIONS:

- *Elderly:* Older individuals tend to be more sensitive to medication side effects such as hypotension and anticholinergic effects. They often require adjustment of medication doses for hepatic or renal dysfunction. Recommended to begin at lower dosage.
- *Pregnancy:* Psychotherapy is the initial choice for most pregnant patients with DD. Category C, not recommended during pregnancy, especially first trimester, as there are no adequate studies during pregnancy.
- *Children:* Not approved by the FDA for use in children. Use only after consultation with psychiatric specialist.

Class: Tricyclic Antidepressants (TCAs)

Older antidepressants that are infrequently used for the primary treatment of dysthymia, and sometimes as an adjunct for patients with co-morbid chronic pain or insomnia.

- TCAs are infrequently used for the treatment of dysthymic disorder due to risk for cardiac arrhythmia and significant side effects. Pre-treatment EKG is indicated in patients with significant cardiac risk factors or in patients older than 50 years of age. Follow up EKGs may be indicated to identify development of conduction changes shortly after initiation of TCA use. Persons with QT prolongation are predisposed to develop ventricular tachycardia.

- TCAs are sometimes used adjunctively off label for sleep problems or neuropathic pain syndromes associated with DD.
- TCAs may be considered for treatment of DD when all other medications fail to work.
- Common adverse effects result from anticholinergic effects (e.g., blurred vision [mydriasis and cycloplegia], dry mucous membranes, elevated IOP, hyperthermia, constipation, and urinary retention).
- Extrapyramidal effects, including tardive dyskinesia, pseudoparkinsonism, akathisia, and dystonia, commonly occur.

amitriptyline   *Elavil*

AVAILABLE FORMS: Tablet, 10, 25, 50, 75, 100 and 150 mg

DOSAGE: Starting dose, 25–50 mg/day; maintenance dose, 100–300 mg/day

ADMINISTRATION: PO, at bedtime or in divided doses

SIDE EFFECTS:

- Cardiotoxicity (particularly in overdose), cardiac arrhythmias, and QT interval prolongation; anticholinergic effects; orthostatic hypotension hypomania; sedation and drowsiness; increased potential for seizures; extrapyramidal effects

(cont.)

amitriptyline (cont.)

DRUG INTERACTIONS:
- *MAOIs:* Risk for extreme hypertension
- *CNS depressants* (e.g., alcohol): TCAs increase effects
- *Direct-acting adrenergic agonists* (e.g., epinephrine): TCAs increase effects
- *Anticholinergic drugs* (e.g., antihistamines): TCAs increase effects. Do not use in combination.
- *SSRIs and other medications:* serotonin syndrome
- Antiarrhythmic agents

PHARMACOKINETICS:
- Nicotine use (smoking) increases drug metabolism and may diminish drug potency
- Blood levels may be checked to ensure that levels are not excessive.

Metabolism: Metabolized by CYP450 2D6 and 1A2, converted to the active metabolite nortriptyline
Half-life: Approx. 15 hr

PRECAUTIONS:
- Adverse effects and side effects are commonly observed before therapeutic effects.
- Many side effects are dose-dependent and may improve over time. Overdose may result in lethal cardiotoxicity or seizure.
- Use with caution in patients having a history of seizure or heart disease.
- Avoid in patients with a history of cardiac arrhythmia. Monitor with EKG.

PATIENT AND FAMILY EDUCATION:
- Should be taken about the same time every day, typically in the evening, with or without food. May cause prolonged sedation. Do not drive until the effect of this medication is known.
- Administration time may be adjusted based on observed sedating or activating drug effects
- May take up to 4–8 weeks to show its maximum effect, but patient may see symptoms of dysthymia improving in as little as 2 weeks.

- If patient plans on becoming pregnant, discuss the benefits versus the risks of using this medicine while pregnant.
- Because this medicine is excreted in the breast milk, nursing mothers should not breastfeed while taking this medicine. Newborns may develop symptoms including feeding or breathing difficulties, seizures, muscle stiffness, jitteriness, or constant crying.
- Do not stop taking this medication unless the health care provider directs. Report symptoms to the health care provider promptly.
- Drug should be tapered gradually.
- Treatment should continue for at least 6–12 months following last reported dysthymic experience.
- Keep these medications out of the reach of children and pets.

SPECIAL POPULATIONS:
- *Elderly:* Older individuals tend to be more sensitive to medication side effects such as hypotension and anticholinergic effects. They often require adjustment of doses for hepatic or renal dysfunction. TCAs have been shown in at least one controlled clinical trial to be more effective than SSRIs in hospitalized geriatric patients, and in patients with melancholia and unipolar depression. However, cardiac side effects and fall risk are of great concern in this population. Side effects may be more pronounced and require decreased dosage.
- *Pregnancy:* Psychotherapy is the initial choice for most pregnant patients with DD. Category C; not recommended in most cases, as there are no adequate studies during pregnancy.
- *Children:* Not recommended for children under the age of 12.

Anafranil   **clomipramine**

AVAILABLE FORMS: Tablet, 25, 50 and 75 mg

DOSAGE: Starting dose, 25–50 mg/day; maintenance dose, typically 100–250 mg/day if used for antidepressive effects

ADMINISTRATION: PO, at bedtime as a single dose (once tolerated)

SIDE EFFECTS: Similar to amitriptyline.
- Anticholinergic effects of dry mouth, constipation, and blurred vision
- Cardiac arrhythmias
- Fatigue, sedation, and weight gain
- Sexual dysfunction

DRUG INTERACTIONS:
- *MAOIs:* Risk for extreme hypertension
- *CNS depressants* (e.g., alcohol): TCAs increase effects

- *Direct-acting adrenergic agonists* (e.g., epinephrine): TCAs increase effects
- *Anticholinergic drugs* (e.g., antihistamines): TCAs increase effects. Do not use in combination.
- Antiarrhythmic agents
- *SSRIs and other medications:* serotonin syndrome

PRECAUTIONS:
- Adverse effects and side effects are commonly observed before therapeutic effects.
- Many side effects are dose dependent and may improve over time.
- Overdose may result in lethal cardiotoxicity.
- Use with caution in patients with a history of seizure or heart disease.
- Avoid in patients with a history of cardiac arrhythmia. Monitor with EKG.

(cont.)

DYSTHYMIC DISORDER: Tricyclic Antidepressants (TCAs)

DYSTHYMIC DISORDER: Tricyclic Antidepressants (TCAs)

clomipramine (*cont.*)

PHARMACOKINETICS:
Metabolism: Metabolized to an inactive form by CYP450 2D6 and 1A2
Half-life: Approx. 24 hr

PATIENT AND FAMILY EDUCATION:
- Should be taken about the same time every day, typically in the evening, and with or without food. May cause prolonged sedation. Do not drive until the effect of this medication is known.
- Administration time may be adjusted based on observed sedating or activating drug effects.
- May take up to 4–8 weeks to show its maximum effect, but patient may see symptoms of dysthymia improving in as little as 2 weeks.
- If patient plans on becoming pregnant, discuss the benefits versus the risks of using this medicine while pregnant.
- Because this medication is excreted in breast milk, nursing mothers should not breastfeed while taking this medicine without prior consultation with a psychiatric nurse practitioner or psychiatrist. Newborns may develop symptoms including feeding or breathing difficulties, seizures, muscle stiffness, jitteriness, or constant crying.
- Do not stop taking this medication unless the health care provider directs. Report symptoms to the health care provider promptly.
- Drug should be tapered gradually.
- Treatment should continue for at least 6–12 months following last reported dysthymic experience.
- Keep these medications out of the reach of children and pets.

SPECIAL POPULATIONS:
- *Elderly:* Older individuals tend to be more sensitive to medication side effects such as hypotension and anticholinergic effects. They often require adjustment of medication doses for hepatic or renal dysfunction. TCAs have been shown in at least one controlled clinical trial to be more effective than SSRIs in hospitalized geriatric patients, and in patients with melancholia and unipolar depression. However, cardiac side effects and fall risk are of great concern in this population. Side effects may be more pronounced and require decreased dosage.
- *Pregnancy:* Psychotherapy is the initial choice for most pregnant patients with DD. Category C; not recommended in most cases, as there are no adequate studies during pregnancy.
- *Children:* Not recommended for children under the age of 12.

despiramine   *Norpramin*

AVAILABLE FORMS: Tablet, 10, 25, 50, 75, 100 and 150 mg

DOSAGE: Starting dose, 25–50 mg/day; maintenance dose, typically 75–300 mg/day if used for antidepressant effect

ADMINISTRATION: PO, in divided doses; may be administered as single dose once tolerated

SIDE EFFECTS: Similar to amitriptyline.
- Cardiac arrhythmias
- Fatigue, sedation, and weight gain
- sexual dysfunction

DRUG INTERACTIONS:
- *MAOIs:* Risk for extreme hypertension
- *CNS depressants* (e.g., alcohol): TCAs increase effects
- *Direct-acting adrenergic agonists* (e.g., epinephrine): TCAs increase effects
- *Anticholinergic drugs* (e.g., antihistamines): TCAs increase effects
- Antiarrhythmic agents
- *SSRIs and other medications:* serotonin syndrome

PHARMACOKINETICS:
Metabolism: Metabolized to an inactive form by CYP450 2D6 and 1A2
Half-life: Approx. 24 hr

PRECAUTIONS:
- Drug overdose has resulted in higher death rate in comparison to other TCAs. Overdose may result in lethal cardiotoxicity or seizure.
- Avoid in patients with a family history of cardiac arrhythmias and/or seizures.
- Monitor for cardiac effects with EKG.

PATIENT AND FAMILY EDUCATION:
- Should be taken about the same time every day, typically in the evening, with or without food. May cause prolonged sedation. Do not drive until the effect of this medication is known.
- Administration time may be adjusted based on observed sedating or activating drug effects.
- May take up to 4–8 weeks to show its maximum effect, but patient may see symptoms of dysthymia improving in as little as 2 weeks.
- If patient plans on becoming pregnant, discuss the benefits versus the risks of using this medicine while pregnant.
- Because this medicine is excreted in the breast milk, nursing mothers should not breastfeed while taking this medicine without prior consultation with a psychiatric nurse practitioner or psychiatrist. Newborns may develop symptoms including feeding or breathing difficulties, seizures, muscle stiffness, jitteriness, or constant crying.

(cont.)

despiramine (*cont.*)

- Do not stop taking this medication unless the health care provider directs. Report symptoms to the health care provider promptly.
- Drug should be tapered gradually.
- Treatment should continue for at least 6–12 months following last reported dysthymic experience.
- Keep these medications out of the reach of children and pets.

SPECIAL POPULATIONS:
- *Elderly:* Older individuals tend to be more sensitive to medication side effects such as hypotension and anticholinergic effects. They often require adjustment of medication doses for hepatic or renal dysfunction. TCAs have been shown in at least one controlled clinical trial to be more effective than SSRIs in hospitalized geriatric patients, and in patients with melancholia and unipolar depression. However, cardiac side effects and fall risk are of great concern in this population. Side effects may be more pronounced and require decreased dosage
- *Pregnancy:* Psychotherapy is the initial choice for most pregnant patients with DD. Category C; not recommended in most cases, as there are no adequate studies during pregnancy.
- *Children:* Not recommended for children under the age of 12.

Tofranil   **imipramine**

AVAILABLE FORMS: Capsule, 75, 100, 125 and 150 mg; tablet, 10, 25 and 50 mg

DOSAGE: Starting dose, 25–50 mg/day; maintenance dose, typically in divided doses; 75–300 mg/day if used for antidepressant effect

ADMINISTRATION: Oral formulations require tid-qid dosing

SIDE EFFECTS: Similar to amitriptyline.
- Cardiac arrhythmias
- Fatigue, sedation, and weight gain
- Sexual dysfunction

DRUG INTERACTIONS:
- *MAOIs:* Risk for extreme hypertension
- *CNS depressants* (e.g., alcohol): TCAs increase effects
- *Direct-acting adrenergic agonists* (e.g., epinephrine): TCAs increase effects
- *Anticholinergic drugs* (e.g., antihistamines): TCAs increase effects. Do not use in combination.
- *SSRIs and other medications:* serotonin syndrome

PHARMACOKINETICS:
Metabolism: Metabolized to the active metabolite desipramine form by CYP450 2D6. Also metabolized by CYP450 1A2
Half-life: Approx. 2–3 days

PRECAUTIONS: Overdose may result in lethal cardiotoxicity or seizure
- Use with caution in patients having a history of seizure or heart disease
- Avoid in patients with a history of cardiac arrhythmia. Monitor with EKG

PATIENT AND FAMILY EDUCATION:
- Should be taken about the same time every day, with or without food. May cause prolonged sedation. Do not drive until the effect of this medication is known.
- Administration time may be adjusted based on observed sedating or activating drug effects

- May take up to 4–8 weeks to show its maximum effect, but patient may see symptoms of dysthymia improving in as little as 2 weeks.
- If patient plans on becoming pregnant, discuss the benefits versus the risks of using this medicine while pregnant.
- Because this medicine is excreted in the breast milk, nursing mothers should not breastfeed while taking this medicine without prior consultation with a psychiatric nurse practitioner or psychiatrist. Newborns may develop symptoms including feeding or breathing difficulties, seizures, muscle stiffness, jitteriness, or constant crying.
- Do not stop taking this medication unless the health care provider directs. Report symptoms to the health care provider promptly.
- Drug should be tapered gradually.
- Treatment should continue for at least 6–12 months following last reported dysthymic experience.
- Keep these medications out of the reach of children and pets.

SPECIAL POPULATIONS:
- *Elderly:* Older individuals tend to be more sensitive to medication side effects such as hypotension and anticholinergic effects. They often require adjustment of medication doses for hepatic or renal dysfunction. TCAs have been shown in at least one controlled clinical trial to be more effective than SSRIs in hospitalized geriatric patients, and in patients with melancholia and unipolar depression. However, cardiac side effects and fall risk are of great concern in this population. Side effects may be more pronounced and require decreased dosage
- *Pregnancy:* Psychotherapy is the initial choice for most pregnant patients with DD. Category D; not recommended in pregnancy, as there are no adequate studies during pregnancy.
- *Children:* Not recommended for children under the age of 12.

DYSTHYMIC DISORDER: Tricyclic Antidepressants (TCAs)

nortriptyline   *Pamelor*

AVAILABLE FORMS: Capsule, 10, 25, 50 and 75 mg; oral solution, 10 mg/5 mL (480 mL)

DOSAGE: Starting dose, 25 mg/day; maintenance dose, typically 50–200 mg/day if used for antidepressive effects

ADMINISTRATION: PO, in 3–4 divided doses. May be given once per day once tolerated

SIDE EFFECTS: Similar to amitriptyline.
- Cardiac arrhythmias
- Fatigue, sedation, and weight gain
- Sexual dysfunction

DRUG INTERACTIONS:
- *MAOIs:* Risk for extreme hypertension
- *CNS depressants* (e.g., alcohol): TCAs increase effects
- *Direct-acting adrenergic agonists* (e.g., epinephrine): TCAs increase effects
- *Anticholinergic drugs* (e.g., antihistamines): TCAs increase effects

PHARMACOKINETICS:
Metabolism: Metabolized to an inactive form by CYP450 2D6
Half-life: Approx. 36 hr

PRECAUTIONS:
- Adverse effects and side effects are commonly observed before therapeutic effects.
- Many side effects are dose-dependent and may improve over time.
- Overdose may result in lethal cardiotoxicity.
- Monitor with routine EKG.

PATIENT AND FAMILY EDUCATION:
- Should be taken about the same time every day, with or without food. May cause prolonged sedation. Do not drive until the effect of this medication are known.
- Administration time may be adjusted based on observed sedating or activating drug effects.
- May take up to 4–8 weeks to show its maximum effect, but patient may see symptoms of dysthymia improving in as little as 2 weeks.
- If patient plans on becoming pregnant, discuss the benefits versus the risks of using this medicine while pregnant.
- Because this medicine is excreted in the breast milk, nursing mothers should not breastfeed while taking this medicine without prior consultation with a psychiatric nurse practitioner or psychiatrist. Newborns may develop symptoms including feeding or breathing difficulties, seizures, muscle stiffness, jitteriness, or constant crying.
- Do not stop taking this medication unless the health care provider directs. Report symptoms to the health care provider promptly.
- Drug should be tapered gradually.
- Treatment should continue for at least 6–12 months following last reported dysthymic experience.
- Keep these medications out of the reach of children and pets.

SPECIAL POPULATIONS:
- *Elderly:* Older individuals tend to be more sensitive to medication side effects such as hypotension and anticholinergic effects. They often require adjustment of medication doses for hepatic or renal dysfunction. TCAs have been shown in at least one controlled clinical trial to be more effective than SSRIs in hospitalized geriatric patients, and in patients with melancholia and unipolar depression. However, cardiac side effects and fall risk are of great concern in this population. Side effects may be more pronounced and require decreased dosage
- *Pregnancy:* Psychotherapy is the initial choice for most pregnant patients with DD. Category D; not recommended in pregnancy, as there are no adequate studies of use during pregnancy.
- *Children:* Not recommended for children under the age of 12.

Class: Monoamine Oxidase Inhibitors (MAOIs)

Older antidepressants that are rarely used, but may be an option when other medical therapy has failed.
- MAOIs are rarely used for dysthymia now due to serious side effects and interactions with other medications and foods.
- May be particularly effective in patients with atypical features such as reactive mood and sensitivity to rejection.
- Should only be prescribed by a psychiatrist who is experienced in their use.

phenelzine   *Nardil*

AVAILABLE FORM: Tablet, 15 mg

DOSAGE: Starting dose, 15 mg/day; maintenance dose, 15–90 mg/day in divided doses

ADMINISTRATION: PO, bid-tid dosing

SIDE EFFECTS:
- Orthostatic hypotension
- Hypertensive crisis, secondary to excessive consumption of dietary tyramine (e.g., soft cheeses, aged fish, aged meat, and avocados)

(cont.)

phenelzine (cont.)

- CNS stimulation
- Orthostatic hypotension
- Sexual dysfunction

DRUG INTERACTIONS:
- *High potential for interactions*: Do not use with other MAOI or antidepressants.
- Avoid products containing sympathomimetic stimulants or dextromethorphan.
- Concurrent use with antihypertensive agents may lead to exaggeration of hypotensive effects.
- Examples of drugs to avoid include alpha$_1$-agonists, amphetamines, buproprion, buspirone, dextromethorphan, linezolid, meperidine, methyldopa, methylphenidate, mirtazapine, SSRIs, SARIs, SNRIs, and TCAs.
- *SSRIs, SNRIs, and TCAs:* Risk for extreme hypertension
- *Indirect-acting adrenergic agonists* (e.g., ephedrine): Increase MAOI effects
- Antihypertensive drugs may dangerously lower blood pressure.

PHARMACOKINETICS:
Duration of action: 2–3 weeks following discontinuation
Half-life: Approx. 11 hr, but irreversible MAO inhibition prolongs effects

PRECAUTIONS:
- Not approved by the FDA for the treatment of depression in children 16 years of age or under.
- *Diabetic patients:* Use with caution and monitor blood glucose
- *Glaucoma:* Potential increase in IOP
- *Patients at risk for seizure disorders:* May lower seizure threshold.
- Patients with hyperthyroidism or being treated with thyroid hormone experienced increased risk of proarrhythmias.

- Generally well tolerated in elderly patients with controlled diet.
- Adverse effects and side effects are commonly observed before therapeutic effects.
- Dietary restrictions require substantial patient adherence.

PATIENT AND FAMILY EDUCATION:
- Should be taken about the same time every day, with or without food.
- Substantial education required on dietary changes and importance of dietary adherence.
- Advise all health care providers of use of MAOI prior to initiating new medications.
- Administration time may be adjusted based on observed sedating or activating drug effects.
- May take up to 4–8 weeks to show its maximum effect, but some may see symptoms of dysthymia improving in as little as 2 weeks.
- Do not take if risk of pregnancy or pregnant.
- Because this medicine is excreted in the breast milk, nursing mothers should not breastfeed while taking this medication. Newborns may develop symptoms including feeding or breathing difficulties, seizures, muscle stiffness, jitteriness, or constant crying.
- Report potential side effects to the health care provider promptly.
- Keep these medications out of the reach of children and pets.

SPECIAL POPULATIONS:
- *Elderly:* Requires 1/3 drug dose in adult patients over 65 years old. Due to common need for polypharmacy, not recommended.
- *Pregnancy:* Psychotherapy is the initial choice for most pregnant patients with DD. Generally not recommended during pregnancy.
- *Children:* Not recommended for children less than 16 years of age

---

Marplan   **isocarboxazid**

AVAILABLE FORM: Tablet, 10 mg

DOSAGE: Starting dose, 20 mg/day; maintenance dose, 20–60 mg/day, in divided doses

ADMINISTRATION: PO, tid-qid dosing

SIDE EFFECTS:
- Hypertensive crisis, secondary to excessive consumption of dietary tyramine (e.g., soft cheeses, aged fish, aged meat, and avocados)
- CNS stimulation
- Orthostatic hypotension
- Sexual dysfunction

DRUG INTERACTIONS:
- *SSRIs, SNRIs, and TCAs:* Risk for extreme hypertension
- *Indirect-acting adrenergic agonists* (e.g., ephedrine): Increase MAOI effects

- Antihypertensive drugs may dangerously lower blood pressure

PHARMACOKINETICS:
Duration of action: 2–3 weeks following discontinuation due to irreversible MAO inhibition

PRECAUTIONS:
- Adverse effects and side effects are commonly observed before therapeutic effects
- Dietary restrictions require substantial patient adherence

PATIENT AND FAMILY EDUCATION:
- Should be taken about the same time every day, with or without food.
- Substantial education required on dietary changes and importance of dietary adherence.
- Advise all health care providers of use of an MAOI prior to initiating new medications.

(cont.)

DYSTHYMIC DISORDER: Monoamine Oxidase Inhibitors (MAOIs)

isocarboxazid (cont.)

- Administration time may be adjusted based on observed sedating or activating drug effects.
- May take up to 4–8 weeks to show its maximum effect, but some may see symptoms of dysthymia improving in as little as 2 weeks.
- Do not take if risk of pregnancy or pregnant.
- Because this medicine is excreted in the breast milk, nursing mothers should not breastfeed while taking this medicine. Newborns may develop symptoms including feeding or breathing difficulties, seizures, muscle stiffness, jitteriness, or constant crying.
- Report potential side effects to the health care provider promptly.
- Keep these medications out of the reach of children and pets.

SPECIAL POPULATIONS:
- *Elderly:* Requires lower drug dose in adult patients older than 65 years. Due to common need for polypharmacy, not recommended.
- *Pregnancy:* Psychotherapy is the initial choice for most pregnant patients with DD. Generally not recommended during pregnancy.
- *Children:* Not recommended for children less than 16 years of age

tranylcypromine *Parnate*

AVAILABLE FORM: Tablet, 10 mg

DOSAGE: Starting dose, 10 mg/day; maintenance dose, 10–60 mg/day in divided doses

ADMINISTRATION: PO, bid-tid dosing

SIDE EFFECTS:
- Hypertensive crisis, secondary to excessive consumption of dietary tyramine (e.g., soft cheeses, aged fish, aged meat, and avocados)
- CNS stimulation
- Orthostatic hypotension
- Sexual dysfunction

DRUG INTERACTIONS:
- *SSRIs, SNRIs, and TCAs:* Risk for extreme hypertension
- *Indirect-acting adrenergic agonists* (e.g., ephedrine): Increase MAOI effects
- Antihypertensive drugs may dangerously lower blood pressure

PHARMACOKINETICS:
Duration of action: 2–3 weeks following discontinuation
Half-life: 1–3 hr, but irreversible MAO inhibition prolongs effects

PRECAUTIONS:
- Adverse effects and side effects are commonly observed before therapeutic effects.
- Dietary restrictions require substantial patient adherence.

PATIENT AND FAMILY EDUCATION:
- Should be taken about the same time every day, with or without food.
- Substantial education required on dietary changes and importance of dietary adherence.
- Advise all health care providers of use of an MAOI prior to initiating new medications.
- Administration time may be adjusted based on observed sedating or activating drug effects.
- May take up to 4–8 weeks to show its maximum effect, but some may see symptoms of dysthymia improving in as little as 2 weeks.
- Do not take if risk of pregnancy or pregnant.
- Because this medicine is excreted in the breast milk, nursing mothers should not breastfeed while taking this medicine. Newborns may develop symptoms including feeding or breathing difficulties, seizures, muscle stiffness, jitteriness, or constant crying.
- Report potential side effects to the health care provider promptly.
- Keep these medications out of the reach of children and pets.

SPECIAL POPULATIONS:
- *Elderly:* Requires lower drug dose in adult patients above 65 years old. Due to common need for polypharmacy, not recommended.
- *Pregnancy:* Psychotherapy is the initial choice for most pregnant patients with DD. Generally not recommended during pregnancy
- *Children:* Not recommended for children less than 16 years of age

Treatment of Psychotic Disorders

- Psychotic disorders are psychiatric disorders that involve delusions and/or perceptual distortions such as auditory or visual hallucinations.
- Psychotic disorders include delusional disorder, schizoaffective disorder, schizophrenia, schizophreniform, and shared psychotic disorder.
- The prevalence rates for psychotic disorders vary with disorder and range from 0.02% in schizophreniform and delusional disorders to 1% lifetime prevalence for schizophrenia.
- Although these disorders account for less than 2% altogether in prevalence, they account for an overall annual cost of $62.7 billion in the USA, with $22.7 billion as health care cost ($7 billion outpatient care, $5 billion psychopharmacological agents, $2.8 billion inpatient care, and $8 billion long-term care). The largest cost is due to unemployment, with only approximately 10% to 15% of affected people being able to maintain full-time employment.
- Genetic, biochemical, and environmental factors are believed to play a role in the development of psychotic disorders.

Delusional Disorder

OVERVIEW

- A psychotic disorder is characterized by fixed irrational, untrue beliefs that are usually about situations that occur in real life and have lasted for at least 1 month, such as the false belief that one is being poisoned or deceived.
- Behavior is not odd or bizarre as in schizophrenia.
- It is characterized by the absence of hallucinations, disorganized speech, catatonic or disorganized behavior, or negative symptoms associated with schizophrenia, such as affective flattening, alogia, or avolition. Tactile and olfactory hallucinations may be present if connected to the delusional theme.
- Delusions are not bizarre, for example, belief that one is being followed, spousal infidelity, or illness.
- Incorrect inference about external reality persists despite evidence to the contrary, and these beliefs are not ordinarily accepted by other members of the person's culture or subculture.
- Subtypes of delusional disorder are based on the predominant delusional theme: erotomanic, grandiose, jealous, persecutory, somatic, mixed, or unspecified.
- Delusions are circumscribed and behavior and functioning are not markedly impaired, although social, marital, or work problems may ensue.
- The individual with delusional disorder is more likely to present to other health care providers, police officers, or lawyers than to mental health providers.
- *Differential diagnosis* includes delirium dementia, psychotic disorder due to general medical condition, substance-induced psychotic disorder, schizophrenia, schizophrenifrom disorder, or mood disorder with psychotic features. The first step is to eliminate medical conditions as a cause of delusions: neurodegenerative disorders, brain tumors, vascular disease, infectious disease (HIV), metabolic disorders, endocrinopathies, vitamin deficiencies (vitamin B12, folate, thiamine, and niacin), medications (adrenocorticotropic hormones, anabolic steroids, and corticosteroids), substances (amphetamines, cocaine, alcohol, cannabis, and hallucinogens), and toxins (mercury, arsenic, manganese, and thallium).
- *Diagnostic workup* includes a thorough history, comprehensive mental status examination, and laboratory analysis. Other medical and psychiatric conditions that commonly present with delusions need to be ruled out. Laboratory workup should include CBC; hepatic, renal, and thyroid function tests; and electrolyte, glucose, vitamin B12, folate, niacin, manganese, and calcium levels. For patients with a history for suspicion, check HIV; RPR; ceruloplasmin; ANA; urine for culture and sensitivity and/or drugs of abuse; and 24-hr urine collections for porphyrins, copper, or heavy metals; and do a pregnancy test for female patients of childbearing age. Any concerns about tumors should be appropriately referred for radiologic evaluation.
- Persons with delusional disorder rarely seek psychiatric help, and the course of the illness is variable. The disorder can wax and wane with full periods of remission, or it can be chronic. The prognosis in the past was thought to be poor although not as poor as the other schizophrenic spectrum disorders. New evidence, however, is presenting a more optimistic prognosis.
- The prevalence of delusional disorder is 0.03%, with an annual incidence of 1 to 3 new cases per 100,000.

Psychopharmacology of Delusional Disorder

- *Atypical antipsychotic drugs* are used as a first-line treatment of delusional disorder with success. Owing to their lower side-effect profile, atypical antipsychotics are prescribed more frequently than conventional or typical antipsychotic medications. However, recent studies have not confirmed atypical drugs to be better than conventional antipsychotics in the treatment of delusional disorder. Lower doses of antipsychotic medications are used with delusional disorder than with schizophrenia. Most commonly used atypical antipsychotic drugs include:
  - Risperidone (*Risperdal*) and olanzapine (*Zyprexa*) usually in low doses. Clozapine (*Clozaril*) has also been used for treatment-resistant cases with some success but requires close monitoring owing to the potential side effect of agranulocytosis.
- *Typical (conventional) antipsychotic drugs* used for the treatment of delusional disorder include the following:
  - Haloperidol (*Haldol*) and pimozide (*Orap*). Until recently, pimozide was touted as the drug of choice for delusional disorder; more recent evidence suggests no difference in improvement with pimozide and other antipsychotics. Also, the evidence suggests no difference in improvement between atypical and conventional antipsychotics in the treatment of patients with delusional disorder.
- If patients fail to respond to drug monotherapy, low-dose combination therapy using drugs from different pharmacological classes may be employed. Depressive symptoms, if present, may be treated with antidepressants. SSRIs have proven helpful with somatic-type delusions.
- Delusional disorder is difficult to treat due to the individual's frequent denial of any existing problem, difficulties in establishing a therapeutic alliance, and social/interpersonal conflicts. Nonetheless, recent evidence suggests that 50% of individuals who are adequately treated recover, and 90% demonstrate at least some improvement.
- Somatic delusions seem to be more responsive to antipsychotic therapy than the other types of delusions, and persecutory delusions respond less well (50% improvement rates with no reports of complete recovery).
- Psychotherapy or CBT may be helpful, either as monotherapy or in combination with an antipsychotic agent.
  - Some form of supportive therapy is helpful with the goal of facilitating treatment adherence, providing education about the illness and treatment, providing social skills training, minimizing risk factors that increase symptoms, and providing realistic guidance in dealing with problems resulting from the illness.
  - CBT may be helpful to individuals with delusional disorder of the persecutory type by helping them to identify maladaptive thoughts and replacing them with alternative, more adaptive attributions.
  - Social skills training directed toward increasing the individual's control and promoting interpersonal competence has also been found to be helpful.
  - Insight-oriented therapy may be indicated rarely and even contraindicated according to the literature. Nonetheless, there are reports of successful treatment with the goals of the development of a therapeutic alliance, containment of projected negative feelings, and development of creative doubt in the internal perception of the negative worldview.

CLASS	DRUG
Antipsychotic Drugs, Atypical (Second Generation)	**First-Line Drug Therapy**
	olanzapine (*Zyprexa, Symbyax Injection*) risperidone (*Risperdal, Risperdal Consta*) clozapine (*Clozaril, Fazaclo*)
Antipsychotic Drugs, Typical (First Generation)	**Second-Line Drug Therapy**
	haloperidol (*Haldol*) pimozide (*Orap*)
Selective Serotonin Reuptake Inhibitors (SSRIs)	**First-Line Drugs Sometimes Helpful for Somatic Delusions**
	fluoxetine (*Prozac, Sarafem*) sertraline (*Zoloft*) escitalopram (*Lexapro*)

DELUSIONAL DISORDER

Class: Antipsychotic Drugs, Atypical (Second Generation)

Zyprexa, Symbyax Injection | **olanzapine**

INDICATIONS: Schizophrenia, monotherapy or combination therapy for acute mixed or manic episodes associated with bipolar I disorder, maintenance monotherapy of bipolar I disorder, agitation associated with schizophrenia or bipolar I disorder.

AVAILABLE FORMS: Tablet, 2.5, 5, 7.5, 10, 15, and 20 mg; orally disintegrating tablet, 5, 10, 15, and 20 mg; IM formulation, 5 mg/mL; each vial contains 10 mg; olanzapine–fluoxetine combination capsule, 6 mg/25 mg, 6 mg/50 mg, 12 mg/25 mg, 12 mg/50 mg

DOSAGE:
- 5 to 10 mg/day, up to a maximum dose of 20 mg/day (PO or IM)
- 6 to 12 mg/olanzapine/25 to 50 mg fluoxetine (olanzapine–fluoxetine combination)

ADMINISTRATION:
- Injectable formulation may be more easily administered to a patient with delusional disorder.
- Tablets may be given with or without food.
- Advise patient to take the missed dose as soon as remembered. Skip the missed dose if it is almost time for the next scheduled dose. Do not take extra medicine to make up the missed dose.
- Store at room temperature away from moisture, heat, and light.

SIDE EFFECTS: Can increase risk for diabetes and dyslipidemia; dizziness, sedation; weight gain; dry mouth, constipation, dyspepsia; peripheral edema; joint pain, back pain, chest pain, extremity pain, abnormal gait, ecchymosis; tachycardia; orthostatic hypotension (usually during initial dose titration); hyperglycemia; increased risk of death and cerebrovascular events in elderly with dementia-related psychosis; TD (rare); rash on exposure to sunlight (rare); neuroleptic malignant syndrome (rare); seizures (rare)

DRUG INTERACTIONS:
- May increase effects of antihypertensive medications
- May antagonize levodopa, dopamine agonists
- May need to reduce dose if given with CYP450 1A2 inhibitors (e.g., fluvoxamine)
- May need to increase dose if given with CYP450 1A2 inducers (e.g., cigarette smoke, carbamazepine)

▶**Alert:** This list may not describe all possible interactions. Instruct clients to provide a list of all the medicines, herbs, nonprescription drugs, or dietary supplements they use.

PHARMACOKINETICS: Metabolites are inactive
Half-life: 21 to 54 hr

PRECAUTIONS:
- Use with caution in patients with conditions that predispose to hypotension (dehydration,

overheating). Watch closely for hypotension if given as an IM formulation.
- Use with caution in patients with prostatic hypertrophy, narrow angle-closure glaucoma, paralytic ileus.
- Use with caution in patients who are at risk for aspiration pneumonia.
- IM formulation is not recommended with parenteral benzodiazepines. If patients need a parenteral benzodiazepine, it should be given at least 1 hr after IM formulation olanzapine (*Zyprexa*).
- Do not use if there is a proven allergy.
- Do not give IM formulation:
  - If patient has unstable medical condition (e.g., AMI, unstable angina pectoris, severe hypotension and/or bradycardia, SSS, or recent heart surgery).
  - If patient has known risks of narrow angle-closure glaucoma.

PATIENT AND FAMILY EDUCATION:
- Take exactly as prescribed by the provider. Do not take in larger or smaller amounts or for longer than recommended.
- Can be taken with or without food.
- For olanzapine orally disintegrating tablets (*Zyprexa Zydis*), keep the tablet in its blister pack until patient is ready to take it. Open the package and peel back the foil from the tablet blister. Do not push a tablet through the foil. Using dry hands, remove the tablet and place it in the mouth and it will begin to dissolve right away.
- Do not swallow the tablet whole. Allow it to dissolve in the mouth without chewing. If desired, drink liquid to help swallow the dissolved tablet.
- *If you have diabetes,* check blood sugar levels on a regular basis while taking olanzapine (*Zyprexa*).
- You can gain weight or have high cholesterol and triglycerides (types of fat) while taking this drug, especially if you teenaged. Your blood will need to be tested often.
- Do not stop taking the drug suddenly without first talking to your provider, even if you feel fine. You may have serious side effects if you stop taking the drug suddenly.
- Call provider if symptoms do not improve, or if they get worse.
- Store at room temperature away from moisture, heat, and light.

SPECIAL POPULATIONS:
- *Elderly:*
  - May tolerate lower doses better. Elderly with dementia-related psychosis treated with atypical antipsychotics are at higher risk of death and cerebrovascular events. It can increase incidence of stroke.
  - If IM formulation is given, the recommended starting dose is 2.5 to 5 mg. A second injection of 2.5 to 5 mg may be given 2 hr after the first injection. No more than

(cont.)

olanzapine (*cont.*)

three injections should be administered within 24 hr.

- *Renal impairment:* No dose adjustment is required for oral formulation. Consider lower starting dose (5 mg) for IM formulation. Not removed by hemodialysis.
- *Hepatic impairment:* Starting oral dose, 5 mg for patients with moderate-to-severe hepatic function impairment; increase dose with caution. Consider lower starting dose (5 mg) for IM formulation. Check patient liver function tests a few times a year.
- *Cardiac impairment:* Use with caution because of risk of orthostatic hypotension.
- *Pregnancy:* Category C. Some animal studies show adverse effects. There are no controlled studies in humans. It should be used only when the potential benefits outweigh potential risks to the fetus. Olanzapine (*Zyprexa*) may be preferable to anticonvulsant mood stabilizers if treatment is required during pregnancy.
- *Lactation:* It is not known if olanzapine (*Zyprexa*) is secreted in human breast milk. It is recommended to either discontinue drug or bottle feed. Infants of women who choose to breastfeed while on this drug should be monitored for possible adverse effect.
- *Children and adolescents:*
  - Probably safe and effective for behavioral disturbances in this population.
  - IM formulation has not been studied in patients younger than 18 years, and is not recommended for use in this population.
  - Should be monitored more frequently than adults.

risperidone
Risperdal, Risperdal Consta

INDICATIONS: Schizophrenia (age 13 and older), monotherapy or combination therapy for acute mixed or manic episodes associated with bipolar I disorder (age 10 and older), treatment of irritability associated with autistic disorder in children and adolescents aged 5 to 16 years.

AVAILABLE FORMS: Tablet, 0.25, 0.5, 1, 2, 3, 4, and 6 mg; orally disintegrating tablet, 0.5, 1, and 2 mg; liquid, 1 mg/mL (30-mL bottle); long-acting depot microspheres formulation for deep IM formulation, 25 mg vial/kit, 37.5 mg vial/kit, 50 mg vial/kit

DOSAGE:
- PO, 2 to 8 mg/day for adults with acute psychosis and bipolar disorder
- PO, 0.5 to 2.0 mg/day for children and elderly
- IM, 25 to 50 mg depot every 2 weeks

ADMINISTRATION:
- Tablets may be given with or without food.
- Advise patient to take the missed dose as soon as remembered. Skip the missed dose if it is almost time for the next scheduled dose. Do not take extra medicine to make up the missed dose.
- Measure the liquid form of risperidone (*Risperdal*) with a special dose-measuring spoon or cup, not a regular tablespoon.
- Do not mix the liquid form with cola or tea.

SIDE EFFECTS: Can increase risk for diabetes and dyslipidemia; extrapyramidal symptoms (dose dependent, use lowest effective dose to minimize); hyperprolactinemia (dose dependent); dizziness, insomnia, headache, anxiety; nausea, sedation, weight gain, constipation, abdominal pain; tachycardia; sexual dysfunction; hyperglycemia; increased risk of death and cerebrovascular events in elderly with dementia-related psychosis; TD (rare); orthostatic hypotension (rare, usually during initial dose titration); neuroleptic malignant syndrome (rare); seizures (rare)

DRUG INTERACTIONS:
- May increase effects of antihypertensive medications
- May antagonize levodopa, dopamine agonists
- Plasma levels of risperidone may be reduced if given in conjunction with carbamazepine
- Plasma levels of risperidone may be increased if given in conjunction with fluoxetine or paroxetine
- Plasma levels of risperidone may be increased if given in conjunction with clozapine (*Clozaril*), but no dose adjustment is required

▶**Alert:** This list may not describe all possible interactions. Instruct client to give a list of all medicines, herbs, nonprescription drugs, or dietary supplements they use.

PHARMACOKINETICS:
- Elimination: 7 to 8 weeks after last injection (long-acting IM formulation)

Metabolism: Metabolites are active; metabolized by CYP450 2D6

Half-life: 20 to 24 hr (oral formulation); 3 to 6 days (long-acting formulation)

PRECAUTIONS:
- Use with caution in patients with conditions that predispose to hypotension (dehydration, overheating).
- Use with caution in patients who are at risk for aspiration pneumonia.
- Priapism has been reported.
- *Do not use if there is a proven allergy.*

PATIENT AND FAMILY EDUCATION:
- Take exactly as prescribed by the provider. Do not take in larger or smaller amounts or for longer than recommended.
- Can be taken with or without food.

(cont.)

risperidone (cont.)

- You may be more sensitive to temperature extremes (very hot or cold conditions) when taking this medication. Avoid getting too cold, or becoming overheated or dehydrated.
- Drink plenty of fluids, especially in hot weather and during exercise.
- Risperidone can cause side effects that may impair your thinking or reactions. Be careful if you drive or do anything that requires you to be awake and alert.
- Risperidone may cause you to have high blood sugar (hyperglycemia). Talk to provider if any signs of hyperglycemia such as increased thirst or urination, excessive hunger, or weakness. If diabetic, check your blood sugar levels on a regular basis.
- Orally disintegrating tablet may contain phenylalanine. Talk to provider before using this form of risperidone if you have PKU.
- *Avoid drinking alcohol.* It can increase some of the side effects.
- *Do not* mix the liquid form with cola or tea.
- *Stop using this medication and call provider immediately* if you have fever, stiff muscles, confusion, sweating, fast or uneven heartbeats, restless muscle movements in face or neck, tremor (uncontrolled shaking), trouble swallowing, feeling light-headed, or fainting.
- Do not stop taking the drug suddenly without first talking to provider, even if you feel fine. You may have serious side effects if you stop taking the drug suddenly.
- Call provider if symptoms do not improve or get worse.
- Store at room temperature away from moisture, light, and heat. Do not freeze the liquid form of risperidone.

SPECIAL POPULATIONS:
- *Elderly:*
  - Initially 0.5 mg orally twice a day, then increase to 0.5 mg twice a day. Titrate once a week for doses above 1.5 mg twice a day.
  - Long-acting risperidone: 25 mg every 2 weeks. Oral administration should be continued for 3 weeks after the first injection.

- Elderly with dementia-related psychosis treated with atypical antipsychotics are at higher risk of death and cerebrovascular events.
- *Lactation:* Drug is secreted in human breast milk. It is recommended to either discontinue drug or bottle feed. Infants of women who choose to breastfeed while on this drug should be monitored for possible adverse effects.
- *Renal impairment:*
  - Initially 0.5 mg orally twice a day for the first week. Increase to 1 mg twice a day during the second week.
  - Long-acting risperidone should not be given to patient with renal function impairment unless s/he can tolerate at least 2 mg/day orally.
  - Long-acting risperidone should be given 25 mg every 2 weeks. Oral administration should be continued for 3 weeks after the first injection.
- *Hepatic impairment:*
  - Initially 0.5 mg orally twice a day for the first week. Increase to 1 mg twice a day during the second week.
  - Long-acting risperidone should not be given to patient with renal function impairment unless s/he can tolerate at least 2 mg/day orally.
  - Long-acting risperidone should be given 25 mg every 2 weeks. Oral administration should be continued for 3 weeks after the first injection.
- *Cardiac impairment:* Use with caution because of risk of orthostatic hypotension. There is a greater risk of stroke if given to elderly patients with atrial fibrillation.
- *Pregnancy:* Category C. Some animal studies show adverse effects. There are no controlled studies in humans. It should be used only when the potential benefits outweigh potential risks to the fetus. Risperidone may be preferable to anticonvulsant mood stabilizers if treatment is required during pregnancy. Effects of hyperprolactinemia on the fetus are unknown.
- *Children and adolescents:* Safe and effective for behavioral disturbances in this population.

Clozaril, FazaClo   **clozapine**

INDICATIONS: Treatment-resistant schizophrenia, reduction in risk of recurrent suicidal behavior in patients with schizophrenia or schizoaffective disorder.

AVAILABLE FORMS: Tablet, 12.5, 25 (scored), 50, and 100 mg (scored); orally disintegrating tablet, 12.5, 25, 50, and 100 mg

DOSAGE: 300 to 450 mg/day

ADMINISTRATION:
- May be given with or without food.
- Take the regular oral tablet with a full glass of water.
- The orally disintegrating tablet (*Fazaclo*) can be taken without water. Advise patients to keep the tablet in its blister pack until ready to take it. The patient should gently peel back the foil from the blister pack and drop the tablet onto dry hand; place the tablet in the mouth; and it

(cont.)

DELUSIONAL DISORDER: Antipsychotic Drugs, Atypical (Second Generation)

clozapine (*cont.*)

will begin to dissolve right away; allow it to dissolve in the mouth without chewing; swallow several times as the tablet dissolves. If desired, advise patients to drink liquid to help swallow the dissolved tablet.
- If one-half of an orally disintegrating tablet is prescribed, advise patients to break the tablet in half and throw the other half away. DO NOT save the other half for later use.
- If patients stop taking clozapine for more than 2 days in a row, caution patients to call providers before starting to take it again.
- Store clozapine at room temperature away from moisture and heat.

SIDE EFFECTS: May increase risk for diabetes and dyslipidemia; weight gain; increase salivation; sweating; dizziness, headache, tachycardia, hypotension; sedation; nausea, dry mouth, constipation; increased risk of death and cerebrovascular events in elderly with dementia-related psychosis; hyperglycemia; agranulocytosis (includes flu-like symptoms or signs of infection); seizure; neuroleptic malignant syndrome (more likely when it is used with another agent); pulmonary embolism (can include deep vein thrombosis or respiratory symptoms); myocarditis; TD (rare).

DRUG INTERACTIONS:
- Risk or severity of bone marrow suppression may be increased if given in conjunction with medications that suppress bone marrow.
- Use with caution if given in conjunction with alcohol, CNS depressants, or general anesthesia.
- May enhance effects of antihypertensive drugs.
- May need to reduce clozapine dose if given in conjunction with CYP450 1A2 inhibitors (e.g., fluvoxamine).
- May need to increase clozapine dose if given in conjunction with CYP450 1A2 inducers (e.g., cigarette smoke).
- CYP450 2D6 inhibitors (e.g., paroxetine, fluoxetine, duloxetine) and CYP450 3A4 inhibitors (e.g., nefazodone, fluvoxamine, fluoxetine) can raise clozapine levels, but usually dosage adjustment is not required.
▶**Alert:** This list may not describe all possible interactions. Instruct clients to provide a list of all the medicines, herbs, nonprescription drugs, or dietary supplements they use.

PHARMACOKINETICS:
Metabolism: Metabolized by multiple CYP450 enzymes including 1A2, 2D6, and 3A4
Half-life: 5 to 16 hr

PRECAUTIONS:
- There is an increased risk of fatal myocarditis, especially during, but not limited to, the first month of therapy. Promptly discontinue clozapine if myocarditis is suspected.

- Life-threatening agranulocytosis can occur. Baseline WBC and ANC should be done before initiation of treatment, during treatment, and for at least 4 weeks after discontinuing treatment.
- Use with caution in patients with glaucoma or enlarged prostate.
- *Do not use in patients with:*
  - Myeloproliferative disorder
  - Uncontrolled seizure
  - Granulocytopenia
  - Paralytic ileus
  - CNS depression
  - Allergic symptoms to clozapine

PATIENT AND FAMILY EDUCATION:
- Clozapine will only be provided in 1- or 2-week supplies, depending on frequency of WBC monitoring. Follow-up visits and weekly blood cell counts are required to monitor therapy and to keep appointments.
- Take prescribed dose with or without food. Take with food if stomach upset occurs.
- Keep tablet in unopened blister pack until just before use. Remove tablet by peeling the foil from the back of the blister and then immediately place the tablet (or half tablet if ordered) in the mouth; allow the tablet to disintegrate; and then swallow with saliva.
- Do not stop taking clozapine when feeling better.
- If medication needs to be discontinued, it will be slowly withdrawn over a period of 1 to 2 weeks unless safety concerns (e.g., low WBC) require a more rapid withdrawal.
- *Immediately report to provider* if any of these conditions occur: altered mental status, change in personality or mood, chest pain, fever, flu-like symptoms, frequent urination, general body discomfort, involuntary body or facial movements, lethargy, mucous membrane sores or other signs of possible infection, muscle rigidity, pounding in the chest, rapid or difficult breathing, rapid or irregular heartbeat, seizures, sore throat, sweating, swelling of feet or ankles, unexplained fatigue, unexplained shortness of breath, unquenchable thirst, weakness, or weight gain.
- *If you have diabetes,* monitor blood glucose more frequently when drug is started or dose is changed and inform your provider of significant changes in readings.
- *If you are taking antihypertensive drugs,* monitor BP at regular intervals.
- *If you have history of seizures or factors predisposing to seizures,* clozapine may cause seizures. Do not engage in any activity in which sudden loss of consciousness could cause serious risk to you or to others (e.g., driving, swimming, climbing).
- *Avoid* strenuous activity during periods of high temperature or humidity.

(cont.)

clozapine (*cont.*)

- *Avoid* alcoholic beverages and sedatives (e.g., diazepam) while taking clozapine.
- Get up slowly from lying or sitting position and avoid sudden position changes to prevent postural hypotension. Hot tubs and hot showers or baths may make dizziness worse.
- Take sips of water, suck on ice chips or sugarless hard candy, or chew sugarless gum if dry mouth occurs.
- Clozapine may impair judgment, thinking, or motor skills, or cause drowsiness. Thus, use with caution while driving or performing other tasks requiring mental alertness until tolerance is determined.

SPECIAL POPULATIONS:
- *Elderly:* May tolerate lower doses better. Elderly with dementia-related psychosis treated with atypical antipsychotics are at higher risk of death and cerebrovascular events.

- *Lactation:* It is not known if clozapine is secreted in human breast milk. It is recommended to either discontinue drug or bottle feed. Infants of women who choose to breastfeed while on this drug should be monitored for possible adverse effect.
- *Renal impairment:* Used with caution.
- *Hepatic impairment:* Used with caution.
- *Cardiac impairment:* Use with caution especially if patient is taking concomitant medication.
- *Pregnancy:* Category B. Animal studies do not show adverse effects. There are no controlled studies in humans. Clozapine should be used only when the potential benefits outweigh potential risks to the fetus.
- *Children and adolescents:* Safety and efficacy have not been established for this population. Should be monitored more frequently than adults.

Class: Antipsychotic Drugs, Typical (First Generation)

Haldol **haloperidol**

INDICATIONS: Psychotic disorders, Tourette's syndrome, schizophrenia, second-line treatment for severe behavior disorders in children, second-line treatment for hyperactive children, bipolar disorder, behavioral disturbances in dementias, delirium (with lorazepam).

AVAILABLE FORMS: Tablet (scored), 0.5, 1, 2, 5, 10, and 20 mg; concentrate, 2 mg/mL; solution, 1 mg/mL; injection, 5 mg/mL (immediate release); decanoate injection, 50 mg haloperidol as 60.5 mg/mL, haloperidol decanoate, 100 mg haloperidol as 141.04 mg/mL haloperidol decanoate

DOSAGE:
- PO, 1 to 20 mg/day
- Immediate-release injection, 2 to 5 mg each dose
- Decanoate injection, 10 to 20 times the effective daily dose of oral formulation, administered every 4 weeks

ADMINISTRATION:
- *PO:* Can give once daily or in divided doses at the beginning of treatment during rapid escalation; increase as needed; can be dosed up to 100 mg/day.
- *Immediate-release injection:* Initial dose: 2 to 5 mg; subsequent doses may be given as often as every hour; patient should be switched to PO administration as soon as possible.
- *Haloperidol decanoate injection:* Initial dose: 10 to 15 times the effective oral dose for patients maintained on low antipsychotic doses (up to equivalent of 10 mg/day oral haloperidol). Initial dose may be as high as 20 times previous oral dose for patients maintained on higher antipsychotic doses; maximum dose is 100 mg.

If higher dose is required, the remainder can be administered 3 to 7 days later. Administer total dose every 4 weeks.
- Patients must stay hydrated.
- Haloperidol is frequently dosed too high. High doses may actually worsen negative symptoms of schizophrenia and increase EPS side effects.

SIDE EFFECTS:
- Neuroleptic-induced deficit syndrome; akathisia; extrapyramidal symptoms, parkinsonism, TD, tardive dystonia; galactorrhea, amenorrhea; dizziness, sedation; dry mouth, constipation, urinary retention, blurred vision; decreased sweating; hypotension, tachycardia, hyperlipidemia; weight gain; rare neuroleptic malignant syndrome; rare seizures; rare jaundice, agranulocytosis, leukopenia. Haloperidol with anticholinergics may increase intraocular pressure; reduces effects of anticoagulants; plasma levels of haloperidol lowered by rifampin; may enhance effects of antihypertensive agents. Haloperidol with lithium may contribute to development of encephalopathic syndrome.

DRUG INTERACTIONS:
- May decrease the effects of levodopa, dopamine agonists
- May increase the effects of antihypertensive drugs except for guanethidine
- Additive effects with CNS depressants; dose of others should be reduced
- May interact with some pressor agents (epinephrine) to lower BP

(cont.)

haloperidol (cont.)

PHARMACOKINETICS:
Half-life: Haloperidol decanoate, approx. 3 weeks; oral, approx. 12 to 36 hr

PRECAUTIONS:
- Discontinue if symptoms of neuroleptic malignant syndrome develop.
- Use with caution in patients with respiratory problems.
- Avoid extreme heat exposure.
- Patients may experience rapid shift to depression if used to treat mania.
- Patients with thyrotoxicosis may experience neurotoxicity.
- Do not use with Lewy body dementia or Parkinson's disease.
- Use with caution in patients with QTc prolongation, hypothyroidism, familial long-QT syndrome.
- Do not use if there is a proven allergy to haloperidol.

PATIENT AND FAMILY EDUCATION:
- Take exactly as prescribed.
- Avoid getting up too fast from a sitting or lying position. Get up slowly and steady yourself to prevent a fall.
- Avoid drinking alcohol.
- *Stop using this medication and call provider immediately* if you have very stiff (rigid) muscles, high fever, sweating, confusion, fast or uneven heartbeats, or tremors; feel like you might pass out; have jerky muscle movements you cannot control, trouble swallowing, problems with speech; have blurred vision, eye pain, or see halos around lights; have increased thirst and urination, excessive hunger, fruity breath odor, weakness, nausea and vomiting; have fever, chills, body aches, flu symptoms; or have white patches or sores inside your mouth or on your lips.
- Do not stop taking the drug suddenly without first talking to provider, even if you feel fine. Serious side effects may result if stop taking the drug suddenly.
- Call provider if symptoms do not improve or get worse.
- Store at room temperature away from moisture and heat.

SPECIAL POPULATIONS:
- *Elderly:* Lower doses should be used and patient should be monitored closely. Do not use in elderly patients with dementia.
- *Renal impairment*: Use with caution.
- *Hepatic impairment*: Use with caution.
- *Cardiac impairment:* Because of risk of orthostatic hypertension, use with caution.
- *Pregnancy:* Category C. Some animal studies show adverse effects; there are no controlled studies in humans.
- *Lactation*: Category C.
- *Children and adolescents:* Safety and efficacy not established. Not intended for use with children younger than 3 years. Generally considered as second line, not first line.

pimozide   *Orap*

DELUSIONAL DISORDER: Antipsychotic Drugs, Typical (First Generation)

INDICATIONS: Suppress motor and phonic tics in Tourette's syndrome, or for psychotic disorders in patients who have failed to respond satisfactorily to standard treatment.

AVAILABLE FORMS: Tablet (scored), 1 and 2 mg

DOSAGE: Initial dose, 1 to 2 mg/day in divided doses; can increase dose every other day; maximum dose, 10 mg/day or 0.2 mg/kg per day. *Children:* Initial dose, 0.05 mg/kg per day at night; can increase every 3 days; maximum dose, 10 mg/day or 0.2 mg/kg per day

ADMINISTRATION:
- Take by mouth with or without food, usually once a day at bedtime.

SIDE EFFECTS: Motor side effects from blockage of D2 in striatum; elevations in prolactin from blockage of D2 in the pituitary; worsening of negative and cognitive symptoms due to blockage of D2 receptors in the mesocortical and mesolimbic dopamine pathways; sedation, blurred vision, constipation, dry mouth; weight gain; dizziness, and hypotension; possible increased incidence of diabetes or dyslipidemia with conventional antipsychotics is unknown; neuroleptic-induced deficit syndrome; akathisia; extrapyramidal symptoms, parkinsonism, TD; galactorrhea, amenorrhea; sexual dysfunction

DRUG INTERACTIONS:
- May decrease the effects of levodopa and other dopamine agonists.
- May increase QTc prolongation of other QTc prolonging drugs.
- May increase the effects of antihypertensive drugs.
- Pimozide levels may be increased by CYP450 3A4 inhibitors, such as fluoxetine, sertraline, fluvoxamine, and nefazodone, and foods such as grapefruit juice.
- Pimozide and fluoxetine may cause bradycardia.
- Additive effects may occur if combined with CNS depressants.
- Some neuroleptics and lithium have caused an encephalopathic syndrome similar to NMS in a few patients.
- Pimozide and epinephrine may lower BP.

(cont.)

pimozide (cont.)

PHARMACOKINETICS:
Metabolism: Metabolized by CYP450 3A and to a lesser extent by CYP450 1A2
Half-life: Approx. 55 hr

PRECAUTIONS:
- With signs of neuroleptic malignant syndrome, treatment must be discontinued immediately.
- Use caution in patients with alcohol withdrawal or convulsive disorders because seizure threshold is lowered.
- Other disorders and overdose may be masked by antiemetic properties of this drug.
- Epinephrine with some pressors may lower BP.
- Use with caution in Parkinson's disease or Lewy body dementia.
- Pimozide, at higher doses, may prolong QTc interval; use with caution with drugs that can induce bradycardia (beta-blockers, calcium channel blockers, clonidine, digitalis).
- Use with caution in patients with hypokalemia and/or hypomagnesemia, or those taking drugs that can induce hypokalemia and/or magnesemia (diuretics, stimulant laxatives, IV amphotericin B, glucocorticoids, and tetracosactide).
- Due to potential elongation of QTc interval, it can potentially cause arrhythmias or sudden death.
- *Do not use* if patient is in a coma or has CNS depression.
- Do not use if patient is taking another drug with QTc prolongation (thioridazine, antiarrhythmics, moxifloxacin, or sparfloxacin).
- Do not use if there is a history of QTc prolongation, cardiac arrhythmias, recent AMI, uncompensated heart failure.
- *Avoid use* if patient is taking drugs that inhibit pimozide metabolism (macrolide antibiotics, azole antifungal agents, protease inhibitors, nefazodone, fluvoxamine, fluoxetine, sertraline).
- *Do not use* if there is a proven allergy to pimozide or sensitivity to any phenothiazine.

PATIENT AND FAMILY EDUCATION:
- Take exactly as prescribed by the provider. Do not take in larger or smaller amounts or for longer than recommended.
- Can be taken with or without food.
- *Avoid becoming overheated or dehydrated during exercise and in hot weather.* You may be more prone to heat stroke.
- *Avoid getting up too fast from a sitting or lying position.* Get up slowly and steady yourself to prevent a fall.
- *Avoid drinking alcohol.*

- *Stop using this medication and call provider immediately* if you have very stiff (rigid) muscles, high fever, sweating, confusion, fast or uneven heartbeats, tremors; feel like you might pass out; have jerky muscle movements you cannot control, trouble swallowing, problems with speech; have blurred vision, eye pain, or see halos around lights; have increased thirst and urination, excessive hunger, fruity breath odor, weakness, nausea and vomiting; have fever, chills, body aches, flu symptoms; or have white patches or sores inside your mouth or on your lips.
- Do not stop taking drug suddenly without first talking to provider, even if you feel fine. You may have serious side effects if you stop taking the drug suddenly.
- Call provider if your symptoms do not improve or if they get worse.
- Store at room temperature away from moisture and heat.

SPECIAL POPULATIONS:
- *Elderly:* May tolerate lower doses better and are more sensitive to adverse effects. Not approved for treatment of elderly patients with dementia-related psychosis; such patients are at increased risk of cardiovascular events and death.
- *Renal impairment:* Use with caution.
- *Liver impairment:* Use with caution.
- *Cardiac impairment:* QTc interval should be evaluated prior to initiation of treatment with pimozide as it causes QTc prolongation, which may be enhanced by bradycardia and hypokalemia. Use with caution with medications that also prolong QTc interval. Avoid in patients with a known history of QTc prolongation (recent AMI and uncompensated heart failure).
- *Pregnancy:* Category C. Some animal studies show adverse effect; there are no controlled studies in humans. Psychotic symptoms may worsen during pregnancy, necessitating some form of treatment. Atypical antipsychotics may be preferable.
- *Lactation:* It is not known if it is secreted in human breast milk, but assumed so. Not recommended for use because of potential cardiovascular effects or tumorigenicity in infants. Either discontinue drug or bottle feed.
- *Children and adolescents:* Safety and efficacy established for patients older than 12 years. Similar preliminary safety established for patients aged 2–12 years. Generally used as second-line treatment after trials with atypical and other conventional antipsychotics.

DELUSIONAL DISORDER: Antipsychotic Drugs, Typical (First Generation)

Class: Selective Serotonin Reuptake Inhibitors (SSRIs)

fluoxetine	*Prozac, Sarafem*

INDICATIONS: Has the most data in the treatment of bulimia nervosa.

AVAILABLE FORMS: Capsule, 10, 20 and 40 mg; tablet, 10, 15 and 20 mg; pellets, delayed release, enteric coated (*Prozac Weekly*), 90 mg; solution, 5 mL and 120 mL (20 mg/5 mL). *Note:* Availability of certain formulations may be limited to brandname versions of the drug.

DOSAGE: Starting dose, 20 mg/day; maintenance dose, 20–60 mg, adjust in 20 mg increments

ADMINISTRATION:
- PO, with or without food.
- Capsules may be diluted into water or apple juice. Grapefruit juice should not be used due to cytochrome P450 effects.

SIDE EFFECTS:
- May cause CNS depression (sedation, fatigue) or activation (insomnia)
- Tends to be weight neutral or approximately 2 pounds of weight gain in one year
- Nervousness, agitation
- Headache and nausea, particularly early in treatment
- Insomnia
- Excess perspiration
- Serotonin syndrome
- Withdrawal syndrome (including neonatal withdrawal syndrome): Symptoms may include dizziness, muscle aches, headache, nausea, vomiting, gait instability, agitation, and/or "electric shock" sensations
- Diarrhea
- Sexual dysfunction (approx. 50% of men and women)
- Hyponatremia (e.g., in geriatric patients taking diuretics)
- Side effects are most common during the first or second week of therapy. Starting with a lower dosage and gradually increasing, and taking the medication with food will limit some of these side effects.

DRUG INTERACTIONS:
- *MAOIs:* Extreme risk for serotonin syndrome. Requires a 5- to 6-week washout period or longer before use of an MAOI.
- *TCAs:* Plasma levels may be increased by SSRIs, so add with caution in low doses
- *ASA and NSAIDs:* Increased risk of bleeding
- *CNS depressants:* May increase depressant effects
- *SSRIs or SARIs:* May cause serotonin syndrome in combination with other medications such as tramadol, high-dose triptans, or the antibiotic linezolid
- Use with caution in patients taking blood thinners (*Coumadin*), other antidepressants, antihistamines, lithium, TCAs, and certain antibiotics, such as erythromycin, clarithromycin, or azithromycin

PHARMACOKINETICS:
- Highly bound to plasma proteins and have a large volume of distribution.
- Readily absorbed in the GI tract, metabolized in the liver, and excreted in the urine. Dosages may be decreased in patients with liver or kidney disease.
- Caution advised in elderly clients.

Peak plasma levels: Reached in 2–10 hr.

Metabolism: Metabolized in the liver by cytochrome P-450 microsomal enzymes.

Half-life: Variable, but most SSRIs have half-lives of 20–24 hr. A notable exception is fluoxetine (*Prozac*), and its active metabolite, norfluoxetine, which have half-lives of 2–4 days and 8–9 days, respectively. Hence, addition of serotonergic medications to a patient's regimen must not occur until 2–3 weeks after discontinuation of an SSRI (some recommend a 5-week "washout" period for fluoxetine prior to initiation of an MAOI).

PRECAUTIONS:
- Use with caution in patients with liver, kidney, or cardiovascular disease.
- *Elderly:* May require decreased dosage
- Adverse effects and side effects are commonly observed before therapeutic effects
- Many side effects are dose dependent and may improve over time
- Taper discontinuation to avoid withdrawal symptoms (although fluoxetine has fewer withdrawal symptoms than other SSRIs due to long half-life).

PATIENT AND FAMILY EDUCATION:
- Should be taken about the same time every day, morning or evening; can be taken with or without food (with food if there is any stomach upset).
- May start with half of lowest effective dose for 3–7 days, then increase to lowest effective dose to diminish side effects.
- Administration time may be adjusted based on observed sedating or activating drug effects.
- May take up to 4–8 weeks to show its maximum effect at this dose, but some may see symptoms of dysthymia improving in as little as 2 weeks.
- If plans on becoming pregnant or is pregnant, discuss the benefits versus the risks of using this medicine while pregnant.
- Because this medicine is excreted in the breast milk, nursing mothers should not breastfeed while taking this medicine without prior consultation with a psychiatric nurse practitioner or psychiatrist. Newborns may develop symptoms including feeding or breathing difficulties, seizures, muscle stiffness, jitteriness, or constant crying.
- Do not stop taking this medication unless the health care provider directs. Report side effects or worsening symptoms to the health care provider promptly.
- The medication should be tapered gradually when changing or discontinuing therapy.

(cont.)

fluoxetine (cont.)

- Dosage should be adjusted to reach remission of symptoms and treatment should continue for at least 6–12 months following last reported dysthymic experience.

SPECIAL POPULATIONS:
- *Elderly:* Avoid use in the elderly if possible. Older individuals tend to be more sensitive to medication side effects such as hypotension and anticholinergic effects. They often require adjustment of medication doses for hepatic or renal dysfunction. SSRIs with shorter half-lives or less P-450 inhibition may be more desirable (e.g., citalopram) for geriatric populations. SSRIs have been associated with increased risk of falls in nursing home residents and neurologic effects in patients with Parkinson's disease.

Geriatric patients are more prone to SSRI-induced hyponatremia.
- *Pregnancy:* Psychotherapy is the initial choice for most pregnant patients with DD. Most SSRIs are Category C drugs, due to adverse effects observed in animal studies. Thus, an individual risk-benefit analysis must be done to determine appropriate treatment in pregnant women with DD.
- *Children:* It has been approved by the FDA for use in children with depression. Initial SSRI dosing in children typically begins at approx. 50% adult dosing. Increasing doses may require more gradual increments, and discontinuation may require a more gradual taper. Psychiatric consultation is recommended due to black box warning of increased suicidal ideation using SSRI therapy in children.

Zoloft **sertraline**

AVAILABLE FORMS: Tablet, 25, 50 and 100 mg; concentrate solution, 20 mg/mL (60 mL)

DOSAGE: Starting dose, 50 mg/day; maintenance dose, 50–200 mg

ADMINISTRATION: PO, with or without food. Concentrate solution must be diluted immediately prior to use with water or juice (other than grapefruit juice).

SIDE EFFECTS: Displays some inhibition of dopamine reuptake, which may be beneficial to some patients (e.g., those experiencing hypersomnia, low energy, or mood reactivity), but problematic to others (e.g., causing overactivation in patients with panic disorder). May see a little more GI side effect (diarrhea) than others in class
- Nervousness, headache and nausea, insomnia; serotonin syndrome; dry mouth, easy bruising, or excess perspiration; diarrhea.
- Withdrawal syndrome (including neonatal withdrawal syndrome): Symptoms may include dizziness, muscle aches, headache, nausea, vomiting, gait instability, agitation, and/or "electric shock" sensations.
- Sexual dysfunction (more than 50% of men and women)
- Hyponatremia (e.g., in geriatric patients taking diuretics)
- Side effects are most common during the first or second week of therapy. Starting with a lower dosage and gradually increasing it, and taking the medication with food will limit some of these side effects.

DRUG INTERACTIONS:
- *MAOIs:* Extreme risk for serotonin syndrome. Allow 2-week washout period post-MAOI prior to initiation
- *TCAs:* Plasma levels may be increased by SSRIs, so add with caution in low doses
- *ASA and NSAIDs:* Increased risk of bleeding

- *CNS depressants:* May increase depressant effects
- *SSRIs or SARIs:* May cause serotonin syndrome in combination with other medications such as tramadol, high-dose triptans, or the antibiotic linezolid.
- Use with caution in patients taking blood thinners (*Coumadin*), other antidepressants, antihistamines, lithium, TCAs, and certain antibiotics, such as erythromycin, clarithromycin, or azithromycin.

PHARMACOKINETICS:
- Highly bound to plasma proteins and have a large volume of distribution.
- Readily absorbed in the GI tract, metabolized in the liver, and excreted in the urine. Dosages may be decreased in patients with liver or kidney disease.
- Caution advised in elderly clients.

Metabolism: Metabolized in the liver by cytochrome P-450 microsomal enzymes.

Peak plasma levels: 2–10 hr.

Half-life: Variable, but most SSRIs have half-lives of 20–24 hr. A notable exception is fluoxetine (*Prozac*), and its active metabolite, norfluoxetine, which have half-lives of 2–4 days and 8–9 days, respectively. Hence, addition of serotonergic medications to a patient's regimen must not occur until 2–3 weeks after discontinuation of an SSRI (some recommend a 5-week "washout" period for fluoxetine prior to initiation of an MAOI).

PRECAUTIONS:
- May cause sedation and mental clouding.
- Use with caution in patients with liver, kidney, or cardiovascular disease.
- Adverse effects and side effects are commonly observed before therapeutic effects.
- Many side effects are dose dependent and may improve over time.
- Taper discontinuation to avoid withdrawal symptoms. *(cont.)*

DELUSIONAL DISORDER: Selective Serotonin Reuptake Inhibitors (SSRIs)

DELUSIONAL DISORDER: Selective Serotonin Reuptake Inhibitors (SSRIs)

sertraline (*cont.*)

- *Elderly:* May require decreased dosage.

PATIENT AND FAMILY EDUCATION:
- Should be taken about the same time every day, morning or evening, and can be taken with or without food (with food if there is any stomach upset).
- May start with half of lowest effective dose for 3–7 days, then increase to lowest effective dose to diminish side effects.
- Administration time may be adjusted based on observed sedating or activating drug effects.
- May take up to 4–8 weeks to show its maximum effect at this dose, but some may see symptoms of dysthymia improving in as little as 2 weeks.
- If patient plans on becoming pregnant or is pregnant, discuss the benefits versus the risks of using this medicine while pregnant.
- Because this medicine is excreted in the breast milk, nursing mothers should not breastfeed while taking this medicine without prior consultation with a psychiatric nurse practitioner or psychiatrist. Newborns may develop symptoms including feeding or breathing difficulties, seizures, muscle stiffness, jitteriness, or constant crying.
- Do not stop taking this medication unless the health care provider directs. Report side effects or worsening symptoms to the health care provider promptly.
- The medication should be tapered gradually when changing or discontinuing therapy.
- Dosage should be adjusted to reach remission of symptoms and treatment should continue for at least 6–12 months following last reported dysthymic experience.
- Caution is advised when using this drug in the elderly because they may be more sensitive to the effects of the drug. Elderly patients should receive a lower starting dose.
- Keep these medications out of the reach of children and pets.

SPECIAL POPULATIONS:
- *Elderly:* Older individuals tend to be more sensitive to medication side effects such as hypotension and anticholinergic effects. They often require adjustment of medication doses for hepatic or renal dysfunction. SSRIs with shorter half-lives or less P-450 inhibition may be more desirable (e.g., citalopram) for geriatric populations than SSRIs with longer half-lives (e.g., fluoxetine). SSRIs have been associated with increased risk of falls in nursing home residents and neurologic effects in patients with Parkinson's disease. Elderly patients are more prone to SSRI-induced hyponatremia.
- *Pregnancy:* Psychotherapy is the initial choice for most pregnant patients with DD. Most SSRIs are Category C drugs, due to adverse effects observed in animal studies. Sertraline has been found to have lower cord blood levels than other SSRIs, although the clinical significance is unknown. Thus, an individual risk-benefit analysis must be done to determine appropriate treatment in pregnant women with DD. If continued during pregnancy, SSRI dosage may need to be increased to maintain euthymia due to physiologic changes associated with pregnancy.
- *Children:* Initial SSRI dosing in children typically begins at approx. 50% adult dosing. Increasing doses may require more gradual increments, and discontinuation may require a more gradual taper. Psychiatric consultation is recommended due to black box warning of increased suicidal ideation using SSRI therapy in children.

escitalopram   *Lexapro*

AVAILABLE FORMS: Tablet, 5, 10, and 20 mg; solution: 1 mg/mL (240 mL)

DOSAGE: Starting dose, 10 mg/day; maintenance dose, 10–20 mg

ADMINISTRATION: Oral, once daily, with or without food

SIDE EFFECTS:
- *CNS:* Headache, agitation or restlessness, insomnia, sedation, changes in sexual desire, sexual performance and sexual satisfaction; excess perspiration; withdrawal syndrome if not tapered; lower incidence of side effects than citalopram;
- *GI:* Nausea, constipation, dry mouth

DRUG INTERACTIONS:
- *MAOIs:* Extreme risk for serotonin syndrome. Allow 2-week washout period post-MAOI prior to initiation
- *TCAs:* Plasma levels may be increased by SSRIs, so add with caution in low doses
- *ASA and NSAIDs:* Increased risk of bleeding
- *CNS depressants:* May increase depressant effects
- *SSRIs or SARIs:* May cause serotonin syndrome in combination with other medications such as tramadol, high-dose triptans, or the antibiotic linezolid.
- Use with caution in patients taking blood thinners (*Coumadin*), other antidepressants, antihistamines, lithium, TCAs, and certain antibiotics, such as erythromycin, clarithromycin, or azithromycin.

PHARMACOKINETICS:
- Metabolized in the liver by cytochrome P-450 microsomal enzymes. Paroxetine, fluoxetine, and sertraline may have greater P-450 enzyme effect than citalopram and escitalopram.
- Highly bound to plasma proteins and have a large volume of distribution.
- Absorbed in the GI tract, metabolized in the liver, and excreted in the urine. Dosages may

(cont.)

escitalopram (*cont.*)

be decreased in patients with liver or kidney disease.

■ Caution advised in elderly clients.

Peak plasma levels: 2–10 hr

Half-life: Variable, but most have half-lives of 20–24 hr. Notable exception is fluoxetine (*Prozac*), and its active metabolite, norfluoxetine, which have half-lives of 2–4 days and 8–9 days, respectively. Hence, addition of serotonergic medications to a patient's regimen must not occur until 2–3 weeks after discontinuation of an SSRI (some recommend a 5-week "washout" period for fluoxetine prior to initiation of an MAOI).

PRECAUTIONS:

■ May cause sedation and mental clouding
■ Use with caution in patients with liver, kidney, or cardiovascular disease
■ *Elderly:* May require decreased dosage
■ Adverse effects and side effects are commonly observed before therapeutic effects
■ Many side effects are dose-dependent and may improve over time
■ Taper discontinuation to avoid withdrawal symptoms

PATIENT AND FAMILY EDUCATION:

■ Should be taken about the same time every day, morning or evening, and can be taken with or without food (with food if there any stomach upset).
■ May start with half of lowest effective dose for 3–7 days, then increase to lowest effective dose to diminish side effects.
■ Administration time may be adjusted based on observed sedating or activating drug effects
■ May take up to 4–8 weeks to reach its full effect at this dose, but some may see symptoms of depression improving in as little as 2 weeks.
■ If planning or are pregnant, discuss benefits versus risks of using this medicine while pregnant.
■ Because this medicine is excreted in the breast milk, nursing mothers should not breastfeed while taking this medicine without prior consultation with a psychiatric nurse practitioner or psychiatrist. Newborns may develop symptoms including feeding or breathing difficulties, seizures, muscle stiffness, jitteriness, or constant crying.
■ Do not stop taking this medication unless the health care provider directs. Report side effects or worsening symptoms to the health care provider promptly.
■ The medication should be tapered gradually when changing or discontinuing therapy.
■ Dosage should be adjusted to reach remission of symptoms and treatment should continue for at least 4–9 months following remission of symptoms.
■ Caution is advised when using this drug in the elderly because they may be more sensitive to the effects of the drug. Elderly patients should receive a lower starting dose.
■ Keep these medications out of the reach of children and pets.

SPECIAL POPULATIONS:

■ *Elderly:* Older individuals tend to be more sensitive to medication side effects such as hypotension and anticholinergic effects. They often require adjustment of medication doses for hepatic or renal dysfunction. SSRIs with shorter half-lives or less P-450 inhibition may be more desirable (e.g., citalopram, escitalopram) for geriatric populations than SSRIs with longer half-lives (e.g., fluoxetine). SSRIs have been associated with increased risk of falls in nursing home residents and neurologic effects in patients with Parkinson's disease. Elderly patients are more prone to SSRI-induced hyponatremia. Paroxetine shows greater anticholinergic and sedating effects than other SSRIs.
■ *Pregnancy:* Psychotherapy is the initial choice for most pregnant patients with mild to moderate MDD. Most SSRIs are category C drugs due to adverse effects observed in animal studies. Thus, an individual risk-benefit analysis must be done to determine appropriate treatment in pregnant women with MDD. Paroxetine is a category D drug. If continued during pregnancy, SSRI dosage may need to be increased to maintain euthymia due to physiologic changes associated with pregnancy.
■ *Children:* Initial SSRI dosing in children typically begins at approx. 50% of adult dosing. Increasing doses may require more gradual increments, and discontinuation may require a more gradual taper. Psychiatric consultation is recommended due to black box warning of increased suicidal ideation using SSRI therapy in children.

DELUSIONAL DISORDER: Selective Serotonin Reuptake Inhibitors (SSRIs)

Schizoaffective Disorder

OVERVIEW

- Schizoaffective disorder is a combination of symptoms of a thought disorder or other psychotic symptoms such as hallucinations or delusions (schizophrenia component) and those of a mood disorder (depressive or manic component).
- It is classified by one of five subtypes: manic, depressive, mixed (manic and depressive), other, and not otherwise specified.
- It tends to be episodic with a more favorable outcome than that of schizophrenia and with less severe residual and negative symptoms.
- Incidence of schizoaffective disorder in the USA is 2 per 10,000.
- *Differential diagnosis* includes psychotic disorder due to a general medical condition (delirium or dementia), substance-induced psychotic disorder, substance-induced delirium, schizophrenia, bipolar disorder, and major depression with psychotic symptoms.
- The distinguishing feature is that psychosis must occur during periods without mood symptoms.
- *Diagnostic workup* includes a complete physical examination, thorough mental status examination, laboratory studies (CBC, rapid plasma reagent, thyroid function, UA, pregnancy test if female and of childbearing age, lipid panel, HIV test). If neurologic findings are abnormal, a CT or MRI, and/or EEG may be indicated. Psychological testing may assist with diagnosis.
- Individuals with the bipolar subtype are thought to have a prognosis similar to those with bipolar type I, whereas the prognosis of people with the depressive subtype is thought to be similar to that of people with schizophrenia.

Psychopharmacology of Schizoaffective Disorder

Overview

- *Second-generation (atypical) antipsychotics* are the first-line treatment for schizoaffective disorder.
- Consistent evidence has demonstrated that risperidone (*Risperdal*), olanzapine (*Zyprexa*), quetiapine (*Seroquel*), ziprasidone (*Geodon*), aripiprazole (*Abilify*), asenapine (*Saphris*), and paliperidone (*Invega*) are efficacious in the treatment of global psychopathology and the positive symptoms of the schizophrenic spectrum disorders including schizoaffective disorder. Less consistent evidence has demonstrated that the negative symptoms improve as well.
- *Second-line treatment:* First-generation (typical or conventional) antipsychotics. Although haloperidol (*Haldol*) was previously regarded as a first-line treatment for patients with schizoaffective disorder, it is now regarded as a second- or third-line treatment since atypical antipsychotics generally have a more tolerable side-effect profile.
- In addition to an antipsychotic agent, antidepressant medications may be prescribed for the depressive symptoms. Mood stabilizers may be used to treat mixed symptoms occurring in schizoaffective disorder. Any of the SSRIs may be used for the depressive symptoms, but the most evidence available is for fluoxetine (*Prozac*).
- Lithium (*Eskalith, Lithobid,* lithium carbonate) has proven helpful as an adjunct to the antipsychotic agents. It has limited effectiveness as monotherapy in treating schizoaffective disorders. When combined with an antipsychotic agent, lithium augments the antipsychotic response in general and negative symptoms specifically.
- Valproate (*Depakote*) studies have reported positive and negative results. Although the evidence base is limited because most studies have few patients, one study compared valproate (*Depakote*) with olanzapine (*Zyprexa*), valproate (*Depakote*) with risperidone (*Risperdal*), olanzapine (*Zyprexa*) with placebo, and risperidone (*Risperdal*) with placebo, and concluded that the valproate (*Depakote*) groups improved significantly more rapidly over the first 2 weeks of treatment than the antipsychotic group alone.
- CBT, modified for this population, focuses on symptom management, symptom recovery in acute psychosis, relapse prevention, and early intervention. Patients are taught coping strategies, attention switching or attention narrowing especially useful for dealing with hallucinations, modified self-statements and internal dialog, reattribution, awareness training, de-arousing techniques, increased activity levels, social engagement and disengagement, and reality testing techniques.
- ECT has been suggested as a treatment for resistant schizoaffective disorders; however, the evidence has been limited to case studies and uncontrolled studies. In general, antipsychotic treatment alone has produced better outcomes than ECT.
- Emphasis is being placed on early identification of any of the schizophrenic spectrum disorders including schizoaffective disorders. Earlier identification allows for earlier intervention and not requiring patients and/or families to reach a high threshold of risk, disruption, or deterioration before accessing treatment. There is evidence that if symptoms are treated prior to the onset of a psychotic episode, full-blown consequences (such as schizoaffective disorder or schizophrenia) may be delayed or even prevented.

CLASS	DRUG
Antipsychotic Drugs, Atypical (Second Generation)	**First-Line Drug Therapy**
	aripiprazole (*Abilify, Abilify Discmelt ODT, Abilify Liquid, Abilify IM Injection*) clozapine (*Clozaril, Fazaclo*) olanzapine (*Zyprexa*) risperidone (*Risperdal, Risperdal Consta*) quetiapine (*Seroquel, Seroquel XR*) ziprasidone (*Geodon, Geodon IM Injection*) paliperidone (*Invega*) asenapine (*Saphris*)
Antipsychotic Drugs, Typical (First Generation)	**Second-Line Drug Therapy**
	haloperidol (*Haldol*) fluphenazine (*Prolixin*)
Selective Serotorin Reuptake (SSRIs)	**Adjunct Treatment for Mood**
	fluoxetine (*Prozac*) paroxetine (*Paxil*) sertraline (*Zoloft*)
Mood Stabilizers	**Adjunct Treatment for Mood**
	lithium (*Eskalith, Lithobid, lithium carbonate*) valproate (*Depakote*)

Class: Antipsychotic Drugs, Atypical (Second Generation)

Abilify, Abilify Discmelt ODT, Abilify Liquid, Abilify IM Injection — **aripiprazole**

INDICATIONS: Schizophrenia (patients 13 years and older), manic and mixed episodes associated with bipolar I disorder, adjunctive treatment to antidepressants for MDD, agitation associated with schizophrenia or bipolar disorder, manic or mixed.

AVAILABLE FORMS: Tablet, 2, 5, 10, 15, 20, and 30 mg; tablet, orally disintegrating, 10 and 15 mg; solution, oral, 1 mg/mL; IM injection, solution, 9.75 mg/1.3 mL

DOSAGE: 10 to 15 mg/day, up to 15 to 30 mg/day. Dosages exceeding 10 to 15 mg/day have not demonstrated greater efficacy.

ADMINISTRATION:
- Tablets may be given with or without food.
- Parenteral administration is intended for IM use only; inject slowly, deep into muscle mass. *IM injection has not been evaluated in children.*
- *Do not give IV or SC.*
- Oral solution may be substituted for tablets on a mg-per-mg basis up to a 25 mg dose. Patients receiving 30 mg tablets should receive 25 mg of the solution.
- Dosing for the orally disintegrating tablet is the same as the oral tablet.
- Do not open the orally disintegrating tablets until ready to administer. The orally disintegrating tablet should be taken without liquid. Do not split the orally disintegrating tablet.
- Use oral aripiprazole 10 to 30 mg/day instead of IM aripiprazole as soon as possible if ongoing therapy is indicated.

SIDE EFFECTS: Nausea, vomiting; dizziness, insomnia, akathisia, activation; headache, asthenia; sedation; weight gain; constipation; orthostatic hypotension (occasionally during initial phase); increased risk of death and cerebrovascular events in elderly with dementia-related psychosis; TD; neuroleptic malignant syndrome (rare); seizures (rare)

DRUG INTERACTIONS:
- CYP450 3A4 inhibitors (e.g., nefazodone, fluvoxamine, fluoxetine), CYP40 2D6 inhibitors (e.g., paroxetine, fluoxetine, duloxetine), and quinidine may increase plasma levels of aripiprazole.
- Carbamazepine and other CYP450 3A4 inducers may decrease plasma levels of aripiprazole.
- May enhance effects of antihypertensive medications.
- May antagonize levodopa and dopamine agonists.

▶**Alert:** This list may not describe all possible interactions. Instruct clients to provide a list of all medicines, herbs, nonprescription drugs, or dietary supplements they use. Also instruct clients to inform if they smoke, drink alcohol, or use illegal drugs.

PHARMACOKINETICS:
- About 25% of a single oral dose is excreted in urine (less than 1% unchanged) and 55% in feces (18% as unchanged drug)

Metabolism: Primarily metabolized by CYP450 2D6 and CYP450 3A4

Half-life: 75 hr (aripiprazole) and 94 hr (active metabolite)

(cont.)

aripiprazole (*cont.*)

PRECAUTIONS:
- Dysphagia is associated with use of aripiprazole. Use with caution in patients who are at risk for aspiration pneumonia.
- Use with caution in patients with conditions that may develop hypotension (dehydration, overheating, etc.).
- *DO NOT USE in patients who are allergic to aripiprazole.*

PATIENT AND FAMILY EDUCATION:
- Store aripiprazole at 59° to 86°F. Can be used for up to 6 months after opening. Protect injection from light by storing in carton until use.
- If patient becomes pregnant, contact provider. Discuss the benefits and risks of using aripiprazole orally disintegrating tablets while pregnant.
- Discuss with provider if you have any of these conditions. A dose adjustment or special tests to safely take aripiprazole may be needed:
  - Liver or kidney disease
  - Heart disease, high BP, heart rhythm problems
  - History of heart attack or stroke
  - History of low WBC
  - History of breast cancer
  - Seizures or epilepsy
  - Personal or family history of diabetes
  - Trouble swallowing
  - PKU
- Talk to provider if any signs of hyperglycemia such as increased thirst or urination, excessive hunger, or weakness. If you have diabetes, check blood sugar levels on a regular basis while taking aripiprazole.

SPECIAL POPULATIONS:
- *Elderly:* Generally dosage adjustment is not required. Elderly with dementia-related psychosis treated with atypical antipsychotics are at higher risk of death and cerebrovascular events.
- *Renal impairment*: No dosage adjustment needed.
- *Hepatic impairment*: No dosage adjustment required.
- *Cardiac impairment:* Use with caution because of the risk of orthostatic hypotension
- *Pregnancy:* Category C. It is not known if aripiprazole orally disintegrating tablets can cause harm to the fetus.
- *Lactation:* Although there are no data on the excretion of aripiprazole into human milk, it is suggested that women receiving aripiprazole should not breastfeed.
- *Children and adolescents:* Aripiprazole is approved for schizophrenia (age 13 and older) and manic/mixed episodes (age 10 and older). They should be monitored more frequently than adults and may tolerate lower doses better.
- ▶**Alert:** Not approved for children with depression.

clozapine   *Clozaril, Fazaclo*

INDICATIONS: Treatment-resistant schizophrenia, reduction in risk of recurrent suicidal behavior in patients with schizophrenia or schizoaffective disorder.

AVAILABLE FORMS: Tablet, 12.5, 25 (scored), 50, and 100 mg (scored); orally disintegrating tablet, 12.5, 25, 50 and 100 mg

DOSAGE: 300 to 450 mg/day

ADMINISTRATION:
- May be given with or without food.
- Take the regular oral tablet with a full glass of water.
- The orally disintegrating tablet (*FazaClo*) can be taken without water. Advise patients to keep the tablet in its blister pack until ready to take it. The patient should gently peel back the foil from the blister pack and drop the tablet onto dry hand; place the tablet in the mouth; it will begin to dissolve right away; allow it to dissolve in the mouth without chewing; swallow several times as the tablet dissolves. If desired, advise patients to drink liquid to help swallow the dissolved tablet.
- If one-half of an orally disintegrating tablet is prescribed, advise patients to break the tablet in half and throw the other half away. DO NOT save the other half for later use.
- If patients stop taking clozapine for more than 2 days in a row, caution patients to call providers before starting to take it again.
- Store clozapine at room temperature away from moisture and heat.

SIDE EFFECTS: May increase risk for diabetes and dyslipidemia; weight gain; increase salivation; sweating; dizziness, headache, tachycardia, hypotension; sedation; nausea, dry mouth, constipation; increased risk of death and cerebrovascular events in elderly with dementia-related psychosis; hyperglycemia; agranulocytosis (includes flu-like symptoms or signs of infection); seizure; neuroleptic malignant syndrome (more likely when it is used with another agent); pulmonary embolism (can include deep vein thrombosis or respiratory symptoms); myocarditis; TD (rare).

DRUG INTERACTIONS:
- Risk or severity of bone marrow suppression may be increased if given in conjunction with medications that suppress bone marrow.
- Use with caution if given in conjunction with alcohol, CNS depressants, or general anesthesia.

(cont.)

clozapine (*cont.*)

- May enhance effects of antihypertensive drugs.
- May need to reduce clozapine dose if given in conjunction with CYP450 1A2 inhibitors (e.g., fluvoxamine).
- May need to increase clozapine dose if given in conjunction with CYP450 1A2 inducers (e.g., cigarette smoke).
- CYP450 2D6 inhibitors (e.g., paroxetine, fluoxetine, duloxetine) and CYP450 3A4 inhibitors (e.g., nefazodone, fluvoxamine, fluoxetine) can raise clozapine levels, but usually dosage adjustment is not required.

▶**Alert:** This list may not describe all possible interactions. Instruct clients to provide a list of all the medicines, herbs, nonprescription drugs, or dietary supplements they use.

PHARMACOKINETICS:
Metabolism: Metabolized by multiple CYP450 enzymes including 1A2, 2D6, and 3A4
Half-life: 5 to 16 hr

PRECAUTIONS:
- There is an increased risk of fatal myocarditis, especially during, but not limited to, the first month of therapy. Promptly discontinue clozapine if myocarditis is suspected.
- Life-threatening agranulocytosis can occur. Baseline WBC and ANC should be done before initiation of treatment, during treatment, and for at least 4 weeks after discontinuing treatment.
- Use with caution in patients with glaucoma or enlarged prostate.
- *Do not use in patients with:*
  - Myeloproliferative disorder
  - Uncontrolled seizure
  - Granulocytopenia
  - Paralytic ileus
  - CNS depression
  - Allergic symptoms to clozapine

PATIENT AND FAMILY EDUCATION:
- Clozapine will only be provided in 1- or 2-week supplies, depending on frequency of WBC monitoring. Follow-up visits and weekly blood cell counts are required to monitor therapy and to keep appointments.
- Take prescribed dose with or without food. Take with food if stomach upset occurs.
- Keep tablet in unopened blister pack until just before use. Remove tablet by peeling the foil from the back of the blister and then immediately place the tablet (or half tablet if ordered) in the mouth; allow the tablet to disintegrate; and then swallow with saliva.
- Do not stop taking clozapine when feeling better.
- If medication needs to be discontinued, it will be slowly withdrawn over a period of 1 to 2 weeks unless safety concerns (e.g., low WBC) require a more rapid withdrawal.
- *Immediately report to provider* if any of these conditions occur: altered mental status, change in personality or mood, chest pain, fever, flu-like symptoms, frequent urination, general body discomfort, involuntary body or facial movements, lethargy, mucous membrane sores or other signs of possible infection, muscle rigidity, pounding in the chest, rapid or difficult breathing, rapid or irregular heartbeat, seizures, sore throat, sweating, swelling of feet or ankles, unexplained fatigue, unexplained shortness of breath, unquenchable thirst, weakness, or weight gain.
- *If you have diabetes,* monitor blood glucose more frequently when drug is started or dose is changed and inform your provider of significant changes in readings.
- *If you are taking antihypertensive drugs,* monitor BP at regular intervals.
- *If you have history of seizures or factors predisposing to seizures,* clozapine may cause seizures. Do not engage in any activity in which sudden loss of consciousness could cause serious risk to you or to others (e.g., driving, swimming, climbing).
- *Avoid* strenuous activity during periods of high temperature or humidity.
- *Avoid* alcoholic beverages and sedatives (e.g., diazepam) while taking clozapine.
- Get up slowly from lying or sitting position and avoid sudden position changes to prevent postural hypotension. Hot tubs and hot showers or baths may make dizziness worse.
- Take sips of water, suck on ice chips or sugarless hard candy, or chew sugarless gum if dry mouth occurs.
- Clozapine may impair judgment, thinking, or motor skills, or cause drowsiness. Thus, use with caution while driving or performing other tasks requiring mental alertness until tolerance is determined.

SPECIAL POPULATIONS:
- *Elderly:* May tolerate lower doses better. Elderly with dementia-related psychosis treated with atypical antipsychotics are at higher risk of death and cerebrovascular events.
- *Renal impairment:* Used with caution.
- *Hepatic impairment:* Used with caution.
- *Cardiac impairment:* Use with caution especially if patient is taking concomitant medication.
- *Pregnancy:* Category B. Animal studies do not show adverse effects. There are no controlled studies in humans. Clozapine should be used only when the potential benefits outweigh potential risks to the fetus.
- *Lactation:* It is not known if clozapine is secreted in human breast milk. It is recommended to either discontinue drug or bottle feed. Infants of women who choose to breastfeed while on this drug should be monitored for possible adverse effect.
- *Children and adolescents:* Safety and efficacy have not been established for this population. Should be monitored more frequently than adults.

SCHIZOAFFECTIVE DISORDER: Antipsychotic Drugs, Atypical (Second Generation)

olanzapine   *Zyprexa*

▶ **Note:** Olanzapine and the SSRI fluoxetine are available in fixed-dose combination under the trade name *Symbyax*.

INDICATIONS: Schizophrenia, monotherapy or combination therapy for acute mixed or manic episodes associated with bipolar I disorder, maintenance monotherapy of bipolar I disorder, agitation associated with schizophrenia or bipolar I disorder.

AVAILABLE FORMS: Tablet, 2.5, 5, 7.5, 10, 15, and 20 mg; orally disintegrating tablet, 5, 10, 15, and 20 mg; IM formulation, 5 mg/mL, each vial contains 10 mg; olanzapine–fluoxetine combination capsule, 6 mg/25 mg, 6 mg/50 mg, 12 mg/25 mg, 12 mg/50 mg

DOSAGE:
- 10 to 20 mg/day (PO or IM)
- 6 to 12 mg/olanzapine/25 to 50 mg fluoxetine (olanzapine–fluoxetine combination)

ADMINISTRATION:
- Tablets may be given with or without food.
- Advise patient to take the missed dose as soon as remembered. Skip missed dose if almost time for the next scheduled dose. Do not take extra medicine to make up the missed dose.
- Store at room temperature away from moisture, heat, and light.

SIDE EFFECTS: Can increase risk for diabetes; dyslipidemia; dizziness, sedation; weight gain; dry mouth, constipation, dyspepsia; peripheral edema; joint pain, back pain, chest pain, extremity pain, abnormal gait, ecchymosis; tachycardia; orthostatic hypotension (usually during initial dose titration); hyperglycemia; increased risk of death and cerebrovascular events in elderly with dementia-related psychosis; TD (rare); rash on exposure to sunlight (rare); neuroleptic malignant syndrome (rare); seizures (rare)

DRUG INTERACTIONS:
- May increase effects of antihypertensive medications
- May antagonize levodopa and dopamine agonists
- May need to reduce dose if given with CYP450 1A2 inhibitors (e.g., fluvoxamine)
- May need to increase dose if given with CYP450 1A2 inducers (e.g., cigarette smoke, carbamazepine)

▶ **Alert:** This list may not describe all possible interactions. Instruct clients to give a list of all the medicines, herbs, nonprescription drugs, or dietary supplements they use.

PHARMACOKINETICS:
Metabolism: Metabolites are inactive
Half-life: 21 to 54 hr

PRECAUTIONS:
- Use with caution in patients with conditions that predispose to hypotension (dehydration,

overheating). Watch closely for hypotension if given IM formulation.
- Use with caution in patients with prostatic hypertrophy, narrow angle-closure glaucoma, paralytic ileus.
- Use with caution in patients who are at risk for aspiration pneumonia.
- IM formulation is not recommended with parenteral benzodiazepines. If patients need a parenteral benzodiazepine, it should be given at least 1 hr after IM formulation olanzapine.
- *Do not use if there is a proven allergy.*
- *Do not give IM formulation:*
  - If patient has unstable medical condition (e.g., AMI, unstable angina pectoris, severe hypotension and/or bradycardia, SSS, recent heart surgery).
  - If patient has known risks of narrow angle-closure glaucoma.

PATIENT AND FAMILY EDUCATION:
- Take exactly as prescribed by the provider. Do not take in larger or smaller amounts or for longer than recommended.
- Can be taken with or without food.
- For olanzapine orally disintegrating tablets, keep the tablet in its blister pack until patient is ready to take it. Open the package and peel back the foil from the tablet blister. Do not push a tablet through the foil. Using dry hands, remove the tablet and place it in the mouth and it will begin to dissolve right away.
- Do not swallow the tablet whole. Allow it to dissolve in mouth without chewing. If desired, drink liquid to help swallow the dissolved tablet.
- *If you have diabetes,* check blood sugar levels on a regular basis.
- *You can gain weight* or have high cholesterol and triglycerides while taking this drug, especially if teenaged. Your blood will need to be tested often.
- Do not stop taking the drug suddenly without first talking to provider, even if you feel fine. You may have serious side effects if you stop taking the drug suddenly.
- Call your provider if symptoms do not improve or get worse.
- Store at room temperature away from moisture, heat, and light.

SPECIAL POPULATIONS:
- *Elderly:*
  - May tolerate lower doses better. Elderly with dementia-related psychosis treated with atypical antipsychotics are at higher risk of death and cerebrovascular events. It can increase incidence of stroke.
  - If IM formulation is given, the recommended starting dose is 2.5 to 5 mg. A second injection of 2.5 to 5 mg may be given 2 hr after the first injection. No more than three injections should be administered within 24 hr.

(cont.)

olanzapine (*cont.*)

- *Renal impairment*: No dose adjustment is required for oral formulation. Consider lower starting dose (5 mg) for IM formulation. Not removed by hemodialysis.
- *Hepatic impairment*: Starting oral dose: 5 mg for patients with moderate-to-severe hepatic function impairment; increase dose with caution. Consider lower starting dose (5 mg) for IM formulation. Check patient liver function tests a few times a year.
- *Cardiac impairment*: Use with caution because of risk of orthostatic hypotension.
- *Pregnancy:* Category C. Some animal studies show adverse effects. There are no controlled studies in humans. Should be used only when the potential benefits outweigh potential risks to the fetus. This drug may be preferable to anticonvulsant mood stabilizers if treatment is required during pregnancy.
- *Lactation*: It is not known if this drug is secreted in human breast milk. It is recommended to either discontinue drug or bottle feed. Infants of women who choose to breastfeed while on this drug should be monitored for possible adverse effect.
- *Children and adolescents:*
  - Probably safe and effective for behavioral disturbances in this population.
  - IM formulation has not been studied in patients younger than 18 years and is not recommended for use in this population.
  - Should be monitored more frequently than adults.

Risperdal, Risperdal Consta   **risperidone**

INDICATIONS: Schizophrenia (age 13 and older), monotherapy or combination therapy for acute mixed or manic episodes associated with bipolar I disorder (age 10 and older), and treatment of irritability associated with autistic disorder in children and adolescents aged 5 to 16 years.

AVAILABLE FORMS: Tablet, 0.25, 0.5, 1, 2, 3, 4, and 6 mg; orally disintegrating tablet, 0.5, 1, and 2 mg; liquid, 1 mg/mL (30-mL bottle); long-acting depot microspheres formulation for deep IM formulation, 25 mg vial/kit, 37.5 mg vial/kit, 50 mg vial/kit

DOSAGE:
- 2 to 8 mg/day PO for adults with acute psychosis and bipolar disorder
- 0.5 to 2.0 mg/day PO for children and elderly
- 25 to 50 mg depot IM every 2 weeks

ADMINISTRATION:
- Tablets may be given with or without food.
- Advise patient to take the missed dose as soon as remembered. Skip the missed dose if almost time for the next scheduled dose. Do not take extra medicine to make up the missed dose.
- Measure the liquid form of risperidone with a special dose-measuring spoon or cup, not a regular tablespoon.
- Do not mix the liquid form with cola or tea.

SIDE EFFECTS: Can increase risk for diabetes and dyslipidemia; extrapyramidal symptoms (dose dependent); hyperprolactinemia (dose dependent); dizziness, insomnia, headache, anxiety; nausea, sedation, weight gain, constipation, abdominal pain; tachycardia; sedation; sexual dysfunction; hyperglycemia; increased risk of death and cerebrovascular events in elderly with dementia-related psychosis; TD (rare); orthostatic hypotension (rare, usually during initial dose titration); neuroleptic malignant syndrome (rare); seizures (rare)

DRUG INTERACTIONS:
- May increase effects of antihypertensive medications
- May antagonize levodopa and dopamine agonists
- Plasma levels of risperidone may be reduced if given in conjunction with carbamazepine.
- Plasma levels of risperidone may be increased if given in conjunction with fluoxetine or paroxetine
- Plasma levels of risperidone may be increased if given in conjunction with clozapine, but no dose adjustment is required.

▶**Alert:** This list may not describe all possible interactions. Instruct clients to provide a list of all the medicines, herbs, nonprescription drugs, or dietary supplements they use.

PHARMACOKINETICS:
Elimination: 7 to 8 weeks after last injection (long-acting formulation)
Metabolism: Metabolites are active; metabolized by CYP450 2D6
Half-life: 20 to 24 hr (oral formulation); 3 to 6 days (long-acting formulation)

PRECAUTIONS:
- Use with caution in patients with conditions that predispose to hypotension (dehydration, overheating).
- Use with caution in patients who are at risk for aspiration pneumonia.
- Priapism has been reported.
- Do not use if there is a proven allergy.

PATIENT AND FAMILY EDUCATION:
- Take exactly as prescribed by the provider. Do not take in larger or smaller amounts or for longer than recommended.

(cont.)

SCHIZOAFFECTIVE DISORDER: Antipsychotic Drugs, Atypical (Second Generation)

risperidone (*cont.*)

- Can be taken with or without food.
- You may be more sensitive to temperature extremes (very hot or cold conditions) when taking this medication. Avoid getting too cold, or becoming overheated or dehydrated.
- Drink plenty of fluids, especially in hot weather and during exercise.
- Risperidone can cause side effects that may impair thinking or reactions. Be careful if you drive or do anything that requires you to be awake and alert.
- Risperidone may cause high blood sugar (hyperglycemia). Talk to your provider if any signs of hyperglycemia such as increased thirst or urination, excessive hunger, or weakness. If diabetic, check blood sugar levels on a regular basis.
- The risperidone orally disintegrating tablet may contain phenylalanine. Talk to your provider before using this form of risperidone if you have PKU.
- *Avoid drinking alcohol.* It can increase some of the side effects.
- *Do not* mix the liquid form with cola or tea.
- *Stop using this medication and call provider immediately* if you have fever, stiff muscles, confusion, sweating, fast or uneven heartbeats, restless muscle movements in face or neck, tremor (uncontrolled shaking), trouble swallowing, feeling light-headed, or fainting.
- Do not stop taking the drug suddenly without first talking to provider, even if you feel fine. You may have serious side effects if you stop taking the drug suddenly.
- Call provider if symptoms do not improve or get worse.
- Store at room temperature away from moisture, light, and heat. Do not freeze the liquid form of risperidone.

SPECIAL POPULATIONS:
- *Elderly:*
  - Initially 0.5 mg orally a day; then increase to 0.5 mg twice a day. Titrate once a week for doses above 1.5 mg twice a day.
  - Long-acting risperidone: 25 mg every 2 weeks. Oral administration should be continued for 3 weeks after the first injection.

- Elderly with dementia-related psychosis treated with atypical antipsychotics are at higher risk of death and cerebrovascular events.
- *Renal impairment*:
  - Initially 0.5 mg orally twice a day for the first week. Increase to 1 mg twice a day during the second week.
  - Long-acting risperidone should not be given to patients with renal function impairment unless s/he can tolerate at least 2 mg/day orally.
  - Long-acting risperidone should be given 25 mg every 2 weeks. Oral administration should be continued for 3 weeks after the first injection.
- *Hepatic impairment*:
  - Initially 0.5 mg orally twice a day for the first week. Increase to 1 mg twice a day during the second week.
  - Long-acting risperidone should not be given to patients with hepatic function impairment unless s/he can tolerate at least 2 mg/day orally.
  - Long-acting risperidone should be given 25 mg every 2 weeks. Oral administration should be continued for 3 weeks after the first injection.
- *Cardiac impairment:* Use with caution because of risk of orthostatic hypotension. There is a greater risk of stroke if given to elderly patients with atrial fibrillation.
- *Pregnancy:* Category C. Some animal studies show adverse effects. There are no controlled studies in humans. It should be used only when the potential benefits outweigh potential risks to the fetus. Risperidone may be preferable to anticonvulsant mood stabilizers if treatment is required during pregnancy. Effects of hyperprolactinemia on the fetus are unknown.
- *Lactation:* Drug is secreted in human breast milk. It is recommended to either discontinue the drug or bottle feed. Infants of women who choose to breastfeed while on this drug should be monitored for possible adverse effect.
- *Children and adolescents:*
  - Safe and effective for behavioral disturbances in this population.
  - Risperidone is the most frequently used atypical antipsychotic medication in this population.

quetiapine   *Seroquel, Seroquel XR*

INDICATIONS: Schizophrenia, depressive episodes associated with bipolar disorder, monotherapy or combination therapy for acute manic episodes associated with bipolar I disorder, acute and maintenance treatment of schizophrenia.

AVAILABLE FORMS: Tablet, 25, 50, 100, 200, 300, and 400 mg; extended-release tablet, 200, 300, and 400 mg

DOSAGE:
- 400 to 800 mg/day in one (*Seroquel XR*) or two (*Seroquel*) doses for schizophrenia and bipolar mania
- 300 mg once per day for bipolar depression

ADMINISTRATION:
- Tablets may be given with or without food.
- Take this medicine with a full glass of water.

(cont.)

...

quetiapine (*cont.*)

- Advise patient not to crush, chew, or break an extended-release tablet. Swallow the pill whole. Breaking the pill may cause too much of the drug to be released at one time.
- Advise patient to take the missed dose as soon as remembered. Skip the missed dose if it is almost time for the next scheduled dose. Do not take extra medicine to make up the missed dose.

SIDE EFFECTS: Can increase risk for diabetes and dyslipidemia; dizziness; sedation; weight gain; dry mouth, constipation, dyspepsia, abdominal pain; tachycardia; hyperglycemia; increased risk of death and cerebrovascular events in elderly with dementia-related psychosis; orthostatic hypotension (usually during initial dose titration); neuroleptic malignant syndrome (rare); seizures (rare)

DRUG INTERACTIONS:
- May increase effects of antihypertensive medications.
- Plasma levels of quetiapine may be increased if given in conjunction with CYP450 3A4 and CYP450 2D6 inhibitors. However, no dose adjustment is required.
▶**Alert:** This list may not describe all possible interactions. Instruct clients to provide a list of all the medicines, herbs, nonprescription drugs, or dietary supplements they use.

PHARMACOKINETICS:
Metabolism: Metabolites are inactive
Half-life: 6 to 7 hr

PRECAUTIONS:
- Use with caution in patients who are at risk for aspiration pneumonia.
- Manufacturer recommends to examine for cataracts before and every 6 months after starting quetiapine.
- Do not use if there is a proven allergy.

PATIENT AND FAMILY EDUCATION:
- Take exactly as prescribed by the provider. Do not take in larger or smaller amounts or for longer than recommended.
- Can be taken with or without food.
- Quetiapine can cause side effects that may impair thinking or reactions. Be careful if you drive or do anything that requires you to be awake and alert.
- Quetiapine may cause high blood sugar (hyperglycemia). Talk to provider if any signs of hyperglycemia such as increased thirst or urination, excessive hunger, or weakness. If diabetic, check blood sugar levels on a regular basis.
- Avoid becoming overheated or dehydrated during exercise and in hot weather. You may be more prone to heat stroke.
- Avoid getting up too fast from a sitting or lying position. Get up slowly and steady yourself to prevent a fall.

- Avoid drinking alcohol.
- Stop using this medication and call provider immediately if you have very stiff (rigid) muscles, high fever, sweating, confusion, fast or uneven heartbeats, tremors; feel like you might pass out; have jerky muscle movements you cannot control, trouble swallowing, problems with speech; have blurred vision, eye pain, or see halos around lights; have increased thirst and urination, excessive hunger, fruity breath odor, weakness, nausea and vomiting; have fever, chills, body aches, flu symptoms; or have white patches or sores inside your mouth or on your lips.
- Do not stop taking the drug suddenly without first talking to provider, even if you feel fine. You may have serious side effects if you stop taking the drug suddenly.
- Call provider if symptoms do not improve or get worse.
- Store at room temperature away from moisture and heat.

SPECIAL POPULATIONS:
- Elderly:
  - Generally a lower dose is used (e.g., 25 to 100 mg twice a day). Higher dose can be used if tolerated.
  - Elderly with dementia-related psychosis treated with atypical antipsychotics are at higher risk of death and cerebrovascular events.
- Renal impairment: No dose adjustment is required.
- Hepatic impairment: May need to reduce dose.
- Cardiac impairment: Use with caution because of risk of orthostatic hypotension.
- Pregnancy: Category C. Some animal studies show adverse effects. There are no controlled studies in humans. It should be used only when the potential benefits outweigh potential risks to the fetus. Quetiapine may be preferable to anticonvulsant mood stabilizers if treatment is required during pregnancy.
- Lactation: It is not known if drug is secreted in human breast milk. It is recommended to either discontinue drug or bottle feed. Infants of women who choose to breastfeed while on this drug should be monitored for possible adverse effect.
- Children and adolescents:
  - Not officially recommended for patients younger than 18 years.
  - Probably safe and effective for behavioral disturbances in this population.
  - Should be monitored more frequently than adults. May tolerate lower doses better.
  - Watch for activation of suicidal ideation. Inform parents or guardian of this risk so that they can help monitor the risk.

SCHIZOAFFECTIVE DISORDER: Antipsychotic Drugs, Atypical (Second Generation)

ziprasidone   *Geodon, Geodon IM Injection*

INDICATIONS: Schizophrenia, delaying relapse in schizophrenia, acute agitation in schizophrenia (IM), acute agitation in schizophrenia, acute mania/mixed mania, other psychotic disorders, bipolar maintenance, bipolar depression, behavioral disturbances in dementia.

AVAILABLE FORMS: Tablet, 20, 40, 60, and 80 mg; injection, 20 mg/mL

DOSAGE:
- 40 to 200 mg/day in divided doses, PO for schizophrenia
- 80 to 160 mg/day in divided doses, PO for bipolar
- 10 to 20 mg IM (doses of 10 mg may be administered every 2 hr, doses of 20 mg may be administered every 4 hr with MDD 40 mg). It is not to be administered for more than 3 consecutive days.

ADMINISTRATION:
- Take this medication with a meal.
- Dosing at 20 to 40 twice a day is too low and activating, perhaps due to potent 5HT2C antagonist properties. Reduce activation by increasing the dose to 60 to 80 mg twice a day.
- Best efficacy in schizophrenia and bipolar disorder is at doses greater than 120 mg/day.
- BMI monthly for 3 months, then quarterly.
- Monitor fasting triglycerides monthly for several months in patients at high risk for metabolic complications.
- BP, fasting plasma glucose, fasting lipids within 3 months and then annually, but earlier and more frequently for patients with diabetes or who have gained more than 5% of initial weight.

SIDE EFFECTS: Dizziness, sedation, and hypotension especially at high doses; motor side effects (rare); possible increased incidence of diabetes or dyslipidemia is unknown

DRUG INTERACTIONS:
- May enhance effects of antihypertensive drugs
- May antagonize levodopa and dopamine agonists
- May enhance QTc prolongation of other drugs capable of prolonging QTc interval

PHARMACOKINETICS:
Mean half-life: 6.6 hr
Protein binding: Greater than 99%
Metabolism: Metabolized by CYP450 3A4

PRECAUTIONS:
- Prolongs QTc interval more than some other antipsychotics.
- Use with caution in patients with conditions that predispose to hypotension (dehydration, overheating).
- Priapism has been reported.
- Dysphagia has been associated with antipsychotic use, and should be used cautiously in patients at risk for aspiration pneumonia.
- Do not use if patient is taking agents capable of prolonging QTc interval (pimozide, thioridazine, selected antiarrhythmics, moxifloxacin, sparfloxacin).
- Do not use if there is a history of QTc prolongation, cardiac arrhythmia, recent AMI, uncompensated heart failure.
- Do not use if there is a proven allergy to ziprasidone.

PATIENT AND FAMILY EDUCATION:
- *Take with a meal* of a few hundred calories (e.g., turkey sandwich and a piece of fruit) to enhance absorption.
- *Avoid becoming overheated or dehydrated during exercise and in hot weather.* You may be more prone to heat stroke.
- *Avoid getting up too fast from a sitting or lying position.* Get up slowly and steady yourself to prevent a fall.
- *Avoid drinking alcohol.*
- *Stop using this medication and call provider immediately* if you have very stiff (rigid) muscles, high fever, sweating, confusion, fast or uneven heartbeats, tremors; feel like you might pass out; have jerky muscle movements you cannot control, trouble swallowing, problems with speech; have blurred vision, eye pain, or see halos around lights; have increased thirst and urination, excessive hunger, fruity breath odor, weakness, nausea and vomiting; have fever, chills, body aches, flu symptoms; or have white patches or sores inside your mouth or on your lips.
- Do not stop taking the drug suddenly without first talking to your provider, even if you feel fine. You may have serious side effects if you stop taking the drug suddenly.
- Call provider if symptoms do not improve or get worse.
- Store at room temperature away from moisture and heat.

SPECIAL POPULATIONS:
- *Elderly:* Some patients may tolerate lower doses better. Elderly patients with dementia-related psychosis treated with atypical antipsychotics are at an increased risk of death compared to placebo.
- *Renal impairment:* No dose adjustment is necessary.
- *Hepatic impairment:* No dose adjustment is necessary.
- *Cardiac impairment:* Contraindicated in patients with a known history of QTc prolongation, recent AMI, and uncompensated heart failure.
- *Pregnancy:* Category C. Some animal studies show adverse effects; there are no controlled studies in humans.
- *Lactation:* It is not known whether it is secreted in human breast milk. Recommend either to discontinue drug or to bottle feed.
- *Children and adolescents:* Not recommended for patients younger than 18 years of age. Early data suggest that it may be safe and effective for behavioral disturbances in children and adolescents.

Invega   **paliperidone**

INDICATIONS: Schizophrenia, bipolar disorder, other psychotic disorders, behavioral responses in dementia, behavioral disturbances in children and adolescents, disorders associated with impulse control.

AVAILABLE FORMS: Tablet (extended-release), 3, 6, and 9 mg

DOSAGE: 6 mg/day; maximum dose: 12 mg/day

ADMINISTRATION: Initial dose, 6 mg/day taken in the morning; can increase by 3 mg/day every 5 days

SIDE EFFECTS: Dizziness; hypotension; motor side effects especially at high doses; elevation in prolactin; weight gain; may increase risk for diabetes and dyslipidemia; rare TD (much less than conventional antipsychotics); sedation; hypersalivation; orthostatic hypotension; tachycardia; hyperglycemia associated with ketoacidosis or osmolar coma or death has been reported in patients taking atypical antipsychotics. *Elderly patients with dementia-related psychosis:* Increased risk of death and cerebrovascular events; neuroleptic malignant syndrome (rare); seizures (rare)

DRUG INTERACTIONS:
- May increase effects of antihypertensive agents.
- May decrease the effects of levodopa and dopamine agonists.
- May increase QTc prolongation of other drugs that also increase the QTc interval.

PHARMACOKINETICS:
- Active metabolite of risperidone
Half-life: Approx. 23 hr

PRECAUTIONS:
- Use with caution with conditions that predispose to hypotension (dehydration, overheating).
- Use with caution in patients at risk for aspiration pneumonia since dysphagia has been associated with antipsychotic use.
- Prolongs QTc interval.
- Priapism reported with other antipsychotics including risperidone; paliperidone is an active metabolite of risperidone.
- *Do not use* if patient is taking other medications or has conditions that prolong QTc interval (pimozide, thioridazine, selected antiarrhythmics, recent AMI, and uncompensated heart failure).
- *Do not use* if patient has preexisting severe GI narrowing.
- *Do not use if allergic to or sensitive* to paliperidone or risperidone.

PATIENT AND FAMILY EDUCATION:
- Take exactly as prescribed by the provider. Do not take in larger or smaller amounts or for longer than recommended.
- *Avoid becoming overheated or dehydrated during exercise and in hot weather.* You may be more prone to heat stroke.
- *Avoid getting up too fast from a sitting or lying position.* Get up slowly and steady yourself to prevent a fall.
- *Avoid drinking alcohol.*
- *Stop using this medication and call provider immediately* if you have very stiff (rigid) muscles, high fever, sweating, confusion, fast or uneven heartbeats, tremors; feel like you might pass out; have jerky muscle movements you cannot control, trouble swallowing, problems with speech; have blurred vision, eye pain, or see halos around lights; have increased thirst and urination, excessive hunger, fruity breath odor, weakness, nausea and vomiting; have fever, chills, body aches, flu symptoms; or have white patches or sores inside mouth or on lips.
- Do not stop taking the drug suddenly without first talking to provider, even if you feel fine. You may have serious side effects if you stop taking the drug suddenly.
- Call provider if your symptoms do not improve or get worse.
- Store at room temperature away from moisture and heat.

SPECIAL POPULATIONS:
- *Elderly:* They may tolerate lower doses better and are more sensitive to adverse effects. Not approved for treatment of elderly patients with dementia-related psychosis; such patients are at increased risk of cardiovascular events and death.
- *Renal impairment:* For mild impairment, maximum dose recommended is 6 mg/day. For moderate-to-severe impairment, maximum dose recommended is 3 mg/day.
- *Hepatic impairment:* No dose adjustment recommended for mild-to-moderate impairment. Use in patients with severe impairment has not been studied.
- *Cardiac impairment:* Use with caution due to risk of orthostatic hypotension.
- *Pregnancy:* Category C. Animal studies show adverse effects; there are no controlled studies in humans. Psychotic symptoms may worsen during pregnancy and necessitate some form of treatment. Paliperidone may be preferable to anticonvulsant mood stabilizers and conventional antipsychotics. Effects of hyperprolactinemia on the fetus are unknown.
- *Lactation:* Some drugs may be found in mother's breast milk; it is recommended that either the drug be discontinued or infant be bottle fed. Infants who are breastfed while mother is on paliperidone need to be monitored for adverse effects.
- *Children and adolescents:* Safety and efficacy are not established for paliperidone for children and adolescents. Children and adolescents will need to be monitored more closely than adults.

SCHIZOAFFECTIVE DISORDER: Antipsychotic Drugs, Atypical (Second Generation)

asenapine   *Saphris*

INDICATIONS: Schizophrenia, manic or mixed episodes associated with bipolar disorder I.

AVAILABLE FORMS: Sublingual tablets, 5 mg, 10 mg

DOSAGE:
- Initial, 5 mg bid; increase to 10 mg bid
- Can decrease back to 5 mg bid based on tolerability

ADMINISTRATION:
- *Place the tablet under the tongue* and allow to dissolve completely. Tablet dissolves within seconds.
- Do not eat or drink anything for 10 to 30 min after administration.
- Tablets should not be crushed, chewed, or swallowed.

SIDE EFFECTS: Akathisia; oral hypoesthesia (numbness); somnolence; dizziness; other extrapyramidal symptoms excluding akathisia; weight gain; insomnia; headache; may induce orthostatic hypotension and syncope in some patients, especially early in treatment; rare neuroleptic malignant syndrome; rare TD

DRUG INTERACTIONS:
- May enhance effects of certain antihypertensive drugs because of its alpha-1-adrenergic antagonism with potential for inducing hypotension.
- Inhibitor of P450 2D6 and may contribute to increased levels.
- Appears to decrease prolactin from baseline.

PHARMACOKINETICS:
- Metabolized primarily through CYP 1A2
- Rapidly absorbed within 0.5 to 1.5 hr
Half-life: Approx. 24 hr

PRECAUTIONS:
- Caution should be used when taken in combination with other centrally acting drugs or alcohol.
- Caution should be used with other drugs that are both substrates and inhibitors for CYP 2D6.
- May cause transient increases in serum transaminase; therefore it needs to be monitored during the initial months.
- Elderly patients with dementia-related psychosis treated with antipsychotic drugs are at an increased risk of death. Asenapine is not approved for the treatment of patients with dementia-related psychosis.
- Patients with a preexisting low WBC or a history of drug-induced leukopenia/neutropenia should have their CBC monitored frequently during the first few months of therapy, and asenapine should be discontinued at the first sign of decline in WBC in the absence of other causative factors.
- The use of asenapine should be avoided in combination with other drugs known to prolong the QTc interval including Class 1A antiarrhythmics (e.g., quinidine, procainamide) or Class 3

antiarrhythmics (e.g., amiodarone, sotalol), antipsychotic medications (e.g., ziprasidone, chlorpromazine, thioridazine), and antibiotics (e.g., gatifloxacin, moxifloxacin).
- Like other drugs that antagonize dopamine D2 receptors, asenapine can elevate prolactin levels, and the elevation can persist during chronic administration.
- As with other antipsychotic drugs, asenapine should be used with caution in patients with a history of seizures or with conditions that potentially lower the seizure threshold, e.g., Alzheimer's dementia. Conditions that lower the seizure threshold may be more prevalent in patients 65 years or older.

PATIENT AND FAMILY EDUCATION:
- Take exactly as prescribed by the provider. Do not take in larger or smaller amounts or for longer than recommended.
- Asenapine tablets must be placed under tongue and allowed to dissolve. Do not crush, chew, or swallow.
- No eating or drinking for at least 10 min—30 min is better—after the drug dissolves.
- *Avoid drinking alcohol.*
- *Stop using this medication and call provider immediately* if you have very stiff (rigid) muscles, high fever, sweating, confusion, fast or uneven heartbeats, tremors; feel like you might pass out; have jerky muscle movements you cannot control, trouble swallowing, problems with speech; have blurred vision, eye pain, or see halos around lights; have increased thirst and urination, excessive hunger, fruity breath odor, weakness, nausea and vomiting; have fever, chills, body aches, flu symptoms; or have white patches or sores inside your mouth or on your lips.
- Do not stop taking this drug suddenly without first talking to your provider, even if you feel fine. You may have serious side effects if you stop taking the drug suddenly.
- Call provider if symptoms do not improve or get worse.
- Store at room temperature away from moisture and heat.

SPECIAL POPULATIONS:
- *Elderly:* They may tolerate lower doses better and are more sensitive to adverse effects. It is not approved for treatment of elderly patients with dementia-related psychosis, and such patients are at increased risk of cardiovascular events and death.
- *Renal impairment*: No adjustment is needed.
- *Hepatic impairment*: Lower dose for mild-to-moderate impairment. It is not recommended with severe liver impairment.
- *Cardiac impairment:* Use with caution due to risk of orthostatic hypotension and QTc potential prolongation.

(cont.)

asenapine (*cont.*)

- *Pregnancy:* Category C. There are no adequate and well-controlled studies of asenapine in pregnant women. In animal studies, asenapine increased post-implantation loss and decreased pup weight and survival at doses similar to or less than recommended clinical doses. In these studies there was no increase in the incidence of structural abnormalities caused by asenapine. Asenapine should be used during pregnancy only if the potential benefit justifies the potential risk to the fetus.

- *Lactation:* Asenapine is excreted in the milk of rats during lactation. It is not known whether asenapine or its metabolites are excreted in human milk. Because many drugs are excreted in human milk, caution should be exercised when asenapine is administered to a nursing woman. It is recommended that women receiving asenapine should not breastfeed.
- *Children and adolescents*: Safety and effectiveness in children and adolescents has not been established.

Class: Antipsychotic Drugs, Typical (First Generation)

Haldol, Haloperidol decanoate   **haloperidol**

INDICATIONS: Psychotic disorders, Tourette's syndrome, schizophrenia, second-line treatment for severe behavior disorders in children, second-line treatment for hyperactive children, bipolar disorder, behavioral disturbances in dementias, delirium with lorazepam.

AVAILABLE FORMS: Tablet (scored), 0.5, 1, 2, 5, and 10 mg scored, 20 mg scored; concentrate, 2 mg/mL; solution, 1 mg/mL; injection, 5 mg/mL (immediate release); decanoate injection, 50 mg haloperidol as 60.5 mg/mL, haloperidol decanoate, 100 mg haloperidol as 141.04 mg/mL haloperidol decanoate

DOSAGE:
- 1 to 40 mg/day orally
- Immediate-release injection, 2 to 5 mg each dose
- Decanoate injection 10 to 20 times the previous daily dose of oral antipsychotic

ADMINISTRATION:
- *Oral*: Can give once daily or in divided doses at beginning of treatment during rapid escalation; increase as needed; can be dosed up to 100 mg/day
- *Immediate-release injection:* Initial dose, 2 to 5 mg; subsequent doses may be given as often as every hour; patient should be switched to oral administration as soon as possible.
- *Haloperidol decanoate injection:* Initial dose, 10 to 15 times the previous oral dose for patients maintained on low antipsychotic doses (up to equivalent of 10 mg/day oral haloperidol). Initial dose may be as high as 20 times previous oral dose for patients maintained on higher antipsychotic doses. Maximum dose is 100 mg. If higher dose is required, the remainder can be administered 3 to 7 days later. Administer total dose every 4 weeks.
- Stay hydrated.
▶**Alert:** Haloperidol is frequently dosed too high. High doses may actually worsen negative symptoms of schizophrenia.

SIDE EFFECTS: Neuroleptic-induced deficit syndrome; akathisia; EPS, parkinsonism, TD, tardive dystonia; galactorrhea, amenorrhea; dizziness, sedation; dry mouth, constipation, urinary retention, blurred vision; decreased sweating; hypotension, tachycardia, hyperlipidemia; weight gain; rare neuroleptic malignant syndrome; seizures (rare); jaundice (rare), agranulocytosis, leukopenia; haloperidol with anticholinergics may increase intraocular pressure; reduces effects of anticoagulants; plasma levels of haloperidol lowered by rifampin; may enhance effects of antihypertensive agents; haloperidol with lithium may contribute to development of encephalopathic syndrome

DRUG INTERACTIONS:
- May decrease the effects of levodopa and dopamine agonists.
- May increase the effects of antihypertensive drugs except for guanethidine.
- Additive effects with CNS depressants; dose of other should be reduced.
- May interact with some pressor agents (epinephrine) to lower BP.

PHARMACOKINETICS:
Half-life: Haloperidol decanoate, approx. 3 weeks; oral, approx. 12 to 36 hr

PRECAUTIONS:
- Discontinue if symptoms of neuroleptic malignant syndrome develop.
- Use with caution in patients with respiratory problems.
- Avoid extreme heat exposure.
- May experience rapid shift to depression if used to treat mania.
- Patients with thyrotoxicosis may experience neurotoxicity.
- Do not use with Lewy body dementia or Parkinson's disease.
- Use with caution in patients with QTc prolongation, hypothyroidism, familial long-QT syndrome.
- Do not use if patient is comatose.
- Do not use if there is a proven allergy to haloperidol.

(cont.)

SCHIZOAFFECTIVE DISORDER: Antipsychotic Drugs, Typical (First Generation)

haloperidol (*cont.*)

PATIENT AND FAMILY EDUCATION:
- Take exactly as prescribed.
- Avoid getting up too fast from a sitting or lying position. Get up slowly and steady yourself to prevent a fall.
- *Avoid drinking alcohol.*
- *Stop using this medication and call provider immediately* if you have very stiff (rigid) muscles, high fever, sweating, confusion, fast or uneven heartbeats, tremors; feel like you might pass out; have jerky muscle movements you cannot control, trouble swallowing, problems with speech; have blurred vision, eye pain, or see halos around lights; have increased thirst and urination, excessive hunger, fruity breath odor, weakness, nausea and vomiting; have fever, chills, body aches, flu symptoms; or have white patches or sores inside your mouth or on your lips.
- Do not stop taking the drug suddenly without first talking to your provider, even if you feel fine. You may have serious side effects if you stop taking the drug suddenly.
- Call provider if symptoms do not improve or get worse.
- Store at room temperature away from moisture and heat.

SPECIAL POPULATIONS:
- *Elderly:* Lower doses should be used and patient should be monitored closely. Do not use in elderly patients with dementia.
- *Renal impairment*: Use with caution.
- *Hepatic impairment*: Use with caution.
- *Cardiac impairment:* Because of the risk of orthostatic hypertension, use with caution.
- *Pregnancy:* Category C. Some animal studies show adverse effects; there are no controlled studies in humans.
- *Lactation*: Category C. Not recommended for use in women who breastfeed or plan to breastfeed while on this drug.
- *Children and adolescents*: Safety and efficacy are not established. Not intended for use with children younger than 3 years. Generally consider as second line, not first line.

fluphenazine   *Prolixin*

INDICATIONS: Psychotic and bipolar disorders

AVAILABLE FORMS: Tablet, 1, 2.5 (scored), 5 (scored), and 10 mg (scored); decanoate for long-acting IM or SC administration, 25 mg/mL; short-acting IM injection, 2.5 mg/mL; elixir, 2.5 mg/5 mL; concentrate, 5 mg/mL

DOSAGE:
- *Oral*: Initial, 0.5 to 10 mg/day in divided doses; maximum, 40 mg/day
- *IM (short-acting)*: Initial, 1.25 mg; 2.5 to 10 mg/day can be given in divided doses every 6 to 8 hr; maximum dose, generally 10 mg/day
- *Fluphenazine decanoate (long-acting)*: Initial, 12.5 to 25 mg (0.5–1 mL); subsequent doses and intervals determined in accordance with the patient's response; generally no more than 50 mg/2 mL given at intervals not longer than 4 weeks

ADMINISTRATION:
- Oral solution should not be mixed with drinks containing caffeine, tannic acid (tea), or pectinates (apple juice).
- 12.5 mg/mL every 2 weeks is equivalent to 10 mg daily of oral fluphenazine.
- Decanoate onset of action is at 24 to 72 hr after administration with significant antipsychotic actions evident within 48 to 96 hr.

SIDE EFFECTS: Motor side effects from blockage of D2 in striatum; elevations in prolactin from blockage of D2 in the pituitary; worsening of negative and cognitive symptoms due to blockage of D2 receptors in the mesocortical and mesolimbic dopamine pathways; sedation, blurred vision, constipation, dry mouth; sedation, weight gain; dizziness, and hypotension; possible increased incidence of diabetes or dyslipidemia with conventional antipsychotics is unknown; neuroleptic-induced deficit syndrome; akathisia; extrapyramidal symptoms, parkinsonism, TD; galactorrhea, amenorrhea; sexual dysfunction; priapism; decreased sweating, depression; hypotension, tachycardia, syncope

DRUG INTERACTIONS:
- May decrease the effects of levodopa and dopamine agonists.
- May increase effects of antihypertensive drugs except for guanethidine, whose actions may be antagonized by fluphenazine.
- Concurrent use with CNS depressants may produce additive effects.
- Additive anticholinergic effects may occur if used with atropine or related compounds.
- Alcohol and diuretics increase the risk of hypotension.
- Some patients on neuroleptics and lithium developed an encephalopathic syndrome similar to NMS.
- Use with epinephrine may lower BP.

PHARMACOKINETICS:
Half-life: Oral formulation, approx. 15 hr; IM formulation, approx. 6.8 to 9.6 days

PRECAUTIONS:
- May decrease the effects of levodopa and dopamine agonist.
- May increase the effects of antihypertensive drugs.
- Additive effects may occur if combined with CNS depressants. *(cont.)*

fluphenazine (*cont.*)

- Some neuroleptics and lithium have caused an encephalopathic syndrome similar to NMS in some patients.
- Fluphenazine and epinephrine may lower BP.
- Additive anticholinergic effects may occur if used with atropine or related compounds.
- Alcohol and diuretics may increase the risk of hypotension.
- Do not use if in a comatose state.
- Do not use if patient is taking cabergoline, pergolide, or metrizamide.
- Do not use if there is proven allergy or sensitivity to fluphenazine.

PATIENT AND FAMILY EDUCATION:
- Avoid this medication if you have an allergy to aspirin. Inform your provider of all drug allergies.
- Take exactly as prescribed by the provider. Do not take in larger or smaller amounts or for longer than recommended.
- Can be taken with or without food.
- *Avoid becoming overheated or dehydrated during exercise and in hot weather.* You may be more prone to heat stroke.
- *Avoid getting up too fast from a sitting or lying position.* Get up slowly and steady yourself to prevent a fall.
- *Avoid drinking alcohol.*
- *Stop using this medication and call provider immediately* if you have very stiff (rigid) muscles, high fever, sweating, confusion, fast or uneven heartbeats, tremors; feel like you might pass out; have jerky muscle movements you cannot control, trouble swallowing, problems with speech; have blurred vision, eye pain, or see halos around lights; have increased thirst and urination, excessive hunger, fruity breath odor, weakness, nausea and vomiting; have fever, chills, body aches, flu symptoms; or have white patches or sores inside your mouth or on your lips.

- Do not stop taking the drug suddenly without first talking to your provider, even if you feel fine. You may have serious side effects if you stop taking the drug suddenly.
- Call provider if symptoms do not improve or get worse.
- Store at room temperature away from moisture and heat.

SPECIAL POPULATIONS:
- *Elderly:* Lower initial dose (1–2.5 mg/day) and slower titration. Elderly are more susceptible to adverse effects. It is not approved for treatment of elderly patients with dementia-related psychosis, and such patients are at increased risk of cardiovascular events and death.
- *Renal impairment*: Use with caution and with slower titration.
- *Hepatic impairment*: Use with caution and with slower titration.
- *Cardiac impairment:* Cardiovascular toxicity can occur, especially orthostatic hypotension.
- *Pregnancy:* Category C. Some animal studies have demonstrated adverse effects; there are no controlled studies in humans. Infants whose mothers took a phenothiazine during pregnancy have exhibited EPS, jaundice, hyperreflexia, hyporeflexia. Psychotic symptoms may worsen during pregnancy, necessitating some form of treatment. Atypical antipsychotics may be preferable.
- *Lactation:* Milk crosses to the infant through breast milk and dystonia, TD, and sedation have been observed in the infant. Recommend discontinuing drug or bottle feed.
- *Children and adolescents*: Safety and efficacy of fluphenazine is not established for children and adolescents. Decanoate and enanthate injectable formulations are contraindicated in children younger than 12 years. It is generally considered second-line treatment after trial with atypical antipsychotics.

Class: Selective Serotonin Reuptake Inhibitors (SSRIs)

Prozac, Sarafem	**fluoxetine**

INDICATIONS: Has the most data in the treatment of bulimia nervosa.

AVAILABLE FORMS: Capsule, 10, 20 and 40 mg; tablet, 10, 15 and 20 mg; pellet, delayed release, enteric coated (*Prozac Weekly*), 90 mg; solution, 5 mL and 120 mL (20 mg/5 mL). *Note:* Availability of certain formulations may be limited to brandname versions of the drug.

DOSAGE: Starting dose, 20 mg/day; maintenance dose, 20–60 mg, adjust in 20 mg increments

ADMINISTRATION:
- PO, with or without food.
- Capsules may be diluted into water or apple juice. Grapefruit juice should not be used due to cytochrome P450 effects.

SIDE EFFECTS:
- May cause CNS depression (sedation, fatigue) or activation (insomnia)
- Tends to be weight neutral or approximately 2 pounds of weight gain in one year
- Nervousness, agitation
- Headache and nausea, particularly early in treatment
- Insomnia
- Excess perspiration
- Serotonin syndrome
- Withdrawal syndrome (including neonatal withdrawal syndrome): Symptoms may include dizziness, muscle aches, headache, nausea, vomiting, gait instability, agitation, and/or "electric shock" sensations
- Diarrhea

(cont.)

SCHIZOAFFECTIVE DISORDER: Selective Serotonin Reuptake Inhibitors (SSRIs)

- Sexual dysfunction (approx. 50% of men and women)
- Hyponatremia (e.g., in geriatric patients taking diuretics)
- Side effects are most common during the first or second week of therapy. Starting with a lower dosage and gradually increasing, and taking the medication with food will limit some of these side effects.

DRUG INTERACTIONS:
- *MAOIs:* Extreme risk for serotonin syndrome. Requires a 5- to 6-week washout period or longer before use of an MAOI.
- *TCAs:* Plasma levels may be increased by SSRIs, so add with caution in low doses
- *ASA and NSAIDs:* Increased risk of bleeding
- *CNS depressants:* May increase depressant effects
- *SSRIs or SARIs:* May cause serotonin syndrome in combination with other medications such as tramadol, high-dose triptans, or the antibiotic linezolid
- Use with caution in patients taking blood thinners (*Coumadin*), other antidepressants, antihistamines, lithium, TCAs, and certain antibiotics, such as erythromycin, clarithromycin, or azithromycin

PHARMACOKINETICS:
- Highly bound to plasma proteins and have a large volume of distribution.
- Readily absorbed in the GI tract, metabolized in the liver, and excreted in the urine. Dosages may be decreased in patients with liver or kidney disease.
- Caution advised in elderly clients.

Peak plasma levels: Reached in 2–10 hr.
Metabolism: Metabolized in the liver by cytochrome P-450 microsomal enzymes.
Half-life: Variable, but most SSRIs have half-lives of 20–24 hr. A notable exception is fluoxetine (*Prozac*), and its active metabolite, norfluoxetine, which have half-lives of 2–4 days and 8–9 days, respectively. Hence, addition of serotonergic medications to a patient's regimen must not occur until 2–3 weeks after discontinuation of an SSRI (some recommend a 5-week "washout" period for fluoxetine prior to initiation of an MAOI).

PRECAUTIONS:
- Use with caution in patients with liver, kidney, or cardiovascular disease.
- *Elderly:* May require decreased dosage
- Adverse effects and side effects are commonly observed before therapeutic effects
- Many side effects are dose dependent and may improve over time
- Taper discontinuation to avoid withdrawal symptoms (although fluoxetine has fewer withdrawal symptoms than other SSRIs due to long half-life).

PATIENT AND FAMILY EDUCATION:
- Should be taken about the same time every day, morning or evening; can be taken with or without food (with food if there is any stomach upset).
- May start with half of lowest effective dose for 3–7 days, then increase to lowest effective dose to diminish side effects.
- Administration time may be adjusted based on observed sedating or activating drug effects.
- May take up to 4–8 weeks to show its maximum effect at this dose, but some may see symptoms of dysthymia improving in as little as 2 weeks.
- If patient plans on becoming pregnant or is pregnant, discuss the benefits versus the risks of using this medicine while pregnant.
- Because this medicine is excreted in the breast milk, nursing mothers should not breastfeed while taking this medicine without prior consultation with a psychiatric nurse practitioner or psychiatrist. Newborns may develop symptoms including feeding or breathing difficulties, seizures, muscle stiffness, jitteriness, or constant crying.
- Do not stop taking this medication unless the health care provider directs. Report side effects or worsening symptoms to the health care provider promptly.
- The medication should be tapered gradually when changing or discontinuing therapy.
- Dosage should be adjusted to reach remission of symptoms and treatment should continue for at least 6–12 months following last reported dysthymic experience.

SPECIAL POPULATIONS:
- *Elderly:* Avoid use in the elderly if possible. Older individuals tend to be more sensitive to medication side effects such as hypotension and anticholinergic effects. They often require adjustment of medication doses for hepatic or renal dysfunction. SSRIs with shorter half-lives or less P-450 inhibition may be more desirable (e.g., citalopram) for geriatric populations. SSRIs have been associated with increased risk of falls in nursing home residents and neurologic effects in patients with Parkinson's disease. Geriatric patients are more prone to SSRI-induced hyponatremia.
- *Pregnancy:* Psychotherapy is the initial choice for most pregnant patients with DD. Most SSRIs are Category C drugs, due to adverse effects observed in animal studies. Thus, an individual risk-benefit analysis must be done to determine appropriate treatment in pregnant women with DD.
- *Children:* It has been approved by the FDA for use in children with depression. Initial SSRI dosing in children typically begins at approx. 50% adult dosing. Increasing doses may require more gradual increments, and discontinuation may require a more gradual taper. Psychiatric consultation is recommended due to black box warning of increased suicidal ideation using SSRI therapy in children.

Paxil, Paxil CR   **paroxetine**

AVAILABLE FORMS: Tablet, 10, 20, 30 and 40 mg; suspension, 10 mg/5 mL (250 mL); controlled-release enteric coated tablet, 12.5, 25 and 37.5 mg.
▶ **Note:** Controlled-release (CR) formulations dissolve in lower intestine and minimize GI distress. Some formulations may be only available as trade name formulations.

DOSAGE: starting dose, 20 mg/day; maintenance dose, 20–60 mg.

ADMINISTRATION: PO, with or without food. Controlled release tables must remain intact and not be split or crushed prior to administration.

SIDE EFFECTS: Due to short-half life, may see greater withdrawal side effects than other drugs in its class. Also may see more weight gain than other medications in its class.
- May cause CNS depression (sedation, fatigue) or activation (insomnia)
- Weight gain
- Nervousness
- Headache and nausea, particularly early in treatment
- Dry mouth
- Excess perspiration
- Serotonin syndrome
- Withdrawal syndrome (including neonatal withdrawal syndrome): Symptoms may include dizziness, muscle aches, headache, nausea, vomiting, gait instability, agitation, and/or "electric shock" sensations.
- Diarrhea
- Sexual dysfunction (approx. 50% of men and women)
- Hyponatremia (e.g., in geriatric patients taking diuretics)
- Side effects are most common during the first or second week of therapy. Starting with a lower dosage and gradually increasing, and taking the medication with food will limit some of these side effects.

DRUG INTERACTIONS:
- *MAOIs:* Extreme risk for serotonin syndrome. Allow 2-week washout period post-MAOI prior to initiation
- *TCAs:* Plasma levels may be increased by SSRIs, so add with caution in low doses
- *ASA and NSAIDs:* Increased risk of bleeding
- *CNS depressants:* May increase depressant effects
- *SSRIs or SARIs:* May cause serotonin syndrome in combination with other medications such as tramadol, high-dose triptans, or the antibiotic linezolid.
- Use with caution in patients taking blood thinners (*Coumadin*), other antidepressants, antihistamines, lithium, TCAs, and certain antibiotics, such as erythromycin, clarithromycin, or azithromycin.

PHARMACOKINETICS:
- Highly bound to plasma proteins and have a large volume of distribution.
- Readily absorbed in the GI tract, metabolized in the liver, and excreted in the urine. Dosages may be decreased in patients with liver or kidney disease.
- Caution advised in elderly clients.
Metabolism: Metabolized in the liver by cytochrome P-450 microsomal enzymes.
Peak plasma levels: Reached in 2–10 hr.
Half-life: Variable, but most SSRIs have half-lives of 20–24 hr. A notable exception is fluoxetine (*Prozac*), and its active metabolite, norfluoxetine, which have half-lives of 2–4 days and 8–9 days, respectively. Hence, addition of serotonergic medications to a patient's regimen must not occur until 2–3 weeks after discontinuation of an SSRI (some recommend a 5-week "washout" period for fluoxetine prior to initiation of an MAOI).

PRECAUTIONS:
- May cause sedation and mental clouding.
- Use with caution in patients with liver, kidney, or cardiovascular disease.
- *Elderly:* May require decreased dosage.
- Adverse effects and side effects are commonly observed before therapeutic effects.
- Many side effects are dose dependent and may improve over time.
- Taper discontinuation to avoid withdrawal symptoms.

PATIENT AND FAMILY EDUCATION:
- Should be taken about the same time every day, morning or evening, and can be taken with or without food (with food if there is any stomach upset).
- May start with half of lowest effective dose for 3–7 days, then increase to lowest effective dose to diminish side effects.
- Administration time may be adjusted based on observed sedating or activating drug effects.
- May take up to 4–8 weeks to show its maximum effect at this dose, but some may see symptoms of dysthymia improving in as little as 2 weeks.
- If patient plans on becoming pregnant or is pregnant, discuss the benefits versus the risks of using this medicine while pregnant.
- Because this medicine is excreted in the breast milk, nursing mothers should not breastfeed while taking this medicine without prior consultation with a psychiatric nurse practitioner or psychiatrist. Newborns may develop symptoms including feeding or breathing difficulties, seizures, muscle stiffness, jitteriness, or constant crying.
- Do not stop taking this medication unless the health care provider directs. Report side effects or worsening symptoms to the health care provider promptly.
- The medication should be tapered gradually when changing therapy or discontinuing.

(cont.)

SCHIZOAFFECTIVE DISORDER: Selective Serotonin Reuptake Inhibitors (SSRIs)

paroxetine (cont.)

- Dosage should be adjusted to reach remission of symptoms and treatment should continue for at least 6–12 months following last reported dysthymic experience.
- Caution is advised when using this drug in the elderly because they may be more sensitive to the effects of the drug. Elderly patients should receive a lower starting dose.

SPECIAL POPULATIONS:
- *Elderly:* ▶ **Caution:** Older individuals tend to be more sensitive to medication side effects such as hypotension and anticholinergic effects. Often require adjustment of medication doses for hepatic or renal dysfunction. SSRIs with shorter half-lives or less P-450 inhibition may be more desirable (e.g., citalopram) for geriatric populations than SSRIs with longer half-lives (e.g., fluoxetine). SSRIs have been associated with increased risk of falls in nursing home residents and neurologic effects in patients with Parkinson's disease. Elderly patients are more prone to SSRI-induced hyponatremia. Paroxetine shows greater anticholinergic and sedating effects than other SSRIs
- *Pregnancy:* Psychotherapy is the initial choice for most pregnant patients with DD. Most SSRIs are Category C drugs, due to adverse effects observed in animal studies. Thus, an individual risk-benefit analysis must be done to determine appropriate treatment in pregnant women with DD. Paroxetine is a Category D drug. If continued during pregnancy, SSRI dosage may need to be increased to maintain euthymia due to physiologic changes associated with pregnancy.
- *Children:* Initial SSRI dosing in children typically begins at approx. 50% adult dosing. Increasing doses may require more gradual increments, and discontinuation may require a more gradual taper. Psychiatric consultation is recommended due to black box warning of increased suicidal ideation using SSRI therapy in children.

sertraline   *Zoloft*

AVAILABLE FORMS: Tablet, 25, 50 and 100 mg; concentrate solution, 20 mg/mL (60 mL)

DOSAGE: Starting dose, 50 mg/day; maintenance dose, 50–200 mg

ADMINISTRATION: PO, with or without food. Concentrate solution must be diluted immediately prior to use with water or juice (other than grapefruit juice).

SIDE EFFECTS: Displays some inhibition of dopamine reuptake, which may be beneficial to some patients (e.g., those experiencing hypersomnia, low energy, or mood reactivity), but problematic to others (e.g., causing overactivation in patients with panic disorder). May see a little more GI side effect (diarrhea) than others in class
- Nervousness, headache and nausea, insomnia; serotonin syndrome; dry mouth, easy bruising, or excess perspiration; diarrhea.
- Withdrawal syndrome (including neonatal withdrawal syndrome): Symptoms may include dizziness, muscle aches, headache, nausea, vomiting, gait instability, agitation, and/or "electric shock" sensations.
- Sexual dysfunction (more than 50% of men and women)
- Hyponatremia (e.g., in geriatric patients taking diuretics)
- Side effects are most common during the first or second week of therapy. Starting with a lower dosage and gradually increasing it, and taking the medication with food will limit some of these side effects.

DRUG INTERACTIONS:
- *MAOIs:* Extreme risk for serotonin syndrome. Allow 2-week washout period post-MAOI prior to initiation
- *TCAs:* Plasma levels may be increased by SSRIs, so add with caution in low doses
- *ASA and NSAIDs:* Increased risk of bleeding
- *CNS depressants:* May increase depressant effects
- *SSRIs or SARIs:* May cause serotonin syndrome in combination with other medications such as tramadol, high-dose triptans, or the antibiotic linezolid.
- Use with caution in patients taking blood thinners (*Coumadin*), other antidepressants, antihistamines, lithium, TCAs, and certain antibiotics, such as erythromycin, clarithromycin, or azithromycin.

PHARMACOKINETICS:
- Highly bound to plasma proteins and have a large volume of distribution.
- Readily absorbed in the GI tract, metabolized in the liver, and excreted in the urine. Dosages may be decreased in patients with liver or kidney disease.
- Caution advised in elderly clients.

Metabolism: Metabolized in the liver by cytochrome P-450 microsomal enzymes.

Peak plasma levels: 2–10 hr

Half-life: Variable, but most SSRIs have half-lives of 20–24 hr. A notable exception is fluoxetine (*Prozac*), and its active metabolite, norfluoxetine, which have half-lives of 2–4 days and 8–9 days, respectively. Hence, addition of serotonergic medications to a patient's regimen must not occur until 2–3 weeks

(cont.)

sertraline (cont.)

after discontinuation of an SSRI (some recommend a 5-week "washout" period for fluoxetine prior to initiation of an MAOI).

PRECAUTIONS:
- May cause sedation and mental clouding.
- Use with caution in patients with liver, kidney, or cardiovascular disease.
- Adverse effects and side effects are commonly observed before therapeutic effects.
- Many side effects are dose dependent and may improve over time.
- Taper discontinuation to avoid withdrawal symptoms.
- *Elderly:* May require decreased dosage.

PATIENT AND FAMILY EDUCATION:
- Should be taken about the same time every day, morning or evening, and can be taken with or without food (with food if there is any stomach upset).
- May start with half of lowest effective dose for 3–7 days, then increase to lowest effective dose to diminish side effects.
- Administration time may be adjusted based on observed sedating or activating drug effects.
- May take up to 4–8 weeks to show its maximum effect at this dose, but some may see symptoms of dysthymia improving in as little as 2 weeks.
- If patient plans on becoming pregnant or is pregnant, discuss the benefits versus the risks of using this medicine while pregnant.
- Because this medicine is excreted in the breast milk, nursing mothers should not breastfeed while taking this medicine without prior consultation with a psychiatric nurse practitioner or psychiatrist. Newborns may develop symptoms including feeding or breathing difficulties, seizures, muscle stiffness, jitteriness, or constant crying.
- Do not stop taking this medication unless the health care provider directs. Report side effects or worsening symptoms to the health care provider promptly.
- The medication should be tapered gradually when changing or discontinuing therapy.

- Dosage should be adjusted to reach remission of symptoms and treatment should continue for at least 6–12 months following last reported dysthymic experience.
- Caution is advised when using this drug in the elderly because they may be more sensitive to the effects of the drug. Elderly patients should receive a lower starting dose.
- Keep these medications out of the reach of children and pets.

SPECIAL POPULATIONS:
- *Elderly:* Older individuals tend to be more sensitive to medication side effects such as hypotension and anticholinergic effects. They often require adjustment of medication doses for hepatic or renal dysfunction. SSRIs with shorter half-lives or less P-450 inhibition may be more desirable (e.g., citalopram) for geriatric populations than SSRIs with longer half-lives (e.g., fluoxetine). SSRIs have been associated with increased risk of falls in nursing home residents and neurologic effects in patients with Parkinson's disease. Elderly patients are more prone to SSRI-induced hyponatremia.
- *Pregnancy:* Psychotherapy is the initial choice for most pregnant patients with DD. Most SSRIs are Category C drugs, due to adverse effects observed in animal studies. Sertraline has been found to have lower cord blood levels than other SSRIs, although the clinical significance is unknown. Thus, an individual risk-benefit analysis must be done to determine appropriate treatment in pregnant women with DD. If continued during pregnancy, SSRI dosage may need to be increased to maintain euthymia due to physiologic changes associated with pregnancy.
- *Children:* Initial SSRI dosing in children typically begins at approx. 50% adult dosing. Increasing doses may require more gradual increments, and discontinuation may require a more gradual taper. Psychiatric consultation is recommended due to black box warning of increased suicidal ideation using SSRI therapy in children.

Class: Mood Stabilizers

Eskalith, Lithobid	lithium

AVAILABLE FORMS: Capsule, 150, 300 and 600 mg; slow-release tablet, 300 mg; controlled-release tablet, 300 and 450 mg; syrup, 300 mg (8 mEq/5 mL)

DOSAGE: *Adults:* 300–600 mg/day to qid or 900 mg controlled-release tablets every 12 hr. Increase dosage based on blood levels. Recommended therapeutic lithium levels are 1–1.5 mEq/L for acute mania and 0.6–1.2 mEq/L for maintenance therapy.

ADMINISTRATION:
- PO
- Give the drug after meals with plenty of water to minimize GI upset.
- Do not crush controlled-release tablets.

SIDE EFFECTS:
- *CNS:* Fatigue, lethargy, coma, epileptiform seizures, tremors, drowsiness, headache, confusion, restlessness, dizziness, psychomotor retardation, blackouts, EEG changes, impaired speech, ataxia, incoordination

(cont.)

lithium (*cont.*)

- *CV:* Arrhythmias, bradycardia, reversible EKG changes, hypotension.
- *EENT:* Tinnitus, blurred vision.
- *GI:* Vomiting, anorexia, diarrhea, thirst, nausea, metallic taste, dry mouth, abdominal pain, flatulence, indigestion.
- *GU:* Polyuria, renal toxicity with long-term use, glycosuria, decreased creatinine clearance, albuminuria.
- *Hematologic:* Leukocytosis with leukocyte count of 14,000 to 18,000/mm.
- *Metabolic:* Transient hyperglycemia, goiter, hypothyroidism, hyponatremia.
- *Musculoskeletal:* Muscle weakness.
- *Skin:* Pruritus, rash, diminished or absent sensation, drying and thinning of hair, psoriasis, acne, alopecia.
- *Other:* Ankle and wrist edema

DRUG INTERACTIONS:
- ACE inhibitors, aminophylline, sodium bicarbonate, urine alkalizers, calcium channel blockers (verapamil), carbamazepine, fluoxetine, methyldopa, NSAIDs, probenecid, neuromuscular blockers, thiazide diuretics.
- Diuretics, especially loop diuretics, may inhibit lithium elimination and increase lithium toxicity.
- Caffeine may decrease lithium levels and drug effects. Advise patients who ingest large amounts of caffeine.

PHARMACOKINETICS:
- Probably alters chemical transmitters in the CNS, possibly by interfering with ionic pump mechanisms in brain cells, and may compete with or replace sodium ions. With PO dose onset the duration of action is unknown. The peak action is between 30 min and 1 hr.

Half-life: 18 hr (adolescents) to 36 hr (elderly).

PRECAUTIONS:
- May increase glucose and creatinine levels. May decrease sodium, T3, T4, and protein-bound iodine levels.
- May increase WBC and neutrophil counts.
- Contraindicated if therapy can't be closely monitored.
- Avoid using in pregnant patients unless benefits outweigh risks.
- Use with caution in patients receiving neuromuscular blockers and diuretics; in elderly or debilitated patients; and in patients with thyroid disease, seizure disorder, infection, renal or CV disease, severe debilitation or dehydration, or sodium depletion.

▶**Alert:** Drug has a narrow therapeutic margin of safety. Determining drug level is crucial to the safe use of the drug. Don't use the drug in patients who can't have regular tests done. Monitor levels 8–12 hr after the first dose, the morning before the second dose is given, two or three times weekly

for the first month, and then weekly to monthly during maintenance therapy.
- When the drug level is less than 1.5 mEq/L, adverse reactions are usually mild.
- Monitor baseline EKG, thyroid studies, renal studies, and electrolyte levels.
- Check fluid intake and output, especially when surgery is scheduled.
- Weigh patient daily; check for edema or sudden weight gain.
- Adjust fluid and salt ingestion to compensate if excessive loss occurs from protracted diaphoresis or diarrhea. Under normal conditions, patient's fluid intake should be 2 to 3 L daily, with a balanced diet with adequate salt intake.
- Check urine specific gravity and report levels below 1.005, which may indicate diabetes insipidus.
- Drug alters glucose tolerance in diabetics. Monitor glucose level closely.
- Perform outpatient follow-up of thyroid and renal functions every 6–12 months. Palpate thyroid to check for enlargement.

PATIENT AND FAMILY EDUCATION:
- Tell the patient to take the drug with plenty of water and after meals to minimize GI upset.
- Explain the importance of having regular blood tests to determine drug levels; even slightly high values can be dangerous.
- Warn patients and caregivers to expect transient nausea, large amounts of urine, thirst, and discomfort during the first few days of therapy and to watch for evidence of toxicity (diarrhea, vomiting, tremor, drowsiness, muscle weakness, incoordination).
- Instruct patients to withhold one dose and call the prescriber if signs and symptoms of toxicity appear, but not to stop drug abruptly.
- Warn patients to avoid hazardous activities that require alertness and good psychomotor coordination until the CNS effects of drug are known.
- Tell patients not to switch brands or take other prescription or OTC drugs without the prescriber's guidance.
- Tell patients to wear or carry medical identification at all times.

SPECIAL POPULATIONS:
- *Elderly:* Initial dose reduction and possibly lower maintenance doses due to age-related changes and sensitivity to side effects.
- *Pregnancy:* Category D. Positive evidence of fetal harm has been demonstrated.
- *Children:* Not approved in children less than 12 years of age; use with caution and monitor closely for side effects and suicidality. Children may experience more frequent and severe side effects.

| *Depacon, Depakene, Depakote, Depakote ER, Depakote Sprinkle* | **valproate sodium, valproic acid, divalproex sodium** |

AVAILABLE FORMS: *Valproate sodium:* Syrup, 250 mg/5 mL; capsule, 250 mg; tablet (extended release), 250 and 500 mg. *Divalproex sodium:* Capsule (sprinkle), 125 mg; tablet (delayed-release), 125, 250 and 500 mg; tablet (extended-release), 250 and 500 mg

DOSAGE: *Adults:* Initially, 750 mg *Depakote* daily PO in divided doses, or 25 mg/kg *Depakote ER* once daily. Adjust dosage based on patient's response; maximum dose of 60 mg/kg daily.

ADMINISTRATION:
- Give PO drug with food or milk to reduce adverse GI effects.
- Do not mix syrup with carbonated beverages as the mixture may be irritating to oral mucosa.
- Capsules may be swallowed whole or opened and contents sprinkled on a teaspoonful of soft food. Patient should swallow the capsule immediately without chewing.
- Monitor drug level, and adjust dosage as needed.

SIDE EFFECTS:
- *CNS:* Asthenia, dizziness, headache, insomnia, nervousness, somnolence, tremor, abnormal thinking, amnesia, ataxia, depression, emotional upset, fever, sedation.
- *CV:* Chest pain, edema, hypertension, hypotension, tachycardia.
- *EENT:* Blurred vision, diplopia, nystagmus, pharyngitis, rhinitis, tinnitus
- *GI:* Abdominal pain, anorexia, diarrhea, dyspepsia, nausea, vomiting, pancreatitis, constipation, increased appetite.
- *Hematologic:* Bone marrow suppression, hemorrhage, thrombocytopenia, bruising, petechiae.
- *Hepatic:* Hepatotoxicity.
- *Metabolic:* Hyperammonemia, weight gain.
- *Musculoskeletal:* Back and neck pain.
- *Respiratory:* Bronchitis, dyspnea.
- *Skin:* Alopecia, flu syndrome, infection, erythema multiforme, hypersensitivity reactions, Stevens-Johnson syndrome, rash, photosensitivity reactions, pruritus

DRUG INTERACTIONS: Aspirin, chlorpromazine, clonazepam, topiramate, cimetidine, erythromycin, felbamate, carbamazepine, lamotrigine, phenobarbital, phenytoin, rifampin, warfarin, zidovudine. Alcohol use is discouraged.

PHARMACOKINETICS:
Peak action: Oral, between 15 min and 4 hr. Facilitates the effects of the inhibitory neurotransmitter GABA.
Half-life: 6–16 hr

PRECAUTIONS:
- May increase ammonia, ALT, AST, and bilirubin lab levels.

- May increase eosinophil count and bleeding time. May decrease platelet, RBC, and WBC.
- May cause false-positive results for urine ketone levels.
- Contraindicated in patients hypersensitive to the drug, with hepatic disease or significant hepatic dysfunction, and, with a UCD.
- Safety and efficacy of *Depakote ER* in children less than 10 years have not been established.
- Obtain liver function test results, platelet count, and PT and INR before starting therapy, and monitor these values periodically.
- Adverse reactions may not be caused by valproic acid alone because it is usually used with other anticonvulsants.
- When changing the drug from *Depakote* to *Depakote ER* for adults and children aged 10 and above with seizures, ensure that the extended-release dose is 8–20% higher than the regular dose administered previously. The manufacturer's PI should be checked for more details.
- Divalproex sodium has a lower risk of adverse GI reactions.
- Never withdraw a drug suddenly as this may worsen seizures. Call the prescriber at once if adverse reactions develop.
- Patients at high risk for hepatotoxicity include those with congenital metabolic disorders, mental retardation, or organic brain disease; those taking multiple anticonvulsants; and children younger than 2 years of age.
- Notify the prescriber if tremors occur; a dosage reduction may be needed.
- weight gain is common. Monitor BMI and assess for pre-diabetes and dyslipidemia.
- sedation is common.
- When changing the drug from a brand-name to a generic one for patients, caution must be exercised as breakthrough seizures may occur.
- May cause thrombocytopenia or tremors

▶**Alert:** Sometimes fatal, hyperammonemic encephalopathy may occur when starting valproate therapy in patients with UCD. Evaluate patients with UCD risk factors before starting valproate therapy. Patients who develop symptoms of unexplained hyperammonemic encephalopathy during valproate therapy should stop taking the drug, undergo prompt appropriate treatment, and be evaluated for underlying UCD.

▶**Alert:** Fatal hepatotoxicity may follow nonspecific symptoms, such as malaise, fever, and lethargy. If these symptoms occur during therapy, notify the prescriber at once because the patient who might be developing hepatic dysfunction must stop taking the drug.

▶**Alert:** Life-threatening pancreatitis has been reported following initiation of therapy as well as after prolonged use. Monitor the patient for developing symptoms and discontinue treatment if pancreatitis is suspected.

(cont.)

valproate sodium, valproic acid, divalproex sodium (*cont.*)

PATIENT AND FAMILY EDUCATION:
- Take the drug with food or milk to reduce adverse GI effects.
- It may take several weeks or longer to optimize mood stabilizing effects
- Capsules may either be swallowed whole or carefully opened and contents sprinkled on a teaspoonful of soft food. Swallow the capsule immediately without chewing.
- Keep drugs out of children's reach.
- Warn about the consequences of stopping drug therapy abruptly.
- Avoid driving and indulging in other potentially hazardous activities that require mental alertness until the drug's effects on the CNS are known.
- Call the prescriber if malaise, weakness, lethargy, facial swelling, loss of appetite, or vomiting occurs.
- Instruct women to inform the prescriber if they become pregnant or have plans to start a family during the course of therapy.

SPECIAL POPULATIONS:
- *Elderly:* Caution is advised when using this drug in the elderly due to more sensitivity to the drug. Initiate treatment at a lower dose and then escalate the dose more slowly.
- *Pregnancy:* Category D. This medication should only be used when required utmost during pregnancy as the drug is secreted into breast milk. Increased risk of neural tube defects (1 in 20) and other major birth defects have been reported, especially when the fetus is exposed during first 12 weeks of pregnancy.
- *Children:* Caution must be exercised when using this drug in a child or adolescent as a balance must be established between the potential risks and the clinical need. The drug is not recommended for use in children or adolescents under 18 years of age who are suffering from bipolar disorder.

Schizophrenia

OVERVIEW
- A chronic, severe, and disabling brain disorder characterized by disordered thoughts, delusions, hallucinations, and bizarre or catatonic behavior.
- According to the *DSM-IV-TR*, the diagnosis of schizophrenia is given if two or more of the following symptoms present for a significant portion of time during a 1-month period (or less if successfully treated): delusions, hallucinations, disorganized speech, grossly disorganized or catatonic behavior, negative symptoms.
- Only one symptom is required for schizophrenia if delusions are bizarre or hallucinations consist of a voice keeping up a running commentary on a person's behavior or thoughts, or two or more voices conversing with each other.
- Usually one or more major areas of functioning such as work, interpersonal relations, self-care, and school are markedly below the level achieved prior to the onset.
- *Differential diagnosis*: Psychotic disorder due to a general medical condition, delirium or dementia, substance-induced psychotic disorder, substance-induced delirium, substance-induced persisting dementia, substance-related disorders, brief psychotic disorder, delusional disorder, schizophreniform disorder, psychotic disorder not otherwise specified, schizoaffective disorder, mood disorder with psychotic features, mood disorder with catatonic features, depressive disorder not otherwise specified, bipolar disorder not otherwise specified,

pervasive developmental disorders (e.g., autistic disorder), childhood presentations combining disorganized speech (from a communication disorder) and disorganized behavior (from ADHD), schizotypal personality disorder, schizoid personality disorder, or paranoid personality disorder.
- *Diagnostic workup*: Physical and mental status examination, CBC, hepatic, renal and thyroid function tests, electrolytes, glucose, B12, folate, and calcium level. For patients with a history for suspicion: check HIV, RPR, ceruloplasmin, ANA, urine for culture and sensitivity and/or drugs of abuse, and 24-hr urine collections for porphyrins, copper, or heavy metals, pregnancy test for female patients of childbearing age.
- Schizophrenia has been found to run in families. People who have first-degree relatives (a parent, sibling) or second-degree relatives (grandparents, aunts, uncles, cousins) with this disorder develop schizophrenia more often than the general population. The identical twin of a person with schizophrenia has the highest risk (40–65%) of developing this disorder.
- Several genes have been found to be strongly associated with schizophrenia. However, current scientific evidence suggests that interactions between genes and the environment are necessary to develop schizophrenia. Environmental risk factors (e.g., exposure to viruses or malnutrition in the womb, problems during birth), and psychosocial factors (e.g., stressful conditions) increase the risk of schizophrenia.

- Schizophrenia occurs in 1% of the general population, affects men and women equally, and occurs at similar rates in all ethnic groups worldwide. Onset of symptoms typically emerges in men in their late teens and early 20s and in women in their mid-20s to early 30s.
- Individuals with schizophrenia are found to abuse alcohol and/or drugs more often than the general population. Abusing substances can reduce the effectiveness of treatment. Patients may need higher doses of psychotropic medication if they smoke.
- Patients with schizophrenia attempt suicide much more often than people in the general population; about 10% succeed, especially young adult males.

Psychopharmacology of Schizophrenia

- *Second-generation (atypical) antipsychotic drugs*: These are used as a first-line treatment of schizophrenia due to fewer side effects when compared with conventional or typical antipsychotic medications.
  - Commonly used *second-generation* atypical antipsychotic drugs include aripiprazole (*Abilify*), clozapine (*Clozaril*), olanzapine (*Zyprexa*), quetiapine (*Seroquel*), quetiapine fumarate (*Seroquel XR*), risperidone (*Risperdal*), long-acting risperidone (*Risperdal Consta*), ziprasidone (*Geodon*), and paliperidone (*Invega*). A newer atypical antipsychotic is asenapine (*Saphris*) and is getting good reviews as effective for schizophrenia especially if there is a mood component involved.
  - Clozapine (*Clozaril*) is the drug of choice for treatment-resistant schizophrenia (little or no symptomatic response to at least 2 antipsychotic trials of an adequate duration—at least 6 weeks—and at a therapeutic dose range), and it has a lower risk of TD. However, due to the potential side effect of agranulocytosis (loss of WBC), a blood test is required weekly for the first 6 months, and biweekly for the next 6 months. Monitoring can be done monthly if no hematological problems are found after 1 year of clozapine treatment.
- *First-generation (typical or conventional) antipsychotic drugs:*
  - Commonly used *first-generation* (typical or conventional) antipsychotic drugs: haloperidol (*Haldol*), fluphenazine (*Prolixin*), thioridazine (*Mellaril*), trifluoperazine (*Stelazine*)
  - Low-dose, high-potency antipsychotics such as haloperidol IM 2 to 5 mg have been found to be safe and effective in managing agitated psychiatric patients. Subsequent doses may be needed within 1 hr depending on responses.
- *Short-acting benzodiazepine:* A low dose of a short-acting benzodiazepine (e.g., lorazepam 0.5–2 mg every 1h IM or IV prn) is effective in decreasing agitation during the acute phase, and may reduce the amount of antipsychotic needed to control patients' psychotic symptoms.
- ECT in combination with antipsychotic medications can be considered for patients with schizophrenia who do not respond to antipsychotic agents. The rate and number of ECT varies from patient to patient depending on their clinical responses and side effects.
- Social skills training aimed to improve the way patients with schizophrenia interact with others (e.g., poor eye contact, odd facial expressions, inaccurate or lack of perceptions of emotions in other people) has been found to be effective in reducing relapse rate.
- CBT helps patients with schizophrenia acquire some insight into their illness and appears to be effective in reducing the severity of symptoms and decreasing the risk of relapse.
- DBT combines cognitive and behavioral theories. Patients with schizophrenia may benefit from DBT to improve interpersonal skills.
- Individual psychotherapy focuses on forming a therapeutic alliance between therapists and patients with schizophrenia. A good therapeutic alliance is likely to help patients with schizophrenia remain in therapy, increase adherence to treatments, and have positive outcomes at 2-year follow-up evaluations.
- Personal therapy, a recently developed form of individual treatment, uses social skills and relaxation exercises, self-reflection, self-awareness, exploration of vulnerability and stress, and psychoeducation to enhance personal and social adjustment of patients with schizophrenia. Patients who receive personal therapy have shown better social adjustment and a lower rate of relapse after 3 years than those not receiving it.
- Many patients with schizophrenia benefit from art therapy because it helps them communicate with and share their inner word with others.
- Employment programs that include individualized job development, rapid placement, ongoing job supports, and integration of mental health and vocational services have been found to be effective in helping patients with schizophrenia to achieve employment.

SCHIZOPHRENIA

CLASS	DRUG
Antipsychotic Drugs, Atypical (Second Generation)	**First-Line Drug Therapy**
	aripiprazole (*Abilify, Abilify Discmelt ODT, Abilify Liquid, Abilify IM Injection*) clozapine (*Clozaril, Fazaclo*) olanzapine (*Zyprexa*) quetiapine (*Seroquel, Seroquel XR*) risperidone (*Risperdal, Risperdal Consta*) ziprasidone (*Geodon, Geodon IM Injections*) paliperidone (*Invega*) asenapine (*Saphris*)
Antipsychotic Drugs, Typical (First Generation)	**Second-Line Drug Therapy**
	haloperidol (*Haldol*) fluphenazine (*Prolixin*) thioridazine (*Mellaril*) trifluoperazine (Stelazine)
Benzodiazepines (BZDs)	**During Acute Phase**
	lorazepam (*Ativan*)

Class: Antipsychotic Drugs, Atypical (Second Generation)

aripiprazole — *Abilify, Abilify Discmelt ODT, Abilify Liquid, Abilify IM Injection*

INDICATIONS: Schizophrenia (13 years and older), manic and mixed episodes associated with bipolar I disorder, adjunctive treatment to antidepressants for MDD, agitation associated with schizophrenia or bipolar disorder, manic or mixed.

AVAILABLE FORMS: Tablet, 2, 5, 10, 15, 20, and 30 mg; tablet, orally disintegrating, 10, and 15 mg; solution, oral, 1 mg/mL; IM injection, solution, 9.75 mg/1.3 mL

DOSAGE: 15 to 30 mg/day

ADMINISTRATION:
- Tablets may be given with or without food.
- Parenteral administration is intended for IM use only; inject slowly, deep into muscle mass.
- *IM injection has not been evaluated in children.*
- *Do not give IV or SC.*
- Oral solution may be substituted for tablets on a mg-per-mg basis up to a 25 mg dose. Patients receiving 30 mg tablets should receive 25 mg of solution.
- Dosing for the orally disintegrating tablet is the same as the oral tablet.
- Do not open the orally disintegrating tablets until ready to administer. The orally disintegrating tablet should be taken without liquid. Do not split the orally disintegrating tablet.
- Use oral aripiprazole 10 to 30 mg/day instead of IM aripiprazole as soon as possible if ongoing therapy is indicated.

SIDE EFFECTS: Nausea, vomiting; dizziness, insomnia, akathisia, activation; headache, asthenia, sedation; constipation; orthostatic hypotension (occasionally during initial phase); increased risk of death and cerebrovascular events in elderly with dementia-related psychosis; TD;

neuroleptic malignant syndrome (rare); seizures (rare)

DRUG INTERACTIONS:
- CYP450 3A4 inhibitors (e.g., nefazodone, fluvoxamine, fluoxetine), CYP450 2D6 inhibitors (e.g., paroxetine, fluoxetine, duloxetine), and quinidine may increase plasma levels of aripiprazole.
- Carbamazepine and other CYP450 3A4 inducers may decrease plasma levels of aripiprazole.
- Aripiprazole may enhance effects of antihypertensive medications.
- Aripiprazole may antagonize levodopa and dopamine agonists.
- ▶**Alert:** This list may not describe all possible interactions. Instruct clients to provide a list of all medicines, herbs, nonprescription drugs, or dietary supplements they use. Also instruct clients to inform if they smoke, drink alcohol, or use illegal drugs.

PHARMACOKINETICS:
Excretion: About 25% of a single oral dose is excreted in urine (less than 1% unchanged) and 55% in feces (18% as unchanged drug)
Metabolism: Primarily metabolized by CYP450 2D6 and CYP450 3A4
Half-life: 75 hr (aripiprazole) and 94 hr (active aripiprazole metabolite)

PRECAUTIONS:
- Dysphagia is associated with use of aripiprazole. Use with caution in patients who are at risk for aspiration pneumonia.
- Use with caution in patients with conditions that may develop hypotension (dehydration, overheating, etc.).
- Do not use in patients who are allergic to aripiprazole.

(cont.)

aripiprazole (cont.)

PATIENT AND FAMILY EDUCATION:

- Store aripiprazole at 59° to 86°F. It can be used for up to 6 months after opening. Protect injection from light by storing in carton until use.
- If you become pregnant, contact provider. You will need to discuss the benefits and risks of using aripiprazole orally disintegrating tablets while you are pregnant.
- Discuss with provider if you have any of these conditions. A dose adjustment or special tests to safely take aripiprazole may be needed:
  - Liver or kidney disease
  - Heart disease, high BP, heart rhythm problems
  - History of heart attack or stroke
  - History of low WBC counts
  - History of breast cancer
  - Seizures or epilepsy
  - Personal or family history of diabetes
  - Trouble swallowing.
  - PKU
- Talk to provider if you have signs of hyperglycemia such as increased thirst or urination, excessive hunger, or weakness. If you have diabetes, check blood sugar levels on a regular basis while taking aripiprazole.

SPECIAL POPULATIONS:

- *Elderly:* Dosage adjustment is generally not required. Elderly with dementia-related psychosis treated with atypical antipsychotics are at higher risk of death and cerebrovascular events.
- *Renal impairment:* No dosage adjustment is needed.
- *Hepatic impairment:* No dosage adjustment is required.
- *Cardiac impairment:* Use with caution because of the risk of orthostatic hypotension.
- *Pregnancy:* It is not known if aripiprazole orally disintegrating tablets can cause harm to the fetus.
- *Lactation:* Although there are no data on the excretion of aripiprazole into human milk, it is suggested that women receiving aripiprazole should not breastfeed.
- *Children and adolescents:* Aripiprazole is approved for schizophrenia (age 13 and older) and manic/mixed episodes (age 10 and older). Should be monitored more frequently than adults. May tolerate lower doses better.

Clozaril, Fazaclo   **clozapine**

INDICATIONS: Treatment-resistant schizophrenia, reduction in risk of recurrent suicidal behavior in patients with schizophrenia or schizoaffective disorder.

AVAILABLE FORMS: Tablet, 12.5, 25 (scored), 50, and 100 mg (scored); orally disintegrating tablet, 12.5, 25, 50, and 100 mg

DOSAGE: 300 to 450 mg/day

ADMINISTRATION:

- Tablets may be given with or without food.
- Take the regular oral tablet with a full glass of water.
- The orally disintegrating tablet (*Fazaclo*) can be taken without water. Advise patients to keep the tablet in its blister pack until ready to take. The patient should gently peel back the foil from the blister pack and drop the tablet onto dry hand; place the tablet in mouth; it will begin to dissolve right away; allow it to dissolve in the mouth without chewing; swallow several times as the tablet dissolves. If desired, advise patients to drink liquid to help swallow the dissolved tablet.
- If one-half of an orally disintegrating tablet is prescribed, advise patients to break the tablet in half and throw the other half away. DO NOT save the other half for later use.
- If patients stop taking clozapine for more than 2 days in a row, caution patients to call providers before starting to take it again.

- Store clozapine at room temperature away from moisture and heat.

SIDE EFFECTS: May increase risk for diabetes and dyslipidemia; increase salivation; sweating; weight gain; dizziness, sedation, headache, tachycardia, hypotension; nausea, dry mouth, constipation; increased risk of death and cerebrovascular events in elderly with dementia-related psychosis; hyperglycemia; agranulocytosis (includes flu-like symptoms or signs of infection); seizure; neuroleptic malignant syndrome (more likely when it is used with another agent); pulmonary embolism (can include deep vein thrombosis or respiratory symptoms); myocarditis; TD (rare)

DRUG INTERACTIONS:

- Risk or severity of bone marrow suppression may be increased if given in conjunction with medications that suppress bone marrow.
- Use with caution if given in conjunction with alcohol, CNS depressants, or general anesthesia.
- May enhance effects of antihypertensive drugs.
- May need to reduce clozapine dose if given in conjunction with CYP450 1A2 inhibitors (e.g., fluvoxamine).
- May need to increase clozapine dose if given in conjunction with CYP450 1A2 inducers (e.g., cigarette smoke).
- CYP450 2D6 inhibitors (e.g., paroxetine, fluoxetine, and duloxetine) and CYP450 3A4 inhibitors (e.g., nefazodone, fluvoxamine, and

(cont.)

SCHIZOPHRENIA: Antipsychotic Drugs, Atypical (Second Generation)

clozapine (*cont.*)

fluoxetine) can raise clozapine levels, but usually dosage adjustment is not required.

▶**Alert:** This list may not describe all possible interactions. Instruct clients to provide a list of all the medicines, herbs, nonprescription drugs, or dietary supplements they use.

PHARMACOKINETICS:

Metabolism: Metabolized by multiple CYP450 enzymes including 1A2, 2D6, and 3A4
Half-life: 5 to 16 hr

PRECAUTIONS:

- Increased risk of fatal myocarditis, especially during, but not limited to, the first month of therapy. Promptly discontinue clozapine if myocarditis is suspected.
- Life-threatening agranulocytosis can occur. Baseline WBC and ANC should be done before initiation of treatment, during treatment, and for at least 4 weeks after discontinuing treatment.
- Use with caution in patients with glaucoma or enlarged prostate.
- *Do not use in patients with:*
  - Myeloproliferative disorder
  - Uncontrolled seizure
  - Granulocytopenia
  - Paralytic ileus
  - CNS depression
  - Allergic symptoms to clozapine

PATIENT AND FAMILY EDUCATION:

- Clozapine will only be provided in 1- or 2-week supplies, depending on frequency of WBC monitoring. Follow-up visits and weekly blood cell counts are required to monitor therapy and to keep appointments.
- Take prescribed dose with or without food. Take with food if stomach upset occurs.
- Keep tablet in unopened blister until just before use. Remove tablet by peeling the foil from the back of the blister and then immediately place the tablet (or half tablet if ordered) in mouth, allow the tablet to disintegrate, and then swallow with saliva.
- Do not stop taking clozapine when feeling better.
- If medication needs to be discontinued, it will be slowly withdrawn over a period of 1 to 2 weeks unless safety concerns (e.g., low WBC) require a more rapid withdrawal.
- *Immediately report to provider* if any of these conditions occur: altered mental status, change in personality or mood, chest pain, fever, flu-like symptoms, frequent urination, general body discomfort, involuntary body or facial movements, lethargy, mucous membrane sores or other signs of possible infection, muscle rigidity,

pounding in the chest, rapid or difficult breathing, rapid or irregular heartbeat, seizures, sore throat, sweating, swelling of feet or ankles, unexplained fatigue, unexplained shortness of breath, unquenchable thirst, weakness, or weight gain.

- *If you have diabetes,* monitor blood glucose more frequently when drug is started or dose is changed and inform provider of significant changes in readings.
- *If you are taking antihypertensive drugs,* monitor BP at regular intervals.
- *If you have history of seizures or factors predisposing to seizures,* clozapine may cause seizures. Do not engage in any activity in which sudden loss of consciousness could cause serious risk to you or others (e.g., driving, swimming, climbing).
- *Avoid* strenuous activity during periods of high temperature or humidity.
- *Avoid* alcoholic beverages and sedatives (e.g., diazepam) while taking clozapine.
- Get up slowly from lying or sitting position and avoid sudden position changes to prevent postural hypotension. Hot tubs and hot showers or baths may make dizziness worse.
- Take sips of water, suck on ice chips or sugarless hard candy, or chew sugarless gum if dry mouth occurs.
- Clozapine may impair your judgment, thinking, or motor skills, or it may cause drowsiness. Thus, use with caution while driving or performing other tasks requiring mental alertness until tolerance is determined.

SPECIAL POPULATIONS:

- *Elderly:* May tolerate lower doses better. Elderly with dementia-related psychosis treated with atypical antipsychotics are at higher risk of death and cerebrovascular events.
- *Renal impairment*: Used with caution.
- *Hepatic impairment*: Used with caution.
- *Cardiac impairment:* Use with caution especially if patient is taking concomitant medication.
- *Pregnancy:* Category B. Animal studies do not show adverse effects. There are no controlled studies in humans. Clozapine should be used only when the potential benefits outweigh potential risks to the fetus.
- *Lactation:* It is not known if clozapine is secreted in human breast milk. It is recommended to either discontinue drug or bottle feed. Infants of women who choose to breastfeed while on this drug should be monitored for possible adverse effect.
- *Children and adolescents:* Safety and efficacy have not been established for this population. Should be monitored more frequently than adults.

▶**Note:** Fixed-dose olanzapine/fluoxetine is marketed under the trade name *Symbyax*.

INDICATIONS: Schizophrenia, monotherapy or combination therapy for acute mixed or manic episodes associated with bipolar I disorder, maintenance monotherapy of bipolar I disorder, agitation associated with schizophrenia or bipolar I disorder.

AVAILABLE FORMS: Tablet, 2.5, 5, 7.5, 10, 15, and 20 mg; orally disintegrating tablet, 5, 10, 15, and 20 mg; IM formulation, 5 mg/mL (each vial contains 10 mg); olanzapine–fluoxetine combination capsule, 6 mg/25 mg, 6 mg/50 mg, 12 mg/25 mg, 12 mg/50 mg

DOSAGE:
- 10 to 20 mg/day (PO or IM)
- 6 to 12 mg/olanzapine/25 to 50 mg fluoxetine (olanzapine–fluoxetine combination)

ADMINISTRATION:
- Tablets may be given with or without food.
- Advise patient to take the missed dose as soon as remembered. Skip missed dose if it is almost time for the next scheduled dose. Do not take extra medicine to make up the missed dose.
- Store at room temperature away from moisture, heat, and light.

SIDE EFFECTS: Can increase risk for diabetes and dyslipidemia; dizziness, sedation; weight gain; dry mouth, constipation, dyspepsia; peripheral edema; joint pain, back pain, chest pain, extremity pain, abnormal gait, ecchymosis; tachycardia; orthostatic hypotension (usually during initial dose titration); hyperglycemia; increased risk of death and cerebrovascular events in elderly with dementia-related psychosis; TD (rare); rash on exposure to sunlight (rare); neuroleptic malignant syndrome (rare); seizures (rare)

DRUG INTERACTIONS:
- May increase effects of antihypertensive medications
- May antagonize levodopa and dopamine agonists
- May need to reduce dose if given with CYP450 1A2 inhibitors (e.g., fluvoxamine)
- May need to increase dose if given with CYP450 1A2 inducers (e.g., cigarette smoke, carbamazepine)

▶**Alert:** This list may not describe all possible interactions. Instruct clients to provide a list of all the medicines, herbs, nonprescription drugs, or dietary supplements they use.

PHARMACOKINETICS:
Metaboliam: Metabolites are inactive
Half-life: 21 to 54 hr

PRECAUTIONS:
- Use with caution in patients with conditions that predispose to hypotension (dehydration,

overheating). Watch closely for hypotension if given IM formulation.
- Use with caution in patients with prostatic hypertrophy, narrow angle-closure glaucoma, paralytic ileus.
- Use with caution in patients who are at risk for aspiration pneumonia.
- IM formulation is not recommended to be given with parenteral benzodiazepines. If patients need a parenteral benzodiazepine, it should be given at least 1 hr after IM formulation olanzapine.
- *Do not use if there is a proven allergy.*
- *Do not give IM formulation:*
  - If patient has unstable medical condition (e.g., AMI, unstable angina pectoris, severe hypotension and/or bradycardia, sick sinus syndrome, recent heart surgery).
  - If patient has known risks of narrow angle-closure glaucoma.

PATIENT AND FAMILY EDUCATION:
- Take exactly as prescribed by the provider. Do not take in larger or smaller amounts or for longer than recommended.
- Can be taken with or without food.
- For olanzapine orally disintegrating tablets, keep the tablet in its blister pack until patient is ready to take it. Open the package and peel back the foil from the tablet blister. Do not push a tablet through the foil. Using dry hands, remove the tablet and place it in the mouth; it will begin to dissolve right away.
- Do not swallow the tablet whole. Allow it to dissolve in the mouth without chewing. If desired, drink liquid to help swallow the dissolved tablet.
- *If you have diabetes,* check blood sugar levels on a regular basis while taking olanzapine.
- You can gain weight or have high cholesterol and triglycerides while taking this drug, especially if teenaged. Your blood will need to be tested often.
- Do not stop taking the drug suddenly without first talking to provider, even if you feel fine. You may have serious side effects if you stop taking the drug suddenly.
- Call provider if symptoms do not improve or get worse.
- Store at room temperature away from moisture, heat, and light.

SPECIAL POPULATIONS:
- *Elderly:*
  - May tolerate lower doses better. Elderly with dementia-related psychosis treated with atypical antipsychotics are at higher risk of death and cerebrovascular events. It can increase incidence of stroke.
  - If IM formulation is given, the recommended starting dose is 2.5 to 5 mg. A second injection of 2.5 to 5 mg may be given 2 hr after the

(cont.)

olanzapine (cont.)

first injection. No more than three injections should be administered within 24 hr.

- *Renal impairment*: No dose adjustment is required for oral formulation. Consider lower starting dose (5 mg) for IM formulation. It is not removed by hemodialysis.
- *Hepatic impairment*: Starting oral dose 5 mg for patients with moderate-to-severe hepatic function impairment; increase dose with caution. Consider lower starting dose (5 mg) for IM formulation. Check patient liver function tests a few times a year.
- *Cardiac impairment:* Use with caution because of risk of orthostatic hypotension.
- *Pregnancy:* Category C. Some animal studies show adverse effects. There are no controlled studies in humans. Should be used only when the potential benefits outweigh potential risks

to the fetus. Olanzapine may be preferable to anticonvulsant mood stabilizers if treatment is required during pregnancy.

- *Lactation*: It is not known if olanzapine is secreted in human breast milk. It is recommended to either discontinue drug or bottle feed. Infants of women who choose to breastfeed while on this drug should be monitored for possible adverse effect.
- *Children and adolescents:*
  - Probably safe and effective for behavioral disturbances in this population.
  - IM formulation has not been studied in patients younger than 18 years, and is not recommended for use in this population.
  - Should be monitored more frequently than adults.

quetiapine   *Seroquel, Seroquel XR*

INDICATIONS: Schizophrenia, depressive episodes associated with bipolar disorder, monotherapy or combination therapy for acute manic episodes associated with bipolar I disorder, acute and maintenance treatment of schizophrenia.

AVAILABLE FORMS: Tablet, 25, 50, 100, 200, 300, and 400 mg; extended-release tablet, 200, 300, and 400 mg

DOSAGE:
- 400 to 800 mg/day in one (*Seroquel XR*) or two (*Seroquel*) doses for schizophrenia and bipolar mania
- 300 mg once per day for bipolar depression

ADMINISTRATION:
- Tablets may be given with or without food.
- Take this medicine with a full glass of water.
- Advise patient not to crush, chew, or break an extended-release tablet. Swallow the pill whole. Breaking the pill may cause too much of the drug to be released at one time.
- Advise patient to take the missed dose as soon as remembered. Skip the missed dose if it is almost time for the next scheduled dose. Do not take extra medicine to make up the missed dose.

SIDE EFFECTS: Can increase risk for diabetes and dyslipidemia; dizziness, sedation; dry mouth, constipation, dyspepsia, abdominal pain, weight gain; tachycardia; hyperglycemia; increased risk of death and cerebrovascular events in elderly with dementia-related psychosis; orthostatic hypotension (usually during initial dose titration); neuroleptic malignant syndrome (rare); seizures (rare)

DRUG INTERACTIONS:
- May increase effects of antihypertensive medications

- Plasma levels of quetiapine may be increased if given in conjunction with CYP450 3A4 and CYP450 2D6 inhibitors. However, no dose adjustment is required.

▶**Alert:** This list may not describe all possible interactions. Instruct clients to provide a list of all the medicines, herbs, nonprescription drugs, or dietary supplements they use.

PHARMACOKINETICS:
Metabolism: Metabolites are inactive
Half-life: 6 to 7 hr

PRECAUTIONS:
- Use with caution in patients who are at risk for aspiration pneumonia.
- Manufacturer recommends to examine for cataracts before and every 6 months after starting quetiapine.
- *Do not use if there is a proven allergy.*

PATIENT AND FAMILY EDUCATION:
- Take exactly as prescribed by the provider. Do not take in larger or smaller amounts or for longer than recommended.
- Can be taken with or without food.
- Quetiapine can cause side effects that may impair thinking or reactions. Be careful if you drive or do anything that requires you to be awake and alert.
- Quetiapine may cause high blood sugar (hyperglycemia). Talk to provider if any signs of hyperglycemia such as increased thirst or urination, excessive hunger, or weakness. If diabetic, check blood sugar levels on a regular basis.
- Avoid becoming overheated or dehydrated during exercise and in hot weather. You may be more prone to heat stroke.
- Avoid getting up too fast from a sitting or lying position. Get up slowly and steady yourself to prevent a fall.

(cont.)

quetiapine (cont.)

- *Avoid drinking alcohol.*
- *Stop using this medication and call provider immediately* if you have very stiff (rigid) muscles, high fever, sweating, confusion, fast or uneven heartbeats, tremors; feel like you might pass out; have jerky muscle movements you cannot control, trouble swallowing, problems with speech; have blurred vision, eye pain, or see halos around lights; have increased thirst and urination, excessive hunger, fruity breath odor, weakness, nausea and vomiting; have fever, chills, body aches, flu symptoms; or have white patches or sores inside your mouth or on your lips.
- Do not stop taking the drug suddenly without first talking to provider, even if you feel fine. You may have serious side effects if you stop taking the drug suddenly.
- Call provider if symptoms do not improve or get worse.
- Store at room temperature away from moisture and heat.

SPECIAL POPULATIONS:
- *Elderly:* Generally lower dose is used (e.g., 25–100 mg twice a day). Higher dose can be used if tolerated. Elderly with dementia-related psychosis treated with atypical antipsychotics are at higher risk of death and cerebrovascular events.

- *Renal impairment*: No dose adjustment is required.
- *Hepatic impairment*: Dose may need to be reduced.
- *Cardiac impairment:* Use with caution because of risk of orthostatic hypotension.
- *Pregnancy:* Category C. Some animal studies show adverse effects. There are no controlled studies in humans. It should be used only when the potential benefits outweigh potential risks to the fetus. Quetiapine may be preferable to anticonvulsant mood stabilizers if treatment is required during pregnancy.
- *Lactation*: It is not known if the drug is secreted in human breast milk. It is recommended to either discontinue drug or bottle feed. Infants of women who choose to breastfeed while on this drug should be monitored for possible adverse effects.
- *Children and adolescents:*
  - Not officially recommended for patients younger than 18 years.
  - Probably safe and effective for behavioral disturbances in this population.
  - Should be monitored more frequently than adults. May tolerate lower doses better.
  - Watch for activation of suicidal ideation. Inform parents or guardian of this risk so they can help monitor the risk.

Risperdal, Risperdal Consta   **risperidone**

INDICATIONS: Schizophrenia (age 13 and older), monotherapy or combination therapy for acute mixed or manic episodes associated with bipolar I disorder (age 10 and older), treatment of irritability associated with autistic disorder in children and adolescents aged 5 to 16 years.

AVAILABLE FORMS: Tablet, 0.25, 0.5, 1, 2, 3, 4, and 6 mg; orally disintegrating tablet, 0.5, 1, and 2 mg; liquid, 1 mg/mL (30-mL bottle); long-acting depot microspheres formulation for deep IM formulation, 25 mg vial/kit, 37.5 mg vial/kit, 50 mg vial/kit

DOSAGE:
- 2 to 8 mg/day PO for adults with acute psychosis and bipolar disorder
- 0.5 to 2.0 mg/day PO for children and elderly
- 25 to 50 mg depot IM every 2 weeks

ADMINISTRATION:
- Tablets may be given with or without food.
- Advise patient to take the missed dose as soon as remembered. Skip the missed dose if almost time for the next scheduled dose. Do not take extra medicine to make up for the missed dose.
- Measure the liquid form of risperidone with a special dose-measuring spoon or cup, not a regular tablespoon.

- Do not mix the liquid form with cola or tea.

SIDE EFFECTS: Can increase risk for diabetes and dyslipidemia; extrapyramidal symptoms (dose dependent); hyperprolactinemia (dose dependent); dizziness, insomnia, headache, anxiety; weight gain; nausea, sedation, constipation, abdominal pain; tachycardia; sexual dysfunction; hyperglycemia; increased risk of death and cerebrovascular events in elderly with dementia-related psychosis; TD (rare); orthostatic hypotension (rare, usually during initial dose titration); neuroleptic malignant syndrome (rare); seizures (rare)

DRUG INTERACTIONS:
- May increase effects of antihypertensive medications
- May antagonize levodopa and dopamine agonists
- Plasma levels of risperidone may be reduced if given in conjunction with carbamazepine.
- Plasma levels of risperidone may be increased if given in conjunction with fluoxetine or paroxetine
- Plasma levels of risperidone may be increased if given in conjunction with clozapine (*Clozaril*), but no dose adjustment is required.
- ▶**Alert:** This list may not describe all possible interactions. Instruct clients to provide a list of all

(cont.)

SCHIZOPHRENIA: Antipsychotic Drugs, Atypical (Second Generation)

risperidone (*cont.*)

the medicines, herbs, nonprescription drugs, or dietary supplements they use.

PHARMACOKINETICS:

Elimination: 7 to 8 weeks after last injection (long-acting formulation)

Metabolism: Metabolites are active; metabolized by CYP450 2D6

Half-life: 20 to 24 hr (oral formulation); 3 to 6 days (long-acting formulation)

PRECAUTIONS:

- Use with caution in patients with conditions that predispose to hypotension (dehydration, overheating).
- Use with caution in patients who are at risk for aspiration pneumonia.
- Priapism has been reported.
- *Do not use if there is a proven allergy.*

PATIENT AND FAMILY EDUCATION:

- Take exactly as prescribed by the provider. Do not take in larger or smaller amounts or for longer than recommended.
- Can be taken with or without food.
- You may be more sensitive to temperature extremes (very hot or cold conditions) when taking this medication. Avoid getting too cold, or becoming overheated or dehydrated.
- Drink plenty of fluids, especially in hot weather and during exercise.
- Risperidone can cause side effects that may impair your thinking or reactions. Be careful if you drive or do anything that requires you to be awake and alert.
- Risperidone may cause high blood sugar (hyperglycemia). Talk to provider if any signs of hyperglycemia, such as increased thirst or urination, excessive hunger, or weakness. If diabetic, check blood sugar levels on a regular basis.
- The risperidone orally disintegrating tablet may contain phenylalanine. Talk to provider before using this form of risperidone if you have PKU.
- *Avoid drinking alcohol.* It can increase some of the side effects.
- *Do not* mix the liquid form with cola or tea.
- *Stop using this medication and call provider immediately* if you have fever, stiff muscles, confusion, sweating, fast or uneven heartbeats, restless muscle movements in face or neck, tremor (uncontrolled shaking), trouble swallowing, light-headedness, or fainting.
- Do not stop taking the drug suddenly without first talking to your provider, even if you feel fine. You may have serious side effects if you stop taking the drug suddenly.
- Call provider if symptoms do not improve or get worse.
- Store at room temperature away from moisture, light, and heat. Do not freeze the liquid form of risperidone.

SPECIAL POPULATIONS:

- *Elderly:*
  - Initially, 0.5 mg orally a day, then increase to 0.5 mg twice a day. Titrate once a week for doses above 1.5 mg twice a day.
  - Long-acting risperidone: 25 mg every 2 weeks. Oral administration should be continued for 3 weeks after the first injection.
  - Elderly with dementia-related psychosis treated with atypical antipsychotics are at higher risk of death and cerebrovascular events.
- *Renal impairment:*
  - Initially 0.5 mg orally twice a day for the first week. Increase to 1 mg twice a day during the second week.
  - Long-acting risperidone should not be given to patients with hepatic function impairment unless s/he can tolerate at least 2 mg/day orally.
  - Long-acting risperidone should be given 25 mg every 2 weeks. Oral administration should be continued for 3 weeks after the first injection.
- *Hepatic impairment:*
  - Initially 0.5 mg orally twice a day for the first week. Increase to 1 mg twice a day during the second week.
  - Long-acting risperidone should not be given to patients with hepatic function impairment unless s/he can tolerate at least 2 mg/day orally.
  - Long-acting risperidone should be given 25 mg every 2 weeks. Oral administration should be continued for 3 weeks after the first injection.
- *Cardiac impairment:* Use with caution because of risk of orthostatic hypotension. There is a greater risk of stroke if given to elderly patients with atrial fibrillation.
- *Pregnancy:* Category C. Some animal studies show adverse effects. There are no controlled studies in humans. Should be used only when the potential benefits outweigh potential risks to the fetus. Risperidone may be preferable to anticonvulsant mood stabilizers if treatment is required during pregnancy. Effects of hyperprolactinemia on the fetus are unknown.
- *Lactation:* Drug is secreted in human breast milk. It is recommended to either discontinue drug or bottle feed. Infants of women who choose to breastfeed while on this drug should be monitored for possible adverse effect.
- *Children and adolescents:*
  - Safe and effective for behavioral disturbances in this population.
  - Risperidone is the most frequently used atypical antipsychotic medication in this population.

Geodon, Geodon IM Injection   **ziprasidone**

INDICATIONS: Schizophrenia, delaying relapse in schizophrenia, acute agitation in schizophrenia (IM), acute mania/mixed mania, other psychotic disorders, bipolar maintenance, bipolar depression, behavioral disturbances in dementia.

AVAILABLE FORMS: Tablet, 20, 40, 60, and 80 mg; injection, 20 mg/mL

DOSAGE:
- 40 to 200 mg/day in divided doses, PO for schizophrenia
- 80 to 160 mg/day in divided doses, PO for bipolar
- 10 to 20 mg IM (doses of 10 mg may be administered every 2 hr; doses of 20 mg may be administered every 4 hr with MDD). Not to be administered for more than 3 consecutive days.

ADMINISTRATION:
- Take this medication with a meal.
- Dosing at 20 to 40 twice a day is too low and activating, perhaps due to potent 5HT2C antagonist properties. Reduce activation by increasing the dose to 60 to 80 mg twice a day.
- Best efficacy in schizophrenia and bipolar disorder is at doses greater than 120 mg/day.
- BMI monthly for 3 months, then quarterly.
- Monitor fasting triglycerides monthly for several months in patients at high risk for metabolic complications.
- BP, fasting plasma glucose, fasting lipids within 3 months and then annually, but earlier and more frequently for patients with diabetes or who have gained more than 5% of initial weight.

SIDE EFFECTS: Dizziness, sedation, and hypotension especially at high doses; motor side effects (rare); possible increased incidence of diabetes or dyslipidemia is unknown

DRUG INTERACTIONS:
- May enhance the effects of antihypertensive drugs
- May antagonize levodopa and dopamine agonists
- May enhance QTc prolongation of other drugs capable of prolonging QTc interval

PHARMACOKINETICS:
Protein binding: Greater than 99%
Metabolism: Metabolized by CYP450 3A4
Half-life: 6.6 hr

PRECAUTIONS:
- Prolongs QTc interval more than some other antipsychotics.
- Use with caution in patients with conditions that predispose to hypotension (dehydration, overheating).
- Priapism has been reported.
- Dysphagia has been associated with antipsychotic use, and should be used cautiously in patients at risk for aspiration pneumonia.
- Do not use if patient is taking agents capable of prolonging QTc interval (pimozide, thioridazine, selected antiarrhythmics, moxifloxacin, sparfloxacin).
- Do not use if there is a history of QTc prolongation, cardiac arrhythmia, recent AMI, uncompensated heart failure.
- Do not use if there is a proven allergy to ziprasidone.

PATIENT AND FAMILY EDUCATION:
- *Take with a meal* of a few hundred calories (turkey sandwich and a piece of fruit) to enhance the absorption
- *Avoid becoming overheated or dehydrated during exercise and in hot weather.* You may be more prone to heat stroke.
- *Avoid getting up too fast from a sitting or lying position.* Get up slowly and steady yourself to prevent a fall.
- *Avoid drinking alcohol.*
- *Stop using this medication and call provider immediately* if you have very stiff (rigid) muscles, high fever, sweating, confusion, fast or uneven heartbeats, tremors; feel like you might pass out; have jerky muscle movements you cannot control, trouble swallowing, problems with speech; have blurred vision, eye pain, or see halos around lights; have increased thirst and urination, excessive hunger, fruity breath odor, weakness, nausea and vomiting; have fever, chills, body aches, flu symptoms; or have white patches or sores inside your mouth or on your lips.
- Do not stop taking the drug suddenly without first talking to your provider, even if you feel fine. You may have serious side effects if you stop taking the drug suddenly.
- Call provider if symptoms do not improve or get worse.
- Store at room temperature away from moisture and heat.

SPECIAL POPULATIONS:
- *Elderly:* Some patients may tolerate lower doses better. Elderly patients with dementia-related psychosis treated with atypical antipsychotics are at an increased risk of death compared to placebo.
- *Renal impairment:* No dose adjustment is necessary.
- *Hepatic impairment:* No dose adjustment is necessary.
- *Cardiac impairment:* Contraindicated in patients with a known history of QTc prolongation, recent AMI, and uncompensated heart failure.
- *Pregnancy:* Category C. Some animal studies show adverse effects. There are no controlled studies in humans.
- *Lactation:* It is not known if it is secreted in human breast milk. Recommend either to discontinue drug or to bottle feed.
- *Children and adolescents:* Not recommended for patients younger than 18 years. Early data suggest that it may be safe and effective for behavioral disturbances in children and adolescents.

SCHIZOPHRENIA: Antipsychotic Drugs, Atypical (Second Generation)

paliperidone   *Invega*

INDICATIONS: Schizophrenia, bipolar disorder, other psychotic disorders, behavioral responses in dementia, behavioral disturbances in children and adolescents, disorders associated with problems with impulse control.

AVAILABLE FORMS: Tablet (extended-release), 3, 6, and 9 mg

DOSAGE:
- 6 mg/day
- Maximum dose, 12 mg/day

ADMINISTRATION:
- Initial dose, 6 mg/day taken in the morning
- Can increase by 3 mg/day every 5 days

SIDE EFFECTS: Dizziness; sedation; hypotension; motor side effects especially at high doses; elevation in prolactin; may increase risk for diabetes and dyslipidemia; rare TD (much less than conventional antipsychotics); sedation, hypersalivation; weight gain; orthostatic hypotension; tachycardia; hyperglycemia associated with ketoacidosis or osmolar coma or death has been reported in patients taking atypical antipsychotics; in elderly patients with dementia-related psychosis, there is an increased risk of death and cerebrovascular events; rare neuroleptic malignant syndrome; rare seizures

DRUG INTERACTIONS:
- May increase effects of antihypertensive agents
- May decrease the effects of levodopa and dopamine agonists
- May increase QTc prolongation of other drugs that also increase the QTc interval

PHARMACOKINETICS: Active   metabolite   of risperidone
Half-life: Approx. 23 hr

PRECAUTIONS:
- Use with caution with conditions that predispose to hypotension (dehydration, overheating).
- Use with caution in patients at risk for aspiration pneumonia since dysphagia has been associated with antipsychotic use.
- Prolongs QTc interval.
- Priapism reported with other antipsychotics including risperidone, and paliperidone is an active metabolite of risperidone.
- *Do not use* if patient is taking other medications or has conditions that prolong QTc interval (pimozide, thioridazine, selected antiarrhythmics, recent AMI, uncompensated heart failure).
- *Do not use* if patient has preexisting severe GI narrowing.
- *Do not use if allergic to or sensitive to* paliperidone or risperidone.

PATIENT AND FAMILY EDUCATION:
- Take exactly as prescribed by the provider. Do not take in larger or smaller amounts or for longer than recommended.
- *Avoid becoming overheated or dehydrated during exercise and in hot weather.* You may be more prone to heat stroke.
- *Avoid getting up too fast from a sitting or lying position.* Get up slowly and steady yourself to prevent a fall.
- *Avoid drinking alcohol.*
- *Stop using this medication and call provider immediately* if you have very stiff (rigid) muscles, high fever, sweating, confusion, fast or uneven heartbeats, tremors; feel like you might pass out; have jerky muscle movements you cannot control, trouble swallowing, problems with speech; have blurred vision, eye pain, or see halos around lights; have increased thirst and urination, excessive hunger, fruity breath odor, weakness, nausea and vomiting; have fever, chills, body aches, flu symptoms; or have white patches or sores inside your mouth or on your lips.
- Do not stop taking the drug suddenly without first talking to provider, even if you feel fine. You may have serious side effects if you stop taking the drug suddenly.
- Call provider if symptoms do not improve or get worse.
- Store at room temperature away from moisture and heat.

SPECIAL POPULATIONS:
- *Elderly:* They may tolerate lower doses better and are more sensitive to adverse effects. Not approved for treatment of elderly patients with dementia-related psychosis, and such patients are at increased risk of cardiovascular events and death.
- *Renal impairment*: For mild impairment, maximum dose recommended is 6 mg/day. For moderate-to-severe impairment, maximum dose recommended is 3 mg/day.
- *Hepatic impairment*: No dose adjustment recommended for mild-to-moderate impairment. Use in patients with severe impairment has not been studied.
- *Cardiac impairment:* Use with caution due to risk of orthostatic hypotension.
- *Pregnancy:* Category C. Animal studies show adverse effects; there are no controlled studies in humans. Psychotic symptoms may worsen during pregnancy and necessitate some form of treatment. Paliperidone may be preferable to anticonvulsant mood stabilizers and conventional antipsychotics. Effects of hyperprolactinemia on the fetus are unknown.
- *Lactation:* Some drugs may be found in mother's breast milk, and it is recommended that either the drug be discontinued or infant be bottle fed. Infants who are breastfed while mother is on paliperidone need to be monitored for adverse effects.
- *Children and adolescents*: Safety and efficacy are not established for paliperidone for children and adolescents. Children and adolescents will need to be monitored more closely than adults.

Saphris   **asenapine**

INDICATIONS: Schizophrenia, manic or mixed episodes associated with bipolar disorder I.

AVAILABLE FORMS: Sublingual tablets, 5 and 10 mg

DOSAGE:
- Initial, 5 mg bid; increase to 10 mg bid
- Can decrease back to 5 mg bid based on tolerability

ADMINISTRATION:
- *Place the tablet under the tongue* and allow to dissolve completely. Tablet dissolves within seconds.
- Do not eat or drink anything for 10 to 30 min after administration.
- Tablets should not be crushed, chewed, or swallowed.

SIDE EFFECTS: Akathisia; oral hypoesthesia (or numbness); somnolence; dizziness; other extrapyramidal symptoms excluding akathisia; weight gain; insomnia; headache; may induce orthostatic hypotension and syncope in some patients, especially early in treatment; rare neuroleptic malignant syndrome; rare TD

DRUG INTERACTIONS:
- May enhance effects of certain antihypertensive drugs because of its alpha-1-adrenergic antagonism with potential for inducing hypotension.
- Inhibitor of P450 2D6 and may contribute to increased levels.
- Appears to decrease prolactin from baseline.

PHARMACOKINETICS:
- Metabolized primarily through CYP 1A2
- Rapidly absorbed within 0.5 to 1.5 hr
Half-life: Approx. 24 hr

PRECAUTIONS:
- Caution should be used when taken in combination with other centrally acting drugs or alcohol.
- Caution should be used with other drugs that are both substrates and inhibitors for CYP 2D6.
- May cause transient increases in serum transaminase; therefore it needs to be monitored during the initial months.
- Elderly patients with dementia-related psychosis treated with antipsychotic drugs are at an increased risk of death. Asenapine is not approved for the treatment of patients with dementia-related psychosis.
- Patients with a preexisting low WBC or a history of drug-induced leukopenia/neutropenia should have their CBC monitored frequently during the first few months of therapy, and asenapine should be discontinued at the first sign of decline in WBC in the absence of other causative factors.
- The use of asenapine should be avoided in combination with other drugs known to prolong the QTc interval including Class 1A antiarrhythmics (e.g., quinidine, procainamide) or Class 3

antiarrhythmics (e.g., amiodarone, sotalol), antipsychotic medications (e.g., ziprasidone, chlorpromazine, thioridazine), and antibiotics (e.g., gatifloxacin, moxifloxacin).
- Like other drugs that antagonize dopamine D2 receptors, asenapine can elevate prolactin levels, and the elevation can persist during chronic administration.
- As with other antipsychotic drugs, asenapine should be used with caution in patients with a history of seizures or with conditions that potentially lower the seizure threshold, e.g., Alzheimer's dementia. Conditions that lower the seizure threshold may be more prevalent in patients 65 years or older.

PATIENT AND FAMILY EDUCATION:
- Take exactly as prescribed by the provider. Do not take in larger or smaller amounts or for longer than recommended.
- Asenapine tablets must be placed under tongue and allowed to dissolve. Do not crush, chew, or swallow.
- No eating or drinking for at least 10 min—30 min is better—after the drug dissolves.
- *Avoid drinking alcohol.*
- *Stop using this medication and call provider immediately* if you have very stiff (rigid) muscles, high fever, sweating, confusion, fast or uneven heartbeats, tremors; feel like you might pass out; have jerky muscle movements you cannot control, trouble swallowing, problems with speech; have blurred vision, eye pain, or see halos around lights; have increased thirst and urination, excessive hunger, fruity breath odor, weakness, nausea and vomiting; have fever, chills, body aches, flu symptoms; or have white patches or sores inside your mouth or on your lips.
- Do not stop taking this drug suddenly without first talking to your provider, even if you feel fine. You may have serious side effects if you stop taking the drug suddenly.
- Call provider if symptoms do not improve or get worse.
- Store at room temperature away from moisture and heat.

SPECIAL POPULATIONS:
- *Elderly:* May tolerate lower doses better and may be more sensitive to adverse effects. It is not approved for treatment of elderly patients with dementia-related psychosis, and such patients are at increased risk of cardiovascular events and death.
- *Renal impairment:* No adjustment is needed.
- *Hepatic impairment:* Lower dose for mild-to-moderate impairment. It is not recommended with severe liver impairment.
- *Cardiac impairment:* Use with caution due to risk of orthostatic hypotension and QTc potential prolongation.
- *Pregnancy:* Category C. There are no adequate and well-controlled studies of asenapine in

(cont.)

SCHIZOPHRENIA: Antipsychotic Drugs, Atypical (Second Generation)

asenapine *(cont.)*

pregnant women. In animal studies, asenapine increased post-implantation loss and decreased pup weight and survival at doses similar to or less than recommended clinical doses. In these studies there was no increase in the incidence of structural abnormalities caused by asenapine. Asenapine should be used during pregnancy only if the potential benefit justifies the potential risk to the fetus.

- *Lactation:* Asenapine is excreted in the milk of rats during lactation. It is not known whether asenapine or its metabolites are excreted in human milk. Because many drugs are excreted in human milk, caution should be exercised when asenapine is administered to a nursing woman. It is recommended that women receiving asenapine should not breastfeed.
- *Children and adolescents:* Safety and effectiveness in children and adolescents has not been established.

Class: Antipsychotic Drugs, Typical (First Generation)

haloperidol   *Haldol, Haloperidol decanoate*

INDICATIONS: Psychotic disorders, Tourette's syndrome, schizophrenia, second-line treatment for severe behavior disorders in children, second-line treatment for hyperactive children, bipolar disorder, behavioral disturbances in dementias, delirium with lorazepam.

AVAILABLE FORMS: Tablet (scored), 0.5, 1, 2, 5, 10, and 20 mg; concentrate, 2 mg/mL; solution, 1 mg/mL; injection, 5 mg/mL (immediate release); decanoate injection, 50 mg haloperidol as 60.5 mg/mL, haloperidol decanoate, 100 mg haloperidol as 141.04 mg/mL haloperidol decanoate

DOSAGE:
- 1 to 40 mg/day orally
- Immediate-release injection, 2 to 5 mg each dose
- Decanoate injection 10 to 20 times the previous daily dose of oral antipsychotic

ADMINISTRATION:
- *Oral:* Can give once daily or in divided doses at beginning of treatment during rapid escalation; increase as needed; can be dosed up to 100 mg/day
- *Immediate-release injection:* Initial dose, 2 to 5 mg; subsequent doses may be given as often as every hour; patient should be switched to oral administration as soon as possible.
- *Haloperidol decanoate injection:* Initial dose, 10 to 15 times the previous oral dose for patients maintained on low antipsychotic doses (up to equivalent of 10 mg/day oral haloperidol). Initial dose may be as high as 20 times previous oral dose for patients maintained on higher antipsychotic doses. Maximum dose is 100 mg. If higher dose is required, the remainder can be administered 3 to 7 days later. Administer total dose every 4 weeks.
- Stay hydrated.
- ▶ **Alert:** Haloperidol is frequently dosed too high. High doses may actually worsen negative symptoms of schizophrenia.

SIDE EFFECTS: Neuroleptic-induced deficit syndrome; akathisia; EPS, parkinsonism, TD, tardive dystonia; galactorrhea, amenorrhea; dizziness, sedation; dry mouth, constipation, urinary retention, blurred vision; decreased sweating; hypotension, tachycardia, hyperlipidemia; weight gain; rare neuroleptic malignant syndrome; seizures (rare); jaundice (rare), agranulocytosis, leukopenia; haloperidol with anticholinergics may increase intraocular pressure; reduces effects of anticoagulants; plasma levels of haloperidol lowered by rifampin; may enhance effects of antihypertensive agents; haloperidol with lithium may contribute to development of encephalopathic syndrome

DRUG INTERACTIONS:
- May decrease the effects of levodopa and dopamine agonists.
- May increase the effects of antihypertensive drugs except for guanethidine.
- Additive effects with CNS depressants; dose of other should be reduced.
- May interact with some pressor agents (epinephrine) to lower BP.

PHARMACOKINETICS:
Half-life: Haloperidol decanoate, approx. 3 weeks; oral, approx. 12 to 36 hr

PRECAUTIONS:
- Discontinue if symptoms of neuroleptic malignant syndrome develop.
- Use with caution in patients with respiratory problems.
- Avoid extreme heat exposure.
- May experience rapid shift to depression if used to treat mania.
- Patients with thyrotoxicosis may experience neurotoxicity.
- Do not use with Lewy body dementia or Parkinson's disease.
- Use with caution in patients with QTc prolongation, hypothyroidism, familial long-QT syndrome.
- Do not use if patient is comatose.
- Do not use if there is a proven allergy to haloperidol.

PATIENT AND FAMILY EDUCATION:
- Take exactly as prescribed.
- Avoid getting up too fast from a sitting or lying position. Get up slowly and steady yourself to prevent a fall.

(cont.)

haloperidol (cont.)

- *Avoid drinking alcohol.*
- *Stop using this medication and call provider immediately if you have very stiff (rigid) muscles, high fever, sweating, confusion, fast or uneven heartbeats, tremors; feel like you might pass out; have jerky muscle movements you cannot control, trouble swallowing, problems with speech; have blurred vision, eye pain, or see halos around lights; have increased thirst and urination, excessive hunger, fruity breath odor, weakness, nausea and vomiting; have fever, chills, body aches, flu symptoms; or have white patches or sores inside your mouth or on your lips.*
- Do not stop taking the drug suddenly without first talking to your provider, even if you feel fine. You may have serious side effects if you stop taking the drug suddenly.
- Call provider if symptoms do not improve or get worse.
- Store at room temperature away from moisture and heat.

SPECIAL POPULATIONS:

- *Elderly:* Lower doses should be used and patient should be monitored closely. Do not use in elderly patients with dementia.
- *Renal impairment:* Use with caution.
- *Hepatic impairment:* Use with caution.
- *Cardiac impairment:* Because of the risk of orthostatic hypertension, use with caution.
- *Pregnancy:* Category C. Some animal studies show adverse effects; there are no controlled studies in humans.
- *Lactation:* Category C. Not recommended for use in women who breastfeed or plan to breastfeed while on this drug.
- *Children and adolescents:* Safety and efficacy are not established. Not intended for use with children younger than 3 years. Generally consider as second line, not first line.

Prolixin　　　**fluphenazine**

INDICATIONS: Psychotic and bipolar disorders

AVAILABLE FORMS: Tablet, 1, 2.5 (scored), 5 (scored), and 10 mg (scored); decanoate for long-acting IM or SC administration, 25 mg/mL; short-acting IM injection, 2.5 mg/mL; elixir, 2.5 mg/5 mL; concentrate, 5 mg/mL

DOSAGE:

- *Oral:* Initial, 0.5 to 10 mg/day in divided doses; maximum, 40 mg/day
- *IM (short-acting):* Initial, 1.25 mg; 2.5 to 10 mg/day can be given in divided doses every 6 to 8 hr; maximum dose, generally 10 mg/day
- *Fluphenazine decanoate (long-acting):* Initial, 12.5 to 25 mg (0.5–1 mL); subsequent doses and intervals determined in accordance with the patient's response; generally no more than 50 mg/2 mL given at intervals not longer than 4 weeks

ADMINISTRATION:

- Oral solution should not be mixed with drinks containing caffeine, tannic acid (tea), or pectinates (apple juice).
- 12.5 mg/mL every 2 weeks is equivalent to 10 mg daily of oral fluphenazine.
- Decanoate onset of action is at 24 to 72 hr after administration with significant antipsychotic actions evident within 48 to 96 hr.

SIDE EFFECTS: Motor side effects from blockage of D2 in striatum; elevations in prolactin from blockage of D2 in the pituitary; worsening of negative and cognitive symptoms due to blockage of D2 receptors in the mesocortical and mesolimbic dopamine pathways; sedation, blurred vision, constipation, dry mouth; sedation, weight gain; dizziness, and hypotension; possible increased incidence of diabetes or dyslipidemia with conventional antipsychotics is unknown; neuroleptic-induced deficit syndrome; akathisia; extrapyramidal symptoms, parkinsonism, TD; galactorrhea, amenorrhea; sexual dysfunction; priapism; decreased sweating, depression; hypotension, tachycardia, syncope

DRUG INTERACTIONS:

- May decrease the effects of levodopa and dopamine agonists.
- May increase effects of antihypertensive drugs except for guanethidine, whose actions may be antagonized by fluphenazine.
- Concurrent use with CNS depressants may produce additive effects.
- Additive anticholinergic effects may occur if used with atropine or related compounds.
- Alcohol and diuretics increase the risk of hypotension.
- Some patients on neuroleptics and lithium developed an encephalopathic syndrome similar to NMS.
- Use with epinephrine may lower BP.

PHARMACOKINETICS:
Half-life: Oral formulation, approx. 15 hr; IM formulation, approx. 6.8 to 9.6 days

PRECAUTIONS:

- May decrease the effects of levodopa and dopamine agonist.
- May increase the effects of antihypertensive drugs.
- Additive effects may occur if combined with CNS depressants.
- Some neuroleptics and lithium have caused an encephalopathic syndrome similar to NMS in some patients.

(cont.)

SCHIZOPHRENIA: Antipsychotic Drugs, Typical (First Generation)

fluphenazine (cont.)

- Fluphenazine and epinephrine may lower BP.
- Additive anticholinergic effects may occur if used with atropine or related compounds.
- Alcohol and diuretics may increase the risk of hypotension.
- Do not use if in a comatose state.
- Do not use if patient is taking cabergoline, pergolide, or metrizamide.
- Do not use if there is proven allergy or sensitivity to fluphenazine.

PATIENT AND FAMILY EDUCATION:
- Avoid this medication if you have an allergy to aspirin. Inform your provider of all drug allergies.
- Take exactly as prescribed by the provider. Do not take in larger or smaller amounts or for longer than recommended.
- Can be taken with or without food.
- *Avoid becoming overheated or dehydrated during exercise and in hot weather.* You may be more prone to heat stroke.
- *Avoid getting up too fast from a sitting or lying position.* Get up slowly and steady yourself to prevent a fall.
- *Avoid drinking alcohol.*
- *Stop using this medication and call provider immediately* if you have very stiff (rigid) muscles, high fever, sweating, confusion, fast or uneven heartbeats, tremors; feel like you might pass out; have jerky muscle movements you cannot control, trouble swallowing, problems with speech; have blurred vision, eye pain, or see halos around lights; have increased thirst and urination, excessive hunger, fruity breath odor, weakness, nausea and vomiting; have fever, chills, body aches, flu symptoms; or have white patches or sores inside your mouth or on your lips.
- Do not stop taking the drug suddenly without first talking to your provider, even if you feel fine. You may have serious side effects if you stop taking the drug suddenly.
- Call provider if symptoms do not improve or get worse.
- Store at room temperature away from moisture and heat.

SPECIAL POPULATIONS:
- *Elderly:* Lower initial dose (1–2.5 mg/day) and slower titration. Elderly are more susceptible to adverse effects. It is not approved for treatment of elderly patients with dementia-related psychosis, and such patients are at increased risk of cardiovascular events and death.
- *Renal impairment*: Use with caution and with slower titration.
- *Hepatic impairment*: Use with caution and with slower titration.
- *Cardiac impairment:* Cardiovascular toxicity can occur, especially orthostatic hypotension.
- *Pregnancy:* Category C. Some animal studies have demonstrated adverse effects; there are no controlled studies in humans. Infants whose mothers took a phenothiazine during pregnancy have exhibited EPS, jaundice, hyperreflexia, hyporeflexia. Psychotic symptoms may worsen during pregnancy, necessitating some form of treatment. Atypical antipsychotics may be preferable.
- *Lactation:* Milk crosses to the infant through breast milk and dystonia, TD, and sedation have been observed in the infant. Recommend discontinuing drug or bottle feed.
- *Children and adolescents*: Safety and efficacy of fluphenazine is not established for children and adolescents. Decanoate and enanthate injectable formulations are contraindicated in children younger than 12 years. It is generally considered second-line treatment after trial with atypical antipsychotics.

thioridazine *Mellaril*

INDICATIONS: Treatment-resistant schizophrenia.

AVAILABLE FORMS: Tablet, 10, 15, 25, 50, 100, 150, and 200 mg; liquid, 30 mg/mL, 100 mg/mL; suspension, 5 mg/mL, 20 mg/mL

DOSAGE: 200 to 800 mg in divided doses

ADMINISTRATION:
- 50 to 100 mg 3 times a day; increase gradually; maximum 800 mg/day in divided doses
- Start low and go slow as QTc prolongation is dose dependent

SIDE EFFECTS: Motor side effects due to blocking of D2 in the striatum; elevations in prolactin due to blocking of D2 in the pituitary; worsening of negative and cognitive symptoms; sedation, blurred vision, constipation, dry mouth; weight gain; dizziness, hypotension; increased incidence of diabetes or dyslipidemia; potentially dangerous QTc prolongation; neuroleptic malignant syndrome (rare); jaundice (rare); agranulocytosis; seizure (rare); ventricular arrhythmias and sudden death; increased risk of death and cerebrovascular events in elderly patients with dementia-related psychosis

DRUG INTERACTIONS:
- May decrease effects of levodopa and dopamine agonists.
- May increase effects of antihypertensive drugs.
- May enhance QTc prolongation interval of other drugs that do the same.
- Paroxetine, fluoxetine, duloxetine, bupropion, sertraline, citalopram, and other CYP450 2D6 agents can raise thioridazine to dangerous levels.

(cont.)

thioridazine (*cont.*)

- Fluvoxamine, propranolol, and pindolol can inhibit metabolism and raise to dangerous levels.
- When used with a barbiturate, it may cause respiratory depression/arrest.
- Additive effects between thioridazine and CNS depressants.
- Increased risk of hypotension with alcohol and diuretics.
- Epinephrine may lower BP.
- Encephalopathic syndrome similar to neuroleptic malignant syndrome may develop when used with lithium.

PHARMACOKINETICS:
- CYP450 2D6 metabolizes thioridazine
Half-life: Approx. 10 hr

PRECAUTIONS:
- With signs of neuroleptic malignant syndrome, treatment must be discontinued immediately.
- *Do not augment* with other psychotropic agents.
- QTc prolongation may lead to torsades de pointes-type arrhythmia or sudden death.
- Use with caution in patients with respiratory disorders, glaucoma, or urinary problems.
- Anti-emetic effect can mask overdose.
- Use with caution in alcohol withdrawal or convulsive disorders because it may lower seizure threshold.
- Do not use epinephrine in case of overdose as it may lower BP.
- Use with caution with parkinsonism or Lewy body dementia.
- Monitor for pigmentary retinopathy especially at higher doses.
- Use with caution in patients with bradycardia or those who are taking drugs that can induce bradycardia (beta-blockers, clonidine, digitalis).
- Use with caution in patients with hypokalemia and/or magnesemia (diuretic, stimulant laxatives, IV amphotericin B, glucocorticoids, tetracosactide).
- *Do not use* if patient suffers from the following conditions: coma, extremes of hypotension or hypertension, QTc interval greater than 450 msec or taking an agent that also prolongs QTc, cardiac arrhythmia, recent AMI, uncompensated heart failure, or taking drugs that inhibit thioridazine metabolism (CYP450 inhibitors).

PATIENT AND FAMILY EDUCATION:
- Take exactly as prescribed by the provider. Do not take in larger or smaller amounts or for longer than recommended.
- Can be taken with or without food.
- *Avoid becoming overheated or dehydrated during exercise and in hot weather.* You may be more prone to heat stroke.
- *Avoid getting up too fast from a sitting or lying position.* Get up slowly and steady yourself to prevent a fall.
- *Avoid drinking alcohol.*
- *Stop using this medication and call provider immediately* if you have very stiff (rigid) muscles, high fever, sweating, confusion, fast or uneven heartbeats, tremors; feel like you might pass out; have jerky muscle movements you cannot control, trouble swallowing, problems with speech; have blurred vision, eye pain, or see halos around lights; have increased thirst and urination, excessive hunger, fruity breath odor, weakness, nausea and vomiting; have fever, chills, body aches, flu symptoms; or have white patches or sores inside your mouth or on your lips.
- Do not stop taking drug suddenly without first talking to provider, even if you feel fine. You may have serious side effects if you stop taking the drug suddenly.
- Call provider if symptoms do not improve or get worse.
- Store at room temperature away from moisture and heat.
- Caution is needed in taking this medication if you have any of the following conditions: narrow-angle glaucoma, prostatic hypertrophy, or cardiovascular disease.
- Annual eye examinations are recommended.

SPECIAL POPULATIONS:
- *Elderly:* They may tolerate lower doses better, and are more sensitive to adverse effects. It is not approved for treatment of elderly patients with dementia-related psychosis, and such patients are at increased risk of cardiovascular events and death.
- *Renal impairment*: Use with caution.
- *Hepatic impairment*: Use with caution.
- *Cardiac impairment*: Avoid in patients with QTc prolongation, recent AMI, and uncompensated heart failure. *Risk/benefit ratio may not justify use* in cardiac impairment.
- *Pregnancy:* Category C. Some animal studies have demonstrated adverse effects; there are no controlled studies in humans. Infants whose mothers took a phenothiazine during pregnancy have exhibited EPS, jaundice, hyperreflexia, or hyporeflexia. Psychotic symptoms may worsen during pregnancy, necessitating some form of treatment. Atypical antipsychotics may be preferable.
- *Lactation:* It is not known if is secreted in human breast milk, but assumed so. Recommended to discontinue thioridazine or bottle feed.
- *Children and adolescents*: Safety and efficacy not established in children and adolescents but risk/benefit ratio may justify use. Start at initial dose of 0.5 mg/kg per day and increase gradually. Maximum dose: 3 mg/kg/day.

SCHIZOPHRENIA: Antipsychotic Drugs, Typical (First Generation)

trifluoperazine   *Stelazine*

INDICATIONS: Schizophrenia (PO, IM), nonpsychotic anxiety (short-term, second-line), other psychotic disorders, bipolar disorder.

AVAILABLE FORMS: Tablet, 1, 2, 5, and 10 mg; vial, 2 mg/mL; concentrate, 10 mg/mL

DOSAGE: 15 to 20 mg/day for psychosis

ADMINISTRATION:
- *Oral:* Typical starting dose is 2–5 mg bid. Most patients show optimum response on 15 to 20 mg daily.
- *IM injection* (for prompt control of severe symptoms): 1 mg to 2 mg (0.5–1 mL) every 4 to 6 h, prn.
- *Concentrate:* Add to 60 mL (2 fl oz) or more of diluent prior to administration. Possible diluents are tomato or fruit juice, milk, simple syrup, orange syrup, carbonated beverages, coffee, tea, water. Semisolid foods such as soup and puddings may also be used.

SIDE EFFECTS: Motor side effects from blockage of D2 in striatum; elevations in prolactin from blockage of D2 in the pituitary; worsening of negative and cognitive symptoms due to blockage of D2 receptors in the mesocortical and mesolimbic dopamine pathways; sedation, blurred vision, constipation, dry mouth; weight gain; dizziness; hypotension, possibility of increased incidence of diabetes or dyslipidemia with conventional antipsychotic is not known.

DRUG INTERACTIONS:
- May increase effects of levodopa and dopamine agonists.
- Increased effects of antihypertensive agents except for guanethidine, which may be antagonized by trifluoperazine.
- Additive effects with CNS depressants.
- Increased risk of hypotension with alcohol and diuretics.
- Lowered BP with epinephrine.
- May reduce effects of anticoagulants.
- Neuroleptics and lithium may contribute to encephalopathic syndrome similar to neuroleptic malignant syndrome.
- Plasma levels of both drugs increased with propranolol.

PHARMACOKINETICS:
Half-life: Approx. 12.5 hr

PRECAUTIONS:
- If neuroleptic malignant syndrome develops, trifluoperazine must be discontinued immediately.
- Use in patients with alcohol withdrawal or convulsive disorders lowers seizure threshold.
- Use with caution with respiratory disorders, glaucoma, or urinary retention.
- Avoid undue exposure to sunlight or extreme heat exposure.

- Signs of other disorders or overdose may be masked by antiemetic effect of trifluoperazine.
- May cause asphyxia through suppression of cough reflex.
- Use of epinephrine may lower BP.
- Use with caution in Parkinson's disease or Lewy body dementia.
- *Do not use* if patient is in a coma or has CNS depression.
- *Do not use* in the presence of blood dyscrasias, bone marrow depression, or liver disease.
- *Do not use* if there is a proven allergy to trifluoperazine or sensitivity to any phenothiazine.

PATIENT AND FAMILY EDUCATION:
- Take exactly as prescribed by the provider. Do not take in larger or smaller amounts or for longer than recommended.
- Can be taken with or without food.
- Do not use alcohol if taking this medication.
- Avoid undue exposure to sunlight or extreme heat exposure.
- Inform prescriber if you have a respiratory disorder, glaucoma, urinary retention, Parkinson's disease, bone marrow suppression, liver disease.
- Inform prescriber of all allergies to medications.

SPECIAL POPULATIONS:
- *Elderly:* Monitor closely and use lower doses. No antipsychotic agent has been approved for treatment of elderly patients with dementia-related psychosis despite their frequent use with the elderly for behavioral disturbances in dementia. Elderly patients treated with antipsychotics are at an increased risk of death and cerebrovascular events.
- *Renal impairment:* Use with caution.
- *Hepatic impairment:* Not recommended for use.
- *Cardiac impairment:* Dose should be lowered. Do not use parenteral administration unless necessary.
- *Pregnancy:* Category C. Some animal studies have demonstrated adverse effects; there are no controlled studies in humans. Infants whose mothers took a phenothiazine during pregnancy have exhibited EPS, jaundice, hyperreflexia, or hyporeflexia. Psychotic symptoms may worsen during pregnancy, necessitating some form of treatment. Atypical antipsychotics may be preferable.
- *Lactation:* Trifluoperazine is found in mother's breast milk. Recommend either to discontinue drug or to bottle feed.
- *Children and adolescents:* Generally consider as second line after trial of atypical antipsychotics. It is not recommended for use in children younger than 6 years of age. Children need to be closely monitored. Initial oral dose is 1 mg; increase gradually; maximum 15 mg/day except in older children with severe symptoms. IM, 1 mg once or twice a day.

Class: Benzodiazepines (BZDs)

Ativan **lorazepam**

INDICATIONS: Anxiety disorders.

AVAILABLE FORMS: Tablets, 0.5, 1, and 2 mg

DOSAGE:
- *Adults:* 2–3 mg/day PO/IM/IV divided bid-tid; 1–2 mg/day PO/IM/IV div bid-tid in elderly patients; maximum dosage is 10 mg/day. Periodically assess the need for treatment and taper the dose gradually to discontinue if prolonged treatment is necessary. Treatment should be limited to as short a period as possible (less than 4 months) and/or undergo re-evaluation for continued use.
- *Children:* 0.05 mg/kg PO/IV q4–8h; maximum dosage is 2 mg/dose. Periodically assess the need for treatment and taper the dose gradually to discontinue if prolonged treatment is necessary.

ADMINISTRATION:
- PO with a glass of water.
- Do not abruptly stop taking the medication.
- Use lowest effective dose for shortest duration.
- Lorazepam can be habit forming; do not increase dosage without guidance from provider.

SIDE EFFECTS:
- *More common:* Drowsiness, lightheadedness, dry mouth, headache, changes in bowel habits, sialorrhea, amnesia, changes in appetite
- *Less common:* Syncope, tachycardia, seizures, respiratory depression, dependency, withdrawal syndrome, suicidal ideation

DRUG INTERACTIONS:
- *Absolute contraindications:* Clarithromycin, fluvoxamine, ketoconazole
- Avoid using calcium channel blockers, erthromycins, tamoxifen, zafirlukast

▶**Alert:** This list may not describe all possible interactions. Instruct clients to provide a list of all medicines, herbs, nonprescription drugs, or dietary supplements they use and advise if they smoke, drink alcohol, or use illegal drugs.

PHARMACOKINETICS:
- BZDs enhance the activity of GABA, a major CNS neurotransmitter, known to open CNS Cl-channels, leading to an inhibition of subsequent CNS neuronal signaling.
- BZDs with similar action can differ in their potency and rate of absorption.

Metabolism: In the liver with the CYP450: exact mechanism is unknown

Excretion: Urine

Half-life: 14 hr

PRECAUTIONS:
- See client as often as necessary to ensure drug is working on the panic attacks, determine compliance, and review side effects.
- Do not abruptly withdraw this drug as it may cause seizures.

- Use with caution on patients with
  - Heart disease
  - Liver disease
  - Seizures (convulsions)
  - Suicidal thoughts, plans, or attempts
  - Unusual or allergic reaction to alprazolam, other medicines, foods, dyes, or preservatives

PATIENT AND FAMILY EDUCATION:
- Instruct client and family to watch for worsening depression or thoughts of suicide. Also watch out for sudden or severe changes in feelings such as feeling anxious, agitated, panicky, irritable, hostile, aggressive, impulsive, severely restless, overly excited and hyperactive, or not being able to sleep. If this happens, especially at the beginning of antidepressant treatment or after a change in dose, call the provider.
- If feeling drowsy or dizzy, do not drive, use machinery, or do anything that needs mental alertness until you know how this medicine affects you.
- Caution patients not to stand or sit up quickly, especially if older. This reduces the risk of dizzy or fainting spells. Alcohol may interfere with the effect of this medicine. Avoid alcoholic drinks.
- Store lorazepam at room temperature away from moisture, heat, and light. Remove any cotton from the bottle of disintegrating tablets, and keep the bottle tightly closed.
- Lorazepam may be habit-forming and *should be used only by the person it was prescribed for.* Lorazepam should never be shared with another person, especially someone who has a history of drug abuse or addiction. Keep the medication in a secure place where others cannot get to it.
- Do not purchase lorazepam on the internet or outside of the USA as dangerous ingredients may be present.

SPECIAL POPULATIONS:
- *Elderly:* Older patients may be more sensitive to the effects of benzodiazepines. The smallest effective dose should be used. Dose adjustment is necessary for patients with liver impairment and/or renal disease due to excessive metabolites excreted by the kidney. Due to increased risk of sedation leading to falls and fractures, benzodiazepines are included on the Beers List of Potentially Inappropriate Medications for Geriatrics.
- *Pregnancy:* Category D; can cause teratogenic fetal effects. Infants born of mothers taking benzodiazepines may be at risk for withdrawal symptoms in the postnatal period.
- *Lactation:* Excreted in human breast milk; infants can become lethargic and lose weight
- *Children:* Not indicated for use with children under 18 years of age.

SCHIZOPHRENIA: Benzodiazepines (BZDs)

Schizophreniform Disorders

OVERVIEW

- Characterized by the presence of the criterion A symptoms of schizophrenia, including delusions, hallucinations, disorganized speech, disorganized or catatonic behavior, and negative symptoms.
- An episode of the disorder (including prodromal, active, and residual phases) lasts at least 1 month but less than 6 months.
- *Differential diagnosis*: Schizophrenia, brief psychotic disorder, substance-induced psychotic disorder, bipolar disorder, and major depression with mood-incongruent features.
- *Diagnostic workup*: Physical and mental status examination, electrolytes, thyroid function tests, drug screen.

- Studies show that relatives of individuals with schizophreniform disorder are at higher risk of having mood disorders than are relatives of individuals with schizophrenia.
- Relatives of individuals with schizophreniform disorder are more likely to have a psychotic mood disorder than are relatives of individuals with bipolar disorders.
- *The cause of schizophreniform disorder remains unknown.* Current biological and epidemiological data suggest that some of the schizophreniform patients are similar to schizophrenia, whereas others have a disorder similar to mood disorder.
- The lifetime prevalence rate of schizophreniform is 0.2%, and a 1-yr prevalence rate is 0.1%.

Psychopharmacology of Schizophreniform Disorder

Overview

- The pharmacotherapy for schizophreniform disorder is similar to that for schizophrenia. Atypical antipsychotic medications are commonly used.
- Antidepressants may help reduce mood disturbances associated with schizophreniform disorder, but patients need to be monitored carefully for possible exacerbations of psychotic symptoms.
- Long-acting medications are found to increase treatment adherence. Paliperidone (*Invega*), a major active metabolite of risperidone and the first oral agent allowing once-daily dosing, was approved by FDA in 2006.
- Ziprasidone (*Geodon*) is available in injection form to help control acute psychotic symptoms. The injections are less likely to cause acute extrapyramidal side effects.

- It is critical to monitor and manage side effects of antipsychotic medications (e.g., extrapyramidal side effects, TD, sedation, postural hypotension, weight gain, and disturbances in sexual function). See details in the schizophrenia section.
- Psychotherapeutic treatment modalities used in the treatment of patients with schizophrenia may be helpful in treating patients with schizophreniform disorder. However, patients with schizophreniform disorder can become frightened in groups in which they are mixed with patients who have chronic schizophrenia.
- Family therapy is proven to be appropriate for patients with schizophreniform disorder and their families.
- In patients with schizophreniform disorder exhibiting impairments in social functioning, rehabilitative strategies similar to those described for patients with schizophrenia may be helpful.

CLASS	DRUG
Antipsychotic Drugs, Atypical (Second Generation)	**First-Line Drug Therapy**
	aripiprazole (*Abilify, Abilify Discmelt ODT, Abilify Liquid, Abilify IM Injection*)
	clozapine (*Clozaril, Fazaclo*)
	olanzapine (*Zyprexa, Zyprexa Zydis*)
	quetiapine (*Seroquel, Seroquel XR*)
	risperidone (*Risperdal, Risperdal Consta*)
	ziprasidone (*Geodon, Geodon IM Injection*)
	paliperidone (*Invega*)
	asenapine (*Saphris*)

Class: Antipsychotic Drugs, Atypical (Second Generation)

Abilify, Abilify Discmelt ODT, Abilify Liquid, Abilify IM Injection   **aripiprazole**

INDICATIONS: Schizophrenia (13 years and older), manic and mixed episodes associated with bipolar I disorder, adjunctive treatment to antidepressants for MDD, agitation associated with schizophrenia or bipolar disorder, manic or mixed.

AVAILABLE FORMS: Tablet, 2, 5, 10, 15, 20, and 30 mg; tablet, orally disintegrating, 10, and 15 mg; solution, oral, 1 mg/mL; IM injection, solution, 9.75 mg/1.3 mL

DOSAGE: 15 to 30 mg/day.

ADMINISTRATION:
- Tablets may be given with or without food.
- Parenteral administration is intended for IM use only; inject slowly, deep into muscle mass. *IM injection has not been evaluated in children.*
- *Do not give IV or SC.*
- Oral solution may be substituted for tablets on a mg-per-mg basis up to a 25 mg dose. Patients receiving 30 mg tablets should receive 25 mg of the solution.
- Dosing for the orally disintegrating tablet is the same as the oral tablet.
- Do not open the orally disintegrating tablets until ready to administer. The orally disintegrating tablet should be taken without liquid. Do not split the orally disintegrating tablet.
- Use oral aripiprazole 10 to 30 mg/day instead of IM aripiprazole as soon as possible if ongoing therapy is indicated.

SIDE EFFECTS: Nausea, vomiting; dizziness, insomnia, akathisia, activation; headache, asthenia; sedation; constipation; *saphris*; orthostatic hypotension (occasionally during initial phase); increased risk of death and cerebrovascular events in elderly with dementia-related psychosis; TD; neuroleptic malignant syndrome (rare); seizures (rare)

DRUG INTERACTIONS:
- CYP450 3A4 inhibitors (e.g., nefazodone, fluvoxamine, fluoxetine), CYP450 2D6 inhibitors (e.g., paroxetine, fluoxetine, duloxetine), and quinidine may increase plasma levels of aripiprazole.
- Carbamazepine and other CYP450 3A4 inducers may decrease plasma levels of aripiprazole.
- Aripiprazole may enhance effects of antihypertensive medications.
- Aripiprazole may antagonize levodopa and dopamine agonists.
- ▶**Alert:** This list may not describe all possible interactions. Instruct clients to provide a list of all the medicines, herbs, nonprescription drugs, or dietary supplements they use. Also instruct clients to inform if they smoke, drink alcohol, or use illegal drugs.

PHARMACOKINETICS:
Excretion: About 25% of a single oral dose is excreted in urine (less than 1% unchanged) and 55% is excreted in feces (18% as unchanged drug). **Metabolism:** Primarily metabolized by CYP450 2D6 and CYP450 3A4.

Half-life: 75 hr (aripiprazole) and 94 hr (active aripiprazole metabolite).

PRECAUTIONS:
- Dysphagia is associated with the use of aripiprazole. Use with caution in patients who are at risk for aspiration pneumonia.
- Use with caution in patients with conditions that may develop hypotension (dehydration, overheating, etc.).
- DO NOT USE in patients who are allergic to aripiprazole.

PATIENT AND FAMILY EDUCATION:
- Store aripiprazole at 59° to 86°F. It can be used for up to 6 months after opening. Protect injection from light by storing in carton until use.
- If you become pregnant, contact provider. You will need to discuss the benefits and risks of using aripiprazole orally disintegrating tablets while pregnant.
- Discuss with your provider if you have any of these conditions. A dose adjustment or special tests to safely take aripiprazole may be needed:
  - Liver or kidney disease
  - Heart disease, high BP, heart rhythm problems
  - History of heart attack or stroke
  - History of low WBC
  - History of breast cancer
  - Seizures or epilepsy
  - A personal or family history of diabetes
  - Trouble swallowing
  - PKU
- Talk to provider if any signs of hyperglycemia such as increased thirst or urination, excessive hunger, or weakness. If you have diabetes, check blood sugar levels on a regular basis while taking aripiprazole.

SPECIAL POPULATIONS:
- *Elderly:* Generally do not require dosage adjustment. Elderly with dementia-related psychosis treated with atypical antipsychotics are at higher risk of death and cerebrovascular events.
- *Renal impairment:* No dosage adjustment is needed.
- *Hepatic impairment:* No dosage adjustment is required.
- *Cardiac impairment:* Use with caution because of the risk of orthostatic hypotension.
- *Pregnancy:* It is not known if aripiprazole orally disintegrating tablets can cause harm to the fetus.
- *Lactation:* Although there are no data on the excretion of aripiprazole into human milk, it is suggested that women receiving aripiprazole should not breastfeed.
- *Children and adolescents:* Approved for schizophrenia (age 13 and older) and manic/mixed episodes (age 10 and older). They should be monitored more frequently than adults and may tolerate lower doses better.
- ▶**Alert:** Not approved for children with depression.

SCHIZOPHRENIFORM DISORDERS: Antipsychotic Drugs, Atypical (Second Generation)

clozapine   *Clozaril, FazaClo*

INDICATIONS: Treatment-resistant schizophrenia, reduction in risk of recurrent suicidal behavior in patients with schizophrenia or schizoaffective disorder.

AVAILABLE FORMS: Tablet, 12.5, 25 (scored), 50, and 100 mg (scored); orally disintegrating tablet, 12.5 mg, 25 mg, 50 mg, 100 mg

DOSAGE: 300 to 450 mg/day

ADMINISTRATION:
- Tablets may be given with or without food.
- Take the regular oral tablet with a full glass of water.
- The orally disintegrating tablet (*FazaClo*) can be taken without water. Advise patients to keep the tablet in its blister pack until ready to take it. The patient should gently peel back the foil from the blister pack and drop the tablet onto dry hand; place the tablet in the mouth; it will begin to dissolve right away; allow it to dissolve in the mouth without chewing; swallow several times as the tablet dissolves. If desired, advise patients to drink liquid to help swallow the dissolved tablet.
- If one-half of an orally disintegrating tablet is prescribed, advise patients to break the tablet in half and throw the other half away. Do not save the other half for later use.
- If patients stop taking clozapine for more than 2 days in a row, caution patients to call providers before starting to take it again.
- Store clozapine at room temperature away from moisture and heat.

SIDE EFFECTS: May increase risk for diabetes and dyslipidemia; increase salivation; sweating; dizziness; sedation; headache; tachycardia; hypotension; nausea, dry mouth, constipation; weight gain; increased risk of death and cerebrovascular events in elderly with dementia-related psychosis; hyperglycemia; agranulocytosis (includes flu-like symptoms or signs of infection); seizure; neuroleptic malignant syndrome (more likely when it is used with another agent); pulmonary embolism (can include deep vein thrombosis or respiratory symptoms); myocarditis; TD (rare).

DRUG INTERACTIONS:
- Risk or severity of bone marrow suppression may be increased if given in conjunction with medications that suppress bone marrow.
- Use with caution if given in conjunction with alcohol, CNS depressants, or general anesthesia.
- May enhance effects of antihypertensive drugs.
- May need to reduce clozapine dose if given in conjunction with CYP450 1A2 inhibitors (e.g., fluvoxamine)
- May need to increase clozapine dose if given in conjunction with CYP450 1A2 inducers (e.g., cigarette smoke)
- CYP450 2D6 inhibitors (e.g., paroxetine, fluoxetine, duloxetine) and CYP450 3A4 inhibitors

(e.g., nefazodone, fluvoxamine, fluoxetine) can raise clozapine levels, but usually dosage adjustment is not required.
▶**Alert:** This list may not describe all possible interactions. Instruct clients to provide a list of all the medicines, herbs, nonprescription drugs, or dietary supplements they use.

PHARMACOKINETICS:
Metabolism: Metabolized by multiple CYP450 enzymes including 1A2, 2D6, and 3A4
Half-life: 5 to 16 hr

PRECAUTIONS:
- There is an increased risk of fatal myocarditis, especially during but not limited to, the first month of therapy. Promptly discontinue clozapine if myocarditis is suspected.
- Life-threatening agranulocytosis can occur. Baseline WBC and ANC should be done before initiation of treatment, during treatment, and for at least 4 weeks after discontinuing treatment.
- Use with caution in patients with glaucoma or enlarged prostate.
- *Do not use in patients with:*
  - Myeloproliferative disorder
  - Uncontrolled seizure
  - Granulocytopenia
  - Paralytic ileus
  - CNS depression
  - Allergic symptoms to clozapine

PATIENT AND FAMILY EDUCATION:
- Clozapine will only be provided in 1- or 2-week supplies, depending on frequency of WBC monitoring. Follow-up visits and weekly blood cell counts are required to monitor therapy and to keep appointments.
- Take prescribed dose with or without food. Take with food if stomach upset occurs.
- Keep tablet in unopened blister until just before use. Remove tablet by peeling the foil from the back of the blister and then immediately place the tablet (or half tablet if ordered) in the mouth, allow the tablet to disintegrate, and then swallow with saliva.
- Do not to stop taking clozapine when feeling better.
- If medication needs to be discontinued, it will be slowly withdrawn over a period of 1 to 2 weeks unless safety concerns (e.g., low WBC) require a more rapid withdrawal.
- *Immediately report to provider* if any of these conditions occur: altered mental status, change in personality or mood, chest pain, fever, flu-like symptoms, frequent urination, general body discomfort, involuntary body or facial movements, lethargy, mucous membrane sores or other signs of possible infection, muscle rigidity, pounding in the chest, rapid or difficult breathing, rapid or irregular heartbeat, seizures, sore throat, sweating, swelling of feet or ankles, unexplained fatigue, unexplained shortness of breath, unquenchable thirst, weakness, or weight gain.

(cont.)

clozapine (cont.)

- *If you have diabetes,* monitor blood glucose more frequently when drug is started or dose is changed and inform your provider of significant changes in readings.
- *If you are taking antihypertensive drugs,* monitor BP at regular intervals.
- *If you have history of seizures or factors predisposing to seizures,* clozapine may cause seizures; do not engage in any activity in which sudden loss of consciousness could cause serious risk to patient or others (e.g., driving, swimming, climbing).
- *Avoid* strenuous activity during periods of high temperature or humidity.
- *Avoid* alcoholic beverages and sedatives (e.g., diazepam) while taking clozapine.
- Get up slowly from lying or sitting position and avoid sudden position changes to prevent postural hypotension. Hot tubs and hot showers or baths may make dizziness worse.
- Take sips of water, suck on ice chips or sugarless hard candy, or chew sugarless gum if dry mouth occurs.
- Clozapine may impair judgment, thinking, or motor skills, or it may cause drowsiness. Thus, use with caution while driving or performing other tasks requiring mental alertness until tolerance is determined.

SPECIAL POPULATIONS:
- *Elderly:* May tolerate lower doses better. Elderly with dementia-related psychosis treated with atypical antipsychotics are at higher risk of death and cerebrovascular events.
- *Renal impairment*: Use with caution.
- *Hepatic impairment*: Use with caution.
- *Cardiac impairment*: Use with caution especially if patient is taking concomitant medication.
- *Pregnancy:* Category B. Animal studies do not show adverse effects. No controlled studies in humans. Clozapine should be used only when the potential benefits outweigh potential risks to the fetus.
- *Lactation*: It is not known if clozapine is secreted in human breast milk. It is recommended to either discontinue drug or bottle feed. Infants of women who choose to breastfeed while on this drug should be monitored for possible adverse effect.
- *Children and adolescents:* Safety and efficacy have not been established for this population. Should be monitored more frequently than adults.

Zyprexa, Zyprexa Zydix   **olanzapine**

▶**Note:** Fixed-dose olanzapine/fluoxetine is marketed under the trade name *Symbyax*.

INDICATIONS: Schizophrenia, monotherapy or combination therapy for acute mixed or manic episodes associated with bipolar I disorder, maintenance monotherapy of bipolar I disorder, agitation associated with schizophrenia or bipolar I disorder.

AVAILABLE FORMS: Tablet, 2.5, 5, 7.5, 10, 15, and 20 mg; orally disintegrating tablet, 5, 10, 15, and 20 mg; IM formulation, 5 mg/mL, each vial contains 10 mg; olanzapine–fluoxetine combination capsule, 6 mg/25 mg, 6 mg/50 mg, 12 mg/25 mg, 12 mg/50 mg

DOSAGE:
- 10 to 20 mg/day (PO or IM)
- 6 to 12 mg/olanzapine/25 to 50 mg fluoxetine (olanzapine–fluoxetine combination)

ADMINISTRATION:
- Tablets may be given with or without food.
- Advise patient to take the missed dose as soon as remembered. Skip the missed dose if it is almost time for the next scheduled dose. Do not take extra medicine to make up for missed dose.
- Store at room temperature away from moisture, heat, and light.

SIDE EFFECTS:
- Can increase risk for diabetes and dyslipidemia; dizziness; sedation; dry mouth, weight gain, constipation, dyspepsia; peripheral edema; joint pain, back pain, chest pain, extremity pain, abnormal gait, ecchymosis; tachycardia; orthostatic hypotension (usually during initial dose titration); hyperglycemia; increased risk of death and cerebrovascular events in elderly with dementia-related psychosis; TD (rare); rash on exposure to sunlight (rare); neuroleptic malignant syndrome (rare); seizures (rare)

DRUG INTERACTIONS:
- May increase effects of antihypertensive medications
- May antagonize levodopa and dopamine agonists
- May need to reduce dose if given with CYP450 1A2 inhibitors (e.g., fluvoxamine)
- May need to increase dose if given with CYP450 1A2 inducers (e.g., cigarette smoke, carbamazepine)

▶**Alert:** This list may not describe all possible interactions. Instruct clients to provide a list of all the medicines, herbs, nonprescription drugs, or dietary supplements they use.

PHARMACOKINETICS:
Metabolism: Metabolites are inactive
Half-life: 21 to 54 hr

(cont.)

SCHIZOPHRENIFORM DISORDERS: Antipsychotic Drugs, Atypical (Second Generation)

olanzapine (*cont.*)

PRECAUTIONS:
- Use with caution in patients with conditions that predispose to hypotension (dehydration, overheating). Watch closely for hypotension if given IM formulation.
- Use with caution in patients with prostatic hypertrophy, narrow angle-closure glaucoma, paralytic ileus.
- Use with caution in patients who are at risk for aspiration pneumonia.
- IM formulation is not recommended to be given with parenteral benzodiazepines. If patients need a parenteral benzodiazepine, it should be given at least 1 hr after IM formulation olanzapine.
- *Do not use if there is a proven allergy.*
- Do not give IM formulation:
  - If patient has unstable medical condition (e.g., AMI, unstable angina pectoris, severe hypotension and/or bradycardia, sick sinus syndrome, recent heart surgery).
  - If patient has known risks of narrow angle-closure glaucoma.

PATIENT AND FAMILY EDUCATION:
- Take exactly as prescribed by the provider. Do not take in larger or smaller amounts or for longer than recommended.
- Can be taken with or without food.
- For orally disintegrating tablets, keep the tablet in its blister pack until patient is ready to take it. Open the package and peel back the foil from the tablet blister. Do not push a tablet through the foil. Using dry hands, remove the tablet and place it in the mouth and it will begin to dissolve right away.
- Do not swallow the tablet whole. Allow it to dissolve in the mouth without chewing. If desired, drink liquid to help swallow the dissolved tablet.
- *If you have diabetes,* check blood sugar levels on a regular basis while taking olanzapine.
- You can gain weight or have high cholesterol and triglycerides while taking this drug, especially if teenaged. Your blood will need to be tested often.
- Do not stop taking the drug suddenly without first talking to your provider, even if you feel fine. You may have serious side effects if you stop taking the drug suddenly.
- Call provider if symptoms do not improve or get worse.
- Store at room temperature away from moisture, heat, and light.

SPECIAL POPULATIONS:
- *Elderly:*
  - May tolerate lower doses better. Elderly with dementia-related psychosis treated with atypical antipsychotics are at higher risk of death and cerebrovascular events. It can increase incidence of stroke.
  - If IM formulation is given, the recommended starting dose is 2.5 to 5 mg. A second injection of 2.5 to 5 mg may be given 2 hr after the first injection. No more than three injections should be administered within 24 hr.
- *Renal impairment*: No dose adjustment is required for oral formulation. Consider lower starting dose (5 mg) for IM formulation. Not removed by hemodialysis.
- *Hepatic impairment*: Starting oral dose 5 mg for patients with moderate-to-severe hepatic function impairment; increase dose with caution. Consider lower starting dose (5 mg) for IM formulation. Check patient liver function a few times a year.
- *Cardiac impairment:* Use with caution because of risk of orthostatic hypotension.
- *Pregnancy:* Category C. Some animal studies show adverse effects. No controlled studies in humans. Should be used only when the potential benefits outweigh potential risks to the fetus. Olanzapine may be preferable to anticonvulsant mood stabilizers if treatment is required during pregnancy.
- *Lactation*: It is not known if olanzapine is secreted in human breast milk. It is recommended to either discontinue drug or bottle feed. Infants of women who choose to breastfeed while on this drug should be monitored for possible adverse effect.
- *Children and adolescents:*
  - Probably safe and effective for behavioral disturbances in this population.
  - IM formulation has not been studied in patients younger than 18 and is not recommended for use in this population.
  - Should be monitored more frequently than adults.

quetiapine   *Seroquel, Seroquel XR*

INDICATIONS: Schizophrenia, depressive episodes associated with bipolar disorder, monotherapy or combination therapy for acute manic episodes associated with bipolar I disorder, acute and maintenance treatment of schizophrenia.

AVAILABLE FORMS: Tablet, 25, 50, 100, 200, 300, and 400 mg; extended-release tablet, 200, 300, and 400 mg

DOSAGE:
- 400 to 800 mg/day in one (*Seroquel XR*) or two (*Seroquel*) doses for schizophrenia and bipolar mania
- 300 mg once per day for bipolar depression

ADMINISTRATION:
- Tablets may be given with or without food.
- Take this medicine with a full glass of water.

(cont.)

quetiapine (*cont.*)

- Advise patient not to crush, chew, or break an extended-release tablet. Swallow the pill whole. Breaking the pill may cause too much of the drug to be released at one time.
- Advise patient to take the missed dose as soon as remembered. Skip the missed dose if it is almost time for the next scheduled dose. Do not take extra medicine to make up for the missed dose.

SIDE EFFECTS: Can increase risk for diabetes and dyslipidemia; dizziness, sedation; dry mouth, constipation, dyspepsia, abdominal pain; weight gain; tachycardia; hyperglycemia; increased risk of death and cerebrovascular events in elderly with dementia-related psychosis; orthostatic hypotension (usually during initial dose titration); neuroleptic malignant syndrome (rare); seizures (rare)

DRUG INTERACTIONS:
- May increase effects of antihypertensive medications
- Plasma levels of quetiapine may be increased if given in conjunction with CYP450 3A and CYP450 2D6 inhibitors. However, no dose adjustment is required.

▶**Alert:** This list may not describe all possible interactions. Instruct clients to provide a list of all the medicines, herbs, nonprescription drugs, or dietary supplements they use.

PHARMACOKINETICS:
Metabolism: Metabolites are inactive
Half-life: 6 to 7 hr

PRECAUTIONS:
- Use with caution in patients who are at risk for aspiration pneumonia.
- Manufacturer recommends examination for cataracts before and every 6 months after starting quetiapine.
- *Do not use if there is a proven allergy.*

PATIENT AND FAMILY EDUCATION:
- Take exactly as prescribed by the provider. Do not take in larger or smaller amounts or for longer than recommended.
- Can be taken with or without food.
- Quetiapine can cause side effects that may impair thinking or reactions. Be careful if you drive or do anything that requires you to be awake and alert.
- Quetiapine may cause high blood sugar (hyperglycemia). Talk to provider if any signs of hyperglycemia such as increased thirst or urination, excessive hunger, or weakness. If diabetic, check blood sugar levels on a regular basis.
- *Avoid becoming overheated or dehydrated during exercise and in hot weather.* You may be more prone to heat stroke.
- *Avoid getting up too fast from a sitting or lying position.* Get up slowly and steady yourself to prevent a fall.
- *Avoid drinking alcohol.*
- *Stop using this medication and call provider immediately* if you have very stiff (rigid) muscles, high fever, sweating, confusion, fast or uneven heartbeats, tremors; feel like you might pass out; have jerky muscle movements you cannot control, trouble swallowing, problems with speech; have blurred vision, eye pain, or see halos around lights; have increased thirst and urination, excessive hunger, fruity breath odor, weakness, nausea and vomiting; have fever, chills, body aches, flu symptoms; or have white patches or sores inside your mouth or on your lips.
- Do not stop taking the drug suddenly without first talking to your provider, even if you feel fine. You may have serious side effects if you stop taking the drug suddenly.
- Call provider if symptoms do not improve or get worse.
- Store at room temperature away from moisture and heat.

SPECIAL POPULATIONS:
- *Elderly:*
  - Generally lower dose is used (e.g., 25–100 mg twice a day). Higher dose can be used if tolerated.
  - Elderly with dementia-related psychosis treated with atypical antipsychotics are at higher risk of death and cerebrovascular events.
- *Renal impairment*: No dose adjustment is required.
- *Hepatic impairment*: May need to reduce dose.
- *Cardiac impairment:* Use with caution because of risk of orthostatic hypotension.
- *Pregnancy:* Category C. Some animal studies show adverse effects. There are no controlled studies in humans. It should be used only when the potential benefits outweigh potential risks to the fetus. Quetiapine may be preferable to anticonvulsant mood stabilizers if treatment is required during pregnancy.
- *Lactation*: It is not known if drug is secreted in human breast milk. It is recommended to either discontinue drug or bottle feed. Infants of women who choose to breastfeed while on this drug should be monitored for possible adverse effect.
- *Children and adolescents:*
  - Not officially recommended for patients younger than 18 years.
  - Probably safe and effective for behavioral disturbances in this population.
  - Should be monitored more frequently than adults. May tolerate lower doses better.
  - Watch for activation of suicidal ideation. Inform parents or guardian of this risk so they can help monitor the risk.

SCHIZOPHRENIFORM DISORDERS: Antipsychotic Drugs, Atypical (Second Generation)

risperidone   *Risperdal, Risperdal Consta*

INDICATIONS: Schizophrenia (age 13 years and older), monotherapy or combination therapy for acute mixed or manic episodes associated with bipolar I disorder (age 10 and older), treatment of irritability associated with autistic disorder in children and adolescents aged 5 to 16 years.

AVAILABLE FORMS: Tablet, 0.25, 0.5, 1, 2, 3, 4, and 6 mg; orally disintegrating tablet, 0.5, 1, and 2 mg; liquid, 1 mg/mL (30 mL bottle); long-acting depot microspheres formulation for deep IM formulation, 25 mg vial/kit, 37.5 mg vial/kit, 50 mg vial/kit

DOSAGE:
- 2 to 8 mg/day PO for adults with acute psychosis and bipolar disorder
- 0.5 to 2.0 mg/day PO for children and elderly
- 25 to 50 mg IM depot every 2 weeks

ADMINISTRATION:
- Tablets may be given with or without food.
- Advise patient to take the missed dose as soon as remembered. Skip the missed dose if it is almost time for the next scheduled dose. Do not take extra medicine to make up for the missed dose.
- Measure the liquid form of risperidone with a special dose-measuring spoon or cup, not a regular tablespoon.
- Do not mix the liquid form with cola or tea.

SIDE EFFECTS: Can increase risk for diabetes and dyslipidemia; extrapyramidal symptoms (dose dependent); hyperprolactinemia (dose dependent); dizziness, insomnia, headache, anxiety; nausea, sedation; weight gain, constipation, abdominal pain; tachycardia; sexual dysfunction; hyperglycemia; increased risk of death and cerebrovascular events in elderly with dementia-related psychosis; TD (rare); orthostatic hypotension (rare, usually during initial dose titration); neuroleptic malignant syndrome (rare); seizures (rare)

DRUG INTERACTIONS:
- May increase effects of antihypertensive medications
- May antagonize levodopa and dopamine agonists
- Plasma levels of risperidone may be reduced if given in conjunction with carbamazepine.
- Plasma levels of risperidone may be increased if given in conjunction with fluoxetine or paroxetine
- Plasma levels of risperidone may be increased if given in conjunction with clozapine, but no dose adjustment is required.

▶**Alert:** This list may not describe all possible interactions. Instruct clients to provide a list of all the medicines, herbs, nonprescription drugs, or dietary supplements they use.

PHARMACOKINETICS:
Elimination: 7 to 8 weeks after last injection (long-acting formulation)
Metabolism: Metabolites are active. Metabolized by CYP450 2D6
Half-life: 20 to 24 hr (oral formulation); 3 to 6 days (long-acting formulation)

PRECAUTIONS:
- Use with caution in patients with conditions that predispose to hypotension (dehydration, overheating).
- Use with caution in patients who are at risk for aspiration pneumonia.
- Priapism has been reported.
- Do not use if there is a proven allergy.

PATIENT AND FAMILY EDUCATION:
- Take exactly as prescribed by the provider. Do not take in larger or smaller amounts or for longer than recommended.
- Can be taken with or without food.
- You may be more sensitive to temperature extremes (very hot or cold conditions) when taking this medication. Avoid getting too cold, or becoming overheated or dehydrated.
- Drink plenty of fluids, especially in hot weather and during exercise.
- Risperidone can cause side effects that may impair thinking or reactions. Be careful if you drive or do anything that requires you to be awake and alert.
- Risperidone may cause high blood sugar (hyperglycemia). Talk to provider if any signs of hyperglycemia such as increased thirst or urination, excessive hunger, or weakness. If diabetic, check blood sugar levels on a regular basis.
- Risperidone orally disintegrating tablet may contain phenylalanine. Talk to provider before using this form of risperidone if you have PKU.
- *Avoid drinking alcohol.* It can increase some of the side effects.
- *Do not* mix the liquid form with cola or tea.
- *Stop using this medication and call provider immediately* if you have fever, stiff muscles, confusion, sweating, fast or uneven heartbeats, restless muscle movements in face or neck, tremor (uncontrolled shaking), trouble swallowing, feeling light-headed, or fainting.
- Do not stop taking the drug suddenly without first talking to your provider, even if you feel fine. You may have serious side effects if you stop taking the drug suddenly.
- Call provider if symptoms do not improve or get worse.
- Store at room temperature away from moisture, light, and heat. Do not freeze the liquid form of risperidone.

SPECIAL POPULATIONS:
- *Elderly:*
  - Initially 0.5 mg orally a day, then increase to 0.5 mg twice a day. Titrate once a week for doses above 1.5 mg twice a day.
  - Long-acting risperidone: 25 mg every 2 weeks. Oral administration should be continued for 3 weeks after the first injection.
  - Elderly with dementia-related psychosis treated with atypical antipsychotics are at higher risk of death and cerebrovascular events.

(cont.)

risperidone (cont.)

- *Renal impairment*:
  - Initially 0.5 mg orally twice a day for the first week. Increase to 1 mg twice a day during the second week.
  - Long-acting risperidone should not be given to patients with renal function impairment unless s/he can tolerate at least 2 mg/day orally.
  - Long-acting risperidone should be given 25 mg every 2 weeks. Oral administration should be continued for 3 weeks after the first injection.
- *Hepatic impairment*:
  - Initially 0.5 mg orally twice a day for the first week. Increase to 1 mg twice a day during the second week.
  - Long-acting risperidone should not be given to patients with hepatic function impairment unless s/he can tolerate at least 2 mg/day orally.
  - Long-acting risperidone should be given 25 mg every 2 weeks. Oral administration should be continued for 3 weeks after the first injection.

- *Cardiac impairment:* Use with caution because of risk of orthostatic hypotension. Can increase the risk of stroke if given to elderly patients with atrial fibrillation.
- *Pregnancy:* Category C. Some animal studies show adverse effects. No controlled studies in humans. Should be used only when the potential benefits outweigh potential risks to the fetus. Risperidone may be preferable to anticonvulsant mood stabilizers if treatment is required during pregnancy. Effects of hyperprolactinemia on the fetus are unknown.
- *Lactation:* Drug is secreted in human breast milk. It is recommended to either discontinue drug or bottle feed. Infants of women who choose to breastfeed while on this drug should be monitored for possible adverse effect.
- *Children and adolescents:*
  - Safe and effective for behavioral disturbances in this population.
  - Risperidone is the most frequently used atypical antipsychotic medication in this population.

Geodon, Geodon IM Injection   **ziprasidone**

INDICATIONS: Schizophrenia, delaying relapse in schizophrenia, acute agitation in schizophrenia (IM), acute mania/mixed mania, other psychotic disorders, bipolar maintenance, bipolar depression, behavioral disturbances in dementia.

AVAILABLE FORMS: Tablet, 20, 40, 60, and 80 mg; injection, 20 mg/mL

DOSAGE:
- 40 to 200 mg/day in divided doses, PO for schizophrenia
- 80 to 160 mg/day in divided doses, PO for bipolar
- 10 to 20 mg IM (doses of 10 mg may be administered every 2 hr, doses of 20 mg may be administered every 4 hr; with MDD 40 mg). Not to be administered for more than 3 consecutive days.

ADMINISTRATION:
- Take this medication with a meal.
- Dosing at 20 to 40 mg twice a day is too low and activating, perhaps due to potent 5HT2C antagonist properties. Reduce activation by increasing the dose to 60 to 80 mg twice a day.
- Best efficacy in schizophrenia and bipolar disorder is at doses greater than 120 mg/day.
- BMI monthly for 3 months, then quarterly.
- Monitor fasting triglycerides monthly for several months in patients at high risk for metabolic complications.
- BP, fasting plasma glucose, fasting lipids within 3 months and then annually, but earlier and more frequently for patients with diabetes or who have gained more than 5% of initial weight.

SIDE EFFECTS:
- Dizziness, sedation, and hypotension especially at high doses
- Motor side effects (rare)

- Possible increased incidence of diabetes or dyslipidemia is unknown

DRUG INTERACTIONS:
- May enhance the effects of antihypertensive drugs
- May antagonize levodopa and dopamine agonists
- May enhance QTc prolongation of other drugs capable of prolonging QTc interval

PHARMACOKINETICS:
Protein binding: Greater than 99%
Metabolism: Metabolized by CYP450 3A4
Half-life: 6.6 hr

PRECAUTIONS:
- Prolongs QTc interval more than some other antipsychotics.
- Use with caution in patients with conditions that predispose to hypotension (dehydration, overheating).
- Priapism has been reported.
- Dysphagia has been associated with antipsychotic use and should be used cautiously in patients at risk for aspiration pneumonia.
- Do not use if patient is taking agents capable of prolonging QTc interval (pimozide, thioridazine, selected antiarrhythmics, moxifloxacin, sparfloxacin).
- Do not use if there is a history of QTc prolongation, cardiac arrhythmia, recent AMI, uncompensated heart failure.
- Do not use if there is a proven allergy to ziprasidone.

PATIENT AND FAMILY EDUCATION:
- *Take with a meal* of a few hundred calories (e.g., turkey sandwich and a piece of fruit) to enhance the absorption.

(cont.)

SCHIZOPHRENIFORM DISORDERS: Antipsychotic Drugs, Atypical (Second Generation)

ziprasidone (cont.)

- *Avoid becoming overheated or dehydrated during exercise and in hot weather.* You may be more prone to heat stroke.
- *Avoid getting up too fast from a sitting or lying position.* Get up slowly and steady yourself to prevent a fall.
- *Avoid drinking alcohol.*
- *Stop using this medication and call provider immediately* if you have very stiff (rigid) muscles, high fever, sweating, confusion, fast or uneven heartbeats, tremors; feel like you might pass out; have jerky muscle movements you cannot control, trouble swallowing, problems with speech; have blurred vision, eye pain, or see halos around lights; have increased thirst and urination, excessive hunger, fruity breath odor, weakness, nausea and vomiting; have fever, chills, body aches, flu symptoms; or have white patches or sores inside your mouth or on your lips.
- Do not stop taking the drug suddenly without first talking to provider, even if you feel fine. You may have serious side effects if you stop taking the drug suddenly.
- Call provider if symptoms do not improve or get worse.

- Store at room temperature away from moisture and heat.

SPECIAL POPULATIONS:
- *Elderly:* Some patients may tolerate lower doses better. Elderly patients with dementia-related psychosis treated with atypical antipsychotics are at an increased risk of death compared to placebo.
- *Renal impairment:* No dose adjustment is necessary.
- *Hepatic impairment:* No dose adjustment is necessary.
- *Cardiac impairment:* Contraindicated in patients with a known history of QTc prolongation, recent AMI, and uncompensated heart failure.
- *Pregnancy:* Category C. Some animal studies show adverse effects. There are no controlled studies in humans.
- *Lactation:* It is not known if it is secreted in human breast milk. Recommend either to discontinue drug or bottle feed.
- *Children and adolescents:* Not recommended for patients younger than 18 years. Early data suggest that it may be safe and effective for behavioral disturbances in children and adolescents.

paliperidone | *Invega*

INDICATIONS: Schizophrenia, bipolar disorder, other psychotic disorders, behavioral responses in dementia, behavioral disturbances in children and adolescents, disorders associated with problems with impulse control.

AVAILABLE FORMS: Tablet (extended-release) 3, 6, and 9 mg

DOSAGE: 6 mg/day; maximum dose, 12 mg/day

ADMINISTRATION:
- Initial dose, 6 mg/day taken in the morning
- Can increase by 3 mg/day every 5 days

SIDE EFFECTS: Dizziness, sedation, and hypotension; motor side effects especially at high doses; elevation in prolactin; may increase risk for diabetes and dyslipidemia; rare TD (much less than conventional antipsychotics); hypersalivation; weight gain; orthostatic hypotension; tachycardia; hyperglycemia associated with ketoacidosis or osmolar coma or death has been reported in patients taking atypical antipsychotics; in elderly patients with dementia-related psychosis, there is an increased risk of death and cerebrovascular events; neuroleptic malignant syndrome (rare); seizures (rare)

DRUG INTERACTIONS:
- May increase effects of antihypertensive agents
- May decrease the effects of levodopa and dopamine agonists
- May increase QTc prolongation of other drugs that also increase the QTc interval

PHARMACOKINETICS:
- Active metabolite of risperidone
Half-life: Approx. 23 hr

PRECAUTIONS:
- Use with caution with conditions that predispose to hypotension (dehydration, overheating).
- Use with caution in patients at risk for aspiration pneumonia since dysphagia has been associated with antipsychotic use.
- Prolongs QTc interval.
- Priapism is reported with other antipsychotic including risperidone, and paliperidone is an active metabolite of risperidone.
- *Do not use* if patient is taking other medications or has conditions that prolong QTc interval (pimozide, thioridazine, selected antiarrhythmics, recent AMI, uncompensated heart failure).
- *Do not use* if patient has preexisting severe GI narrowing.
- *Do not use if allergic to or sensitive to* paliperidone or risperidone.

PATIENT AND FAMILY EDUCATION:
- Take exactly as prescribed by the provider. Do not take in larger or smaller amounts or for longer than recommended.
- *Avoid becoming overheated or dehydrated during exercise and in hot weather.* You may be more prone to heat stroke.
- *Avoid getting up too fast from a sitting or lying position.* Get up slowly and steady yourself to prevent a fall.
- *Avoid drinking alcohol.*
- *Stop using this medication and call provider immediately* if you have very stiff (rigid) muscles, high fever, sweating, confusion, fast or uneven heartbeats, tremors; feel like you might pass out; have

(cont.)

paliperidone (*cont.*)

jerky muscle movements you cannot control, trouble swallowing, problems with speech; have blurred vision, eye pain, or see halos around lights; have increased thirst and urination, excessive hunger, fruity breath odor, weakness, nausea and vomiting; have fever, chills, body aches, flu symptoms; or have white patches or sores inside your mouth or on your lips.

- Do not stop taking the drug suddenly without first talking to your provider, even if you feel fine. You may have serious side effects if you stop taking the drug suddenly.
- Call provider if symptoms do not improve or get worse.
- Store at room temperature away from moisture and heat.

SPECIAL POPULATIONS:

- *Elderly:* May tolerate lower doses better. Are more sensitive to adverse effects. It is not approved for treatment of elderly patients with dementia-related psychosis, and such patients are at increased risk of cardiovascular events and death.
- *Renal impairment:* For more mild impairment, maximum dose recommended is 6 mg/day.

For moderate-to-severe impairment, maximum dose recommended is 3 mg/day.

- *Hepatic impairment:* No dose adjustment recommended for mild-to-moderate impairment. Use in patients with severe impairment has not been studied.
- *Cardiac impairment:* Use with caution due to risk of orthostatic hypotension.
- *Pregnancy:* Category C. Animal studies show adverse effects; there are no controlled studies in humans. Psychotic symptoms may worsen during pregnancy and necessitate some form of treatment. Paliperidone may be preferable to anticonvulsant mood stabilizers and conventional antipsychotics. Effects of hyperprolactinemia on the fetus are unknown.
- *Lactation:* Some drug is found in mother's breast milk, and it is recommended that either the drug be discontinued or infant be bottle fed. Infants who are breastfed while mother is on paliperidone need to be monitored for adverse effects.
- *Children and adolescents:* Safety and efficacy not established for paliperidone for children and adolescents. Children and adolescents will need to be monitored more closely than adults.

Saphris   **asenapine**

INDICATIONS: Schizophrenia, manic or mixed episodes associated with bipolar disorder I.

AVAILABLE FORMS: Sublingual tablets, 5 and 10 mg

DOSAGE:

- Initial dose, 5 mg bid; increase to 10 mg bid
- Can decrease back to 5 mg bid based on tolerability

ADMINISTRATION:

- *Place the tablet under the tongue and allow to dissolve completely.*
- The tablet dissolves within seconds.
- Do not eat or drink anything for 10 to 30 min after administration.
- *Do not crush, chew, or swallow tablets.*

SIDE EFFECTS: Akathisia; oral hypoesthesia (numbness); somnolence; dizziness; other extrapyramidal symptoms excluding akathisia; weight gain; insomnia; headache; may induce orthostatic hypotension and syncope in some patients, especially early in treatment; rare neuroleptic malignant syndrome (rare); TD (rare)

DRUG INTERACTIONS:

- May enhance effects of certain antihypertensive drugs because of its alpha-1-adrenergic antagonism with potential for inducing hypotension
- Inhibitor of P450 CYP2D6 and may contribute to increased levels (paroxetine)
- Appears to decrease prolactin from baseline

PHARMACOKINETICS:

- Metabolized primarily through CP1A2
- Rapidly absorbed within 0.5 to 1.5 hr

Half-life: Approx. 24 hr

PRECAUTIONS:

- Caution should be used when drug is taken in combination with other centrally acting drugs or alcohol.
- Caution should be used with other drugs that are both substrates and inhibitors for CYP2D6; may double the level of paroxetine.
- May cause transient increases in serum transaminase; therefore, this needs to be monitored during the initial months.
- Elderly patients with dementia-related psychosis treated with antipsychotic drugs are at an increased risk of death. Asenapine is not approved for the treatment of patients with dementia-related psychosis.
- Patients with preexisting low WBC or history of drug-induced leukopenia/neutropenia should have their CBC monitored frequently during the first few months of therapy and asenapine should be discontinued at the first sign of decline in WBC in the absence of other causative factors.
- The use of asenapine should be avoided in combination with other drugs known to prolong the QTc interval including Class 1A antiarrhythmics (e.g., quinidine, procainamide) or Class 3 antiarrhythmics (e.g., amiodarone, sotalol), antipsychotic medications (e.g., ziprasidone,

(cont.)

SCHIZOPHRENIFORM DISORDERS: Antipsychotic Drugs, Atypical (Second Generation)

asenapine (*cont.*)

chlorpromazine, thioridazine), and antibiotics (e.g., gatifloxacin, moxifloxacin).
- Like other drugs that antagonize dopamine D2 receptors, asenapine can elevate prolactin levels, and the elevation can persist during chronic administration.
- As with other antipsychotic drugs, asenapine should be used with caution in patients with a history of seizures or with conditions that potentially lower the seizure threshold; e.g., Alzheimer's dementia. Conditions that lower the seizure threshold may be more prevalent in patients 65 years or older.

PATIENT AND FAMILY EDUCATION:
- Take exactly as prescribed by the provider. Do not take in larger or smaller amounts or for longer than recommended.
- Asenapine tablets must be placed under tongue and be allowed to dissolve. Do not crush, chew, or swallow.
- Do not eat or drink for at least 10 min—30 min is better—after the drug dissolves.
- *Avoid drinking alcohol.*
- *Stop using this medication and call provider immediately* if you have very stiff (rigid) muscles, high fever, sweating, confusion, fast or uneven heartbeats, tremors; feel like you might pass out; have jerky muscle movements you cannot control, trouble swallowing, problems with speech; have blurred vision, eye pain, or see halos around lights; have increased thirst and urination, excessive hunger, fruity breath odor, weakness, nausea and vomiting; have fever, chills, body aches, flu symptoms; or have white patches or sores inside your mouth or on your lips.
- Do not stop taking this drug suddenly without first talking to your provider, even if you feel fine. You may have serious side effects if you stop taking the drug suddenly.

- Call provider if symptoms do not improve or get worse.
- Store at room temperature away from moisture and heat.

SPECIAL POPULATIONS:
- *Elderly:* They may tolerate lower doses better and are more sensitive to adverse effects. It is not approved for treatment of elderly patients with dementia-related psychosis, and such patients are at increased risk of cardiovascular events and death.
- *Renal impairment*: No adjustment is needed.
- *Hepatic impairment*: Lower dose for mild-to-moderate impairment. Not recommended with severe liver impairment.
- *Cardiac impairment:* Use with caution due to risk of orthostatic hypotension and QTc potential prolongation.
- *Pregnancy:* Category C. There are no adequate and well-controlled studies of asenapine in pregnant women. In animal studies, asenapine increased postimplantation loss and decreased pup weight and survival at doses similar to or less than recommended clinical doses. In these studies there was no increase in the incidence of structural abnormalities caused by asenapine. Asenapine should be used during pregnancy only if the potential benefit justifies the potential risk to the fetus.
- *Lactation*: Asenapine is excreted in the milk of rats during lactation. It is not known whether asenapine or its metabolites are excreted in human milk. Because many drugs are excreted in human milk, caution should be exercised when asenapine is administered to a nursing woman. Women receiving asenapine are recommended not to breastfeed.
- *Children and adolescents*: Safety and effectiveness in children and adolescents has not been established.

Shared Psychotic Disorder

OVERVIEW
- Also called "folie à deux" (the folly of two), this is a rare disorder characterized by the transfer of delusions from one person (primary) to another person (secondary) with close emotional ties.
- The diagnosis is given if:
  - A delusion develops in an individual in the context of a close relationship with another person(s) who already has an established delusion.
  - The delusion is similar in content to that of the persons who already has an established delusion.
  - The disturbance is not better accounted for by another psychotic disorder (e.g., schizophrenia) or mood disorder with psychotic features

and is not due to the direct physiological effects of a substance (e.g., drug abuse, medication) or a general medical condition.
- Medical conditions associated with the development of delusions (e.g., toxic-metabolic conditions affecting the limbic system and basal ganglia; Huntington's disease), delirium, dementia, substance-related disorders, schizophrenia, mood disorders, OCD, somatoform disorders, paranoid personality disorders are ruled out.
- Physical and mental status examination, x-ray, blood test, drug screen.
- Recent studies suggest that females and males are equally affected, the secondary person can be either younger or older than the primary

person, and the incidence rate in married couples is equal to that in siblings.
- The individual who first has delusion (the primary case) is often chronically ill and is the influential member of a close relationship with a more suggestible individual (the secondary case) who also develops delusion.

- Occurrence of delusion in the secondary case is attributed to the strong influence of the more dominant member.
- The epidemiology remains unclear since most data have been extrapolated from case reports.

Psychopharmacology of Shared Psychotic Disorder

Overview
- The goal of treatment is to relieve the secondary case of the induced delusion and to stabilize the primary person's psychotic disorder.
- Treatment usually necessitates separation of the secondary person from the primary person; however, that tends to be insufficient for recovery.
- Hospitalization may be required for one or both individuals in separate psychiatric units/hospitals to maintain their separateness.
- Two of the atypical antipsychotics have proven especially helpful in the treatment of shared psychotic disorder: aripiprazole (*Abilify*) and quetiapine (*Seroquel*). Aripiprazole is initiated at a dose of 5 to 10 mg PO every day and titrated up by 5 to 10 mg every 3 to 5 days until a 25 to 60 mg daily dose is achieved and symptoms of the psychoses are alleviated. Quetiapine is initiated at 25 to 50 mg twice a day and increased by 50 mg every 3 days until symptom resolution is achieved. Maintenance dose is 200 to 600 mg per day.
- Individual psychotherapy for both primary and secondary partners is required and may be of a long-term nature. Recently, some clinicians are recommending adding conjoint therapy as well to deal with feelings of rejection, inducer-induced dimensions, anger, dependency, hostility, and distorted communication.
- Patient and family education about shared psychosis is also recommended. There are multiple Web sites providing information about the disorder, support programs, and resources.

CLASS	DRUG
Antipsychotic Drugs, Atypical (Second Generation)	**First-Line Drug Therapy**
	aripiprazole (*Abilify, Abilify Discmelt ODT, Abilify Liquid, Abilify IM Injection*) quetiapine (*Seroquel, Seroquel XR*)

SHARED PSYCHOTIC DISORDER

Class: Antipsychotic Drugs, Atypical (Second Generation)

aripiprazole   *Abilify, Abilify Discmelt ODT, Abilify Liquid, Abilify IM Injection*

INDICATIONS: Schizophrenia (13 years and older), manic and mixed episodes associated with bipolar I disorder, adjunctive treatment to antidepressants for MDD, agitation associated with schizophrenia or bipolar disorder, manic or mixed.

AVAILABLE FORMS: Tablet, 2, 5, 10, 15, 20, and 30 mg; tablet, orally disintegrating, 10 and 15 mg; solution, oral, 1 mg/mL; IM injection, solution, 9.75 mg/1.3 mL

DOSAGE: 15 to 30 mg/day

ADMINISTRATION:

- Tablets may be given with or without food.
- Parenteral administration is intended for IM use only; inject slowly, deep into muscle mass. *IM injection has not been evaluated in children.*
- *Do not give IV or SC.*
- Oral solution may be substituted for tablets on a mg-per-mg basis up to a 25 mg dose. Patients receiving 30 mg tablets should receive 25 mg of the solution.
- Dosing for the orally disintegrating tablet is the same as that for the oral tablet.
- Do not open the orally disintegrating tablets until ready to administer. The orally disintegrating tablet should be taken without liquid. Do not split the orally disintegrating tablet.
- Use oral aripiprazole 10 to 30 mg/day instead of IM aripiprazole as soon as possible if ongoing therapy is indicated.

SIDE EFFECTS: Nausea; vomiting; dizziness, insomnia, akathisia, activation; headache, asthenia, sedation; constipation; orthostatic hypotension (occasionally during initial phase); increased risk of death and cerebrovascular events in elderly with dementia-related psychosis; TD; neuroleptic malignant syndrome (rare); seizures (rare)

DRUG INTERACTIONS:

- CYP450 3A4 inhibitors (e.g., nefazodone, fluvoxamine, fluoxetine), CYP40 2D6 inhibitors (e.g., paroxetine, fluoxetine, duloxetine), and quinidine may increase plasma levels of aripiprazole.
- Carbamazepine and other CYP450 3A4 inducers may decrease plasma levels of aripiprazole.
- Aripiprazole may enhance effects of antihypertensive medications.
- Aripiprazole may antagonize levodopa and dopamine agonists.

▶**Alert:** This list may not describe all possible interactions. Instruct clients to provide a list of all the medicines, herbs, nonprescription drugs, or dietary supplements they use and if they smoke, drink alcohol, or use illegal drugs.

PHARMACOKINETICS:

Excretion: About 25% of a single oral dose is excreted in urine (less than 1% unchanged); 55% in feces (18% as unchanged drug).

Metabolism: Primarily metabolized by CYP450 2D6 and CYP450 3A4.

Half-life: 75 hr (aripiprazole) and 94 hr (active aripiprazole metabolite).

PRECAUTIONS:

- Dysphagia is associated with the use of aripiprazole. Use with caution in patients who are at risk for aspiration pneumonia.
- Use with caution in patients with conditions that may develop hypotension (dehydration, overheating, etc.).
- DO NOT USE in patients who are allergic to aripiprazole.

PATIENT AND FAMILY EDUCATION:

- Store aripiprazole at 59° to 86°F. It can be used for up to 6 months after opening. Protect injection from light by storing in carton until use.
- If you become pregnant, contact your provider. You will need to discuss the benefits and risks of using aripiprazole orally disintegrating tablets while you are pregnant.
- Discuss with your provider if you have any of these conditions. A dose adjustment or special tests to safely take aripiprazole may be needed:
  - Liver or kidney disease
  - Heart disease, high BP, heart rhythm problems
  - History of heart attack or stroke
  - History of low WBC
  - History of breast cancer
  - Seizures or epilepsy
  - Personal or family history of diabetes
  - Trouble swallowing
  - PKU
- Talk to provider if any signs of hyperglycemia such as increased thirst or urination, excessive hunger, or weakness. If you have diabetes, check blood sugar levels on a regular basis while taking aripiprazole.

SPECIAL POPULATIONS:

- *Elderly:* Generally does not require dosage adjustment. Elderly with dementia-related psychosis treated with atypical antipsychotics are at higher risk of death and cerebrovascular events.
- *Renal impairment*: No dosage adjustment is needed.
- *Hepatic impairment*: No dosage adjustment is required.
- *Cardiac impairment:* Use with caution because of the risk of orthostatic hypotension.
- *Pregnancy:* It is not known if aripiprazole orally disintegrating tablets can cause harm to the fetus.
- *Lactation:* Although there are no data on the excretion of aripiprazole into human milk, it is

(cont.)

aripiprazole (*cont.*)

suggested that women receiving aripiprazole should not breastfeed.

- *Children and adolescents:* Aripiprazole is approved for schizophrenia (age 13 and older) and manic/mixed episodes (age 10 and older). Should be monitored more frequently than adults. May tolerate lower doses better.

▶**Alert:** Not approved for children with depression.

Seroquel, Seroquel XR   **quetiapine**

INDICATIONS: Schizophrenia, depressive episodes associated with bipolar disorder, monotherapy or combination therapy for acute manic episodes associated with bipolar I disorder, acute and maintenance treatment of schizophrenia.

AVAILABLE FORMS: Tablet, 25, 50, 100, 200, 300, and 400 mg; extended-release tablet, 200, 300, and 400 mg

DOSAGE:

- 400 to 800 mg/day in one (*Seroquel XR*) or two (*Seroquel*) doses for schizophrenia and bipolar mania
- 300 mg once per day for bipolar depression

ADMINISTRATION:

- Tablets may be given with or without food.
- Take this medicine with a full glass of water.
- Advise patient not to crush, chew, or break an extended-release tablet. Swallow the pill whole. Breaking the pill may cause too much of the drug to be released at one time.
- Advise patient to take the missed dose as soon as remembered. Skip the missed dose if almost time for the next scheduled dose. Do not take extra medicine to make up for the missed dose.

SIDE EFFECTS: Can increase risk for diabetes and dyslipidemia; dizziness, sedation; dry mouth, constipation, dyspepsia, abdominal pain; weight gain; tachycardia; hyperglycemia; increased risk of death and cerebrovascular events in elderly with dementia-related psychosis; orthostatic hypotension (usually during initial dose titration); neuroleptic malignant syndrome (rare); seizures (rare)

DRUG INTERACTIONS:

- May increase effects of antihypertensive medications
- Plasma levels of quetiapine may be increased if given in conjunction with CYP450 3A and CYP450 2D6 inhibitors. However, no dose adjustment is required.

▶**Alert:** This list may not describe all possible interactions. Instruct clients to provide a list of all the medicines, herbs, nonprescription drugs, or dietary supplements they use.

PHARMACOKINETICS:
Metabolites: Inactive
Half-life: 6 to 7 hr

PRECAUTIONS:

- Use with caution in patients who are at risk for aspiration pneumonia.
- Examine for cataracts before and every 6 months after starting quetiapine.
- *Do not use if there is a proven allergy.*

PATIENT AND FAMILY EDUCATION:

- Take exactly as prescribed by the provider. Do not take in larger or smaller amounts or for longer than recommended.
- Can be taken with or without food.
- Quetiapine can cause side effects that may impair your thinking or reactions. Be careful if you drive or do anything that requires you to be awake and alert.
- Quetiapine may cause high blood sugar (hyperglycemia). Talk to provider if any signs of hyperglycemia such as increased thirst or urination, excessive hunger, or weakness. If diabetic, check blood sugar levels on a regular basis.
- *Avoid becoming overheated or dehydrated during exercise and in hot weather.* You may be more prone to heat stroke.
- *Avoid getting up too fast from a sitting or lying position.* Get up slowly and steady yourself to prevent a fall.
- *Avoid drinking alcohol.*
- *Stop using this medication and call provider immediately* if you have very stiff (rigid) muscles, high fever, sweating, confusion, fast or uneven heartbeats, tremors; feel like you might pass out; have jerky muscle movements you cannot control, trouble swallowing, problems with speech; have blurred vision, eye pain, or seeing halos around lights; have increased thirst and urination, excessive hunger, fruity breath odor, weakness, nausea and vomiting; have fever, chills, body aches, flu symptoms; or have white patches or sores inside your mouth or on your lips.
- Do not stop taking the drug suddenly without first talking to your provider, even if you feel fine. You may have serious side effects if you stop taking the drug suddenly.
- Call provider if symptoms do not improve or get worse.
- Store at room temperature away from moisture and heat.

SPECIAL POPULATIONS:

- *Elderly:*
  - Generally lower dose is used (e.g., 25–100 mg twice a day); higher dose can be used if tolerated.

(cont.)

SHARED PSYCHOTIC DISORDER: Antipsychotic Drugs, Atypical (Second Generation)

quetiapine (*cont.*)

- Elderly with dementia-related psychosis treated with atypical antipsychotics are at higher risk of death and cerebrovascular events.
- *Renal function impairment*: No dose adjustment is required.
- *Hepatic function impairment*: May need to reduce dose.
- *Cardiac impairment:* Use with caution because of risk of orthostatic hypotension.
- *Pregnancy:* Category C. Some animal studies show adverse effects. There are no controlled studies in humans. It should be used only when the potential benefits outweigh potential risks to the fetus. Quetiapine may be preferable to anticonvulsant mood stabilizers if treatment is required during pregnancy.

- *Lactation*: It is not known if drug is secreted in human breast milk. It is recommended to either discontinue drug or bottle feed. Infants of women who choose to breastfeed while on this drug should be monitored for possible adverse effects.
- *Children and adolescents:*
  - Not officially recommended for patients younger than 18 years.
  - Probably safe and effective for behavioral disturbances in this population.
  - Should be monitored more frequently than adults. May tolerate lower doses better.
  - Watch for activation of suicidal ideation. Inform parents or guardian of this risk so they can help monitor the risk.

Treatment of Anxiety Disorders

OVERVIEW

- Anxiety disorders are the most common type of psychiatric disorders, with an incidence of 18.1% and a lifetime prevalence of 28.8%.
- They account for a $42.3 billion annual cost in the USA, with more than 50% of the total sum directed toward nonpsychiatric medical treatment costs.
- Patients with anxiety disorders also have a high comorbidity with mood disorders.
- Types of anxiety disorders: panic disorder (PD), agoraphobia, generalized anxiety disorder (GAD), obsessive-compulsive disorder (OCD), phobias, and stress disorders (acute and post-traumatic stress).

Panic Disorder (PD)

OVERVIEW

- Sudden feelings of terror that strike without warning.
- Can occur at any time, even during sleep.
- Mimics a heart attack or feeling that death is imminent.
- Per the *DSM-IV*, PD is defined as recurrent, unexpected panic attacks followed by at least 1 month of persistent concern about having another attack, worry about the consequences of panic attacks, and a change in behavior as a result of the attacks.
- *Differential diagnoses* include thyroid disorders, diabetic hyper- or hypoglycemia, cardiac arrhythmias, cerebral lesions, PTSD, drug interactions, or adverse effects.
- *Diagnostic workup* includes physical and mental evaluation.
- PD has been found to run in families; this may mean that inheritance (genes) plays a strong role in determining who will get it. However, many people who have no family history of the disorder develop it.
- Often, the first attacks are triggered by physical illnesses, a major life stress, or medications that increase activity in the part of the brain involved in fear reactions.
- Women are twice as likely as men to develop PD.
- PD typically strikes in the late teen years or young adulthood.
- Individuals with PD have a suicide rate 18 times higher than the general population.
- The rate of substance abuse (especially stimulants, cocaine, and hallucinogens) in persons with PD is 7–28%, 4–14 times greater than that of the general population.
- Pregnant mothers with PD are more likely to have infants of smaller birth weight for gestational age.
- PD patients are nearly twice as likely to develop CAD, and those with known coronary disease can experience myocardial ischemia during their panic episodes.

Psychopharmacology of Panic Disorder

OVERVIEW

- SSRIs are the most commonly used medications for PD.
    - They include fluoxetine *(Prozac)*, sertraline *(Zoloft)*, paroxetine *(Paxil)*, fluvoxamine *(Luvox)*, citalopram *(Celexa)*, and escitalopram *(Lexapro)*
    - Take up to 4 weeks to reach maximum therapeutic efficacy.
    - If these do not help or if more immediate symptomatic relief is necessary, use of BZDs may be considered if the person does not have a history of drug dependence.
- SNRIs are also used as first line therapy for PD.
- BZDs are associated with dependence and addiction.
    - Used on a temporary basis and for immediate relief.
- MAOIs, such as phenelzine *(Nardil)*, tranylcypromine *(Parnate)*, and isocarboxazid *(Marplan)*, are only used when all other drugs do not work.
    - MAOIs are the most effective medications for PD, but they have serious side effects and interactions with other drugs and foods.
    - Should only be prescribed by a psychiatrist experienced in their use.
- Behavioral therapies should be used together with drug therapy. These include CBT, exposure therapy, relaxation techniques, pleasant mental imagery, and cognitive restructuring (learning to recognize and replace panic-inducing thoughts). Behavioral treatment appears to have long-lasting benefits.
- Regular exercise, adequate sleep, and regularly scheduled meals may help reduce the frequency of the attacks. Caffeine and other stimulants should be reduced or eliminated.

PANIC DISORDER

CLASS	DRUG
Selective Serotonin Reuptake Inhibitors (SSRIs)	**First-Line Drug Therapy**
	sertraline (*Zoloft*) fluoxetine (*Prozac*) paroxetine (*Paxil, Paxil CR*); paroxetine mesylate (*Pexeva*) fluvoxamine (*Luvox CR*) citalopram (*Celexa*) escitalopram (*Lexapro*)
Serotonin Norepinephrine Reuptake Inhibitors (SNRIs)	**First-Line Drug Therapy**
	venlafaxine (*Effexor, Effexor XR*) desvenlafaxine (*Pristiq*) duloxetine (*Cymbalta*)
Tricyclic Antidepressants (TCAs)	**Drugs for Treatment Resistant Cases**
	imipramine (*Tofranil*) desipramine (*Norpramin*) nortriptyline (*Pamelor*)
Benzodiazepines (BZDs)	**Drugs Used Only In First Weeks While Establishing Levels of SSRIs or SNRIs**
	alprazolam (*Xanax/Xanax XR/Niravam*) lorazepam (*Ativan*) clonazepam (*Klonopin*)
Serotonin 1A Agonist	**Drug for Augmentation**
	buspirone (*BuSpar*)

Class: Selective Serotonin Reuptake Inhibitors (SSRIs)

- Should be taken about the same time every day, morning or evening, and can be taken with or without food.
- This medicine may take up to 4 weeks to fully effective, but patient may see symptoms of depression improving in as little as 1–2 weeks.
- If patient plans on becoming pregnant, discuss the benefits versus the risks of using this medicine while pregnant. Confirm pregnancy risk category of the specific drug. Because this medicine is excreted in the breast milk, nursing mothers should not breastfeed while taking this medicine.
- This medication should be used only when clearly needed during pregnancy.

- If this medication is used during the last 3 months of pregnancy, the newborn may develop symptoms, including feeding or breathing difficulties, seizures, muscle stiffness, jitteriness, or constant crying.
- This medication should not be stopped unless the health care provider directs. Report any adverse symptoms to the health care provider promptly.
- This drug passes into breast milk. Because of the potential risk to the infant, breastfeeding while using this drug is not recommended.
- Caution should be exercised when using this drug on the elderly because they may be more sensitive to the effects of the drug.

sertraline   *Zoloft*

INDICATIONS: Primarily to treat depression but may also be used for OCD, PD, PTSD, PMDD, or social anxiety

AVAILABLE FORMS: Tablets: 25, 50, and 100 mg

DOSAGE: Starting dose, 25 mg once daily, increase dose incrementally 25 mg per week. Maximum dose, 200 mg daily

ADMINISTRATION:
- PO with a glass of water
- Take with or without food
- Take at regular intervals
- Caution patients not to stop taking drug except on provider's advice.

- May be prescribed for children as young as 6 years for selected conditions (25 mg/day); *precautions do apply.*
- Instruct patients to take missed dose as soon as possible. If it is almost time for the next dose, advise to take only that dose.

SIDE EFFECTS:
- *Most common*: Dizziness, headache, insomnia, somnolence, and change in sex drive or performance.
- *Less common*: Allergic reactions (skin rash, itching, or hives); swelling of the face, lips, or tongue; feeling faint or lightheaded; falls; hallucination; loss of contact with reality; seizures; suicidal

(cont.)

sertraline (cont.)

thoughts or other mood changes; unusual bleeding or bruising; feeling unusually weak or tired; vomiting; change in appetite; indigestion; nausea; diarrhea; increased sweating; tremors

DRUG INTERACTIONS: This medicine may interact with the following medications:

- Absolute contraindications include MAOIs such as phenelzine (*Nardil*), tranylcypromine (*Parnate*), isocarboxazid (*Marplan*), and selegiline (*Eldepryl*).
- Avoid using with SNRI agents, triptans, and other SSRI agents
- Caution with aspirin, NSAIDs (e.g., ibuprofen or naproxen), COX inhibitors, and other anti-inflammatory drugs, St. John's wort.

▶**Alert:** This list may not describe all possible interactions. Instruct patients to provide a list of all medicines, herbs, nonprescription drugs, or dietary supplements used, and if they smoke, drink alcohol, or use illegal drugs.

PHARMACOKINETICS:

- Metabolized in the liver by CYP P450 (CYP) enzymes.
- They are highly bound to plasma proteins and have a large volume of distribution.
- May take 2–6 weeks to fully effective
- Addition of serotonergic medications to a patient's regimen must not occur until 2–3 weeks after discontinuation of an SSRI (some recommend a 5-week "washout" period prior to initiation of an MAOI).

Metabolism: Liver: CYP 2C19, 2D6, 3A4 substrate; 2D6 (weak), 3A4 (weak) inhibitor

Excretion: Urine 40–45% (none unchanged), feces 40–45% (12–14% unchanged)

Half-life: 26 hr

PRECAUTIONS:

- See patients as often as necessary to ensure that the drug is working on the panic attacks, determine compliance, and review side effects.
- Make sure patients realize that they need to take prescribed doses even if they do not feel better right away. It can take several weeks before they feel the full effect of the drug.
- Instruct patients and families to watch for worsening depression or thoughts of suicide. Also, watch for sudden or severe changes in feelings such as feeling anxious, agitated, panicky, irritated, hostile, aggressive, impulsive, severely restless, overly excited, hyperactive, or not being able to sleep. If this happens, especially at the beginning of antidepressant treatment or after a change in dose, patient should call the health care provider.
- Drowsiness or dizziness may occur. Patients should not drive or use machinery or do anything that needs mental alertness until the effect of this medicine is determined.
- Caution patients not to stand or sit up quickly, especially if older. This reduces the risk of dizzy or fainting spells. Alcohol may interfere with the effect of this medicine. Avoid alcoholic drinks.
- Caution patients not to treat themselves for coughs, colds, or allergies without consulting the health care provider. Some ingredients can increase possible side effects.
- Caution should be exercised in the following:
  - Bipolar disorder or a family history of bipolar disorder
  - Diabetes
  - Heart disease
  - Liver disease
  - Electroconvulsive therapy
  - Seizures (convulsions)
  - Suicidal thoughts, plans, or attempts by patients or a family member
  - An unusual or allergic reaction to sertraline, other medicines, foods, dyes, or preservatives
  - Pregnancy or trying to get pregnant
  - Breastfeeding

PATIENT AND FAMILY EDUCATION:

- Store at room temperature. Take any unused, expired medication to the local pharmacy on give-back day. Avoid throwing the medication into the environment.
- Advise client to alert the provider if worsening anxiety, aggressiveness, impulsivity, or restlessness; worsening depression or thoughts of suicide; agitation, panic, irritability, hostile, aggressive or impulsive feelings/actions, severe restlessness, over excitation and hyperactivity; or not being able to sleep
- Patients or families should report any severe, abrupt onset or changes in symptoms to health professionals. This may be reflective of increased risk of suicidal thinking.
- Caution for the concomitant use of NSAIDs, aspirin, warfarin, and any other drugs that alter platelets.
- Caution patients not to treat themselves for coughs, colds, or allergies without consulting the health care provider. Some ingredients can increase possible side effects.
- *For dry mouth:* Chewing sugarless gum or sucking hard candy and drinking plenty of water may help. Contact your provider if the problem persists or is severe.
- Should be taken about the same time every day, morning or evening, and can be taken with or without food.
- This medicine may take up to 4 weeks to fully effective, but patient may see symptoms of depression improving in as little as 1–2 weeks.
- If patient plans on becoming pregnant, discuss the benefits versus the risks of using this medicine while pregnant. Confirm pregnancy risk category of the specific drug. Because this medicine is excreted in the breast milk, nursing mothers should not breastfeed while taking this medicine.
- This medication should be used only when clearly needed during pregnancy.

(cont.)

PANIC DISORDER: Selective Serotonin Reuptake Inhibitors (SSRIs)

sertraline (*cont.*)

- If this medication is used during the last 3 months of pregnancy, the newborn may develop symptoms, including feeding or breathing difficulties, seizures, muscle stiffness, jitteriness, or constant crying.
- This medication should not be stopped unless the health care provider directs. Report any adverse symptoms to the health care provider promptly.
- This drug passes into breast milk. Because of the potential risk to the infant, breastfeeding while using this drug is not recommended.
- Caution should be exercised when using this drug on the elderly because they may be more sensitive to the effects of the drug.

SPECIAL POPULATIONS:
- *Elderly:* Increased risk for hyponatremia.
- *Hepatic impairment:* Dose adjustment is necessary.
- *Pregnancy:* Category C; risks are associated with all SSRIs for neonatal complications if used in the third trimester.
- *Lactation:* Adverse reactions have not been reported; however, long-term effects have not been studied, and the manufacturer recommends caution.
- *Children:* Approved for use in children aged 12 years or older; however, monitoring for increased suicidal ideation is critical.

fluoxetine   *Prozac*

INDICATIONS: Used to treat MDDs, OCD, bulimia nervosa, and PD.

AVAILABLE FORMS: Capsule, 10, 20, and 40 mg; capsule, delayed release, 90 mg; solution, 20 mg/5 mL

DOSAGE: Immediate release (*Prozac*): Daily: starting dose 10 mg PO, daily for 7 days; maximum, 60 mg/day. Capsule, delayed release (*Prozac*): weekly: 90 mg oral, once weekly, 7 days after last daily dose of 20 mg; extended release, not recommended for acute treatment

ADMINISTRATION:
- PO with a glass of water
- Take with or without food
- Take at regular intervals
- Caution patients not to stop taking drug except on provider's advice.
- Capsules may be prescribed for children as young as 7 years for selected conditions; *precautions do apply.*
- Delayed release capsule is not prescribed for children.
- Do not prescribe delayed release capsule for acute treatment.
- Instruct patients to take missed dose as soon as possible. If almost time for next dose, advise to take only that dose.

SIDE EFFECTS:
- *Most common:* Dizziness, headache, insomnia, somnolence, or change in sex drive or performance.
- *Less common:* Allergic reactions (skin rash; itching, or hives); swelling of the face, lips, or tongue; psoriasis; arthralgias; anorexia; feeling faint or lightheaded, nausea; dry mouth; constipation; dyspepsia; suicidal thoughts or other mood changes; unusual bleeding or bruising; fatigue; tremor; change in appetite; diarrhea; increased sweating; indigestion; nausea; tremors

DRUG INTERACTIONS: Most of the interactions occur with OTC cough and cold preparations. This medicine may also interact with the following medications.
- Absolute contraindications include MAOIs such as phenelzine (*Nardil*), tranylcypromine (*Parnate*), isocarboxazid (*Marplan*), and selegiline (*Eldepryl*).
- Avoid using with other SSRIs due to serotonin effect; SNRI drugs such as desvenlafaxine (*Pristiq*) and venlafaxine (*Effexor*); drugs with sympathomimetic properties such as phenylpropanolamine, pseudoephedrine, St. John's wort, haloperidol; and diazepam (*Valium*), any other antidepressants; and clopidogrel (*Plavix*).
- Exercise caution with cold medications; arrhythmia medications such as flecainide and aspirin; other NSAIDs; and drugs used for analgesia with opioid properties
- This list may not describe all possible interactions. Instruct patients to provide a list of all medicines, herbs, nonprescription drugs, or dietary supplements used, and if they smoke, drink alcohol, or use illegal drugs

PHARMACOKINETICS:
Metabolism: Liver: CYP450 2C19, 2D6 (primary) substrate; 2C19, 3A4 (weak) inhibitor; Info: active metabolite
Excretion: Urine 80% (11.6% unchanged), feces 15%
Half-life: 4–6 days (fluoxetine), 9.3 days (norfluoxetine)

PRECAUTIONS:
- See patients as often as necessary to ensure that the drug is working, determine compliance, and review side effects.
- Make sure patients realize that they need to take prescribed doses even if they do not feel better right away. It can take several weeks before they feel the full effect of the drug.
- Instruct patients and families to watch for worsening depression or thoughts of suicide; sudden or severe changes in feelings such as feeling anxious, agitated, panicky, irritated,

(cont.)

hostile, aggressive, impulsive, severely restless, overly excited, hyperactive; or not being able to sleep. If this happens, especially at the beginning of antidepressant treatment or after a change in dose, patient should call the health care provider.

- Drowsiness or dizziness may occur; do not drive or use machinery or do anything that needs mental alertness until the effects of this medicine are known.
- Caution patients not to stand or sit up quickly, especially if older. This reduces the risk of dizzy or fainting spells. Alcohol may interfere with the effect of this medicine. Avoid alcoholic drinks.
- Caution patients not to treat themselves for coughs, colds, or allergies without asking health care professional for advice. Some ingredients can increase possible side effects.
- Dry mouth: Chewing sugarless gum, sucking hard candy, and drinking plenty of water may help. Contact health care provider if the problem persists or is severe.
- Caution should be exercised in the following:
  - Bipolar disorder or a family history of bipolar disorder
  - Diabetes
  - Heart disease
  - Liver disease
  - Electroconvulsive therapy
  - Seizures (convulsions)
  - Suicidal thoughts, plans, or attempts by patient or family member
  - An unusual or allergic reaction to fluoxetine, other medicines, foods, dyes, or preservatives
  - Pregnancy or trying to get pregnant
  - Breastfeeding

PATIENT AND FAMILY EDUCATION:
- Store at room temperature. Take any unused, expired medication to the local pharmacy on give-back day. Avoid throwing the medication into the environment.
- Discuss any worsening anxiety, aggressiveness, impulsivity, or restlessness
- Report any severe, abrupt onset or changes in symptoms to health professionals. May be reflective of increased risk of suicidal thinking.

- Caution for the concomitant use of NSAIDs, aspirin, warfarin, and any other drugs that alter platelets.
- Should be taken about the same time every day, morning or evening, and can be taken with or without food.
- This medicine may take up to 4 weeks to fully effective, but patient may see symptoms of depression improving in as little as 1–2 weeks.
- If patient plans on becoming pregnant, discuss the benefits versus the risks of using this medicine while pregnant. Confirm pregnancy risk category of the specific drug. Because this medicine is excreted in the breast milk, nursing mothers should not breastfeed while taking this medicine.
- This medication should be used only when clearly needed during pregnancy.
- If this medication is used during the last 3 months of pregnancy, the newborn may develop symptoms, including feeding or breathing difficulties, seizures, muscle stiffness, jitteriness, or constant crying.
- This medication should not be stopped unless the health care provider directs. Report any adverse symptoms to the health care provider promptly.
- This drug passes into breast milk. Because of the potential risk to the infant, breastfeeding while using this drug is not recommended.
- Caution should be exercised when using this drug on the elderly because they may be more sensitive to the effects of the drug.

SPECIAL POPULATIONS:
- *Elderly:* No actual contraindications exist, but due to the long half-life of the drug, it has been placed on the Beers List of Potentially Inappropriate Medications for Geriatrics.
- *Pregnancy:* Category C; this is the longest used SSRI in pregnant women. Every attempt should be made to discontinue in the third trimester secondary to development of neonatal distress upon delivery.
- *Lactation:* Not approved for lactation and breastfeeding.
- *Children:* Approved in pediatric population only for MDD and OCD. Monitoring for increased suicidal ideation is critical.

Paxil, Paxil CR, Pexeva   **paroxetine, paroxetine mesylate**

INDICATIONS: Used to treat MDDs, OCD, bulimia nervosa, and PD.

AVAILABLE FORMS: *Pexeva*: Tablet, 20, 30, and 40 mg; *Paxil*: Tablet, 10, 20, 30, and 40 mg; suspension 10 mg/5 mL, *Paxil CR:* Tablet, 12.5, 25, and 37.5 mg

DOSAGE:
- *Pexeva* and *Paxil*: 20 mg PO every morning, 10 mg in elderly patients; increase 10 mg/day

weekly; maximum, 50 mg/day; 40 mg/day in elderly patients
- *Paxil CR*: 12.5 mg PO, daily; increase 12.5 mg/day weekly; maximum, 75 mg/day; 50 mg/day in elderly patients
- No proven additional benefits at doses greater than 20 mg/day

ADMINISTRATION:
- PO with a glass of water
- Do not break/crush or chew

(cont.)

PANIC DISORDER: Selective Serotonin Reuptake Inhibitors (SSRIs)

paroxetine, paroxetine mesylate (cont.)

- Take with or without food
- Take at regular intervals
- Caution patients not to stop taking drug except on provider's advice.
- May be prescribed for children as young as 7 years for selected conditions; *precautions do apply.*
- Instruct patients to take missed dose as soon as possible. If it is almost time for the next dose, advise to take only that dose.

SIDE EFFECTS:

- *Most common*: Somnolence; headache; asthenia; dizziness; dry mouth; tremor; anorexia; nervousness; anxiety; abnormal vision; change in appetite; change in sex drive or performance; diarrhea; constipation; increased sweating; indigestion and nausea.
- *Less common*: Suicidality, worsening depression, serotonin syndrome, seizures, hyponatremia, extrapyramidal symptoms, priapism, and acute angle glaucoma.

DRUG INTERACTIONS: Most of the interactions occur with OTC cough and cold preparations.

- Absolute contraindications include MAOIs such as phenelzine (*Nardil*), tranylcypromine (*Parnate*), isocarboxazid (*Marplan*), and selegiline (*Eldepryl*).
- Avoid using with other SSRIs due to serotonin effect; SNRI drugs such as desvenlafaxine (*Pristiq*) and venlafaxine (*Effexor*); drugs with sympathomimetic properties such as phenylpropanolamine, pseudoephedrine, St. John's wort, haloperidol; and diazepam (*Valium*), any other antidepressants; and clopidogrel (*Plavix*).
- Exercise caution with cold medications, arrhythmia medications such as flecainide, aspirin, and other NSAIDs, and drugs used for analgesia with opioid properties.

▶**Alert**: This list may not describe all possible interactions. Instruct patients to provide a list of all medicines, herbs, nonprescription drugs, or dietary supplements used, and if they smoke, drink alcohol, or use illegal drugs

PHARMACOKINETICS:

Metabolism: Liver extensively; CYP450 2D6 substrate; 2D6 inhibitor
Excretion: Urine 64% (2% unchanged), feces 36% (less than 1% unchanged)
Half-life: 21 hr

PRECAUTIONS:

- See patients as often as necessary to ensure that the drug is working on the panic attacks, determine compliance, and review side effects.
- Make sure patients realize that they need to take prescribed doses even if they do not feel better right away. It can take several weeks before they feel the full effect of the drug.
- Instruct patients and families to watch for worsening depression or thoughts of suicide; also sudden or severe changes in feelings such

as feeling anxious, agitated, panicky, irritated, hostile, aggressive, impulsive, severely restless, overly excited, hyperactive, or not being able to sleep. If this happens, especially at the beginning of antidepressant treatment or after a change in dose, patient should call the health care provider.
- Drowsiness or dizziness: Patients should not drive or use machinery or do anything that requires mental alertness until the effects of this drug are known.
- Caution patients not to stand or sit up quickly, especially if older. This reduces the risk of dizzy or fainting spells. Alcohol may interfere with the effect of this medicine. Avoid alcoholic drinks.
- Caution patients not to treat themselves for coughs, colds, or allergies without asking health care professional for advice. Some ingredients can increase possible side effects.
- Dry mouth: Chewing sugarless gum, sucking hard candy, and drinking plenty of water may help. Contact health care provider if problem persists or is severe.
- Caution should be exercised in the following:
  - Bipolar disorder or a family history of bipolar disorder
  - Diabetes
  - Heart disease
  - Liver disease
  - Electroconvulsive therapy
  - Seizures (convulsions)
  - Suicidal thoughts, plans, or attempts by patients or a family member
  - An unusual or allergic reaction to paroxetine, other medicines, foods, dyes, or preservatives
  - Pregnancy or trying to get pregnant
  - Breastfeeding

PATIENT AND FAMILY EDUCATION:

- Store at room temperature. Take any unused medication after the expiration date to the local pharmacy on drug give-back day. Avoid throwing the medication into the environment.
- Shake the liquid form of paroxetine well just before you measure a dose. To be sure you get the correct dose, measure the liquid with a marked measuring spoon or medicine cup, not with a regular tablespoon. If there is no dose-measuring device available, ask the pharmacist for one.
- Should be taken about the same time every day, morning or evening, and can be taken with or without food.
- This medicine may take up to 4 weeks to fully effective, but patient may see symptoms of depression improving in as little as 1–2 weeks.
- If patient plans on becoming pregnant, discuss the benefits versus the risks of using this medicine while pregnant. Confirm pregnancy risk category of the specific drug. Because this medicine

(cont.)

paroxetine, paroxetine mesylate (*cont.*)

is excreted in the breast milk, nursing mothers should not breastfeed while taking this medicine.
- This medication should be used only when clearly needed during pregnancy.
- If this medication is used during the last 3 months of pregnancy, the newborn may develop symptoms, including feeding or breathing difficulties, seizures, muscle stiffness, jitteriness, or constant crying.
- This medication should not be stopped unless the health care provider directs. Report any adverse symptoms to the health care provider promptly.
- This drug passes into breast milk. Because of the potential risk to the infant, breastfeeding while using this drug is not recommended.
- Caution should be exercised when using this drug on the elderly because they may be more sensitive to the effects of the drug.

SPECIAL POPULATIONS:
- *Elderly:* Due to increased C_{min} concentrations, up to 70–80% in the elderly, the initial dose should be reduced.
- *Renal and hepatic impairment:* The initial dose should be reduced in patients with severe renal and/or hepatic impairment. Titration upward should be slow and at intervals.
- *Pregnancy:* Category D. First trimester teratogenicity, neonatal withdrawal and serotonin syndrome in third trimester, persistent pulmonary HTN if greater than 20-weeks gestation.
- *Lactation:* Considered generally safe; substantial human data show no or minimal risk to breast milk production or to the infant.
- *Children:* Paxil CR is not indicated for children. Monitoring for increased suicidal ideation is critical if using regular *Paxil*.

Luvox CR   **fluvoxamine**

INDICATIONS: Used to treat OCD, social anxiety disorder

AVAILABLE FORMS: Capsule, extended release, 100 and 150 mg

DOSAGE: Start with 100 mg PO nightly, increase by 50 mg/day weekly; maximum, 300 mg/day

ADMINISTRATION:
- PO with a glass of water
- Take with or without food
- Take at regular intervals
- Caution patients not to stop taking drug except on provider's advice
- Not prescribed for children
- Instruct patients to take missed dose as soon as possible. If it is almost time for next dose, advise to take only that dose.

SIDE EFFECTS:
- *Most common:* Somnolence; headache; asthenia; dizziness; dry mouth; tremor; anorexia; nervousness; anxiety; abnormal vision; change in appetite; change in sex drive or performance; diarrhea; constipation; increased sweating; indigestion; nausea; and tremors.
- *Less common:* Suicidality, worsening depression, serotonin syndrome, seizures, hyponatremia, extrapyramidal symptoms, priapism, and acute angle glaucoma.

DRUG INTERACTIONS: Most of the interactions occur with OTC cough and cold preparations.
- Absolute contraindications include MAOIs such as phenelzine (*Nardil*), tranylcypromine (*Parnate*), isocarboxazid (*Marplan*), and selegiline (*Eldepryl*).
- Avoid using with other SSRIs due to serotonin effect; SNRI drugs such as desvenlafaxine (*Pristiq*) and venlafaxine (*Effexor*); drugs with

sympathomimetic properties such as phenylpropanolamine, pseudoephedrine, St. John's wort, haloperidol; and diazepam (*Valium*), any other antidepressants; clopidogrel (*Plavix*); amoxicillin; erythromycins; and lansoprazole (*Prevacid*).
- Exercise caution with cold medications, NSAIDs, and drugs used for analgesia with opioid properties.
- ▶**Alert**: This list may not describe all possible interactions. Instruct patients to provide a list of all medicines, herbs, nonprescription drugs, or dietary supplements used, and if they smoke, drink alcohol, or use illegal drugs.

PHARMACOKINETICS:
Metabolism: Liver extensively; CYP450 1A2, 2D6 inhibitor
Excretion: Urine primarily (2% unchanged)
Half-life: 16.3 hr, 25.9 hr (elderly)

PRECAUTIONS:
- See patients as often as necessary to ensure that the drug is working on the panic attacks, determine compliance, and review side effects.
- Make sure patients realize that they need to take prescribed doses even if they do not feel better right away. It can take several weeks before they feel the full effect of the drug.
- Instruct patients and families to watch for worsening depression or thoughts of suicide. Also watch for sudden or severe changes in feelings such as feeling anxious, agitated, panicky, irritated, hostile, aggressive, impulsive, severely restless, overly excited, hyperactive, or not being able to sleep. If this happens, especially at the beginning of antidepressant treatment or after a change in dose, patient should call the health care provider.

(cont.)

PANIC DISORDER: Selective Serotonin Reuptake Inhibitors (SSRIs)

fluvoxamine (*cont.*)

- Drowsiness or dizziness. The patients should not drive or use machinery or do anything that needs mental alertness until the effects of this medicine are known.
- Caution patients not to stand or sit up quickly, especially if older. This reduces the risk of dizzy or fainting spells. Alcohol may interfere with the effect of this medicine. Avoid alcoholic drinks.
- Caution patients not to treat themselves for coughs, colds, or allergies without asking health care professional for advice. Some ingredients can increase possible side effects.
- Dry mouth: Chewing sugarless gum, sucking hard candy, and drinking plenty of water may help. Contact health care provider if the problem persists or is severe.
- Caution should be exercised in the following:
  - Bipolar disorder or a family history of bipolar disorder
  - Diabetes
  - Heart disease
  - Liver disease
  - Electroconvulsive therapy
  - Seizures (convulsions)
  - Suicidal thoughts, plans, or attempts by patients or a family member
  - An unusual or allergic reaction to fluvoxamine, other medicines, foods, dyes, or preservatives
  - Pregnancy or trying to get pregnant
  - Breastfeeding

PATIENT AND FAMILY EDUCATION:
- Store at room temperature. Take any unused medication after the expiration date to the local pharmacy on drug give-back day. Avoid throwing the medication into the environment.
- Should be taken about the same time every day, morning or evening, and can be taken with or without food.
- This medicine may take up to 4 weeks to fully effective, but patient may see symptoms of depression improving in as little as 1–2 weeks.
- If patient plans on becoming pregnant, discuss the benefits versus the risks of using this medicine while pregnant. Confirm pregnancy risk category of the specific drug. Because this medicine is excreted in the breast milk, nursing mothers should not breastfeed while taking this medicine.
- This medication should be used only when clearly needed during pregnancy.
- If this medication is used during the last 3 months of pregnancy, the newborn may develop symptoms, including feeding or breathing difficulties, seizures, muscle stiffness, jitteriness, or constant crying.
- This medication should not be stopped unless the health care provider directs. Report any adverse symptoms to the health care provider promptly.
- This drug passes into breast milk. Because of the potential risk to the infant, breastfeeding while using this drug is not recommended.
- Caution should be exercised when using this drug on the elderly because they may be more sensitive to the effects of the drug.

SPECIAL POPULATIONS:
- *Elderly:* Due to increased C_{min} concentrations, up to 70–80% in the elderly, the initial dose should be reduced.
- *Renal and hepatic impairment:* The initial dose should be reduced in patients with severe renal and/or hepatic impairment. Titration upward should be slow and at intervals.
- *Pregnancy:* Category D. First trimester teratogenicity, neonatal withdrawal and serotonin syndrome in third trimester, persistent pulmonary HTN if greater than 20-weeks gestation.
- *Lactation:* Considered generally safe; substantial human data show no or minimal risk to breast milk production or to the infant.
- *Children:* Not indicated for children.

citalopram   *Celexa*

INDICATIONS: Used to treat MDD

AVAILABLE FORMS: Tablet, 10, 20, and 40 mg; oral solution, 10 mg/5 mL

DOSAGE: Starting dose, 20 mg once daily; increase dose incrementally 20 mg only once per week. Most patients reach efficacy at 40 mg daily; however, some may need 60 mg/day.

ADMINISTRATION:
- PO with a glass of water.
- Take with or without food
- Take at regular intervals
- Caution patients not to stop taking drug except on provider's advice.
- Not prescribed for children.
- Instruct patients to take missed dose as soon as possible. If it is almost time for next dose, advise to take only that dose.

SIDE EFFECTS:
- *Most common*: Somnolence; headache; asthenia; dizziness; dry mouth; tremor; anorexia; nervousness; anxiety; abnormal vision; change in appetite; change in sex drive or performance; diarrhea; constipation; increased sweating; indigestion; and nausea.
- *Less common*: Suicidality, worsening depression, serotonin syndrome, seizures, hyponatremia,

(cont.)

citalopram (*cont.*)

extrapyramidal symptoms, priapism, and acute angle glaucoma.

DRUG INTERACTIONS: Most of the interactions occur with OTC cough and cold preparations. This medicine may also interact with the following medications.

- Absolute contraindications include MAOIs such as phenelzine (*Nardil*), tranylcypromine (*Parnate*), isocarboxazid (*Marplan*), and selegiline (Eld*epryl*).
- Avoid using with other SSRIs due to serotonin effect; SNRI drugs such as desvenlafaxine (*Pristiq*) and venlafaxine (*Effexor*); drugs with sympathomimetic properties such as phenylpropanolamine, pseudoephedrine, St. John's wort, haloperidol; diazepam (*Valium*), any other antidepressants; and clopidogrel (*Plavix*); amoxicillin, erythromycins; and lansoprazole (Pre*vacid*).
- Exercise caution with cold medications, NSAIDs, and drugs used for analgesia with opioid properties.
- ▶**Alert:** This list may not describe all possible interactions. Instruct patients to provide a list of all medicines, herbs, nonprescription drugs, or dietary supplements used, and if they smoke, drink alcohol, or use illegal drugs.

PHARMACOKINETICS:
Metabolism: Extensively metabolized in the liver in CYP450 2C19, 3A4 substrate; 2D6 (weak) inhibitor
Excretion: Urine primarily (10% unchanged), feces.
Half-life: 35 hr

PRECAUTIONS:

- See patients as often as necessary to ensure that the drug is working on the panic attacks, determine compliance, and review side effects.
- Make sure patients realize that they need to take prescribed doses even if they do not feel better right away. It can take several weeks before they feel the full effect of the drug.
- Instruct patients and families to watch for worsening depression or thoughts of suicide. Also watch for sudden or severe changes in feelings such as feeling anxious, agitated, panicky, irritated, hostile, aggressive, impulsive, severely restless, overly excited, hyperactive, or not being able to sleep. If this happens, especially at the beginning of antidepressant treatment or after a change in dose, patient should call the health care provider.
- Drowsiness or dizziness: Patients should not drive or use machinery or do anything that requires mental alertness until the effects of this medicine are known.
- Caution patients not to stand or sit up quickly, especially if older. This reduces the risk of dizzy or fainting spells. Alcohol may interfere with the effect of this medicine. Avoid alcoholic drinks.

- Caution patients not to treat themselves for coughs, colds, or allergies without asking health care professional for advice. Some ingredients can increase possible side effects.
- Dry mouth: Chewing sugarless gum, sucking hard candy, and drinking plenty of water may help. Contact health care provider if the problem persists or is severe.
- Caution should be exercised in the following:
  - Bipolar disorder or a family history of bipolar disorder
  - Diabetes
  - Heart disease
  - Liver disease
  - Electroconvulsive therapy
  - Seizures (convulsions)
  - Suicidal thoughts, plans, or attempts by patients or a family member
  - An unusual or allergic reaction to citalopram, other medicines, foods, dyes, or preservatives
  - Pregnancy or trying to get pregnant
  - Breastfeeding

PATIENT AND FAMILY EDUCATION:

- Store at room temperature. Take any unused medication after the expiration date to the local pharmacy on drug give-back day. Avoid throwing the medication into the environment.
- Try to take the medicine at the same time each day. Follow the directions on the prescription label. To get the correct dose of liquid citalopram, measure the liquid with a marked measuring spoon or medicine cup, not with a regular tablespoon. If there is no dose-measuring device available, ask the pharmacist for one.
- Should be taken about the same time every day, morning or evening, and can be taken with or without food.
- This medicine may take up to 4 weeks to fully effective, but patient may see symptoms of depression improving in as little as 1–2 weeks.
- If patient plans on becoming pregnant, discuss the benefits versus the risks of using this medicine while pregnant. Confirm pregnancy risk category of the specific drug. Because this medicine is excreted in the breast milk, nursing mothers should not breastfeed while taking this medicine.
- This medication should be used only when clearly needed during pregnancy.
- If this medication is used during the last 3 months of pregnancy, the newborn may develop symptoms, including feeding or breathing difficulties, seizures, muscle stiffness, jitteriness, or constant crying.
- This medication should not be stopped unless the health care provider directs. Report any adverse symptoms to the health care provider promptly.
- This drug passes into breast milk. Because of the potential risk to the infant, breastfeeding while using this drug is not recommended.

(cont.)

citalopram (*cont.*)

- Caution should be exercised when using this drug on the elderly because they may be more sensitive to the effects of the drug.

SPECIAL POPULATIONS:
- *Elderly:* A dose of 20 mg daily is recommended for geriatric patients.
- *Renal and hepatic impairment:* The initial dose should be reduced in patients with severe renal and/or hepatic impairment. Half-life is doubled in patients with hepatic impairment. Titration upward should be slow and at intervals.
- *Pregnancy:* Category C; potential for persistent pulmonary HTN if greater than 20-weeks gestation.
- *Lactation:* Excreted in human breast milk, some reports of infant somulence
- *Children:* Not indicated for children.

escitalopram   *Lexapro*

INDICATIONS: Used to treat MDD, GAD.

AVAILABLE FORMS: Tablet, 5, 10, and 20 mg; oral solution, 5 mg/5 mL

DOSAGE: Starting dose, 10 mg PO daily; may increase after 1 week to a maximum of 20 mg/day. Dose in the elderly should stay at 10 mg/day. Children (12–17 years old), start with 10 mg PO daily, may increase after 3 weeks; maximum, 20 mg/day

ADMINISTRATIWON:
- PO with a glass of water
- Take with or without food
- Take at regular intervals.
- Caution patients not to stop taking drug except on provider's advice.
- Safety not established for children younger than 18 years old in GAD.
- Instruct patients to take missed dose as soon as possible. If it is almost time for next dose, advise to take only that dose.

SIDE EFFECTS:
- *Most common*: Somnolence; headache; asthenia; dizziness; dry mouth; tremor; anorexia; nervousness; anxiety; abnormal vision; change in appetite; change in sex drive or performance; diarrhea; constipation; increased sweating; indigestion; nausea; tremors.
- *Less common*: Suicidality, worsening depression, serotonin syndrome, seizures, hyponatremia, extrapyramidal symptoms, priapism, and acute angle glaucoma.

DRUG INTERACTIONS: Most of the interactions occur with OTC cough and cold preparations. This medicine may also interact with the following medications.
- Absolute contraindications include MAOIs such as phenelzine (*Nardil*), tranylcypromine (*Parnate*), isocarboxazid (*Marplan*), and selegiline (*Eldepryl*).
- Avoid using with other SSRIs due to serotonin effect; SNRI drugs such as desvenlafaxine (*Pristiq*) and venlafaxine (*Effexor*); drugs with sympathomimetic properties such as phenylpropanolamine, pseudoephedrine, St. John's wort, haloperidol, and diazepam (*Valium*), any other antidepressants; and clopidogrel (*Plavix*), amoxicillin, erythromycins, lansoprazole (*Prevacid*)
- Exercise caution with cold medications, NSAIDs, and drugs used for analgesia with opioid properties.

▶**Alert:** This list may not describe all possible interactions. Instruct patients to provide a list of all medicines, herbs, nonprescription drugs, or dietary supplements used, and if they smoke, drink alcohol, or use illegal drugs.

PHARMACOKINETICS:
Metabolism: Liver; CYP450: 2C19, 2D6, 3A4 substrate; 2D6 (weak) inhibitor
Excretion: Only 10% excreted in urine
Half-life: 27–32 hr, but is increased by 50% in elderly patients

PRECAUTIONS:
- See patients as often as necessary to ensure that the drug is working on the panic attacks, determine compliance, and review side effects.
- Make sure patients realize that they need to take prescribed doses even if they do not feel better right away. It can take several weeks before they feel the full effect of the drug.
- Instruct patients and families to watch for worsening depression or thoughts of suicide. Also, watch for sudden or severe changes in feelings such as feeling anxious, agitated, panicky, irritated, hostile, aggressive, impulsive, severely restless, overly excited, hyperactive, or not being able to sleep. If this happens, especially at the beginning of antidepressant treatment or after a change in dose, patient should call the health care provider.
- Drowsiness or dizziness: Patients should not drive or use machinery or do anything that needs mental alertness until the effects of this medicine are known.
- Caution patients not to stand or sit up quickly, especially if older. This reduces the risk of dizzy or fainting spells. Alcohol may interfere with the effect of this medicine. Avoid alcoholic drinks.

(cont.)

- Caution patients not to treat themselves for coughs, colds, or allergies without asking health care professional for advice. Some ingredients can increase possible side effects.
- Dry mouth: Chewing sugarless gum, sucking hard candy, and drinking plenty of water may help. Contact health care provider if the problem persists or is severe.
- Caution should be exercised in the following:
  - Bipolar disorder or a family history of bipolar disorder
  - Diabetes
  - Heart disease
  - Liver disease
  - Electroconvulsive therapy
  - Seizures (convulsions)
  - Suicidal thoughts, plans, or attempts by patients or a family member
  - An unusual or allergic reaction to citalopram, other medicines, foods, dyes, or preservatives
  - Pregnancy or trying to get pregnant
  - Breastfeeding

PATIENT AND FAMILY EDUCATION:
- Store at room temperature. Take any unused medication after the expiration date to the local pharmacy on drug give-back day. Avoid throwing the medication into the environment.
- Try to take the medicine at the same time each day. Follow the directions on the prescription label. To get the correct dose of liquid escitalopram, measure the liquid with a marked measuring spoon or medicine cup, not with a regular tablespoon. If there is no dose-measuring device available, ask the pharmacist for one.
- Should be taken about the same time every day, morning or evening, and can be taken with or without food.
- This medicine may take up to 4 weeks to fully effective, but patient may see symptoms

of depression improving in as little as 1–2 weeks.
- If patient plans on becoming pregnant, discuss the benefits versus the risks of using this medicine while pregnant. Confirm pregnancy risk category of the specific drug. Because this medicine is excreted in the breast milk, nursing mothers should not breastfeed while taking this medicine.
- This medication should be used only when clearly needed during pregnancy.
- If this medication is used during the last 3 months of pregnancy, the newborn may develop symptoms, including feeding or breathing difficulties, seizures, muscle stiffness, jitteriness, or constant crying.
- This medication should not be stopped unless the health care provider directs. Report any adverse symptoms to the health care provider promptly.
- This drug passes into breast milk. Because of the potential risk to the infant, breastfeeding while using this drug is not recommended.
- Caution should be exercised when using this drug on the elderly because they may be more sensitive to the effects of the drug.

SPECIAL POPULATIONS:
- *Elderly:* A dose of 10 mg daily is recommended for geriatric patients. The initial dose should be reduced in patients with severe renal and/or hepatic impairment. Titration upward should be slow and at intervals.
- *Pregnancy:* Category C; potential for persistent pulmonary HTN if greater than 20-weeks gestation.
- *Lactation:* Excreted in human breast milk, some reports of infant somulence.
- *Children:* May be given to children older than 12 years of age. Monitoring of suicidal ideations is important.

Class: Serotonin and Norepinephrine Reuptake Inhibitors (SNRIs)

- Should be taken about the same time every day, morning or evening, and can be taken with or without food.
- May take up to 4 weeks to be fully effective, but patient may see symptoms of depression improving in as little as 1–2 weeks.
- If patient plans on becoming pregnant, discuss the benefits versus the risks of using this medicine while pregnant. This medication should be used only when clearly needed during pregnancy.
- If this medication is used during the last 3 months of pregnancy, the newborn may have

feeding or breathing difficulties, seizures, muscle stiffness, jitteriness, or constant crying.
- This medication should not be stopped unless the health care provider directs. Report any adverse symptoms to the health care provider promptly.
- This drug passes into breast milk. Because of the potential risk to the infant, breastfeeding while using this drug is not recommended.
- Caution should be exercised when using this drug on the elderly because they may be more sensitive to the effects of the drug.

venlafaxine   *Effexor, Effexor XR*

INDICATIONS: Used to treat MDD, GAD, PD and social anxiety disorder

AVAILABLE FORMS: Tablet, 25, 37.5, 50, 75, and 100 mg; extended-release capsule, 37.5, 75, and 150 mg

DOSAGE: *Effexor*: starting dose, 37.5 mg oral bid with dose increases every 4 days for a maximum of 375 mg. *Effexor XR*: starting dose, 37.5–75 mg daily with increases 75 mg/day every 4–7 days for a maximum of 225 mg/day

ADMINISTRATION:
- PO with a glass of water.
- Take with food; *Effexor XR* may be sprinkled on applesauce.
- Do not crush, cut, or chew capsules.
- Take at regular intervals.
- Caution patients not to stop taking drug except on provider's advice.
- Not prescribed for children.
- Instruct patients to take missed dose as soon as possible. If it is almost time for the next dose, advise to take only that dose.

SIDE EFFECTS:
- *Most common*: Somnolence; headache; asthenia; dizziness; dry mouth; tremor; anorexia; nervousness; anxiety; abnormal vision; change in appetite; change in sex drive or performance; diarrhea; constipation; increased sweating; indigestion; and nausea.
- *Less common*: Suicidality, worsening depression, serotonin syndrome, seizures, hyponatremia, extrapyramidal symptoms, priapism, and acute angle glaucoma.

DRUG INTERACTIONS: Most of the interactions occur with OTC cough and cold preparations. This medicine may also interact with the following medications.
- Absolute contraindications include cisapride, phenothiazines, MAOIs such as phenelzine (*Nardil*), tranylcypromine (*Parnate*), isocarboxazid (*Marplan*), and selegiline (*Eldepryl*).
- Avoid using with other SSRIs due to serotonin effect; SNRI drugs such as desvenlafaxine (*Pristiq*) and venlafaxine (*Effexor*); drugs with sympathomimetic properties such as phenylpropanolamine, pseudoephedrine, St. John's wort, haloperidol; diazepam (*Valium*), and any other antidepressants.
- Exercise caution with cold medications, NSAIDs and drugs used for analgesia with opioid properties.
▶**Alert**: This list may not describe all possible interactions. Instruct patients to provide a list of all medicines, herbs, nonprescription drugs, or dietary supplements used, and if they smoke, drink alcohol, or use illegal drugs.

PHARMACOKINETICS:
- Potent inhibitors of neuronal serotonin and norepinephrine reuptake and weak inhibitors of dopamine reuptake.
- Demonstrate slightly higher efficacy than the SSRI class due to the dual effect.
- Relative to SSRIs, SNRI agents seem to be more effective in treating chronic pain issues that coexist with depression and may produce more stimulative effects.
- Highly bound to plasma proteins and have a large volume of distribution.

Metabolism: Liver extensively; CYP450 2D6 substrate; 2D6 (weak) inhibitor; converted to active metabolite (O-desmethylvenlafaxine)
Excretion: Urine 87% (5% unchanged)
Half-life: 5 hr (venlafaxine), 11 hr (O-desmethyl venlafaxine)

PRECAUTIONS:
- See patients as often as necessary to ensure that the drug is working on the panic attacks, determine compliance, and review side effects.
- Make sure patients realize that they need to take prescribed doses even if they do not feel better right away. It can take several weeks before they feel the full effect of the drug.
- Instruct patients and families to watch for worsening depression or thoughts of suicide. Also watch for sudden or severe changes in feelings such as feeling anxious, agitated, panicky, irritated, hostile, aggressive, impulsive, severely restless, overly excited, hyperactive, or not being able to sleep. If this happens, especially at the beginning of antidepressant treatment or after a change in dose, patient should call the health care provider.
- Drowsiness or dizziness. The patient should not drive or use machinery or do anything that needs mental alertness until the effects of this medicine are known.
- Caution patients not to stand or sit up quickly, especially if older. This reduces the risk of dizzy or fainting spells. Alcohol may interfere with the effect of this medicine. Avoid alcoholic drinks.
- Caution patients not to treat themselves for coughs, colds, or allergies without asking health care professional. Some ingredients can increase possible side effects.
- Dry mouth: Chewing sugarless gum, sucking hard candy, and drinking plenty of water may help. Contact health care provider if the problem persists or is severe.
- Caution should be exercised in the following:
  - Bipolar disorder or a family history of bipolar disorder
  - Diabetes
  - Heart disease
  - Liver disease
  - Seizures (convulsions)
  - Suicidal thoughts, plans, or attempts by patients or a family member
  - An unusual or allergic reaction to venlafaxine, other medicines, foods, dyes, or preservatives

(cont.)

venlafaxine (cont.)

- Pregnancy or trying to get pregnant
- Breastfeeding

PATIENT AND FAMILY EDUCATION:
- Store at room temperature. Take any unused medication after the expiration date to the local pharmacy on drug give-back day. Avoid throwing medication into the environment.
- Try to take the medicine at the same time each day. Follow the directions on the prescription label.
- Should be taken about the same time every day, morning or evening and can be taken with or without food.
- May take up to 4 weeks to be fully effective, but patient may see symptoms of depression improving in as little as 1–2 weeks.
- If patient plans on becoming pregnant, discuss the benefits versus the risks of using this medicine while pregnant. Because this medicine is excreted in the breast milk, nursing mothers should not breastfeed while taking this medicine.
- This medication should be used only when clearly needed during pregnancy. Discuss the risks and benefits with your doctor.

- If this medication is used during the last 3 months of pregnancy, newborn may have feeding or breathing difficulties, seizures, muscle stiffness, jitteriness, or constant crying.
- This medication should not be stopped unless health care provider directs. Report any adverse symptoms to health care provider promptly.
- This drug passes into breast milk. Because of the potential risk to the infant, breastfeeding while using this drug is not recommended.
- Caution should be exercised when using this drug on the elderly because they may be more sensitive to the effects of the drug.

SPECIAL POPULATIONS:
- *Elderly:* The initial dose should be reduced in patients with severe renal and/or hepatic impairment. Titration upward should be slow and at intervals.
- *Pregnancy:* Category C. Potential for persistent pulmonary HTN if greater than 20-weeks gestation.
- *Lactation:* Excreted in human breast milk, caution should be taken.
- *Children:* Not indicated for children.

Pristiq | **desvenlafaxine**

INDICATIONS: Used to treat MDD, GAD, PD, and social anxiety disorder

AVAILABLE FORMS: Extended-release capsule, 50 and 100 mg

DOSAGE: Starting dose, 50 mg PO, daily. Doses greater than 50 mg/day are rarely more effective, may increase adverse drug reaction risk; consider 50 mg every other day if poorly tolerated in elderly

ADMINISTRATION:
- PO with a glass of water.
- Do not crush, cut, or chew capsules.
- Take at regular intervals.
- Caution patients not to stop taking drug except on provider's advice.
- Not prescribed for children.
- Instruct patients to take missed dose as soon as possible. If it is almost time for the next dose, advise to take only that dose.

SIDE EFFECTS:
- *Most common:* Nausea, vomiting, headache, insomnia, dizziness, somnolence, decreased libido and sexual dysfunction, palpitations, nervousness, and hypertension.
- *Less common:* Worsening depression, suicidality, hypersensitivity reactions.

DRUG INTERACTIONS: Most of the interactions occur with OTC cough and cold preparations. This medicine may also interact with the following medications.

- Absolute contraindications include MAOIs such as phenelzine (*Nardil*), tranylcypromine (*Parnate*), isocarboxazid (Ma*rplan)*, and selegiline (Eld*epryl*).
- Avoid using with other SSRIs due to serotonin effect; SNRI drugs such as desvenlafaxine (*Pristiq*) and venlafaxine (*Effexor*), and all triptan agents. Exercise caution with cold medications, NSAIDs, and drugs used for analgesia with opioid properties.
- ▶Alert: This list may not describe all possible interactions. Instruct patients to provide a list of all medicines, herbs, nonprescription drugs, or dietary supplements used, and if they smoke, drink alcohol, or use illegal drugs.

PHARMACOKINETICS:
- SNRI agents are potent inhibitors of neuronal serotonin and norepinephrine reuptake and weak inhibitors of dopamine reuptake.
- Demonstrate slightly higher efficacy than the SSRI class due to the dual effect.
- Relative to SSRIs, SNRI agents seem to be more effective in treating chronic pain issues that coexist with depression and may produce more stimulative effects.
- They are highly bound to plasma proteins and have a large volume of distribution.

Metabolism: Liver inactivation via CYP 3A4;

Excretion: Urine 64–69% (45% unchanged); 11 hr (O-desmethylvenlafaxine)

PANIC DISORDER: Serotonin and Norepinephrine Reuptake Inhibitors (SNRIs)

(cont.)

desvenlafaxine (*cont.*)

Half-life: 11 hr, 13–14 hr (moderate to severe hepatic impairment), 13–18 hr (mild to severe renal impairment), 23 hr (ESRD)

PRECAUTIONS:
- See patients as often as necessary to ensure that the drug is working on the panic attacks, determine compliance, and review side effects.
- Make sure patients realize that they need to take prescribed doses even if they do not feel better right away. It can take several weeks before they feel the full effect of the drug.
- Instruct patients and families to watch for worsening depression or thoughts of suicide. Also watch for sudden or severe changes in feelings such as feeling anxious, agitated, panicky, irritated, hostile, aggressive, impulsive, severely restless, overly excited, hyperactive, or not being able to sleep. If this happens, especially at the beginning of antidepressant treatment or after a change in dose, patient should call the health care provider.
- Drowsiness or dizziness: Patients should not drive or use machinery or do anything that needs mental alertness until the effects of this medicine are known.
- Caution patients not to stand or sit up quickly, especially if older. This reduces the risk of dizzy or fainting spells. Alcohol may interfere with the effect of this medicine. Avoid alcoholic drinks.
- Caution patients not to treat themselves for coughs, colds, or allergies without asking health care professional for advice. Some ingredients can increase possible side effects.
- Dry mouth: Chewing sugarless gum, sucking hard candy, and drinking plenty of water may help. Contact health care provider if the problem persists or is severe.
- Caution should be exercised in the following:
  - Bipolar disorder or a family history of bipolar disorder
  - Diabetes
  - Heart disease
  - Liver disease
  - Seizures (convulsions)
  - Suicidal thoughts, plans, or attempts by patients or a family member
  - An unusual or allergic reaction to venlafaxine, other medicines, foods, dyes, or preservatives
  - Pregnancy or trying to get pregnant
  - Breastfeeding

PATIENT AND FAMILY EDUCATION:
- Store at room temperature. Take any unused medication after the expiration date to the local pharmacy on drug give-back day. Avoid throwing the medication into the environment. Try to take the medicine at the same time each day. Follow the directions on the prescription label.
- Should be taken about the same time every day, morning or evening and can be taken with or without food.
- May take up to 4 weeks to be fully effective, but patient may see symptoms of depression improving in as little as 1–2 weeks.
- If patient plans on becoming pregnant, discuss the benefits versus the risks of using this medicine while pregnant. This medicine is excreted in breast milk; nursing mothers should not breastfeed while taking this medicine.
- This medication should be used only when clearly needed during pregnancy. Discuss the risks and benefits with your doctor.
- If this medication is used during the last 3 months of pregnancy, newborn may have feeding or breathing difficulties, seizures, muscle stiffness, jitteriness, or constant crying.
- This medication should not be stopped unless the health care provider directs. Report any adverse symptoms to the health care provider promptly.
- This drug passes into breast milk. Because of the potential risk to the infant, breastfeeding while using this drug is not recommended.
- Caution should be exercised when using this drug on the elderly because they may be more sensitive to the effects of the drug.

SPECIAL POPULATIONS:
- *Elderly:* The initial dose should be reduced in patients with severe renal and/or hepatic impairment. Titration upward should be slow and at intervals.
- *Pregnancy:* Category C; potential for persistent pulmonary HTN if greater than 20-weeks gestation.
- *Lactation:* Excreted in human breast milk, caution should be taken.
- *Children:* Not indicated for children.

duloxetine   *Cymbalta*

INDICATIONS: Used to treat MDD anGAD.

AVAILABLE FORMS: Capsule, enteric coated, 20, 30, and 60 mg

DOSAGE: Starting dose, 30 mg daily for 1 week; increase by 30 mg increments weekly. Can use a maximum of 120 mg daily; however, more than 60 mg is rarely more effective and can increase side effects. Maximum dose is 60 mg daily; do not cut/crush/chew/sprinkle

ADMINISTRATION:
- PO with a glass of water.
- Do not crush, cut, chew, or sprinkle capsules.

(cont.)

duloxetine (*cont.*)

- Take at regular intervals.
- Caution patients not to stop taking drug except on provider's advice.
- Not prescribed for children.
- Instruct patients to take missed dose as soon as possible. If it is almost time for the next dose, advise to take only that dose.

SIDE EFFECTS:
- *Most common*: Nausea, vomiting, headache, insomnia, dizziness, somnolence, decreased libido and sexual dysfunction, palpitations, nervousness, hypertension, and hot flashes.
- *Less common*: Worsening depression, suicidality, hypersensitivity reactions.

DRUG INTERACTIONS:
There are many drug–drug interactions. Most of the interactions occur with OTC cough and cold preparations. This medicine may also interact with the following medications.
- Absolute contraindications include MAOIs such as phenelzine (*Nardil*), tranylcypromine (*Parnate*), isocarboxazid (*Marplan*), and selegiline (*Eldepryl*), phenothiazines
- Avoid using with ciprofloxacin (*Cipro*) and other SSRIs due to serotonin effect; SNRI drugs such as desvenlafaxine (*Pristiq*) and venlafaxine (*Effexor*), caffeine.

▶ **Alert**: This list may not describe all possible interactions. Instruct patients to provide a list of all medicines, herbs, nonprescription drugs, or dietary supplements used, and if they smoke, drink alcohol, or use illegal drugs.

PHARMACOKINETICS:
Metabolism: Extensively metabolized in the liver by the CYP 1A2 and 2D6 into inactive metabolites
Excretion: Urine 70% (less than 1% unchanged)
Half-life: 12 hr

PRECAUTIONS:
- See patients as often as necessary to ensure that the drug is working on the panic attacks, determine compliance, and review side effects.
- Make sure patients realize that they need to take prescribed doses even if they do not feel better right away. It can take several weeks before they feel the full effect of the drug.
- Instruct patients and families to watch for worsening depression or thoughts of suicide. Also, watch for sudden or severe changes in feelings such as feeling anxious, agitated, panicky, irritated, hostile, aggressive, impulsive, severely restless, overly excited, hyperactive, or not being able to sleep. If this happens, especially at the beginning of antidepressant treatment or after a change in dose, patient should call the health care provider.
- Drowsiness or dizziness. The patient should not drive or use machinery or do anything that needs mental alertness until the effects of this medicine are known.

- Caution patients not to stand or sit up quickly, especially if older. This reduces the risk of dizzy or fainting spells. Alcohol may interfere with the effect of this medicine. Avoid alcoholic drinks.
- Caution patients not to treat themselves for coughs, colds, or allergies without asking health care professional for advice. Some ingredients can increase possible side effects.
- Dry mouth: Chewing sugarless gum, sucking hard candy, and drinking plenty of water may help. Contact health care provider if the problem persists or is severe.
- Caution should be exercised in the following:
  - Bipolar disorder or a family history of bipolar disorder
  - Diabetes
  - Heart disease
  - Liver disease
  - Seizures (convulsions)
  - Suicidal thoughts, plans, or attempts by patients or a family member
  - An unusual or allergic reaction to venlafaxine, other medicines, foods, dyes, or preservatives
  - Pregnancy or trying to get pregnant
  - Breastfeeding

PATIENT AND FAMILY EDUCATION:
- Store at room temperature. Take any unused medication after the expiration date to the local pharmacy on give-back day. Avoid throwing the medication into the environment. Try to take the medicine at the same time each day. Follow the directions on the prescription label.
- Should be taken about the same time every day, morning or evening and can be taken with or without food.
- May take up to 4 weeks to be fully effective, but patient may see symptoms of depression improving in as little as 1–2 weeks.
- If patient plans on becoming pregnant, discuss the benefits versus the risks of using this medicine while pregnant. Because this medicine is excreted in the breast milk, nursing mothers should not breastfeed while taking this medicine.
- This medication should be used only when clearly needed during pregnancy. Discuss the risks and benefits with your doctor.
- If this medication is used during the last 3 months of pregnancy, newborn may have feeding or breathing difficulties, seizures, muscle stiffness, jitteriness, or constant crying.
- This medication should not be stopped unless the health care provider directs. Report any adverse symptoms to the health care provider promptly.
- This drug passes into breast milk. Because of the potential risk to the infant, breastfeeding while using this drug is not recommended.
- Caution should be exercised when using this drug on the elderly because they may be more sensitive to the effects of the drug.

(cont.)

PANIC DISORDER: Serotonin and Norepinephrine Reuptake Inhibitors (SNRIs)

duloxetine (*cont.*)

SPECIAL POPULATIONS:
- *Elderly:* The initial dose should be reduced in patients with severe renal and/or hepatic impairment. Titration upward should be slow and at intervals. Higher dose may be required in the treatment of anxiety disorders in geriatric patients; however, this patient population is

more at risk of developing hyponatremia from SSRIs and SNRIs.
- *Pregnancy:* Category C; potential for persistent pulmonary HTN if greater than 20-weeks gestation.
- *Lactation:* Excreted in human breast milk, caution should be taken.
- *Children:* Not indicated for children.

Class: Tricyclic Antidepressants (TCAs)

Due to the class side effects, especially on the cardiac system, TCAs should be used only if the SSRI or SNRI classes fail to show any improvement in symptom profile.

imipramine pamoate   *Tofranil, Tofranil PM*

INDICATIONS: Used to treat adults with depression/anxiety

AVAILABLE FORMS: *Tofranil* tablets, 25 and 50 mg; *Tofranil PM* capsule, 75, 100, 125, and 150 mg

DOSAGE: *Adults:* Start: 25–75 mg PO nightly and increase by 25–50 mg/day every 3–4 days; maximum, 300 mg/day; 100 mg/day in elderly patients. Can be given in divided doses. Must taper dose gradually to discontinue. *Children: For depression:* Start: 1.5 mg/kg/day PO divided tid, increase by 1–1.5 mg/kg/day every 3–4 days. Maximum: 5 mg/kg/day. *Greater than 12 years old:* Start: 30–40 mg/day PO divided qd-tid and increase by 10–25 mg/day every 3–4 days; maximum, 100 mg day.

ADMINISTRATION:
- PO with a glass of water.
- Do not crush, cut, or chew extended-release tablets.
- Do not abruptly stop taking the medication.
- Prescribed for children except when used for nocturnal enuresis and depression in children as young as 6 years.
- Use lowest effective dose for shortest duration.

SIDE EFFECTS:
- *More common:* Drowsiness, dizziness, constipation; nausea/vomiting, urinary retention or frequency, libido changes, weight gain, general nervousness, and galactorrhea.
- *Less common:* Cardiac arrhythmias, extrapyramidal symptoms, clotting disturbances, worsening depression, suicidiality, hyperthermia, and hypertension

DRUG INTERACTIONS: This medicine may interact with the following medications:
- Absolute contraindications include class IA antiarrhythmics, MAOIs such as phenelzine (*Nardil*), tranylcypromine (*Parnate*), isocarboxazid (*Marplan*), and selegiline (*Eldepryl*).
- Avoid using with cimetadine, amiodarone, clarithromycin, haloperidol, and St. John's wort.
- ▶**Alert**: This list may not describe all possible interactions. Instruct patients provide a list of all medicines, herbs, nonprescription drugs, or

dietary supplements used, and if they smoke, drink alcohol, or use illegal drugs.

PHARMACOKINETICS:
- TCAs are thought to work by inhibiting reuptake of norepinephrine and serotonin in the CNS, which potentiates the neurotransmitters. They also have significant anticholinergics, antihistaminic, and alpha-adrenergic activity on the cardiac system. These classes of antidepressants also possess class 1A antiarrhythmic activity, which can lead to depression of cardiac conduction potentially resulting in heart block or ventricular arrhythmias.

Metabolism: Extensively by the liver within the CYP450: 1A2, 2C19, 2D6 (primary), 3A4 substrate
Excretion: Primarily in urine, up to 5% unchanged, also excreted in the bile/feces
Half-life: 11–25 hr

PRECAUTIONS:
- See patients as often as necessary to ensure that the drug is working on the panic attacks, determine compliance, and review side effects.
- Instruct patients and families to watch for worsening depression or thoughts of suicide. Also watch for sudden or severe changes in feelings such as feeling anxious, agitated, panicky, irritated, hostile, aggressive, impulsive, severely restless, overly excited, hyperactive, or not being able to sleep. If this happens, especially at the beginning of antidepressant treatment or after a change in dose, patient should call the health care provider.
- Drowsiness or dizziness: Patients should not drive or use machinery or do anything that needs mental alertness until one knows the effects of this medicine. Other medications that cause drowsiness can add to the drowsiness of imipramine.
- Caution patients not to stand or sit up quickly, especially if older. This reduces the risk of dizzy or fainting spells. Alcohol may interfere with the effect of this medicine. Avoid alcoholic drinks.
- Do not abruptly withdraw this drug as it may cause headache, nausea and malaise.
- Advise to protect skin from ultraviolet light due to increased skin sensitivity.

(cont.)

PANIC DISORDER: Tricyclic Antidepressants (TCAs)

imipramine pamoate (*cont.*)

- Grapefruit and grapefruit juice may interact with imipramine.
- Caution should be exercised in the following:
  - MDD, psychosis, or bipolar affective disorder
  - Contraindicated in patients with a recent myocardial infarction
  - Blood dyscrasias
  - Respiratory disease
  - Heart disease
  - Liver disease
  - Seizures (convulsions)
  - Suicidal thoughts, plans, or attempts by patients or a family member
  - An unusual or allergic reaction to imipramine, other medicines, foods, dyes, or preservatives

PATIENT AND FAMILY EDUCATION:
- Store imipramine at room temperature, away from moisture and heat.
- Stopping this medication suddenly could result in unpleasant side effects.

- Take the missed dose as soon as remembered. If it is almost time for the next dose, skip the missed dose and take the medicine at the next regularly scheduled time. *Do not* take extra medicine to make up the missed dose.

SPECIAL POPULATIONS:
- *Elderly:* Older patients may be more sensitive to the effects of TCAs. The smallest effective dose should be used. Dose adjustment is necessary for patients with liver impairment.
- *Pregnancy:* Category D. Some clinical reports of congenital malformations, but no direct causal link.
- *Lactation:* Excreted in human breast milk, alternative medications are recommended.
- *Children: Tofranil* is indicated for children with nocturnal enuresis and older than 6 years or with depression. Monitor for suicidal ideation with depression. *Tofranil PM* is not approved for children.

Norpramin   **desipramine**

INDICATIONS: Used to treat adults with depression/anxiety

AVAILABLE FORMS: Tablet, 10, 25, 50, 75, 100, and 150 mg

DOSAGE: Starting dose, 25–75 mg PO daily, with a maximum of 300 mg/day. May be given in divided doses; must taper slowly to discontinue.

ADMINISTRATION:
- PO with a glass of water.
- Do not abruptly stop taking the medication.
- Not prescribed for children.
- Use lowest effective dose for shortest duration.

SIDE EFFECTS:
- *More common:* Drowsiness, dizziness, constipation; nausea/vomiting, urinary retention or frequency, libido changes, weight gain, general nervousness, galactorrhea, rash, andurticaria.
- *Less common:* Cardiac arrhythmias, extrapyramidal symptoms, clotting disturbances, worsening depression, suicidiality, hyperthermia, and hypertension

DRUG INTERACTIONS: This medicine may interact with the following medications:
- Absolute contraindications include class IA antiarrhythmics, MAOIs such as phenelzine (*Nardil*), tranylcypromine (*Parnate*), isocarboxazid (*Marplan*), and selegiline (*Eldepryl*).
- Avoid using with cimetadine, amiodarone, clarithromycin, erythromycin, haldoperidol, and St. John's wort.

▶**Alert**: This list may not describe all possible interactions. Instruct patients to provide a list of all medicines, herbs, nonprescription drugs, or dietary supplements used, and if they smoke, drink alcohol, or use illegal drugs.

PHARMACOKINETICS:
- TCAs are thought to work by inhibiting reuptake of norepinephrine and serotonin in the CNS, which potentiates the neurotransmitters. They also have significant anticholinergics, antihistaminic, and alpha-adrenergic activity on the cardiac system. These classes of antidepressants also possess class 1A antiarrhythmic activity, which can lead to depression of cardiac conduction potentially resulting in heart block or ventricular arrhythmias.

Metabolism: Primarily in the liver via the CYP450: 2C19, 2D6 (primary) substrate
Excretion: Urine
Half-life: 12–27 hr

PRECAUTIONS:
- See patients as often as necessary to ensure that the drug is working on the panic attacks, determine compliance, and review side effects.
- Instruct patients and families to watch for worsening depression or thoughts of suicide. Also watch for sudden or severe changes in feelings such as feeling anxious, agitated, panicky, irritated, hostile, aggressive, impulsive, severely restless, overly excited, hyperactive, or not being able to sleep. If this happens, especially at the beginning of antidepressant treatment or after a change in dose, patient should call the health care provider.
- Drowsiness or dizziness: Patients should not drive or use machinery or do anything that needs mental alertness until the effects of this medicine are known. Other medications that cause drowsiness can add to the drowsiness of desipramine.
- Caution patients not to stand or sit up quickly, especially if older. This reduces the risk of dizzy or fainting spells. Alcohol may interfere
(cont.)

PANIC DISORDER: Tricyclic Antidepressants (TCAs)

desipramine (cont.)

with the effect of this medicine. Avoid alcoholic drinks.
- Do not abruptly withdraw this drug as it may cause headache, nausea and malaise.
- Advise to protect skin from ultraviolet light due to increased skin sensitivity.
- Grapefruit and grapefruit juice may interact with imipramine.
- Caution should be exercised in the following:
  - MDD, psychosis, or bipolar affective disorder
  - Contraindicated in patients with a recent myocardial infarction
  - Blood dyscrasias
  - Respiratory disease
  - Heart disease
  - Liver disease
  - Seizures (convulsions)
  - Psychoses or schizophrenia
  - Suicidal thoughts, plans, or attempts by patients or a family member
  - An unusual or allergic reaction to desipramine, other medicines, foods, dyes, or preservatives

PATIENT AND FAMILY EDUCATION:
- Store imipramine at room temperature away from moisture and heat.
- Stopping this medication suddenly could result in unpleasant side effects.
- Take the missed dose as soon as remembered. If it is almost time for the next dose, skip the missed dose and take the medicine at the next regularly scheduled time. *Do not* take extra medicine to make up the missed dose.

SPECIAL POPULATIONS:
- *Elderly:* Older patients may be more sensitive to the effects of TCAs. The smallest effective dose should be used (beginning at 10–25 mg/day). Dose adjustment is necessary for patients with liver impairment.
- *Pregnancy:* Category C; unknown effects as there is limited study.
- *Lactation:* Excreted in human breast milk; use caution
- *Children:* Not indicated for children; used off-label in children 6–12 years of age; however, alternative medications are preferred.

nortriptyline   *Pamelor*

INDICATIONS: Used to treat adults with depression/anxiety

AVAILABLE FORMS: Capsules, 10, 25, 50, and 75 mg; oral solution, 10 mg/5 mL

DOSAGE: *Adults:* Starting dose, 25–50 mg PO nightly and increase by 25–50 mg/day every 2–3 days. *Elderly*: 10–25 mg PO nightly and increase by 10–25 mg/day every 2–3 days; maximum, 150 mg/day. May be given in divided doses. Must taper the dose gradually to discontinue. *Children (6–12 years old, unlabeled use)*: Starting dose, 1–3 mg/kg/day PO divided tid-qid (less than 12 years old). Starting dose, 30–50 mg/day PO divided qd-qid; maximum, 150 mg/day. Alternative dosing, 1–3 mg/kg/day PO divided daily and tid.

ADMINISTRATION:
- PO with a glass of water.
- Do not abruptly stop taking the medication.
- Approved for children with enuresis and depression as young as 6 years old.
- Use lowest effective dose for shortest duration.

SIDE EFFECTS:
- *More common:* Drowsiness, dizziness, constipation; nausea/vomiting, urinary retention or frequency, libido changes, weight gain, general nervousness, galactorrhea, gynecomastia, rash, and urticaria.
- *Less common*: Cardiac arrhythmias, extrapyramidal symptoms, clotting disturbances, worsening depression, suicidality, hyperthermia, and hypertension

DRUG INTERACTIONS: This medicine may interact with the following medications:

- Absolute contraindications include class IA antiarrhythmics, MAOIs such as phenelzine (*Nardil*), tranylcypromine (*Parnate*), isocarboxazid (*Marplan*), and selegiline (*Eldepryl*).
- Avoid using with cimetidine, amiodarone, clarithromycin, erythromycin, haldoperidol, and St. John's wort.
▶**Alert:** This list may not describe all possible interactions. Instruct patients to provide a list of all medicines, herbs, nonprescription drugs, or dietary supplements used, and if they smoke, drink alcohol, or use illegal drugs.

PHARMACOKINETICS:
- TCAs are thought to work by inhibiting reuptake of norepinephrine and serotonin in the CNS, which potentiates the neurotransmitters. They also have significant anticholinergic, antihistaminic, and alpha-adrenergic activity on the cardiac system. These classes of antidepressants also possess class 1A antiarrhythmic activity, which can lead to depression of cardiac conduction potentially resulting in heart block or ventricular arrhythmias
Metabolism: Extensively metabolized by liver CYP 2D6 substrate
Excretion: Urine primarily, feces
Half-life: 18–44 hr

PRECAUTIONS:
- See patients as often as necessary to ensure that the drug is working on the panic attacks, determine compliance, and review side effects.
- Instruct patients and families to watch for worsening depression or thoughts of suicide. Also watch for sudden or severe changes in feelings
(cont.)

PANIC DISORDER: Tricyclic Antidepressants (TCAs)

nortriptyline (*cont.*)

such as feeling anxious, agitated, panicky, irritated, hostile, aggressive, impulsive, severely restless, overly excited, hyperactive, or not being able to sleep. If this happens, especially at the beginning of antidepressant treatment or after a change in dose, patient should call the health care provider.

- Drowsiness or dizziness: Patients should not drive or use machinery or do anything that needs mental alertness until the effects of this medicine are known. Other medications that cause drowsiness can add to the drowsiness of imipramine.
- Caution patients not to stand or sit up quickly, especially if older. This reduces the risk of dizzy or fainting spells. Alcohol may interfere with the effect of this medicine. Avoid alcoholic drinks.
- Do not abruptly withdraw this drug as it may cause headache, nausea, and malaise.
- Advise to protect skin from ultraviolet light due to increased skin sensitivity.
- Grapefruit and grapefruit juice may interact with imipramine.
- Caution should be exercised in the following:
  - MDD, psychosis, or bipolar affective disorder
  - Contraindicated in patients with a recent myocardial infarction
  - Blood dyscrasias
  - Respiratory disease
  - Heart disease

- Liver disease
- Seizures (convulsions)
- Suicidal thoughts, plans, or attempts by patients or a family member
- An unusual or allergic reaction to imipramine, other medicines, foods, dyes, or preservatives

PATIENT AND FAMILY EDUCATION:
- Store nortriptyline at room temperature away from moisture and heat.
- Stopping this medication suddenly could result in unpleasant side effects.
- Take the missed dose as soon as remembered. If it is almost time for the next dose, skip the missed dose and take the medicine at the next regularly scheduled time. *Do not* take extra medicine to make up the missed dose.

SPECIAL POPULATIONS:
- *Elderly:* Older patients may be more sensitive to the effects of TCAs. The smallest effective dose should be used. Dose adjustment is necessary for patients with liver impairment.
- *Pregnancy:* Category D; some clinical reports of congenital malformations, but no direct causal link. Alternative medications are recommended.
- *Lactation:* Excreted in human breast milk, bottle feed if possible or use with caution.
- *Children:* This drug is indicated for children with nocturnal enuresis and older than 6 years or with depression. Monitor for suicidal ideation with depression.

Class: Benzodiazepines (BZDs)

Xanax, Xanax XR, Niravam   **alprazolam**

INDICATIONS: Short-acting BZD used to treat GADs and PD. May be used as a short-term adjunct to an SSRI while waiting for the therapeutic effects of the SSRI to develop.

AVAILABLE FORMS: Tablet, 0.25, 0.5, 1, and 2 mg; extended-release capsule, 0.5, 1, and 2 mg; melt, 0.5, 1, 2, and 3 mg

DOSAGE: *Xanax:* Starting dose, 0.25 to 0.5 mg up to 2–3 times daily; maximum, 4 mg daily. Can be increased every 3–4 days. Treatment should be limited to as short a period as possible (less than 4 months) and/or re-evaluated for continued use. *Xanax XR:* Starting dose, 0.5–1 mg PO, daily; can increase up to 1 mg/day every 3–4 days. *Niravam (melt):* Starting dose, 0.25–0.5 mg up to 2–3 times daily; maximum, 4 mg daily. Can be increased every 3–4 days.

ADMINISTRATION:
- PO with a glass of water.
- Do not crush, cut, or chew extended-release tablets.
- Orally disintegrating (*Niravam*) has special instructions.

- Concentrated liquid must be measured with a special dose-measuring spoon or cup.
- Do not abruptly stop taking the medication.
- Not prescribed for children.
- Use lowest effective dose for shortest duration.
- Alprazolam can be habit forming; do not increase dosage without guidance from the health care provider.

SIDE EFFECTS:
- *More common:* Drowsiness, lightheadedness, dry mouth; headache, changes in bowel habits, sialorrhea, amnesia, and changes in appetite.
- *Less common:* Syncope, tachycardia, seizures, respiratory depression, dependency, withdrawal syndrome, and suicidal ideation.

DRUG INTERACTIONS: This medicine may interact with the following medications:
- Absolute contraindications include clarithromycin, fluvoxamine, and ketoconazole.
- Avoid using calcium channel blockers, erythromycins, tamoxifen, and zafirlukast.
- ▶**Alert:** This list may not describe all possible interactions. Instruct patients to provide a list
(cont.)

PANIC DISORDER: Benzodiazepines (BZDs)

alprazolam (*cont.*)

of all medicines, herbs, nonprescription drugs, or dietary supplements used, and if they smoke, drink alcohol, or use illegal drugs.

PHARMACOKINETICS:
- BZDs enhance the activity of GABA, a major CNS neurotransmitter, known to open CNS Cl- channels leading to an inhibition of subsequent CNS neuronal signaling. BZDs with similar action can differ in their potency and rate of absorption.

Metabolism: Liver in the CYP450 3A4
Excretion: Urine
Half-life: 11.2 hr, 16.3 hr (elderly), 19.7 hr (alcoholic liver disease)

PRECAUTIONS:
- See patients as often as necessary to ensure that the drug is working on the panic attacks, determine compliance, and review side effects.
- Instruct patients and families to watch for worsening depression or thoughts of suicide. Also watch out for sudden or severe changes in feelings such as feeling anxious, agitated, panicky, irritated, hostile, aggressive, impulsive, severely restless, overly excited, hyperactive, or not being able to sleep. If this happens, especially at the beginning of antidepressant treatment or after a change in dose, patient should call the health care provider.
- Drowsiness or dizziness: Patients should not drive or use machinery or do anything that needs mental alertness until the effects of this medicine are known.
- Caution patients not to stand or sit up quickly, especially if older. This reduces the risk of dizzy or fainting spells. Alcohol may interfere with the effect of this medicine. Avoid alcoholic drinks.
- Do not abruptly withdraw this drug as it may cause seizures.
- Caution should be exercised in the following:
  - MDD, psychosis, or bipolar affective disorder
  - Respiratory disease

- Heart disease
- Liver disease
- Seizures (convulsions)
- Suicidal thoughts, plans, or attempts by patients or a family member
- An unusual or allergic reaction to alprazolam, other medicines, foods, dyes, or preservatives

PATIENT AND FAMILY EDUCATION:
- Store alprazolam at room temperature away from moisture, heat, and light. Remove any cotton from the bottle of disintegrating tablets, and keep the bottle tightly closed.
- Alprazolam may be habit forming and *should be used only by the person it was prescribed for.* Alprazolam should never be shared with another person, especially someone who has a history of drug abuse or addiction. Keep the medication in a secure place where others cannot get to it.
- Do not purchase alprazolam on the Internet or outside of the USA as dangerous ingredients may be present. Some purchases of alprazolam from the Internet have been found to contain haloperidol (*Haldol*), an antipsychotic drug.

SPECIAL POPULATIONS:
- *Elderly:* Older patients may be more sensitive to the effects of BZDs. The smallest effective dose should be used. Dose adjustment is necessary for patients with liver impairment and/or renal disease due to excessive metabolites excreted by the kidney. Due to increased risk of sedation leading to falls and fractures, BZDs are included on the Beers List of Potentially Inappropriate Medications for Geriatrics.
- *Pregnancy:* Category D; can cause teratogenic fetal effects. Infants born to mothers taking BZDs may be at risk for withdrawal symptoms in the postnatal period.
- *Lactation:* Excreted in human breast milk; infants can become lethargic and lose weight.
- *Children:* Not indicated for use in children younger than 18 years.

lorazepam   *Ativan*

PANIC DISORDER: Benzodiazepines (BZDs)

INDICATIONS: Used to treat GADs and PD

AVAILABLE FORMS: Tablet, 0.5, 1, and 2 mg

DOSAGE: *Adults:* 2–3 mg/day PO/IM/IV divided bid-tid; 1–2 mg/day PO/IM/IV div bid-tid in elderly patients; maximum, 10 mg/day. Periodically assess the need for treatment and taper the dose gradually to discontinue if prolonged treatment is necessary. Treatment should be limited to as short a period as possible (less than 4 months) and/or re-evaluated for continued use. *Children:* 0.05 mg/kg PO/IV q4–8 hr; maximum, 2 mg/dose. Periodically assess the need for treatment and taper the dose

gradually to discontinue if prolonged treatment is necessary

ADMINISTRATION:
- PO with a glass of water.
- Do not abruptly stop taking the medication.
- Use lowest effective dose for shortest duration.
- Lorazepam can be habit forming; do not increase dosage without guidance from the health care provider.

SIDE EFFECTS:
- *More common:* Drowsiness, lightheadedness, dry mouth; headache, changes in bowel habits, sialorrhea, amnesia, and changes in appetite.

(cont.)

lorazepam (*cont.*)

- *Less common*: Syncope, tachycardia, seizures, respiratory depression, dependency, withdrawal syndrome, and suicidal ideation.

DRUG INTERACTIONS: This medicine may interact with the following medications:
- Absolute contraindications include clarithromycin, fluvoxamine, and ketoconazole.
- Avoid using with calcium channel blockers, erythromycins, tamoxifen, and zafirlukast.
▶**Alert**: This list may not describe all possible interactions. Instruct patients to provide a list of all medicines, herbs, nonprescription drugs, or dietary supplements used, and if they smoke, drink alcohol, or use illegal drugs.

PHARMACOKINETICS:
- BZDs enhance the activity of GABA, a major CNS neurotransmitter, known to open CNS Cl⁻ channels leading to an inhibition of subsequent CNS neuronal signaling. BZDs with similar action can differ in their potency and rate of absorption.
Metabolism: Liver with the CYP450 exact mechanism is unknown
Excretion: Urine
Half-life: 14 hr

PRECAUTIONS:
- See patients as often as necessary to ensure that the drug is working on the panic attacks, determine compliance, and review side effects.
- Instruct patients and families to watch for worsening depression or thoughts of suicide. Also watch out for sudden or severe changes in feelings such as feeling anxious, agitated, panicky, irritated, hostile, aggressive, impulsive, severely restless, overly excited, hyperactive, or not being able to sleep. If this happens, especially at the beginning of antidepressant treatment or after a change in dose, patient should call the health care provider.
- Drowsiness or dizziness: Patients should not drive or use machinery or do anything that needs mental alertness until the effects of this medicine are known.
- Caution patients not to stand or sit up quickly, especially if older. This reduces the risk of

dizzy or fainting spells. Alcohol may interfere with the effect of this medicine. Avoid alcoholic drinks.
- Do not abruptly withdraw this drug as it may cause seizures.
- Caution should be exercised in the following:
  - Heart disease
  - Liver disease
  - Seizures (convulsions)
  - Suicidal thoughts, plans, or attempts by patients or a family member
  - An unusual or allergic reaction to alprazolam, other medicines, foods, dyes, or preservatives

PATIENT AND FAMILY EDUCATION:
- Store lorazepam at room temperature away from moisture, heat, and light. Remove any cotton from the bottle of disintegrating tablets, and keep the bottle tightly closed.
- Lorazepam may be habit forming and *should be used only by the person it was prescribed for.* Lorazepam should never be shared with another person, especially someone who has a history of drug abuse or addiction. Keep the medication in a secure place where others cannot get to it.
- Do not purchase lorazepam on the Internet or outside of the USA as dangerous ingredients may be present.

SPECIAL POPULATIONS:
- *Elderly:* Older patients may be more sensitive to the effects of BZDs. The smallest effective dose should be used. Dose adjustment is necessary for patients with liver impairment and/or renal disease due to excessive metabolites excreted by the kidney. Due to increased risk of sedation leading to falls and fractures, BZDs are included on the Beers List of Potentially Inappropriate Medications for Geriatrics.
- *Pregnancy:* Category D; can cause teratogenic fetal effects. Infants born to mothers taking BZDs may be at risk for withdrawal symptoms in the postnatal period.
- *Lactation:* Excreted in human breast milk; infants can become lethargic and lose weight
- *Children:* Not indicated for use in children younger than 18 years.

Klonopin   **clonazepam**

INDICATIONS: Used to treat GADs and PD

AVAILABLE FORMS: Tablet, 0.5, 1, and 2 mg; wafer melt, 0.125, 0.25, 0.5, 1.2 mg

DOSAGE: *Adults:* Starting dose, 0.25 mg PO bid; increase by 0.25–0.5 mg/day every 3 days; may start lower in elderly patients; maximum, 4 mg/day; treatment should be limited to as short a period as possible (less than 4 months) and/or re-evaluated for continued use. To discontinue, taper

by 0.25 mg/day q3 days if greater than 4 to 6 weeks fo continuous use

ADMINISTRATION:
- PO with a glass of water.
- Do not abruptly stop taking the medication.
- Use lowest effective dose for shortest duration.
- Clonazepam can be habit forming, do not increase dosage without guidance from the health care provider.

(cont.)

PANIC DISORDER: Benzodiazepines (BZDs)

clonazepam (cont.)

SIDE EFFECTS:
- *More common:* Drowsiness, lightheadedness, dry mouth; headache, changes in bowel habits, sialorrhea, amnesia, and changes in appetite.
- *Less common:* Syncope, tachycardia, seizures, respiratory depression, dependency, withdrawal syndrome, and suicidal ideation.

DRUG INTERACTIONS: This medicine may interact with the following medications:
- Absolute contraindications include clarithromycin, fluvoxamine, and ketoconazole.
- Avoid using with calcium channel blockers, erythromycins, tamoxifen, and zafirlukast.

▶**Alert:** This list may not describe all possible interactions. Instruct patients to provide a list of all medicines, herbs, nonprescription drugs, or dietary supplements used, and if they smoke, drink alcohol, or use illegal drugs.

PHARMACOKINETICS:
- BZDs enhance the activity of GABA, a major CNS neurotransmitter, known to open CNS Cl⁻ channels leading to an inhibition of subsequent CNS neuronal signaling. BZDs with similar action can differ in their potency and rate of absorption.

Metabolism: Extensively metabolized in liver CYP450 3A4
Excretion: Urine
Half-life: 20–50 hr

PRECAUTIONS:
- See patients as often as necessary to ensure that the drug is working on the panic attacks, determine compliance, and review side effects.
- Instruct patients and families to watch for worsening depression or thoughts of suicide. Also watch out for sudden or severe changes in feelings such as feeling anxious, agitated, panicky, irritated, hostile, aggressive, impulsive, severely restless, overly excited, hyperactive, or not being able to sleep. If this happens, especially at the beginning of antidepressant treatment or after a change in dose, patient should call the health care provider.
- Drowsiness or dizziness: Patients should not drive or use machinery or do anything that needs mental alertness until the effects of this medicine are known.
- Caution patients not to stand or sit up quickly, especially if older. This reduces the risk of dizzy or fainting spells. Alcohol may interfere with the effect of this medicine. Avoid alcoholic drinks.
- Do not abruptly withdraw this drug as it may cause seizures.
- Caution should be exercised in the following:
  - Heart disease
  - Liver disease
  - Seizures (convulsions)
  - Suicidal thoughts, plans, or attempts by patients or a family member
  - An unusual or allergic reaction to alprazolam, other medicines, foods, dyes, or preservatives

PATIENT AND FAMILY EDUCATION:
- Store clonazepam at room temperature away from moisture, heat, and light. Remove any cotton from the bottle of disintegrating wafers, and keep the bottle tightly closed.
- Clonazepam may be habit forming and *should be used only by the person it was prescribed for.* Clonazepam should never be shared with another person, especially someone who has a history of drug abuse or addiction. Keep the medication in a secure place where others cannot get to it.

SPECIAL POPULATIONS:
- *Elderly:* Older patients may be more sensitive to the effects of BZDs. The smallest effective dose should be used. Dose adjustment is necessary for patients with liver impairment and/or renal disease due to excessive metabolites excreted by the kidney. Due to increased risk of sedation leading to falls and fractures, BZDs are included on the Beers List of Potentially Inappropriate Medications for Geriatrics.
- *Pregnancy:* Category D; can cause teratogenic fetal effects. Infants born to mothers taking BZDs may be at risk for withdrawal symptoms in the postnatal period.
- *Lactation:* Excreted in human breast milk; infants can become lethargic and lose weight.
- *Children:* Not indicated for use in children except for treatment of seizures.

Class: Anxiolytics/Sedatives/Hypnotics

buspirone	*BuSpar*

INDICATIONS: Anxiolytic non-BZD that is used to treat GAD and PD

AVAILABLE FORMS: Tablet, 5, 10, 15, and 30 mg

DOSAGE: *Adults:* Starting dose, 7.5 mg PO bid, then increase by 5 mg/day every 2–3 days; maximum, 60 mg/day. *Children (6–17 years old):* Starting dose, 15–60 mg/day PO divide bid; maximum, 60 mg/day

ADMINISTRATION:
- PO with a glass of water.
- While discontinuation symptoms are minimal with *BuSpar*, it should not be stopped abruptly.

(cont.)

buspirone (cont.)

- There is little potential for abuse, tolerance, and physical or psychological dependence.

SIDE EFFECTS:
- *More common:* Dizziness, drowsiness, headache, nervousness, dry mouth; decreased concentration, and weakness.
- *Less common:* Serotonin syndrome, extrpyramidal symptoms, hostility, and depression.

DRUG INTERACTIONS: This medicine may interact with the following medications:
- Absolute contraindications include MAOIs such as phenelzine (*Nardil*), tranylcypromine (*Parnate*), isocarboxazid (*Marplan*), and selegiline (*Eldepryl*).
- Monitor treatment with amiodarone, dilitazem, erythromycins, verapamil
▶ **Alert:** This list may not describe all possible interactions. Instruct patients to provide a list of all medicines, herbs, nonprescription drugs, or dietary supplements used, and if they smoke, drink alcohol, or use illegal drugs.

PHARMACOKINETICS:
- The only drug of this anxiolytic, non-BZD class that is not chemically related to BZDs, barbiturates, or other sedative/anxiolytic drugs. It seems to have a high affinity for serotonin (5-HT1A) receptors but does not affect GABA binding. There is a moderate affinity for brain serotonin and D2-dopamine receptors.
Metabolism: Liver; CYP450 3A4
Excretion: Urine, feces
Half-life: 2–3 hr

PRECAUTIONS:
- See patients as often as necessary to ensure that the drug is working on the panic attacks, determine compliance, and review side effects.
- Instruct patients and families to watch for worsening depression or thoughts of suicide. Also watch out for sudden or severe changes in feelings such as feeling anxious, agitated, panicky, irritated, hostile, aggressive, impulsive, severely restless, overly excited, hyperactive, or not being able to sleep. If this happens, especially at the beginning of antidepressant treatment or after a change in dose, patient should call the health care provider.
- Drowsy or dizzy. Do not drive, use machinery, or do anything that needs mental alertness until the effects of this medicine are known.
- Caution patients not to stand or sit up quickly, especially if older. This reduces the risk of dizzy or fainting spells. Alcohol may interfere with the effect of this medicine. Avoid alcoholic drinks.
- Caution should be exercised in the following:
  - Renal disease
  - Liver disease
  - Suicidal thoughts, plans, or attempts by patients or a family member
  - An unusual or allergic reaction to buspirone, other medicines, foods, dyes, or preservatives

PATIENT AND FAMILY EDUCATION:
- Store buspirone at room temperature away from moisture, heat, and light.

SPECIAL POPULATIONS:
- *Elderly:* Because buspirone is less sedating, older patients may tolerate it better than BZDs. The smallest effective dose should be used. Dose adjustment is necessary for patients with mild liver impairment and/or renal disease due to excessive metabolites excreted by the kidney. Use is contraindicated in patients with severe liver or kidney disease.
- *Pregnancy:* Category B; no teratogenic effects noted in animal studies; however, limited human data available. Use with caution.
- *Lactation:* Safety is unknown.
- *Children:* Indicated for children 6–17 years of age.

Agoraphobia Disorder

OVERVIEW
- Type of anxiety related to fear related to not being able to get out of places if a panic attack occurs.
- Thought to be a complication of PD
- Places are avoided that may potentiate a panic attack, particularly crowded places
- Common situations and places that are avoided include sporting events, elevators, bridges, shopping malls, and airplanes
- Patient may eventually become "trapped" at home
- Treatment involves medication and therapy that helps patient confront fears

- Starts in late adolescence and early adulthood; more common in women than men; between 1% and 5% will develop agoraphobia in lifetime
- Risk factors include history of panic attacks, experiencing a stressful event, including physical or sexual abuse in childhood, being a nervous or anxious person, or having a substance abuse disorder
- Individuals with agoraphobia are very limited in their ability to have a normal life, finding it difficult to attend school, visit family, or hold a job; these individuals become dependent on others for simple tasks such as grocery shopping

AGORAPHOBIA

Psychopharmacology of Agoraphobia Disorder

OVERVIEW

- *SSRIs*: Drugs in this category that are commonly used to treat agoraphobia include: fluoxetine (*Prozac, Prozac Weekly*), paroxetine (*Paxil, Paxil CR*), and sertraline (*Zoloft*)
- *BZDs (anti-anxiety agents)*: Used as an adjunct to aid in treatment of agoraphobia, providing coverage while therapeutic SSRI levels are obtained. BZDs can also help with the initial side effects of the selected SSRI, but should be withdrawn as soon as possible.
- *TCAs*: May be helpful. Due to the side effect profile, they are less well tolerated than SSRIs
- *MAOIs*: MAOIs such as phenelzine (*Nardil*), tranylcypromine (*Parnate*), and isocarboxazid (*Marplan*) are only used when all the other drugs

do not work. These should be prescribed only by a psychiatrist who is experienced in their use.

- CBT is an important component of agoraphobia treatment. The cognitive portion of this therapy involves learning about agoraphobia, and how to control it.
- The behavioral component of CBT involves changing unwanted or unhealthy behaviors through desensitization. This technique allows patients to safely confront places and situations that cause fear and anxiety. A therapist accompanies patients on excursions such as shopping or driving a car. Through gradual practice, patients may learn that deep-seated fears are not realistic and anxiety may decrease over time.

CLASS	DRUG
Selective Serotonin Reuptake Inhibitors (SSRIs)	**First-Line Drug Therapy**
	sertraline (*Zoloft*)
	fluoxetine (*Prozac*)
	paroxetine (*Paxil, Paxil CR*)
	paroxetine mesylate (*Pexeva*)
	fluvoxamine (*Luvox CR*)
	citalopram (*Celexa*)
	escitalopram (*Lexapro*)
Tricyclic Antidepressants (TCAs)	**Drugs for Treatment of Resistant Cases**
	imipramine (*Tofranil*)
	desipramine (*Norpramin*)
	nortriptyline (*Pamelor*)
Benzodiazepines (BZDs)	**Drugs Used Only in First Weeks While Establishing Levels of SSRI or SNRI**
	alprazolam (*Xanax/Xanax XR/Niravam*)
	lorazepam (*Ativan*)
	clonazepam (*Klonopin*)

AGORAPHOBIA DISORDER

Class: Selective Serotonin Reuptake Inhibitors (SSRIs)

sertraline   *Zoloft*

INDICATIONS: Used to treat primarily depression but may also be used for OCD, PD, posttrauma stress, PMDD, or social anxiety.

AVAILABLE FORMS: Tablet, 25, 50, and 100 mg

DOSAGE: Starting dose, 25 mg once daily, increase dose incrementally 25 mg per week; maximum, 200 mg daily.

ADMINISTRATION:
- PO with a glass of water.
- Take with or without food.
- Take at regular intervals.
- Caution patients not to stop taking drug except on provider's advice.
- May be prescribed for children as young as 6 years for selected conditions (25 mg/day); *precautions do apply.*

- Instruct patients to take missed dose as soon as possible. If it is almost time for the next dose, advise to take only that dose.

SIDE EFFECTS:
- *Most common*: Dizziness, headache, insomnia, somnolence, and change in sex drive or performance.
- *Less common*: Allergic reactions like skin rash, itching, or hives; swelling of the face, lips, or tongue; feeling faint or lightheaded; falls; hallucination; loss of contact with reality; seizures; suicidal thoughts or other mood changes; unusual bleeding or bruising; unusually weak or tired; vomiting; change in appetite; diarrhea; increased sweating; indigestion; nausea; tremors.

(cont.)

AGORAPHOBIA DISORDER: SSRIs

sertraline (*cont.*)

DRUG INTERACTIONS: This medicine may interact with the following medications:
- Absolute contraindications include MAOIs such as phenelzine (*Nardil*), tranylcypromine (*Parnate*), isocarboxazid (*Marplan*), and selegiline (*Eldepryl*).
- Avoid using with SNRI agents, triptans, and other SSRI agents
- Caution with aspirin, NSAIDs (e.g., ibuprofen or naproxen), COX inhibitors, and other anti-inflammatory drugs, St. John's wort.

▶**Alert**: This list may not describe all possible interactions. Instruct patients to provide a list of all medicines, herbs, nonprescription drugs, or dietary supplements used, and if they smoke, drink alcohol, or use illegal drugs.

PHARMACOKINETICS:
- SSRIs are metabolized in the liver by CYP P450 (CYP) enzymes.
- They are highly bound to plasma proteins and have a large volume of distribution.
- May take 2–6 weeks to fully effective
- Addition of serotonergic medications to a patient's regimen must not occur until 2–3 weeks after discontinuation of an SSRI (some recommend a 5-week "washout" period prior to initiation of an MAOI).

Metabolism: Liver; CYP 2C19, 2D6, 3A4 substrate; 2D6 (weak), 3A4 (weak) inhibitor

Excretion: Urine 40–45% (none unchanged); feces 40–45% (12–14% unchanged)

Half-life: 26 hr

PRECAUTIONS:
- See patients as often as necessary to ensure that the drug is working on the panic attacks, determine compliance, and review side effects.
- Make sure patients realize that they need to take prescribed doses even if they do not feel better right away. It can take several weeks before they feel the full effect of the drug.
- Instruct patients and families to watch for worsening depression or thoughts of suicide. Also, watch out for sudden or severe changes in feelings such as feeling anxious, agitated, panicky, irritated, hostile, aggressive, impulsive, severely restless, overly excited, hyperactive, or not being able to sleep. If this happens, especially at the beginning of antidepressant treatment or after a change in dose, patient should call the health care provider.
- Drowsiness or dizziness: Patients should not drive or use machinery or do anything that needs mental alertness until the effects of this medicine are known.

- Caution patients not to stand or sit up quickly, especially if older. This reduces the risk of dizzy or fainting spells. Alcohol may interfere with the effect of this medicine. Avoid alcoholic drinks.
- Caution patients not to treat themselves for coughs, colds, or allergies without asking health care professional for advice. Some ingredients can increase possible side effects.
- For dry mouth, chewing sugarless gum or sucking hard candy and drinking plenty of water may help. Contact health care provider if the problem persists or is severe.
- Caution should be exercised in the following:
  - Bipolar disorder or a family history of bipolar disorder
  - Diabetes
  - Heart disease
  - Liver disease
  - Electroconvulsive therapy
  - Seizures (convulsions)
  - Suicidal thoughts, plans, or attempts by patients or a family member
  - An unusual or allergic reaction to sertraline, other medicines, foods, dyes, or preservatives
  - Pregnancy or trying to get pregnant
  - Breastfeeding

PATIENT AND FAMILY EDUCATION:
- Store at room temperature. Take any unused medication after the expiration date to the local pharmacy on drug give-back day. Avoid throwing the medication into the environment.
- Discuss any worsening anxiety, aggressiveness, impulsivity, or restlessness
- Patients or families should report any severe, abrupt onset or changes in symptoms to health professionals. This may be reflective of increased risk of suicidal thinking.
- Caution for the concomitant use of NSAIDs, aspirin, warfarin, and any other drugs that alter platelets.

SPECIAL POPULATIONS:
- *Elderly:* Increased risk for hyponatremia.
- *Hepatic impairment:* Dose adjustment necessary.
- *Pregnancy:* Category C; risks are associated with all SSRIs for neonatal complications if used in the third trimester.
- *Lactation:* Adverse reactions have not been reported; however, long-term effects have not been studied, and the manufacturer recommends caution.
- *Children:* Approved for use in children aged 12 years or older; however, monitoring for increased suicidal ideation is critical.

AGORAPHOBIA DISORDER: Selective Serotonin Reuptake Inhibitors (SSRIs)

fluoxetine | *Prozac*

INDICATIONS: Used to treat MDDs, OCD, bulimia nervosa, and PD.

AVAILABLE FORMS: Capsule, 10, 20, and 40 mg; capsule, delayed release (*Prozac Weekly*), 90 mg; solution, 20 mg/5 mL

DOSAGE: Immediate release (*Prozac Daily*): Starting dose, 10 mg PO, daily for 7 days; maximum, 60 mg/day. Capsule, delayed release (*Prozac Weekly*): 90 mg oral, once weekly, 7 days after last daily dose of 20 mg. Extended release, not recommended for acute treatment.

ADMINISTRATION:
- PO with a glass of water
- Take with or without food
- Take at regular intervals
- Caution patients not to stop taking drug except on provider's advice.
- *Prozac Daily* may be prescribed for children as young as 7 years for selected conditions; *precautions do apply.*
- *Prozac Weekly* is not prescribed for children.
- Do not prescribe *Prozac Weekly* for acute treatment.
- Instruct patients to take missed dose as soon as possible. If it is almost time for the next dose, advise to take only that dose.

SIDE EFFECTS:
- *Most common*: Dizziness, headache, insomnia, somnolence, and change in sex drive or performance.
- *Less common*: Allergic reactions like skin rash, itching, or hives; swelling of the face, lips, or tongue; psoriasis; arthralgias; anorexia; feeling faint or lightheaded, falls; nausea; dry mouth; constipation; dyspepsia; suicidal thoughts or other mood changes; unusual bleeding or bruising; fatigue; tremor; change in appetite; diarrhea; increased sweating; indigestion.

DRUG INTERACTIONS: Most of the interactions occur with OTC cough and cold preparations. This medicine may also interact with the following medications.
- Absolute contraindications include MAOIs such as phenelzine (*Nardil*), tranylcypromine (*Parnate*), isocarboxazid (*Marplan*), and selegiline (*Eldepryl*).
- Avoid using with other SSRIs due to serotonin effect; SNRI drugs such as desvenlafaxine (*Pristiq*) and venlafaxine (*Effexor*); drugs with sympathomimetic properties such as phenylpropanolamine, pseudoephedrine, St. John's wort, haloperidol; and diazepam (*Valium*); any other antidepressants; and clopidogrel (*Plavix*).
- Exercise caution with cold medications, arrhythmia medications such as flecainide, aspirin, and other NSAIDs, and drugs used for analgesia with opioid properties.
- ▶**Alert**: This list may not describe all possible interactions. Instruct patients to provide a list

of all medicines, herbs, nonprescription drugs, or dietary supplements used, and if they smoke, drink alcohol, or use illegal drugs.

PHARMACOKINETICS:
Metabolism: Liver; CYP450 2C19, 2D6 (primary) substrate; 2C19, 3A4 (weak) inhibitor; active metabolite
Excretion: Urine 80% (11.6% unchanged), feces 15%
Half-life: 4–6 days (fluoxetine), 9.3 days (norfluoxetine)

PRECAUTIONS:
- See patients as often as necessary to ensure that the drug is working on the panic attacks, determine compliance, and review side effects.
- Make sure patients realize that they need to take prescribed doses even if they do not feel better right away. It can take several weeks before they feel the full effect of the drug.
- Instruct patients and families to watch for worsening depression or thoughts of suicide. Also watch out for sudden or severe changes in feelings such as feeling anxious, agitated, panicky, irritated, hostile, aggressive, impulsive, severely restless, overly excited, hyperactive, or not being able to sleep. If this happens, especially at the beginning of antidepressant treatment or after a change in dose, patient should call the health care provider.
- Drowsiness or dizziness: Patients should not drive or use machinery or do anything that needs mental alertness until the effects of this medicine are known.
- Caution patients not to stand or sit up quickly, especially if older. This reduces the risk of dizzy or fainting spells. Alcohol may interfere with the effect of this medicine. Avoid alcoholic drinks.
- Caution patients not to treat themselves for coughs, colds, or allergies without asking health care professional for advice. Some ingredients can increase possible side effects.
- Dry mouth: Chewing sugarless gum, sucking hard candy, and drinking plenty of water may help. Contact health care provider if the problem persists or is severe.
- Caution should be exercised in the following:
  - Bipolar disorder or a family history of bipolar disorder
  - Diabetes
  - Heart disease
  - Liver disease
  - Electroconvulsive therapy
  - Seizures (convulsions)
  - Suicidal thoughts, plans, or attempts by patients or a family member
  - An unusual or allergic reaction to fluoxetine, other medicines, foods, dyes, or preservatives
  - Pregnancy when trying to get pregnant
  - Breastfeeding

(cont.)

fluoxetine (*cont.*)

PATIENT AND FAMILY EDUCATION:
- Store at room temperature. Take any unused medication after the expiration date to the local pharmacy on drug give-back day. Avoid throwing medication into the environment.
- Discuss any worsening anxiety, aggressiveness, impulsivity, or restlessness.
- Report any severe, abrupt onset or changes in symptoms to health professionals. May be reflective of increased risk of suicidal thinking.
- Caution for the concomitant use of NSAIDs, aspirin, warfarin, and any other drugs that alter platelets.

SPECIAL POPULATIONS:
- *Elderly:* No actual contraindications exist, but due to the long half-life of the drug, it has been placed on the Beers List of Potentially Inappropriate Medications for Geriatrics.
- *Pregnancy:* Category C; this is the longest used SSRI in pregnant women. Every attempt should be made to discontinue in the third trimester secondary to development of neonatal distress upon delivery.
- *Lactation:* Not approved for lactation and breastfeeding.

Paxil, Paxil CR, Pexeva   **paroxetine, paroxetine mesylate**

INDICATIONS: Used to treat MDDs, OCD, bulimia nervosa, and PD.

AVAILABLE FORMS: *Pexeva*: Tablet, 20, 30, and 40 mg; *Paxil*: Tablet, 10, 20, 30, and 40 mg; suspension, 10 mg/5 mL; *Paxil CR*: Tablet, 12.5, 25, and 37.5 mg

DOSAGE: *Pexeva* and *Paxil*: 20 mg PO every morning, 10 mg in elderly patients; increase 10 mg/day weekly; maximum, 50 mg/day; 40 mg/day in elderly patients. *Paxil CR*: 12.5 mg PO, daily, increase 12.5 mg/day weekly; maximum, 75 mg/day; 50 mg/day in elderly patients. No proven additional benefits at doses greater than 20 mg/day

ADMINISTRATION:
- PO with a glass of water
- Do not break/crush or chew
- Take with or without food
- Take at regular intervals
- Caution patients not to stop taking drug except on provider's advice.
- May be prescribed for children as young as 7 years for selected conditions; *precautions do apply.*
- Instruct patients to take missed dose as soon as possible. If it is almost time for the next dose, advise to take only that dose.

SIDE EFFECTS:
- *Most common*: Somnolence; headache; asthenia; dizziness; sweating; dry mouth; tremor; anorexia; nervousness; anxiety; abnormal vision; change in appetite; change in sex drive or performance; diarrhea; constipation; indigestion; and nausea.
- *Less common*: Suicidality, worsening depression, serotonin syndrome, seizures, hyponatremia, extrapyramidal symptoms, priapism, and acute angle glaucoma.

DRUG INTERACTIONS: Most of the interactions occur with OTC cough and cold preparations. This medicine may also interact with the following medications.
- Absolute contraindications include MAOIs such as phenelzine (*Nardil*), tranylcypromine

(*Parnate*), isocarboxazid (*Marplan*), and selegiline (*Eldepryl*).
- Avoid using with other SSRIs due to serotonin effect; SNRI drugs such as desvenlafaxine (*Pristiq*) and venlafaxine (*Effexor*); drugs with sympathomimetic properties such as phenylpropanolamine, pseudoephedrine, St. John's wort, haloperidol; and diazepam (*Valium*); any other antidepressants; clopidogrel (*Plavix*).
- Exercise caution with cold medications, arrhythmia medications such as flecainide, aspirin, and other NSAIDs, and drugs used for analgesia with opioid properties.

▶**Alert**: This list may not describe all possible interactions. Instruct patients to provide a list of all medicines, herbs, nonprescription drugs, or dietary supplements used, and if they smoke, drink alcohol, or use illegal drugs.

PHARMACOKINETICS:
Metabolism: Liver extensively; CYP450 2D6 substrate; 2D6 inhibitor
Excretion: Urine 64% (2% unchanged); feces 36% (less than 1% unchanged)
Half-life: 21 hr

PRECAUTIONS:
- See patients as often as necessary to ensure that the drug is working on the panic attacks, determine compliance, and review side effects.
- Make sure patients realize that they need to take prescribed doses even if they do not feel better right away. It can take several weeks before they feel the full effect of the drug.
- Instruct patients and families to watch for worsening depression or thoughts of suicide. Also watch out for sudden or severe changes in feelings such as feeling anxious, agitated, panicky, irritated, hostile, aggressive, impulsive, severely restless, overly excited, hyperactive, or not being able to sleep. If this happens, especially at the beginning of antidepressant treatment or after a change in dose, patient should call the health care provider.

(cont.)

AGORAPHOBIA DISORDER: Selective Serotonin Reuptake Inhibitors (SSRIs)

paroxetine, paroxetine mesylate (*cont.*)

- Drowsiness or dizziness: Patients should not drive or use machinery or do anything that needs mental alertness until the effects of this medicine are known.
- Caution patients not to stand or sit up quickly, especially if older. This reduces the risk of dizzy or fainting spells. Alcohol may interfere with the effect of this medicine. Avoid alcoholic drinks.
- Caution patients not to treat themselves for coughs, colds, or allergies without asking health care professional for advice. Some ingredients can increase possible side effects.
- Dry mouth: Chewing sugarless gum, sucking hard candy, and drinking plenty of water may help. Contact health care provider if the problem persists or is severe.
- Caution should be exercised in the following:
  - Bipolar disorder or a family history of bipolar disorder
  - Diabetes
  - Heart disease
  - Liver disease
  - Electroconvulsive therapy
  - Seizures (convulsions)
  - Suicidal thoughts, plans, or attempts by patients or a family member
  - An unusual or allergic reaction to paroxetine, other medicines, foods, dyes, or preservatives
  - Pregnancy or trying to get pregnant
  - Breastfeeding

PATIENT AND FAMILY EDUCATION:
- Store at room temperature. Take any unused medication after the expiration date to the local pharmacy on drug give-back day. Avoid throwing the medication into the environment.
- Shake the liquid form of paroxetine well just before you measure a dose. To be sure you get the correct dose, measure the liquid with a marked measuring spoon or medicine cup, not with a regular tablespoon. If there is no dose-measuring device available, ask the pharmacist for one.

SPECIAL POPULATIONS:
- *Elderly:* Due to increased C_{min} concentrations, up to 70–80% in the elderly, the initial dose should be reduced.
- *Renal and hepatic impairment:* The initial dose should be reduced in patients with severe renal and/or hepatic impairment. Titration upward should be slow and at intervals.
- *Pregnancy:* Category D; first trimester teratogenicity, neonatal withdrawal and serotonin syndrome in third trimester, persistent pulmonary HTN if greater than 20-weeks gestation.
- *Lactation:* Considered generally safe; substantial human data show no or minimal risk to breast milk production or to the infant.
- *Children: Paxil CR* is not indicated for children. Monitoring for increased suicidal ideation is critical if using regular *Paxil*.

citalopram   *Celexa*

INDICATIONS: Used to treat MDD

AVAILABLE FORMS: Tablet, 10, 20, and 40 mg; oral solution, 10 mg/5 mL

DOSAGE: Starting dose, 20 mg once daily, increase dose incrementally 20 mg only once per week. Most patients reach efficacy at 40 mg daily; however, some may need 60 mg/day.

ADMINISTRATION:
- PO with a glass of water.
- Take with or without food.
- Take at regular intervals.
- Caution patients not to stop taking drug except on provider's advice.
- Not prescribed for children.
- Instruct patients to take missed dose as soon as possible. If it is almost time for the next dose, advise to take only that dose.

SIDE EFFECTS:
- *Most common:* Somnolence; headache; asthenia; dizziness; sweating; dry mouth; tremor; anorexia; nervousness; anxiety; abnormal vision; change in appetite; change in sex drive or performance; diarrhea; constipation; indigestion; and nausea

- *Less common:* Suicidality, worsening depression, serotonin syndrome, seizures, hyponatremia, extrapyramidal symptoms, priapism, and acute angle glaucoma.

DRUG INTERACTIONS: Most of the interactions occur with OTC cough and cold preparations. This medicine may also interact with the following medications.
- Absolute contraindications include MAOIs such as phenelzine (*Nardil*), tranylcypromine (*Parnate*), isocarboxazid (*Marplan*), and selegiline (*Eldepryl*).
- Avoid using with other SSRIs due to serotonin effect; SNRI drugs such as desvenlafaxine (*Pristiq*) and venlafaxine (*Effexor*); drugs with sympathomimetic properties such as phenyl-propanolamine, pseudoephedrine, St. John's wort, haloperidol; and diazepam (*Valium*), any other antidepressants; and clopidogrel (*Plavix*), amoxicillin, erythromycins, lansoprazole (*Prevacid*)
- Exercise caution with cold medications, NSAIDs, and drugs used for analgesia with opioid properties.
- ▶ **Alert**: This list may not describe all possible interactions. Instruct patients to provide a list
(cont.)

citalopram (*cont.*)

of all medicines, herbs, nonprescription drugs, or dietary supplements used, and if they smoke, drink alcohol, or use illegal drugs.

PHARMACOKINETICS:
Metabolism: Extensively metabolized in the liver in CYP450 2C19, 3A4 substrate; 2D6 (weak) inhibitor
Excretion: Urine primarily (10% unchanged); feces
Half-life: 35 hr

PRECAUTIONS:
- See patients as often as necessary to ensure that the drug is working on the panic attacks, determine compliance, and review side effects.
- Make sure patients realize that they need to take prescribed doses even if they do not feel better right away. It can take several weeks before they feel the full effect of the drug.
- Instruct patients and families to watch for worsening depression or thoughts of suicide. Also watch out for sudden or severe changes in feelings such as feeling anxious, agitated, panicky, irritated, hostile, aggressive, impulsive, severely restless, overly excited, hyperactive, or not being able to sleep. If this happens, especially at the beginning of antidepressant treatment or after a change in dose, patient should call the health care provider.
- Drowsiness or dizziness: Patients should not drive or use machinery or do anything that needs mental alertness until the effects of this medicine are known.
- Caution patients not to stand or sit up quickly, especially if older. This reduces the risk of dizzy or fainting spells. Alcohol may interfere with the effect of this medicine. Avoid alcoholic drinks.
- Caution patients not to treat themselves for coughs, colds, or allergies without asking health care professional for advice. Some ingredients can increase possible side effects.
- Dry mouth: Chewing sugarless gum, sucking hard candy, and drinking plenty of water may

help. Contact health care provider if the problem persists or is severe.
- Caution should be exercised in the following:
  - Bipolar disorder or a family history of bipolar disorder
  - Diabetes
  - Heart disease
  - Liver disease
  - Electroconvulsive therapy
  - Seizures (convulsions)
  - Suicidal thoughts, plans, or attempts by patients or a family member
  - An unusual or allergic reaction to citalopram, other medicines, foods, dyes, or preservatives
  - Pregnancy or trying to get pregnant
  - Breastfeeding

PATIENT AND FAMILY EDUCATION:
- Store at room temperature. Take any unused medication after the expiration date to the local pharmacy on drug give-back day. Avoid throwing the medication into the environment.
- Try to take the medicine at the same time each day.
- Follow the directions on the prescription label. To get the correct dose of liquid citalopram, measure the liquid with a marked measuring spoon or medicine cup, not with a regular tablespoon. If there is no dose-measuring device available, ask the pharmacist for one.

SPECIAL POPULATIONS:
- *Elderly:* A dose of 20 mg daily is recommended for geriatric patients.
- *Renal and hepatic impairment:* The initial dose should be reduced in patients with severe renal and/or hepatic impairment. Half-life is doubled in patients with hepatic impairment. Titration upward should be slow and at intervals.
- *Pregnancy:* Category C; potential for persistent pulmonary HTN if greater than 20-weeks gestation—excreted in human breast milk, some reports of infant somulence.
- *Children:* Not indicated for use children.

Lexapro   **escitalopram**

INDICATIONS: MDD and GAD

AVAILABLE FORMS: Tablet, 5, 10, and 20 mg; oral solution, 5 mg/5 mL

DOSAGE: *Adults:* Starting dose, 10 mg PO daily, may increase after 1 week to a maximum of 20 mg/day. *Elderly:* Dose should stay at 10 mg/day. *Children (12–17 years old):* Starting dose, 10 mg PO daily, may increase after 3 weeks; maximum, 20 mg/day

ADMINISTRATION:
- PO with a glass of water.
- Take with or without food.

- Take at regular intervals.
- Caution patients not to stop taking drug except on provider's advice.
- Safety not established for children younger than 18 years old in GAD.
- Instruct patients to take missed dose as soon as possible. If it is almost time for the next dose, advise to take only that dose.

SIDE EFFECTS:
- *Most common:* Somnolence; headache; asthenia; dizziness; sweating; dry mouth; tremor; anorexia; nervousness; anxiety; abnormal vision; change in appetite; change in sex drive

(cont.)

AGORAPHOBIA DISORDER: Selective Serotonin Reuptake Inhibitors (SSRIs)

escitalopram (*cont.*)

or performance; diarrhea; constipation; indigestion; and nausea.

- *Less common*: Suicidality, worsening depression, serotonin syndrome, seizures, hyponatremia, extrapyramidal symptoms, priapism, and acute angle glaucoma.

DRUG INTERACTIONS: Most of the interactions occur with OTC cough and cold preparations. This medicine may also interact with the following medications.

- Absolute contraindications include MAOIs such as phenelzine (*Nardil*), tranylcypromine (*Parnate*), isocarboxazid (*Marplan*), and selegiline (*Eldepryl*).
- Avoid using with other SSRIs due to serotonin effect; SNRI drugs such as desvenlafaxine (*Pristiq*) and venlafaxine (*Effexor*); drugs with sympathomimetic properties such as phenylpropanolamine, pseudoephedrine, St. John's wort, haloperidol; diazepam (*Valium*); any other antidepressants; clopidogrel (*Plavix*); amoxicillin; erythromycins; lansoprazole (*Prevacid*)
- Exercise caution with cold medications, NSAIDs, and drugs used for analgesia with opioid properties.

▶**Alert:** This list may not describe all possible interactions. Instruct patients to provide a list of all medicines, herbs, nonprescription drugs, or dietary supplements used, and if they smoke, drink alcohol, or use illegal drugs.

PHARMACOKINETICS:
Metabolism: Liver; CYP450: 2C19, 2D6, 3A4 substrate; 2D6 (weak) inhibitor
Excretion: Only 10% excreted in urine
Half-life: 27–32 hr, but is increased by 50% in elderly patients

PRECAUTIONS:
- See patients as often as necessary to ensure that the drug is working on the panic attacks, determine compliance, and review side effects.
- Make sure patients realize that they need to take prescribed doses even if they do not feel better right away. It can take several weeks before they feel the full effect of the drug.
- Instruct patients and families to watch for worsening depression or thoughts of suicide. Also, watch out for sudden or severe changes in feelings such as feeling anxious, agitated, panicky, irritated, hostile, aggressive, impulsive, severely restless, overly excited, hyperactive, or not being able to sleep. If this happens, especially at the beginning of antidepressant treatment or after a change in dose, patient should call the health care provider.
- Drowsiness or dizziness: Patients should not drive or use machinery or do anything that needs mental alertness until the effects of this medicine are known.
- Caution patients not to stand or sit up quickly, especially if older. This reduces the risk of dizzy or fainting spells. Alcohol may interfere with the effect of this medicine. Avoid alcoholic drinks.
- Caution patients not to treat themselves for coughs, colds, or allergies without asking health care professional for advice. Some ingredients can increase possible side effects.
- Dry mouth: Chewing sugarless gum, sucking hard candy, and drinking plenty of water may help. Contact health care provider if the problem persists or is severe.
- Caution should be exercised in the following:
  - Bipolar disorder or a family history of bipolar disorder
  - Diabetes
  - Heart disease
  - Liver disease
  - Electroconvulsive therapy
  - Seizures (convulsions)
  - Suicidal thoughts, plans, or attempts by patients or a family member
  - An unusual or allergic reaction to citalopram, other medicines, foods, dyes, or preservatives
  - Pregnancy or trying to get pregnant
  - Breastfeeding

PATIENT AND FAMILY EDUCATION:
- Store at room temperature. Take any unused medication after the expiration date to the local pharmacy on drug give-back day. Avoid throwing the medication into the environment.
- Try to take the medicine at the same time each day. Follow the directions on the prescription label. To get the correct dose of liquid escitalopram, measure the liquid with a marked measuring spoon or medicine cup, not with a regular tablespoon. If there is no dose-measuring device available, ask the pharmacist for one.

SPECIAL POPULATIONS:
- *Elderly:* A dose of 10 mg daily is recommended for geriatric patients. The initial dose should be reduced in patients with severe renal and/or hepatic impairment. Titration upward should be slow and at intervals.
- *Pregnancy:* Category C; potential for persistent pulmonary HTN if greater than 20-weeks gestation—excreted in human breast milk, some reports of infant somulence.
- *Children:* May be given to children older than 12 years of age. Monitoring of suicidal ideations is important.

Class: Tricyclic Antidepressants (TCAs)

- Due to the class side effects, especially on the cardiac system, TCAs should be used only if the SSRI or SNRI classes fail to show any improvement in symptom profile.

Tpfranil, Tofranil PM	imipramine pamoate

INDICATIONS: Used to treat adults with depression/anxiety

AVAILABLE FORMS: *Tofranil:* Tablet, 25, and 50 mg. *Tofranil PM:* Capsule, 75, 100, 125 and 150 mg

DOSAGE: *Adults:* Starting dose, 25–75 mg PO nightly and increase by 25–50 mg/day every 3–4 days; maximum, 300 mg/day; 100 mg/day in elderly patients. Can be given in divided doses. Must taper dose gradually to discontinue. *Children: For depression:* Starting dose, 1.5 mg/kg/day PO divided tid; increase by 1–1.5 mg/kg/day every 3–4 days; maximum, 5 mg/kg/day. *Greater than 12 years old:* Starting dose, 30–40 mg/day PO divided qd-tid and increase by 10–25 mg/day every 3–4 days; max, 100 mg/day

ADMINISTRATION:
- PO with a glass of water.
- Do not crush, cut, or chew extended-release tablets.
- Do not abruptly stop taking the medication.
- Not prescribed for children except when used for nocturnal enuresis and depression in children as young as 6 years.
- Use lowest effective dose for shortest duration.

SIDE EFFECTS:
- *More common:* Drowsiness, dizziness, constipation, nausea/vomiting, urinary retention or frequency, libido changes, weight gain, general nervousness, and galactorrhea.
- *Less common:* Cardiac arrhythmias, extrapyramidal symptoms, clotting disturbances, worsening depression, suicidiality, and hyperthermia, hypertension.

DRUG INTERACTIONS: This medicine may interact with the following medications:
- Absolute contraindications include class IA antiarrhythmics, MAOIs such as phenelzine (*Nardil*), tranylcypromine (*Parnate*), isocarboxazid (*Marplan*), and selegiline (*Eldepryl*).
- Avoid using with cimetadine, amiodarone, clarithromycin, haloperidol, and St. John's wort.
▶**Alert:** This list may not describe all possible interactions. Instruct patients to provide a list of all medicines, herbs, nonprescription drugs, or dietary supplements used, and if they smoke, drink alcohol, or use illegal drugs.

PHARMACOKINETICS:
- TCAs are thought to work by inhibiting reuptake of norepinephrine and serotonin in the CNS, which potentiates the neurotransmitters. They also have significant anticholinergics, antihistaminic, and alpha-adrenergic activity

on the cardiac system. These classes of antidepressants also possess class 1A antiarrhythmic activity, which can lead to depression of cardiac conduction potentially resulting in heart block or ventricular arrhythmias.
Metabolism: Extensively by the liver within the CYP450: 1A2, 2C19, 2D6 (primary), 3A4 substrate
Excretion: Primarily in urine, up to 5% unchanged, also excreted in the bile/feces.
Half-life: 11–25 hr

PRECAUTIONS:
- See patients as often as necessary to ensure that the drug is working on the panic attacks, determine compliance, and review side effects.
- Instruct patients and families to watch for worsening depression or thoughts of suicide. Also watch out for sudden or severe changes in feelings such as feeling anxious, agitated, panicky, irritated, hostile, aggressive, impulsive, severely restless, overly excited, hyperactive, or not being able to sleep. If this happens, especially at the beginning of antidepressant treatment or after a change in dose, patient should call the health care provider.
- Drowsiness or dizziness: Patients should not drive or use machinery or do anything that needs mental alertness until the effects of this medicine are known. Other medications that cause drowsiness can add to the drowsiness of imipramine.
- Caution patients not to stand or sit up quickly, especially if older. This reduces the risk of dizzy or fainting spells. Alcohol may interfere with the effect of this medicine. Avoid alcoholic drinks.
- Do not abruptly withdraw this drug as it may cause headache, nausea, and malaise
- Advise to protect skin from ultraviolet light due to increased skin sensitivity.
- Grapefruit and grapefruit juice may interact with imipramine.
- Caution should be exercised in the following:
  - MDD, psychosis, or bipolar affective disorder
  - Contraindicated in patients with a recent myocardial infarction
  - Blood dyscrasias
  - Respiratory disease
  - Heart disease
  - Liver disease
  - Seizures (convulsions)
  - Suicidal thoughts, plans, or attempts by patients or a family member
  - An unusual or allergic reaction to imipramine, other medicines, foods, dyes, or preservatives
  (cont.)

imipramine pamoate (*cont.*)

PATIENT AND FAMILY EDUCATION:
- Store imipramine at room temperature away from moisture and heat.
- Stopping this medication suddenly could result in unpleasant side effects.
- Take the missed dose as soon as remembered. If it is almost time for the next dose, skip the missed dose and take the medicine at the next regularly scheduled time. *Do not* take extra medicine to make up the missed dose.

SPECIAL POPULATIONS:
- *Elderly:* Older patients may be more sensitive to the effects of TCAs. The smallest effective dose

should be used. Dose adjustment is necessary for patients with liver impairment
- *Pregnancy:* Category D; some clinical reports of congenital malformations, but no direct causal link.
- *Lactation:* Excreted in human breast milk, alternative medications are recommended.
- *Children: Tofranil* is indicated for children older than 6 years with nocturnal enuresis or with depression. Monitor for suicidal ideation with depression. *Tofranil PM* is not approved for use in children.

desipramine   *Norpramin*

INDICATIONS: Used to treat adults with depression/anxiety

AVAILABLE FORMS: Tablet, 10, 25, 50, 75, 100, and 150 mg

DOSAGE: Starting dose, 25–75 mg PO daily; maximum, 300 mg/day. May be given in divided doses; must taper slowly to discontinue

ADMINISTRATION:
- PO with a glass of water.
- Do not abruptly stop taking the medication.
- Not prescribed for children.
- Use lowest effective dose for shortest duration.

SIDE EFFECTS:
- *More common:* Drowsiness, dizziness, constipation; nausea/vomiting, urinary retention or frequency, libido changes, weight gain, general nervousness, galactorrhea, rash, and urticaria.
- *Less common*: Cardiac arrhythmias, extrapyramidal symptoms, clotting disturbances, worsening depression, suicidiality, hyperthermia, and hypertension

DRUG INTERACTIONS: This medicine may interact with the following medications:
- Absolute contraindications include class IA antiarrhythmics, MAOIs such as phenelzine (*Nardil*), tranylcypromine (*Parnate*), isocarboxazid (*Marplan*), and selegiline (*Eldepryl*).
- Avoid using with cimetadine, amiodarone, clarithromycin, erythromycin, haldoperidol, and St. John's wort.
- ▶**Alert:** This list may not describe all possible interactions. Instruct patients to provide a list of all medicines, herbs, nonprescription drugs, or dietary supplements used, and if they smoke, drink alcohol, or use illegal drugs.

PHARMACOKINETICS:
- TCAs are thought to work by inhibiting reuptake of norepinephrine and serotonin in the CNS, which potentiates the neurotransmitters. They also have significant anticholinergics,

antihistaminic, and alpha-adrenergic activity on the cardiac system. These classes of antidepressants also possess class 1A antiarrhythmic activity, which can lead to depression of cardiac conduction potentially resulting in heart block or ventricular arrhythmias.
Metabolism: Primarily in the liver via the CYP450: 2C19, 2D6 (primary) substrate
Excretion: Urine
Half-life: 12–27 hr

PRECAUTIONS:
- See patients as often as necessary to ensure that the drug is working on the panic attacks, determine compliance, and review side effects.
- Instruct patients and families to watch for worsening depression or thoughts of suicide. Also watch out for sudden or severe changes in feelings such as feeling anxious, agitated, panicky, irritated, hostile, aggressive, impulsive, severely restless, overly excited, hyperactive, or not being able to sleep. If this happens, especially at the beginning of antidepressant treatment or after a change in dose, patient should call the health care provider.
- Drowsiness or dizziness: Patients should not drive or use machinery or do anything that needs mental alertness until the effects of this medicine are known. Other medications that cause drowsiness can add to the drowsiness of desipramine.
- Caution patients not to stand or sit up quickly, especially if older. This reduces the risk of dizzy or fainting spells. Alcohol may interfere with the effect of this medicine. Avoid alcoholic drinks.
- Do not abruptly withdraw this drug as it may cause headache, nausea, and malaise
- Advise to protect skin from ultraviolet light due to increased skin sensitivity
- Grapefruit and grapefruit juice may interact with imipramine.
- Caution should be exercised in the following:
  - MDD, psychosis, or bipolar affective disorder

(cont.)

desipramine *(cont.)*

- Contraindicated in patients with a recent myocardial infarction
- Blood dyscrasias
- Respiratory disease
- Heart disease
- Liver disease
- Seizures (convulsions)
- Psychoses or schizophrenia
- Suicidal thoughts, plans, or attempts by patients or a family member
- An unusual or allergic reaction to desipramine, other medicines, foods, dyes, or preservatives

PATIENT AND FAMILY EDUCATION:
- Store imipramine at room temperature away from moisture and heat.
- Stopping this medication suddenly could result in unpleasant side effects.

- Take the missed dose as soon as remembered. If it is almost time for the next dose, skip the missed dose and take the medicine at the next regularly scheduled time. *Do not* take extra medicine to make up the missed dose.

SPECIAL POPULATIONS:
- *Elderly:* Older patients may be more sensitive to the effects of TCAs. The smallest effective dose should be used (beginning at 10–25 mg/day). Dose adjustment is necessary for patients with liver impairment.
- *Pregnancy:* Category C; unknown effects as there is limited study.
- *Lactation:* Excreted in human breast milk, use caution.
- *Children:* Not indicated for children; used off-label in children 6–12 years; however, alternative medications are preferred.

Pamelor   **nortriptyline**

INDICATIONS: Used to treat adults with depression/anxiety

AVAILABLE FORMS: Capsule, 10, 25, 50, and 75 mg; oral solution, 10 mg/5 mL

DOSAGE: *Adults:* Starting dose, 25–50 mg PO nightly and increase by 25–50 mg/day every 2–3 days. *Elderly*: 10–25 mg PO nightly and increase by 10–25 mg/day every 2–3 days. Maximum, 150 mg/day. May be given in divided doses. Must taper the dose gradually to discontinue. *Children: (6–12 years, unlabeled use)*: Starting dose, 1–3 mg/kg/day PO divided tid-qid. *Greater than 12 years*: Starting dose, 30–50 mg/day PO divided qd-qid; maximum, 150 mg/day. *Alternative dosing*: 1–3 mg/kg/day PO divided daily and tid.

ADMINISTRATION:
- PO with a glass of water.
- Do not abruptly stop taking the medication.
- Approved in children with enuresis and depression as young as 6 years.
- Use lowest effective dose for shortest duration.

SIDE EFFECTS:
- *More common:* Drowsiness, dizziness, constipation; nausea/vomiting, urinary retention or frequency, libido changes, weight gain, general nervousness, galactorrhea, gynecomastia, rash, and urticaria.
- *Less common*: Cardiac arrhythmias, extrapyramidal symptoms, clotting disturbances, worsening depression, suicidiality, hyperthermia, and hypertension.

DRUG INTERACTIONS: This medicine may interact with the following medications:
- Absolute contraindications include class IA antiarrhythmics, MAOIs such as phenelzine

(*Nardil*), tranylcypromine (*Parnate*), isocarboxazid (*Marplan*), and selegiline (*Eldepryl*).
- Avoid using with cimetidine, amiodarone, clarithromycin, erythromycin, haldoperidol, St. John's wort.

▶**Alert:** This list may not describe all possible interactions. Instruct patients to provide a list of all medicines, herbs, nonprescription drugs, or dietary supplements used, and if they smoke, drink alcohol, or use illegal drugs.

PHARMACOKINETICS:
- TCAs are thought to work by inhibiting reuptake of norepinephrine and serotonin in the CNS, which potentiates the neurotransmitters. They also have significant anticholinergic, antihistaminic, and alpha-adrenergic activity on the cardiac system. These classes of antidepressants also possess class 1A antiarrhythmic activity, which can lead to depression of cardiac conduction potentially resulting in heart block or ventricular arrhythmias.

Metabolism: Extensively metabolized by liver CYP 2D6 substrate

Excretion: Urine primarily, feces

Half-life: 18–44 hr

PRECAUTIONS:
- See patients as often as necessary to ensure that the drug is working on the panic attacks, determine compliance, and review side effects.
- Instruct patients and families to watch for worsening depression or thoughts of suicide. Also watch out for sudden or severe changes in feelings such as feeling anxious, agitated, panicky, irritated, hostile, aggressive, impulsive, severely restless, overly excited, hyperactive, or not being able to sleep. If this happens, especially at the beginning of antidepressant treatment or after

(cont.)

AGORAPHOBIA DISORDER: Tricyclic Antidepressants (TCAs)

nortriptyline (*cont.*)

a change in dose, patient should call the health care provider.

- Drowsiness or dizziness: Patients should not drive or use machinery or do anything that needs mental alertness until the effects of this medicine are known. Other medications that cause drowsiness can add to the drowsiness of imipramine.
- Caution patients not to stand or sit up quickly, especially if older. This reduces the risk of dizzy or fainting spells. Alcohol may interfere with the effect of this medicine. Avoid alcoholic drinks.
- Do not abruptly withdraw this drug as it may cause headache, nausea, and malaise.
- Advise to protect skin from ultraviolet light due to increased skin sensitivity.
- Grapefruit and grapefruit juice may interact with imipramine.
- Caution should be exercised in the following:
  - MDD, psychosis, or bipolar affective disorder
  - Contraindicated in patients with a recent myocardial infarction
  - Blood dyscrasias
  - Respiratory disease
  - Heart disease
  - Liver disease
  - Seizures (convulsions)
  - Suicidal thoughts, plans, or attempts by patients or a family member

- An unusual or allergic reaction to imipramine, other medicines, foods, dyes, or preservatives

PATIENT AND FAMILY EDUCATION:
- Store nortriptyline at room temperature away from moisture and heat.
- Stopping this medication suddenly could result in unpleasant side effects.
- Take the missed dose as soon as remembered. If it is almost time for the next dose, skip the missed dose and take the medicine at the next regularly scheduled time. *Do not* take extra medicine to make up the missed dose.

SPECIAL POPULATIONS:
- *Elderly:* Older patients may be more sensitive to the effects of TCAs. The smallest effective dose should be used. Dose adjustment is necessary for patients with liver impairment.
- *Pregnancy:* Category D; some clinical reports of congenital malformations, but no direct causal link. Alternative medications are recommended.
- *Lactation:* Excreted in human breast milk, bottle feed if possible or use with caution.
- *Children:* This drug is indicated for children greater than 6 years old with nocturnal enuresis or with depression. Monitor for suicidal ideation with depression.

Class: Benzodiazepines (BZDs)

alprazolam   *Xanax, Xanax XR, Niravam*

INDICATIONS: Short-acting BZD used to treat GADs and PD. May be used as a short-term adjunct to an SSRI while waiting for the therapeutic effects of the SSRI to develop.

AVAILABLE FORMS: Tablet, 0.25, 0.5, 1, and 2 mg; extended-release capsule 0.5, 1, and 2 mg; melt, 0.5, 1, 2, and 3 mg

DOSAGE: *Xanax:* Starting dose, 0.25 to 0.5 mg up to 2–3 times daily; maximum, 4 mg daily. Can be increased every 3–4 days. Treatment should be limited to as short a period as possible (less than 4 months) and/or re-evaluated for continued use. *Xanax XR:* Starting dose 0.5–1 mg PO, daily, can increase up to 1 mg/day every 3–4 days. *Niravam (melt):* Starting dose, 0.25 to 0.5 mg up to 2–3 times daily; maximum, 4 mg daily. Can be increased every 3–4 days.

ADMINISTRATION:
- PO with a glass of water.
- Do not crush, cut, or chew extended-release tablets.
- Orally disintegrating (*Niravam*) has special instructions.
- Concentrated liquid must be measured with a special dose-measuring spoon or cup.
- Do not abruptly stop taking the medication.
- Not prescribed for children.
- Use lowest effective dose for shortest duration.

- Alprazolam can be habit forming; do not increase dosage without guidance from the health care provider.

SIDE EFFECTS:
- *More common:* Drowsiness, lightheadedness, dry mouth; headache, changes in bowel habits, sialorrhea, amnesia, and changes in appetite.
- *Less common:* Syncope, tachycardia, seizures, respiratory depression, dependency, withdrawal syndrome, and suicidal ideation.

DRUG INTERACTIONS: This medicine may interact with the following medications:
- Absolute contraindications include clarithromycin, fluvoxamine, and ketoconazole.
- Avoid using with calcium channel blockers, erythromycins, tamoxifen, and zafirlukast.
- ▶**Alert:** This list may not describe all possible interactions. Instruct patients to provide a list of all medicines, herbs, nonprescription drugs, or dietary supplements used, and if they smoke, drink alcohol, or use illegal drugs.

PHARMACOKINETICS:
- BZDs enhance the activity of GABA, a major CNS neurotransmitter, known to open CNS Cl⁻ channels leading to an inhibition of subsequent CNS neuronal signaling. BZDs with similar action can differ in their potency and rate of absorption.

(cont.)

alprazolam *(cont.)*

Metabolism: By the liver in the CYP450 3A4
Excretion: Urine
Half-life: 11.2 hr, 16.3 hr (elderly), 19.7 hr (alcoholic liver disease)

PRECAUTIONS:
- See patients as often as necessary to ensure that the drug is working on the panic attacks, determine compliance, and review side effects.
- Instruct patients and families to watch for worsening depression or thoughts of suicide. Also watch out for sudden or severe changes in feelings such as feeling anxious, agitated, panicky, irritated, hostile, aggressive, impulsive, severely restless, overly excited, hyperactive, or not being able to sleep. If this happens, especially at the beginning of antidepressant treatment or after a change in dose, patient should call the health care provider.
- Drowsiness or dizziness: Patients should not drive or use machinery or do anything that needs mental alertness until the effects of this medicine are known.
- Caution patients not to stand or sit up quickly, especially if older. This reduces the risk of dizzy or fainting spells. Alcohol may interfere with the effect of this medicine. Avoid alcoholic drinks.
- Do not abruptly withdraw this drug as it may cause seizures.
- Caution should be exercised in the following:
  - MDD, psychosis, or bipolar affective disorder
  - Respiratory disease
  - Heart disease
  - Liver disease
  - Seizures (convulsions)
  - Suicidal thoughts, plans, or attempts by patients or a family member
  - An unusual or allergic reaction to alprazolam, other medicines, foods, dyes, or preservatives

PATIENT AND FAMILY EDUCATION:
- Store alprazolam at room temperature away from moisture, heat, and light. Remove any cotton from the bottle of disintegrating tablets, and keep the bottle tightly closed.
- Alprazolam may be habit forming and *should be used only by the person it was prescribed for.* Alprazolam should never be shared with another person, especially someone who has a history of drug abuse or addiction. Keep the medication in a secure place where others cannot get to it.
- Do not purchase alprazolam on the Internet or outside of the USA as dangerous ingredients may be present. Some purchases of alprazolam from the Internet have been found to contain haloperidol *(Haldol)*, an antipsychotic drug.

SPECIAL POPULATIONS:
- *Elderly:* Older patients may be more sensitive to the effects of BZDs. The smallest effective dose should be used. Dose adjustment is necessary for patients with liver impairment and/or renal disease due to excessive metabolites excreted by the kidney. Due to increased risk of sedation leading to falls and fractures, BZDs are included on the Beers List of Potentially Inappropriate Medications for Geriatrics.
- *Pregnancy*: Category D; can cause teratogenic fetal effects. Infants born to mothers taking BZDs may be at risk for withdrawal symptoms in the postnatal period.
- *Lactation:* Excreted in human breast milk, infants can become lethargic and lose weight.
- *Children:* Not indicated for use in children younger than 18 years.

Ativan **lorazepam**

INDICATIONS: Used to treat GADs and PD

AVAILABLE FORMS: Tablet, 0.5, 1, 2 mg

DOSAGE: *Adults:* 2–3 mg/day PO/IM/IV divided bid-tid; 1–2 mg/day PO/IM/IV divided bid-tid in elderly patients; maximum, 10 mg/day. Periodically assess the need for treatment and taper the dose gradually to discontinue if prolonged treatment is necessary. Treatment should be limited to as short a period as possible (less than 4 months) and/or re-evaluated for continued use. *Children:* 0.05 mg/kg PO/IV q4–8 hr; maximum, 2 mg/dose.

ADMINISTRATION:
- PO with a glass of water.
- Do not abruptly stop taking the medication.
- Use lowest effective dose for shortest duration.

- Lorazepam can be habit forming, do not increase dosage without guidance from the health care provider.

SIDE EFFECTS:
- *More common:* Drowsiness, lightheadedness, dry mouth; headache, changes in bowel habits, sialorrhea, amnesia, and changes in appetite.
- *Less common*: Syncope, tachycardia, seizures, respiratory depression, dependency, withdrawal syndrome, and suicidal ideation.

DRUG INTERACTIONS: This medicine may interact with the following medications:
- Absolute contraindications include clarithromycin, fluvoxamine, and ketoconazole.
- Avoid using with calcium channel blockers, erythromycins, tamoxifen, and zafirlukast.

(cont.)

AGORAPHOBIA DISORDER: Benzodiazepines (BZDs)

lorazepam (*cont.*)

▶**Alert**: This list may not describe all possible interactions. Instruct patients to provide a list of all medicines, herbs, nonprescription drugs, or dietary supplements used, and if they smoke, drink alcohol, or use illegal drugs.

PHARMACOKINETICS:
- BZDs enhance the activity of GABA a major CNS neuroinhibitor. Although the exact physiologic action is unknown, the thought is that different BZDs act on different receptors in the CNS. BZDs with similar action can differ in their potency and rate of absorption.

Metabolism: Liver with the CYP450, exact mechanism is unknown
Excretion: Urine
Half-life: 14 hr

PRECAUTIONS:
- See patients as often as necessary to ensure that the drug is working on the panic attacks, determine compliance, and review side effects.
- Instruct patients and families to watch for worsening depression or thoughts of suicide. Also watch out for sudden or severe changes in feelings such as feeling anxious, agitated, panicky, irritated, hostile, aggressive, impulsive, severely restless, overly excited, hyperactive, or not being able to sleep. If this happens, especially at the beginning of antidepressant treatment or after a change in dose, patient should call the health care provider.
- Drowsiness or dizziness: Patients should not drive or use machinery or do anything that needs mental alertness until the effects of this medicine are known.
- Caution patients not to stand or sit up quickly, especially if older. This reduces the risk of dizzy or fainting spells. Alcohol may interfere with the effect of this medicine. Avoid alcoholic drinks.
- Do not abruptly withdraw this drug as it may cause seizures.

- Caution should be exercised in the following:
  - Heart disease
  - Liver disease
  - Seizures (convulsions)
  - Suicidal thoughts, plans, or attempts by patients or a family member
  - An unusual or allergic reaction to alprazolam, other medicines, foods, dyes, or preservatives

PATIENT AND FAMILY EDUCATION:
- Store lorazepam at room temperature away from moisture, heat, and light. Remove any cotton from the bottle of disintegrating tablets, and keep the bottle tightly closed.
- Lorazepam may be habit forming and *should be used only by the person it was prescribed for.* Lorazepam should never be shared with another person, especially someone who has a history of drug abuse or addiction. Keep the medication in a secure place where others cannot get to it.
- Do not purchase lorazepam on the Internet or outside of the USA as dangerous ingredients may be present.

SPECIAL POPULATIONS:
- *Elderly:* Older patients may be more sensitive to the effects of BZDs. The smallest effective dose should be used. Dose adjustment is necessary for patients with liver impairment and/or renal disease due to excessive metabolites excreted by the kidney. Due to increased risk of sedation leading to falls and fractures, BZDs are included on the Beers List of Potentially Inappropriate Medications for Geriatrics.
- *Pregnancy:* Category D; can cause teratogenic fetal effects. Infants born to mothers taking BZDs may be at risk for withdrawal symptoms in the postnatal period.
- *Lactation:* Excreted in human breast milk, infants can become lethargic and lose weight.
- *Children:* Not indicated for use in children younger than 18 years.

clonazepam — *Klonopin*

INDICATIONS: For treating GADs and PD

AVAILABLE FORMS: Tablet, 0.5, 1, and 2 mg; wafer melt, 0.125, 0.25, 0.5, and 1.2 mg

DOSAGE: *Adults:* start at 0.25 mg PO bid, increase by 0.25–0.5 mg/day every 3 days; may start lower in elderly patients; maximum, 4 mg/day; treatment should be limited to as short a period as possible (less than 4 months) and/or re-evaluated for continued use. To discontinue taper by 0.25 mg/day q3 days if greater than 4 to 6 weeks continuous use.

ADMINISTRATION:
- PO with a glass of water.
- Do not abruptly stop taking the medication.

- Use lowest effective dose for shortest duration
- Clonazepam can be habit-forming; do not increase dosage without guidance from the health care provider

SIDE EFFECTS:
- *More common:* Drowsiness, lightheadedness, dry mouth; headache, changes in bowel habits, sialorrhea, amnesia, and changes in appetite.
- *Less common:* Syncope, tachycardia, seizures, respiratory depression, dependency, withdrawal syndrome, and suicidal ideation.

DRUG INTERACTIONS: This medicine may interact with the following medications:

(cont.)

clonazepam (cont.)

- Absolute contraindications include clarithromycin, fluvoxamine, and ketoconazole.
- Avoid using with calcium channel blockers, erythromycins, tamoxifen, and zafirlukast.

▶**Alert**: This list may not describe all possible interactions. Instruct patients to provide a list of all medicines, herbs, nonprescription drugs, or dietary supplements used, and if they smoke, drink alcohol, or use illegal drugs.

PHARMACOKINETICS:

- BZDs enhance the activity of GABA, a major CNS neuroinhibitor. Although the exact physiologic action is unknown, the thought is that different BZDs act on different receptors in the CNS. BZDs with similar action can differ in potency and rate of absorption.

Metabolism: Extensively metabolized in liver CYP450 3A4

Excretion: Urine

Half-life: 20–50 hr

PRECAUTIONS:

- See patients as often as necessary to ensure that the drug is working on the panic attacks, determine compliance, and review side effects.
- Instruct patients and families to watch for worsening depression or thoughts of suicide. Also watch out for sudden or severe changes in feelings such as feeling anxious, agitated, panicky, irritated, hostile, aggressive, impulsive, severely restless, overly excited, hyperactive, or not being able to sleep. If this happens, especially at the beginning of antidepressant treatment or after a change in dose, patient should call the health care provider.
- Drowsiness or dizziness: Patients should not drive or use machinery or do anything that needs mental alertness until the effects of this medicine are known.
- Caution patients not to stand or sit up quickly, especially if older. This reduces the risk of dizzy or fainting spells. Alcohol may interfere with the effect of this medicine. Avoid alcoholic drinks.
- Do not abruptly withdraw this drug as it may cause seizures.
- Caution should be exercised in the following:
  - Heart disease
  - Liver disease
  - Seizures (convulsions)
  - Suicidal thoughts, plans, or attempts by patients or a family member
  - An unusual or allergic reaction to alprazolam, other medicines, foods, dyes, or preservatives

PATIENT AND FAMILY EDUCATION:

- Store clonazepam at room temperature away from moisture, heat, and light. Remove any cotton from the bottle of disintegrating wafers, and keep the bottle tightly closed.
- Clonazepam may be habit forming and *should be used only by the person it was prescribed for.* Clonazepam should never be shared with another person, especially someone who has a history of drug abuse or addiction. Keep the medication in a secure place where others cannot get to it.

SPECIAL POPULATIONS:

- *Elderly:* Older patients may be more sensitive to the effects of BZDs. The smallest effective dose should be used. Dose adjustment is necessary for patients with liver impairment and/or renal disease due to excessive metabolites excreted by the kidney. Due to increased risk of sedation leading to falls and fractures, BZDs are included on the Beers List of Potentially Inappropriate Medications for Geriatrics.
- *Pregnancy:* Category D; can cause teratogenic fetal effects. Infants born to mothers taking BZDs may be at risk for withdrawal symptoms in the postnatal period.
- *Lactation:* Excreted in human breast milk; infants can become lethargic and lose weight.
- *Children:* Not indicated for use in children except for treatment of seizures.

Generalized Anxiety Disorder (GAD)

OVERVIEW

- GAD is defined as excessive worry more often than not for 6 months or more about everyday life.
- Individuals who experience GAD may experience physical symptoms in relation to their anxiety. It can also affect general mental well-being and ability to function socially.
- GAD is *most commonly* identified first in primary care due to presenting physical complaints without pathophysiology.
- Onset of GAD can be found in early childhood and then later on in adulthood. More women

(6.6%) than men (3.6%) experience GAD in their lifetimes.

- When diagnosing GAD, the health care provider must routinely consider medical conditions; drug use including all prescribed and OTC; and other mind-altering substances.
- Consider other psychiatric disorders such as PD, OCD, and social phobia. Concomitant depression also needs to be considered as contributing to the GAD symptoms.
- Behavioral therapies should be used together with drug therapy. These include CBT, exposure, relaxation techniques, pleasant mental

GENERALIZED ANXIETY DISORDER

imagery, and cognitive restructuring (learning to recognize and replace panic-inducing thoughts). Behavioral treatment appears to have long-lasting benefits.

- Regular exercise, adequate sleep, and regularly scheduled meals may help reduce the frequency of the attacks. Caffeine and other stimulants should be reduced or eliminated.

Psychopharmacology of GAD

OVERVIEW

- SSRIs are the *most common* first-line agents used with GAD.
- TCAs can be effective in treating GADs; however, the initial side effects of the drugs when first initiated (jitteriness and insomnia) can reduce patient adherence to therapy. These medications are generally reserved for GAD resistant to treatment with SSRIs and SNRIs.
- SNRI has FDA approval for treatment of GAD
- The non-BZD anxiolytic agent buspirone can be efficacious for the anxiety component, but has

no effect on depression and should not be used if concomitant depression is present.

- BZDs are generally the most efficacious in patients who only have anxiety symptoms; however, the health care provider needs to be cautious while using these agents for treating the elderly. Additionally, patients may become physically dependent with long-term use. These drugs may be used as part of an initial treatment regimen and then discontinued as a long-term treatment plan has developed.

CLASS	DRUG
Selective Serotonin Reuptake Inhibitors (SSRIs)	**First-Line Drug Therapy**
	escitalopram (*Lexapro*) sertraline (*Zoloft*) paroxetine (*Paxil, Paxil PR*) paroxetine mesylate (*Pexeva*)
Serotonin and Norepinephrine Reuptake Inhibitors (SNRIs)	**First-Line Drug Therapy**
	venlafaxine (*Effexor, Effexor XR*) duloxetine (*Cymbalta*)
Calcium Channel Moderator	**Drug for Augmentation**
	pregabalin (*Lyrica*)
Tricyclic Antidepressants (TCAs)	**Drugs for Treatment Resistant Cases**
	imipramine (*Tofranil, Tofranil PM*)) desipramine (*Norpramin*)
Benzodiazepines (BZDs)	**Drugs Used Only in First Weeks While Establishing Levels of SSRI or SNRI**
	alprazolam (*Xanax/Xanax XR/Niravam*) clonazepam (*Klonopin*) lorazepam (*Ativan*) diazepam (*Valium*)
Antihistamines	**Drug Augmentation**
	hydroxyzine (*Vistaril*)
Anxiolytics	**Drug Augmentation**
	buspirone (*BuSpar*)

Class: Selective Serotonin Reuptake Inhibitors (SSRIs)

escitalopram   *Lexapro*

INDICATIONS: For treating MDD and GAD

AVAILABLE FORMS: Tablet, 5, 10, and 20 mg; oral solution, 5 mg/5 mL

DOSAGE: *Adults:* Starting dose, 10 mg PO, daily, may increase after 1 week to a maximum of 20 mg/day. Dose should stay at 10 mg/day. *Children (12–17 yr);* start at 10 mg PO, daily, may increase after 3 weeks; maximum, 20 mg/day

ADMINISTRATION:
- PO with a glass of water.
- Take with or without food
- Take at regular intervals
- Caution patients not to stop taking drug except on provider's advice.
- Safety not established for children younger than 18 years in GAD.

(cont.)

escitalopram (*cont.*)

- Instruct patients to take missed dose as soon as possible. If it is almost time for the next dose, advise to take only that dose.

SIDE EFFECTS:
- *Most common*: Somnolence; headache; asthenia; dizziness; sweating; dry mouth; tremor; anorexia; nervousness; anxiety; abnormal vision; change in appetite; change in sex drive or performance; diarrhea; constipation; indigestion; and nausea;
- *Less common*: Suicidality, worsening depression, serotonin syndrome, seizures, hyponatremia, extrapyramidal symptoms, priapism, and acute angle glaucoma.

DRUG INTERACTIONS: Most of the interactions occur with OTC cough and cold preparations. This medicine may also interact with the following medications.
- Absolute contraindications include MAOIs such as phenelzine (*Nardil*), tranylcypromine (*Parnate*), isocarboxazid (*Marplan*), and selegiline (*Eldepryl*).
- Avoid using with other SSRIs due to serotonin effect; SNRI drugs such as desvenlafaxine (*Pristiq*) and venlafaxine (*Effexor*); drugs with sympathomimetic properties such as phenylpropanolamine; pseudoephedrine; St. John's wort; haloperidol; and diazepam (*Valium*); any other antidepressants; and clopidogrel (*Plavix*); amoxicillin; erythromycins; and lansoprazole (*Prevacid*).
- Exercise caution with cold medications, NSAIDs, and drugs used for analgesia with opioid properties.
▶**Alert:** This list may not describe all possible interactions. Instruct patients to provide a list of all medicines, herbs, nonprescription drugs, or dietary supplements used, and if they smoke, drink alcohol, or use illegal drugs.

PHARMACOKINETICS:
Metabolism: Liver; CYP450: 2C19, 2D6, 3A4 substrate; 2D6 (weak) inhibitor
Excretion: Only 10% excreted in urine
Half-life: 27–32 hr, but is increased by 50% in elderly patients

PRECAUTIONS:
- See patients as often as necessary to ensure that the drug is working on the panic attacks, determine compliance, and review side effects.
- Make sure patients realize that they need to take prescribed doses even if they do not feel better right away. It can take several weeks before they feel the full effect of the drug.
- Instruct patients and families to watch for worsening depression or thoughts of suicide. Also watch out for sudden or severe changes in feelings such as feeling anxious, agitated, panicky, irritated, hostile, aggressive, impulsive, severely restless, overly excited, hyperactive, or not being able to sleep. If this happens, especially at the

beginning of antidepressant treatment or after a change in dose, patient should call the health care provider.
- Drowsiness or dizziness: Patients should not drive or use machinery or do anything that needs mental alertness until the effects of this medicine are known.
- Caution patients not to stand or sit up quickly, especially if older. This reduces the risk of dizzy or fainting spells. Alcohol may interfere with the effect of this medicine. Avoid alcoholic drinks.
- Caution patients not to treat themselves for coughs, colds, or allergies without asking health care professional for advice. Some ingredients can increase possible side effects.
- Dry mouth: Chewing sugarless gum, sucking hard candy, and drinking plenty of water may help. Contact health care provider if the problem persists or is severe.
- Caution should be exercised in the following:
  - Bipolar disorder or a family history of bipolar disorder
  - Diabetes
  - Heart disease
  - Liver disease
  - Electroconvulsive therapy
  - Seizures (convulsions)
  - Suicidal thoughts, plans, or attempts by patients or a family member
  - An unusual or allergic reaction to citalopram, other medicines, foods, dyes, or preservatives
  - Pregnancy or trying to get pregnant
  - Breastfeeding

PATIENT AND FAMILY EDUCATION:
- Store at room temperature. Take any unused medication after the expiration date to the local pharmacy on drug give-back day. Avoid throwing the medication into the environment.
- Try to take the medicine at the same time each day. Follow the directions on the prescription label. To get the correct dose of liquid escitalopram, measure the liquid with a marked measuring spoon or medicine cup, not with a regular tablespoon. If there is no dose-measuring device available, ask the pharmacist for one.

SPECIAL POPULATIONS:
- *Elderly:* A dose of 10 mg daily is recommended for geriatric patients. The initial dose should be reduced in patients with severe renal and/or hepatic impairment. Titration upward should be slow and at intervals.
- *Pregnancy:* Category C; potential for persistent pulmonary HTN if greater than 20-weeks gestation
- *Lactation:* Excreted in human breast milk, some reports of infant somulence.
- *Children:* May be given to children older than 12 years of age. Monitoring of suicidal ideations is important.

sertraline   *Zoloft*

INDICATIONS: Used to treat primarily depression but may also be used for OCD, PD, posttrauma stress, PMDD, or social anxiety.

AVAILABLE FORMS: Tablet, 25, 50, and 100 mg

DOSAGE: Starting dose, 25 mg once daily, increase dose incrementally 25 mg per week; maximum, 200 mg daily.

ADMINISTRATION:
- PO with a glass of water.
- Take with or without food
- Take at regular intervals
- Caution patients not to stop taking drug except on provider's advice.
- May be prescribed for children as young as 6 years for selected conditions (25 mg/day); *precautions do apply.*
- Instruct patients to take missed dose as soon as possible. If it is almost time for the next dose, advise to take only that dose.

SIDE EFFECTS:
- *Most common*: Dizziness, headache, insomnia, somnolence, and change in sex drive or performance.
- *Less common*: Allergic reactions (skin rash; itching, or hives); swelling of the face, lips, or tongue; feeling faint or lightheaded; falls; hallucination; loss of contact with reality; seizures; suicidal thoughts or other mood changes; unusual bleeding or bruising; unusually weak or tired; vomiting; change in appetite; diarrhea; increased sweating; indigestion; nausea; tremors

DRUG INTERACTIONS: This medicine may interact with the following medications:
- Absolute contraindications include MAOIs such as phenelzine (*Nardil*), tranylcypromine (*Parnate*), isocarboxazid (*Marplan*), and selegiline (*Eldepryl*).
- Avoid using with SNRI agents, triptans, and and other SSRI agents.
- Caution with aspirin, NSAIDs (e.g., ibuprofen or naproxen), COX inhibitors, and other anti-inflammatory drugs, St. John's wort.
- ▶**Alert**: This list may not describe all possible interactions. Instruct patients to provide a list of all medicines, herbs, nonprescription drugs, or dietary supplements used, and if they smoke, drink alcohol, or use illegal drugs.

PHARMACOKINETICS:
- SSRIs are metabolized in the liver by CYP P450 (CYP) enzymes.
- They are highly bound to plasma proteins and have a large volume of distribution.
- May take 2–6 weeks to fully effective
- Addition of serotonergic medications to a patient's regimen must not occur until 2–3 weeks after discontinuation of an SSRI (some recommend a 5-week "washout" period prior to initiation of an MAOI).

Metabolism: Liver; CYP 2C19, 2D6, 3A4 substrate; 2D6 (weak), 3A4 (weak) inhibitor
Excretion: Urine 40–45% (none unchanged), feces 40–45% (12–14% unchanged)
Half-life: 26 hr

PRECAUTIONS:
- See patients as often as necessary to ensure that the drug is working on the panic attacks, determine compliance, and review side effects.
- Make sure patients realize that they need to take prescribed doses even if they do not feel better right away. It can take several weeks before they feel the full effect of the drug.
- Instruct patients and families to watch for worsening depression or thoughts of suicide. Also, watch out for sudden or severe changes in feelings such as feeling anxious, agitated, panicky, irritated, hostile, aggressive, impulsive, severely restless, overly excited, hyperactive, or not being able to sleep. If this happens, especially at the beginning of antidepressant treatment or after a change in dose, patient should call the health care provider.
- Drowsiness or dizziness: Patients should not drive or use machinery or do anything that needs mental alertness until the effects of this medicine are known.
- Caution patients not to stand or sit up quickly, especially if older. This reduces the risk of dizzy or fainting spells. Alcohol may interfere with the effect of this medicine. Avoid alcoholic drinks.
- Caution patients not to treat themselves for coughs, colds, or allergies without asking health care professional for advice. Some ingredients can increase possible side effects.
- For dry mouth: Chewing sugarless gum or sucking hard candy and drinking plenty of water may help. Contact health care professional if the problem persists or is severe.
- Caution should be exercised in the following:
  - Bipolar disorder or a family history of bipolar disorder
  - Diabetes
  - Heart disease
  - Liver disease
  - Electroconvulsive therapy
  - Seizures (convulsions)
  - Suicidal thoughts, plans, or attempts by patients or a family member
  - An unusual or allergic reaction to sertraline, other medicines, foods, dyes, or preservatives
  - Pregnancy or whentrying to get pregnant
  - Breastfeeding

PATIENT AND FAMILY EDUCATION:
- Store at room temperature. Take any unused medication after the expiration date to the local pharmacy on drug give-back day. Avoid throwing the medication into the environment.
- Discuss any worsening anxiety, aggressiveness, impulsivity, or restlessness with health care professional.

(cont.)

sertraline (*cont.*)

- Patients or families should report any severe, abrupt onset or changes in symptoms to health professionals. This may be reflective of increased risk of suicidal thinking.
- Caution for the concomitant use of NSAIDs, aspirin, warfarin, and any other drugs that alter platelets.

SPECIAL POPULATIONS:
- *Elderly:* Increased risk for hyponatremia
- *Hepatic impairment:* Dose adjustment necessary

- *Pregnancy:* Category C; risks are associated with all SSRIs for neonatal complications if used in the third trimester.
- *Lactation:* Adverse reactions have not been reported; however, long-term effects have not been studied, and the manufacturer recommends caution.
- *Children:* Approved for use in children aged 12 years or older; however, monitoring for increased suicidal ideation is critical.

Paxil, Paxil CR, Pexeva

paroxetine, paroxetine mesylate

INDICATIONS: Used to treat MDD, OCD, bulimia nervosa, and PD

AVAILABLE FORMS: *Pexeva:* Tablet, 20, 30, and 40 mg; *Paxil:* Tablet, 10, 20, 30, and 40 mg; suspension, 10 mg/5 mL; *Paxil CR:* Tablet, 12.5, 25, and 37.5 mg

DOSAGE: *Pexeva* and *Paxil:* 20 mg PO every morning, 10 mg in elderly patients; increase 10 mg/day weekly; maximum 50 mg/day; 40 mg/day in elderly patients. *Paxil CR:* 12.5 mg PO, daily, increase 12.5 mg/day weekly; maximum 75 mg/day; 50 mg/day in elderly patients. No proven additional benefits at doses greater than 20 mg/day.

ADMINISTRATION:
- PO with a glass of water
- Do not cut/crush or chew
- Take with or without food.
- Take at regular intervals.
- Caution patients not to stop taking drug except on provider's advice.
- May be prescribed for children as young as 7 years for selected conditions; *precautions do apply.*
- Instruct patients to take missed dose as soon as possible. If it is almost time for the next dose, advise to take only that dose.

SIDE EFFECTS:
- *Most common:* Somnolence; headache; asthenia; dizziness; sweating; dry mouth; tremor; anorexia; nervousness; anxiety; abnormal vision; change in appetite; change in sex drive or performance; diarrhea; constipation; indigestion; and nausea
- *Less common:* Suicidality, worsening depression, serotonin syndrome, seizures, hyponatremia, extrapyramidal symptoms, priapism, and acute angle glaucoma.

DRUG INTERACTIONS: Most of the interactions occur with OTC cough and cold preparations. This medicine may also interact with the following medications.
- Absolute contraindications include MAOIs such as phenelzine (*Nardil*), tranylcypromine (*Parnate*), isocarboxazid (*Marplan*), and selegiline (*Eldepryl*).

- Avoid using with other SSRIs due to serotonin effect; SNRI drugs such as desvenlafaxine (*Pristiq*) and venlafaxine (*Effexor*); drugs with sympathomimetic properties such as phenylpropanolamine, pseudoephedrine, St. John's wort, haloperidol; diazepam (*Valium*); any other antidepressants; and clopidogrel (*Plavix*).
- Exercise caution with cold medications, arrhythmia medications such as flecainide, aspirin, and other NSAIDs, and drugs used for analgesia with opioid properties.
▶**Alert:** This list may not describe all possible interactions. Instruct patients to provide a list of all medicines, herbs, nonprescription drugs, or dietary supplements used, and if they smoke, drink alcohol, or use illegal drugs.

PHARMACOKINETICS:
Metabolism: Liver extensively; CYP450 2D6 substrate; 2D6 inhibitor
Excretion: Urine 64% (2% unchanged), feces 36% (less than 1% unchanged)
Half-life: 21 hr

PRECAUTIONS:
- See patients as often as necessary to ensure that the drug is working on the panic attacks, determine compliance, and review side effects.
- Make sure patients realize that they need to take prescribed doses even if they do not feel better right away. It can take several weeks before they feel the full effect of the drug.
- Instruct patients and families to watch for worsening depression or thoughts of suicide. Also, watch out for sudden or severe changes in feelings such as feeling anxious, agitated, panicky, irritated, hostile, aggressive, impulsive, severely restless, overly excited, hyperactive, or not being able to sleep. If this happens, especially at the beginning of antidepressant treatment or after a change in dose, patient should call the health care provider.
- Drowsiness or dizziness: Patients should not drive or use machinery or do anything that needs mental alertness until the effects of this medicine are known.
- Caution patients not to stand or sit up quickly, especially if older. This reduces the risk of dizzy

(cont.)

paroxetine, paroxetine mesylate (*cont.*)

or fainting spells. Alcohol may interfere with the effect of this medicine. Avoid alcoholic drinks.
- Caution patients not to treat themselves for coughs, colds, or allergies without asking health care professional for advice. Some ingredients can increase possible side effects.
- Dry mouth: Chewing sugarless gum, sucking hard candy, and drinking plenty of water may help. Contact health care provider if the problem persists or is severe.
- Caution should be exercised in the following:
  - Bipolar disorder or a family history of bipolar disorder
  - Diabetes
  - Heart disease
  - Liver disease
  - Electroconvulsive therapy
  - Seizures (convulsions)
  - Suicidal thoughts, plans, or attempts by patients or a family member
  - An unusual or allergic reaction to paroxetine, other medicines, foods, dyes, or preservatives
  - Pregnancy or trying to get pregnant
  - Breastfeeding

PATIENT AND FAMILY EDUCATION:
- Store at room temperature. Take any unused medication after the expiration date to the local pharmacy on drug give-back day. Avoid throwing the medication into the environment.
- Shake the liquid form of paroxetine well just before you measure a dose. To get the correct dose, measure the liquid with a marked measuring spoon or medicine cup, not with a regular tablespoon. If there is no dose-measuring device available, ask the pharmacist for one.

SPECIAL POPULATIONS:
- *Elderly:* Due to increased C_{min} concentrations, up to 70–80% in the elderly, the initial dose should be reduced.
- *Renal and hepatic impairment:* The initial dose should be reduced in patients with severe renal and/or hepatic impairment. Titration upward should be slow and at intervals.
- *Pregnancy:* Category D; first trimester teratogenicity, neonatal withdrawal and serotonin syndrome in third trimester, persistent pulmonary HTN if greater than 20-weeks gestation.
- *Lactation:* Considered generally safe; substantial human data show no or minimal risk to breast milk production or to the infant.
- *Children: Paxil CR* is not indicated for children. Monitoring for increased suicidal ideation is critical if using regular *Paxil*.

Class: Serotonin and Norepinephrine Reuptake Inhibitors (SNRIs)

venlafaxine   *Effexor, Effexor XR*

INDICATIONS: Used to treat MDD, GAD, PD, and social anxiety disorder

AVAILABLE FORMS: Tablet, 25, 37.5, 50, 75, and 100 mg; extended-release capsule, 37.5, 75, and 150 mg

DOSAGE: *Effexor:* Starting dose, 37.5 mg PO bid with dose increases every 4 days up to a maximum of 375 mg. *Effexor XR:* Starting dose, 37.5–75 mg daily with increases of 75 mg/day every 4–7 days up to a maximum of 225 mg/day.

ADMINISTRATION:
- PO with a glass of water.
- Take with food; *Effexor XR* may be sprinkled on applesauce.
- Do not crush, cut, or chew capsules.
- Take at regular intervals.
- Caution patients not to stop taking drug except on provider's advice.
- Not prescribed for children.
- Instruct patients to take missed dose as soon as possible. If it is almost time for the next dose, advise to take only that dose.

SIDE EFFECTS:
- *Most common:* Somnolence; headache; asthenia; dizziness; sweating; dry mouth; tremor; anorexia; nervousness; anxiety; abnormal vision; change in appetite; change in sex drive or performance; diarrhea; constipation; indigestion; and nausea.
- *Less common:* Suicidality, worsening depression, serotonin syndrome, seizures, hyponatremia, extrapyramidal symptoms, priapism, and acute angle glaucoma.

DRUG INTERACTIONS: Most of the interactions occur with OTC cough and cold preparations. This medicine may also interact with the following medications.
- Absolute contraindications include cisapride, phenothiazines, MAOIs such as phenelzine (*Nardil*), tranylcypromine (*Parnate*), isocarboxazid (*Marplan*), and selegiline (*Eldepryl*).
- Avoid using with other SSRIs due to serotonin effect; SNRI drugs such as desvenlafaxine (*Pristiq*) and venlafaxine (*Effexor*); drugs with sympathomimetic properties such as phenylpropanolamine, pseudoephedrine, St. John's wort, haloperidol; diazepam (*Valium*); and any other antidepressants.
- Exercise caution with cold medications, NSAIDs, and drugs used for analgesia with opioid properties.

▶**Alert**: This list may not describe all possible interactions. Instruct patients to provide a list

(cont.)

venlafaxine (cont.)

of all medicines, herbs, nonprescription drugs, or dietary supplements used, and if they smoke, drink alcohol, or use illegal drugs.

PHARMACOKINETICS:
- SNRI agents are potent inhibitors of neuronal serotonin and norepinephrine reuptake and weak inhibitors of dopamine reuptake.
- Demonstrate slightly higher efficacy than the SSRI class due to the dual effect.
- Relative to SSRIs, SNRI agents seem to be more effective in treating chronic pain issues which coexist with depression and may produce more stimulative effects.
- They are highly bound to plasma proteins and have a large volume of distribution.

Metabolism: Liver extensively; CYP450 2D6 substrate; 2D6 (weak) inhibitor; converted to active metabolite (O-desmethylvenlafaxine)

Excretion: Urine 87% (5% unchanged)

Half-life: 5 hr (venlafaxine), 11 hr (O-desmethyl-venlafaxine)

PRECAUTIONS:
- See patients as often as necessary to ensure that the drug is working on the panic attacks, determine compliance, and review side effects.
- Make sure patients realize that they need to take prescribed doses even if they do not feel better right away. It can take several weeks before they feel the full effect of the drug.
- Instruct patients and families to watch for worsening depression or thoughts of suicide. Also, watch out for sudden or severe changes in feelings such as feeling anxious, agitated, panicky, irritated, hostile, aggressive, impulsive, severely restless, overly excited, hyperactive, or not being able to sleep. If this happens, especially at the beginning of antidepressant treatment or after a change in dose, patient should call the health care provider.
- Drowsiness or dizziness: Patients should not drive or use machinery or do anything that needs mental alertness until the effects of this medicine are known.
- Caution patients not to stand or sit up quickly, especially if older. This reduces the risk of

dizzy or fainting spells. Alcohol may interfere with the effect of this medicine. Avoid alcoholic drinks.
- Caution patients not to treat themselves for coughs, colds, or allergies without asking health care professional for advice. Some ingredients can increase possible side effects.
- Dry mouth: Chewing sugarless gum, sucking hard candy, and drinking plenty of water may help. Contact health care provider if the problem persists or is severe.
- Caution should be exercised in the following:
  - Bipolar disorder or a family history of bipolar disorder
  - Diabetes
  - Heart disease
  - Liver disease
  - Seizures (convulsions)
  - Suicidal thoughts, plans, or attempts by patients or a family member
  - An unusual or allergic reaction to venlafaxine, other medicines, foods, dyes, or preservatives
  - Pregnancy or trying to get pregnant
  - Breastfeeding

PATIENT AND FAMILY EDUCATION:
- Store at room temperature. Take any unused medication after the expiration date to the local pharmacy on drug give-back day. Avoid throwing the medication into the environment.
- Try to take the medicine at the same time each day. Follow the directions on the prescription label.

SPECIAL POPULATIONS:
- *Elderly:* The initial dose should be reduced in patients with severe renal and/or hepatic impairment. Titration upward should be slow and at intervals.
- *Pregnancy:* Category C; potential for persistent pulmonary HTN if greater than 20-weeks gestation.
- *Lactation:* Excreted in human breast milk, caution should be taken.
- *Children:* Not indicated for children.

Cymbalta   **duloxetine**

INDICATIONS: Used to treat MDD and GAD

AVAILABLE FORMS: Capsule, enteric coated, 20, 30, and 60 mg

DOSAGE: Starting dose, 30 mg daily for 1 week, increase by 30 mg increments weekly. Can use a maximum of 120 mg daily; however, greater than 60 mg is rarely more effective and can increase side effects. Maximum dose is 60 mg total daily.

ADMINISTRATION:
- PO with a glass of water.
- Do not crush, cut, chew, or sprinkle capsules.

- Take at regular intervals.
- Caution patients not to stop taking drug except on provider's advice.
- Not prescribed for children.
- Instruct patients to take missed dose as soon as possible. If it is almost time for the next dose, advise to take only that dose.

SIDE EFFECTS:
- *Most common*: Nausea, vomiting, headache, insomnia, dizziness, somnolence, decreased libido and sexual dysfunction, palpitations, nervousness, hypertension, and hot flashes.

(cont.)

GENERALIZED ANXIETY DISORDER: Serotonin and Norepinephrine Reuptake Inhibitors (SNRIs)

duloxetine (*cont.*)

- *Less common*: Worsening depression, suicidality, and hypersensitivity reactions.

DRUG INTERACTIONS: There are many drug–drug interactions. Most of the interactions occur with OTC cough and cold preparations. This medicine may also interact with the following medications.
- Absolute contraindications include MAOIs such as phenelzine (*Nardil*), tranylcypromine (*Parnate*), isocarboxazid (*Marplan*), and selegiline (*Eldepryl*), and phenothiazines.
- Avoid using with ciprofloxacin (*Cipro*), other SSRIs due to serotonin effect, SNRI drugs such as desvenlafaxine (*Pristiq*) and venlafaxine (*Effexor*), caffeine.
▶**Alert**: This list may not describe all possible interactions. Instruct patients to provide a list of all medicines, herbs, nonprescription drugs, or dietary supplements used, and if they smoke, drink alcohol, or use illegal drugs.

PHARMACOKINETICS:
Metabolism: Extensively metabolized in the liver by the CYP 1A2 and 2D6 into inactive metabolites
Excretion: Urine 70% (less than 1% unchanged)
Half-life: 12 hr

PRECAUTIONS:
- See patients as often as necessary to ensure that the drug is working on the panic attacks, determine compliance, and review side effects.
- Make sure patients realize that they need to take prescribed doses even if they do not feel better right away. It can take several weeks before they feel the full effect of the drug.
- Instruct patients and families to watch for worsening depression or thoughts of suicide. Also, watch out for sudden or severe changes in feelings such as feeling anxious, agitated, panicky, irritated, hostile, aggressive, impulsive, severely restless, overly excited, hyperactive, or not being able to sleep. If this happens, especially at the beginning of antidepressant treatment or after a change in dose, patient should call the health care provider.
- Drowsiness or dizziness: Patients should not drive or use machinery or do anything that needs mental alertness until the effects of this medicine are known.
- Caution patients not to stand or sit up quickly, especially if older. This reduces the risk of

dizzy or fainting spells. Alcohol may interfere with the effect of this medicine. Avoid alcoholic drinks.
- Caution patients not to treat themselves for coughs, colds, or allergies without asking health care professional for advice. Some ingredients can increase possible side effects.
- Dry mouth: Chewing sugarless gum, sucking hard candy, and drinking plenty of water may help. Contact health care provider if the problem persists or is severe.
- Caution should be exercised in the following:
  - Bipolar disorder or a family history of bipolar disorder
  - Diabetes
  - Heart disease
  - Liver disease
  - Seizures (convulsions)
  - Suicidal thoughts, plans, or attempts by patients or a family member
  - An unusual or allergic reaction to venlafaxine, other medicines, foods, dyes, or preservatives
  - Pregnancy or trying to get pregnant
  - Breastfeeding

PATIENT AND FAMILY EDUCATION:
- Store at room temperature. Take any unused medication after the expiration date to the local pharmacy on drug give-back day. Avoid throwing the medication into the environment.
- Try to take the medicine at the same time each day. Follow the directions on the prescription label.

SPECIAL POPULATIONS:
- *Elderly:* The initial dose should be reduced in patients with severe renal and/or hepatic impairment. Titration upward should be slow and at intervals. Higher dose may be required in the treatment of anxiety disorders in geriatric patients; however, this patient population is more at risk of developing hyponatremia from SSRIs and SNRIs.
- *Pregnancy:* Category C; potential for persistent pulmonary HTN if greater than 20-weeks gestation
- *Lactation:* Excreted in human breast milk, caution should be taken.
- *Children:* Not indicated for children.

Class: Calcium Channel Moderators

pregabalin   *Lyrica*

INDICATIONS: Adjunctive therapy used to treat GAD of more than 6 months duration

AVAILABLE FORMS: Capsule, oral solution

DOSAGE: Starting dose, 75 mg two times a day (150 mg/day); may be increased to 150 mg two times a day (300 mg/day) within 1 week based

on efficacy and tolerability. The dose may be increased to a maximum of 300 mg two times a day (600 mg/day). The recommended dose range of *Lyrica* as an adjunctive treatment of GAD is 150 to 600 mg/day although there is little efficacy in doses greater than 300 mg/day.

(cont.)

pregabalin (cont.)

ADMINISTRATION:
- PO with a glass of water.
- Do not crush, cut, chew, or sprinkle capsules
- Caution patients not to stop taking drug except on provider's advice.
- Not prescribed for children.
- Instruct patients to take missed dose as soon as possible. If it is almost time for the next dose, advise to take only that dose.

SIDE EFFECTS:
- *Most common*: Dizziness, somnolence, ataxia, peripheral edema, weight gain, blurred vision, arthralgias, dry mouth, and headache.
- *Less common*: Severe skin reactions, thrombocytopenia, suicidality.

DRUG INTERACTIONS: Because pregabalin does not bind to plasma proteins, there are few drug–drug interactions. Caution should be exercised with OTC cold preparations. This medicine may also interact with the following medications.
- Avoid using alternative ginko biloba. Monitor treatment with sevelamer.
▶**Alert**: This list may not describe all possible interactions. Instruct patients to provide a list of all medicines, herbs, nonprescription drugs, or dietary supplements used, and if they smoke, drink alcohol, or use illegal drugs.

PHARMACOKINETICS: Pregabalin is predominantly excreted unchanged in the urine, undergoes negligible metabolism in humans (less than 2% of a dose recovered in urine as metabolites), and does not bind to plasma proteins. The exact mechanism of action unknown; binds alpha-2-delta subunit of calcium channels reducing neurotransmitter release; produces antinociceptive and antiseizure effects. Does not bind to GABA or BZD receptors.

PRECAUTIONS:
- See patients as often as necessary to ensure that the drug is working on generalized anxiety, to determine compliance, and review side effects.
- Make sure patients realize that they need to take prescribed doses even if they do not feel better

right away. It can take several weeks before they feel the full effect of the drug.
- Drowsiness or dizziness: Patients should not drive or use machinery or do anything that needs mental alertness until the effects of this medicine are known.
- Caution patients not to stand or sit up quickly, especially if older. This reduces the risk of dizzy or fainting spells. Alcohol may interfere with the effect of this medicine. Avoid alcoholic drinks.
- Caution patients not to treat themselves for coughs, colds, or allergies without asking health care professional for advice. Some ingredients can increase possible side effects.
- Dry mouth: Chewing sugarless gum, sucking hard candy, and drinking plenty of water may help. Contact health care provider if the problem persists or is severe.
- Caution should be exercised in the following:
  - Past history of angioedema
  - Renal disease
  - Liver disease
  - Suicidal thoughts, plans, or attempts by patients or a family member
  - An unusual or allergic reaction to pregabalin, other medicines, foods, dyes, or preservatives
  - Pregnancy or trying to get pregnant
  - Breastfeeding

PATIENT AND FAMILY EDUCATION:
- Store at room temperature. Take any unused medication after the expiration date to the local pharmacy on drug give-back day. Avoid throwing the medication into the environment.
- Try to take the medicine at the same time each day. Follow the directions on the prescription label.

SPECIAL POPULATIONS:
- *Elderly:* The dose titration should be according to the patient's creatinine clearance. Titration upward should be slow and at intervals.
- *Pregnancy:* Category C; limited human data on exposure during pregnancy.
- *Lactation:* Excreted in human breast milk, caution should be taken.
- *Children:* Not approved for use with children.

Class: Tricyclic Antidepressants (TCAs)

Due to the class side effects, especially on the cardiac system, TCAs should be used only if the SSRI or SNRI classes fail to show any improvement in symptom profile.

Tofranil, Tofranil PM	imipramine pamoate

INDICATIONS: Used to treat adults with depression/anxiety

AVAILABLE FORMS: *Tofranil:* Tablet, 25 and 50 mg; *Tofranil PM:* Capsule, 75, 100, 125, and 150 mg

DOSAGE: *Adults:* Starting dose, 25–75 mg PO nightly and increase by 25–50 mg/day every 3–4 days; maximum, 300 mg/day; 100 mg/day in elderly patients. Can be given in divided doses. Must taper dose gradually to discontinue. *Children*
(cont.)

imipramine pamoate (cont.)

with depression: Starting dose, 1.5 mg/kg/day PO divided tid, increase by 1–1.5 mg/kg/day every 3–4 days; maximum, 5 mg/kg/day. (greater than 12 years), starting dose, 30–40 mg/day PO divided qd-tid and increase by 10–25 mg/day every 3–4 days; maximum, 100 mg/day.

ADMINISTRATION:
- PO with a glass of water.
- Do not crush, cut, or chew extended-release tablets.
- Do not abruptly stop taking the medication.
- Not prescribed for children except when used for nocturnal enuresis and depression in children as young as 6 years.
- Use lowest effective dose for shortest duration.

SIDE EFFECTS:
- *More common:* Drowsiness, dizziness, constipation; nausea/vomiting, urinary retention or frequency, libido changes, weight gain, general nervousness, and galactorrhea.
- *Less common:* Cardiac arrhythmias, extrapyramidal symptoms, clotting disturbances, worsening depression, suicidality, hyperthermia, hypertension.

DRUG INTERACTIONS: This medicine may interact with the following medications:
- Absolute contraindications include class 1A antiarrhythmics, MAOIs such as phenelzine (*Nardil*), tranylcypromine (*Parnate*), isocarboxazid (*Marplan*), and selegiline (*Eldepryl*).
- Avoid using with cimetidine, amiodarone, clarithromycin, haloperidol, and St. John's wort.

▶**Alert:** This list may not describe all possible interactions. Instruct patients to provide a list of all medicines, herbs, nonprescription drugs, or dietary supplements used, and if they smoke, drink alcohol, or use illegal drugs.

PHARMACOKINETICS:
- TCAs are thought to work by inhibiting reuptake of norepinephrine and serotonin in the CNS, which potentiates the neurotransmitters. They also have significant anticholinergics, antihistaminic, and alpha-adrenergic activity on the cardiac system. These classes of antidepressants also possess class 1A antiarrhythmic activity, which can lead to depression of cardiac conduction potentially resulting in heart block or ventricular arrhythmias.

Metabolism: Extensively by the liver within the CYP450: 1A2, 2C19, 2D6 (primary), 3A4 substrate
Excretion: Primarily in urine, up to less than 5% unchanged, also excreted in the bile/feces
Half-life: 11–25 hr

PRECAUTIONS:
- See patients as often as necessary to ensure that the drug is working on the panic attacks, determine compliance, and review side effects.
- Instruct patients and their families to watch for worsening depression or thoughts of suicide. Also, watch out for sudden or severe changes in feelings such as feeling anxious, agitated, panicky, irritated, hostile, aggressive, impulsive, severely restless, overly excited, hyperactive, or not being able to sleep. If this happens, especially at the beginning of antidepressant treatment or after a change in dose, patient should call the health care provider.
- Drowsiness or dizziness: Patients should not drive or use machinery or do anything that needs mental alertness until the effects of this medicine are known. Other medications that cause drowsiness can add to the drowsiness of imipramine.
- Caution patients not to stand or sit up quickly, especially if older. This reduces the risk of dizzy or fainting spells. Alcohol may interfere with the effect of this medicine. Avoid alcoholic drinks.
- Do not abruptly withdraw this drug as it may cause headache, nausea, and malaise.
- Advise to protect skin from ultraviolet light due to increased skin sensitivity.
- Grapefruit and grapefruit juice may interact with imipramine.
- Caution should be exercised in the following:
  - MDD, psychosis, or bipolar affective disorder
  - Contraindicated in patients with a recent myocardial infarction
  - Blood dyscrasias
  - Respiratory disease
  - Heart disease
  - Liver disease
  - Seizures (convulsions)
  - Suicidal thoughts, plans, or attempts by patients or a family member
  - An unusual or allergic reaction to imipramine, other medicines, foods, dyes, or preservatives

PATIENT AND FAMILY EDUCATION:
- Store imipramine at room temperature away from moisture and heat.
- Stopping this medication suddenly could result in unpleasant side effects.
- Take the missed dose as soon as remembered. If it is almost time for the next dose, skip the missed dose and take the medicine at the next regularly scheduled time. *Do not* take extra medicine to make up the missed dose.

SPECIAL POPULATIONS:
- *Elderly:* Older patients may be more sensitive to the effects of TCAs. The smallest effective dose should be used. Dose adjustment is necessary for patients with liver impairment.
- *Pregnancy:* Category D; some clinical reports of congenital malformations, but no direct causal link.
- *Lactation:* Excreted in human breast milk; alternative medications are recommended.
- *Children: Tofranil* is indicated for children less than 6 years old with nocturnal enuresis or with depression. Monitor for suicidal ideation with depression. *Tofranil PM* is not approved for use in children.

Norpramin   **desipramine**

AVAILABLE FORMS: Tablet, 10, 25, 50, 75, 100, and 150 mg

DOSAGE: Starting dose, 25–75 mg PO, daily; maximum, 300 mg/day. May be given in divided doses; must taper slowly to discontinue.

ADMINISTRATION:
- PO with a glass of water.
- Do not abruptly stop taking the medication.
- Not prescribed for children.
- Use lowest effective dose for shortest duration.

SIDE EFFECTS:
- *More common:* Drowsiness, dizziness, constipation, nausea/vomiting, urinary retention or frequency, libido changes, weight gain, general nervousness, galactorrhea, rash, and urticaria.
- *Less common:* Cardiac arrhythmias, extrapyramidal symptoms, clotting disturbances, worsening depression, suicidality, hyperthermia, and hypertension.

DRUG INTERACTIONS: This medicine may interact with the following medications:
- Absolute contraindication include class 1A antiarrhythmics, MAOIs such as phenelzine (*Nardil*), tranylcypromine (*Parnate*), isocarboxazid (*Marplan*), and selegiline (*Eldepryl*).
- Avoid using with cimetidine, amiodarone, clarithromycin, erythromycin, haldoperidol, and St. John's wort.

▶**Alert**: This list may not describe all possible interactions. Instruct patients to provide a list of all medicines, herbs, nonprescription drugs, or dietary supplements used, and if they smoke, and drink alcohol, or use illegal drugs.

PHARMACOKINETICS:
- TCAs are thought to work by inhibiting reuptake of norepinephrine and serotonin in the CNS, which potentiates the neurotransmitters. They also have significant anticholinergics, antihistaminic, and alpha-adrenergic activity on the cardiac system. These classes of antidepressants also possess class 1A antiarrhythmic activity, which can lead to depression of cardiac conduction potentially resulting in heart block or ventricular arrhythmias.

Metabolism: Primarily in the liver via the CYP450: 2C19, 2D6 (primary) substrate

Excretion: Urine

Half-life: 12–27 hr

PRECAUTIONS:
- See patients as often as necessary to ensure that the drug is working on the panic attacks, determine compliance, and review side effects.
- Instruct patients and families to watch for worsening depression or thoughts of suicide. Also watch out for sudden or severe changes in feelings such as feeling anxious, agitated, panicky, irritated, hostile, aggressive, impulsive, severely

restless, overly excited, hyperactive, or not being able to sleep. If this happens, especially at the beginning of antidepressant treatment or after a change in dose, patient should call the health care provider.
- Drowsiness or dizziness: Patients should not drive or use machinery or do anything that needs mental alertness until the effects of this medicine are known. Other medications that cause drowsiness can add to the drowsiness of desipramine.
- Caution patients not to stand or sit up quickly, especially if older. This reduces the risk of dizzy or fainting spells. Alcohol may interfere with the effect of this medicine. Avoid alcoholic drinks.
- Do not abruptly withdraw this drug as it may cause headache, nausea, and malaise.
- Advise to protect skin from ultraviolet light due to increased skin sensitivity.
- Grapefruit and grapefruit juice may interact with imipramine.
- Caution should be exercised in the following:
  - MDD, psychosis, or bipolar affective disorder
  - Contraindicated in patients with a recent myocardial infarction
  - Blood dyscrasias
  - Respiratory disease
  - Heart disease
  - Liver disease
  - Seizures (convulsions)
  - Psychoses or schizophrenia
  - Suicidal thoughts, plans, or attempts by patients or a family member
  - An unusual or allergic reaction to desipramine, other medicines, foods, dyes, or preservatives

PATIENT AND FAMILY EDUCATION:
- Store imipramine at room temperature away from moisture and heat.
- Stopping this medication suddenly could result in unpleasant side effects.
- Take the missed dose as soon as remembered. If it is almost time for the next dose, skip the missed dose and take the medicine at the next regularly scheduled time. *Do not* take extra medicine to make up the missed dose.

SPECIAL POPULATIONS:
- *Elderly:* Older patients may be more sensitive to the effects of TCAs. The smallest effective dose should be used (beginning at 10–25 mg/day). Dose adjustment is necessary for patients with liver impairment.
- *Pregnancy:* Category C; unknown effects as there is limited study.
- *Lactation:* Excreted in human breast milk; use caution.
- *Children:* Not indicated for children; used off-label in children 6–12 years old; however, alternative medications are preferred.

GENERALIZED ANXIETY DISORDER: Tricyclic Antidepressants (TCAs)

Class: Benzodiazepines (BZDs)

alprazolam   *Xanax, Xanax XR, and Niravam*

INDICATIONS: Short-acting BZD used to treat GADs and PD. May be used as a short-term adjunct to an SSRI while waiting for the therapeutic effects of the SSRI to develop.

AVAILABLE FORMS: Tablet, 0.25, 0.5, 1, and 2 mg; extended-release capsule, 0.5, 1, and 2 mg; melt, 0.5, 1, 2, and 3 mg

DOSAGE: *Xanax:* Starting dose, 0.25 to 0.5 mg up to 2–3 times daily; maximum, 4 mg daily. Can be increased every 3–4 days. Treatment should be limited to as short a period as possible (less than 4 months) and/or re-evaluated for continued use. *Xanax XR:* Starting dose, 0.5–1 mg PO, daily, can increase up to 1 mg/day every 3–4 days. *Niravam (melt):* Starting dose, 0.25 to 0.5 mg up to 2–3 times daily; maximum, 4 mg daily. Can be increased every 3–4 days.

ADMINISTRATION:
- PO with a glass of water.
- Do not crush, cut, or chew extended-release tablets.
- Orally disintegrating *(Niravam)* has special instructions.
- Concentrated liquid must be measured with a special dose measuring spoon or cup.
- Do not abruptly stop taking the medication.
- Not prescribed for children.
- Use lowest effective dose for shortest duration.
- Alprazolam can be habit forming, do not increase dosage without guidance from the health care provider.

SIDE EFFECTS:
- *Most common:* Drowsiness, lightheadedness, dry mouth; headache, changes in bowel habits, sialorrhea, amnesia, and changes in appetite.
- *Less common:* Syncope, tachycardia, seizures, respiratory depression, dependency, withdrawal syndrome, and suicidal ideation.

DRUG INTERACTIONS: This medicine may interact with the following medications:
- Absolute contraindications include clarithromycin, fluvoxamine, and ketoconazole.
- Avoid using with calcium channel blockers, erythromycins, tamoxifen, and zafirlukast.
- ▶**Alert:** This list may not describe all possible interactions. Instruct patients to provide a list of all medicines, herbs, nonprescription drugs, or dietary supplements used, and if they smoke, drink alcohol, or use illegal drugs.

PHARMACOKINETICS:
- BZDs enhance the activity of GABA, a major CNS neurotransmitter, known to open CNS Cl^- channels leading to an inhibition of subsequent CNS neuronal signaling. BZDs with similar action can differ in their potency and rate of absorption.
Metabolism: By the liver in the CYP450 3A4
Excretion: Urine

Half-life: 11.2 hr, 16.3 hr (elderly), 19.7 hr (alcoholic liver disease), respectively

PRECAUTIONS:
- See patients as often as necessary to ensure that the drug is working on the panic attacks, determine compliance, and review side effects.
- Instruct patients and families to watch for worsening depression or thoughts of suicide. Also, watch out for sudden or severe changes in feelings such as feeling anxious, agitated, panicky, irritated, hostile, aggressive, impulsive, severely restless, overly excited, hyperactive, or not being able to sleep. If this happens, especially at the beginning of antidepressant treatment or after a change in dose, patient should call the health care provider.
- Drowsiness or dizziness: Patients should not drive or use machinery or do anything that needs mental alertness until the effects of this medicine are known.
- Caution patients not to stand or sit up quickly, especially if older. This reduces the risk of dizzy or fainting spells. Alcohol may interfere with the effect of this medicine. Avoid alcoholic drinks.
- Do not abruptly withdraw this drug as it may cause seizures.
- Caution should be exercised in the following:
  - MDD, psychosis, or bipolar affective disorder
  - Respiratory disease
  - Heart disease
  - Liver disease
  - Seizures (convulsions)
  - Suicidal thoughts, plans, or attempts by patients or a family member
  - An unusual or allergic reaction to alprazolam, other medicines, foods, dyes, or preservatives

PATIENT AND FAMILY EDUCATION:
- Store alprazolam at room temperature away from moisture, heat, and light. Remove any cotton from the bottle of disintegrating tablets, and keep the bottle tightly closed.
- Alprazolam may be habit forming and *should be used only by the person it was prescribed for.* Alprazolam should never be shared with another person, especially someone who has a history of drug abuse or addiction. Keep the medication in a secure place where others cannot get to it.
- Do not purchase alprazolam on the Internet or outside of the USA as dangerous ingredients may be present. Some purchases of alprazolam from the Internet have been found to contain haloperidol *(Haldol)*, an antipsychotic drug.

SPECIAL POPULATIONS:
- *Elderly:* Older patients may be more sensitive to the effects of BZDs. The smallest effective dose should be used. Dose adjustment is necessary for patients with liver impairment and/or renal disease due to excessive metabolites excreted *(cont.)*

alprazolam (cont.)

by the kidney. Due to increased risk of sedation leading to falls and fractures, BZDs are included on the Beers List of Potentially Inappropriate Medications for Geriatrics.

- *Pregnancy:* Category D; can cause teratogenic fetal effects. Infants born to mothers taking BZDs may be at risk for withdrawal symptoms in the postnatal period.
- *Lactation:* Excreted in human breast milk; infants can become lethargic and lose weight
- *Children:* Not indicated for use in children younger than 18 years.

Klonopin   **clonazepam**

INDICATIONS: Used to treat GAD and PD

AVAILABLE FORMS: Tablet, 0.5, 1, and 2 mg; wafer melt, 0.125, 0.25, 0.5, and 1.2 mg

DOSAGE: *Adults:* Starting dose, 0.25 mg PO bid, increase by 0.25–0.5 mg/day every 3 days; may start lower in elderly patients; maximum, 4 mg/day; treatment should be limited to as short a period as possible (less than 4 months) and/or re-evaluated for continued use. To discontinue, taper by 0.25 mg/day q3 days if greater than 4 to 6 weeks continuous use

ADMINISTRATION:
- PO with a glass of water.
- Do not abruptly stop taking the medication.
- Use lowest effective dose for shortest duration.
- Clonazepam can be habit forming, do not increase dosage without guidance from the health care provider.

SIDE EFFECTS:
- *More common:* Drowsiness, lightheadedness, dry mouth; headache, changes in bowel habits, sialorrhea, amnesia, and changes in appetite.
- *Less common:* Syncope, tachycardia, seizures, respiratory depression, dependency, withdrawal syndrome, and suicidal ideation.

DRUG INTERACTIONS: This medicine may interact with the following medications:
- Absolute contraindications include clarithromycin, fluvoxamine, and ketoconazole.
- Avoid using with calcium channel blockers, erythromycins, tamoxifen, and zafirlukast.
▶**Alert:** This list may not describe all possible interactions. Instruct patients to provide a list of all medicines, herbs, nonprescription drugs, or dietary supplements used, and if they smoke, drink alcohol, or use illegal drugs.

PHARMACOKINETICS:
- BZDs enhance the activity of GABA, a major CNS neurotransmitter, known to open CNS Cl⁻ channels leading to an inhibition of subsequent CNS neuronal signaling. BZDs with similar action can differ in their potency and rate of absorption.
Metabolism: Extensively metabolized in liver CYP450 3A4
Excretion: Urine
Half-life: 20–50 hr

PRECAUTIONS:
- See patients as often as necessary to ensure that the drug is working on the panic attacks, determine compliance, and review side effects.
- Instruct patients and their families to watch for worsening depression or thoughts of suicide. Also, watch out for sudden or severe changes in feelings such as feeling anxious, agitated, panicky, irritated, hostile, aggressive, impulsive, severely restless, overly excited, hyperactive, or not being able to sleep. If this happens, especially at the beginning of antidepressant treatment or after a change in dose, patient should call the health care provider.
- Drowsy or dizzy: Do not drive, use machinery, or do anything that needs mental alertness until the effects of this medicine are known.
- Caution patients not to stand or sit up quickly, especially if older. This reduces the risk of dizzy or fainting spells. Alcohol may interfere with the effect of this medicine. Avoid alcoholic drinks.
- Do not abruptly withdraw this drug as it may cause seizures.
- Caution should be exercised in the following:
  - Heart disease
  - Liver disease
  - Seizures (convulsions)
  - Suicidal thoughts, plans, or attempts by patients or a family member
  - An unusual or allergic reaction to alprazolam, other medicines, foods, dyes, or preservatives

PATIENT AND FAMILY EDUCATION:
- Store clonazepam at room temperature away from moisture, heat, and light. Remove any cotton from the bottle of disintegrating wafers, and keep the bottle tightly closed.
- Clonazepam may be habit forming and *should be used only by the person it was prescribed for.* Clonazepam should never be shared with another person, especially someone who has a history of drug abuse or addiction. Keep the medication in a secure place where others cannot get to it.

SPECIAL POPULATIONS:
- *Elderly:* Older patients may be more sensitive to the effects of BZDs. The smallest effective dose should be used. Dose adjustment is necessary for patients with liver impairment and/or renal disease due to excessive metabolites excreted

(cont.)

GENERALIZED ANXIETY DISORDER: Benzodiazepines (BZDs)

clonazepam (*cont.*)

by the kidney. Due to increased risk of sedation leading to falls and fractures, BZDs are included on the Beers List of Potentially Inappropriate Medications for Geriatrics.

- *Pregnancy:* Category D; can cause teratogenic fetal effects. Infants born to mothers taking

BZDs may be at risk for withdrawal symptoms in the postnatal period.

- *Lactation:* Excreted in human breast milk; infants can become lethargic and lose weight.
- *Children:* Not indicated for use with children except for treatment of seizures.

lorazepam   *Ativan*

INDICATIONS: Used to treat GAD and PD

AVAILABLE FORMS: Tablet, 0.5, 1, and 2 mg

DOSAGE: *Adults*: 2–3 mg/day PO/IM/IV divided bid-tid; 1–2 mg/day PO/IM/IV divided bid-tid in elderly patients; maximum, 10 mg/day. Periodically assess the need for treatment and taper the dose gradually to discontinue if prolonged treatment is necessary. Treatment should be limited to as short a period as possible (less than 4 months) and/or re-evaluated for continued use. *Children*: 0.05 mg/kg PO/IV q4–8 hr; maximum, 2 mg/dose. Periodically assess the need for treatment and taper the dose gradually to discontinue if prolonged treatment is necessary.

ADMINISTRATION:
- PO with a glass of water.
- Do not abruptly stop taking the medication.
- Use lowest effective dose for shortest duration.
- Lorazepam can be habit forming; do not increase dosage without guidance from the health care provider.

SIDE EFFECTS:
- *More common:* Drowsiness, lightheadedness, dry mouth; headache, changes in bowel habits, sialorrhea, amnesia, and changes in appetite.
- *Less common*: Syncope, tachycardia, seizures, respiratory depression, dependency, withdrawal syndrome, and suicidal ideation.

DRUG INTERACTIONS: This medicine may interact with the following medications.
- Absolute contraindications include clarithromycin, fluvoxamine, and ketoconazole.
- Avoid using with calcium channel blockers, erythromycins, tamoxifen, and zafirlukast.
▶**Alert**: This list may not describe all possible interactions. Instruct patients to provide a list of all medicines, herbs, nonprescription drugs, or dietary supplements used, and if they smoke, drink alcohol, or use illegal drugs.

PHARMACOKINETICS:
- BZDs enhance the activity of GABA, a major CNS neurotransmitter, known to open CNS Cl⁻ channels leading to an inhibition of subsequent CNS neuronal signaling. BZDs with similar action can differ in their potency and rate of absorption.
Metabolism: Liver with the CYP450; exact mechanism unknown
Excretion: Urine
Half-life: 14 hr

PRECAUTIONS:
- See patients as often as necessary to ensure that the drug is working on the panic attacks, determine compliance, and review side effects.
- Instruct patients and their families to watch for worsening depression or thoughts of suicide. Also, watch out for sudden or severe changes in feelings such as feeling anxious, agitated, panicky, irritated, hostile, aggressive, impulsive, severely restless, overly excited, hyperactive, or not being able to sleep. If this happens, especially at the beginning of antidepressant treatment or after a change in dose, patient should call the health care provider.
- Drowsiness or dizziness: Patients should not drive or use machinery or do anything that needs mental alertness until the effects of this medicine are known.
- Caution patients not to stand or sit up quickly, especially if older. This reduces the risk of dizzy or fainting spells. Alcohol may interfere with the effect of this medicine. Avoid alcoholic drinks.
- Do not abruptly withdraw this drug as it may cause seizures.
- Caution should be exercised in the following:
  - Heart disease
  - Liver disease
  - Seizures (convulsions)
  - Suicidal thoughts, plans, or attempts by patients or a family member
  - An unusual or allergic reaction to alprazolam, other medicines, foods, dyes, or preservatives

PATIENT AND FAMILY EDUCATION:
- Store lorazepam at room temperature away from moisture, heat, and light. Remove any cotton from the bottle of disintegrating tablets, and keep the bottle tightly closed.
- Lorazepam may be habit forming and *should be used only by the person it was prescribed for.* Lorazepam should never be shared with another person, especially someone who has a history of drug abuse or addiction. Keep the medication in a secure place where others cannot get to it.
- Do not purchase lorazepam on the Internet or outside of the USA as dangerous ingredients may be present.

SPECIAL POPULATIONS:
- *Elderly:* Older patients may be more sensitive to the effects of BZDs. The smallest effective dose should be used. Dose adjustment is necessary for patients with liver impairment and/or renal disease due to excessive metabolites excreted
(cont.)

lorazepam (*cont.*)

by the kidney. Due to increased risk of sedation leading to falls and fractures, BZDs are included on the Beers List of Potentially Inappropriate Medications for Geriatrics.

- *Pregnancy:* Category D; can cause teratogenic fetal effects. Infants born to mothers taking

BZDs may be at risk for withdrawal symptoms in the postnatal period.

- *Lactation:* Excreted in human breast milk; infants can become lethargic and lose weight.
- *Children:* Not indicated for use in children younger than 18 years.

Valium   **diazepam**

INDICATIONS: Short-acting BZD to treat GAD and PD

AVAILABLE FORMS: Tablet, 2, 5, and 10 mg

DOSAGE: *Adults:* 2–10 mg PO bid-qid; alternate, 2–10 mg IM/IV q3–4 hr prn

ADMINISTRATION:
- PO with a glass of water.
- Do not abruptly stop taking the medication.
- Not prescribed for children.
- Use lowest effective dose for shortest duration.
- Diazepam can be habit forming, do not increase dosage without guidance from the health care provider.

SIDE EFFECTS:
- Syncope, tachycardia, seizures, respiratory depression, coma, dependency, abuse, withdrawal if abrupt discontinuation, suicidal ideation, and hypomania/mania
- *Common:* Drowsiness, lightheadedness, dry mouth; depression, headache, constipation; diarrhea; confusion, nausea, vomiting, insomnia, tachycardia, nasal congestion, blurred vision, hypotension, rigidity, sialorrhea, dermatitis, syncope, ataxia, amnesia, impaired coordination, irritability, altered libido, dysarthria, appetite change, weight changes, and urinary hesitancy

DRUG INTERACTIONS: This medicine may interact with the following medications:
- Absolute contraindications include clarithromycin, fluvoxamine, and ketoconazole.
- Avoid using with calcium channel blockers, erythromycins, tamoxifen, and zafirlukast.

▶**Alert**: This list may not describe all possible interactions. Instruct patients to provide a list of all medicines, herbs, nonprescription drugs, or dietary supplements used, and if they smoke, drink alcohol, or use illegal drugs.

PHARMACOKINETICS:
- BZDs enhance the activity of GABA, a major CNS neuroinhibitor. Although the exact physiologic action is unknown, the thought is that different BZDs act on different receptors in the CNS. BZDs with similar action can differ in their potency and rate of absorption.

Metabolism: Extensively metabolized by the liver within the CYP450: 2C19, 3A4 substrate. Active metabolites include desmethyldiazepam.

Excretion: Urine
Half-life: 30–60 hr (diazepam); 30–100 hr (desmethyldiazepam)

PRECAUTIONS:
- See patients as often as necessary to ensure that the drug is working on the panic attacks, determine compliance, and review side effects.
- Instruct patients and families to watch for worsening depression or thoughts of suicide. Also watch out for sudden or severe changes in feelings such as feeling anxious, agitated, panicky, irritated, hostile, aggressive, impulsive, severely restless, overly excited, hyperactive, or not being able to sleep. If this happens, especially at the beginning of antidepressant treatment or after a change in dose, patient should call the health care provider.
- Drowsiness or dizziness: Patients should not drive or use machinery or do anything that needs mental alertness until the effects of this medicine are known.
- Caution patients not to stand or sit up quickly, especially if older. This reduces the risk of dizzy or fainting spells. Alcohol may interfere with the effect of this medicine. Avoid alcoholic drinks.
- Do not abruptly withdraw this drug as it may cause seizures.
- Caution should be exercised in the following:
    - MDD, psychosis, or bipolar affective disorder
    - Respiratory disease
    - Heart disease
    - Liver disease
    - Seizures (convulsions)
    - Suicidal thoughts, plans, or attempts by patients or a family member
    - An unusual or allergic reaction to diazepam, other medicines, foods, dyes, or preservatives

PATIENT AND FAMILY EDUCATION:
- Store diazepam at room temperature away from moisture, heat, and light. Remove any cotton from the bottle of disintegrating tablets, and keep the bottle tightly closed.
- Diazepam may be habit forming and *should be used only by the person it was prescribed for.* Diazepam should never be shared with another person, especially someone who has a history of drug abuse or addiction. Keep the medication in a secure place where others cannot get to it.

(cont.)

GENERALIZED ANXIETY DISORDER: Benzodiazepines (BZDs)

diazepam (*cont.*)

- Do not purchase diazepam on the Internet or outside of the USA as dangerous ingredients may be present. Some purchases of alprazolam from the Internet have been found to contain haloperidol (*Haldol*), an antipsychotic drug.

SPECIAL POPULATIONS:
- *Elderly:* Older patients may be more sensitive to the effects of BZDs. The smallest effective dose should be used. Dose adjustment is necessary for patients with liver impairment and/or renal

disease due to excessive metabolites excreted by the kidney.
- *Pregnancy:* Category D; can cause teratogenic fetal effects. Infants born to mothers taking BZDs may be at risk for withdrawal symptoms in the postnatal period.
- *Lactation:* Excreted in human breast milk; infants can become lethargic and lose weight.
- *Children:* Not indicated for use in children younger than 18 years.

Class: Antihistamines

hydroxyzine   *Vistaril*

INDICATIONS: Anxiolytic non-BZD used to treat GADs and PD

AVAILABLE FORMS: Capsule, suspension, and injections

DOSAGE: *Adults:* 50–100 mg PO every 6 hr as needed; maximum, 600 mg daily. *Pediatric (6–12 years)*: 12.5–25 mg PO q6–8 hr prn; Alternative: 0.5–1 mg/kg IM q4–6 hr prn; (*older than 12 years*), see adult dosing.

ADMINISTRATION:
- PO with a glass of water.
- No concern about discontinuation symptoms.
- Little potential for abuse, tolerance, and physical or psychological dependence.

SIDE EFFECTS: Wheezing, dyspnea, seizures, dry mouth, drowsiness, dizziness, ataxia, weakness, slurred speech, headache, agitation, bitter taste, and nausea

DRUG INTERACTIONS: This medicine may interact with the following medications.
- Absolute contraindications include potassium chloride, urinary acidifiers.
- Avoid using with all MAOIs.
▶**Alert**: This list may not describe all possible interactions. Instruct patients to provide a list of all medicines, herbs, nonprescription drugs, or dietary supplements used, and if they smoke, drink alcohol, or use illegal drugs.

PHARMACOKINETICS:
- Hydroxyzine suppresses regions of the subcortical areas of the CNS. It antagonizes central and peripheral histamine H1 peripheral receptors.
Metabolism: By the liver, where it is converted to the active metabolite cetirizine
Excretion: Primarily by the urine
Half-life: 20–25 hr

PRECAUTIONS:
- See patients as often as necessary to ensure that the drug is working on general anxiety, determine compliance, and review side effects.

- Instruct patients and families to watch for worsening depression or thoughts of suicide. Also, watch out for sudden or severe changes in feelings such as feeling anxious, agitated, panicky, irritated, hostile, aggressive, impulsive, severely restless, overly excited, hyperactive, or not being able to sleep.
- Drowsiness or dizziness: Patients should not drive or use machinery or do anything that needs mental alertness until the effects of this medicine are known.
- Caution patients not to stand or sit up quickly, especially if older. This reduces the risk of dizzy or fainting spells. Alcohol may interfere with the effect of this medicine. Avoid alcoholic drinks.
- Hydroxyzine potentiates other CNS depressant; this must be taken into consideration when administering other agents concurrently.
- Caution should be exercised in the following:
  - Renal disease
  - Suicidal thoughts, plans, or attempts by patients or a family member
  - An unusual or allergic reaction to hydroxyzine, other medicines, foods, dyes, or preservatives

PATIENT AND FAMILY EDUCATION:
- Store hydroxyzine at room temperature away from moisture, heat, and light.
- Take this medicine with a full glass of water.
- Measure liquid medicine with a special dose-measuring spoon or cup, not a regular tablespoon. If there is no dose-measuring device available, ask the pharmacist for one.
- Take the missed dose as soon as remembered. If it is almost time for the next dose, wait until then to take the medicine and skip the missed dose. *Do not* take extra medicine to make up the missed dose.

SPECIAL POPULATIONS:
- *Elderly:* Older patients may be more sensitive to the effects of hydroxyzine. The smallest effective dose should be used. Dose adjustment is
(cont.)

hydroxyzine (*cont.*)

necessary for patients with mild renal disease due to excessive metabolites excreted by the kidney. Due to its strong anticholinergic properties, the drug is included in the Beers List of Potentially Inappropriate Medications for Geriatrics.

- *Pregnancy:* Category C; no teratogenic effects noted in animal studies; however, limited human data are available. Use with caution.
- *Lactation:* Safety is unknown.
- *Children:* Can be used in children as young as 6 years.

Class: Anxiolytics

BuSpar   **buspirone**

INDICATIONS: Anxiolytic non-BZD used to treat GAD and PD

AVAILABLE FORMS: Tablet, 5, 10, 15, and 30 mg

DOSAGE: *Adults:* Starting dose, 7.5 mg PO bid, then increase by 5 mg/day every 2–3 days; maximum, 60 mg/day. *Children (6–17 yr)*: dose, 15–60 mg/day PO divided bid; maximum, 60 mg/day

ADMINISTRATION:
- PO with a glass of water.
- While discontinuation symptoms are minimal from *BuSpar*, it should not be stopped abruptly.
- There is little potential for abuse, tolerance, and physical or psychological dependence.

SIDE EFFECTS:
- *More common:* Dizziness, drowsiness headache, nervousness, dry mouth; decreased concentration, and weakness.
- *Less common*: Serotonin syndrome, extrapyramidal symptoms, hostility, and depression.

DRUG INTERACTIONS: This medicine may interact with the following medications:
- Absolute contraindications include MAOIs such as phenelzine (*Nardil*), tranylcypromine (*Parnate*), isocarboxazid (*Marplan*), and selegiline (*Eldepryl*).
- Monitor treatment with amiodarone, dilitazem, erythromycins, and verapamil.
- ▶**Alert**: This list may not describe all possible interactions. Instruct patients to provide a list of all medicines, herbs, nonprescription drugs, or dietary supplements used, and if they smoke, drink alcohol, or use illegal drugs.

PHARMACOKINETICS:
- The only drug of this anxiolytic, non-BZD class that is not chemically related to BZDs, barbiturates, or other sedative/anxiolytic drugs. It seems to have a high affinity for serotonin (5-HT1A) receptors but does not affect GABA binding. There is a moderate affinity for brain serotonin and D2-dopamine receptors.

Metabolism: Liver; CYP450 3A4
Excretion: Urine, feces
Half-life: 2–3 hr

PRECAUTIONS:
- See patients as often as necessary to ensure that the drug is working on the panic attacks, determine compliance, and review side effects.
- Instruct patients and families to watch for worsening depression or thoughts of suicide. Also, watch out for sudden or severe changes in feelings such as feeling anxious, agitated, panicky, irritated, hostile, aggressive, impulsive, severely restless, overly excited, hyperactive, or not being able to sleep. If this happens, especially at the beginning of antidepressant treatment or after a change in dose, patient should call the health care provider.
- Drowsiness or dizziness: Patients should not drive or use machinery or do anything that needs mental alertness until the effects of this medicine are known.
- Caution patients not to stand or sit up quickly, especially if older. This reduces the risk of dizzy or fainting spells. Alcohol may interfere with the effect of this medicine. Avoid alcoholic drinks.
- Caution should be exercised in the following:
  - Renal disease
  - Liver disease
  - Suicidal thoughts, plans, or attempts by patients or a family member
  - An unusual or allergic reaction to buspirone, other medicines, foods, dyes, or preservatives

PATIENT AND FAMILY EDUCATION:
- Store buspirone at room temperature away from moisture, heat, and light.

SPECIAL POPULATIONS:
- *Elderly:* Because buspirone is less sedating, older patients may tolerate it better than BZDs. The smallest effective dose should be used. Dose adjustment is necessary for patients with mild liver impairment and/or renal disease due to excessive metabolites excreted by the kidney. Use is contraindicated in patients with severe liver or kidney disease.
- *Pregnancy:* Category B; no teratogenic effects noted in animal studies; however, limited human data are available. Use with caution.
- *Lactation:* Safety is unknown.
- *Children:* Indicated for children 6–17 years of age.

Obsessive–Compulsive Disorder (OCD)

OVERVIEW

- Type of anxiety disorder where unreasonable thoughts and fears (obsessions) lead to repetitive behaviors (compulsions).
- Patients realize that the obsessions are not reasonable and may try to ignore or stop the obsessions causing increases in anxiety. They ultimately feel driven to perform compulsive acts in an effort to relieve the anxiety.
- The disorder may center on a theme, such as the fear of contamination by germs. To ease the fear, the person compulsively washes hands so much that dermatitis develops. Despite the person's efforts, the distressing thoughts of obsession returns, leading to more ritualistic behavior causing a vicious cycle characteristic of OCD.
- OCD is a chronic condition; therefore, treatment is continued for life.

- Treatment can be difficult, may not offer a cure, and may be needed for the rest of the person's life.
- OCD treatment can help bring symptoms under control so that they do not control the person's life. The two main treatments for OCD include psychotherapy and medication.
- CBT has been shown to be the most effective form of therapy for OCD and involves retraining thought patterns and routines so that compulsive behaviors are no longer needed to relieve anxiety.
- One CBT approach is exposure and response prevention. This involves gradually exposing person to a feared object or obsession, such as something dirty, while teaching the patient ways to cope with the resulting anxiety.

Psychopharmacology of OCD

- SSRIs are the *most common* first-line agents used with OCD, increasing the level of serotonin lacking in patients.
- TCAs (most specifically clomipramine) can be effective in treating OCD; however, the initial side effects of the drugs when first initiated (jitteriness and insomnia) can reduce patient adherence to therapy.
- It is not unusual to try several medications before finding one that works. To control symptoms, medications from different pharmacologic categories may be combined. Consult with a specialist as necessary.

- Behavioral therapies should be used together with drug therapy. These include CBT, exposure, relaxation techniques, pleasant mental imagery, and cognitive restructuring (learning to recognize and replace panic-inducing thoughts). Behavioral treatment appears to have long-lasting benefits.
- Regular exercise, adequate sleep, and regularly scheduled meals may help reduce the frequency of the attacks. Caffeine and other stimulants should be reduced or eliminated.

CLASS	DRUG
Selective Serotonin Reuptake Inhibitors (SSRIs)	First-Line Drug Therapy
	fluoxetine (*Prozac*)
	sertraline (*Zoloft*)
	paroxetine (*Paxil, Paxil CR*))
	paroxetine mesylate (*Pexeva*)
	fluvoxamine (*Luvox CR*)
	citalopram (*Celexa*)
Tricyclic Antidepressants (TCAs)	Drugs for Treatment Resistant Cases
	clomipramine (*Anafranil*)

OBSESSIVE–COMPULSIVE DISORDER

Class: Selective Serotonin Reuptake Inhibitors (SSRIs)

Prozac   **fluoxetine**

INDICATIONS: Used to treat MDD, OCD, bulimia nervosa, and PD

AVAILABLE FORMS: Capsule, 10, 20, and 40 mg; capsule, delayed release (*Prozac Weekly*), 90 mg; solution, 20 mg/5 mL

DOSAGE: *Immediate release* (Prozac Daily), starting dose 10 mg PO, daily for 7 days; maximum, 60 mg/day. *Capsule, delayed release (Prozac Weekly)*: 90 mg oral, once weekly, 7 days after last daily dose of 20 mg. *Extended release*: Not recommended for acute treatment

ADMINISTRATION:
- PO with a glass of water.
- Take with or without food.
- Take at regular intervals.
- Caution patients not to stop taking drug except on provider's advice.
- *Prozac Daily* may be prescribed for children as young as 7 years for selected conditions; *precautions do apply.*
- *Prozac Weekly* is not prescribed for children.
- Do not prescribe *Prozac Weekly* for acute treatment.
- Instruct patients to take missed dose as soon as possible. If it is almost time for the next dose, advise to take only that dose.

SIDE EFFECTS:
- *Most common*: Dizziness, headache, insomnia, somnolence, and change in sex drive or performance.
- *Less common*: Allergic reactions like skin rash; itching; or hives; swelling of the face; lips; or tongue; psoriasis; arthralgias; anorexia; feeling faint or lightheaded; falls nausea; dry mouth; constipation; dyspepsia; suicidal thoughts or other mood changes; unusual bleeding or bruising; fatigue; tremor; change in appetite; diarrhea; increased sweating; indigestion; and nausea.

DRUG INTERACTIONS: Most of the interactions occur with OTC cough and cold preparations. This medicine may also interact with the following medications.
- Absolute contraindications include MAOIs such as phenelzine (*Nardil*), tranylcypromine (*Parnate*), isocarboxazid (*Marplan*), and selegiline (*Eldepryl*).
- Avoid using with other SSRIs due to serotonin effect; SNRI drugs such as desvenlafaxine (*Pristiq*) and venlafaxine (*Effexor*); drugs with sympathomimetic properties such as phenylpropanolamine, pseudoephedrine, St. John's wort, haloperidol; and diazepam (*Valium*), any other antidepressants; and clopidogrel (*Plavix*).
- Exercise caution with cold medications, arrhythmia medications such as flecainide, aspirin, and other NSAIDs, and drugs used for analgesia with opioid properties.

▶**Alert**: This list may not describe all possible interactions. Instruct patients to provide a list of all medicines, herbs, nonprescription drugs, or dietary supplements used, and if they smoke, drink alcohol, or use illegal drugs.

PHARMACOKINETICS:
Metabolism: Liver; CYP450 2C19, 2D6 (primary) substrate; 2C19, 3A4 (weak) inhibitor; active metabolite
Excretion: Urine 80% (11.6% unchanged), feces 15%
Half-life: 4–6 days (fluoxetine), 9.3 days (norfluoxetine)

PRECAUTIONS:
- See patients as often as necessary to ensure that the drug is working on the panic attacks, determine compliance, and review side effects.
- Make sure patients realize that they need to take prescribed doses even if they do not feel better right away. It can take several weeks before they feel the full effect of the drug.
- Instruct patients and their families to watch for worsening depression or thoughts of suicide. Also watch out for sudden or severe changes in feelings such as feeling anxious, agitated, panicky, irritated, hostile, aggressive, impulsive, severely restless, overly excited, hyperactive, or not being able to sleep. If this happens, especially at the beginning of antidepressant treatment or after a change in dose, patient should call the health care provider.
- Drowsiness or dizziness: Patients should not drive or use machinery or do anything that needs mental alertness until the effects of this medicine are known.
- Caution patients not to stand or sit up quickly, especially if older. This reduces the risk of dizzy or fainting spells. Alcohol may interfere with the effect of this medicine. Avoid alcoholic drinks.
- Caution patients not to treat themselves for coughs, colds, or allergies without asking health care professional for advice. Some ingredients can increase possible side effects.
- Dry mouth: Chewing sugarless gum, sucking hard candy, and drinking plenty of water may help. Contact health care provider if the problem persists or is severe.
- Caution should be exercised in the following:
  - Bipolar disorder or a family history of bipolar disorder
  - Diabetes
  - Heart disease
  - Liver disease
  - Electroconvulsive therapy
  - Seizures (convulsions)
  - Suicidal thoughts, plans, or attempts by patients or a family member
  - An unusual or allergic reaction to fluoxetine, other medicines, foods, dyes, or preservatives
  - Pregnancy or trying to get pregnant
  - Breastfeeding

(cont.)

OBSESSIVE–COMPULSIVE DISORDER: Selective Serotonin Reuptake Inhibitors (SSRIs)

fluoxetine (*cont.*)

PATIENT AND FAMILY EDUCATION:
- Store at room temperature. Take any unused medication after the expiration date to the local pharmacy on drug give-back day. Avoid throwing the medication into the environment.
- Discuss any worsening anxiety, aggressiveness, impulsivity, or restlessness.
- Report any severe, abrupt onset or changes in symptoms to health professionals. May be reflective of increased risk of suicidal thinking.
- Caution for the concomitant use of NSAIDs, aspirin, warfarin, and any other drugs that alter platelets.

SPECIAL POPULATIONS:
- *Elderly:* No actual contraindications exist, but due to the long half-life of the drug, it has been placed on the Beers List of Potentially Inappropriate Medications for Geriatrics.
- *Pregnancy:* Category C; this is the longest used SSRI in pregnant women. Every attempt should be made to discontinue in the third trimester secondary to development of neonatal distress upon delivery.
- *Lactation:* Not approved.
- *Children:* Approved in pediatric population only for MDD and OCD. Monitoring for increased suicidal ideation is critical.

sertraline   *Zoloft*

INDICATIONS: Used primarily to treat depression but may also be used for OCD, PD, posttrauma stress, PMDD, or social anxiety

AVAILABLE FORMS: Tablet, 25, 50, and 100 mg

DOSAGE: Starting dose, 25 mg once daily; increase dose incrementally 25 mg per week; maximum, 200 mg daily.

ADMINISTRATION:
- PO with a glass of water.
- Take with or without food
- Take at regular intervals
- Caution patients not to stop taking drug except on provider's advice.
- May be prescribed for children as young as 6 years for selected conditions (25 mg/day); *precautions do apply.*
- Instruct patients to take missed dose as soon as possible. If it is almost time for the next dose, advise to take only that dose.

SIDE EFFECTS:
- *Most common:* Dizziness, headache, insomnia, somnolence, and change in sex drive or performance.
- *Less common:* Allergic reactions like skin rash; itching; or hives; swelling of the face; lips; or tongue; feeling faint or lightheaded; falls; hallucination; loss of contact with reality; seizures; suicidal thoughts or other mood changes; unusual bleeding or bruising; unusually weak or tired; vomiting; change in appetite; diarrhea; increased sweating; indigestion; nausea; and tremors.

DRUG INTERACTIONS: This medicine may interact with the following medications:
- Absolute contraindications include MAOIs such as phenelzine (*Nardil*), tranylcypromine (*Parnate*), isocarboxazid (*Marplan*), and selegiline (*Eldepryl*).
- Avoid using with SNRI agents, triptans, and and other SSRI agents.

- Caution with aspirin, NSAIDs (e.g., ibuprofen or naproxen), COX inhibitors, and other antiinflammatory drugs, St. John's wort.
- ▶**Alert:** This list may not describe all possible interactions. Instruct patients to provide a list of all medicines, herbs, nonprescription drugs, or dietary supplements used, and if they smoke, drink alcohol, or use illegal drugs.

PHARMACOKINETICS:
- SSRIs are metabolized in the liver by CYP P450 (CYP) enzymes.
- Highly bound to plasma proteins and have a large volume of distribution.
- May take 2–6 weeks for the drug to be fully effective.
- Addition of serotonergic medications to a patient's regimen must not occur until 2–3 weeks after discontinuation of an SSRI (some recommend a 5-week "washout" period prior to initiation of an MAOI).

Metabolism: Liver; CYP 2C19, 2D6, 3A4 substrate; 2D6 (weak), 3A4 (weak) inhibitor
Excretion: Urine 40–45% (none unchanged), feces 40–45% (12–14% unchanged)
Half-life: 26 hr

PRECAUTIONS:
- See patients as often as necessary to ensure that the drug is working on the panic attacks, determine compliance, and review side effects.
- Make sure patients realize that they need to take prescribed doses even if they do not feel better right away. It can take several weeks before they feel the full effect of the drug.
- Instruct patients and their families to watch for worsening depression or thoughts of suicide. Also, watch out for sudden or severe changes in feelings such as feeling anxious, agitated, panicky, irritated, hostile, aggressive, impulsive, severely restless, overly excited, hyperactive, or not being able to sleep. If this happens, especially at the beginning of antidepressant

(cont.)

sertraline (cont.)

treatment or after a change in dose, patient should call the health care provider.

- Drowsy or dizzy: Do not drive, use machinery, or do anything that needs mental alertness until the effects of this medicine are known.
- Caution patients not to stand or sit up quickly, especially if older. This reduces the risk of dizzy or fainting spells. Alcohol may interfere with the effect of this medicine. Avoid alcoholic drinks.
- Caution patients not to treat themselves for coughs, colds, or allergies without asking health care professional for advice. Some ingredients can increase possible side effects.
- Dry mouth: Chewing sugarless gum or sucking hard candy and drinking plenty of water may help. Contact health care provider if the problem persists or is severe.
- Caution should be exercised in the following:
  - Bipolar disorder or a family history of bipolar disorder
  - Diabetes
  - Heart disease
  - Liver disease
  - Electroconvulsive therapy
  - Seizures (convulsions)
  - Suicidal thoughts, plans, or attempts by patients or a family member
  - An unusual or allergic reaction to sertraline, other medicines, foods, dyes, or preservatives

- Pregnancy or trying to get pregnant
- Breastfeeding

PATIENT AND FAMILY EDUCATION:

- Store at room temperature. Take any unused medication after the expiration date to the local pharmacy on drug give-back day. Avoid throwing the medication into the environment.
- Discuss any worsening anxiety, aggressiveness, impulsivity, or restlessness with provider.
- Patients or families should report any severe, abrupt onset or changes in symptoms to health professionals. This may be reflective of increased risk of suicidal thinking.
- Caution for the concomitant use of NSAIDs, aspirin, warfarin, and any other drugs that alter platelets.

SPECIAL POPULATIONS:

- *Elderly:* Increased risk for hyponatremia
- *Hepatic impairment:* Dose adjustment necessary.
- *Pregnancy:* Category C; risks are associated with all SSRIs for neonatal complications if used in the third trimester.
- *Lactation:* Adverse reactions have not been reported; however, long-term effects have not been studied and the manufacturer recommends caution.
- *Children:* Approved for use in children aged 12 years or older; however, monitoring for increased suicidal ideation is critical.

Paxil, Paxil CR, Pexeva | **paroxetine, paroxetine mesylate**

INDICATIONS: Used to treat MDD, OCD, bulimia nervosa, and PD.

AVAILABLE FORMS: *Pexeva*: Tablet, 20, 30, and 40 mg; *Paxil*: Tablet, 10, 20, 30, and 40 mg; suspension 10 mg/5 mL; *Paxil CR*: Tablet, 12.5, 25, and 37.5 mg

DOSAGE: *Pexeva* and *Paxil*: 20 mg PO every morning, 10 mg in elderly patients; increase 10 mg/day weekly; maximum 50 mg/day; 40 mg/day in elderly patients. *Paxil CR*: 12.5 mg PO, daily, increase 12.5 mg/day weekly; maximum, 75 mg/day; 50 mg/day in elderly patients. No proven additional benefits at doses greater than 20 mg/day

ADMINISTRATION:

- PO with a glass of water.
- Do not break/crush or chew.
- Take with or without food.
- Take at regular intervals.
- Caution patients not to stop taking drug except on provider's advice.
- May be prescribed for children as young as 7 years for selected conditions; *precautions do apply.*
- Instruct patients to take missed dose as soon as possible. If it is almost time for the next dose, advise to take only that dose.

SIDE EFFECTS:

- *Most common:* Somnolence; headache; asthenia; dizziness; sweating; dry mouth; tremor; anorexia; nervousness; anxiety; abnormal vision; change in appetite; change in sex drive or performance; diarrhea; constipation; indigestion; and nausea.
- *Less common:* Suicidality, worsening depression, serotonin syndrome, seizures, hyponatremia, extrapyramidal symptoms, priapism, and acute angle glaucoma.

DRUG INTERACTIONS: Most of the interactions occur with OTC cough and cold preparations. This medicine may also interact with the following medications.

- Absolute contraindications include MAOIs such as phenelzine (*Nardil*), tranylcypromine (*Parnate*), isocarboxazid (*Marplan*), and selegiline (*Eldepryl*).
- Avoid using with other SSRIs due to serotonin effect; SNRI drugs such as desvenlafaxine (*Pristiq*) and venlafaxine (*Effexor*); drugs with sympathomimetic properties such as phenylpropanolamine, pseudoephedrine, St. John's wort, haloperidol; diazepam (*Valium*); any other antidepressants; and clopidogrel (*Plavix*).

(cont.)

OBSESSIVE–COMPULSIVE DISORDER: Selective Serotonin Reuptake Inhibitors (SSRIs)

paroxetine, paroxetine mesylate (*cont.*)

- Exercise caution with cold medications, arrhythmia medications such as flecainide, aspirin, and other NSAIDs, and drugs used for analgesia with opioid properties.
- ▶**Alert**: This list may not describe all possible interactions. Instruct patients to provide a list of all medicines, herbs, nonprescription drugs, or dietary supplements used, and if they smoke, drink alcohol, or use illegal drugs.

PHARMACOKINETICS:
Metabolism: Liver extensively; CYP450 2D6 substrate; 2D6 inhibitor
Excretion: Urine 64% (2% unchanged), feces 36% (less than 1% unchanged)
Half-life: 21 hr

PRECAUTIONS:
- See patients as often as necessary to ensure that the drug is working on the panic attacks, determine compliance, and review side effects.
- Make sure patients realize that they need to take prescribed doses even if they do not feel better right away. It can take several weeks before they feel the full effect of the drug.
- Instruct patients and families to watch for worsening depression or thoughts of suicide. Also, watch for sudden or severe changes in feelings such as feeling anxious, agitated, panicky, irritated, hostile, aggressive, impulsive, severely restless, overly excited, hyperactive, or not being able to sleep. If this happens, especially at the beginning of antidepressant treatment or after a change in dose, patient should call the health care provider.
- Drowsiness or dizziness: Patients should not drive or use machinery or do anything that needs mental alertness until the effects of this medicine are known.
- Caution patients not to stand or sit up quickly, especially if older. This reduces the risk of dizzy or fainting spells. Alcohol may interfere with the effect of this medicine. Avoid alcoholic drinks.
- Caution patients not to treat themselves for coughs, colds, or allergies without asking health care professional for advice. Some ingredients can increase possible side effects.

- Dry mouth: Chewing sugarless gum, sucking hard candy, and drinking plenty of water may help. Contact health care provider if the problem persists or is severe.
- Caution should be exercised in the following:
  - Bipolar disorder or a family history of bipolar disorder
  - Diabetes
  - Heart disease
  - Liver disease
  - Electroconvulsive therapy
  - Seizures (convulsions)
  - Suicidal thoughts, plans, or attempts by patients or a family member
  - An unusual or allergic reaction to paroxetine, other medicines, foods, dyes, or preservatives
  - Pregnancy or trying to get pregnant
  - Breastfeeding

PATIENT AND FAMILY EDUCATION:
- Store at room temperature. Take any unused medication after the expiration date to the local pharmacy on drug give-back day. Avoid throwing the medication into the environment.
- Shake the liquid form of paroxetine well just before you measure a dose. To get the correct dose, measure the liquid with a marked measuring spoon or medicine cup, not with a regular tablespoon. If a dose-measuring device is not available, ask the pharmacist for one.

SPECIAL POPULATIONS:
- *Elderly:* Due to increased C_{min} concentrations, up to 70–80% in the elderly, the initial dose should be reduced.
- *Renal and hepatic impairment:* The initial dose should be reduced in patients with severe renal and/or hepatic impairment. Titration upward should be slow and at intervals.
- *Pregnancy:* Category D; first trimester teratogenicity, neonatal withdrawal and serotonin syndrome in third trimester, persistent pulmonary HTN if greater than 20-weeks gestation.
- *Lactation:* Considered generally safe; substantial human data show no or minimal risk to breast milk production or to the infant.
- *Children:* Paxil CR is not indicated for children. Monitoring for increased suicidal ideation is critical if using regular *Paxil*.

fluvoxamine   *Luvox CR*

INDICATIONS: Used to treat OCD, social anxiety disorder

AVAILABLE FORMS: Capsule, extended-release, 100 mg, 150 mg

DOSAGE: Starting, 100 mg PO nightly; increase by 50 mg/day weekly; maximum, 300 mg/day

ADMINISTRATION:
- PO with a glass of water.
- Take with or without food
- Take at regular intervals
- Caution patients not to stop taking drug except on provider's advice.
- Not prescribed for children.

(cont.)

fluvoxamine (*cont.*)

- Instruct patients to take missed dose as soon as possible. If it is almost time for the next dose, advise to take only that dose.

SIDE EFFECTS:
- *Most common*: Somnolence; headache; asthenia; dizziness; sweating; dry mouth; tremor; anorexia; nervousness; anxiety; abnormal vision; change in appetite; change in sex drive or performance; diarrhea; constipation; indigestion; and nausea.
- *Less common*: Suicidality, worsening depression, serotonin syndrome, seizures, hyponatremia, extrapyramidal symptoms, priapism, and acute angle glaucoma.

DRUG INTERACTIONS: Most of the interactions occur with OTC cough and cold preparations. This medicine may also interact with the following medications.
- Absolute contraindications include MAOIs such as phenelzine (*Nardil*), tranylcypromine (*Parnate*), isocarboxazid (*Marplan*), and selegiline (*Eldepryl*).
- Avoid using with other SSRIs due to serotonin effect; SNRI drugs such as desvenlafaxine (*Pristiq*) and venlafaxine (*Effexor*); drugs with sympathomimetic properties such as phenylpropanolamine, pseudoephedrine, St. John's wort, haloperidol; diazepam (*Valium*), any other antidepressants; clopidogrel (*Plavix*), amoxicillin, erythromycins, and lansoprazole (*Prevacid*).
- Exercise caution with cold medications, NSAIDs, and drugs used for analgesia with opioid properties.
▶**Alert**: This list may not describe all possible interactions. Instruct patients to provide a list of all medicines, herbs, nonprescription drugs, or dietary supplements used, and if they smoke, drink alcohol, or use illegal drugs.

PHARMACOKINETICS:
Metabolism: Liver extensively; CYP450 1A2, 2D6 inhibitor
Excretion: Urine primarily (2% unchanged)
Half-life: 16.3 hr, 25.9 hr (elderly)

PRECAUTIONS:
- See patients as often as necessary to ensure that the drug is working on the panic attacks, determine compliance, and review side effects.
- Make sure patients realize that they need to take prescribed doses even if they do not feel better right away. It can take several weeks before they feel the full effect of the drug.
- Instruct patients and families to watch for worsening depression or thoughts of suicide. Also watch out for sudden or severe changes in feelings such as feeling anxious, agitated, panicky, irritated, hostile, aggressive, impulsive, severely restless, overly excited, hyperactive, or not being able to sleep. If this happens, especially at the beginning of antidepressant treatment or after a change in dose, patient should call the health care provider.
- Drowsiness or dizziness: Patients should not drive or use machinery or do anything that needs mental alertness until the effects of this medicine are known.
- Caution patients not to stand or sit up quickly, especially if older. This reduces the risk of dizzy or fainting spells. Alcohol may interfere with the effect of this medicine. Avoid alcoholic drinks.
- Caution patients not to treat themselves for coughs, colds, or allergies without asking health care professional for advice. Some ingredients can increase possible side effects.
- Dry mouth: Chewing sugarless gum, sucking hard candy, and drinking plenty of water may help. Contact health care provider if the problem persists or is severe.
- Caution should be exercised in the following:
  - Bipolar disorder or a family history of bipolar disorder
  - Diabetes
  - Heart disease
  - Liver disease
  - Electroconvulsive therapy
  - Seizures (convulsions)
  - Suicidal thoughts, plans, or attempts by patients or a family member
  - An unusual or allergic reaction to fluvoxamine, other medicines, foods, dyes, or preservatives
  - Pregnancy or trying to get pregnant
  - Breastfeeding

PATIENT AND FAMILY EDUCATION:
- Store at room temperature. Take any unused medication after the expiration date to the local pharmacy on drug give-back day. Avoid throwing the medication into the environment.

SPECIAL POPULATIONS:
- *Elderly:* Due to increased C_{min} concentrations, up to 70–80% in the elderly, the initial dose should be reduced.
- *Renal and hepatic impairment:* The initial dose should be reduced in patients with severe renal and/or hepatic impairment. Titration upward should be slow and at intervals.
- *Pregnancy:* Category D; first trimester teratogenicity, neonatal withdrawal and serotonin syndrome in third trimester, persistent pulmonary HTN if more than 20-weeks gestation.
- *Lactation:* Considered generally safe; substantial human data show no or minimal risk to breast milk production or to the infant.
- *Children:* Not indicated for children.

OBSESSIVE–COMPULSIVE DISORDER: Selective Serotonin Reuptake Inhibitors (SSRIs)

citalopram   *Celexa*

INDICATIONS: Used for MDD

AVAILABLE FORMS: Tablet, 10, 20, and 40 mg; oral solution, 10 mg/5 mL

DOSAGE: Starting dose, 20 mg once daily, increase dose incrementally 20 mg only once per week. Most patients reach efficacy at 40 mg daily; however, some may need 60 mg/day.

ADMINISTRATION:
- PO with a glass of water.
- Take with or without food.
- Take at regular intervals.
- Caution patients not to stop taking drug except on provider's advice.
- Not prescribed for children.
- Instruct patients to take missed dose as soon as possible. If it is almost time for the next dose, advise to take only that dose.

SIDE EFFECTS:
- *Most common*: Somnolence; headache; asthenia; dizziness; sweating; dry mouth; tremor; anorexia; nervousness; anxiety; abnormal vision; change in appetite; change in sex drive or performance; diarrhea; constipation; indigestion; and nausea.
- *Less common*: Suicidality, worsening depression, serotonin syndrome, seizures, hyponatremia, extrapyramidal symptoms, priapism, and acute angle glaucoma.

DRUG INTERACTIONS: Most of the interactions occur with OTC cough and cold preparations. This medicine may also interact with the following medications.
- Absolute contraindications include MAOIs such as phenelzine (*Nardil*), tranylcypromine (*Parnate*), isocarboxazid (*Marplan*), and selegiline (*Eldepryl*).
- Avoid using with other SSRIs due to serotonin effect; SNRI drugs such as desvenlafaxine (*Pristiq*) and venlafaxine (*Effexor*); drugs with sympathomimetic properties such as phenylpropanolamine, pseudoephedrine, St. John's wort, haloperidol; diazepam (*Valium*), any other antidepressants; and clopidogrel (*Plavix*), amoxicillin, erythromycins, and lansoprazole (*Prevacid*).
- Exercise caution with cold medications, NSAIDs, and drugs used for analgesia with opioid properties.
- ▶Alert: This list may not describe all possible interactions. Instruct patients to provide a list of all medicines, herbs, nonprescription drugs, or dietary supplements used, and if they smoke, drink alcohol, or use illegal drugs.

PHARMACOKINETICS:
Metabolism: Extensively metabolized in the liver in CYP450 2C19, 3A4 substrate; 2D6 (weak) inhibitor
Excretion: Urine primarily (10% unchanged), feces
Half-life: 35 hr

PRECAUTIONS:
- See patients as often as necessary to ensure that the drug is working on the panic attacks, determine compliance, and review side effects.
- Make sure patients realize that they need to take prescribed doses even if they do not feel better right away. It can take several weeks before they feel the full effect of the drug.
- Instruct patients and their families to watch for worsening depression or thoughts of suicide. Also watch out for sudden or severe changes in feelings such as feeling anxious, agitated, panicky, irritated, hostile, aggressive, impulsive, severely restless, overly excited, hyperactive, or not being able to sleep. If this happens, especially at the beginning of antidepressant treatment or after a change in dose, patient should call the health care provider.
- Drowsiness or dizziness: Patients should not drive or use machinery or do anything that needs mental alertness until the effects of this medicine are known.
- Caution patients not to stand or sit up quickly, especially if older. This reduces the risk of dizzy or fainting spells. Alcohol may interfere with the effect of this medicine. Avoid alcoholic drinks.
- Caution patients not to treat themselves for coughs, colds, or allergies without asking health care professional for advice. Some ingredients can increase possible side effects.
- Dry mouth: Chewing sugarless gum, sucking hard candy, and drinking plenty of water may help. Contact health care provider if the problem persists or is severe.
- Caution should be exercised in the following:
  - Bipolar disorder or a family history of bipolar disorder
  - Diabetes
  - Heart disease
  - Liver disease
  - Electroconvulsive therapy
  - Seizures (convulsions)
  - Suicidal thoughts, plans, or attempts by patients or a family member
  - An unusual or allergic reaction to citalopram, other medicines, foods, dyes, or preservatives
  - Pregnancy or trying to get pregnant
  - Breastfeeding

PATIENT AND FAMILY EDUCATION:
- Store at room temperature. Take any unused medication after the expiration date to the local pharmacy on drug give-back day. Avoid throwing the medication into the environment.
- Try to take the medicine at the same time each day. Follow the directions on the prescription label. To get the correct dose of liquid citalopram, measure the liquid with a marked measuring spoon or medicine cup, not with a regular tablespoon. If there is no dose-measuring device available, ask the pharmacist for one.

(cont.)

citalopram (*cont.*)

SPECIAL POPULATIONS:
- *Elderly:* A dose of 20 mg daily is recommended for geriatric patients.
- *Renal and hepatic impairment:* The initial dose should be reduced in patients with severe renal and/or hepatic impairment. Half-life is doubled in patients with hepatic impairment. Titration upward should be slow and at intervals.

- *Pregnancy:* Category C; potential for persistent pulmonary HTN if more than 20-weeks gestation.
- *Lactation:* Excreted in human breast milk, some reports of infant somulence.
- *Children:* Not indicated for children.

Class: Tricyclic Antidepressants (TCAs)

Due to the class side effects, especially on the cardiac system, TCAs should be used only if the SSRI or SNRI classes fail to show any improvement in symptom profile

Aanafranil — **clomipramine**

INDICATIONS: Used to treat obsessions and OCD

AVAILABLE FORMS: Capsules

DOSAGE: *Adults:* Starting dose, 25 mg PO daily, then increase by 25 mg/day every 4–7 days; maximum, 100 mg/day in first 2 weeks. Maintenance dose, generally 250 mg/day; taper dose gradually to discontinue. *Children:* 100–200 mg PO nightly; starting dose, 25 mg PO daily, then increase by 25 mg/day every 4–7 days; maximum, 3 mg/kg/day up to 100 mg/day in first 2 weeks; maintenance dose, up to 200 mg/day.

ADMINISTRATION:
- PO with a glass of water and on a full stomach to minimize GI side effects.
- Do not abruptly stop taking the medication.
- Approved for children 10 years and above.
- Re-evaluate periodically the need for the medication.

SIDE EFFECTS:
- *More common:* Drowsiness, dizziness, constipation; nausea/vomiting, urinary retention or frequency, libido changes, weight gain, general nervousness, and galactorrhea.
- *Less common:* Cardiac arrhythmias, extrapyramidal symptoms, clotting disturbances, worsening depression, suicidality, hyperthermia, and hypertension.

DRUG INTERACTIONS: This medicine may interact with the following medications:
- Absolute contraindications include class 1A antiarrhythmics, MAOIs like phenelzine (*Nardil*), tranylcypromine (*Parnate*), isocarboxazid (*Marplan*), and selegiline (*Eldepryl*).
- Avoid using with cimetadine, amiodarone, clarithromycin, haloperidol, and St. John's wort.
- ▶ **Alert:** This list may not describe all possible interactions. Instruct patients to provide a list of all medicines, herbs, nonprescription drugs, or dietary supplements used, and if they smoke, drink alcohol, or use illegal drugs.

PHARMACOKINETICS:
- TCAs are thought to work by inhibiting reuptake of norepinephrine and serotonin in the CNS, which potentiates the neurotransmitters. They also have significant anticholinergics, antihistaminic, and alpha-adrenergic activity on the cardiac system. These classes of antidepressants also possess class 1A antiarrhythmic activity, which can lead to depression of cardiac conduction potentially resulting in heart block or ventricular arrhythmias

Metabolism: Extensively metabolized in the liver within CYP450: 1A2, 2C19, 2D6 (primary), 3A4 substrate

Excretion: Urine 66%, feces

Half-life: 32 hr (clomipramine), 69 hr (desmethylclomipramine); half-life may be prolonged at upper end of dosing range due to accumulation

PRECAUTIONS:
- See patients as often as necessary to ensure that the drug is working on the OCD, determine compliance, and review side effects.
- Instruct patients and families to watch for worsening depression or thoughts of suicide. Also, watch out for sudden or severe changes in feelings such as feeling anxious, agitated, panicky, irritated, hostile, aggressive, impulsive, severely restless, overly excited, hyperactive, or not being able to sleep. If this happens, especially at the beginning of antidepressant treatment or after a change in dose, patient should call the health care provider.
- Drowsiness or dizziness: Patients should not drive or use machinery or do anything that needs mental alertness until the effects of this medicine are known. Other medications that cause drowsiness can add to the drowsiness of chlorimipramine.
- Caution patients not to stand or sit up quickly, especially if older. This reduces the risk of dizzy or fainting spells. Alcohol may interfere

(cont.)

clomipramine (*cont.*)

with the effect of this medicine. Avoid alcoholic drinks.

- Do not abruptly withdraw this drug as it may cause headache, nausea, and malaise.
- Advise to protect skin from ultraviolet light due to increased skin sensitivity.
- Grapefruit and grapefruit juice may interact with chlorimipramine.
- Caution should be exercised in the following:
  - MDD, psychosis, or bipolar affective disorder
  - Contraindicated in patients with a recent myocardial infarction
  - Blood dyscrasias
  - Respiratory disease
  - Heart disease
  - Liver disease
  - Seizures (convulsions)
  - Psychoses or schizophrenia
  - Suicidal thoughts, plans, or attempts by patients or a family member
  - An unusual or allergic reaction to desipramine, other medicines, foods, dyes, or preservatives

PATIENT AND FAMILY EDUCATION:

- Store chloramipramine at room temperature away from moisture and heat.
- Stopping this medication suddenly could result in unpleasant side effects.
- Take the missed dose as soon as remembered. If it is almost time for the next dose, skip the missed dose and take the medicine at the next regularly scheduled time. *Do not* take extra medicine to make up the missed dose.

SPECIAL POPULATIONS:

- *Elderly:* Older patients may be more sensitive to the effects of TCAs. The smallest effective dose should be used. Caution in administration with significant renal and/or liver disease. Dose adjustments may be necessary. Monitor creatinine and liver functions.
- *Pregnancy:* Category C; unknown effects as there is limited study.
- *Lactation:* Excreted in human breast milk; use caution.
- *Children:* Approved for children 10 years and older.

Phobias

OVERVIEW

- An overwhelming and unreasonable fear of something that poses minimal real danger (e.g., large, open spaces, certain social situations, or more specific items, such as snakes, elevators or flying).
- A phobia is long-lasting, causes intense physical and psychological distress, and can affect ability to function normally.
- Not all phobias require treatment, but if a phobia affects normal functioning in daily life, a person may require treatment.
- Phobias are diagnosed in 13% of population in the USA.
  - Social phobia usually develops early in life, most often between the ages of 11 and 15, and almost never after age 25. Specific phobias having to do with the environment or personal injury also first appear in childhood—as early as age 5. Fear of tunnels, elevators, bridges, flying, or driving and other situational phobias usually develop by the mid-20s.
  - Phobias affect both sexes, but women and girls are twice as likely to have social phobia than men and boys. Women are also more likely to be diagnosed with agoraphobia, while men are less likely to seek help for anxiety-related disorders.
- If someone in a person's immediate family has a specific phobia, they are more likely to develop the same phobia.

- Having a phobia may cause other problems, including:
  - The person may avoid social situations and public places. Financial, professional and interpersonal problems can result from social phobia.
  - Depression; avoiding enjoyable activities may lead a person to become depressed.
  - Substance abuse; some people with phobias turn to alcohol or other drugs to deal with stress.
- The goal of phobia treatment is to reduce fear and anxiety to help the person better manages reactions to the object or situation that causes them.
  - *Behavior therapy*
  - *Desensitization or exposure therapy:* Used to change the response to the object or situation that is feared. Gradual repeated exposure to the cause of phobia may help person control their anxiety. For example, if a person is afraid of spiders, therapy may progress from simply thinking about spiders to looking at pictures of spiders, to going outside to look at actual spiders, and finally to touching a spider
  - *Cognitive-behavioral therapy:* Involves working with a therapist to learn ways to view and cope with the feared object or situation differently. The person can learn alternative beliefs about the specific fear. Special emphasis is made on learning to develop control of thoughts and feelings.

Acute treatment: Specific phobias usually are treated with behavioral therapy. Social phobias may be treated with antidepressants or beta-blockers, along with behavior therapy. Agoraphobia, especially when it is accompanied by a PD, is usually treated with SSRIs and behavior therapy.

Chronic treatment: Childhood fears, such as fear the dark, monsters, or being left alone, are common, and most children outgrow them. However, if a child has a persistent, excessive fear that limits ability to function in daily life, the child may need treatment.

Psychopharmacology of Phobias

CLASS	DRUG
Beta-Blockers	**Drugs Used for Short-Term Treatment**
	propranolol (*Inderal*)
Benzodiazepines (BZDs)	**Drugs Used for Short-Term Treatments**
	alprazolam (*Xanax/Xanax XR/Niravam*)
	lorazepam (*Ativan*)
	diazepam (*Valium*)
	chlordiazepoxide (*Librium*)
Selective Serotonin Reuptake Inhibitors (SSRIs)	**First-Line Drug Therapy**
	sertraline (*Zoloft*)
	fluoxetine (*Prozac*)
	paroxetine (*Paxil*)
	paroxetine mesylate (*Pexeva*)
	fluvoxamine (*Luvox*)
	citalopram (*Celexa*)
	escitalopram (*Lexapro*)
Serotonin and Norepinephrine Reuptake Inhibitors (SNRIs)	**First-Line Drug Therapy**
	venlafaxine (*Effexor, Effexor XR*)
Tricyclic Antidepressants (TCAs)	**Drugs for Treatment Resistant Cases**
	imipramine (*Tofranil*)
	desipramine (*Norpramin*)
	clomipramine (*Anafranil*)

PHOBIAS

Class: Beta-Blockers

Inderal	**propranolol**

INDICATIONS: Primarily used as cardiac drug but also useful for treating "stage fright." Due to its ability to slow heart rate, it can produce a calming effect and decrease anxiousness prior to a performance.

AVAILABLE FORMS: Tablets and oral solution

DOSAGE: Single dose of 5–10 mg orally taken 20–30 min prior to the anxiety-producing event.

ADMINISTRATION:
- PO with a glass of water.
- Not appropriate for children.

SIDE EFFECTS:
- *More common:* Fatigue, dizziness, constipation; bradycardia, hypotension, depression, insomnia, weakness, disorientation, nausea, diarrhea; allergic reaction, purpura, alopecia, and impotence.

- *Less common:* Congestive heart failure, severe bradycardia, bronchospasm, exfoliative skin disorders, and Raynaud's phenomena.

DRUG INTERACTIONS: This medicine may interact with the following medications:
- Absolute contraindications include thoridazine.
- Avoid using with cimetadine, central alpha-2 agonists, COX-2 inhibitors, fibric acid derivatives, opioid analgesics, insulin, and NSAIDs.
▶**Alert:** This list may not describe all possible interactions. Instruct patients to provide a list of all medicines, herbs, nonprescription drugs, or dietary supplements used, and if they smoke, drink alcohol, or use illegal drugs.

PHARMACOKINETICS:
- Beta-blockers such as propranolol nonselectively antagonize beta-1 and beta-2 adrenergic receptors. Beta-1-antagonism in the heart

(cont.)

PHOBIAS: Beta-Blockers

proparanolol (cont.)

results in a slower heart rate and decreased force of contraction.

Metabolism: Liver extensively; CYP 1A2, 2C19, and 2D6 (primary)

Excretion: Urine (less than 1% unchanged)

Half-life: 3–5 hr, 8–11 hr (ER)

PRECAUTIONS:

- Advise clients to take a trial dose at home so they can predict the drug's effects when encountering the phobic situation.
- Drowsiness or dizziness: Patients should not drive or use machinery or do anything that needs mental alertness until the effects of this medicine are known.
- Caution patients not to stand or sit up quickly, especially if older. This reduces the risk of dizzy or fainting spells. Alcohol may interfere with the effect of this medicine. Avoid alcoholic drinks.
- Caution should be exercised in the following:
  - Respiratory disease—especially asthma
  - Heart disease
  - Diabetes mellitus
  - Liver disease

- An unusual or allergic reaction to propranolol, other medicines, foods, dyes, or preservatives

PATIENT AND FAMILY EDUCATION:

- Store propranolol at room temperature away from moisture, heat, and light.
- Always take this medication with a full glass of water.
- To get the correct dose, measure the liquid with a marked measuring spoon or medicine cup, not with a regular tablespoon. If a dose-measuring device is not available, ask the pharmacist for one.

SPECIAL POPULATIONS:

- *Elderly:* Exercise caution with propranolol *(Inderal)* in the elderly due to decreased end-organ function, along with other drug therapy. Dose adjustment is necessary for patients with liver impairment and/or renal disease due to excessive metabolites excreted by the kidneys.
- *Pregnancy:* Category C.
- *Lactation:* Excreted in human breast milk, caution advised.
- *Children:* Not indicated for children.

Class: Benzodiazepines (BZDs)

alprazolam   *Xanax, Xanax XR, and Niravam*

INDICATIONS: Short-acting BZD used to treat GADs and PD. May be used as a short-term adjunct to an SSRI while waiting for the therapeutic effects of the SSRI to develop.

AVAILABLE FORMS: Tablet, 0.25, 0.5, 1, and 2 mg; extended-release capsule, 0.5, 1, and 2 mg; melt, 0.5, 1, 2, and 3 mg

DOSAGE: *Xanax:* Starting dose, 0.25 to 0.5 mg up to 2–3 times daily; maximum, 4 mg daily. Can be increased every 3–4 days. Treatment should be limited to as short a period as possible (less than 4 months) and/or re-evaluated for continued use. *Xanax XR:* Starting dose 0.5–1 mg PO, daily, can increase up to 1 mg/day every 3–4 days. *Niravam (melt):* Starting dose, 0.25 to 0.5 mg up to 2–3 times daily; maximum, 4 mg daily. Can be increased every 3–4 days.

ADMINISTRATION:

- PO with a glass of water.
- Do not crush, cut, or chew extended-release tablets.
- Orally disintegrating form *(Niravam)* has special instructions.
- Concentrated liquid must be measured with a special dose-measuring spoon or cup.
- Do not abruptly stop taking the medication.
- Not prescribed for children.
- Use lowest effective dose for shortest duration.

- Alprazolam can be habit forming; do not increase dosage without guidance from the health care provider.

SIDE EFFECTS:

- *More common:* Drowsiness, lightheadedness, dry mouth; headache, changes in bowel habits, sialorrhea, amnesia, and changes in appetite.
- *Less common:* Syncope, tachycardia, seizures, respiratory depression, dependency, withdrawal syndrome, and suicidal ideation.

DRUG INTERACTIONS: This medicine may interact with the following medications:

- Absolute contraindications include clarithromycin, fluvoxamine, and ketoconazole.
- Avoid using with calcium channel blockers, erythromycins, tamoxifen, and zafirlukast.

▶**Alert:** This list may not describe all possible interactions. Instruct patients to provide a list of all medicines, herbs, nonprescription drugs, or dietary supplements used, and if they smoke, drink alcohol, or use illegal drugs.

PHARMACOKINETICS:

- BZDs enhance the activity of GABA, a major CNS neurotransmitter, known to open CNS Cl⁻ channels leading to an inhibition of subsequent CNS neuronal signaling. BZDs with similar action can differ in their potency and rate of absorption.

(cont.)

PHOBIAS: Benzodiazepines (BZDs)

alprazolam (cont.)

Metabolism: By the liver in the CYP450 3A4
Excretion: Urine
Half-life: 11.2 hr, 16.3 hr (elderly), 19.7 hr (alcoholic liver disease)

PRECAUTIONS:
- See patients as often as necessary to ensure that the drug is working on the panic attacks, determine compliance, and review side effects.
- Instruct patients and their families to watch for worsening depression or thoughts of suicide. Also watch out for sudden or severe changes in feelings such as feeling anxious, agitated, panicky, irritated, hostile, aggressive, impulsive, severely restless, overly excited, hyperactive, or not being able to sleep. If this happens, especially at the beginning of antidepressant treatment or after a change in dose, patient should call the health care provider.
- Drowsiness or dizziness: Patients should not drive or use machinery or do anything that needs mental alertness until the effects of this medicine are known.
- Caution patients not to stand or sit up quickly, especially if older. This reduces the risk of dizzy or fainting spells. Alcohol may interfere with the effect of this medicine. Avoid alcoholic drinks.
- Do not abruptly withdraw this drug as it may cause seizures.
- Caution should be exercised in the following:
  - MDD, psychosis, or bipolar affective disorder
  - Respiratory disease
  - Heart disease
  - Liver disease
  - Seizures (convulsions)
  - Suicidal thoughts, plans, or attempts by patients or a family member
  - An unusual or allergic reaction to alprazolam, other medicines, foods, dyes, or preservatives

PATIENT AND FAMILY EDUCATION:
- Store alprazolam at room temperature away from moisture, heat, and light. Remove any cotton from the bottle of disintegrating tablets, and keep the bottle tightly closed.
- Alprazolam may be habit forming and *should be used only by the person it was prescribed for.* Alprazolam should never be shared with another person, especially someone who has a history of drug abuse or addiction. Keep the medication in a secure place where others cannot get to it.
- Do not purchase alprazolam on the Internet or outside of the USA as dangerous ingredients may be present. Some purchases of alprazolam from the Internet have been found to contain haloperidol *(Haldol)*, an antipsychotic drug.

SPECIAL POPULATIONS:
- *Elderly:* Older patients may be more sensitive to the effects of BZDs. The smallest effective dose should be used. Dose adjustment is necessary for patients with liver impairment and/or renal disease due to excessive metabolites excreted by the kidney. Due to increased risk of sedation leading to falls and fractures, BZDs are included on the Beers List of Potentially Inappropriate Medications for Geriatrics.
- *Pregnancy:* Category D; can cause teratogenic fetal effects. Infants born to mothers taking BZDs may be at risk for withdrawal symptoms in the postnatal period.
- *Lactation:* Excreted in human breast milk; infants can become lethargic and lose weight
- *Children:* Not indicated for use in children younger than 18 years.

Ativan **lorazepam**

INDICATIONS: Used to treat GADs and PD

AVAILABLE FORMS: Tablet, 0.5, 1, and 2 mg

DOSAGE: *Adults:* 2–3 mg/day PO/IM/IV divided bid-tid; 1–2 mg/day PO/IM/IV divided bid-tid in elderly patients; maximum, 10 mg/day. Periodically assess the need for treatment and taper the dose gradually to discontinue if prolonged treatment is necessary. Treatment should be limited to as short a period as possible (less than 4 months) and/or re-evaluated for continued use. *Children:* 0.05 mg/kg PO/IV q4–8 hr; maximum, 2 mg/dose. Periodically assess the need for treatment and taper the dose gradually to discontinue if prolonged treatment is necessary.

ADMINISTRATION:
- PO with a glass of water.
- Do not abruptly stop taking the medication.
- Use lowest effective dose for shortest duration.
- Lorazepam can be habit forming; do not increase dosage without guidance from the health care provider.

SIDE EFFECTS:
- *More common:* Drowsiness, lightheadedness, dry mouth; headache, changes in bowel habits, sialorrhea, amnesia, and changes in appetite.
- *Less common:* Syncope, tachycardia, seizures, respiratory depression, dependency, withdrawal syndrome, and suicidal ideation.

DRUG INTERACTIONS: This medicine may interact with the following medications:
- Absolute contraindications include clarithromycin, fluvoxamine, and ketoconazole.
- Avoid using with calcium channel blockers, erythromycins, tamoxifen, and zafirlukast.

(cont.)

PHOBIAS: Benzodiazepines (BZDs)

lorazepam (cont.)

▶**Alert**: This list may not describe all possible interactions. Instruct patients to provide a list of all medicines, herbs, nonprescription drugs, or dietary supplements used, and if they smoke, drink alcohol, or use illegal drugs.

PHARMACOKINETICS:
- BZDs enhance the activity of GABA, a major CNS neurotransmitter, known to open CNS Cl⁻ channels leading to an inhibition of subsequent CNS neuronal signaling. BZDs with similar action can differ in their potency and rate of absorption.

Metabolism: Liver with the CYP450; exact mechanism is unknown
Excretion: Urine
Half-life: 14 hr

PRECAUTIONS:
- See patients as often as necessary to ensure that the drug is working on the panic attacks, determine compliance, and review side effects.
- Instruct patients and their families to watch for worsening depression or thoughts of suicide. Also watch out for sudden or severe changes in feelings such as feeling anxious, agitated, panicky, irritated, hostile, aggressive, impulsive, severely restless, overly excited, hyperactive, or not being able to sleep. If this happens, especially at the beginning of antidepressant treatment or after a change in dose, patient should call the health care provider.
- Drowsiness or dizziness: Patients should not drive or use machinery or do anything that needs mental alertness until the effects of this medicine are known.
- Caution patients not to stand or sit up quickly, especially if older. This reduces the risk of dizzy or fainting spells. Alcohol may interfere with the effect of this medicine. Avoid alcoholic drinks.
- Do not abruptly withdraw this drug as it may cause seizures.

- Caution should be exercised in the following:
  - Heart disease
  - Liver disease
  - Seizures (convulsions)
  - Suicidal thoughts, plans, or attempts by patients or a family member
  - An unusual or allergic reaction to alprazolam, other medicines, foods, dyes, or preservatives

PATIENT AND FAMILY EDUCATION:
- Store lorazepam at room temperature away from moisture, heat, and light. Remove any cotton from the bottle of disintegrating tablets, and keep the bottle tightly closed.
- Lorazepam may be habit forming and *should be used only by the person it was prescribed for.* Lorazepam should never be shared with another person, especially someone who has a history of drug abuse or addiction. Keep the medication in a secure place where others cannot get to it.
- Do not purchase lorazepam on the Internet or outside of the USA as dangerous ingredients may be present.

SPECIAL POPULATIONS:
- *Elderly:* Older patients may be more sensitive to the effects of BZDs. The smallest effective dose should be used. Dose adjustment is necessary for patients with liver impairment and/or renal disease due to excessive metabolites excreted by the kidney. Due to increased risk of sedation leading to falls and fractures, BZDs are included on the Beers List of Potentially Inappropriate Medications for Geriatrics.
- *Pregnancy:* Category D; can cause teratogenic fetal effects. Infants born to mothers taking BZDs may be at risk for withdrawal symptoms in the postnatal period.
- *Lactation:* Excreted in human breast milk; infants can become lethargic and lose weight.
- *Children:* Not indicated for use in children younger than 18 years.

diazepam   *Valium*

INDICATIONS: Short-acting BZD used to treat GADs and PD

AVAILABLE FORMS: Tablet, 2, 5, and 10 mg

DOSAGE: *Adults:* 2–10 mg PO bid-qid; alternative, 2–10 mg IM/IV q3–4 hr prn.

ADMINISTRATION:
- PO with a glass of water.
- Do not abruptly stop taking the medication.
- Not prescribed for children.
- Use lowest effective dose for shortest duration.
- Diazepam can be habit forming; do not increase dosage without guidance from the health care provider.

SIDE EFFECTS:
- Syncope, tachycardia, seizures, respiratory depression, coma, dependency, abuse, withdrawal if abrupt D/C, suicidal ideation, and hypomania/mania
- *Common reactions:* Drowsiness, lightheadedness, dry mouth; depression, headache, constipation; diarrhea; confusion, nausea, vomiting, insomnia, tachycardia, nasal congestion, blurred vision, hypotension, rigidity, sialorrhea, dermatitis, syncope, ataxia, amnesia, impaired coordination, irritability, altered libido, dysarthria, appetite change, weight changes, and urinary hesitancy

(cont.)

diazepam (cont.)

DRUG INTERACTIONS: This medicine may interact with the following medications:
- Absolute contraindications include clarithromycin, fluvoxamine, and ketoconazole.
- Avoid using with calcium channel blockers, erythromycins, tamoxifen, and zafirlukast.

▶**Alert:** This list may not describe all possible interactions. Instruct patients to provide a list of all medicines, herbs, nonprescription drugs, or dietary supplements used, and if they smoke, drink alcohol, or use illegal drugs.

PHARMACOKINETICS:
- BZDs enhance the activity of GABA, a major CNS neurotransmitter, known to open CNS Cl⁻channels leading to an inhibition of subsequent CNS neuronal signaling. BZDs with similar action can differ in their potency and rate of absorption.

Metabolism: Extensively metabolized by the liver within the CYP450: 2C19, 3A4 substrate. The active metabolites include desmethyldiazepam.

Excretion: Urine

Half-life: 30–60 hr (diazepam), 30–100 hr (desmethyldiazepam)

PRECAUTIONS:
- See patients as often as necessary to ensure that the drug is working on the panic attacks, determine compliance, and review side effects.
- Instruct patients and their families to watch for worsening depression or thoughts of suicide. Also, watch out for sudden or severe changes in feelings such as feeling anxious, agitated, panicky, irritated, hostile, aggressive, impulsive, severely restless, overly excited, hyperactive, or not being able to sleep. If this happens, especially at the beginning of antidepressant treatment or after a change in dose, patient should call the health care provider.
- Drowsiness or dizziness: Patients should not drive or use machinery or do anything that needs mental alertness until the effects of this medicine are known.
- Caution patients not to stand or sit up quickly, especially if older. This reduces the risk of dizzy or fainting spells. Alcohol may interfere

with the effect of this medicine. Avoid alcoholic drinks.
- Do not abruptly withdraw this drug as it may cause seizures.
- Caution should be exercised in the following:
  - MDD, psychosis, or bipolar affective disorder
  - Respiratory disease
  - Heart disease
  - Liver disease
  - Seizures (convulsions)
  - Suicidal thoughts, plans, or attempts by patients or a family member
  - An unusual or allergic reaction to diazepam, other medicines, foods, dyes, or preservatives

PATIENT AND FAMILY EDUCATION:
- Store diazepam at room temperature away from moisture, heat, and light. Remove any cotton from the bottle of disintegrating tablets, and keep the bottle tightly closed.
- Diazepam may be habit forming and *should be used only by the person it was prescribed for.* Diazepam should never be shared with another person, especially someone who has a history of drug abuse or addiction. Keep the medication in a secure place where others cannot get to it.
- Do not purchase diazepam on the Internet or outside of the USA as dangerous ingredients may be present. Some purchases of alprazolam from the Internet have been found to contain haloperidol *(Haldol)*, an antipsychotic drug.

SPECIAL POPULATIONS:
- *Elderly:* Older patients may be more sensitive to the effects of BZDs. The smallest effective dose should be used. Dose adjustment is necessary for patients with liver impairment and/or renal disease due to excessive metabolites excreted by the kidneys.
- *Pregnancy:* Category D; can cause teratogenic fetal effects. Infants born to mothers taking BZDs may be at risk for withdrawal symptoms in the postnatal period.
- *Lactation:* Excreted in human breast milk, infants can become lethargic and lose weight.
- *Children:* Not indicated for use in children younger than 18 years.

Librium | **chlordiazepoxide**

INDICATIONS: Used to treat GADs

AVAILABLE FORMS: Capsule

DOSAGE: *Anxiety, mild–moderate*: 5–10 mg PO tid-qid; Start with 5 mg daily to bid in elderly or debilitated patients, then gradually increase to 5 mg PO bid-qid. *Anxiety, severe*: 20–25 mg PO tid-qid; start with 5 mg daily to bid in elderly or debilitated patients, then gradually increase to 5 mg PO bid-qid. *Children (greater than 6 years)*: start with 5 mg PO bid. May increase the dose to 10 mg bid-tid.

- Periodically assess the need for treatment and taper the dose gradually to discontinue if prolonged treatment is necessary.

ADMINISTRATION:
- PO with a glass of water.
- Do not abruptly stop taking the medication.
- Use lowest effective dose for shortest duration.
- Chlordiazepoxide can be habit forming; do not increase dosage without guidance from the health care provider.

(cont.)

PHOBIAS: Benzodiazepines (BZDs)

chlordiazepoxide (*cont.*)

SIDE EFFECTS:

- *More common:* Drowsiness, ataxia, confusion, skin eruptions, edema, menstrual irregularities, nausea, constipation; extrapyramidal effects, libido changes, and paradoxical stimulation.
- *Less common:* Dependency abuse, withdrawal if abruptly stopped after long-term use, syncope, hepatic impairment, and blood dyscrasias.

DRUG INTERACTIONS: This medicine may interact with the following medications:

- Avoid using with cimetadine, clarithromycin, and ketoconazole.

▶ **Alert:** This list may not describe all possible interactions. Instruct patients to provide a list of all medicines, herbs, nonprescription drugs, or dietary supplements used, and if they smoke, drink alcohol, or use illegal drugs.

PHARMACOKINETICS:

- BZDs enhance the activity of GABA, a major CNS neurotransmitter, known to open CNS Cl⁻ channels leading to an inhibition of subsequent CNS neuronal signaling. BZDs with similar action can differ in their potency and rate of absorption.

Metabolism: Extensively metabolized by the liver in the CYP450 particularly the 3A4 (partial) substrate

Excretion: Urine (3–6% unchanged)

Half-life: 5–30 hr (chlordiazepoxide), 3–200 hr (active metabolites)

PRECAUTIONS:

- See patients as often as necessary to ensure that the drug is working on the panic attacks, determine compliance, and review side effects.
- Instruct patients and families to watch for worsening depression or thoughts of suicide. Also watch out for sudden or severe changes in feelings such as feeling anxious, agitated, panicky, irritated, hostile, aggressive, impulsive, severely restless, overly excited, hyperactive, or not being able to sleep. If this happens, especially at the beginning of antidepressant treatment or after a change in dose, patient should call the health care provider.

- Drowsiness or dizziness: Patients should not drive or use machinery or do anything that needs mental alertness until the effects of this medicine are known.
- Caution patients not to stand or sit up quickly, especially if older. This reduces the risk of dizzy or fainting spells. Alcohol may interfere with the effect of this medicine. Avoid alcoholic drinks.
- Do not abruptly withdraw this drug as it may cause seizures.
- Caution should be exercised in the following:
  - Heart disease
  - Liver disease
  - Seizures (convulsions)
  - Suicidal thoughts, plans, or attempts by patients or a family member
  - An unusual or allergic reaction to diazepam, other medicines, foods, dyes, or preservatives

PATIENT AND FAMILY EDUCATION:

- Store chlordiazepoxide at room temperature away from moisture, heat, and light. Remove any cotton from the bottle of disintegrating tablets, and keep the bottle tightly closed.
- Chlordiazepoxide may be habit forming and *should be used only by the person it was prescribed for.* Chlordiazepoxide should never be shared with another person, especially someone who has a history of drug abuse or addiction. Keep the medication in a secure place where others cannot get to it.

SPECIAL POPULATIONS:

- *Elderly:* Older patients may be more sensitive to the effects of BZDs. The smallest effective dose should be used. Dose adjustment is necessary for patients with liver impairment and/or renal disease due to excessive metabolites excreted by the kidneys.
- *Pregnancy:* Category D; can cause teratogenic fetal effects. Infants born to mothers taking BZDs may be at risk for withdrawal symptoms in the postnatal period.
- *Lactation:* Excreted in human breast milk; infants can become lethargic and lose weight.
- *Children:* Not indicated for use in children younger than 6 years.

Class: Selective Serotonin Reuptake Inhibitors (SSRIs)

| sertraline | *Zoloft* |

INDICATIONS: Used primarily for depression but may also be used for OCD, PD, posttrauma stress, PMDD, and social anxiety

AVAILABLE FORMS: Tablet, 25, 50, and 100 mg

DOSAGE: Starting dose, 25 mg once daily, increase dose incrementally 25 mg per week; maximum, 200 mg daily.

ADMINISTRATION:

- PO with a glass of water.
- Take with or without food.
- Take at regular intervals.
- Caution patients not to stop taking drug except on provider's advice.
- May be prescribed for children as young as 6 years for selected conditions (25 mg/day); *precautions do apply.*

(cont.)

sertraline (cont.)

- Instruct patients to take missed dose as soon as possible. If it is almost time for the next dose, advise to take only that dose.

SIDE EFFECTS:

- *Most common*: Dizziness, headache, insomnia, somnolence, and change in sex drive or performance.
- *Less common*: Allergic reactions like skin rash; itching; or hives; swelling of the face; lips; or tongue; feeling faint or lightheaded; falls; hallucination; loss of contact with reality; seizures; suicidal thoughts or other mood changes; unusual bleeding or bruising; unusually weak or tired; vomiting; change in appetite; diarrhea; increased sweating; indigestion; nausea; tremors.

DRUG INTERACTIONS: This medicine may interact with the following medications:

- Absolute contraindications include MAOIs such as phenelzine (*Nardil*), tranylcypromine (*Parnate*), isocarboxazid (*Marplan*), and selegiline (*Eldepryl*).
- Avoid using with SNRI agents, triptans, and and other SSRI agents.
- Caution with aspirin, NSAIDs (e.g., ibuprofen or naproxen), COX inhibitors, and other anti-inflammatory drugs, St. John's wort.

▶**Alert**: This list may not describe all possible interactions. Instruct patients to provide a list of all medicines, herbs, nonprescription drugs, or dietary supplements used, and if they smoke, drink alcohol, or use illegal drugs.

PHARMACOKINETICS:

- SSRIs are metabolized in the liver by CYP P450 (CYP) enzymes.
- They are highly bound to plasma proteins and have a large volume of distribution.
- May take 2–6 weeks for the drug to be fully effective
- Addition of serotonergic medications to a patient's regimen must not occur until 2–3 weeks after discontinuation of an SSRI (some recommend a 5-week "washout" period prior to initiation of an MAOI).

Metabolism: Liver; CYP 2C19, 2D6, 3A4 substrate; 2D6 (weak), 3A4 (weak) inhibitor

Excretion: Urine 40–45% (none unchanged), feces 40–45% (12–14% unchanged)

Half-life: 26 hr

PRECAUTIONS:

- See patients as often as necessary to ensure that the drug is working on the panic attacks, determine compliance, and review side effects.
- Make sure patients realize that they need to take prescribed doses even if they do not feel better right away. It can take several weeks before they feel the full effect of the drug.
- Instruct patients and their families to watch for worsening depression or thoughts of suicide. Also, watch out for sudden or severe changes in feelings such as feeling anxious, agitated, panicky, irritated, hostile, aggressive, impulsive,

severely restless, overly excited, hyperactive, or not being able to sleep. If this happens, especially at the beginning of antidepressant treatment or after a change in dose, patient should call the health care provider.

- Drowsiness or dizziness: Patients should not drive or use machinery or do anything that needs mental alertness until the effects of this medicine are known.
- Caution patients not to stand or sit up quickly, especially if older. This reduces the risk of dizzy or fainting spells. Alcohol may interfere with the effect of this medicine. Avoid alcoholic drinks.
- Caution patients not to treat themselves for coughs, colds, or allergies without asking health care professional for advice. Some ingredients can increase possible side effects.
- For dry mouth, chewing sugarless gum or sucking hard candy and drinking plenty of water may help. Contact health care provider if the problem persists or is severe.
- Caution should be exercised in the following:
  - Bipolar disorder or a family history of bipolar disorder
  - Diabetes
  - Heart disease
  - Liver disease
  - Electroconvulsive therapy
  - Seizures (convulsions)
  - Suicidal thoughts, plans, or attempts by patients or a family member
  - An unusual or allergic reaction to sertraline, other medicines, foods, dyes, or preservatives
  - Pregnancy or trying to get pregnant
  - Breastfeeding

PATIENT AND FAMILY EDUCATION:

- Store at room temperature. Take any unused medication after the expiration date to the local pharmacy on drug give-back day. Avoid throwing the medication into the environment.
- Discuss any worsening anxiety, aggressiveness, impulsivity, or restlessness with provider.
- Patients or families should report any severe, abrupt onset or changes in symptoms to health professionals. This may be reflective of increased risk of suicidal thinking.
- Caution for the concomitant use of NSAIDs, aspirin, warfarin, and any other drugs that alter platelets.

SPECIAL POPULATIONS:

- *Elderly:* Increased risk for hyponatremia.
- *Hepatic impairment:* Dose adjustment is necessary.
- *Pregnancy:* Category C; risks are associated with all SSRIs for neonatal complications if used in the third trimester.
- *Lactation:* Adverse reactions have not been reported; however, long-term effects have not been studied, and the manufacturer recommends caution.
- *Children:* Approved for use in children 12 years and older; however, monitoring for increased suicidal ideation is critical.

PHOBIAS: Selective Serotonin Reuptake Inhibitors (SSRIs)

fluoxetine   *Prozac*

INDICATIONS: Used to treat MDDs, OCD, bulimia nervosa, and PD

AVAILABLE FORMS: Capsule, 10, 20, and 40 mg; capsule, delayed release (*Prozac Weekly*): 90 mg; solution, 20 mg/5 mL

DOSAGE: *Immediate release (Prozac Daily):* Starting dose 10 mg PO, daily for 7 days; maximum, 60 mg/day. *Capsule, delayed release (Prozac Weekly):* 90 mg oral, once weekly, 7 days after last daily dose of 20 mg. *Extended release:* Not recommended for acute treatment.

ADMINISTRATION:
- PO with a glass of water
- Take with or without food
- Take at regular intervals
- Caution patients not to stop taking drug except on provider's advice.
- *Prozac Daily* may be prescribed for children as young as 7 years for selected conditions; *precautions do apply.*
- *Prozac Weekly* is not prescribed for children.
- Do not prescribe *Prozac Weekly* for acute treatment.
- Instruct patients to take missed dose as soon as possible. If it is almost time for the next dose, advise to take only that dose.

SIDE EFFECTS:
- *Most common:* Dizziness, headache, insomnia, somnolence, and change in sex drive or performance.
- *Less common:* Allergic reactions (skin rash; itching, or hives); swelling of the face, lips, or tongue allergic reactions like skin rash, psoriasis; arthralgias; anorexia; feeling faint or lightheaded, falls nausea; dry mouth; constipation; dyspepsia; suicidal thoughts or other mood changes; unusual bleeding or bruising; fatigue; tremor; change in appetite; diarrhea; increased sweating; indigestion; and nausea.

DRUG INTERACTIONS: Most of the interactions occur with OTC cough and cold preparations. This medicine may also interact with the following medications.
- Absolute contraindications include MAOIs such as phenelzine (*Nardil*), tranylcypromine (*Parnate*), isocarboxazid (*Marplan*), and selegiline (*Eldepryl*).
- Avoid using with other SSRIs due to serotonin effect; SNRI drugs such as desvenlafaxine (*Pristiq*) and venlafaxine (*Effexor*); drugs with sympathomimetic properties such as phenylpropanolamine, pseudoephedrine, St. John's wort, haloperidol; diazepam (*Valium*), any other antidepressants; and clopidogrel (*Plavix*).
- Exercise caution with cold medications, arrhythmia medications such as flecainide, aspirin, and other NSAIDs, and drugs used for analgesia with opioid properties.

▶**Alert:** This list may not describe all possible interactions. Instruct patients to provide a list of all medicines, herbs, nonprescription drugs, or dietary supplements used, and if they smoke, drink alcohol, or use illegal drugs.

PHARMACOKINETICS:
Metabolism: Liver; CYP450 2C19, 2D6 (primary) substrate; 2C19, 3A4 (weak) inhibitor; active metabolite
Excretion: Urine 80% (11.6% unchanged), feces 15%
Half-life: 4–6 days (fluoxetine), 9.3 days (norfluoxetine)

PRECAUTIONS:
- See patients as often as necessary to ensure that the drug is working on the panic attacks, determine compliance, and review side effects.
- Make sure patients realize that they need to take prescribed doses even if they do not feel better right away. It can take several weeks before they feel the full effect of the drug.
- Instruct patients and families to watch for worsening depression or thoughts of suicide. Also, watch out for sudden or severe changes in feelings such as feeling anxious, agitated, panicky, irritated, hostile, aggressive, impulsive, severely restless, overly excited, hyperactive, or not being able to sleep. If this happens, especially at the beginning of antidepressant treatment or after a change in dose, patient should call the health care provider.
- Drowsiness or dizziness: Patients should not drive or use machinery or do anything that needs mental alertness until the effects of this medicine are known.
- Caution patients not to stand or sit up quickly, especially if older. This reduces the risk of dizzy or fainting spells. Alcohol may interfere with the effect of this medicine. Avoid alcoholic drinks.
- Caution patients not to treat themselves for coughs, colds, or allergies without asking the health care professional for advice. Some ingredients can increase possible side effects.
- Dry mouth: Chewing sugarless gum, sucking hard candy, and drinking plenty of water may help. Contact health care provider if the problem persists or is severe.
- Caution should be exercised in the following:
  - Bipolar disorder or a family history of bipolar disorder
  - Diabetes
  - Heart disease
  - Liver disease
  - Electroconvulsive therapy
  - Seizures (convulsions)
  - Suicidal thoughts, plans, or attempts by patients or a family member
  - An unusual or allergic reaction to fluoxetine, other medicines, foods, dyes, or preservatives
  - Pregnancy or trying to get pregnant
  - Breastfeeding

(cont.)

fluoxetine (cont.)

PATIENT AND FAMILY EDUCATION:
- Store at room temperature. Take any unused medication after the expiration date to the local pharmacy on drug give-back day. Avoid throwing the medication into the environment.
- Discuss any worsening anxiety, aggressiveness, impulsivity, or restlessness with provider.
- Report any severe, abrupt onset or changes in symptoms to health professionals. May be reflective of increased risk of suicidal thinking.
- Caution for the concomitant use of NSAIDs, aspirin, warfarin, and any other drugs that alter platelets.

SPECIAL POPULATIONS:
- *Elderly:* No actual contraindications exist, but due to the long half-life of the drug, it has been placed on the Beers List of Potentially Inappropriate Medications for Geriatrics
- *Pregnancy:* Category C; this is the longest SSRI used in pregnant women. Every attempt should be made to discontinue in the third trimester secondary to development of neonatal distress upon delivery.
- *Lactation:* Not approved for lactation and breastfeeding.
- *Children:* Approved in pediatric population only for MDD and OCD. Monitoring for increased suicidal ideation is critical.

Paxil, Paxil CR, Pexeva | **paroxetine, paroxetine mesylate**

INDICATIONS: Used to treat MDDs, OCD, bulimia nervosa, and PD.

AVAILABLE FORMS: *Pexeva*: Tablet, 20, 30, and 40 mg; *Paxil*: Tablet, 10, 20, 30, and 40 mg; suspension; 10 mg/5 mL; *Paxil CR*: Tablet, 12.5, 25, and 37.5 mg

DOSAGE: *Pexeva* and *Paxil*: 20 mg PO every morning, 10 mg in elderly patients; increase 10 mg/day weekly; maximum, 50 mg/day; 40 mg/day in elderly patients. *Paxil CR*: 12.5 mg PO, daily, increase 12.5 mg/day weekly; maximum, 75 mg/day; 50 mg/day in elderly patients. No proven additional benefits at doses greater than 20 mg/day.

ADMINISTRATION:
- PO with a glass of water.
- Do not cut/crush or chew.
- Take with or without food.
- Take at regular intervals.
- Caution patients not to stop taking drug except on provider's advice.
- May be prescribed for children as young as 7 years for selected conditions; *precautions do apply.*
- Instruct patients to take missed dose as soon as possible. If it is almost time for the next dose, advise to take only that dose.

SIDE EFFECTS:
- *Most common*: Somnolence; headache; asthenia; dizziness; sweating; dry mouth; tremor; anorexia; nervousness; anxiety; abnormal vision; change in appetite; change in sex drive or performance; diarrhea; constipation; indigestion; and nausea.
- *Less common*: Suicidality, worsening depression, serotonin syndrome, seizures, hyponatremia, extrapyramidal symptoms, priapism, and acute angle glaucoma.

DRUG INTERACTIONS: Most of the interactions occur with OTC cough and cold preparations. This medicine may also interact with the following medications.

- Absolute contraindications include MAOIs such as phenelzine (*Nardil*), tranylcypromine (*Parnate*), isocarboxazid (*Marplan*), and selegiline (*Eldepryl*).
- Avoid using with other SSRIs due to serotonin effect; SNRI drugs such as desvenlafaxine (*Pristiq*) and venlafaxine (*Effexor*); drugs with sympathomimetic properties such as phenylpropanolamine, pseudoephedrine, St. John's wort, haloperidol; diazepam (*Valium*), any other antidepressants; and clopidogrel (*Plavix*).
- Exercise caution with cold medications, arrhythmia medications such as flecainide, aspirin, and other NSAIDs, and drugs used for analgesia with opioid properties.

▶**Alert**: This list may not describe all possible interactions. Instruct patients to provide a list of all medicines, herbs, nonprescription drugs, or dietary supplements used, and if they smoke, drink alcohol, or use illegal drugs.

PHARMACOKINETICS:
Metabolism: Liver extensively; CYP450 2D6 substrate; 2D6 inhibitor
Excretion: Urine 64% (2% unchanged), feces 36% (less than 1% unchanged)
Half-life: 21 hr

PRECAUTIONS:
- See patients as often as necessary to ensure that the drug is working on the panic attacks, determine compliance, and review side effects.
- Make sure patients realize that they need to take prescribed doses even if they do not feel better right away. It can take several weeks before they feel the full effect of the drug.
- Instruct patients and families to watch for worsening depression or thoughts of suicide. Also watch out for sudden or severe changes in feelings such as feeling anxious, agitated, panicky, irritated, hostile, aggressive, impulsive, severely restless, overly excited, hyperactive, or not being able to sleep. If this happens, especially at the beginning of antidepressant treatment or after

(cont.)

PHOBIAS: Selective Serotonin Reuptake Inhibitors (SSRIs)

paroxetine, paroxetine mesylate (cont.)

a change in dose, patient should call the health care provider.

- Drowsiness or dizziness: Patients should not drive or use machinery or do anything that needs mental alertness until the effects of this medicine are known.
- Caution patients not to stand or sit up quickly, especially if older. This reduces the risk of dizzy or fainting spells. Alcohol may interfere with the effect of this medicine. Avoid alcoholic drinks.
- Caution patients not to treat themselves for coughs, colds, or allergies without asking health care professional for advice. Some ingredients can increase possible side effects.
- Dry mouth: Chewing sugarless gum, sucking hard candy, and drinking plenty of water may help. Contact health care provider if the problem persists or is severe.
- Caution should be exercised in the following:
    - Bipolar disorder or a family history of bipolar disorder
    - Diabetes
    - Heart disease
    - Liver disease
    - Electroconvulsive therapy
    - Seizures (convulsions)
    - Suicidal thoughts, plans, or attempts by patients or a family member
    - An unusual or allergic reaction to paroxetine, other medicines, foods, dyes, or preservatives

- Pregnancy or trying to get pregnant
- Breastfeeding

PATIENT AND FAMILY EDUCATION:
- Store at room temperature. Take any unused medication after the expiration date to the local pharmacy on drug give-back day. Avoid throwing the medication into the environment.
- Shake the liquid form of paroxetine well just before you measure a dose. To get the correct dose, measure the liquid with a marked measuring spoon or medicine cup, not with a regular tablespoon. If a dose-measuring device is not available, ask the pharmacist for one.

SPECIAL POPULATIONS:
- *Elderly:* Due to increased C_{min} concentrations, up to 70–80% in the elderly, the initial dose should be reduced.
- *Renal and hepatic impairment:* The initial dose should be reduced in patients with severe renal and/or hepatic impairment. Titration upward should be slow and at intervals.
- *Pregnancy:* Category D; first trimester teratogenicity, neonatal withdrawal and serotonin syndrome in third trimester, persistent pulmonary HTN if more than 20-weeks gestation.
- *Lactation:* Considered generally safe; substantial human data show no or minimal risk to breast milk production or to the infant.
- *Children: Paxil CR* is not indicated for children. Monitoring for increased suicidal ideation is critical if using regular *Paxil*.

fluvoxamine   *Luvox CR*

INDICATIONS: Used to treat OCD, social anxiety disorder

AVAILABLE FORMS: Capsule, extended release, 100 and 150 mg

DOSAGE: Starting dose, 100 mg PO nightly, increase by 50 mg/day weekly; maximum, 300 mg/day

ADMINISTRATION:
- PO with a glass of water.
- Take with or without food.
- Take at regular intervals.
- Caution patients not to stop taking drug except on provider's advice.
- Not prescribed for children.
- Instruct patients to take missed dose as soon as possible. If it is almost time for the next dose, advise to take only that dose.

SIDE EFFECTS:
- *Most common:* Somnolence; headache; asthenia; dizziness; sweating; dry mouth; tremor; anorexia; nervousness; anxiety; abnormal vision; change in appetite; change in sex drive or performance; diarrhea; constipation; indigestion; and nausea

- *Less common:* Suicidality, worsening depression, serotonin syndrome, seizures, hyponatremia, extrapyramidal symptoms, priapism, and acute angle glaucoma.

DRUG INTERACTIONS: Most of the interactions occur with OTC cough and cold preparations. This medicine may also interact with the following medications.
- Absolute contraindications include MAOIs such as phenelzine (*Nardil*), tranylcypromine (*Parnate*), isocarboxazid (*Marplan*), and selegiline (*Eldepryl*).
- Avoid using with other SSRIs due to serotonin effect; SNRI drugs such as desvenlafaxine (*Pristiq*) and venlafaxine (*Effexor*); drugs with sympathomimetic properties such as phenylpropanolamine, pseudoephedrine, St. John's wort, haloperidol; and diazepam (*Valium*), any other antidepressants; clopidogrel (*Plavix*), amoxicillin, erythromycins, and lansoprazole (*Prevacid*).
- Exercise caution with cold medications, NSAIDs, and drugs used for analgesia with opioid properties.

▶**Alert:** This list may not describe all possible interactions. Instruct patients to provide a list
(cont.)

fluvoxamine (*cont.*)

of all medicines, herbs, nonprescription drugs, or dietary supplements used, and if they smoke, drink alcohol, or use illegal drugs.

PHARMACOKINETICS:
Metabolism: Liver extensively; CYP450 1A2, 2D6 inhibitor
Excretion: Urine primarily (2% unchanged)
Half-life: 16.3 hr, 25.9 hr (elderly)

PRECAUTIONS:
- See patients as often as necessary to ensure that the drug is working on the panic attacks, determine compliance, and review side effects.
- Make sure patients realize that they need to take prescribed doses even if they do not feel better right away. It can take several weeks before they feel the full effect of the drug.
- Instruct patients and families to watch for worsening depression or thoughts of suicide. Also watch out for sudden or severe changes in feelings such as feeling anxious, agitated, panicky, irritated, hostile, aggressive, impulsive, severely restless, overly excited, hyperactive, or not being able to sleep. If this happens, especially at the beginning of antidepressant treatment or after a change in dose, patient should call the health care provider.
- Drowsiness or dizziness: Patients should not drive or use machinery or do anything that needs mental alertness until the effects of this medicine are known.
- Caution patients not to stand or sit up quickly, especially if older. This reduces the risk of dizzy or fainting spells. Alcohol may interfere with the effect of this medicine. Avoid alcoholic drinks.
- Caution patients not to treat themselves for coughs, colds, or allergies without asking health care professional for advice. Some ingredients can increase possible side effects.

- Dry mouth: Chewing sugarless gum, sucking hard candy, and drinking plenty of water may help. Contact health care provider if the problem persists or is severe.
- Caution should be exercised in the following:
  - Bipolar disorder or a family history of bipolar disorder
  - Diabetes
  - Heart disease
  - Liver disease
  - Electroconvulsive therapy
  - Seizures (convulsions)
  - Suicidal thoughts, plans, or attempts by patients or a family member
  - An unusual or allergic reaction to fluvoxamine, other medicines, foods, dyes, or preservatives
  - Pregnancy or trying to get pregnant
  - Breastfeeding

PATIENT AND FAMILY EDUCATION:
- Store at room temperature. Take any unused medication after the expiration date to the local pharmacy on drug give-back day. Avoid throwing the medication into the environment.

SPECIAL POPULATIONS:
- *Elderly:* Due to increased C_{min} concentrations, up to 70–80% in the elderly, the initial dose should be reduced.
- *Renal and hepatic impairment:* Initial dose should be reduced in patients with severe renal and/or hepatic impairment. Titration upward should be slow and at intervals.
- *Pregnancy:* Category D; first trimester teratogenicity, neonatal withdrawal and serotonin syndrome in third trimester, persistent pulmonary HTN if more than 20-weeks gestation.
- *Lactation:* Considered generally safe; substantial human data show no or minimal risk to breast milk production or to the infant.
- *Children:* Not indicated for children.

Celexa   **citalopram**

INDICATIONS: Used to treat MDD

AVAILABLE FORMS: Tablet, 10, 20, and 40 mg; oral solution, 10 mg/5 mL

DOSAGE: Starting dose, 20 mg once daily, increase dose incrementally 20 mg only once per week. Most patients reach efficacy at 40 mg daily; however, some may need 60 mg/day.

ADMINISTRATION:
- PO with a glass of water.
- Take with or without food
- Take at regular intervals
- Caution patients not to stop taking drug except on provider's advice.
- Not prescribed for children.
- Instruct patients to take missed dose as soon as possible. If it is almost time for the next dose, advise to take only that dose.

SIDE EFFECTS:
- *Most common:* Somnolence; headache; asthenia; dizziness; sweating; dry mouth; tremor; anorexia; nervousness; anxiety; abnormal vision; change in appetite; change in sex drive or performance; diarrhea; constipation; indigestion; and nausea
- *Less common:* Suicidality, worsening depression, serotonin syndrome, seizures, hyponatremia, extrapyramidal symptoms, priapism, and acute angle glaucoma.

DRUG INTERACTIONS: Most of the interactions occur with OTC cough and cold preparations. This medicine may also interact with the following medications.
- Absolute contraindications include MAOIs such as phenelzine (*Nardil*), tranylcypromine
(cont.)

PHOBIAS: Selective Serotonin Reuptake Inhibitors (SSRIs)

citalopram (*cont.*)

(*Parnate*), isocarboxazid (*Marplan*), and selegiline (*Eldepryl*).

- Avoid using with other SSRIs due to serotonin effect; SNRI drugs such as desvenlafaxine (*Pristiq*) and venlafaxine (*Effexor*); drugs with sympathomimetic properties such as phenylpropanolamine, pseudoephedrine, St. John's wort, haloperidol; and diazepam (*Valium*), any other antidepressants; clopidogrel (*Plavix*), amoxicillin, erythromycins, and lansoprazole (*Prevacid*).
- Exercise caution with cold medications, NSAIDs, and drugs used for analgesia with opioid properties.
- ▶**Alert**: This list may not describe all possible interactions. Instruct patients to provide a list of all medicines, herbs, nonprescription drugs, or dietary supplements used, and if they smoke, drink alcohol, or use illegal drugs.

PHARMACOKINETICS:
Metabolism: Extensively metabolized in the liver in CYP450 2C19, 3A4 substrate; 2D6 (weak) inhibitor
Excretion: Urine primarily (10% unchanged), feces.
Half-life: 35 hr

PRECAUTIONS:
- See patients as often as necessary to ensure that the drug is working on the panic attacks, determine compliance, and review side effects.
- Make sure patients realize that they need to take prescribed doses even if they do not feel better right away. It can take several weeks before they feel the full effect of the drug.
- Instruct patients and families to watch for worsening depression or thoughts of suicide. Also watch out for sudden or severe changes in feelings such as feeling anxious, agitated, panicky, irritated, hostile, aggressive, impulsive, severely restless, overly excited, hyperactive, or not being able to sleep. If this happens, especially at the beginning of antidepressant treatment or after a change in dose, patient should call the health care provider.
- Drowsiness or dizziness: Patients should not drive or use machinery or do anything that needs mental alertness until the effects of this medicine are known.
- Caution patients not to stand or sit up quickly, especially if older. This reduces the risk of dizzy or fainting spells. Alcohol may interfere

with the effect of this medicine. Avoid alcoholic drinks.
- Caution patients not to treat themselves for coughs, colds, or allergies without asking health care professional for advice. Some ingredients can increase possible side effects.
- Dry mouth: Chewing sugarless gum, sucking hard candy, and drinking plenty of water may help. Contact health care provider if the problem persists or is severe.
- Caution should be exercised in the following:
  - Bipolar disorder or a family history of bipolar disorder
  - Diabetes
  - Heart disease
  - Liver disease
  - Electroconvulsive therapy
  - Seizures (convulsions)
  - Suicidal thoughts, plans, or attempts by patients or a family member
  - An unusual or allergic reaction to citalopram, other medicines, foods, dyes, or preservatives
  - Pregnancy or trying to get pregnant
  - Breastfeeding

PATIENT AND FAMILY EDUCATION:
- Store at room temperature. Take any unused medication after the expiration date to the local pharmacy on drug give-back day. Avoid throwing the medication into the environment.
- Try to take the medicine at the same time each day. Follow the directions on the prescription label. To get the correct dose of liquid citalopram, measure the liquid with a marked measuring spoon or medicine cup, not with a regular tablespoon. If there is no dose-measuring device available, ask the pharmacist for one.

SPECIAL POPULATIONS:
- *Elderly:* A dose of 20 mg daily is recommended for geriatric patients.
- *Renal and hepatic impairment:* The initial dose should be reduced in patients with severe renal and/or hepatic impairment. Half-life is doubled in patients with hepatic impairment. Titration upward should be slow and at intervals.
- *Pregnancy:* Category C; potential for persistent pulmonary HTN if more than 20-weeks gestation
- *Lactation:* excreted in human breast milk, some reports of infant somulence.
- *Children:* Not indicated for children.

escitalopram *Lexapro*

INDICATIONS: Used to treat MDD, GAD

AVAILABLE FORMS: Tablet, 5, 10, and 20 mg; oral solution, 5 mg/5 mL

DOSAGE: *Adults:* Starting dose, 10 mg PO, daily, may increase after 1 week to a maximum of 20

mg/day. *Elderly:* Dose should stay at 10 mg/day. *Children (12–17 years):* start with 10 mg PO, daily, may increase after 3 weeks; maximum, 20 mg/day

ADMINISTRATION:
- PO with a glass of water.
- Take with or without food

(cont.)

escitalopram (*cont.*)

- Take at regular intervals
- Caution patients not to stop taking drug except on provider's advice.
- Safety not established for children younger than 18 years old in GAD. Instruct patients to take missed dose as soon as possible. If it is almost time for the next dose, advise to take only that dose.

SIDE EFFECTS:
- *Most common*: Somnolence; headache; asthenia; dizziness; sweating; dry mouth; tremor; anorexia; nervousness; anxiety; abnormal vision; change in appetite; change in sex drive or performance; diarrhea; constipation; indigestion; and nausea.
- *Less common*: Suicidality, worsening depression, serotonin syndrome, seizures, hyponatremia, extrapyramidal symptoms, priapism, and acute angle glaucoma.

DRUG INTERACTIONS: Most of the interactions occur with OTC cough and cold preparations. This medicine may also interact with the following medications.
- Absolute contraindications include MAOIs such as phenelzine (*Nardil*), tranylcypromine (*Parnate*), isocarboxazid (*Marplan*), and selegiline (*Eldepryl*).
- Avoid using with other SSRIs due to serotonin effect; SNRI drugs such as desvenlafaxine (*Pristiq*) and venlafaxine (*Effexor*); drugs with sympathomimetic properties such as phenylpropanolamine, pseudoephedrine, St. John's wort, haloperidol; and diazepam (*Valium*); any other antidepressants; and clopidogrel (*Plavix*); amoxicillin; erythromycins; lansoprazole (*Prevacid*)
- Exercise caution with cold medications, NSAIDs, and drugs used for analgesia with opioid properties.
- ▶**Alert**: This list may not describe all possible interactions. Instruct patients to provide a list of all medicines, herbs, nonprescription drugs, or dietary supplements used, and if they smoke, drink alcohol, or use illegal drugs.

PHARMACOKINETICS:
Metabolism: Liver; CYP450: 2C19, 2D6, 3A4 substrate; 2D6 (weak) inhibitor
Excretion: Only 10% excreted in urine
Half-life: 27–32 hr, but is increased by 50% in elderly patients

PRECAUTIONS:
- See patients as often as necessary to ensure that the drug is working on the panic attacks, determine compliance, and review side effects.
- Make sure patients realize that they need to take prescribed doses even if they do not feel better right away. It can take several weeks before they feel the full effect of the drug.
- Instruct patients and families to watch for worsening depression or thoughts of suicide. Also watch out for sudden or severe changes in feelings such as feeling anxious, agitated, panicky, irritated, hostile, aggressive, impulsive, severely

restless, overly excited, hyperactive, or not being able to sleep. If this happens, especially at the beginning of antidepressant treatment or after a change in dose, patient should call the health care provider.
- Drowsiness or dizziness: Patients should not drive or use machinery or do anything that needs mental alertness until the effects of this medicine are known.
- Caution patients not to stand or sit up quickly, especially if older. This reduces the risk of dizzy or fainting spells. Alcohol may interfere with the effect of this medicine. Avoid alcoholic drinks.
- Caution patients not to treat themselves for coughs, colds, or allergies without asking health care professional for advice. Some ingredients can increase possible side effects.
- Dry mouth: Chewing sugarless gum, sucking hard candy, and drinking plenty of water may help. Contact health care provider if the problem persists or is severe.
- Caution should be exercised in the following:
  - Bipolar disorder or a family history of bipolar disorder
  - Diabetes
  - Heart disease
  - Liver disease
  - Electroconvulsive therapy
  - Seizures (convulsions)
  - Suicidal thoughts, plans, or attempts by patients or a family member
  - An unusual or allergic reaction to citalopram, other medicines, foods, dyes, or preservatives
  - Pregnancy or trying to get pregnant
  - Breastfeeding

PATIENT AND FAMILY EDUCATION:
- Store at room temperature. Take any unused medication after the expiration date to the local pharmacy on drug give-back day. Avoid throwing the medication into the environment.
- Try to take the medicine at the same time each day. Follow the directions on the prescription label. To get the correct dose of liquid escitalopram, measure the liquid with a marked measuring spoon or medicine cup, not with a regular tablespoon. If there is no dose-measuring device available, ask the pharmacist for one.

SPECIAL POPULATIONS:
- *Elderly:* A dose of 10 mg daily is recommended for geriatric patients. The initial dose should be reduced in patients with severe renal and/or hepatic impairment. Titration upward should be slow and at intervals.
- *Pregnancy:* Category C; potential for persistent pulmonary HTN if more than 20-weeks gestation
- *Lactation:* Excreted in human breast milk; some reports of infant somulence.
- *Children:* May be given to children older than 12 years of age. Monitoring of suicidal ideations is important.

PHOBIAS: Selective Serotonin Reuptake Inhibitors (SSRIs)

Class: Serotonin and Norepinephrine Reuptake Inhibitors (SNRIs)

venlafaxine	*Effexor, Effexor XR*

INDICATIONS: Used to treat MDD, GAD, PD, and social anxiety disorder

AVAILABLE FORMS: Tablet, 25, 37.5, 50, 75, and 100 mg; extended-release capsule, 37.5, 75, and 150 mg

DOSAGE: *Effexor*: Starting dose, 37.5 mg oral bid, with dose increases every 4 days for a maximum of 375 mg. *Effexor XR*: Starting dose, 37.5–75 mg daily with increases of 75 mg/day every 4–7 days for a maximum of 225 mg/day

ADMINISTRATION:

- PO with a glass of water.
- With food, *Effexor XR* may be sprinkled on applesauce.
- Do not crush, cut, or chew capsules.
- Take at regular intervals.
- Caution patients not to stop taking drug except on provider's advice.
- Not prescribed for children.
- Instruct patients to take missed dose as soon as possible. If it is almost time for the next dose, advise to take only that dose.

SIDE EFFECTS:

- *Most common*: Somnolence; headache; asthenia; dizziness; sweating; dry mouth; tremor; anorexia; nervousness; anxiety; abnormal vision; change in appetite; change in sex drive or performance; diarrhea; constipation; indigestion; and nausea
- *Less common*: Suicidality, worsening depression, serotonin syndrome, seizures, hyponatremia, extrapyramidal symptoms, priapism, and acute angle glaucoma.

DRUG INTERACTIONS: Most of the interactions occur with OTC cough and cold preparations. This medicine may also interact with the following medications.

- Absolute contraindications include cisapride, phenothiazines, MAOIs such as phenelzine (*Nardil*), tranylcypromine (*Parnate*), isocarboxazid (*Marplan*), and selegiline (*Eldepryl*).
- Avoid using with other SSRIs due to serotonin effect; SNRI drugs such as desvenlafaxine (*Pristiq*) and venlafaxine (*Effexor*); drugs with sympathomimetic properties such as phenylpropanolamine, pseudoephedrine, St. John's wort, haloperidol; and diazepam (*Valium*); and any other antidepressants.
- Exercise caution with cold medications, NSAIDs, and drugs used for analgesia with opioid properties.

▶**Alert:** This list may not describe all possible interactions. Instruct patients to provide a list of all medicines, herbs, nonprescription drugs, or dietary supplements used, and if they smoke, drink alcohol, or use illegal drugs.

PHARMACOKINETICS:

- SNRI agents are potent inhibitors of neuronal serotonin and norepinephrine reuptake, and weak inhibitors of dopamine reuptake.
- Demonstrate slightly higher efficacy than the SSRI class due to the dual effect.
- Relative to SSRIs, SNRI agents seem to be more effective in treating chronic pain issues that coexist with depression and may produce more stimulative effects
- They are highly bound to plasma proteins and have a large volume of distribution.

Metabolism: Liver extensively; CYP450 2D6 substrate; 2D6 (weak) inhibitor; converted to active metabolite (O-desmethylvenlafaxine)

Excretion: Urine 87% (5% unchanged)

Half-life: 5 hr (venlafaxine), 11 hr (O-desmethylvenlafaxine)

PRECAUTIONS:

- See patients as often as necessary to ensure that the drug is working on the panic attacks, determine compliance, and review side effects.
- Make sure patients realize that they need to take prescribed doses even if they do not feel better right away. It can take several weeks before they feel the full effect of the drug.
- Instruct patients and families to watch for worsening depression or thoughts of suicide. Also watch out for sudden or severe changes in feelings such as feeling anxious, agitated, panicky, irritated, hostile, aggressive, impulsive, severely restless, overly excited, hyperactive, or not being able to sleep. If this happens, especially at the beginning of antidepressant treatment or after a change in dose, patient should call the health care provider.
- Drowsiness or dizziness: Patients should not drive or use machinery or do anything that needs mental alertness until the effects of this medicine are known.
- Caution patients not to stand or sit up quickly, especially if older. This reduces the risk of dizzy or fainting spells. Alcohol may interfere with the effect of this medicine. Avoid alcoholic drinks.
- Caution patients not to treat themselves for coughs, colds, or allergies without asking health care professional for advice. Some ingredients can increase possible side effects.
- Dry mouth: Chewing sugarless gum, sucking hard candy, and drinking plenty of water may help. Contact health care provider if the problem persists or is severe.
- Caution should be exercised in the following:
  - Bipolar disorder or a family history of bipolar disorder
  - Diabetes
  - Heart disease
  - Liver disease
  - Seizures (convulsions)
  - Suicidal thoughts, plans, or attempts by patients or a family member
  - An unusual or allergic reaction to venlafaxine, other medicines, foods, dyes, or preservatives

(cont.)

venlafaxine (*cont.*)

» Pregnancy or trying to get pregnant
» Breastfeeding

PATIENT AND FAMILY EDUCATION:
- Store at room temperature. Take any unused medication after the expiration date to the local pharmacy on drug give-back day. Avoid throwing the medication into the environment. Try to take the medicine at the same time each day. Follow the directions on the prescription label.

SPECIAL POPULATIONS:
- *Elderly:* The initial dose should be reduced in patients with severe renal and/or hepatic impairment. Titration upward should be slow and at intervals.
- *Pregnancy:* Category C; potential for persistent pulmonary HTN if more than 20-weeks gestation
- *Lactation:* Excreted in human breast milk, caution should be taken.
- *Children:* Not indicated for children.

Class: Tricyclic Antidepressants (TCAs)

Due to the class side effects, especially on the cardiac system, TCAs should be used only if the SSRI or SNRI classes fail to show any improvement in symptom profile.

Tofranil, Tofranil PM	**imipramine pamoate**

INDICATIONS: Used to treat adults with depression/anxiety

AVAILABLE FORMS: *Tofranil:* Tablet, 25, and 50 mg; *Tofranil PM:* Capsule, 75, 100, 125, and 150 mg

DOSAGE: *Adults:* Start, 25–75 mg PO nightly and increase by 25–50 mg/day every 3–4 days; maximum, 300 mg/day. *Elderly:* 100 mg/day. Can be given in divided doses. Must taper dose gradually to discontinue. *Children: For depression:* Start, 1.5 mg/kg/day PO divided tid, increase by 1–1.5 mg/kg/day every 3–4 days; maximum, 5 mg/kg/day. *More than 12 years:* Start, 30–40 mg/day PO divided qd-tid and increase by 10–25 mg/day every 3–4 days; maximum, 100 mg/day

ADMINISTRATION:
- PO with a glass of water.
- Do not crush, cut, or chew extended-release tablets.
- Do not abruptly stop taking the medication.
- Not prescribed for children except when used for nocturnal enuresis and depression in children as young as 6 years.
- Use lowest effective dose for shortest duration.

SIDE EFFECTS:
- *More common:* Drowsiness, dizziness, constipation; nausea/vomiting, urinary retention or frequency, libido changes, weight gain, general nervousness, and galactorrhea.
- *Less common:* Cardiac arrhythmias, extrapyramidal symptoms, clotting disturbances, worsening depression, suicidality, hyperthermia, and hypertension.

DRUG INTERACTIONS: This medicine may interact with the following medications:
- Absolute contraindications include class 1A antiarrhythmics, MAOIs such as phenelzine (*Nardil*), tranylcypromine (*Parnate*), isocarboxazid (*Marplan*), and selegiline (*Eldepryl*).

- Avoid using with cimetidine, amiodarone, clarithromycin, haldoperidol, and St. John's wort.
▶**Alert:** This list may not describe all possible interactions. Instruct patients to provide a list of all medicines, herbs, nonprescription drugs, or dietary supplements used, and if they smoke, drink alcohol, or use illegal drugs.

PHARMACOKINETICS:
- TCAs are thought to work by inhibiting reuptake of norepinephrine and serotonin in the CNS, which potentiates the neurotransmitters. They also have significant anticholinergics, antihistaminic, and alpha-adrenergic activity on the cardiac system. These classes of antidepressants also possess class 1A antiarrhythmic activity, which can lead to depression of cardiac conduction potentially resulting in heart block or ventricular arrhythmias.

Metabolism: Extensively by the liver within the CYP450: 1A2, 2C19, 2D6 (primary), 3A4 substrate

Excretion: Primarily in urine, up to less than 5% unchanged, also excreted in the bile/feces

Half-life: 11–25 hr

PRECAUTIONS:
- See patients as often as necessary to ensure that the drug is working on the panic attacks, determine compliance, and review side effects.
- Instruct patients and families to watch for worsening depression or thoughts of suicide. Also, watch out for sudden or severe changes in feelings such as feeling anxious, agitated, panicky, irritated, hostile, aggressive, impulsive, severely restless, overly excited, hyperactive, or not being able to sleep. If this happens, especially at the beginning of antidepressant treatment or after a change in dose, patient should call the health care provider.
- Drowsiness or dizziness: Patients should not drive or use machinery or do anything that needs
(cont.)

PHOBIAS: Tricyclic Antidepressants (TCAs)

imipramine pamoate *(cont.)*

mental alertness until the effects of this medicine are known. Other medications that cause drowsiness can add to the drowsiness of imipramine.
- Caution patients not to stand or sit up quickly, especially if older. This reduces the risk of dizzy or fainting spells. Alcohol may interfere with the effect of this medicine. Avoid alcoholic drinks.
- Do not abruptly withdraw this drug as it may cause headache, nausea, and malaise
- Advise to protect skin from ultraviolet light due to increased skin sensitivity.
- Grapefruit and grapefruit juice may interact with imipramine.
- Caution should be exercised in the following:
  - MDD, psychosis, or bipolar affective disorder
  - Contraindicated in patients with a recent myocardial infarction
  - Blood dyscrasias
  - Respiratory disease
  - Heart disease
  - Liver disease
  - Seizures (convulsions)
  - Suicidal thoughts, plans, or attempts by patients or a family member
  - An unusual or allergic reaction to imipramine, other medicines, foods, dyes, or preservatives

PATIENT AND FAMILY EDUCATION:
- Store imipramine at room temperature away from moisture and heat.
- Stopping this medication suddenly could result in unpleasant side effects.
- Take the missed dose as soon as remembered. If it is almost time for the next dose, skip the missed dose and take the medicine at the next regularly scheduled time. *Do not* take extra medicine to make up the missed dose.

SPECIAL POPULATIONS:
- *Elderly:* Older patients may be more sensitive to the effects of TCAs. The smallest effective dose should be used. Dose adjustment is necessary for patients with liver impairment
- *Pregnancy:* Category D; some clinical reports of congenital malformations, but no direct causal link.
- *Lactation:* Excreted in human breast milk; alternative medications are recommended.
- *Children: Tofranil* is indicated for children less than 6 years old with nocturnal enuresis or with depression. Monitor for suicidal ideation with depression. *Tofranil PM* is not approved for use in children.

desipramine   *Norpramin*

INDICATIONS: Used to treat adults with depression/anxiety

AVAILABLE FORMS: Tablet, 10, 25, 50, 75, 100, and 150 mg

DOSAGE: Start, 25–75 mg PO, daily with a maximum of 300 mg/day. May be given in divided doses; must taper slowly to discontinue

ADMINISTRATION:
- PO with a glass of water.
- Do not abruptly stop taking the medication.
- Not prescribed for children.
- Use lowest effective dose for shortest duration.

SIDE EFFECTS:
- *More common:* Drowsiness, dizziness, constipation; nausea/vomiting, urinary retention or frequency, libido changes, weight gain, general nervousness, galactorrhea, rash, and urticaria.
- *Less common:* Cardiac arrhythmias, extrapyramidal symptoms, clotting disturbances, worsening depression, suicidality, hyperthermia, and hypertension.

DRUG INTERACTIONS: This medicine may interact with the following medications:
- Absolute contraindications include class 1A antiarrhythmics, MAOIs such as phenelzine (*Nardil*), tranylcypromine (*Parnate*), isocarboxazid (*Marplan*), and selegiline (*Eldepryl*).
- Avoid using with cimetidine, amiodarone, clarithromycin, erythromycin, haldoperidol, and St. John's wort.

▶**Alert**: This list may not describe all possible interactions. Instruct patients to provide a list of all medicines, herbs, nonprescription drugs, or dietary supplements used, and if they smoke, drink alcohol, or use illegal drugs.

PHARMACOKINETICS:
- TCAs are thought to work by inhibiting reuptake of norepinephrine and serotonin in the CNS, which potentiates the neurotransmitters. They also have significant anticholinergics, antihistaminic, and alpha-adrenergic activity on the cardiac system. These classes of antidepressants also possess class 1A antiarrhythmic activity, which can lead to depression of cardiac conduction potentially resulting in heart block or ventricular arrhythmias.

Metabolism: Primarily in the liver via the CYP450: 2C19, 2D6 (primary) substrate
Excretion: Urine
Half-life: 12–27 hr

PRECAUTIONS:
- See patients as often as necessary to ensure that the drug is working on the panic attacks, determine compliance, and review side effects.
- Instruct patients and their families to watch for worsening depression or thoughts of suicide. Also watch out for sudden or severe changes in feelings such as feeling anxious, agitated, panicky, irritated, hostile, aggressive, impulsive, severely restless, overly excited, hyperactive, or not being able to sleep. If this happens, especially
(cont.)

PHOBIAS: Tricyclic Antidepressants (TCAs)

desipramine (cont.)

at the beginning of antidepressant treatment or after a change in dose, patient should call the health care provider.

- Drowsiness or dizziness: Patients should not drive or use machinery or do anything that needs mental alertness until the effects of this medicine are known. Other medications that cause drowsiness can add to the drowsiness of desipramine.
- Caution patients not to stand or sit up quickly, especially if older. This reduces the risk of dizzy or fainting spells. Alcohol may interfere with the effect of this medicine. Avoid alcoholic drinks.
- Do not abruptly withdraw this drug as it may cause headache, nausea, and malaise.
- Advise to protect skin from ultraviolet light due to increased skin sensitivity.
- Grapefruit and grapefruit juice may interact with imipramine.
- Caution should be exercised in the following:
  - MDD, psychosis, or bipolar affective disorder
  - Contraindicated in patients with a recent myocardial infarction
  - Blood dyscrasias
  - Respiratory disease
  - Heart disease
  - Liver disease
  - Seizures (convulsions)
  - Psychoses or schizophrenia
  - Suicidal thoughts, plans, or attempts by patients or a family member
  - An unusual or allergic reaction to desipramine, other medicines, foods, dyes, or preservatives

PATIENT AND FAMILY EDUCATION:
- Store imipramine at room temperature away from moisture and heat.
- Stopping this medication suddenly could result in unpleasant side effects.
- Take the missed dose as soon as remembered. If it is almost time for the next dose, skip the missed dose and take the medicine at the next regularly scheduled time. *Do not* take extra medicine to make up the missed dose.

SPECIAL POPULATIONS:
- *Elderly:* Older patients may be more sensitive to the effects of TCAs. The smallest effective dose should be used (beginning at 10–25 mg/day). Dose adjustment is necessary for patients with liver impairment.
- *Pregnancy:* Category C; unknown effects as there is limited study.
- *Lactation:* Excreted in human breast milk; use caution
- *Children:* Not indicated for children. Used off-label in children 6–12 years; however, alternative medications are preferred.

Anafranil clomipramine

INDICATIONS: Used to treatment of obsessions and OCD

AVAILABLE FORMS: Capsules

DOSAGE: *Adults:* Start, 25 mg PO, daily, then increase by 25 mg/day every 4–7 days; maximum, 100 mg/day in first 2 weeks. Maintenance dose, generally 250 mg/day. Taper dose gradually to discontinue. *Children:* 100–200 mg PO nightly; start, 25 mg PO, daily, then increase by 25 mg/day every 4–7 days; maximum, 3 mg/kg/day up to 100 mg/day in first 2 weeks; maintenance, up to 200 mg/day.

ADMINISTRATION:
- PO with a glass of water and on a full stomach to minimize GI side effects.
- Do not abruptly stop taking the medication.
- Approved for children 10 years old and above.
- Re-evaluate periodically the need for the medication.

SIDE EFFECTS:
- *More common:* Drowsiness, dizziness, constipation; nausea/vomiting, urinary retention or frequency, libido changes, weight gain, general nervousness, and galactorrhea.
- *Less common:* Cardiac arrhythmias, extrapyramidal symptoms, clotting disturbances, worsening depression, suicidality, hyperthermia, and hypertension.

DRUG INTERACTIONS: This medicine may interact with the following medications:
- Absolute contraindications include class 1A antiarrhythmics, MAOIs such as phenelzine (*Nardil*), tranylcypromine (*Parnate*), isocarboxazid (*Marplan*), and selegiline (*Eldepryl*).
- Avoid using with cimetidine, amiodarone, clarithromycin, haldoperidol, and St. John's wort.
▶ **Alert**: This list may not describe all possible interactions. Instruct patients to provide a list of all medicines, herbs, nonprescription drugs, or dietary supplements used, and if they smoke, drink alcohol, or use illegal drugs.

PHARMACOKINETICS:
- TCAs are thought to work by inhibiting reuptake of norepinephrine and serotonin in the CNS, which potentiates the neurotransmitters. They also have significant anticholinergics, antihistaminic, and alpha-adrenergic activity on the cardiac system. These classes of antidepressants also possess class 1A antiarrhythmic activity, which can lead to depression of cardiac conduction potentially resulting in heart block or ventricular arrhythmias.

Metabolism: Extensively metabolized in the liver within CYP450: 1A2, 2C19, 2D6 (primary), 3A4 substrate

Excretion: Urine 66%, feces

(cont.)

PHOBIAS: Tricyclic Antidepressants (TCAs)

clomipramine (cont.)

Half-life: 32 hr (clomipramine), 69 hr (desmethylclomipramine). Half-life may be prolonged at upper end of dosing range due to accumulation.

PRECAUTIONS:

- See patients as often as necessary to ensure that the drug is working on the obsessive compulsive disorder, determine compliance, and review side effects.
- Instruct patients and families to watch for worsening depression or thoughts of suicide. Also watch out for sudden or severe changes in feelings such as feeling anxious, agitated, panicky, irritated, hostile, aggressive, impulsive, severely restless, overly excited, hyperactive, or not being able to sleep. If this happens, especially at the beginning of antidepressant treatment or after a change in dose, patient should call the health care provider.
- Drowsiness or dizziness: Patients should not drive or use machinery or do anything that needs mental alertness until the effects of this medicine are known. Other medications that cause drowsiness can add to the drowsiness of chlorimipramine.
- Caution patients not to stand or sit up quickly, especially if older. This reduces the risk of dizzy or fainting spells. Alcohol may interfere with the effect of this medicine. Avoid alcoholic drinks.
- Do not abruptly withdraw this drug as it may cause headache, nausea, and malaise.
- Advise to protect skin from ultraviolet light due to increased skin sensitivity.
- Grapefruit and grapefruit juice may interact with chlorimipramine.
- Caution should be exercised in the following:
  - MDD, psychosis, or bipolar affective disorder
  - Contraindicated in patients with a recent myocardial infarction
  - Blood dyscrasias
  - Respiratory disease
  - Heart disease
  - Liver disease
  - Seizures (convulsions)
  - Psychoses or schizophrenia
  - Suicidal thoughts, plans, or attempts by patients or a family member
  - An unusual or allergic reaction to desipramine, other medicines, foods, dyes, or preservatives

PATIENT AND FAMILY EDUCATION:

- Store chlorimipramine at room temperature away from moisture and heat.
- Stopping this medication suddenly could result in unpleasant side effects.
- Take the missed dose as soon as remembered. If it is almost time for the next dose, skip the missed dose and take the medicine at the next regularly scheduled time. *Do not* take extra medicine to make up the missed dose.

SPECIAL POPULATIONS:

- *Elderly:* Older patients may be more sensitive to the effects of TCAs. The smallest effective dose should be used. Caution in administration with significant renal and/or liver disease. Dose adjustments may be necessary. Monitor creatinine and liver functions.
- *Pregnancy:* Category C; unknown effects as there is limited study.
- *Lactation:* Excreted in human breast milk; use caution
- *Children:* Approved for children 10 years and older.

Stress Disorder

OVERVIEW

Acute Stress Disorder (ASD) / Post-Traumatic Stress Disorder (PTSD)

Acute Care

- ASD is the exposure to an extreme stressor in life. The event can be something that is life-threatening, horrifying, or terrifying in nature.
- Symptoms will emerge soon after the event, but can also abate more quickly.
- Can have dissociative symptoms; however, these tend to be more prominent in PTSD.
- Patients with ASD will revisit the event frequently, but also try to avoid reminders.
- ASD is a "temporal" diagnosis used with anyone who is symptomatic 2–30 days duration of symptoms.

- Persons who develop ASD may develop PTSD, especially if they have underlying psychological issues before the stress event.
- Predisposing factors to develop ASD include older age, previous exposure to trauma, biological vulnerability, lack of support networks, people whose perception and interpretation is skewed toward personal responsibility of the events, or negative worldviews.
- Women are twice as likely as men to develop ASD.
- More than 10% of men and 6% of women report experiencing four or more types of trauma.
- Symptoms of ASD: Psychic numbing, less aware about surroundings, derealization, depersonalization, dissociative amnesia, general depression symptoms may also be present.

STRESS DISORDER

Chronic Care
- Individuals diagnosed with PTSD must be exposed to a traumatic event.
- Traumatic events include military combat, rape, torture, genocide, or natural or workplace disasters. Additionally, long-term abuse, domestic violence, stalking, cult membership, and hostage situations can also cause PTSD.
- Lifetime prevalence is higher in urban depressed areas and Native Americans on reservations. Military veterans are also at higher risk for developing PTSD.
- Biochemical changes can be found in the amygdale and hippocampus, which affect the link between fear and memory.

- Societies that are highly authoritarian and that glorify violence seem to have a higher incidence of PTSD.
- Persons who work in occupations with high exposure to traumatic events can develop secondary PTSD.
- An individual's sense of vulnerability with regard to cognitive and emotional responses to trauma can influence reaction to a traumatic event.
- Most individuals diagnosed with PTSD also have another psychiatric diagnosis of anxiety disorder (30–60%), dissociative mood disorders (26–85%), borderline personality disorder (40–60%), and/or substance abuse disorder (60–80%).

Psychopharmacology of ASD and PTSD

- Drug therapy is similar for both ASD and PTSD. The goal of medication is to alleviate or at least control the symptoms affecting daily life. Drugs must be used in conjunction with cognitive therapies, both individual and group.
- Drugs are not effective in all individuals, especially those with long-standing PTSD.
- SSRI is the drug of choice for treatment of both ASD and PTSD. Selection of a specific SSRI is generally based on the side effect profile and tolerability; however, fluoxetine has shown greater efficacy in decreasing arousal, avoidance, and numbing in women.

- TCA, specifically amitriptyline and imipramine, show efficacy in helping with insomnia and nightmares. Others have not been as effective.
- Anxiety symptoms can be temporarily relieved with alprazolam or clonazepam; however, a concern exists for long-term use due to the addictive potential.
- CISD is an important aspect of prevention and helps to weaken the acute stress reaction.
- Along with medication, CBT, psychodynamic psychotherapy, discussion groups, and family therapy are all key components of treatment.

CLASS	DRUG
Selective Serotonin Reuptake Inhibitors (SSRIs)	**First-Line Drug Therapy**
	sertraline (*Zoloft*)
	fluoxetine (*Prozac*)
	paroxetine (*Paxil, Paxil CR*)
	paroxetine mesylate (*Pexeva*)
	fluvoxamine (*Luvox CR*)
	citalopram (*Celexa*)
	escitalopram (*Lexapro*)
Serotonin and Norepinephrine Reuptake Inhibitors (SNRIs)	**First-Line Drug Therapy**
	venlafaxine (*Effexor, Effexor XR*)
Tricyclic Antidepressants (TCAs)	**Drugs for Treatment Resistant Cases**
	imipramine (*Tofranil*)
	amitriptyline (*Elavil*)
Benzodiazepines (BZDs)	**Drugs Used Only in First Weeks While Establishing Levels of SSRI or SNRI**
	alprazolam (*Xanax/Xanax XR/Niravam*)
	lorazepam (*Ativan*)
	clonazepam (*Klonopin*)

STRESS DISORDER

Class: Selective Serotonin Reuptake Inhibitors (SSRIs)

sertraline   *Zoloft*

INDICATIONS: Used primarily to treat depression but may also be used for OCD, PD, posttrauma stress, PMDD, or social anxiety

AVAILABLE FORMS: Tablet, 25, 50, and 100 mg

DOSAGE: Starting dose, 25 mg once daily; increase dose incrementally 25 mg per week; maximum, 200 mg daily

ADMINISTRATION:
- PO with a glass of water.
- Take with or without food.
- Take at regular intervals.
- Caution patients not to stop taking drug except on provider's advice.
- May be prescribed for children as young as 6 years for selected conditions (25 mg/day); *precautions do apply.*
- Instruct patients to take missed dose as soon as possible. If it is almost time for the next dose, advise to take only that dose.

SIDE EFFECTS:
- *Most common*: Dizziness, headache, insomnia, somnolence, and change in sex drive or performance.
- *Less common*: Allergic reactions (skin rash; itching, or hives); swelling of the face, lips, or tongue; feeling faint or lightheaded; falls; hallucination; loss of contact with reality; seizures; suicidal thoughts or other mood changes; unusual bleeding or bruising; unusually weak or tired; vomiting; change in appetite; diarrhea; increased sweating; indigestion; nausea; tremors.

DRUG INTERACTIONS: This medicine may interact with the following medications:
- Absolute contraindications include MAOIs such as phenelzine (*Nardil*), tranylcypromine (*Parnate*), isocarboxazid (*Marplan*), and selegiline (*Eldepryl*).
- Avoid using with SNRI agents, triptans, and other SSRI agents.
- Caution with aspirin, NSAIDs (e.g., ibuprofen or naproxen), COX inhibitors, and other anti-inflammatory drugs, St. John's wort.
▶**Alert:** This list may not describe all possible interactions. Instruct patients to provide a list of all medicines, herbs, nonprescription drugs, or dietary supplements used, and if they smoke, drink alcohol, or use illegal drugs.

PHARMACOKINETICS:
- SSRIs are metabolized in the liver by CYP P450 (CYP) enzymes.
- They are highly bound to plasma proteins and have a large volume of distribution.
- Addition of serotonergic medications to a patient's regimen must not occur until 2–3 weeks after discontinuation of an SSRI (some recommend a 5-week "washout" period prior to initiation of an MAOI).

Metabolism: Liver; CYP 2C19, 2D6, 3A4 substrate; 2D6 (weak), 3A4 (weak) inhibitor
Excretion: Urine 40–45% (none unchanged); feces 40–45% (12–14% unchanged)
Half-life: 26 hr

PRECAUTIONS:
- See patients as often as necessary to ensure that the drug is working on the panic attacks, determine compliance, and review side effects.
- Make sure patients realize that they need to take prescribed doses even if they do not feel better right away. It can take several weeks before they feel the full effect of the drug.
- Instruct patients and families to watch for worsening depression or thoughts of suicide. Also, watch out for sudden or severe changes in feelings such as feeling anxious, agitated, panicky, irritated, hostile, aggressive, impulsive, severely restless, overly excited, hyperactive, or not being able to sleep. If this happens, especially at the beginning of antidepressant treatment or after a change in dose, patient should call the health care provider.
- Drowsiness or dizziness: Patients should not drive or use machinery or do anything that needs mental alertness until the effects of this medicine are known.
- Caution patients not to stand or sit up quickly, especially if older. This reduces the risk of dizzy or fainting spells. Alcohol may interfere with the effect of this medicine. Avoid alcoholic drinks.
- Caution patients not to treat themselves for coughs, colds, or allergies without asking health care professional for advice. Some ingredients can increase possible side effects.
- For dry mouth, chewing sugarless gum or sucking hard candy and drinking plenty of water may help. Contact your health care provider if the problem persists or is severe.
- Caution should be exercised in the following:
  - Bipolar disorder or a family history of bipolar disorder
  - Diabetes
  - Heart disease
  - Liver disease
  - Electroconvulsive therapy
  - Seizures (convulsions)
  - Suicidal thoughts, plans, or attempts by patients or a family member
  - An unusual or allergic reaction to sertraline, other medicines, foods, dyes, or preservatives
  - Pregnancy or trying to get pregnant
  - Breastfeeding

PATIENT AND FAMILY EDUCATION:
- Store at room temperature. Take any unused medication after the expiration date to the local pharmacy on drug give-back day. Avoid throwing the medication into the environment.
- Discuss any worsening anxiety, aggressiveness, impulsivity, or restlessness.

(cont.)

sertraline (*cont.*)

- Patients or families should report any severe, abrupt onset or changes in symptoms to health professionals. This may be reflective of increased risk of suicidal thinking.
- Caution for the concomitant use of NSAIDs, aspirin, warfarin, and any other drugs that alter platelets.

SPECIAL POPULATIONS:
- *Elderly:* Increased risk for hyponatremia
- *Hepatic impairment:* Dose adjustment necessary

- *Pregnancy:* Category C; risks are associated with all SSRIs for neonatal complications if used in the third trimester.
- *Lactation:* Adverse reactions have not been reported; however, long-term effects have not been studied, and the manufacturer recommends caution.
- *Children:* Approved for use in children aged 12 years or older; however, monitoring for increased suicidal ideation is critical.

Prozac **fluoxetine**

INDICATIONS: Used to treat MDDs, OCD, bulimia nervosa, and PD

AVAILABLE FORMS: Capsule, 10, 20, and 40 mg; capsule, delayed release (*Prozac Weekly*), 90 mg; solution, 20 mg/5 mL

DOSAGE: *Immediate release* (*Prozac Daily*): Starting dose, 10 mg PO, daily for 7 days; maximum, 60 mg/day. *Capsule, delayed release* (*Prozac Weekly*): 90 mg oral, once weekly, 7 days after last daily dose of 20 mg. *Extended release:* Not recommended for acute treatment

ADMINISTRATION:
- PO with a glass of water
- Take with or without food
- Take at regular intervals
- Caution patients not to stop taking drug except on provider's advice.
- *Prozac Daily* may be prescribed for children as young as 7 years for selected conditions; *precautions do apply.*
- *Prozac Weekly* is not prescribed for children
- Do not prescribe *Prozac Weekly* for acute treatment.
- Instruct patients to take missed dose as soon as possible. If it is almost time for the next dose, advise to take only that dose.

SIDE EFFECTS:
- *Most common:* Dizziness, headache, insomnia, somnolence, and change in sex drive or performance.
- *Less common:* Allergic reactions (skin rash; itching, or hives); swelling of the face, lips, or tongue; psoriasis; arthralgias; anorexia; feeling faint or lightheaded, falls nausea; dry mouth; constipation; dyspepsia; suicidal thoughts or other mood changes; unusual bleeding or bruising; fatigue; tremor; change in appetite; diarrhea; increased sweating; indigestion; and nausea.

DRUG INTERACTIONS: Most of the interactions occur with OTC cough and cold preparations. This medicine may also interact with the following medications.
- Absolute contraindications include MAOIs such as phenelzine (*Nardil*), tranylcypromine

(*Parnate*), isocarboxazid (*Marplan*), and selegiline (*Eldepryl*).
- Avoid using with other SSRIs due to serotonin effect; SNRI drugs such as desvenlafaxine (*Pristiq*) and venlafaxine (*Effexor*); drugs with sympathomimetic properties such as phenylpropanolamine, pseudoephedrine, St. John's wort, haloperidol; and diazepam (*Valium*), any other antidepressants; and clopidogrel (*Plavix*).
- Exercise caution with cold medications, arrhythmia medications such as flecainide, aspirin, and other NSAIDs, and drugs used for analgesia with opioid properties.
▶**Alert:** This list may not describe all possible interactions. Instruct patients to provide a list of all medicines, herbs, nonprescription drugs, or dietary supplements used, and if they smoke, drink alcohol, or use illegal drugs.

PHARMACOKINETICS:
Metabolism: Liver; CYP450 2C19, 2D6 (primary) substrate; 2C19, 3A4 (weak) inhibitor; active metabolite
Excretion: Urine 80% (11.6% unchanged), feces 15%
Half-life: 4–6 days (fluoxetine), 9.3 days (norfluoxetine)

PRECAUTIONS:
- See patients as often as necessary to ensure that the drug is working on the panic attacks, determine compliance, and review side effects.
- Make sure patients realize that they need to take prescribed doses even if they do not feel better right away. It can take several weeks before they feel the full effect of the drug.
- Instruct patients and families to watch for worsening depression or thoughts of suicide. Also, watch out for sudden or severe changes in feelings such as feeling anxious, agitated, panicky, irritated, hostile, aggressive, impulsive, severely restless, overly excited, hyperactive, or not being able to sleep. If this happens, especially at the beginning of antidepressant treatment or after a change in dose, patient should call the health care provider.
- Drowsiness or dizziness: Patients should not drive or use machinery or do anything that
(cont.)

STRESS DISORDER: Selective Serotonin Reuptake Inhibitors (SSRIs)

fluoxetine (*cont.*)

needs mental alertness until the effects of this medicine are known.

- Caution patients not to stand or sit up quickly, especially if older. This reduces the risk of dizzy or fainting spells. Alcohol may interfere with the effect of this medicine. Avoid alcoholic drinks.
- Caution patients not to treat themselves for coughs, colds, or allergies without asking health care professional for advice. Some ingredients can increase possible side effects.
- Dry mouth: Chewing sugarless gum, sucking hard candy, and drinking plenty of water may help. Contact health care provider if the problem persists or is severe.
- Caution should be exercised in the following:
  - Bipolar disorder or a family history of bipolar disorder
  - Diabetes
  - Heart disease
  - Liver disease
  - Electroconvulsive therapy
  - Seizures (convulsions)
  - Suicidal thoughts, plans, or attempts by patients or a family member
  - An unusual or allergic reaction to fluoxetine, other medicines, foods, dyes, or preservatives
  - Pregnancy or trying to get pregnant
  - Breastfeeding

PATIENT AND FAMILY EDUCATION:

- Store at room temperature. Take any unused medication after the expiration date to the local pharmacy on drug give-back day. Avoid throwing the medication into the environment.
- Discuss any worsening anxiety, aggressiveness, impulsivity, or restlessness.
- Report any severe, abrupt onset or changes in symptoms to health professionals. May be reflective of increased risk of suicidal thinking.
- Caution for the concomitant use of NSAIDs, aspirin, warfarin, and any other drugs that alter platelets.

SPECIAL POPULATIONS:

- *Elderly:* No actual contraindications exist, but due to the long half-life of the drug, it has been placed on the Beers List of Potentially Inappropriate Medications for Geriatrics.
- *Pregnancy:* Category C; this is the longest used SSRI in pregnant women. Every attempt should be made to discontinue in the third trimester secondary to development of neonatal distress upon delivery.
- *Lactation:* Not approved for lactation and breastfeeding.
- *Children:* Approved in pediatric population only for MDD and OCD. Monitoring for increased suicidal ideation is critical.

paroxetine, paroxetine mesylate   *Paxil, Paxil CR, Pexeva*

INDICATIONS: Used to treat MDDs, OCD, bulimia nervosa, and PD

AVAILABLE FORMS: *Pexeva*: Tablet, 20, 30, and 40 mg; *Paxil*: Tablet, 10, 20, 30, and 40 mg; suspension, 10 mg/5 mL; *Paxil CR*: Tablet, 12.5, 25, and 37.5 mg

DOSAGE: *Pexeva* and *Paxil*: 20 mg PO every morning, 10 mg in elderly patients; increase 10 mg/day weekly; maximum, 50 mg/day; 40 mg/day in elderly patients. *Paxil CR*: 12.5 mg PO, daily, increase 12.5 mg/day weekly; maximum, 75 mg/day; 50 mg/day in elderly patients. No proven additional benefits at doses greater than 20 mg/day

ADMINISTRATION:

- PO with a glass of water
- Do not cut, crush, or chew
- Take with or without food
- Take at regular intervals
- Caution patients not to stop taking drug except on provider's advice.
- May be prescribed for children as young as 7 years for selected conditions; *precautions do apply.*
- Instruct patients to take missed dose as soon as possible. If it is almost time for the next dose, advise to take only that dose.

SIDE EFFECTS:

- *Most common*: Somnolence; headache; asthenia; dizziness; sweating; dry mouth; tremor; anorexia;

nervousness; anxiety; abnormal vision; change in appetite; change in sex drive or performance; diarrhea; constipation; indigestion; and nausea.

- *Less common*: Suicidality, worsening depression, serotonin syndrome, seizures, hyponatremia, extrapyramidal symptoms, priapism, and acute angle glaucoma.

DRUG INTERACTIONS: Most of the interactions occur with OTC cough and cold preparations. This medicine may also interact with the following medications.

- Absolute contraindications include MAOIs such as phenelzine (*Nardil*), tranylcypromine (*Parnate*), isocarboxazid (*Marplan*), and selegiline (*Eldepryl*).
- Avoid using with other SSRIs due to serotonin effect; SNRI drugs such as desvenlafaxine (*Pristiq*) and venlafaxine (*Effexor*); drugs with sympathomimetic properties such as phenylpropanolamine, pseudoephedrine, St. John's wort, haloperidol; and diazepam (*Valium*), any other antidepressants; and clopidogrel (*Plavix*).
- Exercise caution with cold medications, arrhythmia medications such as flecainide, aspirin, and other NSAIDs, and drugs used for analgesia with opioid properties.

▶**Alert**: This list may not describe all possible interactions. Instruct patients to provide a list

(cont.)

paroxetine, paroxetine mesylate (*cont.*)

of all medicines, herbs, nonprescription drugs, or dietary supplements used, and if they smoke, drink alcohol, or use illegal drugs.

PHARMACOKINETICS:
Metabolism: Liver extensively; CYP450 2D6 substrate; 2D6 inhibitor
Excretion: Urine 64% (2% unchanged), feces 36% (less than 1% unchanged)
Half-life: 21 hr

PRECAUTIONS:
- See patients as often as necessary to ensure that the drug is working on the panic attacks, determine compliance, and review side effects.
- Make sure patients realize that they need to take prescribed doses even if they do not feel better right away. It can take several weeks before they feel the full effect of the drug.
- Instruct patients and families to watch for worsening depression or thoughts of suicide. Also watch out for sudden or severe changes in feelings such as feeling anxious, agitated, panicky, irritated, hostile, aggressive, impulsive, severely restless, overly excited, hyperactive, or not being able to sleep. If this happens, especially at the beginning of antidepressant treatment or after a change in dose, patient should call the health care provider.
- Drowsiness or dizziness: Patients should not drive or use machinery or do anything that needs mental alertness until the effects of this medicine are known.
- Caution patients not to stand or sit up quickly, especially if older. This reduces the risk of dizzy or fainting spells. Alcohol may interfere with the effect of this medicine. Avoid alcoholic drinks.
- Caution patients not to treat themselves for coughs, colds, or allergies without asking health care professional for advice. Some ingredients can increase possible side effects.
- Dry mouth: Chewing sugarless gum, sucking hard candy, and drinking plenty of water may help. Contact health care provider if the problem persists or is severe.

- Caution should be exercised in the following:
  - Bipolar disorder or a family history of bipolar disorder
  - Diabetes
  - Heart disease
  - Liver disease
  - Electroconvulsive therapy
  - Seizures (convulsions)
  - Suicidal thoughts, plans, or attempts by patients or a family member
  - An unusual or allergic reaction to paroxetine, other medicines, foods, dyes, or preservatives
  - Pregnancy or trying to get pregnant
  - Breastfeeding

PATIENT AND FAMILY EDUCATION:
- Store at room temperature. Take any unused medication after the expiration date to the local pharmacy on drug give-back day. Avoid throwing the medication into the environment.
- Shake the liquid form of paroxetine well just before measure a dose. To get the correct dose, measure the liquid with a marked measuring spoon or medicine cup, not with a regular tablespoon. If a dose-measuring device is not available, ask the pharmacist for one.

SPECIAL POPULATIONS:
- *Elderly:* Due to increased C_{min} concentrations, up to 70–80% in the elderly, the initial dose should be reduced.
- *Renal and hepatic impairment:* Initial dose should be reduced in patients with severe renal and/or hepatic impairment. Titration upward should be slow and at intervals.
- *Pregnancy:* Category D; first trimester teratogenicity, neonatal withdrawal and serotonin syndrome in third trimester; persistent pulmonary HTN if more than 20-weeks gestation.
- *Lactation:* Considered generally safe; substantial human data show no or minimal risk to breast milk production or to the infant.
- *Children:* Paxil CR is not indicated for children. Monitoring for increased suicidal ideation is critical if using regular *Paxil.*

Luvox CR **fluvoxamine**

INDICATIONS: Used to treat OCD, social anxiety disorder

AVAILABLE FORMS: Capsule, extended release, 100, and 150 mg

DOSAGE: Starting dose, 100 mg PO nightly, increase by 50 mg/day weekly; maximum, 300 mg/day

ADMINISTRATION:
- PO with a glass of water.
- Take with or without food.
- Take at regular intervals.
- Caution patients not to stop taking drug except on provider's advice.
- Not prescribed for children.

- Instruct patients to take missed dose as soon as possible. If it is almost time for the next dose, advise to take only that dose.

SIDE EFFECTS:
- *Most common:* Somnolence; headache; asthenia; dizziness; sweating; dry mouth; tremor; anorexia; nervousness; anxiety; abnormal vision; change in appetite; change in sex drive or performance; diarrhea; constipation; indigestion; and nausea.
- *Less common:* Suicidality, worsening depression, serotonin syndrome, seizures, hyponatremia, extrapyramidal symptoms, priapism, and acute angle glaucoma. *(cont.)*

STRESS DISORDER: Selective Serotonin Reuptake Inhibitors (SSRIs)

fluvoxamine (*cont.*)

DRUG INTERACTIONS: Most of the interactions occur with OTC cough and cold preparations. This medicine may also interact with the following medications.

- Absolute contraindications include MAOIs such as phenelzine (*Nardil*), tranylcypromine (*Parnate*), isocarboxazid (*Marplan*), and selegiline (*Eldepryl*).
- Avoid using with other SSRIs due to serotonin effect; SNRI drugs such as desvenlafaxine (*Pristiq*) and venlafaxine (*Effexor*); drugs with sympathomimetic properties such as phenylpropanolamine, pseudoephedrine, St. John's wort, haloperidol; diazepam (*Valium*), any other antidepressants; clopidogrel (*Plavix*), amoxicillin, erythromycins, and lansoprazole (*Prevacid*).
- Exercise caution with cold medications, NSAIDs, and drugs used for analgesia with opioid properties.
▶**Alert**: This list may not describe all possible interactions. Instruct patients to provide a list of all medicines, herbs, nonprescription drugs, or dietary supplements used, and if they smoke, drink alcohol, or use illegal drugs.

PHARMACOKINETICS:
Metabolism: Liver extensively; CYP450 1A2, 2D6 inhibitor
Excretion: urine primarily (2% unchanged)
Half-life: 16.3 hr, 25.9 hr (elderly)

PRECAUTIONS:
- See patients as often as necessary to ensure that the drug is working on the panic attacks, determine compliance, and review side effects.
- Make sure patients realize that they need to take prescribed doses even if they do not feel better right away. It can take several weeks before they feel the full effect of the drug.
- Instruct patients and families to watch for worsening depression or thoughts of suicide. Also, watch out for sudden or severe changes in feelings such as feeling anxious, agitated, panicky, irritated, hostile, aggressive, impulsive, severely restless, overly excited, hyperactive, or not being able to sleep. If this happens, especially at the beginning of antidepressant treatment or after a change in dose, patient should call the health care provider.
- Drowsiness or dizziness: Patients should not drive or use machinery or do anything that needs mental alertness until the effects of this medicine are known.

- Caution patients not to stand or sit up quickly, especially if older. This reduces the risk of dizzy or fainting spells. Alcohol may interfere with the effect of this medicine. Avoid alcoholic drinks.
- Caution patients not to treat themselves for coughs, colds, or allergies without asking health care professional for advice. Some ingredients can increase possible side effects.
- Dry mouth: Chewing sugarless gum, sucking hard candy, and drinking plenty of water may help. Contact health care provider if the problem persists or is severe.
- Caution should be exercised in the following:
  - Bipolar disorder or a family history of bipolar disorder
  - Diabetes
  - Heart disease
  - Liver disease
  - Electroconvulsive therapy
  - Seizures (convulsions)
  - Suicidal thoughts, plans, or attempts by patients or a family member
  - An unusual or allergic reaction to fluvoxamine, other medicines, foods, dyes, or preservatives
  - Pregnancy or trying to get pregnant
  - Breastfeeding

PATIENT AND FAMILY EDUCATION:
- Store at room temperature. Take any unused medication after the expiration date to the local pharmacy on drug give-back day. Avoid throwing the medication into the environment.

SPECIAL POPULATIONS:
- *Elderly:* Due to increased C_{min} concentrations, up to 70–80% in the elderly, the initial dose should be reduced.
- *Renal and hepatic impairment:* The initial dose should be reduced in patients with severe renal and/or hepatic impairment. Titration upward should be slow and at intervals.
- *Pregnancy:* Category D; first trimester teratogenicity, neonatal withdrawal and serotonin syndrome in third trimester, persistent pulmonary HTN if more than 20-weeks gestation.
- *Lactation:* Considered generally safe; substantial human data show no or minimal risk to breast milk production or to the infant.
- *Children:* Not indicated for children.

citalopram · *Celexa*

INDICATIONS: Used to treat MDD

AVAILABLE FORMS: Tablet, 10, 20, and 40 mg; oral solution, 10 mg/5 mL

DOSAGE: Starting dose, 20 mg once daily, increase dose incrementally 20 mg only once per week. Most patients reach efficacy at 40 mg daily; however, some may need 60 mg/day.

ADMINISTRATION:
- PO with a glass of water.
- Take with or without food.

(cont.)

citalopram (*cont.*)

- Take at regular intervals.
- Caution patients not to stop taking drug except on provider's advice.
- Not prescribed for children.
- Instruct patients to take missed dose as soon as possible. If it is almost time for the next dose, advise to take only that dose.

SIDE EFFECTS:

- *Most common*: Somnolence; headache; asthenia; dizziness; sweating; dry mouth; tremor; anorexia; nervousness; anxiety; abnormal vision; change in appetite; change in sex drive or performance; diarrhea; constipation; indigestion; and nausea.
- *Less common*: Suicidality, worsening depression, serotonin syndrome, seizures, hyponatremia, extrapyramidal symptoms, priapism, and acute angle glaucoma.

DRUG INTERACTIONS: Most of the interactions occur with OTC cough and cold preparations. This medicine may also interact with the following medications.

- Absolute contraindications include MAOIs such as phenelzine (*Nardil*), tranylcypromine (*Parnate*), isocarboxazid (*Marplan*), and selegiline (*Eldepryl*).
- Avoid using with other SSRIs due to serotonin effect; SNRI drugs such as desvenlafaxine (*Pristiq*) and venlafaxine (*Effexor*); drugs with sympathomimetic properties such as phenylpropanolamine, pseudoephedrine, St. John's wort, haloperidol; diazepam (*Valium*), any other antidepressants; clopidogrel (*Plavix*), amoxicillin, erythromycins, and lansoprazole (*Prevacid*).
- Exercise caution with cold medications, NSAIDs, and drugs used for analgesia with opioid properties.

▶ Alert: This list may not describe all possible interactions. Instruct patients to provide a list of all medicines, herbs, nonprescription drugs, or dietary supplements used, and if they smoke, drink alcohol, or use illegal drugs.

PHARMACOKINETICS:

Metabolism: Extensively metabolized in the liver in CYP450 2C19, 3A4 substrate; 2D6 (weak) inhibitor

Excretion: Urine primarily (10% unchanged), feces.

Half-life: 35 hr

PRECAUTIONS:

- See patients as often as necessary to ensure that the drug is working on the panic attacks, determine compliance, and review side effects.
- Make sure patients realize that they need to take prescribed doses even if they do not feel better right away. It can take several weeks before they feel the full effect of the drug.
- Instruct patients and families to watch for worsening depression or thoughts of suicide. Also watch out for sudden or severe changes in feelings such as feeling anxious, agitated, panicky, irritated, hostile, aggressive, impulsive, severely restless, overly excited, hyperactive, or not being able to sleep. If this happens, especially at the beginning of antidepressant treatment or after a change in dose, patient should call the health care provider.
- Drowsiness or dizziness: Patients should not drive or use machinery or do anything that needs mental alertness until the effects of this medicine are known.
- Caution patients not to stand or sit up quickly, especially if older. This reduces the risk of dizzy or fainting spells. Alcohol may interfere with the effect of this medicine. Avoid alcoholic drinks.
- Caution patients not to treat themselves for coughs, colds, or allergies without asking health care professional for advice. Some ingredients can increase possible side effects.
- Dry mouth: Chewing sugarless gum, sucking hard candy, and drinking plenty of water may help. Contact health care provider if the problem persists or is severe.
- Caution should be exercised in the following:
  - Bipolar disorder or a family history of bipolar disorder
  - Diabetes
  - Heart disease
  - Liver disease
  - Electroconvulsive therapy
  - Seizures (convulsions)
  - Suicidal thoughts, plans, or attempts by patients or a family member
  - An unusual or allergic reaction to citalopram, other medicines, foods, dyes, or preservatives
  - Pregnancy or trying to get pregnant
  - Breastfeeding

PATIENT AND FAMILY EDUCATION:

- Store at room temperature. Take any unused medication after the expiration date to the local pharmacy on drug give-back day. Avoid throwing the medication into the environment.
- Try to take the medicine at the same time each day. Follow the directions on the prescription label. To get the correct dose of liquid citalopram, measure the liquid with a marked measuring spoon or medicine cup, not with a regular tablespoon. If there is no dose-measuring device available, ask the pharmacist for one.

SPECIAL POPULATIONS:

- *Elderly:* A dose of 20 mg daily is recommended for geriatric patients.
- *Renal and hepatic impairment:* Initial dose should be reduced in patients with severe renal and/or hepatic impairment. Half-life is doubled in patients with hepatic impairment. Titration upward should be slow and at intervals.

(cont.)

STRESS DISORDER: Selective Serotonin Reuptake Inhibitors (SSRIs)

citalopram (*cont.*)

- *Pregnancy:* Category C; potential for persistent pulmonary HTN if more than 20-weeks gestation.
- *Lactation:* Excreted in human breast milk, some reports of infant somulence.
- *Children:* Not indicated for children.

escitalopram   *Lexapro*

INDICATIONS: Used to treat MDD, GAD

AVAILABLE FORMS: Tablet, 5, 10, and 20 mg; oral solution, 5 mg/5 mL

DOSAGE: *Adults:* Starting dose, 10 mg PO daily, may increase after 1 week to a maximum of 20 mg/day. Dose should stay at 10 mg/day. *Children (12–17 yr):* start, 10 mg PO daily, may increase after 3 weeks; maximum, 20 mg/day

ADMINISTRATION:
- PO with a glass of water.
- Take with or without food.
- Take at regular intervals.
- Caution patients not to stop taking drug except on provider's advice.
- Safety not established for children younger than 18 years old in GAD.
- Instruct patients to take missed dose as soon as possible. If it is almost time for the next dose, advise to take only that dose.

SIDE EFFECTS:
- *Most common:* Somnolence; headache; asthenia; dizziness; sweating; dry mouth; tremor; anorexia; nervousness; anxiety; abnormal vision; change in appetite; change in sex drive or performance; diarrhea; constipation; indigestion; and nausea.
- *Less common:* Suicidality, worsening depression, serotonin syndrome, seizures, hyponatremia, extrapyramidal symptoms, priapism, and acute angle glaucoma.

DRUG INTERACTIONS: Most of the interactions occur with OTC cough and cold preparations. This medicine may also interact with the following medications.
- Absolute contraindications include MAOIs such as phenelzine (*Nardil*), tranylcypromine (*Parnate*), isocarboxazid (*Marplan*), and selegiline (*Eldepryl*).
- Avoid using with other SSRIs due to serotonin effect; SNRI drugs such as desvenlafaxine (*Pristiq*) and venlafaxine (*Effexor*); drugs with sympathomimetic properties such as phenylpropanolamine, pseudoephedrine, St. John's wort, haloperidol; diazepam (*Valium*), and any other antidepressants; clopidogrel (*Plavix*), anamoxicillin; erythromycins, and lansoprazole (*Prevacid*).
- Exercise caution with cold medications, NSAIDs, and drugs used for analgesia with opioid properties.
- ▶ **Alert:** This list may not describe all possible interactions. Instruct patients to provide a list of all medicines, herbs, nonprescription drugs, or dietary supplements used, and if they smoke, drink alcohol, or use illegal drugs.

PHARMACOKINETICS:
Metabolism: Liver; CYP450: 2C19, 2D6, 3A4 substrate; 2D6 (weak) inhibitor
Excretion: Only 10% excreted in urine
Half-life: 27–32 hr, but is increased by 50% in elderly patients

PRECAUTIONS:
- See patients as often as necessary to ensure that the drug is working on the panic attacks, determine compliance, and review side effects.
- Make sure patients realize that they need to take prescribed doses even if they do not feel better right away. It can take several weeks before they feel the full effect of the drug.
- Instruct patients and families to watch for worsening depression or thoughts of suicide. Also watch out for sudden or severe changes in feelings such as feeling anxious, agitated, panicky, irritated, hostile, aggressive, impulsive, severely restless, overly excited, hyperactive, or not being able to sleep. If this happens, especially at the beginning of antidepressant treatment or after a change in dose, patient should call the health care provider.
- Drowsiness or dizziness: Patients should not drive or use machinery or do anything that needs mental alertness until the effects of this medicine are known.
- Caution patients not to stand or sit up quickly, especially if older. This reduces the risk of dizzy or fainting spells. Alcohol may interfere with the effect of this medicine. Avoid alcoholic drinks.
- Caution patients not to treat themselves for coughs, colds, or allergies without asking health care professional for advice. Some ingredients can increase possible side effects.
- Dry mouth: Chewing sugarless gum, sucking hard candy, and drinking plenty of water may help. Contact health care provider if the problem persists or is severe.
- Caution should be exercised in the following:
  - Bipolar disorder or a family history of bipolar disorder
  - Diabetes
  - Heart disease
  - Liver disease
  - Electroconvulsive therapy
  - Seizures (convulsions)
  - Suicidal thoughts, plans, or attempts by patients or a family member

(cont.)

escitalopram (*cont.*)

- An unusual or allergic reaction to citalopram, other medicines, foods, dyes, or preservatives
- Pregnancy or trying to get pregnant
- Breastfeeding

PATIENT AND FAMILY EDUCATION:
- Store at room temperature. Take any unused medication after the expiration date to the local pharmacy on drug give-back day. Avoid throwing the medication into the environment.
- Try to take the medicine at the same time each day. Follow the directions on the prescription label. To get the correct dose of liquid escitalopram, measure the liquid with a marked measuring spoon or medicine cup, not with a regular tablespoon. If there is no dose-measuring device available, ask the pharmacist for one.

SPECIAL POPULATIONS:
- *Elderly:* A dose of 10 mg daily is recommended for geriatric patients. The initial dose should be reduced in patients with severe renal and/or hepatic impairment. Titration upward should be slow and at intervals.
- *Pregnancy:* Category C; potential for persistent pulmonary HTN if more than 20-weeks gestation
- *Lactation:* excreted in human breast milk, some reports of infant somulence.
- *Children:* May be given to children older than 12 years of age. Monitoring of suicidal ideations is important.

Class: Serotonin and Norepinephrine Reuptake Inhibitors (SNRIs)

Effexor, Effexor XR   **venlafaxine**

INDICATIONS: Used to treat MDD, GAD, PD, and social anxiety disorder

AVAILABLE FORMS: Tablet, 25, 37.5, 50, 75, and 100 mg; extended-release capsule, 37.5, 75, and 150 mg

DOSAGE: *Effexor:* Starting dose, 37.5 mg oral bid with dose increases every 4 days for a maximum of 375 mg. *Effexor XR:* Starting dose, 37.5–75 mg daily with increases 75 mg/day every 4–7 days for a maximum of 225 mg/day

ADMINISTRATION:
- PO with a glass of water.
- Take with food; *Effexor XR* may be sprinkled on applesauce.
- Do not crush, cut, or chew capsules.
- Take at regular intervals.
- Caution patients not to stop taking drug except on provider's advice.
- Not prescribed for children.
- Instruct patients to take missed dose as soon as possible. If it is almost time for the next dose, advise to take only that dose.

SIDE EFFECTS:
- *Most common:* Somnolence; headache; asthenia; dizziness; sweating; dry mouth; tremor; anorexia; nervousness; anxiety; abnormal vision; change in appetite; change in sex drive or performance; diarrhea; constipation; indigestion; and nausea.
- *Less common:* Suicidality, worsening depression, serotonin syndrome, seizures, hyponatremia, extrapyramidal symptoms, priapism, and acute angle glaucoma.

DRUG INTERACTIONS: Most of the interactions occur with OTC cough and cold preparations. This medicine may also interact with the following medications.

- Absolute contraindications include cisapride, phenothiazines, MAOIs such as phenelzine (*Nardil*), tranylcypromine (*Parnate*), isocarboxazid (*Marplan*), and selegiline (*Eldepryl*).
- Avoid using with other SSRIs due to serotonin effect; SNRI drugs such as desvenlafaxine (*Pristiq*) and venlafaxine (*Effexor*); drugs with sympathomimetic properties such as phenylpropanolamine, pseudoephedrine, St. John's wort, haloperidol; and diazepam (*Valium*), any other antidepressants.
- Exercise caution with cold medications, NSAIDs, and drugs used for analgesia with opioid properties.
- ▶**Alert**: This list may not describe all possible interactions. Instruct patients to provide a list of all medicines, herbs, nonprescription drugs, or dietary supplements used, and if they smoke, drink alcohol, or use illegal drugs.

PHARMACOKINETICS:
- SNRI agents are potent inhibitors of neuronal serotonin and norepinephrine reuptake and weak inhibitors of dopamine reuptake.
- Demonstrate slightly higher efficacy than the SSRI class due to the dual effect.
- Relative to SSRIs, SNRI agents seem to be more effective in treating chronic pain issues which coexist with depression and may produce more stimulative effects
- They are highly bound to plasma proteins and have a large volume of distribution.

Metabolism: Liver extensively; CYP450 2D6 substrate; 2D6 (weak) inhibitor; converted to active metabolite (O-desmethylvenlafaxine)
Excretion: Urine 87% (5% unchanged)
Half-life: 5 hr (venlafaxine), 11 hr (O-desmethylvenlafaxine)

(cont.)

venlafaxine (*cont.*)

PRECAUTIONS:
- See patients as often as necessary to ensure that the drug is working on the panic attacks, determine compliance, and review side effects.
- Make sure patients realize that they need to take prescribed doses even if they do not feel better right away. It can take several weeks before they feel the full effect of the drug.
- Instruct patients and families to watch for worsening depression or thoughts of suicide. Also, watch out for sudden or severe changes in feelings such as feeling anxious, agitated, panicky, irritated, hostile, aggressive, impulsive, severely restless, overly excited, hyperactive, or not being able to sleep. If this happens, especially at the beginning of antidepressant treatment or after a change in dose, patient should call the health care provider.
- Drowsiness or dizziness: Patients should not drive or use machinery or do anything that needs mental alertness until the effects of this medicine are known.
- Caution patients not to stand or sit up quickly, especially if older. This reduces the risk of dizzy or fainting spells. Alcohol may interfere with the effect of this medicine. Avoid alcoholic drinks.
- Caution patients not to treat themselves for coughs, colds, or allergies without asking health care professional for advice. Some ingredients can increase possible side effects.
- Dry mouth: Chewing sugarless gum, sucking hard candy, and drinking plenty of water may help. Contact health care provider if the problem persists or is severe.

- Caution should be exercised in the following:
  - Bipolar disorder or a family history of bipolar disorder
  - Diabetes
  - Heart disease
  - Liver disease
  - Seizures (convulsions)
  - Suicidal thoughts, plans, or attempts by patients or a family member
  - An unusual or allergic reaction to venlafaxine, other medicines, foods, dyes, or preservatives
  - Pregnancy or trying to get pregnant
  - Breastfeeding

PATIENT AND FAMILY EDUCATION:
- Store at room temperature. Take any unused medication after the expiration date to the local pharmacy on drug give-back day. Avoid throwing the medication into the environment.
- Try to take the medicine at the same time each day. Follow the directions on the prescription label.

SPECIAL POPULATIONS:
- *Elderly:* The initial dose should be reduced in patients with severe renal and/or hepatic impairment. Titration upward should be slow and at intervals.
- *Pregnancy:* Category C; potential for persistent pulmonary HTN if greater than 20-weeks gestation
- *Lactation:* excreted in human breast milk; caution should be taken.
- *Children:* Not indicated for children.

Class: Tricyclic Antidepressants (TCAs)

Due to the class side effects, especially on the cardiac system, TCAs should be used only if the SSRI or SNRI classes fail to show any improvement in symptom profile.

imipramine pamoate   *Tofranil, Tofranil PM*

INDICATIONS: Used to treat adults with depression/anxiety

AVAILABLE FORMS: *Tofranil:* Tablet, 25, and 50 mg. *Tofranil PM:* Capsule, 75, 100, 125, and 150 mg

DOSAGE: *Adults:* Start, 25–75 mg PO nightly and increase by 25–50 mg/day every 3–4 days; maximum, 300 mg/day; 100 mg/day in elderly patients. Can be given in divided doses. Must taper dose gradually to discontinue. *Children: For depression:* Start, 1.5 mg/kg/day PO divided tid increase by 1–1.5 mg/kg/day every 3–4 days; maximum, 5 mg/kg/day. *Greater than 12 years*: Start, 30–40 mg/day PO divided qd-tid and increase by 10–25 mg/day every 3–4 days; maximum, 100 mg/day

ADMINISTRATION:
- PO with a glass of water.
- Do not crush, cut, or chew extended-release tablets.
- Do not abruptly stop taking the medication.
- Prescribed for children except when used for nocturnal enuresis and depression in children as young as 6 years.
- Use lowest effective dose for shortest duration.

SIDE EFFECTS:
- *More common:* Drowsiness, dizziness, constipation; nausea/vomiting, urinary retention or frequency, libido changes, weight gain, general nervousness, and galactorrhea.

(cont.)

imipramine pamoate (*cont.*)

- *Less common*: Cardiac arrhythmias, extrapyramidal symptoms, clotting disturbances, worsening depression, suicidality, hyperthermia, and hypertension.

DRUG INTERACTIONS: This medicine may interact with the following medications:
- Absolute contraindications include class 1A antiarrhythmics, MAOIs such as phenelzine (*Nardil*), tranylcypromine (*Parnate*), isocarboxazid (*Marplan*), and selegiline (*Eldepryl*).
- Avoid using with cimetadine, amiodarone, clarithromycin, haloperidol, and St. John's wort.

▶**Alert**: This list may not describe all possible interactions. Instruct patients to provide a list of all medicines, herbs, nonprescription drugs, or dietary supplements used, and if they smoke, drink alcohol, or use illegal drugs.

PHARMACOKINETICS:
- TCAs are thought to work by inhibiting reuptake of norepinephrine and serotonin in the CNS, which potentiates the neurotransmitters. They also have significant anticholinergics, antihistaminic, and alpha-adrenergic activity on the cardiac system. These classes of antidepressants also possess class 1A antiarrhythmic activity, which can lead to depression of cardiac conduction potentially resulting in heart block or ventricular arrhythmias

Metabolism: Extensively by the liver within the CYP450: 1A2, 2C19, 2D6 (primary), 3A4 substrate

Excretion: Primarily in urine, up to less than 5% and also excreted in the bile/feces.

Half-life: 11–25 hr

PRECAUTIONS:
- See patients as often as necessary to ensure that the drug is working on the panic attacks, determine compliance, and review side effects.
- Instruct patients and families to watch for worsening depression or thoughts of suicide. Also, watch out for sudden or severe changes in feelings such as feeling anxious, agitated, panicky, irritated, hostile, aggressive, impulsive, severely restless, overly excited, hyperactive, or not being able to sleep. If this happens, especially at the beginning of antidepressant treatment or after a change in dose, patient should call the health care provider.
- Drowsiness or dizziness: Patients should not drive or use machinery or do anything that needs mental alertness until the effects of this medicine are known. Other medications that

cause drowsiness can add to the drowsiness of imipramine.
- Caution patients not to stand or sit up quickly, especially if older. This reduces the risk of dizzy or fainting spells. Alcohol may interfere with the effect of this medicine. Avoid alcoholic drinks.
- Do not abruptly withdraw this drug as it may cause headache, nausea, and malaise
- Advise to protect skin from ultraviolet light due to increased skin sensitivity.
- Grapefruit and grapefruit juice may interact with imipramine.
- Caution should be exercised in the following:
  - MDD, psychosis, or bipolar affective disorder
  - Contraindicated in patients with a recent myocardial infarction
  - Blood dyscrasias
  - Respiratory disease
  - Heart disease
  - Liver disease
  - Seizures (convulsions)
  - Suicidal thoughts, plans, or attempts by patients or a family member
  - An unusual or allergic reaction to imipramine, other medicines, foods, dyes, or preservatives

PATIENT AND FAMILY EDUCATION:
- Store imipramine at room temperature away from moisture and heat.
- Stopping this medication suddenly could result in unpleasant side effects.
- Take the missed dose also as soon as remembered. If it is almost time for the next dose, skip the missed dose and take the medicine at the next regularly scheduled time. *Do not* take extra medicine to make up the missed dose.

SPECIAL POPULATIONS:
- *Elderly:* Older patients may be more sensitive to the effects of TCAs. The smallest effective dose should be used. Dose adjustment is necessary for patients with liver impairment
- *Pregnancy:* Category D; some clinical reports of congenital malformations, but no direct causal link.
- *Lactation:* Excreted in human breast milk; alternative medications are recommended.
- *Children: Tofranil* is indicated for children older than 6 years with nocturnal enuresis or with depression. Monitor for suicidal ideation with depression. *Tofranil PM* is not approved for children.

Elavil   **amitriptyline**

INDICATIONS: Used to treat adults with depression/anxiety

AVAILABLE FORMS: Tablet, 10, 25, , 50, 75, 100, and 150 mg

DOSAGE: *Adults:* Start, 25–75 mg PO nightly and increase by 25–50 mg/day every 2–3 days; lower starting dose, 10–25 mg PO nightly in elderly patients; increase 10–25 mg/day every 2–3 days; maximum, 300 mg/day. *Children (9–12 years*
(cont.)

STRESS DISORDER: Tricyclic Antidepressants (TCAs)

amitriptyline (cont.)

old): 1–3 mg/kg/day PO divided tid; start, 1 mg/kg/day PO div tid 3 days, increase by 0.5 mg/kg/day every 2–3 days. *Older than 12 years*: 50–100 mg/day PO divided qd-tid; start, 10 mg PO tid and 20 mg nightly; increase 10–25 mg/day every 2–3 days; maximum pediatric dose, 200 mg/day. For all populations, the medication can be given in divided doses. Must taper dose gradually to discontinue.

ADMINISTRATION:
- PO with a glass of water.
- Do not abruptly stop taking the medication.
- Use lowest effective dose for shortest duration.

SIDE EFFECTS:
- *Most common*: Drowsiness, dry mouth, dizziness, constipation; blurred vision, palpitations, tachycardia, lack of coordination, appetite increased, nausea/vomiting, sweating, weakness, disorientation, confusion, restlessness, insomnia, anxiety/agitation, urinary retention, urinary frequency, rash/urticaria, pruritus, weight gain, libido changes, impotence, gynecomastia, galactorrhea, tremor, hypo/hyperglycemia, paresthesias, and photosensitivity.
- *Less common*: Hypertension or orthostatic hypotension, ventricular arrhythmias, and extrapyramidal symptoms thrombocytopenia.

DRUG INTERACTIONS: This medicine may interact with the following medications.
- Absolute contraindications include class 1A antiarrhythmics and all MAOIs.
- Avoid using with amiodarone, cimetadine, clarithromycin, haldoperidol, St. John's wort.
▶**Alert**: This list may not describe all possible interactions. Instruct patients to provide a list of all medicines, herbs, nonprescription drugs, or dietary supplements used, and if they smoke, drink alcohol, or use illegal drugs.

PHARMACOKINETICS:
- TCAs are thought to work by inhibiting reuptake of norepinephrine and serotonin in the CNS, which potentiates the neurotransmitters. They also have significant anticholinergics, antihistaminic, and alpha-adrenergic activity on the cardiac system. These classes of antidepressants also possess class 1A antiarrhythmic activity, which can lead to depression of cardiac conduction potentially resulting in heart block or ventricular arrhythmias
Metabolism: Extensively by the liver within the CYP450: 1A2, 2D6 (primary), 3A4 substrate; active metabolites include nortriptyline
Excretion: Primarily in urine (18% unchanged), feces
Half-life: 10–26 hr (amitriptyline), 18–44 hr (nortriptyline)

PRECAUTIONS:
- See patients as often as necessary to ensure that the drug is working on the panic attacks, determine compliance, and review side effects.

- Instruct patients and families to watch for worsening depression or thoughts of suicide. Also, watch out for sudden or severe changes in feelings such as feeling anxious, agitated, panicky, irritated, hostile, aggressive, impulsive, severely restless, overly excited, hyperactive, or not being able to sleep. If this happens, especially at the beginning of antidepressant treatment or after a change in dose, patient should call the health care provider.
- Drowsiness or dizziness: Patients should not drive or use machinery or do anything that needs mental alertness until the effects of this medicine are known. Other medications that cause drowsiness can add to the drowsiness of imipramine.
- Caution patients not to stand or sit up quickly, especially if older. This reduces the risk of dizzy or fainting spells. Alcohol may interfere with the effect of this medicine. Avoid alcoholic drinks.
- Do not abruptly withdraw this drug as it may cause headache, nausea, and malaise.
- Advise to protect skin from ultraviolet light due to increased skin sensitivity.
- Grapefruit and grapefruit juice may interact with imipramine.
- Caution should be exercised in the following:
  - MDD, psychosis, or bipolar affective disorder
  - Contraindicated in patients with a recent myocardial infarction
  - Blood dyscrasias
  - Respiratory disease
  - Heart disease
  - Liver disease
  - Seizures (convulsions)
  - Suicidal thoughts, plans, or attempts by patients or a family member
  - An unusual or allergic reaction to imipramine, other medicines, foods, dyes, or preservatives

PATIENT AND FAMILY EDUCATION:
- Store amitriptyline at room temperature away from moisture and heat.
- Stopping this medication suddenly could result in unpleasant side effects.
- Take the missed dose as soon as remembered. If it is almost time for the next dose, skip the missed dose and take the medicine at the next regularly scheduled time. *Do not* take extra medicine to make up the missed dose.

SPECIAL POPULATIONS:
- *Elderly*: Older patients may be more sensitive to the effects of TCAs. The smallest effective dose should be used. Dose adjustment is necessary for patients with liver impairment. Due to its strong anticholinergic properties, amitriptyline is included in the Beers List of Potentially Inappropriate Medications for Geriatrics.
- *Pregnancy*: Category C
- *Lactation*: Excreted in human breast milk
- *Children*: Monitor closely for suicidal ideation with children.

Class: Benzodiazepines (BZDs)

Xanax, Xanax XR, and Niravam   **alprazolam**

INDICATIONS: Short-acting BZD used to treat GAD and PD. May be used as a short-term adjunct to an SSRI while waiting for the therapeutic effects of the SSRI to develop.

AVAILABLE FORMS: Tablet, 0.25, 0.5, 1, and 2 mg; Extended-release capsule, 0.5, 1, 2; melt 0.5, 1, 2, and 3 mg

DOSAGE: *Xanax*: Starting dose, 0.25 to 0.5 mg up to 2–3 times daily; maximum, 4 mg daily. Can be increased every 3–4 days. Treatment should be limited to as short a period as possible (less than 4 months) and/or re-evaluated for continued use. *Xanax XR*: Starting dose 0.5–1 mg PO, daily, can increase up to 1 mg/day every 3–4 days. *Niravam (melt)*: Starting dose, 0.25 to 0.5 mg up to 2–3 times daily; maximum, 4 mg daily. Can be increased every 3–4 days.

ADMINISTRATION:
- PO with a glass of water.
- Do not crush, cut, or chew extended-release tablets.
- Orally disintegrating *(Niravam)*, has special instructions.
- Concentrated liquid must be measured with a special dose-measuring spoon or cup.
- Do not abruptly stop taking the medication.
- Not prescribed for children.
- Use lowest effective dose for shortest duration.
- Alprazolam can be habit forming, do not increase dosage without guidance from the health care provider.

SIDE EFFECTS:
- *More common:* Drowsiness, lightheadedness, dry mouth; headache, changes in bowel habits, sialorrhea, amnesia, and changes in appetite.
- *Less common*: Syncope, tachycardia, seizures, respiratory depression, dependency, withdrawal syndrome, and suicidal ideation.

DRUG INTERACTIONS: This medicine may interact with the following medications.
- Absolute contraindications include clarithromycin, fluvoxamine, and ketoconazole.
- Avoid using with calcium channel blockers, erythromycins, tamoxifen, and zafirlukast.

▶**Alert**: This list may not describe all possible interactions. Instruct patients to provide a list of all medicines, herbs, nonprescription drugs, or dietary supplements used, and if they smoke, drink alcohol, or use illegal drugs.

PHARMACOKINETICS:
- BZDs enhance the activity of GABA, a major CNS neurotransmitter, known to open CNS Cl⁻ channels leading to an inhibition of subsequent CNS neuronal signaling. BZDs with similar action can differ in their potency and rate of absorption.

Metabolism: By the liver in the CYP450 3A4
Excretion: Urine
Half-life: 11.2 hr, 16.3 hr (elderly), 19.7 hr (alcoholic liver disease)

PRECAUTIONS:
- See patients as often as necessary to ensure that the drug is working on the panic attacks, determine compliance, and review side effects.
- Instruct patients and families to watch for worsening depression or thoughts of suicide. Also, watch out for sudden or severe changes in feelings such as feeling anxious, agitated, panicky, irritated, hostile, aggressive, impulsive, severely restless, overly excited, hyperactive, or not being able to sleep. If this happens, especially at the beginning of antidepressant treatment or after a change in dose, patient should call the health care provider.
- Drowsiness or dizziness: Patients should not drive or use machinery or do anything that needs mental alertness until the effects of this medicine are known.
- Caution patients not to stand or sit up quickly, especially if older. This reduces the risk of dizzy or fainting spells. Alcohol may interfere with the effect of this medicine. Avoid alcoholic drinks.
- Do not abruptly withdraw this drug as it may cause seizures.
- Caution should be exercised in the following:
  - MDD, psychosis, or bipolar affective disorder
  - Respiratory disease
  - Heart disease
  - Liver disease
  - Seizures (convulsions)
  - Suicidal thoughts, plans, or attempts by patients or a family member
  - An unusual or allergic reaction to alprazolam, other medicines, foods, dyes, or preservatives

PATIENT AND FAMILY EDUCATION:
- Store alprazolam at room temperature away from moisture, heat, and light. Remove any cotton from the bottle of disintegrating tablets, and keep the bottle tightly closed.
- Alprazolam may be habit forming and *should be used only by the person it was prescribed for.* Alprazolam should never be shared with another person, especially someone who has a history of drug abuse or addiction. Keep the medication in a secure place where others cannot get to it.
- Do not purchase alprazolam on the Internet or outside of the USA as dangerous ingredients may be present. Some purchases of alprazolam from the Internet have been found to contain haloperidol *(Haldol)*, an antipsychotic drug.

SPECIAL POPULATIONS:
- *Elderly:* Older patients may be more sensitive to the effects of BZDs. The smallest effective dose
(cont.)

STRESS DISORDER: Benzodiazepines (BZDs)

alprazolam (*cont.*)

should be used. Dose adjustment is necessary for patients with liver impairment and/or renal disease due to excessive metabolites excreted by the kidney. Due to increased risk of sedation leading to falls and fractures, BZDs are included on the Beers List of Potentially Inappropriate Medications for Geriatrics.

- *Pregnancy:* Category D; can cause teratogenic fetal effects. Infants born to mothers taking BZDs may be at risk for withdrawal symptoms in the postnatal period.
- *Lactation:* Excreted in human breast milk; infants can become lethargic and lose weight
- *Children:* Not indicated for use with children younger than 18 years.

lorazepam   *Ativan*

INDICATIONS: Use to treat GAD and PD

AVAILABLE FORMS: Tablet, 0.5, 1, and 2 mg

DOSAGE: *Adults:* 2–3 mg/day PO/IM/IV divided bid-tid; 1–2 mg/day PO/IM/IV divided bid-tid in elderly patients; maximum, 10 mg/day. Periodically assess the need for treatment and taper the dose gradually to discontinue if prolonged treatment is necessary. Treatment should be limited to as short a period as possible (less than 4 months) and/or re-evaluated for continued use. *Children:* 0.05 mg/kg PO/IV q4–8 hr; maximum, 2 mg/dose. Periodically assess the need for treatment and taper the dose gradually to discontinue if prolonged treatment is necessary.

ADMINISTRATION:
- PO with a glass of water.
- Do not abruptly stop taking the medication.
- Use lowest effective dose for shortest duration
- Lorazepam can be habit forming; do not increase dosage without guidance from the health care provider.

SIDE EFFECTS:
- *More common:* Drowsiness, lightheadedness, dry mouth; headache, changes in bowel habits, sialorrhea, amnesia, and changes in appetite.
- *Less common:* Syncope, tachycardia, seizures, respiratory depression, dependency, withdrawal syndrome, and suicidal ideation.

DRUG INTERACTIONS: This medicine may interact with the following medications.
- Absolute contraindications include clarithromycin, fluvoxamine, and ketoconazole.
- Avoid using with calcium channel blockers, erythromycins, tamoxifen, and zafirlukast.
▶**Alert:** This list may not describe all possible interactions. Instruct patients to provide a list of all medicines, herbs, nonprescription drugs, or dietary supplements used, and if they smoke, drink alcohol, or use illegal drugs.

PHARMACOKINETICS:
- BZDs enhance the activity of GABA, a major CNS neurotransmitter, known to open CNS Cl⁻ channels leading to an inhibition of subsequent CNS neuronal signaling. BZDs with similar action can differ in their potency and rate of absorption.
Metabolism: In the liver with the CYP450, exact mechanism is unknown

Excretion: Urine
Half-life: 14 hr

PRECAUTIONS:
- See patients as often as necessary to ensure that the drug is working on the panic attacks, determine compliance, and review side effects.
- Instruct patients and families to watch for worsening depression or thoughts of suicide. Also, watch out for sudden or severe changes in feelings such as feeling anxious, agitated, panicky, irritated, hostile, aggressive, impulsive, severely restless, overly excited, hyperactive, or not being able to sleep. If this happens, especially at the beginning of antidepressant treatment or after a change in dose, patient should call the health care provider.
- Drowsiness or dizziness: Patients should not drive or use machinery or do anything that needs mental alertness until the effects of this medicine are known.
- Caution patients not to stand or sit up quickly, especially if older. This reduces the risk of dizzy or fainting spells. Alcohol may interfere with the effect of this medicine. Avoid alcoholic drinks.
- Do not abruptly withdraw this drug as it may cause seizures.
- Caution should be exercised in the following:
  - Heart disease
  - Liver disease
  - Seizures (convulsions)
  - Suicidal thoughts, plans, or attempts by patients or a family member
  - An unusual or allergic reaction to alprazolam, other medicines, foods, dyes, or preservatives

PATIENT AND FAMILY EDUCATION:
- Store lorazepam at room temperature away from moisture, heat, and light. Remove any cotton from the bottle of disintegrating tablets, and keep the bottle tightly closed.
- Lorazepam may be habit forming and *should be used only by the person it was prescribed for.* Lorazepam should never be shared with another person, especially someone who has a history of drug abuse or addiction. Keep the medication in a secure place where others cannot get to it.
- Do not purchase lorazepam on the Internet or outside of the USA as dangerous ingredients may be present.

(cont.)

STRESS DISORDER: Benzodiazepines (BZDs)

lorazepam (*cont.*)

SPECIAL POPULATIONS:
- *Elderly:* Older patients may be more sensitive to the effects of BZDs. The smallest effective dose should be used. Dose adjustment is necessary for patients with liver impairment and/or renal disease due to excessive metabolites excreted by the kidney. Due to increased risk of sedation leading to falls and fractures, BZDs are included on the Beers List of Potentially Inappropriate Medications for Geriatrics.

- *Pregnancy:* Category D; can cause teratogenic fetal effects. Infants born to mothers taking BZDs may be at risk for withdrawal symptoms in the postnatal period.
- *Lactation:* Excreted in human breast milk; infants can become lethargic and lose weight.
- *Children:* Not indicated for use with children younger than 18 years.

Klonopin **clonazepam**

INDICATIONS: Use to treat GADs and PD

AVAILABLE FORMS: Tablet, 0.5, 1, and 2 mg; wafer melt, 0.125, 0.25, 0.5, and 1.2 mg

DOSAGE: Start at 0.25 mg PO bid, increase by 0.25–0.5 mg/day every 3 days; may start lower in elderly patients; maximum, 4 mg/day; treatment should be limited to as short a period as possible (less than 4 months) and/or re-evaluated for continued use. To discontinue, taper by 0.25 mg/day q3 days if less than 4 to 6 weeks continuous use

ADMINISTRATION:
- PO with a glass of water.
- Do not abruptly stop taking the medication.
- Use lowest effective dose for shortest duration.
- Clonazepam can be habit forming; do not increase dosage without guidance from the health care provider.

SIDE EFFECTS:
- *More common:* Drowsiness, lightheadedness, dry mouth; headache, changes in bowel habits, sialorrhea, amnesia, and changes in appetite.
- *Less common:* Syncope, tachycardia, seizures, respiratory depression, dependency, withdrawal syndrome, and suicidal ideation.

DRUG INTERACTIONS: This medicine may interact with the following medications.
- Absolute contraindications include clarithromycin, fluvoxamine, and ketoconazole.
- Avoid using with calcium channel blockers, erythromycins, tamoxifen, and zafirlukast.
- ▶ **Alert**: This list may not describe all possible interactions. Instruct patients to provide a list of all medicines, herbs, nonprescription drugs, or dietary supplements used, and if they smoke, drink alcohol, or use illegal drugs.

PHARMACOKINETICS:
- BZDs enhance the activity of GABA, a major CNS neurotransmitter, known to open CNS Cl^- channels leading to an inhibition of subsequent CNS neuronal signaling. BZDs with similar action can differ in their potency and rate of absorption.
Metabolism: Extensively metabolized in liver CYP450 3A4

Excretion: Urine
Half-life: 20–50 hr

PRECAUTIONS:
- See patients as often as necessary to ensure that the drug is working on the panic attacks, determine compliance, and review side effects.
- Instruct patients and families to watch for worsening depression or thoughts of suicide. Also watch out for sudden or severe changes in feelings such as feeling anxious, agitated, panicky, irritated, hostile, aggressive, impulsive, severely restless, overly excited, hyperactive, or not being able to sleep. If this happens, especially at the beginning of antidepressant treatment or after a change in dose, patient should call the health care provider.
- Drowsiness or dizziness: Patients should not drive or use machinery or do anything that needs mental alertness until the effects of this medicine are known.
- Caution patients not to stand or sit up quickly, especially if older. This reduces the risk of dizzy or fainting spells. Alcohol may interfere with the effect of this medicine. Avoid alcoholic drinks.
- Do not abruptly withdraw this drug as it may cause seizures.
- Caution should be exercised in the following:
  - Heart disease
  - Liver disease
  - Seizures (convulsions)
  - Suicidal thoughts, plans, or attempts by patients or a family member
  - An unusual or allergic reaction to alprazolam, other medicines, foods, dyes, or preservatives

PATIENT AND FAMILY EDUCATION:
- Store clonazepam at room temperature away from moisture, heat, and light. Remove any cotton from the bottle of disintegrating wafers, and keep the bottle tightly closed.
- Clonazepam may be habit forming and *should be used only by the person it was prescribed for.* Clonazepam should never be shared with another person, especially someone who has a history of drug abuse or addiction. Keep the
(cont.)

STRESS DISORDER: Benzodiazepines (BZDs)

clonazepam (*cont.*)

medication in a secure place where others cannot get to it.

SPECIAL POPULATIONS:

- *Elderly:* Older patients may be more sensitive to the effects of BZDs. The smallest effective dose should be used. Dose adjustment is necessary for patients with liver impairment and/or renal disease due to excessive metabolites excreted by the kidney. Due to increased risk of sedation leading to falls and fractures, BZDs are included on the Beers List of Potentially Inappropriate Medications for Geriatrics.
- *Pregnancy:* Category D; can cause teratogenic fetal effects. Infants born to mothers taking BZDs may be at risk for withdrawal symptoms in the postnatal period.
- *Lactation:* Excreted in human breast milk; infants can become lethargic and lose weight.
- *Children:* Not indicated for use in children except for treatment of seizures.

Attention Deficit Hyperactivity Disorder (ADHD)

OVERVIEW

- ADHD is a common medical disorder that affects the lives of approximately 7.8% of school-aged children in the USA. It is also estimated that 4.4% of adults are also affected.
- ADHD is believed to be caused by an imbalance of two naturally occurring chemical messengers in the brain.
- The disorder is classified into three general subtypes: predominantly hyperactive-impulsive, predominantly inattentive, and combined. The combined type is the most common form.
- ADHD may result in difficulties with focusing on tasks, organizing and prioritizing work, and impulse control.
- When treated, the symptoms of ADHD-inattention (e.g., lack of focus, inability to listen and follow instructions) and behavioral symptoms (e.g., hyperactivity, impulsivity) can be managed.
- In one study of 84 children of 31 adults diagnosed with ADHD, 57% of children were reported to have ADHD when one of their parents was diagnosed with the disorder.
- It is well established that ADHD can be associated with other psychiatric disorders. Many patients with ADHD may also meet criteria for ODD, substance abuse, depression, mania, and a significant portion will develop conduct disorder.
- Dopamine influences behaviors such as risk taking and impulsivity, whereas norepinephrine modulates attention, arousal, and mood. Dopamine and norepinephrine are likely involved in the pathophysiology of ADHD, but further study is needed. Current research suggests that rather than acting specifically on dopamine, stimulants create a calming effect by increasing serotonin levels.
- Recent genome scan studies suggest that ADHD is complex. ADHD has been associated with markers at chromosomes 4, 5, 6, 8, 11, 16, and 17. These genes showed statistically significant evidence for association with ADHD (the dopamine 4 and 5 receptors, the dopamine transporter, the enzyme dopamine hydroxylase, the serotonin transporter gene, the serotonin 1B receptor, and the synaptosomal associated protein 25 gene).
- Nongenetic causes of ADHD are also neurobiological in nature, consisting of such factors as perinatal stress and low birth weight, traumatic brain injury, maternal smoking during pregnancy, and severe early deprivation.
- There is also no correlation between a child's sex and cognitive, psychosocial, school, or family functioning.

TREATMENT FOR ADHD
Acute Care

- Health care providers should be familiar with the multiple medications available to treat ADHD. Stimulant medications are first-line agents. Atomoxetine (*Strattera*) is a second-line agent and has been shown to be effective in placebo-controlled trials. Other medications with less extensive evidence to support their use include alpha-2-agonists (*Intuniv*).

Chronic Care

- Behavior modification, also called behavior therapy, is recommended as part of a total treatment plan for ADHD.
- It is based upon rewarding an individual for desired behaviors and having consequences for undesired behaviors. Rewards and point systems are effective when used consistently at school and home.
- It can help build self-esteem and guide the patient toward good behavior patterns.
- Create schedules and follow routines daily.
- Keep tasks simple.
- Help the child become organized.
- Use brief and clear instructions.
- Limit distractions (e.g., TV, radio, games) when the child is doing homework.
- Set SMART goals to track the child's progress:
  S = *Specific*: Develop specific goals that are clearly stated
  M = *Measurable*: A goal is measurable if progress is made toward reaching it
  A = *Agreed upon*: Talk about the goal with the child and agree upon actions
  R = *Realistic*: The goals should be within reach
  T = *Timely*: A timely goal is one that can be achieved within a time frame that is meaningful

CLASS	DRUG
Amphetamines	
	Short-Acting Stimulants dextroamphetamine/amphetamine (*Adderall*) dextroamphetamine (*Dexedrine* and *Dextrostat*)
	Long-Acting Stimulants dextroamphetamine (*Spansule*) dextroamphetamine/amphetamine (*Adderall XR*) lisdexamfetamine (*Vyvanse*)
Methylphenidates (Amphetamine Derivatives)	
	Short-Acting Stimulants dexmethylphenidate (*Focalin*) methylphenidate (*Methylin*) methylphenidate (*Ritalin SR* and *LA*)
	Intermediate-Acting Stimulants methylphenidate (*Metadate ER* and *CD*) methylphenidate (*Methylin ER*) methylphenidate (*Ritalin SR* and *LA*)
	Long-Acting Stimulants methylphenidate (*Concerta*) methylphenidate transdermal (*Daytrana Patch*) dexmethylphenidate (*Foaclin XR*)
Selective Norepinephrine Reuptake Inhibitors (SNRIs)	**Nonstimulant** atomoxetine (*Strattera*)
Selective Alpha-2a-Adrenergic Receptor Agonist (SARIs)	**Nonstimulant** guanfacine (*Intuniv*)

Class: Amphetamines—Short-Acting

▶ **Note:** This class of medications are controlled substances.

■ Although some children benefit from daily stimulant therapy, weekend and summer "drug holidays" are suggested for children whose ADHD symptoms predominantly affect schoolwork, or to limit adverse effects (e.g., appetite suppression, abdominal pain, headache, insomnia, irritability, tics).

Short-acting preparations:

■ Often used as initial treatment in small children (less than 16 kg), but have disadvantage of bid to tid dosing to control symptoms throughout the day.

dextroamphetamine/amphetamine	*Adderall*

INDICATIONS: Stimulant indicated for the treatment of ADHD of children and adults

AVAILABLE FORMS: Capsule, 5, 7.5, 10, 12.5, 15, 20, and 30 mg

DOSAGE: Dosage should be individualized according to the therapeutic needs and response of the patient. All stimulant preparations should be administered at the lowest effective dosage. *Children: 3 to 5 yr old*: 2.5 to 40 mg/day PO divided daily tid; start, 2.5 mg qam, increase 2.5 mg/day every week, give divided doses at 4- to 6-hr intervals, doses greater than 40 mg/day rarely more effective. *Greater than 6 yr old*: 5 to 40 mg/day PO divided daily tid; start, 5 mg PO qam or bid, increase 5 mg/day every week, give divided doses at 4- to 6-hr intervals, doses greater than 40 mg/day rarely more effective. *Adults*: 5 to 40 mg/day PO divided daily tid; start, 5 mg PO qam or bid,

increase 5 mg/day every week, give divided doses at 4- to 6-hr intervals, doses greater than 40 mg/day rarely more effective.

ADMINISTRATION: Swallow capsules whole with water or other liquids. If patient cannot swallow the capsule, open it and sprinkle the medicine over a spoonful of applesauce. Swallow all of the applesauce and medicine mixture without chewing immediately. Follow with a drink of water or other liquid. Never chew or crush the capsule or the medicine inside the capsule. It can be taken with or without food.

SIDE EFFECTS: Decreased appetite; dizziness; dry mouth; irritability; insomnia; upper abdominal pain; nausea and/or vomiting; weight loss; headaches; anxiety; psychiatric events (increase in manic states for bipolar patients, aggression, tics, tremors); long-term growth suppression (patients
(cont.)

dextroamphetamine/amphetamine (*cont.*)

should be monitored throughout treatment; if there appears to be growth suppression, the treatment should be discontinued); rash; pyrexia; palpitations, tachycardia, elevated BP, sudden death, MI, cardiomyopathy; Stevens-Johnson syndrome and toxic epidermal necrolysis; impotence, libido changes

DRUG INTERACTIONS: Urinary acidifying agents; MAOIs; adrenergic blockers; antihistamines; antihypertensives; veratrum alkaloids; ethosuximide; TCAs; meperidine; phenobarbital; phenytoin; chlorpromazine; *Haldol*; lithium; norepinephrine; propoxyphene

PHARMACOKINETICS:
- Absorbed by the GI tract.
- Amphetamines are noncatecholamine sympathomimetic amines with CNS-stimulant activity.
- The mode of therapeutic action in ADHD is not known. Amphetamines are thought to block the reuptake of norepinephrine and dopamine into the presynaptic neuron and increase the release of these monoamines into the extraneural space.
Excretion: Urine
Half-life: 9 to 14 hr

PRECAUTIONS:
- Advanced arteriosclerosis, symptomatic cardiovascular disease, moderate-to-severe HTN
- Hyperthyroidism
- Known hypersensitivity or idiosyncratic reaction to sympathomimetic amines
- Glaucoma
- Agitated states
- Patients with a history of drug abuse: Amphetamines have a high potential for abuse. Administration of Amphetamines for an extended period of time may lead to drug dependence. Particular attention should be paid to the possibility of subjects obtaining this class of medication for nontherapeutic use or

distribution to others, and the drugs should be prescribed or dispensed sparingly.
- During or within 14 days following the administration of MAOIs, hypertensive crisis may result.
- Preexisting psychosis
- Seizure history; some studies have shown the potential for lowering the seizure threshold

PATIENT AND FAMILY EDUCATION:
- Store at room temperature, protected from light.
- Keep out of reach of children.
- Seek medical care for any signs of heart problems (chest pain, shortness of breath), fainting, psychotic symptoms, overdose, or any other concerns.
- Routinely assess weight and BP.
- Treatment should be initiated at low dosages and then titrated over 2 to 4 wk until an adequate response is achieved or unacceptable adverse effects occur.
- If one stimulant is not effective, another should be attempted before second-line medications are considered. Although some children benefit from daily stimulant therapy, weekend and summer "drug holidays" are suggested for children whose ADHD symptoms predominantly affect schoolwork or to limit adverse effects (e.g., appetite suppression, abdominal pain, headache, insomnia, irritability, tics).

SPECIAL POPULATIONS:
- *Elderly:* Caution with polypharmacy and comorbid conditions
- *Pregnancy:* Category C; based on animal data, they may cause fetal harm
- *Lactation:* Possibly unsafe
- *Children:* Has not been studied in children younger than 6 yr; should not be used in children younger than 3 yr.

Dexedrine, Dextrostat   **dextroamphetamine**

INDICATIONS: Stimulant indicated for the treatment of ADHD of children and adults

AVAILABLE FORMS: Capsule, 5, 10, and 15 mg

DOSAGE: Dosage should be individualized according to the therapeutic needs and response of the patient. All stimulant preparations should be administered at the lowest effective dosage. *Children: Less than 6 yr old:* 5 to 40 mg PO qam; start, 5 mg PO qam, increase 5 mg/day every week; maximum, 60 mg/day; doses greater than 40 mg/day rarely more effective. *Adults:* 5 to 40 mg qam; start, 5 mg PO qam, increase 5 mg/day every week; maximum, 60 mg/day; doses greater than 40 mg/day rarely more effective.

ADMINISTRATION: Do not crush or chew; can be taken without regard to food

SIDE EFFECTS: Decreased appetite; dizziness; dry mouth; irritability; insomnia; upper abdominal pain; nausea and/or vomiting; weight loss; headaches; anxiety; psychiatric events (increase in manic states for bipolar patients, aggression, tics, tremors); long-term growth suppression (patients should be monitored throughout treatment, if there appears to be growth suppression, the treatment should be discontinued); rash; pyrexia; palpitations, tachycardia, elevated BP, sudden death, MI, cardiomyopathy; Stevens-Johnson syndrome and toxic epidermal necrolysis; impotence, libido changes

DRUG INTERACTIONS: Urinary acidifying agents; MAOIs; adrenergic blockers; antihistamines; antihypertensives; veratrum alkaloids; ethosuximide; TCAs; meperidine; phenobarbital; phenytoin; chlorpromazine; *Haldol*; lithium; norepinephrine; propoxyphene

(cont.)

ATTENTION DEFICIT HYPERACTIVITY DISORDER: Amphetamines—Short-Acting

dextroamphetamine (cont.)

PHARMACOKINETICS:
- Absorbed by the GI tract.
- Amphetamines are noncatecholamine sympathomimetic amines with CNS-stimulant activity.
- The mode of therapeutic action in ADHD is not known. Amphetamines are thought to block the reuptake of norepinephrine and dopamine into the presynaptic neuron and increase the release of these monoamines into the extraneural space.

Metabolism: Liver, excreted in the urine
Half-life: 10.25 to 12 hr

PRECAUTIONS:
- Advanced arteriosclerosis, symptomatic cardiovascular disease, moderate-to-severe HTN
- Hyperthyroidism
- Known hypersensitivity or idiosyncratic reaction to sympathomimetic amines
- Glaucoma
- Agitated states
- Patients with a history of drug abuse: Amphetamines have a high potential for abuse. Administration of Amphetamines for an extended period of time may lead to drug dependence. Particular attention should be paid to the possibility of subjects obtaining this class of medication for nontherapeutic use or distribution to others, and the drugs should be prescribed or dispensed sparingly.
- During or within 14 days following the administration of MAOIs, hypertensive crisis may result.
- Preexisting psychosis

- Seizure history: Some studies have shown the potential for lowering the seizure threshold

PATIENT AND FAMILY EDUCATION:
- Store at room temperature, protected from light.
- Keep out of reach of children.
- Seek medical care for any signs of heart problems (chest pain, shortness of breath), fainting, psychotic symptoms, overdose, or any other concerns.
- Routinely assess weight and BP.
- Treatment should be initiated at low dosages and then titrated over 2 to 4 wk until an adequate response is achieved or unacceptable adverse effects occur.
- If one stimulant is not effective, another should be attempted before second-line medications are considered. Although some children benefit from daily stimulant therapy, weekend and summer "drug holidays" are suggested for children whose ADHD symptoms predominantly affect schoolwork, or to limit adverse effects (e.g., appetite suppression, abdominal pain, headache, insomnia, irritability, tics).

SPECIAL POPULATIONS:
- *Elderly:* Caution with polypharmacy and comorbid conditions
- *Pregnancy:* Category C; based on animal data, they may cause fetal harm
- *Lactation:* Possibly unsafe
- *Children:* Has not been studied in children younger than 6 yr; should not be used in children younger than 3 yr.

Class: Amphetamines—Long-Acting

▶**Note:** This class of medications are controlled substances.
- Although some children benefit from daily stimulant therapy, weekend and summer "drug holidays" are suggested for children whose ADHD symptoms predominantly affect schoolwork, or to limit adverse effects (e.g., appetite suppression, abdominal pain, headache, insomnia, irritability, tics).

Long-acting preparations:
- Offer greater convenience, confidentiality, and compliance with single daily dosing, but may have greater problematic effects on evening appetite and sleep.

dextroamphetamine   *Spansule*

INDICATIONS: Stimulant indicated for the treatment of ADHD of children and adults

AVAILABLE FORMS: Capsule, 5, 10, and 15 mg

DOSAGE: Dosage should be individualized according to the therapeutic needs and response of the patient. All stimulant preparations should be administered at the lowest effective dosage. *Children: Over 6 yr:* 5 to 40 mg PO qam; start, 5 mg PO qam, increase 5 mg/day every week; maximum, 60 mg/day; doses greater than 40 mg/day are rarely more effective. *Adults:* 5 to 40 mg qam; start, 5 mg PO qam, increase 5 mg/day every week; maximum, 60 mg/day; doses greater than 40 mg/day are rarely more effective

ADMINISTRATION: Do not crush or chew; can be taken with or without food.

SIDE EFFECTS: Decreased appetite; dizziness; dry mouth; irritability; insomnia; upper abdominal pain; nausea and/or vomiting; weight loss; headaches; anxiety; psychiatric events (increase in manic states for bipolar patients, aggression, tics, tremors); long-term growth suppression (patients should be monitored throughout treatment, if there appears to be growth suppression, the

(cont.)

dextroamphetamine (*cont.*)

treatment should be discontinued); rash; pyrexia; palpitations, tachycardia, elevated BP, sudden death, MI, cardiomyopathy; Stevens-Johnson syndrome and toxic epidermal necrolysis; impotence, libido changes

DRUG INTERACTIONS: Urinary acidifying agents; MAOIs; adrenergic blockers; antihistamines; antihypertensives; veratrum alkaloids; ethosuximide; TCAs; meperidine; phenobarbital; phenytoin; chlorpromazine; *Haldol*; lithium; norepinephrine; propoxyphene

PHARMACOKINETICS:
- Absorbed by the GI tract.
- Amphetamines are noncatecholamine sympathomimetic amines with CNS-stimulant activity.
- The mode of therapeutic action in ADHD is not known. Amphetamines are thought to block the reuptake of norepinephrine and dopamine into the presynaptic neuron and increase the release of these monoamines into the extraneural space.

Metabolism: Liver, excreted in the urine
Half-life: 10.25–12 hr

PRECAUTIONS:
- Advanced arteriosclerosis, symptomatic cardiovascular disease, moderate-to-severe HTN
- Hyperthyroidism
- Known hypersensitivity or idiosyncratic reaction to sympathomimetic amines
- Glaucoma
- Agitated states
- Patients with a history of drug abuse; Amphetamines have a high potential for abuse. Administration of Amphetamines for an extended period of time may lead to drug dependence. Particular attention should be paid to the possibility of subjects obtaining this class of medication for nontherapeutic use or

distribution to others, and the drugs should be prescribed or dispensed sparingly.
- During or within 14 days following the administration of MAOIs, hypertensive crisis may result.
- Preexisting psychosis
- Seizure history: Some studies have shown the potential for lowering the seizure threshold

PATIENT AND FAMILY EDUCATION:
- Store at room temperature, protected from light.
- Keep out of reach of children.
- Seek medical care for any signs of heart problems (chest pain, shortness of breath), fainting, psychotic symptoms, overdose, or any other concerns.
- Routinely assess weight and BP.
- Treatment should be initiated at low dosages and then titrated over 2 to 4 wk until an adequate response is achieved or unacceptable adverse effects occur.
- If one stimulant is not effective, another should be attempted before second-line medications are considered. Although some children benefit from daily stimulant therapy, weekend and summer "drug holidays" are suggested for children whose ADHD symptoms predominantly affect schoolwork or to limit adverse effects (e.g., appetite suppression, abdominal pain, headache, insomnia, irritability, tics).

SPECIAL POPULATIONS:
- *Elderly:* Caution with polypharmacy and comorbid conditions; has not been studied for use in this population
- *Pregnancy:* Category C; based on animal data, they may cause fetal harm
- *Lactation:* Possibly unsafe
- *Children:* Has not been studied in children younger than 6 yr; should not be used in children younger than 3 yr.

Adderall XR

INDICATIONS: Stimulant indicated for the treatment of ADHD of children and adults

AVAILABLE FORMS: Capsule, 5, 10, 15, 20, 25, and 30 mg

DOSAGE: Dosage should be individualized according to the therapeutic needs and response of the patient. All stimulant preparations should be administered at the lowest effective dosage. *Children: 6 to 12 yr:* 10 mg qam; start, 5 to 10 mg PO qam, increase 5 to 10 mg/day every week; maximum, 30 mg/day; may convert from IR to ER at same total daily dose qam. *13 to 17 yr old:* 10 to 20 mg/day PO qam; start, 10 mg PO qam, increase 10 mg/day daily; maximum, 40 mg/day; may convert from IR to ER at same total daily dose qam, doses greater than 20 mg/day rarely more effective.

dextroamphetamine/amphetamine

Adults: 5 to 40 mg/day PO divided daily tid; start, 20 mg PO qam, increase 10 mg/day every week; maximum, 60 mg/day; doses greater than 20 mg/day rarely more effective.

ADMINISTRATION: Swallow capsules whole with water or other liquid. If patient cannot swallow the capsule, open and sprinkle the medicine over a spoonful of applesauce. Swallow all of the applesauce and medicine mixture without chewing immediately. Follow with a drink of water or other liquid. Never chew or crush the capsule or the medicine inside the capsule. It can be taken with or without food.

SIDE EFFECTS: Decreased appetite; dizziness; dry mouth; irritability; insomnia; upper abdominal pain; nausea and/or vomiting; weight loss;
(cont.)

ATTENTION DEFICIT HYPERACTIVITY DISORDER: Amphetamines—Long-Acting

dextroamphetamine/amphetamine (cont.)

headaches; anxiety; psychiatric events (increase in manic states for bipolar patients, aggression, tics, tremors); long-term growth suppression (patients should be monitored throughout treatment, if there appears to be growth suppression, the treatment should be discontinued); rash; pyrexia; palpitations, tachycardia, elevated BP, sudden death, MI, cardiomyopathy; Stevens-Johnson syndrome and toxic epidermal necrolysis; impotence, libido changes

DRUG INTERACTIONS: Urinary acidifying agents; MAOIs; adrenergic blockers; antihistamines; antihypertensives; veratrum alkaloids; ethosuximide; TCAs; meperidine; phenobarbital; phenytoin; chlorpromazine; *Haldol*; lithium; norepinephrine; propoxyphene

PHARMACOKINETICS:
- Absorbed by the GI tract.
- Amphetamines are noncatecholamine sympathomimetic amines with CNS-stimulant activity.
- The mode of therapeutic action in ADHD is not known. Amphetamines are thought to block the reuptake of norepinephrine and dopamine into the presynaptic neuron and increase the release of these monoamines into the extraneural space.

Excretion: Urine
Half-life: 9–14 hr

PRECAUTIONS:
- Advanced arteriosclerosis, symptomatic cardiovascular disease, moderate-to-severe HTN
- Hyperthyroidism
- Known hypersensitivity or idiosyncratic reaction to sympathomimetic amines
- Glaucoma
- Agitated states
- Patients with a history of drug abuse: Amphetamines have a high potential for abuse. Administration of Amphetamines for an extended period of time may lead to drug dependence. Particular attention should be paid

to the possibility of subjects obtaining this class of medication for nontherapeutic use or distribution to others, and the drugs should be prescribed or dispensed sparingly.
- During or within 14 days following the administration of MAOIs, hypertensive crisis may result.
- Preexisting psychosis
- Seizure history: Some studies have shown the potential for lowering the seizure threshold

PATIENT AND FAMILY EDUCATION:
- Store at room temperature, protected from light.
- Keep out of reach of children.
- Seek medical care for any signs of heart problems (chest pain, shortness of breath), fainting, psychotic symptoms, overdose, or any other concerns.
- Routinely assess weight and BP.
- Treatment should be initiated at low dosages and then titrated over 2 to 4 wk until an adequate response is achieved or unacceptable adverse effects occur.
- If one stimulant is not effective, another should be attempted before second-line medications are considered. Although some children benefit from daily stimulant therapy, weekend and summer "drug holidays" are suggested for children whose ADHD symptoms predominantly affect schoolwork, or to limit adverse effects (e.g., appetite suppression, abdominal pain, headache, insomnia, irritability, tics).

SPECIAL POPULATIONS:
- *Elderly:* Caution with polypharmacy and comorbid conditions; has not been studied for use in this population
- *Pregnancy:* Category C; based on animal data, they may cause fetal harm
- *Lactation:* Possibly unsafe
- *Children:* Has not been studied in children younger than 6 yr old; should not be used in children younger than 3 yr.

lisdexamfetamine · *Vyvanse*

INDICATIONS: Stimulant indicated for the treatment of ADHD of children and adults

AVAILABLE FORMS: Capsule, 20, 30, 40, 50, 60, and 70 mg

DOSAGE: Dosage should be individualized according to the therapeutic needs and response of the patient. All stimulant preparations should be administered at the lowest effective dosage. *Children: 6 to 12 yr old:* 30 mg PO qam; maximum, 70 mg/day; may increase dose 10 to 20 mg/day every week; use lowest effective dose. *Adults:* 30 mg qam; maximum, 70 mg/day; may increase dose 10 to 20 mg/day every week; use lowest effective dose.

ADMINISTRATION: Swallow capsules whole with water or other liquids. If patient cannot swallow the capsule, open it and mix with water. Follow with a drink of water or other liquid. It can be taken with or without food.

SIDE EFFECTS: Decreased appetite; dizziness; dry mouth; irritability; insomnia; upper abdominal pain; nausea and/or vomiting; weight loss; headaches; anxiety; psychiatric events: increase in manic states for bipolar patients, aggression, tics, tremors; long-term growth suppression: patients should be monitored throughout treatment; if there appears to be growth suppression, the treatment
(cont.)

lisdexamfetamine (*cont.*)

should be discontinued; rash; pyrexia; palpitations, tachycardia, elevated BP, sudden death, MI, cardiomyopathy; Stevens-Johnson syndrome and toxic epidermal necrolysis; impotence, libido changes

DRUG INTERACTIONS: Urinary acidifying agents; MAOIs; adrenergic blockers; antihistamines; antihypertensives; veratrum alkaloids; ethosuximide; TCAs; meperidine; phenobarbital; phenytoin; chlorpromazine; *Haldol*; lithium; norepinephrine; propoxyphene

PHARMACOKINETICS:
- Absorbed by the GI tract.
- Amphetamines are noncatecholamine sympathomimetic amines with CNS-stimulant activity.
- The mode of therapeutic action in ADHD is not known. Amphetamines are thought to block the reuptake of norepinephrine and dopamine into the presynaptic neuron and increase the release of these monoamines into the extraneural space.
- Prodrug converted to dextroamphetamine

Metabolism: Liver; mainly excreted in the urine
Half-life: 12 hr

PRECAUTIONS:
- Advanced arteriosclerosis, symptomatic cardiovascular disease, moderate-to-severe HTN
- Hyperthyroidism
- Known hypersensitivity or idiosyncratic reaction to sympathomimetic amines
- Glaucoma
- Agitated states
- Patients with a history of drug abuse: Amphetamines have a high potential for abuse. Administration of Amphetamines for an extended period of time may lead to drug dependence. Particular attention should be paid to the possibility of subjects obtaining this class of medication for nontherapeutic use or

distribution to others, and the drugs should be prescribed or dispensed sparingly.
- During or within 14 days following the administration of MAOIs, hypertensive crisis may result.
- Preexisting psychosis
- Seizure history: Some studies have shown the potential for lowering the seizure threshold

PATIENT AND FAMILY EDUCATION:
- Store at room temperature, protected from light.
- Keep out of reach of children.
- Seek medical care for any signs of heart problems (chest pain, shortness of breath), fainting, psychotic symptoms, overdose, or any other concerns.
- Routinely assess weight and BP.
- Treatment should be initiated at low dosages and then titrated over 2 to 4 wk until an adequate response is achieved or unacceptable adverse effects occur.
- If one stimulant is not effective, another should be attempted before second-line medications are considered. Although some children benefit from daily stimulant therapy, weekend and summer "drug holidays" are suggested for children whose ADHD symptoms predominantly affect schoolwork, or to limit adverse effects (e.g., appetite suppression, abdominal pain, headache, insomnia, irritability, tics).

SPECIAL POPULATIONS:
- *Elderly:* Caution with polypharmacy and comorbid conditions; has not been studied for use in this population
- *Pregnancy:* Category C; based on animal data, they may cause fetal harm
- *Lactation:* Possibly unsafe
- *Children:* Has not been studied in children younger than 6 yr; should not be used in children younger than 3 yr.

Class: Methylphenidates—Short-Acting

▶ **Note:** This class of medications is a controlled substance.

Focalin   **dexmethylphenidate**

INDICATIONS: Stimulant indicated for the treatment of ADHD of children and adults

AVAILABLE FORMS: Capsule, 2.5, 5, and 10 mg

DOSAGE: Dosage should be individualized according to the therapeutic needs and response of the patient. All stimulant preparations should be administered at the lowest effective dosage. *Children: Older than 6 yr:* 2.5 to 10 mg PO bid; start, 2.5 mg PO bid, increase 5 to 10 mg/day every 7 days; maximum, 20 mg/day; to convert from methylphenidate start at 50% of current methylphenidate daily dose; space doses at least 4 hr apart. *Adults:* 2.5 to 10 mg bid, 2.5 mg PO bid,

increase 5 to 10 mg/day every 7 days; maximum, 20 mg/day; to convert from methylphenidate start at 50% of current methylphenidate daily dose; space doses at least 4 hr apart.

ADMINISTRATION: Do not crush or chew; may be given with or without food

SIDE EFFECTS: Decreased appetite; dizziness; dry mouth; irritability; insomnia; upper abdominal pain; nausea and/or vomiting; weight loss; headaches; anxiety; psychiatric events: increase in manic states for bipolar patients, aggression, tics, tremors; long-term growth suppression: patients should be monitored throughout treatment, if there
(cont.)

dexmethylphenidate (cont.)

appears to be growth suppression, the treatment should be discontinued; rash; pyrexia; palpitations, tachycardia, elevated BP, sudden death, mi, cardiomyopathy; Stevens-Johnson syndrome and toxic epidermal necrolysis; impotence, libido changes

DRUG INTERACTIONS: Urinary acidifying agents; MAOIs; adrenergic blockers; antihistamines; antihypertensives; veratrum alkaloids; ethosuximide; TCAs; meperidine; phenobarbital; phenytoin; chlorpromazine; *Haldol*; lithium; norepinephrine; propoxyphene

PHARMACOKINETICS:
- Absorbed by the GI tract.
- Amphetamines are noncatecholamine sympathomimetic amines with CNS-stimulant activity.
- The mode of therapeutic action in ADHD is not known. Amphetamines are thought to block the reuptake of norepinephrine and dopamine into the presynaptic neuron and increase the release of these monoamines into the extraneural space.

Metabolism: Liver, excreted in the urine
Half-life: 2–4.5 hr

PRECAUTIONS:
- Advanced arteriosclerosis, symptomatic cardiovascular disease, moderate-to-severe HTN
- Hyperthyroidism
- Known hypersensitivity or idiosyncratic reaction to sympathomimetic amines
- Glaucoma
- Agitated states
- Patients with history of drug abuse: Amphetamines have a high potential for abuse. Administration of Amphetamines for an extended period of time may lead to drug dependence. Particular attention should be paid to the possibility of subjects obtaining this class of medication for nontherapeutic use or

distribution to others, and the drugs should be prescribed or dispensed sparingly.
- During or within 14 days following the administration of MAOIs, hypertensive crisis may result.
- Preexisting psychosis
- Seizure history: Some studies have shown the potential for lowering the seizure threshold.

PATIENT AND FAMILY EDUCATION:
- Store at room temperature, protected from light.
- Keep out of reach of children.
- Seek medical care for any signs of heart problems (chest pain, shortness of breath), fainting, psychotic symptoms, overdose, or any other concerns.
- Routinely assess weight and BP.
- Treatment should be initiated at low dosages and then titrated over 2 to 4 wk until an adequate response is achieved, or unacceptable adverse effects occur.
- If one stimulant is not effective, another should be attempted before second-line medications are considered. Although some children benefit from daily stimulant therapy, weekend and summer "drug holidays" are suggested for children whose ADHD symptoms predominantly affect schoolwork, or to limit adverse effects (e.g., appetite suppression, abdominal pain, headache, insomnia, irritability, tics).

SPECIAL POPULATIONS:
- *Elderly:* Caution with polypharmacy and comorbid conditions; has not been studied for use in this population
- *Pregnancy:* Category C; based on animal data, they may cause fetal harm
- *Lactation:* Possibly unsafe
- *Children:* Has not been studied in children younger than 6 yr; should not be used in children younger than 3 yr.

methylphenidate   *Methylin*

INDICATIONS: Stimulant indicated for the treatment of ADHD of children and adults

AVAILABLE FORMS: Capsule, 5, 10, and 20 mg; chewable, 2.5, 5, and 10 mg; liquid, 5 mg/5 mL, 10 mg/5 mL

DOSAGE: Dosage should be individualized according to the therapeutic needs and response of the patient. All stimulant preparations should be administered at the lowest effective dosage. *Children: Older than 6 yr:* 0.3 to 2 mg/kg/day PO divided bid to tid; start, 0.3 mg/kg PO bid or 2.5 to 5 mg PO bid, increase 0.1 mg/kg/dose or 5 to 10 mg/day every 7 days; maximum, 2 mg/kg/day up to 60 mg/day. *Adults:* 5 to 15 mg PO bid to tid; start, 5 to 10 mg PO bid; increase 10 mg/day every 7 days.

ADMINISTRATION: Duration 3 to 5 hr; give 30 to 45 min before meals, last dose before 6 pm.

SIDE EFFECTS: Decreased appetite; dizziness; dry mouth; irritability; insomnia; upper abdominal pain; nausea and/or vomiting; weight loss; headaches; anxiety; psychiatric events: increase in manic states for bipolar patients, aggression, tics, tremors; long-term growth suppression: patients should be monitored throughout treatment; if there appears to be growth suppression, the treatment should be discontinued; rash; pyrexia; palpitations, tachycardia, elevated BP, sudden death, MI, cardiomyopathy; Stevens-Johnson syndrome and toxic epidermal necrolysis; impotence, libido changes

DRUG INTERACTIONS: Urinary acidifying agents; MAOIs; adrenergic blockers; antihistamines; antihypertensives; veratrum alkaloids; ethosuximide; TCAs; meperidine; phenobarbital; phenytoin; chlorpromazine; *Haldol*; lithium; norepinephrine; propoxyphene   *(cont.)*

methylphenidate (*cont.*)

PHARMACOKINETICS:
- Absorbed by the GI tract.
- Amphetamines are noncatecholamine sympath-omimetic amines with CNS-stimulant activity.
- The mode of therapeutic action in ADHD is not known. Amphetamines are thought to block the reuptake of norepinephrine and dopamine into the presynaptic neuron and increase the release of these monoamines into the extraneural space.

Metabolism: Liver, excreted in urine
Half-life: 2–3 hr

PRECAUTIONS:
- Advanced arteriosclerosis, symptomatic cardiovascular disease, moderate-to-severe HTN.
- Hyperthyroidism
- Known hypersensitivity or idiosyncratic reaction to sympathomimetic amines
- Glaucoma
- Agitated states
- Patients with a history of drug abuse: Amphetamines have a high potential for abuse. Administration of Amphetamines for an extended period of time may lead to drug dependence. Particular attention should be paid to the possibility of subjects obtaining this class of medication for nontherapeutic use or distribution to others, and the drugs should be prescribed or dispensed sparingly.
- During or within 14 days following the administration of MAOIs, hypertensive crisis may result.
- Preexisting psychosis

- Seizure history: Some studies have shown the potential for lowering the seizure threshold

PATIENT AND FAMILY EDUCATION:
- Store at room temperature, protected from light.
- Keep out of reach of children.
- Seek medical care for any signs of heart problems (chest pain, shortness of breath), fainting, psychotic symptoms, overdose, or any other concerns.
- Routinely assess weight and BP.
- Treatment should be initiated at low dosages and then titrated over 2 to 4 wk until an adequate response is achieved or unacceptable adverse effects occur.
- If one stimulant is not effective, another should be attempted before second-line medications are considered. Although some children benefit from daily stimulant therapy, weekend and summer "drug holidays" are suggested for children whose ADHD symptoms predominantly affect schoolwork, or to limit adverse effects (e.g., appetite suppression, abdominal pain, headache, insomnia, irritability, tics).

SPECIAL POPULATIONS:
- *Elderly:* Caution with polypharmacy and comorbid conditions; has not been studied for use in this population
- *Pregnancy:* Category C; based on animal data, they may cause fetal harm
- *Lactation:* Possibly unsafe
- *Children:* Has not been studied in children younger than 6 yr old: should not be used in children younger than 3 yr.

Ritalin SR and LA   methylphenidate

INDICATIONS: Stimulant indicated for the treatment of ADHD of children and adults

AVAILABLE FORMS: Capsule, 10, 20, 30, and 40 mg

DOSAGE: Dosage should be individualized according to the therapeutic needs and response of the patient. All stimulant preparations should be administered at the lowest effective dosage. *Children: Older than 6 yr:* 20 to 40 mg PO qam; start, 20 mg PO qam; increase 10 mg/day every 7 days; maximum, 60 mg/day. *Adults:* 20 to 40 mg qam; start, 20 mg PO qam; increase 10 mg/day every 7 days; maximum, 60 mg/day.

ADMINISTRATION: *Ritalin LA* capsules may be opened and sprinkled on soft food; may sprinkle on applesauce immediately before use; do not crush/chew; to switch from bid IR form use same total daily dose.

SIDE EFFECTS: Decreased appetite; dizziness; dry mouth; irritability; insomnia; upper abdominal pain; nausea and/or vomiting; weight loss; headaches; anxiety; psychiatric events: increase in manic states for bipolar patients, aggression, tics, tremors; long-term growth suppression: patients should be monitored throughout treatment, if there appears to be growth suppression, the treatment should be discontinued; rash; pyrexia; palpitations, tachycardia, elevated BP, sudden death, MI, cardiomyopathy; Stevens-Johnson syndrome and toxic epidermal necrolysis; impotence, libido changes

DRUG INTERACTIONS: Urinary acidifying agents; MAOIs; adrenergic blockers; antihistamines; antihypertensives; veratrum alkaloids; ethosuximide; TCAs; meperidine; phenobarbital; phenytoin; chlorpromazine; *Haldol*; lithium; norepinephrine; propoxyphene

PHARMACOKINETICS:
- Absorbed by the GI tract.
- Amphetamines are noncatecholamine sympath-omimetic amines with CNS-stimulant activity.
- The mode of therapeutic action in ADHD is not known. Amphetamines are thought to block the reuptake of norepinephrine and dopamine into the presynaptic neuron and increase the release of these monoamines into the extraneural space.

Metabolism: Liver, excreted mainly in the urine
Half-life: 3–4 hr

(cont.)

ATTENTION DEFICIT HYPERACTIVITY DISORDER: Methylphenidates—Short-Acting

methylphenidate (*cont.*)

PRECAUTIONS:
- Advanced arteriosclerosis, symptomatic cardio-vascular disease, moderate-to-severe HTN
- Hyperthyroidism
- Known hypersensitivity or idiosyncratic reaction to sympathomimetic amines
- Glaucoma
- Agitated states
- Patients with a history of drug abuse: Amphetamines have a high potential for abuse. Administration of Amphetamines for an extended period of time may lead to drug dependence. Particular attention should be paid to the possibility of subjects obtaining this class of medication for nontherapeutic use or distribution to others, and the drugs should be prescribed or dispensed sparingly.
- During or within 14 days following the administration of MAOIs, hypertensive crisis may result.
- Preexisting psychosis
- Seizure history: Some studies have shown the potential for lowering the seizure threshold.

PATIENT AND FAMILY EDUCATION:
- Store at room temperature, protected from light.
- Keep out of reach of children.
- Seek medical care for any signs of heart problems (chest pain, shortness of breath), fainting, psychotic symptoms, overdose, or any other concerns.
- Routinely assess weight and BP.
- Treatment should be initiated at low dosages and then titrated over 2 to 4 wk until an adequate response is achieved or unacceptable adverse effects occur.
- If one stimulant is not effective, another should be attempted before second-line medications are considered. Although some children benefit from daily stimulant therapy, weekend and summer "drug holidays" are suggested for children whose ADHD symptoms predominantly affect schoolwork, or to limit adverse effects (e.g., appetite suppression, abdominal pain, headache, insomnia, irritability, tics).

SPECIAL POPULATIONS:
- *Elderly:* Caution with polypharmacy and comorbid conditions; has not been studied for use in this population
- *Pregnancy:* Category C; based on animal data, they may cause fetal harm
- *Lactation:* Possibly unsafe
- *Children:* Has not been studied in children younger than 6 yr; should not be used in children younger than 3 yr.

Class: Methylphenidates—Intermediate-Acting

▶**Note:** This class of medications is a controlled substance.

methylphenidate   *Metadate ER and CD*

INDICATIONS: Stimulant indicated for the treatment of ADHD of children and adults

AVAILABLE FORMS: Capsule, 10, 20, 30, 40, 50, and 60 mg

DOSAGE: Dosage should be individualized according to the therapeutic needs and response of the patient. All stimulant preparations should be administered at the lowest effective dosage. *Children: Older than 6 yr:* 20 to 60 mg PO qam; start, 20 mg PO qam; increase 10 to 20 mg/day every, 7 days; maximum, 60 mg/day. *Adults:* 20 to 60 mg PO qam; start, 20 mg PO qam; increase 10 to 20 mg/day every 7 days; maximum, 60 mg/day.

ADMINISTRATION: *Metadate* may be opened and sprinkled on soft food; initial titration with IR form recommended; give before meal

SIDE EFFECTS: Decreased appetite; dizziness; dry mouth; irritability; insomnia; upper abdominal pain; nausea and/or vomiting; weight loss; headaches; anxiety; psychiatric events: increase in manic states for bipolar patients, aggression, tics, tremors; long-term growth suppression: patients should be monitored throughout treatment, if there appears to be growth suppression, the treatment should be discontinued; rash; pyrexia; palpitations, tachycardia, elevated BP, sudden death, MI, cardiomyopathy; Stevens-Johnson syndrome and toxic epidermal necrolysis; impotence, libido changes

DRUG INTERACTIONS: Urinary acidifying agents; MAOIs; adrenergic blockers; antihistamines; antihypertensives; veratrum alkaloids; ethosuximide; TCAs; meperidine; phenobarbital; phenytoin; chlorpromazine; *Haldol*; lithium; norepinephrine; propoxyphene

PHARMACOKINETICS:
- Absorbed by the GI tract.
- Amphetamines are noncatecholamine sympathomimetic amines with CNS-stimulant activity.
- The mode of therapeutic action in ADHD is not known. Amphetamines are thought to block the reuptake of norepinephrine and dopamine into the presynaptic neuron and increase the release of these monoamines into the extraneural space.

Metabolism: Liver, mainly excreted in the urine
Half-life: 3–4 hr

(cont.)

methylphenidate (*cont.*)

PRECAUTIONS:

- Advanced arteriosclerosis, symptomatic cardiovascular disease, moderate-to-severe HTN
- Hyperthyroidism
- Known hypersensitivity or idiosyncratic reaction to sympathomimetic amines
- Glaucoma
- Agitated states
- Patients with a history of drug abuse: Amphetamines have a high potential for abuse. Administration of Amphetamines for an extended period of time may lead to drug dependence. Particular attention should be paid to the possibility of subjects obtaining this class of medication for nontherapeutic use or distribution to others, and the drugs should be prescribed or dispensed sparingly.
- During or within 14 days following the administration of MAOIs, hypertensive crisis may result.
- Preexisting psychosis
- Seizure history: Some studies have shown the potential for lowering the seizure threshold

PATIENT AND FAMILY EDUCATION:

- Store at room temperature, protected from light.
- Keep out of reach of children.
- Seek medical care for any signs of heart problems (chest pain, shortness of breath), fainting, psychotic symptoms, overdose, or any other concerns.
- Routinely assess weight and BP.
- Treatment should be initiated at low dosages and then titrated over 2 to 4 wk until an adequate response is achieved or unacceptable adverse effects occur.
- If one stimulant is not effective, another should be attempted before second-line medications are considered. Although some children benefit from daily stimulant therapy, weekend and summer "drug holidays" are suggested for children whose ADHD symptoms predominantly affect schoolwork, or to limit adverse effects (e.g., appetite suppression, abdominal pain, headache, insomnia, irritability, tics).

SPECIAL POPULATIONS:

- *Elderly:* Caution with polypharmacy and comorbid conditions; has not been studied for use in this population
- *Pregnancy:* Category C; based on animal data, they may cause fetal harm
- *Lactation:* Possibly unsafe
- *Children:* Has not been studied in children younger than 6 yr; should not be used in children younger than 3 yr.

Class: Methylphenidates—Long-Acting

▶ **Note:** This class of medications is a controlled substance.

	Concerta	methylphenidate

INDICATIONS: Stimulant indicated for the treatment of ADHD of children and adults

AVAILABLE FORMS: Capsule, 18, 27, 36, and 54 mg

DOSAGE: Dosage should be individualized according to the therapeutic needs and response of the patient. All stimulant preparations should be administered at the lowest effective dosage. *Children: 6 to 12 yr old:* 1 tab PO qam; start, 18 mg PO daily, increase 18 mg/day every 7 days; maximum, 54 mg/day. *Older than 13 yr:* 1 tab PO qam; start, 18 mg PO daily, increase 18 mg/day every 7 days; maximum, 2 mg/kg/day or 72 mg/day. *Adults: 18 to 65 yr:* 1 tab PO qam; start, 18 to 36 mg PO daily, increase 18 mg/day every 7 days; maximum, 72 mg/day.

ADMINISTRATION: *Concerta* capsules may be opened and sprinkled on soft food, initial titration with IR form recommended; give before meals

SIDE EFFECTS: Decreased appetite; dizziness; dry mouth; irritability; insomnia; upper abdominal pain; nausea and/or vomiting; weight loss; headaches; anxiety; psychiatric events (increase in manic states for bipolar patients, aggression, tics, tremors); long-term growth suppression (patients should be monitored throughout treatment, if there appears to be growth suppression, the treatment should be discontinued); rash; pyrexia; palpitations, tachycardia, elevated BP, sudden death, MI, cardiomyopathy; Stevens-Johnson syndrome and toxic epidermal necrolysis; impotence, libido changes

DRUG INTERACTIONS: Urinary acidifying agents; MAOIs; adrenergic blockers; antihistamines; antihypertensives; veratrum alkaloids; ethosuximide; TCAs; meperidine; phenobarbital; phenytoin; chlorpromazine; *Haldol*; lithium; norepinephrine; propoxyphene

PHARMACOKINETICS:

- Absorbed by the GI tract.
- Amphetamines are noncatecholamine sympathomimetic amines with CNS-stimulant activity.
- The mode of therapeutic action in ADHD is not known. Amphetamines are thought to block the reuptake of norepinephrine and dopamine into the presynaptic neuron and increase the release of these monoamines into the extraneural space.

Metabolism: Liver; mainly excreted in the urine
Half-life: 3.5 hr

(cont.)

ATTENTION DEFICIT HYPERACTIVITY DISORDER: Methylphenidates—Long-Acting

methylphenidate (cont.)

PRECAUTIONS:

- Advanced arteriosclerosis, symptomatic cardio-vascular disease, moderate-to-severe HTN
- Hyperthyroidism
- Known hypersensitivity or idiosyncratic reaction to sympathomimetic amines
- Glaucoma
- Agitated states
- Patients with a history of drug abuse: Amphetamines have a high potential for abuse. Administration of Amphetamines for an extended period of time may lead to drug dependence. Particular attention should be paid to the possibility of subjects obtaining this class of medication for nontherapeutic use or distribution to others, and the drugs should be prescribed or dispensed sparingly.
- During or within 14 days following the administration of MAOIs, hypertensive crisis may result.
- Preexisting psychosis
- Seizure history: Some studies have shown the potential for lowering the seizure threshold

PATIENT AND FAMILY EDUCATION:

- Store at room temperature, protected from light.
- Keep out of reach of children.
- Seek medical care for any signs of heart problems (chest pain, shortness of breath), fainting, psychotic symptoms, overdose, or any other concerns.
- Routinely assess weight and BP.
- Treatment should be initiated at low dosages and then titrated over 2 to 4 wk until an adequate response is achieved or unacceptable adverse effects occur.
- If one stimulant is not effective, another should be attempted before second-line medications are considered. Although some children benefit from daily stimulant therapy, weekend and summer "drug holidays" are suggested for children whose ADHD symptoms predominantly affect schoolwork, or to limit adverse effects (e.g., appetite suppression, abdominal pain, headache, insomnia, irritability, tics).

SPECIAL POPULATIONS:

- *Elderly:* Caution with polypharmacy and comorbid conditions; has not been studied for use in this population
- *Pregnancy:* Category C; based on animal data, they may cause fetal harm
- *Lactation:* Possibly unsafe
- *Children:* Has not been studied in children younger than 6 yr; should not be used in children younger than 3 yr.

---

methylphenidate transdermal   *Daytrana Patch*

INDICATIONS: Stimulant indicated for the treatment of ADHD of children and adults

AVAILABLE FORMS: Transdermal patch, 10, 15, 20, and 30 mg/9 hr patch

DOSAGE: Dosage should be individualized according to the therapeutic needs and response of the patient. All stimulant preparations should be administered at the lowest effective dosage. *Children: Older than 6 yr:* 1 patch daily × 9 hr, off × 15 hr; start, 10 mg/9 hr patch daily, may increase to next size patch every 7 days; maximum, 30 mg/9 hr patch daily. *Adults: 18 to 65 yr old:* 1 patch daily × 9 hr, off × 15 hr; start, 10 mg/9 hr patch daily, may increase to next size patch every 7 days; maximum, 30 mg/9 hr patch daily.

ADMINISTRATION: Use same titration when converting from PO; apply to hip 2 hr before desired effect; drug effects may persist 5 hr after patch removal; rotate sites; do not alter/cut patch.

SIDE EFFECTS: Decreased appetite; dizziness; dry mouth; irritability; insomnia; upper abdominal pain; nausea and/or vomiting; weight loss; headaches; anxiety; psychiatric events: increase in manic states for bipolar patients, aggression, tics, tremors; long-term growth suppression: patients should be monitored throughout treatment, if there appears to be growth suppression, the treatment should be discontinued; rash; pyrexia; palpitations, tachycardia, elevated BP, sudden death, MI, cardiomyopathy; Stevens-Johnson syndrome and toxic epidermal necrolysis; impotence, libido changes; skin irritation

DRUG INTERACTIONS: Urinary acidifying agents; MAOIs; adrenergic blockers; antihistamines; antihypertensives; veratrum alkaloids; ethosuximide; TCAs; meperidine; phenobarbital; phenytoin; chlorpromazine; *Haldol*; lithium; norepinephrine; propoxyphene

PHARMACOKINETICS:

- Absorbed by the GI tract.
- Amphetamines are noncatecholamine sympathomimetic amines with CNS-stimulant activity.
- The mode of therapeutic action in ADHD is not known. Amphetamines are thought to block the reuptake of norepinephrine and dopamine into the presynaptic neuron and increase the release of these monoamines into the extraneural space.

Metabolism: Liver, mainly excreted in the urine
Half-life: 3.5 hr

PRECAUTIONS:

- Advanced arteriosclerosis, symptomatic cardiovascular disease, moderate-to-severe HTN
- Hyperthyroidism

(cont.)

methylphenidate transdermal (*cont.*)

- Known hypersensitivity or idiosyncratic reaction to sympathomimetic amines
- Glaucoma
- Agitated states
- Patients with a history of drug abuse: Amphetamines have a high potential for abuse: administration of Amphetamines for an extended period of time may lead to drug dependence. Particular attention should be paid to the possibility of subjects obtaining this class of medication for nontherapeutic use or distribution to others, and the drugs should be prescribed or dispensed sparingly.
- During or within 14 days following the administration of MAOIs, hypertensive crisis may result.
- Preexisting psychosis
- Seizure history: Some studies have shown the potential for lowering the seizure threshold.

PATIENT AND FAMILY EDUCATION:
- Store at room temperature, protected from light.
- Keep out of reach of children.
- Seek medical care for any signs of heart problems (chest pain, shortness of breath), fainting, psychotic symptoms, overdose, or any other concerns.

- Routinely assess weight and BP.
- Treatment should be initiated at low dosages and then titrated over 2 to 4 wk until an adequate response is achieved or unacceptable adverse effects occur.
- If one stimulant is not effective, another should be attempted before second-line medications are considered. Although some children benefit from daily stimulant therapy, weekend and summer "drug holidays" are suggested for children whose ADHD symptoms predominantly affect schoolwork, or to limit adverse effects (e.g., appetite suppression, abdominal pain, headache, insomnia, irritability, tics).

SPECIAL POPULATIONS:
- *Elderly:* Caution with polypharmacy and comorbid conditions; has not been studied for use in this population
- *Pregnancy:* Category C; based on animal data, they may cause fetal harm
- *Lactation:* Possibly unsafe
- *Children:* Has not been studied in children younger than 6 yr; should not be used in children younger than 3 yr.
- Nonstimulants

Class: Selective Norepinephrine Reuptake Inhibitors (SNRIs)

Strattera   **atomoxetine**

INDICATIONS: Stimulant indicated for the treatment of ADHD of children aged 6 and above and adults. Although nonstimulants are considered second-line therapy, they may be a safer alternative than stimulants for patients with a history of substance abuse.

AVAILABLE FORMS: Capsule, 10, 18, 25, 40, 60, 80, and 100 mg

DOSAGE: Dosage should be individualized according to the therapeutic needs and response of the patient. *Children: Older than 6 yr:* Less than 70 kg; start, 0.5 mg/kg PO qam × 3 days, then increase to 1.2 mg/kg PO qam; maximum, 1.4 mg/kg/day, doses greater than 0.5 mg/kg/day may be divided bid. *Greater than 6 yr:* greater than 70 kg; start, 40 mg PO qam × 3 days, then increase to 80 mg PO qam, may increase to 100 mg/day after 2 to 4 wk if needed; maximum, 100 mg/day. *Adults:* 80 mg qam; start, 40 mg PO qam × 3 days, then increase to 80 mg PO qam, may increase to 100 mg/day after 2 to 4 wk if needed. Maximum: 100 mg/day; taking with food may alleviate GI side effects, requires slower titration if patient is poor CYP2D6 metabolizer or on strong CYP2D6 inhibitor periodically reassess need for treatment during maintenance.

SIDE EFFECTS: Nausea and/or vomiting; fatigue; decreased appetite; abdominal pain; somnolence;

constipation; dry mouth; insomnia; priapism; urinary hesitancy or retention or dysuria; dysmenorrhea; hot flashes; severe liver injury; serious cardiovascular events (MI, stroke, sudden death); rapid heart rate and increased BP; suicidal ideation; allergic reactions; decreased growth. *Dispose of patch properly*: Remnants of medication may remain on patch and can be dangerous to children or animals.

DRUG INTERACTIONS: MAOIs; CYP2D6 inhibitors; BP agents; albuterol and other beta-2 agonists: action of albuterol on cardiovascular system can be potentiated

PHARMACOKINETICS:
- The precise mechanism by which atomoxetine produces its therapeutic effect is unknown.
- Its therapeutic effect may be related to selective inhibition of the presynaptic norepinephrine transporter.
- Minimally affected by food intake.
- Maximal plasma concentration is reached within 1 to 2 hr after dosing
- Mainly excreted in the urine (80%)

Half-life: Approx. 5 hr

PRECAUTIONS:
- Hypersensitivity to atomoxetine or other constituents of the product

(cont.)

atomoxetine (cont.)

- Use within 2 wk of taking or discontinuing MAOIs
- Narrow angle glaucoma

PATIENT AND FAMILY EDUCATION:
- Do not crush, open, or chew capsules.
- Avoid touching a broken capsule: If powder gets into eyes it is a known ocular irritant and needs to be flushed out immediately.
- Can be taken with or without food.
- Do not double the dose if a day is missed.
- Call poison control/seek medical attention for overdose.
- Seek medical attention for chest pain, shortness of breath, elevated BP, erections that last more than 4 hr, or any other concerning symptoms.
- Children, adolescents, or adults who are being considered for treatment with atomoxetine should have a careful history (including assessment for a family history of sudden death or ventricular arrhythmia) and physical exam to assess for the presence of cardiac disease, and should receive further cardiac evaluation if findings suggest such disease (e.g., electrocardiogram and echocardiogram). Patients who develop symptoms such as exertional chest pain, unexplained syncope, or other symptoms suggestive of cardiac disease during atomoxetine treatment should undergo a prompt cardiac evaluation.
- Store at room temperature.
- Routinely assess weight and BP.

SPECIAL POPULATIONS:
- *Elderly:* Safety has not been studied in geriatric patients
- *Pregnancy:* Category C
- *Lactation:* Safety unknown
- *Children:* Has not been studied in children younger than 6 yr; should not be used in children younger than 3 yr.

Class: Selective Alpha-2A-Adrenergic Receptor Agonist (SARIs)

guanfacine   *Intuniv*

INDICATIONS: Selective alpha-2a-adrenergic receptor agonist indicated for the treatment of ADHD of children and adolescents aged 6 to 17

AVAILABLE FORMS: Capsule, 1, 2, 3, and 4 mg

DOSAGE: *Children:* 6 to 17 yr: 1 to 4 mg PO daily; start, 1 mg PO daily, increase by 1 mg/day every week; alternate, 0.05 to 0.12 mg/kg PO daily. *Adults:* Not for adult use.

ADMINISTRATION: Do not give with high fat meals; do not cut/crush/chew; taper dose by 1 mg/day every 3 to 7 days to discontinue.

SIDE EFFECTS: Somnolence; headache; fatigue; upper abdominal pain; nausea; irritability; dizziness; hypotension; decreased appetite; dry mouth; constipation; syncope; AV block, bradycardia, sinus arrhythmia; dyspepsia; chest pain; asthma; emotional lability, anxiety, depression, insomnia, nightmares, sleep changes

DRUG INTERACTIONS: CYP3A4/5 inhibitors; CUP3A4 inducers; valproic acid; antihypertensive medications; CNS depressants

PHARMACOKINETICS:
- Guanfacine is a selective alpha-2a-adrenergic receptor agonist that has a 15 to 20 times higher affinity for this receptor subtype than for the alpha-2b or alpha-2c subtypes.
- It is a known antihypertensive agent: By stimulating alpha-2a-adrenergic receptors, guanfacine reduces sympathetic nerve impulses from the vasomotor center to the heart and blood vessels, resulting in decreased peripheral vascular resistance and a reduction in heart rate.
- Time to peak plasma concentration is 5 hr.

Metabolism: Liver, excreted in urine.
Half-life: 18 hr

PRECAUTIONS:
- Hypersensitivity to guanfacine or concomitant use with other products containing guanfacine (*Tenex*).
- Not for use in children younger than 6 yr; safety beyond 2 yr of treatment has not been established
- Adult and geriatric populations—not labeled for use

PATIENT AND FAMILY EDUCATION:
- Swallow whole with water, milk, or other liquid.
- Store at room temperature.
- Do not take with a high fat meal—plasma concentrations will increase.
- Use with caution when operating heavy equipment or machinery until response to treatment is known.
- Avoid use with alcohol.
- Avoid dehydration and becoming overheated.
- Have BP and heart rate assessed while taking.
- Taper dose by 1 mg/day every 3 to 7 days to D/C (abrupt cessation may cause increased plasma catecholamines, rebound HTN, nervousness/anxiety).

SPECIAL POPULATIONS:
- *Elderly:* There is no adult dosing for this medication
- *Pregnancy:* Category B
- *Lactation:* Safety unknown
- *Children:* For use in ages 6 to 17

Autism Spectrum Disorder (ASD)

- ASD is a range of complex neurodevelopment disorders.
- The condition is characterized by social impairments, communication difficulties, and restricted, repetitive, and stereotyped patterns of behavior.
- Autistic disorder, sometimes called autism or classical ASD, is the most severe form of ASD, while other conditions along the spectrum include a milder form known as Asperger syndrome, the rare condition called Rett syndrome, and Childhood Disintegrative Disorder and Pervasive Developmental Disorder Not Otherwise Specified (usually referred to as PDD-NOS).
- Although ASD varies significantly in character and severity, it occurs in all ethnic and socioeconomic groups and affects every age group.
- It is estimated that 3 to 6 out of every 1,000 persons will have ASD. That would equate to approximately 1 in every 166 births. Males are four times more likely to have ASD than females.
- The most distinguishing feature is impaired social interaction.
- Starting in infancy, a baby with ASD may be unresponsive to people or may focus intently on one item for long periods of time. A child with ASD may appear to develop normally physically but then withdraw and become indifferent to social engagement.
- Children with ASD appear to have a higher than normal risk for certain co-occurring conditions, including fragile X syndrome, tuberous sclerosis, epileptic seizures, Tourette's syndrome, learning disabilities, and ADD.
- About 20–30% of children with ASD develop epilepsy by the time they enter adulthood.
- The specific cause of ASD is unknown. There may be a link between genetics and the environment.
- Identical twin studies have shown that if one twin is affected, there is a 90% chance the other twin will be affected with ASD.
- There are also a number of studies in progress to determine the specific genetic factors associated with the development of ASD. In families with one child with ASD, the risk of having a

second child with the disorder is approximately 5%, or 1 in 20.
- Patients with autism have normal life expectancies. With early intervention and appropriate treatment, some autistic patients can function productively and attain some degree of independence. Most patients require lifelong assistance.

NEUROBIOLOGY
- Research has identified a number of genes associated with ASD.
- Studies of patients with ASD have found irregularities in the cerebellum.
- Other studies suggest that people with ASD have abnormal levels of serotonin or other neurotransmitters in the brain. These abnormalities suggest that ASD could result from the disruption of normal brain development early in fetal development caused by defects in genes that control brain growth and that regulate how brain cells communicate with each other, possibly due to the influence of environmental factors on gene function.
- Theories that parental practices and vaccine use being responsible for ASD have been disproved.

SYMPTOMS
- Failure to respond to their name
- Often avoid eye contact
- Inability to understand social cues (e.g., tone of voice, facial expressions, body language)
- Lack empathy
- Repetitive movements (e.g., rocking, twirling, or self-abusing behaviors like head-banging and biting)
- Delayed speech
- Refer to themselves by name instead of "I" or "Me"

TREATMENT
- Treatment needs to be initiated early in childhood to obtain the most benefit.
- Treatment may consist of medication (to control anxiety, depression, seizures, etc.), behavior modifications, learning accommodations, and other alternative therapy (e.g., dietary restrictions).

Psychopharmacology for ASD

Overview
- There are a number of medications frequently used for individuals with autism to address certain behaviors or symptoms. Some have studies to support their use, while others do not. SSRIs have been effective in treating depression, obsessive–compulsive behaviors, and anxiety that present in some individuals with ASD.
- Elevated levels of serotonin in the bloodstream of one-third of individuals with autism led researchers to conclude that SSRIs could

potentially reverse some of the symptoms of serotonin dysregulation found in autism.
- Three drugs that have been studied are clomipramine (*Anafranil*), fluvoxamine (*Luvox*), and fluoxetine (*Prozac*). Studies have shown that they may reduce the frequency and intensity of repetitive behaviors and may decrease irritability, tantrums, and aggressive behavior. Some children have also shown improvements in eye contact and responsiveness.

AUTISM SPECTRUM DISORDER

- SSRIs (e.g., fluoxetine) may be used in adolescents with depression or anxiety that cannot be managed through a structured environment or behavioral methods. They do not treat the core features of autism, but may lessen anxiety or depression. Use should only be suggested by a specialist.
- Other drugs, such as *Elavil*, *Wellbutrin*, *Valium*, *Ativan*, and *Xanax* have not been studied as much but may have a role in treating behavioral symptoms. However, all these drugs have potential side effects, which should be discussed with qualified professionals before treatment is started.
- Antipsychotic medications have been the most widely studied of the psychopharmacologic agents in autism for the past 35 years. Originally developed for treating schizophrenia, these drugs have been found to decrease hyperactivity, stereotypical behaviors, withdrawal, and aggression in individuals with autism.
- Five that have been approved by the FDA are clozapine (*Clozaril*), risperidone (*Risperdal*), olanzapine (*Zyprexa*), quetiapine (*Seroquel*), and aripiprazole (*Abilify*).
- Only risperidone (*Risperdal*) has been researched in a controlled study of adults with autism and was approved in 2006 by the FDA for the treatment of autism. Like the antidepressants, these drugs all have potential side effects, including sedation, which need to be carefully monitored by a qualified professional with experience in autism. It is essential that pediatric patients needing treatment with SSRI, TCAs, other antidepressants, antipsychotics, or benzodiazepines be referred to a specialist for management. This therapy continues to be studied and should only be prescribed in a specialist setting.
- Stimulant medications, such as *Ritalin*, *Adderall*, and *Dexedrine*, used to treat hyperactivity in children with ADHD, have also been prescribed for children with ASD. Despite few studies, anecdotal evidence shows that stimulant medications may increase focus and decrease impulsivity and hyperactivity in autism, particularly in children who are not as severely affected as others. However, dosages need to be carefully monitored because behavioral side effects are often dose related.
- Stimulant use is less frequently effective in the treatment of children with autism (approximately 30% respond) than children with ADHD (approximately 80–90% respond). Weight and BP monitoring is required with their use.

CHRONIC TREATMENT OF ASD
Behavior Modification
There are several methods of behavior modification that are used to treat inappropriate, repetitive, and aggressive behavior and to provide autistic patients with skills necessary to function in their environment. Most types of behavior modification are based on the theory that rewarded behavior is more likely to be repeated than behavior that is ignored. This theory is called applied behavior analysis (ABA).

Successful behavior modification must involve the following:
- Highly structured, skill-oriented activities that are based on the patient's needs and interests.
- Intense, one-on-one training with a therapist
- Extensive caregiver involvement.
- *Sensory integration therapy* is a type of behavior modification that focuses on helping autistic patients cope with sensory stimulation. Treatment may include having the patient handle materials with different textures or listen to different sounds.
- *Play therapy* is a type of behavior modification that is used to improve emotional development. This type of therapy improves social skills and learning. Play therapy involves adult–child interaction that is controlled by the child.
- *Social stories* can also be used to improve undeveloped social skills. Stories are designed to help autistic patients understand the feelings, ideas, points of view of others, or to suggest an alternate response to a particular situation. They also may be used to help patients understand and cope with their own feelings.

Dietary Modifications
It is thought that autism is not caused by diet, and the use of dietary modifications and supplements to treat the disorder remain controversial. Changing the diet or adding vitamin supplements may improve digestion and eliminate food intolerances or allergies, which may contribute to behavioral problems in autistic patients. This may alleviate negative behaviors in the autistic patient.

Researchers have found elevated levels of proteins found in wheat, oats, and rye (gluten) and casein (protein in dairy products) byproducts in patients with autism, suggesting that the incomplete breakdown or excessive absorption of these substances may affect brain function.
- Studies have shown that vitamins A, B, and D, magnesium may improve behavior, eye contact, attention span, and learning in autistic patients. Vitamin C has been shown to improve depression and lessen the severity of symptoms in patients with autism.

CLASS	NAME
Selective Serotonin Reuptake Inhibitors (SSRIs)	
	fluvoxamine (*Luvox*)
	fluoxetine (*Prozac*)
Tricyclic Antidepressants (TCAs)	
	amitriptyline (*Elavil*)
Benzodiazepines (BZDs)	
	lorazepam (*Ativan*)
	diazepam (*Valium*)
Norepinepherine/Dopamine Reuptake Inhibitors (NDRIs)	
	buproprion HCl (*Wellbutrin*)
Antipsychotics, Atypical (Second-Generation)	
	clozapine (*Clozaril*)
	risperidone (*Risperdal*)
	olanzapine (*Zyprexa*)
	quetiapine (*Seroquel*)
	aripiprazole (*Abilify*)
Amphetamine Derivatives	
	Short-Acting Stimulants
	dextroamphetamine/amphetamine (*Adderall*)
	dextroamphetamine (*Dexedrine and DextroStat*)
	Long-Acting Stimulants
	dextroamphetamine (*Dexedrine Spansule*)
	dextroamphetamine/amphetamine (*Adderall XR*)
	lisdexamfetamine (*Vyvanse*)
Methylphenidates	
	Short-Acting Stimulants
	dexmethylphenidate (*Focalin*)
	methylphenidate (*Methylin*)
	methylphenidate (*Ritalin SR and LA*)
	Intermediate-Acting Stimulants
	methylphenidate (*Metadate CD and ER*)
	methylphenidate (*Ritalin SR and LA*)
	Long-Acting Stimulants
	methylphenidate (*Concerta*)
	methylphenidate transdermal (*Daytrana Patch*)
	dexmethylphenidate (*Focalin XR*)

Class: Selective Serotonin Reuptake Inhibitors (SSRIs)

- Examples in research that have been used for autism treatment are clonipramine, fluvoxamine, and fluoxetine.

- Use of this class of medicine for the treatment of autism should be done by specialists.

Luvox	**fluvoxamine**

INDICATIONS: To treat depression, anxiety, and OCD in children and adults

AVAILABLE FORMS: Capsule, 25, 50, and 100 mg

DOSAGE: Titrated to least effective dose. *Children: 8 to 11 yr:* 50 to 200 mg PO daily divided bid; start, 25 mg PO qhs, increase 25 mg every 4 to 7 days; maximum, 200 mg/day. *12 to 17 yr:* 50 to 200 mg PO daily divided bid; start, 25 mg PO qhs, increase 25 mg every 4 to 7 days; maximum, 300 mg/day. *Adults:* 50 to 150 mg bid; start, 50 mg PO qhs, increase 50 mg every 4 to 7 days; maximum, 300 mg/day; divide doses greater than 100 mg.

ADMINISTRATION: Consider lower dose in females in this age group; taper dose gradually to discontinue

SIDE EFFECTS: Worsening depression/mania or suicidal thoughts; serotonin syndrome; neuroleptic malignant syndrome; extrapyramidal symptoms; withdrawal syndrome; seizures; priapism; anaphylactic reactions; altered platelet function;

(cont.)

fluvoxamine (cont.)

neonatal persistent pulmonary HTN (greater than 20-wks gestation); neonatal serotonin syndrome (third trimester); neonatal withdrawal (third trimester); nausea/vomiting; headaches; insomnia or somnolence; dizziness; tremor; ejaculatory dysfunction; decreased libido; vision changes

DRUG INTERACTIONS: *Zanaflex;* MAOIs; *Lotronex; Orap; Mellaril; Tegretol; Plavix; Zyvox; Clozaril; Rozerem; Dilantin; Prilosec; Ultram;* benzodiazepines; triptans; TCAs; *Coumadin; Theophylline; Inderal;* St. John's wort; *Quinidine; Cognex*

PHARMACOKINETICS:
- Selectively inhibits serotonin reuptake
Metabolism: Liver extensively—CYP450
Half-life: 15.6 hr

PRECAUTIONS:
- Hypersensitivity to drug class
- Hyponatremia

- Hepatic involvement
- Avoid volume depletion
- Seizure disorder
- Bleeding risks
- Smoking habit changes

PATIENT AND FAMILY EDUCATION:
- Avoid abrupt withdrawal.
- Monitor for worsening depression/suicidal ideations.
- Keep out of reach of children.
- Store at room temperature

SPECIAL POPULATIONS:
- *Elderly:* Caution with use due to polypharmacy and comorbid conditions
- *Pregnancy:* Category C, except for greater than 20-wk gestation.
- *Lactation:* Probably safe
- *Children:* For ages 8 to 17

---

fluoxetine   *Prozac*

INDICATIONS: To treat depression, anxiety, and obsessive–compulsive disorder in children and adults.

AVAILABLE FORMS: Capsule, 10, 20, 40 mg; liquid, 20 mg/5 mL

DOSAGE: Titrated to least effective dose. *Children: 7 to 17 yr:* 10–20 mg PO daily; start, 10 mg PO daily x 7 days; slower titration in lower weight pediatric patients. *Adults:* 20 to 80 mg qam, 20 mg PO qam, increase after several weeks as needed to achieve desired effect; maximum, 80 mg/day.

ADMINISTRATION: May be given with or without food; taper gradually.

SIDE EFFECTS: Worsening depression/mania or suicidal thoughts; serotonin syndrome; neuroleptic malignant syndrome; extrapyramidal symptoms; withdrawal syndrome; seizures; priapism; anaphylactic reactions; altered platelet function; neonatal persistent pulmonary HTN (greater than 20-wks gestation); neonatal serotonin syndrome (third trimester); neonatal withdrawal (third trimester); nausea/vomiting; headaches; insomnia or somnolence; dizziness; tremor; ejaculatory dysfunction; decreased libido; vision changes

DRUG INTERACTIONS: *Zanaflex;* MAOIs; *Lotronex; Orap; Mellaril; Tegretol; Plavix; Zyvox; Clozaril; Rozerem; Dilantin; Prilosec; Ultram;* benzodiazepines; triptans; TCAs; *Coumadin; Theophylline; Inderal;* St. John's wort; *Quinidine; Cognex*

PHARMACOKINETICS:
- Selectively inhibits serotonin reuptake
Metabolism: Liver extensively, CYP450. Excreted by the kidneys; it has long half-life after administration for acute (1–3 days) and chronic (4–6 days) administration, and has non-linear kinetics. Fluoxetine has a half-life of 4–16 days after acute and chronic administration, and has linear kinetics. Steady state levels after prolonged dosing are similar to levels seen at 4–5 wks.
Half-life: 4 to 6 days

PRECAUTIONS:
- Hypersensitivity to drug class
- Hyponatremia
- Hepatic involvement
- Avoid volume depletion
- Seizure disorder
- Bleeding risks
- Smoking habit changes

PATIENT AND FAMILY EDUCATION:
- Avoid abrupt withdrawal.
- Monitor for worsening depression/suicidal ideations.
- Keep out of reach of children.
- Store at room temperature.

SPECIAL POPULATIONS:
- *Elderly:* Caution with use due to polypharmacy and comorbid conditions
- *Pregnancy:* Category C, except for greater than 20-wks gestation
- *Lactation:* Safety unknown
- *Children:* For ages 7 to 17

Class: Tricyclic Antidepressants (TCAs)

▶ **Alert:** Use of this class of medication for the treatment of autism should be done only by specialists

Elavil	amitriptyline

INDICATIONS: Treatment of depression and chronic pain

AVAILABLE FORMS: Tablet, 10, 25, 50, 75, 100, 125, and 150 mg

DOSAGE: Lowest effective dose. *Children: 9 to 12 yr:* 1 to 3 mg/kg/day PO divided tid; start, 1 mg/kg/day PO divided tid × 3 days, increase 0.5 mg/kg/day every 2 to 3 days; maximum, 5 mg/kg/day up to 200 mg/day; taper dose gradually to discontinue. *Greater than 12 yr:* 50 to 100 mg/day PO divided daily tid; start, 10 mg PO tid and 20 mg qhs; increase 10 to 25 mg/day every 2 to 3 days; maximum, 200 mg/day; taper dose gradually to discontinue. *Adults:* 50 to 150 mg qhs: start: 25 to 75 mg PO qhs, increase 25 to 50 mg/day every 2 to 3 days; 10 to 25 mg PO qhs in elderly patients, increase 10 to 25 mg/day every 2 to 3 days; maximum, 300 mg/day; may give in divided doses; taper dose gradually to discontinue.

ADMINISTRATION: Can be given with or without food

SIDE EFFECTS: Syncope; arrhythmias; QT prolongation; torsades de pointes; MI; CVA; tardive dyskinesia; ataxia; leukopenia; thrombocytopenia; SIADH; hyperthermia; drowsiness; dry mouth; dizziness; constipation; blurred vision; palpitations; tachycardia; incoordination; appetite increase; nausea/vomiting; sweating; weakness; disorientation; confusion; restlessness; insomnia; anxiety/agitation; urinary retention; urinary frequency; rash/urticaria; pruritus; weight gain; libido changes; impotence; gynecomastia; galactorrhea; tremor; hypo/hyperglycemia; paresthesias; photosensitivity

DRUG INTERACTIONS: Antiarrhythmics; cisapride; flumazenil; yohimbe; MAOIs; cimetidine; potassium salts; methadone; clarithromycin; St. John's wort

PHARMACOKINETICS:
- Inhibits norepinephrine and serotonin reuptake
- CYP450 use

Metabolism: Liver extensively
Half-life: 10 to 26 hr

PRECAUTIONS:
- Hypersensitivity to drug class
- Recent MI
- Caution in patient less than 25 yr old
- Cardiovascular disease
- BPH
- Urinary retention
- Glaucoma
- Increased ocular pressure
- Seizure
- Diabetes
- Thyroid conditions
- Asthma
- Parkinson's
- Hepatic impairment
- Schizophrenia
- Bipolar disorder
- Caution with ECT therapy
- Alcoholism
- Suicide risk
- GI obstruction

PATIENT AND FAMILY EDUCATION:
- Avoid abrupt withdrawal.
- Report adverse effects.
- Report use of SSRI within 5 days of initiation.
- Report use of cold medicine or OTC preparations to provider before use.
- Monitor serum drug levels; EKG; BP, HR if dose is greater than 3 mg/kg/24 hr (peds); symptoms of suicidality, clinical worsening, and/or unusual behavior changes, especially during initial treatment or after dose changes

SPECIAL POPULATIONS:
- *Elderly:* Caution with use due to polypharmacy and comorbid conditions
- *Pregnancy:* Category C
- *Lactation:* Probably safe
- *Children:* For ages 9 to 17

Class: Benzodiazepines (BZDs)

▶ **Alert:** Use of this class of medication for the treatment of autism should only be done by specialists.

Ativan	lorazepam

INDICATIONS: Indicated for anxiety, sedation, status epilepticus, and chemotherapy-related nausea/vomiting

AVAILABLE FORMS: PO, IV, IM: 0.5, 1, 2 mg

DOSAGE: Lowest effective dose. *Children:* 0.05 mg/kg PO/IV every 4 to 8 hr; maximum, 2 mg/dose; periodically reassess need for treatment; taper dose gradually to discontinue if prolonged treatment. *Adults:* 2 to 6 mg/day PO/IM/IV divided bid to tid; start, 2 to 3 mg/day PO/IM/IV divided bid to tid; 1 to 2 mg/day PO/IM/IV divided bid to tid in elderly patients; maximum, 10 mg/day; periodically assess

(cont.)

AUTISM SPECTRUM DISORDER: Benzodiazepines (BZDs)

lorazepam (cont.)

need for treatment; taper dose gradually to discontinue if prolonged treatment.

ADMINISTRATION: Can be given with or without food. Avoid use in neonates: Serious, potentially fatal "gasping syndrome" may occur.

SIDE EFFECTS: Sedation; dizziness; weakness; unsteadiness; local injection site reaction; respiratory depression; hypoventilation (IV); hypotension; dependency, abuse; withdrawal syndrome; respiratory failure; respiratory depression; seizures; depression; suicidality; anaphylactic reaction; hypersensitivity reaction; blood dyscrasias; hepatic encephalopathy exacerbation; gangrene (intra-arterial)

DRUG INTERACTIONS: Sodium oxybate; aripiprazole; dexmedetomidine; probenicid; propofol; valproic acid derivatives

PHARMACOKINETICS:
- Binds to benzodiazepine receptors
- Enhances GABA effects
Metabolism: Liver, excreted in urine
Half-life: 14 hr

PRECAUTIONS:
- Hypersensitivity to drug/class
- Intra-arterial administration

- Glaucoma, acute angle-closure
- Renal failure
- Hepatic failure
- Alcohol intoxication
- CNS depression
- Respiratory impairment, severe (IV)
- Psychosis
- Depression
- Avoid abrupt withdrawal, pregnancy, breastfeeding, Caution if renal impairment, hepatic impairment, hepatic encephalopathy, impaired pulmonary function, Caution in elderly or debilitated patients, pediatric patients, Caution if alcohol or drug abuse history

PATIENT AND FAMILY EDUCATION:
- Watch for respiratory depression
- Habit-forming/dependence possible
- Store at room temperature

SPECIAL POPULATIONS:
- *Elderly:* Caution with use due to polypharmacy and comorbid conditions
- *Pregnancy:* Category D
- *Lactation:* Probably unsafe
- *Children:* Avoid use in neonates due to potential fatal "gasping syndrome"

diazepam   *Valium*

INDICATIONS: Indicated for anxiety, sedation, status epilepticus, and chemotherapy-related nausea/vomiting

AVAILABLE FORMS: PO, IV, IM: 2, 5, 10 mg (IM and IV form only available in generic)

DOSAGE: Lowest effective dose. *Children: 6 months to 12 yr:* 0.12 to 0.8 mg/kg/day PO divided every 6 to 8h; alternative, 0.04 to 0.2 mg/kg IM/IV every 2 to 4 hr prn; maximum, 0.6 mg/kg/8 hr IM/IV. *Older than 12 yr:* 2 to 10 mg PO bid to qid; alternative: 2 to 10 mg IM/IV every 3 to 4 hr prn.

ADMINISTRATION: Can be given with or without food, caution with "purple glove" syndrome if given IV

SIDE EFFECTS: Sedation; dizziness; weakness; unsteadiness; local injection site reaction; respiratory depression; hypoventilation (IV); hypotension; dependency, abuse; withdrawal syndrome; respiratory failure; respiratory depression; seizures; depression; suicidality; anaphylactic reaction; hypersensitivity reaction; blood dyscrasias; hepatic encephalopathy exacerbation; gangrene (intra-arterial)

DRUG INTERACTIONS: Sodium oxybate; aripiprazole; dexmedetomidine; probenicid; propofol; valproic acid derivatives

PHARMACOKINETICS:
- Binds to benzodiazepine receptors
- Enhances GABA effects

Metabolism: Liver, excreted in the urine
Half-life: 30 to 60 hr

PRECAUTIONS:
- Hypersensitivity to drug/class
- Intra-arterial administration
- Glaucoma, acute angle-closure
- Renal failure
- Hepatic failure
- Alcohol intoxication
- CNS depression
- Respiratory impairment, severe (IV)
- Psychosis
- Depression
- Avoid abrupt withdrawal, pregnancy, breastfeeding, Caution if renal impairment, hepatic impairment, hepatic encephalopathy, impaired pulmonary function, Caution in elderly or debilitated patients, pediatric patients, Caution if alcohol or drug abuse history

PATIENT AND FAMILY EDUCATION:
- Watch for respiratory depression
- Habit-forming/dependence possible
- Store at room temperature
- Monitor CBC and LFTs for prolonged treatment

SPECIAL POPULATIONS:
- *Elderly:* Caution with use due to polypharmacy and comorbid conditions
- *Pregnancy:* Category D
- *Lactation:* Probably unsafe
- *Children:* For ages 6 months and above

Class: Norepinepherine/Dopamine Reuptake Inhibitors (NDRIs)

▶ **Alert:** Use of this class of medication for the treatment of autism should only be done by specialists

Wellbutrin	buproprion HCl

INDICATIONS: Major depression of adults; ADHD in adults and children older than 6 yr, used for smoking cessation

AVAILABLE FORMS: Tablet; 75, 100 mg

DOSAGE: *Children: Older than 6 yr:* 1.4 to 6 mg/kg/divided bid; maximum, 150 mg/dose, 450 mg/day. *Adults:* 100 mg PO tid; start, 100 mg PO bid, increase after 3 days; maximum, 150 mg/dose, 450 mg/day.

ADMINISTRATION: Can give with or without food

SIDE EFFECTS: Dry mouth; headache; agitation; nausea; dizziness; constipation; tremor; sweating; abnormal dreams; insomnia; tinnitus; pharyngitis; anorexia; weight loss; infection; abdominal pain; diarrhea; anxiety; flatulence; rash; palpitations; myalgia/arthralgia; chest pain; blurred vision; urinary frequency; suicidality; depression, worsening; psychiatric disorder exacerbation; behavioral disturbances; agitation; psychosis; hallucinations; Paranoia; mania; seizures; hepatotoxicity; arrhythmias; tachycardia; HTN, severe; elevated intraocular pressure; migraine; Stevens-Johnson syndrome; erythema multiforme; anaphylactic/anaphylactoid reactions

DRUG INTERACTIONS: MAOIs
- Gingko biloba
- *Phenergan* with codeine
- Linezolid
- Ethanol

PHARMACOKINETICS:
- Mechanism for smoking cessation unknown
- Exact mechanism of action for depression unknown

- Inhibits neuronal uptake of norepinephrine and dopamine

Metabolism: Liver, excreted mainly in the urine
Half-life: 21 hr

PRECAUTIONS:
- Hypersensitivity to drug/class
- MAO inhibitor use within 14 days
- Seizure disorder
- Bulimia
- anorexia
- Abrupt alcohol, BZD or sedative D/C
- Caution if seizure threshold lowered, head injury/intracranial lesion, alcohol or drug abuse, psychiatric disorder, bipolar disorder, suicidality history, suicidal ideation
- Caution in patients less than 25 yr, elderly patients
- Caution if diabetes mellitus, cirrhosis, severe, hepatic impairment, renal impairment, recent MI, HTN

PATIENT AND FAMILY EDUCATION:
- Metabolized by the liver/CYP450
- Store at room temperature
- Monitor for worsening psychiatric complaints

SPECIAL POPULATIONS:
- *Elderly:* Caution with use due to polypharmacy and comorbid conditions
- *Pregnancy:* Category C
- *Lactation:* Probably unsafe
- *Children:* For ages 6 to 17

Class: Antipsychotics, Atypical (Second-Generation)

▶ **Alert:** The use of this class of medication for the treatment of autism should only be done by a specialist.

Clozaril	clozapine

INDICATIONS: Schizophrenia, bipolar disorder, and autistic irritability for children 5 yr of age and above.

AVAILABLE FORMS: Tablet, 25 and 100 mg

DOSAGE: Taper to goal dose. *Children:* Not for pediatric use. *Adults:* 150 to 300 mg bid; start, 12.5 mg PO daily, bid, increase 25 to 50 mg/day every 3 to 7 days; maximum, 900 mg/day; taper dose gradually over 1 to 2 wk to discontinue.

ADMINISTRATION: Restricted distribution in the USA.

SIDE EFFECTS: Hypotension, severe; syncope; extrapyramidal symptoms, severe; tardive dyskinesia; neuroleptic malignant syndrome; hyperglycemia, severe; diabetes mellitus; seizures; priapism; stroke; TIA; QT prolongation; hypersensitivity reaction; anaphylactic reaction; angioedema; erythema multiforme; leukopenia; neutropenia; agranulocytosis; suicidality; somnolence; increased appetite; fatigue; rhinitis; URI; nausea/vomiting; cough; urinary incontinence; salivation; constipation; fever; dystonia; abdominal pain; anxiety; dizziness; dry mouth; tremor; rash; akathisia; dyspepsia; tachycardia; hyperprolactinemia/gynecomastia; weight gain

(cont.)

AUTISM SPECTRUM DISORDER: Antipsychotics, Atypical (Second-Generation)

clozapine (cont.)

DRUG INTERACTIONS: Triptorelin; ginseng; *Haldol*; sodium oxybate; ziprasidone. Caution with diabetes and HTN medications.

PHARMACOKINETICS:
- Exact mechanism of action unknown
- Antagonizes dopamine D2 receptors and serotonin 5-HT2 receptors

Metabolism: Liver, excreted in urine and feces
Half-life: 4–66 hr

PRECAUTIONS:
- Hypersensitivity to drug/class
- Caution if renal impairment, hepatic impairment, dementia, Parkinson's disease, neuroleptic malignant syndrome history, seizure history, cardiac disease, cerebrovascular disease, hypotension, hypovolemia, dehydration, aspiration pneumonia risk, May impair body temperature regulation, PKU (phenylalanine-containing forms), diabetes mellitus or diabetes mellitus risk, Caution in elderly patients, pediatric or

adolescent patients, drug-induced leukopenia or neutropenia history, suicide risk

PATIENT AND FAMILY EDUCATION:
- Drug effects can linger 7–8 wk after last dose.
- Monitor CBC, glucose, and cholesterol throughout treatment course—WBC/ANC at baseline, then every week × 6 months, then every 2 wk × 6 months, then every 4 wk for treatment duration and every week × 4 wk after D/C; fasting glucose at baseline if diabetes risk factors, then periodically; see package insert for additional recommendations based on results of WBC/ANC monitoring
- Restricted distribution in the USA—permission granted through the FDA.

SPECIAL POPULATIONS:
- *Elderly:* Caution with use due to polypharmacy and comorbid conditions.
- *Pregnancy:* Category B.
- *Lactation:* Probably unsafe.
- *Children:* Not for use in children.

risperidone   *Risperdal*

INDICATIONS: Schizophrenia, bipolar disorder, and autistic irritability for children 5 yr of age and above.

AVAILABLE FORMS: Tablet, 0.25, 0.5, 1, 2, 3, and 4 mg; solution, 1/mL

DOSAGE: Weight-based with a taper to goal dose. *Children: 5 to 16 yr, 15 to 20 kg*: dose, 0.5 to 1 mg/day PO divided daily bid; start, 0.25 mg PO daily × 4 days, then increase 0.25 mg/day every 2 wk prn; maximum, 1 mg/day; discontinue if ANC less than 1,000; consider discontinuation if unexplained decrease in WBC. *5 to 16 yr old, greater than 20 kg*: dose, 0.5 to 2.5 mg/day PO divided daily bid; start, 0.5 mg/day PO divided daily bid × 4 days, then increase 0.5 mg/day every 2 wk as needed; maximum, if below 45 kg, 2.5 mg/day; if more than 45 kg, 3 mg/day. Discontinue if ANC less than 1,000; consider discontinuation if unexplained decrease in WBC. *Adults:* No dosing for autistic patients

ADMINISTRATION: Can give with or without food.

SIDE EFFECTS: Hypotension, severe; syncope; extrapyramidal symptoms, severe; tardive dyskinesia; neuroleptic malignant syndrome; hyperglycemia, severe; diabetes mellitus; seizures; priapism; stroke; TIA; QT prolongation; hypersensitivity reaction; anaphylactic reaction; angioedema; erythema multiforme; leukopenia; neutropenia; agranulocytosis; suicidality; somnolence; increased appetite; fatigue; rhinitis; URI; nausea/vomiting; cough; urinary incontinence; salivation; constipation; fever; extrapyramidal effects; dystonia; abdominal pain; anxiety; dizziness; dry mouth; tremor; rash; akathisia; dyspepsia; tachycardia; hyperprolactinemia/gynecomastia; weight gain

DRUG INTERACTIONS: Triptorelin; ginseng; *Haldol*; sodium oxybate; ziprasidone. Caution with diabetes and HTN medications

PHARMACOKINETICS:
- Exact mechanism of action unknown.
- Antagonizes dopamine D2 receptors and serotonin 5-HT2 receptors.

Metabolism: Liver, excreted mainly in urine.
Half-life: 20 hr (PO), 3 to 6 days (IM). Drug effects may persist 7 to 8 wk after last dose.

PRECAUTIONS:
- Hypersensitivity to drug/class; Caution if renal impairment; hepatic impairment; dementia; Parkinson's disease; neuroleptic malignant syndrome history; seizure history; cardiac disease; cerebrovascular disease; hypotension; hypovolemia; dehydration; aspiration pneumonia risk; PKU (phenylalanine-containing forms); diabetes mellitus; diabetes mellitus risk; drug-induced leukopenia or neutropenia history; leukopenia; suicide risk.
- May impair body temperature regulation.

PATIENT AND FAMILY EDUCATION:
- Drug effects can linger 7 to 8 wk after last dose.
- Monitor CBC, glucose, and cholesterol throughout treatment course.

SPECIAL POPULATIONS:
- *Elderly:* Caution with use due to polypharmacy and comorbid conditions; not for use if over 65 yr of age.
- *Pregnancy:* Category C
- *Lactation:* Probably unsafe
- *Children:* Age 5 to 17
- *Other:* No dosing guidelines for adults with autism; only for schizophrenia.

Zyprexa   **olanzapine**

INDICATIONS: Schizophrenia, bipolar disorder, and autistic irritability for children 5 yr of age and above.

AVAILABLE FORMS: Tablet, 2.5, 5, 7.5, 10, 15, and 20 mg

DOSAGE: Weight-based with a taper to goal dose. *Children: 13 to 17 yr:* 10 mg PO daily; start, 2.5 to 5 mg PO daily; maximum, 20 mg/day. Not first-line treatment due to increase in weight gain, hyperlipidemia. Periodically reassess need for treatment; discontinue if ANC less than 1,000; consider discontinuation if unexplained decrease in WBC. *Adults:* 10 mg daily; start, 5 to 10 mg PO daily; 2.5 to 5 mg PO daily in nonsmoker, elderly, debilitated, or female patients, or if predisposed to hypotension; may increase 5 mg/day every week; maximum, 20 mg/day. Doses greater than 10 mg/day rarely more effective; periodically reassess need for treatment; discontinue if ANC less than 1,000; consider discontinuation if unexplained decrease in WBC.

ADMINISTRATION: Can be given with or without food

SIDE EFFECTS: Hypotension, severe; syncope; extrapyramidal symptoms, severe; tardive dyskinesia; neuroleptic malignant syndrome; hyperglycemia, severe; diabetes mellitus; seizures; priapism; stroke; TIA; QT prolongation; hypersensitivity reaction; anaphylactic reaction; angioedema; erythema multiforme; leukopenia; neutropenia; agranulocytosis; suicidality; somnolence; increased appetite; fatigue; rhinitis; URI; nausea/vomiting; cough; urinary incontinence; salivation; constipation; fever; extrapyramidal effects; dystonia; abdominal pain; anxiety; dizziness; dry mouth; tremor; rash; akathisia; dyspepsia; tachycardia; hyperprolactinemia/gynecomastia; weight gain

DRUG INTERACTIONS: Triptorelin; ginseng; *Haldol*; sodium oxybate; ziprasidone. Caution with diabetes and HTN medications

PHARMACOKINETICS:
- Exact mechanism of action unknown
- Antagonizes dopamine D2 receptors and serotonin 5-HT2 receptors

Metabolism: Liver/CYP450
Half-life: 21–54 hr

PRECAUTIONS:
- Hypersensitivity to drug/class
- Caution if renal impairment, hepatic impairment, dementia, Parkinson's disease, neuroleptic malignant syndrome history, seizure history, cardiac disease, cerebrovascular disease, hypotension, hypovolemia, dehydration, aspiration pneumonia risk; PKU (phenylalanine-containing forms), diabetes mellitus, diabetes mellitus risk, drug-induced leukopenia or neutropenia history, leukopenia, suicide risk.

▶**Caution:** May impair body temperature regulation.

PATIENT AND FAMILY EDUCATION:
- Drug effects can linger 7 to 8 wk after last dose.
- Monitor CBC, glucose, and cholesterol throughout treatment course.

SPECIAL POPULATIONS:
- *Elderly:* Caution with use due to polypharmacy and comorbid conditions
- *Pregnancy:* Category C
- *Lactation:* Probably unsafe
- *Children:* Use in ages 13 to 17

Seroquel   **quetiapine**

INDICATIONS: Schizophrenia, bipolar disorder, and autistic irritability for children 5 yr of age and above.

FORMS: Tablet, 25, 50, 100, 200, 300, and 400 mg

DOSAGE: Weight-based with a taper to goal dose. *Children: 10 to 17 yr:* 400 to 600 mg/day PO divided bid–tid; start, 25 mg bid ×1 day, then 50 mg bid ×1 day, then increase by 100 mg/day up to 200 mg PO bid by day 5, then may increase by 50 to 100 mg/day prn; maximum, 800 mg/day. Periodically reassess need for treatment; discontinue if ANC less than 1,000; consider discontinuing if unexplained decrease in WBC. *Adults:* 150 to 750 mg divided bid–tid; start, 25 mg PO bid, then increase by 50 to 150 mg/day up to 300 to 400 mg/day PO divided bid–tid by day 4, then adjust dose by 50 to 100 mg/day at intervals more than 2 days prn; start, 25 mg PO qpm in elderly or debilitated patients, then increase by 25 to 50 mg/day; maximum, 800

mg/day. Periodically reassess need for treatment; discontinue if ANC less than 1,000; consider discontinuing if unexplained decrease in WBC.

ADMINISTRATION: Can give with or without food.

SIDE EFFECTS: Hypotension, severe; syncope; extrapyramidal symptoms, severe; tardive dyskinesia; neuroleptic malignant syndrome; hyperglycemia, severe; diabetes mellitus; seizures; priapism; stroke; TIA; QT prolongation; hypersensitivity reaction; anaphylactic reaction; angioedema; erythema multiforme; leukopenia; neutropenia; agranulocytosis; suicidality; somnolence; increased appetite; fatigue; rhinitis; URI; nausea/vomiting; cough; urinary incontinence; salivation; constipation; fever; extrapyramidal effects; dystonia; abdominal pain; anxiety; dizziness; dry mouth; tremor; rash; akathisia; dyspepsia; tachycardia; hyperprolactinemia/gynecomastia; weight gain.

(cont.)

AUTISM SPECTRUM DISORDER: Antipsychotics, Atypical (Second-Generation)

quetiapine (cont.)

DRUG INTERACTIONS: Triptorelin; ginseng; *Haldol*; sodium oxybate; ziprasidone. Caution with diabetes and HTN medications.

PHARMACOKINETICS:
- Exact mechanism of action unknown.
- Antagonizes dopamine D2 receptors and serotonin 5-HT2 receptors
Metabolism: Liver/CYP450
Half-life: 6 hr

PRECAUTIONS:
- Hypersensitivity to drug/class.
- Caution if renal impairment, hepatic impairment, dementia, Parkinson's disease, neuroleptic malignant syndrome history, seizure history, cardiac disease, cerebrovascular disease, hypotension, hypovolemia, dehydration, aspiration pneumonia risk, PKU (phenylalanine-containing forms), diabetes mellitus, diabetes mellitus risk, drug-induced leukopenia or neutropenia history, leukopenia, suicide risk.
▶**Caution:** May impair body temperature regulation.

PATIENT AND FAMILY EDUCATION:
- Drug effects can linger 7 to 8 wk after last dose.
- Monitor CBC, glucose, and cholesterol throughout treatment course.

SPECIAL POPULATIONS:
- *Elderly:* Caution with use due to polypharmacy and comorbid conditions
- *Pregnancy:* Category C
- *Lactation:* Safety unknown
- *Children:* Use for ages 10 to 17

aripiprazole   *Abilify*

AVAILABLE FORMS: Tablet, 2, 5, 10, 15, 20, and 30 mg; tablet, orally disintegrating: 10 and 15 mg; solution, oral, 1 mg/mL

DOSAGE: 10–15 mg/day, up to 15–30 mg/day. Dosages exceeding 10–15 mg/day have not demonstrated greater efficacy

ADMINISTRATION:
- Tablets may be given with or without food.
- Parenteral administration is intended for IM use only; inject slowly, deep into the muscle mass. IM injection has not been evaluated in children.
- Do not give IV or SC.
- Oral solution may be substituted for tablets on a mg-per-mg basis up to a 25 mg dose. Patients receiving 30 mg tablets should receive 25 mg of the solution.
- Dosing for the orally disintegrating tablet is the same as the oral tablet.
- Do not open the orally disintegrating tablets until ready to administer. The orally disintegrating tablet should be taken without liquid. Do not split the orally disintegrating tablet.
- Use oral aripiprazole 10–30 mg/day instead of IM aripiprazole as soon as possible if ongoing therapy is indicated.

SIDE EFFECTS: Nausea, vomiting; dizziness, insomnia, akathisia, activation; headache, asthenia; sedation; weight gain; constipation; orthostatic hypotension (occasionally during initial phase); increased risk of death and cerebrovascular events in elderly with dementia-related psychosis; tardive dyskinesia; neuroleptic malignant syndrome (rare); seizures (rare)

DRUG INTERACTIONS:
- CYP450 3A4 inhibitors (e.g., nefazodone, fluvoxamine, fluoxetine), CYP40 2D6 inhibitors (e.g., paroxetine, fluoxetine, duloxetine), and quinidine may increase plasma levels of aripiprazole
- Carbamazepine and other CYP450 3A4 inducers may decrease plasma levels of aripiprazole
- Aripiprazole may enhance effects of antihypertensive medications
- Aripiprazole may antagonize levodopa, dopamine agonists
▶**Alert:** This list may not describe all possible interactions. Instruct the patient to provide a list of all the medicines, herbs, nonprescription drugs, or dietary supplements being used. Also instruct clients to inform health care providers if they smoke, drink alcohol, or use illegal drugs.

PHARMACOKINETICS:
- Primarily metabolized by CYP450 2D6 and CYP450 3A4
- About 25% of a single oral dose is excreted in urine (less than 1% unchanged) and 55% in feces (18% as unchanged drug).
Mean elimination half-life: 75 hr (aripiprazole) and 94 hr (active metabolite)

PRECAUTIONS:
- Dysphagia is associated with the use of aripiprazole. Use with caution in patients who are at risk for aspiration pneumonia
- Use with caution in patients with conditions who may develop hypotension (dehydration, overheating etc.)
▶**Alert:** Patients who are allergic to aripiprazole.

PATIENT AND FAMILY EDUCATION:
- Store aripiprazole at 59–86°F. An opened bottle can be used for up to 6 months. Protect solution from light by storing in a carton until use.
- If pregnant, contact the health care provider. Discuss the benefits and risks of using aripiprazole orally-disintegrating tablets while pregnant.
- Dose adjustment or special tests to safely take aripiprazole may be needed with: liver or
(cont.)

aripiprazole (*cont.*)

kidney disease; heart disease, high blood pressure, heart rhythm problems; history of heart attack or stroke; history of high WBC counts; history of breast cancer; seizures or epilepsy; personal or family history of diabetes; problems swallowing; PKU.

- Contact health care provider if signs of hyperglycemia such as increased thirst or urination, excessive hunger, or weakness. If diabetic, check blood sugar levels on a regular basis while taking aripiprazole.

SPECIAL POPULATIONS:

- *Elderly:* Dosage adjustment is generally not required. Elderly with dementia-related psychosis who are treated with atypical antipsychotics such as aripiprazole are at a higher risk of death and cerebrovascular events.

- *Renal impairment*: No dosage adjustment is needed.
- *Hepatic impairment*: No dosage adjustment required.
- *Cardiac impairment*: Use with caution because of the risk of orthostatic hypotension
- *Pregnancy:* Category C. It is not known if aripiprazole orally disintegrating tablets can cause harm to the fetus.
- *Lactation*: Although there are no data on the excretion of aripiprazole into human milk, it is suggested that women receiving aripiprazole should not breast-feed.
- *Children and adolescents:* Aripiprazole is approved for children with schizophrenia (aged 13 and older) and manic/mixed episodes (age 10 and older). Should be monitored more frequently than adults. May tolerate lower doses better.

▶**Alert:** Not approved for children with depression.

Class: Amphetamine Derivatives (Short- and Long-Acting)

▶**Note:** This class of medication is a controlled substance.

- Short-acting preparations are often used as initial treatment in small children (less than 16 kg), but have disadvantage of bid–tid dosing to control symptoms throughout the day.

- Long-acting preparations offer greater convenience, confidentiality, and compliance with single daily dosing, but may have greater problematic effects on evening appetite and sleep.

Class: Amphetamines—Short-Acting

Adderall	dextroamphetamine/amphetamine

INDICATIONS: Treatment of ADHD of children and adults

AVAILABLE FORMS: Capsule, 5, 7.5, 10, 12.5, 15, 20, and 30 mg

DOSAGE: Dosage should be individualized according to the therapeutic needs and responses of the patient. All stimulant preparations should be administered at the lowest effective dosage. *Children: 3 to 5 yr:* 2.5 to 40 mg/day PO divided daily tid; start, 2.5 mg qam, increase 2.5 mg/day every week, give divided doses at 4- to 6-hr intervals, doses greater than 40 mg/day rarely more effective. *Older than 6 yr:* 5 to 40 mg/day PO divided daily tid; start, 5 mg PO qam or bid, increase 5 mg/day every week, give divided doses at 4- to 6-hr intervals, doses greater than 40 mg/day rarely more effective. *Adults:* 5 to 40 mg/day PO divided daily tid; start, 5 mg PO qam or bid, increase 5 mg/day every week, give divided doses at 4- to 6-hr intervals, doses greater than 40 mg/day rarely more effective.

ADMINISTRATION: Swallow capsules whole; take with water or other liquid. If patient cannot swallow the capsule, open and sprinkle the medicine over a spoonful of applesauce. Swallow all of the applesauce and medicine mixture without chewing immediately. Follow with a drink of water or other liquid. Never chew or crush the capsule or the medicine inside the capsule. It can be taken with or without food.

SIDE EFFECTS: Decreased appetite; dizziness; dry mouth; irritability; insomnia; upper abdominal pain; nausea and/or vomiting; weight loss; headaches; anxiety; psychiatric events: increase in manic states for bipolar patients, aggression, tics, tremors; long-term growth suppression: patients should be monitored throughout treatment; if there appears to be growth suppression, the treatment should be discontinued; rash; pyrexia; palpitations, tachycardia, elevated BP, sudden death, MI, cardiomyopathy; Stevens-Johnson syndrome and toxic epidermal necrolysis; impotence, libido changes

DRUG INTERACTIONS: Urinary acidifying agents; MAOIs; adrenergic blockers; antihistamines; antihypertensives; veratrum alkaloids; ethosuximide; TCAs; meperidine; phenobarbital; phenytoin; chlorpromazine; *Haldol*; lithium; norepinephrine; propoxyphene

(cont.)

AUTISM SPECTRUM DISORDER: Amphetamines—Short-Acting

dextroamphetamine/amphetamine (cont.)

PHARMACOKINETICS:
- Absorbed by the GI tract.
- Amphetamines are noncatecholamine sympathomimetic amines with CNS-stimulant activity.
- The mode of therapeutic action in ADHD is not known. Amphetamines are thought to block the reuptake of norepinephrine and dopamine into the presynaptic neuron and increase the release of these monoamines into the extraneural space.

Metabolism: Excreted in the urine
Half-life: 9–14 hr

PRECAUTIONS:
- Advanced arteriosclerosis, symptomatic cardiovascular disease, moderate-to-severe HTN
- Hyperthyroidism
- Known hypersensitivity or idiosyncratic reaction to sympathomimetic amines
- Glaucoma
- Agitated states
- Patients with a history of drug abuse: Amphetamines have a high potential for abuse. Administration of Amphetamines for an extended period of time may lead to drug dependence. Particular attention should be paid to the possibility of patients obtaining this class of medication for nontherapeutic use or distribution to others, and the drugs should be prescribed or dispensed sparingly.
- During or within 14 days following the administration of MAOIs, hypertensive crisis may result.
- Preexisting psychosis

- Seizure history: Some studies have shown the potential for lowering the seizure threshold

PATIENT AND FAMILY EDUCATION:
- Store at room temperature, protected from light.
- Keep out of reach of children.
- Seek medical care for any signs of heart problems (chest pain, shortness of breath), fainting, psychotic symptoms, overdose, or any other concerns.
- Routinely assess weight and BP.
- Treatment should be initiated at low dosages and then titrated over 2 to 4 wk until an adequate response is achieved or unacceptable adverse effects occur.
- If one stimulant is not effective, another should be attempted before second-line medications are considered. Although some children benefit from daily stimulant therapy, weekend and summer "drug holidays" are suggested for children whose ADHD symptoms predominantly affect schoolwork, or to limit adverse effects (e.g., appetite suppression, abdominal pain, headache, insomnia, irritability, tics).

SPECIAL POPULATIONS:
- *Elderly:* Caution with polypharmacy and comorbid conditions; has not been studied for use in this population
- *Pregnancy:* Category C; based on animal data, they may cause fetal harm
- *Lactation:* Possibly unsafe
- *Children:* Has not been studied in children younger than 6 yr; should not be used in children younger than 3 yr.

dextroamphetamine   *Dexedrine, Dextrostat*

INDICATIONS: Stimulant indicated for the treatment of ADHD of children and adults

AVAILABLE FORMS: Capsule, 5, 10, and 15 mg

DOSAGE: Dosage should be individualized according to the therapeutic needs and responses of the patient. All stimulant preparations should be administered at the lowest effective dosage. *Children: Older than 6 yr:* 5 to 40 mg PO qam; start, 5 mg PO qam, increase 5 mg/day every week; maximum, 60 mg/day; doses greater than 40 mg/day rarely more effective. *Adults:* 5 to 40 mg qam; start, 5 mg PO qam, increase 5 mg/day every week; maximum, 60 mg/day; doses greater than 40 mg/day rarely more effective.

ADMINISTRATION: Do not crush or chew; can be taken with or without food.

SIDE EFFECTS: Decreased appetite; dizziness; dry mouth; irritability; insomnia; upper abdominal pain; nausea and/or vomiting; weight loss; headaches; anxiety; psychiatric events: increase in manic states for bipolar patients, aggression, tics, tremors; long-term growth suppression: patients should be monitored throughout treatment, if there

appears to be growth suppression, the treatment should be discontinued; rash; pyrexia; palpitations, tachycardia, elevated BP, sudden death, MI, cardiomyopathy; Stevens-Johnson syndrome and toxic epidermal necrolysis; impotence, libido changes

DRUG INTERACTIONS: Urinary acidifying agents; MAOIs; adrenergic blockers; antihistamines; antihypertensives; veratrum alkaloids; ethosuximide; TCAs; meperidine; phenobarbital; phenytoin; chlorpromazine; *Haldol;* lithium; norepinephrine; propoxyphene

PHARMACOKINETICS:
- Absorbed by the GI tract.
- Amphetamines are noncatecholamine sympathomimetic amines with CNS-stimulant activity.
- The mode of therapeutic action in ADHD is not known. Amphetamines are thought to block the reuptake of norepinephrine and dopamine into the presynaptic neuron and increase the release of these monoamines into the extraneural space.

Metabolism: Liver; excreted in the urine
Half-life: 10.25–12 hr

(cont.)

dextroamphetamine (cont.)

PRECAUTIONS:
- Advanced arteriosclerosis, symptomatic cardio-vascular disease, moderate-to-severe HTN
- Hyperthyroidism
- Known hypersensitivity or idiosyncratic reaction to sympathomimetic amines
- Glaucoma
- Agitated states
- Patients with a history of drug abuse: Amphetamines have a high potential for abuse. Administration of Amphetamines for an extended period of time may lead to drug dependence. Particular attention should be paid to the possibility of patients obtaining this class of medication for nontherapeutic use or distribution to others, and the drugs should be prescribed or dispensed sparingly.
- During or within 14 days following the administration of MAOIs, hypertensive crisis may result.
- Preexisting psychosis
- Seizure history: Some studies have shown the potential for lowering the seizure threshold

PATIENT AND FAMILY EDUCATION:
- Store at room temperature, protected from light.
- Keep out of reach of children.
- Seek medical care for any signs of heart problems (chest pain, shortness of breath), fainting, psychotic symptoms, overdose, or any other concerns.
- Routinely assess weight and BP.
- Treatment should be initiated at low dosages and then titrated over 2 to 4 wk until an adequate response is achieved or unacceptable adverse effects occur.
- If one stimulant is not effective, another should be attempted before second-line medications are considered. Although some children benefit from daily stimulant therapy, weekend and summer "drug holidays" are suggested for children whose ADHD symptoms predominantly affect schoolwork, or to limit adverse effects (e.g., appetite suppression, abdominal pain, headache, insomnia, irritability, tics).

SPECIAL POPULATIONS:
- *Elderly:* Caution with polypharmacy and comorbid conditions; has not been studied for use in this population
- *Pregnancy:* Category C; based on animal data, they may cause fetal harm
- *Lactation:* Possibly unsafe
- *Children:* Has not been studied in children younger than 6 yr; should not be used in children younger than 3 yr.

Class: Amphetamines—Long-Acting

Dexedrine Spansule	dextroamphetamine

INDICATIONS: Treatment of ADHD of children and adults

AVAILABLE FORMS: Capsule, 5, 10, and 15 mg

DOSAGE: Dosage should be individualized according to the therapeutic needs and responses of the patient. All stimulant preparations should be administered at the lowest effective dosage. *Children: Older than 6 yr:* 5 to 40 mg PO qam; start, 5 mg PO qam, increase 5 mg/day every week; maximum, 60 mg/day; doses greater than 40 mg/day rarely more effective. *Adults:* 5 to 40 mg qam; start, 5 mg PO qam, increase 5 mg/day every week; maximum, 60 mg/day; doses greater than 40 mg/day rarely more effective.

ADMINISTRATION: Do not crush or chew, can be taken with or without food.

SIDE EFFECTS: Decreased appetite; dizziness; dry mouth; irritability; insomnia; upper abdominal pain; nausea and/or vomiting; weight loss; headaches; anxiety; psychiatric events: increase in manic states for bipolar patients, aggression, tics, tremors; long-term growth suppression: patients should be monitored throughout treatment, if there appears to be growth suppression, the treatment should be discontinued; rash; pyrexia; palpitations, tachycardia, elevated BP, sudden death, MI, cardiomyopathy; Stevens-Johnson syndrome and toxic epidermal necrolysis; impotence, libido changes

DRUG INTERACTIONS: Urinary acidifying agents; MAOIs; adrenergic blockers; antihistamines; antihypertensives; veratrum alkaloids; ethosuximide; TCAs; meperidine; phenobarbital; phenytoin; chlorpromazine; *Haldol*; lithium; norepinephrine; propoxyphene

PHARMACOKINETICS:
- Absorbed by the GI tract.
- Amphetamines are noncatecholamine sympathomimetic amines with CNS-stimulant activity.
- The mode of therapeutic action in ADHD is not known. Amphetamines are thought to block the reuptake of norepinephrine and dopamine into the presynaptic neuron and increase the release of these monoamines into the extraneural space.

Metabolism: Liver; excreted in the urine
Half-life: 10.25–12 hr

PRECAUTIONS:
- Advanced arteriosclerosis, symptomatic cardiovascular disease, moderate-to-severe HTN
- Hyperthyroidism
- Known hypersensitivity or idiosyncratic reaction to sympathomimetic amines

(cont.)

AUTISM SPECTRUM DISORDER: Amphetamines—Long-Acting

dextroamphetamine (cont.)

- Glaucoma
- Agitated states
- Patients with a history of drug abuse: Amphetamines have a high potential for abuse. Administration of Amphetamines for an extended period of time may lead to drug dependence. Particular attention should be paid to the possibility of patients obtaining this class of medication for nontherapeutic use or distribution to others, and the drugs should be prescribed or dispensed sparingly.
- During or within 14 days following the administration of MAOIs, hypertensive crisis may result.
- Preexisting psychosis
- Seizure history: Some studies have shown the potential for lowering the seizure threshold

PATIENT AND FAMILY EDUCATION:
- Store at room temperature, protected from light.
- Keep out of reach of children.
- Seek medical care for any signs of heart problems (chest pain, shortness of breath), fainting, psychotic symptoms, overdose, or any other concerns.
- Routinely assess weight and BP.

- Treatment should be initiated at low dosages and then titrated over 2 to 4 wk until an adequate response is achieved or unacceptable adverse effects occur.
- If one stimulant is not effective, another should be attempted before second-line medications are considered. Although some children benefit from daily stimulant therapy, weekend and summer "drug holidays" are suggested for children whose ADHD symptoms predominantly affect schoolwork, or to limit adverse effects (e.g., appetite suppression, abdominal pain, headache, insomnia, irritability, tics).

SPECIAL POPULATIONS:
- *Elderly:* Caution with polypharmacy and comorbid conditions; has not been studied for use in this population
- *Pregnancy:* Category C; based on animal data, may cause fetal harm
- *Lactation:* Possibly unsafe
- *Children:* Has not been studied in children younger than 6 yr; should not be used in children younger than 3 yr.

---

dextroamphetamine/amphetamine   *Adderall XR*

INDICATIONS: Treatment of ADHD of children and adults

AVAILABLE FORMS: Capsule, 5, 10, 15, 20, 25, and 30 mg ER

DOSAGE: Dosage should be individualized according to the therapeutic needs and response of the patient. All stimulant preparations should be administered at the lowest effective dosage. *Children: 6 to 12 yr old:* 10 mg qam, start: 5 to 10 mg PO qam, increase 5 to 10 mg/day every week; maximum, 30 mg/day; may convert from IR to ER at same total daily dose qam. *13 to 17 yr old:* 10 to 20 mg/day PO qam; start, 10 mg PO qam, increase 10 mg/day every week; maximum, 40 mg/day; may convert from IR to XR at same total daily dose qam; doses greater than 20 mg/day rarely more effective. *Adults:* 5 to 40 mg/day PO divided daily tid; start, 20 mg PO qam, increase 10 mg/day every week; maximum, 60 mg/day; may convert from IR to XR at same total daily dose qam; doses greater than 20 mg/day rarely more effective.

ADMINISTRATION: Swallow capsules whole with water or other liquid. If patient cannot swallow the capsule, open and sprinkle the medicine over a spoonful of applesauce. Swallow all of the applesauce and medicine mixture without chewing immediately. Follow with a drink of water or other liquid. Never chew or crush the capsule or the medicine inside the capsule. It can be taken with or without food.

SIDE EFFECTS: Decreased appetite; dizziness; dry mouth; irritability; insomnia; upper abdominal pain; nausea and/or vomiting; weight loss; headaches; anxiety; psychiatric events: increase in manic states for bipolar patients, aggression, tics, tremors; long-term growth suppression: patients should be monitored throughout treatment, if there appears to be growth suppression, the treatment should be discontinued; rash; pyrexia; palpitations, tachycardia, elevated BP, sudden death, MI, cardiomyopathy; Stevens-Johnson syndrome and toxic epidermal necrolysis; impotence, libido changes

DRUG INTERACTIONS: Urinary acidifying agents; MAOIs; adrenergic blockers; antihistamines; antihypertensives; veratrum alkaloids; ethosuximide; TCAs; meperidine; phenobarbital; phenytoin; chlorpromazine; *Haldol;* lithium; norepinephrine; propoxyphene

PHARMACOKINETICS:
- Absorbed by the GI tract.
- Amphetamines are noncatecholamine sympathomimetic amines with CNS-stimulant activity.
- The mode of therapeutic action in ADHD is not known. Amphetamines are thought to block the reuptake of norepinephrine and dopamine into the presynaptic neuron and increase the release of these monoamines into the extraneural space.

Metabolism: Excreted in the urine
Half-life: 9–14 hr

(cont.)

dextroamphetamine/amphetamine (*cont.*)

PRECAUTIONS:
- Advanced arteriosclerosis, symptomatic cardiovascular disease, moderate-to-severe HTN
- Hyperthyroidism
- Known hypersensitivity or idiosyncratic reaction to sympathomimetic amines
- Glaucoma
- Agitated states
- Patients with a history of drug abuse: Amphetamines have a high potential for abuse. Administration of Amphetamines for an extended period of time may lead to drug dependence. Particular attention should be paid to the possibility of patients obtaining this class of medication for nontherapeutic use or distribution to others, and the drugs should be prescribed or dispensed sparingly.
- During or within 14 days following the administration of MAOIs, hypertensive crisis may result.
- Preexisting psychosis
- Seizure history: Some studies have shown the potential for lowering the seizure threshold

PATIENT AND FAMILY EDUCATION:
- Store at room temperature, protect from light.
- Keep out of reach of children.
- Seek medical care for any signs of heart problems (chest pain, shortness of breath), fainting, psychotic symptoms, overdose, or any other concerns.
- Routinely assess weight and BP.
- Treatment should be initiated at low dosages and then titrated over 2 to 4 wk until an adequate response is achieved or unacceptable adverse effects occur.
- If one stimulant is not effective, another should be attempted before second-line medications are considered. Although some children benefit from daily stimulant therapy, weekend and summer "drug holidays" are suggested for children whose ADHD symptoms predominantly affect schoolwork, or to limit adverse effects (e.g., appetite suppression, abdominal pain, headache, insomnia, irritability, tics).

SPECIAL POPULATIONS:
- *Elderly:* Caution with polypharmacy and comorbid conditions; has not been studied for use in this population
- *Pregnancy:* Category C; based on animal data, may cause fetal harm
- *Lactation:* Possibly unsafe
- *Children:* Has not been studied in children younger than 6 yr; should not be used in children younger than 3 yr.

Vyvanse   **lisdexamfetamine**

INDICATIONS: Stimulant indicated for the treatment of ADHD of children and adults

AVAILABLE FORMS: Capsule, 20, 30, 40, 50, 60, and 70 mg

DOSAGE: Dosage should be individualized according to the therapeutic needs and response of the patient. All stimulant preparations should be administered at the lowest effective dosage. *Children: 6 to 12 yr:* 30 mg PO qam; maximum, 70 mg/day. May increase dose 10 to 20 mg/day every week; use lowest effective dose. *Adults:* 30 mg qam; maximum, 70 mg/day. May increase dose 10 to 20 mg/day every week; use lowest effective dose.

ADMINISTRATION: Swallow capsules whole with water or other liquid. If patient cannot swallow the capsule, open and mix with water. Follow with a drink of water or other liquid. It can be taken with or without food.

SIDE EFFECTS: Decreased appetite; dizziness; dry mouth; irritability; insomnia; upper abdominal pain; nausea and/or vomiting; weight loss; headaches; anxiety; psychiatric events: increase in manic states for bipolar patients, aggression, tics, tremors; long-term growth suppression: patients should be monitored throughout treatment, if there appears to be growth suppression, the treatment should be discontinued; rash; pyrexia; palpitations, tachycardia, elevated BP, sudden death, MI, cardiomyopathy; Stevens-Johnson syndrome and toxic epidermal necrolysis; impotence, libido changes

DRUG INTERACTIONS: Urinary acidifying agents; MAOIs; adrenergic blockers; antihistamines; antihypertensives; veratrum alkaloids; ethosuximide; TCAs; meperidine; phenobarbital; phenytoin; chlorpromazine; *Haldol*; lithium; norepinephrine; propoxyphene

PHARMACOKINETICS:
- Absorbed by the GI tract.
- Amphetamines are noncatecholamine sympathomimetic amines with CNS-stimulant activity.
- The mode of therapeutic action in ADHD is not known. Amphetamines are thought to block the reuptake of norepinephrine and dopamine into the presynaptic neuron and increase the release of these monoamines into the extraneural space.
- Prodrug converted to dextroamphetamine
Metabolism: Liver; mainly excreted in the urine
Half-life: 12 hr

PRECAUTIONS:
- Advanced arteriosclerosis, symptomatic cardiovascular disease, moderate-to-severe HTN
- Hyperthyroidism
- Known hypersensitivity or idiosyncratic reaction to sympathomimetic amines
- Glaucoma

(cont.)

AUTISM SPECTRUM DISORDER: Amphetamines—Long-Acting

lisdexamfetamine (cont.)

- Agitated states
- Patients with a history of drug abuse: Amphetamines have a high potential for abuse. Administration of Amphetamines for an extended period of time may lead to drug dependence. Particular attention should be paid to the possibility of patients obtaining this class of medication for nontherapeutic use or distribution to others, and the drugs should be prescribed or dispensed sparingly.
- During or within 14 days following the administration of MAOIs, hypertensive crisis may result.
- Preexisting psychosis
- Seizure history: Some studies have shown the potential for lowering the seizure threshold.

PATIENT AND FAMILY EDUCATION:
- Store at room temperature, protected from light.
- Keep out of reach of children.
- Seek medical care for any signs of heart problems (chest pain, shortness of breath), fainting, psychotic symptoms, overdose, or any other concerns.
- Routinely assess weight and BP.

- Treatment should be initiated at low dosages and then titrated over 2 to 4 wk until an adequate response is achieved or unacceptable adverse effects occur.
- If one stimulant is not effective, another should be attempted before second-line medications are considered. Although some children benefit from daily stimulant therapy, weekend and summer "drug holidays" are suggested for children whose ADHD symptoms predominantly affect schoolwork, or to limit adverse effects (e.g., appetite suppression, abdominal pain, headache, insomnia, irritability, tics).

SPECIAL POPULATIONS:
- *Elderly:* Caution with polypharmacy and comorbid conditions; has not been studied for use in this population.
- *Pregnancy:* Category C; based on animal data, may cause fetal harm
- *Lactation:* Possibly unsafe
- *Children:* Has not been studied in children younger than 6 yr; should not be used in children younger than 3 yr.

Class: Methylphenidates—Short-Acting

dexmethylphenidate   *Focalin*

INDICATIONS: Treatment of ADHD of children and adults

AVAILABLE FORMS: Capsule, 2.5, 5, and 10 mg

DOSAGE: Dosage should be individualized according to the therapeutic needs and responses of the patient. All stimulant preparations should be administered at the lowest effective dosage. *Children: Older than 6 yr:* 2.5 to 10 mg PO bid; start, 2.5 mg PO bid, increase 5 to 10 mg/day every 7 days; maximum, 20 mg/day. To convert from methylphenidate, start at 50% of current methylphenidate daily dose; space doses at least 4 hr apart. *Adults:* 2.5 to 10 mg bid, 2.5 mg PO bid, increase 5 to 10 mg/day every 7 days; maximum, 20 mg/day. To convert from methylphenidate start at 50% of current methylphenidate daily dose; space doses at least 4 hr apart.

ADMINISTRATION: Do not crush or chew, may be given with or without food.

SIDE EFFECTS: Decreased appetite; dizziness; dry mouth; irritability; insomnia; upper abdominal pain; nausea and/or vomiting; weight loss; headaches; anxiety; psychiatric events: increase in manic states for bipolar patients, aggression, tics, tremors; long-term growth suppression: patients should be monitored throughout treatment, if there appears to be growth suppression, the treatment should be discontinued; rash; pyrexia; palpitations; tachycardia, elevated BP, sudden death, MI, cardiomyopathy; Stevens-Johnson syndrome

and toxic epidermal necrolysis; impotence, libido changes

DRUG INTERACTIONS: Urinary acidifying agents; MAOIs; adrenergic blockers; antihistamines; antihypertensives; veratrum alkaloids; ethosuximide; TCAs; meperidine; phenobarbital; phenytoin; chlorpromazine; *Haldol*; lithium; norepinephrine; propoxyphene

PHARMACOKINETICS:
- Absorbed by the GI tract.
- Amphetamines are noncatecholamine sympathomimetic amines with CNS-stimulant activity.
- The mode of therapeutic action in ADHD is not known. Amphetamines are thought to block the reuptake of norepinephrine and dopamine into the presynaptic neuron and increase the release of these monoamines into the extraneural space.

Metabolism: Liver; excreted in the urine
Half-life: 2–4.5 hr

PRECAUTIONS:
- Advanced arteriosclerosis, symptomatic cardiovascular disease, moderate-to-severe HTN
- Hyperthyroidism
- Known hypersensitivity or idiosyncratic reaction to sympathomimetic amines
- Glaucoma
- Agitated states
- Patients with a history of drug abuse: Amphetamines have a high potential for abuse.
(cont.)

dexmethylphenidate (*cont.*)

Administration of Amphetamines for an extended period of time may lead to drug dependence. Particular attention should be paid to the possibility of patients obtaining this class of medication for nontherapeutic use or distribution to others, and the drugs should be prescribed or dispensed sparingly.
- During or within 14 days following the administration of MAOIs, hypertensive crisis may result.
- Preexisting psychosis
- Seizure history: Some studies have shown the potential for lowering the seizure threshold

PATIENT AND FAMILY EDUCATION:
- Store at room temperature, protected from light.
- Keep out of reach of children.
- Seek medical care for any signs of heart problems (chest pain, shortness of breath), fainting, psychotic symptoms, overdose, or any other concerns.
- Routinely assess weight and BP.
- Treatment should be initiated at low dosages and then titrated over 2 to 4 wk until an

adequate response is achieved or unacceptable adverse effects occur.
- If one stimulant is not effective, another should be attempted before second-line medications are considered. Although some children benefit from daily stimulant therapy, weekend and summer "drug holidays" are suggested for children whose ADHD symptoms predominantly affect schoolwork or to limit adverse effects (e.g., appetite suppression, abdominal pain, headache, insomnia, irritability, tics).

SPECIAL POPULATIONS:
- *Elderly:* Caution with polypharmacy and comorbid conditions; has not been studied for use in this population
- *Pregnancy:* Category C; based on animal data, may cause fetal harm
- *Lactation:* Possibly unsafe
- *Children:* Has not been studied in children younger than 6 yr; should not be used in children younger than 3 yr.

Methylin   **methylphenidate**

INDICATIONS: Treatment of ADHD of children and adults

AVAILABLE FORMS: Capsule, 5, 10, and 20 mg; chewable, 2.5, 5, and 10 mg; liquid, 5 and 10 mg/5 mL

DOSAGE: Dosage should be individualized according to the therapeutic needs and responses of the patient. All stimulant preparations should be administered at the lowest effective dosage. *Children: Older than 6 yr:* 0.3 to 2 mg/kg/day PO divided bid–tid; start, 0.3 mg/kg PO bid or 2.5 to 5 mg PO bid, increase 0.1 mg/kg/dose or 5 to 10 mg/day every 7 days; maximum, 2 mg/kg/day up to 60 mg/day. *Adults:* 5 to 15 mg PO bid–tid; start, 5 to 10 mg PO bid; increase 10 mg/day every 7 days.

ADMINISTRATION: Duration 3 to 5 hr; give 30 to 45 min before meals, last dose before 6 pm.

SIDE EFFECTS: Decreased appetite; dizziness; dry mouth; irritability; insomnia; upper abdominal pain; nausea and/or vomiting; weight loss; headaches; anxiety; psychiatric events: increase in manic states for bipolar patients, aggression, tics, tremors; long-term growth suppression: patients should be monitored throughout treatment, if there appears to be growth suppression, the treatment should be discontinued; rash; pyrexia; palpitations, tachycardia, elevated BP, sudden death, MI, cardiomyopathy; Stevens-Johnson syndrome and toxic epidermal necrolysis; impotence, libido changes

DRUG INTERACTIONS: Urinary acidifying agents; MAOIs; adrenergic blockers; antihistamines; antihypertensives; veratrum alkaloids; ethosuximide; TCAs; meperidine; phenobarbital; phenytoin;

chlorpromazine; *Haldol*; lithium; norepinephrine; propoxyphene

PHARMACOKINETICS:
- Absorbed by the GI tract.
- Noncatecholamine sympathomimetic amines with CNS-stimulant activity.
- The mode of therapeutic action in ADHD is not known; thought to block the reuptake of norepinephrine and dopamine into the presynaptic neuron and increase the release of these monoamines into the extraneural space.

Metabolism: Liver; excreted in urine
Half-life: 2–3 hr

PRECAUTIONS:
- Advanced arteriosclerosis, symptomatic cardiovascular disease, moderate-to-severe HTN
- Hyperthyroidism
- Known hypersensitivity or idiosyncratic reaction to sympathomimetic amines
- Glaucoma
- Agitated states
- Patients with a history of drug abuse: Have a high potential for abuse. Administration for an extended period of time may lead to drug dependence. Particular attention should be paid to the possibility of patients obtaining this class of medication for nontherapeutic use or distribution to others, and the drugs should be prescribed or dispensed sparingly.
- During or within 14 days following the administration of MAOIs, hypertensive crisis may result.
- Preexisting psychosis
- Seizure history: Some studies have shown the potential for lowering the seizure threshold

(cont.)

methylphenidate (cont.)

PATIENT AND FAMILY EDUCATION:
- Store at room temperature, protected from light.
- Keep out of reach of children.
- Seek medical care for any signs of heart problems (chest pain, shortness of breath), fainting, psychotic symptoms, overdose, or any other concerns.
- Routinely assess weight and BP.
- Treatment should be initiated at low dosages and then titrated over 2 to 4 wk until an adequate response is achieved or unacceptable adverse effects occur.
- If one stimulant is not effective, another should be attempted before second-line medications are considered. Although some children benefit from daily stimulant therapy, weekend and summer "drug holidays" are suggested for children whose ADHD symptoms predominantly affect schoolwork or to limit adverse effects (e.g., appetite suppression, abdominal pain, headache, insomnia, irritability, tics).

SPECIAL POPULATIONS:
- *Elderly:* Caution with polypharmacy and comorbid conditions; has not been studied for use in this population
- *Pregnancy:* Category C; based on animal data, may cause fetal harm
- *Lactation:* Possibly unsafe
- *Children:* Has not been studied in children younger than 6 yr; should not be used in children younger than 3 yr.

methylphenidate   *Ritalin SR and LA*

INDICATIONS: Treatment of ADHD of children and adults

AVAILABLE FORMS: Capsule, 10, 20, 30, and 40 mg

DOSAGE: Dosage should be individualized according to the therapeutic needs and response of the patient. All stimulant preparations should be administered at the lowest effective dosage. *Children: Older than 6 yr:* 20 to 40 mg PO qam; start, 20 mg PO qam; increase 10 mg/day every 7 days; maximum, 60 mg/day. *Adults:* 20 to 40 mg qam; start, 20 mg PO qam; increase 10 mg/day every 7 days; maximum, 60 mg/day.

ADMINISTRATION: *Ritalin LA* capsules may be opened and sprinkled on soft food; may sprinkle on applesauce immediately before use; do not crush/chew; to switch from bid SR form, use same total daily dose.

SIDE EFFECTS: Decreased appetite; dizziness; dry mouth; irritability; insomnia; upper abdominal pain; nausea and/or vomiting; weight loss; headaches; anxiety; psychiatric events: increase in manic states for bipolar patients, aggression, tics, tremors; long-term growth suppression: patients should be monitored throughout treatment, if there appears to be growth suppression, the treatment should be discontinued; rash; pyrexia; palpitations; tachycardia, elevated BP, sudden death, MI, cardiomyopathy; Stevens-Johnson syndrome and toxic epidermal necrolysis; impotence, libido changes

DRUG INTERACTIONS: Urinary acidifying agents; MAOIs; adrenergic blockers; antihistamines; antihypertensives; veratrum alkaloids; ethosuximide; TCAs; meperidine; phenobarbital; phenytoin; chlorpromazine; *Haldol;* lithium; norepinephrine; propoxyphene

PHARMACOKINETICS:
- Absorbed by the GI tract.
- Noncatecholamine sympathomimetic amines with CNS-stimulant activity.
- The mode of therapeutic action in ADHD is not known; thought to block the reuptake of norepinephrine and dopamine into the presynaptic neuron and increase the release of these monoamines into the extraneural space.

Metabolism: Liver; excreted mainly in the urine
Half-life: 3–4 hr

PRECAUTIONS:
- Advanced arteriosclerosis, symptomatic cardiovascular disease, moderate-to-severe HTN
- Hyperthyroidism
- Known hypersensitivity or idiosyncratic reaction to sympathomimetic amines
- Glaucoma
- Agitated states
- Patients with a history of drug abuse: Have a high potential for abuse. Administration for an extended period of time may lead to drug dependence. Particular attention should be paid to the possibility of patients obtaining this class of medication for nontherapeutic use or distribution to others, and the drugs should be prescribed or dispensed sparingly.
- During or within 14 days following the administration of MAOIs, hypertensive crisis may result.
- Preexisting psychosis
- Seizure history: Some studies have shown the potential for lowering the seizure threshold

PATIENT AND FAMILY EDUCATION:
- Store at room temperature, protected from light.
- Keep out of reach of children.
- Seek medical care for any signs of heart problems (chest pain, shortness of breath), fainting, psychotic symptoms, overdose, or any other concerns.
- Routinely assess weight and BP.
- Treatment should be initiated at low dosages and then titrated over 2 to 4 wk until an adequate response is achieved or unacceptable adverse effects occur.

(cont.)

methylphenidate (cont.)

- If one stimulant is not effective, another should be attempted before second-line medications are considered. Although some children benefit from daily stimulant therapy, weekend and summer "drug holidays" are suggested for children whose ADHD symptoms predominantly affect schoolwork, or to limit adverse effects (e.g., appetite suppression, abdominal pain, headache, insomnia, irritability, tics).

SPECIAL POPULATIONS:
- *Elderly:* Caution with polypharmacy and comorbid conditions; has not been studied for use in this population
- *Pregnancy:* Category C; based on animal data, may cause fetal harm
- *Lactation:* Possibly unsafe
- *Children:* Has not been studied in children younger than 6 yr; should not be used in children younger than 3 yr.

Class: Methylphenidate—Intermediate-Acting

Metadate CD and ER   methylphenidate

INDICATIONS: Treatment of ADHD of children and adults

AVAILABLE FORMS: Capsule, 10, 20, 30, 40, 50, and 60 mg

DOSAGE: Dosage should be individualized according to the therapeutic needs and responses of the patient. All stimulant preparations should be administered at the lowest effective dosage. *Children: Older than 6 yr:* 20 to 60 mg PO qam; start, 20 mg PO qam; increase 10 to 20 mg/day every 7 days; maximum, 60 mg/day. *Adults:* 20 to 60 mg PO qam; start, 20 mg PO qam; increase 10 to 20 mg/day every 7 days; maximum, 60 mg/day.

ADMINISTRATION: *Metadate* may be opened and sprinkled on soft food, initial titration with ER form recommended; give before meal

SIDE EFFECTS: Decreased appetite; dizziness; dry mouth; irritability; insomnia; upper abdominal pain; nausea and/or vomiting; weight loss; headaches; anxiety; psychiatric events: increase in manic states for bipolar patients, aggression, tics, tremors; long-term growth suppression: patients should be monitored throughout treatment, if there appears to be growth suppression, the treatment should be discontinued; rash; pyrexia; palpitations, tachycardia, elevated BP, sudden death, MI, cardiomyopathy; Stevens-Johnson syndrome and toxic epidermal necrolysis; impotence; libido changes

DRUG INTERACTIONS: Urinary acidifying agents; MAOIs; adrenergic blockers; antihistamines; antihypertensives; veratrum alkaloids; ethosuximide; TCAs; meperidine; phenobarbital; phenytoin; chlorpromazine; *Haldol*; lithium; norepinephrine; propoxyphene

PHARMACOKINETICS:
- Absorbed by the GI tract.
- Noncatecholamine sympathomimetic amines with CNS-stimulant activity.
- The mode of therapeutic action in ADHD is not known; thought to block the reuptake of norepinephrine and dopamine into the presynaptic neuron and increase the release of these monoamines into the extraneural space.

Metabolism: Liver; mainly excreted in the urine
Half-life: 3–4 hr

PRECAUTIONS:
- Advanced arteriosclerosis, symptomatic cardiovascular disease, moderate-to-severe HTN
- Hyperthyroidism
- Known hypersensitivity or idiosyncratic reaction to sympathomimetic amines
- Glaucoma
- Agitated states
- Patients with a history of drug abuse: Have a high potential for abuse. Administration for an extended period of time may lead to drug dependence. Particular attention should be paid to the possibility of patients obtaining this class of medication for nontherapeutic use or distribution to others, and the drugs should be prescribed or dispensed sparingly.
- During or within 14 days following the administration of MAOIs, hypertensive crisis may result.
- Preexisting psychosis
- Seizure history: Some studies have shown the potential for lowering the seizure threshold

PATIENT AND FAMILY EDUCATION:
- Store at room temperature, protected from light.
- Keep out of reach of children.
- Seek medical care for any signs of heart problems (chest pain, shortness of breath), fainting, psychotic symptoms, overdose, or any other concerns.
- Routinely assess weight and BP.
- Treatment should be initiated at low dosages and then titrated over 2 to 4 wk until an adequate response is achieved or unacceptable adverse effects occur.
- If one stimulant is not effective, another should be attempted before second-line medications are considered. Although some children benefit from daily stimulant therapy, weekend and summer "drug holidays" are suggested for children whose ADHD symptoms predominantly affect schoolwork, or to limit adverse effects (e.g., appetite suppression,

(cont.)

methylphenidate (cont.)

abdominal pain, headache, insomnia, irritability, tics).

SPECIAL POPULATIONS:
- *Elderly:* Caution with polypharmacy and comorbid conditions; has not been studied for use in this population

- *Pregnancy:* Category C; based on animal data, may cause fetal harm
- *Lactation:* Possibly unsafe
- *Children:* Has not been studied in children younger than 6 yr; should not be used in children younger than 3 yr.

methylphenidate   *Ritalin SR and LA*

INDICATIONS: Treatment of ADHD of children and adults

AVAILABLE FORMS: Capsule, 10, 20, 30, and 40 mg

DOSAGE: Dosage should be individualized according to the therapeutic needs and response of the patient. All stimulant preparations should be administered at the lowest effective dosage. *Children: Older than 6 yr:* 20 to 40 mg PO qam; start, 20 mg PO qam; increase 10 mg/day every 7 days; maximum, 60 mg/day. *Adults:* 20 to 40 mg qam; start, 20 mg PO qam; increase 10 mg/day every 7 days; maximum, 60 mg/day.

ADMINISTRATION: *Ritalin LA* capsules may be opened and sprinkled on soft food; may sprinkle on applesauce immediately before use; do not crush/chew; to switch from bid SR form, use same total daily dose.

SIDE EFFECTS: Decreased appetite; dizziness; dry mouth; irritability; insomnia; upper abdominal pain; nausea and/or vomiting; weight loss; headaches; anxiety; psychiatric events: increase in manic states for bipolar patients, aggression, tics, tremors; long-term growth suppression: patients should be monitored throughout treatment, if there appears to be growth suppression, the treatment should be discontinued; rash; pyrexia; palpitations, tachycardia, elevated BP, sudden death, MI, cardiomyopathy; Stevens-Johnson syndrome and toxic epidermal necrolysis; impotence, libido changes

DRUG INTERACTIONS: Urinary acidifying agents; MAOIs; adrenergic blockers; antihistamines; antihypertensives; veratrum alkaloids; ethosuximide; TCAs; meperidine; phenobarbital; phenytoin; chlorpromazine; *Haldol;* lithium; norepinephrine; propoxyphene

PHARMACOKINETICS:
- Absorbed by the GI tract.
- Noncatecholamine sympathomimetic amines with CNS-stimulant activity.
- The mode of therapeutic action in ADHD is not known; thought to block the reuptake of norepinephrine and dopamine into the presynaptic neuron and increase the release of these monoamines into the extraneural space.

Metabolism: Liver; excreted mainly in the urine
Half-life: 3–4 hr

PRECAUTIONS:
- Advanced arteriosclerosis, symptomatic cardiovascular disease, moderate-to-severe HTN

- Hyperthyroidism
- Known hypersensitivity or idiosyncratic reaction to sympathomimetic amines
- Glaucoma
- Agitated states
- Patients with a history of drug abuse: Have a high potential for abuse. Administration for an extended period of time may lead to drug dependence. Particular attention should be paid to the possibility of patients obtaining this class of medication for nontherapeutic use or distribution to others, and the drugs should be prescribed or dispensed sparingly.
- During or within 14 days following the administration of MAOIs, hypertensive crisis may result.
- Preexisting psychosis
- Seizure history: Some studies have shown the potential for lowering the seizure threshold

PATIENT AND FAMILY EDUCATION:
- Store at room temperature, protected from light.
- Keep out of reach of children.
- Seek medical care for any signs of heart problems (chest pain, shortness of breath), fainting, psychotic symptoms, overdose, or any other concerns.
- Routinely assess weight and BP.
- Treatment should be initiated at low dosages and then titrated over 2 to 4 wk until an adequate response is achieved or unacceptable adverse effects occur.
- If one stimulant is not effective, another should be attempted before second-line medications are considered. Although some children benefit from daily stimulant therapy, weekend and summer "drug holidays" are suggested for children whose ADHD symptoms predominantly affect schoolwork, or to limit adverse effects (e.g., appetite suppression, abdominal pain, headache, insomnia, irritability, tics).

SPECIAL POPULATIONS:
- *Elderly:* Caution with polypharmacy and comorbid conditions; has not been studied for use in this population
- *Pregnancy:* Category C; based on animal data, may cause fetal harm
- *Lactation:* Possibly unsafe
- *Children:* Has not been studied in children younger than 6 yr; should not be used in children younger than 3 yr.

Class: Methylphenidate—Long-Acting

Concerta   **methylphenidate**

INDICATIONS: Treatment of ADHD of children and adults

AVAILABLE FORMS: Capsule, 18, 27, 36, and 54 mg

DOSAGE: Dosage should be individualized according to the therapeutic needs and response of the patient. All stimulant preparations should be administered at the lowest effective dosage. *Children: 6 to 12 yr old:* 1 tab PO qam; start, 18 mg PO daily, increase 18 mg/day every 7 days; maximum, 54 mg/day. *Older than 13 yr:* 1 tab PO qam; start, 18 mg PO daily, increase 18 mg/day every 7 days; maximum, 2 mg/kg/day or 72 mg/day. *Adults: 18 to 65 yr old:* 1 tab PO qam; start, 18 to 36 mg PO daily, increase 18 mg/day every 7 days; maximum, 72 mg/day.

ADMINISTRATION: *Concerta* may be opened and sprinkled on soft food; give before meal

SIDE EFFECTS: Decreased appetite; dizziness; dry mouth; irritability; insomnia; upper abdominal pain; nausea and/or vomiting; weight loss; headaches; anxiety; psychiatric events: increase in manic states for bipolar patients, aggression, tics, tremors; long-term growth suppression: patients should be monitored throughout treatment, if there appears to be growth suppression, the treatment should be discontinued; rash; pyrexia; palpitations, tachycardia, elevated BP, sudden death, MI, cardiomyopathy; Stevens-Johnson syndrome and toxic epidermal necrolysis; impotence, libido changes

DRUG INTERACTIONS: Urinary acidifying agents; MAOIs; adrenergic blockers; antihistamines; antihypertensives; veratrum alkaloids; ethosuximide; TCAs; meperidine; phenobarbital; phenytoin; chlorpromazine; *Haldol*; lithium; norepinephrine; propoxyphene

PHARMACOKINETICS:
- Absorbed by the GI tract.
- Noncatecholamine sympathomimetic amines with CNS-stimulant activity.
- The mode of therapeutic action in ADHD is not known; thought to block the reuptake of norepinephrine and dopamine into the presynaptic neuron and increase the release of these monoamines into the extraneural space.

Metabolism: Liver; mainly excreted in the urine
Half-life: 3.5 hr

PRECAUTIONS:
- Advanced arteriosclerosis, symptomatic cardiovascular disease, moderate-to-severe HTN
- Hyperthyroidism
- Known hypersensitivity or idiosyncratic reaction to sympathomimetic amines
- Glaucoma
- Agitated states
- Patients with a history of drug abuse: Have a high potential for abuse. Administration for an extended period of time may lead to drug dependence. Particular attention should be paid to the possibility of patients obtaining this class of medication for nontherapeutic use or distribution to others, and the drugs should be prescribed or dispensed sparingly.
- During or within 14 days following the administration of MAOIs, hypertensive crisis may result.
- Preexisting psychosis
- Seizure history: Some studies have shown the potential for lowering the seizure threshold

PATIENT AND FAMILY EDUCATION:
- Store at room temperature, protected from light.
- Keep out of reach of children.
- Seek medical care for any signs of heart problems (chest pain, shortness of breath), fainting, psychotic symptoms, overdose, or any other concerns.
- Routinely assess weight and BP.
- Treatment should be initiated at low dosages and then titrated over 2 to 4 wk until an adequate response is achieved or unacceptable adverse effects occur.
- If one stimulant is not effective, another should be attempted before second-line medications are considered. Although some children benefit from daily stimulant therapy, weekend and summer "drug holidays" are suggested for children whose ADHD symptoms predominantly affect schoolwork, or to limit adverse effects (e.g., appetite suppression, abdominal pain, headache, insomnia, irritability, tics).

SPECIAL POPULATIONS:
- *Elderly:* Caution with polypharmacy and comorbid conditions; has not been studied for use in this population
- *Pregnancy:* Category C; based on animal data, may cause fetal harm
- *Lactation:* Possibly unsafe
- *Children:* Has not been studied in children younger than 6 yr; should not be used in children younger than 3 yr.

Daytrana Patch   **methylphenidate transdermal**

INDICATIONS: Treatment of ADHD of children and adults

AVAILABLE FORMS: Transdermal patch, 10, 15, 20, and 30 mg/9 hr patch

DOSAGE: Dosage should be individualized according to the therapeutic needs and response of the patient. All stimulant preparations should be administered at the lowest effective dosage. *Children: Older than 6 yr:* 1 patch daily ×9 hr,
(cont.)

AUTISM SPECTRUM DISORDER: Methylphenidate—Long-Acting

methylphenidate transdermal (*cont.*)

off ×15 h; start, 10 mg/9 hr patch daily, may increase to next size patch every 7 days; maximum, 30 mg/9 hr patch daily. *Adults: 18 to 65 yr:* 1 patch daily ×9 hr, off ×15 hr; start, 10 mg/9 hr patch daily, may increase to next size patch every 7 days; maximum, 30 mg/9 hr patch daily.

ADMINISTRATION: Apply to hip 2 hr before desired effect; drug effects may persist 5 hr after patch removal; rotate sites; do not alter/cut patch.

SIDE EFFECTS: Decreased appetite; dizziness; dry mouth; irritability; insomnia; upper abdominal pain; nausea and/or vomiting; weight loss; headaches; anxiety; psychiatric events: increase in manic states for bipolar patients, aggression, tics, tremors; long-term growth suppression: patients should be monitored throughout treatment, if there appears to be growth suppression, the treatment should be discontinued; rash; pyrexia; palpitations, tachycardia, elevated BP, sudden death, MI, cardiomyopathy; Stevens-Johnson syndrome and toxic epidermal necrolysis; impotence, libido changes; Skin irritation

DRUG INTERACTIONS: Urinary acidifying agents; MAOIs; adrenergic blockers; antihistamines; antihypertensives; veratrum alkaloids; ethosuximide; TCAs; meperidine; phenobarbital; phenytoin; chlorpromazine; *Haldol*; lithium; norepinephrine; propoxyphene

PHARMACOKINETICS:
- Absorbed by the GI tract.
- Noncatecholamine sympathomimetic amines with CNS-stimulant activity.
- The mode of therapeutic action in ADHD is not known; thought to block the reuptake of norepinephrine and dopamine into the presynaptic neuron and increase the release of these monoamines into the extraneural space.

Metabolism: Liver; mainly excreted in the urine
Half-life: 3.5 hr

PRECAUTIONS:
- Advanced arteriosclerosis, symptomatic cardiovascular disease, moderate-to-severe HTN
- Hyperthyroidism
- Known hypersensitivity or idiosyncratic reaction to sympathomimetic amines
- Glaucoma
- Agitated states
- Patients with a history of drug abuse: Have a high potential for abuse. Administration for an extended period of time may lead to drug dependence. Particular attention should be paid to the possibility of patients obtaining this class of medication for nontherapeutic use or distribution to others, and the drugs should be prescribed or dispensed sparingly.
- During or within 14 days following the administration of MAOIs, hypertensive crisis may result.
- Preexisting psychosis
- Seizure history: Some studies have shown the potential for lowering the seizure threshold

PATIENT AND FAMILY EDUCATION:
- Store at room temperature, protected from light.
- Keep out of reach of children.
- Seek medical care for any signs of heart problems (chest pain, shortness of breath), fainting, psychotic symptoms, overdose, or any other concerns.
- Routinely assess weight and BP.
- Treatment should be initiated at low dosages and then titrated over 2 to 4 wk until an adequate response is achieved or unacceptable adverse effects occur.
- Dispose of properly away from children or animals (remnant medication may persist on patch)
- If one stimulant is not effective, another should be attempted before second-line medications are considered. Although some children benefit from daily stimulant therapy, weekend and summer "drug holidays" are suggested for children whose ADHD symptoms predominantly affect schoolwork, or to limit adverse effects (e.g., appetite suppression, abdominal pain, headache, insomnia, irritability, tics).

SPECIAL POPULATIONS:
- *Elderly:* Caution with polypharmacy and comorbid conditions; has not been studied for use in this population
- *Pregnancy:* Category C; based on animal data, may cause fetal harm
- *Lactation:* Possibly unsafe
- *Children:* Has not been studied in children younger than 6 yr; should not be used in children younger than 3 yr.

dexmethylphenidate   *Focalin*

INDICATIONS: Treatment of ADHD of children and adults

AVAILABLE FORMS: Capsule, 2.5, 5, and 10 mg

DOSAGE: Dosage should be individualized according to the therapeutic needs and responses of the patient. All stimulant preparations should be administered at the lowest effective dosage. *Children: Older than 6 yr:* 2.5 to 10 mg PO bid; start, 2.5 mg PO bid, increase 5 to 10 mg/day every 7 days; maximum, 20 mg/day. To convert from methylphenidate, start at 50% of current methylphenidate daily dose; space doses at least 4 hr apart. *Adults:* 2.5 to 10 mg bid, 2.5 mg PO bid, increase 5 to 10 mg/day every 7 days; maximum, 20 mg/day. To convert from methylphenidate start at 50% of current methylphenidate daily dose; space doses at least 4 hr apart.

(cont.)

dexmethylphenidate (cont.)

ADMINISTRATION: Do not crush or chew, may be given with or without food.

SIDE EFFECTS: Decreased appetite; dizziness; dry mouth; irritability; insomnia; upper abdominal pain; nausea and/or vomiting; weight loss; headaches; anxiety; psychiatric events: increase in manic states for bipolar patients, aggression, tics, tremors; long-term growth suppression: patients should be monitored throughout treatment, if there appears to be growth suppression, the treatment should be discontinued; rash; pyrexia; palpitations, tachycardia, elevated BP, sudden death, MI, cardiomyopathy; Stevens-Johnson syndrome and toxic epidermal necrolysis; impotence, libido changes

DRUG INTERACTIONS: Urinary acidifying agents; MAOIs; adrenergic blockers; antihistamines; antihypertensives; veratrum alkaloids; ethosuximide; TCAs; meperidine; phenobarbital; phenytoin; chlorpromazine; *Haldol*; lithium; norepinephrine; propoxyphene

PHARMACOKINETICS:
- Absorbed by the GI tract.
- Amphetamines are noncatecholamine sympathomimetic amines with CNS-stimulant activity.
- The mode of therapeutic action in ADHD is not known. Amphetamines are thought to block the reuptake of norepinephrine and dopamine into the presynaptic neuron and increase the release of these monoamines into the extraneural space.

Metabolism: Liver; excreted in the urine
Half-life: 2–4.5 hr

PRECAUTIONS:
- Advanced arteriosclerosis, symptomatic cardiovascular disease, moderate-to-severe HTN
- Hyperthyroidism
- Known hypersensitivity or idiosyncratic reaction to sympathomimetic amines
- Glaucoma
- Agitated states
- Patients with a history of drug abuse: Amphetamines have a high potential for abuse.

Administration of Amphetamines for an extended period of time may lead to drug dependence. Particular attention should be paid to the possibility of patients obtaining this class of medication for nontherapeutic use or distribution to others, and the drugs should be prescribed or dispensed sparingly.
- During or within 14 days following the administration of MAOIs, hypertensive crisis may result.
- Preexisting psychosis
- Seizure history: Some studies have shown the potential for lowering the seizure threshold

PATIENT AND FAMILY EDUCATION:
- Store at room temperature, protected from light.
- Keep out of reach of children.
- Seek medical care for any signs of heart problems (chest pain, shortness of breath), fainting, psychotic symptoms, overdose, or any other concerns.
- Routinely assess weight and BP.
- Treatment should be initiated at low dosages and then titrated over 2 to 4 wk until an adequate response is achieved or unacceptable adverse effects occur.
- If one stimulant is not effective, another should be attempted before second-line medications are considered. Although some children benefit from daily stimulant therapy, weekend and summer "drug holidays" are suggested for children whose ADHD symptoms predominantly affect schoolwork or to limit adverse effects (e.g., appetite suppression, abdominal pain, headache, insomnia, irritability, tics).

SPECIAL POPULATIONS:
- *Elderly:* Caution with polypharmacy and comorbid conditions; has not been studied for use in this population
- *Pregnancy:* Category C; based on animal data, may cause fetal harm
- *Lactation:* Possibly unsafe
- *Children:* Has not been studied in children younger than 6 yr; should not be used in children younger than 3 yr.

Substance Abuse

OVERVIEW

- In the *DSM-IV*, substance abuse is defined as a maladaptive pattern of substance use that poses a hazard to health.
- Differential diagnoses include hypoglycemia, electrolyte imbalance, head injury/trauma, stroke, psychosis, neurological disorder.
- ICD Code: 304.90 (substance abuse)
- Diagnostic workup includes physical and mental evaluation.
- There is no single cause of substance abuse, though there are numerous theoretical causes related to genetics and biochemistry.
- Males are twice as likely as females to abuse substances.

ACUTE TREATMENT

- Detox either as an outpatient or inpatient depending on the drug being abused
- Inpatient treatment often includes psychotherapy
- Treat agitation
- Focus on patients nutrition, replacing fluids and electrolytes as indicated
- Exercise plan

CHRONIC TREATMENT

- Psychotherapy
- Family counseling
- Alcoholics anonymous

CLASS	DRUG
Nicotinic Receptor Agonists	
	nicotine, nicotine transdermal system, nicotine polacrilex (*Nicotrol NS, Nicotrol Inhaler, Commit, Habitrol, NicoDerm, Nicotrol ProStep, Nicorette Gum, Nicorette DS*) varenicline (*Chantix*)
Opioid Antagonists	
	naltrexone hydrochloride (*Revia, Vivitrol*)
Substance Abuse Deterrents	
	disulfiram (*Antabuse*) acamprosate calcium (*Campral*)
Vitamins	
	B complex (*Vitamin B1/Thiamine Hydrochloride*)
Norepinephrine/Dopamine Reuptake Inhibitors (NDRIs)	
	bupropion (*Wellbutrin, Zyban*)

SUBSTANCE ABUSE

Class: Nicotinic Receptor Agonists

Nicotrol NS, Nicotrol Inhaler, Commit,
Habitrol, NicoDerm, Nicotrol ProStep,
Nicorette Gum, Nicorette DS

**nicotine,
nicotine transdermal system,
nicotine polacrilex**

INDICATIONS: Used to treat nicotine dependence

AVAILABLE FORMS: Gum, 2 and 4 mg; lozenges, 2 and 4 mg; spray, 0.5 mg; inhaler, 4 mg; transdermal patch, 7, 14, and 21; 5, 10, and 15; and 11 and 22 mg/day

DOSAGE: *Oral:* Chew one piece of gum during urge to smoke. Repeat as needed up to 30 pieces/day. *Inhaler:* Spray twice in each nostril every hour up to 40 times daily. *Topical:* Apply one transdermal patch every 24 hr as follows: *Habitrol and*

Nicoderm: 21 mg/day for 6 wk, then 14 mg/day for 2 wk, then 7 mg/day for 2 wk. For patients with CV disease, weigh less that 45 kg, or smoke less than ½ pack per day: 14 mg/day for 6 wk the 7 mg/day for 4 wk. *Prostep:* 22 mg/day for 4–8 wk, then 11 mg/day for 2 to 4 wk. For patients with CV disease, weigh less that 45 kg, or smoke less than ½ pack per day: 11 mg/day for 4–8 wk. *Nicotrol:* Wear patch for 16 hr/day. 15 mg/day for 4–12 wk, then 10 mg/day for 2 to 4 wk, then 5 mg/day for 2 to 4 wk

(cont.)

SUBSTANCE ABUSE

nicotine, nicotine transdermal system, nicotine polacrilex (cont.)

ADMINISTRATION:
- Chew gum as directed.
- Remove old patch before applying new one.
- Apply patch to nonhairy skin surface.
- Patches are heat sensitive; store at or below 30°C.

SIDE EFFECTS: Headaches, dizziness, lightheadedness; insomnia, irritability; tachycardia, palpitations; sore mouth, throat, tingling of tongue; skin rash, pruritus; runny nose, nasal irritation, watery eyes

DRUG INTERACTIONS:
- May increase metabolism of caffeine, theophylline, insulin, propranolol, acetaminophen
- Coffee and cola may decrease absorption of gum

PHARMACOKINETICS:
Half-life: 30–120 min

PRECAUTIONS: Contraindicated immediately post-MI, severe angina pectoris, or life-threatening arrhythmias

PATIENT AND FAMILY EDUCATION:
- Chew gum for 30 min at a time to get full effect.
- Chew only one piece of gum at a time.
- Discontinue use of patch if local skin reaction occurs.
- Smoking while using the patch increases adverse reactions.

SPECIAL POPULATIONS:
- *Elderly:* Use with caution; can cause unsavory side effects such as nausea.
- *Pregnancy:* Category D (nasal spray, transdermal patch); category C (gum)
- *Lactation:* Use only if benefits outweigh the associated risks
- *Children and adolescents*: Safety and efficacy not established; long-term effects in children/adolescents unknown.

---

varenicline   *Chantix*

INDICATIONS: Aid for smoking cessation

AVAILABLE FORMS: Tablet, 0.5 and 1.0 mg

DOSAGE: *Days 1–3:* 0.5 mg once daily. *Days 4–7:* 0.5 mg twice daily. Then 1 mg twice daily until end of treatment. Treatment is for 12 wk.

ADMINISTRATION:
- Patient should set date to quit smoking. Dosing should begin 1 wk prior to this date.
- PO with a glass of water.
- Take after eating.
- Take at regular intervals.
- After 12 wk of initial treatment, patients who stop smoking may continue with an additional 12-wk course of treatment to increase long-term abstinence.
- If patient is unsuccessful after 12 wk of initial treatment, other psychosocial factors should be addressed to promote behavioral change. After addressing these factors, patient may again try a 12-wk regimen.

SIDE EFFECTS: Diarrhea; nausea; insomnia; chest pain; flu-like symptoms; back pain; muscle cramps; disturbance in attention; dizziness; increased urination; nosebleeds; flushing. *Rare*: Serious skin reactions (Steven-Johnsons syndrome and erythema multiforme); accidental injury (traffic accidents, near-miss incidents in traffic)

DRUG INTERACTIONS: No drug interactions. Safety and efficacy of treatment combined with other smoking cessation treatments (bupropion and NRT) has not been established.

PHARMACOKINETICS:
- Absorption and distribution occurs with 3 to 4 hr after oral administrations.

- Oral bioavailability is unaffected by food or time-day dosing
Metabolism: 92% excreted in urine
Half-life: 24 hr

PRECAUTIONS:
- Serious neuropsychiatric events including, but not limited to, depression, suicidal ideation, suicide attempt, and completed suicide have been reported in patients taking this medication.
- Depression has occurred in patients who continued to smoke.
- All patients being treated should be observed for neuropsychiatric symptoms including changes in behavior, hostility, agitation, depressed mood, and suicide-related events, including ideation, behavior, and attempted suicide.
- These symptoms, as well as worsening of preexisting psychiatric illness and completed suicide, have been reported in some patients attempting to quit smoking while taking in the postmarketing experience.
- When symptoms were reported, most were during treatment, but some were following discontinuation of therapy.
- Safety and efficacy in patients with serious psychiatric illness such as schizophrenia, bipolar disorder, and major depressive disorder have not been established.
- Resolution of symptoms after discontinuation was reported, although in some cases the symptoms persisted.
- Ongoing monitoring and supportive care should be provided until symptoms resolve.
- The risks should be weighed against the benefits of its use.
- Increases the likelihood of abstinence from smoking for as long as 1 yr compared to treatment with placebo.

(cont.)

varenicline (cont.)

PATIENT AND FAMILY EDUCATION:
- Advise patients and caregivers that the patient should stop taking *Chantix* and contact a health care provider immediately if agitation, hostility, depressed mood, or changes in behavior or thinking that are not typical for the patient are observed, or if the patient develops suicidal ideation or suicidal behavior.
- Set a quit date and begin treatment 1 wk prior to date.
- May continue with treatment if smoking relapses occur.
- Nausea and insomnia are most often transient. However, if continual, a dosage reduction may be beneficial.
- May experience nicotine withdrawal symptoms such as irritability and depressed mood.
- Immediately discontinue medication and notify health care provider at first sign of skin reaction or rash with lesions on mouth.

- Caution when driving or operative machinery.
- May experience vivid, unusual, or strange dreams.

SPECIAL POPULATIONS:
- *Elderly:* No dosage adjustments are indicated; however, renal function should be monitored and doses adjusted when indicated.
- *Hepatic impairment:* No dosage adjustments are needed.
- *Renal impairment:* For patients with mild-to-moderate impairment, dosage adjustments are not necessary. For patients with severe renal impairments, the recommended starting dose is 0.5 mg once daily for 1 wk and then titrated to 0.5 mg twice daily. For patients with end-stage renal disease; the recommended dosage is 0.5 mg once daily.
- *Pregnancy:* Category C
- *Lactation:* May be excreted in breast milk.
- *Children:* Safety and efficacy has not been established.

Class: Opioid Antagonists

Revia, Vivitrol | **naltrexone hydrochloride**

INDICATIONS: Narcotic drug and alcohol addictions

AVAILABLE FORMS: Tablet, 50 mg

DOSAGE: 50 mg once daily for up to 12 wk

ADMINISTRATION:
- PO with glass of water
- May be taken with or without food
- Carry ID card or medical ID bracelet stating that you are taking medication
- *Missed dose:* Take the medication as soon as remembered. If it is almost time for the next dose, skip the missed dose and wait until next regularly scheduled dose. Do not take extra medicine to make up the missed dose.

SIDE EFFECTS: Visual changes; palpitations; mood changes; nausea and/or abdominal pain, anorexia; tinnitus; pruritus or rash, jaundice; wheezing, difficulty breathing; nervousness, irritability; dizziness, insomnia; polyuria; fatigue, muscle weakness; sexual side effects

DRUG INTERACTIONS:
- Lethargy and somnolence has occurred with concurrent use of thioridazine.
- May experience limited or no benefit from opioid-containing medicines such as cold and cough preparations, antidiarrheal preparations, and opioid analgesics.

PHARMACOKINETICS:
- Pure opioid receptor antagonist
- Subject to significant first-pass metabolism
Half-life: 4 hr

PRECAUTIONS:
- Do not initiate treatment until confirmed abstinence from opioids for 7 to 10 days.
- Urine drug screen is often not sufficient proof that patient is opioid-free; therefore, health care provider may choose to give naloxone challenge before treatment.
- Attempts by patient to overcome blocking effects by using large amounts of opiates may result in life-endangering opioid intoxication.

PATIENT AND FAMILY EDUCATION:
- Use caution when driving or operating machinery.
- Do not use narcotic drugs or alcohol when taking medication.
- Ask health care providers prior to taking any OTC medication for cold symptoms.

SPECIAL POPULATIONS:
- *Elderly:* Use with caution.
- *Hepatic impairment:* Use with caution due to hepatotoxic effects.
- *Renal impairment:* Use with caution
- *Pregnancy:* Category C; caution when using for nursing mothers
- *Children:* Safety and effectiveness has not been established.

SUBSTANCE ABUSE: Opioid Antagonists

Class: Substance Abuse Deterrents

disulfiram   *Antabuse*

INDICATIONS: Aids in the management of alcohol dependence

AVAILABLE FORMS: Tablet, 250 and 500 mg

DOSAGE:
▶ **Note:** Should never be administered until patient has been abstinent from alcohol for at least 12 hr.
- 500 mg daily given in single dose for 1 to 2 wk; then maintenance dose of 250 mg daily. Maintenance therapy may be required for months to years.

ADMINISTRATION:
- PO with a full glass of water
- May be taken with or without food
- *Missed dose:* Take as soon as remembered. Skip the missed dose if it is almost time for the next scheduled dose. Do not take extra medicine.

SIDE EFFECTS:
- *Disulfiram-alcohol reaction:* Small amounts of alcohol while taking disulfiram could result in the following (varies with each individual): flushing, throbbing in head and neck, throbbing headache, respiratory difficulty, nausea, copious vomiting, sweating, thirst, chest pain, palpitation, dyspnea, hyperventilation, tachycardia, hypotension, syncope, marked uneasiness, weakness, vertigo, blurred vision, and confusion.
- In severe reactions, there may be respiratory depression, CV collapse, arrhythmias, MI, acute CHF, unconsciousness, convulsions, and death

DRUG INTERACTIONS:
- Medications containing alcohol are contraindicated.
- Used with caution with phenytoin and its congeners due to variation in therapeutic levels.
- Dosage of oral anticoagulants may need to be adjusted; prothrombin times may be prolonged.
- When taken concurrently with isoniazid, should be observed for changes in gait or mental status.

PHARMACOKINETICS:
Half-life: 4–10 hr

PRECAUTIONS:
- Never administer to someone intoxicated or without patient's knowledge.
- Because of possibility of accidental disulfiram-alcohol reaction, treatment is contraindicated for patients with the following conditions: DM, hypothyroidism, epilepsy, brain injury, renal and hepatic insufficiency.
- Patients with history of rubber allergy should be evaluated for hypersensitivity to thiuram derivatives before receiving disulfiram.

PATIENT AND FAMILY EDUCATION:
- Must be fully informed of disulfiram-alcohol reaction.
- Avoid alcohol in disguised forms (mouthwash, cologne, cough mixtures).
- Reactions may occur with alcohol up to 14 days after discontinuation.
- Carry ID card or bracelet that states patient is receiving disulfiram and the symptoms that may occur as a result of disulfiram-alcohol reaction.

SPECIAL POPULATIONS:
- *Elderly:* Use with caution.
- *Renal impairment:* Contraindicated.
- *Hepatic impairment:* Contraindicated
- *Pregnancy:* Safety has not been established.
- *Lactation:* Contraindicated
- *Children:* Safety and effectiveness has not been established

acamprosate calcium   *Campral*

INDICATIONS: Maintenance of alcohol abstinence with patients who are abstinent at beginning of treatment.

AVAILABLE FORMS: Enteric-coated tablet, 333 mg

DOSAGE: 666 mg three times daily; tablets are 333 mg each. A lower dosage may be effective for some patients.

ADMINISTRATION:
- PO with a glass of water
- Take without food
- Take at regular intervals
- *Missed dose:* Take as soon as remembered. If it is almost time for next dose, wait until next regularly scheduled dose. Do not take extra medicine to make up the missed dose.

SIDE EFFECTS: Anorexia, diarrhea, flatulence, nausea; anxiety, depressed mood; dizziness; dry mouth; insomnia, somnolence; pruritus, sweating, rash; headache, weight gain; abdominal pain; rhinitis

DRUG INTERACTIONS: No drug interactions. Drinking alcohol with treatment does not have effect on pharmacokinetics.

PHARMACOKINETICS:
- Excreted in the urine; does not undergo metabolism
Half-life: 20–33 hr

PRECAUTIONS:
- Acute overdose can result in diarrhea and hypercalcemia

PATIENT AND FAMILY EDUCATION:
- Use caution when driving or operating machinery.
- In the event of relapse, notify health care provider and continue taking medication as prescribed.

(cont.)

acamprosate calcium (*cont.*)

SPECIAL POPULATIONS:
- *Elderly:* No dosage adjustments are indicated; however, renal function should be monitored and doses when indicated.
- *Renal impairment:* Moderate renal impairment requires dose reduction. Contraindicated for patient with severe renal impairment.

- *Pregnancy:* Category C
- *Lactation:* It is unknown whether medication is excreted in breast milk.
- *Children*: Safety and efficacy have not been established.

Class: Vitamins

Vitamin B1/ Thiamine Hydrochloride	B complex

INDICATIONS: Treat and prevent thiamine deficiency, including thiamine-specific deficiency Wernicke–Korsakoff syndrome

AVAILABLE FORMS: Tablets, 50, 100, and 250 mg; enteric-coated tablet, 20 mg; injectable, 100 mg/mL

DOSAGE: 1 to 2 mg of thiamine per day is commonly used. Daily RDAs:
- *Infants: 0 to 6 months:* 0.2 mg; *infants 7 to 12 months*: 0.3 mg.
- *Children:* 1 to 3 yr, 0.5 mg; *4–8 yr*, 0.6 mg.
- *Males: 9 to 13 yr*, 0.9 mg; *14 yr and older*, 1.2 mg.
- *Females: 9 to 13 yr*, 0.9 mg; *14–18 yr*, 1 mg; *over 18 yr*, 1.1 mg; *pregnant women*, 1.4 mg; *breastfeeding women*, 1.5 mg.

ADMINISTRATION:
- PO with a glass of water.
- May be taken with or without food.
- Do not crush or chew enteric-coated pills; swallow whole.

SIDE EFFECTS: Feeling of warmth, restlessness; nausea; pruritus

DRUG INTERACTIONS: None indicated.

PHARMACOKINETICS: Widely distributed. Eliminated in urine.

PRECAUTIONS: Watch for anaphylaxis reaction

PATIENT AND FAMILY EDUCATION:
- Take medication at same time every day

SPECIAL POPULATIONS:
- *Elderly:* No contraindications
- *Renal impairment:* Use with caution
- *Hepatic impairment*: Use with caution
- *Pregnancy:* Category A
- *Lactation:* Contraindicated; excreted in breast milk
- *Children and adolescents*: Iron toxicity may occur if ingested by children; store out of reach and in child-proof bottles.

Class: Norepinephrine/Dopamine Reuptake Inhibitors (NDRIs)

Wellbutrin, Zyban	bupropion

INDICATIONS: Smoking cessation treatment

AVAILABLE FORMS: Tablet, 150 mg

DOSAGE: Recommended maximum dose is 150 mg twice daily. Dosing should begin at 150 mg daily for the first 3 days.

ADMINISTRATION:
- PO with glass of water
- Swallow tablet whole; do not crush, divide, or chew.

SIDE EFFECTS: Flu-like symptoms; dyspepsia, flatulence, constipation, diarrhea; hypoglycemia/hyperglycemia; sweating; visual disturbances; urinary frequency; anorexia, nausea; myalgia; insomnia; anxiety, nervousness; dizziness, disturbed concentration; rhinitis, sinusitis; rash, pruritus; taste perversion, dry mouth

DRUG INTERACTIONS:
- Contraindicated in patients treated with any medication containing bupropion
- Concurrent use with MAOI is contraindicated. MAOI must be discontinued for at least 14 days prior to initiation of *Zyban*.

PHARMACOKINETICS:
- Extensively metabolized
- **Half-life:** 3–4 hr

PRECAUTIONS:
- Contraindicated in patients with seizure disorder, bulimia or anorexia nervosa, and patients undergoing abrupt discontinuation of alcohol or sedatives

PATIENT AND FAMILY EDUCATION:
- Do not take if you have taken a MAOI in the last 14 days.
- Call health care provider if new or worsening symptoms in mood or behavior including suicidal ideations.
- Do not smoke if using this mediation with another nicotine product.

SPECIAL POPULATIONS:
- *Elderly:* Use with caution
- *Renal impairment:* Use with caution
- *Hepatic impairment*: Use with caution
- *Pregnancy:* Category B
- *Lactation:* It is unknown whether medication is excreted in breast milk
- *Children and adolescents*: Safety and efficacy has not been established.

Substance Dependence

OVERVIEW
- Commonly referred to as addiction
- Per the *DSM-IV*, substance dependence is defined as a tolerance to a substance that leads to withdrawal when the substance is eliminated or significantly reduced.

CLASS	DRUG
Nicotine Replacement Therapy	
	nicotine, nicotine transdermal system, nicotine polacrilex (*Nicotrol NS, Nicotrol Inhaler, Commit, Habitrol, Nicoderm, Nicotrol ProStep, Nicorette Gum, Nicorette DS*)
Benzodiazepines (BZDs)	
	chlordiazepoxide (*Librium*)
	diazepam (*Valium*)
	lorazepam (*Ativan*)
	oxazepam (*Serax*)
Partial Opioid Agonists	
	buprenorphine HO (*Subutex*)
	buprenorphine HCl and naloxone HCl dihydrate (*Suboxone*)
	methadone HCl (*Methadose Oral Concentrate*)
Alpha-Agonists	
	clonidine (*Catapres, Catapres-TTS*)
Anticholinergic Drugs	
	dicyclomine (*Bentyl*)
NSAIDs	
	ibuprofen (*Motrin*)
Antidiarrheal Drugs	
	loperamide (*Imodium*)
Opioid Antagonists	
	naltrexone (*Revia*)
Alcohol Antagonists	
	disulfiram (*Antabuse*)
Substance Abuse Deterrents	
	acamprosate calcium (*Campral*)
Vitamins	
	B complex (*Vitamin B1/Thiamine Hydrochloride*)
Antidepressants	
	bupropion HCl (*Wellbutrin, Zyban*)
Nicotinic Receptor Agonists	
	varenicline (*Chantix*)

Class: Nicotine Replacement Therapy

nicotine, nicotine transdermal system, nicotine polacrilex — *Nicotrol NS, Nicotrol Inhaler, Commit, Habitrol, Nicoderm, Nicotrol ProStep, Nicorette Gum, Nicorette DS*

INDICATIONS: Commonly used to treat tobacco dependence

AVAILABLE FORMS: Gum, 2 and 4 mg; lozenges, 2 and 4 mg; spray, 0.5 mg; inhaler, 4 mg; transdermal patch, 7, 14, and 21; 5, 10, and 15; and 11 and 22 mg/day

DOSAGE: *Oral:* Chew one piece of gum during urge to smoke. Repeat as needed up to 30 pieces/day. *Inhaler:* Spray twice in each nostril every hour up to 40 times daily. *Topical:* Apply one transdermal patch every 24 hr as follows: *Habitrol and Nicoderm:* 21 mg/day for 6 wk, then 14 mg/day for

(cont.)

nicotine transdermal system, nicotine polacrilex (*cont.*)

2 wk, then 7 mg/day for 2 wk. For patients with CV disease, weigh less that 45 kg or smoke less than ½ pack per day: 14 mg/day for 6 wk, then 7 mg/day for 4 wk. *Prostep:* 22 mg/day for 4–8 wk, then 11 mg/day for 2 to 4 wk. For patients with CV disease, weigh less that 45 kg or smoke less than ½ pack per day: 11 mg/day for 4–8 wk. *Nicotrol:* Wear patch for 16 hr/day. 15 mg/day for 4–12 wk, then 10 mg/day for 2 to 4 wk, then 5 mg/day for 2 to 4 wk.

ADMINISTRATION:
- Chew gum as directed.
- Remove old patch before applying new one.
- Apply patch to nonhairy skin surface.
- Patches are heat sensitive; store at or below 30°C.

SIDE EFFECTS:
Headaches, dizziness, lightheadedness; insomnia, irritability; tachycardia, palpitations; sore mouth, throat, tingling of tongue; skin rash, pruritus; runny nose, nasal irritation, watery eyes

DRUG INTERACTIONS:
- May increase metabolism of caffeine, theophylline, insulin, propranolol, acetaminophen.
- Coffee and cola may decrease absorption of gum.

PHARMACOKINETICS:
Half-life: 30–120 min

PRECAUTIONS:
- Contraindicated immediately post-MI, severe angina pectoris, or life-threatening arrhythmias

PATIENT AND FAMILY EDUCATION:
- Chew gum for 30 min at a time to get full effect.
- Chew only one piece of gum at a time.
- Discontinue use of patch if local skin reaction occurs.
- Smoking while using the patch increases adverse reactions.

SPECIAL POPULATIONS:
- *Elderly:* Use with caution
- *Renal impairment:* No contraindications
- *Hepatic impairment:* No contraindications
- *Pregnancy:* Category D (nasal spray, transdermal patch); category C (gum)
- *Lactation:* Use only if benefits outweigh the risk associated
- *Children and adolescents:* Safety and efficacy not established; long-term effects in children/adolescents are unknown

Class: Benzodiazepines (BZDs)

Librium   chlordiazepoxide

INDICATIONS:
To prevent withdrawal from alcohol; used on a temporary (tapering) basis

AVAILABLE FORMS:
Capsule, 5, 10, and 25 mg; injectable, 100 mg/5 mL

DOSAGE:
10 to 40 mg/day in 3 to 4 divided doses

ADMINISTRATION:
- PO with a full glass of water.
- May be taken with or without food.
- Write prescription for the shortest duration possible to prevent potential dependence.
- *Missed dose:* Take as soon as remembered. Skip the missed dose if it is almost time for the next scheduled dose. Do not take extra medicine.

SIDE EFFECTS:
Depression, fatigue, sedation; dizziness, slurred speech, weakness; confusion; nervousness, hyperexcitability; hypersalivation, dry mouth; hallucinations (rare)

DRUG INTERACTIONS:
Increased CNS depressive effects when taken with other CNS depressants

PHARMACOKINETICS:
Half-life: 24–48 hr

PRECAUTIONS:
- Use with caution in patients with pulmonary impairment/disease.
- History of substance abuse increases risk of dependency.
- Some patients present with disinhibiting behaviors after administration.

- Since dependence may develop, use with caution in patients with history of substance abuse.

PATIENT AND FAMILY EDUCATION:
- Take exactly as prescribed. Do not take in larger or smaller amounts or for longer than recommended.
- Can be taken with or without food.
- Exercise caution when driving or operating machinery due to sedative effects of medication.
- Do not drink alcohol.
- Do not stop taking the drug abruptly.

SPECIAL POPULATIONS:
- *Elderly:* Use with caution; may require smaller dosage due to sedative effects.
- *Renal impairment:* Use with caution; may require smaller dosage: 10 to 20 mg/day initially in two to four doses; increase as needed
- *Hepatic impairment:* Use with caution; may require smaller dosage: 10 to 20 mg/day in two to four doses initially; increase as needed. Because of sedative properties and increased risk of fall and fracture, BZDs are included on the Beers List of Potentially Inappropriate Medications for Geriatrics.
- *Lactation:* It is unknown if medication is secreted in breast milk; discontinue drug or bottle feed.
- *Children and adolescents:* Not recommended in children under 6. Initial 10 to 20 mg/day in two to four doses: may increase to 20 to 30 mg/day in two to three doses if needed

diazepam   *Valium*

INDICATIONS: Alcohol dependence and withdrawal

AVAILABLE FORMS: Tablet, 2, 5, or 10 mg; liquid, 5 mg/5 mL; concentrate, 5 mg/5 mL

DOSAGE: 4–40 mg/day in divided doses

ADMINISTRATION:
- PO with a full glass of water.
- May be taken with or without food.
- Write prescription for the shortest duration possible to prevent potential dependence.
- *Missed dose:* Take as soon as remembered. Skip the missed dose if it is almost time for the next scheduled dose. Do not take extra medicine.

SIDE EFFECTS: depression, fatigue, sedation; dizziness, slurred speech, weakness; confusion; nervousness, hyperexcitability; hypersalivation, dry mouth; hallucinations (rare)

DRUG INTERACTIONS:
- Increased CNS depressive effects when taken with other CNS depressants.
- Cimetidine may reduce the clearance and raise levels of diazepam.
- Flumazenil may cause seizures.

PHARMACOKINETICS:
Half-life: 20–50 hr

PRECAUTIONS:
- Use with caution in patients with pulmonary impairment/disease.
- History of substance abuse increases risk of dependency; use with caution in patients with history of substance abuse.

- Some patients present with disinhibiting behaviors after administration.

PATIENT AND FAMILY EDUCATION:
- Take exactly as prescribed. Do not take in larger or smaller amounts or for longer than recommended.
- Can be taken with or without food.
- Exercise caution when driving or operating machinery due to sedative effects of medication.
- Do not drink alcohol.
- Do not stop taking the drug abruptly.

SPECIAL POPULATIONS:
- *Elderly:* Use with caution due to sedative effects. Initial dose 2 to 2.5 mg, one to two times/day; increase as needed.
- *Renal impairment:* Use with caution. Initial dose 2 to 2.5 mg, one to two times/day; increase as needed. Because of sedative properties and increase risk of fall and fracture, BZDs are included on the Beers List of Potentially Inappropriate Medications for Geriatrics.
- *Hepatic impairment:* Use with caution. Initial dose 2 to 2.5 mg, one to two times/day; increase as needed.
- *Pregnancy:* Category D
- *Lactation:* It is unknown if medication is secreted in breast milk; discontinue drug or bottle feed.
- *Children and adolescents:* Long-term effects of diazepam in children/adolescents are unknown; should give low dosage and monitor frequently.

lorazepam   *Ativan*

INDICATIONS: Treatment of alcohol withdrawal

AVAILABLE FORMS: Tablet, 0.5, 1, and 2 mg; liquid, 0.5 and 2 mg/5 mL; injection, 1 mg/0.5 mL, 2 mg/mL, and 4 mg/mL

DOSAGE: *Oral:* 2 to 6 mg/day in divided doses; *injection:* 4 mg given slowly

ADMINISTRATION:
- PO with a full glass of water.
- May be taken with or without food.
- Write prescription for the shortest duration possible to prevent potential dependence.
- *Missed dose:* Take as soon as remembered. Skip the missed dose if it is almost time for the next scheduled dose. Do not take extra medicine.

SIDE EFFECTS: Depression, fatigue, sedation; dizziness, slurred speech, weakness; confusion; nervousness, hyperexcitability; hypersalivation, dry mouth; hallucinations (rare)

DRUG INTERACTIONS:
- Increased CNS depressive effects when taken with other CNS depressants.

- Valproate and probenecid may reduce clearance and raise plasma concentrations.
- Oral contraceptives may increase clearance and reduce plasma concentrations.
- Flumazenil may cause seizures.

PHARMACOKINETICS:
- No active metabolites
Half-life: 10–20 hr

PRECAUTIONS:
- Use with caution in patients with pulmonary impairment/disease.
- History of substance abuse increases risk of dependency; use with caution in patients with history of substance abuse.
- Some patients present with disinhibiting behaviors after administration.
- Do not use with patients with narrow-angle glaucoma.
- Some depressed patients may experience a worsening of suicidal thoughts.

PATIENT AND FAMILY EDUCATION:
- Take exactly as prescribed. Do not take in larger or smaller amounts or for longer than recommended.

(cont.)

lorazepam (*cont.*)

- Can be taken with or without food.
- Exercise caution when driving or operating machinery due to sedative effects of medication.
- Do not drink alcohol.
- Do not stop taking the drug abruptly.

SPECIAL POPULATIONS:
- *Elderly:* Use with caution due to sedative effects; 1 to 2 mg/day in two to three doses.
- *Renal impairment:* Use with caution. 1 to 2 mg/day in two to three doses. Because of sedative properties and increased risk of fall and

fracture, BZDs are included on the Beers List of Potentially Inappropriate Medications for Geriatrics.
- *Hepatic impairment*: Because of its short half-life, it is a preferred BZD for those with liver disease.
- *Pregnancy:* Category D
- *Lactation:* Some drug is found in mother's breast milk; discontinue drug or bottle feed.
- *Children and adolescents:* Under age 12: Safety and efficacy not established. Long-term effects in children/adolescents unknown.

Serax | **oxazepam**

INDICATIONS: Treatment of alcohol withdrawal

AVAILABLE FORMS: Capsule, 10, 15, and 30 mg; tablet, 15 mg

DOSAGE: 30 to 60 mg/day in three to four divided doses

ADMINISTRATION:
- PO with a full glass of water.
- May be taken with or without food.
- Write prescription for the shortest duration possible in order to prevent potential dependence.
- *Missed dose:* Take as soon as remembered. Skip the missed dose if it is almost time for the next scheduled dose. Do not take extra medicine.

SIDE EFFECTS: Depression, fatigue, sedation; dizziness, slurred speech, weakness; confusion; nervousness, hyperexcitability; hypersalivation, dry mouth; hallucinations (rare)

DRUG INTERACTIONS: Increased CNS depressive effects when taken with other CNS depressants

PHARMACOKINETICS:
- No active metabolites
Half-life: 3–21 hr

PRECAUTIONS:
- Use with caution in patients with pulmonary impairment/disease.
- History of substance abuse increases risk of dependency; use with caution in patients with history of substance abuse.
- Some patients present with disinhibiting behaviors after administration.

- Do not use with patients with narrow-angle glaucoma.
- Some depressed patients may experience of worsening of suicidal thoughts.

PATIENT AND FAMILY EDUCATION:
- Take exactly as prescribed. Do not take in larger or smaller amounts or for longer than recommended.
- Can be taken with or without food.
- Exercise caution when driving or operating machinery due to sedative effects of medication.
- Do not drink alcohol.
- Do not stop taking the drug abruptly.

SPECIAL POPULATIONS:
- *Elderly:* Use with caution due to sedative effects. Initial dose 30 mg in three divided doses: Can increase up to 60 mg/day in three to four doses if needed.
- *Renal impairment:* Use with caution. May increase drug levels.
- *Hepatic impairment*: Use with caution. May increase drug levels. Because of its short half-life, it is a preferred BZD for those with liver disease. Because of sedative properties and increased risk of fall and fracture, BZDs are included on the Beers List of Potentially Inappropriate Medications for Geriatrics
- *Pregnancy:* Category D
- *Lactation:* Some drug is found in mother's breast milk; discontinue drug or bottle feed
- *Children and adolescents*: Under 6: Safety and efficacy not established. Long-term effects for children/adolescents unknown.

Class: Partial Opioid Agonists

Subutex
Suboxone | **buprenorphine HO**
buprenorphine HCl and naloxone HCl dihydrate

INDICATIONS: Used to treat opiate dependence
▶ **Note**: Under the Drug Addiction Treatment Act of 2000 (DATA) codified at 21 U.S.C. 823(g), prescription use of this product in the treatment of opioid dependence is limited to physicians who meet certain qualifying requirements, and have

notified the Secretary of HHS of their intent to prescribe this product for the treatment of opioid dependence

AVAILABLE FORMS: Sublingual tablets: *Subutex:* 2 and 8 mg; *Suboxone*: 2 mg/0.5 mg and 8 mg/2 mg
(cont.)

buprenorphine HO buprenorphine HCl and naloxone HCl dihydrate (*cont.*)

DOSAGE: *Subutex:* 8 mg on day 1, then 16 mg on day 2, then adjust dose daily until opiate-withdrawal effects are suppressed, then *Suboxone* for maintenance: 4–24 mg/day until determined by provider.

ADMINISTRATION:
- Place under tongue until dissolved.
- For doses requiring more than one tablet, place both tablets under tongue at the same time.
- Do not swallow tablets.
- *Missed dose:* Take as soon as remembered. Skip the missed dose if it is almost time for the next scheduled dose. Do not take extra medicine.

SIDE EFFECTS: Sedation, drowsiness, headache; insomnia, nausea, sweating; hypotension

DRUG INTERACTIONS:
- Opiates and other CNS depressants will increase sedation.
- Diazepam may cause respiratory distress or cardiac arrest.
- Macrolide antibiotics may increase drug levels.

PHARMACOKINETICS:
Metabolism: Liver by CYP3A4
Half-life: 37 hr

PRECAUTIONS:
- Watch for respiratory depression.
- Supervise ambulation due to sedative effects.

PATIENT AND FAMILY EDUCATION:
- Do not drive or engage in other hazardous activities until response to drug is known.
- Avoid alcohol or other CNS depressants.

SPECIAL POPULATIONS:
- *Elderly:* Use with caution due to sedative effects.
- *Renal impairment:* Use with caution.
- *Hepatic impairment*: Use with caution; may require lower dosage
- *Pregnancy:* Category B
- *Lactation:* Safety has not been established
- *Children and adolescents*: Safety has not been established

methadone HCl   *Methadose Oral Concentrate*

INDICATIONS: Detoxification treatment of opioid and maintenance treatment for opiate dependence.
▶**Note**: Outpatient maintenance and outpatient detoxification treatment may be provided only by OTPs certified by the Federal SAMHSA and registered by the DEA.

AVAILABLE FORMS: Oral concentrate, 10 mg/1 mL

DOSAGE: *Short-term detoxification:* Titrated to a daily dose of 40 mg in divided doses. *Maintenance treatment:* 80 to 120 mg/day

ADMINISTRATION:
- PO with a full glass of water.
- May be taken with or without food.
- *Missed dose:* Take as soon as remembered. Skip the missed dose if it is almost time for the next scheduled dose. Do not take extra medicine.

SIDE EFFECTS: Dizziness, sedation; nausea, vomiting, sweating; bradycardia, palpitations; dysphoria, euphoria; respiratory depression, pulmonary edema

DRUG INTERACTIONS:
- May experience withdrawal symptoms when given opioid antagonists, mixed agonist/antagonists, and partial agonists.
- Antiretroviral agents result in increased clearance and decreased plasma levels.
- Rifampin may cause decrease in serum levels and possible withdrawal symptoms.
- Phenytoin may cause up to 50% decrease in serum levels, leading to withdrawal symptoms.
- St. John's wort, phenobarbital, and carbamazepine may result in withdrawal symptoms.

PHARMACOKINETICS:
Half-life: 8–59 hr

PRECAUTIONS:
- Death has been reported when methadone is abused in conjunction with BZDs.
- Caution should be used when giving drugs capable of inducing electrolyte disturbance that may prolong the QT interval.
- Should not be abruptly discontinued.
- Use with caution in hypothyroidism, Addison's disease, and prostatic hypertrophy and respiratory insufficiency.
- May result in hypotension in patients who have inability to maintain stable blood pressure.
- Use with extreme caution with head injuries.

PATIENT AND FAMILY EDUCATION:
- Take exactly as prescribed. Do not take in larger or smaller amounts or for longer than recommended.
- Can be taken with or without food.
- Exercise caution when driving or operating machinery due to sedative effects of medication.
- Do not drink alcohol.
- Do not stop taking the drug abruptly.

SPECIAL POPULATIONS:
- *Elderly:* Use with caution due to sedative effects.
- *Renal impairment:* Use with caution
- *Hepatic impairment:* Use with caution
- *Pregnancy:* Category C. There are no controlled studies of methadone use in pregnant women that can be used to establish safety.
- *Lactation:* Some drug is found in mother's breast milk; discontinue drug or bottle feed
- *Children and adolescents*: Safety and efficacy has not been established

Class: Alpha-Agonists

Catapres, Catapres-TTS   **clonidine**

INDICATIONS: Controlling withdrawal symptoms for opiates or alcohol

AVAILABLE FORMS: Tablet, 0.1, 0.2, and 0.3 mg; topical (7-day administration), 0.1 mg/24 hr, 0.2 mg/24 hr, and 0.3 mg/24 hr

DOSAGE: *Oral:* 0.1 to 0.3 mg given in divided doses prn as needed. Maximum dose is dependent on clinical response but should not exceed 0.6 mg. *Topical:* Apply once every 7 days.

ADMINISTRATION: *Oral:* Take with a full glass of water; may be taken with or without food. *Topical:* Apply patch on skin without hair. Leave in place for 7 days.

SIDE EFFECTS: Dry mouth; sedation, dizziness; constipation; weakness, fatigue; insomnia, headache, impotence, loss of libido; major depression; hypotension; nervousness, agitation; nausea, vomiting

DRUG INTERACTIONS:
- Do not give with beta-blocker due to CV symptoms.
- Increased sedative and depressive symptoms when given with another CNS depressant.
- Administration with drugs that affect sinus node or AV function may result in bradycardia or AV block.

PHARMACOKINETICS:
Metabolism: Liver, excreted by kidney
Half-life: 12–16 hr

PRECAUTIONS:
- There have been rare cases of hypertensive crisis, and stroke after abrupt discontinuation.
- If used with a beta-blocker, the beta-blocker should be stopped several days before tapering drug.

PATIENT AND FAMILY EDUCATION:
- Make position changes slowly, and in stages. Dangle feet over bed prior to standing.
- Lie down immediately if feeling faint or dizzy.
- Avoid potentially hazardous activities until effect of medication has been determined.
- *Missed dose:* Take as soon as remembered. If it is almost time for next dose, wait until next regularly scheduled dose. Do not take extra medicine to make up the missed dose.

SPECIAL POPULATIONS:
- *Elderly:* Use with caution due to sedative effects.
- *Renal impairment:* Use with caution. May require smaller dosage
- *Hepatic impairment*: Use with caution
- *Pregnancy:* Category C
- *Lactation:* Some drug is found in mother's breast milk; discontinue drug or bottle feed.
- *Children and adolescents*: Safety and efficacy not established for children under 12; children are more likely to experience CNS depression with overdose

Class: Anticholinergic Drugs

Bentyl   **dicyclomine**

INDICATIONS: Abdominal cramping associated with opiate-withdrawal

AVAILABLE FORMS: Capsule, 10 and 20 mg; liquid, 10 mg/5 mL syrup, 20 mg/2 mL syrup

DOSAGE: 40 mg four times daily. May begin with 20 mg four times daily and increase after 1 wk to reduce side effects

ADMINISTRATION:
- PO with glass of water.
- Measure liquid medicine with a special dose-measuring spoon or cup, not a regular table spoon.

SIDE EFFECTS: Confusion, disrupted thoughts; palpitations and/or arrhythmias; decreased urination; drowsiness, dizziness; blurred vision; nausea and/or vomiting; anorexia; pruritus or rash; stuffy nose, dry mouth

DRUG INTERACTIONS:
- The following medications may exacerbate side effects: amantadine, antiarrhythmic agents of class 1, antihistamines, antipsychotic agents, BZDs, MAOIs, narcotic analgesics, nitrites and

nitrates, sympathomimetic agents, and tricyclic antidepressants.
- May antagonize the effects of antiglaucoma agents.
- Should be avoided when intraocular pressure is present and when taking corticosteroids.
- May affect GI absorption of digoxin.
- May antagonize the effects of metoclopramide.
- Avoid simultaneous use of antacids.

PHARMACOKINETICS:
Half-life: 1.8 hr

PRECAUTIONS:
- May increase risk of heatstroke by decreasing sweating.

PATIENT AND FAMILY EDUCATIONS:
- Use caution when driving or operating machinery.
- Avoid drinking alcohol.
- Avoid become overheated or dehydrated during exercise and hot weather.
- Tell health care provider about all prescription and OTC medications due to interaction.

(cont.)

dicyclomine (*cont.*)

SPECIAL POPULATIONS:
- *Elderly:* Use caution; dosage should start at the low end.
- *Renal impairment:* Use with caution.
- *Hepatic impairment*: Use with caution
- *Pregnancy:* Category B.
- *Lactation:* Contraindicated

- *Children and adolescents*: Safety and efficacy has not been established
- *Other:* Use with caution in patients with the following: autonomic neuropathy, hepatic/renal disease, ulcerative colitis, hyperthyroidism, hypertension, coronary heart disease, heart failure, cardiac tachyarrhythmia, hiatal hernia, and prostatic hypertrophy

Class: NSAIDs

ibuprofen   *Motrin*

INDICATIONS: Generalized pain associated with opiate withdrawal

AVAILABLE FORMS: Tablet, 400, 600, and 800 mg

DOSAGE: 1200 to 3200 mg daily divided as follows: 300 mg qid or 400, 600, or 800 mg tid or qid; maximum, not to exceed 3200 mg/day

ADMINISTRATION:
- PO with meals or milk to reduce GI upset.
- *Missed dose:* Take as soon as remembered. Skip the missed dose if it is almost time for the next scheduled dose. Do not take extra medicine.

SIDE EFFECTS: Heartburn, nausea, vomiting; constipation, bloating; GI ulceration, occult blood loss

DRUG INTERACTIONS:
- Heparin may prolong bleeding time.
- May increase lithium toxicity.
- Garlic, ginger, and ginkgo may increase bleeding time.

PHARMACOKINETICS:
Metabolism: Liver, eliminated in urine
Half-life: 2–4 hr

PRECAUTIONS:
- Watch for toxic hepatitis, peptic ulcer disease, and anaphylaxis

PATIENT AND FAMILY EDUCATION:
- Notify health care provider immediately of passage of dark tarry stools, coffee ground emesis, or other GI distress.
- Do not take with aspirin.
- Avoid alcohol and NSAIDs.

SPECIAL POPULATIONS:
- *Elderly:* No contraindications
- *Renal impairment:* Use with caution
- *Hepatic impairment*: Use with caution; may require smaller dosage
- *Pregnancy:* Category B
- *Lactation:* No contraindication
- *Children and adolescents*: Safe use under age 6 has not been established

Class: Antidiarrheal Drugs

loperamide   *Imodium*

INDICATIONS: Diarrhea associated with opiate withdrawal

AVAILABLE FORMS: Capsule, 2 mg

DOSAGE: 4 mg (2 capsules) followed by 2 mg (1 capsule) after each unformed stool. Daily dose should not exceed 16 mg (8 capsules). Clinical improvement is usually observed within 48 hr.

ADMINISTRATION:
- PO with a full glass of water.
- May be taken with or without food.
- *Missed dose:* Take as soon as remembered. Skip the missed dose if it is almost time for the next scheduled dose. Do not take extra medicine.

SIDE EFFECTS: Anaphylactic reactions (rare); stomach pain/bloating; diarrhea that is bloody, watery, or worsening; flu-like symptoms with skin reaction/rash; dizziness; fatigue; constipation; mild stomach pain; mild skin pruritus, rash

DRUG INTERACTIONS: When given concurrently with saquinavir, the therapeutic efficacy of saquinavir should be closely monitored.

PHARMACOKINETICS:
Half-life: 11 hr

PRECAUTIONS:
- Discontinue if constipation, abdominal distention, or ileus develop

PATIENT AND FAMILY EDUCATION:
- Do not take if stools are bloody, black, or tarry.
- Do not use this medication to treat diarrhea caused by antibiotic use.
- Drink extra water to prevent dehydration.
- It may take up to 48 hr for symptoms to improve.
- Call health care provider if symptoms do not improve after treatment for 10 days.
- Exercise caution when driving or operating machinery.

(cont.)

loperamide (cont.)

SPECIAL POPULATIONS:
- *Elderly:* No dosage adjustments required
- *Renal impairment:* No dosage adjustments required
- *Hepatic impairment:* Use with caution; monitor for signs of CNS toxicity
- *Pregnancy:* Category C
- *Lactation:* Contraindicated
- *Children and adolescents*: Use with caution; monitor fluid and electrolyte balance

Class: Opioid Antagonists

Revia   **naltrexone**

INDICATIONS: Narcotic drug and alcohol addictions

AVAILABLE FORMS: Tablet, 50 mg

DOSAGE: 50 mg once daily for up to 12 wk; dosing must be individualized and may be increased if tolerated and no withdrawal signs are present

ADMINISTRATION:
- PO with glass of water.
- May be taken with or without food.
- Carry ID card or medical ID bracelet stating that you are taking medication.
- *Missed dose:* Take the medication as soon as remembered. If it is almost time for the next dose, skip the missed dose and wait until next regularly scheduled dose. Do not take extra medicine to make up the missed dose.

SIDE EFFECTS: Visual changes; palpitations; mood changes; nausea and/or abdominal pain, anorexia; tinnitus; pruritus or rash, jaundice; wheezing, difficulty breathing; nervousness, irritability; dizziness, insomnia; polyuria; fatigue, muscle weakness; sexual side effects

DRUG INTERACTIONS:
- Lethargy and somnolence have occurred with concurrent use of thioridazine.
- May experience limited or no benefit from opioid-containing medicines such as cold and cough preparations, antidiarrheal preparations, and opioid analgesics.

PHARMACOKINETICS:
- Pure opioid receptor antagonist
- Subject to significant first-pass metabolism
Half-life: 4 hr

PRECAUTIONS:
- Do not initiate treatment until confirmed abstinence from opioids for 7 to 10 days.
- Urine drug screen is often not sufficient proof that patient is opioid free; therefore, health care provider may choose to give naloxone challenge before treatment.
- Attempts by patient to overcome blocking effects by using large amounts of opiates may result in life-endangering opioid intoxication.

PATIENT AND FAMILY EDUCATION:
- Use caution when driving or operating machinery.
- Do not use narcotic drugs or alcohol when taking medication.
- Ask health care providers before taking OTC medication for cold symptoms.

SPECIAL POPULATIONS:
- *Elderly:* Use with caution.
- *Hepatic impairment*: Use caution due to hepatotoxic effects.
- *Renal impairment:* Use with caution
- *Pregnancy:* Category C
- *Lactation:* Contraindicated
- *Children*: Safety and effectiveness has not been established

Class: Alcohol Antagonist

Antabuse   **disulfiram**

INDICATIONS: Aid in the management of alcohol dependence

AVAILABLE FORMS: Tablet, 250 and 500 mg

DOSAGE:
- Should never be administered until patient has been abstinent from alcohol for at least 12 hr.
- 500 mg daily is given in a single dose for 1 to 2 wk. Then patient is placed on maintenance dose of 250 mg daily. Maintenance therapy may be required for months to years.

ADMINISTRATION:
- PO with a full glass of water.
- May be taken with or without food.
- *Missed dose:* Take as soon as remembered. Skip the missed dose if it is almost time for the next scheduled dose. Do not take extra medicine.

SIDE EFFECTS: Disulfiram-alcohol reaction: Small amounts of alcohol while taking disulfiram could result in the following and will vary with each individual: flushing, throbbing in head and neck,

(cont.)

disulfiram (*cont.*)

throbbing headache, respiratory difficulty, nausea, copious vomiting, sweating, thirst, chest pain, palpitation, dyspnea, hyperventilation, tachycardia, hypotension, syncope, marked uneasiness, weakness, vertigo, blurred vision, and confusion. In severe reactions, there may be respiratory depression, CV collapse, arrhythmias, MI, acute CHF, unconsciousness, convulsions, and death

DRUG INTERACTIONS:
- Medications containing alcohol are contraindicated.
- Use with caution for patients taking phenytoin and its congeners due to variation in therapeutic levels.
- Dosage of oral anticoagulants may need to be adjusted; prothrombin times may be prolonged.
- With concurrent use of isoniazid, patients should be observed for changes in gait or mental status.

PHARMACOKINETICS:
Half-life: 4–10 hr

PRECAUTIONS:
- Never administer to someone intoxicated or without patient's knowledge.
- Because of possibility of accidental disulfiram-alcohol reaction, treatment is contraindicated

for patients with the following conditions: DM, hypothyroidism, epilepsy, brain injury, renal and hepatic insufficiency.
- Patients with history of rubber allergy should be evaluated for hypersensitivity to thiuram derivatives before receiving disulfiram.

PATIENT AND FAMILY EDUCATION:
- Must be fully informed of disulfiram-alcohol reaction.
- Avoid alcohol in disguised forms (mouthwash, cologne, cough mixtures).
- Reactions may occur with alcohol up to 14 days after discontinuation.
- Carry ID card or bracelet that states that the patient is receiving disulfiram and the symptoms that may occur as a result of disulfiram-alcohol reaction.

SPECIAL POPULATIONS:
- *Elderly:* Use with caution.
- *Renal impairment:* Contraindicated
- *Hepatic impairment:* Contraindicated
- *Pregnancy:* Safety has not been established.
- *Lactation:* Contraindicated
- *Children:* Safety and effectiveness has not been established

Class: Substance Abuse Deterrents

acamprosate calcium   *Campral*

INDICATIONS: Maintenance of alcohol abstinence with patients in alcohol dependence who are abstinent at beginning of treatment.

AVAILABLE FORMS: Enteric-coated tablet, 333 mg

DOSAGE: 666 mg three times daily (tablets are 333 mg each). A lower dosage may be effective for some patients.

ADMINISTRATION:
- PO with a glass of water.
- Take without food.
- Take at regular intervals.
- *Missed dose:* Take as soon as remembered. If it is almost time for next dose, wait until next regularly scheduled dose. Do not take extra medicine to make up the missed dose.

SIDE EFFECTS: Anorexia, diarrhea, flatulence, nausea; anxiety, depressed mood; dizziness; dry mouth; insomnia, somnolence; pruritus, sweating, rash; headache, weight gain; abdominal pain; rhinitis

DRUG INTERACTIONS: No drug interactions. Drinking alcohol during treatment does not have effect on pharmacokinetics.

PHARMACOKINETICS:
- Excreted in the urine; does not undergo metabolism
Half-life: 20–33 hr

PRECAUTIONS:
- Acute overdose can result in diarrhea and hypercalcemia.

PATIENT AND FAMILY EDUCATION:
- Use caution when driving or operating machinery.
- In the event of relapse, notify health care provider and continue taking medication as prescribed.

SPECIAL POPULATIONS:
- *Elderly:* No dosage adjustments are indicated; however, renal function should be monitored and doses when indicated.
- *Renal impairment:* Moderate renal impairment requires dose reduction. Contraindicated for patient with severe renal impairment.
- *Pregnancy:* Category C
- *Lactation:* It is unknown whether medication is excreted in breast milk.
- *Children:* Safety and efficacy have not been established.

Class: Vitamins

Vitamin B1/Thiamine Hydrochloride   **B complex**

INDICATIONS: Treat and prevent thiamine deficiency, including thiamine-specific deficiency Wernicke-Korsakoff syndrome (common in patients diagnosed with alcoholism)

AVAILABLE FORMS: Tablet, 50, 100, and 250 mg; enteric-coated tablet, 20 mg; injectable, 100 mg/mL

DOSAGE: 1 to 2 mg of thiamine per day is commonly used. The daily RDAs:
- *Infants: 0 to 6 months,* 0.2 mg; *7 to 12 months,* 0.3 mg.
- *Children: 1 to 3 yr,* 0.5 mg; *4–8 yr,* 0.6 mg.
- *Males: 9 to 13 yr,* 0.9 mg. *14 yr and older,* 1.2 mg.
- *Females: 9 to 13 yr,* 0.9 mg; *14–18 yr,* 1 mg; *over 18 yr,* 1.1 mg; *pregnant women,* 1.4 mg; *lactating women,* 1.5 mg.

ADMINISTRATION:
- PO with a glass of water.
- May be taken with or without food.
- Do not crush or chew enteric-coated pills. Swallow whole.

SIDE EFFECTS: Feeling of warmth, restlessness, nausea, pruritus

DRUG INTERACTIONS: None

PHARMACOKINETICS: Widely distributed. Eliminated in urine.

PRECAUTIONS:
- Watch for anaphylaxis reaction

PATIENT AND FAMILY EDUCATION:
- Take medication at same time every day

SPECIAL POPULATIONS:
- *Elderly:* No contraindication.
- *Renal impairment:* Use with caution
- *Hepatic impairment:* Use with caution
- *Pregnancy:* Category A
- *Lactation:* Contraindicated, excreted in breast milk
- *Children and adolescents:* Iron toxicity may occur; store out of reach and in child-proof bottles

Class: Antidepressants

Wellbutrin, Zyban   **bupropion HCl**

INDICATIONS: Aid to smoking cessation treatment

AVAILABLE FORMS: Tablet, 150 mg

DOSAGE: Recommended maximum dose is 150 mg twice daily. Dosing should begin at 150 mg daily for the first 3 days.

ADMINISTRATION:
- PO with glass of water.
- Swallow tablet whole; do not crush, break, or chew.

SIDE EFFECTS: Flu-like symptoms; dyspepsia, flatulence, constipation, diarrhea; hypoglycemia/hyperglycemia; sweating; visual disturbances; urinary frequency; anorexia, nausea; myalgia; insomnia; anxiety, nervousness; dizziness, disturbed concentration; rhinitis, sinusitis; rash, pruritus; taste perversion, dry mouth

DRUG INTERACTIONS:
- Contraindicated in patients treated with any medication containing bupropion
- Concurrent use of MAOIs is contraindicated. MAOI must be discontinued for at least 14 days prior to initiation of *Zyban.*

PHARMACOKINETICS:
- Extensively metabolized
- **Half-life**: 3–4 hr

PRECAUTIONS:
- Contraindicated in patients with seizure disorder, bulimia, or anorexia nervosa
- Contraindicated in patients undergoing abrupt discontinuation of alcohol or sedatives

PATIENT AND FAMILY EDUCATION:
- Do not take if you have taken a MAOI in the last 14 days
- Call health care provider if any new or worsening symptoms in mood or behavior including suicidal ideations.
- Do not smoke if using this medication with another nicotine product.

SPECIAL POPULATIONS:
- *Elderly:* Use with caution
- *Renal impairment:* Use with caution
- *Hepatic impairment:* Use with caution
- *Pregnancy:* Category B
- *Lactation:* It is unknown whether medication is excreted in breast milk.
- *Children and adolescents:* Safety and efficacy has not been established.

SUBSTANCE DEPENDENCE: Vitamins/Antidepressants

Class: Nicotinic Receptor Agonists

varenicline	*Chantix*

INDICATIONS: Aid for smoking cessation

AVAILABLE FORMS: Tablet, 0.5 and 1.0 mg

DOSAGE: Days 1 to 3: 0.5 mg once daily; Days 4–7: 0.5 mg twice daily then 1 mg twice daily, until end of treatment. Treatment is for 12 wk.

ADMINISTRATION:
- Patient should set a date to quit smoking. Dosing should begin 1 wk prior to that date.
- PO with a glass of water.
- Take after eating.
- Take at regular intervals.
- After 12 wks of initial treatment, patients who stop smoking may continue with an additional 12 wk course of treatment to increase long-term abstinence.
- If patient is unsuccessful after 12 wks of initial treatment, other psychosocial factors should be addressed to promote behavioral change. After addressing these factors, patient may again try a 12-wk regimen.

SIDE EFFECTS: Diarrhea; nausea; insomnia; chest pain; flu-like symptoms; pack pain; muscle cramps; disturbance in attention; dizziness; increased urination; nosebleeds; flushing. *Rare:* serious skin reactions (Steven-Johnsons syndrome and erythema multiforme); accidental injury (traffic accidents, near-miss incidents in traffic)

DRUG INTERACTIONS: None. Safety and efficacy of treatment combined with other smoking cessation treatments (bupropion and NRT) has not been established.

PHARMACOKINETICS:
- Absorption and distribution occurs with 3 to 4 hr after oral administration.
- Oral bioavailability is unaffected by food or time-day dosing.
Metabolism: 92% excreted in urine
Half-life: 24 hr

PRECAUTIONS:
- Serious neuropsychiatric events including, but not limited to, depression, suicidal ideation, suicide attempt, and completed suicide have been reported in patients taking this medication.
- Depression has occurred in patients who continued to smoke.
- All patients being treated should be observed for neuropsychiatric symptoms including changes in behavior, hostility, agitation, depressed mood, and suicide-related events, including ideation, behavior, and attempted suicide.
- These symptoms, as well as worsening of preexisting psychiatric illness and completed suicide, have been reported in some patients attempting to quit smoking while taking *Chantix* in the postmarketing experience.

- Most symptoms were reported during treatment, but some were following discontinuation of therapy.
- Safety and efficacy in patients with serious psychiatric illness such as schizophrenia, bipolar disorder, and major depressive disorder has not been established.
- Resolution of symptoms after discontinuation was reported, although in some cases the symptoms persisted.
- Ongoing monitoring and supportive care should be provided until symptoms resolve.
- The risks should be weighed against the benefits of use.
- Increases the likelihood of abstinence from smoking for as long as 1 yr compared to treatment with placebo.

PATIENT AND FAMILY EDUCATION:
- Set a smoking-quit date and begin treatment 1 wk prior to date.
- May continue treatment if smoking relapses occur.
- Nausea and insomnia are most often transient. However, if continual, a dosage reduction may be beneficial.
- Discontinue medication immediately and notify health care provider if experiencing a change in mood including depression, mania, psychosis, irritability, agitation, anxiety, or homicidal/suicidal ideations and at first sign of skin reaction or rash with lesions on mouth.
- May experience nicotine-withdrawal symptoms such as irritability and depressed mood.
- Exercise caution when driving or operative machinery.
- May experience vivid, unusual, or strange dreams.

SPECIAL POPULATIONS:
- *Elderly:* No dosage adjustments are indicated; however, renal function should be monitored and doses adjusted when indicated.
- *Hepatic impairment:* No dosage adjustments are needed
- *Renal impairment:* For patients with mild-to-moderate impairment, dosage adjustments are not necessary. For patients with severe renal impairments, the recommended starting dose is 0.5 mg once daily for 1 wk and then titrated to 0.5 mg twice daily. For patients with end-stage renal disease, the recommended dosage is 0.5 mg once daily.
- *Pregnancy:* Category C
- *Lactation:* May be excreted in breast milk
- *Children:* Safety and efficacy has not been established.

Treatment of Eating Disorders

10

OVERVIEW

- Genetics and family history play a significant role in the development of eating disorders among patients. According to Franco (2010, p. 5), "first-degree relatives and monozygotic twin offspring of patients with anorexia nervosa have higher rates of anorexia nervosa and bulimia nervosa."

- Although certain biologic factors are implicated in the pathophysiology of eating disorders, the exact causes and mechanisms remain unclear.
- There are three main categories of eating disorders: Anorexia Nervosa (AN), Bulimia Nervosa (BN), and Eating Disorder Not Otherwise Specified (EDNOS).

Anorexia Nervosa

OVERVIEW

- "The essential features of anorexia nervosa are refusal to maintain a minimally normal body weight, intense fear of gaining weight, and significant disturbance in the perception of the shape or size of one's body" (Franco, 2010, p. 6).
- The patient affected by anorexia nervosa tends to exhibit symptoms such as depressed mood, social withdrawal, irritability, insomnia, and decreased libido.
- Obsessive–compulsive characteristics such as thoughts of food, hoarding food, picking or pulling apart small portions of food, or collecting recipes are often displayed.
- Parents who have anorexia nervosa increase the lifetime risk of this illness in their children at a rate that is 10-fold that of the general population.
- Endogenous opioids, diminished norepinephrine activity and turnover, and polymorphism of the promoter region of serotonin 2a receptor are associated with anorexia nervosa.
- In general, pharmacotherapy has limited usefulness in the treatment of anorexia nervosa.
- "Current American Psychiatric Association guidelines do not recommend pharmacotherapy but note that other associated psychiatric conditions may be treated" (Mayhew, 2009, p. 296).
- Second-generation antipsychotics, SSRIs, and TCAs are the drug classification selections used to treat depression, anxiety, and/or

- obsessive–compulsive symptomatology associated with anorexia nervosa.

Acute Treatment
- The acute treatment of anorexia nervosa involves hospitalization.
- A hospital stay may be needed if:
  - The person has lost a lot of weight (below 30% of ideal body weight for age and height).
  - Weight loss continues despite outpatient treatment.
  - Medical complications, such as arrhythmias, changes in mental status or mental status problems, or hypokalemia, develop.
  - The person has severe depression or thinks about committing suicide (Mayo Clinic Staff, 2009; The Victorian of Newport Beach, 2010).

Chronic Treatment
- One-on-one therapy
- Group therapy
- Body image groups
- Nutritional education
- Assistance with preparing and consuming meals in a group
- Twelve-step support groups
- Highly monitored and structured living arrangements
- Supervised group outings to Restaurants (Mayo Clinic Staff, 2009; The Victorian of Newport Beach, 2010)

CLASS	DRUG
Tricyclic Antidepressants (TCAs)	**Drugs Sometimes Useful to Treat Symptomatology**
	amitriptyline (*Apo-Amitriptyline, Elavil*)
	clomipramine (*Anafranil*)
Selective Serotonin Reuptake Inhibitors (SSRIs)	**Drugs Sometimes Useful to Treat Symptomatology**
	citalopram (*Celexa*)
	fluoxetine (*Prozac*)
	sertraline (*Zoloft*)
Antipsychotics, Atypical (Second-Generation)	**Drugs Sometimes Useful to Treat Symptomatology**
	quetiapine (*Seroquel*)

ANOREXIA NERVOSA

Class: Tricyclic Antidepressants (TCAs)

amitriptyline   *Apo-Amitriptyline, Elavil*

▶**Note**: The use of amitriptyline for the treatment of anorexia nervosa is an off-label use for all age groups.

AVAILABLE FORMS: Tablet, 10, 25, 50, 75, 100, and 150 mg

DOSAGE: *Children: 6 to 12 yr:* Not recommended for treatment of anorexia nervosa in this age group. *Adults:* 25 to 150 mg/day as a single dose at bedtime or in divided doses. *Elderly:* 10 to 25 mg at bedtime initially; then increase by 10 to 25 mg at weekly intervals

ADMINISTRATION: Give with food or milk if GI distress occurs.

SIDE EFFECTS: Dizziness; dry mouth; orthostatic hypotension; headache; nausea; heartburn

DRUG INTERACTIONS:
- CNS depressants may increase sedation, respiratory depression, and hypotensive effects.
- Antithyroid agents may increase risk of agranulocytosis.
- Phenothiazines may increase sedative, anticholinergic effects.
- Sympathomimetics may increase cardiac effects.
- MAOIs may increase risk of hypertensive crisis, hyperpyresis, and seizures.

PHARMACOKINETICS:
Onset: 4–6 wk
Peak: 2–12 hr
Metabolism: Metabolized in the liver to primary active metabolite, nortriptyline. CYP enzymes responsible for the metabolism of amitriptyline are CY1A2, CYP2C19, CYP2D6, and CYP3A4.

Excretion: Within 24 hr, approximately 25–50% of a dose of amitriptyline is excreted in the urine as inactive metabolites; small amounts are excreted in the bile.
Half-life: 10–26 hr

PRECAUTIONS:
Contraindications: Acute recovery period after MI; within 14 days of MAOI use
Cautions: Prostatic hypertrophy; history of urinary retention or obstruction; glaucoma; diabetes mellitus; hyperthyroidism; history of seizure disorders; cardiac/hepatic/renal disease; schizophrenia; increased IOP; hiatal hernia

PATIENT AND FAMILY EDUCATION:
- Change positions slowly to avoid hypotensive effect.
- Wear sunscreen due to increased propensity for photosensitivity.
- Do not abruptly discontinue medication.
- Avoid tasks that require alertness or advanced motor skills until response to medication is established.
- Sip tepid water to relieve dry mouth.

SPECIAL POPULATIONS:
- *Elderly*: Increased risk of toxicity. Increased sensitivity to anticholinergic effects. Caution in those with cardiovascular disease.
- *Pregnancy*: Category C; crosses placenta.
- *Lactation*: Enters breast milk. Not recommended for breastfeeding mothers.
- *Children*: More sensitive to increased dosage and toxicity. Increased risk of suicidal ideation. Worsening of depression.

clomipramine   *Anafranil*

▶**Note**: The use of clomipramine for the treatment of anorexia nervosa is an off-label use for all age groups.

AVAILABLE FORMS: Capsule, 25, 50, and 75 mg

DOSAGE: *Children: 10 yr and older*: 25 mg/day initially; then increase up to a maximum of 3 mg/kg/day or 200 mg, whichever is smaller. *Adults:* 25 mg/day initially; then increase to 100 mg/day during the first 2 wk of treatment. *Elderly:* 25 mg/day initially; then increase to 100 mg/day during the first 2 wk of treatment.

ADMINISTRATION:
- This drug should be given in divided doses with meals to reduce GI side effects.
- The goal of this initial titration phase is to minimize side effects by permitting tolerance to side effects to develop or by allowing the patient time to adapt if tolerance does not develop.

SIDE EFFECTS: Drowsiness; fatigue; dry mouth; blurred vision; constipation; sexual dysfunction; orthostatic hypotension; impaired concentration; urinary retention

DRUG INTERACTIONS:
- Alcohol and other CNS depressants may increase CNS, respiratory depression, and hypotensive effects.
- Antithyroid agents may increase the risk of agranulocytosis.
- MAOIs may increase risk of neuroleptic malignant syndrome, seizures, hyperpyresis, and hypertensive crisis.
- Sympathomimetics may increase the risk of cardiac effects.
- Grapefruit juice may increase serum concentration and toxicity.

PHARMACOKINETICS:
Onset: 2 wk
Peak: 2–6 hr
Metabolism: Metabolized in the liver to active desmethylclomipramine. The CYP enzymes responsible for the metabolism of clomipramine are CYP1A2, CYP2C19, and CYP2D6.

(cont.)

clomipramine (cont.)

Excretion: Two-thirds is excreted in the form of water-soluble conjugates in the urine and approximately one-third is excreted in the feces.
Half-life: 20–30 hr

PRECAUTIONS:
Contraindications: Acute recovery period after MI; within 14 days of MAOI use
Cautions: Prostatic hypertrophy; history of urinary retention or obstruction; glaucoma; diabetes mellitus; hyperthyroidism; history of seizure disorders; cardiac/hepatic/renal disease; schizophrenia; increased IOP; hiatal hernia

PATIENT AND FAMILY EDUCATION:
- May cause dry mouth, constipation, and blurred vision.
- Change positions slowly to avoid hypotensive effect.
- Avoid tasks that require alertness or advanced motor skills until response to medication is established.
- Do not abruptly discontinue medication.
- Increase fluid intake to combat dry mouth and constipation.

SPECIAL POPULATIONS:
- *Elderly*: Increased risk of toxicity. Increased sensitivity to anticholinergic effects. Caution in those with cardiovascular disease.
- *Pregnancy:* Category C; crosses placenta.
- *Lactation:* Enters breast milk. Not recommended for nursing mothers.
- *Children:* More sensitive to increased dosage and toxicity. Increased risk of suicidal ideation. Worsening of depression.

Class: Selective Serotonin Reuptake Inhibitors (SSRIs)

Celexa **citalopram**

AVAILABLE FORMS: Oral solution, 10 mg/5 mL; tablet, 10, 20, and 40 mg

DOSAGE: *Children:* The safety and effectiveness of this drug to treat depression associated with Eating Disorder Not Otherwise Specified have not been established in children under 18 years of age. *Adults:* 20 mg initially once daily in the morning or evening; then increase in 20-mg increments at intervals of no less than 1 wk. *Elderly:* 20 mg/day initially; then slowly increase to 40 mg/day for nonresponding patients only.

ADMINISTRATION:
- Give with or without food.
- Scored tablets may be crushed.

SIDE EFFECTS: Nausea; dry mouth; drowsiness; tremor; diarrhea; abnormal ejaculation; decreased libido; agitation

DRUG INTERACTIONS: Linezolid or MAOIs may cause serotonin syndrome

PHARMACOKINETICS:
Onset: 1–2 wk
Peak: 4 hr
Metabolism: Citalopram is metabolized in the liver into DCT, DDCT, and citalopram-*N*-oxide. The CYP enzymes responsible for the metabolism of citalopram are CYP2C19 and CYP3A4.

Excretion: Primarily excreted in the urine.
Half-life: 35 hr

PRECAUTIONS:
Contraindications: Sensitivity to citalopram; MAOI use within 14 days
Cautions: Hepatic/renal impairment; history of seizures; mania; hypomania

PATIENT AND FAMILY EDUCATION:
- Do not stop taking medication abruptly or increase dosage without notifying health care provider.
- Avoid alcohol use.
- Avoid tasks that require alertness and motor skills until response to drug is established.

SPECIAL POPULATIONS:
- *Elderly*: More sensitive to anticholinergic effects. More likely to experience dizziness, sedation, confusion, hypotension, and hyperexcitability. Generally able to tolerate citalopram better than other SSRIs.
- *Pregnancy:* Category C
- *Lactation:* Distributed in breast milk. Not recommended for breastfeeding mothers.
- *Children:* May cause increased anticholinergic effects and hyperexcitability.

Prozac **fluoxetine**

AVAILABLE FORMS: Capsule, 10, 20, and 40 mg; oral solution, 20 mg/5 mL; tablet, 10 and 20 mg

DOSAGE: *Children: 7 yr and older:* 5 to 10 mg/day initially; then titrate upward as needed. Usual dosage is 20 mg/day. *Adults:* 20 mg/day each morning initially; then gradually increase to maximum of 80 mg/day in two equally divided doses in morning and at noon. *Elderly:* 10 mg/day initially; then increase by 10 to 20 mg every 2 wk.

ADMINISTRATION: Give with food or milk if GI distress occurs.

(cont.)

ANOREXIA NERVOSA: Selective Serotonin Reuptake Inhibitors (SSRIs)

fluoxetine (cont.)

SIDE EFFECTS: Headache; asthenia; insomnia; drowsiness; nausea; diarrhea; dry mouth; constipation; fatigue; vomiting; rash

DRUG INTERACTIONS:
- Alcohol and other CNS depressants may increase hypotensive, CNS, and respiratory depressant effects.
- Antithyroid agents may increase risk of agranulocytosis.
- MAOIs and TCAs may increase anticholinergic and sedative effects.
- Medication prolonging QT interval may have additive effect.

PHARMACOKINETICS:
Onset: 2–4 wk
Peak: 6–8 hr
Metabolism: Extensively metabolized in the liver to the metabolite, norfluoxetine. The CYP enzymes responsible for the metabolism of fluoxtine are CYP2C19 and CYP2D6.

Excretion: Primarily excreted in the urine.
Half-life: 2–3 days

PRECAUTIONS:
Contraindications: Use within 14 days of MAOIs.
Cautions: Seizure disorders; cardiac dysfunction; diabetes; risk for suicide

PATIENT AND FAMILY EDUCATION:
- Do not abruptly discontinue medication.
- Avoid tasks that require alertness and motor skills until response to drug is established.
- Avoid alcohol use.
- Take last dose of drug before 4 pm to avoid insomnia.

SPECIAL POPULATIONS:
- *Elderly:* Susceptible to anticholinergic effects
- *Pregnancy:* Category C; crosses the placenta.
- *Lactation:* Distributed in breast milk. Not recommended for breastfeeding mothers.
- *Children:* Safety and efficacy has not been established.

sertraline   *Zoloft*

AVAILABLE FORMS: Tablet, 25, 50, and 100 mg; oral concentrate, 20 mg/mL

DOSAGE: *Children: 6 yr and older:* 25 mg/day initially; then increase 25 to 50 mg/day at 7-day intervals up to 200 mg/day. *Adults:* 50 mg/day initially; then increase by 50 mg/day at 7-day intervals up to 200 mg/day. *Elderly:* 25 mg/day initially; then increase 25 to 50 mg/day at 7-day intervals up to 200 mg/day

ADMINISTRATION:
- Give with food or milk if GI distress occurs.
- Oral concentrate must be diluted with 4 oz of water, ginger ale, lemon/lime soda, or orange juice only and administered immediately after mixing.

SIDE EFFECTS: Headache; nausea; diarrhea; insomnia; drowsiness; dry mouth; dyspepsia; diaphoresis; sexual dysfunction; hot flashes; chills

DRUG INTERACTIONS:
- May increase the concentration and risk of toxicity of highly protein-bound medications such as digoxin and warfarin.
- MAOIs may cause neuroleptic malignant syndrome, hypertensive crisis, hyperpyrexia, seizures, and serotonin syndrome.
- May increase the concentration and risk of toxicity of TCAs.

PHARMACOKINETICS:
Onset: 1 wk
Peak: 4.5–8.4 hr

Metabolism: Metabolized by the liver into the metabolite, *N*-desmethylsertraline. The CYP enzyme responsible for the metabolism of sertraline is CYP3A4.
Excretion: Excreted in both urine and feces.
Half-life: 26 hr

PRECAUTIONS:
Contraindications: MAOI use within 14 days
Cautions: Seizure disorders; cardiac disease; recent MI; hepatic impairment; suicidal patients

PATIENT AND FAMILY EDUCATION:
- Dry mouth may be relieved by sugarless gum and/or sips of tepid water.
- Report signs/symptoms of headache, fatigue, tremor, and sexual dysfunction.
- Avoid tasks that require alertness and/or motor skills until response to drug has been established.
- Take with food if nausea occurs.
- Inform health care provider if pregnancy occurs.
- Avoid alcohol use.
- Do not take OTC medications without consulting with health care provider.

SPECIAL POPULATIONS:
- *Elderly:* No age-related precautions necessary
- *Pregnancy:* Category C
- *Lactation:* Not distributed in breast milk.
- *Children:* Safety and efficacy of this drug has not been established.

Class: Antipsychotics, Atypical (Second-Generation)

Seroquel | quetiapine

AVAILABLE FORMS: Tablet, 25, 50, 100, 200, 300, and 400 mg

DOSAGE: *Children: 13 yr and older:* The total daily dose for the initial 5 days of therapy is 50 mg (Day 1), 100 mg (Day 2), 200 mg (Day 3), 300 mg (Day 4), and 400 mg (Day 5). After Day 5, the dose should be adjusted within the recommended dose range of 400 to 600 mg/day based on response and tolerability. *Adults:* 25 mg twice daily initially, with increases in total daily dose of 25 to 50 mg divided in to two or three doses on the second and third days, as tolerated, to a total dose range of 300 to 400 mg daily by the fourth day. Can be given at a maximum dose of 800 mg/day. *Elderly:* 25 mg/day initially. The dose should be increased daily in increments of 25 to 50 mg/day to an effective dose, depending on the clinical response and tolerability of the patient.

ADMINISTRATION: Can be taken with or without food

SIDE EFFECTS: Palpitations; blurred vision; dry mouth; palpitations; fatigue; asthenia; somnolence; dizziness; cough; orthostatic hypotension; hypertension

DRUG INTERACTIONS:
- Alcohol and other CNS depressants may increase CNS depression.
- May increase hypotensive effects of antihypertensives.
- May increase the clearance of hepatic enzyme inducers such as phenytoin.
- May decrease total free thyroxine (T4) serum levels.
- May increase serum cholesterol, triglycerides, AST, ALT, WBC count, and gamma-GGT levels.
- May produce false-positive pregnancy test result.

PHARMACOKINETICS:
Onset: Unknown
Peak: 1.5 hr

Metabolism: Metabolized by the liver into the metabolite, *N*-desalkyl-quetiapine. The CYP enzymes responsible for the metabolism of quetiapine are CYP2D6 and CYP3A4.
Excretion: Primarily excreted in the urine (73%), and the remaining amount of the drug is excreted in the feces (27%).
Half-life: 6 hr

PRECAUTIONS:
Contraindications: None known
Cautions: Alzheimer's dementia; history of breast cancer; cardiovascular disease; cerebrovascular disease; dehydration; hepatic impairment; seizures; hypothyroidism

PATIENT AND FAMILY EDUCATION:
- Drink fluids often, especially during physical activity.
- Avoid exposure to extreme heat.
- Take medication as ordered; do not stop taking or increase dosage without consulting the health care provider.
- Avoid alcohol.
- Change positions slowly to reduce hypotensive effect.
- Avoid tasks that require alertness and motor skills until response to drug is established.

SPECIAL POPULATIONS:
- *Elderly:* No age-related precautions noted, but lower initial and target dosages should be prescribed. Elderly with dementia-related psychosis are at increased risk for death.
- *Pregnancy:* Category C
- *Lactation:* Unknown if drug is distributed in breast milk. Not recommended for breastfeeding mothers.
- *Children:* Increased risk of suicidal thinking and behavior in children and adolescents with major depressive disorder and other psychiatric disorders.

Bulimia Nervosa

OVERVIEW
- In bulimia nervosa, "the essential features are binge eating and inappropriate compensatory behavior such as fasting, vomiting, overusing laxatives, or excessive exercising to prevent weight gain" (Franco, 2010, p. 6).
- Binge eating is usually elicited by dysphoria, interpersonal stressors, extreme hunger after episodes of fasting, or destructive thoughts about one's perception of body weight, shape, and food.
- Patients with bulimia nervosa are typically within normal body weight range and limit their total caloric consumption between binge

eating sessions, which are most often done in secrecy (Franco, 2010).
- Patients with bulimia nervosa have higher rates of substance abuse, affective disorders, and obesity among their family members (Franco, 2010).

TREATMENT
- Pharmacotherapy recommended by the American Psychiatric Association for the treatment of bulimia nervosa includes SSRIs, benzodiazepines, anticonvulsants, and TCAs.
- These medications also help to manage disorders associated with bulimia nervosa such as

depression and deficits in impulse regulation, self-esteem, and behavior.
- SSRIs are typically considered first-line therapy for bulimia nervosa.
- "Fluoxetine (*Prozac*) 60 (milligrams orally once daily in the morning) is the only drug approved by the FDA for bulimia, and it should be given for at least 9 to 12 months" (Mayhew, 2009, p. 296).

Acute Treatment
- Bulimia can usually be treated outside of the hospital.
- If an individual has a severe form of bulimia and serious health complications, they may require treatment in a hospital.
- When needed, hospitalization may be on a medical or psychiatric ward.

- Specialized eating disorder clinics may offer intensive inpatient treatment, or eating disorder programs may offer day treatment, rather than full inpatient hospitalization (Mayo Clinic Staff, 2010).

Chronic Treatment
- Assertiveness training
- Behavioral modification techniques
- Biofeedback mechanisms
- Cognitive therapy
- Exposure/desensitization therapy
- Hypnosis
- Insight-oriented therapy
- Relaxation techniques/therapy (Reuters, 2010)

CLASS	DRUG
Selective Serotonin Reuptake Inhibitors (SSRIs)	**First-Line Drug Therapy**
	*fluoxetine (*Prozac*) citalopram (*Celexa*) sertraline (*Zoloft*)
Benzodiazepines (BZDs)	
	alprazolam (*Xanax IR* and *ER*) clonazepam (*Klonopin*) diazepam (*Valium*)
Mood-Stabilizing Anticonvulsants	**Second-Line Drug Therapy**
	carbamazepine (*Tegretol*) zonisamide (*Zonegran*)
Tricyclic Antidepressants (TCAs)	**Third-Line Drug Therapy**
	amitriptyline (*Elavil, Endep, Vanatrip*) clomipramine (*Anafranil*)

*FDA-approved for bulimia nervosa

Class: Selective Serotonin Reuptake Inhibitors (SSRIs)

fluoxetine	*Prozac*

▶**Note**: This is the only FDA approved drug to treat bulimia nervosa.

AVAILABLE FORMS: Capsule, 10, 20, and 40 mg; oral solution, 20 mg/5 mL; tablet, 10 and 20 mg

DOSAGE: *Children: 7 yr and older:* 5 to 10 mg/day initially; then titrate upward as needed. Usual dosage is 20 mg/day. *Adults:* 20 mg/day each morning initially; then gradually increase to maximum of 80 mg/day in two equally divided doses in morning and at noon. *Elderly:* 10 mg/day initially; then increase by 10 to 20 mg every 2 wk.

ADMINISTRATION: Give with food or milk if GI distress occurs.

SIDE EFFECTS: Headache; asthenia; insomnia; drowsiness; nausea; diarrhea; dry mouth; constipation; fatigue; vomiting; rash

DRUG INTERACTIONS:
- Alcohol and other CNS depressants may increase hypotensive, CNS, and respiratory depressant effects.
- Antithyroid agents may increase risk of agranulocytosis.
- MAOIs and TCAs may increase anticholinergic and sedative effects.
- Medication prolonging QT interval may have additive effect.

PHARMACOKINETICS:
Onset: 2–4 wk
Peak: 6–8 hr
Metabolism: Extensively metabolized in the liver to the metabolite, norfluoxetine. The CYP enzymes responsible for the metabolism of Fluoxetine are CYP2C19 and CYP2D6.

(cont.)

fluoxetine (cont.)

Excretion: Primarily excreted in the urine.
Half-life: 2–3 days

PRECAUTIONS:
Contraindications: Use within 14 days of MAOIs
Cautions: Seizure disorders; cardiac dysfunction; diabetes; risk for suicide

PATIENT AND FAMILY EDUCATION:
- Do not abruptly discontinue medication.
- Avoid tasks that require alertness and motor skills until response to drug is established.

- Avoid alcohol use.
- Take last dose of drug before 4 pm to avoid insomnia.

SPECIAL POPULATIONS:
- *Elderly*: Susceptible to anticholinergic effects
- *Pregnancy*: Category C
- *Lactation:* Crosses the placenta. Distributed in breast milk. Not recommended for breastfeeding mothers.
- *Children*: Safety and efficacy of this drug not established.

Celexa   **citalopram**

AVAILABLE FORMS: Oral solution, 10 mg/5 mL; tablet, 10, 20, and 40 mg

DOSAGE: *Children:* The safety and effectiveness of this drug to treat depression associated with Eating Disorder Not Otherwise Specified have not been established in children under age 18. *Adults:* 20 mg initially once daily in the morning or evening; then increase in 20-mg increments at intervals of no less than 1 wk. *Elderly:* 20 mg/day initially; then slowly increase to 40 mg/day for nonresponding patients only.

ADMINISTRATION:
- Give with or without food.
- Scored tablets may be crushed.

SIDE EFFECTS: Nausea; dry mouth; drowsiness; tremor; diarrhea; abnormal ejaculation; decreased libido; agitation

DRUG INTERACTIONS:
- Linezolid or MAOIs may cause serotonin syndrome

PHARMACOKINETICS:
Onset: 1–2 wk
Peak: 4 hr
Metabolism: Metabolized in the liver into DCT, DDCT, and citalopram-*N*-oxide. The CYP enzymes

responsible for the metabolism of citalopram are CYP2C19 and CYP3A4.
Excretion: Primarily excreted in the urine.
Half-life: 35 hr

PRECAUTIONS:
Contraindications: Sensitivity to citalopram; MAOI use within 14 days
Cautions: Hepatic/renal impairment; history of seizures; mania; hypomania

PATIENT AND FAMILY EDUCATION:
- Do not stop taking medication abruptly or increase dosage without notifying health care provider.
- Avoid alcohol use.
- Avoid tasks that require alertness and motor skills until response to drug is established.

SPECIAL POPULATIONS:
- *Elderly*: More sensitive to anticholinergic effects. More likely to experience dizziness, sedation, confusion, hypotension, and hyperexcitability. Generally able to tolerate citalopram better than other SSRIs
- *Pregnancy:* Category C
- *Lactation:* Distributed in breast milk. Not recommended for breastfeeding mothers.
- *Children*: May cause increased anticholinergic effects and hyperexcitability

---

Zoloft   **sertraline**

AVAILABLE FORMS: Tablet, 25, 50, and 100 mg; oral concentrate, 20 mg/mL

DOSAGE: *Children: 6 yr and older:* 25 mg/day initially; then increase 25 to 50 mg/day at 7-day intervals up to 200 mg/day. *Adults:* 50 mg/day initially; then increase by 50 mg/day at 7-day intervals up to 200 mg/day. *Elderly:* 25 mg/day initially; then increase 25 to 50 mg/day at 7-day intervals up to 200 mg/day.

ADMINISTRATION:
- Give with food or milk if GI distress occurs.
- Oral concentrate must be diluted with 4 oz of water, ginger ale, lemon/lime soda, or orange

juice only and administered immediately after mixing.

SIDE EFFECTS: Headache; nausea; diarrhea; insomnia; drowsiness; dry mouth; dyspepsia; diaphoresis; sexual dysfunction; hot flashes; chills

DRUG INTERACTIONS:
- May increase the concentration and risk of toxicity of highly protein-bound medications such as digoxin and warfarin.
- MAOIs may cause neuroleptic malignant syndrome, hypertensive crisis, hyperpyrexia, seizures, and serotonin syndrome.
- May increase the concentration and risk of toxicity of TCAs.

(cont.)

BULIMIA NERVOSA: Selective Serotonin Reuptake Inhibitors (SSRIs)

sertraline (*cont.*)

PHARMACOKINETICS:
Onset: 1 wk
Peak: 4.5–8.4 hr
Metabolism: Metabolized by the liver into the metabolite, *N*-desmethylsertraline. The CYP enzyme responsible for the metabolism of sertraline is CYP3A4.
Excretion: Excreted in both urine and feces.
Half-life: 26 hr

PRECAUTIONS:
Contraindications: MAOI use within 14 days
Cautions: Seizure disorders; cardiac disease; recent MI; hepatic impairment; suicidal patients

PATIENT AND FAMILY EDUCATION:
- Dry mouth may be relieved by sugarless gum and/or sips of tepid water.
- Report signs/symptoms of headache, fatigue, tremor, and sexual dysfunction.
- Avoid tasks that require alertness and/or motor skills until response to drug has been established.
- Take with food if nausea occurs.
- Inform health care provider if pregnancy occurs.
- Avoid alcohol use.
- Do not take OTC medications without consulting with health care provider.

SPECIAL POPULATIONS:
- *Elderly*: No age-related precautions necessary
- *Pregnancy*: Category C
- *Lactation:* Not distributed in breast milk.
- *Children*: Safety and efficacy of this drug has not been established.

Class: Benzodiazepines (BZDs)

alprazolam   *Xanax IR and ER*

AVAILABLE FORMS: Oral solution, 1 mg/mL; orally disintegrating tablet, 0.25, 0.5, 1, and 2 mg; tablet, 0.25, 0.5, 1, and 2 mg

DOSAGE: *Children:* The safety and efficacy of this drug for the treatment of eating disorders has not been established for children younger than 12 years of age. *Adults:* 0.25 to 0.5 mg three times daily, may titrate every 3 to 4 hr with a maximum of 4 mg/day in divided doses (immediate-release); 0.25 to 0.5 mg three times daily with a maximum of 4 mg/day in divided doses (orally disintegrating). *Elderly*: 0.25 mg two to three times daily initially; then gradually increase to optimum therapeutic response.

ADMINISTRATION:
- May give IR tablets without regard to meals, and tablets may be crushed.
- Administer once daily and do not crush, chew, or break ER tablets. These must be swallowed whole.
- Place orally disintegrating tablet on tongue and allow to dissolve completely. No water necessary.
- Limit duration of treatment to as short a period as necessary (less than 4 months) to minimize potential for abuse.

SIDE EFFECTS: Ataxia; light-headedness; slurred speech; confusion; constipation; depression; anger; paradoxical reactions (nervousness, irritability, insomnia)

DRUG INTERACTIONS:
- Potentiated effects when used in conjunction with other CNS depressants.
- Fluvoxamine, ketoconazole, and nefazodone may inhibit hepatic metabolism and increase serum concentrations.

PHARMACOKINETICS:
Onset: 15–45 min
Peak: 2 hr
Metabolism: Primarily metabolized by the liver into the metabolites, 4-hydroxyalprazolam and α-hydroxyalprazolam. The CYP enzyme responsible for the metabolism of alprazolam is CYP3A4.
Excretion: Primarily excreted in the urine.
Half-life: 6–27 hr

PRECAUTIONS:
Contraindications: Acute alcohol intoxication with depressed vital signs; acute angle-closure glaucoma; myasthenia gravis; severe COPD; history of addictions or drug abuse
Cautions: Renal/hepatic impairment

PATIENT AND FAMILY EDUCATION:
- If dizziness occurs, change positions slowly from recumbent to sitting position before standing.
- Avoid tasks that require alertness and motor skills until response to drug is established.
- Smoking should be discontinued since it reduces the drug's effectiveness.
- Sour, hard candy, gum, and sips of tepid water alleviate dry mouth.
- Avoid alcohol use.
- Do not abruptly discontinue this medication after long-term therapy.

SPECIAL POPULATIONS:
- *Elderly*: Use small doses initially with gradual titration to avoid ataxia or excessive sedation. Because benzodiazepines have sedating properties, all medications in this drug class are listed on the beers list of potentially inappropriate medications for geriatrics.

(cont.)

alprazolam (cont.)

- *Pregnancy:* Category D; chronic ingestion during pregnancy may produce neonatal withdrawal syndrome. CNS depression in neonates.

- *Lactation:* Crosses placenta. Distributed in breast milk. Not recommended for breastfeeding mothers.
- *Children:* Safety and efficacy of this drug has not established.

Klonopin   **clonazepam**

AVAILABLE FORMS: Tablet, 0.5, 1, and 2 mg; orally disintegrating tablet, 0.125, 0.25, 0.5, 1, and 2 mg

DOSAGE: *Children:* The safety and effectiveness of this drug to treat panic disorder associated with bulimia nervosa have not been established in children under 18 years of age. *Adults:* 0.25 mg twice daily initially; then increase in increments of 0.125 to 0.25 mg twice daily every 3 days with a maximum of 4 mg/day. *Elderly:* 0.25 mg twice daily initially; then increase in increments of 0.125 to 0.25 mg twice daily every 3 days with a maximum of 4 mg/day.

ADMINISTRATION:
- Give with or without food.
- Tablets may be crushed.
- Limit duration of treatment to as short a period as necessary (less than 4 months) to minimize potential for abuse.

SIDE EFFECTS: Drowsiness; behavioral disturbances; rash; ankle or facial edema; nocturia; dysuria; changes in appetite or weight; dry mouth; sore gums; paradoxical CNS reactions

DRUG INTERACTIONS:
- Alcohol and other CNS depressants may increase CNS depressant effect.
- Azole antifungals may increase serum concentration and toxicity.

PHARMACOKINETICS:
Onset: 20–60 min
Peak: Unknown
Metabolism: Primarily metabolized by the liver into the metabolite, 7-aminoclonazepam. The CYP

enzyme responsible for the metabolism of clonazepam is CYP3A4.
Excretion: Primarily excreted in the urine.
Half-life: 18–50 hr

PRECAUTIONS:
Contraindications: Narrow-angle glaucoma; significant hepatic disease; history of addictions or drug abuse
Cautions: Renal/hepatic impairment; chronic respiratory disease

PATIENT AND FAMILY EDUCATION:
- Avoid tasks that require alertness and motor skills until response to drug is established.
- Smoking reduces drug effectiveness.
- Do not abruptly discontinue medication after long-term therapy.
- Avoid alcohol use.

SPECIAL POPULATIONS:
- *Elderly:* Usually more sensitive to CNS effects. Use low dosage initially and increase gradually. Because benzodiazepines have sedating properties, all medications in this drug class are listed on the Beers List of Potentially Inappropriate Medications for Geriatrics.
- *Pregnancy:* Category D; crosses placenta. Enters breast milk. Chronic ingestion during pregnancy may produce withdrawal symptoms and CNS depression in neonates.
- *Lactation:* Not recommended for breastfeeding mothers.
- *Children:* Safety and efficacy not established in children for treatment of panic disorder associated with bulimia nervosa.

Valium   **diazepam**

AVAILABLE FORMS: Solution for injection, 5 mg/mL; oral concentrate, 5 mg/mL; oral solution, 5 mg/5 mL; rectal gel, 5 mg/mL; tablet, 2, 5, and 10 mg

DOSAGE: *Children:* The safety and effectiveness of this drug to treat anxiety disorders associated with bulimia nervosa have not been established in children under 18 years of age. *Adults:* 2 to 10 mg two to four times daily (tablets, oral concentrate, oral solution); 2 to 10 mg repeated every 3 to 4 hr as needed (IV, IM). *Elderly:* 1 to 2 mg once or twice daily (tablets, oral concentrate, oral solution); 2 to 10 mg repeated every 3 to 4 hr as needed (IV, IM).

ADMINISTRATION:
- For oral forms of this drug, give with or without food.
- Dilute oral concentrate with water, juice, or carbonated beverages.
- Oral forms of this drug may be mixed in semisolid food.
- Tablets may be crushed.
- Limit duration of treatment to as short a period as necessary (less than 4 months) to minimize potential for abuse.

SIDE EFFECTS: Drowsiness; fatigue; ataxia; slurred speech; orthostatic hypotension; headache;

(cont.)

diazepam (*cont.*)

constipation; nausea; blurred vision; paradoxical CNS reactions

DRUG INTERACTIONS:
- Alcohol and other CNS depressants may increase CNS depression.
- Fluvoxamine, itraconazole, and ketoconazole may increase serum concentration and toxicity.

PHARMACOKINETICS:
Onset: 30–60 min
Peak: 1–2 hr
Metabolism: Primarily metabolized by the liver into the following metabolites: *N*-desmethyldiazepam, temazepam, *N*-desmethyldiazepam, and oxazepam. The CYP enzymes responsible for the metabolism of diazepam are CYP2C19 and CYP3A4.
Excretion: Primarily excreted in the urine.
Half-life: 20–70 hr

PRECAUTIONS:
Contraindications: Angle-closure glaucoma; coma; preexisting CNS depression; respiratory depression; severe, uncontrolled pain; history of addictions or drug abuse
Cautions: Those receiving other CNS depressants; renal/hepatic impairment; hypoalbuminemia

PATIENT AND FAMILY EDUCATION:
- Avoid alcohol use.
- Limit caffeine intake.
- Avoid tasks that require alertness and motor skills until response to drug is established.
- May be habit forming.

SPECIAL POPULATIONS:
- *Elderly*: Use small initial doses with gradual increases to avoid ataxia and excessive sedation. Because benzodiazepines have sedating properties, all medications in this drug class are listed on the Beers List of Potentially Inappropriate Medications for Geriatrics.
- *Pregnancy*: Category D; crosses placenta. May increase risk of fetal abnormalities, if administered during the first trimester of pregnancy. Chronic ingestion during pregnancy may produce withdrawal symptoms in neonates. CNS depression in neonates.
- *Lactation*: Distributed in breast milk. Not recommended for breastfeeding mothers.
- *Children*: The safety and effectiveness of this drug to treat anxiety disorders associated with bulimia nervosa have not been established in children under 18 years of age.

Class: Mood Stabilizing Anticonvulsants

carbamazepine   *Tegretol*

AVAILABLE FORMS: Suspension, 100 mg/5 mL; tablet, 200 mg; chewable tablet, 100 mg; extended-release capsules, 100, 200, and 300 mg; extended-release tablets, 100, 200, and 400 mg

DOSAGE: *Children: 12 yr and older:* 200 mg twice daily initially; then increase dosage by 200 mg/day at weekly intervals. *Adults:* 200 mg twice daily initially; then increase dosage by 200 mg/day at weekly intervals. *Elderly:* 100 mg once or twice daily initially; then increase dosage by 100 mg/day at weekly intervals.

ADMINISTRATION:
- Store oral suspension and tablets at room temperature.
- Give with meals to reduce the risk of GI distress.
- Shake oral suspension well.
- Do not administer with grapefruit juice.
- Do not crush extended-release capsules or tablets.

SIDE EFFECTS: Drowsiness; dizziness; nausea; vomiting; visual abnormalities; dry mouth; tongue irritation; headache; fluid retention; diaphoresis; constipation; behavioral changes in children

DRUG INTERACTIONS:
- May decrease effects of anticoagulants, clarithromycin, dilitiazem, erythromycin, estrogens, propoxyphene, quinidine, and steroids.
- May increase CNS depressant effects of antipsychotic medications, haloperidol, and TCAs.
- May increase metabolism of other anticonvulsants, barbiturates, benzodiazepines, and valproic acid.
- Cimetidine, itraconazole, ketoconazole, and isoniazid may increase serum concentration and toxicity of drug.
- May increase the metabolism of isoniazid.
- MAOIs may cause seizures and hypertensive crisis.

PHARMACOKINETICS:
Onset: 3–5 wk
Peak: 1.5 hr (oral suspension); 4–5 hr (tablets)
Metabolism: Primarily metabolized by the liver into the metabolite, carbamazepine-10, 11-epoxide. The CYP enzyme responsible for the metabolism of diazepam is CYP3A4.
Excretion: Excreted by the urine (72%) and feces (28%).
Half-life: 25–60 hr

PRECAUTIONS:
Contraindications: Concomitant use of MAOIs; history of myelosuppression; hypersensitivity to TCAs
Cautions: Mental illness; increased IOP; cardiac/hepatic/renal impairment

(cont.)

carbamazepine (cont.)

PATIENT AND FAMILY EDUCATION:
- Do not abruptly discontinue this drug after long-term use.
- Avoid tasks that require alertness and motor skills until response to drug is established.
- Report visual disturbances.
- Report for frequent blood tests during the first 3 months of therapy and at monthly intervals thereafter for 2 to 3 years.
- Do not take oral suspension simultaneously with other liquid medicine.
- Do not take with grapefruit juice.

SPECIAL POPULATIONS:
- *Elderly*: More susceptible to confusion, agitation, AV block, bradycardia, and syndrome of inappropriate antidiuretic hormone
- *Pregnancy:* Category D; crosses placenta. Accumulates in fetal tissue.
- *Lactation:* Distributed in breast milk. Not recommended for breastfeeding mothers.
- *Children*: Behavioral changes more likely to occur.

Zonegran   **zonisamide**

AVAILABLE FORMS: Capsule, 25, 50, and 100 mg

DOSAGE: *Children: 2 to 16 yr:* Not recommended for children younger than 16 years of age. *Adults:* Initially 100 mg once daily initially; then increase to 200 mg once daily initially after 2 wks. Further increases to 300 mg once daily and 400 mg once daily can be made with a minimum of 2 wks between adjustments. Maximum dose: 600 mg once daily. *Elderly:* Initially 100 mg once daily initially; then increase to 200 mg once daily initially after 2 wks. Further increases to 300 mg once daily and 400 mg once daily can be made with a minimum of 2 wks between adjustments.

ADMINISTRATION:
- May give with or without food.
- Do not crush or break capsules. Swallow capsules whole.
- Do not give to patients allergic to sulfonamides.

SIDE EFFECTS: Drowsiness; dizziness; fatigue; confusion; irritability; impaired memory/concentration; diplopia; insomnia; speech difficulties; dyspepsia; diarrhea

DRUG INTERACTIONS:
- Alcohol and CNS depressants may increase sedative effect.
- Carbamazepine, phenobarbital, phenytoin, and valproic acid may increase metabolism and decrease effect of drug.
- May increase BUN and serum creatinine.

PHARMACOKINETICS:
Onset: 4 days
Peak: 2 hr
Metabolism: Metabolized in the liver into metabolites, *N*-acetyl zonisamide and 2-sulfamoylacetyl phenol. The CYP enzyme responsible for the metabolism of zonisamide is CYP3A4.
Excretion: Primarily excreted in the urine.
Half-life: 21 hr

PRECAUTIONS:
Contraindications: Allergy to sulfonamides
Cautions: Renal and hepatic impairment

PATIENT AND FAMILY EDUCATION:
- Avoid tasks that require alertness and motor skills until response to drug is established.
- Avoid alcohol.
- Instruct patient to report if rash, back/abdominal pain, blood in urine, fever, sore throat, ulcers in mouth, or if easy bruising occur.

SPECIAL POPULATIONS:
- *Elderly*: No age-related precautions, but lower doses recommended.
- *Pregnancy:* Category C
- *Lactation:* Not known if distributed in breast milk. Not recommended for breastfeeding patients.
- *Children*: Safety and efficacy of this drug not established in children younger than 16 years of age.

Class: Tricyclic Antidepressants (TCAs)

Elavil, Endep, Vanatrip   **amitriptyline**

AVAILABLE FORMS: Tablet, 10, 25, 50, 75, 100, and 150 mg

DOSAGE: *Children: 6 yr and older:* 1 to 5 mg/kg/day in divided doses. *Adults:* 25 to 150 mg/day as a single dose at bedtime or in divided doses. *Elderly:* 10 to 25 mg at bedtime initially; then increase by 10 to 25 mg at weekly intervals

ADMINISTRATION: Give with food or milk if GI distress occurs.

SIDE EFFECTS: Dizziness; dry mouth; orthostatic hypotension; headache; nausea; heartburn

DRUG INTERACTIONS:
- CNS depressants may increase sedation, respiratory depression, and hypotensive effects.
- Antithyroid agents may increase risk of agranulocytosis.
- Phenothiazines may increase sedative, anticholinergic effects.

(cont.)

BULIMIA NERVOSA: Tricyclic Antidepressants (TCAs)

amitriptyline (*cont.*)

- Sympathomimetics may increase cardiac effects.
- MAOIs may increase risk of hypertensive crisis, hyperpyresis, and seizures.

PHARMACOKINETICS:
Onset: 4–6 wk
Peak: 2–12 hr
Metabolism: Metabolized in the liver to its primary active metabolite, nortriptyline. The CYP enzymes responsible for the metabolism of amitriptyline are CY1A2, CYP2C19, CYP2D6, and CYP3A4.
Excretion: Within 24 hr, approximately 25% to 50% is excreted in the urine as inactive metabolites; small amounts are excreted in the bile.
Half-life: 10–26 hr

PRECAUTIONS:
Contraindications: Acute recovery period after MI; within 14 days of MAOI use
Cautions: Prostatic hypertrophy; history of urinary retention or obstruction; glaucoma; diabetes mellitus; hyperthyroidism; history of seizure disorders; cardiac/hepatic/renal disease; schizophrenia; increased IOP; hiatal hernia

PATIENT AND FAMILY EDUCATION:
- Change positions slowly to avoid hypotensive effect.
- Wear sunscreen due to increased propensity for photosensitivity.
- Do not abruptly discontinue medication.
- Avoid tasks that require alertness or advanced motor skills until response to medication is established.
- Sip tepid water to relieve dry mouth.

SPECIAL POPULATIONS:
- *Elderly:* Increased risk of toxicity. Increased sensitivity to anticholinergic effects. Caution in those with cardiovascular disease.
- *Pregnancy:* Category C; crosses placenta.
- *Lactation:* Enters breast milk. Not recommended for breastfeeding mothers.
- *Children:* More sensitive to increased dosage and toxicity. Increased risk of suicidal ideation. Worsening of depression.

clomipramine   *Anafranil*

AVAILABLE FORMS: Capsules, 25, 50, and 75 mg

DOSAGE: *Children: 10 yr and older:* 25 mg/day initially; then increase up to a maximum of 3 mg/kg/day or 200 mg, whichever is smaller. *Adults:* 25 mg/day initially; then increase to 100 mg/day during the first 2 wk of treatment. *Elderly:* 25 mg/day initially; then increase to 100 mg/day during the first 2 wk of treatment.

ADMINISTRATION:
- This drug should be given in divided doses with meals to reduce GI side effects.
- The goal of this initial titration phase is to minimize side effects by permitting tolerance to side effects to develop or allowing the patient time to adapt if tolerance does not develop.

SIDE EFFECTS: Drowsiness; fatigue; dry mouth; blurred vision; constipation; sexual dysfunction; orthostatic hypotension; impaired concentration; urinary retention

DRUG INTERACTIONS:
- Alcohol and other CNS depressants may increase CNS and respiratory depression, and hypotensive effects.
- Antithyroid agents may increase the risk of agranulocytosis.
- MAOIs may increase risk of neuroleptic malignant syndrome, seizures, hyperpyresis, and hypertensive crisis.
- Sympathomimetics may increase the risk of cardiac effects.
- Grapefruit juice may increase serum concentration and toxicity.

PHARMACOKINETICS:
Onset: 2 wk
Peak: 2–6 hr
Metabolism: Metabolized in the liver to active desmethylclomipramine. The CYP enzymes responsible for the metabolism are CYP1A2, CYP2C19, and CYP2D6.
Excretion: Two-thirds is excreted in the form of water-soluble conjugates in the urine and approximately one-third is excreted in the feces.
Half-life: 20–30 hr

PRECAUTIONS:
Contraindications: Acute recovery period after MI; within 14 days of MAOI use
Cautions: Prostatic hypertrophy; history of urinary retention or obstruction; glaucoma; diabetes mellitus; hyperthyroidism; history of seizure disorders; cardiac/hepatic/renal disease; schizophrenia; increased IOP; hiatal hernia

PATIENT AND FAMILY EDUCATION:
- May cause dry mouth, constipation, and blurred vision.
- Change positions slowly to avoid hypotensive effect.
- Avoid tasks that require alertness or advanced motor skills until response to medication is established.
- Do not abruptly discontinue medication.
- Increase fluid intake to combat dry mouth and constipation.

(cont.)

clomipramine (cont.)

SPECIAL POPULATIONS:

- *Elderly*: Increased risk of toxicity. Increased sensitivity to anticholinergic effects. Caution in those with cardiovascular disease.
- *Pregnancy*: Category C; crosses placenta.

- *Lactation:* Enters breast milk. Not recommended for breastfeeding mothers.
- *Children*: More sensitive to increased dosage and toxicity. Increased risk of suicidal ideation. Worsening of depression.

Eating Disorder Not Otherwise Specified (EDNOS)

OVERVIEW

- Patients classified as having an Eating Disorder Not Otherwise Specified (EDNOS) typically have normal body weights and use inappropriate compensatory behaviors (i.e., self-induced vomiting, excess laxative use) after eating small amounts of food.
- Other characteristics include repetitious chewing and spitting out, but not swallowing, large amounts of food (Franco, 2010).
- Female patients have regular menses.
- Polymorphism of the melanocortin 4 receptor genes, polymorphism in the agouti-related peptide gene, and polymorphism of the ghrelin receptor gene are associated with bulimia nervosa and EDNOS such as binge eating (Franco, 2010).

TREATMENT

- Pharmacology is very similar to the treatment of bulimia nervosa.
- Binge eating disorder is a common eating disorder that falls in this particular category.

- SSRIs are primarily used to reduce eating attacks and demonstrate some weight loss.

Acute Treatment

- Can usually be treated outside of the hospital.
- When serious health complications occur as a result of binge eating, individuals may require treatment in a hospital.
- When needed, hospitalization may be on a medical or psychiatric ward.
- Specialized eating disorder clinics may offer intensive inpatient treatment or eating disorder programs may offer day treatment, rather than full inpatient hospitalization (Mayo Clinic Staff, 2010).

Chronic Treatment

- Assertiveness training
- Behavioral modification techniques
- Biofeedback mechanisms
- Cognitive-therapy
- Exposure/desensitization therapy
- Hypnosis
- Insight oriented-therapy
- Relaxation techniques/therapy (Reuters, 2010)

CLASS	DRUG
Selective Serotonin Reuptake Inhibitors (SSRIs)	**First-Line Drug Therapy** citalopram (*Celexa*) fluoxetine (*Prozac*) sertraline (*Zoloft*)

EDNOS

Class: Selective Serotonin Reuptake Inhibitors (SSRIs)

Celexa   citalopram

AVAILABLE FORMS: Oral solution, 10 mg/5 mL; tablet, 10, 20, and 40 mg

DOSAGE: *Children:* The safety and effectiveness of this drug to treat depression associated with Eating Disorder Not Otherwise Specified have not been

established in children under age 18. *Adults:* 20 mg initially once daily in the morning or evening; then increase in 20-mg increments at intervals of no less than 1 wk. *Elderly:* 20 mg/day initially; then slowly increase to 40 mg/day for nonresponding patients only   *(cont.)*

citalopram (*cont.*)

ADMINISTRATION:
- Give with or without food.
- Scored tablets may be crushed.

SIDE EFFECTS: Nausea; dry mouth; drowsiness; tremor; diarrhea; abnormal ejaculation; decreased libido; agitation

DRUG INTERACTIONS: Linezolid or MAOIs may cause serotonin syndrome

PHARMACOKINETICS:
Onset: 1–2 wk
Peak: 4 hr
Metabolism: Metabolized in the liver into DCT, DDCT, and citalopram-*N*-oxide. The CYP enzymes responsible for the metabolism of citalopram are CYP2C19 and CYP3A4.
Excretion: Primarily excreted in the urine.
Half-life: 35 hr

PRECAUTIONS:
Contraindications: Sensitivity to citalopram; MAOI use within 14 days

Cautions: Hepatic/renal impairment; history of seizures; mania; hypomania

PATIENT AND FAMILY EDUCATION:
- Do not stop taking medication abruptly or increase dosage without notifying health care provider.
- Avoid alcohol use.
- Avoid tasks that require alertness and motor skills until response to drug is established.

SPECIAL POPULATIONS:
- *Elderly:* More sensitive to anticholinergic effects. More likely to experience dizziness, sedation, confusion, hypotension, and hyperexcitability. Generally able to tolerate citalopram better than other SSRIs.
- *Pregnancy:* Category C.
- *Lactation:* Distributed in breast milk. Not recommended for breastfeeding mothers.
- *Children:* May cause increased anticholinergic effects and hyperexcitability.

fluoxetine   *Prozac*

AVAILABLE FORMS: Capsule, 10, 20, and 40 mg; oral solution, 20 mg/5 mL; tablet, 10 and 20 mg

DOSAGE: *Children: 7 yr and older:* 5 to 10 mg/day initially; then titrate upward as needed. Usual dosage is 20 mg/day. *Adults:* 20 mg/day each morning initially; then gradually increase to maximum of 80 mg/day in two equally divided doses in morning and at noon. *Elderly:* 10 mg/day initially; then increase by 10 to 20 mg every 2 wk.

ADMINISTRATION: Give with food or milk if GI distress occurs.

SIDE EFFECTS: Headache; asthenia; insomnia; drowsiness; nausea; diarrhea; dry mouth; constipation; fatigue; vomiting; rash

DRUG INTERACTIONS:
- Alcohol and other CNS depressants may increase hypotensive, CNS, and respiratory depressant effects.
- Antithyroid agents may increase risk of agranulocytosis.
- MAOIs and TCAs may increase anticholinergic and sedative effects.
- Medication prolonging QT interval may have additive effect.

PHARMACOKINETICS:
Onset: 2–4 wk
Peak: 6–8 hr
Metabolism: Extensively metabolized in liver to norfluoxetine and inactive metabolites.
Excretion: Slower than most other SSRIs; inactive metabolites are excreted by the kidneys
Half-life: 2–3 days

PRECAUTIONS:
Contraindications: Use within 14 days of MAOIs
Cautions: Seizure disorders; cardiac dysfunction; diabetes; risk for suicide

PATIENT AND FAMILY EDUCATION:
- Do not abruptly discontinue medication.
- Avoid tasks that require alertness and motor skills until response to drug is established.
- Avoid alcohol use.
- Take last dose of drug before 4 pm to avoid insomnia.

SPECIAL POPULATIONS:
- *Elderly:* Susceptible to anticholinergic effects
- *Pregnancy:* Category C; crosses the placenta.
- *Lactation:* Distributed in breast milk. Not recommended for breastfeeding mothers.
- *Children:* Safety and efficacy of this drug has not been established

sertraline   *Zoloft*

AVAILABLE FORMS: Tablet, 25, 50, and 100 mg; oral concentrate, 20 mg/mL

DOSAGE: *Children: 6 yr and older:* 25 mg/day initially; then increase 25 to 50 mg/day at 7-day intervals up to 200 mg/day. *Adults:* 50 mg/day initially; then increase by 50 mg/day at 7-day intervals up to 200 mg/day. *Elderly:* 25 mg/day initially; then increase 25 to 50 mg/day at 7-day intervals up to 200 mg/day

(cont.)

EDNOS: Selective Serotonin Reuptake Inhibitors (SSRIs)

sertraline (*cont.*)

ADMINISTRATION:
- Give with food or milk if GI distress occurs.
- Oral concentrate must be diluted with 4 oz of water, ginger ale, lemon/lime soda, or orange juice only and administered immediately after mixing.

SIDE EFFECTS:
Headache; nausea; diarrhea; insomnia; drowsiness; dry mouth; dyspepsia; diaphoresis; sexual dysfunction; hot flashes; chills

DRUG INTERACTIONS:
- May increase the concentration and risk of toxicity of highly protein-bound medications such as digoxin and warfarin.
- MAOIs may cause neuroleptic malignant syndrome, hypertensive crisis, hyperpyrexia, seizures, and serotonin syndrome.
- May increase the concentration and risk of toxicity of TCAs.

PHARMACOKINETICS:
Onset: 1 wk
Peak: 4.5–8.4 hr
Metabolism: Undergoes extensive first-pass metabolism; extensively metabolized in liver to inactive metabolites
Excretion: Inactive metabolites excreted by kidney
Half-life: 26 hr

PRECAUTIONS:
Contraindications: MAOI use within 14 days
Cautions: Seizure disorders; cardiac disease; recent MI; hepatic impairment; suicidal patients

PATIENT AND FAMILY EDUCATION:
- Dry mouth may be relieved by sugarless gum and/or sips of tepid water.
- Report signs/symptoms of headache, fatigue, tremor, and sexual dysfunction.
- Avoid tasks that require alertness and/or motor skills until response to drug has been established.
- Take with food if nausea occurs.
- Inform health care provider if pregnancy occurs.
- Avoid alcohol use.
- Do not take OTC medications without consulting with health care provider.

SPECIAL POPULATIONS:
- *Elderly:* No age-related precautions necessary
- *Pregnancy:* Category C
- *Lactation:* Not distributed in breast milk.
- *Children:* Safety and efficacy of this drug has not been established.

EDNOS: Selective Serotonin Reuptake Inhibitors (SSRIs)

Dementia and Alzheimer's Disease (AD)

OVERVIEW

- More than 6 million people in the USA suffer from dementia.
- Depression, anxiety, or other behavioral disturbances may accompany dementia.
- Cost of treating dementia in the elderly is estimated to be more than $148 billion annually.
- There are several types of dementia, including vascular, frontal, Lewy body, and AD.

- Reversible causes of dementia should be explored before initiating pharmacologic therapy.
- In the USA, a patient is diagnosed with AD, a form of dementia, every 71 seconds.
- AD accounts for 70% of all dementias; the other 30% is due to other or multiple causes.

CLASS	DRUG
Cholinesterase Inhibitors	**First-Line Drug Therapy** donepezil hydrochloride (*Aricept*) rivastigimine tartrate (*Exelon* and *Exelon patch*) galantamine (*Razadyne* and *Razadyne ER*)
N-Methyl-ᴅ-Aspartate (NMDA) Receptor Antagonist	
	memantine (*Namenda*)

Class: Cholinesterase Inhibitors

Aricept — **donepezil hydrochloride**

INDICATIONS: Used to treat dementia of the Alzheimer's type. Has been proven effective in patients with mild to moderate as well as severe AD.

AVAILABLE FORMS: Tablets, oral solution, rapidly dissolving tablet

DOSAGE:
- Initially 5 mg PO once daily
- Upward titration to 10 mg/day should not occur for at least 4–6 weeks.
- Effective dose range is 5–10 mg/day.

ADMINISTRATION:
- Orally, once daily, just prior to retiring. Swallow tablets whole; do not crush, split, or chew. May be given with or without food.
- Rapidly dissolving tablet: Place on tongue, allow to dissolve, then swallow.
- Oral solution: Measure dose with a calibrated oral syringe.

SIDE EFFECTS: Nausea; vomiting; diarrhea; loss of appetite; weight loss; frequent urination; muscle cramps; joint pain, swelling, or stiffness; pain; excessive tiredness; drowsiness; headache; dizziness; nervousness; depression; confusion; changes in behavior; abnormal dreams; difficulty falling asleep or staying asleep; discoloration or bruising of the skin; red, scaling, itchy skin. *Serious side effects that may require medical attention:* Fainting; slow heartbeat; chest pain; black or tarry stools; red blood in stools; bloody vomit; vomit that looks like coffee grounds; inability to control urination; difficulty urinating or pain when urinating; lower back pain; fever; seizures

DRUG INTERACTIONS: This medicine may interact with the following medications: other cholinesterase inhibitors; neuromuscular blockers; parasympathomimetics; amantadine; amiodarone; amoxapine; anti-retroviral protease inhibitors; antimuscarinics; barbiturates; bosentan; carbamazepine; clozapine; cyclobenzaprine; digoxin; disopyramide; fluoxetine; fluvoxamine; fosphenytoin; fluvoxamine; fosphenytoin; general anesthetics; imatinib, STI-571; ketoconazole; local anesthetics; maprotiline; nefazodone; nilotinib; NSAIDs; olanzapine; orphenadrine; oxcarbazepine; paroxetine; phenothiazines; phenytoin; ranolazine; rifampin; rifapentine; sedating H-1 blockers; sertraline; St. John's wort; tricyclic antidepressants; troglitazone; cimetidine; clarithromycin; dalfopristin; delavirdine; dexamethasone; diltiazem; efavirenz; erythromycin; gefitanib; itraconazole; modafinil; nevirapine; propafenone; quinidine; verapamil; voriconazole

PHARMACOKINETICS:
- Cholinesterase inhibitor—selectively inhibits acetylcholinesterase
- Peak plasma levels are reached in 3–4 hr. *(cont.)*

donepezil hydrochloride (*cont.*)

- Bioavailability of 100%
Half-life: Average 70 hr

PRECAUTIONS: Parasympathetic effects may occur in patients with the following conditions: asthma; coronary disease; peptic ulcer; arrhythmias; epilepsy; parkinsonism; bradycardia and intestinal or urinary tract obstruction could be exacerbated by the stimulation of cholinergic receptors

PATIENT AND FAMILY EDUCATION: Store at controlled room temperature between 15°C and 30°C (59°F–86°F).

SPECIAL POPULATIONS:
- *Hepatic impairment:* No specific dosage adjustments are needed. Adjust dose to patient response and tolerance.
- *Pregnancy:* The uterus could be stimulated along with induction of labor.

rivastigimine tartrate   *Exelon, Exelon Patch*

INDICATIONS:
- Used for the treatment of mild to moderate dementia of the Alzheimer's type.
- Used for the treatment of mild to moderate dementia associated with Parkinson's disease.

AVAILABLE FORMS: Capsule, oral solution, patch

DOSAGE: *Oral:* Starting dose, 1.5 mg PO bid. After 2 weeks, if the dose is well tolerated, may be increased to 3 mg bid. Dose may be increased to 6 mg bid. The maximum dose is 6 mg bid (12 mg/day). *Transdermal:* Starting dose, one 4.6 mg/24-hr patch transdermally daily. After 4 weeks, may increase to the 9.5 mg/24-hr patch. Recommended maintenance dose and maximum dose is 9.5 mg/24 hr.

ADMINISTRATION:
- *Oral*: Should be taken with meals in divided doses in the morning and evening. May be swallowed directly from the syringe provided, or may be mixed with a small amount of water, cold fruit juice, or soda. Oral solution and capsules may be interchanged at equal doses.
- *Patch:* Remove previous transdermal patch before placement of a new one.

SIDE EFFECTS: Nausea; vomiting; loss of appetite; heartburn or indigestion; stomach pain; weight loss; diarrhea; constipation; gas; weakness; dizziness; headache; extreme tiredness; lack of energy; tremor or worsening of tremor; increased sweating; difficulty falling asleep or staying asleep; confusion. *Serious side effects that may require medical attention:* Fainting; black and tarry stools; red blood in stools; bloody vomit; vomit that looks like coffee grounds; difficult or painful urination; seizures; depression; anxiety; aggressive behavior; hearing voices or seeing things that do not exist; uncontrollable movements and muscle contractions; Stevens-Johnson syndrome

DRUG INTERACTIONS: This medicine may interact with the following medications: amantadine; other cholinesterase inhibitors; neuromuscular blockers; orphenadrine; cyclobenzaprine; parasympathomimetics; disopyramide; sedating H-1 blockers; amoxapine; antimuscarinics; clozapine; digoxin; general anesthetics; local anesthetics;

maprotiline; nicotine; NSAIDs; olanzapine; phenothiazines; tricyclic antidepressants

PHARMACOKINETICS: Selective inhibitor of brain acetylcholinesterase and butylcholinesterase
Oral:
- Peak plasma concentrations reached in approximately 1 hr.
- Bioavailability after a 3 mg dose is 36%, indicating a significant first pass effect.
- Should be taken with food to enhance bioavailability.
Topical:
- Peak plasma concentrations are typically reached in 8 hr (range from 8–16 hr).
- Steady state of medication affected by body weight.
- Approximately 50% of the drug load is released from the transdermal system over 24 hr.

PRECAUTIONS: Patients with a carbamate hypersensitivity; rivastigmine is a carbamate derivative

PATIENT AND FAMILY EDUCATION:
Oral:
- Store at 25°C (77°F); excursions permitted to 15–30°C (59°F–86°F).
- Store in a tight container. Store solution in an upright position.
- Do not place rivastigmine solution in the freezer or allow to freeze.
- When oral solution is combined with cold fruit juice or soda, the mixture is stable at room temperature for up to 4 hr.
- Throw away any medication that is outdated or no longer needed.
Patches:
- Apply once daily to clean, dry, hairless, intact skin
- May apply to back, chest, or upper arm
- Rotate application sites daily. Do not apply to the same site more than once every 14 days.
- Apply patch at approximately the same time every day. Remove the old patch before replacing with a new one.
- May wear while swimming, bathing, showering, or in hot weather.
- Avoid excessive sunlight or saunas.

Razadyne IR and ER   **galantamine**

INDICATIONS: Used to treat mild to moderate AD

AVAILABLE FORMS: Immediate-release tablet, extended-release capsule, and oral solution

DOSAGE:
IR tablets: Initially, 4 mg PO bid. After 4 weeks, may increase to 8 mg PO bid. *ER capsules:* 8 mg PO daily in the morning; after 4 weeks may increase to 16 mg PO daily in morning. *Oral solution:* Equivalent to the immediate-release tablets.

ADMINISTRATION:
- Orally
- Take with food to limit drug intolerance

SIDE EFFECTS: Nausea; vomiting; diarrhea; loss of appetite; stomach pain; heartburn; weight loss; extreme tiredness; dizziness; pale skin; headache; uncontrollable shaking of a part of body; depression; difficulty falling asleep or staying asleep; runny nose. *Serious side effects that may require medical attention:* Difficulty urinating; blood in the urine; pain or burning while urinating; seizures; slowed heartbeat; fainting; shortness of breath; black and tarry stools; red blood in the stools; bloody vomit; vomit that looks like coffee grounds

DRUG INTERACTIONS: This medicine may interact with the following medications: cholinesterase inhibitors; conivaptan; fluoxetine; neuromuscular blockers; parasympathomimetics; paroxetine; amantadine; amiodarone; amoxapine; anti-retroviral protease inhibitors; antimuscarinics; aprepitant, fosaprepitant; barbiturates; cimetidine; clarithromycin; clozapine; cyclobenzaprine; delavirdine; digoxin; disopyramide; efavirenz; erythromycin; fluconazole; fluvoxamine; general anesthetics; imatinib, STI-571; itraconazole; ketoconazole; local anesthetics; maprotiline; nefazodone; nilotinib; olanzapine; orphenadrine; phenothiazines; sedating H-1 blockers; St. John's wort; tricyclic antidepressants; troglitazone; troleandomycin; voriconazole; beta-blockers; bosentan; carbamazepine; phenytoin; quinidine; rifabutin; diltiazem; fosphenytoin; nevirapine; nicardipine; NSAIDs; oxcarbazepine; rifampin; rifapentine; terbinafine; verapamil; zafirlukast

PHARMACOKINETICS:
- Cholinesterase inhibitor; reversible inhibitor of acetylcholinesterase
- Peak plasma levels are reached in approximately 1 hr
- Bioavailability is 90%
Half-life: Average 7 hr

PRECAUTIONS:
- If treatment is stopped for several days with the intent to restart, then patient should be started back with the initial dose and then slowly re-titrated to the highest tolerated dose.
- Moderate hepatic impairment.
- Patients should be cautioned about engaging in tasks that require mental alertness such as operating heavy machinery, or driving until reasonably certain that the drug does not affect them adversely.
- Pulmonary disease.
- Use with caution in patients with cardiac disease.
- May exacerbate symptoms of Parkinson's disease.

PATIENT AND FAMILY EDUCATION: Store galantamine at room temperature and away from excess heat and moisture. Throw away any medication that is outdated or no longer needed.

SPECIAL POPULATIONS:
- *Hepatic impairment*: Do not use in patients with severe hepatic dysfunction. Dose should not exceed 16 mg/day PO. Monitor liver function.

Class: *N*-Methyl-D-Aspartate (NMDA) Receptors

Namenda   **memantine**

INDICATIONS: Used to treat moderate to severe AD.

AVAILABLE FORMS: Immediate-release tablet; oral solution; extended-release capsule

DOSAGE: *Oral dosage: Immediate-release tablets or oral solution:* 5 mg PO once daily, titrate slowly to increase the dose by 5 mg/week over a 3-week period to achieve target dose of 10 mg PO bid at week 4. *Extended-release capsules:* 7 mg PO once daily. Increase dose in increments at minimum intervals of 1 wk up to the target dose of 28 mg once daily, making sure previous dose is well tolerated before advancing.

ADMINISTRATION:
- Oral, IV.
- Take with or without food.
- Do not cut/divide/chew.
- May sprinkle contents on applesauce.

SIDE EFFECTS: Extreme tiredness; dizziness; confusion; headache; sleepiness; constipation; vomiting; pain anywhere in the body, especially the back; coughing. *Serious side effects that may require medical attention:* Shortness of breath; hallucination; Stevens-Johnson syndrome; seizures; suicidal ideation

DRUG INTERACTIONS: Dofetilide; procainamide; quinidine; acetazolamide; adefovir; alkalinizing
(cont.)

memantine (*cont.*)

agents; amantadine; antimuscarinics; bromocriptine; cimetidine; dextromethorphan; digoxin; entecavir; ketamine; lamivudine, 3CT; levodopa; metformin; methazolamide; midodrine; morphine; pergolide; pramipexole; quinine; ropinirole; trimethoprim; trospium; vancomycin; amiloride; hydrochlorothiazide; nicotine; ranitidine; triamterene

PHARMACOKINETICS:
Peak concentration: Immediate-release: 3–7 hr; extended-release: 9–12 hr
- Bioavailability 100%
- Can be detected in the CSF 30 min after IV infusion.
Half-life: Average 60–80 hr

PRECAUTIONS:
- Patients with severe hepatic disease; renal failure
- Memantine has not been evaluated in patients with known seizure disorders. Patients who are taking memantine and have seizures or a history of seizure disorder should be monitored closely.

PATIENT AND FAMILY EDUCATION:
- Do not divide, cut, or chew the capsules.

- Contents of capsule may be sprinkled on applesauce.
- Store memantine at room temperature and away from excess heat and moisture.
- Throw away any medication that is outdated or no longer needed.
- Take the missed dose as soon as remembered. However, if it is almost time for the next dose, skip the missed dose and continue regular dosing schedule. Do not take a double dose to make up for a missed one.

SPECIAL POPULATIONS:
- *Hepatic impairment:* In patients with mild to moderate hepatic impairment, no dose adjustments are needed; however, caution is advised when using this drug in patients with severe hepatic dysfunction.
- *Renal impairment:* In patients with CrCl 30 mL/min or greater, no adjustment is needed; if CrCl is 5–29 mL/min based on Cockcroft-Gault equation, a target dose of 5 mg PO twice daily of immediate release is recommended or a target dose of 14 mg/day of the extended release capsule is recommended. If CrCl is less than 5 mL/min, not recommended.

Major Depressive Disorder (MDD) in the Elderly

OVERVIEW
- Prevalence of depression increases with aging.
- More than 30% of adults over 65 years have symptoms of depression.
- Symptoms may include decreased energy, sleep disturbances, weight changes, loss of interest, guilt, poor concentration, and thoughts of suicide.
- ICD9-CM 311, depression, unspecified
- *DSM-IV* Criteria: Presence of 2–4 depressive symptoms of greater than 2 weeks in duration.

- Risk factors include acute stress, anxiety, and illness.
- Differential diagnoses include grief reaction, metabolic disorder, substance abuse or medication induced.

Acute Treatment
- SSRIs are indicated first line for MDDs.
- SNRIs may be considered if SSRIs are ineffective.

Chronic Treatment
- SSRIs and SNRIs are also first-line options for persistent MDDs.

Psychopharmacology of MDD in the Elderly

GENERAL CONSIDERATIONS
- Patients should avoid consuming alcohol while taking this medication.
- Use with caution in patients with history of seizure disorder and/or diabetes.
- Avoid abrupt withdrawal of this class of drug. Dosage should be tapered down prior to discontinuation.

- Monitor closely for clinical worsening and suicide risk.
- Monitor closely for serotonin syndrome.
- Contraindicated if patient has been on an MAOI within 14 days or has taken thioridazine within 5 weeks.

MDD in the ELDERLY

CLASS	DRUG
Selective Serotonin Reuptake Inhibitors (SSRIs)	**First-Line Drug Therapy**
	fluoxetine (*Prozac*)
	paroxetine (*Paxil*)
	citalopram (*Celexa*)
	escitalopram (*Lexapro*)
	sertraline (*Zoloft*)
Serotonin and Norepinephrine Reuptake Inhibitors (SNRIs)	
	duloxetine (*Cymbalta*)
	venlafaxine (*Effexor*)
	desvenlafaxine (*Pristiq*)

Class: Selective Serotonin Reuptake Inhibitors (SSRIs)

Prozac   **fluoxetine**

INDICATIONS: Used to treat MDD

AVAILABLE FORMS: Capsule

DOSAGE: 20–80 mg PO q day

ADMINISTRATION:
- PO with a glass of water.
- May be given with or without food.

SIDE EFFECTS: Worsening depression; suicidality; serotonin syndrome; neuroleptic syndrome; extrapyramidal symptoms; withdrawal syndrome; mania; seizures; hyponatremia; SIADH; hypoglycemia; serum sickness; vasculitis; anaphylactoid reaction; rash, severe; erythema multiforme; pulmonary fibrosis; altered platelet function; priapism; acute narrow angle glaucoma. *Side effects that usually do not require medical attention:* Nausea; headache; insomnia; nervousness; anxiety; asthenia; diarrhea; anorexia; dizziness; dry mouth; tremor; dyspepsia; sweating; ejaculatory dysfunction; constipation; flu syndrome; decreased libido

DRUG INTERACTIONS: This medicine may interact with the following medications: linezolid; all MAOIs; pimozide; thioridazine; almotriptan; clopidogrel; desvenlafaxine; diazepam; duloxetine; triptans; haloperidol

PHARMACOKINETICS:
- Selectively inhibits CNS neuronal uptake of serotonin.
- Highly bound to plasma proteins.
- Peak plasma levels are reached in 6–8 hr.
Half-life: Average 1–3 days

PRECAUTIONS:
- Patients should avoid consuming alcohol while taking this medication.
- Use with caution in patients with history of seizure disorder and/or diabetes.
- Avoid abrupt withdrawal of this class of drug. Dosage should be tapered down prior to discontinuation.
- Monitor closely for clinical worsening and suicide risk.
- Monitor closely for serotonin syndrome.
- Contraindicated if patient has been on an MAOI within 14 days or has taken thioridazine within 5 weeks.
- See patient as often as necessary if long-term use is indicated.
- Patients should be advised not to participate in hazardous tasks until reasonably certain that the drug does not affect them adversely.
- Photosensitivity may occur; sunscreen and protective clothing should be used to protect against ultraviolet light or sunlight until tolerance is determined.

PATIENT AND FAMILY EDUCATION: Store at room temperature between 20°C and 25°C (68°F and 77°F). Throw away any unused medication after the expiration date.

SPECIAL POPULATIONS:
- *Elderly:* Start with lowest dose and titrate up slowly.
- *Hepatic impairment:* Use lowest dose possible in patients with cirrhosis. Monitor closely.

MDD in the ELDERLY: Selective Serotonin Reuptake Inhibitors (SSRIs)

paroxetine   *Paxil*

INDICATIONS: Used to treat MDD

AVAILABLE FORMS: Tablet, suspension

DOSAGE: 20–50 mg PO qd. Start with 10 mg PO q am in elderly patients; increase dose by 10 mg each week until optimal results are obtained. Maximum dose is 50 mg PO q day.

ADMINISTRATION:
- PO with a glass of water.
- May be given with or without food.

SIDE EFFECTS: Worsening depression; suicidality; serotonin syndrome; neuroleptic syndrome; extrapyramidal symptoms; withdrawal syndrome; mania; seizures; hyponatremia; SIADH; hypoglycemia; serum sickness; vasculitis; anaphylactoid reaction; rash, severe; erythema multiforme; pulmonary fibrosis; altered platelet function; priapism; acute narrow angle glaucoma. *Side effects that usually do not require medical attention:* Nausea; headache; insomnia; nervousness; somnolence; asthenia; diarrhea; dizziness; dry mouth; tremor; sweating; ejaculatory dysfunction; constipation; decreased libido; visual changes

DRUG INTERACTIONS: This medicine may interact with the following medications: linezolid; all MAOIs; pimozide; thioridazine; almotriptan; desvenlafaxine; duloxetine; triptans; venlafaxine; St. John's wort; sibutramine; olanzapine/fluoxetine; haloperidol; milnacipran

PHARMACOKINETICS:
- Selectively inhibits CNS neuronal uptake of serotonin.
- Highly bound to plasma proteins.
- Peak plasma levels are reached in 5 hr.
- Bioavailability is 100%.

Half-life: Average 21 hr.

PRECAUTIONS:
- Patients should avoid consuming alcohol while taking this medication.
- Use with caution in patients with history of seizure disorder and/or diabetes.
- Avoid abrupt withdrawal of this class of drug. Dosage should be tapered down prior to discontinuation.
- Monitor closely for clinical worsening and suicide risk.
- Monitor closely for serotonin syndrome.
- Contraindicated if patient has been on an MAOI within 14 days or has taken thioridazine within 5 weeks.
- See patient as often as necessary if long-term use is indicated.
- Patients should be advised not to participate in hazardous tasks until reasonably certain that the drug does not affect them adversely.
- Photosensitivity may occur; sunscreen and protective clothing should be used to protect against ultraviolet light or sunlight until tolerance is determined.

PATIENT AND FAMILY EDUCATION: Store at room temperature between 15°C and 30°C (59°F and 86°F). Store suspension at or below 25°C (77°F). Throw away any unused medication after the expiration date.

SPECIAL POPULATIONS:
- *Elderly:* Start with lowest dose and titrate up slowly.
- *Hepatic impairment:* Use lowest dose possible in patients with cirrhosis. Monitor closely.

citalopram   *Celexa*

INDICATIONS: Used to treat MDD

AVAILABLE FORMS: Tablet, solution, 10 mg/5 mL

DOSAGE: 20–40 mg PO qd in morning or evening

ADMINISTRATION:
- PO with a glass of water.
- May be given with or without food.

SIDE EFFECTS: Worsening depression; suicidality; serotonin syndrome; neuroleptic syndrome; extrapyramidal symptoms; withdrawal syndrome; mania; seizures; hyponatremia; SIADH; hypoglycemia; serum sickness; anaphylactoid reaction; altered platelet function; priapism; acute narrow angle glaucoma; neonatal pulmonary hypertension, withdrawal and serotonin syndrome. *Side effects that usually do not require medical attention:* Nausea; headache; insomnia; somnolence; nervousness; anxiety; asthenia; dyspepsia; diarrhea; anorexia; dry mouth; anorexia; sweating; ejaculatory dysfunction; flu syndrome; decreased libido

DRUG INTERACTIONS: This medicine may interact with the following medications: linezolid; all MAOIs; pimozide; thioridazine; desvenlafaxine; duloxetine; triptans; haloperidol; milnacipran; nefazodone; olanzapine/fluoxetine; sibutramine; SSRIs; St. John's wort; tizanidine; venlafaxine

PHARMACOKINETICS:
- Selectively inhibits CNS neuronal uptake of serotonin.
- 80% protein bound
- Peak plasma levels: No data
- Bioavailability is 80%

Half-life: Average 35 hr

PRECAUTIONS:
- Patients should avoid consuming alcohol while taking this medication.
- Use with caution in patients with history of seizure disorder and/or diabetes.
- Avoid abrupt withdrawal of this class of drug. Dosage should be tapered down prior to discontinuation.

(cont.)

citalopram (cont.)

- Monitor closely for clinical worsening and suicide risk.
- Monitor closely for serotonin syndrome.
- Contraindicated if patient has been on an MAOI within 14 days or has taken thioridazine within 5 weeks.
- See patient as often as necessary if long-term use is indicated.
- Patients should be advised not to participate in hazardous tasks until reasonably certain that the drug does not affect them adversely.
- Photosensitivity may occur; sunscreen and protective clothing should be used to protect against ultraviolet light or sunlight until tolerance is determined.

PATIENT AND FAMILY EDUCATION: Store at room temperature between 15°C and 30°C (59°F and 86°F). Throw away any unused medication after the expiration date.

SPECIAL POPULATIONS:

- *Elderly:* Start with lowest dose and titrate up slowly.
- *Hepatic impairment:* Start with 20 mg PO qd and titrate up to a maximum of 40 mg PO qd slowly. Monitor closely.

Lexapro　　　**escitalopram**

INDICATIONS: Used to treat MDD or generalized anxiety disorder.

AVAILABLE FORMS: Tablet, 10 and 20 mg; oral solution, 1 mg/mL

DOSAGE: Maximum dose for elderly patients, 10 mg PO qd.

ADMINISTRATION:

- PO with a glass of water.
- May be given with or without food.

SIDE EFFECTS: Worsening depression; suicidality; serotonin syndrome; neuroleptic syndrome; extrapyramidal symptoms; withdrawal syndrome; mania; seizures; hyponatremia; SIADH; hypoglycemia; anaphylactoid reaction; altered platelet function; priapism; neonatal pulmonary hypertension, serotonin syndrome and withdrawal. *Side effects that usually do not require medical attention:* Nausea; insomnia; decreased appetite; dizziness; fatigue; dry mouth; impotence; dyspepsia; sweating; ejaculatory dysfunction; constipation; abdominal pain; decreased libido

DRUG INTERACTIONS: This medicine may interact with the following medications: linezolid; all MAOIs; pimozide; thioridazine; almotriptan; clopidogrel; desvenlafaxine; diazepam; duloxetine; triptans; haloperidol; milnacipran; nefazodone; olanzapine/fluoxetine; sibutramine; SSRIs; St. John's wort; venlafaxine

PHARMACOKINETICS:

- Selectively inhibits CNS neuronal uptake of serotonin.
- Highly bound to plasma proteins.
- Peak plasma levels: No data available.

Half-life: Average 27–32 hr (increased by 50% in elderly patients)

PRECAUTIONS:

- Patients should avoid consuming alcohol while taking this medication.
- Use with caution in patients with history of seizure disorder and/or diabetes.
- Avoid abrupt withdrawal of this class of drug. Dosage should be tapered down prior to discontinuation.
- Monitor closely for clinical worsening and suicide risk.
- Monitor closely for serotonin syndrome.
- Contraindicated if patient has been on an MAOI within 14 days or has taken thioridazine within 5 weeks.
- See patient as often as necessary if long-term use is indicated.
- Patients should be advised not to participate in hazardous tasks until reasonably certain that the drug does not affect them adversely.
- Photosensitivity may occur; sunscreen and protective clothing should be used to protect against ultraviolet light or sunlight until tolerance is determined.

PATIENT AND FAMILY EDUCATION: Store at 25°C (77°F); excursions are permitted between 15°C and 30°C (59°F and 86°F). Throw away any unused medication after the expiration date.

SPECIAL POPULATIONS:

- *Elderly:* Start with lowest dose and titrate up slowly.
- *Hepatic impairment:* May use 10 mg PO qd in elderly patients with hepatic impairment. Monitor closely.
- *Renal impairment:* Use with caution in patients with renal impairment.

sertraline	Zoloft

INDICATIONS: Used to treat MDD.

AVAILABLE FORMS: Tablet, oral concentrate

DOSAGE: 50 mg PO q day either in the morning or in the evening.

ADMINISTRATION:
- PO with a glass of water.
- May be given with or without food.

SIDE EFFECTS: Worsening depression; suicidality; serotonin syndrome; neuroleptic malignant syndrome; withdrawal syndrome; mania; seizures; hyponatremia; SIADH; hypoglycemia; serum sickness; altered platelet function; priapism; acute narrow angle glaucoma. *Side effects that usually do not require medical attention:* Nausea; headache; insomnia; diarrhea; dry mouth; ejaculatory dysfunction; somnolence; asthenia; tremor; dyspepsia; anorexia; constipation; decreased libido; nervousness; anxiety; rash; blurred vision

DRUG INTERACTIONS: This medicine may interact with the following medications: linezolid; all MAOIs; pimozide; thioridazine; almotriptan; desvenlafaxine; duloxetine; triptans; haloperidol; milnacipran; olanzapine/fluoxetine; sibutramine; SSRIs; St. John's wort; venlafaxine

PHARMACOKINETICS:
- Selectively inhibits CNS neuronal uptake of serotonin.
- Highly bound to plasma proteins.

- Peak plasma levels are reached in 4.5–8.4 hr.
Half-life: Average 26–104 hr.

PRECAUTIONS:
- Patients should avoid consuming alcohol while taking this medication.
- Use with caution in patients with history of seizure disorder and/or diabetes.
- Avoid abrupt withdrawal of this class of drug. Dosage should be tapered down prior to discontinuation.
- Monitor closely for clinical worsening and suicide risk.
- Monitor closely for serotonin syndrome.
- Contraindicated if patient has been on an MAOI within 14 days or has taken thioridazine within 5 weeks.
- See patient as often as necessary if long-term use is indicated.
- Patients should be advised not to participate in hazardous tasks until reasonably certain that the drug does not affect them adversely.

PATIENT AND FAMILY EDUCATION: Store at room temperatures between 15°C and 30°C (59°F and 86°F). Throw away any unused medication after the expiration date.

SPECIAL POPULATIONS:
- *Elderly:* Start with lowest dose and titrate up slowly.
- *Hepatic impairment:* Use lowest dose possible in patients with liver disease. Monitor closely.

Class: Serotonin and Norepinephrine Reuptake Inhibitors (SNRIs)

duloxetine	Cymbalta

INDICATIONS: Used to treat MDD and generalized anxiety disorders.

AVAILABLE FORMS: Capsule

DOSAGE: 30–120 mg PO qd. Increase in 30 mg increments. Doses greater than 60 mg qd are rarely more effective.

ADMINISTRATION:
- PO with a glass of water.
- May be given with or without food.
- No not cut, crush, chew or open capsule.

SIDE EFFECTS: Worsening depression; suicidality; serotonin syndrome; neuroleptic syndrome; extrapyramidal symptoms; withdrawal syndrome; hepatotoxicity; hypertensive crisis; mania; seizures; hyponatremia; SIADH; anaphylaxis; Stevens-Johnson; erythema multiforme; altered platelet function; acute narrow angle glaucoma. *Side effects that usually do not require medical attention:* Nausea; dry mouth; constipation; headache; blurred vision; insomnia; somnolence; anxiety; fatigue; diarrhea; decreased appetite; dizziness; tremor; vomiting; sweating; ejaculatory dysfunction; anorgasmia; hypotension; decreased libido; syncope; yawning;

urinary hesitancy; elevated liver transaminases; weight changes; elevated BP; hyperhidrosis

DRUG INTERACTIONS: This medicine may interact with the following medications: phenothiazines; all MAOIs; triptans; citalopram; ciprofloxacin; caffeine; desvenlafaxine; ergotamine/caffeine; escitalopram; ethanol; flecainide; triptans; haloperidol; amiodarone; fluoxetine; fluvoxamine; linezolid; methoxsalen; mexiletine; milnacipran; olanzapine/fluoxetine; paroxetine; sertraline; sibutramine; tacrine; ticlopidine; venlafaxine; zileuton

PHARMACOKINETICS:
- Exact mechanism of action unknown; is thought to selectively inhibit CNS norepinephrine and serotonin reuptake.
- Highly bound to plasma proteins.
- Peak plasma levels are reached in 6 hr.
Half-life: Average 12 hr.

PRECAUTIONS:
- Patients should avoid consuming alcohol while taking this medication.
- Use with caution in patients with history of seizure disorder and/or diabetes.

(cont.)

duloxetine (*cont.*)

- Avoid abrupt withdrawal of this class of drug. Dosage should be tapered down prior to discontinuation.
- Monitor closely for clinical worsening and suicide risk.
- Monitor closely for serotonin syndrome.
- Contraindicated if patient has been on an MAOI within 14 days or has taken thioridazine within 5 weeks.
- See patient as often as necessary if long-term use is indicated.
- Patients should be advised not to participate in hazardous tasks until reasonably certain that the drug does not affect them adversely.
- Patients should be advised to avoid alcohol concomitantly to avoid liver injury.

PATIENT AND FAMILY EDUCATION:
- Store at 25°C (77°F). Excursions to 15°C and 30°C (59°F and 86°F) permitted.
- Discard any unused medication after the expiration date.

SPECIAL POPULATIONS:
- *Elderly:* Start with lowest dose and titrate up slowly.
- *Hepatic impairment:* Not for use in patients with hepatic insufficiency.
- *Renal impairment:* Not recommended for patients with renal insufficiency (less than 30 mL/min) or end-stage renal disease.

Effexor   **venlafaxine**

INDICATIONS: Used to treat MDD and generalized anxiety disorder.

AVAILABLE FORMS: Tablet, ER capsule

DOSAGE: 37.5–75 mg PO bid or tid. Start with 37.5 mg PO bid and increase dose q4 days. *ER formulation:* dose q day with equivalent bid dose.

ADMINISTRATION:
- PO with a glass of water.
- Take with food.
- Do not cut, crush, chew, open capsule, or place in water.
- Take at same time each day.

SIDE EFFECTS: Worsening depression; suicidality; serotonin syndrome; neuroleptic syndrome; extrapyramidal symptoms; withdrawal syndrome; hepatotoxicity; hypertensive crisis; mania; seizures; arrhythmias; hyponatremia; SIADH; anaphylaxis; interstitial lung disease; pneumonia, eosinophilic; pancreatitis; skin reactions, severe; angioedema; altered platelet function; acute narrow angle glaucoma; growth suppression in children; mydriasis. *Side effects that usually do not require medical attention:* Nausea; dry mouth; constipation; headache; blurred vision; anxiety; insomnia; somnolence; anxiety; vomiting; impotence; infection; hypercholesterolemia; tremor; weight loss; vasodilation; abnormal dreams; yawning; paresthesias; chills

DRUG INTERACTIONS: This medicine may interact with the following medications: phenothiazines; all MAOIs; dronedarone; triptans; antiarrhythmics; asenapine; chloroquine phosphate; citalopram; degarelix; desvenlafaxine; dofetilide; droperidol; haloperidol; duloxetine; erythromycins; escitalopram; flecainide; fluoxetine; ibutilide; iloperidone; linezolid; methadone; milnacipran; nilotinib; olanzapine/fluoxetine; amiodarone; fluvoxamine; linezolid; paliperidone; paroxetine; pimozide; pentamidine; ranolazine; sertraline; sibutramine; sotalol; sunitinib; St. John's wort; telavancin; tetrabenazine; toremifene; ziprasidone

PHARMACOKINETICS:
- Inhibits norepinephrine, serotonin and dopamine reuptake.
- Highly bound to plasma proteins.
- Peak plasma levels are reached in 6 hr.
- Bioavailability is 45%.

Half-life: 5 hr

PRECAUTIONS:
- Patients should avoid consuming alcohol while taking this medication.
- Use with caution in patients with history of seizure disorder and/or diabetes.
- Avoid abrupt withdrawal of this class of drug. Dosage should be tapered down prior to discontinuation.
- Monitor closely for clinical worsening and suicide risk.
- Monitor closely for serotonin syndrome.
- Contraindicated if patient has been on an MAOI within 14 days or has taken thioridazine within 5 weeks.
- See patient as often as necessary if long-term use is indicated.
- Patients should be advised not to participate in hazardous tasks until reasonably certain that the drug does not affect them adversely.
- Patients should be advised to avoid alcohol.
- Patients should be advised that inert components of the tablet will remain intact during GI transit and are eliminated in the feces as an insoluble shell.

PATIENT AND FAMILY EDUCATION: Store 20°C–25°C (68°F–77°F). Excursions to 15°C–30°C (59°F–86°F) permitted. Throw away any unused medication after the expiration date.

(cont.)

MDD in the ELDERLY: Serotonin and Norepinephrine Reuptake Inhibitors (SNRIs)

venlafaxine (*cont.*)

SPECIAL POPULATIONS:
- *Elderly:* No dose adjustment is recommended. Use care with increasing dose.
- *Hepatic impairment:* Decrease dose by 50% for patients with mild to moderate hepatic function impairment.

- *Renal impairment:* Decrease dose by 25%–50% for patients with renal insufficiency.

desvenlafaxine   *Pristiq*

INDICATIONS: Used to treat MDD

AVAILABLE FORMS: Tablet

DOSAGE: 50–100 mg PO qd

ADMINISTRATION:
- PO with a glass of water.
- Take with or without food.
- Do not cut, crush, chew, sprinkle, or place in water.
- Take at same time each day.

SIDE EFFECTS: Worsening depression; suicidality; mania; serotonin syndrome; neuroleptic syndrome; extrapyramidal symptoms; withdrawal syndrome; hepatotoxicity; hypertension; myocardial infarction; seizures; tachycardia; hyponatremia; SIADH; interstitial lung disease; pneumonia, eosinophilic; altered platelet function; glaucoma; hypersensitivity reaction; mydriasis; hypercholesterolemia. *Side effects that usually do not require medical attention:* Nausea; xerostomia; hyperhidrosis; constipation; headache; blurred vision; anxiety; insomnia; somnolence; anxiety; vomiting; fatigue; decreased appetite; tremor; erectile dysfunction; anorgasmia; abnormal ejaculation; chills; abnormal dreams; nervousness; paresthesias; irritability; weight loss; urinary hesitancy; tinnitus; dysgeusia; rash

DRUG INTERACTIONS: This medicine may interact with the following medications: triptans; SSRIs; linezolid; milnacipran; sibutramine; carbamazepine; chlorpromazine; cisplatin; clozapine; cyclophosphamide; desmopressin; diuretics; fluphenazine; glucosamine; haloperidol; hydrocodone/ibuprofen; metformin; NSAIDs; oxcarbazepine; oxytocin; perphenazine; TZDs; promethazine; prochlorperazine; sulfonylureas; thioridazine; thiothixene; trazodone; TCAs; trifluoperazine; valproic acid derivatives; vasopressin; vinca alkaloids; warfarin

PHARMACOKINETICS:
- Inhibits norepinephrine and serotonin reuptake.

- 30% plasma protein binding.
- Peak plasma levels are reached in 7.5 hr.
- Bioavailability is 80%.
Half-life: 11 hr

PRECAUTIONS:
- Patients should avoid consuming alcohol while taking this medication.
- Use with caution in patients with history of seizure disorder and/or diabetes.
- Avoid abrupt withdrawal of this class of drug. Dosage should be tapered down prior to discontinuation.
- Monitor closely for clinical worsening and suicide risk.
- Monitor closely for serotonin syndrome.
- Contraindicated if patient has been on an MAOI within 14 days or has taken thioridazine within 5 weeks.
- See patient as often as necessary if long-term use is indicated.
- Patients should be advised not to participate in hazardous tasks until reasonably certain that the drug does not affect them adversely.
- Patients should be advised to avoid alcohol.
- Patients should be advised that inert components of the tablet will remain intact during GI transit and are eliminated in the feces as an insoluble shell.

PATIENT AND FAMILY EDUCATION: Store 20°C–25°C (68°F–77°F). Excursions to 15–30°C (59°F–86°F) permitted. Throw away any unused medication after the expiration date.

SPECIAL POPULATIONS:
- *Elderly:* No dose adjustment is recommended. Use care with increasing dose.
- *Hepatic impairment:* Dose escalation greater than 100 mg a day is not recommended.
- *Renal impairment:* For patients with severe renal disease, decrease dose to 50 mg every other day.

Generalized Anxiety Disorder (GAD) in the Elderly

OVERVIEW
- Prevalence of anxiety is not as common in older adults.
- May be associated with depression and/or dementia.

- Symptoms may include excessive worry, restlessness, poor concentration, irritability or sleep disturbance typically for longer than 6 months. Typically, at least three symptoms are present.

MDD in the ELDERLY: Serotonin and Norepinephrine Reuptake Inhibitors (SNRIs)

- ICD9-CM 300.02
- *DSM-IV* criteria: 6 months of excessive worry about issues causing distress or impairment.
- Risk factors include acute stress and/or illness.
- Differential diagnoses include grief reaction, posttraumatic stress disorder, depression, metabolic disorder, cardiovascular disease, infection, or substance abuse.

Acute Treatment
- Atypical anxiolytics are indicated first line for generalized anxiety disorder in older adults.
- Typical anxiolytics may be considered if atypical anxiolytics are ineffective.

Chronic Treatment
- Atypical or typical anxiolytics are also first-line options for persistent generalized anxiety disorder.

Psychopharmacology of GAD in the Elderly

GENERAL CONSIDERATIONS
- Atypical anxiolytics are most commonly used medications for generalized anxiety disorder in the elderly population.
- Typical anxiolytics are used with caution in the elderly.
- Patients should avoid consuming alcohol while taking any of these medications.

- Use with caution in patients with history of seizure disorders.
- Avoid abrupt withdrawal of this class of drug. Dosage should be tapered down prior to discontinuation.
- Monitor closely for clinical worsening and suicide risk.

CLASS	DRUG
Serotonin 1A Agonist	**First-Line Drug Therapy**
	buspirone (*BuSpar*)
Selective Serotonin Reuptake Inhibitors (SSRIs)	
	paroxetine (*Paxil*)
	escitalopram (*Lexapro*)
Selective Norepinephrine Reuptake Inhibitors (SNRIs)	
	duloxetine (*Cymbalta*)
Benzodiazepines (BZDs)	**Second-Line Drug Therapy**
	lorazepam (*Ativan*)

Class: Serotonin 1A Agonist

BuSpar   **buspirone**

INDICATIONS: Used for GAD

AVAILABLE FORMS: Tablet

DOSAGE: Initial, 7.5 mg PO bid; increase 5 mg qd every 2–3 days as needed. Do not exceed 60 mg/day.

ADMINISTRATION:
- PO with a glass of water.
- May be given with or without food; should be taken consistently with or without food as food significantly impacts bioavailability.

SIDE EFFECTS: Serotonin syndrome; akathisia; extrapyramidal symptoms; tardive dyskinesia; dystonia; hostility; depression. *Side effects that usually do not require medical attention:* Insomnia; dizziness; drowsiness; nausea; headache; nervousness; fatigue; dry mouth; confusion; blurred vision; abdominal pain; numbness; weakness

DRUG INTERACTIONS: This medicine may interact with the following medications: linezolid; MAOIs; rifampin; sibutramine; amiodarone; azole antifungals; diltiazem; erythromycins; nefazodone; protease inhibitors; telithromycin; verapamil; triptans

PHARMACOKINETICS:
- Atypical anxiolytics: selectively inhibits CNS neuronal uptake of serotonin.
- Highly bound to plasma proteins.
- Peak plasma levels are reached in 40–90 min.
- Bioavailability is 90%.
Half-life: 2–3 hr

PRECAUTIONS:
- Patients should avoid consuming alcohol while taking any of these medications.
- Use with caution in patients with history of seizure disorders.

(cont.)

buspirone (*cont.*)

- Avoid abrupt withdrawal of this class of drug. Dosage should be tapered down prior to discontinuation.
- Monitor closely for clinical worsening and suicide risk.
- See patient as often as necessary if long-term use is indicated.
- Patients should be advised not to participate in hazardous tasks until reasonably certain that the drug does not affect them adversely.

PATIENT AND FAMILY EDUCATION: Store at room temperature. Protect from temperatures greater than 30°C (86°F). Discard any unused medication after the expiration date.

SPECIAL POPULATIONS:
- *Elderly:* Start with lowest dose and titrate up slowly.
- *Hepatic impairment:* High doses of drug accumulate rapidly. Use with caution in patients with hepatic dysfunction. Monitor closely.

Class: Selective Serotonin Reuptake Inhibitors (SSRIs)

paroxetine   *Paxil*

INDICATIONS: Used to treat MDD and GAD

AVAILABLE FORMS: Tablet, suspension

DOSAGE: 20–50 mg PO qd. Start with 10 mg PO q am in elderly patients; increase dose by 10 mg each week until optimal results are obtained. Maximum dose is 50 mg PO q day.

ADMINISTRATION:
- PO with a glass of water.
- May be given with or without food.

SIDE EFFECTS: Worsening depression; suicidality; serotonin syndrome; neuroleptic syndrome; extrapyramidal symptoms; withdrawal syndrome; mania; seizures; hyponatremia; SIADH; hypoglycemia; serum sickness; vasculitis; anaphylactoid reaction; rash, severe; erythema multiforme; pulmonary fibrosis; altered platelet function; priapism; acute narrow angle glaucoma. *Side effects that usually do not require medical attention:* Nausea; headache; insomnia; nervousness; somnolence; asthenia; diarrhea; dizziness; dry mouth; tremor; sweating; ejaculatory dysfunction; constipation; decreased libido; visual changes

DRUG INTERACTIONS: This medicine may interact with the following medications: linezolid; all MAOIs; pimozide; thioridazine; almotriptan; desvenlafaxine; duloxetine; triptans; venlafaxine; St. John's wort; sibutramine; olanzapine/fluoxetine; haloperidol; milnacipran

PHARMACOKINETICS:
- Selectively inhibits CNS neuronal uptake of serotonin.
- Highly bound to plasma proteins.

- Peak plasma levels are reached in 5 hr.
- Bioavailability is 100%.
Half-life: Average 21 hr.

PRECAUTIONS:
- Patients should avoid consuming alcohol while taking any of these medications.
- Use with caution in patients with history of seizure disorders.
- Avoid abrupt withdrawal of this class of drug. Dosage should be tapered down prior to discontinuation.
- Monitor closely for clinical worsening and suicide risk.
- See patient as often as necessary if long-term use is indicated.
- Patients should be advised not to participate in hazardous tasks until reasonably certain that the drug does not affect them adversely.
- Photosensitivity may occur; sunscreen and protective clothing should be used to protect against ultraviolet light or sunlight until tolerance is determined.

PATIENT AND FAMILY EDUCATION:
- Store at room temperature between 15°C and 30°C (59–86°F). Store suspension at or below 25°C (77°F).
- Discard unused medication after the expiration date.

SPECIAL POPULATIONS:
- *Elderly:* Start with lowest dose and titrate up slowly.
- *Hepatic impairment:* Use lowest dose possible in patients with cirrhosis. Monitor closely.

escitalopram   *Lexapro*

INDICATIONS: Used to treat MDD and GAD

AVAILABLE FORMS: Tablet, solution (1 mg/mL)

DOSAGE: 10 mg PO qd. Maximum dose for elderly patients, 10 mg PO qd.

ADMINISTRATION:
- PO with a glass of water.
- May be given with or without food.

SIDE EFFECTS: Worsening depression; suicidality; serotonin syndrome; neuroleptic syndrome;
(cont.)

escitalopram (*cont.*)

extrapyramidal symptoms; withdrawal syndrome; mania; seizures; hyponatremia; SIADH; hypoglycemia; anaphylactoid reaction; altered platelet function; priapism; neonatal pulmonary hypertension, serotonin syndrome and withdrawal. *Side effects that usually do not require medical attention:* Nausea; insomnia; decreased appetite; dizziness; fatigue; dry mouth; impotence; dyspepsia; sweating; ejaculatory dysfunction; constipation; abdominal pain; decreased libido

DRUG INTERACTIONS: This medicine may interact with the following medications: linezolid; all MAOIs; pimozide; thioridazine; almotriptan; clopidogrel; desvenlafaxine; diazepam; duloxetine; triptans; haloperidol; milnacipran; nefazodone; olanzapine/fluoxetine; sibutramine; SSRIs; St. John's wort; venlafaxine

PHARMACOKINETICS:
- Selectively inhibits CNS neuronal uptake of serotonin.
- Highly bound to plasma proteins.
- Peak plasma levels: no data available.
Half-life: Average 27–32 hr (increased by 50% in elderly patients).

PRECAUTIONS:
- Patients should avoid consuming alcohol while taking any of these medications.

- Use with caution in patients with history of seizure disorders.
- Avoid abrupt withdrawal of this class of drug. Dosage should be tapered down prior to discontinuation.
- Monitor closely for clinical worsening and suicide risk.
- See patient as often as necessary if long-term use is indicated.
- Patients should be advised not to participate in hazardous tasks until reasonably certain that the drug does not affect them adversely.
- Photosensitivity may occur; sunscreen and protective clothing should be used to protect against ultraviolet light or sunlight until tolerance is determined.

PATIENT AND FAMILY EDUCATION:
- Store at 25°C (77°F); excursions are permitted between 15°C and 30°C (59–86°F).
- Discard unused medication after the expiration date.

SPECIAL POPULATIONS:
- *Elderly:* Start with lowest dose and titrate up slowly.
- *Hepatic impairment:* May use 10 mg PO qd in elderly patients with hepatic impairment. Monitor closely.
- *Renal impairment:* Use with caution in patients with renal impairment.

Class: Selective Norepinephrine Reuptake Inhibitors (SNRIs)

Cymbalta   **duloxetine**

INDICATIONS: Used to treat MDD and GAD

AVAILABLE FORMS: Capsule

DOSAGE: 30–120 mg PO qd. Increase in 30 mg increments. Doses greater than 60 mg qd are rarely more effective.

ADMINISTRATION:
- PO with a glass of water.
- May be given with or without food.
- Do not cut/crush/chew/sprinkle.

SIDE EFFECTS: Worsening depression; suicidality; serotonin syndrome; neuroleptic syndrome; extrapyramidal symptoms; withdrawal syndrome; hepatotoxicity; hypertensive crisis; mania; seizures; hyponatremia; SIADH; anaphylaxis; Stevens-Johnson; erythema multiforme; altered platelet function; acute narrow angle glaucoma. *Side effects that usually do not require medical attention:* Nausea; dry mouth; constipation; headache; blurred vision; insomnia; somnolence; anxiety; fatigue; diarrhea; decreased appetite; dizziness; tremor; vomiting; sweating; ejaculatory dysfunction; anorgasmia; hypotension; decreased libido; syncope; yawning;

urinary hesitancy; elevated liver transaminases; weight changes; elevated BP; hyperhidrosis

DRUG INTERACTIONS: This medicine may interact with the following medications: phenothiazines; all MAOIs; triptans; citalopram; ciprofloxacin; caffeine; desvenlafaxine; ergotamine/caffeine; escitalopram; ethanol; flecainide; triptans; haloperidol; amiodarone; fluoxetine; fluvoxamine; linezolid; methoxsalen; mexiletine; milnacipran; olanzapine/fluoxetine; paroxetine; sertraline; sibutramine; tacrine; ticlopidine; venlafaxine; zileuton

PHARMACOKINETICS:
- SNRI: Exact mechanism of action unknown; is thought to selectively inhibit CNS norepinephrine and serotonin reuptake.
- Highly bound to plasma proteins.
- Peak plasma levels are reached in 6 hr.
Half-life: Average 12 hr.

PRECAUTIONS:
- Patients should avoid consuming alcohol while taking any of these medications.
- Use with caution when history of seizure disorders.

(cont.)

duloxetine (cont.)

- Avoid abrupt withdrawal of this class of drug. Dosage should be tapered down prior to discontinuation.
- Monitor closely for clinical worsening and suicide risk.
- See patient as often as necessary if long-term use is indicated.
- Patients should be advised not to participate in hazardous tasks until reasonably certain that the drug does not affect them adversely.
- Patients should be advised to avoid alcohol concomitantly to avoid liver injury.

PATIENT AND FAMILY EDUCATION:
- Store at 25°C (77°F). Excursions to 15–30°C (59–86°F) permitted.
- Discard unused medication after the expiration date.

SPECIAL POPULATIONS:
- *Elderly:* Start with lowest dose and titrate up slowly.
- *Hepatic impairment:* Not for use in patients with hepatic insufficiency.
- *Renal impairment:* Not recommended for patients with renal insufficiency (less than 30 mL/min) or end-stage renal disease.

Class: Benzodiazepines (BZDs)

lorazepam	*Ativan*

AVAILABLE FORMS: Tablet

DOSAGE: 1–2 mg PO q day divided bid or tid for elderly patients

ADMINISTRATION:
- PO with a glass of water.
- Drowsiness and/or dizziness will be exacerbated with concomitant alcohol consumption; alcohol should be avoided while taking this medication.

SIDE EFFECTS: Dependency, abuse; respiratory depression; suicidal ideation; seizures; depression; anaphylactic reaction; hypersensitivity reaction; blood dyscrasias; hepatic encephalopathy exacerbation; gangrene (intra-arterial); hypotension. *Side effects that usually do not require medical attention:* Sedation; dizziness; weakness; unsteadiness

DRUG INTERACTIONS: This medicine may interact with the following medications: sodium oxybate (contradicted); aripiprazole; dexmedetomidine; probenecid; propofol; valproic acid derivatives

PHARMACOKINETICS:
- Benzodiazepine, hypnotic: Mechanism of action is thought to occur at the level of the GABA receptor complex.
- Highly bound to plasma proteins.
- Peak plasma levels are reached in 2–4 hr.
Half-life: Average 14 hr

PRECAUTIONS:
- Patients should avoid consuming alcohol while taking any of these medications.

- Use with caution in patients with history of seizure disorders.
- Avoid abrupt withdrawal of this class of drug. Dosage should be tapered down prior to discontinuation.
- Monitor closely for clinical worsening and suicide risk.
- See patient as often as necessary if long-term use is indicated.
- Ensure that patient is aware to not exceed maximum dosage.
- Instruct patient to monitor for behavior changes.
- If drowsy or dizzy, the patient should not drive, use machinery, or attempt to accomplish any task that requires mental alertness.
- Avoid alcohol as concomitant use may exacerbate symptoms.

PATIENT AND FAMILY EDUCATION:
- Store at room temperature between 15°C and 30°C (59–86°F). Protect from moisture.
- Discard unused medication after the expiration date.

SPECIAL POPULATIONS:
- *Elderly:* More sensitive to hypnotics. Use lowest effective dose.
- *Hepatic impairment*: Monitor for drug accumulation in patients with hepatic function impairment.
- *Renal impairment*: Monitor for drug accumulation in patients with renal insufficiency.

12

Treatment of Personality Disorders

Paranoid Personality Disorder

OVERVIEW

- Displays pervasive distrust and suspiciousness. Common beliefs include the following:
  - Others are exploiting or deceiving the person.
  - Friends and associates are untrustworthy.
  - Information confided to others will be used maliciously.
  - There is hidden meaning in remarks or events that others perceive as benign.
  - The spouse or partner is unfaithful.
- Guarded, restricted affect in most patients.
- More common in men than women.
- May develop transient psychotic symptoms, especially during periods of stress.
- Appear aloof and withdrawn.
- Mood may be labile, quickly changing from quietly suspicious to hostile or angry.
- May appear as a prodrome to delusional disorder or schizophrenia.
- Patients are at risk for agoraphobia, major depression, OCD, and substance abuse.
- A genetic contribution to paranoid traits and a possible genetic link between personality disorder and schizophrenia exist. Psychosocial theories implicate projection of negative internal feelings and parental modeling.
- Distrust of professionals may lead to poor compliance with medication or psychotherapy.

Acute Treatment

- While pharmacotherapy for personality disorders is done off label, medications combined with psychotherapy as an adjunct can be useful in initial treatment of the disorders. Short-term use of a benzodiazepine, such as diazepam, can be appropriate if the patient suffers from severe anxiety or agitation where it begins to interfere with normal, daily functioning. Prescribe a benzodiazepine only after screening for suicidal ideations and with assurance of no risk for suicide.
- Low dose of an antipsychotic medication, such as olanzapine or haloperidol, may be appropriate to manage an acute psychotic state or if the patient decompensates into severe agitation or delusional thinking. Antipsychotics have been shown to decrease irritability and aggressive behavior, and may be used for acute and chronic treatment.

Chronic Treatment

- Often resisted by the patient or met with distrust
- Cognitive behavioral therapy or psychotherapy is often preferred to medication
- Combination of low-dose first- or second-generation antipsychotics (like olanzapine or haloperidol) and SSRIs may be warranted
- May respond negatively to unpleasant side effects
- May be offended by the suggestion to take antipsychotic medication
- More effective to delay considering medication until asked by client to address specific symptoms

GENERAL CONSIDERATIONS ABOUT DRUG TREATMENT OF PARANOID PERSONALITY DISORDERS

Medications are in no way curative for any personality disorder. They should be viewed as an adjunct to psychotherapy to facilitate engagement in psychotherapy.

CLASS	DRUG
Selective Serotonin Reuptake Inhibitors (SSRIs)	**First-Line Drugs for Treatment***
	sertraline (*Zoloft*)
	paroxetine hydrochloride (*Paxil, Paxil CR*)
	fluoxetine (*Prozac, Prozac Weekly, Sarafem*)
	escitalopram (*Lexapro*)
Mood-Stabilizing Anticonvulsant**	**Short-Term Treatment**
	valproate sodium (*Depacon, Depakene*), valproic acid (*Depakene*), divalproex sodium (*Depakote, Depakote ER, Depakote Sprinkle*)
Benzodiazepines (BZDs)	**Acute Treatment**
	diazepam (*Diastat, Diazemuls, Diazepam, Intensol, Novo-Dipam, Valium*)
	lorazepam (*Ativan*)
	clonazepam (*Klonopin*)
Antipsychotics, Typical (First Generation)	**Short-Term Treatment for Active Symptoms**
	haloperidol (*Haldol*), haloperidol decanoate (*Haldol Decanoate, Haloperidol LA*), haloperidol lactate (*Haldol, Haldol Concentrate*)
Antipsychotics, Atypical (Second Generation)	
	risperidone (*Risperdal, Risperdal Consta, Risperdal M-Tab)*)
	olanzapine (*Zyprexa, Zydis*)
	quetiapine (*Seroquel*)
	ziprasidone (*Geodon*)

*Because of overdose risk, TCAs and MAOIs are not recommended.
**Should be prescribed only in consultation with a psychiatry/mental health specialist.

Class: Selective Serotonin Reuptake Inhibitors (SSRIs)

sertraline	*Zoloft*

AVAILABLE FORMS: Tablet, 25, 50, and 100 mg; solution, 20 mg/mL (60 mL)

DOSAGE: 25 to 200 mg once daily; treatment of depression, OCD, panic disorder, PTSD, and social anxiety disorder is initiated at 25 to 50 mg once daily. After 1 wk, may increase daily dose by 25 mg and then wait a few weeks before increasing dose further.

ADMINISTRATION: Usually once daily with or without food; take dosage at the same time each day, either in the morning or in the evening; dosage is based on response to therapy; continue taking this medication as prescribed even if patient feels well. Do not stop taking medication without consulting provider. It may take up to 4 wk before the full benefit of this drug takes effect.

SIDE EFFECTS: Sleepiness, nervousness, insomnia, dizziness, nausea, tremor, skin rash, upset stomach, loss of appetite, headache, diarrhea, abnormal ejaculation, dry mouth and weight loss, irregular heartbeats, allergic reactions, and activation of mania in patients with bipolar disorder.

DRUG INTERACTIONS:
- Use with amphetamines, buspirone, dextromethorphan, dihydroergotamine, lithium salts, meperidine, other SSRIs or SSNRIs (duloxetine, venlafaxine), tramadol, trazodone, TCAs, tryptophan may increase the risk of serotonin syndrome.
- Avoid combining drugs that increase the availability of serotonin in the CNS; monitor patient closely if used together.
- SSRIs should never be used in combination with MAOIs. Cimetidine (*Tagamet*) may increase the levels of sertraline in blood by decreased excretion of the drug by the liver.
- Avoid use with pimozide for it may cause cardiac arrhythmias. Increases the blood level of pimozide (*Orap*) by 40%.
- Drug may increase the blood thinning action of warfarin (*Coumadin*). Monitor warfarin when sertraline is started or stopped.

PHARMACOKINETICS:
- Mean peak plasma concentrations of sertraline occurred between 4.5 and 8.4 hr post-dosing.
- The average terminal elimination half-life of plasma sertraline is about 26 hr.
- Based on this pharmacokinetic parameter, steady state sertraline plasma levels should be achieved after approximately 1 wk of once-daily dosing.
- The single dose bioavailability of sertraline tablets is approximately equal to an equivalent dose of solution.
- For the tablet, drug effects were enhanced when administered with food, while the time to reach peak plasma concentration decreased from 8 hr post-dosing to 5.5 hr.

(cont.)

sertraline (cont.)

PRECAUTIONS:
- Antidepressants increased the risk of suicidal thinking and behavior (suicidality) in short-term studies in children and adolescents with depression and other psychiatric disorders.
- The use of sertraline or any other antidepressant in a child or adolescent must balance risk with the clinical need for the antidepressant.
- Patients who are started on therapy should be closely observed for clinical worsening, suicidal thoughts, or unusual changes in behavior
- SSRIs and MAOIs should not be used within 14 days of each other. Life-threatening serotonin syndrome, characterized by hyperthermia, fluctuations in blood pressure, and rigidity of muscles, may occur.
- Do not discontinue drug abruptly; some patients experience symptoms such as abdominal cramps, flu-like symptoms, fatigue, and memory impairment; gradually reduce the dose when therapy is discontinued.

PATIENT AND FAMILY EDUCATION:
- Patients, their families, and their caregivers should do the following:
  - Be alert to the appearance of anxiety, agitation, panic attacks, insomnia, irritability, hostility, aggressiveness, impulsivity, akathisia (psychomotor restlessness), hypomania, mania, other unusual changes in behavior, worsening of depression, and suicidal ideation, especially early during antidepressant treatment and when the dose is adjusted up or down.
  - Caution about risk of serotonin syndrome with the concomitant use of SNRIs and SSRIs, including *Zoloft*, and triptans, tramadol, or other serotonergic agents and NSAIDs.
  - Alert patients that until they learn how they respond to the drug they should be careful doing activities when they need to be alert, such as driving a car or operating machinery.
  - Alert patients to avoid use of aspirin, warfarin, or other drugs that affect coagulation since these agents have been associated with an increased risk of bleeding.
  - Alert patients to avoid alcohol.
  - Ensure that the use of any OTC product is initiated cautiously. Check with health care provider before using any OTC medication.
  - Notify health care provider if become pregnant or intend to become pregnant during therapy.
  - Alert patients to notify their physician if they are breast feeding an infant.

SPECIAL POPULATIONS:
- *Elderly:* Caution is advised when using this drug in the elderly due to more sensitivity to the drug. May require decreased dosage. The elderly are more susceptible to electrolyte imbalance especially if they are also taking diuretics with this medication.
- *Pregnancy:* Avoid using this drug during the third trimester for it leads to adverse effects in the newborn. This medication should only be used when clearly needed during pregnancy.
- *Lactation:* Secreted into breast milk.
- *Children:* Caution when using this drug in child or adolescent; must balance the potential risks with the clinical need.
  ▶**Alert:** Antidepressants increased the risk of suicidal thinking and behavior (suicidality) in short-term studies in children and adolescents with depression and other psychiatric disorders. Caution is advised when using this drug in children because they may be more sensitive to the side effects of the drug, especially loss of appetite and weight loss. It is important to monitor weight and growth in children who are taking this drug.

Paxil, Paxil CR — **paroxetine hydrochloride**

AVAILABLE FORMS: Suspension, 10 mg/5 mL; tablet, 10, 20, 30, and 40 mg; tablet (controlled-release), 12.5 and 25 mg

DOSAGE:
Depression:
- *Adults:* Initially, 20 mg PO daily, preferably in morning, as indicated. If patient does not improve, increase dose by 10 mg daily at intervals of at least 1 wk to a maximum of 50 mg daily. If using controlled-release form, initially, 25 mg PO daily. Increase dose by 12.5 mg daily at weekly intervals to a maximum of 62.5 mg daily.
- *Elderly patients:* Initially, 10 mg PO daily, preferably in morning, as indicated. If patient does not improve, increase dose by 10 mg daily at weekly intervals, to a maximum of 40 mg daily. If using controlled-release form, start therapy at 12.5 mg PO daily. Do not exceed 50 mg daily.

OCD:
- *Adults:* Initially, 20 mg PO daily, preferably in morning. Increase dose by 10 mg daily at weekly intervals. Recommended daily dose is 40 mg. Maximum daily dose is 60 mg.

Panic Disorder:
- *Adults:* Initially, 10 mg PO daily; increase dose by 10 mg at no less than weekly intervals to maximum of 60 mg daily. Or 12.5 mg *Paxil CR* PO as a single daily dose, usually in the morning, with or without food; increase dose at intervals of at least 1 wk by 12.5 mg daily, up to a maximum of 75 mg daily. *Adjust-a-dose:* In elderly or debilitated patients and in those with severe renal or hepatic impairment, the first dose of *Paxil CR* is 12.5 mg daily; increase if indicated. Dosage should not exceed 50 mg daily.

(cont.)

PARANOID PERSONALITY DISORDER: Selective Serotonin Reuptake Inhibitors (SSRIs)

paroxetine hydrochloride (*cont.*)

Social Anxiety Disorder:
- *Adults:* Initially, 20 mg PO daily, preferably in morning. Dosage range is 20 to 60 mg daily; adjust dosage to maintain patient on lowest effective dose. Or 12.5 mg *Paxil CR* PO as a single daily dose, usually in the morning, with or without food; increase dosage at weekly intervals in increments of 12.5 mg daily, up to a maximum of 37.5 mg daily.

ADMINISTRATION: May take with or without food. Do not split or crush controlled-release tablets.

SIDE EFFECTS: Asthenia, dizziness, headache, insomnia, somnolence, tremor, nervousness, suicidal behavior, anxiety, paresthesia, confusion, agitation, palpitations, vasodilation, orthostatic hypotension, lump or tightness in throat, dry mouth, nausea, constipation, diarrhea, flatulence, vomiting, dyspepsia, dysgeusia, increased or decreased appetite, abdominal pain, ejaculatory disturbances, sexual dysfunction, urinary frequency, other urinary disorders, myopathy, myalgia, myasthenia, diaphoresis, rash, pruritus, and sedation

DRUG INTERACTIONS:
- Amphetamines, buspirone, dextromethorphan, dihydroergotamine, lithium salts, meperidine, other SSRIs or SSNRIs (duloxetine, venlafaxine), tramadol, trazodone, TCAs, tryptophan may increase the risk of serotonin syndrome. Avoid combining drugs that increase the availability of serotonin in the CNS; monitor patient closely if used together.
- Cimetidine may decrease hepatic metabolism of paroxetine, leading to risk of adverse reactions. Dosage adjustments may be needed.
- Digoxin may decrease digoxin level. Use together cautiously.
- MAOIs, such as phenelzine, selegiline, tranylcypromine may cause serotonin syndrome. Avoid using within 14 days of MAOI therapy.
- Phenobarbital, phenytoin may alter pharmacokinetics of both drugs. Dosage adjustments may be needed.
- Procyclidine may increase procyclidine level. Watch for excessive anticholinergic effects.
- Sumatriptan may cause weakness, hyperreflexia, and uncoordination. Monitor patient closely.
- Theophylline may decrease theophylline clearance. Monitor theophylline level.
- Thioridazine may prolong QTc interval and increase risk of serious ventricular arrhythmias, such as torsades de pointes, and sudden death. Avoid using together.
- TCAs may inhibit TCA metabolism. Do not administer an SSRI and TCA concurrently discontinue one medication if necessary.
- Triptans may cause serotonin syndrome (restlessness, hallucinations, loss of coordination, fast heartbeat, rapid changes in blood pressure, increased body temperature, overactive reflexes, nausea, vomiting, and diarrhea). Use cautiously, especially at the start of therapy and at dosage increases.
- Warfarin may cause bleeding. Use together cautiously.
- St. John's wort may increase sedative-hypnotic effects. Discourage use together.
- Drug-lifestyle or alcohol—use may alter psychomotor function. Discourage use together.

PHARMACOKINETICS:
- Thought to be linked to drug's inhibition of CNS neuronal uptake of serotonin.
- Oral dose has a peak action of 2 to 8 hr; duration of effect is unknown; onset of action unknown. Oral use of extended release has peak action of 6 to 10 hr with onset and duration of effects unknown.
Half-life: About 24 hr.

PRECAUTIONS:
- Contraindicated in patients hypersensitive to drug, within 14 days of MAOI therapy, and in those taking thioridazine.
- Contraindicated in children and adolescents younger than age 18 for MDD.
- Use cautiously in patients with history of seizure disorders or mania and in those with other severe, systemic illness.
- Use cautiously in patients at risk for volume depletion and monitor them appropriately.
- Using drug in the first trimester may increase the risk of congenital fetal malformations; using drug in the third trimester may cause neonatal complications at birth. Consider the risk versus benefit of therapy.
- Patients taking drug may be at increased risk for developing suicidal behavior, but this has not been definitively attributed to use of the drug.
- Patients taking *Paxil CR* for PMDD should be periodically reassessed to determine the need for continued treatment.
- If signs or symptoms of psychosis occur or increase, expect prescriber to reduce dosage. Record mood changes. Monitor patient for suicidal tendencies and allow only a minimum supply of drug.
- Monitor patient for complaints of sexual dysfunction. In men, they include anorgasmy, erectile difficulties, delayed ejaculation or orgasm, or impotence; in women, they include anorgasmia or difficulty with orgasm.

▶**Alert:** Drug may increase the risk of suicidal thinking and behavior in children, adolescents, and young adults aged 18 to 24 during the first 2 months of treatment, especially in those with MDD or other psychiatric disorder.

▶**Alert:** Do not stop drug abruptly. Withdrawal or discontinuation syndrome may occur if drug is stopped abruptly. Symptoms include headache, myalgia, lethargy, and general flu-like symptoms. Taper drug slowly over 1 to 2 wk.

▶**Alert:** Combining triptans with an SSRI or an SSNRI may cause serotonin syndrome. Signs and *(cont.)*

paroxetine hydrochloride (*cont.*)

symptoms may include restlessness, hallucinations, loss of coordination, fast heartbeat, rapid changes in blood pressure, increased body temperature, overactive reflexes, nausea, vomiting, and diarrhea. Serotonin syndrome may be more likely to occur when starting or increasing the dose of triptan, SSRI, or SSNRI.

PATIENT AND FAMILY EDUCATION:

- Drug may be taken with or without food, usually in the morning.
- Do not break, crush, or chew controlled-release tablets.
- Avoid activities that require alertness and good coordination until effects of drug are known.
- Contact prescriber if patient is a woman of childbearing age and becomes pregnant or plans to become pregnant during therapy or if currently breastfeeding.
- Avoid alcohol and consult prescriber before taking other prescription or OTC drugs or herbal medicines.
- Do not stop taking drug abruptly.
- It may take 4 wk before full therapeutic effects are noticed, and side effects may occur within the first week of treatment.

SPECIAL POPULATIONS:

- *Elderly:* Caution is advised when using this drug in the elderly due to more sensitivity to the drug.
- *Pregnancy:* Avoid using this drug during the third trimester for it leads to adverse effects in the newborn. This medication should only be used when clearly needed during pregnancy.
- *Lactation:* Secreted into breast milk.
- *Children:* Caution when using this drug in a child or adolescent; must balance the potential risks with the clinical need. Not recommended for use under age 18 for MDD.
- ►**Alert:** Antidepressants increased the risk of suicidal thinking and behavior (suicidality) in short-term studies in children and adolescents with depression and other psychiatric disorders. Caution is advised when using this drug in children because they may be more sensitive to the side effects of the drug, especially loss of appetite and weight loss. It is important to monitor weight and growth in children who are taking this drug.

Prozac, Prozac Weekly, Sarafem | **fluoxetine**

AVAILABLE FORMS: Capsule (delayed-release), 90 mg; capsule (pulvules), 10, 20, and 40 mg; oral solution, 20 mg/5 mL; tablet, 10 and 20 mg

DOSAGE:
Depression, OCD:

- *Adults:* Initially, 20 mg PO in the morning; increase dosage based on patient response. Maximum daily dose is 80 mg.
- *Children aged 7 to 17 (OCD):* 10 mg PO daily. After 2 wk, increase to 20 mg daily. Dosage is 20 to 60 mg daily.
- *Children aged 8 to 18 (depression):* 10 mg PO once daily for 1 wk; then increase to 20 mg daily.

Depression in Elderly:

- *Adults aged 65 and older:* Initially, 20 mg PO daily in the morning. Increase dose based on response. Doses may be given bid, morning and noon. Maximum daily dose is 80 mg. Consider using a lower dosage or less-frequent dose in these patients, especially those with systemic illness and are receiving drugs for other illnesses.

Maintenance Therapy for Depression in Stabilized Patients (Not for Newly Diagnosed Depression):

- *Adults:* 90 mg *Prozac* PO once weekly. Start once-weekly doses 7 days after the last daily dose of *Prozac* 20 mg.

Short-Term Treatment of Panic Disorder With or Without Agoraphobia:

- *Adults:* 10 mg PO once daily for 1 wk; then increase dose as needed to 20 mg daily. Maximum daily dose is 60 mg. Adjust dose for patients with renal or hepatic impairment, reduce dose or increase interval.
- For patients with renal or hepatic impairment and those taking several drugs at the same time, reduce dose or increase dosing interval.

ADMINISTRATION:

- Give drug with or without food.
- Avoid giving drug in the afternoon, whenever possible, because doing so commonly causes nervousness and insomnia.
- Delayed-release capsules must be swallowed whole; do not crush or open.

SIDE EFFECTS: Nervousness, somnolence, anxiety, insomnia, headache, drowsiness, tremor, dizziness, asthenia, suicidal behavior, fatigue, fever, palpitations, hot flashes, nasal congestion, pharyngitis, sinusitis, nausea, diarrhea, dry mouth, anorexia, dyspepsia, constipation, abdominal pain, vomiting, flatulence, increased appetite, sexual dysfunction, weight loss, muscle pain, upper respiratory tract, infection, cough, respiratory distress, rash, pruritus, diaphoresis, flu-like syndrome.

DRUG INTERACTIONS:

- Amphetamines, buspirone, dextromethorphan, dihydroergotamine, lithium salts, meperidine, other SSRIs or SSNRIs (duloxetine, venlafaxine), tramadol, trazodone, TCAs, tryptophan may increase risk of serotonin syndrome. Avoid combinations of drugs that increase the availability of serotonin in the CNS; monitor patient closely if used together.

(cont.)

PARANOID PERSONALITY DISORDER: Selective Serotonin Reuptake Inhibitors (SSRIs)

fluoxetine (cont.)

- Benzodiazepines, lithium, TCAs may increase CNS effects. Monitor patient closely.
- Beta-blockers, carbamazepine, flecainide, vinblastine may increase levels of these drugs. Monitor drug levels and monitor patient for adverse reactions.
- Cyproheptadine may reverse or decrease fluoxetine effect. Monitor patient closely.
- Dextromethorphan may cause unusual side effects such as visual hallucinations. Advise use of cough suppressant that does not contain dextromethorphan while taking fluoxetine.
- Highly protein-bound drugs may increase level of fluoxetine or other highly protein-bound drugs. Monitor patient closely.
- Insulin, oral antidiabetics may alter glucose level and antidiabetic requirements. Adjust dosage.
- MAOIs (phenelzine, selegiline, tranylcypromine) may cause serotonin syndrome. Avoid using at the same time and for at least 5 wk after stopping.
- Phenytoin may increase phenytoin level and risk of toxicity. Monitor phenytoin level and adjust dosage.
- Triptans may cause weakness, hyperreflexia, uncoordination, rapid changes in blood pressure, nausea, and diarrhea. Monitor patient closely, especially at the start of treatment and when dosage increases.
- Thioridazine may increase thioridazine level, increasing risk of serious ventricular arrhythmias and sudden death. Avoid using at the same time and for at least 5 wk after stopping.
- Warfarin may increase risk for bleeding. Monitor PT and INR.
- St. John's wort may increase sedative and hypnotic effects; may cause serotonin syndrome. Discourage use.
- Alcohol may increase CNS depression. Discourage use.

PHARMACOKINETICS:
- May be linked to drug's inhibition of CNS neuronal uptake of serotonin. Peak action is 6 to 8 hr with duration and onset of action unknown. **Half-life:** Fluoxetine, 2–3 days; norfluoxetine, 7–9 days.

PRECAUTIONS:
- Contraindicated in patients hypersensitive to drug and in those taking MAOIs within 14 days of starting therapy. MAOIs should not be started within 5 wk of stopping fluoxetine. Avoid using thioridazine with fluoxetine or within 5 wk after stopping fluoxetine.
- Use cautiously in patients at high risk for suicide and in those with history of diabetes mellitus, seizures, mania, or hepatic, renal, or CV disease.
- Use in third trimester of pregnancy may be associated with neonatal complications at birth.

Consider the risk versus benefit of treatment during this time.
- Use antihistamines or topical corticosteroids to treat rashes or pruritus.
- Watch for weight change during therapy, particularly in underweight or bulimic patients.
- Record mood changes. Watch for suicidal tendencies.
- Drug has a long half-life; monitor patient for adverse effects for up to 2 wk after drug is stopped.

▶**Alert:** Drug may increase the risk of suicidal thinking and behavior in children and adolescents with MDD or other psychiatric disorder.

▶**Alert:** Drug may increase the risk of suicidal thinking and behavior in young adults aged 18 to 24 during the first 2 months of treatment.

▶**Alert:** Combining triptans with an SSRI or an SSNRI may cause serotonin syndrome. Signs and symptoms may include restlessness, hallucinations, loss of coordination, fast heartbeat, rapid changes in blood pressure, increased body temperature, overactive reflexes, nausea, vomiting, and diarrhea. Serotonin syndrome may be more likely to occur when starting or increasing the dose of triptan, SSRI, or SSNRI.

PATIENT AND FAMILY EDUCATION:
- Avoid taking drug in the afternoon whenever possible because doing so commonly causes nervousness and insomnia.
- Drug may cause dizziness or drowsiness.
- Avoid driving and other hazardous activities that require alertness and good psychomotor coordination until effects of drug are known.
- Consult prescriber before taking other prescription or OTC drugs.
- Full therapeutic effect may not be seen for 4 wk or longer, yet side effects may occur within the first week.

SPECIAL POPULATIONS:
- *Elderly:* Caution is advised when using this drug in the elderly due to more sensitivity to the drug.
- *Pregnancy:* Avoid using this drug during the third trimester due to adverse effects in the newborn. This medication should only be used when clearly needed during pregnancy.
- *Lactation:* Secreted into breast milk.
- *Children:* Caution when using this drug in a child or adolescent; must balance the potential risks with the clinical need. Not recommended for use under age 18 years for MDD.

▶**Alert:** Antidepressants increased the risk of suicidal thinking and behavior (suicidality) in short-term studies in children and adolescents with depression and other psychiatric disorders. Caution is advised when using this drug in children because they may be more sensitive to the side effects of the drug, especially loss of appetite and weight loss. It is important to monitor weight and growth in children who are taking this drug.

AVAILABLE FORMS: Tablet, capsule, 5, 10, and 20 mg; oral solution, 5 mg/5 mL

DOSAGE: 10 to 20 mg every day

ADMINISTRATION:
- PO with a glass of water
- Take with or without food
- Take at regular intervals, preferably in the morning
- Caution clients not to stop taking drug except on provider's advice
- Instruct client to take missed dose ASAP. If it is almost time for the next dose, advise to take only that dose.

SIDE EFFECTS: Somnolence, dizziness, insomnia, nervousness, dry mouth, constipation, asthenia, diaphoresis, anxiety, headache, drowsiness, anorexia, dyspepsia, suicide risk, fatigue, fever, palpitations, hot flashes, nasal congestion, pharyngitis, sinusitis, nausea, diarrhea, dry mouth, anorexia, dyspepsia, constipation, abdominal pain, vomiting, flatulence, increased appetite, sexual dysfunction, weight loss, muscle pain, upper respiratory tract, infection, cough, respiratory distress, rash, pruritus, diaphoresis, flu-like syndrome.

DRUG INTERACTIONS:
- This medicine may interact with the following medications: cyproheptadine, flecainide, carbamazepine, vinblastine, insulin, oral diabetic agents, lithium, TCAs, phenytoin, tryptophan, warfarin (and other highly protein-bound drugs).
- Concomitant use with SSRIs, SNRIs, or tryptophan is not recommended. Use caution if consuming concomitantly with drugs that affect hemostasis (NSAIDs, aspirin, warfarin).

▶**Alert:** This list may not describe all possible interactions. Instruct clients to provide a list of all the medicines, herbs, nonprescription drugs, or dietary supplements they use. Also instruct clients to inform if they smoke, drink alcohol, or use illegal drugs.

PHARMACOKINETICS: SSRIs are metabolized in the liver by cytochrome P-450 MFO microsomal enzymes. They are highly bound to plasma proteins and have a large volume of distribution. Peak plasma levels are reached in 2–10 hr. Escitalopram's half-life is 27–32 hr. Steady state plasma levels are achieved in 1 wk with escitalopram. Hence, addition of serotonergic medications to a patient's regimen must not occur until 2–3 wk after discontinuation of an SSRI.

PRECAUTIONS:
- *Clinical worsening/suicide risk:* Monitor for clinical worsening, suicidality, and unusual change in behavior, especially during the initial few months of therapy or at times of dose changes.
- *Serotonin syndrome or NMS-like reactions:* Manage with immediate discontinuation and continuing monitoring.

- *Discontinuation of treatment with lexapro:* A gradual reduction in dose rather than abrupt cessation is recommended whenever possible.
- *Seizures:* Prescribe with care in patients with history of seizure.
- *Activation of mania/hypomania:* Use cautiously in patients with a history of mania.
- *Hyponatremia:* Can occur in association with SIADH.
- *Abnormal bleeding:* Use caution in concomitant use with NSAIDs, aspirin, warfarin, or other drugs that affect coagulation.
- *Interference with cognitive and motor performance:* Use caution when operating machinery.
- *Use in patients with concomitant illness:* Use caution in patients with diseases or conditions that produce altered metabolism or hemodynamic response.
- See client as often as necessary to ensure that the drug is working on the panic attacks, determine compliance, and review side effects
- Make sure the client realizes that they need to take prescribed dose even if they do not feel better right away. It can take several weeks before the full effect is felt.
- Instruct client and family to watch for worsening depression or thoughts of suicide. Also watch out for sudden or severe changes in feelings such as feeling anxious, agitated, panicky, irritable, hostile, aggressive, impulsive, severely restless, overly excited and hyperactive, or not being able to sleep. If this happens, especially at the beginning of antidepressant treatment or after a change in dose, patients should call the provider.
- Clients may become drowsy or dizzy and should not drive, use machinery, or do anything that needs mental alertness until the effects of this medicine are known.
- Caution patients not to stand or sit up quickly, especially if an older patient. This reduces the risk of dizzy or fainting spells. Alcohol may interfere with the effect of this medicine. Avoid alcoholic drinks.
- Caution patients not to treat themselves for coughs, colds, or allergies without asking health care professional for advice. Some ingredients can increase possible side effects.
- *Dry mouth:* Chewing sugarless gum or sucking hard candy, and drinking plenty of water may help. Contact the provider if the problem does not go away or is severe.

PRECAUTIONS:
Use with caution on patients with bipolar disorder or a family history of bipolar disorder, diabetes, heart disease, liver disease, seizures (convulsions); those with suicidal thoughts, plans, or attempts by patient or a family member; those with an unusual or allergic reaction to sertraline, other medicines, foods, dyes, or preservatives; and those who are pregnant or trying to get pregnant and who are breastfeeding.

(cont.)

escitalopram *(cont.)*

PATIENT AND FAMILY EDUCATION:
- Avoid taking drug in the afternoon whenever possible because doing so commonly causes nervousness and insomnia.
- The drug may cause dizziness or drowsiness.
- Avoid driving and other hazardous activities that require alertness and good psychomotor coordination until effects of drug are known.
- Consult prescriber before taking other prescription or OTC drugs.
- Full therapeutic effect may not be seen for 4 wk or longer, yet side effects may occur within the first week.

SPECIAL POPULATIONS:
- *Elderly:* Caution is advised when using this drug in the elderly due to more sensitivity to the drug.

- *Pregnancy:* Avoid using this drug during the third trimester for it leads to adverse effects in the newborn. This medication should only be used when clearly needed during pregnancy.
- *Lactation:* Secreted into breast milk.
- *Children:* When using this drug in a child or adolescent; must balance the potential risks with the clinical need. Antidepressants increased the risk of suicidal thinking and behavior (suicidality) in short-term studies in children and adolescents with depression and other psychiatric disorders. Caution is advised when using this drug in children because they may be more sensitive to the side effects of the drug, especially loss of appetite and weight loss. It is important to monitor weight and growth in children who are taking this drug.

Class: Mood-Stabilizing Anticonvulsants

valproate sodium	Depacon, Depakene
valproic acid	Depakene
divalproex sodium	Depakote, Depakote ER, Depakote Sprinkle

▶**Note:** Valproate sodium should only be prescribed for this condition in consultation with a psychiatric/mental health specialist.

AVAILABLE FORMS: *Valproate sodium:* Injection, 100 mg/mL; syrup, 250 mg/5 mL. *Valproic acid:* Capsule, 250 mg; syrup, 200 mg/5 mL; tablet (crushable), 100 mg; tablet (enteric-coated), 200 and 500 mg. *Divalproex sodium:* Capsule (sprinkle), 125 mg; tablet (delayed-release), 125, 250, and 500 mg; tablet (extended-release), 250 and 500 mg

DOSAGE:
Mania:
- *Adults:* Initially, 750 mg *Depakote* daily PO in divided doses, or 25 mg/kg *Depakote ER* once daily. Adjust dosage based on patient's response; maximum dose for either form is 60 mg/kg daily.

To Prevent Migraine Headache:
- *Adults:* Initially, 250 mg delayed-release divalproex sodium PO bid. Some patients may need up to 1,000 mg daily. Or, 500 mg *Depakote ER* PO daily for 1 wk; then 1,000 mg PO daily. *Adjust-a-dose:* For elderly patients, start at lower dosage. Increase dosage more slowly and with regular monitoring of fluid and nutritional intake, and watch for dehydration, somnolence, and other adverse reactions.

ADMINISTRATION:
- *Oral:* Give drug with food or milk to reduce adverse GI effects.
- Do not mix syrup with carbonated beverages; mixture may be irritating to oral mucosa.
- Do not give syrup to patients who need sodium restriction. Check with prescriber.
- Capsules may be swallowed whole or opened and contents sprinkled on a teaspoonful of soft food. Patient should swallow immediately without chewing.
- Monitor drug level and adjust dosage as needed.
- *Incompatibilities:* None reported.

SIDE EFFECTS:
- *CNS:* Asthenia, dizziness, headache, insomnia, nervousness, somnolence, tremor, abnormal thinking, amnesia, ataxia, depression, emotional upset, fever, sedation
- *CV:* Chest pain, edema, hypertension, hypotension, tachycardia
- *EENT:* Blurred vision, diplopia, nystagmus, pharyngitis, rhinitis, tinnitus
- *GI:* Abdominal pain, anorexia, diarrhea, dyspepsia, nausea, vomiting, pancreatitis, constipation, increased appetite
- *Hematologic:* Bone marrow suppression, hemorrhage, thrombocytopenia, bruising, petechiae
- *Hepatic:* Hepatotoxicity
- *Metabolic:* Hyperammonemia, weight gain
- *Musculoskeletal:* Back and neck pain
- *Respiratory:* Bronchitis, dyspnea
- *Skin:* Alopecia, flu syndrome, infection, erythema multiforme, hypersensitivity reactions, Stevens-Johnson syndrome, rash, photosensitivity reactions, pruritus

DRUG INTERACTIONS: Aspirin, chlorpromazine, cimetidine, erythromycin, felbamate, carbamazepine, lamotrigine, phenobarbital, phenytoin, rifampin, warfarin, zidovudine. Alcohol use is discouraged.

PHARMACOKINETICS:
Peak action for oral dose is 15 min to 4 hr. Facilitates the effects of the inhibitory neurotransmitter GABA.
Half-life: 6–16 hr

(cont.)

valproate sodium, valproic acid, divalproex sodium *(cont.)*

PRECAUTIONS:

- May increase ammonia, ALT, AST, and bilirubin lab levels.
- May increase eosinophil count and bleeding time. May decrease platelet, RBC, and WBC counts.
- May cause false-positive results for urine ketone levels.
- Contraindicated in patients hypersensitive to drug and in those with hepatic disease or significant hepatic dysfunction, and in patients with a UCD.
- Safety and efficacy of *Depakote ER* in children younger than age 10 have not been established.
- Obtain liver function test results, platelet count, and PT and INR before starting therapy, and monitor these values periodically.
- Adverse reactions may not be caused by valproic acid alone because it is usually used with other anticonvulsants.
- When converting adults and children aged 10 and older with seizures from *Depakote* to *Depakote ER*, make sure the extended-release dose is 8% to 20% higher than the regular dose taken previously. See manufacturer's package insert for more details.
- Divalproex sodium has a lower risk of adverse GI reactions.
- Never withdraw drug suddenly, because sudden withdrawal may worsen seizures. Call prescriber at once if adverse reactions develop.
- Patients at high risk for hepatotoxicity include those with congenital metabolic disorders, mental retardation, or organic brain disease; those taking multiple anticonvulsants; and children younger than age 2 years.
- Notify prescriber if tremors occur; a dosage reduction may be needed.
- Monitor drug level. Therapeutic level is 50 to 100 mcg/mL.
- When converting patients from a brand-name drug to a generic drug, use caution because breakthrough seizures may occur.

▶**Alert:** Sometimes fatal, hyperammonemic encephalopathy may occur when starting valproate therapy in patients with UCD. Evaluate patients with UCD risk factors before starting valproate therapy. Patients who develop symptoms of unexplained hyperammonemic encephalopathy during valproate therapy should stop drug, undergo prompt appropriate treatment, and be evaluated for underlying UCD.

▶**Alert:** Fatal hepatotoxicity may follow nonspecific symptoms, such as malaise, fever, and lethargy. If these symptoms occur during therapy, notify prescriber at once because patients who might be developing hepatic dysfunction must stop taking drug.

PATIENT AND FAMILY EDUCATION:

- Take drug with food or milk to reduce adverse GI effects.
- Do not chew capsules; irritation of mouth and throat may result.
- Capsules may be either swallowed whole or carefully opened and contents sprinkled on a teaspoonful of soft food. Tell patient to swallow immediately without chewing.
- Avoid driving and other potentially hazardous activities that require mental alertness until drug's CNS effects are known.
- Call prescriber if patient becomes pregnant or plans to become pregnant during therapy.
- Syrup should not be mixed with carbonated beverages; mixture may be irritating to mouth and throat.
- Keep drug out of children's reach.
- Do not stop drug therapy abruptly.
- Call prescriber if malaise, weakness, lethargy, facial swelling, loss of appetite, or vomiting occurs.

SPECIAL POPULATIONS:

- *Elderly:* Caution is advised when using this drug in the elderly due to more sensitivity to the drug.
- *Pregnancy:* Category D. This medication should only be used when clearly needed during pregnancy.
- *Lactation:* Secreted into breast milk.
- *Children:* Caution when using this drug in a child or adolescent; must balance the potential risks with the clinical need. Not recommended for use under age 18 years for MDD.

▶**Alert:** Antidepressants increased the risk of suicidal thinking and behavior (suicidality) in short-term studies in children and adolescents with depression and other psychiatric disorders. Caution is advised when using this drug in children because they may be more sensitive to the side effects of the drug, especially loss of appetite and weight loss. It is important to monitor weight and growth in children who are taking this drug.

Class: Benzodiazepines (BZDs)

Diastat, Diazemuls, Diazepam Intensol, Novo-Dipam, Valium   **diazepam**

▶**ALERT:** Controlled-Substance Schedule IV

AVAILABLE FORMS: Injection, 5 mg/mL; oral solution, 5 mg/5 mL; rectal gel twin packs, 2.5 mg (pediatric), 5 mg (pediatric), 10 and 15 mg (adult), 20 mg (adult); tablet, 2, 5, and 10 mg

DOSAGE:
Anxiety:
- *Adults:* Depending on severity, 2 to 10 mg PO bid to qid, or 2 to 10 mg IM or IV every 3 to 4 hr, as needed.

(cont.)

diazepam (*cont.*)

- *Children: 6 months and older:* 1 to 2.5 mg PO tid or qid, increase gradually, as needed and tolerated.
- *Elderly patients:* Initially, 2 to 2.5 mg once daily or bid; increase gradually.

Acute Alcohol Withdrawal:
- *Adults:* 10 mg PO tid or qid first 24 hr; reduce to 5 mg PO tid or qid, as needed. Or, initially, 10 mg IV or IM. Then, 5 to 10 mg IV or IM every 3 to 4 hr, as needed.

ADMINISTRATION:
- *PO:* When using oral solution, dilute dose just before giving.
- *IV:* The more reliable parenteral route; IM route is not recommended because absorption is variable and injection is painful.
  - Keep emergency resuscitation equipment and oxygen at bedside.
  - Avoid infusion sets or containers made from polyvinyl chloride.
  - If possible, inject directly into a large vein. If not, inject slowly through infusion tubing as near to the insertion site as possible. Give at no more than 5 mg/min. Watch closely for phlebitis at injection site.
  - Monitor respirations every 5 to 15 min and before each dose.
  - Do not store parenteral solution in plastic syringes.
  - *Incompatibilities:* All other IV drugs, most IV solutions.
- *IM:* Use the IM route if IV administration is impossible.
- *Rectal:* Use *Diastat* rectal gel to treat no more than five episodes per month and no more than one episode every 5 days, because tolerance may develop.

▶**Alert:** Only caregivers who can distinguish the distinct cluster of seizures or events from the patient's ordinary seizure activity, who have been instructed and can give the treatment competently, who understand which seizures may be treated with *Diastat*, and who can monitor the clinical response and recognize when immediate professional medical evaluation is needed should give *Diastat* rectal gel.

SIDE EFFECTS: Drowsiness, dysarthria, slurred speech, tremor, transient amnesia, fatigue, ataxia, headache, insomnia, paradoxical anxiety, hallucinations, minor changes in EEG patterns, pain, collapse, bradycardia, hypotension, diplopia, blurred vision, nystagmus, nausea, constipation, diarrhea with rectal form, incontinence, urine retention, neutropenia, jaundice, respiratory depression, apnea, skin rash, phlebitis at injection site, altered libido, physical or psychological dependence.

DRUG INTERACTIONS:
- Cimetidine, disulfiram, fluoxetine, fluvoxamine, hormonal contraceptives, isoniazid, metoprolol, propoxyphene, propranolol, valproic acid, CNS depressants, *Digoxin.*

- Avoid using diltiazem, fluconazole, itraconazole, ketoconazole, or miconazole, as these may increase and prolong diazepam level, CNS depression, and psychomotor impairment.
- Levodopa, phenobarbital, kava, alcohol use may cause additive CNS effects.
- Smoking may decrease effectiveness of drug.

PHARMACOKINETICS: A benzodiazepine that probably potentiates the effects of GABA, depresses the CNS, and suppresses the spread of seizure activity.
- Metabolized by CYP450 2C19, 3A4

Half-life: About 1–12 days

ROUTE	ONSET	PEAK	DURATION
PO	30 min	2 hr	20–80 hr
IV	1–5 min	1–5 min	15–60 min
IM	Unknown	2 hr	Unknown
PR	Unknown	90 min	Unknown

PRECAUTIONS:
- May increase liver function test values. May decrease neutrophil count.
- Contraindicated in patients hypersensitive to drug or soy protein; in patients experiencing shock, coma, or acute alcohol intoxication (parenteral form); in pregnant women, especially in first trimester; and in infants younger than age 6 months (oral form).
- *Diastat* rectal gel is contraindicated in patients with acute angle-closure glaucoma.
- Use cautiously in patients with liver or renal impairment, depression, or chronic open-angle glaucoma. Use cautiously in elderly and debilitated patients.
- Monitor periodic hepatic, renal, and hematopoietic function studies in patients receiving repeated or prolonged therapy.
- Monitor elderly patients for dizziness, ataxia, mental status changes. Patients are at an increased risk for falls.

▶**Alert:** Use of drug may lead to abuse and addiction. Do not withdraw drug abruptly after long-term use; withdrawal symptoms may occur.

PATIENT AND FAMILY EDUCATION:
- Avoid activities that require alertness and good coordination until effects of drug are known.
- Avoid alcohol while taking drug.
- Smoking may decrease drug's effectiveness.
- Do not abruptly stop drug because withdrawal symptoms may occur.
- Avoid use during pregnancy.
- Instruct caregiver on the proper use of *Diastat* rectal gel.

SPECIAL POPULATIONS:
- *Elderly:* Use with caution. May increase risk of falling. Due to sedation and increased risk of falls, all benzodiazepines are placed on beers list of potentially inappropriate medications for geriatrics.
- *Pregnancy:* Avoid use.
- *Children:* Use with caution. Adjust dose carefully.

Ativan   **lorazepam**

INDICATIONS: Anxiety disorders

AVAILABLE FORMS: Tablet, 0.5, 1, and 2 mg

DOSAGE:
- *Adults:* 2–3 mg/day PO/IM/IV divided bid-tid; 1–2 mg/day PO/IM/IV div bid-tid in elderly patients; maximum, 10 mg/day. Periodically assess the need for treatment and taper the dose gradually to discontinue if prolonged treatment is necessary. Treatment should be limited to as short a period as possible (less than 4 months) and/or undergo re-evaluation for continued use.
- *Children:* 0.05 mg/kg PO/IV q4–8h; maximum, 2 mg/dose. Periodically assess the need for treatment and taper the dose gradually to discontinue if prolonged treatment is necessary.

ADMINISTRATION:
- PO with a glass of water.
- Do not abruptly stop taking the medication.
- Use lowest effective dose for shortest duration.
- Lorazepam can be habit forming; do not increase dosage without guidance from the healthcare provider.

SIDE EFFECTS:
- *More common:* Drowsiness, lightheadedness, dry mouth, headache, changes in bowel habits, sialorrhea, amnesia, changes in appetite
- *Less common:* Syncope, tachycardia, seizures, respiratory depression, dependency, withdrawal syndrome, suicidal ideation

DRUG INTERACTIONS:
- *Absolute contraindications:* Clarithromycin, fluvoxamine, ketoconazole
- Avoid using calcium channel blockers, erthromycins, tamoxifen, zafirlukast

▶**Alert:** This list may not describe all possible interactions. Instruct clients to provide a list of all the medicines, herbs, nonprescription drugs, or dietary supplements they use. In addition, instruct clients to inform if they smoke, drink alcohol, or use illegal drugs.

PHARMACOKINETICS:
- Benzodiazepines enhance the activity of the GABA, a major central nervous system neurotransmitter, known to open CNS Cl⁻ channels, leading to an inhibition of subsequent CNS neuronal signaling.
- BZDs with similar action can differ in their potency and rate of absorption.

Metabolism: Liver with the CYP450; exact mechanism unknown

Excretion: Urine

Half-life: 14 hr

PRECAUTIONS:
- See client as often as necessary to ensure the drug is working on the panic attacks, determine compliance, and review side effects.
- Instruct client and family to watch for worsening depression or thoughts of suicide. Also watch out for sudden or severe changes in feelings such as feeling anxious, agitated, panicky, irritable, hostile, aggressive, impulsive, severely restless, overly excited and hyperactive, or not being able to sleep. If this happens, especially at the beginning of antidepressant treatment or after a change in dose, patients should call the provider.
- If feeling drowsy or dizzy, patient should not drive, use machinery, or do anything that needs mental alertness until the effects of this medicine are known.
- Caution patients not to stand or sit up quickly, especially if older. This reduces the risk of dizzy or fainting spells. Alcohol may interfere with the effect of this medicine. Avoid alcoholic drinks.
- Do not abruptly withdraw this drug as it may cause seizures.
- Use with caution on patients with:
  - Heart disease
  - Liver disease
  - Seizures (convulsions)
  - Suicidal thoughts, plans, or attempt by you or a family member
  - An unusual or allergic reaction to alprazolam, other medicines, foods, dyes, or preservatives

PATIENT AND FAMILY EDUCATION:
- Store lorazepam at room temperature away from moisture, heat, and light. Remove any cotton from the bottle of disintegrating tablets, and keep the bottle tightly closed.
- Lorazepam may be habit-forming and *should be used only by the person it was prescribed for.* Lorazepam should never be shared with another person, especially someone who has a history of drug abuse or addiction. Keep the medication in a secure place where others cannot get to it.
- Do not purchase lorazepam on the internet or outside of the United States as dangerous ingredients may be present.

SPECIAL POPULATIONS:
- *Elderly:* Older patients may be more sensitive to the effects of benzodiazepines. The smallest effective dose should be used. Dose adjustment is necessary for patients with liver impairment and/or renal disease due to excessive metabolites excreted by the kidney. Due to increased risk of sedation leading to falls and fractures, benzodiazepines are included on the Beers List of Potentially Inappropriate Medications for Geriatrics.
- *Pregnancy:* Category D; can cause teratogenic fetal effects. Infants born of mothers taking benzodiazepines may be at risk for withdrawal symptoms in the postnatal period.
- *Lactation:* Excreted in human breast milk; infants can become lethargic and lose weight
- *Children:* Not indicated for use with children under 18 years of age.

PARANOID PERSONALITY DISORDER: Benzodiazepines (BZDs)

clonazepam | *Klonopin*

INDICATIONS: Anxiety disorders

AVAILABLE FORMS: Tablet, 0.5, 1, and 2 mg; wafer melt, 0.125, 0.25, 0.5, and 1.2 mg

DOSAGE: *Adults:* Start at 0.25 mg PO bid, increase by 0.25–0.5 mg/day every 3 days; may start lower in elderly patients; maximum, 4 mg/day; treatment should be limited to as short a period as possible (less than 4 months) and/or undergo re-evaluation for continued use. To discontinue, taper by 0.25 mg/day q3 days if more than 4–6 wk continuous use

ADMINISTRATION:
- PO with a glass of water.
- Do not abruptly stop taking the medication.
- Use lowest effective dose for shortest duration.
- Clonazepam can be habit forming; do not increase dosage without guidance from the healthcare provider.

SIDE EFFECTS:
- *More common:* Drowsiness, lightheadedness, dry mouth, headache, changes in bowel habits, sialorrhea, amnesia, changes in appetite
- *Less common:* Syncope, tachycardia, seizures, respiratory depression, dependency, withdrawal syndrome, suicidal ideation

DRUG INTERACTIONS:
- *Absolute contraindications:* Clarithromycin, fluvoxamine, ketoconazole
- Avoid using calcium channel blockers, erthromycins, tamoxifen, zafirlukast

▶**Alert:** This list may not describe all possible interactions. Instruct clients to provide a list of all the medicines, herbs, nonprescription drugs, or dietary supplements they use. In addition, instruct client to inform them if they smoke, drink alcohol, or use illegal drugs.

PHARMACOKINETICS:
- Benzodiazepines enhance the activity of GABA, a major central nervous system neurotransmitter, known to open CNS Cl⁻ channels, leading to an inhibition of subsequent CNS neuronal signaling.
- BZDs with similar action can differ in their potency and rate of absorption.

Metabolism: Extensively metabolized in liver CYP450 3A4

Excretion: Urine

Half-life: 20–50 hr

PRECAUTIONS:
- See client as often as necessary to ensure the drug is working on the panic attacks, determine compliance, and review side effects.
- Instruct client and family to watch for worsening depression or thoughts of suicide. Also watch out for sudden or severe changes in feelings such as feeling anxious, agitated, panicky, irritable, hostile, aggressive, impulsive, severely restless, overly excited and hyperactive, or not being able to sleep. If this happens, especially at the beginning of antidepressant treatment or after a change in dose, patients should call the provider.
- If feeling drowsy or dizzy, the patient should not drive, use machinery, or do anything that needs mental alertness until the effects of this medicine are known.
- Caution patients not to stand or sit up quickly, especially if an older patient. This reduces the risk of dizzy or fainting spells. Alcohol may interfere with the effect of this medicine. Avoid alcoholic drinks.
- Do not abruptly withdraw this drug as it may cause seizures.
- Use with caution on patients with:
  - Heart disease
  - Liver disease
  - Seizures (convulsions)
  - Suicidal thoughts, plans, or attempts by patient or a family member
  - An unusual or allergic reaction to alprazolam, other medicines, foods, dyes, or preservatives

PATIENT AND FAMILY EDUCATION:
- Store clonazepam at room temperature away from moisture, heat, and light. Remove any cotton from the bottle of disintegrating tablets, and keep the bottle tightly closed.
- Clonazepam may be habit-forming and *should be used only by the person it was prescribed for.* Clonazepam should never be shared with another person, especially someone who has a history of drug abuse or addiction. Keep the medication in a secure place where others cannot get to it.

SPECIAL POPULATIONS:
- *Elderly:* Older patients may be more sensitive to the effects of benzodiazepines. The smallest effective dose should be used. Dose adjustment is necessary for patients with liver impairment and/or renal disease due to excessive metabolites excreted by the kidney. Due to increased risk of sedation leading to falls and fractures, benzodiazepines are included on the Beers List of Potentially Inappropriate Medications for Geriatrics.
- *Pregnancy:* Category D; can cause teratogenic fetal effects. Infants born of mothers taking benzodiazepines may be at risk for withdrawal symptoms in the postnatal period.
- *Lactation:* Excreted in human breast milk; infants can become lethargic and lose weight
- *Children:* Not indicated for use with children except for treatment of seizures.

Class: Antipsychotics, Typical (First Generation)

Haldol	**haloperidol**
Haldol Decanoate, Haloperidol LA	**haloperidol decanoate**
Haldol, Haldol Concentrate	**haloperidol lactate**

AVAILABLE FORMS: *Haloperidol:* Tablet, 0.5, 1, 2, 5, 10, and 20 mg. *Haloperidol decanoate:* Injection, 50 and 100 mg/mL. *Haloperidol lactate:* Injection, 5 mg/mL; oral concentrate, 2 mg/mL

DOSAGE:

Psychotic Disorders:

- *Adults and children older than 12 yr:* Dosage varies for each patient. Initially, 0.5 to 5 mg PO bid or tid, or 2 to 5 mg IM lactate every 4 to 8 hr, although hourly administration may be needed until control is obtained. Maximum, 100 mg PO daily.
- *Children, 3 to 12 who weigh 15 to 40 kg (33–88 lb):* Initially, 0.5 mg PO daily divided bid or tid. May increase dose by 0.5 mg at 5- to 7-day intervals depending on therapeutic response and patient tolerance. Maintenance dose: 0.05 mg/kg to 0.15 mg/kg PO daily given in two or three divided doses. Severely disturbed children may need higher doses.

Chronic Psychosis Requiring Prolonged Therapy:

- *Adults:* 50 to 100 mg IM decanoate every 4 wk.

Nonpsychotic Behavior Disorders:

- *Children aged 3 to 12:* 0.05 to 0.075 mg/kg PO daily, in two or three divided doses. Maximum, 6 mg daily.

ADMINISTRATION:

- *PO:* Protect drug from light. Slight yellowing of concentrate is common and does not affect potency. Discard very discolored solutions. Dilute oral dose with water or a beverage such as orange juice, apple juice, tomato juice, or cola immediately before administration.
- *IV:* Only the lactate form can be given IV. Monitor patient receiving single doses higher than 50 mg or total daily doses greater than 500 mg closely for prolonged QTc interval and torsades de pointes. Store at controlled room temperature and protect from light.
- *Incompatibilities:* Allopurinol, amphotericin B cholesteryl sulfate complex, benztropine, cefepime, diphenhydramine, fluconazole, foscarnet, heparin, hydromorphone, hydroxyzine, ketorolac, morphine, nitroprusside sodium, piperacillin and tazobactam sodium, sargramostim.
- *IM:* Protect drug from light. Slight yellowing of injection is common and does not affect potency. Discard very discolored solutions.
- When switching from tablets to decanoate injection, give 10 to 15 times the oral dose once a month (maximum 100 mg).

▶**Alert:** Do not give decanoate form IV.

PHARMACOKINETICS: A butyrophenone that probably exerts antipsychotic effects by blocking postsynaptic dopamine receptors in the brain.

SIDE EFFECTS: Severe extrapyramidal reactions, tardive dyskinesia, NMS, seizures, sedation, drowsiness, lethargy, headache, insomnia, confusion, vertigo, tachycardia, hypotension, hypertension, ECG change, torsades de pointes, with IV use blurred vision, dry mouth, anorexia, constipation, diarrhea, nausea, vomiting, dyspepsia, urine retention, menstrual irregularities, priapism, leucopenia, leukocytosis, jaundice, rash, other skin reactions, diaphoresis, gynecomastia

DRUG INTERACTIONS:

- Anticholinergics, azole antifungals, buspirone, macrolides, carbamazepine, CNS depressants, lithium, methyldopa, rifampin.
- Alcohol use may increase CNS depression. Discourage use together.

PRECAUTIONS:

- May increase liver function test values. May increase or decrease WBC count.
- Contraindicated in patients hypersensitive to drug and in those with parkinsonism, coma, or CNS depression.
- Use cautiously in elderly and debilitated patients; in patients with history of seizures or EEG abnormalities, severe CV disorders, allergies, glaucoma, or urine retention; and in those taking anticonvulsants, anticoagulants, antiparkinsons, or lithium.
- Monitor patient for tardive dyskinesia, which may occur after prolonged use. It may not appear until months or years later and may disappear spontaneously or persist for life, despite ending drug.

▶**Alert:** Watch for signs and symptoms of NMS (extrapyramidal effects, hyperthermia, autonomic disturbance), which is rare but commonly fatal. Do not withdraw drug abruptly unless required by severe adverse reactions.

▶**Alert:** Haldol may contain tartrazine.

▶*Look alike–sound alike:* Do not confuse *Haldol* with *Halcion* or *Halog*.

PATIENT AND FAMILY EDUCATION:

- Avoid activities that require alertness and good coordination until effects of drug are known. Drowsiness and dizziness usually subside after a few weeks.
- Avoid alcohol during therapy.
- To relieve dry mouth, use sugarless gum or hard candy.

SPECIAL POPULATIONS:

- *Elderly:* Caution is advised when using this drug in the elderly due to more sensitivity to the drug.
- *Pregnancy:* Not recommended for use. Effects inconclusive
- *Children:* Caution when using this drug in a child or adolescent; must balance the potential risks with the clinical need. Caution is advised when using this drug in children because they may be more sensitive to the side effects of the drug, especially loss of appetite and weight loss. It is important to monitor weight and growth in children who are taking this drug.

Class: Antipsychotics, Atypical (Second Generation)

risperidone   *Risperdal, Risperdal Consta, Risperdal M-Tab*

AVAILABLE FORMS: Injection, 12.5, 25, 37.5, and 50 mg; solution, 1 mg/mL; tablet, 0.25, 0.5, 1, 2, 3, and 4 mg; tablet (orally disintegrating), 0.5, 1, 2, 3, and 4 mg

DOSAGE:
Schizophrenia:
- *Adults:* Drug may be given once or twice daily. Initial dosing is generally 2 mg/day. Increase dosage at intervals not less than 24 hr, in increments of 1 to 2 mg/day, as tolerated, to a recommended dose of 4 to 8 mg/day. Periodically reassess to determine the need for maintenance treatment with an appropriate dose.
- *Adolescents: 13 to 17 yr:* Start treatment with 0.5 mg once daily, given as a single daily dose in either the morning or evening. Adjust dose, if indicated, at intervals not less than 24 hr, in increments of 0.5 or 1 mg/day, as tolerated, to a recommended dose of 3 mg/day. There are no data to support use beyond 8 wk.

Irritability, Including Aggression, Self-Injury, and Temper Tantrums, Associated With an Autistic Disorder:
- *Children 5 yr and older who weigh 20 kg (44 lb) or more:* Initially, 0.5 mg PO once daily or divided bid. After 4 days, increase dose to 1 mg. Increase dosage further in 0.5 mg increments at intervals of at least 2 wk.
- *Children: 5 yr and older who weigh less than 20 kg:* Initially, 0.25 mg PO once daily or divided bid. After 4 days, increase dose to 0.5 mg. Increase dosage further in 0.25 mg increments at intervals of at least 2 wk. Increase cautiously in children who weigh less than 15 kg (33 lb).

ADMINISTRATION:
PO:
- Give drug with or without food.
- Open package for ODTs immediately before giving by peeling off foil backing with dry hands. Do not push tablets through the foil.
- Phenylalanine contents of ODTs are as follows: 0.5 mg tablet contains 0.14 mg phenylalanine; 1 mg tablet contains 0.28 mg phenylalanine; 2 mg tablet contains 0.56 mg phenylalanine; 3 mg tablet contains 0.63 mg phenylalanine; 4 mg tablet contains 0.84 mg phenylalanine.

IM:
- Continue oral therapy for the first 3 wk of IM injection therapy until injections take effect, then stop oral therapy.
- To reconstitute IM injection, inject premeasured diluent into vial and shake vigorously for at least 10 sec. Suspension appears uniform, thick, and milky; particles are visible, but no dry particles remain. Use drug immediately or refrigerate for up to 6 hr after reconstitution. If more than 2 min pass before injection, shake vigorously again. See manufacturer's package insert for more detailed instructions.

- Refrigerate IM injection kit and protect it from light. Drug can be stored at temperature less than 77° F (25° C) for no more than 7 days before administration.

SIDE EFFECTS:
- Akathisia, somnolence, dystonia, headache, insomnia, agitation, anxiety, pain, parkinsonism, NMS, suicide attempt, dizziness, fever, hallucination, mania, impaired concentration, abnormal thinking and dreaming, tremor, hypoesthesia, fatigue, depression, nervousness, tachycardia, chest pain, orthostatic hypotension, peripheral edema, syncope, hypertension, rhinitis, sinusitis, pharyngitis, ear disorder
- Constipation, nausea, vomiting, dyspepsia, abdominal pain, anorexia, dry mouth, increased saliva, diarrhea.
- Urinary incontinence, increased urination, abnormal orgasm, vaginal dryness, weight gain, hyperglycemia, weight loss.
- Arthralgia, back pain, leg pain, myalgia.
- Coughing, dyspnea, upper respiratory infection.
- Rash, dry skin, photosensitivity reactions, acne, injection site pain
- Tooth disorder, toothache, injury, decreased libido

DRUG INTERACTIONS: Antihypertensives, carbamazepine, clozapine, CNS depressants, dopamine agonists, levodopa, fluoxetine, paroxetine. Alcohol use may cause CNS depression.

PHARMACOKINETICS:
- Blocks dopamine and 5-HT$_2$ receptors in the brain.
- Onset and duration of action with oral dose is unknown
- IM onset of action is 3 wk with peak action at 4 to 6 wk; duration of action at 7 wk.

Peak action: 1 hr
Half-life: 3–20 hr

PRECAUTIONS:
- May increase prolactin level. May decrease hemoglobin level and hematocrit.
- *Sun exposure may increase risk of photosensitivity reactions.*
- Contraindicated in patients hypersensitive to drug and in breastfeeding women.
- Use cautiously in patients with prolonged QT interval, cerebrovascular disease, dehydration, hypovolemia, history of seizures, or conditions that could affect metabolism or hemodynamic responses.
- Use cautiously in patients exposed to extreme heat.
- Use caution in patients at risk for aspiration pneumonia.
- Use IM injection cautiously in those with hepatic or renal impairment.
- Periodically reevaluate drug's risks and benefits, especially during prolonged use.

(cont.)

risperidone (cont.)

- Monitor patient for weight gain.
▶ **Alert:** Obtain baseline BP measurements before starting therapy, and monitor pressure regularly. Watch for orthostatic hypotension, especially during first dosage adjustment.
▶ **Alert:** Fatal cerebrovascular adverse events (stroke, transient ischemic attacks) may occur in elderly patients with dementia. Drug is not safe or effective in these patients.
▶ **Alert:** Monitor patient for tardive dyskinesia, which may occur after prolonged use. It may not appear until months or years later and may disappear spontaneously or persist for life, despite stopping drug.
▶ **Alert:** Watch for evidence of NMS (extrapyramidal effects, hyperthermia, autonomic disturbance), which is rare but can be fatal.
▶ **Alert:** Life-threatening hyperglycemia may occur in patients taking atypical antipsychotics. Monitor patients with diabetes regularly.
▶ **Alert:** Monitor patient for symptoms of metabolic syndrome (significant weight gain and increased BMI, hypertension, hyperglycemia, hypercholesterolemia, and hypertriglyceridemia).

PATIENT AND FAMILY EDUCATION:
- Avoid activities that require alertness until effects of drug are known.
- Rise slowly, avoid hot showers, and use other precautions to avoid fainting when starting therapy.
- Use caution in hot weather to prevent heatstroke.
- Take drug with or without food.
- Keep the ODT in the blister pack until just before taking it. After opening the pack, dissolve the tablet on tongue without cutting or chewing. Use dry hands to peel apart the foil to expose the tablet; do not attempt to push it through the foil.
- Use sunblock and wear protective clothing outdoors.
- Avoid alcohol during therapy.

SPECIAL POPULATIONS:
- *Pregnancy/Lactation:* Advise women not to become pregnant or to breastfeed for 12 wk after the last IM injection.

Zyprexa, Zydis   **olanzapine**

INDICATIONS: Schizophrenia

AVAILABLE FORMS: Injection, 10 mg; tablet, 2.5, 5, 7.5, 10, 15, and 20 mg; tablet (orally disintegrating), 5, 10, 15, and 20 mg

DOSAGE: *Adults:* Initially, 5 to 10 mg PO once daily with the goal 10 mg daily within several days of starting therapy. Adjust dose in 5 mg increments at intervals of 1 wk or more. Most patients respond to 10 to 15 mg daily. Safety of dosages greater than 20 mg daily has not been established.

ADMINISTRATION:
PO:
- Give drug with or without food.
- Do not crush or break ODT.
- Place immediately on patient's tongue after opening package.
- ODT may be given without water.
IM:
- Inspect IM solution for particulate matter and discoloration before administration.
- To reconstitute IM injection, dissolve contents of one vial with 2.1 mL of sterile water for injection to yield a clear yellow 5 mg/mL solution. Store at room temperature and give within 1 hr of reconstitution. Discard any unused solution.

SIDE EFFECTS:
- Somnolence, insomnia, parkinsonism, dizziness, NMS, suicide attempt, abnormal gait, asthenia, personality disorder, akathisia, tremor, articulation impairment, tardive dyskinesia, fever, extrapyramidal events
- Orthostatic hypotension, tachycardia, chest pain, hypertension, ecchymosis, peripheral edema, hypotension
- Amblyopia, rhinitis, pharyngitis, conjunctivitis
- Constipation, dry mouth, dyspepsia, increased appetite, increased salivation, vomiting, thirst
- Hematuria, metrorrhagia, urinary incontinence, UTI, amenorrhea, vaginitis
- Leucopenia
- Hyperglycemia, weight gain
- Joint pain, extremity pain, back pain, neck rigidity, twitching, hypertonia
- Increased cough, dyspnea
- Sweating, injection site pain
- Flu-like syndrome, injury

DRUG INTERACTIONS:
- Antihypertensives, carbamazepine, omeprazole, rifampin, ciprofloxacin, diazepam, dopamine agonists, levodopa, fluoxetine, fluvoxamine, St. John's wort.
- Alcohol use may increase CNS effects. Smoking may increase drug clearance.

PHARMACOKINETICS:
- May block dopamine and $5-HT_2$ receptors. Oral onset of action and duration of action are unknown. Peak action occurs in 6 hr.
- IM onset of action is rapid with duration unknown. Peak action occurs at 15 to 45 min.
Half-life: 21–54 hr

PRECAUTIONS:
- May increase AST, ALT, GGT, CK, triglyceride, and prolactin levels.
- May increase eosinophil count; may decrease WBC count.
- Contraindicated in patients hypersensitive to drug.
- Use cautiously in patients with heart disease, cerebrovascular disease, conditions that

(cont.)

PARANOID PERSONALITY DISORDER: Antipsychotics, Atypical (Second Generation)

olanzapine (cont.)

predispose patient to hypotension, history of seizures or conditions that might lower the seizure threshold, and hepatic impairment.
- Use cautiously in elderly patients, those with a history of paralytic ileus, and those at risk for aspiration pneumonia, prostatic hyperplasia, or angle-closure glaucoma.
- ODTs contain phenylalanine.
- Monitor patient for abnormal body temperature regulation, especially if patient exercises, is exposed to extreme heat, takes anticholinergics, or is dehydrated.
- Obtain baseline and periodic liver function test results.
- Monitor patient for weight gain.
- Monitor patient for tardive dyskinesia, which may occur after prolonged use. It may not appear until months or years later and may disappear spontaneously or persist for life, despite stopping drug.
- Periodically reevaluate the long-term usefulness of olanzapine.
- Drug may increase risk of stroke and death in elderly patients with dementia. Not approved to treat patients with dementia-related psychosis.
- Patient who feel dizzy or drowsy after an IM injection should remain recumbent until assessment for orthostatic hypotension and bradycardia. Patient should rest until the feeling passes.
▶ **Alert:** Drug may increase the risk of suicidal thinking and behavior in young adults aged 18 to 24 during the first 2 months of treatment.
▶ **Alert:** Watch for evidence of NMS (hyperpyrexia, muscle rigidity, altered mental status, autonomic instability), which is rare but commonly fatal. Stop drug immediately; monitor and treat patient as needed.

▶ **Alert:** Drug may cause hyperglycemia. Monitor patients with diabetes regularly. In patients with risk factors for diabetes, obtain fasting blood glucose test results at baseline and periodically.
▶ **Alert:** Monitor patient for symptoms of metabolic syndrome (significant weight gain and increased BMI, hypertension, hyperglycemia, hypercholesterolemia, and hypertriglyceridemia).

PATIENT AND FAMILY EDUCATION:
- Avoid hazardous tasks until full effects of drug are known.
- Warn patients against exposure to extreme heat; drug may impair body's ability to reduce temperature.
- May gain weight.
- Avoid alcohol.
- Rise slowly to avoid dizziness upon standing up quickly.
- ODTs contain phenylalanine.
- To peel foil away from ODT and not to push tablet through. Take tablet immediately, allowing tablet to dissolve on tongue and be swallowed with saliva; no additional fluid is needed.
- Take drug with or without food.
- If women of childbearing age, to notify prescriber if becomes pregnant or plans or suspects pregnancy. Tell patient not to breastfeed during therapy.

SPECIAL POPULATIONS:
- *Elderly:* Caution is advised when using this drug in the elderly because they may be more sensitive to the effects of the drug, especially drowsiness, difficulty urinating, and heart problems.
- *Pregnancy:* This medication should be used only when clearly needed during pregnancy.
- *Lactation:* Do not breastfeed during therapy.
- *Children:* Not approved for use in children and adolescents.

quetiapine   *Seroquel*

AVAILABLE FORMS: Tablet, 25, 50, 100, 200, 300, and 400 mg; extended-release formulation, 200, 300, and 400 mg

DOSAGE:
- Immediate-release tablet: 2 or 3 times daily; extended-release tablets; once daily.
- Dose usually increased slowly over several days or weeks to achieve desired effect.
Bipolar Disorder:
- Initial dose, 50 mg twice daily (100 mg/day). Dose can be increased by 100 mg/day to a daily dose of 400 mg/day. Most patients respond to 400 to 800 mg/day.
- Doses greater than 800 mg/day have not been studied.
Schizophrenia:
- Initial dose, 25 mg twice daily (50 mg/day). Dose can be increased by 25 to 50 mg two or

three times daily. Target dose is 300 to 400 mg/day in two or three doses.
- Patients respond to 150 to 750 mg/day; doses greater than 800 mg/day have not been evaluated.

ADMINISTRATION:
- Avoid eating grapefruit or drinking grapefruit juice while being treated with this medication.
- Can be taken with or without food.

SIDE EFFECTS:
- Constipation, drowsiness, dizziness, stomach pain or upset, weight gain or dry mouth
- Fainting, unusually fast or irregular heartbeat
- Skin rash, itching, trouble breathing
- Fever, persistent sore throat, muscle stiffness, confusion, sweating, uncontrolled muscle movements (e.g., tongue or facial muscles), one-sided muscle weakness, cold sensitivity, trouble urinating, black stools, unusual moods

(cont.)

quetiapine (*cont.*)

- May infrequently make blood sugar level rise, therefore causing or worsening diabetes. This high blood sugar can rarely cause serious (sometimes fatal) conditions such as diabetic coma.
- May also cause significant weight gain and rise in blood cholesterol (or triglyceride) levels. These effects, along with diabetes, may increase risk for developing heart disease.

DRUG INTERACTIONS:
- Used with caution in combination with other centrally acting drugs.
- Caution should be exercised when quetiapine is used concomitantly with drugs known to cause electrolyte imbalance or to increase QT interval.

PHARMACOKINETICS:
- Bioavailability is unknown.
- Food has minimal effects on quetiapine absorption.
- The drug is approximately 83% bound to serum proteins.
- Single and multiple dose studies have demonstrated linear pharmacokinetics in the clinical dose range (up to 375 mg twice daily).
- The drug is eliminated with a mean terminal half-life of approximately 7 hr. The primary route of elimination is through hepatic metabolism.

PRECAUTIONS:
- Black box warning about the use of *Seroquel* in elderly people with psychosis or dementia.
- Elderly people with dementia (Alzheimer's disease is the most common form) who are treated with antipsychotics—including *Seroquel*—are more likely to die of various causes than those who were not treated with those medications.
- *Seroquel* is not approved to treat dementia or dementia-related psychosis, and caution should be used before giving the medication to elderly people with this condition.
- FDA has required the drug to carry the special antidepressant and suicide warning, since it is used to treat bipolar depression.
- Antidepressants may increase the risk of suicidal thinking or behavior in people taking it.

PATIENT AND FAMILY EDUCATION:
- Take this medication by mouth with or without food, usually 2 or 3 times daily or as directed by provider.

- Dosage is based on medical condition and response to therapy. Provider will start with a low dose and gradually increase the dose to reduce the dizziness and lightheadedness that may occur.
- It may take several weeks to notice the full benefit of this drug.
- Use this medication regularly in order to get the most benefit from it.
- Take medication at the same time each day.
- It is important to take this medication exactly as prescribed, even if condition improves.
- Do not stop taking this medication without first consulting provider. Some conditions may become worse when the drug is suddenly stopped.
- May cause withdrawal reactions, especially if it has been used regularly for a long time or in high doses.
- Avoid eating grapefruit or drinking grapefruit juice while on this medication.
- May increase blood sugar levels and worsen diabetes.
- Take precautions to avoid the risk of heat stroke.

SPECIAL POPULATIONS:
- *Elderly*
  - Higher incidence of concomitant illness and concomitant medication in this population, *Seroquel* should be used with caution.
  - The mean plasma clearance of *Seroquel* was reduced by 30% to 50% in elderly subjects when compared to younger patients. The rate of dose titration may thus need to be slower, and the daily therapeutic target dose lower than that used in younger patients.
  - Quetiapine is extensively metabolized by the liver and should be used with caution in patients with mild hepatic impairment, especially during the initial dosing period.
  - Patients with mild hepatic impairment should be started on 25 mg/day. The dose should be increased daily in increments of 25 to 50 mg/day to an effective dose.
- *Pregnancy*: This medication should be used only when clearly needed during pregnancy.
- *Lactation*: It is not known whether this drug passes into breast milk. Because of the possible risk to the infant, breastfeeding while using this drug is not recommended.
- *Children*: Not recommended for children.

Geodon   **ziprasidone**

AVAILABLE FORMS: Capsule, 20 mg (blue/white), 40 mg (blue/blue), 60 mg (white/white), and 80 mg (blue/white)
DOSAGE:
Schizophrenia:
- Start, 20 mg PO bid; maximum, 80 mg bid; give with food; may adjust dose every 2 days prn; doses greater than 40 mg/day rarely more effective;

periodically reassess need for treatment; discontinue if ANC less than 1,000; consider discontinue if unexplained decrease in WBC.
Bipolar Disorder, Manic/Mixed:
- Monotherapy: dose, 40 to 80 mg PO bid; start, 40 mg PO bid ×1 day, then 60 to 80 mg PO bid; maximum, 80 mg bid; for acute treatment, give with food; may adjust dose every 2 days prn; discontinue if ANC
(cont.)

ziprasidone *(cont.)*

less than 1,000; consider discontinuing if unexplained decrease in WBC. Valproate or lithium adjunct: Dose, 40 to 80 mg PO bid; for maintenance treatment, give with food; continue treatment at same dose at which patient initially stabilized; periodically reassess need for treatment; discontinue if ANC less than 1,000; consider discontinuing if unexplained decrease in WBC.

Agitation, Schizophrenia-Associated:
- 10 mg IM every 2 hr prn. Alternative, 20 mg IM every 4 hr prn; maximum, 40 mg/day ×3 days; switch to PO ASAP; discontinue if ANC less than 1,000; consider discontinuing if unexplained decrease in WBC.

Other:
Renal dosing: No adjustment.
- *Renal impairment*: Caution advised with IM use
Hepatic dosing: No adjustment.
- *Pediatric dosing:* Not applicable for this medication.

ADMINISTRATION:
- Administered at an initial daily dose of 20 mg twice daily with food.
- Daily dosage may subsequently be adjusted on the basis of individual clinical status up to 80 mg twice daily.
- Dosage adjustments, if indicated, should generally occur at intervals of not less than 2 days, as steady state is achieved within 1 to 3 days. In order to ensure use of the lowest effective dose, patients should be observed for improvement for several weeks before upward dosage adjustment.

SIDE EFFECTS:
- *Cardiac:* Tachycardia, torsade de pointes (in the presence of multiple confounding factors)
- *Digestive system:* Swollen tongue
- *Reproductive system and breast disorders:* Galactorrhea, priapism
- *Nervous system:* Facial droop, NMS, serotonin syndrome (alone or in combination with serotonergic medicinal products), tardive dyskinesia
- *Psychiatric:* Insomnia, mania/hypomania
- *Skin and subcutaneous tissue:* Allergic reaction (such as allergic dermatitis, angioedema, orofacial edema, urticaria), rash
- *Urogenital system:* Enuresis, urinary incontinence
- *Vascular:* Postural hypotension, syncope

DRUG INTERACTIONS:
- Other drugs besides ziprasidone, that may affect the heart rhythm (QTc prolongation in the EKG), include dofetilide, pimozide, quinidine, sotalol, procainamide, and sparfloxacin among others.
- QTc prolongation can infrequently result in serious, rarely fatal, irregular heartbeats. Anti-Parkinson drugs (e.g., pramipexole, ropinirole), azole antifungals (e.g., ketoconazole, itraconazole), certain blood pressure medications (e.g., beta-blockers such as metoprolol or propranolol, diuretics such as furosemide or hydrochlorothiazide, or alpha-blockers such as doxazosin or prazosin) may interact.

- Drugs that cause drowsiness, including antianxiety drugs (e.g., diazepam), antihistamines that cause drowsiness (e.g., diphenhydramine), antiseizure drugs (e.g., carbamazepine), medicine for sleep (e.g., sedatives), muscle relaxants, narcotic pain relievers (e.g., codeine), other psychiatric medicines (e.g., phenothiazines such as chlorpromazine, or tricyclics such as amitriptyline), tranquilizers.

PHARMACOKINETICS:
- A selective monoaminergic antagonist with high affinity for the serotonin Type 2 (5-HT$_2$), dopamine Type 2 (D2), 1 and 2 adrenergic, and H1 histaminergic receptors.
- Acts as an antagonist at other receptors, but with lower potency.
- Antagonism at receptors other than dopamine and 5-HT$_2$ with similar receptor affinities may explain some of the other therapeutic and side effects of *Geodon*.
- Antagonism of muscarinic M1-5 receptors may explain its anticholinergic effects.
- Antagonism of histamine H1 receptors may explain the somnolence observed with this drug. *Geodon*'s antagonism of adrenergic alpha-1 receptors may explain the orthostatic hypotension observed with this drug.
- Functions as an antagonist at the dopamine D2, 5-HT$_{2A}$, and 5-HT$_{1D}$ receptors, and as an agonist at the 5-HT$_{1A}$ receptor.
- Inhibits synaptic reuptake of serotonin and norepinephrine.

PRECAUTIONS: Monitor patient closely and check potassium levels regularly. Patient should report fainting; dizziness; fast, racing, pounding, or irregular heartbeat; hyperglycemia, especially blurred vision; drowsiness; dry mouth; flushed, dry skin; fruit-like breath odor; increased urination; ketones in urine; loss of appetite; stomachache; nausea or vomiting; tiredness; trouble breathing; unconsciousness; or unusual thirst. Do not use in treatment of dementia-related psychosis.

PATIENT AND FAMILY EDUCATION:
- May cause some people to become drowsy, dizzy, or less alert than they are normally.
- Avoid driving, using machines, or other activities that could be dangerous if are dizzy or are not alert. Avoid use of alcohol.
- Avoid activities involving high temperature or humidity. This medicine may reduce the body's ability to adjust to the heat.

SPECIAL POPULATIONS:
- *Elderly:* Patients with dementia-related psychosis treated with antipsychotic drugs are at an increased risk of death. *Geodon* is not approved for the treatment of dementia-related psychosis.
- *Pregnancy/Lactation:* Safe use in pregnancy and breastfeeding have not been established.
- *Children:* Safe use in pediatric patients has not been established.

Schizoid Personality Disorder

OVERVIEW

- Characterized by a pervasive pattern of detachment from social relationships and a restricted range of emotional expression in interpersonal settings.
- Occurs in 0.5% to 7% of the general populations; occurs more often in males than in females.
- Support for the heritability of this disorder exists.
- Patients avoid treatment; display a constricted affect and little emotion; are aloof and indifferent, reporting no leisure or pleasurable activities; and do not appear troubled by their lack of emotion.
- May have a rich fantasy life, though this is not usually shared with others.
- Accomplished intellectually; may spend hours on the computer, working puzzles, or solving math equations.
- May be indecisive and lack future goals or direction.
- May reside with parent(s) until late in life.

Acute Treatment

Medication is usually not an issue for someone who suffers from this disorder, unless they also have an additional Axis I disorder, such as major depression. Most patients show no additional improvement with the addition of an antidepressant medication unless they are also suffering from suicidal ideation or a major depressive episode. Low dose of an antipsychotic may be appropriate if irritability or aggressive behavior develops.

Chronic Treatment

Long-term treatment of this disorder with medication should be avoided; medication should be prescribed only for acute symptom relief. In addition, prescription of medication may interfere with the effectiveness of certain psychotherapeutic approaches. Consideration of this effect should be taken into account when arriving at a treatment recommendation.

CLASS	DRUG
Selective Serotonin Reuptake Inhibitors (SSRIs)	**First-Line Drug Therapy***
	sertraline (*Zoloft*)
	paroxetine (*Paxil, Paxil CR*)
	fluoxetine (*Prozac, Prozac Weekly, Sarafem*)
	escitalopram (*Lexapro*)
Antipsychotics, Atypical (Second Generation)	
	risperidone (*Risperdal, Risperdal Consta, Risperdal M-Tab*)
	olanzapine (*Zyprexa, Zydis*)
	quetiapine (*Seroquel*)
	ziprasidone (*Geodon*)

Because of overdose risk, TCAs and MAOIs are usually not prescribed.

Class: Selective Serotonin Reuptake Inhibitors (SSRIs)

Zoloft | **sertraline**

AVAILABLE FORMS: Tablet, 25, 50, and 100 mg; oral concentrate, 20 mg/mL

DOSAGE: 25 to 200 mg once daily. *Depression, OCD, panic disorder, PTSD, and social anxiety disorder:* Initiated at 25 to 50 mg once daily. *PMDD:* 50 to 150 mg every day of the menstrual cycle or for 14 days before menstruation.

ADMINISTRATION: Usually once daily with or without food; take dosage at the same time each day, either in the morning or in the evening; dosage is based on response to therapy; continue taking this medication as prescribed even if patient feels well. Do not stop taking medication without consulting provider. It may take up to 4 wk before the full benefit of this drug takes effect.

SIDE EFFECTS: Sleepiness, nervousness, insomnia, dizziness, nausea, tremor, skin rash, upset stomach, loss of appetite, headache, diarrhea, abnormal ejaculation, dry mouth and weight loss, irregular heartbeats, allergic reactions, and activation of mania in patients with bipolar disorder

DRUG INTERACTIONS:
- Hyperthermia, fluctuations in blood pressure, and rigidity of muscles may occur when SSRIs are used in combination with MAOIs. SSRIs should not be used in combination with MAOIs.
- SSRIs and MAOIs should not be used within 14 days of each other.

(cont.)

sertraline (cont.)

- Cimetidine (*Tagamet*) may increase the levels in blood of sertraline by decreased excretion of the drug by the liver.
- Increases the blood level of pimozide (*Orap*) by 40%.
- Avoid use with pimozide for it may cause cardiac arrhythmias.
- Drug may increase the blood thinning action of warfarin (*Coumadin*).
- Monitor warfarin when sertraline is started or stopped.

PHARMACOKINETICS:
- Store at room temperature between 15° and 30°C (59° to 86°F).
- Mean peak plasma concentrations of sertraline occurs between 4.5 and 8.4 hr post-dosing.
- The average terminal elimination half-life of plasma sertraline is about 26 hr.
- Based on this pharmacokinetic parameter, steady state sertraline plasma levels should be achieved after approximately 1 wk of once-daily dosing.
- The single dose bioavailability of sertraline tablets is approximately equal to an equivalent dose of solution.
- For the tablet, drug effects were enhanced when administered with food, while the time to reach peak plasma concentration decreased from 8 hr post-dosing to 5.5 hr.

PRECAUTIONS:
- Antidepressants increased the risk of suicidal thinking and behavior (suicidality) in short-term studies in children and adolescents with depression and other psychiatric disorders.
- The use of sertraline or any other antidepressant in a child or adolescent must balance risk with the clinical need for the antidepressant.
- Patients who are started on therapy should be closely observed for clinical worsening, suicidal thoughts, or unusual changes in behavior.
- Do not discontinue drug abruptly; some patients experience symptoms such as abdominal cramps, flu-like symptoms, fatigue, and memory impairment; gradually reduce the dose when therapy is discontinued.

PATIENT AND FAMILY EDUCATION:
- Advise patients to be alert to the emergence of anxiety, agitation, panic attacks, insomnia, irritability, hostility, aggressiveness, impulsivity, akathisia (psychomotor restlessness), hypomania, mania, other unusual changes in behavior, worsening of depression, and suicidal ideation, especially early during antidepressant treatment and when the dose is adjusted up or down.
- Caution about risk of serotonin syndrome with the concomitant use of SNRIs and SSRIs, including *Zoloft*, and triptans, tramadol, or other serotonergic agents.
- Until they learn how they respond to the drug, patients should be careful doing activities when they need to be alert, such as driving a car or operating machinery.
- Caution about concomitant use of *Zoloft* and NSAIDs, aspirin, warfarin, or other drugs that affect coagulation since these agents have been associated with an increased risk of bleeding.
- Advise against the concomitant use of *Zoloft* and alcohol.
- Initiate the use of any OTC product cautiously. Check with health care provider before using any OTC medicines.
- Notify health care provider if become pregnant or intend to become pregnant during therapy.
- Notify physician if breastfeeding.

SPECIAL POPULATIONS:
- *Elderly:* Caution is advised when using this drug in the elderly due to more sensitivity to the drug. The elderly are more susceptible to electrolyte imbalance especially if they are also taking "water pills" or diuretics with this medication.
- *Pregnancy:* Avoid using this drug during the third trimester for it leads to adverse effects in the newborn. This medication should only be used when clearly needed during pregnancy.
- *Lactation:* Secreted into breast milk.
- *Children:* Caution when using this drug in a child or adolescent; must balance the potential risks with the clinical need.

▶**Alert:** Antidepressants increased the risk of suicidal thinking and behavior (suicidality) in short-term studies in children and adolescents with depression and other psychiatric disorders. Caution is advised when using this drug in children because they may be more sensitive to the side effects of the drug, especially loss of appetite and weight loss. It is important to monitor weight and growth in children who are taking this drug.

paroxetine   *Paxil, Paxil CR*

AVAILABLE FORMS: Suspension, 10 mg/5 mL; tablet, 10, 20, 30, and 40 mg; tablet (controlled-release), 12.5, 25, and 37.5 mg

DOSAGE:
Depression:
- *Adults:* Initially, 20 mg PO daily, preferably in morning, as indicated. If patient does not improve, increase dose by 10 mg daily at intervals of at least 1 wk to a maximum of 50 mg daily. If using controlled-release form, initially 25 mg PO daily. Increase dose by 12.5 mg daily at weekly intervals to a maximum of 62.5 mg daily.
- *Elderly:* Initially, 10 mg PO daily, preferably in morning, as indicated. If patient does not

(cont.)

paroxetine (cont.)

improve, increase dose by 10 mg daily at weekly intervals to a maximum of 40 mg daily. If using controlled-release form, start therapy at 12.5 mg PO daily. Do not exceed 50 mg daily.

OCD:
- *Adults:* Initially, 20 mg PO daily, preferably in morning. Increase dose by 10 mg daily at weekly intervals. Recommended daily dose is 40 mg. Maximum daily dose is 60 mg.

Panic Disorder:
- *Adults:* Initially, 10 mg PO daily. Increase dose by 10 mg at no less than weekly intervals to maximum of 60 mg daily, or 12.5 mg *Paxil CR* PO as a single daily dose, usually in the morning, with or without food; increase dose at intervals of at least 1 wk by 12.5 mg daily, up to a maximum of 75 mg daily. Adjust-a-dose: In elderly or debilitated patients and in those with severe renal or hepatic impairment, the first dose of *Paxil CR* is 12.5 mg daily; increase if indicated. Dosage should not exceed 50 mg daily.

Social Anxiety Disorder:
- *Adults:* Initially, 20 mg PO daily, preferably in morning. Dosage range is 20 to 60 mg daily. Adjust dosage to maintain patient on lowest effective dose. Or, 12.5 mg *Paxil CR* PO as a single daily dose, usually in the morning, with or without food. Increase dosage at weekly intervals in increments of 12.5 mg daily, up to a maximum of 37.5 mg daily.

Generalized Anxiety Disorder:
- *Adults:* 20 mg PO daily initially, increasing by 10 mg per day weekly up to 50 mg daily. Adjust dose: For debilitated patients or those with renal or hepatic impairment taking immediate-release form, initially, 10 mg PO daily, preferably in morning. If patient does not respond after full antidepressant effect has occurred, increase dose by 10 mg per day at weekly intervals to a maximum of 40 mg daily. If using controlled-release form, start therapy at 12.5 mg daily. Do not exceed 50 mg daily.

PTSD:
- *Adults:* Initially, 20 mg PO daily. Increase dose by 10 mg daily at intervals of at least 1 wk. Maximum daily dose is 50 mg PO.

ADMINISTRATION: May take with or without food. Do not split or crush controlled-release tablets.

SIDE EFFECTS: Asthenia, dizziness, headache, insomnia, somnolence, tremor, nervousness, suicidal behavior, anxiety, paresthesia, confusion, agitation, palpitations, vasodilation, orthostatic hypotension, lump or tightness in throat, dry mouth, nausea, constipation, diarrhea, flatulence, vomiting, dyspepsia, dysgeusia, increased or decreased appetite, abdominal pain, ejaculatory disturbances, sexual dysfunction, urinary frequency, other urinary disorders, myopathy, myalgia, myasthenia, diaphoresis, rash, pruritus

DRUG INTERACTIONS:
- Amphetamines, buspirone, dextromethorphan, dihydroergotamine, lithium salts, meperidine, other SSRIs or SSNRIs (duloxetine, venlafaxine), tramadol, trazodone, TCAs, tryptophan) may increase the risk of serotonin syndrome. Avoid combining drugs that increase the availability of serotonin in the CNS; monitor patient closely if used together.
- *Cimetidine.* May decrease hepatic metabolism of paroxetine, leading to risk of adverse reactions. Dosage adjustments may be needed.
- *Digoxin.* May decrease *digoxin* level. Use together cautiously.
- *MAOIs, such as phenelzine, selegiline, tranylcypromine:* May cause serotonin syndrome. Avoid using within 14 days of MAOI therapy.
- *Phenobarbital, phenytoin.* May alter pharmacokinetics of both drugs. Dosage adjustments may be needed.
- *Procyclidine.* May increase procyclidine level. Watch for excessive anticholinergic effects.
- *Sumatriptan.* May cause weakness, hyperreflexia, and uncoordination. Monitor patient closely.
- *Theophylline.* May decrease theophylline clearance. Monitor theophylline level.
- *Thioridazine.* May prolong QTc interval and increase risk of serious ventricular arrhythmias, such as torsades de pointes, and sudden death. Avoid using together.
- *TCAs.* May inhibit TCA metabolism. Dose of TCA may need to be reduced. Monitor patient closely.
- *Triptans.* May cause serotonin syndrome (restlessness, hallucinations, loss of coordination, fast heartbeat, rapid changes in blood pressure, increased body temperature, overactive reflexes, nausea, vomiting, and diarrhea). Use cautiously, especially at the start of therapy and at dosage increases.
- *Warfarin.* May cause bleeding. Use together cautiously.
- *St. John's wort.* May increase sedative-hypnotic effects. Discourage use together.
- *Alcohol use.* May alter psychomotor function. Discourage use together.

PHARMACOKINETICS: Thought to be linked to drug's inhibition of CNS neuronal uptake of serotonin. Oral onset and duration of effect is unknown. Peak action is 2 to 10 hr.
Half-life: About 24 hr

PRECAUTIONS:
- Contraindicated in patients hypersensitive to drug, within 14 days of MAOI therapy, and in those taking thioridazine.
- Contraindicated in children and adolescents younger than age 18 for MDDs.
- Use cautiously in patients with history of seizure disorders or mania and in those with other severe, systemic illness.

(cont.)

paroxetine (cont.)

- Use cautiously in patients at risk for volume depletion and monitor them appropriately.
- Using drug in the first trimester may increase the risk of congenital fetal malformations; using drug in the third trimester may cause neonatal complications at birth. Consider the risk versus benefit of therapy.
- Patients may be at increased risk for developing suicidal behavior, but this has not been definitively attributed to use of the drug.
- Patients taking *Paxil CR* for PMDD should be periodically reassessed to determine the need for continued treatment.
- If signs or symptoms of psychosis occur or increase, expect prescriber to reduce dosage. Record mood changes. Monitor patient for suicidal tendencies, and allow only a minimum supply of drug.

▶**Alert:** Drug may increase the risk of suicidal thinking and behavior in children, adolescents, and young adults aged 18 to 24 during the first 2 months of treatment, especially in those with MDD or other psychiatric disorder.

- Monitor patient for complaints of sexual dysfunction. In men, they include anorgasmy, erectile difficulties, delayed ejaculation or orgasm, or impotence; in women, they include anorgasmia or difficulty with orgasm.

▶**Alert:** Do not stop drug abruptly. Withdrawal or discontinuation syndrome may occur if drug is stopped abruptly. Symptoms include headache, myalgia, lethargy, and general flu-like symptoms. Taper drug slowly over 1 to 2 wk.

▶**Alert:** Combining triptans with an SSRI or an SSNRI may cause serotonin syndrome. Signs and symptoms may include restlessness, hallucinations, loss of coordination, fast heartbeat, rapid changes in blood pressure, increased body temperature, overactive reflexes, nausea, vomiting, and diarrhea. Serotonin syndrome may be more likely to occur when starting or increasing the dose of triptan, SSRI, or SSNRI.

PATIENT AND FAMILY EDUCATION:
- Tell patient that drug may be taken with or without food, usually in the morning.
- Tell patient not to break, crush, or chew controlled-release tablets.
- Warn patient to avoid activities that require alertness and good coordination until effects of drug are known.
- Advise women of childbearing age to contact prescriber if become pregnant or plan to become pregnant during therapy or if are currently breastfeeding.
- Tell patient to avoid alcohol and to consult prescriber before taking other prescription or OTC drugs or herbal medicines.
- Instruct patient not to stop taking drug abruptly.

SPECIAL POPULATIONS:
- *Elderly:* Caution is advised when using this drug in the elderly due to more sensitivity to the drug.
- *Pregnancy:* Avoid using this drug during the third trimester for it leads to adverse effects in the newborn. This medication should only be used when clearly needed during pregnancy.
- *Lactation:* Secreted into breast milk.
- *Children:* Caution when using this drug in a child or adolescent; must balance the potential risks with the clinical need. Not recommended for use under age 18 years for MDD.

▶**Alert:** Antidepressants increased the risk of suicidal thinking and behavior (suicidality) in short-term studies in children and adolescents with depression and other psychiatric disorders. Caution is advised when using this drug in children because they may be more sensitive to the side effects of the drug, especially loss of appetite and weight loss. It is important to monitor weight and growth in children who are taking this drug.

fluoxetine   *Prozac, Prozac Weekly, Sarafem*

AVAILABLE FORMS: Capsule (delayed-release), 90 mg; capsule (pulvule), 10, 20, and 40 mg; oral solution, 20 mg/5 mL; tablet, 10 and 20 mg

DOSAGE:

Depression, OCD:
- *Adults:* Initially, 20 mg PO in the morning; increase dosage based on patient response. Maximum daily dose is 80 mg.

OCD:
- *Children aged 7 to 17:* 10 mg PO daily. After 2 wk, increase to 20 mg daily. Dosage is 20 to 60 mg daily.

Depression:
- *Children aged 8 to 18:* 10 mg PO once daily for 1 wk; then increase to 20 mg daily.
- *Age 65 and older:* Initially, 20 mg PO daily in the morning. Increase dose based on response. Doses may be given bid, morning and noon. Maximum daily dose is 80 mg. Consider using a lower dosage or less-frequent dose in these patients, especially those with systemic illness and those who are receiving drugs for other illnesses.

Maintenance Therapy for Depression in Stabilized Patients (Not for Newly Diagnosed Depression):
- *Adults:* 90 mg *Prozac Weekly* PO once weekly. Start once-weekly doses 7 days after the last daily dose of *Prozac* 20 mg.

Short-Term Treatment of Panic Disorder With or Without Agoraphobia:
- *Adults:* 10 mg PO once daily for 1 wk; then increase dose as needed to 20 mg daily. Maximum daily dose is 60 mg.
- *For patients with renal or hepatic impairment:* Reduce dose or increase interval.

(cont.)

fluoxetine (*cont.*)

ADMINISTRATION:
- Give drug with or without food.
- Avoid giving drug in the afternoon, whenever possible, because doing so commonly causes nervousness and insomnia.
- Delayed-release capsules must be swallowed whole; do not crush or open.

SIDE EFFECTS: Nervousness, somnolence, anxiety, insomnia, headache, drowsiness, tremor, dizziness, asthenia, suicidal behavior, fatigue, fever, palpitations, hot flashes, nasal congestion, pharyngitis, sinusitis, nausea, diarrhea, dry mouth, anorexia, dyspepsia, constipation, abdominal pain, vomiting, flatulence, increased appetite, sexual dysfunction, weight loss, muscle pain, upper respiratory tract, infection, cough, respiratory distress, rash, pruritus, diaphoresis, flu-like syndrome.

DRUG INTERACTIONS:
- Amphetamines, buspirone, dextromethorphan, dihydroergotamine, lithium salts, meperidine, other SSRIs or SSNRIs (duloxetine, venlafaxine), tramadol, trazodone, TCAs, tryptophan.
- May increase risk of serotonin syndrome.
- Avoid combinations of drugs that increase the availability of serotonin in the CNS; monitor patient closely if used together.
- *Benzodiazepines, lithium, TCAs.* May increase CNS effects. Monitor patient closely.
- *Beta-blockers, carbamazepine, flecainide, vinblastine.* May increase levels of these drugs. Monitor drug levels and patient for adverse reactions.
- *Cyproheptadine.* May reverse or decrease fluoxetine effect. Monitor patient closely.
- *Dextromethorphan.* May cause unusual side effects such as visual hallucinations.
- Advise use of cough suppressant that does not contain dextromethorphan while taking fluoxetine.
- *Highly protein-bound drugs.* May increase level of fluoxetine or other highly protein-bound drugs. Monitor patient closely.
- *Insulin, oral antidiabetics.* May alter glucose level and antidiabetic requirements. Adjust dosage. MAOIs (phenelzine, selegiline, tranylcypromine). May cause serotonin syndrome. Avoid using at the same time and for at least 5 wk after stopping.
- *Phenytoin.* May increase phenytoin level and risk of toxicity. Monitor phenytoin level and adjust dosage.
- *Triptans.* May cause weakness, hyperreflexia, uncoordination, rapid changes in blood pressure, nausea, and diarrhea. Monitor patient closely, especially at start of treatment and dosage increases.
- *Thioridazine.* May increase thioridazine level, increasing risk of serious ventricular arrhythmias and sudden death. Avoid using at the same time and for at least 5 wk after stopping.

- *Warfarin.* May increase risk for bleeding. Monitor PT and INR.
- *St. John's wort.* May increase sedative and hypnotic effects; may cause serotonin syndrome. Discourage use together.
- *Alcohol use.* May increase CNS depression. Discourage use together.

PHARMACOKINETICS:
- Thought to be linked to drug's inhibition of CNS neuronal uptake of serotonin. Oral dose onset and duration of effects are unknown. Peak action is 6 to 8 hr.

Half-life: Fluoxetine, 2–3 days; norfluoxetine, 7–9 days.

PRECAUTIONS:
- Contraindicated in patients hypersensitive to drug and in those taking MAOIs within 14 days of starting therapy. MAOIs should not be started within 5 wk of stopping fluoxetine. Avoid using thioridazine with fluoxetine or within 5 wk after stopping fluoxetine.
- Use cautiously in patients at high risk for suicide and in those with history of diabetes mellitus, seizures, mania, or hepatic, renal, or CV disease.
- Use in third trimester of pregnancy may be associated with neonatal complications at birth. Consider the risk versus benefit of treatment during this time.
- Use antihistamines or topical corticosteroids to treat rashes or pruritus.
- Watch for weight change during therapy, particularly in underweight or bulimic patients.
- Record mood changes. Watch for suicidal tendencies.
- Drug has a long half-life; monitor patient for adverse effects for up to 2 wk after drug is stopped.

▶**Alert:** Drug may increase the risk of suicidal thinking and behavior in children and adolescents with MDD or other psychiatric disorder.

▶**Alert:** Drug may increase the risk of suicidal thinking and behavior in young adults aged 18 to 24 during the first 2 months of treatment.

▶**Alert:** Combining triptans with an SSRI or an SSNRI may cause serotonin syndrome. Signs and symptoms may include restlessness, hallucinations, loss of coordination, fast heartbeat, rapid changes in blood pressure, increased body temperature, overactive reflexes, nausea, vomiting, and diarrhea. Serotonin syndrome may be more likely to occur when starting or increasing the dose of triptan, SSRI, or SSNRI.

PATIENT AND FAMILY EDUCATION:
- Tell patient to avoid taking the drug in the afternoon whenever possible because doing so commonly causes nervousness and insomnia.
- Drug may cause dizziness or drowsiness. Warn patient to avoid driving and other hazardous activities that require alertness and good

(cont.)

SCHIZOID PERSONALITY DISORDER: Selective Serotonin Reuptake Inhibitors (SSRIs)

fluoxetine (cont.)

psychomotor coordination until effects of drug are known.
- Tell patient to consult prescriber before taking other prescription or OTC drugs.
- Advise patient that full therapeutic effect may not be seen for 4 wk or longer.

SPECIAL POPULATIONS:
- *Elderly:* Caution is advised when using this drug in the elderly due to more sensitivity to the drug.
- *Pregnancy:* Avoid using this drug during the third trimester for it leads to adverse effects in the newborn. This medication should only be used when clearly needed during pregnancy.

- *Lactation:* Secreted into breast milk.
- *Children:* Caution when using this drug in a child or adolescent; must balance the potential risks with the clinical need. Not recommended for use under age 18 years for MDD.

▶**Alert:** Antidepressants increased the risk of suicidal thinking and behavior (suicidality) in short-term studies in children and adolescents with depression and other psychiatric disorders. Caution is advised when using this drug in children because they may be more sensitive to the side effects of the drug, especially loss of appetite and weight loss. It is important to monitor weight and growth in children who are taking this drug.

escitalopram   *Lexapro*

AVAILABLE FORMS: Tablet, 10 and 20 mg; oral solution, 1 mg/mL

DOSAGE: 10 to 20 mg every day

ADMINISTRATION:
- PO with a glass of water
- Take with or without food
- Take at regular intervals, preferably in the morning
- Caution clients not to stop taking drug except on provider's advice
- Instruct client to take missed dose ASAP. If it is almost time for next dose, advise to take only that dose.

SIDE EFFECTS: Somnolence, dizziness, insomnia, nervousness, dry mouth, constipation, asthenia, diaphoresis, anxiety, headache, drowsiness, anorexia, dyspepsia, suicide risk, fatigue, fever, palpitations, hot flashes, nasal congestion, pharyngitis, sinusitis, nausea, diarrhea, dry mouth, anorexia, dyspepsia, constipation, abdominal pain, vomiting, flatulence, increased appetite, sexual dysfunction, weight loss, muscle pain, upper respiratory tract, infection, cough, respiratory distress, rash, pruritus, diaphoresis, flu-like syndrome.

DRUG INTERACTIONS:
- This medicine may interact with the following: cyproheptadine, flecainide, carbamazepine, vinblastine, insulin, oral diabetic agents, lithium, TCAs, phenytoin, tryptophan, warfarin (and other highly protein-bound drugs).
- Concomitant use with SSRIs, SNRIs, or tryptophan is not recommended.
- Use caution when concomitantly consuming drugs that affect hemostasis (NSAIDs, aspirin, warfarin).
- Instruct clients to provide a list of all the medicines, herbs, nonprescription drugs, or dietary supplements they use.
- Also instruct clients to inform if they smoke, drink alcohol, or use illegal drugs.

▶**Alert:** This list may not describe all possible interactions.

PHARMACOKINETICS:
- SSRIs are metabolized in the liver by cytochrome P-450 MFO microsomal enzymes.
- Highly bound to plasma proteins and have a large volume of distribution. Peak plasma levels are reached in 2 to 10 hr.
- Steady state plasma levels are achieved in 1 wk with escitalopram.
- Hence, addition of serotonergic medications to a patient's regimen must not occur until 2 to 3 wk after discontinuation of an SSRI

Half-life: 27–32 hr

PRECAUTIONS:
- *Clinical worsening/suicide risk:* Monitor for clinical worsening, suicidality, and unusual change in behavior, especially during the initial few months of therapy or at times of dose changes.
- *Serotonin syndrome or NMS-like reactions:* Manage with immediate discontinuation and continuing monitoring.
- *Discontinuation of treatment with Lexapro:* A gradual reduction in dose rather than abrupt cessation is recommended whenever possible.
- *Seizures:* Prescribe with care in patients with history of seizure.
- *Activation of mania/hypomania:* Use cautiously in patients with a history of mania.
- *Hyponatremia:* Can occur in association with SIADH.
- *Abnormal bleeding:* Use caution in concomitant use with NSAIDs, aspirin, warfarin, or other drugs that affect coagulation.
- *Interference with cognitive and motor performance:* Use caution when operating machinery
- *Use in patients with concomitant illness:* Use caution in patients with diseases or conditions that produce altered metabolism or hemodynamic response.
- See client as often as necessary to ensure that the drug is working on the panic attacks, determine compliance, and review side effects.
- Make sure clients realize that they need to take prescribed dose even if they do not feel better

(cont.)

escitalopram (cont.)

right away. It can take several weeks before the full effect is felt.

- Instruct client and family to watch for worsening depression or thoughts of suicide. Also watch for sudden or severe changes in feelings such as feeling anxious, agitated, panicky, irritable, hostile, aggressive, impulsive, severely restless, overly excited and hyperactive, or not being able to sleep. If this happens, especially at the beginning of antidepressant treatment or after a change in dose, patients should call the provider.
- Clients may become drowsy or dizzy and should not drive, use machinery, or do anything that needs mental alertness until the effects of this medicine are known.
- Caution patients not to stand or sit up quickly, especially if an older patient. This reduces the risk of dizzy or fainting spells. Alcohol may interfere with the effect of this medicine. Avoid alcoholic drinks.
- Caution patients not to treat themselves for coughs, colds, or allergies without asking health care professional for advice. Some ingredients can increase possible side effects.
- Dry mouth: Chewing sugarless gum or sucking hard candy, and drinking plenty of water may help. Contact provider if the problem does not go away or is severe.
- Use with caution in patients with bipolar disorder or a family history of bipolar disorder, diabetes, heart disease, liver disease; seizures (convulsions) suicidal thoughts, plans, or attempts by client or a family member; an unusual or allergic reaction to sertraline, other medicines, foods, dyes, or preservatives; those who are receiving electroconvulsive therapy;

and those who are pregnant, trying to get pregnant, or are breastfeeding

PATIENT AND FAMILY EDUCATION:
- Tell patient to avoid taking drug in the afternoon whenever possible because doing so commonly causes nervousness and insomnia.
- Drug may cause dizziness or drowsiness. Warn patient to avoid driving and other hazardous activities that require alertness and good psychomotor coordination until effects of drug are known.
- Tell patient to consult prescriber before taking other prescription or OTC drugs.
- Advise patient that full therapeutic effect may not be seen for 4 wk or longer.

SPECIAL POPULATIONS:
- *Elderly:* Caution is advised when using this drug in the elderly due to more sensitivity to the drug.
- *Pregnancy:* Avoid using this drug during the third trimester for it leads to adverse effects in the newborn. This medication should only be used when clearly needed during pregnancy.
- *Lactation:* Secreted into breast milk.
- *Children:* Caution when using this drug in a child or adolescent; must balance the potential risks with the clinical need. Antidepressants increased the risk of suicidal thinking and behavior (suicidality) in short-term studies in children and adolescents with depression and other psychiatric disorders. Caution is advised when using this drug in children because they may be more sensitive to the side effects of the drug, especially loss of appetite and weight loss. It is important to monitor weight and growth in children who are taking this drug.

Class: Antipsychotics, Atypical (Second Generation)

Risperdal, Risperdal Consta, Risperdal M-Tab   **risperidone**

AVAILABLE FORMS: Injection, 12.5, 25, 37.5, and 50 mg; solution, 1 mg/mL; tablet, 0.25, 0.5, 1, 2, 3, and 4 mg; tablet (orally disintegrating), 0.5, 1, 2, 3, and 4 mg

DOSAGE:
Schizophrenia:
- *Adults:* Drug may be given once or twice daily. Initial dosing is generally 2 mg/day. Increase dosage at intervals not less than 24 hr, in increments of 1 to 2 mg/day, as tolerated, to a recommended dose of 4 to 8 mg/day. Periodically reassess to determine the need for maintenance treatment with an appropriate dose.
- *Adolescents aged 13 to 17:* Start treatment with 0.5 mg once daily, given as a single daily dose either in the morning or in evening. Adjust dose, if indicated, at intervals not less than 24

hr, in increments of 0.5 or 1 mg/day, as tolerated, to a recommended dose of 3 mg/day. There are no data to support use beyond 8 wk.

Irritability, Including Aggression, Self-Injury, and Temper Tantrums, Associated With Autistic Disorder:
- *Adolescents and children aged 5 and older who weigh 20 kg (44 lb) or more:* Initially, 0.5 mg PO once daily or divided bid. After 4 days, increase dose to 1 mg. Increase dosage further in 0.5 mg increments at intervals of at least 2 wk.
- *Children aged 5 and older who weigh less than 20 kg:* Initially, 0.25 mg PO once daily or divided bid. After 4 days, increase dose to 0.5 mg. Increase dosage further in 0.25 mg increments at intervals of at least 2 wk. Increase cautiously in children who weigh less than 15 kg (33 lb).

(cont.)

risperidone (*cont.*)

ADMINISTRATION:

PO:

- Give drug with or without food.
- Open package for ODTs immediately before taking by peeling off foil backing with dry hands. Do not push tablets through the foil.
- Phenylalanine contents of ODTs are as follows: 0.5 mg tablet contains 0.14 mg phenylalanine; 1 mg tablet contains 0.28 mg phenylalanine; 2 mg tablet contains 0.56 mg phenylalanine; 3 mg tablet contains 0.63 mg phenylalanine; 4 mg tablet contains 0.84 mg phenylalanine.

IM:

- Continue oral therapy for the first 3 wk of IM injection therapy until injections take effect, then stop oral therapy.
- To reconstitute IM injection, inject premeasured diluent into vial and shake vigorously for at least 10 sec. Suspension appears uniform, thick, and milky; particles are visible, but no dry particles remain. Use drug immediately, or refrigerate for up to 6 hr after reconstitution. If more than 2 min pass before injection, shake vigorously again. See package insert for more detailed instructions.
- Refrigerate IM injection kit and protect it from light. Drug can be stored at temperature less than 77° F (25° C) for no more than 7 days before administration.

SIDE EFFECTS:

- Akathisia, somnolence, dystonia, headache, insomnia, agitation, anxiety, pain, parkinsonism, NMS, suicide attempt, dizziness, fever, hallucination, mania, impaired concentration, abnormal thinking and dreaming, tremor, hypoesthesia, fatigue, depression, nervousness
- Tachycardia, chest pain, orthostatic hypotension, peripheral edema, syncope, hypertension
- Rhinitis, sinusitis, pharyngitis, ear disorder
- Constipation, nausea, vomiting, dyspepsia, abdominal pain, anorexia, dry mouth, increased saliva, diarrhea
- Urinary incontinence, increased urination, abnormal orgasm, vaginal dryness, weight gain, hyperglycemia, weight loss
- Arthralgia, back pain, leg pain, myalgia
- Coughing, dyspnea, upper respiratory infection
- Rash, dry skin, photosensitivity reactions, acne, injection site pain
- Tooth disorder, toothache, injury, decreased libido

DRUG INTERACTIONS: Antihypertensives, carbamazepine, clozapine, CNS depressants, dopamine agonists, levodopa, fluoxetine, paroxetine. Alcohol use may cause CNS depression.

PHARMACOKINETICS:

- Blocks dopamine and 5-HT$_2$ receptors in the brain
- Onset and duration of action with oral dose is unknown

- Peak action is 1 hr
- IM onset of action is 3 wk with peak action at 4 to 6 wk and duration of action at 7 wk.

Half-life: 3–20 hr

PRECAUTIONS:

- May increase prolactin level. May decrease hemoglobin level and hematocrit.
- *Sun exposure may increase risk of photosensitivity reactions.*
- Contraindicated in patients hypersensitive to drug and in breastfeeding women.
- Use cautiously in patients with prolonged QT interval, cerebrovascular disease, dehydration, hypovolemia, history of seizures, or conditions that could affect metabolism or hemodynamic responses.
- Use cautiously in patients exposed to extreme heat.
- Use caution in patients at risk for aspiration pneumonia.
- Use IM injection cautiously in those with hepatic or renal impairment.
- Periodically reevaluate drug's risks and benefits, especially during prolonged use.
- Monitor patient for weight gain.
- Life-threatening hyperglycemia may occur in patients taking atypical antipsychotics. Monitor patients with diabetes regularly.

▶**Alert:** Obtain baseline BP measurements before starting therapy, and monitor regularly. Watch for orthostatic hypotension, especially during first dosage adjustment.

▶**Alert:** Fatal cerebrovascular adverse events (stroke, transient ischemic attacks) may occur in elderly patients with dementia. Drug is not safe or effective in these patients.

▶**Alert:** Monitor patient for tardive dyskinesia, which may occur after prolonged use. It may not appear until months or years later and may disappear spontaneously or persist for life, despite stopping drug.

▶**Alert:** Watch for evidence of NMS (extrapyramidal effects, hyperthermia, autonomic disturbance), which is rare but can be fatal.

▶**Alert:** Monitor patient for symptoms of metabolic syndrome (significant weight gain and increased BMI, hypertension, hyperglycemia, hypercholesterolemia, and hypertriglyceridemia).

PATIENT AND FAMILY EDUCATION:

- Warn patient to avoid activities that require alertness until effects of drug are known.
- Warn patient to rise slowly, avoid hot showers, and use other precautions to avoid fainting when starting therapy.
- Advise patient to use caution in hot weather to prevent heatstroke.
- Tell patient to take drug with or without food.
- Instruct patient to keep the ODT in the blister pack until just before taking it. After opening the pack, dissolve the tablet on tongue without
(cont.)

risperidone (cont.)

cutting or chewing. Use dry hands to peel apart the foil to expose the tablet; do not attempt to push it through the foil.
- Tell patient to use sunblock and wear protective clothing outdoors.
- Advise patient to avoid alcohol during therapy.

SPECIAL POPULATIONS:
- *Pregnancy/Lactation:* Advise women not to become pregnant or to breastfeed for 12 wk after the last IM injection.

Zyprexa, Zydis   **olanzapine**

AVAILABLE FORMS: Injection, 10 mg; tablet, 2.5, 5, 7.5, 10, 15, and 20 mg; tablet (orally disintegrating), 5, 10, 15, and 20 mg

DOSAGE:
Schizophrenia: *Adults:* Initially, 5 to 10 mg PO once daily with the goal to be at 10 mg daily within several days of starting therapy. Adjust dose in 5 mg increments at intervals of 1 wk or more. Most patients respond to 10 to 15 mg daily. Safety of dosages greater than 20 mg daily has not been established.

ADMINISTRATION:
PO:
- Give drug with or without food.
- Do not crush or break ODT.
- Place immediately on patient's tongue after opening package.
- ODT may be given without water.
IM:
- Inspect IM solution for particulate matter and discoloration before administration.
- To reconstitute IM injection, dissolve contents of one vial with 2.1 mL of sterile water for injection to yield a clear yellow 5 mg/mL solution. Store at room temperature and give within 1 hr of reconstitution. Discard any unused solution.

SIDE EFFECTS:
- Somnolence, insomnia, parkinsonism, dizziness, NMS, suicide attempt, abnormal gait, asthenia, personality disorder, akathisia, tremor, articulation impairment, tardive dyskinesia, fever, extrapyramidal events
- Orthostatic hypotension, tachycardia, chest pain, hypertension, ecchymosis, peripheral edema, hypotension
- Amblyopia, rhinitis, pharyngitis, conjunctivitis
- Constipation, dry mouth, dyspepsia, increased appetite, increased salivation, vomiting, thirst
- Hematuria, metrorrhagia, urinary incontinence, UTI, amenorrhea, vaginitis
- Leucopenia
- Hyperglycemia, weight gain
- Joint pain, extremity pain, back pain, neck rigidity, twitching, hypertonia
- Increased cough, dyspnea
- Sweating, injection site pain
- Flu-like syndrome, injury

DRUG INTERACTIONS:
- Antihypertensives, carbamazepine, omeprazole, rifampin, ciprofloxacin, diazepam, dopamine agonists, levodopa, fluoxetine, fluvoxamine, St. John's wort.
- Alcohol use may increase CNS effects. Smoking may increase drug clearance.

PHARMACOKINETICS:
- May block dopamine and 5-HT$_2$ receptors. Oral onset of action and duration of action are unknown. Peak action occurs in 6 hr.
- IM onset of action is rapid with duration unknown. Peak action occurs at 15 to 45 min.
Half-life: 21–54 hr

PRECAUTIONS:
- May increase AST, ALT, GGT, CK, triglyceride, and prolactin levels.
- May increase eosinophil count; may decrease WBC count.
- Contraindicated in patients hypersensitive to drug.
- Use cautiously in patients with heart disease, cerebrovascular disease, conditions that predispose patient to hypotension, history of seizures or conditions that might lower the seizure threshold, and hepatic impairment.
- Use cautiously in elderly patients, those with a history of paralytic ileus, and those at risk for aspiration pneumonia, prostatic hyperplasia, or angle-closure glaucoma.
- ODTs contain phenylalanine.
- Monitor patient for abnormal body temperature regulation, especially if patient exercises, is exposed to extreme heat, takes anticholinergics, or is dehydrated.
- Obtain baseline and periodic liver function test results.
- Monitor patient for weight gain.
- Monitor patient for tardive dyskinesia, which may occur after prolonged use. It may not appear until months or years later and may disappear spontaneously or persist for life, despite stopping drug.
- Periodically reevaluate the long-term usefulness of olanzapine.
- Drug may increase risk of stroke and death in elderly patients with dementia. Olanzapine is not approved to treat patients with dementia-related psychosis.
- Patients who feel dizzy or drowsy after an IM injection should remain recumbent until assessed

(cont.)

SCHIZOID PERSONALITY DISORDER: Antipsychotics, Atypical (Second Generation)

olanzapine (cont.)

for orthostatic hypotension and bradycardia. Patients should rest until the feeling passes.

▶**Alert:** Drug may increase the risk of suicidal thinking and behavior in young adults aged 18 to 24 during the first 2 months of treatment.

▶**Alert:** Watch for evidence of NMS (hyperpyrexia, muscle rigidity, altered mental status, autonomic instability), which is rare but commonly fatal. Stop drug immediately; monitor and treat patient as needed.

▶**Alert:** Drug may cause hyperglycemia. Monitor patients with diabetes regularly. In patients with risk factors for diabetes, obtain fasting blood glucose test results at baseline and periodically.

▶**Alert:** Monitor patient for symptoms of metabolic syndrome (significant weight gain and increased BMI, hypertension, hyperglycemia, hypercholesterolemia, and hypertriglyceridemia).

PATIENT AND FAMILY EDUCATION:
- Warn patient Avoid hazardous tasks until full effects of drug are known.
- Warn patient against exposure to extreme heat; drug may impair body's ability to reduce temperature.
- Inform patient that he/she may gain weight.

- Advise patient to avoid alcohol.
- Tell patient to rise slowly to avoid dizziness upon standing up quickly.
- Inform patient that ODTs contain phenylalanine.
- Tell patient to peel foil away from ODT, not to push tablet through. Have patient take tablet immediately, allowing tablet to dissolve on tongue and swallowed with saliva; no additional fluid is needed.
- Tell patient to take drug with or without food.
- Urge women of childbearing age to notify prescriber if they become pregnant or plan or suspects pregnancy. Tell patient not to breastfeed during therapy.

SPECIAL POPULATIONS:
- *Elderly:* Caution is advised when using this drug in the elderly because they may be more sensitive to the effects of the drug, especially drowsiness, difficulty urinating, and heart problems.
- *Pregnancy:* This medication should be used only when clearly needed during pregnancy.
- *Lactation:* Patients should not breastfeed during therapy.
- *Children:* Not approved for use in children and adolescents.

---

quetiapine   *Seroquel*

AVAILABLE FORMS: Tablet, 25, 50, 100, 200, 300, and 400 mg; extended-release formulations, 200, 300, and 400 mg

DOSAGE:
- *Immediate-release tablet:* 2 or 3 times daily. Extended-release tablets taken once daily
- The dose usually is increased slowly over several days or weeks to achieve the desired effect.
- Can be taken with or without food.

Bipolar Disorder:
- Initial dose, 50 mg twice daily (100 mg/day).
- The dose can be increased by 100 mg/day to a daily dose of 400 mg/day. Most patients respond to 400 to 800 mg/day.
- Doses greater than 800 mg/day have not been studied.

Schizophrenia:
- Initial dose, 25 mg twice daily (50 mg/day).
- The dose can be increased by 25 to 50 mg two or three times daily. The target dose is 300 to 400 mg/day in two or three doses.
- Patients respond to 150 to 750 mg/day, and doses greater than 800 mg/day have not been evaluated.

ADMINISTRATION:
- Avoid eating grapefruit or drinking grapefruit juice while being treated with this medication.

SIDE EFFECTS:
- Constipation, drowsiness, dizziness, stomach pain or upset, weight gain or dry mouth

- Fainting, unusually fast or irregular heartbeat
- Skin rash, itching, trouble breathing
- Fever, persistent sore throat, muscle stiffness, confusion, sweating, uncontrolled muscle movements (e.g., tongue or facial muscles), one-sided muscle weakness, cold sensitivity, trouble urinating, black stools, unusual moods
- This drug may infrequently make blood sugar level rise, therefore causing or worsening diabetes. This high blood sugar can rarely cause serious (sometimes fatal) conditions such as diabetic coma.
- This drug may also cause significant weight gain and rise in blood cholesterol (or triglyceride) levels. These effects, along with diabetes, may increase risk for developing heart disease.

DRUG INTERACTIONS:
- Used with caution in combination with other centrally acting drugs.
- Caution should be exercised when quetiapine is used concomitantly with drugs known to cause electrolyte imbalance or to increase QT interval.

PHARMACOKINETICS:
- Bioavailability is unknown.
- Food has minimal effects on quetiapine absorption.
- The drug is approximately 83% bound to serum proteins.

(cont.)

quetiapine (cont.)

- Single and multiple dose studies have demonstrated linear pharmacokinetics in the clinical dose range (up to 375 mg twice daily).
- The drug is eliminated with a mean terminal half-life of approximately 7 hr. The primary route of elimination is through hepatic metabolism.

PRECAUTIONS:
- Black box warning about the use of *Seroquel* in elderly people with psychosis or dementia.
- Elderly people with dementia (Alzheimer's disease is the most common form) who are treated with antipsychotics—including *Seroquel*—are more likely to die of various causes than those who were not treated with those medications.
- *Seroquel* is not approved to treat dementia or dementia-related psychosis, and caution should be used before giving the medication to elderly people with this condition.
- FDA has required the drug to carry the special antidepressant and suicide warning, since it is used to treat bipolar depression.
- Antidepressants may increase the risk of suicidal thinking or behavior in people taking it.

PATIENT AND FAMILY EDUCATION:
- Take this medication by mouth with or without food, usually 2 or 3 times daily or as directed by provider.
- Dosage is based on medical condition and response to therapy.
- Provider will start with a low dose and gradually increase the dose to reduce the dizziness and lightheadedness that may occur.
- It may take several weeks to notice the full benefit of this drug.
- Use this medication regularly in order to get the most benefit from it.
- Use it at the same times each day.
- Take this medication exactly as prescribed, even if condition improves.

- Do not stop taking this medication without first consulting provider. Some conditions may become worse when the drug is suddenly stopped.
- Medication may cause withdrawal reactions, especially if it has been used regularly for a long time or in high doses.
- Do not eat grapefruit or drink grapefruit juice while on this medication.
- This drug may increase blood sugar levels and worsen diabetes.
- Patients taking this drug may be more susceptible to heat stroke.

SPECIAL POPULATIONS:
- *Elderly:*
  - Higher incidence of concomitant illness and concomitant medication in this population; *Seroquel* should be used with caution.
  - The mean plasma clearance of *Seroquel* was reduced by 30% to 50% in elderly subjects when compared to younger patients. The rate of dose titration may thus need to be slower, and the daily therapeutic target dose lower than that used in younger patients.
  - Quetiapine is extensively metabolized by the liver and should be used with caution in patients with mild hepatic impairment, especially during the initial dosing period.
  - Patients with mild hepatic impairment should be started on 25 mg/day. The dose should be increased daily in increments of 25 to 50 mg/day to an effective dose.
- *Pregnancy:* This medication should be used only when clearly needed during pregnancy.
- *Lactation:* It is not known whether this drug passes into breast milk. Because of the possible risk to the infant, breastfeeding while using this drug is not recommended.
- *Children:* Not recommended for children

Geodon   **ziprasidone**

AVAILABLE FORMS: Capsule for oral administration in 20 mg (blue/white), 40 mg (blue/blue), 60 mg (white/white), and 80 mg (blue/white); IM

DOSAGE:
Schizophrenia:
- Start, 20 mg PO bid; maximum, 80 mg bid; give with food; may adjust dose every 2 days prn; doses greater than 40 mg/day rarely more effective; periodically reassess need for treatment; discontinue if ANC less than 1,000; consider discontinue if unexplained decrease in WBC.
Bipolar Disorder, Manic/Mixed:
- Monotherapy dose: 40 to 80 mg PO bid; start, 40 mg PO bid ×1 day, then 60 to 80 mg PO bid; maximum, 80 mg bid; for acute treatment, give

with food; may adjust dose every 2 days prn; discontinue if ANC less than 1,000; consider discontinue if unexplained decrease in WBC. *Valproate or lithium adjunct*: 40 to 80 mg PO bid; for maintenance treatment; give with food; continue treatment at same dose at which patient initially stabilized; periodically reassess need for treatment; discontinue if ANC less than 1,000; consider discontinue if unexplained decrease in WBC.
Agitation, Schizophrenia-Associated:
- 10 mg IM every 2 hr prn; alternative, 20 mg IM every 4 hr prn; maximum, 40 mg/day ×3 days; switch to PO ASAP; discontinue if ANC less than 1,000; consider discontinue if unexplained decrease in WBC.

(cont.)

ziprasidone (cont.)

Other:
- *Renal dosing:* No adjustment. *Renal impairment:* Caution advised with IM use. *Hepatic dosing:* No adjustment. *Children:* Not applicable for this medication

ADMINISTRATION:
- Administer at an initial daily dose of 20 mg twice daily with food.
- Daily dosage may subsequently be adjusted on the basis of individual clinical status up to 80 mg twice daily.
- Dosage adjustments, if indicated, should generally occur at intervals of not less than 2 days, as steady state is achieved within 1 to 3 days. In order to ensure use of the lowest effective dose, patients should be observed for improvement for several weeks before upward dosage adjustment.

SIDE EFFECTS:
- *Cardiac:* Tachycardia, torsade de pointes (in the presence of multiple confounding factors)
- *Digestive system:* Swollen tongue
- *Reproductive system/breast disorders:* Galactorrhea, priapism
- *Nervous system:* Facial droop, NMS, serotonin syndrome (alone or in combination with serotonergic medicinal products), tardive dyskinesia
- *Psychiatric:* Insomnia, mania/hypomania
- *Skin and subcutaneous tissue:* Allergic reaction (such as allergic dermatitis, angioedema, orofacial edema, urticaria), rash
- *Urogenital system:* Enuresis, urinary incontinence
- *Vascular:* Postural hypotension, syncope

DRUG INTERACTIONS:
- Other drugs besides ziprasidone that may affect the heart rhythm (QTc prolongation in the EKG) include dofetilide, pimozide, quinidine, sotalol, procainamide, and sparfloxacin among others.
- QTc prolongation can infrequently result in serious, rarely fatal, irregular heartbeats. Anti-Parkinson drugs (e.g., pramipexole, ropinirole), azole antifungals (e.g., ketoconazole, itraconazole), certain blood pressure medications (e.g., beta-blockers such as metoprolol or propranolol, diuretics such as furosemide or hydrochlorothiazide, or alpha-blockers such as doxazosin or prazosin) may interact.
- Patients should advise if they take drugs that cause drowsiness, including antianxiety drugs (e.g., diazepam), antihistamines (e.g., diphenhydramine), antiseizure drugs (e.g., carbamazepine), medicine for sleep (e.g., sedatives), muscle relaxants, narcotic pain relievers (e.g., codeine), other psychiatric medicines (e.g., phenothiazines such as chlorpromazine, or tricyclics such as amitriptyline), tranquilizers.

PHARMACOKINETICS:
- A selective monoaminergic antagonist with high affinity for the serotonin Type 2 (5-HT$_2$), dopamine Type 2 (D2), 1 and 2 adrenergic, and H1 histaminergic receptors.
- Acts as an antagonist at other receptors, but with lower potency.
- Antagonism at receptors other than dopamine and 5-HT$_2$ with similar receptor affinities may explain some of the other therapeutic and side effects of *Geodon.*
- Antagonism of muscarinic M1-5 receptors may explain its anticholinergic effects.
- Antagonism of histamine H1 receptors may explain the somnolence observed with this drug. *Geodon's* antagonism of adrenergic alpha-1 receptors may explain the orthostatic hypotension observed with this drug.
- Functions as an antagonist at the dopamine D2, 5-HT$_{2A}$, and 5-HT$_{1D}$ receptors, and as an agonist at the 5-HT$_{1A}$ receptor.
- Inhibits synaptic reuptake of serotonin and norepinephrine.

PRECAUTIONS: Monitor patient closely and check potassium levels regularly. Patient should report fainting, dizziness, fast, racing, pounding, or irregular heartbeat, hyperglycemia, especially blurred vision; drowsiness; dry mouth; flushed, dry skin; fruit-like breath odor; increased urination; ketones in urine; loss of appetite; stomachache; nausea or vomiting; tiredness; trouble breathing; unconsciousness; or unusual thirst. Do not use in treatment of dementia-related psychosis.

PATIENT AND FAMILY EDUCATION: This medicine may cause some people to become drowsy, dizzy, or less alert than normally. Determine reaction to this medicine before driving, using machines, or do anything else that could be dangerous if you are dizzy or are not alert. Avoid use of alcohol. Avoid activities involving high temperature or humidity. This medicine may reduce body's ability to adjust to the heat.

SPECIAL POPULATIONS:
- *Elderly:* Patients with dementia-related psychosis treated with antipsychotic drugs are at an increased risk of death. *Geodon* is not approved for the treatment of dementia-related psychosis.
- *Pregnancy/Lactation:* Safe use in pregnancy and breastfeeding have not been established.
- *Children:* Safe use in pediatric patients has not been established.

Schizotypal Personality Disorder

OVERVIEW
- Characterized by a pervasive pattern of social and interpersonal deficits marked by acute discomfort with, and reduced capacity for, close relationships as well as by cognitive or perceptual distortions and behavioral eccentricities.
- Incidence is about 3% to 5% of the population.
- Slightly more prevalent in males than in females.
- May experience transient psychotic episodes in response to stress.
- Patients often have an odd appearance that causes others to notice them.
- May be unkempt, disheveled with ill-fitting, ill-matched clothing.
- 10% to 20% of patients with schizotypal personality disorder develop schizophrenia.
- Speech is coherent, but may be loose, digressive or vague, sometimes bizarre.
- May exhibit restricted range of emotion, flat affect, sometimes silly or inappropriate.

- Magical thinking, unfounded beliefs, obsession with parapsychology may be present.
- Patients usually have only one significant relationship with a first-degree relative.
- May exhibit great anxiety around other people who are unfamiliar.
- Rarely are able to succeed in employment without significant support.

Acute Treatment
Some success has been seen with short-term use of anxiolytics, such as benzodiazepines, or antipsychotic medications. Use of SSRIs, especially in conjunction with antipsychotics in this disorder, has been generally met with an increase in psychoses.

Chronic Treatment
Medication is not recommended for long-term therapy.

CLASS	DRUG
Benzodiazepines (BZDs)	**Acute Treatment** diazepam (*Diastat, Diazemuls, Diazepam Intensol, Novo-Dipam, Valium*) lorazepam (*Ativan*) clonazepam (*Klonopin*)
Antipsychotics, Typical (First Generation)	**Short-Term Treatment for Active Symptoms** haloperidol (*Haldol*) haloperidol decanoate (*Haldol Decanoate, Haloperidol LA*) haloperidol lactate (*Haldol, Haldol Concentrate*)
Antipsychotics, Atypical (Second Generation)	risperidone (*Risperdal, Risperdal Consta, Risperdal M-Tab*) olanzapine (*Zyprexa, Zydis*) quetiapine (*Seroquel*) ziprasidone (*Geodon*)

Class: Benzodiazepines (BZDs)
Diastat, Diazemuls, Diazepam Intensol, Novo-Dipam, Valium   **diazepam**

▶ **Alert:** Controlled-substance schedule IV

AVAILABLE FORMS: Injection, 5 mg/mL; oral solution, 5 mg/5 mL; rectal gel twin packs, 2.5 mg (pediatric), 5 mg (pediatric), 10, 15 and 20 mg (adult); tablet, 2, 5, and 10 mg

DOSAGE:
Anxiety:
- *Adults:* Depending on severity, 2 to 10 mg PO bid to qid, or 2 to 10 mg IM or IV every 3 to 4 hr, as needed. *Children: 6 months and older*: 1 to 2.5 mg PO tid or qid, increase gradually, as needed and

tolerated. *Elderly*: Initially, 2 to 2.5 mg once daily or bid; increase gradually.
Acute Alcohol Withdrawal:
- *Adults:* 10 mg PO tid or qid first 24 hr; reduce to 5 mg PO tid or qid, as needed. Or, initially, 10 mg IV or IM. Then, 5 to 10 mg IV or IM every 3 to 4 hr, as needed.
Adjunct Treatment for Seizure Disorders:
- *Adults:* 2 to 10 mg PO bid to qid. *Children: 6 months and older*: 1 to 2.5 mg PO tid or qid initially; increase as needed and as tolerated.
Status Epilepticus, Severe Recurrent Seizures:
- *Adults:* 5 to 10 mg IV or IM initially. Use IM route only if IV access is unavailable. Repeat

(cont.)

diazepam (*cont.*)

every 10 to 15 min, as needed; maximum, 30 mg. Repeat every 2 to 4 hr, if needed. *Children: 5 yr and older:* 1 mg IV every 2 to 5 min; maximum, 10 mg. Repeat every 2 to 4 hr, if needed. *1 month to 5 years:* 0.2 to 0.5 mg IV slowly every 2 to 5 min; maximum, 5 mg. Repeat every 2 to 4 hr, if needed.

Patients on Stable Regimens of Antiepileptic Drugs Who Need Diazepam Intermittently to Control Bouts of Increased Seizure Activity:
- *Adults and children: 12 yr and older:* 0.2 mg/kg PR, rounding up to the nearest available dose form. A second dose may be given 4 to 12 hr later. *Children: 6 to 11 yr:* 0.3 mg/kg PR, rounding up to the nearest available dose form. A second dose may be given 4 to 12 hr later. *Children: 2 to 5 yr:* 0.5 mg/kg PR, rounding up to the nearest available dose form. A second dose may be given 4 to 12 hr later.
- *Adjust dose*: For elderly and debilitated patients, reduce dosage to decrease the likelihood of ataxia and over sedation.

ADMINISTRATION:
PO:
- When using oral solution, dilute dose just before giving.

IV:
- IV route is the more reliable parenteral route; IM route is not recommended because absorption is variable and injection is painful.
- Keep emergency resuscitation equipment and oxygen at bedside.
- Avoid infusion sets or containers made from polyvinyl chloride.
- If possible, inject directly into a large vein. If not, inject slowly through infusion tubing as near to the insertion site as possible. Give at no more than 5 mg/min. Watch closely for phlebitis at injection site.
- Monitor respirations every 5 to 15 min and before each dose.
- Do not store parenteral solution in plastic syringes.
- Incompatible with all other IV drugs, most IV solutions.

IM:
- Use the IM route if IV administration is impossible.

Rectal:
- Use *Diastat* rectal gel to treat no more than five episodes per month and no more than one episode every 5 days because tolerance may develop.

▶**Alert:** Only caregivers who can distinguish the distinct cluster of seizures or events from the patient's ordinary seizure activity, have been instructed and can give the treatment competently, understand which seizures may be treated with *Diastat*, and can monitor clinical response and recognize when immediate professional medical evaluation is needed should give *Diastat* rectal gel.

SIDE EFFECTS:
- *CNS:* Drowsiness, dysarthria, slurred speech, tremor, transient amnesia, fatigue, ataxia, headache, insomnia, paradoxical anxiety, hallucinations, minor changes in EEG patterns, pain
- *CV:* CV collapse, bradycardia, hypotension
- *EENT:* Diplopia, blurred vision, nystagmus
- *GI:* Nausea, constipation, diarrhea with rectal form
- *GU:* Incontinence, urine retention
- *Hematologic*: Neutropenia
- *Hepatic*: Jaundice
- *Respiratory:* Respiratory depression, apnea
- *Skin:* Rash, phlebitis at injection site
- *Other:* Altered libido, physical or psychological dependence

DRUG INTERACTIONS:
- Cimetidine, disulfiram, fluoxetine, fluvoxamine, hormonal contraceptives, isoniazid, metoprolol, propoxyphene, propranolol, valproic acid, CNS depressants, digoxin
- Avoid using diltiazem, fluconazole, itraconazole, ketoconazole, or miconazole, as these may increase and prolong diazepam level, CNS depression, and psychomotor impairment.
- Levodopa, phenobarbital, kava, and alcohol use may cause additive CNS effects. Smoking may decrease effectiveness of drug.

PHARMACOKINETICS:
- A benzodiazepine that probably potentiates the effects of GABA, depresses the CNS, and suppresses the spread of seizure activity.

Half-life: About 1–12 days

ROUTE	ONSET	PEAK	DURATION
PO	30 min	2 hr	20–80 hr
IV	1–5 min	1–5 min	15–60 min
IM	Unknown	2 hr	Unknown
PR	Unknown	90 min	Unknown

PRECAUTIONS:
- May increase liver function test values. May decrease neutrophil count.
- Contraindicated in patients hypersensitive to drug or soy protein; in patients experiencing shock, coma, or acute alcohol intoxication (parenteral form); in pregnant women, especially in first trimester; and in infants younger than age 6 months (oral form).
- *Diastat* rectal gel is contraindicated in patients with acute angle-closure glaucoma.
- Use cautiously in patients with liver or renal impairment, depression, or chronic open-angle glaucoma. Use cautiously in elderly and debilitated patients.
- Monitor periodic hepatic, renal, and hematopoietic function studies in patients receiving repeated or prolonged therapy.
- Monitor elderly patients for dizziness, ataxia, mental status changes; are at increased risk for falls.

(cont.)

diazepam (cont.)

▶ **Alert:** Use of drug may lead to abuse and addiction. Do not withdraw drug abruptly after long-term use; withdrawal symptoms may occur.

PATIENT AND FAMILY EDUCATION:
- Warn patient to avoid activities that require alertness and good coordination until effects of drug are known.
- Tell patient to avoid alcohol while taking drug.
- Notify patient that smoking may decrease drug's effectiveness.

- Warn patient not to abruptly stop drug because withdrawal symptoms may occur.
- Warn women to avoid use during pregnancy.
- Instruct patient's caregiver on the proper use of *Diastat* rectal gel.

SPECIAL POPULATIONS:
- *Elderly:* Use with caution. May increase risk of falling.
- *Pregnancy/Lactation:* Avoid use.
- *Children:* Use with caution. Adjust dose carefully.

Ativan   **lorazepam**

INDICATIONS: Anxiety disorders

AVAILABLE FORMS: Tablet, 0.5, 1 and 2 mg

DOSAGE:
- *Adults:* 2–3 mg/day PO/IM/IV divided bid-tid; 1–2 mg/day PO/IM/IV div bid-tid in elderly patients; maximum, 10 mg/day. Periodically assess the need for treatment and taper the dose gradually to discontinue if prolonged treatment is necessary. Treatment should be limited to as short a period as possible (less than 4 months) and/or undergo re-evaluation for continued use.
- *Children:* 0.05 mg/kg PO/IV q4–8h; maximum, 2 mg/dose. Periodically assess the need for treatment and taper the dose gradually to discontinue if prolonged treatment is necessary.

ADMINISTRATION:
- PO with a glass of water.
- Do not abruptly stop taking the medication.
- Use lowest effective dose for shortest duration.
- Lorazepam can be habit forming; do not increase dosage without guidance from the health care provider.

SIDE EFFECTS:
- *More common:* Drowsiness, lightheadedness, dry mouth, headache, changes in bowel habits, sialorrhea, amnesia, changes in appetite
- *Less common:* Syncope, tachycardia, seizures, respiratory depression, dependency, withdrawal syndrome, suicidal ideation

DRUG INTERACTIONS:
- *Absolute contraindications:* Clarithromycin, fluvoxamine, ketoconazole
- Avoid using calcium channel blockers, erthromycins, tamoxifen, zafirlukast

▶ **Alert:** This list may not describe all possible interactions. Instruct clients to provide a list of all medicines, herbs, nonprescription drugs, or dietary supplements they use. In addition, instruct clients to inform if they smoke, drink alcohol, or use illegal drugs.

PHARMACOKINETICS:
- BZDs enhance the activity of the GABA, a major CNS neurotransmitter, known to open CNS

Cl⁻ channels, leading to an inhibition of subsequent CNS neuronal signaling.
- BZDs with similar action can differ in their potency and rate of absorption.

Metabolism: Liver with the CYP450; exact mechanism is unknown
Excretion: Urine
Half-life: 14 hr

PRECAUTIONS:
- See client as often as necessary to ensure the drug is working on the panic attacks, determine compliance, and review side effects.
- Instruct client and family to watch for worsening depression or thoughts of suicide. Also watch for sudden or severe changes in feelings such as feeling anxious, agitated, panicky, irritable, hostile, aggressive, impulsive, severely restless, overly excited and hyperactive, or not being able to sleep. If this happens, especially at the beginning of antidepressant treatment or after a change in dose, patients should call the provider.
- Patient should not drive, use machinery, or do anything that needs mental alertness until the effects of this medicine are known.
- Caution patients not to stand or sit up quickly, especially if older. This reduces the risk of dizzy or fainting spells. Alcohol may interfere with the effect of this medicine. Avoid alcoholic drinks.
- Do not abruptly withdraw this drug as it may cause seizures.
- Use with caution on patients with heart disease; liver disease; seizures (convulsions); suicidal thoughts, plans, or attempts by patient or family member; an unusual or allergic reaction to alprazolam, other medicines, foods, dyes, or preservatives.

PATIENT AND FAMILY EDUCATION:
- Store lorazepam at room temperature away from moisture, heat, and light. Remove any cotton from the bottle of disintegrating tablets, and keep the bottle tightly closed.
- Lorazepam may be habit-forming and *should be used only by the person it was prescribed for.* Lorazepam should never be shared with another

(cont.)

lorazepam (cont.)

person, especially someone who has a history of drug abuse or addiction. Keep the medication in a secure place where others cannot get to it.

- Do not purchase lorazepam on the internet or outside of the USA as dangerous ingredients may be present.

SPECIAL POPULATIONS:
- *Elderly:* Older patients may be more sensitive to the effects of benzodiazepines. The smallest effective dose should be used. Dose adjustment is necessary for patients with liver impairment and/or renal disease due to excessive

metabolites excreted by the kidney. Due to increased risk of sedation leading to falls and fractures, benzodiazepines are included on the Beers List of Potentially Inappropriate Medications for Geriatrics.
- *Pregnancy:* Category D; can cause teratogenic fetal effects. Infants born of mothers taking benzodiazepines may be at risk for withdrawal symptoms in the postnatal period.
- *Lactation:* Excreted in human breast milk; infants can become lethargic and lose weight
- *Children:* Not indicated for use with children under 18 years of age.

clonazepam · *Klonopin*

INDICATIONS: Anxiety disorders

AVAILABLE FORMS: Tablet, 0.5, 1, and 2 mg, wafer melt, 0.125, 0.25, 0.5, and 1.2 mg

DOSAGE: *Adults:* Start at 0.25 mg PO bid, increase by 0.25–0.5 mg/day every 3 days; may start lower in elderly patients; maximum, 4 mg/day; treatment should be limited to as short a period as possible (less than 4 months) and/or undergo re-evaluation for continued use. To discontinue, taper by 0.25 mg/day q3 days if greater than 4–6 wk continuous use.

ADMINISTRATION:
- PO with a glass of water.
- Do not abruptly stop taking the medication.
- Use lowest effective dose for shortest duration.
- Clonazepam can be habit forming; do not increase dosage without guidance from the healthcare provider.

SIDE EFFECTS:
- *More common:* Drowsiness, lightheadedness, dry mouth, headache, changes in bowel habits, sialorrhea, amnesia, changes in appetite
- *Less common:* Syncope, tachycardia, seizures, respiratory depression, dependency, withdrawal syndrome, suicidal ideation

DRUG INTERACTIONS:
- *Absolute contraindications:* Clarithromycin, fluvoxamine, ketoconazole
- Avoid using calcium channel blockers, erthromycins, tamoxifen, zafirlukast
▶**Alert:** This list may not describe all possible interactions. Instruct clients to provide a list of all medicines, herbs, nonprescription drugs, or dietary supplements they use. In addition, instruct clients to inform if they smoke, drink alcohol, or use illegal drugs.

PHARMACOKINETICS:
- Benzodiazepines enhance the activity of GABA, a major CNS neurotransmitter, known to open CNS Cl⁻ channels, leading to an inhibition of subsequent CNS neuronal signaling.

- BZDs with similar action can differ in their potency and rate of absorption.

Metabolism: Extensively metabolized in liver; CYP450 3A4
Excretion: Urine
Half-life: 20–50 hr

PRECAUTIONS:
- See client as often as necessary to ensure the drug is working on the panic attacks, determine compliance, and review side effects.
- Instruct client and family to watch for worsening depression or thoughts of suicide. Also watch out for sudden or severe changes in feelings such as feeling anxious, agitated, panicky, irritable, hostile, aggressive, impulsive, severely restless, overly excited and hyperactive, or not being able to sleep. If this happens, especially at the beginning of antidepressant treatment or after a change in dose, patients should call the provider.
- Patients should not drive, use machinery, or do anything that needs mental alertness until the effects of this medicine are known.
- Caution patients not to stand or sit up quickly, especially if older. This reduces the risk of dizzy or fainting spells. Alcohol may interfere with the effect of this medicine. Avoid alcoholic drinks.
- Do not abruptly withdraw this drug as it may cause seizures.
- Use with caution on patients with: heart disease; liver disease; seizures (convulsions); suicidal thoughts, plans, or attempts by patient or family member; an unusual or allergic reaction to alprazolam, other medicines, foods, dyes, or preservatives.

PATIENT AND FAMILY EDUCATION:
- Store clonazepam at room temperature away from moisture, heat, and light. Remove any cotton from the bottle of disintegrating tablets, and keep the bottle tightly closed.
- Clonazepam may be habit-forming and *should be used only by the person it was prescribed for.* Clonazepam should never be shared with
(cont.)

clonazepam (*cont.*)

another person, especially someone who has a history of drug abuse or addiction. Keep the medication in a secure place where others cannot get to it.

SPECIAL POPULATIONS:
- *Elderly:* Older patients may be more sensitive to the effects of benzodiazepines. The smallest effective dose should be used. Dose adjustment is necessary for patients with liver impairment and/or renal disease due to excessive metabolites excreted by the kidney. Due to increased risk of sedation leading to falls and fractures, benzodiazepines are included on the Beers List of Potentially Inappropriate Medications for Geriatrics.
- *Pregnancy:* Category D; can cause teratogenic fetal effects. Infants born of mothers taking benzodiazepines may be at risk for withdrawal symptoms in the postnatal period.
- *Lactation:* Excreted in human breast milk; infants can become lethargic and lose weight
- *Children:* Not indicated for use with children except for treatment of seizures.

Class: Antipsychotics, Typical (First Generation)

Haldol	**haloperidol**
Haldol Decanoate, Haloperidol LA	**haloperidol decanoate**
Haldol, Haldol Concentrate	**haloperidol lactate**

AVAILABLE FORMS: Haloperidol: Tablet, 0.5, 1, 2, 5, 10, and 20 mg; haloperidol decanoate injection, 50 and 100 mg/mL; haloperidol lactate injection, 5 mg/mL; oral concentrate, 2 mg/mL

DOSAGE:
Psychotic Disorders:
- *Adults and children older than age 12:* Dosage varies for each patient. Initially, 0.5 to 5 mg PO bid or tid. Or 2 to 5 mg IM lactate every 4 to 8 hr, although hourly administration may be needed until control is obtained. Maximum, 100 mg PO daily.
- *Children: 3 to 12 yr who weigh 15 to 40 kg (33–88 lb):* Initially, 0.5 mg PO daily divided bid or tid. May increase dose by 0.5 mg at 5- to 7-day intervals, depending on therapeutic response and patient tolerance.
- *Adjust dose:* For debilitated patients, initially, 0.5 to 2 mg PO bid or tid; increase gradually, as needed.

Delirium:
- *Adults:* 1 to 2 mg IV lactate every 2 to 4 hr. Severely agitated patients may require higher doses. *Elderly patients:* 0.25 to 0.5 mg IV every 4 hr.

ADMINISTRATION:
PO:
- Protect drug from light. Slight yellowing of concentrate is common and does not affect potency. Discard very discolored solutions.
- Dilute oral dose with water or a beverage such as orange juice, apple juice, tomato juice, or cola immediately before administration.

IV:
- Only the lactate form can be given IV.
- Monitor patient receiving single doses higher than 50 mg or total daily doses greater than 500 mg closely for prolonged QTc interval and torsades de pointes.
- Store at controlled room temperature and protect from light.

- *Incompatibilities:* Allopurinol, amphotericin B cholesteryl sulfate complex, benztropine, cefepime, diphenhydramine, fluconazole, foscarnet, heparin, hydromorphone, hydroxyzine, ketorolac, morphine, nitroprusside sodium, piperacillin and tazobactam sodium, sargramostim

IM:
- Protect drug from light. Slight yellowing of injection is common and does not affect potency. Discard very discolored solutions.
- When switching from tablets to decanoate injection, give 10 to 15 times the oral dose once a month (maximum 100 mg).
- ▶**Alert:** Do not give the decanoate form IV; exerts antipsychotic effects by blocking postsynaptic dopamine receptors in the brain.

SIDE EFFECTS:
- Severe extrapyramidal reactions, tardive dyskinesia, NMS, seizures, sedation, drowsiness, lethargy, headache, insomnia, confusion, vertigo
- Tachycardia, hypotension, hypertension, ECG change, torsades de pointes, with IV use blurred vision, dry mouth, anorexia, constipation, diarrhea, nausea, vomiting, dyspepsia, urine retention, menstrual irregularities, priapism, leucopenia, leukocytosis, jaundice, rash, other skin reactions, diaphoresis; gynecomastia

DRUG INTERACTIONS: Anticholinergics, azole antifungals, buspirone, macrolides, carbamazepine, CNS depressants, lithium, methyldopa, rifampin. Alcohol use may increase CNS depression.

PRECAUTIONS:
- May increase liver function test values; may increase or decrease WBC count.
- Contraindicated in patients hypersensitive to drug and in those with parkinsonism, coma, or CNS depression.
- Use cautiously in elderly and debilitated patients; in patients with history of seizures or EEG abnormalities, severe CV disorders,

(cont.)

haloperidol, haloperidol decanoate, haloperidol lactate (*cont.*)

allergies, glaucoma, or urine retention; and in those taking anticonvulsants, anticoagulants, antiparkinsons, or lithium.

- Monitor patient for tardive dyskinesia, which may occur after prolonged use. It may not appear until months or years later and may disappear spontaneously or persist for life, despite ending drug.

▶**Alert:** Watch for signs and symptoms of NMS (extrapyramidal effects, hyperthermia, autonomic disturbance), which is rare but commonly fatal.

- Do not withdraw drug abruptly unless required by severe adverse reactions.

▶**Alert:** *Haldol* may contain tartrazine.

▶ *Look Alike–Sound Alike:* Do not confuse *Haldol* with *Halcion* or *Halog.*

PATIENT AND FAMILY EDUCATION:

- Patients avoid activities that require alertness and good coordination until effects of drug are known. Drowsiness and dizziness usually subside after a few weeks.
- Avoid alcohol during therapy.
- Dry mouth: Use sugarless gum or hard candy.

SPECIAL POPULATIONS:

- *Elderly:* Contraindicated in patients hypersensitive to drug and in those with parkinsonism, coma, or CNS depression. Use cautiously in elderly and debilitated patients; in patients with history of seizures or EEG abnormalities, severe CV disorders, allergies, glaucoma, or urine retention; and in those taking anticonvulsants, anticoagulants, antiparkinsons, or lithium.
- Caution is advised when using this drug in the elderly due to more sensitivity to the drug.
- *Pregnancy:* Caution is advised when considering use of this medication in anyone who is pregnant or thinking of becoming pregnant.
- *Children:* Caution when using this drug in a child or adolescent; must balance the potential risks with the clinical need. Caution is advised when using this drug in children because they may be more sensitive to the side effects of the drug, especially loss of appetite and weight loss. It is important to monitor weight and growth in children who are taking this drug.

Class: Antipsychotics, Atypical (Second Generation)

risperidone   *Risperdal, Risperdal Consta, Risperdal M-Tab*

AVAILABLE FORMS: Injection, 12.5, 25, 37.5, and 50 mg; solution, 1 mg/mL; tablet, 0.25, 0.5, 1, 2, 3, and 4 mg; tablet (orally disintegrating), 0.5, 1, 2, 3, and 4 mg

DOSAGE:
Schizophrenia:

- *Adults:* Drug may be given once or twice daily. Initial dosing is generally 2 mg/day. Increase dosage at intervals not less than 24 hr, in increments of 1 or 2 mg/day, as tolerated, to a recommended dose of 4 to 8 mg/day. Periodically reassess to determine the need for maintenance treatment with an appropriate dose.
- *Adolescents aged 13 to 17:* Start treatment with 0.5 mg once daily, given as a single daily dose in either the morning or evening. Adjust dose, if indicated, at intervals not less than 24 hr, in increments of 0.5 or 1 mg/day, as tolerated, to a recommended dose of 3 mg/day. There are no data to support use beyond 8 wk.

Irritability, Including Aggression, Self-Injury, and Temper Tantrums, Associated With an Autistic Disorder:

- *Adolescents and children aged 5 and older who weight 20 kg (44 lb) or more:* Initially, 0.5 mg PO once daily or divided bid. After 4 days, increase dose to 1 mg. Increase dosage further in 0.5 mg increments at intervals of at least 2 wk.
- *Children aged 5 and older who weigh less than 20 kg:* Initially, 0.25 mg PO once daily or divided bid. After 4 days, increase dose to 0.5 mg. Increase dosage further in 0.25 mg increments

at intervals of at least 2 wk. Increase cautiously in children who weigh less than 15 kg (33 lb).

ADMINISTRATION:
PO:

- Give drug with or without food.
- Open package for ODTs immediately before giving by peeling off foil backing with dry hands. Do not push tablets through the foil.
- Phenylalanine contents of ODTs are as follows: 0.5 mg tablet contains 0.14 mg phenylalanine; 1 mg tablet contains 0.28 mg phenylalanine; 2 mg tablet contains 0.56 mg phenylalanine; 3 mg tablet contains 0.63 mg phenylalanine; 4 mg tablet contains 0.84 mg phenylalanine.

IM:

- Continue oral therapy for the first 3 wk of IM injection therapy until injections take effect, then stop oral therapy.
- To reconstitute IM injection, inject premeasured diluent into vial and shake vigorously for at least 10 sec. Suspension appears uniform, thick, and milky; particles are visible, but no dry particles remain. Use drug immediately, or refrigerate for up to 6 hr after reconstitution. If more than 2 min pass before injection, shake vigorously again. See manufacturer's package insert for more detailed instructions.
- Refrigerate IM injection kit and protect it from light. Drug can be stored at temperature less than 77° F (25° C) for no more than 7 days before administration.

(cont.)

risperidone (*cont.*)

SIDE EFFECTS:
- Akathisia, somnolence, dystonia, headache, insomnia, agitation, anxiety, pain, parkinsonism, NMS, suicide attempt, dizziness, fever, hallucination, mania, impaired concentration, abnormal thinking and dreaming, tremor, hypoesthesia, fatigue, depression, nervousness
- Tachycardia, chest pain, orthostatic hypotension, peripheral edema, syncope, hypertension
- Rhinitis, sinusitis, pharyngitis, ear disorder
- Constipation, nausea, vomiting, dyspepsia, abdominal pain, anorexia, dry mouth, increased saliva, diarrhea
- Urinary incontinence, increased urination, abnormal orgasm, vaginal dryness, weight gain, hyperglycemia, weight loss
- Arthralgia, back pain, leg pain, myalgia
- Coughing, dyspnea, upper respiratory infection
- Rash, dry skin, photosensitivity reactions, acne, injection site pain
- Tooth disorder, toothache, injury, decreased libido

DRUG INTERACTIONS:
- Antihypertensives, carbamazepine, clozapine, CNS depressants, dopamine agonists, levodopa, fluoxetine, paroxetine. Alcohol use may cause CNS depression.

PHARMACOKINETICS:
- Blocks dopamine and 5-HT$_2$ receptors in the brain.

Half-life: 3–20 hr

ROUTE	ONSET	PEAK	DURATION
PO	Onset is unknown	Peak Action = 1 hr	Duration of effect is Unknown
IM	3 wk	4–6 wk	7 wk

PRECAUTIONS:
- May increase prolactin level. May decrease hemoglobin level and hematocrit.
- *Sun exposure may increase risk of photosensitivity reactions.*
- Contraindicated in patients hypersensitive to drug and in breastfeeding women.
- Use cautiously in patients with prolonged QT interval, cerebrovascular disease, dehydration, hypovolemia, history of seizures, or conditions that could affect metabolism or hemodynamic responses.
- Use cautiously in patients exposed to extreme heat.
- Use caution in patients at risk for aspiration pneumonia.

- Use IM injection cautiously in those with hepatic or renal impairment.
- ▶**Alert:** Obtain baseline BP measurements before starting therapy, and monitor pressure regularly. Watch for orthostatic hypotension, especially during first dosage adjustment.
- ▶**Alert:** Fatal cerebrovascular adverse events (stroke, transient ischemic attacks) may occur in elderly patients with dementia. Drug is not safe or effective in these patients.
- Monitor patient for tardive dyskinesia, which may occur after prolonged use. It may not appear until months or years later and may disappear spontaneously or persist for life, despite stopping drug.
- Life-threatening hyperglycemia may occur in patients taking atypical antipsychotics. Monitor patients with diabetes regularly.
- Monitor patient for weight gain.
- Periodically reevaluate drug's risks and benefits, especially during prolonged use.
- ▶**Alert:** Watch for evidence of NMS (extrapyramidal effects, hyperthermia, autonomic disturbance), which is rare but can be fatal.
- ▶**Alert:** Monitor patient for symptoms of metabolic syndrome (significant weight gain and increased BMI, hypertension, hyperglycemia, hypercholesterolemia, and hypertriglyceridemia).

PATIENT AND FAMILY EDUCATION:
- Warn patient to avoid activities that require alertness until effects of drug are known.
- Warn patient to rise slowly, avoid hot showers, and use other precautions to avoid fainting when starting therapy.
- Advise patient to use caution in hot weather to prevent heatstroke.
- Tell patient to take drug with or without food.
- Instruct patient to keep the ODT in the blister pack until just before taking it. After opening the pack, dissolve the tablet on tongue without cutting or chewing. Use dry hands to peel apart the foil to expose the tablet; do not attempt to push it through the foil.
- Tell patient to use sunblock and wear protective clothing outdoors.
- Advise patient to avoid alcohol during therapy.

SPECIAL POPULATIONS:
- *Pregnancy:* Advise women not to become pregnant or to breastfeed for 12 wk after the last IM injection.

SCHIZOTYPAL PERSONALITY DISORDER: Antipsychotics, Atypical (Second Generation)

olanzapine   *Zyprexa, Zydis*

AVAILABLE FORMS: Injection, 10 mg; tablet, 2.5, 5, 7.5, 10, 15, and 20 mg; tablet (orally disintegrating), 5, 10, 15, and 20 mg

DOSAGE:
Schizophrenia:
- *Adults:* Initially, 5 to 10 mg PO once daily with the goal 10 mg daily within several days of starting therapy. Adjust dose in 5 mg increments at intervals of 1 wk or more. Most patients respond to 10 to 15 mg daily. Safety of dosages greater than 20 mg daily not established.

Short-Term Treatment of Acute Manic Episodes Linked to Bipolar I Disorder:
- *Adults:* Initially, 10 to 15 mg PO daily. Adjust dosage as needed in 5 mg daily increments at intervals of 24 hr or more. Maximum, 20 mg PO daily. Duration of treatment is 3 to 4 wk.

Short-Term Treatment, With Lithium or Valproate, of Acute Manic Episodes Linked to Bipolar I Disorder:
- *Adults:* 10 mg PO once daily. Dosage range is 5 to 20 mg daily. Duration of treatment is 6 wk.
- *Adjust dose:* In elderly or debilitated patients, those predisposed to hypotensive reactions, patients who may metabolize olanzapine more slowly than usual (nonsmoking women older than age 65) or may be more pharmacodynamically sensitive to olanzapine, initially, 5 mg PO. Increase dose cautiously.

Agitation Caused by Schizophrenia and Bipolar I Mania:
- *Adults:* 10 mg IM (range 2.5–10 mg). Subsequent doses of up to 10 mg may be given 2 hr after the first dose or 4 hr after the second dose, up to 30 mg IM daily. If maintenance therapy is required, convert patient to 5 to 20 mg PO daily.
- *Adjust dose:* In elderly patients, give 5 mg IM. In debilitated patients, in those predisposed to hypotension, and in patients sensitive to effects of drug, give 2.5 mg IM.

ADMINISTRATION:
PO:
- Give drug with or without food.
- Do not crush or break ODT.
- Place immediately on patient's tongue after opening package.
- ODT may be given without water.

IM:
- Inspect IM solution for particulate matter and discoloration before administration.
- To reconstitute IM injection, dissolve contents of one vial with 2.1 mL of sterile water for injection to yield a clear yellow 5 mg/mL solution. Store at room temperature and give within 1 hr of reconstitution. Discard any unused solution.

SIDE EFFECTS:
- Somnolence, insomnia, parkinsonism, dizziness, NMS, suicide attempt, abnormal gait, asthenia, personality disorder, akathisia, tremor, articulation impairment, tardive dyskinesia, fever, extrapyramidal events
- Orthostatic hypotension, tachycardia, chest pain, hypertension, ecchymosis, peripheral edema, hypotension
- Amblyopia, rhinitis, pharyngitis, conjunctivitis
- Constipation, dry mouth, dyspepsia, increased appetite, increased salivation, vomiting, thirst
- Hematuria, metrorrhagia, urinary incontinence, UTI, amenorrhea, vaginitis
- Leucopenia
- Hyperglycemia, weight gain
- Joint pain, extremity pain, back pain, neck rigidity, twitching, hypertonia
- Increased cough, dyspnea
- Sweating, injection site pain (*IM*)
- Flu-like syndrome, injury

DRUG INTERACTIONS:
- Antihypertensives, carbamazepine, omeprazole, rifampin, ciprofloxacin, diazepam, dopamine agonists, levodopa, fluoxetine, fluvoxamine, St. John's wort
- Alcohol use may increase CNS effects.
- Smoking may increase drug clearance.

PHARMACOKINETICS:
- May block dopamine and 5-HT$_2$ receptors.
Half-life: 21–54 hr

ROUTE	ONSET	PEAK	DURATION
PO	Unknown	6 hr	Unknown
IM	Rapid	15–45 min	Unknown

PRECAUTIONS:
- May increase AST, ALT, GGT, CK, triglyceride, and prolactin levels.
- May increase eosinophil count; may decrease WBC count.
- Contraindicated in patients hypersensitive to drug.
- Use cautiously in patients with heart disease, cerebrovascular disease, conditions that predispose patient to hypotension, history of seizures or conditions that might lower the seizure threshold, and hepatic impairment.
- Use cautiously in elderly patients, those with a history of paralytic ileus, and those at risk for aspiration pneumonia, prostatic hyperplasia, or angle-closure glaucoma.
- ODTs contain phenylalanine.
- Monitor patient for abnormal body temperature regulation, especially if patient exercises, is exposed to extreme heat, takes anticholinergics, or is dehydrated.
- Obtain baseline and periodic liver function test results.
- Monitor patient for weight gain.
- ▶**Alert:** Watch for evidence of NMS (hyperpyrexia, muscle rigidity, altered mental status, autonomic instability), which is rare but commonly
(cont.)

fatal. Stop drug immediately; monitor and treat patient as needed.
▶**Alert:** Drug may cause hyperglycemia. Monitor patients with diabetes regularly. In patients with risk factors for diabetes, obtain fasting blood glucose test results at baseline and periodically.
▶**Alert:** Monitor patient for symptoms of metabolic syndrome (significant weight gain and increased BMI, hypertension, hyperglycemia, hypercholesterolemia, and hypertriglyceridemia).
- Monitor patient for tardive dyskinesia, which may occur after prolonged use. It may not appear until months or years later and may disappear spontaneously or persist for life, despite stopping drug.
- Periodically reevaluate the long-term usefulness of olanzapine.
- Drug may increase risk of stroke and death in elderly patients with dementia. Olanzapine is not approved to treat patients with dementia-related psychosis.
- Patient who feel dizzy or drowsy after an IM injection should remain recumbent until patient can be assessed for orthostatic hypotension and bradycardia. Patient should rest until the feeling passes.
▶**Alert:** Drug may increase the risk of suicidal thinking and behavior in young adults ages 18 to 24 during the first 2 months of treatment.

PATIENT AND FAMILY EDUCATION:
- Avoid hazardous tasks until full effects of drug are known.
- Avoid exposure to extreme heat; drug may impair body's ability to reduce temperature.
- Patient may gain weight.
- Avoid alcohol.
- Rise slowly to avoid dizziness upon standing up quickly.
- That ODTs contain phenylalanine.
- Peel foil away from ODT; do not push tablet through. Take tablet immediately, allowing tablet to dissolve on tongue and swallow with saliva; no additional fluid is needed.
- Take drug with or without food.
- If a woman of childbearing age, notify prescriber if becomes pregnant or plans or suspects pregnancy. Do not breastfeed during therapy.

SPECIAL POPULATIONS:
- *Elderly:* Caution is advised when using this drug in the elderly because they may be more sensitive to the effects of the drug, especially drowsiness, difficulty urinating, and heart problems.
- *Pregnancy:* This medication should be used only when clearly needed during pregnancy.
- *Lactation:* Do not breastfeed during therapy.

Seroquel   **quetiapine**

AVAILABLE FORMS: Tablet, 25, 50, 100, 200, 300, and 400 mg

DOSAGE:
Bipolar Disorder:
- Initial dose 50 mg twice daily (100 mg/day). The dose can be increased by 100 mg/day to a daily dose of 400 mg/day. Most patients respond to 400 to 800 mg/day. Doses greater than 800 mg/day have not been studied.
Schizophrenia:
- Initial dose 25 mg twice daily (50 mg/day). The dose can be increased by 25 to 50 mg two or three times daily. The target dose is 300 to 400 mg/day in two or three doses. Patients respond to 150 to 750 mg/day, and doses greater than 800 mg/day have not been evaluated.

ADMINISTRATION:
- Taken two or three times daily.
- Dose usually is increased slowly over several days or weeks to achieve the desired effect.
- Can be taken with or without food.
- Avoid eating grapefruit or drinking grapefruit juice while being treated with this medication.

SIDE EFFECTS:
- Constipation, drowsiness, dizziness, stomach pain or upset, weight gain or dry mouth.
- Fainting, unusually fast or irregular heartbeat
- Skin rash, itching, trouble breathing.
- Fever, persistent sore throat, muscle stiffness, confusion, sweating, uncontrolled muscle movements (e.g., tongue or facial muscles), one-sided muscle weakness, cold sensitivity, trouble urinating, black stools, unusual moods
- May infrequently make blood sugar level rise, therefore causing or worsening diabetes
- Patient should check blood sugar level regularly
- May also cause significant weight gain and rise in blood cholesterol (or triglyceride) levels
- These effects, along with diabetes, may increase risk for developing Heart disease

DRUG INTERACTIONS: Used with caution in combination with other centrally acting drugs. Caution should be exercised when used concomitantly with drugs known to cause electrolyte imbalance or to increase QT interval

PHARMACOKINETICS:
- The absolute bioavailability is unknown, but the relative bioavailability from orally
(cont.)

quetiapine (cont.)

administered tablets compared with a solution was nearly complete.

- Food has minimal effects on quetiapine absorption.
- The drug is approximately 83% bound to serum proteins.
- Single and multiple dose studies have demonstrated linear pharmacokinetics in the clinical dose range (up to 375 mg twice daily).
- The drug is eliminated with a mean terminal half-life of approximately 7 hr.
- The primary route of elimination is through hepatic metabolism

PRECAUTIONS:

- The US FDA has issued a black box warning about the use of *Seroquel* in elderly people with psychosis or dementia (a condition involving confusion; disorientation; and a loss of memory, intellect, and judgment).
- Elderly people with dementia (Alzheimer's disease is the most common form) who are treated with antipsychotics—including *Seroquel*—are more likely to die of various causes than those who were not treated with those medications.
- Not approved to treat dementia or dementia-related psychosis, and caution should be used before giving the medication to elderly people with this condition.
- Even though *Seroquel* is not classified as an antidepressant, the FDA has required the drug to carry the special antidepressant and suicide warning, since it is used to treat bipolar depression.
- Antidepressants may increase the risk of suicidal thinking or behavior in people taking it.

PATIENT AND FAMILY EDUCATION:

- Take this medication by mouth with or without food, usually 2 or 3 times daily or as directed by provider.
- Dosage is based on medical condition and response to therapy.
- That provider will start with a low dose and gradually increase the dose to reduce dizziness and lightheadedness that may occur when starting this drug.
- It may take several weeks to notice the full benefit of this drug.

- Take this medication regularly and at the same times each day to get the most benefit from it.
- Take this medication exactly as prescribed, even if feeling better and thinking more clearly.
- Do not stop taking this medication without first consulting the prescriber to avoid withdrawal symptoms (such as trouble sleeping, nausea, diarrhea, irritability) that may occur when suddenly stopping this medication. To prevent withdrawal reactions, the provider may reduce your dose gradually.
- Some conditions may become worse when the drug is suddenly stopped.
- Consult your doctor for more details and report any withdrawal reactions immediately.
- Avoid grapefruit and grapefruit juice while being treated with this medication. Grapefruit may increase the amount of certain medications in the blood stream.
- This drug may increase blood sugar levels and worsen diabetes.
- This drug may increase susceptibility to heat stroke.

SPECIAL POPULATIONS:

- *Elderly:* Use with caution. The mean plasma clearance of the drug was reduced by 30% to 50% in elderly subjects when compared to younger patients. The rate of dose titration may thus need to be slower, and the daily therapeutic target dose lower, than that used in younger patients. Should be used with caution in patients with mild hepatic impairment, especially during the initial dosing period. Patients with mild hepatic impairment should be started on 25 mg/day; dose should be increased daily in increments of 25 to 50 mg/day to an effective dose.
- *Pregnancy:* Use only when clearly needed during pregnancy.
- *Lactation:* It is not known whether this drug passes into breast milk. Because of the possible risk to the infant, breastfeeding while using this drug is not recommended.
- *Children:* Use with caution before using this drug in children. Research inconclusive.

ziprasidone   *Geodon*

AVAILABLE FORMS: IM: Capsule, 20 mg (blue/white), 40 mg (blue/blue), 60 mg (white/white), and 80 mg (blue/white)

DOSAGE:

- *Schizophrenia (20 mg PO bid):* Start, 20 mg PO bid; maximum, 80 mg bid; Give with food; may adjust dose every 2 days prn; doses greater than 40 mg/day rarely more effective; periodically reassess need for treatment; discontinue if ANC

less than 1,000; consider discontinuing if unexplained decrease in WBC.

- *Bipolar disorder, manic/mixed:* Monotherapy, 40 to 80 mg PO bid; start, 40 mg PO bid ×1 day, then 60 to 80 mg PO bid; maximum, 80 mg bid; for acute treatment, give with food; may adjust dose every 2 days prn; discontinuing if ANC less than 1,000; consider discontinue if unexplained decrease in WBC. Valproate or lithium adjunct: 40 to 80 mg PO bid; for maintenance treatment; *(cont.)*

ziprasidone (cont.)

give with food; continue treatment at same dose at which patient initially stabilized; periodically reassess need for treatment; discontinue if ANC less than 1,000; consider discontinuing if unexplained decrease in WBC.

- *Agitation, schizophrenia-associated* (10 mg IM every 2 hr prn): Alternative, 20 mg IM every 4 hr prn; maximum, 40 mg/day ×3 days; switch to PO ASAP; discontinue if ANC less than 1,000; consider discontinuing if unexplained decrease in WBC.
- *Renal impairment:* Caution advised with IM use.
- Pediatric dosing not applicable for this medication

ADMINISTRATION:
- Should be administered at an initial dose of 20 mg twice daily with food.
- In some patients, daily dosage may subsequently be adjusted on the basis of individual clinical status up to 80 mg twice daily.
- Dosage adjustments, if indicated, should generally occur at intervals of not less than 2 days, as steady state is achieved within 1 to 3 days.
- In order to ensure use of the lowest effective dose, patients should be observed for improvement for several weeks before upward dosage adjustment.

SIDE EFFECTS:
- Cardiac: Tachycardia, torsade de pointes (in the presence of multiple confounding factors)
- *GI:* Swollen tongue
- *Reproductive system and breast:* Galactorrhea, priapism
- *CNS:* Facial droop, NMS, serotonin syndrome (alone or in combination with serotonergic medicinal products), tardive dyskinesia
- *Psychiatric:* Insomnia, mania/hypomania
- *Skin:* Allergic reaction (such as allergic dermatitis, angioedema, orofacial edema, urticaria), rash
- *GU*: Enuresis, urinary incontinence
- *Vascular:* Postural hypotension, syncope

DRUG INTERACTIONS:
- Caution when using with other drugs that may affect the heart rhythm (QTc prolongation in the EKG) such as dofetilide, pimozide, quinidine, sotalol, procainamide, and sparfloxacin among others.
- QTc prolongation can infrequently result in serious, rarely fatal, irregular heartbeats.
- Anti-Parkinson drugs (e.g., pramipexole, ropinirole), azole antifungals (e.g., ketoconazole, itraconazole), certain blood pressure medications (e.g., beta-blockers such as metoprolol or propranolol, "water pills" or diuretics such as furosemide or hydrochlorothiazide, or alpha-blockers such as doxazosin or prazosin) may interact with this drug.
- Patients should advise if they take drugs that cause drowsiness, including antianxiety drugs (e.g., diazepam), antihistamines that cause drowsiness (e.g., diphenhydramine), antiseizure drugs

(e.g., carbamazepine), medicine for sleep (e.g., sedatives), muscle relaxants, narcotic pain relievers (e.g., codeine), other psychiatric medicines (e.g., phenothiazines such as chlorpromazine, or tricyclics such as amitriptyline), tranquilizers.

PHARMACOKINETICS:
- Is a selective monoaminergic antagonist with high affinity for the serotonin type 2 (5-HT$_2$), dopamine type 2 (D2), 1 and 2 adrenergic, and H1 histaminergic receptors.
- Acts as an antagonist at other receptors, but with lower potency.
- Antagonism at receptors other than dopamine and 5-HT$_2$ with similar receptor affinities may explain some of the other therapeutic and side effects.
- Antagonism of muscarinic M1-5 receptors may explain its anticholinergic effects.
- Antagonism of histamine H1 receptors.
- Antagonism of adrenergic alpha-1 receptors may explain the orthostatic hypotension observed with this drug.
- Functions as an antagonist at the dopamine D2, 5-HT$_{2A}$, and 5-HT$_{1D}$ receptors, and as an agonist at the 5-HT$_{1A}$ receptor.
- Inhibits synaptic reuptake of serotonin and norepinephrine.

PRECAUTIONS:
- Monitor patient closely and check potassium levels regularly.
- Patient should report fainting; dizziness; fast, racing, pounding, or irregular heartbeat; hyperglycemia, especially blurred vision; drowsiness; dry mouth; flushed, dry skin; fruit-like breath odor; increased urination; ketones in urine; loss of appetite; stomachache; nausea or vomiting; tiredness; trouble breathing; unconsciousness; or unusual thirst.
- Do not use in treatment of dementia-related psychosis.

PATIENT AND FAMILY EDUCATION:
- May cause some people to become drowsy, dizzy, or less alert than normally.
- Make sure the patient knows the reaction to this medicine before driving, using machines, or anything else that could be dangerous if dizzy or not alert.
- Avoid use of alcohol.
- Avoid activities involving high temperature or humidity.
- This medicine may reduce the body's ability to adjust to heat.

SPECIAL POPULATIONS:
- *Elderly:* Patients with dementia-related psychosis treated with antipsychotic drugs are at an increased risk of death. Not approved for the treatment of dementia-related psychosis.
- *Pregnancy/Lactation:* Safe use in pregnancy and breastfeeding have not been established.
- *Children:* Safe use in pediatric patients has not been established.

Antisocial Personality Disorder

OVERVIEW

- Characterized by pattern of disregard for, and violation of, the rights of others with central characteristics of deceit and manipulation; often homicidal.
- Occurs in about 3% of the population and is three times more common in males than females.
- 50% of prison populations are diagnosed with antisocial personality disorder.
- Antisocial behaviors tend to peak in the 20s and diminish significantly after 45 years of age.
- A genetic contribution to antisocial behaviors is strongly supported.
- Childhood histories include enuresis, sleepwalking, and syntonic acts of cruelty.
- Diagnostic criteria include violation of rights of others; lack of remorse for behaviors; shallow emotions; lying; rationalization of own behavior; poor judgment; impulsivity; irritability and aggressiveness; lack of insight; thrill-seeking behaviors; exploitation of people in reationships; poor work history; consistent irresponsbility.
- Often appear confident, self-assured and accomplished, even arrogant.
- Typically maniuplate and exploit those around them.
- Patients often are involved in many relationships, sometimes simultaneously, but cannot sustain long-term commitments. Work history is usually poor.
- At risk for anxiety disorders, substance abuse, somatization disorder, and pathological gambling.

Acute Treatment

Medications are rarely effective in treatment of this disorder; it is one of the most difficult to treat and medications are often abused by individuals with antisocial personality disorder. Occasional, short-term use of antipsychotics or mood stabilizers may be helpful in some individuals. The medications may be useful in decreasing irritability and aggressive behavior.

Chronic Treatment

Some symptoms, criminal behaviors, may improve with age, beginning in the 30s. Long-term medication use is not a good option for management; however, it may be necessary either as monotherapy in a patient resistant to psychotherapy or as an adjunct to psychotherapy. For an adherent patient, pyschotherapy (especially cognitive and behavioral group therapy) with an experienced clinician is the preferred choice for chronic management.

CLASS	DRUG
Antipsychotics, Typical (First Generation)	
	haloperidol (*Haldol*)
Antipsychotics, Atypical (Second Generation)	
	risperidone (*Risperida, Risperidal Consta*)
	olanzapine (*Zyprexa*); Olanzapine/fluoxetine combination (*Symbyax*)
	quetiapine (*Seroquel, Seroquel XR*)
	ziprasidone (*Geodon, Geodon IM Injection*)
Mood Stabilizers	
	lithium (*Eskalith, Lithobid, Carbolith, Duralith Lithizine*)
Mood-Stabilizing Anticonvulsants	
	carbamazepine (*Tegretol Carbatrol, Epitol, Equetro, Tegretol-XR, Tegretol-CR*)
	valproate sodium, valproic acid, divalproex sodium (*Depacon, Depakene, Depakote, Depakote ER, Depakote Sprinkle*)
	topiramate (*Topamax*)
	lamotrigine (*Lamictal, Lamictal XR*)

ANTISOCIAL PERSONALITY DISORDER

Class: Antipsychotics, Typical (First Generation)

Haldol   **haloperidol**

AVAILABLE FORMS: Tablet, 0.5, 1, 2, 5, 10, and 20 mg scored; concentrate, 2 mg/mL; solution, 1 mg/mL; injection, 5 mg/mL (immediate-release); decanoate injection, 50 mg haloperidol as 60.5 mg/mL, haloperidol decanoate, 100 mg haloperidol as 141.04 mg/mL haloperidol decanoate

DOSAGE: 1 to 20 mg/day orally. *Immediate-release injection:* 2 to 5 mg each dose. *Decanoate injection:* 10 to 20 times the effective daily dose of oral formulation, administered every 4 wk

ADMINISTRATION:
- *Oral:* Once daily or in divided doses at the beginning of treatment during rapid escalation; increase as needed; can be dosed up to 100 mg/day.
- *Immediate-release injection:* Initial dose 2 to 5 mg; subsequent doses may be given as often as every hour; patient should be switched to oral administration ASAP.
- *Decanoate injection:* Initial dose 10 to 15 times the effective oral dose for patients maintained on low antipsychotic doses (up to equivalent of 10 mg/day oral haloperidol). Initial dose may be as high as 20 times previous oral dose for patients maintained on higher antipsychotic doses: Maximum, 100 mg. If higher dose is required, the remainder can be administered 3 to 7 days later. Administer total dose every 4 wk.
- Patient must stay hydrated.
- Haloperidol is frequently dosed too high. High doses may actually worsen negative symptoms of schizophrenia and increase EPS side effects.

SIDE EFFECTS: Neuroleptic-induced deficit syndrome; akathisia; EPS, parkinsonism, tardive dyskinesia, tardive dystonia; galactorrhea, amenorrhea; dizziness, sedation; dry mouth, constipation, urinary retention, blurred vision; decreased sweating; hypotension, tachycardia, hyperlipidemia; weight gain; rare NMS; rare seizures; rare jaundice, agranulocytosis, leukopenia; haloperidol with anticholinergics may increase intraocular pressure; reduces effects of anticoagulants; plasma levels of haloperidol lowered by rifampin; may enhance effects of antihypertensive agents; haloperidol with lithium may contribute to development of encephalopathic syndrome

DRUG INTERACTIONS:
- May decrease the effects of levodopa, dopamine agonists
- May increase the effects of antihypertensive drugs except for guanethidine
- Additive effects with CNS depressants, dose of other should be reduced
- May interact with some pressor agents (epinephrine) to lower blood pressure

PHARMACOKINETICS:
Half-life: Haloperidol decanoate, approximately 3 wk; oral half-life, approximately 12 to 36 hr

PRECAUTIONS:
- Discontinue if patient develops symptoms of NMS.
- Use with caution in patients with respiratory problems.
- Avoid extreme heat exposure.
- May experience rapid shift to depression if used to treat mania.
- Patients with thyrotoxicosis may experience neurotoxicity.
- Do not use with Lewy body dementia or Parkinson's disease.
- Use with caution in patients with QTc prolongation, hypothyroidism, familial long-QT syndrome.
- Do not use if there is a proven allergy to haloperidol.

PATIENT AND FAMILY EDUCATION:
- Take exactly as prescribed.
- Avoid getting up too fast from sitting or lying position. Get up slowly and steady yourself to prevent a fall.
- Avoid drinking alcohol.
- *Stop using this medication and call provider immediately* if you have very stiff (rigid) muscles, high fever, sweating, confusion, fast or uneven heartbeats, tremors; feel like you might pass out; have jerky muscle movements you cannot control, trouble swallowing, problems with speech; have blurred vision, eye pain, or seeing halos around lights; have increased thirst and urination, excessive hunger, fruity breath odor, weakness, nausea and vomiting; have fever, chills, body aches, flu symptoms, or have white patches or sores inside mouth or on lips.
- Do not stop taking drug suddenly without first talking to provider, even if you feel fine. May have serious side effects if you stop taking the drug suddenly.
- Call provider if symptoms do not improve, or get worse.
- Store at room temperature away from moisture and heat.

SPECIAL POPULATIONS:
- *Elderly:* Lower doses should be used and patient monitored closely. Do not use in elderly patients with dementia.
- *Renal impairment*: Use with caution.
- *Hepatic impairment*: Use with caution.
- *Cardiac impairment*: Because of risk of orthostatic hypertension, use with caution.
- *Pregnancy:* Category C; some animal studies show adverse effects, no controlled studies in humans.
- *Lactation:* Category C.
- *Children and adolescents*: Safety and efficacy not established. Not intended for use with children under age 3. Generally consider as second line, not first line.

ANTISOCIAL PERSONALITY DISORDER: Antipsychotics, Typical (First Generation)

Class: Antipsychotics, Atypical (Second Generation)

risperidone	*Risperdal, Risperdal Consta*

AVAILABLE FORMS: Tablet, 0.25, 0.5, 1, 2, 3, 4, or 6 mg; ODT, 0.5, 1, or 2 mg; liquid, 1 mg/mL (30 mL bottle); long-acting depot microspheres for deep IM formulation, 25 mg vial/kit, 37.5 mg vial/kit, 50 mg vial/kit

DOSAGE:
- *Adults:* 2 to 8 mg/day orally for acute psychosis and bipolar disorder
- *Children/Elderly:* 0.5 to 2.0 mg/day orally
- 25 to 50 mg depot IM every 2 wk

ADMINISTRATION:
- Tablets may be given with or without food.
- Advise patient to take the missed dose as soon as remembers. Skip the missed dose if almost time for next scheduled dose. Do not take extra medicine to make up the missed dose.
- Measure the liquid form of risperidone with a special dose-measuring spoon or cup, not a regular tablespoon.
- Do not mix the liquid form with cola or tea.

SIDE EFFECTS: Can increase risk for diabetes and dyslipidemia; EPS (dose-dependent, use lowest effective dose to minimize); hyperprolactinemia (dose-dependent); dizziness, insomnia, headache, anxiety; nausea, sedation, weight gain, constipation, abdominal pain; tachycardia; sedation; sexual dysfunction; hyperglycemia; increased risk of death and cerebrovascular events in elderly with dementia-related psychosis; tardive dyskinesia (rare); orthostatic hypotension (rare, usually during initial dose titration); NMS (rare); seizures (rare)

DRUG INTERACTIONS:
- May increase effects of antihypertensive medications.
- May antagonize levodopa, dopamine agonists.
- Plasma levels of risperidone may be reduced if given in conjunction with carbamazepine.
- Plasma levels of risperidone may be increased if given in conjunction with fluoxetine or paroxetine.
- Plasma levels of risperidone may be increased if given in conjunction with clozapine (*Clozaril*), but no dose adjustment is required.

▶**Alert:** This list may not describe all possible interactions. Instruct clients to provide a list of all the medicines, herbs, nonprescription drugs, or dietary supplements they use.

PHARMACOKINETICS:
Elimination: 7–8 wk after last injection (long-acting IM formulation)
Metabolism: Active; metabolized by CYP450 2D6
Half-life: 20–24 hr (oral formulation); 3–6 days (long-acting formulation)

PRECAUTIONS:
- Use with caution in patients with conditions that predispose to hypotension (dehydration, overheating) or are at risk for aspiration pneumonia.
- Priapism has been reported.

- *Do not use if there is a proven allergy.*

PATIENT AND FAMILY EDUCATION:
- Take exactly as prescribed by provider. Do not take in larger or smaller amounts or for longer than recommended.
- Can be taken with or without food.
- May be more sensitive to temperature extremes (very hot or cold conditions) when taking this medication. Avoid getting too cold, or becoming overheated or dehydrated.
- Drink plenty of fluids, especially in hot weather and during exercise.
- Risperidone can cause side effects that may impair thinking or reactions. Be careful when driving or doing anything that requires you to be awake and alert.
- Risperidone may cause high blood sugar (hyperglycemia). Talk to provider if any signs of hyperglycemia such as increased thirst or urination, excessive hunger, or weakness. If diabetic, check blood sugar levels on a regular basis.
- Risperidone ODT may contain phenylalanine. Talk to provider before using this form of risperidone if you have PKU.
- *Avoid drinking alcohol.* It can increase some of the side effects.
- *Do not* mix the liquid form with cola or tea.
- *Stop using this medication and call provider immediately* if you have fever, stiff muscles, confusion, sweating, fast or uneven heartbeats, restless muscle movements in face or neck, tremor (uncontrolled shaking), trouble swallowing, feeling light-headed, or fainting.
- Do not stop taking drug suddenly without first talking to provider, even if you feel fine. May have serious side effects if you stop taking the drug suddenly.
- Call provider if symptoms do not improve or get worse.
- Store at room temperature away from moisture, light, and heat. Do not freeze the liquid form of risperidone.

SPECIAL POPULATIONS:
- *Elderly:*
  - Initially, 0.5 mg orally a day, then increase to 0.5 mg twice a day. Titrate once a week for doses above 1.5 mg twice a day.
  - Long-acting risperidone: 25 mg every 2 wk. Oral administration should be continued for 3 wk after the first injection.
  - Elderly with dementia-related psychosis treated with atypical antipsychotics are at higher risk of death and cerebrovascular events.
- *Renal impairment:*
  - Initially, 0.5 mg orally twice a day for the first week. Increase to 1 mg twice a day during the second week.
  - Long-acting risperidone should not be given to patient with renal function impairment unless s/he can tolerate at least 2 mg/day orally. *(cont.)*

risperidone (*cont.*)

- Long-acting risperidone should be given 25 mg every 2 wk. Oral administration should be continued for 3 wk after the first injection.
- *Hepatic impairment*
  - Initially, 0.5 mg orally twice a day for the first week. Increase to 1 mg twice a day during the second week.
  - Long-acting risperidone should not be given to patient with renal function impairment unless s/he can tolerate at least 2 mg/day orally.
  - Long-acting risperidone should be given 25 mg every 2 wk. Oral administration should be continued for 3 wk after the first injection.
- *Cardiac impairment*: Use with caution because of risk of orthostatic hypotension. Can increase the risk of stroke if given to elderly patients with atrial fibrillation.

- *Pregnancy:* Category C; some animal studies show adverse effects. No controlled studies in humans. Should be used only when the potential benefits outweigh potential risks to the fetus. Risperidone may be preferable to anticonvulsant mood stabilizers if treatment is required during pregnancy. Effects of hyperprolactinemia on the fetus are unknown.
- *Lactation:* Secreted in human breast milk. It is recommended to either discontinue drug or bottlefeed. Infants of women who choose to breastfeed while on this drug should be monitored for possible adverse effects.
- *Children and adolescents*: Safe and effective for behavioral disturbances in this population.

Zyprexa
Symbyax

olanzapine
olanzapine/fluoxetine

AVAILABLE FORMS: Tablet, 2.5, 5, 7.5, 10, 15, and 20 mg; ODT, 5, 10, 15, and 20 mg. *Symbyax* (olanzapine/fluoxetine combination): IM: 5 mg/mL (each vial contains 10 mg olanzapine–fluoxetine); combination capsule, 6 mg/25 mg, 6 mg/50 mg, 12 mg/25 mg, 12 mg/50 mg

DOSAGE:

- 5 to 10 mg/day, up to maximum 20 mg/day (oral or IM)
- 6 to 12 mg/olanzapine/25 to 50 mg fluoxetine (olanzapine–fluoxetine combination)

ADMINISTRATION:

- Injectable formulation may be more easily administered to patient with delusional disorder.
- Tablets may be given with or without food.
- Advise patient to take the missed dose as soon as s/he remembers. Skip the missed dose if almost time for next scheduled dose. Do not take extra medicine to make up the missed dose.
- Store at room temperature away from moisture, heat, and light.

SIDE EFFECTS: Can increase risk for diabetes and dyslipidemia; dizziness, sedation; weight gain; dry mouth, constipation, dyspepsia; peripheral edema; joint pain, back pain, chest pain, extremity pain, abnormal gait, ecchymosis; tachycardia; orthostatic hypotension (usually during initial dose titration); hyperglycemia; increased risk of death and cerebrovascular events in elderly with dementia-related psychosis; tardive dyskinesia (rare); rash on exposure to sunlight (rare); NMS (rare); seizures (rare)

DRUG INTERACTIONS:

- May increase effects of antihypertensive medications
- May antagonize levodopa, dopamine agonists
- May need to reduce dose if given with CYP450 1A2 inhibitors (e.g., fluvoxamine)

- May need to increase dose if given with CYP450 1A2 inducers (e.g., cigarette smoke, carbamazepine)
- ▶ **Alert:** This list may not describe all possible interactions. Instruct clients to provide a list of all the medicines, herbs, nonprescription drugs, or dietary supplements they use.

PHARMACOKINETICS:
Metabolism: Inactive
Half-life: 21–54 hr

PRECAUTIONS:

- Use with caution in patients with conditions that predispose to hypotension (dehydration, overheating). Watch closely for hypotension if given IM formulation.
- Use with caution in patients with prostatic hypertrophy, narrow angle-closure glaucoma, paralytic ileus.
- Use with caution in patients who are at risk for aspiration pneumonia.
- IM formulation is not recommended to be given with parenteral benzodiazepines. If patients need a parenteral benzodiazepine, it should be given at least 1 hr after IM formulation olanzapine (*Zyprexa*).
- Do not use if there is a proven allergy
- Do not give IM formulation:
  - If patient has unstable medical condition (e.g., acute MI, unstable angina pectoris, severe hypotension, and/or bradycardia, sick sinus syndrome, recent heart surgery).
  - If patient has known risks of narrow angle-closure glaucoma.

PATIENT AND FAMILY EDUCATION:

- Take exactly as prescribed by the provider. Do not take in larger or smaller amounts or for longer than recommended.
- Can be taken with or without food.

(cont.)

ANTISOCIAL PERSONALITY DISORDER: Antipsychotics, Atypical (Second Generation)

olanzapine, olanzapine/fluoxetine (*cont.*)

- For olanzapine ODTs, keep the tablet in its blister pack until patient is ready to take it. Open the package and peel back the foil from the tablet blister. Do not push a tablet through the foil. Using dry hands, remove the tablet and place it in mouth and it will begin to dissolve right away.
- Do not swallow the tablet whole. Allow it to dissolve in mouth without chewing. If desired, drink liquid to help swallow the dissolved tablet.
- *If you have diabetes*: Check blood sugar levels on a regular basis while taking olanzapine.
- Can gain weight or have high cholesterol and triglycerides (types of fat) while taking this drug, especially if a teenager. Your blood will need to be tested often.
- Do not stop taking drug suddenly without first talking to provider, even if feeling fine. May have serious side effects if you stop taking the drug suddenly.
- Call provider if symptoms do not improve or get worse.
- Store at room temperature away from moisture, heat, and light.

SPECIAL POPULATIONS:
- *Elderly:*
  - May tolerate lower doses better. Elderly with dementia-related psychosis treated with atypical antipsychotics are at higher risk of death and cerebrovascular events. It can increase incidence of stroke.
  - If IM formulation is given, recommended starting dose is 2.5 to 5 mg. A second injection of 2.5 to 5 mg maybe given 2 hr after the

first injection. No more than three injections should be administered within 24 hr.
- *Renal impairment:* No dose adjustment is required for oral formulation. Consider lower starting dose (5 mg) for IM formulation. Not removed by hemodialysis.
- *Hepatic impairment:* Starting oral dose, 5 mg for patients with moderate-to-severe hepatic function impairment; increase dose with caution. Consider lower starting dose (5 mg) for IM formulation. Liver function tests a few times a year.
- *Cardiac impairment:* Use with caution because of risk of orthostatic hypotension.
- *Pregnancy:* Category C; some animal studies show adverse effects. No controlled studies in humans. Should be used only when the potential benefits outweigh potential risks to the fetus. Olanzapine may be preferable to anticonvulsant mood stabilizers if treatment is required during pregnancy.
- *Lactation:* Unknown if olanzapine is secreted in human breast milk. It is recommended to either discontinue drug or bottlefeed. Infants of women who choose to breastfeed while on this drug should be monitored for possible adverse effect.
- *Children and adolescents:*
  - Probably safe and effective for behavioral disturbances in this population.
  - IM formulation has not been studied in patients under 18 and is not recommended for use in this population.
  - Should be monitored more frequently than adults.

quetiapine   *Seroquel, Seroquel XR*

AVAILABLE FORMS: Tablet, 25, 50, 100, 200, 300, and 400 mg; extended-release tablet, 200, 300, and 400 mg

DOSAGE: 400 to 800 mg/day in 1 dose (*Seroquel XR*) or 2 doses (*Seroquel*) for schizophrenia and bipolar mania. 300 mg once per day for bipolar depression.

ADMINISTRATION:
- Tablets may be given with or without food.
- Take this medicine with a full glass of water.
- Advise patient not to crush, chew, or break an extended-release tablet. Swallow whole. Breaking may cause too much of the drug to be released at one time.
- Advise patient to take the missed dose as soon as remembers. Skip the missed dose if almost time for next scheduled dose. Do not take extra medicine to make up the missed dose.

SIDE EFFECTS: Can increase risk for diabetes and dyslipidemia; dizziness, sedation; dry mouth,

constipation, dyspepsia, abdominal pain, weight gain; tachycardia; hyperglycemia; increased risk of death and cerebrovascular events in elderly with dementia-related psychosis; orthostatic hypotension (usually during initial dose titration); NMS (rare); seizures (rare)

DRUG INTERACTIONS:
- May increase effects of antihypertensive medications
- Plasma levels of quetiapine may be increased if given in conjunction with CYP450 3A4 and CYP450 2D6 inhibitors. However, no dose adjustment is required.
▶**Alert:** This list may not describe all possible interactions. Instruct clients to provide a list of all the medicines, herbs, nonprescription drugs, or dietary supplements they use.

PHARMACOKINETICS:
Metabolism: Inactive
Half-life: 6–7 hr

(cont.)

quetiapine (*cont.*)

PRECAUTIONS:
- Use with caution in patients at risk for aspiration pneumonia.
- Manufacturer recommends to examine for cataracts before and every 6 months after starting quetiapine.
- *Do not use if there is a proven allergy.*

PATIENT AND FAMILY EDUCATION:
- Take exactly as prescribed by provider. Do not take in larger or smaller amounts or longer than recommended.
- Can be taken with or without food.
- Can cause side effects that may impair thinking or reactions. Be careful when driving or doing anything that requires you to be awake and alert.
- May cause high blood sugar (hyperglycemia). Talk to provider if any signs of hyperglycemia such as increased thirst or urination, excessive hunger, or weakness. If diabetic, check blood sugar levels on a regular basis.
- *Avoid becoming overheated or dehydrated during exercise and in hot weather;* may be more prone to heat stroke.
- *Avoid getting up too fast from a sitting or lying position.* Get up slowly and steady yourself to prevent a fall.
- *Avoid drinking alcohol.*
- *Stop using this medication and call provider immediately* if you have very stiff (rigid) muscles, high fever, sweating, confusion, fast or uneven heartbeats, tremors; feel like you might pass out; have jerky muscle movements you cannot control, trouble swallowing, problems with speech; have blurred vision, eye pain, or seeing halos around lights; have increased thirst and urination, excessive hunger, fruity breath odor, weakness, nausea and vomiting; have fever, chills, body aches, flu symptoms, or have white patches or sores inside mouth or on lips.

- Do not stop taking drug suddenly without first talking to provider, even if you feel fine. May have serious side effects if you stop taking the drug suddenly.
- Call provider if symptoms do not improve or get worse.
- Store at room temperature away from moisture and heat.

SPECIAL POPULATIONS:
- *Elderly:* Generally lower dose is used (e.g., 25 to 100 mg twice a day). Higher dose can be used if tolerated. Elderly with dementia-related psychosis treated with atypical antipsychotics are at higher risk of death and cerebrovascular events.
- *Renal impairment:* No dose adjustment is required.
- *Hepatic impairment:* May need to reduce dose.
- *Cardiac impairment:* Use with caution because of risk of orthostatic hypotension.
- *Pregnancy:* Category C; some animal studies show adverse effects. No controlled studies in humans. Should be used only when the potential benefits outweigh potential risks to the fetus. May be preferable to anticonvulsant mood stabilizers if treatment is required during pregnancy.
- *Lactation:* Unknown if drug is secreted in human breast milk. It is recommended to either discontinue drug or bottlefeed. Infants of women who choose to breastfeed while on this drug should be monitored for possible adverse effect.
- *Children and adolescents:* Not officially recommended for patients under age 18. Probably safe and effective for behavioral disturbances in this population. Should be monitored more frequently than adults. May tolerate lower doses better. Watch for activation of suicidal ideation. Inform parents or guardian of this risk so they can help monitor the risk.

Geodon, Geodon IM Injection   **ziprasidone**

AVAILABLE FORMS: Tablet, 20, 40, 60, and 80 mg; injection, 20 mg/mL

DOSAGE:
Schizophrenia: 40 to 200 mg/day in divided doses orally.
Bipolar disorder: 80 to 160 mg/day in divided doses orally
- 10 to 20 mg IM (doses of 10 mg may be administered every 2 hr, doses of 20 mg may be administered every 4 hr with maximum daily dose 40 mg. Not to be administered for more than 3 consecutive days.

ADMINISTRATION:
- Take with a meal.
- Dosing at 20 to 40 twice a day is too low and activating, perhaps due to potent 5-HT$_{2C}$ antagonist

properties. Reduce activation by increasing the dose to 60 to 80 mg twice a day.
- Best efficacy in schizophrenia and bipolar disorder is at doses greater than 120 mg/day.
- BMI monthly for 3 months, then quarterly.
- Monitor fasting triglycerides monthly for several months in patients at high risk for metabolic complications.
- Blood pressure, fasting plasma glucose, fasting lipids within 3 months and then annually, but earlier and more frequently for patients with diabetes or who have gained more than 5% of initial weight.

SIDE EFFECTS: Dizziness, sedation, and hypotension especially at high doses; motor side effects (rare); possible increased incidence of diabetes or dyslipidemia is unknown

(cont.)

ziprasidone (*cont.*)

DRUG INTERACTIONS:
- May enhance the effects of antihypertensive drugs
- May antagonize levodopa, dopamine agonists
- May enhance QTc prolongation of other drugs capable of prolonging QTc interval

PHARMACOKINETICS:
Protein binding: Greater than 99%
Metabolism: CYP450 3A4
Half-life: 6.6 hr

PRECAUTIONS:
- Prolongs QTc interval more than some other antipsychotics.
- Use with caution with conditions that predispose to hypotension (dehydration, overheating).
- Priapism has been reported.
- Dysphagia has been associated with antipsychotic use; use cautiously in patients at risk for aspiration pneumonia.
- Do not use if patient is taking agents capable of prolonging QTc interval (pimozide, thioridazine, selected antiarrhythmics, moxifloxacin, sparfloxacin).
- Do not use if history of QTc prolongation, cardiac arrhythmia, recent acute MI, uncompensated heart failure.
- Do not use if proven allergy to ziprasidone.

PATIENT AND FAMILY EDUCATION:
- Take with a meal of a few hundred calories (turkey sandwich and a piece of fruit) to enhance absorption.
- Avoid becoming overheated or dehydrated during exercise and in hot weather; may be more prone to heat stroke.
- Avoid getting up too fast from a sitting or lying position. Get up slowly and steady yourself to prevent a fall.
- Avoid drinking alcohol.
- Stop using this medication and call provider immediately if you have very stiff (rigid) muscles, high fever, sweating, confusion, fast or uneven heartbeats, tremors; feel like you might pass out; have jerky muscle movements you cannot control, trouble swallowing, problems with speech; have blurred vision, eye pain, or seeing halos around lights; have increased thirst and urination, excessive hunger, fruity breath odor, weakness, nausea and vomiting; have fever, chills, body aches, flu symptoms, or have white patches or sores inside mouth or on lips.
- Do not stop taking drug suddenly without first talking to provider, even if you feel fine. You may have serious side effects if you stop taking the drug suddenly.
- Call provider if symptoms do not improve or get worse.
- Store at room temperature away from moisture and heat.

SPECIAL POPULATIONS:
- *Elderly:* Some patients may tolerate lower doses better. Elderly patients with dementia-related psychosis treated with atypical antipsychotics are at increased risk of death compared to placebo.
- *Renal impairment:* No dose adjustment necessary.
- *Hepatic impairment:* No dose adjustment necessary.
- *Cardiac Impairment:* Contraindicated with known history of QTc prolongation.
- *Pregnancy:* Category C; some animal studies show adverse effects; no controlled studies in humans.
- *Lactation:* Unknown if secreted in human breast milk. Recommend either to discontinue drug or bottlefeed.
- *Children and adolescents:* Not recommended for patients under age 18. Early data suggest that it may be safe and effective for behavioral disturbances in children and adolescents.

Class: Mood Stabilizers

lithium	*Eskalith, Lithobid, Carbolith, Duralith Lithizine*

AVAILABLE FORMS: Capsule, 150, 300, and 600 mg; slow-release tablet, 300 mg; controlled-release tablet, 300 and 450 mg; syrup, 300 mg (8 mEq lithum/5 mL)

DOSAGE: *Adults:* 300 to 600 mg PO up to qid. Or 900 mg controlled-release tablet PO every 12 hr. Increase dosage based on blood levels to achieve optimum dosage. Recommended therapeutic lithium levels are 1 to 1.5 mEq/L for acute mania and 0.6 to 1.2 mEq/L for maintenance therapy.

ADMINISTRATION:
- Give drug after meals with plenty of water to minimize GI upset.
- Do not crush controlled-release tablets.

SIDE EFFECTS: Fatigue, lethargy, coma, epileptiform seizures, tremors, drowsiness, headache, confusion, restlessness, dizziness, psychomotor retardation, blackouts, EEG changes, worsened organic, mental syndrome, impaired speech, ataxia, uncoordination, arrhythmias, bradycardia, reversible ECG changes, hypotension

(cont.)

lithium (cont.)

- Tinnitus, blurred vision
- Vomiting, anorexia, diarrhea, thirst, nausea, metallic taste, dry mouth, abdominal pain, flatulence, indigestion
- Polyuria, renal toxicity with long-term use, glycosuria, decreased creatinine clearance, albuminuria
- Leukocytosis with leukocyte count of 14,000 to 18,000/mm
- Transient hyperglycemia, goiter, hypothyroidism, hyponatremia
- Muscle weakness
- Pruritus, rash, diminished or absent sensation drying and thinning of hair, psoriasis, acne, alopecia
- Ankle and wrist edema

DRUG INTERACTIONS:
- ACE inhibitors, aminophylline, sodium bicarbonate, urine alkalizers, calcium channel blockers (verapamil), carbamazepine, fluoxetine, methyldopa, NSAIDs, probenecid, neuromuscular blockers, thiazide diuretics, diuretics, especially loop diuretics may inhibit lithium elimination and increase lithium toxicity.
- Caffeine may decrease lithium level and drug effect. Advise patients who ingest large amounts of caffeine.

PHARMACOKINETICS:
- Probably alters chemical transmitters in the CNS, possibly by interfering with ionic pump mechanisms in brain cells; may compete with or replace sodium ions. With PO dose, onset and duration of action is unknown.
Peak action: 30 min to 1 hr.
Half-life: 18 hr (adolescents); 36 hr (elderly).

PRECAUTIONS:
- May increase glucose and creatinine levels. May decrease sodium, T_3, T_4, and protein-bound iodine levels.
- May increase WBC and neutrophil counts.
- Contraindicated if therapy cannot be closely monitored.
- Avoid using in pregnant patient unless benefits outweigh risks.
- Use with caution in patients receiving neuromuscular blockers and diuretics; in elderly or debilitated patients; and in patients with thyroid disease, seizure disorder, infection, renal or CV disease, severe debilitation or dehydration, or sodium depletion.
▶**Alert:** Drug has a narrow therapeutic margin of safety. Determining drug level is crucial to safe use of drug. Do not use in patients who cannot have regular tests. Monitor level 8 to 12 hr after first dose, the morning before second dose

is given, two or three times weekly for the first month, and then weekly to monthly during maintenance therapy.
- When drug level is less than 1.5 mEq/L, adverse reactions are usually mild.
- Monitor baseline ECG, thyroid studies, renal studies, and electrolyte levels.
- Check fluid intake and output, especially when surgery is scheduled.
- Weigh patient daily; check for edema or sudden weight gain.
- Adjust fluid and salt ingestion to compensate if excessive loss occurs from protracted diaphoresis or diarrhea. Under normal conditions, patient fluid intake should be 2.5 to 3 L daily; patient should follow a balanced diet with adequate salt intake.
- Check urine-specific gravity and report level below 1.005, which may indicate diabetes insipidus.
- Drug alters glucose tolerance in diabetics. Monitor glucose level closely.
- Perform outpatient follow-up of thyroid and renal functions every 6 to 12 months. Palpate thyroid to check for enlargement.

PATIENT AND FAMILY EDUCATION:
- Take drug with plenty of water and after meals to minimize GI upset.
- Having regular blood tests to determine drug levels is important; even slightly high values can be dangerous.
- Withhold one dose and call prescriber if signs and symptoms of toxicity appear, but do not stop drug abruptly.
- Avoid hazardous activities that require alertness and good psychomotor coordination until CNS effects of drug are known.
- Do not switch brands or take other prescription or OTC drugs without prescriber's guidance.
- Wear or carry medical identification at all times.
- Expect transient nausea, large amounts of urine, thirst, and discomfort during first few days of therapy; watch for evidence of toxicity (diarrhea, vomiting, tremor, drowsiness, muscle weakness, uncoordination).

SPECIAL POPULATIONS:
- *Elderly:* Initial dose reduction and possibly lower maintenance doses due to age-related changes and sensitivity to side effects.
- *Pregnancy:* Category D; positive evidence of fetal harm has been demonstrated.
- *Children:* Not approved under 12 years; use with caution and monitor closely for side effects and suicidality. Children may experience more frequent and severe side effects.

ANTISOCIAL PERSONALITY DISORDER: Mood Stabilizers

Class: Mood-Stabilizing Anticonvulsants

carbamazepine   *Tegretol, Carbatrol, Epitol, Equetro, Tegretol-XR, Tegretol-CR*

AVAILABLE FORMS: Tablet, 200 mg; chewable tablet, 100 mg; XR capsule, 100, 200, 300, and 400 mg; oral suspension, 100 mg/5 mL

DOSAGE: *Adults:* 300 to 600 mg PO up to qid. Or, 900 mg controlled-release tablets PO every 12 hr. Increase dosage based on blood levels to achieve optimum dosage. Recommended therapeutic lithium levels are 1 to 1.5 mEq/L for acute mania and 0.6 to 1.2 mEq/L for maintenance therapy.

ADMINISTRATION:
- Lithium carbonate capsule, 150, 300, and 600 mg; tablet, 300 mg (300 mg equals 8.12 mEq lithium); tablet (controlled-release), 300 and 450 mg
- Lithium citrate syrup (sugarless), 8 mEq lithium/5 mL; 5 mL lithium citrate liquid contains 8 mEq lithium, equal to 300 mg lithium carbonate

SIDE EFFECTS:
- Fatigue, lethargy, coma, epileptiform seizures, tremors, drowsiness, headache, confusion, restlessness, dizziness, psychomotor retardation, blackouts, EEG changes, worsened organic, mental syndrome, impaired speech, ataxia, uncoordination
- Arrhythmias, bradycardia, reversible ECG changes, hypotension
- Tinnitus, blurred vision
- Vomiting, anorexia, diarrhea, thirst, nausea, metallic taste, dry mouth, abdominal pain, flatulence, indigestion
- Polyuria, renal toxicity with long-term use, glycosuria, decreased creatinine clearance, albuminuria
- Leukocytosis with leukocyte count of 14,000 to 18,000/mm
- Transient hyperglycemia, goiter, hypothyroidism, hyponatremia
- Muscle weakness
- Pruritus, rash, diminished or absent sensation
- Drying and thinning of hair, psoriasis, acne, alopecia
- Ankle and wrist edema

DRUG INTERACTIONS:
- ACE inhibitors, aminophylline, sodium bicarbonate, urine alkalizers.
- Calcium channel blockers (verapamil), carbamazepine, fluoxetine, methyldopa, NSAIDs, probenecid.
- Neuromuscular blockers, thiazide diuretics.
- Caffeine may decrease lithium level and drug effect. Advise patient who ingests large amounts of caffeine to tell prescriber before stopping caffeine. Adjust lithium dosage, as needed.

PHARMACOKINETICS: Probably alters chemical transmitters in the CNS, possibly by interfering with ionic pump mechanisms in brain cells, and may compete with or replace sodium ions. With oral doses onset and duration of action is unknown.

Peak action: 30 min to 1 hr
Half-life: 18 hr (adolescents); 36 hr (elderly).

PRECAUTIONS:
- Contraindicated if therapy cannot be closely monitored.
- Avoid using in pregnant patient unless benefits outweigh risks.
- Use with caution in patients receiving neuromuscular blockers and diuretics; in elderly or debilitated patients; and in patients with thyroid disease, seizure disorder, infection, renal or CV disease, severe debilitation or dehydration, or sodium depletion.
- ▶**Alert:** Drug has a narrow therapeutic margin of safety. Determining drug level is crucial to safe use of drug. Do not use drug in patients who cannot have regular tests. Monitor level 8 to 12 hr after first dose, the morning before second dose is given, two or three times weekly for the first month, and then weekly to monthly during maintenance therapy.
- When drug level is less than 1.5 mEq/L, adverse reactions are usually mild.
- Monitor baseline ECG, thyroid studies, renal studies, and electrolyte levels.
- Check fluid intake and output, especially when surgery is scheduled.
- Weigh patient daily; check for edema or sudden weight gain.
- Adjust fluid and salt ingestion to compensate if excessive loss occurs from protracted diaphoresis or diarrhea. Under normal conditions, patient fluid intake should be 2.5 to 3 L daily, and he should follow a balanced diet with adequate salt intake.
- Check urine-specific gravity and report level below 1.005, which may indicate diabetes insipidus.
- Drug alters glucose tolerance in diabetics. Monitor glucose level closely.
- Perform outpatient follow-up of thyroid and renal functions every 6 to 12 months. Palpate thyroid to check for enlargement.

PATIENT AND FAMILY EDUCATION:
- Tell patient to take drug with plenty of water and after meals to minimize GI upset.
- Explain the importance of having regular blood tests to determine drug levels; even slightly high values can be dangerous.
- Warn patient and caregivers to expect transient nausea, large amounts of urine, thirst, and discomfort during first few days of therapy and to watch for evidence of toxicity (diarrhea, vomiting, tremor, drowsiness, muscle weakness, uncoordination).
- Instruct patient to withhold one dose and call prescriber if signs and symptoms of toxicity appear, but not to stop drug abruptly.

(cont.)

carbamazepine (*cont.*)

- Warn patient to avoid hazardous activities that require alertness and good psychomotor coordination until CNS effects of drug are known.
- Tell patient not to switch brands or take other prescription or OTC drugs without prescriber's guidance.
- Tell patient to wear or carry medical identification at all times.

SPECIAL POPULATIONS:
- *Elderly:* Use with caution in men with BPH due to increased urinary retention; monitor for dizziness and falls secondary to sedation.
- *Pregnancy/Lactation:* Do not use if breastfeeding.
- *Children:* Approved for use in epilepsy, therefore safety profile exists. Used off label for aggression.

Depacon, Depakene Depakote Depakote ER, Depakote Sprinkle	**valproate sodium** **valproic acid** **divalproex sodium**

▶**Special Note:** Valproate sodium should only be prescribed for APD in consultation with a psychiatric/mental health specialist.

AVAILABLE FORMS: Injection, 100 mg/mL; syrup, 250 mg/5 mL. *Valproic acid:* capsule, 250 mg; syrup, 200 mg/5 mL; tablet (crushable), 100 mg; tablet (enteric-coated), 200 and 500 mg. *Divalproex sodium:* capsule (sprinkle), 125 mg; tablet (delayed-release), 125, 250, and 500 mg; tablet (extended-release), 250 and 500 mg

DOSAGE:
- **Mania:** *Adults:* Initially, 750 mg *Depakote* daily, PO in divided doses, or 25 mg/kg *Depakote ER* once daily. Adjust dosage based on patient's response; maximum dose for either form is 60 mg/kg daily.
- **To Prevent Migraine Headache:** *Adults:* Initially, 250 mg delayed-release divalproex sodium PO bid. Some patients may need up to 1,000 mg daily. Or 500 mg *Depakote ER* PO daily for 1 wk; then 1,000 mg PO daily. *Adjust-a-dose:* For elderly patients, start at lower dosage. Increase dosage more slowly and with regular monitoring of fluid and nutritional intake, and watch for dehydration, somnolence, and other adverse reactions.

ADMINISTRATION:
- *Oral:* Give drug with food or milk to reduce adverse GI effects.
- Do not mix syrup with carbonated beverages; mixture may be irritating to oral mucosa.
- Do not give syrup to patients who need sodium restriction. Check with prescriber.
- Capsules may be swallowed whole or opened and contents sprinkled on a teaspoonful of soft food. Patient should swallow immediately without chewing.
- Monitor drug level and adjust dosage as needed.
- Incompatibilities: None reported.

SIDE EFFECTS:
- *CNS:* Asthenia, dizziness, headache, insomnia, nervousness, somnolence, tremor, abnormal thinking, amnesia, ataxia, depression, emotional upset, fever, sedation
- *CV:* Chest pain, edema, hypertension, hypotension, tachycardia

- *EENT:* Blurred vision, diplopia, nystagmus, pharyngitis, rhinitis, tinnitus
- *GI:* Abdominal pain, anorexia, diarrhea, dyspepsia, nausea, vomiting, pancreatitis, constipation, increased appetite
- *Hematologic:* Bone marrow suppression, hemorrhage, thrombocytopenia, bruising, petechiae
- *Hepatic:* Hepatotoxicity
- *Metabolic:* Hyperammonemia, weight gain
- *Musculoskeletal:* Back and neck pain
- *Respiratory:* Bronchitis, dyspnea
- *Skin:* Alopecia, flu syndrome, infection, erythema multiforme, hypersensitivity reactions, Stevens-Johnson syndrome, rash, photosensitivity reactions, pruritus

DRUG INTERACTIONS: Aspirin, chlorpromazine, cimetidine, erythromycin, felbamate, carbamazepine, lamotrigine, phenobarbital, phenytoin, rifampin, warfarin, zidovudine. Alcohol use is discouraged.

PHARMACOKINETICS:
Peak action for oral dose is 15 min to 4 hr. Facilitates the effects of the inhibitory neurotransmitter GABA.
Half-life: 6–16 hr

PRECAUTIONS:
- May increase ammonia, ALT, AST, and bilirubin lab levels.
- May increase eosinophil count and bleeding time. May decrease platelet, RBC, and WBC counts.
- May cause false-positive results for urine ketone levels.
- Contraindicated in patients hypersensitive to drug and in those with hepatic disease or significant hepatic dysfunction, and in patients with a UCD.
- Safety and efficacy of *Depakote ER* in children younger than age 10 have not been established.
- Obtain liver function test results, platelet count, and PT and INR before starting therapy, and monitor these values periodically.
- Adverse reactions may not be caused by valproic acid alone because it is usually used with other anticonvulsants.

ANTISOCIAL PERSONALITY DISORDER: Mood-Stabilizing Anticonvulsants

(cont.)

valproate sodium, valproic acid, divalproex sodium (*cont.*)

- When converting adults and children aged 10 and older with seizures from *Depakote* to *Depakote ER*, make sure the extended-release dose is 8% to 20% higher than the regular dose taken previously. See manufacturer's package insert for more details.
- Divalproex sodium has a lower risk of adverse GI reactions.
- Never withdraw drug suddenly, because sudden withdrawal may worsen seizures. Call prescriber at once if adverse reactions develop.
- Patients at high risk for hepatotoxicity include those with congenital metabolic disorders, mental retardation, or organic brain disease; those taking multiple anticonvulsants; and children younger than age 2 years.
- Notify prescriber if tremors occur; a dosage reduction may be needed.
- Monitor drug level. Therapeutic level is 50 to 100 mcg/mL.
- When converting patients from a brand-name drug to a generic drug, use caution because breakthrough seizures may occur.

▶**Alert:** Sometimes fatal, hyperammonemic encephalopathy may occur when starting valproate therapy in patients with UCD. Evaluate patients with UCD risk factors before starting valproate therapy. Patients who develop symptoms of unexplained hyperammonemic encephalopathy during valproate therapy should stop drug, undergo prompt appropriate treatment, and be evaluated for underlying UCD.

▶**Alert:** Fatal hepatotoxicity may follow nonspecific symptoms, such as malaise, fever, and lethargy. If these symptoms occur during therapy, notify prescriber at once because patients who might be developing hepatic dysfunction must stop taking drug.

PATIENT AND FAMILY EDUCATION:
- Take drug with food or milk to reduce adverse GI effects.

- Do not chew capsules; irritation of mouth and throat may result.
- Capsules may be either swallowed whole or carefully opened and contents sprinkled on a teaspoonful of soft food. Tell patient to swallow immediately without chewing.
- Avoid driving and other potentially hazardous activities that require mental alertness until drug's CNS effects are known.
- Women should call prescriber if become pregnant or plan to become pregnant during therapy.
- Syrup should not be mixed with carbonated beverages; mixture may be irritating to mouth and throat.
- Keep drug out of children's reach.
- Do not stop drug therapy abruptly.
- Call prescriber if malaise, weakness, lethargy, facial swelling, loss of appetite, or vomiting occurs.

SPECIAL POPULATIONS:
- *Elderly:* Caution is advised when using this drug in the elderly due to more sensitivity to the drug.
- *Pregnancy:* Category D. This medication should only be used when clearly needed during pregnancy.
- *Lactation:* Secreted into breast milk.
- *Children:* Caution when using this drug in a child or adolescent; must balance the potential risks with the clinical need. Not recommended for use under age 18 years for MDD.

▶**Alert:** Antidepressants increased the risk of suicidal thinking and behavior (suicidality) in short-term studies in children and adolescents with depression and other psychiatric disorders. Caution is advised when using this drug in children because they may be more sensitive to the side effects of the drug, especially loss of appetite and weight loss. It is important to monitor weight and growth in children who are taking this drug.

topiramate   *Topamax*

AVAILABLE FORMS: Tablet, 25, 50, 100, and 200 mg; sprinkle capsules, 15 and 25 mg

DOSAGE:
- *Adults:* 25–50 mg/day for one week initially, then increase by 25–50 mg/day at weekly intervals. Usual maintenance dose 100–200 mg twice daily
- *Elderly:* 25–50 mg/day for one week initially, then increase by 25–50 mg/day at weekly intervals. Usual maintenance dose 100–200 mg twice daily

ADMINISTRATION:
- Do not break tablets.
- Give with or without food.

- Capsules may be swallowed whole or contents sprinkled on teaspoonful of soft food and swallowed immediately. Do not chew.

SIDE EFFECTS: Drowsiness; dizziness; ataxia; nystagmus; diplopia; paresthesia; nausea; tremor; confusion; dyspepsia; depression; weight loss; mood disturbances

DRUG INTERACTIONS:
- Alcohol and other CNS depressants may increase CNS depression.
- Carbamazepine, phenytoin, and valproic acid may decrease serum concentration.
- Carbonic anhydrase inhibitors may increase risk of renal calculi formation.

(cont.)

topiramate (cont.)

PHARMACOKINETICS:
Onset: 4 days
Peak: 2 hr
Duration: 2–3 months
Half-life: 21 hr

PRECAUTIONS:
- *Contraindications*: bipolar disorder
- *Cautions*: Sensitivity to topiramate; hepatic/renal impairment; predisposition to renal calculi

PATIENT AND FAMILY EDUCATION:
- Avoid tasks that require alertness and motor skills until response to drug is established.

- Avoid use of alcohol and other CNS depressants.
- Do not abruptly discontinue this drug.
- Do not break tablets.
- Maintain adequate fluid intake.
- Inform health care provider if blurred vision or eye pain occurs.

SPECIAL POPULATIONS:
- *Elderly:* Age-related renal impairment may require dosage adjustment
- *Pregnancy/Lactation:* Unknown if distributed in breast milk.
- *Children:* Safety and efficacy have not been established in pediatric patients.

Lamictal, Lamictal XR **lamotrigine**

INDICATIONS: Used to treat bipolar disorder in adults.

AVAILABLE FORMS: Tablet, 25, 100, 150, and 200 mg; chewable tablet, 2, 5, and 25 mg

DOSAGE: Starting dose (adults), 25 mg by mouth every day for two weeks; then 50 mg every day for two weeks; then 100 mg every day for one week; maximum, 200 mg/day.

ADMINISTRATION:
- Take as directed; well tolerated in the recommended doses.
- Individuals taking this medicine should carry an identification card to alert medical personnel who might be caring for them.
- Potential carcinogenic, mutagenic, and fertility effects are unknown.
- Not recommended to take potentially hepatotoxic medicines.
- Does not interfere with drug testing using urine samples.

SIDE EFFECTS: Common reactions to the drug include dizziness, headache, diplopia, ataxia, asthenia, nausea, blurred vision, somnolence, rhinitis, rash, pharyngitis, vomiting, cough, flu syndrome, dysmenorrheal, uncoordination, insomnia, diarrhea, fever, abdominal pain, depression, tremor, anxiety, vaginitis, speech disturbance, seizures, weight loss, photosensitivity, nystagmus, constipation, and dry mouth.

DRUG INTERACTIONS:
Avoid using the following drugs:
- Oral progesterone contraceptives (may decrease hormonal contraceptive levels)
- Etonogestrel subdermal implant (may decrease hormonal contraceptive levels)
- Ginkgo biloba, Eun-haeng, fossil tree, ginkyo, icho, ityo, Japanese silver apricot, kew tree, maidenhair tree, salisburia, silver apricot, ginkgo (may decrease anticonvulsant efficacy)
- Medroxyprogesterone acetate (may decrease hormonal contraceptive levels)

- St. John's wort (may decrease lamotrigine levels as clearance is increased)

PHARMACOKINETICS: Metabolized by the liver (CYP450); excreted in the urine (94%) and feces (2%).
Half-life: 25 hr

PRECAUTIONS:
- Discontinue medicine at first sign of a rash. Incidence is 0.8% in children 2–6 years of age and 0.3% in adults. Most life-threatening rashes occur in the first 2–8 weeks of treatment.
- Caution should be exercised when administering this medicine to patient with suicide risk, pregnancy, hepatic impairment, renal impairment, and hypersensitivity to antiepileptic drugs.
- Use in patients under the age of 18 years has not been established.
- Individuals taking opioid containing medicines, such as cough and cold preparations, antidiarrheal preparations, and opioid analgesics may not benefit from these medicines.

PATIENT AND FAMILY EDUCATION:
- Do not stop taking this drug suddenly; it must be tapered by your health care provider.
- Notify your health care provider immediately if your depression symptoms increase.

SPECIAL POPULATIONS:
- *Elderly:* Caution should be exercised when administering this drug to the elderly.
- *Renal impairment:* For moderate to severe impairment, decrease dose by 25%. If there is severe impairment, decrease dose by 50%.
- *Pregnancy:* Category C drug; animal studies show adverse fetal effect(s) but no controlled human studies.
- *Lactation:* Considered unsafe for breastfeeding mothers. Medication administration requires cessation of breastfeeding.
- *Children:* Serious rashes requiring hospitalizations and discontinuance of treatment include the Stevens-Johnson syndrome and rare cases of toxic epidermal necrolysis and rash-related deaths.

ANTISOCIAL PERSONALITY DISORDER: Mood-Stabilizing Anticonvulsants

Borderline Personality Disorder

OVERVIEW

- Characterized by a pervasive pattern of marked impulsivity, unstable interpersonal relationships, and poor self-image that may begin as early as 18 to 30 months of age
- Occurs in about 2% to 3% of the general populations and is five times more common in those with first-degree relatives with the diagnosis
- Most common disorder found in clinical settings
- Found three times more in women than in men
- 50% have been sexually abused; others have experienced physical or verbal abuse and are offspring of alcoholics
- Often formulated as a variant of PTSD.
- Mood disorders in first-degree relatives are strongly linked.
- Intellectual capacity intact and fully oriented to reality most of the time
- Transient psychosis often occurs with stress
- 8% to 10% with this diagnosis commit suicide
- Cutting, burning, and other self-mutilation activities are common
- Tend to use transitional objects (teddy bears, pillows, blankets, dolls, etc.) into adulthood
- Vacillate between clinging behaviors one minute to angry outbursts the next—rarely adhering to what they have agreed
- Diagnostic criteria include:
  - Fear of abandonment, real or perceived
  - Unstable and intense relationships
  - Impulsivity or recklessness
  - Recurrent self-mutilating behavior or suicidal threats/gestures
  - Chronic feelings of emptiness and boredom
  - Labile mood
  - Irritability
  - Polarized thinking about self and others ("splitting")
  - Impaired judgment
  - Lack of insight
  - Transient psychotic symptoms such as hallucinations demanding self-harm
- Pervasive mood is dysphoric
- May experience dissociative episodes
- May experience auditory hallucinations encouraging or demanding self-harm
- Associated with a risk for substance abuse, eating disorders (particularly bulimia), and PTSD
- Suicide is a particular risk in borderline patient

Acute Treatment

Medications are rarely effective in treatment of this disorder. Counseling and psychotherapy are the most useful treatment modalities. Occasional, short-term use of mood stabilizers may be helpful in some individuals.

Chronic Treatment

- Long-term medication use is not a good option for management. Therapy with an experienced clinician is the best choice for chronic management. In patients with comorbid disorders that are known to respond to major depression, panic disorder, and PTSD, however, it is reasonable to continue antidepressant therapy.
- Management of comorbid conditions

CLASS	DRUG
Antipsychotics, Typical (First Generation)	
	haloperidol (*Haldol*)
Antipsychotics, Atypical (Second Generation)	
	risperidone (*Risperda, Risperdal Consta*)
	olanzapine (*Zyprexa)*; Olanzapine/fluoxetine combination (*Symbyax*)
	quetiapine (*Seroquel, Seroquel XR*)
	ziprasidone (*Geodon, Geodon IM Injection*)
Mood Stabilizer	
	lithium (*Eskalith, Lithobid, Carbolith, Duralith Lithizine*)
Mood Stabilizing Anticonvulsants	
	carbamazepine (*Tegretol Carbatrol, Epitol, Equetro, Tegretol-XR, Tegretol-CR*)
	valproate sodium, valproic acid, divalproex sodium (*Depacon, Depakene, Depakote, Depakote ER, Depakote Sprinkle*)
	topiramate (*Topamax*)
	lamotrigine (*Lamictal, Lamictal XR*)

BORDERLINE PERSONALITY DISORDER

Class: Antipsychotics, Typical (First Generation)

Haldol | **haloperidol**

AVAILABLE FORMS: Tablet (scored), 0.5, 1, 2, 5, 10, and 20 mg; concentrate, 2 mg/mL; solution, 1 mg/mL; injection, 5 mg/mL (immediate-release); *haloperidol decanoate:* injection, 50 mg haloperidol as 60.5 mg/mL; *haloperidol decanoate*, 100 mg haloperidol as 141.04 mg/mL

DOSAGE: 1 to 20 mg/day orally. *Immediate-release injection:* 2 to 5 mg each dose. *Decanoate injection:* 10 to 20 times the effective daily dose of oral formulation, administered every 4 wk

ADMINISTRATION:

- *Oral:* Once daily or in divided doses at beginning of treatment during rapid escalation; increase as needed; can be dosed up to 100 mg/day.
- *Immediate-release injection:* Initial dose 2 to 5 mg; subsequent doses may be given as often as every hour; patient should be switched to oral administration ASAP.
- *Haloperidol decanoate injection:* Initial dose 10 to 15 times the effective oral dose for patients maintained on low antipsychotic doses (up to equivalent of 10 mg/day oral haloperidol). Initial dose may be as high as 20 times previous oral dose for patients maintained on higher antipsychotic doses: Maximum, 100 mg. If higher dose required, remainder can be administered 3 to 7 days later. Administer total dose every 4 wk.
- Haloperidol is frequently dosed too high. High doses may actually worsen negative symptoms of schizophrenia and increase EPS side effects.

SIDE EFFECTS: Neuroleptic-induced deficit syndrome; akathisia; EPS, parkinsonism, tardive dyskinesia, tardive dystonia; galactorrhea, amenorrhea; dizziness, sedation; dry mouth, constipation, urinary retention, blurred vision; decreased sweating; hypotension, tachycardia, hyperlipidemia; weight gain; rare NMS; rare seizures; rare jaundice, agranulocytosis, leukopenia; haloperidol with anticholinergics may increase intraocular pressure; reduces effects of anticoagulants; plasma levels of haloperidol lowered by rifampin; may enhance effects of antihypertensive agents; haloperidol with lithium may contribute to development of encephalopathic syndrome

DRUG INTERACTIONS:

- May decrease effects of levodopa, dopamine agonists
- May increase effects of antihypertensive drugs except for guanethidine
- Additive effects with CNS depressants; dose of other should be reduced
- May interact with some pressor agents (epinephrine) to lower blood pressure

PHARMACOKINETICS:
Half-life: Approx. 3 wk (haloperidol decanoate); approx. 12–36 hr (oral)

PRECAUTIONS:

- Discontinue if symptoms of NMS develop.
- Use with caution in patients with respiratory problems.
- Avoid extreme heat exposure.
- May experience rapid shift to depression if used to treat mania.
- Patients with thyrotoxicosis may experience neurotoxicity.
- Do not use with Lewy body dementia or Parkinson's disease.
- Use with caution in patients with QTc prolongation, hypothyroidism, familial long-QT syndrome.
- Do not use if there is a proven allergy to haloperidol.

PATIENT AND FAMILY EDUCATION:

- Take exactly as prescribed.
- Avoid getting up too fast from a sitting or lying position. Get up slowly and steady yourself to prevent a fall.
- Stay hydrated.
- Avoid drinking alcohol.
- *Stop using this medication and call provider immediately* if you have very stiff (rigid) muscles, high fever, sweating, confusion, fast or uneven heartbeats, tremors; feel like you might pass out; have jerky muscle movements you cannot control, trouble swallowing, problems with speech; have blurred vision, eye pain, or seeing halos around lights; have increased thirst and urination, excessive hunger, fruity breath odor, weakness, nausea and vomiting; have fever, chills, body aches, flu symptoms, white patches or sores inside mouth or on lips.
- Do not stop taking drug suddenly without first talking to provider, even if you feel fine. May have serious side effects if you stop taking the drug suddenly.
- Call provider if symptoms do not improve or get worse.
- Store at room temperature away from moisture and heat.

SPECIAL POPULATIONS:

- *Elderly:* Lower doses should be used and patient monitored closely. Do not use in elderly patients with dementia.
- *Renal impairment*: Use with caution.
- *Hepatic impairment*: Use with caution.
- *Cardiac impairment*: Because of risk of orthostatic hypertension use with caution.
- *Pregnancy/Lactation:* Category C; some animal studies show adverse effects, no controlled studies in humans.
- *Children and adolescents:* Safety and efficacy not established. Not intended for use with children under age 3. Generally consider as second line, not first line.

Class: Antipsychotics, Atypical (Second Generation)

risperidone   *Risperdal, Risperdal Consta*

AVAILABLE FORMS: Tablet, 0.25, 0.5, 1, 2, 3, 4, and 6 mg; ODT, 0.5, 1, and 2 mg; liquid, 1 mg/mL (30 mL bottle); long-acting depot microspheres formulation for deep IM formulation, 25 mg vial/kit, 37.5 mg vial/kit, 50 mg vial/kit

DOSAGE:

Acute Psychosis and Bipolar Disorder:
- 2 to 8 mg/day orally for adults
- 0.5 to 2.0 mg/day orally for children and elderly
- 25 to 50 mg depot IM every 2 wk

ADMINISTRATION:
- Tablets may be given with or without food.
- Advise patient to take missed dose as soon as remembers. Skip missed dose if almost time for next scheduled dose. Do not take extra medicine to make up the missed dose.
- Measure the liquid form of risperidone with a special dose-measuring spoon or cup, not a regular tablespoon.
- Do not mix the liquid form with cola or tea.

SIDE EFFECTS: Can increase risk for diabetes and dyslipidemia; EPS (dose-dependent, use lowest effective dose to minimize); hyperprolactinemia (dose-dependent); dizziness, insomnia, headache, anxiety; nausea, sedation, weight gain, constipation, abdominal pain; tachycardia; weight gain; sedation; sexual dysfunction; hyperglycemia; increased risk of death and cerebrovascular events in elderly with dementia-related psychosis; tardive dyskinesia (rare); orthostatic hypotension (rare, usually during initial dose titration); NMS (rare); seizures (rare)

DRUG INTERACTIONS:
- May increase effects of antihypertensive medications.
- May antagonize levodopa, dopamine agonists.
- Plasma levels of risperidone may be reduced if given in conjunction with carbamazepine.
- Plasma levels of risperidone may be increased if given in conjunction with fluoxetine or paroxetine.
- Plasma levels of risperidone may be increased if given in conjunction with clozapine, but no dose adjustment is required.

▶**Alert:** This list may not describe all possible interactions. Instruct clients to provide a list of all the medicines, herbs, nonprescription drugs, or dietary supplements they use.

PHARMACOKINETICS:
Elimination: 7–8 wk after last injection (long-acting IM formulation)
Metabolism: Active; metabolized by CYP450 2D6
Half-life: 20–24 hr (oral formulation); 3–6 days (long-acting formulation)

PRECAUTIONS:
- Use with caution in patients with conditions that predispose to hypotension (dehydration, overheating).

- Use with caution in patients at risk for aspiration pneumonia.
- Priapism has been reported.
- *Do not use if there is a proven allergy.*

PATIENT AND FAMILY EDUCATION:
- Take exactly as prescribed by the provider. Do not take in larger or smaller amounts or for longer than recommended.
- Can be taken with or without food.
- Patient may be more sensitive to temperature extremes (very hot or cold conditions) when taking this medication. Avoid getting too cold, or becoming overheated or dehydrated.
- Drink plenty of fluids, especially in hot weather and during exercise.
- Risperidone can cause side effects that may impair thinking or reactions. Be careful when driving or doing anything that requires you to be awake and alert.
- Risperidone may cause high blood sugar (hyperglycemia). Talk to provider if any signs of hyperglycemia such as increased thirst or urination, excessive hunger, or weakness. If diabetic, check blood sugar levels on a regular basis.
- Risperidone ODT may contain phenylalanine. Talk to provider before using this form of risperidone if you have PKU.
- *Avoid drinking alcohol.* It can increase some of the side effects.
- *Do not* mix the liquid form with cola or tea.
- *Stop using this medication and call provider immediately* if you have fever, stiff muscles, confusion, sweating, fast or uneven heartbeats, restless muscle movements in face or neck, tremor (uncontrolled shaking), trouble swallowing, feeling light-headed, or fainting.
- Do not stop taking drug suddenly without first talking to provider, even if you feel fine. May have serious side effects if you stop taking the drug suddenly.
- Call provider if symptoms do not improve or get worse.
- Store at room temperature away from moisture, light, and heat. Do not freeze the liquid form of risperidone.

SPECIAL POPULATIONS:
- *Elderly:*
  - Initially 0.5 mg PO once a day, then increase to 0.5 mg twice a day. Titrate once a week for doses above 1.5 mg twice a day.
  - Long-acting risperidone: 25 mg every 2 wk. Oral administration should be continued for 3 wk after the first injection.
  - Elderly with dementia-related psychosis treated with atypical antipsychotics are at higher risk of death and cerebrovascular events.
- *Renal impairment:*
  - Initially 0.5 mg PO twice a day for the first week. Increase to 1 mg twice a day during the second week.

(cont.)

risperidone (cont.)

- Long-acting risperidone should not be given to patient with renal function impairment unless s/he can tolerate at least 2 mg/day orally.
- Long-acting risperidone should be given 25 mg every 2 wk. Oral administration should be continued for 3 wk after first injection.
- *Hepatic impairment*
  - Initially 0.5 mg PO twice a day for the first week. Increase to 1 mg twice a day during the second week.
  - Long-acting risperidone should not be given to patient with renal function impairment unless s/he can tolerate at least 2 mg/day orally.
  - Long-acting risperidone should be given 25 mg every 2 wk. Oral administration should be continued for 3 wk after first injection.
- *Cardiac impairment*: Use with caution because of risk of orthostatic hypotension. Can increase

the risk of stroke if given to elderly patients with atrial fibrillation.
- *Pregnancy:* Category C; some animal studies show adverse effects. No controlled studies in humans. Should be used only when the potential benefits outweigh potential risks to the fetus. Risperidone may be preferable to anticonvulsant mood stabilizers if treatment is required during pregnancy. Effects of hyperprolactinemia on the fetus are unknown.
- *Lactation:* Secreted in human breast milk. It is recommended to either discontinue drug or bottlefeed. Infants of women who choose to breastfeed while on this drug should be monitored for possible adverse effects.
- *Children and adolescents:* Safe and effective for behavioral disturbances in this population.

| Zyprexa Symbyax | olanzapine olanzapine/fluoxetine |

AVAILABLE FORMS: Tablet, 2.5, 5, 7.5, 10, 15, and 20 mg; ODT, 5, 10, 15, and 20 mg. *Symbyax* (olanzapine/fluoxetine combination): IM, 5 mg/mL (each vial contains 10 mg olanzapine–fluoxetine); combination capsule, 6 mg/25 mg, 6 mg/50 mg, 12 mg/25 mg, 12 mg/50 mg

DOSAGE: *Oral or IM:* 5 to 10 mg/day, up to a maximum dose of 20 mg/day; *olanzapine–fluoxetine combination:* 6 to 12 mg/olanzapine/25 to 50 mg fluoxetine

ADMINISTRATION:
- Injectable formulation may be easier to administer to a patient with delusional disorder.
- Tablets may be given with or without food.
- Advise patient to take the missed dose as soon as s/he remembers. Skip the missed dose if almost time for next scheduled dose. Do not take extra medicine to make up the missed dose.
- Store at room temperature away from moisture, heat, and light.

SIDE EFFECTS: Can increase risk for diabetes and dyslipidemia; dizziness, sedation; weight gain; dry mouth, constipation, dyspepsia; peripheral edema; joint pain, back pain, chest pain, extremity pain, abnormal gait, ecchymosis; tachycardia; orthostatic hypotension (usually during initial dose titration); hyperglycemia; increased risk of death and cerebrovascular events in elderly with dementia-related psychosis; tardive dyskinesia (rare); rash on exposure to sunlight (rare); NMS (rare); seizures (rare)

DRUG INTERACTIONS:
- May increase effects of antihypertensive medications
- May antagonize levodopa, dopamine agonists
- May need to reduce dose if given with CYP450 1A2 inhibitors (e.g., fluvoxamine)

- May need to increase dose if given with CYP450 1A2 inducers (e.g., cigarette smoke, carbamazepine)
▶**Alert:** This list may not describe all possible interactions. Instruct client to provide a list of all the medicines, herbs, nonprescription drugs, or dietary supplements they use.

PHARMACOKINETICS:
Metabolism: Inactive
Half-life: 21–54 hr

PRECAUTIONS:
- Use with caution in patients with conditions that predispose to hypotension (dehydration, overheating). Watch closely for hypotension if given IM formulation.
- Use with caution in patients with prostatic hypertrophy, narrow angle-closure glaucoma, paralytic ileus.
- Use with caution in patients at risk for aspiration pneumonia.
- IM formulation is not recommended to be given with parenteral benzodiazepines. If patients need a parenteral benzodiazepine, it should be given at least 1 hr after IM formulation olanzapine.
- Do not use if there is a proven allergy.
- Do not give IM formulation:
  - If patient has unstable medical condition (e.g., acute MI, unstable angina pectoris, severe hypotension, and/or bradycardia, sick sinus syndrome, recent heart surgery).
  - If patient has known risks of narrow angle-closure glaucoma.

PATIENT AND FAMILY EDUCATION:
- Take exactly as prescribed by the provider. Do not take in larger or smaller amounts or for longer than recommended.
- Can be taken with or without food.

(cont.)

olanzapine, olanzapine/fluoxetine (*cont.*)

- For olanzapine ODTs, keep the tablet in its blister pack until ready to take it. Open the package and peel back the foil from the tablet blister. Do not push a tablet through the foil. Using dry hands, remove the tablet and place it in mouth; it will begin to dissolve right away.
- Do not swallow the tablet whole. Allow it to dissolve in mouth without chewing. If desired, drink liquid to help swallow the dissolved tablet.
- *If you have diabetes*: Check blood sugar levels on a regular basis while taking olanzapine.
- Can gain weight or have high cholesterol and triglycerides (types of fat) while taking this drug, especially if a teenager. Your blood will need to be tested often.
- Do not stop taking drug suddenly without first talking to provider, even if you feel fine. May have serious side effects if you stop taking the drug suddenly.
- Call provider if symptoms do not improve or get worse.
- Store at room temperature away from moisture, heat, and light.

SPECIAL POPULATIONS:
- *Elderly:*
  - May tolerate lower doses better. Elderly with dementia-related psychosis treated with atypical antipsychotics are at higher risk of death and cerebrovascular events. It can increase incidence of stroke.
  - If IM formulation is given, the recommended starting dose is 2.5 to 5 mg. A second injection of 2.5 to 5 mg maybe given 2 hr after the first injection. No more than three injections should be administered within 24 hr.
- *Renal impairment:* No dose adjustment is required for oral formulation. Consider lower starting dose (5 mg) for IM formulation. Not removed by hemodialysis.
- *Hepatic impairment:* Starting oral dose, 5 mg for patients with moderate-to-severe hepatic function impairment and increase dose with caution. Consider lower starting dose (5 mg) for IM formulation. Check patient liver function tests a few times a year.
- *Cardiac impairment*: Use with caution because of risk of orthostatic hypotension.
- *Pregnancy:* Category C; some animal studies show adverse effects. No controlled studies in humans. Should be used only when the potential benefits outweigh potential risks to the fetus. Olanzapine may be preferable to anticonvulsant mood stabilizers if treatment is required during pregnancy.
- *Lactation:* Unknown if olanzapine is secreted in human breast milk. It is recommended to either discontinue drug or bottlefeed. Infants of women who choose to breastfeed while on this drug should be monitored for possible adverse effect.
- *Children and adolescents:*
  - Probably safe and effective for behavioral disturbances in this population.
  - IM formulation has not been studied in patients under 18 and is not recommended for use in this population.
  - Should be monitored more frequently than adults.

quetiapine | *Seroquel, Seroquel XR*

AVAILABLE FORMS: Tablet, 25, 50, 100, 200, 300, and 400 mg; extended-release tablet, 200, 300, and 400 mg

DOSAGE:
- 400 to 800 mg/day in 1 dose (*Seroquel XR*) or 2 doses (*Seroquel*) for schizophrenia and bipolar mania.
- 300 mg once per day for bipolar depression.

ADMINISTRATION:
- Tablets may be given with or without food.
- Take this medicine with a full glass of water.
- Advise patient not to crush, chew, or break an extended-release tablet. Swallow the pill whole. Breaking the pill may cause too much of the drug to be released at one time.
- Advise patient to take the missed dose as soon as remembers. Skip the missed dose if almost time for next scheduled dose. Do not take extra medicine to make up the missed dose.

SIDE EFFECTS: Can increase risk for diabetes and dyslipidemia; dizziness, sedation; dry mouth, constipation, dyspepsia, abdominal pain; weight gain; tachycardia; hyperglycemia; increased risk of death and cerebrovascular events in elderly with dementia-related psychosis; orthostatic hypotension (usually during initial dose titration); NMS (rare); seizures (rare)

DRUG INTERACTIONS:
- May increase effects of antihypertensive medications
- Plasma levels of quetiapine may be increased if given in conjunction with CYP450 3A4 and CYP450 2D6 inhibitors. However, no dose adjustment is required.
- ▶**Alert:** This list may not describe all possible interactions. Instruct clients to provide a list of all the medicines, herbs, nonprescription drugs, or dietary supplements they use.

PHARMACOKINETICS:
Metabolism: Inactive
Half-life: 6–7 hr

PRECAUTIONS:
- Use with caution in patients who are at risk for aspiration pneumonia.

(cont.)

quetiapine (*cont.*)

- Manufacturer recommends to examine for cataracts before and every 6 months after starting quetiapine.
- Do not use if there is a proven allergy.

PATIENT AND FAMILY EDUCATION:
- Take exactly as prescribed by the provider. Do not take in larger or smaller amounts or for longer than recommended.
- Can be taken with or without food.
- Quetiapine can cause side effects that may impair thinking or reactions. Be careful when driving or doing anything that requires you to be awake and alert.
- Quetiapine may cause high blood sugar (hyperglycemia). Talk to provider if any signs of hyperglycemia such as increased thirst or urination, excessive hunger, or weakness. If are diabetic, check blood sugar levels on a regular basis.
- Avoid becoming overheated or dehydrated during exercise and in hot weather. You may be more prone to heat stroke.
- Avoid getting up too fast from a sitting or lying position. Get up slowly and steady yourself to prevent a fall.
- Avoid drinking alcohol.
- Stop using this medication and call provider immediately if you have very stiff (rigid) muscles, high fever, sweating, confusion, fast or uneven heartbeats, tremors; feel like you might pass out; have jerky muscle movements you cannot control, trouble swallowing, problems with speech; have blurred vision, eye pain, or seeing halos around lights; have increased thirst and urination, excessive hunger, fruity breath odor, weakness, nausea and vomiting; have fever, chills, body aches, flu symptoms, or have white patches or sores inside mouth or on lips.
- Do not stop taking drug suddenly without first talking to provider, even if you feel fine. You may have serious side effects if you stop taking the drug suddenly.
- Call provider if symptoms do not improve or get worse.
- Store at room temperature away from moisture and heat.

SPECIAL POPULATIONS:
- *Elderly:* Generally lower dose is used (e.g., 25 to 100 mg twice a day). Higher dose can be used if tolerated. Elderly with dementia-related psychosis treated with atypical antipsychotics are at higher risk of death and cerebrovascular events.
- *Renal impairment:* No dose adjustment is required.
- *Hepatic impairment:* May need to reduce dose.
- *Cardiac impairment:* Use with caution because of risk of orthostatic hypotension.
- *Pregnancy:* Category C; some animal studies show adverse effects. No controlled studies in humans. Should be used only when the potential benefits outweigh potential risks to the fetus. Quetiapine may be preferable to anticonvulsant mood stabilizers if treatment is required during pregnancy.
- *Lactation:* Unknown if drug is secreted in human breast milk. It is recommended to either discontinue drug or bottlefeed. Infants of women who choose to breastfeed while on this drug should be monitored for possible adverse effect.
- *Children and adolescents:*
  - Not officially recommended for patients under age 18.
  - Probably safe and effective for behavioral disturbances in this population.
  - Should be monitored more frequently than adults. May tolerate lower doses better.
  - Watch for activation of suicidal ideation. Inform parents or guardian of this risk so they can help monitor the risk.

Geodon, Geodon IM Injection **ziprasidone**

AVAILABLE FORMS: Tablet, 20, 40, 60, and 80 mg; injection, 20 mg/mL

DOSAGE:
Schizophrenia:
- 40 to 200 mg/day in divided doses PO
Bipolar Disorder:
- 80 to 160 mg/day in divided doses PO. 10 to 20 mg IM (doses of 10 mg may be administered every 2 hr, doses of 20 mg may be administered every 4 hr); maximum daily dose, 40 mg. Not to be administered for more than 3 consecutive days.

ADMINISTRATION:
- Take with a meal.
- Dosing at 20 to 40 twice a day is too low and activating, perhaps due to potent $5-HT_{2C}$ antagonist properties. Reduce activation by increasing the dose to 60 to 80 mg twice a day.
- Best efficacy in schizophrenia and bipolar disorder is at doses greater than 120 mg/day.
- BMI monthly for 3 months, then quarterly.
- Monitor fasting triglycerides monthly for several months in patients at high risk for metabolic complications.
- Blood pressure, fasting plasma glucose, fasting lipids within 3 months and then annually, but earlier and more frequently for patients with diabetes or who have gained more than 5% of initial weight.

SIDE EFFECTS: Dizziness, sedation, and hypotension especially at high doses; motor side effects (rare); possible increased incidence of diabetes or dyslipidemia is unknown

(cont.)

BORDERLINE PERSONALITY DISORDER: Antipsychotics, Atypical (Second Generation)

ziprasidone (cont.)

DRUG INTERACTIONS:
- May enhance the effects of antihypertensive drugs
- May antagonize levodopa, dopamine agonists
- May enhance QTc prolongation of other drugs capable of prolonging QTc interval

PHARMACOKINETICS:
Protein binding: Greater than 99%
Metabolism: Metabolized by CYP450 3A4
Half-life: 6.6 hr

PRECAUTIONS:
- Prolongs QTc interval more than some other antipsychotics.
- Use with caution in patients with conditions that predispose to hypotension (dehydration, overheating).
- Priapism has been reported.
- Dysphagia has been associated with antipsychotic use, and should be used cautiously in patients at risk for aspiration pneumonia.
- Do not use if patient is taking agents capable of prolonging QTc interval (pimozide, thioridazine, selected antiarrhythmics, moxifloxacin, sparfloxacin).
- Do not use if there is a history of QTc prolongation, cardiac arrhythmia, recent acute MI, uncompensated heart failure.
- Do not use if there is a proven allergy to ziprasidone.

PATIENT AND FAMILY EDUCATION:
- Take with a meal of a few hundred calories (turkey sandwich and a piece of fruit) to enhance the absorption
- Avoid becoming overheated or dehydrated during exercise and in hot weather. You may be more prone to heat stroke.
- Avoid getting up too fast from a sitting or lying position. Get up slowly and steady yourself to prevent a fall.
- Avoid drinking alcohol.

- Stop using this medication and call provider immediately if you have very stiff (rigid) muscles, high fever, sweating, confusion, fast or uneven heartbeats, tremors; feel like you might pass out; have jerky muscle movements you cannot control, trouble swallowing, problems with speech; have blurred vision, eye pain, or seeing halos around lights; have increased thirst and urination, excessive hunger, fruity breath odor, weakness, nausea and vomiting; have fever, chills, body aches, flu symptoms, or have white patches or sores inside mouth or on lips.
- Do not stop taking drug suddenly without first talking to provider, even if you feel fine. You may have serious side effects if you stop taking the drug suddenly.
- Call provider if symptoms do not improve or get worse.
- Store at room temperature away from moisture and heat.

SPECIAL POPULATIONS:
- *Elderly:* Some patients may tolerate lower doses better. Elderly patients with dementia-related psychosis treated with atypical antipsychotics are at an increased risk of death compared to placebo.
- *Renal impairment:* No dose adjustment necessary.
- *Hepatic impairment:* No dose adjustment necessary.
- *Cardiac impairment:* Contraindicated in patients with a known history of QTc prolongation, recent MI
- *Pregnancy:* Category C; some animal studies show adverse effects; no controlled studies in humans.
- *Lactation:* Unknown if secreted in human breast milk. Recommend either to discontinue drug or to bottlefeed.
- *Children and adolescents:* Not recommended for patients under age 18. Early data suggest that it may be safe and effective for behavioral disturbances in children and adolescents.

Class: Mood Stabilizers

lithium	*Eskalith, Lithobid, Carbolith, Duralith Lithizine*

AVAILABLE FORMS: Capsule, 150, 300, and 600 mg; slow-release tablet, 300 mg; controlled-release tablets, 300 and 450 mg; syrup, 300 mg (8 mEq lithium/5 mL)

DOSAGE: *Adults:* 300 to 600 mg PO up to qid. Or 900 mg controlled-release tablets PO every 12 hr. Increase dosage based on blood levels to achieve optimum dosage. Recommended therapeutic lithium levels are 1 to 1.5 mEq/L for acute mania and 0.6 to 1.2 mEq/L for maintenance therapy.

ADMINISTRATION:
- Give drug after meals with plenty of water to minimize GI upset.
- Do not crush controlled-release tablets.

SIDE EFFECTS:
- *CNS:* Fatigue, lethargy, coma, epileptiform seizures, tremors, drowsiness, headache, confusion, restlessness, dizziness, psychomotor retardation, blackouts, EEG changes, worsened organic mental syndrome, impaired speech, ataxia, uncoordination

(cont.)

lithium (*cont.*)

- *CV:* Arrhythmias, bradycardia, reversible ECG changes, hypotension
- *EENT:* Tinnitus, blurred vision
- *GI:* Vomiting, anorexia, diarrhea, thirst, nausea, metallic taste, dry mouth, abdominal pain, flatulence, indigestion
- *GU:* Polyuria, renal toxicity with long-term use, glycosuria, decreased creatinine clearance, albuminuria
- *Hematologic:* Leukocytosis with leukocyte count of 14,000 to 18,000/mm
- *Metabolic:* Transient hyperglycemia, goiter, hypothyroidism, hyponatremia
- *Musculoskeletal:* Muscle weakness
- *Skin:* Pruritus, rash, diminished or absent sensation drying and thinning of hair, psoriasis, acne, alopecia
- *Other:* Ankle and wrist edema

DRUG INTERACTIONS: ACE inhibitors, aminophylline, sodium bicarbonate, urine alkalizers, calcium channel blockers (verapamil), carbamazepine, fluoxetine, methyldopa, NSAIDs, probenecid, neuromuscular blockers, thiazide diuretics. Caffeine may decrease lithium level and drug effect; advise patient who ingests large amounts of caffeine.

PHARMACOKINETICS: Probably alters chemical transmitters in the CNS, possibly by interfering with ionic pump mechanisms in brain cells, and may compete with or replace sodium ions.
Half-life: 18 hr (adolescents); 36 hr (elderly).

ROUTE	ONSET	PEAK	DURATION
PO	Unknown	30 min–3 hr	Unknown

PRECAUTIONS:
- May increase glucose and creatinine levels. May decrease sodium, T_3, T_4, and protein-bound iodine levels.
- May increase WBC and neutrophil counts.
- Contraindicated if therapy cannot be closely monitored.
- Avoid using in pregnant patient unless benefits outweigh risks.
- Use with caution in patients receiving neuromuscular blockers and diuretics; in elderly or debilitated patients; and in patients with thyroid disease, seizure disorder, infection, renal or CV disease, severe debilitation or dehydration, or sodium depletion.

▶**Alert:** Drug has a narrow therapeutic margin of safety. Determining drug level is crucial to safe use of drug. Do not use drug in patients who cannot have regular tests. Monitor level 8 to 12 hr after first dose, the morning before second dose is given, two or three times weekly for the first month, and then weekly to monthly during maintenance therapy.

- When drug level is less than 1.5 mEq/L, adverse reactions are usually mild.
- Monitor baseline ECG, thyroid studies, renal studies, and electrolyte levels.
- Check fluid intake and output, especially when surgery is scheduled.
- Weigh patient daily; check for edema or sudden weight gain.
- Adjust fluid and salt ingestion to compensate if excessive loss occurs from protracted diaphoresis or diarrhea. Under normal conditions, patient fluid intake should be 2.5 to 3 L daily, and patient should follow a balanced diet with adequate salt intake.
- Check urine specific gravity and report level below 1.005, which may indicate diabetes insipidus.
- Drug alters glucose tolerance in diabetics. Monitor glucose level closely.
- Perform outpatient follow-up of thyroid and renal functions every 6 to 12 months. Palpate thyroid to check for enlargement.

PATIENT AND FAMILY EDUCATION:
- Tell patient to take drug with plenty of water and after meals to minimize GI upset.
- Explain the importance of having regular blood tests to determine drug levels; even slightly high values can be dangerous.
- Warn patient and caregivers to expect transient nausea, large amounts of urine, thirst, and discomfort during first few days of therapy and to watch for evidence of toxicity (diarrhea, vomiting, tremor, drowsiness, muscle weakness, uncoordination).
- Instruct patient to withhold one dose and call prescriber if signs and symptoms of toxicity appear, but not to stop drug abruptly.
- Warn patient to avoid hazardous activities that require alertness and good psychomotor coordination until CNS effects of drug are known.
- Tell patient not to switch brands or take other prescription or OTC drugs without prescriber's guidance.
- Tell patient to wear or carry medical identification at all times.

SPECIAL POPULATIONS:
- *Elderly:* Initial dose reduction and possibly lower maintenance doses due to age-related changes and sensitivity to side effects.
- *Pregnancy/Lactation:* Category D. Positive evidence of fetal harm has been demonstrated.
- *Children:* Not approved in patients under 12 years; use with caution and monitor closely for side effects and suicidality. Children may experience more frequent and severe side effects.

Class: Mood Stabilizing Anticonvulsants

carbamazepine   *Tegretol, Carbatrol, Epitol, Equetro, Tegretol-XR, Tegretol CR*

AVAILABLE FORMS: Tablet, 200 mg; chewable tablet, 100 mg; XR capsule, 100, 200, 300, and 400 mg; oral suspension, 100 mg/5 mL

DOSAGE: *Adults:* 300 to 600 mg PO up to qid. Or, 900 mg controlled-release tablets PO every 12 hr. Increase dosage based on blood levels to achieve optimum dosage. Recommended therapeutic lithium levels are 1 to 1.5 mEq/L for acute mania and 0.6 to 1.2 mEq/L for maintenance therapy.

ADMINISTRATION:
- Store at room temperature.
- Give with meals to reduce the risk of GI distress.
- Shake oral suspension well.
- Do not administer with grapefruit juice.
- Do not crush capsules or tablets.

SIDE EFFECTS:
- *CNS:* Fatigue, lethargy, coma, epileptiform seizures, tremors, drowsiness, headache, confusion, restlessness, dizziness, psychomotor retardation, blackouts, EEG changes, worsened organic mental syndrome, impaired speech, ataxia, uncoordination
- *CV:* Arrhythmias, bradycardia, reversible ECG changes, hypotension
- *EENT:* Tinnitus, blurred vision
- *GI:* Vomiting, anorexia, diarrhea, thirst, nausea, metallic taste, dry mouth, abdominal pain, flatulence, indigestion
- *GU:* Polyuria, renal toxicity with long-term use, glycosuria, decreased creatinine clearance, albuminuria
- *Hematologic:* Leukocytosis with leukocyte count of 14,000 to 18,000/mm
- *Metabolic:* Transient hyperglycemia, goiter, hypothyroidism, hyponatremia
- *Musculoskeletal:* Muscle weakness
- *Skin:* Pruritus, rash, diminished or absent sensation, drying and thinning of hair, psoriasis, acne, alopecia
- *Other:* Ankle and wrist edema

DRUG INTERACTIONS: ACE inhibitors, aminophylline, sodium bicarbonate, urine alkalizers, calcium channel blockers (verapamil), carbamazepine, fluoxetine, methyldopa, NSAIDs, probenecid, neuromuscular blockers, thiazide diuretics, caffeine may decrease lithium level and drug effect. Advise patient who ingests large amounts of caffeine to tell prescriber before stopping caffeine. Adjust lithium dosage, as needed.

PHARMACOKINETICS: Probably alters chemical transmitters in the CNS, possibly by interfering with ionic pump mechanisms in brain cells, and may compete with or replace sodium ions.
Half-life: 18 hr (adolescents); 36 hr (elderly).

ROUTE	ONSET	PEAK	DURATION
PO	Unknown	30 min–3 hr	Unknown

PRECAUTIONS:
- Contraindicated if therapy cannot be closely monitored.
- Avoid using in pregnant patient unless benefits outweigh risks.
- Use with caution in patients receiving neuromuscular blockers and diuretics; in elderly or debilitated patients; and in patients with thyroid disease, seizure disorder, infection, renal or CV disease, severe debilitation or dehydration, or sodium depletion.

▶**Alert:** Drug has a narrow therapeutic margin of safety. Determining drug level is crucial to safe use of drug. Do not use drug in patients who cannot have regular tests. Monitor level 8 to 12 hr after first dose, the morning before second dose is given, two or three times weekly for the first month, and then weekly to monthly during maintenance therapy.
- When drug level is less than 1.5 mEq/L, adverse reactions are usually mild.
- Monitor baseline ECG, thyroid studies, renal studies, and electrolyte levels.
- Check fluid intake and output, especially when surgery is scheduled.
- Weigh patient daily; check for edema or sudden weight gain.
- Adjust fluid and salt ingestion to compensate if excessive loss occurs from protracted diaphoresis or diarrhea. Under normal conditions, patient fluid intake should be 2.5 to 3 L daily, and patient should follow a balanced diet with adequate salt intake.
- Check urine specific gravity and report level below 1.005, which may indicate diabetes insipidus.
- Drug alters glucose tolerance in diabetics. Monitor glucose level closely.
- Perform outpatient follow-up of thyroid and renal functions every 6 to 12 months. Palpate thyroid to check for enlargement.

PATIENT AND FAMILY EDUCATION:
- Tell patient to take drug with plenty of water and after meals to minimize GI upset.
- Explain the importance of having regular blood tests to determine drug levels; even slightly high values can be dangerous.
- Warn patient and caregivers to expect transient nausea, large amounts of urine, thirst, and discomfort during first few days of therapy and to watch for evidence of toxicity (diarrhea, vomiting, tremor, drowsiness, muscle weakness, uncoordination).
- Instruct patient to withhold one dose and call prescriber if signs and symptoms of toxicity appear, but not to stop drug abruptly.

(cont.)

carbamazepine (cont.)

- Warn patient to avoid hazardous activities that require alertness and good psychomotor coordination until CNS effects of drug are known.
- Tell patient not to switch brands or take other prescription or OTC drugs without prescriber's guidance.
- Tell patient to wear or carry medical identification at all times.

SPECIAL POPULATIONS:
- *Elderly:* Use with caution in men with BPH due to increased urinary retention; monitor for dizziness and falls secondary to sedation.
- *Pregnancy/Lactation:* Do not use when breastfeeding.
- *Children:* Approved for use in epilepsy, therefore safety profile exists. Used off label for aggression.

Depacon *Depakene* *Depakote, Depakote ER, Depakote Sprinkle*	**valproate sodium** **valproic acid** **divalproex sodium**

▶**Special Note:** Valproate sodium should only be prescribed for this condition in consultation with a psychiatric/mental health specialist.

AVAILABLE FORMS: Injection, 100 mg/mL; syrup, 250 mg/5 mL. *Valproic acid*: Capsule, 250 mg; syrup, 200 mg/5 mL; tablet (crushable), 100 mg; tablet (enteric-coated), 200 and 500 mg. *Divalproex sodium:* Capsules (sprinkle), 125 mg; tablet (delayed-release), 125, 250, and 500 mg; tablet (extended-release), 250 and 500 mg

DOSAGE:
Mania:
- *Adults:* Initially, 750 mg *Depakote* daily PO in divided doses, or 25 mg/kg *Depakote ER* once daily. Adjust dosage based on patient's response; maximum dose for either form is 60 mg/kg daily.

To Prevent Migraine Headache:
- *Adults:* Initially, 250 mg delayed-release divalproex sodium PO bid. Some patients may need up to 1,000 mg daily. Or, 500 mg *Depakote ER* PO daily for 1 wk; then 1,000 mg PO daily. *Adjust-a-dose:* For elderly patients, start at lower dosage. Increase dosage more slowly and with regular monitoring of fluid and nutritional intake, and watch for dehydration, somnolence, and other adverse reactions.

ADMINISTRATION:
- *Oral:* Give drug with food or milk to reduce adverse GI effects.
- Do not mix syrup with carbonated beverages; mixture may be irritating to oral mucosa.
- Do not give syrup to patients who need sodium restriction. Check with prescriber.
- Capsules may be swallowed whole or opened and contents sprinkled on a teaspoonful of soft food. Patient should swallow immediately without chewing.
- Monitor drug level and adjust dosage as needed.
- *Incompatibilities:* None reported.

SIDE EFFECTS:
- *CNS:* Asthenia, dizziness, headache, insomnia, nervousness, somnolence, tremor, abnormal thinking, amnesia, ataxia, depression, emotional upset, fever, sedation
- *CV:* Chest pain, edema, hypertension, hypotension, tachycardia
- *EENT:* Blurred vision, diplopia, nystagmus, pharyngitis, rhinitis, tinnitus
- *GI:* Abdominal pain, anorexia, diarrhea, dyspepsia, nausea, vomiting, pancreatitis, constipation, increased appetite
- *Hematologic:* Bone marrow suppression, hemorrhage, thrombocytopenia, bruising, petechiae
- *Hepatic:* Hepatotoxicity
- *Metabolic:* Hyperammonemia, weight gain
- *Musculoskeletal:* Back and neck pain
- *Respiratory:* Bronchitis, dyspnea
- *Skin:* Alopecia, flu syndrome, infection, erythema multiforme, hypersensitivity reactions, Stevens-Johnson syndrome, rash, photosensitivity reactions, pruritus

DRUG INTERACTIONS: Aspirin, chlorpromazine, cimetidine, erythromycin, felbamate, carbamazepine, lamotrigine, phenobarbital, phenytoin, rifampin, warfarin, zidovudine. Alcohol use is discouraged.

PHARMACOKINETICS: Peak action for oral dose is 15 min to 4 hr. Facilitates the effects of GABA.
Half-life: 6–16 hr

PRECAUTIONS:
- May increase ammonia, ALT, AST, and bilirubin lab levels.
- May increase eosinophil count and bleeding time. May decrease platelet, RBC, and WBC counts.
- May cause false-positive results for urine ketone levels.
- Contraindicated in patients hypersensitive to drug and in those with hepatic disease or significant hepatic dysfunction, and in patients with a UCD.
- Safety and efficacy of *Depakote ER* in children younger than age 10 have not been established.
- Obtain liver function test results, platelet count, and PT and INR before starting therapy, and monitor these values periodically.
- Adverse reactions may not be caused by valproic acid alone because it is usually used with other anticonvulsants.

(cont.)

BORDERLINE PERSONALITY DISORDER: Mood Stabilizing Anticonvulsants

valproate sodium, valproic acid, divalproex sodium (*cont.*)

- When converting adults and children aged 10 and older with seizures from *Depakote* to *Depakote ER*, make sure the extended-release dose is 8% to 20% higher than the regular dose taken previously. See manufacturer's package insert for more details.
- *Divalproex sodium* has a lower risk of adverse GI reactions.
- Never withdraw drug suddenly, because sudden withdrawal may worsen seizures. Call prescriber at once if adverse reactions develop.
- Patients at high risk for hepatotoxicity include those with congenital metabolic disorders, mental retardation, or organic brain disease; those taking multiple anticonvulsants; and children younger than age 2 years.
- Notify prescriber if tremors occur; a dosage reduction may be needed.
- Monitor drug level. Therapeutic level is 50 to 100 mcg/mL.
- When converting patients from a brand-name drug to a generic drug, use caution because breakthrough seizures may occur.

▶**Alert:** Sometimes fatal, hyperammonemic encephalopathy may occur when starting valproate therapy in patients with UCD. Evaluate patients with UCD risk factors before starting valproate therapy. Patients who develop symptoms of unexplained hyperammonemic encephalopathy during valproate therapy should stop drug, undergo prompt appropriate treatment, and be evaluated for underlying UCD.

▶**Alert:** Fatal hepatotoxicity may follow nonspecific symptoms, such as malaise, fever, and lethargy. If these symptoms occur during therapy, notify prescriber at once because patients who might be developing hepatic dysfunction must stop taking drug.

PATIENT AND FAMILY EDUCATION:
- Take drug with food or milk to reduce adverse GI effects.

- Do not chew capsules; irritation of mouth and throat may result.
- Capsules may be either swallowed whole or carefully opened and contents sprinkled on a teaspoonful of soft food. Swallow immediately without chewing.
- Avoid driving and other potentially hazardous activities that require mental alertness until drug's CNS effects are known.
- Women, should call prescriber if become pregnant or plan to become pregnant during therapy.
- Syrup should not be mixed with carbonated beverages; mixture may be irritating to mouth and throat.
- Keep drug out of children's reach.
- Do not stop drug therapy abruptly.
- Call prescriber if malaise, weakness, lethargy, facial swelling, loss of appetite, or vomiting occurs.

SPECIAL POPULATIONS:
- *Elderly:* Caution is advised when using this drug in the elderly due to more sensitivity to the drug.
- *Pregnancy:* Category D. This medication should only be used when clearly needed during pregnancy.
- *Lactation:* Secreted into breast milk.
- *Children:* Caution when using this drug in a child or adolescent; must balance the potential risks with the clinical need. Not recommended for use under age 18 years for MDD.

▶**Alert:** Antidepressants increased the risk of suicidal thinking and behavior (suicidality) in short-term studies in children and adolescents with depression and other psychiatric disorders. Caution is advised when using this drug in children because they may be more sensitive to the side effects of the drug, especially loss of appetite and weight loss. It is important to monitor weight and growth in children who are taking this drug.

topiramate	*Topamax*

AVAILABLE FORMS: Tablet, 25, 50, 100, and 200 mg; sprinkle capsule, 15 and 25 mg

DOSAGE: *Adults:* 25–50 mg/day for one week initially, then increase by 25–50 mg/day at weekly intervals. Usual maintenance dose is 100–200 mg twice daily

ADMINISTRATION:
- Do not break tablets.
- Give with or without food.
- Capsules may be swallowed whole or contents sprinkled on teaspoonful of soft food and swallowed immediately. Do not chew.

SIDE EFFECTS: Drowsiness; dizziness; ataxia; nystagmus; diplopia; paresthesia; nausea; tremor; confusion; dyspepsia; depression; weight loss; mood disturbances

DRUG INTERACTIONS:
- Alcohol and other CNS depressants may increase CNS depression.
- Carbamazepine, phenytoin, and valproic acid may decrease serum concentration.
- Carbonic anhydrase inhibitors may increase risk of renal calculi formation.

PHARMACOKINETICS:
Onset: 4 days
Peak: 2 hr
Duration: 2–3 months
Half-life: 21 hr

(cont.)

topiramate (*cont.*)

PRECAUTIONS:
Contraindications:
- Bipolar disorder

Cautions:
- Sensitivity to topiramate; hepatic/renal impairment; predisposition to renal calculi

PATIENT AND FAMILY EDUCATION:
- Avoid tasks that require alertness and motor skills until response to drug is established.
- Avoid use of alcohol and other CNS depressants.
- Do not abruptly discontinue this drug.

- Do not break tablets.
- Maintain adequate fluid intake.
- Inform health care provider if blurred vision or eye pain occurs.

SPECIAL POPULATIONS:
- *Elderly:* Age-related renal impairment may require dosage adjustment
- *Pregnancy/Lactation:* Unknown if distributed in breast milk.
- *Children:* Safety and efficacy have not been established in pediatric patients.

Lamictal, Lamictal XR   **lamotrigine**

INDICATIONS: Used to treat bipolar disorder in adults.

AVAILABLE FORMS: Tablet, 25, 100, 150, and 200 mg; chewable tablet, 2, 5 and 25 mg

DOSAGE: Starting dose for adults is 25 mg by mouth every day for 2 weeks; then 50 mg every day for 2 weeks; then 100 mg every day for 1 week; maximum, 200 mg/day.

ADMINISTRATION:
- Discontinue medicine at first sign of a rash.
- This medicine should be taken as directed and is well tolerated in the recommended doses. Individuals taking this medicine should carry an identification card to alert medical personnel who might be caring for them.
- The potential carcinogenic, mutagenic, and fertility effects are unknown.
- Category C drug and should be used in pregnancy if the potential benefit outweighs the risk. It is not known if excreted in breast milk so caution should be exercised when it is administered to a nursing women.
- Pediatric use under the age of 18 years has not been established. Individuals taking opioid containing medicines, such as cough and cold preparations, antidiarrheal preparations, and opioid analgesics with lamotrigine may not benefit from these medicines.
- Concomitant use is unknown, but it is not recommended to take potentially hepatotoxic medicines.
- Does not interfere with drug testing using urine samples.

SIDE EFFECTS: Common reactions include dizziness, headache, diplopia, ataxia, asthenia, nausea, blurred vision, somnolence, rhinitis, rash, pharyngitis, vomiting, cough, flu syndrome, dysmenorrheal, uncoordination, insomnia, diarrhea, fever, abdominal pain, depression, tremor, anxiety, vaginitis, speech disturbance, seizures, weight loss, photosensitivity, nystagmus, constipation, and dry mouth.

DRUG INTERACTIONS:
Avoid using the following drugs with this medicine:

- Oral progesterone contraceptives (may decrease hormonal contraceptive levels)
- Etonogestrel subdermal implant (may decrease hormonal contraceptive levels)
- Ginkgo biloba, Eun-haeng, fossil tree, ginkyo, icho, ityo, Japanese silver apricot, kew tree, maidenhair tree, salisburia, silver apricot, ginkgo (may decrease anticonvulsant efficacy)
- Medroxyprogesterone acetate (may decrease hormonal contraceptive levels)
- St. John's wort (may decrease lamotrigine levels as clearance is increased)

PHARMACOKINETICS: Metabolized by the liver (CYP450). Excreted in the urine (94%) and feces (2%). **Half-life:** 25 hr

PRECAUTIONS: Caution should be exercised when administering this medicine to patients with suicide risk, pregnancy, hepatic impairment, renal impairment, and hypersensitivity to antiepileptic drugs.

PATIENT AND FAMILY EDUCATION:
- Do not stop taking this drug suddenly; it must be tapered by your health care provider.
- Notify your health care provider immediately if depression symptoms increase.

SPECIAL POPULATIONS:
- *Elderly:* Caution should be exercised when administering this drug to the elderly.
- *Renal impairment:* For moderate to severe impairment, decrease dose by 25%. If there is severe impairment, decrease dose by 50%.
- *Pregnancy:* Category C drug. Animal studies show adverse fetal effect(s) but no controlled human studies.
- *Lactation:* It is considered unsafe for breastfeeding mothers. Medication administration requires cessation of breastfeeding.
- *Children:* Serious rashes requiring hospitalizations and discontinuance of treatment include the Stevens-Johnson syndrome and rare cases of toxic epidermal necrolysis and rash-related deaths. Incidence is 0.8% in children 2–6 years of age and 0.3% in adults. Most life-threatening rashes occur in the first 2–8 weeks of treatment.

BORDERLINE PERSONALITY DISORDER: Mood Stabilizing Anticonvulsants

Obsessive–Compulsive Personality Disorder

OVERVIEW

- Characterized by pervasive pattern of preoccupation with perfectionism, mental and interpersonal control, and orderliness at the expense of flexibility, openness, and efficiency.
- Occurs in 1% to 2% of the general population.
- Affects twice as many men as women.
- 3% to 10% of patients in mental health settings have the disorder.
- Increased in oldest children and people in professions involving facts, figures, or focus on details.
- Clients often seek treatment because they feel their life is "pleasureless."
- Demeanor is formal and serious.
- Perfectionism typically dates to childhood.

- Emotional range is usually constricted and rigid.
- Have problems with judgment and decision making, as they are obsessed with "getting it right."
- Insight is limited.
- Prefer written rules for every task.
- Often have very low self-esteem and are always harsh, critical and judgmental of themselves.
- Burdened by high and unattainable standards.
- Have much difficulty in relationships, few friends, and little social life.
- People with obsessive–compulsive personality disorder may be at risk for myocardial infarction because of their common type A lifestyles. They may also be at risk for anxiety disorders.

CLASS	DRUG
Tricyclic Antidepressants (TCAs)	**First-Line Drug Therapy**
	clomipramine (*Anafranil*)
	amitriptyline (*Elavil*)
Selective Serotonin Reuptake Inhibitors (SSRIs)	
	sertraline (*Zoloft*)
	paroxetine hydrochloride (*Paxil, Paxil CR*)
	fluoxetine (*Prozac, Prozac Weekly, Sarafem*)
	escitalopram (*Lexapro*)

OCD

Class: Tricyclic Antidepressants (TCAs)

clomipramine   *Anafranil*

AVAILABLE FORMS: Tablet, 25, 50, and 75 mg

DOSAGE: 75 to 300 mg. Generally 150 to 250 mg is the most effective dosage for OCD. 75 to 100 mg dose is usually only used on women weighing in the 100 pound range. Starting dose 25 to 50 mg, which can then be increased by 25 to 50 mg every 1 to 3 days. It takes 6 to 10 wk for the full effect to be realized. A dose close to 250 mg taken over 10 wk, on average, produces the best results.

ADMINISTRATION: Take with or without food. Do not abruptly discontinue medication.

SIDE EFFECTS: Drowsiness, dry mouth, nausea, vomiting, diarrhea, constipation, nervousness, decreased sexual ability, decreased memory or concentration, headache, stuffy nose, change in appetite or weight. *The following side effects should be immediately reported to the clinician:* Uncontrollable shaking of a part of the body, seizures, fast, irregular, or pounding heartbeat, difficulty urinating or loss of bladder control, believing things that are not true, hallucinations (seeing things or hearing voices that do not exist), eye pain, shakiness, difficulty breathing or fast breathing, severe muscle stiffness, unusual tiredness or weakness, sore throat, fever, and other signs of infection.

DRUG INTERACTIONS:

- Drug interactions with other medications, such as anticholinergic medications, arrhythmia medications, or thyroid medications, can cause the body to metabolize the medications differently than intended. Some of these drug interactions can increase the amounts of certain medications in the blood, increasing the risk of side effects or increasing the risk of a QT prolongation.

(cont.)

clomipramine (*cont.*)

- Specific medications that may interact with *Anafranil* include cimetidine (*Tagamet*); guanethidine (*Ismelin*); methylphenidate (Concerta, Ritalin, Daytrana); phenytoin (*Dilantin*); warfarin (*Coumadin*); heart or blood pressure medication such as clonidine (*Catapres*) or digoxin (*Lanoxin*); heart rhythm medications such as flecainide (*Tambocor*), quinidine (*Cardioquin, Quinidex, Quinaglute*); or antipsychotic medications such as chlorpromazine (*Thorazine*), haloperidol (*Haldol*), thioridazine (*Mellaril*), clozapine (*Clozaril*), olanzapine (*Zyprexa, Zydis*), quetiapine (*Seroquel*), risperidone (*Risperdal*), or ziprasidone (*Geodon*).
▶ **Alert:** The list of potential drug interactions is not comprehensive; there may be other medications that interact with *Anafranil*.

PHARMACOKINETICS: Presumed to influence obsessive and compulsive behaviors through its effects on serotonergic neuronal transmission. The actual neurochemical mechanism is unknown, but its capacity to inhibit the reuptake of serotonin (5-HT) is thought to be important.

PRECAUTIONS:
- Contraindicated with recent MI.
- Do not use if MAOI used within past 14 days.
- Do not use if patient is allergic to similar drugs (TCAs).
- Monitor for suicidal thoughts.
- Report new or worsening symptoms of mood or behavior changes, anxiety, panic attacks, insomnia, or feelings of impulsivity, irritability, agitation, hostility aggressiveness, restlessness, hyperactivity, increased depression or suicidal thoughts.

PATIENT AND FAMILY EDUCATION:
- That anxiety symptoms may temporarily worsen when you first start taking clomipramine. If any of these effects persist or worsen, to notify prescriber or pharmacist promptly.

- To relieve dry mouth, suck on (sugarless) hard candy or ice chips, chew (sugarless) gum, drink water or use a saliva substitute.
- To prevent constipation, maintain a diet adequate in fiber, drink plenty of water, and exercise. If you become constipated while using this drug, consult your pharmacist for help in selecting a laxative (e.g., stimulant-type with stool softener).
- Notify your clinician immediately if any of these unlikely but serious side effects occur: mental/mood changes (e.g., confusion, depression, hallucinations, memory problems), enlarged/painful breasts, unwanted breast milk production, irregular/painful menstrual periods, muscle stiffness/twitching, feelings of restlessness, ringing in the ears, sexual problems (e.g., decreased sexual ability, changes in desire), shakiness (tremors), numbness/tingling of the hands/feet, trouble urinating, severe vomiting.
- Notify your clinician immediately if any of these rare but very serious side effects occur: easy bruising/bleeding, signs of infection (e.g., fever, persistent sore throat), unusual/uncontrolled movements (especially of the tongue/face/lips), severe stomach/abdominal pain, dark urine, yellowing of eyes/skin.
- Seek immediate medical attention if any of these rare but very serious side effects occur: black stools, chest pain, fainting, high fever, slow/fast/irregular heartbeat, seizures, vomit that looks like coffee grounds.

SPECIAL POPULATIONS:
- *Elderly:* Lower doses are recommended.
- *Pregnancy:* Category C drug and animal studies have shown adverse fetal effects.
- *Lactation:* Presumed to carry risks.
- *Children and adolescents 12 to 17 years:* There is an increased risk of suicidality in children, adolescents, and young adults. Gradual increase in dose is recommended.

Elavil   **amitriptyline**

AVAILABLE FORMS: Tablet, 10, 25, 50, 75, 100, and 150 mg

DOSAGE: Starting dose 25–50 mg/day; maintenance dose, 100–300 mg/day

ADMINISTRATION: Orally at bedtime or in divided doses

SIDE EFFECTS:
- Cardiotoxicity (particularly in overdose), cardiac arrhythmias, and QT interval prolongation
- Anticholinergic effects
- Orthostatic hypotension
- Hypomania
- Sedation and drowsiness

- Increased potential for seizures
- Extrapyramidal effects

DRUG INTERACTIONS
- *MAOIs:* Risk for extreme hypertension
- *CNS depressants* (e.g., alcohol): TCAs increase effects
- *Direct-acting adrenergic agonists* (e.g., epinephrine): TCAs increase effects
- *Anticholinergic drugs* (e.g., antihistamines): TCAs increase effects. Do not use in combination.
- Antiarrhythmic agents
- *SSRIs and other medications:* serotonin syndrome

PHARMACOKINETICS:
- Nicotine use (smoking) increases drug metabolism and may diminish drug potency

(cont.)

amitriptyline (cont.)

- Metabolized by CYP450 2D6 and 1A2, converted to the active metabolite nortriptyline.
- Blood levels may be checked to ensure that levels are not excessive.

Half-life: Approx. 15 hr

PRECAUTIONS:

- Adverse effects and side effects are commonly observed before therapeutic effects
- Many side effects are dose-dependent and may improve over time
- Overdose may result in lethal cardiotoxicity or seizure
- Use with caution in patients with a history of seizure or heart disease
- Avoid in patients with a history of cardiac arrhythmia.
- Monitor with EKG

PATIENT AND FAMILY EDUCATION:

- Should be taken about the same time every day, typically in the evening, and can be taken with or without food. May cause prolonged sedation. Do not drive until you know the effect of this medication.
- Administration time may be adjusted based on observed sedating or activating drug effects
- May take up to 4–8 weeks to show its maximum effect, but patient may see symptoms of depression improving in as little as 2 weeks.
- If patient plans on becoming pregnant, discuss the benefits versus the risks of using this medicine while pregnant.
- Because this medicine is excreted in the breast milk, nursing mothers should not breastfeed while taking this medicine. Newborns may develop symptoms including feeding or breathing difficulties, seizures, muscle stiffness, jitteriness, or constant crying.
- Do not stop taking this medication unless the health care provider directs. Report symptoms to the health care provider promptly.
- Drug should be tapered gradually when discontinued
- Dosage should be adjusted to reach remission of symptoms and treatment should continue for at least 4–9 months following remission of symptoms
- Keep these medications out of the reach of children and pets.

SPECIAL POPULATIONS:

- *Elderly:* Older individuals tend to be more sensitive to medication side effects such as hypotension and anticholinergic effects. They often require adjustment of doses for hepatic or renal dysfunction. TCAs have been shown in at least one controlled clinical trial to be more effective than SSRIs in hospitalized geriatric patients, and in patients with melancholia and unipolar depression. However, cardiac side effects and fall risk are of great concern in this population. Side effects may be more pronounced and require decreased dosage
- *Pregnancy:* Psychotherapy is the initial choice for most pregnant patients with MDD. Category C. Not recommended in most cases.
- *Children:* Not recommended for children under the age of 12.

Class: Selective Serotonin Reuptake Inhibitors (SSRIs)

sertraline   *Zoloft*

AVAILABLE FORMS: Tablet, 25, 50, and 100 mg; oral concentrate, 20 mg/mL; sertraline should be stored at room temperature between 15° and 30°C (59° to 86°F).

DOSAGE: 25 to 200 mg once daily; treatment of depression, OCD, panic disorder, PTSD, and social anxiety disorder is initiated at 25 to 50 mg once daily. The recommended dose for PMDD is 50 to 150 mg every day of the menstrual cycle or for 14 days before menstruation.

ADMINISTRATION: Usually once daily with or without food; take dosage at the same time each day, either in the morning or evening; dosage is based on response to therapy; continue taking this medication as prescribed even if patient feels well. Do not stop taking medication without consulting provider. It may take up to 4 wk before the full benefit of this drug takes effect.

SIDE EFFECTS: Sleepiness, nervousness, insomnia, dizziness, nausea, tremor, skin rash, upset stomach, loss of appetite, headache, diarrhea, abnormal ejaculation, dry mouth and weight loss, irregular heartbeats, allergic reactions and activation of mania in patients with bipolar disorder.

DRUG INTERACTIONS:

- Hyperthermia, fluctuations in blood pressure and rigidity of muscles may occur when SSRIs are used in combination with MAOI.
- SSRIs should not be used in combination with MAOIs.
- SSRIs and MAOIs should not be used within 14 days of each other.
- Cimetidine (*Tagamet*) may increase the levels in blood of sertraline by decreased excretion of the drug by the liver.
- Increases the blood level of pimozide (*Orap*) by 40%.
- Avoid use with pimozide for it may cause cardiac arrhythmias.
- Drug may increase the blood thinning action of warfarin (*Coumadin*).

(cont.)

sertraline (cont.)

- Monitor warfarin when sertraline is started or stopped.

PHARMACOKINETICS:
- Mean peak plasma concentrations of sertraline occur between 4.5 and 8.4 hr post-dosing.
- The average terminal elimination half-life of plasma sertraline is about 26 hr.
- Based on this pharmacokinetic parameter, steady state sertraline plasma levels should be achieved after approximately 1 wk of once-daily dosing.
- The single dose bioavailability of sertraline tablets is approximately equal to an equivalent dose of solution.
- For the tablet, drug effects were enhanced when administered with food, while the time to reach peak plasma concentration decreased from 8 hr post-dosing to 5.5 hr.

PRECAUTIONS:
- Antidepressants increased the risk of suicidal thinking and behavior (suicidality) in short-term studies in children and adolescents with depression and other psychiatric disorders.
- The use of sertraline or any other antidepressant in a child or adolescent must balance risk with the clinical need for the antidepressant.
- Patients who are started on therapy should be closely observed for clinical worsening, suicidal thoughts, or unusual changes in behavior
- Do not discontinue drug abruptly; some patients experience symptoms such as abdominal cramps, flu-like symptoms, fatigue, and memory impairment; gradually reduce the dose when therapy is discontinued.

PATIENT AND FAMILY EDUCATION:
- Be alert to the emergence of anxiety, agitation, panic attacks, insomnia, irritability, hostility, aggressiveness, impulsivity, akathisia (psychomotor restlessness), hypomania, mania, other unusual changes in behavior, worsening of depression, and suicidal ideation, especially early in antidepressant treatment and when the dose is adjusted up or down.

- Caution about risk of serotonin syndrome with the concomitant use of SNRIs and SSRIs, including *Zoloft*, and triptans, tramadol, or other serotonergic agents.
- Until they learn how they respond to the drug they should be careful doing activities when they need to be alert, such as driving a car or operating machinery.
- Caution about concomitant use of *Zoloft* and NSAIDs, aspirin, warfarin, or other drugs that affect coagulation since these agents have been associated with an increased risk of bleeding.
- Concomitant use of *Zoloft* and alcohol is not advised.
- Ensure that the use of any OTC product is initiated cautiously. Check with health care provider before using any OTC medicine.
- Notify health care provider if become pregnant or intend to become pregnant during therapy.
- Patients should be advised to notify their physician if they are breastfeeding an infant.

SPECIAL POPULATIONS:
- *Elderly:* Caution is advised when using this drug in the elderly due to more sensitivity to the drug.
- The elderly are more susceptible to electrolyte imbalance especially if they are also taking "water pills" or diuretics with this medication.
- *Pregnancy:* Avoid using this drug during the third trimester for it leads to adverse effects in the newborn. This medication should only be used when clearly needed during pregnancy.
- *Lactation:* Secreted into breast milk.
- *Children:* Caution when using this drug in a child or adolescent; must balance the potential risks with the clinical need.

▶**Alert:** Antidepressants increased the risk of suicidal thinking and behavior (suicidality) in short-term studies in children and adolescents with depression and other psychiatric disorders. Caution is advised when using this drug in children because they may be more sensitive to the side effects of the drug, especially loss of appetite and weight loss. It is important to monitor weight and growth in children who are taking this drug.

Paxil, Paxil CR   **paroxetine**

AVAILABLE FORMS: Suspension, 10 mg/5 mL; tablet, 10, 20, 30, and 40 mg; tablet (controlled-release), 12.5, 25, and 37.5 mg

DOSAGE:
Depression:
- *Adults:* Initially 20 mg PO daily, preferably in morning, as indicated. If patient does not improve, increase dose by 10 mg daily at intervals of at least 1 wk to a maximum of 50 mg daily. If using controlled-release form, initially 25 mg PO daily. Increase dose by 12.5 mg daily at weekly intervals to a maximum of 62.5 mg daily.

- *Elderly patients:* Initially 10 mg PO daily, preferably in morning, as indicated. If patient does not improve, increase dose by 10 mg daily at weekly intervals to a maximum of 40 mg daily. If using controlled-release form, start therapy at 12.5 mg PO daily. Do not exceed 50 mg daily.
OCD:
- *Adults:* Initially 20 mg PO daily, preferably in morning. Increase dose by 10 mg daily at weekly intervals. Recommended daily dose is 40 mg; maximum daily dose is 60 mg.

(cont.)

paroxetine (cont.)

Panic Disorder:
- *Adults:* Initially, 10 mg PO daily. Increase dose by 10 mg at no less than weekly intervals to maximum of 60 mg daily. Or, 12.5 mg Paxil CR PO as a single daily dose, usually in the morning, with or without food; increase dose at intervals of at least 1 wk by 12.5 mg daily, up to a maximum of 75 mg daily.
- *Adjust-a-dose:* In elderly or debilitated patients and in those with severe renal or hepatic impairment, the first dose of Paxil CR is 12.5 mg daily; increase if indicated. Dosage should not exceed 50 mg daily.

Social Anxiety Disorder:
- *Adults:* Initially, 20 mg PO daily, preferably in morning. Dosage range is 20 to 60 mg daily. Adjust dosage to maintain patient on lowest effective dose. Or, 12.5 mg Paxil CR PO as a single daily dose, usually in the morning, with or without food. Increase dosage at weekly intervals in increments of 12.5 mg daily, up to a maximum of 37.5 mg daily.

Generalized Anxiety Disorder:
- *Adults:* 20 mg PO daily initially, increasing by 10 mg per day weekly up to 50 mg daily.
- *Adjust-a-dose*: For debilitated patients or those with renal or hepatic impairment taking immediate-release form, initially, 10 mg PO daily, preferably in morning. If patient does not respond after full antidepressant effect has occurred, increase dose by 10 mg per day at weekly intervals to a maximum of 40 mg daily. If using controlled-release form, start therapy at 12.5 mg daily. Do not exceed 50 mg daily

ADMINISTRATION: May take with or without food. Do not split or crush controlled-release tablets.

SIDE EFFECTS: Asthenia, dizziness, headache, insomnia, somnolence, tremor, nervousness, suicidal behavior, anxiety, paresthesia. confusion, agitation, palpitations, vasodilation, orthostatic, hypotension, lump or tightness in throat, dry mouth, nausea, constipation, diarrhea, flatulence, vomiting, dyspepsia, dysgeusia, increased or decreased appetite, abdominal pain, ejaculatory disturbances, sexual dysfunction, urinary frequency, other urinary disorders, myopathy, myalgia, myasthenia, diaphoresis, rash, pruritus

DRUG INTERACTIONS:
- *Amphetamines, buspirone, dextromethorphan, dihydroergotamine, lithium salts, meperidine, other SSRIs or SSNRIs (duloxetine, venlafaxine), tramadol, trazodone, TCAs, tryptophan:* May increase risk of serotonin syndrome. Avoid combining drugs that increase the availability of serotonin in the CNS; monitor patient closely if used together.
- *Cimetidine:* May decrease hepatic metabolism of paroxetine, leading to risk of adverse reactions. Dosage adjustments may be needed.

- *Digoxin:* May decrease digoxin level. Use together cautiously.
- *MAOIs, such as phenelzine, selegiline, tranylcypromine:* May cause serotonin syndrome. Avoid using within 14 days of MAOI therapy.
- *Phenobarbital, phenytoin:* May alter pharmacokinetics of both drugs. Dosage adjustments may be needed.
- *Procyclidine:* May increase procyclidine level. Watch for excessive anticholinergic effects.
- *Sumatriptan:* May cause weakness, hyperreflexia, and uncoordination. Monitor patient closely.
- *Theophylline:* May decrease theophylline clearance. Monitor theophylline level.
- *Thioridazine:* May prolong QTc interval and increase risk of serious ventricular arrhythmias, such as torsades de pointes, and sudden death. Avoid using together.
- *TCAs:* May inhibit TCA metabolism. Dose of TCA may need to be reduced. Monitor patient closely.
- *Triptans:* May cause serotonin syndrome (restlessness, hallucinations, loss of coordination, fast heartbeat, rapid changes in blood pressure, increased body temperature, overactive reflexes, nausea, vomiting, and diarrhea). Use cautiously, especially at the start of therapy and at dosage increases.
- *Warfarin:* May cause bleeding. Use together cautiously.
- *St. John's wort:* May increase sedative–hypnotic effects. Discourage use together.
- *Alcohol use:* May alter psychomotor function. Discourage use together.

PHARMACOKINETICS:
- Thought to be linked to drug's inhibition of CNS neuronal uptake of serotonin.

Half-life: About 24 hr

ROUTE	ONSET	PEAK	DURATION
PO	Unknown	2–8 hr	Unknown
PO (controlled-release)	Unknown	6–10 hr	Unknown

PRECAUTIONS:
- Contraindicated in patients hypersensitive to drug, within 14 days of MAOI therapy, and in those taking thioridazine.
- Contraindicated in children and adolescents younger than age 18 for MDD.
- Use cautiously in patients with history of seizure disorders or mania and in those with other severe, systemic illness.
- Use cautiously in patients at risk for volume depletion and monitor them appropriately.
- Using drug in the first trimester may increase the risk of congenital fetal malformations; using drug in the third trimester may cause neonatal

(cont.)

paroxetine (*cont.*)

complications at birth. Consider the risk versus benefit of therapy.

- Patients taking drug may be at increased risk for developing suicidal behavior, but this has not been definitively attributed to use of the drug.
- Patients taking *Paxil CR* for PMDD should be periodically reassessed to determine the need for continued treatment.
- If signs or symptoms of psychosis occur or increase, expect prescriber to reduce dosage. Record mood changes. Monitor patient for suicidal tendencies and allow only a minimum supply of drug.
- Monitor patient for complaints of sexual dysfunction. In men, they include anorgasmy, erectile difficulties, delayed ejaculation or orgasm, or impotence; in women, they include anorgasmia or difficulty with orgasm.

►**Alert:** Drug may increase the risk of suicidal thinking and behavior in children, adolescents, and young adults aged 18 to 24 during the first 2 months of treatment, especially in those with MDD or other psychiatric disorder.

►**Alert:** Do not stop drug abruptly. Withdrawal or discontinuation syndrome may occur if drug is stopped abruptly. Symptoms include headache, myalgia, lethargy, and general flu-like symptoms. Taper drug slowly over 1 to 2 wk.

►**Alert:** Combining triptans with an SSRI or an SSNRI may cause serotonin syndrome. Signs and symptoms may include restlessness, hallucinations, loss of coordination, fast heartbeat, rapid changes in blood pressure, increased body temperature, overactive reflexes, nausea, vomiting, and diarrhea. Serotonin syndrome may be more likely to occur when starting or increasing the dose of triptan, SSRI, or SSNRI.

PATIENT AND FAMILY EDUCATION:
- That drug may be taken with or without food, usually in morning.
- Do not break, crush, or chew controlled-release tablets.
- Avoid activities that require alertness and good coordination until effects of drug are known.
- If woman of childbearing age, contact prescriber if becomes pregnant or plans to become pregnant during therapy or if currently breastfeeding.
- Avoid alcohol and consult prescriber before taking other prescription or OTC drugs or herbal medicines.
- Do not stop taking drug abruptly.

SPECIAL POPULATIONS:
- *Elderly:* Caution is advised when using this drug in the elderly due to more sensitivity to the drug.
- *Pregnancy:* Avoid using this drug during the third trimester for it leads to adverse effects in the newborn. This medication should only be used when clearly needed during pregnancy.
- *Lactation:* Secreted into breast milk.
- *Children:* Caution is advised when using this drug in a child or adolescent; must balance the potential risks with the clinical need. Not recommended for use under age 18 years for MDD.

►**Alert:** Antidepressants increased the risk of suicidal thinking and behavior (suicidality) in short-term studies in children and adolescents with depression and other psychiatric disorders. Caution is advised when using this drug in children because they may be more sensitive to the side effects of the drug, especially loss of appetite and weight loss. It is important to monitor weight and growth in children who are taking this drug.

Prozac, Prozac Weekly, Sarafem   **fluoxetine**

AVAILABLE FORMS: Capsule (delayed-release), 90 mg; capsule (pulvules), 10, 20, and 40 mg; oral solution, 20 mg/5 mL; tablet, 10 and 20 mg

DOSAGE:
Depression, OCD:
- *Adults:* Initially 20 mg PO in the morning; increase dosage based on patient response. Maximum daily dose is 80 mg.

OCD:
- *Children 7 to 17 yr:* 10 mg PO daily. After 2 wk, increase to 20 mg daily. Dosage is 20 to 60 mg daily.

Depression:
- *Children 8 to 18 yr:* 10 mg PO once daily for 1 wk; then increase to 20 mg daily.
- *Elderly:* Initially, 20 mg PO daily in the morning. Increase dose based on response. Doses may be given bid, morning and noon. Maximum daily dose is 80 mg. Consider using a lower dosage or

less-frequent dose in these patients, especially those with systemic illness and those who are receiving drugs for other illnesses.

Maintenance Therapy for Depression in Stabilized Patients (Not for Newly Diagnosed Depression):
- *Adults:* 90 mg *Prozac Weekly* PO once weekly. Start once-weekly doses 7 days after the last daily dose of *Prozac* 20 mg.

Short-Term Treatment of Panic Disorder With or Without Agoraphobia:
- *Adults:* 10 mg PO once daily for 1 wk; then increase dose as needed to 20 mg daily. Maximum daily dose is 60 mg.
- *Adjust-a-dose:* For patients with renal or hepatic impairment, reduce dose or increase interval.

Anorexia Nervosa in Weight-Restored Patients:
- *Adults:* 40 mg PO daily.

Depression Caused by Bipolar Disorder:
- *Adults:* 20 to 60 mg PO daily.

(cont.)

fluoxetine (*cont.*)

Cataplexy:
- *Adults:* 20 mg PO once or twice daily with CNS stimulant therapy.

Alcohol Dependence:
- *Adults:* 60 mg PO daily.

Premenstrual Dysphoric Disorder:
- *Adults:* 20 mg *Sarafem* PO daily continuously (every day of the menstrual cycle) or intermittently (daily dose starting 14 days before the anticipated onset of menstruation through the first full day of menses and repeating with each new cycle). Maximum daily dose is 80 mg PO.
- *Adjust-a-dose:* For patients with renal or hepatic impairment and those taking several drugs at the same time, reduce dose or increase dosing interval.

ADMINISTRATION:
- Give drug with or without food.
- Avoid giving drug in the afternoon, whenever possible, because doing so commonly causes nervousness and insomnia.
- Delayed-release capsules must be swallowed whole; do not crush or open.

SIDE EFFECTS: Nervousness, somnolence, insomnia, headache, drowsiness, tremor, dizziness, asthenia, fatigue, fever, palpitations, hot flashes, nasal congestion, pharyngitis, sinusitis, nausea, diarrhea, dry mouth, dyspepsia, constipation, abdominal pain, vomiting, flatulence, increased appetite, sexual dysfunction, weight loss, anorexia, suicidal behavior, anxiety muscle pain, upper respiratory tract, infection, cough, respiratory distress, rash, pruritus, diaphoresis; flu-like syndrome.

DRUG INTERACTIONS:
- *Amphetamines, buspirone, dextromethorphan, dihydroergotamine, lithium salts, meperidine, other SSRIs or SSNRIs (duloxetine, venlafaxine), tramadol, trazodone, TCAs, tryptophan:* May increase risk of serotonin syndrome. Avoid combinations of drugs that increase the availability of serotonin in the CNS; monitor patient closely if used together.
- *Benzodiazepines, lithium, TCAs:* May increase CNS effects. Monitor patient closely.
- *Beta-blockers, carbamazepine, flecainide, vinblastine:* May increase levels of these drugs. Monitor drug levels and monitor patient for adverse reactions.
- *Cyproheptadine:* May reverse or decrease fluoxetine effect. Monitor patient closely.
- *Dextromethorphan:* May cause unusual side effects such as visual hallucinations. Advise use of cough suppressant that does not contain dextromethorphan while taking fluoxetine.
- *Highly protein-bound drugs:* May increase level of fluoxetine or other highly protein-bound drugs. Monitor patient closely.
- *Insulin, oral antidiabetics:* May alter glucose level and antidiabetic requirements. Adjust dosage.

- *MAOIs (phenelzine, selegiline, tranylcypromine):* May cause serotonin syndrome. Avoid using at the same time and for at least 5 wk after stopping.
- *Phenytoin:* May increase phenytoin level and risk of toxicity. Monitor phenytoin level and adjust dosage.
- *Triptans:* May cause weakness, hyperreflexia, uncoordination, rapid changes in blood pressure, nausea, and diarrhea. Monitor patient closely, especially at the start of treatment and when dosage increases.
- *Thioridazine:* May increase thioridazine level, increasing risk of serious ventricular arrhythmias and sudden death. Avoid using at the same time and for at least 5 wk after stopping.
- *Warfarin:* May increase risk for bleeding. Monitor PT and INR.
- *St. John's wort:* May increase sedative and hypnotic effects; may cause serotonin syndrome. Discourage use together.
- *Alcohol use:* May increase CNS depression. Discourage use together.

PHARMACOKINETICS: Thought to be linked to drug's inhibition of CNS neuronal uptake of serotonin.
Half-life: Fluoxetine, 2 to 3 days; norfluoxetine, 7 to 9 days.

ROUTE	ONSET	PEAK	DURATION
PO	Unknown	6–8 hr	Unknown

PRECAUTIONS:
- Contraindicated in patients hypersensitive to drug and in those taking MAOIs within 14 days of starting therapy. MAOIs shouldn't be started within 5 wk of stopping fluoxetine. Avoid using thioridazine with fluoxetine or within 5 wk after stopping fluoxetine.
- Use cautiously in patients at high risk for suicide and in those with history of diabetes mellitus, seizures, mania, or hepatic, renal, or CV disease.
- Use in third trimester of pregnancy may be associated with neonatal complications at birth. Consider the risk versus benefit of treatment during this time.
- Use antihistamines or topical corticosteroids to treat rashes or pruritus.
- Watch for weight change during therapy, particularly in underweight or bulimic patients.
- Record mood changes. Watch for suicidal tendencies.
- Drug has a long half-life; monitor patient for adverse effects for up to 2 wk after drug is stopped.
- ▶**Alert:** Drug may increase the risk of suicidal thinking and behavior in children and adolescents with MDD or other psychiatric disorder.
- ▶**Alert:** Drug may increase the risk of suicidal thinking and behavior in young adults ages 18 to 24 during the first 2 months of treatment.

(cont.)

fluoxetine (*cont.*)

▶**Alert:** Combining triptans with an SSRI or an SSNRI may cause serotonin syndrome. Signs and symptoms may include restlessness, hallucinations, loss of coordination, fast heartbeat, rapid changes in blood pressure, increased body temperature, overactive reflexes, nausea, vomiting, and diarrhea. Serotonin syndrome may be more likely to occur when starting or increasing the dose of triptan, SSRI, or SSNRI.

PATIENT AND FAMILY EDUCATION:

- Avoid taking drug in the afternoon whenever possible because doing so commonly causes nervousness and insomnia.
- Drug may cause dizziness or drowsiness. Avoid driving and other hazardous activities that require alertness and good psychomotor coordination until effects of drug are known.
- Consult prescriber before taking other prescription or OTC drugs.
- Full therapeutic effect may not be seen for 4 wk or longer.

SPECIAL POPULATIONS:

- *Elderly:* Caution is advised when using this drug in the elderly due to more sensitivity to the drug.
- *Pregnancy:* Avoid using this drug during the third trimester for it leads to adverse effects in the newborn. This medication should only be used when clearly needed during pregnancy.
- *Lactation:* Secreted into breast milk.
- *Children:* Caution when using this drug in a child or adolescent; must balance the potential risks with the clinical need. Not recommended for use under age 18 years for MDD.

▶**Alert:** Antidepressants increased the risk of suicidal thinking and behavior (suicidality) in short-term studies in children and adolescents with depression and other psychiatric disorders. Caution is advised when using this drug in children because they may be more sensitive to the side effects of the drug, especially loss of appetite and weight loss. It is important to monitor weight and growth in children who are taking this drug.

Lexapro　　　escitalopram

AVAILABLE FORMS: Tablet, 10 and 20 mg; oral solution, 1 mg/mL

DOSAGE: 10 to 20 mg every day

ADMINISTRATION:

- PO with a glass of water.
- Take with or without food.
- Take at regular intervals, preferably in the morning
- Caution clients not to stop taking drug except on provider's advice
- Instruct client to take missed dose ASAP. If it is almost time for the next dose, advise to take only that dose.

SIDE EFFECTS: Somnolence, nervousness, insomnia, headache, drowsiness, tremor, dizziness, asthenia, fatigue, fever, palpitations, hot flashes, dry mouth, nasal congestion, pharyngitis, sinusitis; nausea, diarrhea, dry mouth, dyspepsia, constipation, abdominal pain, vomiting, flatulence, increased appetite, sexual dysfunction, weight loss, anorexia, suicidal behavior and suicide risk, anxiety, muscle pain, upper respiratory tract, infection, cough, respiratory distress, rash, pruritus, diaphoresis; flu-like syndrome.

DRUG INTERACTIONS:

- This medicine may interact with the following medications: Cyproheptadine, flecainide, carbamazepine, vinblastine, insulin, oral diabetic agents, lithium, TCAs, phenytoin, tryptophan, warfarin (and other highly protein-bound drugs).
- Concomitant use with SSRIs, SNRIs, or tryptophan is not recommended.

- Use caution with concomitant use with drugs that affect hemostasis (NSAIDs, aspirin, warfarin).
- Determine use of tobacco, alcohol, or illegal drugs.

▶**Alert:** This list may not describe all possible interactions. Instruct clients to provide a list of all the medicines, herbs, nonprescription drugs, or dietary supplements they use.

PHARMACOKINETICS: SSRIs are metabolized in the liver by cytochrome P-450 MFO microsomal enzymes. They are highly bound to plasma proteins and have a large volume of distribution. Peak plasma levels are reached in 2 to 10 hr. Escitalopram's half-life is 27 to 32 hr. Steady state plasma levels are achieved in 1 wk with escitalopram. Hence, addition of serotonergic medications to a patient's regimen must not occur until 2 to 3 wk after discontinuation of an SSRI

PRECAUTIONS:

- *Clinical worsening/suicide risk:* Monitor for clinical worsening, suicidality and unusual change in behavior, especially, during the initial few months of therapy or at times of dose changes.
- Serotonin syndrome or NMS-like reactions: Manage with immediate discontinuation and continuing monitoring.
- *Discontinuation of treatment with Lexapro:* A gradual reduction in dose rather than abrupt cessation is recommended whenever possible.
- *Seizures:* Prescribe with care in patients with history of seizure.
- *Activation of mania/hypomania:* Use cautiously in patients with a history of mania.

(cont.)

escitalopram (*cont.*)

- *Hyponatremia:* Can occur in association with SIADH.
- *Abnormal bleeding:* Use caution in concomitant use with NSAIDs, aspirin, warfarin, or other drugs that affect coagulation.
- *Interference with cognitive and motor performance:* Use caution when operating machinery.
- *Use in patients with concomitant illness:* Use caution in patients with diseases or conditions that produce altered metabolism or hemodynamic response.
- See client as often as necessary to ensure the drug is working on the panic attacks, determine compliance and review side effects.
- Make sure clients realize that they need to take prescribed dose even if they do not feel better right away. It can take several weeks before clients feel the full effect.
- Instruct client and family to watch for worsening depression or thoughts of suicide. Also watch out for sudden or severe changes in feelings such as feeling anxious, agitated, panicky, irritable, hostile, aggressive, impulsive, severely restless, overly excited and hyperactive, or not being able to sleep. If this happens, especially at the beginning of antidepressant treatment or after a change in dose, they should call the provider
- Clients may become drowsy or dizzy and should not drive, use machinery, or do anything that needs mental alertness until the effects of this medicine are known.
- Caution patients not to stand or sit up quickly, especially if older. This reduces the risk of dizzy or fainting spells. Alcohol may interfere with the effect of this medicine. Avoid alcoholic drinks.
- Caution patients not to treat themselves for coughs, colds or allergies without asking health care professional for advice. Some ingredients can increase possible side effects.
- *Dry mouth:* Chewing sugarless gum or sucking hard candy, and drinking plenty of water may help. Contact provider if the problem does not go away or is severe.

PRECAUTIONS: Use with caution on patients with bipolar disorder or a family history of bipolar disorder; diabetes; heart disease; liver disease; seizures (convulsions); suicidal thoughts, plans, or attempts by client or a family member; an unusual or allergic reaction to sertraline, other medicines, foods, dyes, or preservatives; patients receiving electroconvulsive therapy; are pregnant or trying to get pregnant, and are breastfeeding.

PATIENT AND FAMILY EDUCATION:
- Avoid taking drug in the afternoon whenever possible because doing so commonly causes nervousness and insomnia.
- Drug may cause dizziness or drowsiness. Warn patient to avoid driving and other hazardous activities that require alertness and good psychomotor coordination until effects of drug are known.
- Consult prescriber before taking other prescription or OTC drugs.
- Full therapeutic effect may not be seen for 4 wk or longer.

SPECIAL POPULATIONS:
- *Elderly:* Caution is advised when using this drug in the elderly due to more sensitivity to the drug.
- *Pregnancy:* Avoid using this drug during the third trimester for it leads to adverse effects in the newborn. This medication should only be used when clearly needed during pregnancy.
- *Lactation:* Secreted into breast milk.
- *Children:* Caution when using this drug in a child or adolescent; must balance the potential risks with the clinical need.

▶**Alert:** Antidepressants increased the risk of suicidal thinking and behavior (suicidality) in short-term studies in children and adolescents with depression and other psychiatric disorders. Caution is advised when using this drug in children because they may be more sensitive to the side effects of the drug, especially loss of appetite and weight loss. It is important to monitor weight and growth in children who are taking this drug.

Other Personality Disorders

Histrionic Personality Disorder

OVERVIEW
- Characterized by excessive emotionality and attention-seeking behaviors.
- Occurs in 2% to 3% of the general population and 10% to 15% of the clinical populations.
- More often seen in women than men.
- Patients usually seek treatment for depression, unexplained physical problems or difficulty in relationships.
- May display "la belle indifference," a seemingly indifferent detachment, while describing dramatic physical symptoms.
- Speech is colorful and theatrical, though descriptions are vague and lacking in detail.
- Overly concerned with appearance.
- Often exhibit flirtatious or even seductive behaviors in social as well as professional settings.
- Very expressive, gregarious, and effusive.

- Rapid shifts in moods and emotions.
- Self-absorbed with little regard for others.
- May fabricate unbelievable stories or create public scenes to attract attention.
- Temper tantrums or crying outbursts are common.
- Histrionic personality disorder is associated particularly with somatoform disorders.

Acute and Chronic Treatment
No body of treatment research exists for histrionic personality disorder. Two meta-analyses of psychotherapeutic treatments for personality disorders suggest that these conditions respond to both psychodynamic therapy and cognitive–behavioral therapy. None of the studies focused specifically on histrionic personality disorder.

PSYCHOPHARMACOLOGY
No medications are thought to be useful, so psychotherapy must be considered the cornerstone of treatment.

Narcissistic Personality Disorder

OVERVIEW
- Characterized by grandiosity (in fantasy or behavior), need for admiration, and lack of empathy.
- Occurs in 1% to 2% of the general population and 2% to 16% of the clinical population.
- 50% to 75% of patients are men.
- May display an arrogant or haughty attitude.
- Express envy of others' successes, believing it to rightfully be theirs.
- Often preoccupied with fantasies of unlimited success, power, brilliance, beauty, or ideal love to reinforce their sense of superiority.
- Often compare themselves favorably with famous or privileged people.
- Thought processing intact, but insight is limited or poor.
- View their problems to be the fault of others.
- Underlying self-esteem is fragile and vulnerable; patients are hypersensitive to criticism.
- Form and exploit relationships to elevate their own status.
- Work performance is poor, as they view themselves superior to others.
- Narcissistic personality disorder patients are at risk for anorexia nervosa and substance abuse as well as experiencing depression.

Acute and Chronic Treatment
Personality disorders are typically some of the most challenging mental disorders to treat, since they are, by definition, an integral part of what defines an individual and their self-perceptions. Treatment most often focuses on increasing coping skills and interpersonal relationship skills through psychotherapy. External Axis I disorders may be treated as warranted.

PSYCHOPHARMACOLOGY
Medications are not used to treat narcissistic personality disorders. Psychotherapy, cognitive therapy, and group therapies are considered the cornerstones of treatment.

Avoidant Personality Disorder

OVERVIEW
- Characterized by a pattern of social discomfort and reticence, low self-esteem, and hypersensitivity to negative evaluation.
- Occurs in 0.5% to 1% of the general population and 10% of the clinical population.
- Equally common in men and women.
- Report being overly inhibited as children.
- Intensely avoid unfamiliar situations and people.
- May appear sad and anxious, describing themselves as socially awkward, shy, fearful, and easily devastated by criticism.
- Unusually fearful of rejection, though they strongly desire social acceptance and human companionship.
- May perform well on the job as they are constantly seeking approval.
- Avoidant personality disorder is associated with anxiety disorders (especially social phobia).

Acute and Chronic Treatment
As with all personality disorders, psychotherapy is the treatment of choice for avoidant personality disorder.

PSYCHOPHARMACOLOGY
Medications should only be prescribed for specific and acute Axis I diagnoses or problems suffered by the individual. Antianxiety agents and antidepressants should be prescribed only when there is a clear Axis I diagnosis in conjunction with the personality disorder. Clinicians should resist the temptation to overprescribe to someone with this disorder, because they often present with complaints of anxiety in social situations or a feeling of disconnectedness with their feelings. The anxiety in this instance is clearly situationally related and medication may actually interfere with effective psychotherapeutic treatment.

Dependent Personality Disorder

OVERVIEW

- Characterized by an excessive need to be taken care of that leads to clinging, submissive behavior.
- Occurs in 15% of the population.
- Three times more prevalent in women.
- Runs in families and especially in youngest children.
- Often seek treatment for depression, anxiety, or somatic symptoms.
- Pessimistic and self-critical; feelings are easily hurt.
- Commonly report feeling unhappy or depressed.
- Preoccupied with unrealistic fears of being left alone.
- Extreme difficulty with decision making.
- Perceive themselves unable to function outside of a relationship with someone who will tell them what to do.
- Difficulty initiating tasks or daily routines.
- Hold onto relationships with desperation, even poor ones.
- Dependent personality disorder carries a risk for anxiety disorders and adjustment disorder.

Acute and Chronic Treatment

Clinicians should be aware that individuals with dependent personality disorder will often present with a number of physical or somatic complaints.

PSYCHOPHARMACOLOGY

- While appropriate medications need to be prescribed as necessary, the clinician should carefully monitor medication intake and maintenance to ensure the patient is not abusing it. Physical complaints should not be minimized or dismissed, as is often the case with someone who suffers from this disorder, but they must not also be encouraged. A simple, matter-of-fact approach works best in this case.
- Clinicians in general should be wary of the therapeutic relationship with a person suffering from dependent personality disorder. The needs of the individual can be great and overwhelming at times, and the patient will often try to test the limits of the frame set for therapy. Burnout among therapists treating this disorder is common, because of the client's demands for constant reassurance and attention, especially between therapy sessions. A clear explanation at the onset of therapy about how treatment is to be conducted, including a discussion of appropriate times and needs for contacting the clinician in between sessions, is vitally important. While rapport and a close therapeutic relationship must be established, the boundaries in therapy must also be constantly and clearly delineated.
- The most effective psychotherapeutic approach is one that focuses on solutions to specific life problems the patient is presently experiencing. Long-term therapy, while ideal for many personality disorders, is contraindicated in this instance since it reinforces a dependent relationship upon the therapist.

Depressive Personality Disorder

OVERVIEW

- Characterized by patterns of depressive cognitions and behaviors in various contexts.
- Occur equally in men and women.
- Generally respond well to treatment with antidepressant medications.
- Similar behavior characteristics as those seen with major depression (moodiness, brooding, pessimism, joylessness, etc.), but less severe and of shorter duration.
- Patients do not generally present with insomnia, loss of appetite, recurrent thoughts of death or disinterest in activities seen in major depression.
- Patients exhibit sad, gloomy, or dejected affect.
- Express chronic unhappiness, cheerlessness, and hopelessness regardless of situation.
- Do not display a sense of humor and have difficulty relaxing.
- Brood and worry over daily life and often repress anger.
- Negative thinking pervades even positive experiences.
- Judgment and decision making are overshadowed by pessimism.
- Self-esteem is low with strong feelings of worthlessness and inadequacy.
- Feel dependent on approval from others.
- Self-critical and critical of others.
- Tend to be followers rather than leaders.

Acute and Chronic Treatment

Cognitive restructuring techniques, such as thought stopping or positive self-talk can enhance self-esteem, which appears to be at the core of this personality disorder. Limited success with medication management, except with comorbid conditions, has been noted.

Treatment of Sleep Disorders

13

OVERVIEW

- Types of sleep disorders include primary insomnia, primary hypersomnia, narcolepsy, nightmare disorder, sleep terror disorder, sleep-walking disorder.

- Sleep disorders occur in 50% of adults. Predominant between ages 18 and 64. Prevalence is 1.5 times greater in females.
- Cost of treating sleep disorders is greater than 42 billion dollars annually.

Primary Insomnia

OVERVIEW

- 40% of patients with psychiatric disorders have a high comorbidity for insomnia.
- Trouble for one month falling asleep or maintaining sleep.
- Associated with physical factors and physiologic disorders excluding anxiety or depression.
- Patient complains of not feeling rested and may relate that this impacts day-to-day functioning.
- Physiologic changes associated with pregnancy may disrupt sleep; medications should be avoided.
- Medications should be used only for short-term management in older adults.
- Use of BZDs or sedative-hypnotics increases risk of confusion, delirium, and/or falls in older adults.
- Predominant between ages of 18 and 64.
- Accounts for 16% of all insomnia complaints.
- Risk factors associated with insomnia include acute stress, depression, anxiety, medications, obesity, and age.
- Differential diagnoses include substance abuse and thyroid dysfunction.

Acute Treatment

- Hypnotics are the first line of therapy for acute insomnia.
- New-generation hypnotics may be used without limit on the term of use.
- BZDs are rarely used for treatment of insomnia and, if used, should be used only for short-term insomnia as related to situational anxiety.

Chronic Treatment

- Hypnotics are first-line option for chronic insomnia.
- New-generation hypnotics may be used without limit on the term of use.
- BZDs are not indicated for treatment of chronic insomnia.

Psychopharmacology of Primary Insomnia

GENERAL CONSIDERATIONS

- *Non-BZDs:* Most commonly used medications for primary insomnia. Should this class of drug not be helpful, short-term use of BZDs may be considered if the patient does not have a history of drug dependence and tolerance.
- *BZD medications:* Short-term use only; associated with dependence/addiction.
- To promote sleep: Avoid diet high in protein and alcohol 3–6 hr before sleep; avoid caffeine or nicotine 12 hr before sleep; avoid use of OTC antihistamine to induce sleepiness.
- Exercise regularly 5–6 hr before bedtime; create a calm, cool quiet atmosphere for sleep. If unable to sleep for 30 min leave bedroom and engage in a quiet activity such as light reading.

CLASS	DRUG
Non-Benzodiazepine GABA Receptor Agonists	**First-Line Drug Therapy**
	eszopiclone *(Lunesta)*
	zaleplon *(Sonata)*
	ramelteon *(Rozerem)*
	zolpidem *(Ambien)*
Benzodiazepines (BZDs)	**Second-Line Drug Therapy**
	flurazepam *(Dalmane)*
	temazepam *(Restoril)*
	triazolam *(Halcion)*

Class: Non-Benzodiazepine GABA Receptor Agonists

eszopiclone *Lunesta*

INDICATIONS: Treatment of insomnia in the non-depressed patient.

AVAILABLE FORMS: Tablet, 1, 2, and 3 mg

DOSAGE: 2 mg PO immediately before patient is ready for sleep. May increase to 3 mg if clinically indicated in non-elderly patients.

ADMINISTRATION:
- PO with a glass of water.
- Drowsiness and/or dizziness will be exacerbated with concomitant alcohol consumption; alcohol should be avoided while taking this medication.
- Caution clients not to stop taking drug abruptly if used long-term.

SIDE EFFECTS:
- Hallucinations; behavior changes; SSRI-treated patients taking eszopiclone may experience impaired concentration, aggravated depression, and manic reaction
- *Side effects that usually do not require medical attention*: Unpleasant taste; nausea; daytime drowsiness; headache; vomiting; dizziness; infection; pain; pharyngitis

DRUG INTERACTIONS:
- This medicine may interact with the following medications: antifungals; rifampin; ritonavir; SSRIs; CNS depressants (including alcohol)

PHARMACOKINETICS:
- Non-BZDs hypnotic. Mechanism of action is thought to occur at the level of the GABA receptor complex.
- Weakly bound to plasma proteins.
- Peak plasma levels are reached in 1 hr.
- Bioavailability is 80%.

Half-life: Average is 6 hr.

PRECAUTIONS:
- See patient as often as necessary if long-term use is indicated.
- Ensure that patient is aware he/she is not to exceed maximum dosage and is not taking other CNS depressant medications.
- Instruct patient to monitor for behavior changes.
- If patient is drowsy or dizzy, patient should not drive, use machinery, or attempt to accomplish any task that requires mental alertness.
- Avoid alcohol as concomitant use may exacerbate symptoms.

PATIENT AND FAMILY EDUCATION: Store at room temperature between 15°C and 30°C (59°F–86°F). Throw away any unused medication after the expiration date. An FDA-approved patient medication guide, which is available with the product information, must be dispensed with this medication.

SPECIAL POPULATIONS:
- *Elderly*: Recommended starting dose for elderly patients who have difficulty falling asleep is 1 mg. For elderly patients who have difficulty staying asleep, the recommended dose is 1–2 mg.
- *Hepatic impairment:* The starting dose should be 1 mg in patients with severe hepatic impairment. Monitor closely.
- *Pregnancy*: Category C.
- *Lactation*: No human studies have been performed. Not recommended in breastfeeding mothers.
- *Children*: Safety and efficacy have not been established.

zaleplon *Sonata*

INDICATIONS: Short-term (7–10 days) treatment insomnia in the nondepressed patient.

AVAILABLE FORM: Capsule

DOSAGE: 5–10 mg PO immediately before patient is ready for sleep.

ADMINISTRATION:
- PO with a glass of water.
- Avoid taking within 2 hr of a fatty meal.
- Drowsiness and/or dizziness will be exacerbated with concomitant alcohol consumption; alcohol should be avoided while taking this medication.

SIDE EFFECTS:
- Hallucinations; behavior changes; SSRI-treated patients taking zaleplon may experience impaired concentration, aggravated depression, and manic reaction; may cause amnesia. In most cases, memory problems can be avoided

if zaleplon is taken only when the patient is able to get more than 4 hr of sleep before being active.
- *Side effects that usually do not require medical attention*: Nausea; daytime drowsiness; headache; vomiting; dizziness; diarrhea

DRUG INTERACTIONS: This medicine may interact with the following medications: antifungals; chlorpromazine; flumazenil; clarithromycin; rifamycin; ritonavir; SSRIs; CNS depressants (including alcohol); amiodarone; verapamil

PHARMACOKINETICS: Non-BZDs hypnotic of the pyrazolopyrimidines class. Mechanism of action is thought to occur at the level of the GABA-BZ receptor complex.
- Peak plasma levels are reached in 1 hr.
- Bioavailability is 30%.

Half-life: Average is 1 hr.

(cont.)

zaleplon (*cont.*)

PRECAUTIONS:
- Ensure that patient is aware he/she is not to exceed maximum dosage.
- Patient should not take this medication unless prepared to sleep for at least 4 hr.
- Instruct patient to monitor for behavior changes.
- If patient is drowsy or dizzy, patient should not drive, use machinery, or attempt to accomplish any task that requires mental alertness.
- Avoid alcohol as concomitant use may exacerbate symptoms.

PATIENT AND FAMILY EDUCATION: Store at room temperature. Throw away any unused medication after the expiration date. An FDA-approved patient medication guide, which is available with the product information, must be dispensed with this medication.

SPECIAL POPULATIONS:
- *Elderly*: More sensitive to hypnotics. Use no more than 5 mg.
- *Hepatic impairment:* Modify dosage accordingly in patients with hepatic function impairment
- *Pregnancy*: Category C.
- *Lactation*: No human studies have been performed. Not recommended in breastfeeding mothers.
- *Children*: Safety and efficacy have not been established.

Rozerem **ramelteon**

INDICATIONS: Treatment of insomnia characterized by difficulty with sleep onset in the nondepressed patient.

AVAILABLE FORM: Tablet

DOSAGE: 8 mg PO taken within 30 min of going to bed.

ADMINISTRATION:
- PO with a glass of water.
- Take at least 2 hr after a meal.
- Drowsiness and/or dizziness will be exacerbated with concomitant alcohol consumption; alcohol and CNS depressants should be avoided while taking this medication.

SIDE EFFECTS:
- Hallucinations; behavior changes; insomnia; SSRI-treated patients taking ramelteon may experience impaired concentration, aggravated depression, and manic reaction
- *Side effects that usually do not require medical attention:* Nausea; daytime drowsiness; headache; vomiting; dizziness; diarrhea; fatigue

DRUG INTERACTIONS: This medicine may interact with the following medications: antifungals; fluvoxamine; rifampin; SSRIs; CNS depressants (including alcohol)

PHARMACOKINETICS:
- Non-BZDs hypnotic. Mechanism of action: melatonin receptor agonist.
- Highly bound to plasma proteins.
- Peak plasma levels are reached in 0.75 hr.
- Bioavailability is only 1.8%.
- Metabolized by CYP450 1A2 and 3A4

Half-life: Average is 1–2.6 hr.

PRECAUTIONS:
- See patient as often as necessary if long-term use is indicated.
- Ensure that patient is aware he/she is not to exceed maximum dosage.
- Instruct patient to monitor for behavior changes.
- If patient is drowsy or dizzy, patient should not drive, use machinery, or attempt to accomplish any task that requires mental alertness.
- Avoid alcohol and CNS depressants as concomitant use may exacerbate symptoms.

PATIENT AND FAMILY EDUCATION:
- Store at 25°C (77°F); drug will remain stable between 15°C and 30°C (59°F–77°F).
- Discard unused medication after expiration date.
- An FDA-approved patient medication guide, which is available with the product information, must be dispensed with this medication.

SPECIAL POPULATIONS:
- *Elderly*: Impaired hepatic function: Do not use in patients with impaired hepatic function.
- *Pregnancy*: Category C.
- *Lactation*: No human studies have been performed. Not recommended in breastfeeding mothers.
- *Children*: Safety and efficacy have not been established.

Ambien **zolpidem**

INDICATIONS: Treatment of insomnia in the nondepressed patient.

AVAILABLE FORM: Tablet

DOSAGE: 5–10 mg PO immediately before patient is ready for sleep. May use 12.5 mg *Ambien ER* in patients who have difficulty staying asleep.

ADMINISTRATION:
- PO with a glass of water.
- Take at least 2 hr after a meal.
- Drowsiness and/or dizziness will be exacerbated with concomitant alcohol consumption; alcohol should be avoided while taking this medication.

(cont.)

zolpidem (*cont.*)

- Caution clients not to stop taking drug abruptly if used long-term.

SIDE EFFECTS:
- Hallucinations, sedation; behavior changes; SSRI-treated patients taking zolpidem may experience impaired concentration, aggravated depression, and manic reaction
- *Side effects that usually do not require medical attention:* Nausea; daytime drowsiness; headache; vomiting; dizziness; diarrhea

DRUG INTERACTIONS: This medicine may interact with the following medications: antifungals; chlorpromazine; flumazenil; imipramine; rifamycin; ritonavir; SSRIs; CNS depressants (including alcohol)

PHARMACOKINETICS:
- Non-BZDs hypnotic of the imidazopyridine class. Mechanism of action is thought to occur at the level of the GABA receptor complex.
- Highly bound to plasma proteins.
- Peak plasma levels are reached in 1.6 hr.
- Bioavailability is 100%.
- **Half-life:** Average is 2.6 hr.

PRECAUTIONS:
- See patient as often as necessary if long-term use is indicated.

- Ensure that patient is aware he/she is not to exceed maximum dosage.
- Instruct patient to monitor for behavior changes.
- If patient is drowsy or dizzy, patient should not drive, use machinery, or attempt to accomplish any task that requires mental alertness.
- Avoid alcohol as concomitant use may exacerbate symptoms.

PATIENT AND FAMILY EDUCATION:
- Store at room temperature between 20°C and 25°C (59°F–77°F).
- Discard unused medication after the expiration date.
- An FDA-approved patient medication guide, which is available with the product information, must be dispensed with this medication.

SPECIAL POPULATIONS:
- *Elderly:* More sensitive to hypnotics. Use no more than 5 mg.
- *Hepatic impairment:* Modify dosage accordingly.
- *Pregnancy:* Category C.
- *Lactation:* No human studies have been performed. Not recommended in breastfeeding mothers.
- *Children:* Safety and efficacy have not been established.

Class: Benzodiazepines (BZDs)

flurazepam   *Dalmane*

INDICATIONS: Treatment of insomnia.

AVAILABLE FORMS: Capsule, 15 and 30 mg

DOSAGE: 15–30 mg PO immediately before patient is ready for sleep.

ADMINISTRATION:
- PO with a glass of water.
- Drowsiness and/or dizziness will be exacerbated with concomitant alcohol consumption; alcohol should be avoided while taking this medication.
- Caution clients not to stop taking drug abruptly if used long-term.

SIDE EFFECTS:
- Hallucinations; behavior changes
- *Side effects that usually do not require medical attention:* Nausea; daytime drowsiness; headache; vomting; dizziness; diarrhea; dry mouth; nervousness

DRUG INTERACTIONS: This medicine may interact with the following medications: antifungals; CNS depressants (including alcohol); digoxin; macrolides; phenytoin

PHARMACOKINETICS:
- BZD, hypnotic.
- Mechanism of action is thought to occur at the level of the GABA receptor complex.
- Highly bound to plasma proteins.
- Peak plasma levels are reached in 0.50–2 hr.
- Metabolized by CYP450 3A4 and excreted through the urine
- Half-life of patent drug average is 2–3 hr, half-life of metabolite is 40–114 hr.

PRECAUTIONS:
- See patient as often as necessary if long-term use is indicated.
- Ensure that patient is aware he/she is not to exceed maximum dosage.
- Instruct patient to monitor for behavior changes.
- If patient is drowsy or dizzy, patient should not drive, use machinery, or attempt to accomplish any task that requires mental alertness.
- Avoid alcohol as concomitant use may exacerbate symptoms.

PATIENT AND FAMILY EDUCATION:
- Store at room temperature between 20°C and 25°C (59°F–77°F).

(cont.)

flurazepam (cont.)

- Discard unused medication after the expiration date.

SPECIAL POPULATIONS:
- *Elderly*: More sensitive to hypnotics. Use lowest effective dose, maximum 15 mg. Due to sedation and increased risk of falls, all BZDs are placed on Beers List of Potentially Inappropriate Medications for Geriatrics.

- Modify dosage accordingly in patients with hepatic function impairment, typical 15 mg maximum dose.
- *Pregnancy*: Category X. Absolute contraindication.
- *Lactation*: No human studies have been performed. Not recommended in breastfeeding mothers. Drug is excreted in breast milk.
- *Children*: Not for use in children less than 15 years of age.

Restoril **temazepam**

INDICATIONS: Treatment of insomnia.

AVAILABLE FORMS: Capsule, 7.5, 15, and 30 mg

DOSAGE: 15–30 mg/day PO immediately before patient is ready for sleep.

ADMINISTRATION:
- PO with a glass of water.
- Drowsiness and/or dizziness will be exacerbated with concomitant alcohol consumption; alcohol should be avoided while taking this medication.
- Caution clients not to stop taking drug abruptly if used long-term.

SIDE EFFECTS:
- Hallucinations; behavior changes
- *Side effects that usually do not require medical attention*: Nausea; daytime drowsiness; headache; vomiting; dizziness; diarrhea; dry mouth; nervousness

DRUG INTERACTIONS: This medicine may interact with the following medications: antifungals; CNS depressants (including alcohol); digoxin; macrolides; phenytoin

PHARMACOKINETICS:
- BZD, hypnotic.
- Mechanism of action is thought to occur at the level of the GABA receptor complex.
- Highly bound to plasma proteins.
- Peak plasma levels are reached in 1.2–1.6 hr.
- Metabolized by CYP450 2B6, 2C19, 3A4
Half-life: Average is 20–40 hr.

PRECAUTIONS:
- See patient as often as necessary if long-term use is indicated.
- Ensure that patient is aware he/she is not to exceed maximum dosage.
- Instruct patient to monitor for behavior changes.
- If patient is drowsy or dizzy, patient should not drive, use machinery, or attempt to accomplish any task that requires mental alertness.
- Avoid alcohol as concomitant use may exacerbate symptoms.

PATIENT AND FAMILY EDUCATION:
- Store at room temperature between 20°C and 25°C (59°F–77°F).
- Discard unused medication after the expiration date.

SPECIAL POPULATIONS:
- *Elderly*: More sensitive to hypnotics. Use lowest effective dose, recommended 7.5 mg/day. Due to sedation and increased risk of falls, all BZDs are placed on Beers List of Potentially Inappropriate Medications for Geriatrics.
- *Hepatic impairment*: Modify dosage accordingly.
- *Pregnancy*: Category X.
- *Lactation*: No human studies have been performed. Not recommended in breastfeeding mothers. Drug is excreted in breast milk.
- *Children*: Not for use in children less than 18 years of age.

Halcion **triazolam**

INDICATIONS: Treatment of insomnia.

AVAILABLE FORMS: Tablet, 0.125 and 0.25 mg

DOSAGE: 0.125–0.5 mg PO immediately before patient is ready for sleep.

ADMINISTRATION:
- PO with a glass of water.
- Drowsiness and/or dizziness will be exacerbated with concomitant alcohol consumption; alcohol should be avoided while taking this medication.
- Caution clients not to stop taking drug abruptly if used long-term.

SIDE EFFECTS:
- Hallucinations; behavior changes
- *Side effects that usually do not require medical attention*: Nausea; daytime drowsiness; headache; vomiting; dizziness; diarrhea; dry mouth; nervousness

DRUG INTERACTIONS: This medicine may interact with the following medications: antifungals; CNS depressants (including alcohol); digoxin; macrolides; phenytoin

(cont.)

PRIMARY INSOMNIA: Benzodiazepines (BZDs)

triazolam (*cont.*)

PHARMACOKINETICS:
- BZD, hypnotic.
- Mechanism of action is thought to occur at the level of the GABA receptor complex.
- Highly bound to plasma proteins.
- Peak plasma levels are reached in 1–2 hr.
- Metabolized by CYP450 3A4.

Half-life: Average is 1.5–5.5 hr.

PRECAUTIONS:
- See patient as often as necessary if long-term use is indicated.
- Ensure that patient is aware he/she is not to exceed maximum dosage.
- Instruct patient to monitor for behavior changes.
- If patient is drowsy or dizzy, patient should not drive, use machinery, or attempt to accomplish any task that requires mental alertness.
- Avoid alcohol as concomitant use may exacerbate symptoms.

PATIENT AND FAMILY EDUCATION:
- Store at room temperature between 20°C and 25°C (59°F–77°F).
- Throw away any unused medication after the expiration date.

SPECIAL POPULATIONS:
- *Elderly*: More sensitive to hypnotics. Use lowest effective dose, typically 0.125 mg. Due to sedation and increased risk of falls, all BZDs are placed on Beers List of Potentially Inappropriate Medications for Geriatrics.
- *Hepatic impairment:* Modify dosage accordingly.
- *Pregnancy*: Category X. Absolute contraindication.
- *Lactation*: No human studies have been performed. Not recommended in breastfeeding mothers. Drug is excreted in breast milk.
- *Children*: Not for use in children less than 18 years of age.

Primary Hypersomnia

OVERVIEW
- Reoccurring excessive daytime sleepiness or prolonged nighttime sleep impacting activities of daily living without central origin.
- Three categories of hypersomnia include insufficient nighttime sleep, fragmented nighttime sleep, and increased drive to sleep.
- May present as monosymptomatic or polysymptomatic.
- Monosymptomatic presents as solely excessive daytime sleepiness without abnormal night time awakenings.
- Polysymptomatic presents with abnormally long night time sleeping and sleep drunkenness upon awakening.
- Most common onset is during adolescence.
- Rarely presents after age 30.
- Affects males and females equally.
- Idiopathic. No genetic, environmental or other relating factors identified.
- Responds poorly to treatment.

Psychopharmacology of Primary Hypersomnia

Acute Treatment
- Trial stimulants at the lowest dose to produce optimal alertness and minimize side effects in combination with lifestyle modifications and regular work routine. Typically requires long-term treatment.

Chronic Treatment
- Stimulants (non-amphetamine or amphetamine) at the lowest dose to produce optimal alertness.
- Re-evaluate as indicated to ensure treatment compliance and relief of symptomatology.

GENERAL CONSIDERATIONS
- Most commonly used medications for primary hypersomnia
- Proper use of this medicine:
  - Medication should be taken at the time of day appropriate for wakefulness.
  - Can be taken with or without food.
  - When taken with meal, absorption may be delayed by 1 hr.

CLASS	DRUG
Stimulants, Non-Amphetamine	**First-Line Drug Therapy**
	modafinil *(Provigil)*
	armodafinil *(Nuvigil)*
Amphetamines	**Second-Line Drug Therapy**
	amphetamine/dextroamphetamine *(Adderall)*
	dextroamphetamine *(Dextrostat)*
	methylphenidate *(Ritalin)*

Class: Stimulants, Non-Amphetamine

Provigil   **modafinil**

INDICATIONS: Used primarily to treat sleep disorders that result in excessive sleepiness such as narcolepsy, obstructive sleep apnea, hypopnea syndrome, and shift work sleep disorder.

AVAILABLE FORMS: Tablet, 100 and 200 mg

DOSAGE: 200 mg PO when prepared for long period of wakefulness. Maximum, 400–800 mg.

ADMINISTRATION:
- PO with a glass of water
- Take with or without food

SIDE EFFECTS:
- Hypertension; arrhythmia; cataplexy; dysmenorrhea; dyspnea; infection; abnormal thinking; weight loss; UTI
- *Side effects that usually do not require medical attention*: Anxiety; back pain; diarrhea; dizziness; dyspepsia; headache; insomnia; nausea; nervousness; rhinitis

DRUG INTERACTIONS: Drug may interact with the following medications: antifungals; CNS depressants (including alcohol); MAOIs; macrolides; phenytoin; estrogen; cyclosporine; SSRIs; TCAs; CNS stimulants; carbamazepine

PHARMACOKINETICS:
- Rapid absorption in absence of food.
- Peak plasma levels are reached in 2–4 hr.
- Steady state reached within 2–4 days of dosing.
Half-life: Average is 15 hr once steady state is reached.

PRECAUTIONS:
- See client as often as necessary to ensure drug is promoting wakefulness, determine compliance, and review side effects.

- Advise patient to report any new rashes immediately.
- Discontinue drug immediately if any rash is reported.
- Advise patient of risk for transient psychosis-like symptoms (ideas of reference, paranoid delusions, and auditory hallucinations).
- May experience transient palpitations and EKG changes.
- Avoid using in clients with left ventricular hypertrophy or mitral valve prolapse.

PATIENT AND FAMILY EDUCATION:
- Do not operate heavy machinery or equipment until reasonably certain that drug will not affect ability to engage in such activities.
- Discontinue medication immediately if rash is noted and follow up with provider.
- May experience palpitations.
- Have patient monitor BP at home and notify provider of persistent BP elevations.
- Store at room temperature between 20°C and 25°C (68°F–77°F).

SPECIAL POPULATIONS:
- *Elderly*: More sensitive to stimulants. Use lowest effective dose.
- *Hepatic impairment:* Modify dosage by one-half accordingly.
- *Pregnancy*: Category C.
- *Lactation*: No human studies have been performed. Not recommended in breastfeeding mothers.
- *Children*: Not for use in pediatric patients.

Nuvigil   **armodafinil**

INDICATIONS: Used primarily to treat sleep disorders that result in excessive sleepiness such as narcolepsy, obstructive sleep apnea, hypopnea syndrome, and shift work sleep disorder.

AVAILABLE FORMS: Tablet, 50, 150, and 250 mg

DOSAGE: 150–250 mg PO when prepared for long period of wakefulness.

ADMINISTRATION:
- PO with a glass of water
- Take without food

SIDE EFFECTS:
- Hypertension; arrhythmia; cataplexy; dysmenorrhea; dyspnea; infection; abnormal thinking; weight loss; UTI
- *Side effects that usually do not require medical attention*: Anxiety; back pain; diarrhea; dizziness;
(cont.)

armodafinil (*cont.*)

dyspepsia; headache; insomnia; nausea; nervousness; rhinitis

DRUG INTERACTIONS: Drug may interact with the following medications: antifungals; CNS depressants (including alcohol); MAOIs; macrolides; phenytoin; estrogen; cyclosporine; SSRIs; TCAs; CNS stimulants; carbamazepine; phenobarbital

PHARMACOKINETICS:
- Rapid absorption in absence of food.
- Peak plasma levels are reached in 2 hr in the fasted state.
- Steady state reached within 7 days of dosing.
Half-life: Average is 15 hr once steady state is reached.

PRECAUTIONS:
- See client as often as necessary to ensure drug is promoting wakefulness, determine compliance, and review side effects.
- Advise patient to report any new rashes immediately.
- Discontinue drug immediately if any rash is reported.
- Advise patient of risk for transient psychosis-like symptoms (ideas of reference, paranoid delusions, and auditory hallucinations.

- May experience transient palpitations and EKG changes.
- Avoid using in clients with left ventricular hypertrophy or mitral valve prolapsed.

PATIENT AND FAMILY EDUCATION:
- Do not operate heavy machinery or equipment until reasonably certain that drug will not affect ability to engage in such activities.
- Discontinue medication immediately if rash is noted and follow up with provider.
- May experience palpitations.
- Have patient monitor BP at home and notify provider of persistent BP elevations.
- Store at room temperature between 20°C and 25°C (68°F–77°F).

SPECIAL POPULATIONS:
- *Elderly*: Clearance reduced in older adults. Use lowest effective dose.
- *Hepatic impairment:* Modify dosage by one-half accordingly.
- *Pregnancy*: Category C.
- *Lactation*: No human studies have been performed. Not recommended in breastfeeding mothers.
- *Children*: Not for use in pediatric patients.

Class: Amphetamines

amphetamine/dextroamphetamine   *Adderall*

INDICATIONS: Used primarily to treat narcolepsy and ADHD.

AVAILABLE FORMS: Immediate-release tablet, 5, 7.5, 10, 12.5, 15, and 20 mg; extended-release tablet, 5, 10, 15, 20, 25, and 30 mg

DOSAGE: 5–60 mg PO q day or divided tid to be taken when prepared for long period of wakefulness. Start with 10 mg PO qam; increase 10 mg/day q week. Give divided doses of immediate-release formulations at 4–6 hr intervals.

ADMINISTRATION:
- PO with a glass of water
- Take with or without food

SIDE EFFECTS:
- Palpitations; stroke; myocardial infarction; sudden death in patients with structural cardiac defects; hypertension; arrhythmia; overstimulation; restlessness; seizures; infection; abnormal thinking; weight loss; somnolence; changes in libido; urticaria; Stevens-Johnson syndrome; toxic epidermal necrolysis; impotence
- *Side effects that usually do not require medical attention*: Anxiety; insomnia; diarrhea; constipation; dizziness; insomnia; nausea; nervousness; rhinitis; dry mouth
- *Contraindications:* Advanced arteriosclerosis, symptomatic cardiovascular disease, moderate

to severe hypertension, hyperthyroidism, glaucoma, history of drug abuse, agitated states or within 14 days of MAOIs.

DRUG INTERACTIONS: Drug may interact with the following medications: antifungals; CNS depressants (including alcohol); MAOIs; adrenergic blockers; SSRIs; antihypertensives; CNS stimulants; TCAs; antihistamines; meperidine; phenytoin; haloperidol; methenamine; phenothiazines; propoxyphene

PHARMACOKINETICS:
- Stimulant; blocks reuptake of NE and dopamine into the presynaptic neuron and increases the release of these monoamines into the extraneuronal space.
- Food prolongs time to maximum concentration by 2.5 hr.
- Peak plasma levels are reached in 3 hr.
Half-life: Average is 12 hr (mean half-life average shortened by 1–2 hr in children).

PRECAUTIONS:
- See client as often as necessary to ensure drug is promoting positive cognitive and behavioral results.
- Advise patient to report any new rashes immediately.
- Discontinue drug immediately if any rashes are reported.

(cont.)

amphetamine/dextroamphetamine (*cont.*)

- Advise patient of risk for transient psychosis-like symptoms (ideas of reference, paranoid delusions, and auditory hallucinations) and aggressive behaviors.
- Client may develop drug tolerance or dependence.
- May experience transient palpitations and EKG changes.
- Avoid using in clients with left ventricular hypertrophy or mitral valve prolapse.
- May lower seizure threshold.
- Potential for growth inhibition in pediatric clients.
- Advise patient not to suddenly discontinue, taper off.

PATIENT AND FAMILY EDUCATION:
- Do not operate heavy machinery or equipment until reasonably certain that drug will not affect ability to engage in such activities.
- Discontinue medication immediately if rash is noted and follow up with provider.

- Store at room temperature between 15°C and 30°C (59°F–86°F). Throw away any unused medication after the expiration date.
- May experience palpitations.
- Have patient monitor BP at home and notify provider of persistent BP elevations.
- Discontinue or hold medication in presence of chest pain and do not restart until reassessed by provider.
- May experience transient blurred vision.

SPECIAL POPULATIONS:
- *Elderly*: More sensitive to stimulants. Use lowest effective dose.
- *Hepatic impairment:* Modify dosage by one-half accordingly.
- *Pregnancy:* Category C.
- *Lactation:* Excreted in breast milk. No human studies have been performed. Not recommended in breastfeeding mothers.
- *Children:* For use in children 12 years of age or older.

Dextrostat | **dextroamphetamine**

INDICATIONS: Used primarily to treat primary hypersomnia, narcolepsy, and ADHD.

AVAILABLE FORMS: Tablet, 5, 10, and 15 mg

DOSAGE: 5–60 mg/day q day or divided tid to be taken when prepared for long period of wakefulness. Start with 10 mg PO qam; increase 10 mg/day q week. Give divided doses at 4–6 hr intervals.

ADMINISTRATION:
- PO with a glass of water
- Take with or without food

SIDE EFFECTS:
- Palpitations; stroke; myocardial infarction; sudden death in patients with structural cardiac defects; hypertension; arrhythmia; overstimulation; restlessness; seizures; infection; abnormal thinking; weight loss; somnolence; changes in libido; urticaria; Stevens-Johnson syndrome; toxic epidermal necrolysis; impotence
- *Side effects that usually do not require medical attention:* Anxiety; insomnia; diarrhea; constipation; dizziness; insomnia; nausea; nervousness; rhinitis; dry mouth
- *Contraindications:* Advanced arteriosclerosis, symptomatic cardiovascular disease, moderate to severe hypertension, hyperthyroidism, glaucoma, history of drug abuse, agitated states or within 14 days of MAOIs.

DRUG INTERACTIONS: Drug may interact with the following medications: antifungals; CNS depressants (including alcohol); MAOIs; adrenergic blockers; SSRIs; antihypertensives; CNS

stimulants; TCAs; antihistamines; meperidine; phenytoin; haloperidol; methenamine; phenothiazines; propoxyphene

PHARMACOKINETICS:
- Stimulant; blocks reuptake of NE and dopamine into the presynaptic neuron and increases the release of these monoamines into the extraneuronal space.
- Food prolongs time to maximum concentration by 2.5 hr.
- Peak plasma levels are reached in 3 hr.

Half-life: Average is 12 hr (mean half-life average shortened by 1–2 hr in children).

PRECAUTIONS:
- See client as often as necessary to ensure drug is promoting positive cognitive and behavioral results.
- Advise patient to report any new rashes immediately.
- Discontinue drug immediately if any rash is reported.
- Advise patient of risk for transient psychosis-like symptoms (ideas of reference, paranoid delusions, and auditory hallucinations) and aggressive behaviors.
- Client may develop drug tolerance or dependence.
- May experience transient palpitations and EKG changes.
- Avoid using in clients with left ventricular hypertrophy or mitral valve prolapse.
- May lower seizure threshold.
- Potential for growth inhibition in pediatric clients.
- Advise patient not to suddenly discontinue, taper off.

(cont.)

PRIMARY HYPERSOMNIA: Amphetamines

dextroamphetamine *(cont.)*

PATIENT AND FAMILY EDUCATION:
- Do not operate heavy machinery or equipment until reasonably certain that drug will not affect ability to engage in such activities.
- Discontinue medication immediately if rash is noted and follow up with provider.
- Store at room temperature between 15°C and 30°C (59°F–86°F). Throw away any unused medication after the expiration date.
- May experience palpitations.
- Have patient monitor BP at home and notify provider of persistent BP elevations.
- Discontinue or hold medication in presence of chest pain and do not restart until reassessed by provider.
- May experience transient blurred vision.

SPECIAL POPULATIONS:
- *Elderly:* More sensitive to stimulants. Use lowest effective dose.
- *Hepatic impairment:* Modify dosage by one-half accordingly.
- *Pregnancy:* Category C.
- *Lactation:* Excreted in breast milk. No human studies have been performed. Not recommended in breastfeeding mothers.
- *Children:* For use in children 12 years of age or older.

methylphenidate   *Ritalin*

INDICATIONS: Used primarily to treat narcolepsy.

AVAILABLE FORMS: Immediate-release tablet, 5, 10, and 20 mg; sustained release capsule and transdermal patches, 10, 20, 30, and 40 mg

DOSAGE: 20–60 mg/day in two or three divided doses. Start with 10 mg PO qam; increase 10 mg/day q week. Give divided doses at 4–6 hr intervals.

ADMINISTRATION:
- PO with a glass of water
- 30–45 min before meals

SIDE EFFECTS:
- Palpitations; stroke; myocardial infarction; sudden death in patients with structural cardiac defects; hypertension; arrhythmia; overstimulation; restlessness; seizures; infection; abnormal thinking; weight loss; somnolence; changes in libido; urticaria; Stevens-Johnson syndrome; toxic epidermal necrolysis; impotence
- *Side effects that usually do not require medical attention:* Anxiety; insomnia; diarrhea; constipation; dizziness; insomnia; nausea; nervousness; rhinitis; dry mouth
- *Contraindications:* Advanced arteriosclerosis, symptomatic cardiovascular disease, moderate to severe hypertension, hyperthyroidism, glaucoma, history of drug abuse, agitated states or within 14 days of MAOIs.

DRUG INTERACTIONS: Drug may interact with the following medications: CNS depressants (including alcohol); MAOIs; SSRIs; antihypertensives; CNS stimulants; TCAs; phenytoin; warfarin

PHARMACOKINETICS:
- Stimulant; blocks reuptake of NE and dopamine into the presynaptic neuron and increases the release of these monoamines into the extraneuronal space.
- Food prolongs time to maximum concentration by 2.5 hr.
- Peak plasma levels of immediate-release formulations are reached in 3 hr.

Half-life: Average is 12 hr (mean half-life average shortened by 1–2 hr in children).

PRECAUTIONS:
- See client as often as necessary to ensure drug is promoting positive cognitive and behavioral results.
- Advise patient to report any new rashes immediately.
- Discontinue drug immediately if any rash is reported.
- Advise patient of risk for transient psychosis-like symptoms (ideas of reference, paranoid delusions, and auditory hallucinations) and aggressive behaviors.
- Client may develop drug tolerance or dependence.
- May experience transient palpitations and EKG changes.
- Avoid using in clients with left ventricular hypertrophy or mitral valve prolapse.
- May lower seizure threshold.
- Potential for growth inhibition in pediatric clients.
- Advise patient not to suddenly discontinue medication, taper off.

PATIENT AND FAMILY EDUCATION:
- Do not operate heavy machinery or equipment until reasonably certain that drug will not affect their ability to engage in such activities.
- Discontinue medication immediately if rash is noted and follow up with provider.
- Store at room temperature between 15°C and 30°C (59°F–86°F). Throw away any unused medication after the expiration date.
- May experience palpitations.
- Have patient monitor BP at home and notify provider of persistent BP elevations.
- Discontinue or hold medication in presence of chest pain and do not restart until reassessed by provider.
- May experience transient blurred vision.

(cont.)

methylphenidate *(cont.)*

SPECIAL POPULATIONS:
- *Elderly:* More sensitive to stimulants. Use lowest effective dose.
- *Hepatic impairment:* Modify dosage by one-half accordingly.
- *Pregnancy:* Category C.

- *Lactation:* Excreted in breast milk. No human studies have been performed. Not recommended in breastfeeding mothers.
- *Children:* For use in children 12 years of age or older.

Narcolepsy

OVERVIEW
- Chronic REM sleep disorder of central origin characterized by excessive daytime sleepiness
- Classic presenting symptoms include excessive daytime sleepiness, sleep paralysis, cataplexy and hypnagogic hallucinations
- Nocturnal sleep disturbances are common
- At risk for motor vehicle accidents and injury
- Male to female ratio is 1.64: 1
- First-degree relatives have a 10- to 40-fold higher risk than the general population.

- Age of peak presentation is 15
- Reported in children as young as 2
- Frequently familial
- Associated with specific HLA haplotypes
- Possible autoimmune etiology
- Stimulant drugs are most commonly used medications; include both non-amphetamine and amphetamine drugs
- Regular exercise, consistent schedules, and regularly scheduled meals may improve symptoms.

Psychopharmacology of Narcolepsy

Acute Treatment
- Trial stimulants at the lowest dose to produce optimal alertness and minimize side effects in combination with lifestyle modifications and regular work routine. Typically requires long-term treatment.

Chronic Treatment
- Stimulants (non-amphetamine or amphetamine) at the lowest dose to produce as optimal alertness.
- Re-evaluate as indicated to ensure treatment compliance and relief of symptomatology.

CLASS	DRUG
Stimulants, Non-Amphetamine	**First–Line Drug Therapy**
	modafinil *(Provigil)*
	armodafinil *(Nuvigil)*
Amphetamines	**Second-Line Drug Therapy**
	amphetamine/dextroamphetamine *(Adderall)*
	dextroamphetamine *(Dextrostat)*
	methylphenidate *(Ritalin)*

Class: Stimulants, Non-Amphetamine

Provigil   **modafinil**

INDICATIONS: Used primarily to treat sleep disorders that result in excessive sleepiness such as narcolepsy, obstructive sleep apnea, hypopnea syndrome, and shift work sleep disorder.

AVAILABLE FORM: Tablet

DOSAGE: 200 mg PO when prepared for long periods of wakefulness. Maximum dose is 400 mg. Rarely more effective with dosing greater than 200 mg.

ADMINISTRATION:
- PO with a glass of water
- Take with or without food

SIDE EFFECTS:
- Hypertension; arrhythmia; cataplexy; dysmenorrhea; dyspnea; infection; abnormal thinking; weight loss; UTI
- *Side effects that usually do not require medical attention:* Anxiety; back pain; diarrhea; dizziness;
(cont.)

modafinil (*cont.*)

dyspepsia; headache; insomnia; nausea; nervousness; rhinitis

DRUG INTERACTIONS: Drug may interact with the following medications: antifungals; CNS depressants (including alcohol); MAOIs; macrolides; phenytoin; estrogen; cyclosporine; SSRIs; TCAs; CNS stimulants; carbamazepine

PHARMACOKINETICS:
- Stimulant, exact mechanism of action unknown. Believed to have similar wake-promoting actions as sympathomimetic agents.
- Rapid absorption in absence of food.
- Peak plasma levels are reached in 2–4 hr.
- Steady state reached within 2–4 days of dosing.
Half-life: Average is 15 hr once steady state is reached.

PRECAUTIONS:
- See client as often as necessary to ensure drug is promoting wakefulness, determine compliance, and review side effects.
- Advise patient to report any new rashes immediately.
- Discontinue drug immediately if any rash is reported.
- Advise patient of risk for transient psychosis-like symptoms (ideas of reference, paranoid delusions, and auditory hallucinations).

- May experience transient palpitations and EKG changes.
- Avoid using in clients with left ventricular hypertrophy or mitral valve prolapse.

PATIENT AND FAMILY EDUCATION:
- Do not operate heavy machinery or equipment until reasonably certain that drug will not affect ability to engage in such activities.
- Discontinue medication immediately if rash is noted and follow up with provider.
- May experience palpitations.
- Have patient monitor BP at home and notify provider of persistent BP elevations.
- Store at room temperature between 20°C and 25°C (68°F–77°F).

SPECIAL POPULATIONS:
- *Elderly*: More sensitive to stimulants. Use lowest effective dose.
- *Hepatic impairment:* Modify dosage by one-half accordingly.
- *Pregnancy*: Category C.
- *Lactation*: No human studies have been performed. Not recommended in breastfeeding mothers.
- *Children*: Not for use in pediatric patients.

armodafinil   *Nuvigil*

INDICATIONS: Used primarily to treat sleep disorders that result in excessive sleepiness such as narcolepsy, obstructive sleep apnea, hypopnea syndrome, and shift work sleep disorder.

AVAILABLE FORM: Tablet

DOSAGE: 150–250 mg PO when prepared for long period of wakefulness.

ADMINISTRATION:
- PO with a glass of water
- Take without food

SIDE EFFECTS:
- Hypertension; arrhythmia; cataplexy; dysmenorrhea; dyspnea; infection; abnormal thinking; weight loss; UTI
- *Side effects that usually do not require medical attention*: Anxiety; back pain; diarrhea; dizziness; dyspepsia; headache; insomnia; nausea; nervousness; rhinitis

DRUG INTERACTIONS: Drug may interact with the following medications: antifungals; CNS depressants (including alcohol); MAOIs; macrolides; phenytoin; estrogen; cyclosporine; SSRIs; TCAs; CNS stimulants; carbamazepine; phenobarbital

PHARMACOKINETICS:
- Stimulant; exact mechanism of action unknown. Believed to have similar wake-promoting actions as sympathomimetic agents.
- Rapid absorption in absence of food.
- Peak plasma levels are reached in 2 hr in the fasted state.
- Steady state reached within 7 days of dosing.
Half-life: Average is 15 hr once steady state is reached.

PRECAUTIONS:
- See client as often as necessary to ensure drug is promoting wakefulness, determine compliance, and review side effects.
- Advise patient to report any new rashes immediately.
- Discontinue drug immediately if any rash is reported.
- Advise patient of risk for transient psychosis-like symptoms (ideas of reference, paranoid delusions, and auditory hallucinations).
- May experience transient palpitations and EKG changes.
- Avoid using in clients with left ventricular hypertrophy or mitral valve prolapsed.

(cont.)

armodafinil (cont.)

PATIENT AND FAMILY EDUCATION:
- Do not operate heavy machinery or equipment until reasonably certain that drug will not affect ability to engage in such activities.
- Discontinue medication immediately if rash is noted and follow up with provider.
- May experience palpitations.
- Have patient monitor BP at home and notify provider of persistent BP elevations.
- Store at room temperature between 20°C and 25°C (68°F–77°F).

SPECIAL POPULATIONS:
- *Elderly*: Clearance reduced in older adults. Use lowest effective dose.
- *Hepatic impairment*: Modify dosage by one-half accordingly.
- *Pregnancy*: Category C.
- *Lactation*: No human studies have been performed. Not recommended in breastfeeding mothers.
- *Children*: Not for use in pediatric patients.

Class: Amphetamines

Adderall	**amphetamine/dextroamphetamine**

INDICATIONS: Used primarily to treat narcolepsy and ADHD.

AVAILABLE FORMS: Tablet

DOSAGE: 5–60 mg PO q day or divided tid to be taken when prepared for long period of wakefulness. Start with 10 mg PO qam; increase 10 mg/day q week. Give divided doses at 4–6 hr intervals.

ADMINISTRATION:
- PO with a glass of water
- Take with or without food

SIDE EFFECTS:
- Palpitations; stroke; myocardial infarction; sudden death in patients with structural cardiac defects; hypertension; arrhythmia; overstimulation; restlessness; seizures; infection; abnormal thinking; weight loss; somnolence; changes in libido; urticaria; Stevens-Johnson syndrome; toxic epidermal necrolysis; impotence
- *Side effects that usually do not require medical attention*: Anxiety; insomnia; diarrhea; constipation; dizziness; insomnia; nausea; nervousness; rhinitis; dry mouth
- *Contraindications*: Advanced arteriosclerosis, symptomatic cardiovascular disease, moderate to severe hypertension, hyperthyroidism, glaucoma, history of drug abuse, agitated states or within 14 days of MAOIs.

DRUG INTERACTIONS: Drug may interact with the following medications: antifungals; CNS depressants (including alcohol); MAOIs; adrenergic blockers; SSRIs; antihypertensives; CNS stimulants; TCAs; antihistamines; meperidine; phenytoin; haloperidol; methenamine; phenothiazines; propoxyphene

PHARMACOKINETICS:
- Stimulant; blocks reuptake of NE and dopamine into the presynaptic neuron and increases the release of these monoamines into the extraneuronal space.
- Food prolongs time to maximum concentration by 2.5 hr.

- Peak plasma levels are reached in 3 hr.
Half-life: Average is 12 hr (mean half-life average shortened by 1–2 hr in children).

PRECAUTIONS:
- See client as often as necessary to ensure drug is promoting positive cognitive and behavioral results.
- Advise patient to report any new rashes immediately.
- Discontinue drug immediately if any rash is reported.
- Advise patient of risk for transient psychosis-like symptoms (ideas of reference, paranoid delusions, and auditory hallucinations) and aggressive behaviors.
- Client may develop drug tolerance or dependence.
- May experience transient palpitations and EKG changes.
- Avoid using in clients with left ventricular hypertrophy or mitral valve prolapse.
- May lower seizure threshold.
- Potential for growth inhibition in pediatric clients.
- Advise patient not to suddenly discontinue, taper off.

PATIENT AND FAMILY EDUCATION:
- Do not operate heavy machinery or equipment until reasonably certain that drug will not affect ability to engage in such activities.
- Discontinue medication immediately if rash is noted and follow up with provider.
- Store at room temperature between 15°C and 30°C (59°F–86°F). Throw away any unused medication after the expiration date.
- May experience palpitations.
- Have patient monitor BP at home and notify provider of persistent BP elevations.
- Discontinue or hold medication in presence of chest pain and do not restart until reassessed by provider.
- May experience transient blurred vision.

(cont.)

amphetamine/dextroamphetamine (cont.)

SPECIAL POPULATIONS:
- *Elderly*: More sensitive to stimulants. Use lowest effective dose.
- *Hepatic impairment:* Modify dosage by one-half accordingly.
- *Pregnancy*: Category C.

- *Lactation*: Excreted in breast milk. No human studies have been performed. Not recommended in breastfeeding mothers.
- *Children*: For use in children 12 years of age or older.

dextroamphetamine   *Dextrostat*

INDICATIONS: Used primarily to treat primary hypersomnia, narcolepsy, and ADHD.

AVAILABLE FORM: Tablet

DOSAGE: 5–60 mg PO q day or divided tid to be taken when prepared for long period of wakefulness. Start with 10 mg PO qam; increase 10 mg/day q week. Give divided doses at 4–6 hr intervals.

ADMINISTRATION:
- PO with a glass of water
- Take with or without food

SIDE EFFECTS:
- Palpitations; stroke; myocardial infarction; sudden death in patients with structural cardiac defects; hypertension; arrhythmia; overstimulation; restlessness; seizures; infection; abnormal thinking; weight loss; somnolence; changes in libido; urticaria; Stevens-Johnson syndrome; toxic epidermal necrolysis; impotence
- *Side effects that usually do not require medical attention:* Anxiety; insomnia; diarrhea; constipation; dizziness; insomnia; nausea; nervousness; rhinitis; dry mouth
- *Contraindications:* Advanced arteriosclerosis, symptomatic cardiovascular disease, moderate to severe hypertension, hyperthyroidism, glaucoma, history of drug abuse, agitated states or within 14 days of MAOIs.

DRUG INTERACTIONS: May interact with the following medications: antifungals; CNS depressants (including alcohol); MAOIs; adrenergic blockers; SSRIs; antihypertensives; CNS stimulants; TCAs; antihistamines; meperidine; phenytoin; haloperidol; methenamine; phenothiazines; propoxyphene

PHARMACOKINETICS:
- Stimulant; blocks reuptake of NE and dopamine into the presynaptic neuron and increases the release of these monoamines into the extraneuronal space.
- Food prolongs time to maximum concentration by 2.5 hr.
- Peak plasma levels are reached in 3 hr.

Half-life: Average is 12 hr (mean half-life average shortened by 1–2 hr in children).

PRECAUTIONS:
- See client as often as necessary to ensure drug is promoting positive cognitive and behavioral results.
- Advise patient to report any new rashes immediately.
- Discontinue drug immediately if any rash is reported.
- Advise patient of risk for transient psychosis-like symptoms (ideas of reference, paranoid delusions, and auditory hallucinations) and aggressive behaviors.
- Client may develop drug tolerance or dependence.
- May experience transient palpitations and EKG changes.
- Avoid using in clients with left ventricular hypertrophy or mitral valve prolapse.
- May lower seizure threshold.
- Potential for growth inhibition in pediatric clients.
- Advise patient not to suddenly discontinue, taper off.

PATIENT AND FAMILY EDUCATION:
- Do not operate heavy machinery or equipment until reasonably certain that drug will not affect ability to engage in such activities.
- Discontinue medication immediately if rash is noted and follow up with provider.
- Store at room temperature between 15°C and 30°C (59°F–86°F). Throw away any unused medication after the expiration date.
- May experience palpitations.
- Have patient monitor BP at home and notify provider of persistent BP elevations.
- Discontinue or hold medication in presence of chest pain and do not restart until reassessed by provider.
- May experience transient blurred vision.

SPECIAL POPULATIONS:
- *Elderly*: More sensitive to stimulants. Use lowest effective dose.
- *Hepatic impairment:* Modify dosage by one-half accordingly.
- *Pregnancy*: Category C.
- *Lactation*: Excreted in breast milk. No human studies have been performed. Not recommended in breastfeeding mothers.
- *Children*: For use in children 12 years of age or older.

Ritalin **methylphenidate**

INDICATIONS: Used primarily to treat narcolepsy and ADHD.

AVAILABLE FORM: Tablet

DOSAGE: 5–15 mg PO bid. Start with 10 mg PO qam; increase 10 mg/day q week. Give divided doses at 4–6 hr intervals.

ADMINISTRATION:
- PO with a glass of water
- 30–45 min before meals

SIDE EFFECTS:
- Palpitations; stroke; myocardial infarction; sudden death in patients with structural cardiac defects; hypertension; arrhythmia; overstimulation; restlessness; seizures; infection; abnormal thinking; weight loss; somnolence; changes in libido; urticaria; Stevens-Johnson syndrome; toxic epidermal necrolysis; impotence
- *Side effects that usually do not require medical attention:* Anxiety; insomnia; diarrhea; constipation; dizziness; insomnia; nausea; nervousness; rhinitis; dry mouth
- *Contraindications:* Advanced arteriosclerosis, symptomatic cardiovascular disease, moderate to severe hypertension, hyperthyroidism, glaucoma, history of drug abuse, agitated states or within 14 days of MAOIs.

DRUG INTERACTIONS: Drug may interact with the following medications: CNS depressants (including alcohol); MAOIs; SSRIs; antihypertensives; CNS stimulants; TCAs; phenytoin; warfarin

PHARMACOKINETICS:
- Stimulant; blocks reuptake of NE and dopamine into the presynaptic neuron and increases the release of these monoamines into the extraneuronal space.
- Food prolongs time to maximum concentration by 2.5 hr.
- Peak plasma levels are reached in 3 hr.

Half-life: Average is 12 hr (mean half-life average shortened by 1–2 hr in children).

PRECAUTIONS:
- See client as often as necessary to ensure drug is promoting positive cognitive and behavioral results.
- Advise patient to report any new rashes immediately.
- Discontinue drug immediately if any rash is reported.
- Advise patient of risk for transient psychosis-like symptoms (ideas of reference, paranoid delusions, and auditory hallucinations) and aggressive behaviors.
- Client may develop drug tolerance or dependence.
- May experience transient palpitations and EKG changes.
- Avoid using in clients with left ventricular hypertrophy or mitral valve prolapse.
- May lower seizure threshold.
- Potential for growth inhibition in pediatric clients.
- Advise patient not to suddenly discontinue medication, taper off.

PATIENT AND FAMILY EDUCATION:
- Do not operate heavy machinery or equipment until reasonably certain that drug will not affect ability to engage in such activities.
- Discontinue medication immediately if rash is noted and follow up with provider.
- Store at room temperature between 15°C and 30°C (59°F–86°F). Throw away any unused medication after the expiration date.
- May experience palpitations.
- Have patient monitor BP at home and notify provider of persistent BP elevations.
- Discontinue or hold medication in presence of chest pain and do not restart until reassessed by provider.
- May experience transient blurred vision.

SPECIAL POPULATIONS:
- *Elderly:* More sensitive to stimulants. Use lowest effective dose.
- *Hepatic impairment:* Modify dosage by one-half accordingly.
- *Pregnancy:* Category C.
- *Lactation:* Excreted in breast milk. No human studies have been performed. Not recommended in breastfeeding mothers.
- *Children:* For use in children 12 years of age or older.

Nightmare Disorder

OVERVIEW
- Associated with rapid eye movement sleep
- Occurs at any age
- Patient is arousable from sleep and describes bizarre dream plot.
- Exacerbated by stress
- Occurs equally in males and females; in 20–39% of children between ages 5 to 12 and in 5–8% of adults
- Risk factors include stress, sleep deprivation, psychiatric and neurologic disorders in adults and medications affecting neurotransmitter levels such as antidepressants, narcotics, or barbiturates.

NIGHTMARE DISORDER

Psychopharmacology of Nightmare Disorder

Patient Teaching
- Reassure parents that disorder should resolve with maturity.
- Reinforce the need for security to parents.
- Adult patients should decrease stressors.

Acute Treatment
- Comfort and reassurance. Behavioral strategies or counseling if episodes are frequent and severe

Chronic Treatment
- No FDA-approved medications.
- Referral to psychiatrist may be indicated if psychiatric disturbance is suspected
- Referral to sleep lab if history does not correlate with clinical findings to rule out sleep disordered breathing, parasomnia, or restless legs syndrome

Sleep Terror Disorder

OVERVIEW
- Also referred to as pavor nocturnus (night terrors)
- Sleep disturbance arising from slow wave sleep non-REM sleep Stage III or IV
- Occurs 60–90 min after onset of sleep in children
- Patient does not remember the event and is often confused and disoriented afterward.
- Screaming, sitting upright in bed; Frequently will have pallor, pupil dilation, tachycardia and sweating
- Occurs most often in children age 4 to 12; occurs in 3% of children ages 18 months to adolescence
- Typically a strong family history of parasomnias
- Exacerbated by stress and fatigue
- Predominant in males
- Adults likely to have psychopathology such as substance abuse and affective disorders

Psychopharmacology of Sleep Terror Disorder

Acute Treatment
- No FDA-approved medications for sleep terror disorder.

Chronic Treatment
- For persistent symptoms tricyclic antidepressants or BZDs may improve symptoms.
- Use lowest dose possible to control symptoms.

CLASS	DRUG
Benzodiazepines (BZDs)	**First-Line Drug Therapy**
	alprazolam *(Xanax)*
	diazepam *(Valium)*
Tricyclic Antidepressants (TCAs)	**Second-Line Drug Therapy**
	imipramine *(Tofranil)*
Serotonin Antagonist and Reuptake Inhibitors (SARIs)	
	trazodone *(Oleptro, Desyrel)*

Class: Benzodiazepines (BZDs)

alprazolam *Xanax*

INDICATIONS: Off-label use to treat sleep terror disorder.

AVAILABLE FORMS: Tablet, 0.25, 0.5, 1, and 2 mg

DOSAGE: 0.5–1.0 mg PO immediately before patient is ready for sleep.

ADMINISTRATION:
- PO with a glass of water.
- Drowsiness and/or dizziness will be exacerbated with concomitant alcohol consumption; alcohol should be avoided while taking this medication.
- Caution clients not to stop taking drug abruptly if used long-term.

SIDE EFFECTS:
- Syncope; tachycardia; seizures; respiratory depression; suicidal ideation; dependency; hypomania/mania
- *Side effects that usually do not require medical attention:* Nausea; daytime drowsiness; headache;
(cont.)

alprazolam (cont.)

vomiting; dizziness; diarrhea; dry mouth; nervousness; constipation; blurred vision; nasal congestion; depression; hypotension; ataxia; altered libido; appetite change; urinary hesitancy; sialorrhea; amnesia; dermatitis

DRUG INTERACTIONS: This medicine may interact with the following medications: chloramphenicol; conivaptan; cyclosporine; CNS depressants (including alcohol); antifungals; protease inhibitors; macrolides; isoniazid; efavirenz; delavirdine

PHARMACOKINETICS:
- BZD, hypnotic. Mechanism of action is thought to occur at the level of the GABA receptor complex.
- Highly bound to plasma proteins.
- Peak plasma levels are reached in 2 hr.
- Metabolized in the liver by CYP450 3A4
Half-life: Average is 11.2 hr.

PRECAUTIONS:
- See patient as often as necessary if long-term use is indicated.
- Ensure that patient is aware not to exceed maximum dosage.

- Instruct patient to monitor for behavior changes.
- If patient is drowsy or dizzy, patient should not drive, use machinery, or attempt to accomplish any task that requires mental alertness.
- Avoid alcohol as concomitant use may exacerbate symptoms.

PATIENT AND FAMILY EDUCATION: Store at room temperature between 20°C and 25°C (59°F–77°F). Throw away any unused medication after the expiration date.

SPECIAL POPULATIONS:
- *Elderly*: More sensitive to hypnotics. Use lowest effective dose. Due to sedation and increased risk of falls, all BZDs are placed on Beers List of Potentially Inappropriate Medications for Geriatrics.
- *Hepatic impairment:* Modify dosage accordingly.
- *Pregnancy*: Category D.
- *Lactation*: No human studies have been performed. Available data demonstrate potential or adverse effects to breast milk production. Not recommended in breastfeeding mothers.
- *Children*: Not for use in children.

Valium | **diazepam**

INDICATIONS: Off-label use to treat sleep terror disorder.

AVAILABLE FORMS: Tablet, 2, 5, and 10 mg

DOSAGE: 2–10 mg PO immediately before patient is ready for sleep.

ADMINISTRATION:
- PO with a glass of water.
- Drowsiness and/or dizziness will be exacerbated with concomitant alcohol consumption; alcohol should be avoided while taking this medication.
- Caution clients not to stop taking drug abruptly if used long-term.

SIDE EFFECTS:
- Syncope; bradycardia; seizure exacerbation; respiratory depression; suicidal ideation; dependency; hypomania/mania; psychosis; jaundice; blood dyscrasias
- *Side effects that usually do not require medical attention*: Nausea; daytime drowsiness; headache; vomiting; dizziness; diarrhea; dry mouth; nervousness; constipation; blurred vision; nasal congestion; depression; hypotension; ataxia; altered libido; appetite change; urinary retention; fatigue; phlebitis; muscle weakness; venous thrombosis; blurred vision; diplopia; dermatitis; elevated LFTs; hypersalivation; tremor; amnesia; dysarthria

DRUG INTERACTIONS: This medicine may interact with the following medications:

chloramphenicol; conivaptan; cyclosporine; CNS depressants (including alcohol); antifungals; protease inhibitors; macrolides; isoniazid; efavirenz; delavirdine; cimetidine; clarithromycin; fluoxetine; gefitinib; imatinib; esomeprazole; felbamate; nefazodone; olanzapine/fluoxetine; omeprazole; naproxen/esomeprazole

PHARMACOKINETICS:
- BZD, hypnotic. Mechanism of action is thought to occur at the level of the GABA receptor complex.
- Highly bound to plasma proteins.
- Metabolized by CYP450 2C19, 3A4
- Peak plasma levels are reached in 1–1.5 hr.
Half-life: Average is 30–60 hr.

PRECAUTIONS:
- See patient as often as necessary if long-term use is indicated.
- Ensure that patient is aware not to exceed maximum dosage.
- Instruct patient to monitor for behavior changes.
- If patient is drowsy or dizzy, patient should not drive, use machinery, or attempt to accomplish any task that requires mental alertness.
- Avoid alcohol as concomitant use may exacerbate symptoms.

PATIENT AND FAMILY EDUCATION: Store at room temperature between 20°C and 25°C (59°F–77°F). Throw away any unused medication after the expiration date.

(cont.)

SLEEP TERROR DISORDER: Benzodiazepines (BZDs)

diazepam (cont.)

SPECIAL POPULATIONS:
- *Elderly*: More sensitive to hypnotics. Use lowest effective dose. Due to sedation and increased risk of falls, all BZDs are placed on Beers List of Potentially Inappropriate Medications for Geriatrics.
- *Hepatic impairment*: Modify dosage accordingly.
- *Pregnancy*: Category D.
- *Lactation*: Excreted in breast milk. Not recommended for use in breastfeeding mothers.
- *Children*: Not for use in children.

Class: Tricyclic Antidepressants (TCAs)

imipramine   *Tofranil*

INDICATIONS: Off-label use to treat sleep terror disorder.

AVAILABLE FORMS: Tablet, 10, 25, and 50 mg; capsule, 75, 100, 125, and 150 mg

DOSAGE: *Adults:* Starting dose, 75 mg/day; may be increased to maximum of 150 mg/day. *Children:* 0.2–3.0 mg/kg PO immediately before patient is ready for sleep. Increase dose by 50% every 2–3 days to a maximum dose of 5 mg/kg/day.

ADMINISTRATION:
- PO with a glass of water.
- Drowsiness and/or dizziness will be exacerbated with concomitant alcohol consumption; alcohol should be avoided while taking this medication.
- Caution clients not to stop taking drug abruptly if used long-term.

SIDE EFFECTS:
- Hypertension; hypotension; syncope; ventricular arrhythmias; QT prolongation; torsades de pointes; AV block; MI; stroke; seizures; extrapyramidal symptoms; ataxia; tardive dyskinesia; paralytic ileus; increased intraocular pressure; blood dyscrasias; hallucinations; depression; mania; suicidality; SIADH; hepatitis; angioedema; psychosis; hyperthermia
- *Side effects that usually do not require medical attention*: Nausea; daytime drowsiness; headache; vomiting; dizziness; diarrhea; dry mouth; restlessness; constipation; blurred vision; nasal congestion; altered libido; appetite change; urinary hesitancy; increased appetite; amnesia; urticaria; gynecomastia; galactorrhea; paresthesias; photosensitivity; impotence

DRUG INTERACTIONS: This medicine may interact with the following medications: antiarrhythmics; dronedarone; dopamine; dobutamine; cimetidine; asenapine; flumazenil; isoproterenol; MAOIs; pimozide; potassium salts; paliperidone; pazopanib; pentamidine; NE; epinephrine; nilotinib; yohimbe; clarithromycin; haldol; propoxyphene; ranolazine; sibutramine; sotalol; St. John's wort; toremifene

PHARMACOKINETICS:
- Metabolized in the liver via CYP 2D6
- Peak plasma levels are reached in 2–5 hr.
Half-life: Average is 11–25 hr.

PRECAUTIONS:
- See patient as often as necessary if long-term use is indicated.
- Ensure that patient is aware not to exceed maximum dosage. Assess to ensure not at risk for suicide.
- Instruct patient to monitor for behavior changes.
- If patient is drowsy or dizzy, patient should not drive, use machinery, or attempt to accomplish any task that requires mental alertness.
- Avoid alcohol as concomitant use may exacerbate symptoms.

PATIENT AND FAMILY EDUCATION: Store at room temperature between 20°C and 25°C (59°F–77°F). Throw away any unused medication after the expiration date.

SPECIAL POPULATIONS:
- *Elderly*: More sensitive to TCAs; 100 mg should be maximum dose.
- *Hepatic impairment*: Modify dosage accordingly.
- *Pregnancy*: Category D.
- *Lactation*: Probably safe. Limited information in animals and/or humans demonstrates no risk/minimal risk of adverse effects to infant/breast milk; caution advised.
- *Children*: Older than 6 years of age, start with 1–3 mg/kg at hs. Increase 1–1.5 mg/kg q 3–4 days; maximum dose is 5 mg/kg/24 hr.

Class: Serotonin Antagonist and Reuptake Inhibitors (SARIs)

trazodone   *Oleptro, Desyrel*

INDICATIONS: Off-label use to treat sleep terror disorder.

AVAILABLE FORM: Tablet

DOSAGE: 25–50 mg PO immediately before patient is ready for sleep. Maximum dose, 200 mg qd. *Children: (6–12 years)*: Starting dose, 1.5–2 mg/kg/day

(cont.)

trazodone (*cont.*)

ADMINISTRATION:
- PO with a glass of water.
- Drowsiness and/or dizziness will be exacerbated with concomitant alcohol consumption; alcohol should be avoided while taking this medication.
- Caution clients not to stop taking drug abruptly if used long-term.

SIDE EFFECTS:
- Hypotension, orthostatic; ventricular arrhythmias; QT prolongation; hypertension; MI; priapism; serotonin syndrome; depression; suicidality; SIADH; hyponatremia; confusion; ataxia; syncope
- *Side effects that usually do not require medical attention:* Somnolence; xerostomia; headache; dizziness; nausea; vomiting; blurred vision; fatigue; diarrhea; constipation; edema; myalgia; nasal congestion; weight changes; tremor; malaise

DRUG INTERACTIONS: This medicine may interact with the following medications: linezolid; MAOIs; pimozide; sibutramine; sodium oxybate; St. John's wort; toremifene; antifungals; protease inhibitors; imatinib; warfarin

PHARMACOKINETICS:
- Exact mechanism of action unknown. Is thought to inhibit serotonin reuptake.
- Peak plasma levels are reached in 0.5–2 hr.

Half-life: Average is 3–6 hr.

PRECAUTIONS:
- See patient as often as necessary if long-term use is indicated.
- Ensure that patient is aware is not to exceed maximum dosage.
- Instruct patient to monitor for behavior changes.
- If patient is drowsy or dizzy, patient should not drive, use machinery, or attempt to accomplish any task that requires mental alertness.
- Avoid alcohol as concomitant use may exacerbate symptoms.

PATIENT AND FAMILY EDUCATION: Store at room temperature between 20°C and 25°C (59°F–77°F). Throw away any unused medication after the expiration date.

SPECIAL POPULATIONS:
- *Elderly:* More sensitive to TCAs. Use lowest effective dose.
- *Hepatic impairment:* Modify dosage accordingly.
- *Pregnancy:* Category C.
- *Lactation:* Probably safe. Limited information in animals and/or humans demonstrates no risk/minimal risk of adverse effects to infant/breast milk; caution advised.
- *Children:* Older than 6 years, start with 1.5–6 mg/kg/ at hs. Increase slowly q3–4 days. Maximum dose is 6 mg/kg/24 hr.

Sleepwalking Disorder

OVERVIEW
- Arousal from deep non-REM sleep results in sleepwalking occurring in Stage IV sleep, usually 1–2 hr into sleep
- May involve complex motor activity such as eating or driving
- Precipitated by fever, stress, sleep deprivation, and medications
- Occurs most often in school-aged children
- Genetic component linked with *HLA* gene
- No gender predominance
- Occurs typically between ages 3 and 10; affects 10–20% of all children and 1–4% of adults with somnambulism as a child

Psychopharmacology of Sleepwalking Disorder

Acute Treatment
- No FDA-approved medications.
- For adults with history of injurious NREM parasomnia, BZDs may be helpful.

Chronic Treatment
- For persistent symptoms, BZDs may improve symptoms.
- Use lowest dose possible to control symptoms.

CLASS	DRUG
Benzodiazepines (BZDs)	
	clonazepam *(Klonopin)* diazepam *(Valium)*
Tricyclic Antidepressants (TCAs)	
	imipramine pamoate *(Tofranil, Tofranil PM)* clomipramine *(Anafranil)*

Class: Benzodiazepines (BZDs)

clonazepam   *Klonopin*

INDICATIONS: Off-label use to treat sleep terror disorder.

AVAILABLE FORMS: Tablet, 0.5, 1, and 2 mg; disintegrating wafers, 0.125, 0.25, 0.5, 1, and 2 mg

DOSAGE: 0.5–2 mg PO immediately before patient is ready for sleep.

ADMINISTRATION:
- PO with a glass of water.
- Drowsiness and/or dizziness will be exacerbated with concomitant alcohol consumption; alcohol should be avoided while taking this medication.
- Caution clients not to stop taking drug abruptly if used long-term.

SIDE EFFECTS:
- Respiratory depression; hepatotoxicity; depression; suicidal ideations; seizure exacerbation; hypotension; elevated LFTs
- *Side effects that usually do not require medical attention*: Drowsiness; impaired coordination; nervousness; confusion; constipation; diarrhea; dry mouth; headache; impaired memory; rash; slurred speech; visual changes; fatigue; dysuria

DRUG INTERACTIONS: May interact with the following medications: chloramphenicol; cimetidine; clarithromycin; conivaptan; cyclosporine; delavirdine; imatinib; antifungals; protease inhibitors; telithromycin; valproic acid; propofol

PHARMACOKINETICS:
- BZD, hypnotic. Mechanism of action is thought to occur at the GABA receptor complex.

- Highly bound to plasma proteins.
- Peak plasma levels are reached in 1–4 hr.
Half-life: Average is 20–50 hr.

PRECAUTIONS:
- See patient as often as necessary if long-term use is indicated.
- Ensure that patient is aware not to exceed maximum dosage.
- Instruct patient to monitor for behavior changes.
- If patient is drowsy or dizzy, patient should not drive, use machinery, or attempt to accomplish any task that requires mental alertness.
- Avoid alcohol as concomitant use may exacerbate symptoms.

PATIENT AND FAMILY EDUCATION: Store at room temperature between 20°C and 25°C (59°F–77°F). Discard unused medication after the expiration date.

SPECIAL POPULATIONS:
- *Elderly*: More sensitive to hypnotics. Use lowest effective dose. Due to sedation and increased risk of falls, all BZDs are placed on Beers List of Potentially Inappropriate Medications for Geriatrics.
- *Hepatic impairment*: Modify dosage accordingly.
- *Pregnancy*: Category D.
- *Lactation*: Safety unknown. Caution advised.
- *Children*: Start with 0.01–0.03 mg/kg at hs. Increase by 0.25–0.5 mg q3 days until symptoms controlled. Maximum dose is 0.1–0.2 mg/kg/day.

diazepam   *Valium*

INDICATIONS: Off-label use to treat sleep terror disorder.

AVAILABLE FORMS: Tablet

DOSAGE: 2–10 mg PO immediately before patient is ready for sleep.

ADMINISTRATION:
- PO with a glass of water.
- Drowsiness and/or dizziness will be exacerbated with concomitant alcohol consumption; alcohol should be avoided while taking this medication.

- Caution clients not to stop taking drug abruptly if used long-term.

SIDE EFFECTS:
- Syncope; bradycardia; seizure exacerbation; respiratory depression; suicidal ideation; dependency; hypomania/mania; psychosis; jaundice; blood dyscrasias
- *Side effects that usually do not require medical attention*: Nausea; daytime drowsiness; headache; vomiting; dizziness; diarrhea; dry mouth; nervousness; constipation; blurred vision; nasal congestion; depression; hypotension; ataxia; altered
(cont.)

diazepam (cont.)

libido; appetite change; urinary retention; fatigue; phlebitis; muscle weakness; venous thrombosis; blurred vision; diplopia; dermatitis; elevated LFTs; hypersalivation; tremor; amnesia; dysarthria

DRUG INTERACTIONS: This medicine may interact with the following medications: chloramphenicol; conivaptan; cyclosporine; CNS depressants (including alcohol); antifungals; protease inhibitors; macrolides; isoniazid; efavirenz; delavirdine; cimetidine; clarithromycin; fluoxetine; gefitinib; imatinib; esomeprazole; felbamate; nefazodone; olanzapine/fluoxetine; omeprazole; naproxen/esomeprazole

PHARMACOKINETICS:
- BZD, hypnotic. Mechanism of action is thought to occur at the level of the GABA receptor complex.
- Highly bound to plasma proteins.
- Peak plasma levels are reached in 1–1.5 hr.
Half-life: Average is 30–60 hr.

PRECAUTIONS:
- See patient as often as necessary if long-term use is indicated.

- Ensure that patient is aware not to exceed maximum dosage.
- Instruct patient to monitor for behavior changes.
- If patient is drowsy or dizzy, patient should not drive, use machinery, or attempt to accomplish any task that requires mental alertness.
- Avoid alcohol as concomitant use may exacerbate symptoms.

PATIENT AND FAMILY EDUCATION: Store at room temperature between 20°C and 25°C (59°F–77°F). Throw away any unused medication after the expiration date.

SPECIAL POPULATIONS:
- *Elderly:* More sensitive to hypnotics. Use lowest effective dose.
- *Hepatic impairment:* Modify dosage accordingly.
- *Pregnancy:* Category D.
- *Lactation:* Excreted in breast milk. Not recommended for use in breastfeeding mothers.
- *Children:* Not for use in children.

Class: Tricyclic Antidepressants (TCAs)

Tofranil, Tofranil PM   imipramine pamoate

INDICATIONS: Used for the treatment of adults with depression/anxiety

AVAILABLE FORMS: *Tofranil:* Tablet, 25 and 50 mg; *Tofranil PM:* Capsule, 75, 100, 125, and 150 mg

DOSAGE: *Adults:* Start, 25–75 mg PO nightly and increase by 25–50 mg/day every 3–4 days; maximum, 300 mg/day; 100 mg/day in elderly patients. Can be given in divided doses. Must taper dose gradually to discontinue. *Children less than 12 yr:* Start, 1.5 mg/kg/day PO divided tid, increase by 1–1.5 mg/kg/day every 3–4 days; maximum, 5 mg/kg/day. *Older than 12 years:* Start, 30–40 mg/day PO divided qd-tid and increase by 10–25 mg/day every 3–4 days; maximum, 100 mg/day

ADMINISTRATION:
- PO with a glass of water.
- Do not crush, cut or chew extended-release tablets
- Do not abruptly stop taking the medication.
- Approved for pediatric patients except when used for nocturnal enuresis and depression for as young as 6 years.
- Use lowest effective dose for shortest duration

SIDE EFFECTS:
- *More common:* Drowsiness; dizziness; constipation; nausea/vomiting; urinary retention or frequency; libido changes; weight gain; general nervousness; galactorrhea,

- *Less common:* Cardiac arrhythmias; extrapyramidal symptoms; clotting disturbances; worsening depression; suicidiality; hyperthermia; hypertension

DRUG INTERACTIONS:
- Absolute contraindications include class IA antiarrhythmics, MAOIs such as phenetzine (*Nardil*), tranylcypromine (*Parnate*), isocarboxazid (*Marplan*), and selegiline (*Eldepryl*)
- Avoid using with cimetadine, amiodarone, clarithromycin, haldoperidol, St. John's wort
- Instruct clients to advise if they smoke, drink alcohol, or use illegal drugs.
▶**Alert:** This list may not describe all possible interactions. Instruct clients to provide a list of all the medicines, herbs, non-prescription drugs, or dietary supplements they use.

PHARMACOKINETICS: Tricyclic antidepressants are thought to work by inhibiting reuptake of NE and serotonin in the CNS, which potentiates the neurotransmitters. They also have significant anticholinergics, antihistaminic and alpha adrenergic activity on the cardiac system. These classes of antidepressants also possess class 1A antiarrhythmic activity, which can lead to depression of cardiac conduction potentially resulting in heart block or ventricular arrhythmias
Metabolism: Extensively by the liver within the CYP450: 1A2, 2C19, 2D6 (primary), 3A4 substrate

SLEEPWALKING DISORDER: Tricyclic Antidepressants (TCAs)

(cont.)

imipramine pamoate (cont.)

Excretion: Primarily in urine, less than 5% unchanged, also excreted in the bile/feces.
Half-life: 11–25 hr

PRECAUTIONS:

- See client as often as necessary to ensure the drug is working on the panic attacks, determine compliance, and review side effects
- Instruct client and family to watch for worsening depression or thoughts of suicide. Also watch out for sudden or severe changes in feelings such as feeling anxious, agitated, panicky, irritable, hostile, aggressive, impulsive, severely restless, overly excited and hyperactive, or not being able to sleep. If this happens, especially at the beginning of antidepressant treatment or after a change in dose, they should call the provider.
- Drowsy or dizzy: Do not drive, use machinery, or do anything that needs mental alertness until the effects of this medicine are known. Other medications that cause drowsiness can add to the drowsiness of imipramine.
- Caution patients not to stand or sit up quickly, especially if older. This reduces the risk of dizzy or fainting spells. Alcohol may interfere with the effect of this medicine. Avoid alcoholic drinks.
- Do not abruptly withdraw this drug as it may cause headache, nausea and malaise
- Advise to protect skin from ultraviolet light due to increased skin sensitivity.
- Grapefruit and grapefruit juice may interact with imipramine.
- Use with caution on patients with:
  - Major depressive disorder, psychosis, or bipolar affective disorder
  - A recent myocardial infarction

- Blood dyscrasias
- Respiratory disease
- Heart disease
- Liver disease
- Seizures (convulsions)
- Suicidal thoughts, plans, or attempts by patient or a family member
- An unusual or allergic reaction to imipramine, other medicines, foods, dyes, or preservatives

PATIENT AND FAMILY EDUCATION:

- Store imipramine at room temperature away from moisture and heat.
- Stopping this medication suddenly could cause unpleasant side effects.
- Take the missed dose as soon as remembered. If it is almost time for next dose, skip the missed dose and take the medicine at the next regularly scheduled time. *Do not* take extra medicine to make up the missed dose.

SPECIAL POPULATIONS:

- *Elderly*: Older patients may be more sensitive to the effects of tricyclic antidepressants. The smallest effective dose should be used. Dose adjustment necessary for patient with liver impairment
- *Pregnancy*: Category D; some clinical reports of congenital malformations, but no direct causal link.
- *Lactation*: Excreted in human breast milk, alternative medications are recommended
- *Children*: Tofranil is indicated for children older than 6 years with nocturnal enuresis or depression. Monitor closely for suicidal ideation with depression. *Tofranil PM* is not approved for children.

clomipramine   *Anafranil*

INDICATIONS: Used for the treatment of obsessions and OCD

AVAILABLE FORMS: Capsule

DOSAGE: Start, 25 mg PO daily then increase by 25 mg/day every 4–7 days; maximum, 100 mg/day in first 2 weeks. Maintenance dose, generally 250 mg/day. Taper dose gradually to discontinue. *Children:* 100–200 mg PO nightly; start, 25 mg PO daily then increase by 25 mg/day every 4–7 days; maximum, 3 mg/kg/day up to 100 mg/day in first 2 weeks. Maintenance dose up to 200 mg/day.

ADMINISTRATION:

- PO with a glass of water and on a full stomach to minimize GI side effects.
- Do not abruptly stop taking the medication.
- Approved for children 10 years old and above.
- Re-evaluate periodically the need for the medication.

SIDE EFFECTS:

- *More common:* Drowsiness, dizziness, constipation, nausea/vomiting, urinary retention or frequency, libido changes, weight gain, general nervousness, galactorrhea
- *Less common:* Cardiac arrhythmias, extrapyramidal symptoms, clotting disturbances, worsening depression, suicidality, hyperthermia, hypertension

DRUG INTERACTIONS:

- Absolute contraindications include class IA antiarrhythmics, MAOIs like phenetzine (*Nardil*), tranylcypromine (*Parnate*), isocarboxazid (*Marplan*), and selegiline (*Eldepryl*)
- Avoid using with cimetadine, amiodarone, clarithromycin, haloperidol, St. John's wort
- This list may not describe all possible interactions. Instruct clients to provide a list of all the medicines, herbs, nonprescription drugs, or dietary supplements they use.

(cont.)

SLEEPWALKING DISORDER: Tricyclic Antidepressants (TCAs)

clomipramine *(cont.)*

- Also, instruct clients to advise if they smoke, drink alcohol, or use illegal drugs.

PHARMACOKINETICS: Tricyclic antidepressants are thought to work by inhibiting reuptake of NE and serotonin in the CNS, which potentiates the neurotransmitters. They also have significant anticholinergics, antihistaminic and alpha-adrenergic activity on the cardiac system. These classes of antidepressants also possess class 1A antiarrhythmic activity, which can lead to depression of cardiac conduction potentially resulting in heart block or ventricular arrhythmias
Metabolism: Extensively metabolized in the liver within CYP450: 1A2, 2C19, 2D6 (primary), 3A4 substrate
Excretion: Urine 66%, feces
Half-life: 32 hr (clomipramine), 69 hr (desmethyl-clomipramine). Half-life may be prolonged at upper end of dosing range due to accumulation

PRECAUTIONS:
- See client as often as necessary to ensure the drug is working on OCD, determine compliance, and review side effects.
- Instruct client and family to watch for worsening depression or thoughts of suicide. Also, watch out for sudden or severe changes in feelings such as feeling anxious, agitated, panicky, irritable, hostile, aggressive, impulsive, severely restless, overly excited and hyperactive, or not being able to sleep. If this happens, especially at the beginning of antidepressant treatment or after a change in dose, they should call the provider
- Drowsy or dizzy: Do not drive, use machinery, or do anything that needs mental alertness until the effects of this medicine are known. Other medications that cause drowsiness can add to the drowsiness of chlorimipramine.
- Caution patients not to stand or sit up quickly, especially if older. This reduces the risk of dizzy or fainting spells. Alcohol may interfere with the effect of this medicine. Avoid alcoholic drinks.

- Do not abruptly withdraw this drug as it may cause headache, nausea and malaise.
- Advise to protect skin from ultraviolet light due to increased skin sensitivity.
- Grapefruit and grapefruit juice may interact with chlorimipramine.
- Use with caution on patients with:
  - Major depressive disorder, psychosis, or bipolar affective disorder
  - Recent myocardial infarction
  - Blood dyscrasias
  - Respiratory disease
  - Heart disease
  - Liver disease
  - Seizures (convulsions)
  - Psychoses or schizophrenia
  - Suicidal thoughts, plans, or attempts by patient or a family member
  - An unusual or allergic reaction to desipramine, other medicines, foods, dyes, or preservatives

PATIENT AND FAMILY EDUCATION:
- Store chlorimipramine at room temperature away from moisture and heat.
- Stopping this medication suddenly could cause unpleasant side effects.
- Take the missed dose as soon as remembered. If it is almost time for next dose, skip the missed dose and take the medicine at the next regularly scheduled time. *Do not* take extra medicine to make up the missed dose.

SPECIAL POPULATIONS:
- *Elderly*: Older patients may be more sensitive to the effects of tricyclic antidepressants. The smallest effective dose should be used. Caution in administration with significant renal and/or liver disease. Dose adjustments may be necessary. Monitor creatinine and liver functions.
- *Pregnancy*: Category C; unknown effects as there is limited study.
- *Lactation*: Excreted in human breast milk, use caution
- *Children*: Approved for children 10 years and older.

SLEEPWALKING DISORDER: Tricyclic Antidepressants (TCAs)

14

Dissociative Disorders

Depersonalization Disorder

OVERVIEW

- A depersonalization disorder occurs when an individual feels detached from one's mental processes or body.
- Symptoms include a sense of automation, of going through the motions of life but not experiencing it as though one were in a movie; i.e., feeling as if one was in a movie or dream or in an out-of-body experience.
- Individuals also feel as if they are floating on the ceiling looking down at themselves, or as if their body is dissolving, or as it they are robots, or on autopilot.
- This disorder is often comorbid with anxiety disorders, panic disorders, clinical depression, and bipolar disorder.
- Sufferers of this condition are able to distinguish between their own internal processes and the reality of the external world; they are not psychotic and are not harmful to society.
- The individual with this disorder feels as though time is "passing" them by and they are not in the present.

- Exacerbating factors include negative effects, stress, subjective threatening, social interaction and unfamiliar environments.
- Factors that diminish symptoms include comfort from interpersonal interactions, physical/emotional stimulation, and relaxation.
- These individuals have fears of losing control; they have trouble emotionally connecting with others and with maintaining attention. Therefore, they have some cognitive disruptions in their daily life.
- Their sense of other people is that they are unfamiliar or mechanical.
- Onset for this disorder is during the teenage years or early 20s.
- This disorder is found equally in men and women, with prevalence in the general population of 2.4%.
- This disorder has to be differentiated from epilepsy, migraine headaches, schizophrenia, panic disorder, acute stress disorder, and drug-abuse.

Psychopharmacology of Depersonalization Disorder

- No treatment recommendations or guidelines exist for depersonalization disorder, and it remains largely resistant to treatment.
- A variety of psychotherapeutic techniques have been used, such as cognitive behavioral therapy, but none have established efficacy to date.
- Clinical pharmacotherapy research is studying the effects of SSRIs, anticonvulsants, and opioid antagonists, but no recommendations have been put forth at this time.
- Subjects given benzodiazepines in a research study reported slight or definite improvement in depersonalization disorders but they mainly targeted the comorbid anxiety and stress and not the depersonalization disorder itself. To date, no clinical trials have included the use of benzodiazepines to validate their efficacy. Medications that might be used include lorazepam (*Ativan*), and alprazolam (*Xanax*).
- Some small studies were done using SSRIs using fluoxetine, but the studies failed to show improvement in the subjects studied.
- SSRI treatment created an overall improvement, but only by treating the anxiety and

depression. SSRIs have also been used in combination with lamotrigine, an anticonvulsant. Some SSRIs that might be used include fluoxetine (*Prozac*), sertraline (*Zoloft*), and paroxetine (*Paxil*).
- A TCA, clomipramine, was found to show significant improvement in depersonalization disorders. TCAs that might be used include amitriptyline (*Elavil*), and doxepin (*Sinequan*).
- Stimulants like methylphenidate (*Ritalin*) have been used with some benefit in some patients as have MAOIs like phenelzine (*Nardil*). Behavioral health specialists prescribe this medication.
- Naloxone, an opiate antagonist, was reported to improve symptoms, but there are no long-term studies. Naltrexone showed favorable improvements in the individuals, with an average decrease in 30% of the symptoms. Behavioral health specialists would prescribe this medication.
- Unfortunately, there are very few well-designed studies comparing different medications for depersonalization disorders.

CLASS	DRUG
Benzodiazepines (BZDs)	**Short-Term Use Until Other Agents Begin Effects**
	alprazolam (*Xanax, Niravam*) lorazepam (*Ativan*) clorazepate (*Tranxene*)
Selective Serotonin Reuptake Inhibitors (SSRIs)	**First-Line Drugs Used to Treat Comorbid Anxiety and Depression Commonly Seen With This Disorder**
	sertraline (*Zoloft*) fluoxetine (*Prozac, Sarafem*) paroxetine (*Paxil, Pexeva, Paxil CR*)
Tricyclic Antidepressants (TCAs)	**Used for Comorbid Depression Commonly Seen With This Disorder**
	clomipramine (*Anafranil*) amitriptyline (*Elavil*) doxepin (*Sinequan, Silenor*)
Amphetamine Derivatives (Psychostimulants)	**Used to Increase Focus**
	methylphenidate (*Ritalin, Concerta, Metadate CD, Metadate ER, Methylin, Methylin ER*)
Mood-Stablizing Anticonvulsants	**Used to Treat Comorbid Mood Disorders Such as Bipolar Disorder**
	lamotrigine (*Lamictal, Lamictal XR*)
Opioid Antagonists	**Used to Treat Condition With Some Degree of Success**
	naloxone (*Narcan*) naltrexone (*ReVia, Vivitrol*)

Class: Benzodiazepines (BZDs)

alprazolam   *Xanax, Niravam*

▶Schedule IV drug that requires a prescription. Maximum number of refills is 5 refills/6 mo.

INDICATIONS: Used to treat anxiety.

AVAILABLE FORMS: Tablet, 0.25, 0.5, 1, and 2 mg.

DOSAGE: *Adults:* 0.25–0.5 mg PO tid; maximum, 4 mg/day. Start at 0.25 mg PO tid. *Children:* Currently unavailable or not applicable.

ADMINISTRATION: The tablet is taken PO.

SIDE EFFECTS: Changes in appetite, changes in sexual desire, constipation, dizziness, drowsiness, dry mouth, increased saliva production, lightheadedness, tiredness, trouble concentrating, unsteadiness, weight changes.

DRUG INTERACTIONS: The following drugs are contraindicated: Chloramphenicol, clarithromycin, conivaptan, cyclosporin, delavirdine, efavirenz, fluvoxamine, imatinib, isoniazid, itraconazole, ketoconazole, posaconazole, protease inhibitors, sodium oxybate, telithromycin, and voriconazole (may increase benzodiazepine levels, risk of CNS depression, and psychomotor impairment).

PHARMACOKINETICS: Metabolized in the liver (CYP450 2C19, 3A4) and excreted in the urine.
Half-life: 11.2 hr (adults); 16.3 hr (elderly). It binds to benzodiazepine receptors and enhances GABA effects.

PRECAUTIONS: Serious reactions to the drug include syncope, tachycardia, seizures, respiratory depression, coma, suicidal ideation, and hypomania/mania.

PATIENT AND FAMILY EDUCATION:
- Inform provider about glaucoma, hepatic or renal impairment, drug-abuse history, salivary flow decrease (interferes with ODT absorption), or pregnancy.
- Do not stop taking this medication abruptly or decrease the dose without consulting the provider.
- Take the missed dose as soon as remembered. If it is time for the next dose, skip the missed dose and resume usual dosing schedule. Do not double the dose to catch up.

SPECIAL POPULATIONS
- *Elderly*: 0.25 mg PO bid or tid. Use lowest most effective dose. Due to sedative properties and increased risk of falls, all benzodiazepines are included on Beers List of Potentially Inappropriate Medications for Geriatrics.
- *Renal impairment:* No adjustment needed.
- *Hepatic impairment:* With advanced hepatic disease, start at 0.25 mg PO bid a day or tid and titrate gradually.
- *Pregnancy*: Contraindicated in pregnancy.
- *Children*: Pediatric dosing is currently unavailable.

Ativan   **lorazepam**

▶Schedule IV drug and requires prescription. Maximum number of refills is 5 refills/6 mo.

INDICATIONS: Used to treat anxiety.

AVAILABLE FORMS: Tablet, 0.5, 1, and 2 mg.

DOSAGE: *Adults*: For procedural sedation: 0.05 mg/kg IM ×1; maximum, 4 mg/dose given 2 hr before operation. IV, can be given at 0.044–0.05 mg/kg ×1; maximum, 4 mg/dose; 2 mg/dose in elderly given 15–20 min prior to hypnosis. *Children:* 0.05 mg/kg PO, IM or IV ×1; maximum dosage is 2 mg/dose. Give PO dose 1 hr prior to procedures; give IM more than 2 hr, and IV 15–20 min prior to procedure.

ADMINISTRATION: Can be given PO, IM, and IV. Take this medication with or without food at the same time every day. Do not suddenly stop taking this drug without notifying provider.

SIDE EFFECTS: Dizziness, weakness, unsteadiness, nausea, constipation, and fatigue.

DRUG INTERACTIONS: Sodium oxybate (*Xyrem*) is contraindicated and is known to increase benzodiazepine levels, risk of CNS depression, and psychomotor impairment.

PHARMACOKINETICS: Metabolized by the liver (CYP450). The drug enhances GABA effects.
Half-life: 14 hr.

PRECAUTIONS: Avoid abrupt withdrawal for long-term use, avoid use of alcohol, avoid use in depressed patients, avoid intra-arterial administration and avoid in drug-abuse patients.

PATIENT AND FAMILY EDUCATION:
- Inform provider of liver or kidney problems, alcohol or drug consumption, glaucoma, lung problems, or treatment for psychiatric disorders.
- Do not stop taking this medication abruptly or decrease the dose without consulting provider.
- Take the missed dose as soon as remembered. If it is time for the next dose, skip the missed dose and resume usual dosing schedule. Do not double the dose to catch up.

SPECIAL POPULATIONS
- *Elderly*: Caution is advised. Because of its sedative properties and increased risk of falls, all benzodiazepines are included on Beers List of Potentially Inappropriate Medications for Geriatrics
- *Renal impairment:* No adjustment is needed if using the oral form; however, dose may need to be adjusted if using the IV form.
- *Hepatic impairment:* Hepatic involvement may require decreasing the dose; in hepatic failure, use should be avoided.
- *Pregnancy/Lactation:* Do not use during pregnancy or during breastfeeding.
- *Children*: No adjustment is needed if using the oral form for impaired renal function. However, the dose may need to be adjusted for renal impairment if using the IV form. Hepatic involvement may require decreasing the dose, and in hepatic failure, use should be avoided.

Tranxene   **clorazepate**

▶Schedule IV drug. Maximum number of refills is 5 refills/6 mo.

INDICATIONS: Used to treat anxiety.

AVAILABLE FORMS: Tablet, 3.75, 7.5, and 15 mg

DOSAGE: *Adults*: 15–60 mg dose PO every day divided into bid or tid or 15–30 mg at bedtime. *Children: 9–12 year old:* Starts at 7.5 mg PO bid a day, increasing 7.5 mg every week; maximum, 60 mg/day. Alternatively, dose can begin at 0.3 mg/kg/day PO divided into bid or qid. *Over 12 years old:* Starting dose is 7.5 mg PO tid, increasing to 7.5 every week; maximum, 90 mg/day.

ADMINISTRATION: Take this medicine exactly as prescribed. Do not change the dose without consulting health care provider. Do not stop taking the drug without advice of the health care provider.

SIDE EFFECTS: Drowsiness, dizziness, various GI complaints, nervousness, blurred vision, dry mouth, headache, and confusion.

DRUG INTERACTIONS: Sodium oxybate (*Xyrem*) is contraindicated and is known to increase benzodiazepine levels, risk of CNS depression, and psychomotor impairment. Since this drug is a CNS depressant, the concomitant use of other CNS depressant drugs is contraindicated.

PHARMACOKINETICS: Metabolized in the liver (CYP450) and excreted primarily through the urine and feces.
Half-life: 40–50 hr

PRECAUTIONS: Serious reactions to the drug include hepatotoxicity, respiratory depression, seizure exacerbation, suicidality, dependency, and abuse.

PATIENT AND FAMILY EDUCATION:
- Avoid taking this drug if there is a known hypersensitivity to the drug or if there is acute narrow-angle glaucoma.
- Do not discontinue the drug without notifying the health care provider.
- Do not drive, operate heavy machinery, or do other dangerous activities until the effect of this drug is known.
- Avoid becoming pregnant while on this drug; if pregnancy occurs, alert health care provider immediately.

(cont.)

DEPERSONALIZATION DISORDER: Benzodiazepines (BZDs)

clorazepate (cont.)

SPECIAL POPULATIONS:
- *Elderly*: The elderly or debilitated patients need to start at 7.5–15 mg/day. Because of its sedative property and increased risk of falls, all benzodiazepines are included on Beers List of Potentially Inappropriate Medications for Geriatrics
- *Renal impairment*: No adjustment needed.

- *Hepatic impairment*: Not defined at this time.
- *Pregnancy*: FDA category C but trimester-specific or population-specific risks.
- *Lactation*: Probably safe during lactation but caution advised.
- *Children*: Pediatric dosing is currently unavailable or not applicable.

Class: Selective Serotonin Reuptake Inhibitors (SSRIs)

sertraline   *Zoloft*

INDICATIONS: Used to treat anxiety and depression.

AVAILABLE FORMS: Tablet, 25, 50, and 100 mg; oral solution, 20 mg/mL

DOSAGE: *Adults:* 25–200 mg PO every day. Usual initial dose is 25–50 mg PO every day for depression and 25 mg PO every day for anxiety. After 1 week, may increase daily dose by 25, and then wait for a few weeks before increasing dose further.

ADMINISTRATION: Administered PO. Never stop an antidepressant medicine without first talking to a health care provider. Do not start new medicines without notifying the health care provider. Take this medicine, usually once daily. Tablet form can be taken with or without food; capsule form is usually taken with food after breakfast or after evening meal. It may take 4 weeks before an effect is noticed.

SIDE EFFECTS: Common side effects include nausea, headache, insomnia, diarrhea, dry mouth, ejaculatory dysfunction, somnolence, asthenia, tremor, dyspepsia, anorexia, constipation, libido decrease, nervousness, anxiety, rash, and abnormal vision.

DRUG INTERACTIONS: The following drugs may interact with sertraline: Linezolid (*Zyvox*) may increase the risk of serotonin syndrome and neuroleptic syndrome. MAOIs are contraindicated within 5 weeks of sertraline use because they may increase the risk of serotonin syndrome and neuroleptic syndrome. Pimozide (*Orap*) may increase the risk of bradycardia, increase pimozide levels, and increase risk of QT prolongation and cardiac arrhythmias. Thioridazine (*Mellaril*) may increase risk of QT prolongation, cardiac arrhythmias, SIADH, hyponatremia, serotonin syndrome, neuroleptic and malignant syndrome. Cimetidine (*Tagamet*) may increase the sertraline levels in blood by decreasing metabolism of the drug by the liver.

PHARMACOKINETICS: Metabolized by the liver (CYP450; 2C9, 2D6, 3A4) and is excreted in the urine (40–50%) and in the feces (40–45%).
Half-life: 26 hr. This drug selectively inhibits serotonin reuptake.

PRECAUTIONS: Black box warning states that there is an increased risk of suicidality in children, adolescents, and young adults especially during the first months of treatment. Caution should be exercised in patients with seizure disorders, disulfiram use, patients younger than 25 years of age, patients with liver impairment, hyponatremic patients, patients using alcohol, and those with mania/hypomania.

PATIENT AND FAMILY EDUCATION:
- Notify the provider if there is increased depression while taking this drug.
- Notify the health care provider if there is hypoglycemia, seizures or mania, glaucoma, or abnormal bleeding/bruising.

SPECIAL POPULATIONS:
- *Elderly*: Caution must be exercised in the use of this drug. May require decreased dosage.
- *Renal impairment*: No adjustment needed.
- *Hepatic impairment:* Patients with hepatic impairment may need to have decreased dosing and/or frequency.
- *Pregnancy*: FDA category C but trimester-specific.
- *Children*: Not approved in pediatric patients except in OCD.

fluoxetine   *Prozac, Sarafem*

INDICATIONS: Used for depression.

AVAILABLE FORMS: Capsule, 10, 20, and 40 mg; suspension, 20 mg/5 mL

DOSAGE: *Adults:* 20–80 mg PO qam. Starting dose is 20 mg PO qam and may be increased after several weeks. Maximum is 80 mg/day. Doses more than 20 mg/day may be divided into bid a day dosing. *Children: (8–18 yr):* 10–20 mg PO every day starting with 10 mg PO every day for 7 days.

ADMINISTRATION: Administered PO. Never stop an antidepressant medicine without first talking to a health care provider. Do not start new medicines without notifying the health care provider. Take this medicine, usually once daily. Tablet form can be taken with or without food; capsule form is usually
(cont.)

fluoxetine (cont.)

taken with food after breakfast or after evening meal. It may take 4 weeks before an effect is noticed.

SIDE EFFECTS: Common reactions include nausea, headache, insomnia, nervousness, anxiety, asthenia, diarrhea, anorexia, dizziness, dry mouth, tremor, dyspepsia, sweating, ejaculatory dysfunction, constipation, flu syndrome, libido decrease, rash, and abnormal vision.

DRUG INTERACTIONS:
- The following drugs may interact with fluoxetine: linezolid (*Zyvox*) may increase the risk of serotonin syndrome, neuroleptic syndrome, and in combination with fluvoxamine (*Luvox*) may increase rasagiline (*Azilect*) levels, risk of adverse effects
- MAOIs: Contraindicated within 5 weeks of sertraline use because it may increase the risk of serotonin syndrome, neuroleptic syndrome and in combination with fluvoxamine may increase rasagiline levels, risk of adverse effects
- Pimozide (*Orap*) may increase the risk of bradycardia, increase pimozide levels, risk of QT prolongation, cardiac arrhythmias, and thioridazine (*Mellaril*) may increase thioridazine levels, risk of QT prolongation, cardiac arrhythmias, risk of SIADH, hyponatremia, serotonin syndrome, neuroleptic and malignant syndrome.

PHARMACOKINETICS: Metabolized by the liver (CYP450, 2C19 and 2D6) and excreted in the urine (80%) and feces (15%).

Half-life: 4–6 days. The drug selectively inhibits serotonin reuptake.

PRECAUTIONS: Caution is recommended in patients younger than 25 years old. Caution should also be exercised in those with the following conditions: diabetes mellitus, hyponatremia, seizures, mania/hypomania, or those with volume depletion.

PATIENT AND FAMILY EDUCATION:
- Report any increase in depression as the risk of suicidality in children, adolescents, and young adults increases with major depressive or other psychiatric disorders especially during the first months of treatment.
- Advise health care provider if there is glaucoma, hypoglycemia, or abnormal bleeding tendencies.

SPECIAL POPULATIONS:
- *Elderly:* Caution should be used in the use of this drug with the elderly.
- *Renal impairment:* No adjustment is needed for those with kidney disease.
- *Hepatic impairment:* Dose may need to be decreased in patients with liver disease.
- *Pregnancy:* FDA category C but trimester-specific.
- *Lactation:* The safety in lactation is unknown.
- *Children:* Use of this drug in children carries the risk of suicide.

Paxil, Pexeva, Paxil CR　　**paroxetine**

INDICATIONS: Used to treat anxiety and depression.

AVAILABLE FORMS: Tablet, 10, 20, 30, and 40 mg; controlled-release tablet, 12.5, and 25 mg; suspension 10 mg/5 mL

DOSAGE: *Adults:* Depression: 20–50 mg PO each day. Starting dose is usually 20 mg PO qam; maximum 50 mg/day. Anxiety 20 mg PO qam; maximum 50 mg/day.

ADMINISTRATION: Administered PO. Never stop an antidepressant medicine without first talking to a health care provider. Do not start new medicines without notifying the health care provider. Take this medicine, usually once daily. Tablet form can be taken with or without food; capsule form is usually taken with food after breakfast or after evening meal. It may take 4 weeks before an effect is noticed.

SIDE EFFECTS: Nausea, somnolence, headache, asthenia, dizziness, constipation, libido decrease, diarrhea, sedation, sweating, dry mouth, ejaculatory dysfunction, tremor, anorexia, nervousness, anxiety, and abnormal vision.

DRUG INTERACTIONS: The following drugs may interact with *Paxil*:
- Linezolid (*Zyvox*) may increase the risk of serotonin syndrome, neuroleptic syndrome, and in combination with fluvoxamine (*Luvox*) may increase rasagiline (*Azilect*) levels, risk of adverse effects
- MAOIs: Contraindicated within 5 weeks of sertraline use because it may increase the risk of serotonin syndrome, neuroleptic syndrome and in combination with fluvoxamine (*Luvox*) may increase rasagiline (*Azilect*) levels, risk of adverse effects
- Pimozide (*Orap*) may increase the risk of bradycardia, increase pimozide levels, risk of QT prolongation, cardiac arrhythmias
- Thioridazine (*Mellaril*) may increase thioridazine levels, risk of QT prolongation, cardiac arrhythmias, risk of SIADH, hyponatremia, serotonin syndrome, neuroleptic and malignant syndrome.

PHARMACOKINETICS: Metabolized in the liver (CYP450, 2D6) and is excreted in the urine (64%) and feces (36%).
Half-life: 21 hr

(cont.)

paroxetine (cont.)

PRECAUTIONS: There is an increased risk of suicidality in younger patients and young adults.

PATIENT AND FAMILY EDUCATION:
- Inform health care provider if there is seizure disorder, renal/liver impairment, glaucoma, alcohol addition or a bleeding disorder.
- That it may take 4 weeks before full therapeutic effects are noticed
- Side effects may occur within the first week of treatment.

SPECIAL POPULATIONS
- *Elderly*: Dosage is usually reduced in half for elderly patients to 10 mg PO qam and a maximum dose of 40 mg/day for treatment of anxiety and depression.
- *Renal impairment:* Renal dose adjustment may be required. In adult dosing, if the CrCl is below 30, then the initial dose is started at 10 mg every day.
- *Hepatic impairment:* Reduced dosing may be required in children. In adults with severe impairment the dose is started at 10 mg every day.
- *Pregnancy*: There is positive evidence of human fetal risk.
- *Lactation:* There is minimal risk to the baby during lactation.
- *Children*: Caution should be exercised and patients closely monitored for the duration of treatment.

Class: Tricyclic Antidepressants (TCAs)

clomipramine   *Anafranil*

AVAILABLE FORMS: Capsule, 25, 50, and 75 mg.

DOSAGE: *Adults:* 150–300 mg PO at bedtime. Initial dosing is 25 mg PO every day with increments 25 mg/day every 4–7 days; maximum, 100 mg/day in first 2 weeks. *Children over 10 yr:* 100–200 mg PO at bedtime. Initial dose is 25 mg PO every day and increase 25 mg/day every 4–7 days; maximum 3 mg/kg/day up to 100 mg/day in first 2 weeks and up to 200 mg/day.

ADMINISTRATION: Take this medicine PO with or without food. Do not take more or less of the drug or take it more frequently than prescribed. Avoid eating grapefruit or drinking grapefruit juice while being treated with this drug. Take this drug at the same time every day. Do not suddenly stop taking this drug; talk to the health care provider if desire to discontinue.

SIDE EFFECTS: Common reactions to the drug include the following: dry mouth, drowsiness, tremor, dizziness, headache, constipation, ejaculatory dysfunction, fatigue, nausea/vomiting, sweating, insomnia, appetite changes, weight changes, impotence, dyspepsia, libido changes, blurred vision, nervousness, urinary frequency, diarrhea, myoclonus, impaired memory, anxiety/agitation, paresthesias, rash/urticaria, palpitations/tachycardia, pruritus, concentration difficulty, galactorrhea, and urinary retention.

DRUG INTERACTIONS:
- The following drugs are contraindicated with amitriptyline: antiarrhythmics class IA such as procainamide, quinidine gluconate, quinidine sulfate, disopyramide (*Norpace*) may increase risk of QT prolongation)
- Cisapride (*Propulsid*) may increase risk of QT prolongation, cardiac arrhythmias, dronedarone (*Multaq*) may increase TCA levels and risk of adverse effects, increase risk of QT prolongation, cardiac arrhythmias, flumazenil (*Romazicon*) may increase risk of cardiac arrhythmias, seizures
- MAOIs such as selegiline (*Eldepryl/Zelapar*), procarbazine (*Matulane*), phenelzine (*Nardil*), tranylcypromine (*Parnate*), isocarboxazid (*Marplan*), selegiline transdermal (*Eldepryl/Zelapar*), rasagiline (*Azilect*) may result in CNS overstimulation, hyperpyrexia, seizures, death
- Pimozide (*Orap*) may increase risk of CNS depression, and psychomotor impairment, QT prolongation, arrhythmias, anticholinergic effects, hyperpyrexia; potassium salts such as potassium acid phosphate, and potassium citrate, potassium chloride, potassium iodide, potassium phosphate/sodium phosphate, potassium acid, phosphate/sodium acid phosphate, and potassium phosphate are contraindicated for solid potassium dose forms
- Weigh risk/benefit of thyroid protection with solid iodide salt forms, may delay solid potassium passage through GI tract, increase risk of ulcerative/stenotic lesions

PHARMACOKINETICS:
- Metabolized in the liver extensively (CYP450, 1A2, 2C19, 2D6) and is excreted in the urine (66%) and in the feces.
- The exact mechanism of action is unknown. It inhibits norepinephrine and serotonin reuptake.

Half-life: 32 hr.

PATIENT AND FAMILY EDUCATION:
- Do not stop taking this medicine without notifying the health care provider.
- Anxiety symptoms may temporarily worsen when first starting clomipramine.
- Notify doctor or pharmacist promptly, if any of these effects persist or worsen.
- To relieve dry mouth, suck on (sugarless) hard candy or ice chips, chew (sugarless) gum, drink water, or use a saliva substitute.

(cont.)

DEPERSONALIZATION DISORDER: Tricyclic Antidepressants (TCAs)

clomipramine (cont.)

- To prevent constipation, maintain a diet adequate in fiber, drink plenty of water, and exercise. In case of constipation, consult pharmacist for help in selecting a laxative (e.g., stimulant-type with stool softener).
- Inform clinician immediately if any of these unlikely but serious side effects occur: mental/mood changes (e.g., confusion, depression, hallucinations, memory problems), enlarged/painful breasts, unwanted breast milk production, irregular/painful menstrual periods, muscle stiffness/twitching, feelings of restlessness, ringing in the ears, sexual problems (e.g., decreased sexual ability, changes in desire), shakiness (tremors), numbness/tingling of the hands/feet, trouble urinating, severe vomiting.
- Inform clinician immediately if any of these rare but very serious side effects occur: easy bruising/bleeding, signs of infection (e.g., fever, persistent sore throat), unusual/uncontrolled movements (especially of the tongue/face/lips), severe stomach/abdominal pain, dark urine, yellowing of eyes/skin.
- Seek immediate medical attention if any of these rare but very serious side effects occur: black stools, chest pain, fainting, high fever, slow/fast/irregular heartbeat, seizures, vomit that looks like coffee grounds.

SPECIAL POPULATIONS:
- *Elderly:* Caution should be exercised.
- *Renal impairment:* Significant caution is warranted with renal impairment.
- *Hepatic impairment:* Caution is advised in children with hepatic impairment.
- *Pregnancy/Lactation:* This is a category C drug; animal studies have shown adverse fetal effects. Using this drug during lactation is presumed to carry risks.
- *Children:* There is an increased risk of suicidality in children, adolescents, and young adults.

Elavil   **amitriptyline**

AVAILABLE FORMS: Tablet, 10, 25, 50, 75, 100, and 150 mg

DOSAGE: *Adults:* Between 50 and 150 mg PO at bedtime. Dosage can be increased by 25–50 mg/day every 2–3 days until desired effect occurs. Maximum dosage, 300 mg/day. *Children 9 to 12 yr:* 1–3 mg/kg/day PO tid with gradual increases of 0.5 mg/kg/day every 2–3 days. Maximum dosage for children, 5 mg/kg/day up to 200 mg/day.

SIDE EFFECTS: Common reactions include drowsiness, dry mouth, dizziness, constipation, blurred vision, palpitations, tachycardia, uncoordination, appetite increase, nausea/vomiting, sweating, weakness, disorientation, confusion, restlessness, insomnia, anxiety/agitation, urinary retention/frequency, rash/urticaria, pruritus, weight gain, libido changes, impotence, gynecomastia, galactorrhea, tremor, hypo/hyperglycemia, paresthesias, and photosensitivity.

DRUG INTERACTIONS:
- The following drugs are contraindicated with amitriptyline: antiarrhythmics class 1A such as procainamide, quinidine gluconate, quinidine sulfate, disopyramide (*Norpace*) may increase risk of QT prolongation)
- Cisapride (*Propulsid*) may increase risk of QT prolongation, cardiac arrhythmias, dronedarone (*Multaq*) may increase TCA levels and risk of adverse effects, increase risk of QT prolongation, cardiac arrhythmias, flumazenil (*Romazicon*) may increase risk of cardiac arrhythmias, seizures
- MAOIs such as selegiline (*Eldepryl/Zelapar*), procarbazine (*Matulane*), phenelzine (*Nardil*),

tranylcypromine (*Parnate*), isocarboxazid (*Marplan*), selegiline transdermal (*Eldepryl/Zelapar*), rasagiline (*Azilect*) may result in CNS overstimulation, hyperpyrexia, seizures, death
- Pimozide (*Orap*) may increase risk of CNS depression, and psychomotor impairment, QT prolongation, arrhythmias, anticholinergic effects, hyperpyrexia; potassium salts such as potassium acid phosphate, and potassium citrate, potassium chloride, potassium iodide, potassium phosphate/sodium phosphate, potassium acid, phosphate/sodium acid phosphate, and potassium phosphate are contraindicated for solid potassium dose forms
- Weigh risk/benefit of thyroid protection with solid iodide salt forms, may delay solid potassium passage through GI tract, increase risk of ulcerative/stenotic lesions

PHARMACOKINETICS: Metabolized extensively in the liver (CYP450, 1A2, 2D6) and is excreted in urine (18% unchanged) and feces.
Half-life: 10–26 hr

PRECAUTIONS: Use caution in patients with the following conditions: cardiovascular disease, urinary retention, prostatic hypertrophy, glaucoma, seizure disorders, thyroid disease, schizophrenia, bipolar disorder, alcohol abuse, GI/GU obstruction, Parkinson's disease, diabetes mellitus, asthma, and increased intracranial pressure.

PATIENT AND FAMILY EDUCATION:
- Do not stop taking this medicine without notifying the health care provider.
- Anxiety symptoms may temporarily worsen when first starting clomipramine.

(cont.)

DEPERSONALIZATION DISORDER: Tricyclic Antidepressants (TCAs)

amitriptyline (cont.)

- Notify doctor or pharmacist promptly if any of these effects persist or worsen.
- To relieve dry mouth, suck on (sugarless) hard candy or ice chips, chew (sugarless) gum, drink water, or use a saliva substitute.
- To prevent constipation, maintain a diet adequate in fiber, drink plenty of water, and exercise. In case of constipation, consult pharmacist for help in selecting a laxative (e.g., stimulant-type with stool softener).
- Inform clinician immediately if any of these unlikely but serious side effects occur: mental/mood changes (e.g., confusion, depression, hallucinations, memory problems), enlarged/painful breasts, unwanted breast milk production, irregular/painful menstrual periods, muscle stiffness/twitching, feelings of restlessness, ringing in the ears, sexual problems (e.g., decreased sexual ability, changes in desire), shakiness (tremors), numbness/tingling of the hands/feet, trouble urinating, severe vomiting.
- Inform clinician immediately if any of these rare but very serious side effects occur: easy bruising/bleeding, signs of infection (e.g., fever, persistent sore throat), unusual/uncontrolled movements (especially of the tongue/face/lips), severe stomach/abdominal pain, dark urine, yellowing of eyes/skin.
- Seek immediate medical attention if any of these rare but very serious side effects occur: black stools, chest pain, fainting, high fever, slow/fast/irregular heartbeat, seizures, vomit that looks like coffee grounds.

SPECIAL POPULATIONS:
- *Elderly:* Elderly patients may need a reduced dosage. 10–25 mg each day with increases of 10–25 mg at bedtime every 2–3 days may be sufficient.
- *Renal impairment:* No adjustment is given for patients with renal impairment.
- *Hepatic impairment:* Dosing in the presence of hepatic dysfunction is not given; caution is advised.
- *Pregnancy:* Safety not established. Use with caution.
- *Children:* There is an increased risk of suicidality in children, adolescents, and young adults with major depressive or other psychiatric conditions.

| doxepin | *Sinequan, Silenor* |

INDICATIONS: Used for anxiety/depression

AVAILABLE FORMS: Capsule, 10, 25, 50, 75, 100, and 150 mg; solution, 10 mg/mL

DOSAGE: *Adults:* 150–300 mg PO at bedtime. The initial dose is 25–75 mg PO at bedtime. Maximum, 300 mg/day. *Children:* Dosing is currently unavailable or not applicable.

ADMINISTRATION: Take this medication regularly in order to get the most benefit and at the same time every day. Do not stop taking this medication without consulting the health care provider. If this medicine should be taken only once a day, take at bedtime to reduce daytime sleepiness.

SIDE EFFECTS: Common reactions include drowsiness, dry mouth, dizziness, constipation, blurred vision, palpitations, tachycardia, uncoordination, appetite increase, nausea/vomiting, sweating, weakness, disorientation, confusion, restlessness, insomnia, anxiety/agitation, urinary retention/frequency, rash/urticaria, pruritus, weight gain, libido changes, impotence, gynecomastia, galactorrhea, tremor, hypo/hyperglycemia, paresthesias, and photosensitivity.

DRUG INTERACTIONS:
- The following drugs are contraindicated with doxepin: antiarrhythmics class 1A such as procainamide, quinidine gluconate, quinidine sulfate, disopyramide (*Norpace*) may increase risk of QT prolongation)

- Cisapride (*Propulsid*) may increase risk of QT prolongation, cardiac arrhythmias; dronedarone (*Multaq*) may increase TCA levels and risk of adverse effects, increase risk of QT prolongation, cardiac arrhythmias; flumazenil (*Romazicon*) may increase risk of cardiac arrhythmias, seizures
- MAOIs such as selegiline (*Eldepryl/Zelapar*), procarbazine (*Matulane*), phenelzine (*Nardil*), tranylcypromine (*Parnate*), isocarboxazid (*Marplan*), selegiline transdermal (*Eldepryl/Zelapar*), rasagiline (*Azilect*) may result in CNS overstimulation, hyperpyrexia, seizures, death.
- Pimozide (*Orap*) may increase risk of CNS depression, and psychomotor impairment, QT prolongation, arrhythmias, anticholinergic effects, hyperpyrexia; potassium salts such as potassium acid phosphate, and potassium citrate, potassium chloride, potassium iodide, potassium phosphate/sodium phosphate, potassium acid, phosphate/sodium acid phosphate, and potassium phosphate are contraindicated for solid potassium dose forms.
- Weigh risk/benefit of thyroid protection with solid iodide salt forms, may delay solid potassium passage through GI tract, increase risk of ulcerative/stenotic lesions.

PHARMACOKINETICS:
- Metabolized extensively in the liver (CYP450, 2C9/19, 2D6) and is excreted in the urine.
- The exact mechanism of action is unknown; inhibits norepinephrine and serotonin reuptake.

(cont.)

DEPERSONALIZATION DISORDER: Tricyclic Antidepressants (TCAs)

doxepin (cont.)

Half-life: 6–8 hr

PRECAUTIONS: Exercise caution when using this medicine in patients with prostatic hypertrophy, myocardial infarction, urinary retention, GI/GU obstruction, cardiovascular disease, asthma, diabetes mellitus, Parkinson's disease, schizophrenia, bipolar disorder, thyroid disease, increased intracranial pressure, and alcohol abuse.

PATIENT AND FAMILY EDUCATION:
- Do not stop taking this medicine without notifying the health care provider.
- Anxiety symptoms may temporarily worsen when first starting clomipramine.
- Notify doctor or pharmacist promptly if any of these effects persist or worsen.
- To relieve dry mouth, suck on (sugarless) hard candy or ice chips, chew (sugarless) gum, drink water, or use a saliva substitute.
- To prevent constipation, maintain a diet adequate in fiber, drink plenty of water, and exercise. In case of constipation, consult pharmacist for help in selecting a laxative (e.g., stimulant-type with stool softener).
- Inform clinician immediately if any of these unlikely but serious side effects occur: mental/mood changes (e.g., confusion, depression, hallucinations, memory problems), enlarged/painful breasts, unwanted breast milk production, irregular/painful menstrual periods, muscle stiffness/twitching, feelings of restlessness, ringing in the ears, sexual problems (e.g., decreased sexual ability, changes in desire), shakiness (tremors), numbness/tingling of the hands/feet, trouble urinating, severe vomiting.
- Inform clinician immediately if any of these rare but very serious side effects occur: easy bruising/bleeding, signs of infection (e.g., fever, persistent sore throat), unusual/uncontrolled movements (especially of the tongue/face/lips), severe stomach/abdominal pain, dark urine, yellowing of eyes/skin.
- Seek immediate medical attention if any of these rare but very serious side effects occur: black stools, chest pain, fainting, high fever, slow/fast/irregular heartbeat, seizures, vomit that looks like coffee grounds.

SPECIAL POPULATIONS
- *Elderly:* Exercise caution. Elderly patients may need a reduced dosage.
- *Renal impairment:* No adjustment for renal impairment.
- *Hepatic impairment:* There is no dosing defined with hepatic impairment.
- *Pregnancy:* This is a category C drug. Animal studies show adverse fetal effects but there have been no controlled human studies.
- *Lactation:* It is unsafe to breast feed and use this drug.
- *Children:* There is an increased risk for suicidality in children, adolescents, and young adults with major depressive or other psychiatric disorders.

Class: Amphetamine Derivatives (Psychostimulants)

Ritalin, Concerta, Metadate CD, Metadate ER, Methylin, Methylin ER   **methylphenidate**

▶ Schedule II drug that requires prescription. No refills or verbal order allowed.

INDICATIONS: Used to increase focus during hypnotic sessions.

AVAILABLE FORMS: Tablet, 5, 10, 15, and 20 mg; extended-release tablet, 10, 20, 30, 40, and 60 mg

DOSAGE: *Adults:* 5–15 mg of immediate-release formulation PO bid or tid. *Children over 6 yr:* 0.3–2 mg/kg/day PO bid or tid. Dose can be increased 0.1 mg/kg/dose or 5–10 mg/day every 7 days; maximum, 2 mg/kg/day up to 60 mg/day. Duration is 3–5 hr

ADMINISTRATION: PO

SIDE EFFECTS: Some common side effects include nervousness, insomnia, anorexia, abdominal pain, weight loss, tachycardia, nausea, motor tics, headache, palpitations, dizziness, fever, rash, urticaria, depression, drowsiness, dyskinesia, angina, blood pressure changes, visual disturbances, and elevated liver transaminases.

PHARMACOKINETICS:
- Metabolized in the liver (CYP450) and excreted in the urine.
- Stimulates CNS activity and blocks the reuptake and increases release of norepinephrine and dopamine in extraneuronal space.

Half-life: 2–3 hr

PRECAUTIONS: Caution should be exercised due to drug dependence. Other serious reactions include aggressive behavior, stroke, sudden death, seizures, arrhythmias, myocardial infarction, exfoliative dermatitis, erythema multiforme, erythema multiforme, thrombocytopenic purpura, leucopenia, neuroleptic malignant syndrome, cerebral arteritis, and hepatic coma

PATIENT AND FAMILY EDUCATION:
- Take 30–45 min before meals, last dose before 6 p.m.
- Inform health care provider if used an MAOI within 14 days, if there is hypertension, bipolar disorder, hyperthyroidism, phenylketonuria,

(cont.)

DEPERSONALIZATION DISORDER: Amphetamine Derivatives (Psychostimulants) glaucoma, heart disease, Tourette's syndrome, or psychosis.

SPECIAL POPULATIONS
- *Elderly:* May need reduced dosage.
- *Renal impairment:* Not defined.

- *Hepatic impairment:* Not defined.
- *Pregnancy:* Category C.
- *Lactation:* Probably safe during lactation.
- *Children:* Dosages for children are available.

Class: Mood-Stablizing Anticonvulsants

lamotrigine *Lamictal, Lamictal XR*

INDICATIONS: Used to treat bipolar disorder in adults.

AVAILABLE FORMS: Tablet, 25, 100, 150, and 200 mg; chewable tablet, 2, 5, and 25 mg.

DOSAGE: *Adults:* Starting dose, 25 mg PO every day for 2 weeks; then 50 mg every day for 2 weeks; then 100 mg every day for 1 week; maximum, 200 mg/day.

ADMINISTRATION:
- Discontinue medicine at first sign of a rash.
- This medicine should be taken as directed and is well tolerated in the recommended doses. Individuals taking this medicine should carry an identification card to alert medical personnel who might be caring for them.
- The potential carcinogenic, mutagenic, and fertility effects are unknown.
- Naltrexone is a category C drug; use in pregnancy if the potential benefit outweighs the risk. It is unknown if naltrexone is excreted in breast milk so caution should be exercised when administered to a nursing woman.
- Use for children under age 18 years has not been established. Individuals taking opioid containing medicines, such as cough and cold preparations, antidiarrheal preparations, and opioid analgesics with naltrexone may not benefit from these medicines.
- The concomitant use of naltrexone and disulfiram is unknown, but it is not recommended to take two potentially hepatotoxic medicines.
- Naltrexone does not interfere with drug testing using urine samples.

SIDE EFFECTS: Common reactions to the drug include dizziness, headache, diplopia, ataxia, asthenia, nausea, blurred vision, somnolence, rhinitis, rash, pharyngitis, vomiting, cough, flu syndrome, dysmenorrheal, uncoordination, insomnia, diarrhea, fever, abdominal pain, depression, tremor, anxiety, vaginitis, speech disturbance, seizures, weight loss, photosensitivity, nystagmus, constipation, and dry mouth.

DRUG INTERACTIONS: Avoid using the following drugs with this medicine:
- Oral progesterone contraceptives (may decrease hormonal contraceptive levels)

- Etonogestrel subdermal implant (may decrease hormonal contraceptive levels)
- Ginkgo biloba, Eun-haeng, fossil tree, ginkyo, icho, ityo, Japanese silver apricot, kew tree, maidenhair tree, salisburia, silver apricot (may decrease anticonvulsant efficacy)
- Medroxyprogesterone acetate (may decrease hormonal contraceptive levels)
- St. John's wort (may decrease lamotrigine levels as clearance is increased)

PHARMACOKINETICS: Metabolized by the liver (CYP450). It is excreted in urine 94% and feces 2%. **Half-life:** 25 hr

PRECAUTIONS: Caution should be exercised when administering this medicine to patients with suicide risk, hepatic impairment, renal impairment, and hypersensitivity to antiepileptic drugs and to pregnant women

PATIENT AND FAMILY EDUCATION:
- Do not stop taking this drug suddenly; it must be tapered by health care provider.
- Notify the health care provider immediately if depression symptoms increase.

SPECIAL POPULATIONS:
- *Elderly:* Caution should be exercised.
- *Renal impairment:* If the creatinine clearance is 10–50, decrease dose by 25%. If the creatinine clearance is less than 10, give 100 mg every other day. Give 100 mg after dialysis or 100 mg every other day.
- *Hepatic impairment:* For moderate to severe impairment, decrease dose by 25%. If severe impairment, decrease dose by 50%.
- *Pregnancy:* Category C drug; animal studies show adverse fetal effect(s) but no controlled human studies.
- *Lactation:* It is considered unsafe for breastfeeding mothers. Medication administration requires cessation of breastfeeding.
- *Children:* Serious rashes requiring hospitalizations and in case of Stevens-Johnson syndrome and rare cases of toxic epidermal necrolysis and rash-related deaths, treatment should be discontinued. Incidence is 0.8% in children 2–6 years of age and 0.3% in adults. Most life-threatening rashes occur in first 2–8 weeks of treatment.

Class: Opioid Antagonists

Narcan   **naloxone**

AVAILABLE FORMS: Injection, 0.4 mg

DOSAGE: *Adults:* 0.4–2 mg IM/SC/ETT every 2–3 min when needed. 0.005 mg/kg IV, then 0.0025–0.16 mg/kg/hr IV, continuous infusion. May repeat every 1–2 hr if symptoms recur, question diagnosis if no response after 10 mg. *Children:* 0.1 mg/kg IV every 2–3 min or 0.1 mg/kg IM every 3–8 min when needed. May repeat every 1–2 hr if symptoms recur for under 1 mo olds. *For 1 mo–5 yr and under 20 kg:* 0.1 mg/kg IV every 2–3 min when needed or 0.1 mg/kg IO/IM/SC/ETT every 3–8 min when needed. May repeat every 1–2 hr if symptoms recur. *Over 5 years of age or over 20 kg:* 2 mg IV every 3–8 min when needed or 0.0005 mg/kg IV 1, then 0.0025–0.16 mg/kg/hour continuous IV. May repeat 1–2 hr if symptoms recur.

ADMINISTRATION: SC, IM, or IV

SIDE EFFECTS: Common reactions include tachycardia, hypertension, hypotension, nausea, vomiting, tremor, withdrawal symptoms, diaphoresis, pulmonary edema, and irritability (pediatric).

DRUG INTERACTIONS: This medicine may also interact with:
- Topiramate (may increase risk of CNS depression, and psychomotor impairment)
- Tramadol and tramadol/acetaminophen (may not reverse all symptoms of overdose, increase risk of seizures).

- This drug blocks effects of all opioids, including opioid-containing cough suppressants and opioid analgesics

PHARMACOKINETICS:
- Metabolized in the liver (CYP450). The drug is excreted in the urine.
- The drug antagonizes the various opioid receptors.

Half-life: 64 min

PRECAUTIONS: Caution is advised in patients with cardiovascular disease, opioid addiction, hepatic impairment, or renal impairment, in patients on cardiotoxic drugs.

PATIENT AND FAMILY EDUCATION:
- Stop using naloxone and call the doctor if chest pain, lightheadedness, seizure, or difficulty breathing develops.

SPECIAL POPULATIONS:
- *Renal impairment:* No adjustment is needed.
- *Hepatic impairment:* Caution is advised in children with hepatic impairment; dosing not defined.
- *Pregnancy:* Category C drug.
- *Lactation:* Safety in lactation is unknown. Caution is advised.
- *Children:* Dose adjustment may be required in children with renal impairment, but no specific pediatric dosing adjustments are defined. Caution is advised in children with hepatic impairment.

ReVia, Vivitrol   **naltrexone**

INDICATIONS: Used primarily in the management of alcohol dependence and opioid addiction but is being tested for use in depersonalization disorders.

AVAILABLE FORMS: Tablet and injection, 25, 50, and 100 mg

DOSAGE: In studies, average dose of 120 mg per day was used for 6–10 weeks.

ADMINISTRATION:
- Take with a full glass of water.
- Take without food unless stomach upset occurs.
- Do not stop taking drug without provider's advice.
- Do not take opioids while on this medicine.

SIDE EFFECTS: Depression, sedation/somnolence, suicidal attempt/ideation, skin rash, pharyngitis, hepatocellular injury, aches, pains, change in sex drive or performance, feeling anxious, dizzy, restlesness, fearful, headache, loss of appetite, nausea, runny nose, sinus problems, sneezing, stomach cramps, and trouble sleeping

DRUG INTERACTIONS: This medicine may also interact with the following medications:

- Topiramate (*Topamax*) may increase risk of CNS depression, and psychomotor impairment
- Tramadol (*Rybix/Ryzolt/Ultram*) and tramadol/acetaminophen may not reverse all symptoms of overdose, increase risk of seizures, block effects of all opioids, including opioid-containing cough suppressants and opioid analgesics

PHARMACOKINETICS: Opioid antagonists such as naltrexone are metabolized in the liver. They are completely absorbed from the GI tract. Elimination is primarily by glomerular filtration. naltrexone and its metabolites may undergo enterohepatic recirculation. Elimination from the system takes 5 to 10 days. Initial peak is within 2 hr, followed by a second peak 2 to 3 days later. Measurable levels can occur for more than 1 mo after initial dosing. Exposure is 3- to 4-fold higher with im administration compared to oral administration.

PRECAUTIONS:
- Do not drive, operate machinery, or do anything that requires mental alertness until it is known how this drug exerts its effects.
- Caution individuals not to stand or sit up quickly, as dizziness is a side effect of this medicine.

(cont.)

naltrexone (*cont.*)

- Check liver enzyme levels before beginning treatment and periodically thereafter.
- Tell individual not to take any medicine that contains opioids during treatment as this could cause serious injury, coma, or death.
- Avoid pregnancy and nursing while taking this medicine.

PATIENT AND FAMILY EDUCATION:
- Take medication with a full glass of water but without regard to meals. If stomach upset occurs, take with food.
- Wear medical identification indicating naltrexone use.
- This drug may increase sensitivity to lower doses of opioids; large doses of heroin or any other opiate may cause coma and death.
- Do not take this medicine within 7 to 10 days of taking any opioid drug.
- Exercise caution when driving or performing other tasks requiring mental alertness and coordination.
- Stop taking the medicine if any of the following develops: allergic reaction, stomach pain lasting more than a few days, white bowel movements, dark urine, or yellowing of eyes.
- Combine with psychotherapy or other counseling methods for full treatment effect.
- Notify health care provider if there is shortness of breath, coughing, or wheezing as *Vivitrol* injections may cause allergic pneumonia.
- Nausea may result after a *Vivitrol* injection.

SPECIAL POPULATIONS:
- *Elderly*: Trials of subjects over 65 years of age did not include sufficient numbers to determine the safety and efficacy in the geriatric population.
- *Renal impairment:* Caution advised in renal impairment.
- *Hepatic impairment:* Caution advised in children with hepatic impairment. Contraindicated in acute hepatitis and hepatic failure.
- *Pregnancy*: Category C.
- *Lactation*: Nursing mothers should not take this medicine as it has a potential for serious adverse effects in infants.
- *Children*: The safety and efficacy of this medicine has not been established in the pediatric population.

Dissociative Identity Disorder

OVERVIEW
- A dissociative identity disorder occurs when a person displays multiple distinct identities or personalities, each perceiving and interacting with the environment in their own way.
- The average age for initial development is 5.9 years; children have a pronounced ability to dissociate so an abused child slips into a state of mind in which it seems that the abuse is not really happening to him or her, but to somebody else.
- Each personality must take control of the individual's behavior with an associated memory loss of the other personality.
- This disorder seems to be entirely confined to North America; reports from other continents are rare.
- Functioning can vary from normal to severely impaired.
- A multitude of symptoms can occur such as phobias, anger, panic/anxiety attacks, depression, memory loss, distortion of time, headaches/body pains, flashbacks of abuse/trauma, and lack of intimacy and personal connections.
- Children with this disorder can have conduct problems, difficulty paying attention in school, and hallucinations.
- The symptoms may mimic epilepsy, schizophrenia, anxiety disorders, mood disorders, post traumatic stress disorder, personality disorders, and eating disorders.
- The antecedents to the occurrence of this disorder are some overwhelming stress or trauma. A high percentage of individuals report child abuse.
- The progression of the disorder begins with a child being harmed by a trusted caregiver; the memories go into the subconscious and split off the event from memory and are later manifested as a separate personality; as the child continues to undergo trauma, different personalities develop, and as a result dissociation becomes the coping mechanism for further stressful events.
- Incidence in the USA is 10% prevalence among the mentally ill and 1% among the general population.
- This disorder is diagnosed in a sizable minority individuals in drug-abuse treatment facilities.
- The symptoms of this disorder have a considerable overlap with borderline personality disorder.
- Some people with dissociative disorders have a tendency toward self-persecution, self-sabotage, and even violence.
- There is usually a host personality who may be unaware of the presence of the other personalities, which can number as many as a 100.

Psychopharmacology of Dissociative Identity Disorder

- There are no specific drugs to treat dissociative identity disorders.
- Psychotherapy sessions attempt to reconnect the identities into a single functioning identity.
- Treatment may also include psychotherapy and medications for comorbid disorders.
- Some behavioral therapists may use responding to only one identity to address the disorder.
- Individuals with primary dissociative symptoms or post-traumatic stress disorder recover with treatment; those with comorbid addictions,

and personality, mood, or eating disorders face a longer, complicated treatment. Individuals with this condition commonly attempt suicide.
- Prior to the administration of a benzodiazepine, patients should be sufficiently screened to ensure they are not at risk for suicide.
- Sometimes, a mood stabilizer (like lithium) is the most effective treatment; however, this drug should only be prescribed for dissociative identity disorder by a psychiatric specialist.

CLASS	DRUG
Selective Serotonin Reuptake Inhibitors (SSRIs)	**First-Line Drugs Used to Treat Comorbid Depression Commonly Seen With This Disorder**
	sertraline (*Zoloft*) fluoxetine (*Prozac, Sarafem*) paroxetine (*Paxil, Pexeva, Paxil CR*) citalopram (*Celexa*) escitalopram (*Lexapro*)
Serotonin and Norepinephrine Reuptake Inhibitors (SNRIs)	**Second-Line Drugs Used to Treat Comorbid Depression Commonly Seen With This Disorder**
	venlafaxine (*Effexor*) duloxetine (*Cymbalta*) desvenlafaxine (*Pristiq*)
Noradrenergic and Specific Serotonergic Antidepressants (NaSSAs)	
	mirtazapine (*Remeron, Remeron SolTab*) clomipramine (*Anafranil*)
Norepinephrine and Dopamine Reuptake Inhibitors (NDRIs)	
	bupropion HCL (*Wellbutrin, Zyban, Wellbutrin SR, Wellbutrin XL*)
Serotonin Antagonist and Reuptake Inhibitors (SARIs)	
	trazodone (*Desyrel, Oleptro*)
Benzodiazepines (BZDs)	**Used Short Term Until Other Agents Begin Effects**
	diazepam (*Valium, Diastat, Di-Tran, T-Quil, Valrelease, Vaz epam, Zetran*) lorazepam (*Ativan, Alzapam*) alprazolam (*Xanax, Niravam*)

Class: Selective Serotonin Reuptake Inhibitors (SSRIs)

Zoloft | sertraline

INDICATIONS: Used to treat depression.

AVAILABLE FORMS: Tablet, 25, 50, and 100 mg; concentrate, 20 mg/mL

DOSAGE: *Adults*: 25–200 mg PO every day. Usual initial dose, 25–50 mg PO every day. After 1 week, may increase daily dose by 25 mg and then wait for a few weeks before increasing dose further.

ADMINISTRATION:
- Administered PO.
- Store sertraline in a tightly closed container and keep away from excess heat and moisture.
- Take the medicine exactly as it is prescribed.
- Do not take the medicine in larger amounts, or take it for longer than recommended by the health care provider.

(cont.)

DISSOCIATIVE IDENTITY DISORDER

DISSOCIATIVE IDENTITY DISORDER

sertraline (cont.)

- Take the sertraline tablet with water.
- Sertraline may be taken with or without food.
- Try to take the medicine at the same time each day.

SIDE EFFECTS: Common side effects include nausea, headache, insomnia, diarrhea, dry mouth, ejaculatory dysfunction, somnolence, asthenia, tremor, dyspepsia, anorexia, constipation, libido decrease, nervousness, anxiety, rash, and abnormal vision.

DRUG INTERACTIONS: The following drugs may interact with sertraline: Linezolid (*Zyvox*) may increase the risk of serotonin syndrome and neuroleptic syndrome. MAOIs are contraindicated within 5 weeks of sertraline use because they may increase the risk of serotonin syndrome and neuroleptic syndrome. Pimozide (*Orap*) may increase the risk of bradycardia, increase pimozide levels, and increase risk of QT prolongation and cardiac arrhythmias. Thioridazine (*Mellaril*) may increase risk of QT prolongation, cardiac arrhythmias, SIADH, hyponatremia, serotonin syndrome, neuroleptic and malignant syndrome. Cimetidine (*Tagamet*) may increase the sertraline levels in blood by decreasing metabolism of the drug by the liver.

PHARMACOKINETICS:
- Metabolized by the liver (CYP450; 2C9, 2D6, 3A4) and is excreted in the urine (40–50%) and in the feces (40–45%).
- Selectively inhibits serotonin reuptake.
Half-life: 26 hr

PRECAUTIONS:
- Black box warning states that there is an increased risk of suicidality in children, adolescents, and young adults especially during the first months of treatment.
- Caution should be exercised in patients with seizure disorders, disulfiram use, patients younger than 25 years of age, patient with liver impairment, hyponatremic patients, patients using alcohol, and those with mania/hypomania.
- MAOIs should not be used within 14 days of sertraline to reduce the chance of the serotonin syndrome.
- Cimetidine may increase the effects of sertraline.
- Warfarin may result in increased bleeding.

PATIENT AND FAMILY EDUCATION:
- Inform provider if increased depression while taking this drug.
- Notify the health care provider if hypoglycemia, seizures or mania, glaucoma, or abnormal bleeding/bruising.
- Avoid alcohol while taking this drug.
- Store sertraline in a tightly closed container and keep away from excess heat and moisture.
- Therapeutic effects may take 4 weeks to fully develop, but side effects may be noticeable within 1 week of beginning therapy.

SPECIAL POPULATIONS:
- *Elderly*: Caution must be exercised. May require decreased dosage.
- *Renal impairment:* No adjustment needed.
- *Hepatic impairment:* Patients with hepatic impairment may need to have decreased dosing and/or frequency.
- *Pregnancy*: Category C, but trimester-specific.
- *Children*: Not approved in pediatric patients except in OCD.

fluoxetine   *Prozac, Sarafem*

INDICATIONS: Used to treat depression.

AVAILABLE FORMS: Capsule, 10, 20, and 40 mg; syrup, 20 mg/5 mL; tablet, 10 mg

DOSAGE: *Adults:* 20–80 mg PO qam. Starting dose 20 mg PO qam; may be increased after several weeks. Maximum, 80 mg/day. Doses more than 20 mg/day may be divided into bid dosing. Pediatric dosing in 8–18 year olds is 10–20 mg PO every day starting with 10 mg PO every day for 7 days.

ADMINISTRATION:
- The drug is given PO.
- Do not take fluoxetine with grapefruit juice, as it may increase blood levels of the drug.
- Avoid use of herbs that have a sedative effect.
- Fluoxetine may increase the levels of phenytoin and TCAs. Alcohol should be avoided while using fluoxetine.
- Use of buspirone, bromocriptine, levodopa, dextromethorphan, lithium, meperidine, nefazodone, paroxetine, pentazocine, sertraline, sumatriptan, tramadol, trazodone, tryptophan, and venlafaxine can cause a serotonin syndrome.
- Never give a double dose of the medicine.
- Fluoxetine can be taken with or without food.
- Caution while driving, riding a bicycle, or operating machinery, as this drug causes drowsiness.

SIDE EFFECTS: Common reactions include nausea, headache, insomnia, nervousness, anxiety, asthenia, diarrhea, anorexia, dizziness, dry mouth, tremor, dyspepsia, sweating, ejaculatory dysfunction, constipation, flu syndrome, libido decrease, rash, and abnormal vision.

DRUG INTERACTIONS: The following drugs may interact with fluoxetine:
- Linezolid (*Zyvox*) may increase the risk of serotonin syndrome, neuroleptic syndrome, and in combination with fluvoxamine (*Luvox*) may increase rasagiline (*Azilect*) levels
- MAOIs contraindicated within 5 weeks of fluoxetine use because it may increase the risk of
(cont.)

fluoxetine (*cont.*)

serotonin syndrome, neuroleptic syndrome and in combination with fluvoxamine (*Luvox*) may increase rasagiline (*Azilect*) levels, and risk of adverse effects
- Pimozide (*Orap*) may increase the risk of bradycardia, increase pimozide levels, risk of QT prolongation, cardiac arrhythmias
- Thioridazine (*Mellaril*) may increase thioridazine levels, risk of QT prolongation, cardiac arrhythmias, and may increase risk of SIADH, hyponatremia, serotonin syndrome, and neuroleptic and malignant syndrome.

PHARMACOKINETICS:
- Metabolized by the liver (CYP450, 2C19 and 2D6) and excreted in the urine (80%) and feces (15%).
- Selectively inhibits serotonin reuptake.

Half-life: 4–6 days

PRECAUTIONS: Caution is recommended in patients younger than 25 years. Caution should also be exercised with the following conditions: diabetes mellitus, hyponatremia, seizures, mania/hypomania, or volume depletion.

PATIENT AND FAMILY EDUCATION:
- Increased risk of suicidality in children, adolescents, and young adults with major depressive or other psychiatric disorders especially during the first months of treatment.
- Inform health care provider of glaucoma, hypoglycemia, or abnormal bleeding tendencies.
- Therapeutic effects may take 4 weeks to fully develop, but side effects may be noticeable within 1 week of beginning therapy.

SPECIAL POPULATIONS:
- *Elderly*: Caution should be used.
- *Renal impairment:* No adjustment is needed for those with kidney disease.
- *Hepatic impairment:* Dose may need to be decreased in patients with liver disease.
- *Pregnancy*: Category C, but trimester-specific.
- *Lactation*: Safety in lactation is unknown.
- *Children*: Use of this drug in children carries the risk of suicide.

Paxil, Pexeva, Paxil CR   **paroxetine**

INDICATIONS: Used to treat depression.

AVAILABLE FORMS: Tablet, 10, 20, 30, and 40 mg; controlled-release tablet, 12.5, and 25 mg; suspension, 10 mg/5 mL

DOSAGE: *Adults:* 20–50 mg PO each day. Starting dose usually 20 mg PO qam; maximum 50 mg/day.

ADMINISTRATION:
- Administer PO.
- Take the medicine at the same time each day.
- Do not crush, chew, or break a controlled-release tablet.
- Swallow the pill whole. Breaking the pill would cause too much of the drug to be released at one time.
- Shake the liquid form of paroxetine well just before measuring a dose.
- To ensure the correct dose, measure liquid with a marked measuring spoon or medicine cup.
- Store paroxetine at room temperature away from moisture and heat.

SIDE EFFECTS: Nausea, somnolence, headache, asthenia, sedation, dizziness, constipation, libido decrease, diarrhea, sweating, dry mouth, ejaculatory dysfunction, tremor, anorexia, nervousness, anxiety, and abnormal vision.

DRUG INTERACTIONS: The following drugs may interact with paroxetine:
- Linezolid (*Zyvox*) may increase the risk of serotonin syndrome, neuroleptic syndrome, and in combination with fluvoxamine (*Luvox*) may increase rasagiline (*Azilect*) levels, and risk of adverse effects

- MAOIs are contraindicated within 5 weeks of paroxetine use because it may increase the risk of serotonin syndrome, neuroleptic syndrome and in combination with fluvoxamine (*Luvox*) may increase rasagiline levels, and risk of adverse effects
- Pimozide (*Orap*) may increase the risk of bradycardia, increase pimozide levels, risk of QT prolongation, cardiac arrhythmias
- Thioridazine (*Mellaril*) may increase thioridazine (*Mellaril*) levels, risk of QT prolongation, and cardiac arrhythmia, risk of SIADH, hyponatremia, serotonin syndrome, neuroleptic and malignant syndrome.

PHARMACOKINETICS: Metabolized in the liver (CYP450, 2D6) and is excreted in the urine (64%) and feces (36%).

Half-life: 21 hr

PRECAUTIONS: Increased risk of suicidality in younger patients and young adults. Caution should be exercised in the use of this drug in patients with bleeding risk, alcohol use, mania/hypomania, hyponatremia, volume depletion, seizure disorder, glaucoma (angle closure), renal impairment, and hepatic impairment

PATIENT AND FAMILY EDUCATION:
- Inform health care provider of seizure disorder, renal/liver impairment, glaucoma, alcohol use, or a bleeding disorder.
- Therapeutic effects may not be noticed for 4 weeks
- Side effects may occur within the first week of treatment.

(cont.)

DISSOCIATIVE IDENTITY DISORDER: Selective Serotonin Reuptake Inhibitors (SSRIs)

paroxetine (*cont.*)

- Report any increase in risk of suicidality in children, adolescents, and young adults with major depressive or other psychiatric disorders especially during the first months of treatment.

SPECIAL POPULATIONS:
- *Elderly*: Dosage is usually reduced in half for elderly patients to 10 mg PO qam and a maximum dose of 40 mg/day.
- *Renal impairment:* Renal dose adjustment may be required. In adult dosing, if CrCl is below 30, then initial dose is started at 10 mg every day.
- *Hepatic impairment:* Reduced dosing may be required in children. In adults with severe impairment, dose is started at 10 mg every day.
- *Pregnancy*: There is positive evidence of human fetal risk.
- *Lactation*: There is minimal risk during lactation to the baby.
- *Children*: Caution should be exercised in people under 25 years of age.

---

citalopram	*Celexa*

INDICATIONS: Used to treat depression.

AVAILABLE FORMS: Tablet, capsule, 10, 20, and 40 mg

DOSAGE: *Adults*: 20–40 mg PO every day. Initial dose usually 20 mg PO every day; maximum dose, 60 mg/day.

ADMINISTRATION:
- Administered PO.
- Take the missed dose as soon as remembered. However, if almost time for the next regularly scheduled dose, skip the missed dose and take the next one as directed. Do not take extra medicine to make up the missed dose.
- Take the medication exactly as it was prescribed.
- Take the medicine at the same time each day.
- Use the marked measuring spoon or medicine cup for the liquid.

SIDE EFFECTS: Nausea, somnolence, headache, asthenia, dizziness, constipation, libido decrease, diarrhea, sweating, dry mouth, ejaculatory dysfunction, tremor, anorexia, nervousness, anxiety, and abnormal vision.

DRUG INTERACTIONS: The following drugs may interact with citalopram:
- Linezolid (*Zyvox*) may increase the risk of serotonin syndrome, neuroleptic syndrome, and in combination with fluvoxamine (*Luvox*) may increase rasagiline (*Azilect*) levels, and risk of adverse effects
- MAOIs are contraindicated within 5 weeks of citalopram use because it may increase the risk of serotonin syndrome, neuroleptic syndrome and in combination with fluvoxamine (*Luvox*) may increase rasagiline (*Azilect*) levels and the risk of adverse effects
- Pimozide (*Orap*) may increase the risk of bradycardia, increase pimozide (*Orap*) levels, risk of QT prolongation, cardiac arrhythmias
- Thioridazine (*Mellaril*) may increase thioridazine (*Mellaril*) levels, risk of QT prolongation, cardiac arrhythmias, risk of SIADH, hyponatremia, serotonin syndrome, neuroleptic and malignant syndrome.

PHARMACOKINETICS: Metabolized extensively in the liver (CYP450 2C19 and 3A4) and is excreted primarily in the urine and some in feces. It selectively inhibits serotonin reuptake.

PRECAUTIONS: Caution should be exercised in patients with seizure disorders, hepatic/renal impairment, mania, or volume depletion or in those who use alcohol.

PATIENT AND FAMILY EDUCATION:
- Inform health care provider if increasing depression occurs especially during the first months of treatment.
- Inform health care provider of glaucoma, hypoglycemia, or abnormal bleeding tendencies.
- Therapeutic effects may take 4 weeks to develop fully, but side effects may be noticeable within 1 week of beginning therapy.

SPECIAL POPULATIONS:
- *Elderly*: The dosage is adjusted for the elderly to a maximum of 60 mg/day.
- *Renal impairment:* No adjustment is recommended but caution is advised.
- *Hepatic impairment:* Patients with hepatic impairment should take 20 mg every day to a maximum of 40 mg daily.
- *Pregnancy*: Caution is advised for pregnant women who are over 20 weeks gestation.
- *Children*: Caution should be exercised and patients closely monitored through duration of treatment.

DISSOCIATIVE IDENTITY DISORDER: Selective Serotonin Reuptake Inhibitors (SSRIs)

Lexapro	escitalopram

INDICATIONS: Used to treat depression.

AVAILABLE FORMS: Tablet, 5, 10, and 20 mg; oral solution, 5 mg/5 mL

DOSAGE: *Adults:* Starting dose, 10 mg PO every day; may be increased after a week to maximum of 20 mg/day.

ADMINISTRATION:
- Administered PO.
- Take the missed dose as soon as remembered. However, if almost time for the next regularly scheduled dose, skip the missed dose and take the next one as directed. Do not take extra medicine to make up the missed dose.
- Take the medicine as prescribed.
- Take each dose with a full glass of water.
- Take the medicine at the same time every day.
- Use the measuring spoon or cup rather than a household spoon to measure the medicine.

SIDE EFFECTS: Nausea, somnolence, headache, asthenia, dizziness, constipation, libido decrease, diarrhea, sweating, dry mouth, ejaculatory dysfunction, tremor, anorexia, nervousness, anxiety, and abnormal vision.

DRUG INTERACTIONS: The following drugs may interact with escitalopram:
- Linezolid (*Zyvox*) may increase the risk of serotonin syndrome, neuroleptic syndrome, and in combination with fluvoxamine (*Luvox*) may increase rasagiline (*Azilect*) levels, and risk of adverse effects
- MAOIs are contraindicated within 5 weeks of escitalopram use because it may increase the risk of serotonin syndrome, neuroleptic syndrome and in combination with fluvoxamine (*Luvox*) may increase rasagiline (*Azilect*) levels, and risk of adverse effects
- Pimozide (*Orap*) may increase the risk of bradycardia, increase pimozide (*Orap*) levels, risk of QT prolongation, cardiac arrhythmias

- Thioridazine may increase thioridazine (*Mellaril*) levels, risk of QT prolongation, cardiac arrhythmias, risk of SIADH, hyponatremia, serotonin syndrome, neuroleptic and malignant syndrome.

PHARMACOKINETICS: Metabolized in the liver (CYP450 2C19, 2D6, and 3A4) and is excreted in the urine.
Half-life: 27–32 hr; half-life is increased 50% in the elderly.

PRECAUTIONS:
- Caution should be exercised in patients with seizure disorders, hepatic/renal impairment, mania, or volume depletion or in those who use alcohol.
- Increase in the risk of suicidality in children, adolescents, and young adults with major depressive or other psychiatric disorders especially during the first months of treatment.
- Assess patient for glaucoma, hypoglycemia, or abnormal bleeding tendencies.
- Therapeutic effects may take 4 weeks to fully develop, but side effects may be noticeable within 1 week of beginning therapy.

PATIENT AND FAMILY EDUCATION:
- Inform health care provider of alcohol use, seizures, or hepatic/renal involvement.

SPECIAL POPULATIONS:
- *Elderly:* Dosage is usually half of the adult dose; initial dose is 10 mg/day.
- *Renal impairment:* Mild to moderate impairment, no adjustments needed; in severe impairment, caution is advised.
- *Hepatic impairment:* The dose is decreased to a maximum of 10 mg/day.
- *Pregnancy:* Category C, but trimester-specific.
- *Lactation:* Safety is unknown during lactation.
- *Children:* Suicidality is a concern in young children, adolescents, and young adults.

Class: Serotonin and Norepinephrine Reuptake Inhibitors (SNRIs)

Effexor	venlafaxine

AVAILABLE FORMS: Tablet, capsule, 25, 37.5, 50, 75, 100, and 150 mg, including extended-release formulations

DOSAGE: Dosage ranges 37.5 to 75 mg PO bid to tid. Initial dose 37.5 mg PO bid (or 37.5 mg once daily for extended-release formulations) increasing the dose every 4 days. Maximum dose 375 mg/day.

ADMINISTRATION:
- This drug should be taken with food.
- Take this medication exactly as it was prescribed
- Do not take the medicine in larger amounts, or take it for longer than recommended.

- Take this medication with a full glass of water and food.
- Take this medicine at the same time every day.
- It may take 4 weeks or longer for the symptoms to improve.
- Store this medicine away from moisture and heat.

SIDE EFFECTS: Common reactions include:
- *CNS:* Headache, somnolence, insomnia, paresthesias, nervousness, asthenia, chills, sweating
- *CV:* Hypertension, dizziness
- *EENT:* Blurred vision anorexia

(cont.)

venlafaxine (*cont.*)

- *GI*: Nausea, diarrhea, dry mouth constipation, tremors
- *GU*: Ejaculation
- *Skin*: Rash

PHARMACOKINETICS: Metabolized in the liver (CYP450 2D6) and excreted in the urine (87%). **Half-life:** 5 hr

PRECAUTIONS: Exercise caution in patients with seizure, mania, hypertension, hyperthyroidism, heart failure, recent myocardial infarction, bleeding disorder, hypovolemia, hyponatremia, dehydration, increased intracranial pressure, and glaucoma.

PATIENT AND FAMILY EDUCATION:
- Avoid abrupt cessation of drug because rapid discontinuation may cause problems.
- Inform health care provider about any other medications being used.

- Not all antidepressant medicines prescribed for children are FDA approved; talk to the health care provider about this.

SPECIAL POPULATIONS:
- *Elderly*: Exercise caution in elderly patients.
- *Renal impairment:* If CrCl is 10–70, decrease dose by 25–50%. If CrCl is below 10, decrease dose by 50%.
- *Hepatic impairment:* If moderate impairment, decrease dose by 50%. Severe impairment is not defined.
- *Pregnancy*: Category C drug but trimester-specific or population-specific risks exist.
- *Lactation*: Safety is unknown in lactating mothers.
- *Children*: There is an increased risk of suicide in children, adolescents, and young adults.

---

duloxetine	*Cymbalta*

AVAILABLE FORMS: Capsule, 20, 30, and 60 mg

DOSAGE: *Adults:* Start at 30 mg PO every day for 1 week; increase dose at 30 mg increments until desired effect is accomplished. Maximum, 120 mg/day. Doses over 60 mg/day are rarely effective and may increase adverse effect incidence. Pediatric dosing is currently unavailable or not applicable.

ADMINISTRATION:
- Do not cut, crush, chew or sprinkle.
- Take this medication exactly as it was prescribed.
- Do not take the medicine in larger amounts, or take it for longer than recommended by the doctor.
- Take with a full glass of water.
- Take this medicine at the same time every day.
- It may take 4 weeks or longer for the symptoms to improve.
- Store this medicine away from moisture and heat.

SIDE EFFECTS: Common side effects include:
- *CNS*: Insomnia, dizziness, somnolence, libido decrease, tremor, anxiety, headache
- *CV*: Fatigue, yawning, hypertension, hypotension, and syncope
- *EENT*: Blurred vision
- *GI*: Dry mouth, constipation, nausea, diarrhea, decrease appetite, vomiting
- *GU*: Erectile dysfunction, ejaculatory dysfunction, anorgasmia, urinary hesitancy
- *Metabolic*: Weight changes, hot flashes, sweating

PHARMACOKINETICS: Metabolized extensively in the liver (CYP450 1A2 and 2D6); excreted in the urine (70%) and feces (20%) (less than 1% unchanged). **Half-life**: 12 hr

PRECAUTIONS: Caution should be exercised in the use of this drug with patients with the following conditions: alcohol abuse, seizures, mania, suicidal tendencies, hypertension, GI motility disorder, glaucoma, hypovolemia, dehydration, obstructive uropathy, smoking habit changes, bleeding risk, and creatinine clearance less than 30.

PATIENT AND FAMILY EDUCATION:
- Avoid abrupt withdrawal while on this drug; it must be tapered down over time.
- Talk to health care provider about any other medications that one might be taking.
- Not all antidepressant medicines prescribed for children are FDA approved; talk to the health care provider about this.

SPECIAL POPULATIONS:
- *Elderly*: Caution should be exercised.
- *Renal impairment:* Use lower start dose, and gradual titration in diabetics. If CrCl is below 30, do not use this medicine.
- *Hepatic impairment:* Do not use this medicine if hepatic impairment is present.
- *Pregnancy*: Category C; trimester-specific or population-specific risks exist.
- *Children*: There is an increased risk of suicide in children, adolescents, and young adults with major depressive or other psychiatric disorders.

Pristiq **desvenlafaxine**

INDICATIONS: Used to treat a major depressive disorder.

AVAILABLE FORMS: Tablet, extended-release tablet, 50 and 100 mg

DOSAGE: *Adults:* Begin with 50 mg PO every day. Doses greater than 50 mg/day are rarely more effective. Pediatric dosing is currently unavailable or not applicable.

ADMINISTRATION:
- This drug is administered PO and may be taken with or without food. Do not cut, crush, chew or sprinkle.
- Take this medication exactly as prescribed.
- Do not take the medicine in larger amounts, or longer than recommended by the doctor.
- Take this medication with a full glass of water at the same time every day.
- It may take 4 weeks or longer for symptoms to improve.
- Store away from moisture and heat.
- Since this tablet is made with a shell that is not absorbed or melted in the body, part of this medicine may be found in the stool.
- Do not stop taking this medicine without consulting health care provider.

SIDE EFFECTS: Common reactions include nausea/vomiting, headache, insomnia, hyperhidrosis, insomnia, dizziness, constipation, somnolence, diarrhea, fatigue, decreased appetite, tremor, mydriasis, erectile dysfunction, anorgasmia, anxiety, blurred vision, libido decrease, abnormal ejaculation, chills, abnormal dreams, palpitations/nervousness, paresthesias, irritability, hypertension, hyperlipidemia, weight loss, urinary hesitancy, tinnitus, rash, and dysgeusia.

PHARMACOKINETICS: Metabolized in the liver (CYP450, 3A4). It is excreted in the urine (64–59%) and 45% is unchanged.

Half-life: 11 hr; 13–14 hr for moderately severe hepatic impairment and 23 hr for mild to severe renal impairment.

PRECAUTIONS: Caution should be exercised in patients with hyperlipidemia, hypovolemia, bleeding risk, cerebrovascular disease, hypertension, mania, cardiovascular disease, dehydration, glaucoma, hyponatremia, increased intracranial pressure, or seizure disorders, and to pregnant women.

PATIENT AND FAMILY EDUCATION:
- Do not cut/crush/chew the drug.
- Do not abruptly stop taking the medicine; contact the health care provider who will taper doses.
- Talk to the health care provider about any other medications that are being taken.
- Not all antidepressant medicines prescribed for children are FDA approved; talk to the health care provider about this.

SPECIAL POPULATIONS:
- *Elderly:* Consider 50 mg every other day if poorly tolerated.
- *Renal impairment:* If creatinine clearance is 30–50, then maximum dose per day is 50 mg. If creatinine clearance is below 30 or if end-stage renal disease is present, then the dosage is 50 mg every other day.
- *Hepatic impairment:* If there is hepatic impairment present, then the maximum dosage is 100 mg/day.
- *Pregnancy:* Category C; semester-specific or population-specific risks exist.
- *Lactation:* Safety is unknown for use in breast-feeding women; caution is advised.
- *Children:* There is an increased risk of suicidality in children, adolescents, and young adults with major depressive or other psychiatric disorders especially during the first months of treatment with an antidepressive drug versus a placebo.

Class: Noradrenergic and Specific Serotonergic Antidepressants (NaSSAs)

Remeron, Remeron SolTab **mirtazapine**

AVAILABLE FORMS: Tablet, 15, 30, and 45 mg

DOSAGE: *Adults:* 15–45 mg PO at bedtime. Initial dose is usually 15 mg PO at bedtime. Pediatric dosing is currently unavailable or not applicable.

ADMINISTRATION:
- Given PO; regular tablet is given with water.
- To take the disintegrating tablets (*Remeron SolTab*), keep the tablet in its blister pack until ready to use. Open the package and peel the foil from the tablet blister. Do not push a tablet through the foil or it may break the tablet. Using

dry hands, remove the tablet, place in mouth, and let it dissolve. Do not swallow the tablet whole. Do not chew it. Swallow several times and flush it away with water.

SIDE EFFECTS: Common side effects include the following: somnolence, dry mouth, decreased appetite, hypercholesteremia, constipation, weight gain, sedation, asthenia, dizziness, hyperglyceridemia, influenza-like symptoms, abnormal dreams, abnormal thinking, tremor, confusion, peripheral edema, myalgia, back pain, urinary frequency

(cont.)

mirtazapine (cont.)

PHARMACOKINETICS: Metabolized extensively in the liver (CYP450 1A2, 2C9, 2D6, and 3A4) and excreted in the urine (75%) and feces (15%).

PRECAUTIONS: Caution should be exercised if the patient has the following conditions: bipolar disorder, hypotension, cerebrovascular diagnosis, hypovolemia, seizure disorder, dehydration, smoking habit changes, and phenylketonuria.

PATIENT AND FAMILY EDUCATION: Avoid discontinuing the drug without tapering the dosage. Talk to the health care provider about any other medications in use. Mirtazapine is not FDA approved for use in children.

SPECIAL POPULATIONS:
- *Elderly*: Caution should be exercised.
- *Renal impairment:* Dosage has not been defined
- *Hepatic impairment:* Dosage has not been defined.
- *Pregnancy*: Category C; animal studies show adverse fetal effects, but no controlled human studies have been conducted.
- *Children*: There is an increased risk of suicidality in children, adolescents, and young adults especially during the first months of treatment. Mirtazapine is not FDA approved for use in children.

---

clomipramine   *Anafranil*

AVAILABLE FORMS: Tablets, 25, 50, and 75 mg

DOSAGE: Starting dose, 25–50 mg/day; maintenance dose, typically 100–250 mg/day if used for antidepressive effects

ADMINISTRATION: PO, at bedtime as a single dose (once tolerated)

SIDE EFFECTS: Similar to amitriptyline.
- Anticholinergic effects of dry mouth, constipation, and blurred vision
- Cardiac arrhythmias
- Fatigue, sedation, and weight gain
- Sexual dysfunction

DRUG INTERACTIONS:
- *MAOIs:* Risk for extreme hypertension
- *CNS depressants* (e.g., alcohol): TCAs increase effects
- *Direct-acting adrenergic agonists* (e.g., epinephrine): TCAs increase effects
- *Anticholinergic drugs* (e.g., antihistamines): TCAs increase effects. Do not use in combination.
- *SSRIs and other medications:* serotonin syndrome
- *Antiarrhythmic agents*

PRECAUTIONS:
- Adverse effects and side effects commonly observed before therapeutic effects
- Many side effects are dose dependent and may improve over time
- Overdose may result in lethal cardiotoxicity
- Use with caution in patients with a history of seizure or heart disease
- Avoid in patients with a history of cardiac arrhythmia.
- Monitor with EKG.

PHARMACOKINETICS
Metabolism: Metabolized to an inactive form by CYP450 2D6 and 1A2
Half-life: Approx. 24 hr

PATIENT AND FAMILY EDUCATION:
- Should be taken about the same time every day, typically in the evening, and can be taken with or without food. May cause prolonged sedation. Do not drive until the effect of this medication is known.
- Administration time may be adjusted based on observed sedating or activating drug effects
- May take up to 4–8 weeks to show its maximum effect, but patient may see symptoms of depression improving in as little as 2 weeks.
- If patient plans on becoming pregnant, discuss benefits versus risks of using this medicine while pregnant.
- Because this medication is excreted in breast milk, nursing mothers should not breastfeed while taking this medicine without prior consultation with a psychiatric nurse practitioner or psychiatrist. Newborns may develop symptoms including feeding or breathing difficulties, seizures, muscle stiffness, jitteriness, or constant crying.
- Do not stop taking this medication unless the health care provider directs. Report symptoms to the health care provider promptly.
- Drug should be tapered gradually when discontinued. Dosage should be adjusted to reach remission of symptoms and treatment should continue for at least 4–9 months following remission of symptoms.
- Keep these medications out of the reach of children and pets.

SPECIAL POPULATIONS:
- *Elderly:* Older individuals tend to be more sensitive to side effects such as hypotension and anticholinergic effects. Often require adjustment of medication doses for hepatic or renal dysfunction. TCAs have been shown in at least one controlled clinical trial to be more effective than SSRIs in hospitalized geriatric patients, and in

(cont.)

clomipramine (*cont.*)

patients with melancholia and unipolar depression. However, cardiac side effects and fall risk are of great concern in this population. Side effects may be more pronounced and require decreased dosage

- *Pregnancy:* Psychotherapy is the initial choice for most pregnant patients with MDD. Category C; not recommended in most cases.
- *Children:* Not recommended for children under the age of 12.

Class: Norepinephrine and Dopamine Reuptake Inhibitors (NDRIs)

Wellbutrin, Zyban, Wellbutrin SR, and Wellbutrin XL   **bupropion HCL**

INDICATIONS: Used to treat major depressive disorders.

AVAILABLE FORMS: Tablet, 75, 100, 150, 200 (*Luvox*), and 300 mg, including sustained release and extended-release formulations.

DOSAGE: *Adults:* Starting 150 mg PO a day and increasing dose after 3 days. Maximum is 450 mg/day in divided doses (150 mg tid maximum dose for immediate-release formulation). Pediatric dosing is currently unavailable or not applicable.

ADMINISTRATION: Avoid or minimize alcohol use. Do not cut/chew/crush.

SIDE EFFECTS: Psychiatric disorder exacerbation, behavioral disturbances, agitation, psychosis, hallucinations, paranoia, mania, seizures, hepatotoxicity, arrhythmias, tachycardia, weight loss, hypertension, migraine, Stevens Johnson syndrome, erythema multiforme, and anaphylaxis.

PHARMACOKINETICS: Metabolized by the liver (CYP450 2B6, and 2D6) and is excreted in the urine 87% (0.5 % unchanged) and the feces 10%. This drug works by inhibiting neuronal uptake of norepinephrine and dopamine.

PRECAUTIONS: Caution should be exercised if patients have seizures, bulimia, anorexia, head injury/intracranial lesion, bipolar disorder, psychiatric disorder, diabetes mellitus, renal impairment, cirrhosis, myocardial infarction, hypertension, or suicidality history.

PATIENT AND FAMILY EDUCATION: If depression worsens while taking this drug, please inform the health care provider immediately.

SPECIAL POPULATIONS:
- *Elderly:* Test creatinine at baseline and continuously thereafter. May require decreased dosages
- *Renal impairment:* Caution advised with renal impairment; consider decreasing the dose.
- *Hepatic impairment:* In mild to moderate cirrhosis, consider decreasing the dose frequently and/or amount. In severe cirrhosis, the maximum is 100 mg/day or 150 mg every 4 hr.
- *Pregnancy:* Category C; animal studies show adverse fetal effect(s), but no controlled human studies have been conducted.
- *Lactation:* The use of this drug in breastfeeding mothers is possibly unsafe. Available animal and/or human data demonstrates potential or actual adverse effects to infant/breast milk production.
- *Children:* There is an increased risk in children, adolescents, and young adults with major depressive or other psychiatric disorders especially during the first months of treatment with antidepressants versus placebo.

Class: Serotonin Antagonist and Reuptake Inhibitors (SARIs)

Desyrel, Oleptro   **trazodone**

INDICATIONS: Used to treat major depressive disorders.

AVAILABLE FORMS: Tablet, 50, 100, 150 (*Luvox*), and 300 mg

DOSAGE: *Adults:* Start with 25–50 mg PO bid or tid with increases of 50 mg/day every 3–4 days. Maximum dose 400 mg/day (outpatient) to 600 mg/day (inpatient). *Children*: Start, 1.5–2 mg/kg/day PO divided tid; increase dose every 3–4 days. *12–18 years:* 50 mg PO bid or tid; starting dose 25 mg PO bid or tid with increases in dose every 3–4 days. Maximum dose 6 mg/kg/day or 400 mg/day (outpatient). *(Unlabeled) Pediatric Dose: Children 6–12 yr:* 1.5 mg–6 mg/kg/day PO divided by tid.

ADMINISTRATION: Do not crush/chew the tablet. May give on an empty stomach. Dose must be tapered prior to discontinuing, so notify the health care provider if wish to discontinue.

(cont.)

trazodone (cont.)

SIDE EFFECTS: The most common reactions to this drug include somnolence, xerostomia, headache, sedation, dizziness, nausea/vomiting, blurred vision, fatigue, diarrhea, constipation, edema, abdominal discomfort, myalgia/arthralgia, nasal congestion, weight changes, confusion, ataxia, sexual dysfunction, syncope, tremor, ocular irritation, malaise, and hypertension.

PHARMACOKINETICS: Metabolized extensively in the liver (CYP450 3A4) and excreted in the urine 75% (less than 1% unchanged) and in the feces 20% of the time.
Half-life: 3–6 hr (first phase) and 5–9 hr (second phase)

PRECAUTIONS: Caution is advised in patients with hyponatremia, bipolar disorder, priapism, bleeding risk, volume depletion, alcohol use, cardiac disease, and QT prolongation.

PATIENT AND FAMILY EDUCATION: Notify the health care provider if feeling more depressed after initiation of therapy. Do not use alcohol while taking this drug. Do not stop taking this drug without talking to the health care provider.

SPECIAL POPULATIONS:
- *Elderly*: Exercise caution in the use of this drug.
- *Renal impairment:* Renal dosing is not defined.
- *Hepatic impairment:* Caution is advised in hepatic impairment.
- *Pregnancy*: Animal studies show adverse fetal effect(s), but no controlled human studies have been conducted.
- *Lactation:* There is limited information in animals and/or humans that demonstrates no risk/minimal risk of adverse effects to infant/breast milk production.
- *Children*: There is an increased risk of suicidality in children, adolescents, and young adults with major depressive or other psychiatric disorders especially during the first months of treatment with antidepressants versus placebo.

Class: Benzodiazepines (BZDs)

diazepam   *Valium, Diastat, Di-Tran, T-Quil, Valrelease, Vaz epam, Zetran*

▶Schedule IV drug that requires prescription. Maximum of five refills/6 mo

INDICATIONS: Used to promote relaxation during hypnosis.

AVAILABLE FORMS: Tablet, 2, 5, and 10 mg

DOSAGE: *Adults*: 2–10 mg bid–qid (maximum dose 40 mg/day). *Children over 12 years:* 2–10 mg PO bid or qid. Alternatively, 2–10 mg IM/IV every 3–4 hr when needed.

ADMINISTRATION: May be given PO, IV/IM. Avoid abrupt cessation; taper dose gradually. Monitor complete blood count and liver profile if prolonged treatment. Diazepam can be taken with or without food. Never give a double dose.

SIDE EFFECTS: Drowsiness, impaired motor functions, impaired coordination, impaired balance, fatigue, depression, anterograde amnesia and reflex tachycardia.

PHARMACOKINETICS: Metabolized almost exclusively in the liver (CYP450 2C19, 3A4 substrate).
Half-life: 30–60 hr

PRECAUTIONS: Respiratory depression, bradycardia, hypotension, seizures, hallucinations, psychosis, jaundice, neutropenia, blood dyscrasias, depression, and abuse.

PATIENT AND FAMILY EDUCATION:
- Be sure and tell the health care provider all of the medicines that one is taking as this drug has numerous contraindicated medicines.
- Grapefruit and grapefruit juice can slow down the breakdown of diazepam.
- Avoid alcohol use and herbs with sedative effects.
- Cimetidine, oral contraceptives, disulfiram, fluoxetine, isoniazid, ketoconazole, rifampin, metoprolol, probenecid, propoxyphene, propranolol, and valproic acid may prolong the effects of diazepam.
- Determine response to the medicine before riding a bike, driving a car, or operating machinery.
- Store in a tightly closed container and keep at room temperature away from excess heat and moisture.

SPECIAL POPULATIONS:
- *Elderly*: Exercise caution in the use of the drug. Because of its sedative property and increased risk of falls, all benzodiazepines are included on Beers List of Potentially Inappropriate Medications for Geriatrics.
- *Renal impairment:* Caution advised.
- *Hepatic impairment:* Contraindicated in severe impairment.
- *Pregnancy*: Positive evidence of human fetal risk in pregnant females.
- *Lactation:* Evidence of risk during breastfeeding.
- *Children*: No specific precautions other than monitoring of vital signs.

Ativan, Alzapam   **lorazepam**

▶Schedule IV drug and requires prescription. Maximum number of refills is 5 refills/6 mo.

INDICATIONS: Used for sedation during hypnosis.

AVAILABLE FORMS: Tablet, 0.5, 1, and 2 mg

DOSAGE: *Adults:* Procedural sedation: 0.05 mg/kg IM ×1; maximum dose 4 mg/dose given 2 hr before operation. *Elderly:* IV, 0.044–0.05 mg/kg ×1; maximum dose 4 mg/dose; 2 mg/dose 15–20 min prior to hypnosis. *Children:* 0.05 mg/kg PO, IM or IV ×1; maximum dosage 2 mg/dose.

- Give PO 1 hr prior to procedures; give IM more than 2 hr, prior dose and IV 15–20 min prior to procedure.

ADMINISTRATION: Can be given PO, IM, and IV. Missed doses need to be given as soon as possible; however, if it is time for the next dose, do not administer a double dose. This drug can be taken with food to help prevent stomach irritation.

SIDE EFFECTS: Dizziness, weakness, unsteadiness, nausea, constipation, and fatigue.

PHARMACOKINETICS:

- The drug enhances GABA effects which inhibits the transmission of nerve signals and thus reduces nervous excitation.
- Metabolized by the liver (CYP450)

Half-life: 14 hr.

PRECAUTIONS: Avoid abrupt withdrawal for long-term use, avoid use of alcohol, avoid use in depressed patients, avoid intra-arterial administration, and avoid use in drug-abuse patients.

PATIENT AND FAMILY EDUCATION:

- Tell health care provider if there are problems with the liver or kidneys, alcohol or drug

consumption, glaucoma, lung problems, or if treated for psychiatric disorders.

- Grapefruit juice should be avoided as it slows the body's breakdown of the drug and can lead to dangerous concentrations in the blood.
- Herbs with sedative effects should be avoided.
- Alcoholic beverages should be avoided. Lithium with lorazepam can cause body temperature to drop.
- Use of central nervous system depressants can cause respiratory depression.
- Birth control pills, theophylline, caffeine, and other stimulants can reduce the effects of lorazepam.
- Heparin, macrolide antibiotics, probenecid, quetiapine, and valproic acid can increase the effects of lorazepam.
- Store in a tightly closed container and keep at room temperature away from excess heat and moisture.

SPECIAL POPULATIONS:

- *Elderly:* Caution is advised. Because of its sedative property and increased risk of falls, all benzodiazepines are included on Beers List of Potentially Inappropriate Medications for Geriatrics.
- *Renal impairment:* No adjustment is needed if using the oral form; however, dose may need to be adjusted if using the IV form.
- *Hepatic impairment:* May require decreasing the dose, and in hepatic failure, use should be avoided. Impaired liver function.
- *Pregnancy:* Category D. This drug should not be used in women who are pregnant. Lorazepam is associated with an increased risk of birth defects.
- *Lactation:* Should not be used if breastfeeding.
- *Children:* Safety has not been established in children under 12; long-terms effects are unknown.

Xanax, Niravam   **alprazolam**

▶Schedule IV drug that requires a prescription. Maximum number of refills is 5 refills/6 mo.

INDICATIONS: Used to achieve sedation during hypnosis.

AVAILABLE FORMS: Tablet, 0.25, 0.5, 1, and 2 mg

DOSAGE: *Adults:* 0.25–0.5 mg PO tid. Maximum 4 mg/day. The dose should be started at 0.25 mg PO tid.

ADMINISTRATION: Take PO. Do not increase the dose, take it more frequently, or use for a longer period. Do not discontinue abruptly without contacting health care provider.

SIDE EFFECTS: Changes in appetite, changes in sexual desire, constipation, dizziness, drowsiness, dry mouth, increased saliva production, lightheadedness, tiredness, trouble concentrating, unsteadiness, and weight changes.

PHARMACOKINETICS:

- Metabolized in the liver (CYP450) and is excreted in the urine.
- Binds to BZD receptors and enhances GABA effects.

Half-life: 11.2 hr (adults); 16.3 hr (elderly)

PRECAUTIONS: Serious reactions include syncope, tachycardia, seizures, respiratory depression, coma, suicidal ideation, and hypomania/mania.

PATIENT AND FAMILY EDUCATION: Inform health care provider of glaucoma, hepatic or renal impairment, drug-abuse history, salivary flow decrease (interferes with ODT absorption), or pregnancy.

SPECIAL POPULATIONS:

- *Elderly:* Give 0.25 mg PO bid or tid. Use lowest most effective dose. Because of its sedative

(cont.)

DISSOCIATIVE IDENTITY DISORDER: Benzodiazepines (BZDs)

alprazolam (*cont.*)

property and increased risk of falls, all benzodiazepines are included on Beers List of Potentially Inappropriate Medications for Geriatrics.
- *Renal impairment:* No adjustment needed.

- *Hepatic impairment:* With advanced hepatic disease, start at 0.25 mg PO bid or tid and titrate gradually.
- *Pregnancy:* Category D; contraindicated in pregnancy.
- *Children:* Pediatric dosing currently unavailable.

Dissociative Fugue Disorder

OVERVIEW
- A dissociative fugue occurs when a person impulsively wanders or travels away from home and upon arrival in the new location is unable to remember his/her past.
- The individual's personal identity is lost because that person is confused about who he/she is and he/she establishes a new identity.
- The travel from home generally occurs following a stressful event or the reappearance of an event or person representing an earlier life trauma.
- The person in the fugue appears to be functioning normally. However, after the fugue experience, the individual may not be able to recall what happened during the fugue state.
- The condition is usually diagnosed when relatives find their lost family member living in another community with a new identity.
- Commonly, individuals who experience the onset of dissociative fugue are found wandering in a dazed or confused state, unable to recall

their own identity or recognize their own relatives or daily surroundings. Often, they suffer from some post-traumatic stress
- The condition is usually short lived, but may last from days to months or longer.
- This condition is not related to the direct physiological effects of ingestion of a drug substance or a medical condition.
- About 2 of 1,000 people in the USA are affected.
- Often, diagnosis is made retroactively when the person abruptly returns to prefugue identity.
- Dissociative fugue is often mistaken for malingering because both conditions give individuals an excuse to avoid accountability.
- Most fugues seem to represent disguised wish fulfillment, e.g., an escape from overwhelming stresses. Other fugues are related to feelings of rejection or separation or may develop as an alternative to suicidal or homicidal impulses.
- After the fugue state, the individual may experience depression, discomfort, grief, shame, intense conflict, suicidal or aggressive tendencies.

Psychopharmacology of Dissociative Fugue Disorder

- There is no medication to treat dissociative fugue. The treatment for dissociative amnesia is therapy aimed at helping the person restore lost memories as soon as possible. If a person is not able to recall the memories, hypnosis or a medication called thiopental (*Pentothal*) can sometimes help restore the memories. Efforts to restore memories of what happened during the fugue itself are usually unsuccessful. However, if patients also suffer from other illnesses such as depression and/or anxiety, they may benefit from treatment with antidepressants or antianxiety medication.
- Psychotherapy may help people explore their patterns of handling the types of situations, conflicts, and moods that triggered the fugue to prevent subsequent fugues. Psychotherapy is helpful for the person who has traumatic past events to resolve.

- Cognitive therapy may be used to focus on changing the dysfunctional thinking patterns and resulting feelings and behaviors.
- Family therapy helps to teach the family about the disorder and its causes and helps the family to recognize symptoms of recurrence.
- Creative therapy allows the individual to explore and express thoughts and feelings in a safe and creative way.
- Clinical hypnosis uses intense relaxation and focused attention to achieve an altered state of consciousness. Hypnosis is often used in the treatment of dissociative fugue. Hypnosis can help the client/patient recall his/her true identity and remember the events of the past. The use of this method is controversial due to the risk of creating false memories.

CLASS	DRUG
Selective Serotonin Reuptake Inhibitors (SSRIs)	**First Line Agent That Can be Used to Treat Comorbid Depression and Anxiety** fluoxetine (*Prozac, Sarafem*) sertraline (*Zoloft*) paroxetine (*Paxil, Pexeva, Paxil CR*) citalopram (*Celexa*) escitalopram (*Lexapro*)

Class: Selective Serotonin Reuptake Inhibitors (SSRIs)

Prozac, Sarafem   **fluoxetine**

INDICATIONS: Used to treat depression.

AVAILABLE FORMS: Capsule, 10, 20, and 40 mg; suspension, 20 mg/5 mL

DOSAGE: *Adults:* 20–80 mg PO qam. Starting dose 20 mg PO qam and may be increased after several weeks. Maximum 80 mg/day. Doses more than 20 mg/day may be divided into bid dosing. *Children: 8–18 yr:* 10–20 mg PO every day starting with 10 mg PO every day for 7 days.

ADMINISTRATION:
- Give PO.
- Take this medication exactly as it was prescribed.
- Do not take the medication in larger amounts, or take it for longer than recommended by the doctor. Do not break, chew, or open an extended-release capsule.
- Swallow the pill whole. It is specially made to release medicine slowly in the body. Breaking the pill would cause too much of the drug to be released at one time.
- Measure the liquid form with a special dose-measuring spoon or cup, not a regular tablespoon.
- It may take 4 weeks or longer before patient starts feeling better.
- Do not stop using fluoxetine without first talking to provider.

SIDE EFFECTS: Common reactions include nausea, headache, insomnia, nervousness, anxiety, asthenia, diarrhea, anorexia, dizziness, dry mouth, tremor, dyspepsia, sweating, ejaculatory dysfunction, constipation, flu syndrome, libido decrease, rash, and abnormal vision.

DRUG INTERACTIONS:
- Linezolid (*Zyvox*) may increase the risk of serotonin syndrome, neuroleptic syndrome, and in combination with fluvoxamine (*Mellaril*) may increase rasagiline (*Azilect*) levels, and increase the risk of adverse effects
- MAOIs are contraindicated within 5 weeks of fluoxetine use because it may increase the risk of serotonin syndrome, neuroleptic syndrome and in combination with fluvoxamine (*Luvox*)

may increase rasagiline (*Azilect*) levels, and increase risk of adverse effects
- Pimozide (*Orap*) may increase the risk of bradycardia, increase pimozide (*Orap*) levels, risk of QT prolongation, cardiac arrhythmias
- Thioridazine (*Mellaril*) may increase thioridazine (*Mellaril*) levels, risk of QT prolongation, cardiac arrhythmias, risk of SIADH, hyponatremia, serotonin syndrome, neuroleptic and malignant syndrome.

PHARMACOKINETICS: Metabolized by the liver (CYP450, 2C19 and 2D6) and excreted in the urine (80%) and feces (15%). The drug selectively inhibits serotonin reuptake.
Half-life: 4–6 days

PRECAUTIONS: Caution is recommended in patients younger than 25 years old. Caution should also be exercised in those with the following conditions: diabetes mellitus, hyponatremia, seizures, mania/hypomania, or volume depletion.

PATIENT AND FAMILY EDUCATION:
- Report any increase the risk of suicidality in children, adolescents, and young adults with major depressive or other psychiatric disorders especially during the first months of treatment.
- Be sure and inform the health care provider of glaucoma, hypoglycemia, or abnormal bleeding tendencies.
- It may take 4 weeks before full therapeutic effects are noticed, and side effects may occur within the first week of treatment. Side effects from the medication may improve once the body adjusts to the medication.
- If deciding to stop taking antidepressants, gradually reduce the dose over a period of several weeks. It is important to discuss quitting or changing the medications with the health care provider first.
- Antianxiety drugs carry a risk of addiction so they are not as desirable for long-term use.
- This drug may cause dizziness and sleepiness so make sure that patients do not drive, operate machinery, or ride a bike prior evaluation.

(cont.)

fluoxetine (cont.)

SPECIAL POPULATIONS:
- *Elderly:* Caution should be exercised.
- *Renal impairment:* No adjustment is needed for those with kidney disease.
- *Hepatic impairment:* Dose may need to be decreased in patients with liver disease.

- *Pregnancy:* Category C; trimester specific.
- *Lactation:* Safety in lactation is unknown.
- *Children:* Use of this drug in children carries the risk of suicide.

sertraline　　*Zoloft*

AVAILABLE FORMS: Tablet, 25, 50, and 100 mg; concentrate, 20 mg/mL

DOSAGE: *Adults:* 25–200 mg PO every day. Usual initial dose 25–50 mg PO every day. After 1 week, may increase daily dose by 25, and then wait a few weeks before increasing dose further.

ADMINISTRATION:
- Administered PO.
- Store sertraline in a tightly closed container and keep away from excess heat and moisture.
- Take the medicine exactly as prescribed. Do not take in larger amounts, or for longer than recommended by the prescriber.
- Take sertraline tablet with water.
- May be taken with or without food.
- Take the medicine at the same time each day.

SIDE EFFECTS: Common side effects include nausea, headache, insomnia, diarrhea, dry mouth, ejaculatory dysfunction, somnolence, asthenia, tremor, dyspepsia, anorexia, constipation, libido decrease, nervousness, anxiety, rash, and abnormal vision.

DRUG INTERACTIONS: Linezolid (*Zyvox*) may increase the risk of serotonin syndrome and neuroleptic syndrome. MAOIs are contraindicated within 5 weeks of sertraline use because they may increase the risk of serotonin syndrome and neuroleptic syndrome. Pimozide (*Orap*) may increase the risk of bradycardia, increase pimozide levels, and increase risk of QT prolongation and cardiac arrhythmias. Thioridazine (*Mellaril*) may increase risk of QT prolongation, cardiac arrhythmias, SIADH, hyponatremia, serotonin syndrome, neuroleptic and malignant syndrome. Cimetidine (*Tagamet*) may increase the sertraline levels in blood by decreasing metabolism of the drug by the liver.

PHARMACOKINETICS: Metabolized in the liver (CYP450; 2C9, 2D6, 3A4) and is excreted in the urine (40–50%) and in the feces (40–45%). This drug selectively inhibits serotonin reuptake. **Half-life:** 26 hr.

PRECAUTIONS:
- Black box warning states that there is an increased risk of suicidality in children, adolescents, and young adults especially during the first months of treatment.
- Caution should be exercised in patients with seizure disorders, with disulfiram use, patients younger than 25 years of age, with liver impairment, hyponatremic patients, alcohol use, and those with mania/hypomania.

PATIENT AND FAMILY EDUCATION:
- Inform provider if increased depression while taking this drug.
- Notify provider if one is hypoglycemic, suffers from seizures or mania, has glaucoma, or has abnormal bleeding/bruising.
- If a dose is missed, take as soon as remembered. If nearly time for the next dose, skip the missed dose and continue with the regular dosing schedule.
- Because sertraline can cause drowsiness and dizziness, make sure to know reaction to the medicine prior to driving, riding a bike, or operating machinery.
- It may take 4 weeks before full therapeutic effects are noticed, and side effects may occur within the first week of treatment.

SPECIAL POPULATIONS:
- *Elderly:* Caution must be exercised in the use of this drug. May require decreased dosage.
- *Renal impairment:* No adjustment needed.
- *Hepatic impairment:* May need to have decreased dosing and/or frequency.
- *Pregnancy:* Category C; trimester-specific.
- *Children:* Not approved in pediatric patients except in OCD.

paroxetine　　*Paxil, Pexeva, Paxil CR*

AVAILABLE FORMS: Tablet, 10, 20, 30, and 40 mg; controlled-release tablet, 12.5 and 25 mg; suspension, 10 mg/5 mL

DOSAGE: *Adults:* 20–50 mg PO each day. Starting dose usually 20 mg PO qam. Maximum 50 mg/day.

ADMINISTRATION:
- Administered PO.
- Take at the same time each day.
- Do not crush, chew, or break a controlled-release tablet.

(cont.)

paroxetine (*cont.*)

- Swallow the pill whole. Breaking the pill would cause too much of the drug to be released at one time.
- Shake the liquid form of paroxetine well just before measuring a dose.
- To get the correct dose, measure the liquid with a marked measuring spoon or medicine cup.
- Store paroxetine at room temperature away from moisture and heat.

SIDE EFFECTS: Nausea, somnolence, headache, asthenia, dizziness, sedation, constipation, libido decrease, diarrhea, sweating, dry mouth, ejaculatory dysfunction, tremor, anorexia, nervousness, anxiety, and abnormal vision.

DRUG INTERACTIONS:
- Linezolid (*Zyvox*) may increase the risk of serotonin syndrome, neuroleptic syndrome, and in combination with fluvoxamine (*Luvox*) may increase rasagiline (*Azilect*) levels, and increase risk of adverse effects
- MAOIs are contraindicated within 5 weeks of paroxetine use because it may increase the risk of serotonin syndrome, neuroleptic syndrome, and in combination with fluvoxamine (*Luvox*) may increase rasagiline (*Azilect*) levels, and increase the risk of adverse effects
- Pimozide (*Orap*) may increase the risk of bradycardia, increase pimozide (*Orap*) levels, risk of QT prolongation, cardiac arrhythmias
- Thioridazine (*Mellaril*) may increase thioridazine (*Mellaril*) levels, risk of QT prolongation, cardiac arrhythmias, risk of SIADH, hyponatremia, serotonin syndrome, neuroleptic, and malignant syndrome.

PHARMACOKINETICS: Metabolized in the liver (CYP450, 2D6) and is excreted in the urine (64%) and feces (36%).
Half-life: 21 hr

PRECAUTIONS: There is an increased risk of suicidality in younger patients and young adults.

PATIENT AND FAMILY EDUCATION:
- Advise health care provider if there is a seizure disorder, renal/liver impairment, glaucoma, alcohol use, or a bleeding disorder.
- Tell the provider if there is increased depression while taking this drug.
- Notify provider of hypoglycemia, seizures or mania, glaucoma, or abnormal bleeding/bruising.
- If a dose is missed, take as soon as remembered. If nearly time for the next dose, skip the missed dose and continue with the regular dosing schedule.
- Because sertraline can cause drowsiness and dizziness, make sure to know reaction to the medicine prior to driving, riding a bike, or operating machinery.
- It may take 4 weeks before full therapeutic effects are noticed; side effects may occur within the first week of treatment.

SPECIAL POPULATIONS:
- *Elderly*: Dosage is usually reduced in half to 10 mg PO qam and a maximum dose is 40 mg/day.
- *Renal impairment:* Dose adjustment may be required. In adult dosing, if the CrCl is below 30, then the initial dose is started at 10 mg every day.
- *Hepatic impairment:* Reduced dosing may be required in children. In adults with severe impairment, the dose is started at 10 mg every day.
- *Pregnancy*: There is positive evidence of human fetal risk.
- *Lactation:* There is minimal risk during lactation.
- *Children*: Caution should be exercised and patients closely monitored for the duration of treatment.

Celexa **citalopram**

INDICATIONS: Used to treat depression.

AVAILABLE FORMS: Tablet and capsule, 10, 20, and 40 mg

DOSAGE: *Adults*: 20–40 mg PO every day. Initial dose usually 20 mg PO every day. Maximum 60 mg/day.

ADMINISTRATION:
- Administered PO.
- Take the missed dose as soon as remembered. However, if almost time for the next regularly scheduled dose, skip the missed dose and take the next one as directed. Do not take extra medicine to make up the missed dose.
- Take the medication exactly as it was prescribed.
- Take the medicine at the same time each day.
- Use the marked measuring spoon or medicine cup for the liquid.

SIDE EFFECTS: Nausea, somnolence, headache, asthenia, dizziness, constipation, libido decrease, diarrhea, sweating, dry mouth, ejaculatory dysfunction, tremor, anorexia, nervousness, anxiety, and abnormal vision.

DRUG INTERACTIONS:
- Linezolid (*Zyvox*) may increase the risk of serotonin syndrome, neuroleptic syndrome, and in combination with fluvoxamine (*Luvox*) may increase rasagiline (*Azilect*) levels, and increase risk of adverse effects
- MAOIs are contraindicated within 5 weeks of citalopram use because it may increase the risk of serotonin syndrome, neuroleptic syndrome, and in combination with fluvoxamine (*Luvox*) may increase rasagiline (*Azilect*) levels, risk of adverse effects

(cont.)

DISSOCIATIVE FUGUE DISORDER: Selective Serotonin Reuptake Inhibitors (SSRIs)

citalopram (*cont.*)

- Pimozide (*Orap*) may increase the risk of brady-cardia, increase pimozide (*Orap*) levels, risk of QT prolongation, cardiac arrhythmias
- Thioridazine (*Mellaril*) may increase thiorida-zine (*Mellaril*) levels, risk of QT prolongation, cardiac arrhythmias, increase risk of SIADH, hyponatremia, serotonin syndrome, and neuro-leptic and malignant syndrome.

PHARMACOKINETICS: Metabolized extensively in the liver (CYP450 2C19 and 3A4) and is excreted primarily in the urine and some in feces. It selec-tively inhibits serotonin reuptake.

PRECAUTIONS: Caution should be exercised in patients with seizure disorders, hepatic/renal impairment, mania, volume depletion or in those who use alcohol.

PATIENT AND FAMILY EDUCATION:
- Tell the provider if there is increased depression while taking this drug.
- Notify provider of hypoglycemia, seizures or mania, glaucoma, or abnormal bleeding/bruising.

- If a dose is missed, take as soon as remembered. If nearly time for the next dose, skip the missed dose and continue with the regular dosing schedule.
- Because sertraline can cause drowsiness and dizziness, make sure to know reaction to the medicine prior to driving, riding a bike, or oper-ating machinery.
- It may take 4 weeks before full therapeutic effects are noticed, and side effects may occur within the first week of treatment.

SPECIAL POPULATIONS:
- *Elderly*: The dosage is adjusted for the elderly to a maximum of 60 mg/day.
- *Renal impairment:* No adjustment is recom-mended but caution is advised.
- *Hepatic impairment:* Patients with hepatic impairment should take 20 mg every day to a maximum of 40 mg daily.
- *Pregnancy*: Caution is advised for pregnant indi-viduals who are over 20 weeks gestation.
- *Children*: Caution should be used and patients closely monitored for duration of treatment.

escitalopram   *Lexapro*

INDICATIONS: Used to treat depression.

AVAILABLE FORMS: Tablet and capsule, 5, 10, and 20 mg; oral solution, 20 mg/mL

DOSAGE: *Adults:* Starting dose 10 mg PO every day, which may be increased after a week to maxi-mum of 20 mg/day.

ADMINISTRATION:
- Administered PO.
- Take the medicine as it was prescribed.
- Take each dose with a full glass of water.
- Take the medicine at the same time every day.
- Use the measuring spoon or cup rather than a household spoon to measure the medicine.

SIDE EFFECTS: Nausea, somnolence, headache, asthenia, dizziness, constipation, libido decrease, diarrhea, sweating, dry mouth, ejaculatory dys-function, tremor, anorexia, nervousness, anxiety, and abnormal vision.

DRUG INTERACTIONS:
- Linezolid (*Zyvox*) may increase the risk of serotonin syndrome, neuroleptic syndrome, and in combination with fluvoxamine (*Luvox*) may increase rasagiline (*Azilect*) levels, risk of adverse effects
- MAOIs are contraindicated within 5 weeks of escitalopram use because it may increase the risk of serotonin syndrome, neuroleptic syn-drome, and in combination with fluvoxamine (*Luvox*) may increase rasagiline (*Azilect*) levels, risk of adverse effects

- Pimozide (*Orap*) may increase the risk of brady-cardia, increase pimozide (*Orap*) levels, risk of QT prolongation, cardiac arrhythmias
- Thioridazine (*Mellaril*) may increase thiorida-zine (*Mellaril*) levels, risk of QT prolongation, cardiac arrhythmias, risk of SIADH, hypona-tremia, serotonin syndrome, neuroleptic and malignant syndrome.
- *Lactation:* Safety is unknown during lactation.

PHARMACOKINETICS: Metabolized in the liver (CYP450 2C19, 2D6, and 3A4) and is excreted in the urine.
Half-life: 27–32 hr; half-life is increased 50% in the elderly

PRECAUTIONS: Caution should be exercised in patients with seizure disorders, hepatic/renal impairment, mania, or volume depletion, or in those who use alcohol.

PATIENT AND FAMILY EDUCATION:
- Tell health care provider of alcohol use or sei-zures, or hepatic/renal involvement.
- Tell provider if increased depression while tak-ing this drug.
- Notify provider of hypoglycemia, seizures or mania, glaucoma, or abnormal bleeding/bruising.
- If a dose is missed, take as soon as remembered. If nearly time for the next dose, skip the missed dose and continue with the regular dosing schedule.
- Because sertraline can cause drowsiness and dizziness, make sure to know reaction to the
(cont.)

escitalopram (*cont.*)

medicine prior to driving, riding a bike, or operating machinery.

- It may take 4 weeks before full therapeutic effects are noticed, and side effects may occur within the first week of treatment.

SPECIAL POPULATIONS:

- *Elderly*: Dosage is usually half of the adult dose; initial dose is 10 mg/day.

- *Renal impairment:* Mild to moderate impairment, no adjustments are needed; in severe impairment, caution is advised.
- *Hepatic impairment:* The dose is decreased to a maximum of 10 mg/day.
- *Pregnancy*: Category C; trimester-specific.
- *Children*: Suicidality is a concern in young children, adolescents, and young adults.

Dissociative Amnesia Disorder

OVERVIEW

- Inability to remember important personal information, which is usually associated with a traumatic event in their lives cannot be explained by normal forgetfulness.
- The dissociation is a protective activation of altered states of consciousness in reaction to overwhelming psychological trauma so when the individual returns to baseline, access to the dissociative information is diminished. The memories are encoded in the individual's mind but are not conscious, i.e., they have been repressed.
- There are two types of memory tracings: explicit and implicit. Explicit memories include facts and experiences that are consciously stored and available for immediate recall. Implicit memories are independent of conscious memory. Explicit memory tracings are not well developed in children and may account for more implicit memory tracings being laid down. Trauma may result in implicit memory.
- Loss of memory creates gaps in the individual's personal history.
- Generally a problem in adulthood, dissociative amnesia can be found in children and adolescents.
- *Generalized amnesia* is the most extreme form of dissociative amnesia and refers to failure to recall one's entire life.
- *Localized amnesia* involves a lack of memory for certain time periods such as those experienced in battle.

- *Continuous amnesia* occurs when the individual has no memory of events up to and including the present time.
- *Systematized amnesia* involves the loss of memory for certain categories of information such as certain places or persons.
- Symptoms of dissociative amnesia cause clinically significant distress or impairment in social, occupational, or other important areas of functioning.
- If episode is associated with traumatic events and once the individual is removed from the traumatic situation, the amnesia may clear.
- Length of an event of dissociative amnesia may be a few months or several years.
- Once memories are recovered, they may not be recognized as personal memories.
- Loss of memory creates gaps in the individual's personal history.
- Various treatments are available for individuals with psychogenic amnesia although no well-controlled studies on the effectiveness of different treatments exist.
- Psychoanalysis uses dream analysis and other psychoanalytic methods to retrieve memories. Individuals may also be placed in threatening situations where they are overwhelmed with intense emotion.
- With the help of psychotherapy and family members' historical perspective, most patients recover their memories completely.

Psychopharmacology of Dissociative Amnesia Disorder

- Psychoanalysis is used to analyze dreams and to retrieve memories. Sometimes individuals are placed in threatening situations to bring the issues to the forefront in order to recover the memories of the stressful time. The treatment for dissociative amnesia is therapy aimed at helping the person restore lost memories as soon as possible. If a person is not able to recall the memories, hypnosis or a medication called thiopental (*Pentothal*) can sometimes help to restore the memories. Psychotherapy can help

an individual deal with the trauma associated with the recalled memories.

- Hypnosis is often used in treatment and can help the client/patient recall his/her true identity and remember the events of the past. Psychotherapy is helpful for the person who has traumatic, past events to resolve.
- Relaxation is used in conjunction with benzodiazepines and other hypnotic medications in an attempt for the individual to be able to recall memories. Psychotherapy and hearing

biographies from family members usually result in the complete recovery of memories.

- While not as popular, abreaction can be used in conjunction with midazolam (*Versed*) to recover memories. It is thought to either depress the function of the cerebral cortex, making the memory more tolerable when expressed, or relieve the strength of the emotion attached to a memory that is so intense it suppresses memory function.

- Individuals with dissociative amnesia can have comorbid disorders of mood disorders, anxiety disorders, or post-traumatic stress disorders and should be treated with pharmacological agents. In severe cases, the new antiepileptic agents in combination with SNRIs (serotonin/norepinephrine reuptake inhibitors), SSRIs (serotonin reuptake inhibitors), and atypical neuroleptics are used.

CLASS	DRUG
Barbiturates	**First-Line Drugs Used for Hypnosis for Recall of Memories**
	thiopental sodium (*Pentothal*)
Benzodiazepines (BZDs)	**Drugs Used to Promote Relaxation During Hypnosis**
	midazolam (*Versed*)
	diazepam (*Valium, Diastat, Di-Tran, T-Quil, Valrelease, Vazepam, Zetran*)
	lorazepam (*Ativan, Alzapam*)
	oxazepam (*Serax*)
	clorazepate (*Tranxene*)
	alprazolam (*Xanax, Niravam*)
	chlordiazepoxide (*Librium*)
Amphetamine Derivatives (Psychostimulants)	
	Drugs Used to Reduce inhibitions
	methylphenidate (*Ritalin, Concerta, Metadate CD, Metadate ER, Methylin, Methylin ER*)

Class: Barbiturates

thiopental sodium   *Pentothal*

INDICATIONS Used as the sole anesthetic agents for brief (15 min) procedures, to provide hypnosis with other agents for analgesia or muscle relaxation, for control of convulsions, and for narcoanalysis and narcosynthesis in psychiatric disorders. In dissociative amnesia, it helps to desensitize patients with phobias and assist in the recall of painful repressed memories. Anesthetists or anesthesiologists would be best trained to use this medication for treatment of amnesia

AVAILABLE FORMS: Liquid for IV infusion; diluent may be supplied in a separate container

DOSAGE:
- There is no fixed dosage, and the drug is titrated against patient requirements as governed by age, sex, and body weight.
- Younger patients require relatively larger doses than middle-aged or elderly persons.
- Adult females require less than adult males.
- Obese patients require a larger dose.
- The dosage can range from 250 mg to 25 g and the concentration can range from 2% to 2.5%.
▶ **Warning:** The 2.5 g and larger sizes contain adequate medication for several patients.

ADMINISTRATION:
- Premedication with an anticholinergic agent may precede administration of thiopental sodium.
- *Pentothal* (thiopental sodium for injection, USP) is injected IV at a slow rate of 100 mg/mm (4 mL/min of a 2.5% solution) with the patient counting backward from 100. When the patient becomes confused, but before actual sleep is produced, the injection is discontinued.
- Alternatively, may be administered by rapid IV drip using a 0.2% concentration in 5% dextrose. At this concentration, the rate of administration should not exceed 50 mL/min.
- Allow the patient to return to a semidrowsy state where conversation is coherent.
- It is advisable to inject a small "test" dose of 25 to 75 mg (1 to 3 mL of a 2.5% solution) to assess tolerance or unusual sensitivity to drug and pause for at least 60 sec to see if respiratory depression occurs.
- Momentary apnea after each injection is typical.
- Extravascular infiltration should be avoided by ensuring that the needle is within the lumen of the vein prior to injection of pentothal.
- Avoid intra-arterial injection by palpating for the pulsing vessel prior to sticking the patient.

(cont.)

thiopental sodium (*cont.*)

- Do not administer pentothal if the precipitate is not clear.
- Store at room temperature 15°C to 30°C.
- Keep reconstituted solution in a cool place.

SIDE EFFECTS: Respiratory depression, myocardial depression, cardiac arrhythmias, prolonged somnolence and recovery, laryngospasm, bronchospasm, immune hemolytic anemia with renal failure, radial nerve palsy, urticaria, shivering, sneezing, and coughing.

DRUG INTERACTIONS: *Contraindicated with the following*: probenecid (prolonged action of thiopental), diazoxide (hypotension), zimelidine (thiopental antagonism), opioid analgesics (decreased antinociceptive), aminophylline (thiopental antagonism), midazolam (synergistic reaction), azole antifungals (may decrease antifungal efficacy), etravirine (may decrease etravirine levels), pazopanib (may decrease pazopanib levels), protease inhibitors (may decrease protease inhibitor levels), ranolazine (may decrease ranolazine levels), and sodium oxybate (may increase risk of CNS and respiratory depression).
- Co-administration of pentoxifylline and thiopental causes death by acute pulmonary edema in rats due to increased pulmonary vascular permeability.
- Instruct individuals not to smoke, drink alcohol, or use illegal drugs as in combination with pentobarbital; these agents could cause serious consequences such as respiratory depression.
- Solutions of succinylcholine, tubocurarine, or other drugs with an acid pH should not be mixed with thiopental sodium solutions.
▶**Alert:** This list may not describe all possible interactions. Instruct individuals to provide a list of all the medicines, herbs, nonprescription drugs, or dietary supplements they use so as to evaluate interactions.

PHARMACOKINETICS:
- Largely degraded in the liver and to a smaller extent in the kidney and brain.
- Hypnosis is produced within 30 to 40 sec of IV injection.
- Approximately 80% of the drug in the blood is bound to plasma protein.
- Products of thiopental are excreted in the urine.

▶Schedule IV drug; requires a prescription with a maximum of 5 refills/6 mo.

INDICATIONS: Used for relaxation during hypnotic sessions.

AVAILABLE FORMS: Injection form, 1, 2, and 5 mg/ mL; preservative-free solution

- Acts on the GABA receptor in the brain and spinal cord and inhibits this receptor to decrease neuronal activity.

Half-life: The elimination phase after a single IV dose is 3–11.5 hr, decreased in children, with an onset of action of 5–30 min

PRECAUTIONS:
- Keep resuscitative and endotracheal intubation equipment and oxygen readily available. Maintain patency of airway at all times.
- Avoid extravasation or intra-arterial injection.
- May be habit forming.
- Use within 24 hr after reconstitution. Discard unused portions.
- Administer only clear reconstituted solutions

PATIENT AND FAMILY EDUCATION: Be sure and tell the health care provider of any of the following:
- Allergy to barbiturates
- Porphyria (South African)
- Acute intermittent porphyria
- Liver problems/disease
- Kidney problems/disease
- Pregnancy
- Asthma
- Myasthenia gravis
- Endocrine disorders
- Advanced cardiac disease
- Hangover from administration of thiopental can last for up to 36 hr so patient should not drive or operate heavy machinery or children should not ride bicycle for 36 hr after administration.

SPECIAL POPULATIONS:
- *Elderly*: Advanced cardiac disease, increased intracranial pressure, ophthalmoplegia, asthma, myasthenia gravis, endocrine insufficiency (pituitary, thyroid, adrenal, pancreas)
- *Renal impairment:* Caution should be used and renal function checked prior to beginning treatment with dose adjustment as necessary.
- *Hepatic impairment:* Caution should be used and liver function checked prior to beginning treatment with dose adjustment as necessary.
- *Pregnancy*: Category C (given only if needed)
- *Children*: Best results occurred with children over 12 years of age and over 50 kg in weight (30 mg/ kg/PR). Maximum is 1 g dose.

Class: Benzodiazepines (BZDs)

Versed	midazolam

DOSAGE:
Procedural IV Dosing:
- *Adults under 60 yr:* 1 mg IV every 2–3 min with a maximum of 2.5 mg/dose. Cumulative doses over 5 mg are rarely needed. *Over 60 yr:* Maximum dose 1.5 mg total. Cumulative doses over 3.5 mg are rarely needed. *Children:*

(cont.)

DISSOCIATIVE AMNESIA DISORDER: Benzodiazepines (BZDs)

midazolam (*cont.*)

6 mo to 5 yr: 0.05–0.1 mg/kg ×1; repeat every 2–3 min as needed. Maximum 0.6 mg/kg total. Cumulative dose rarely over 6 mg. *Children 6 to 12 yr:* 0.025–0.05 mg/kg ×1; repeat every 2–3 min before procedure. Maximum dose 0.4 mg. Cumulative dose rarely above 10 mg. *Children over 12 yr:* 0.5–2 mg IV ×1; repeat every 2–3 min when needed. Cumulative dose above 10 mg is rarely needed.

PO:
- *Children over 6 yr:* 0.25–0.5 mg/kg PO ×1 with a maximum of 20 mg. Give 20–30 min before procedure. *Under 6 yr:* May need up to 1 mg/kg/dose.

IM
- *Children over 6 yr:* 0.1–0.15 mg/kg IM ×1 with maximum of 0.5 mg/kg total. Cumulative dosing over 10 mg rarely needed. Give 15–30 min before procedure.

ADMINISTRATION:
- Given by slow IV administration (more than 2 min) with careful attention to proper venous placement to avoid extravasation.
- Do not give rapid IV injection in neonates as severe hypotension and seizures were reported.
- This drug can also be given IM.

SIDE EFFECTS: Nausea, vomiting, and reduced heart rate. Serious side effects include difficulty breathing, irregular heart rate, allergic reactions, respiratory depression and/or cardiac arrest, airway obstruction, oxygen desaturation, apnea and sometimes death.

DRUG INTERACTIONS:
- The sedative effect of IV midazolam is accentuated by any other drugs that may depress the central nervous system, particularly narcotics such as morphine.
- Caution is also advised when midazolam is administered concomitantly with drugs that are known to inhibit the P450 34A enzyme system such as cimetidine (*Tagamet*), erythromycin, diltiazem (*Cardizem*), verapamil (*Calan/Isoptin/Verelan*), ketoconazole, and itraconazole (*Sporanox*).
- Both cimetidine and ranitidine increased the mean steady-state concentration of blood level for midazolam.
- Erythromycin doubled the half-life of midazolam.
- No significant adverse interactions have been noted with commonly used premedications or drugs used during anesthesia including atropine, scopolamine, diazepam, hydroxyzine, succinylcholine, or topical local anesthetics.

PHARMACOKINETICS:
- Metabolized by the liver (CYP450: 3A4 substrate) and excreted in the urine.
- Drug binds to benzodiazepine receptors and enhances GABA effects.

Half-life: 2.5 hr

PRECAUTIONS:
- Use only in hospital/ambulatory care setting with continuous respiratory and cardiac monitoring, appropriate ventilation/intubation equipment, and personnel trained/skilled in airway management.
- One dedicated person other than practitioner performing the procedure should continuously monitor deeply sedated pediatric patients.
- Reactions such as agitation, involuntary movements, hyperactivity, and combativeness have been reported in adult and pediatric patients.
- Should such reactions occur, caution should be exercised before continuing administration.

PATIENT AND FAMILY EDUCATION:
- Tell practitioner if pregnant or nursing.
- Midazolam is associated with a high incidence of partial or complete impairment of recall for the next several hours.
- Do not mix alcohol or any other depressant drug and midazolam without the health care provider's knowledge.
- Do not operate hazardous machinery or motor vehicle until the effects of the drug have subsided or until one full day after anesthesia.

SPECIAL POPULATIONS:
- *Elderly:* Glaucoma, angle closure, COPD, and congestive heart failure are contraindications to use. IV dosing of midazolam should be decreased for elderly or debilitated patients. Because of its sedative property and increased risk of falls, all benzodiazepines are included on Beers List of Potentially Inappropriate Medications for Geriatrics.
- *Renal impairment:* Caution should be used and renal function checked prior to beginning treatment with dose adjustment as necessary.
- *Hepatic impairment:* Caution should be used and liver function checked prior to beginning treatment with dose adjustment as necessary.
- *Pregnancy:* Category D; has shown positive evidence of human fetal risk.
- *Lactation:* Safety unknown as there is inadequate literature to assess risk.
- *Children:* Caution in neonates as rapid IV injection can cause severe hypotension and seizures.

DISSOCIATIVE AMNESIA DISORDER: Benzodiazepines (BZDs)

Valium, Diastat, Di-Tran, T-Quil, Valrelease, Vazepam, Zetran | **diazepam**

▶Schedule IV drug that requires prescription. Maximum of 5 refills/6 mo.

INDICATIONS: Used to promote relaxation during hypnosis.

AVAILABLE FORMS: Tablet, 2, 5, and 10 mg

DOSAGE: *Adults:* 2–10 mg bid–qid (maximum 40 mg/day). *Children over 12 yr:* 2–10 mg PO bid or qid. Alternatively, 2–10 mg IM/IV every 3–4 hr when needed.

ADMINISTRATION: May be given PO, IV, or IM. Avoid abrupt cessation; taper dose gradually. Monitor complete blood count and liver transaminase levels if prolonged treatment. Diazepam can be taken with or without food. Never give a double dose.

SIDE EFFECTS: Drowsiness, impaired motor functions, impaired coordination, impaired balance, fatigue, depression, anterograde amnesia and reflex tachycardia, respiratory depression, bradycardia, hypotension, seizures, hallucinations, psychosis, jaundice, neutropenia, blood dyscrasias, depression, and drug-abuse

DRUG INTERACTIONS: Cimetidine (*Tagamet*), oral contraceptives, disulfiram (*Antabuse*), fluoxetine (*Prozac/Sarafem*), isoniazid, ketoconazole, rifampin (*Rifadin*), metoprolol (*Lopressor/Toprol-XL*), probenecid, propoxyphene (*Darvon*), propranolol (*Inderal*), and valproic acid (*Depakene/Stavzor*) may prolong the effects of diazepam

PHARMACOKINETICS: Metabolized almost exclusively in the liver (CYP450 2C19, 3A4 substrate).
Half-life: 30–60 hr

PRECAUTIONS: Allergy to diazepam, glaucoma, breathing problems, kidney or liver disease, seizures, or a history of drug or alcohol addiction, mental illness, depression, or suicidal thoughts are contraindications for using this drug.

PATIENT AND FAMILY EDUCATION:
- Tell health care provider all of the medicines being taken as this drug has numerous contraindicated medicines.
- Grapefruit and grapefruit juice can slow down the breakdown of diazepam.
- Avoid alcohol use and herbs with sedative effects.
- Know response to the medicine before riding a bike, driving a car, or operating machinery.
- Store in a tightly closed container and keep at room temperature away from excess heat and moisture.
- Never take more of this medicine than the doctor has prescribed. Do not use this medication if allergic to diazepam, or in cases of myasthenia gravis, severe liver disease, narrow-angle glaucoma, severe breathing problems, or sleep apnea
- Use an effective form of birth control while using this product.
- Do not stop this drug without knowledge of the doctor.

SPECIAL POPULATIONS:
- *Elderly*: Caution should be exercised. The sedative effects of diazepam may last longer in older adults. Because of sedative effects and increased risk of falls, all benzodiazepines are included on Beers List of Potentially Inappropriate Medications for Geriatrics.
- *Renal impairment:* Caution advised.
- *Hepatic impairment:* Contraindicated in severe impairment.
- *Pregnancy*: Category D. Positive evidence of human fetal risk in pregnant females.
- *Lactation*: Avoid use.
- *Children*: No specific precautions other than monitoring of vital signs. Do not give this medication to a child younger than 6 mo.

Ativan, Alzapam | **lorazepam**

▶Schedule IV drug. Maximum number of refills is 5 refills/6 mo.

INDICATIONS: Used for sedation during hypnosis.

AVAILABLE FORMS: Tablet, 0.5, 1, and 2 mg

DOSAGE: *Adults:* PO: 2–3 mg/day divided in 2–3 dosing; maximum 10 mg/day. *Procedural sedation:* 0.05 mg/kg IM; maximum 4 mg/dose given 2 hr before operation. IV: 0.044–0.05 mg/kg ×1; maximum 4 mg/dose; 2 mg/dose in elderly given 15–20 min prior to hypnosis. *Children:* IM or IV: 0.05 mg/kg PO, ×1; maximum 2 mg/dose. Give PO dose 1 hr prior to procedures; give IM dose more than 2 hr and IV 15–20 min prior to procedure.

ADMINISTRATION:
- Can be given PO, IM, and IV. Missed doses need to be given as soon as possible; however, if it is time for the next dose, do not administer a double dose.
- This drug can be taken with food to help prevent stomach irritation.
- Smoking can decrease the effectiveness of this drug.
- If a dose is missed, it should be taken as soon as possible. If it is time for the next dose, skip the missed dose and resume usual dosing schedule.

SIDE EFFECTS: Dizziness, weakness, and unsteadiness. A few other side effects include nausea, constipation, and fatigue.

DRUG INTERACTIONS:
- The administration of lorazepam (*Ativan*) and sodium oxybate (*Xyrem*) has been contraindicated as this combination may increase the risk of CNS and respiratory depression.

(cont.)

lorazepam (cont.)

- The following drugs should be used with great caution because they may increase the risk of CNS depression: aripiprazole (*Abilify*), dexmedetomidine (*Precedex*), and propofol (*Diprivan*).
- Probenecid may increase lorazepam (*Ativan*) levels and risk of toxicity. Before taking drugs that cause drowsiness such as antihistamines (diphenhydramine), anti-seizure drugs (carbamazepine), medicine for sleep (sedatives), muscle relaxants, narcotic pain relievers (codeine), psychiatric medicines (phenothiazines such as chlorpromazine, or tricyclics such as amitriptyline), and/or tranquilizers, notify health care provider.

PHARMACOKINETICS:
- Metabolized by the liver (CYP450)
- Enhances GABA effects, which inhibit transmission of nerve signals and thus reduces nervous excitation.

Half-life: 14 hr

PRECAUTIONS: Avoid abrupt withdrawal for long-term use, use of alcohol, in depressed patients, avoid intra-arterial administration, use in drug-abuse patients.

PATIENT AND FAMILY EDUCATION:
- Notify health care provider if problems with liver, kidneys, alcohol or drug consumption, glaucoma, lung problems, or if treated for psychiatric disorders.
- Grapefruit juice should be avoided as it slows the body's breakdown of the drug and can lead to dangerous concentrations.

- Herbs with sedative effects should be avoided.
- Alcoholic beverages should be avoided. Lithium with lorazepam can cause children's body temperature to drop.
- Use of CNS depressants can cause respiratory depression.
- Birth control pills, theophylline, caffeine, and other stimulants can reduce the effects of lorazepam.
- Heparin, macrolide antibiotics, probenecid, quetiapine, and valproic acid can increase the effects of lorazepam.
- Store in a tightly closed container and keep at room temperature away from excess heat and moisture.

SPECIAL POPULATIONS:
- *Elderly*: Caution is advised. Because of sedative effect and increased risk of falls, all benzodiazepines are included on Beers List of Potentially Inappropriate Medications for Geriatrics.
- *Renal impairment:* No adjustment is needed if using the oral form; however, dose may need to be adjusted if using the IV form.
- *Hepatic impairment:* May require decreasing the dose; if patient has hepatic failure, use should be avoided.
- *Pregnancy*: Category D. Should not be used in women who are pregnant. Lorazepam is associated with an increased risk of birth defects.
- *Lactation:* Should not be used in women who are breastfeeding.
- *Children*: Safety not established in children less than 12 years old.

oxazepam   *Serax*

INDICATIONS: Used for sedation during hypnosis and to treat anxiety.

AVAILABLE FORMS: Capsule, 10, 15, and 30 mg

DOSAGE: *Adults:* Anxiety: 10–30 mg PO 3 to qid; *Elderly:* 10–15 mg PO 3 or qid.

ADMINISTRATION:
- If discontinuing the drug, health care provider will gradually taper.
- Dose may need to be gradually decreased in order to avoid side effects such as seizures.
- When used for an extended period, this medication may not work as well and may require different dosing.
- Stop smoking while taking this drug as it may decrease the effectiveness of oxazepam.

SIDE EFFECTS: Clumsiness or unsteadiness, confusion, unusual risk behaviors, hyperactivity, hallucinations, jaundice, lightheadedness, dizziness drowsiness, and slurred speech.

DRUG INTERACTIONS:
- Oxazepam should not be used with sodium oxybate as it may increase the risk of CNS and respiratory depression.
- Probenecid may should be used with great caution; may increase the risk of CNS depression (aripiprazole, dexmedetomidine, and propofol). May increase oxazepam levels and risk of toxicity. Before taking drugs that cause drowsiness such as antihistamines (diphenhydramine), anti-seizure drugs (carbamazepine), medicine for sleep (sedatives), muscle relaxants, narcotic pain relievers (codeine), psychiatric medicines (phenothiazines such as chlorpromazine, or tricyclics such as amitriptyline), and/or tranquilizers the health care provider needs to be notified.

PHARMACOKINETICS: Metabolized in the liver (CYP450) Enhances the GABA effects.
Half-life: 8.2 hr

(cont.)

DISSOCIATIVE AMNESIA DISORDER: Benzodiazepines (BZDs)

oxazepam (*cont.*)

PRECAUTIONS: Monitor CBC and liver profiles. Serious reactions include leukopenia, hepatic impairment, and abuse.

PATIENT AND FAMILY EDUCATION:
- Tell the provider if treated for another psychiatric illness such as depression.
- Refrain from driving or operating dangerous machinery until the effect of this drug is known.
- Do not discontinue drug abruptly as this can cause serious problems.
- There is a potential for dependence on the drug, so consult health care provider before either increasing the dose or abruptly discontinuing it.
- If pregnant during therapy or intend to become pregnant, communicate this information to the health care provider.
- Avoid alcohol while taking this drug.

SPECIAL POPULATIONS:
- *Elderly*: Caution should be exercised and the initial dose should be the lowest possible due to the drowsiness effect. Because of its sedative property and increased risk of falls, all benzodiazepines are included on Beers List of Potentially Inappropriate Medications for Geriatrics.
- *Renal impairment*: No adjustment is needed at the present time.
- *Hepatic impairment*: Adjustments have not been defined at this time.
- *Pregnancy*: Category D; do not use unless benefits outweigh risks.
- *Lactation*: Caution advised with breastfeeding.
- *Children*: The safety and effectiveness of this drug has not been established in children less than 6 years of age. Absolute dosage for pediatric patients 6 to 12 years of age has not been established.

Tranxene　　**clorazepate**

▶Schedule IV drug and requires prescription. Maximum number of refills is 5 refills/6 mo.

INDICATIONS: Used to achieve sedation during hypnosis and to relieve anxiety.

AVAILABLE FORMS: Tablet, 3.75, 7.5, and 15 mg

DOSAGE: *Adults:* 15–60 mg dose PO every day divided into bid or tid or 15–30 mg at bedtime. *Children 9–12 yr:* Start 7.5 mg PO bid, increase 7.5 mg every week. Maximum 60 mg/day. Alternatively, dose can begin at 0.3 mg/kg/day PO divided into bid or qid. *Over 12 yr:* Starting dose 7.5 mg PO tid, increasing to 7.5 every week. Maximum 90 mg/day.

ADMINISTRATION: Taken PO. Do not abruptly stop taking this drug. To discontinue this drug, talk to the health care provider.

SIDE EFFECTS: Drowsiness, dizziness, various GI complaints, nervousness, blurred vision, dry mouth, headache, and confusion.

DRUG INTERACTIONS:
- Avoid sodium oxybate as it can increase CNS and respiratory depression.
- Chloramphenicol, cimetidine (*Tagamet*), clarithromycin (*Biaxin*), conivaptan (*Vaprisol*), cyclosporine (*Gengraf/Neoral*), delavirdine (*Rescriptor*), imatinib (*Gleevec*), isoniazid, itraconazole (*Sporanox*), ketoconazole, nefazodone (*Serzone*), posaconazole (*Noxafil*), protease inhibitors, telithromycin (*Ketek*), and voriconazole (*Vfend*) may increase benzodiazepine levels, risk CNS depression, and psychomotor impairment.
- The action of benzodiazepines may be potentiated by barbiturates, narcotics, phenothiazines, MAOIs, or other antidepressants.

PHARMACOKINETICS:
- Metabolized in the liver (CYP450) and excreted primarily through the urine and feces.

- This drug has depressant effects on the central nervous system by binding to benzodiazepine receptors and enhancing GABA effects.
Half-life: 40–50 hr

PRECAUTIONS: Serious reactions to the drug include hepatotoxicity, respiratory depression, seizure exacerbation, suicidality, dependency, and abuse.

PATIENT AND FAMILY EDUCATION:
- Do not abruptly stop taking the drug; the dose must be tapered.
- May increase the risk of suicidal thoughts and behavior; be alert for the emergence or worsening of signs and symptoms of depression, unusual changes in mood or behavior, or emergence of suicidal thoughts.
- Do not drive, operate heavy machinery, or do other dangerous activities until it is known how clorazepate exerts its effects.
- Do not drink alcohol or take other drugs that may cause sleepiness or dizziness while taking clorazepate without first talking to provider.

SPECIAL POPULATIONS:
- *Elderly*: The elderly or debilitated patients need to start at 7.5–15 mg/day. Because of the sedative effect and increased risk of falls, all benzodiazepines are included on Beers List of Potentially Inappropriate Medications for Geriatrics.
- *Renal impairment*: No adjustment needed.
- *Hepatic impairment*: Not defined at this time.
- *Pregnancy*: Category D; trimester-specific or population-specific risks. There is an increased risk of congenital malformations associated with the use of this drug during the first trimester of pregnancy.
- *Children*: Pediatric dosing is currently unavailable or not applicable. It is not recommended for children under 9 years of age.

DISSOCIATIVE AMNESIA DISORDER: Benzodiazepines (BZDs)

alprazolam — *Xanax, Niravam*

▶Schedule IV drug that requires a prescription. Maximum number of refills is 5 refills/6 mo.

INDICATIONS: Used to achieve sedation during hypnosis and to treat anxiety.

AVAILABLE FORMS: Tablet, 0.25, 0.5, 1, and 2 mg.

DOSAGE: *Adults:* 0.25–0.5 mg PO tid; maximum, 4 mg/day. The dose should be started at 0.25 mg PO tid.

ADMINISTRATION: Taken PO. Keep alprazolam out of the light in a dry and tightly closed container. Store at room temperature.

SIDE EFFECTS: Changes in appetite, changes in sexual desire, constipation, dizziness, drowsiness, dry mouth, increased saliva production, lightheadedness, tiredness, trouble concentrating, unsteadiness, and weight changes.

DRUG INTERACTIONS:
- Avoid sodium oxybate as it can increase CNS and respiratory depression. Chloramphenicol, cimetidine (*Tagamet*), clarithromycin (*Biaxin*), conivaptan (*Vaprisol*), cyclosporine (*Gengraf/Neoral*), delavirdine (*Rescriptor*), imatinib (*Gleevec*), isoniazid, itraconazole (*Sporanox*), ketoconazole, nefazodone (*Serzone*), posaconazole (*Noxafil*), protease inhibitors, telithromycin (*Ketek*), and voriconazole (*Vfend*) may increase benzodiazepine levels, risk of CNS depression, and psychomotor impairment.
- The action of benzodiazepines may be potentiated by barbiturates, narcotics, phenothiazines, MAOIs, or other antidepressants.

PHARMACOKINETICS: Metabolized in the liver (CYP450) and is excreted in the urine. It binds to benzodiazepine receptors and enhances GABA effects.

Half-life: 11.2 hr (adults); 16.3 hr (elderly)

PRECAUTIONS: Serious reactions to the drug include syncope, tachycardia, seizures, respiratory depression, coma, suicidal ideation, and hypomania/mania.

PATIENT AND FAMILY EDUCATION:
- Tell the health care provider of glaucoma, hepatic or renal impairment, drug-abuse history, salivary flow decrease (interferes with ODT absorption), or pregnancy.
- Missed doses should be taken as soon as possible; however, if it is too close to next dose, then it should be skipped.
- Take medicine as prescribed and do not abruptly stop it without first discussing with health care provider.
- Before taking this medicine tell health care provider if medical history of liver disease, kidney disease, lung/breathing problems, drug or alcohol abuse, or any allergies.
- Do not drive, operate heavy machinery or perform dangerous activities until it is known how this medicine will exert its effects.
- This drug may be habit forming and should be used only by the person for whom it was prescribed.

SPECIAL POPULATIONS:
- *Elderly*: Give 0.25 mg PO bid or tid. Use lowest most effective dose. Because of sedative property and increased risk of falls, all benzodiazepines are included on Beers List of Potentially Inappropriate Medications for Geriatrics.
- *Renal impairment:* No adjustment needed.
- *Hepatic impairment:* With advanced hepatic disease, start at 0.25 mg PO bid or tid and titrate gradually.
- *Pregnancy*: Category D; contraindicated in pregnancy.
- *Children*: Pediatric dosing currently unavailable.

chlordiazepoxide — *Librium*

INDICATIONS: Used to achieve sedation during hypnosis and to relieve anxiety.

AVAILABLE FORMS: Capsule, 5, 10, and 25 mg

DOSAGE: *Adults:* 5–10 mg PO tid to qid. *Children:* 5 mg bid or qid; may be increased to 10 mg bid or tid.

ADMINISTRATION:
- Administered PO.
- Use exactly as prescribed.
- Do not increase the dose; take it more frequently or use it for a longer period of time.
- The drug should not be stopped abruptly, but tapered off slowly.
- When used for an extended period of time this medicine may not work as well and may require different dosing.

SIDE EFFECTS: Some common side effects are drowsiness, ataxia, confusion, skin eruptions, edema, menstrual irregularities, nausea, constipation, extrapyramidal effects, libido changes, or paradoxical stimulation.

DRUG INTERACTIONS:
- Avoid sodium oxybate as it can increase CNS and respiratory depression. Chloramphenicol, cimetidine (*Tagamet*), clarithromycin (*Biaxin*), conivaptan (*Vaprisol*), cyclosporine (*Gengraf/Neoral*), delavirdine (*Rescriptor*), imatinib (*Gleevec*), isoniazid, itraconazole (*Sporanox*), ketoconazole, nefazodone (*Serzone*), posaconazole (*Noxafil*), protease inhibitors, telithromycin (*Ketek*), and voriconazole (*Vfend*) may increase benzodiazepine levels, risk CNS depression, and psychomotor impairment.
- The action of benzodiazepines may be potentiated by barbiturates, narcotics, phenothiazines, MAOIs or other antidepressants. be used if

(cont.)

DISSOCIATIVE AMNESIA DISORDER: Benzodiazepines (BZDs)

chlordiazepoxide (*cont.*)

depression, porphyria, suicidal ideation, alcohol/drug-abuse, or psychosis is present

PHARMACOKINETICS: Metabolized in the liver (CYP450) and excreted in the urine. Binds to BZD receptors and enhances GABA effects.
Half-life: 5–30 hr

PRECAUTIONS: In general concomitant administration of chlordiazepoxide and other psychotropic drugs is not recommended. Caution should be exercised in administering chlordiazepoxide to patients with a history of psychosis, depression, suicidal ideation, porphyria, or alcohol/drug abuse.

PATIENT AND FAMILY EDUCATION:
- Tell health care provider of glaucoma, hepatic or renal impairment, drug-abuse history, salivary flow decrease (interferes with ODT absorption), or pregnancy.
- Take medicine as prescribed and do not abruptly stop it without first consulting with provider.
- Before taking this medicine, tell provider if medical history of liver disease, kidney

disease, lung/breathing problems, drug or alcohol abuse or any allergies.
- Do not drive, operate heavy machinery, or perform dangerous activities until it is known how this medicine will exerts its effects.
- This drug may be habit forming and should be used only by the person for whom it was prescribed.

SPECIAL POPULATIONS:
- *Elderly*: Start with 5 mg every day bid and then gradually increase to 5 mg PO bid or qid. Because of sedative effects and increased risk of falls, all benzodiazepines are included on Beers List of Potentially Inappropriate Medications for Geriatrics.
- *Renal impairment:* Adjust dose to 50% of the normal dosage if CrCl is below 10.
- *Hepatic impairment:* Caution advised in children with hepatic impairment.
- *Pregnancy*: Category D; positive evidence of human fetal risk.
- *Lactation:* Probably safe for breastfeeding mothers.
- *Children*: The use of this drug in children younger than 6 years of age is not recommended.

Class: Amphetamine Derivatives (Psychostimulants)

Ritalin, Concerta, Metadate CD, Metadate ER, Methylin, Methylin ER   **methylphenidate**

▶Schedule II drug that requires prescription. No refills or verbal order allowed.

INDICATIONS: Used to increase focus during hypnotic sessions.

AVAILABLE FORMS: Tablet, 18, 27, 36, and 54 mg

DOSAGE: *Adults*: 5–15 mg PO bid or tid. *Children over 6 yr*: 0.3–2 mg/kg/day PO bid or tid. Dose can be increased 0.1 mg/kg/dose or 5–10 mg/day every 7 days. Maximum dose is 2 mg/kg/day up to 60 mg/day. Duration is 3–5 hr

ADMINISTRATION:
- Administered PO; can be taken with or without food.
- Take the drug each day in the morning.
- Must be swallowed whole with liquids; must not be chewed, divided, or crushed.
- The tablet shell is nonabsorbable and may be noticed in the stool; patients should not be concerned.

SIDE EFFECTS: Some common side effects include nervousness, insomnia, anorexia, upper abdominal pain, weight loss, tachycardia, nausea, motor tics, headache, palpitations, dizziness, fever, rash, urticaria, depression, drowsiness, dyskinesia, angina, blood pressure changes, visual disturbances, and elevated liver transaminases.

DRUG INTERACTIONS:
- The following drugs are contraindicated to be used with methylphenidate: *anorexiants*, e.g., phentermine (*Adipex-P*), diethylpropion, phendimetrazine (*Bontril PDM*), and benzphetamine (*Didrex*) increase risk of cardiovascular and CNS stimulatory effects; *MAOIs, nonselective*, e.g., procarbazine (*Matulane*), phenelzine (*Nardil*), tranylcypromine (*Parnate*), isocarboxazid (*Marplan*), selegiline (*Eldepryl/Zelapar*) transdermal (result in hypertensive crisis), and sibutramine (*Meridia*) may increase the risk of adverse effects due to additive effects.
- Other drugs that need to be avoided: linezolid (*Zyvox*) may increase hypertensive effects, pimozide (*Orap*) may cause motor/phonic tics, venlafaxine (*Effexor*) may result in greater than expected weight loss.

PHARMACOKINETICS:
- Metabolized in the liver (CYP450) and excreted in the urine.
- Stimulates CNS activity; blocks the reuptake and increases release of norepinephrine and dopamine in extraneuronal space.
Half-life: 2–3 hr

PRECAUTIONS: Caution should be exercised due to drug dependence. Other serious reactions include aggressive behavior, stroke, sudden death, seizures, arrhythmias, myocardial infarction,
(cont.)

methylphenidate (*cont.*)

exfoliative dermatitis, erythema multiforme, erythema multiforme, thrombocytopenic purpura, leucopenia, neuroleptic malignant syndrome, cerebral arteritis, and hepatic coma

PATIENT AND FAMILY EDUCATION:
- Take 30–45 min before meals; take last dose before 6 p.m.
- Tell health care provider if taken; MAOI within 14 days, have hypertension, bipolar disorder, hyperthyroidism, phenylketonuria, glaucoma, heart disease, Tourette's syndrome, or psychosis.
- May increase the effects of TCAs and guanethidine. May alter the effects of blood thinners and seizure medicines.
- Avoid alcohol and caffeinated beverages such as coffee, tea, and colas.
- Avoid foods rich in tyramine such as aged cheeses, bologna, chicken liver, chocolate, pepperoni, raisins, salami, soy sauce, and yeast extracts.

- Tell the health care provider before any type of surgery or dental procedure is performed.
- Store methylphenidate in a tightly closed container and keep at room temperature away from excess heat and moisture.
- Until the effects of this medicine are known, do not operate potentially hazardous machinery or vehicles.

SPECIAL POPULATIONS:
- *Elderly*: May need reduced dosage.
- *Renal impairment:* Not defined.
- *Hepatic impairment*: Not defined.
- *Pregnancy*: Category C but safety has not been established in pregnancy
- *Lactation:* Safety has not been established.
- *Children*: Dosages for children are available. Methylphenidate should not be used in children under 6 years of age, since safety and efficacy in this age group have not been established.

DISSOCIATIVE AMNESIA DISORDER: Amphetamine Derivatives (Psychostimulants)

References

Acute Stress Syndrome, Encyclopedia of Mental Health. Retrieved September 15, 2010, from http://www.minddisorders.com/A-Br/Acute-stress-disorder.html

Agoraphobia. (2000). In *Diagnostic and statistical manual of mental disorders* (DSM-IV-TR, 4th ed.). Arlington, VA: American Psychiatric Association. Retrieved September 10, 2010, from http://www.psychiatryonline.com

Agoraphobia. (2007). In Moore, D. P., et al. *Handbook of medical psychiatry*. Philadelphia, PA: Mosby. Retrieved September 10, 2010, from http://www.mdconsult.com/das/book/body/125211023-6/0/1243/85.html?tocnode=52436571&fromURL=85.html#4-u1.0-B0-323-02911-6..X5001-5--section6_797

Allen, M. H., Currier, G. W., Carpenter, D., Ross, R. W., Docherty, J. P. (2005). The expert consensus guideline series: Treatment of behavioral emergencies 2005. *Journal of Psychiatric Practice, 11* (Suppl. 1), 1–108.

Allugulander, C. (2009). General anxiety disorder: Between now and DSM-V. *Psychiatric Clinics of North America, 32*, 611–628.

American Psychiatric Association Steering Committee on Practice Guidelines. (2004). Practice guidelines for the treatment of patients with acute stress disorder and posttraumatic stress disorder.

American Psychiatric Association. (2000). *Diagnostic and statistical manual of mental disorders* (4th ed., text rev.). Washington, DC: Author.

American Psychiatric Association. (2010). *Practice guideline for the treatment of patients with obsessive-compulsive disorder*. Arlington, VA: Author. Retrieved September 10, 2010, from http//www.psych.org

American Psychological Association. (2010). *The publication manual of the American Psychological Association* (6th ed.). Washington, DC: Author.

Anxiety disorders. National Institute of Mental Health. Retrieved September 10, 2010, from http://www.nimh.nih.gov/publicat/anxiety.cfm#anx3

Anxiety disorders. National Institute of Mental Health. Retrieved September 10, 2010, from http://www.nimh.nih.gov/health/publications/anxiety-disorders/complete-publication.shtml

Autism Society. (2009, March). *Treatment options*. Bethesda, MD: Author.

Azzaro, A. J., Ziemniak, J., Kemper, E., Campbell, B. J., & VanDenBerg, C. (2007). Selegiline transdermal system: An examination of the potential for CYP450-dependent pharmacokinetic interactions with 3 psychotropic medications. *The Journal of Clinical Pharmacology, 47*(2), 146–158.

Bandelow, B., Zohar, J., Hollander, E., Kasper, S., Moller, H. J., Zohar, J., et al. (2008). World federation of societies of biological psychiatry: Guidelines for the pharmacological treatment of anxiety, obsessive-compulsive and post-traumatic stress disorders—First revision. *The World of Journal of Biological Psychiatry, 9*(4), 248–312.

Barley, R. (2010). *Anatomy of the brain*. Retrieved July 25, 2010 from http://biology.about.com/od/humananatomybiology/a/anatomybrain.htm

Bellinier, T. J. (2002). Continuum of care: Stabilizing the acutely agitated patient. *American Journal of Health-System Pharmacy, 59*(Suppl. 5), S12–S18.

Bourine, M. (2003). Use of paroxetine for the treatment of depression and anxiety disorders in the elderly: A review. *Human Psychopharmacology of Clinical and Experimental, 18*, 185–190.

Bozorg, A. M. & Benbadis, S. R. (2008). Narcolepsy. *Medscape*. Retrieved March 11, 2009, from http://emedicine.medscape.com/article/1188433-overview

Brielmaier, B. D. (2006). Eszopiclone (Lunesta): A new nonbenzodiazepine hypnotic agent. *Proceedings, 19*(1), 54–59.

Bruce T. J., & Saeed, S. A. (1999). Social anxiety disorder: A common unrecognized social disorder. *American Family Physician, 60*(8), 2311–2322.

Burns, C. E. (2004). Sleep and rest. In Burns, C. E., Dunn, A. M., Brady, M. A., Starr, N. B., & Blosser, C. G. (Eds.), *Pediatric primary pare* (pp. 331–343). Philadelphia, PA: Saunders.

Callen, R. R. (2009, April 15). Current strategies in the diagnosis and treatment of childhood attention-deficit/hyperactivity disorder. *American Family Physician, 657*–665.

Ciechanowski, P. Overview of phobic disorders in adults. Retrieved September 10, 2010, from http://www.uptodate.com/home/index.html

Ciechanowski, P. Overview of obsessive-compulsive disorder. Retrieved September 10, 2010, from http://www.uptodate.com/home/index.html

Clinical Pharmacology. (2010). Retrieved September 28, 2010 from http://www.clinicalpharmacology.com

Cooper, J., Carty J., & Creamer, M. (2005). Pharmacotherapy for posttraumatic stress disorder: Empirical review and recommendations. *Australian and New Zealand Journal of Psychiatry, 39*, 674–682.

Cupp, M., & Tracey, T. (1998). Cytochrome P450: New nomenclature and clinical implications. *American Academy of Family Practice January 1, 1998*. Retrieved November 30, 2010, from http://www.aafp.org/afp/980101ap/cupp.html

Currier, G. W., & Medori, R. (2006). Orally versus intramuscular administered antipsychotic drugs in psychiatric emergencies. *Journal of Psychiatric Practice. 12*(1), 30–40.

Diagnostic and Statistical Manual of Mental Disorders (4th ed.). (2000). Washington, DC: American Psychiatric Press, Inc.

Eli Lilly and Company. (2008, September 24). Strattera Package Insert. *Straterra Package Insert*. Indianapolis, IN: Eli Lilly and Company.

Epocrates. (2010). Retrieved August 17, 2010 from http://www.epocrates.com

Epocrates. (2010). Retrieved September 22, 2010 from http www.epocrates.com

Epocrates. (2010). Retrieved September 30, 2010, from www.epocrates.com

Facts & Comparisons. (2010). Wolters Kluwer Health, Hard Copy.

Fava, G. A., Grandi, S., Rafanelli, C., Ruini, C., Conti, S., Belluardo, P. (2001). Long-term outcome of social phobia treated by exposure. *Psychological Medicine*, 31, 899–905.

Fischer, J. (2007). Posttraumatic stress disorder needs to be recognized in primary care. *Annals of Internal Medicine*, 146(8), 617–620.

Franco, K. N. (2010, August 1). *Eating disorders*. Cleveland Clinic for Continuing Education. Retrieved September 28, 2010, from http://www.cleveland clinicmeded.com/medicalpubs/diseasemanage ment/psychiatry-psychology/eating-disorders/

Fricchione, G. (2004). Generalized anxiety disorder. *New England Journal of Medicine*, 351, 675–682.

Guilleminault, C., Palombini, L., Pelayo, R., & Chervin, R. D. (2004). Sleepwalking and sleep terrors in prepubertal children: What triggers them? *Pediatrics*, 111, 17–25.

Gupta, A., Chatelain, P., Massingham, R., Jonsson E. N., & Hammarlund-Udenaes, M. (2006). Brain distribution of cetirizine enantiomers: Comparison of three different tissue-to-plasma partition coefficients: K(p), K(p,u), and K(p,uu). *Drug Metabolism and Disposition*, 34(2), 318–323.

Gupta, A., Chatelain, P., Massingham, R., Jonsson E. N., & Hammarlund-Udenaes, M. (2006). Brain distribution of cetirizine enantiomers: Comparison of three different tissue-to-plasma partition coefficients: K(p), K(p,u), and K(p,uu). *Drug Metabolism and Disposition*, 34(2), 318–323.

Hales, R. E., Yudofsky, S. C., & Gabbard, G. O. (Eds.). (2008). Obsessive-compulsive disorder. In *The American Psychiatric Publishing Textbook of Psychiatry* (5th ed.). Arlington, VA: American Psychiatric Publishing Inc.

Hall, G., Gallagher, M., & Dougherty, J. (2009). Integrating roles for successful dementia management. *The Nurse Practitioner*, 34(11), 35–41.

Hisaka, A., Ohno, Y., Yamamoto, T., & Suzuki, H. (2010). Theoretical considerations on quantitative prediction of drug-drug interactions. *Drug Metabolism and Pharmacokinetics*, 25(1), 48–61.

Hodgson, B. B., & Kizior, R. J. (2011). *Saunders' nursing drug handbook 2011*. St. Louis, MO: Elsevier Saunders.

Hollander, E., & Simeon, D. (2008). Panic disorders. In Hales, R. E., et al. (Eds.), *The American Psychiatric Publishing Textbook of Psychiatry* (5th ed.). Arlington, VA: American Psychiatric Association.

Horn, J. R., & Hansten, P. D. (2008). Get to know an enzyme: CYP3A4. Pharmacy Times. Retrieved July 28, 2010, from http://www.pharmacytimes.com/ issue/pharmacy/2008/2008–09/2008–09-8687

International Classification of Sleep Disorders: Diagnostic and Coding Manual (2nd ed.) (2005). Westchester, IL: American Academy of Sleep Medicine.

Kendler, K. S., Gardner, C. O., Annas, P., Neale, M. C., Eaves, L. J., Lichtenstein, P. (2008). A longitudinal twin study of fears from middle childhood to early adulthood: Evidence for a developmentally dynamic genome. *Archives of General Psychiatry*, 65(4), 421–429.

Kothare, S. V., & Kaleyias, J. (2008). Narcolepsy and other hypersomnias in children. *Neurology*, 6, 666–675.

Lamberg, L. (2002). Psychiatric emergencies call for comprehensive assessment and treatment. *Journal of American Medical Association*, 288(6), 686–687.

Lehman, A. H., Lieberman, J. A., Dixon, L. B., McGlashan, T. H., Miller, A. L., Perkins, D. O., et al.

(2004). Practice guidelines for the treatment of patients with schizophrenia, 2nd edition. *American Journal of Psychiatry*, 61(Suppl. 2), 1–56.

Lehne, R. A. (2007). *Pharmacology for nursing care* (7th ed.). St. Louis: Saunders Elsevier. 100–104.

Let's talk facts about phobias. American Psychiatric Association. Retrieved September 10, 2010, from http://healthyminds.org/multimedia/phobias.pdf

Llorente Fernández, E., Parés, L., Ajuria, I., Bandres, F., Castanyer, B., Campos F., et al. (2010). State of the art in therapeutic drug monitoring. *Clinical Chemistry and Laboratory Medicine*, 48(4), 437–446.

Lukens, T. W., Wolf, S. J., Edlow, J. A., Shahabuddin, S., Allen, M. H., Currier, G. W., et al. ACEP Clinical Policies Subcommittee on Critical Issues (trunc). (2006). Clinical policy: Critical issues in the diagnosis and management of the adult psychiatric patient in the emergency department. *Annals of Emergency Medicine*, 47(1), 79–99.

MacDonald, L., Foster, B. C., & Akhtar, H. (2009). Food and therapeutic product interactions—A therapeutic perspective. *Journal of Pharmacy and Pharmaceutical Sciences*, 12(3), 367–377.

Management of Alzheimer's disease and related dementias. (2010). Agency for Health Care Research and Quality. Retrieved on September 20, 2010 from, http://guideline.gov/syntheses/ synthesis.aspx?f=rss&id=16414

Mancini, C. Social phobia in children and adolescents. Canadian Psychiatric Association. Retrieved September 10, 2010, from http://ww1.cpa-apc. org:8080/Publications/Archives/Bulletin/2001/ May/Social.asp

Marder, S. R. (2006). A review of agitation in mental illness: Treatment guidelines and current therapies. *Journal of Clinical Psychiatry*, 67 (Suppl. 10), 13–21.

Marshall, R., Spitzer, R., & Liebowitz, M. (1999). Review and critique of the new DSM-IV diagnosis of acute stress disorder. *American Journal of Psychiatry*, 156(11), 1677.

Mayhew, M. S. (2009). Medical management of eating disorders [Electronic version]. *The Journal of Nurse Practitioners*, 5(4), 296–297.

Mayo Clinic Staff. (2009). *Anorexia nervosa: Treatments and drugs*. Mayo Clinic. Retrieved October 3, 2010, from http://www.mayoclinic.com/health/anorexia/ DS00606/DSECTION=treatments-and-drugs

Mayo Clinic Staff. (2010). *Bulimia nervosa: Treatments and drugs*. Mayo Clinic. Retrieved October 5, 2010, from http://www.mayoclinic.com/health/ bulimia/DS00607/DSECTION=treatments-and-drugs

Medical Management Institute. (2008). *International Classification of Diseases 9th Revision—Clinical Modification (ICD-9-CM) for Physicians*. Salt Lake City, UT: Author.

National Institute of Health. (2010). Retrieved September 28, 2010 from http://www.ncbi.nlm.nih.gov/pubmed health/PMH0001066; http://ww.ncbi.nlm.nih.gov/ pubmedhealth/PMH0000190;http://www.ncbi.nlm. nih.gov/pubmedhealth/PMH0001006; http://www. ncbi.nlm.nih.gov/pubmedhealth/PMH0000250

National Institute of Neurological Disorders and Stroke. (2002). *Autism Fact Sheet*. Bethesda, MD: Author.

Newell, C. (2010). Early recognition of eating disorders [Electronic version]. *Practice Nurse*, 39(12), 20–25.

Norden, J. (2007). *Understanding the brain: Parts I, II, & III.* Chantilly, VA: The Teaching Company.

Obsessive-compulsive disorder. (2000). In *Diagnostic and Statistical Manual of Mental Disorders DSM-IV-TR.* Arlington, VA: American Psychiatric Association.

Pagel, J. F. (2000). Nightmares and disorders of dreaming. *American Family Physician, 61,* 2037–2044.

Perlis, R. H., Mischoulon, D., Smoller, J. W., Wan, Y. J., Lamon-Fava, S., Lin K.M., et al. (2003). Serotonin transporter polymorphisms and adverse effects with fluoxetine treatment. *Biological Psychiatry, 54*(9), 879–883.

Plante, D. T., & Winkelman, J. W. (2006). Parasomnias. *Psychiatric Clinics of North America, 29,* 969–987.

Pliszka, S. (2003). *Neuroscience for the mental health clinician.* New York: The Guilford Press.

Pliszka, S. (2007, July). Practice parameter for the assessment and treatment. *Journal of the American Academy of Child and Adolescent Psychiatry,* 894–921.

Porter, R. S., Kaplan, J. L., & Homeier, B. P. (2010). Merck Manual Medical Library. Retrieved September 17, 2010, from http://www.merck.com/mmhe/sec06/ch081/ch081g.html

Posttraumatic Stress Disorder. Encyclopedia of mental health. Retrieved September 15, 2010, from http://www.minddisorders.com/Ob-Ps/Post-traumatic-stress-disorder.html

Preda, A. (2009). Primary hypersomnia: Treatment and medication. Emedicine. Retrieved July 28, 2010, from http://emedicine.medscape.com/article/291699-treatment

Pridmore, S. Clinical practice guidelines management of anxiety disorders: Principles of diagnosis and management of anxiety. *Canadian Journal of Psychiatry, 51*(S2), 9–21.

Reuters, T. (2010). *Bulimia nervosa.* Retrieved October 5, 2010, from http://www.drugs.com/cg/bulimia-nervosa.html

Richardson, W. H., Slone, C. M., & Michels, J.E. (2007). Herbal drugs of abuse: An emerging problem. *Emergency Medicine Clinics of North America, 25,* 435.

Sharma, S. (2007). Primary hypersomnia. Medscape. Retrieved March 11, 2009, from http://emedicine.medscape.com/article/291699-overview

Shearer, S. L. (2007). Recent advances in the understanding and treatment of anxiety disorders. *Primary Care: Clinics in Office Practice, 34*:475.

Shire US Inc. (2009, August). Intuniv Package Insert. *Intuniv Package Insert.* Wayne, PA: Shire US Inc.

Shire US, Inc. (2010). *A parent's guide to being aware.* Wayne, PA: Shire US, Inc.

Shire US, Inc. (2010, April). Vyvanse Package Insert. *Vyvanse.* Wayne, PA: Shire US, Inc.

Silber, M. (2001). Sleep disorders. *Neurologic Clinics, 19,* 173–186.

Simpson, H., Foa, E. B., Liebowitz, M. R., Ledley, D. R., Huppert, J. D., Cahill, S., et al. (2008). A randomized, controlled trial of cognitive-behavioral therapy for augmenting pharmacotherapy in obsessive-compulsive disorder. *American Journal of Psychiatry, 165,* 621.

Social phobia (Social anxiety disorder). National Institute of Mental Health. Retrieved September 10, 2010, from http://www.nimh.nih.gov/health/topics/social-phobia/index.shtml

Social phobia. (1994). In *Diagnostic and Statistical Manual of Mental Disorders DSM-IV-TR.* Washington, DC: American Psychiatric Association.

Specific phobias. (1994). In *Diagnostic and Statistical Manual of Mental Disorders DSM-IV-TR.* Washington, DC: American Psychiatric Association.

Stahl, S. (2008). *Stahl's essential psychopharmacology: Neuroscientific basis and practical applications* (3rd ed.). Cambridge, UK: Cambridge University Press.

Stahl, S. (2009). *The prescriber's guide: Stahl's Essential psychopharmacology* (3rd ed.). Cambridge, UK: Cambridge University Press.

Substance Abuse and Mental Health Services Administration, Office of Applied Studies. (2008). *Drug abuse warning network, 2006: National estimates of drug-related emergency department visits.* DAWN Series D-30, DHHS Publication No. (SMA) 08–4339. Rockville, MD: Author.

The Victorian of Newport Beach. (2010). *Eating disorder treatment: Anorexia nervosa info.* Retrieved October 3, 2010, from http://www.eatingdisordertreatment.com/about-eating-disorders/anorexia-nervosa-information-symptoms-and-treatment-of-anorexia

Thiedke, C. C. (2001). Sleep disorders and sleep problems in childhood. *American Family Physician, 63,* 277–284.

Ting, L., & Malhotra, A. (2005). Disorders of sleep: An overview. *Primary Care: Clinics in Office Practice, 32,* 305–318.

United States National Library of Medicine. (2008). National Institutes of Health. Retrieved July 28, 2010, from http://www.ncbi.nlm.nih.gov/pubmedhealth/PMH0000182#a601251-storageConditions

WHO. (2004). *Scientific facts on psychoactive drugs.* Retrieved July 25, 2010 from http://www.greenfacts.org/en/psychoactive-drugs/index.htm#7

Williams, S. M. (2005). *Clinical neuroanatomy for undergraduates.* Retrieved July 25, 2010 from http://www.fas.harvard.edu/~bok_cen/sfn/2005/Duke.pdf

Index

▶KEY: Drug classifications, bold italics; drug tables, bold; generic names, lower case; trade names, italics.

▶KEY: Drug classifications, bold italics; drug tables, bold; generic names, lower case; trade names, italics.

▶KEY: Drug classifications, bold italics; drug tables, bold; generic names, lower case; trade names, italics.

▶KEY: Drug classifications, bold italics; drug tables, bold; generic names, lower case; trade names, italics.

▶KEY: Drug classifications, bold italics; drug tables, bold; generic names, lower case; trade names, italics.

▶KEY: Drug classifications, bold italics; drug tables, bold; generic names, lower case; trade names, italics.

▶KEY: Drug classifications, bold italics; drug tables, bold; generic names, lower case; trade names, italics.

►KEY: Drug classifications, bold italics; drug tables, bold; generic names, lower case; trade names, italics.

▶KEY: Drug classifications, bold italics; drug tables, bold; generic names, lower case; trade names, italics.

▶KEY: Drug classifications, bold italics; drug tables, bold; generic names, lower case; trade names, italics.

▶KEY: Drug classifications, bold italics; drug tables, bold; generic names, lower case; trade names, italics.

▶KEY: Drug classifications, bold italics; drug tables, bold; generic names, lower case; trade names, italics.

▶KEY: Drug classifications, bold italics; drug tables, bold; generic names, lower case; trade names, italics.